BUILDING No. 41,

OCCUPIED JOINTLY BY THE

CENTENNIAL CATALOGUE COMPANY,

AND

S. M. Pettengill & Co., Newspaper Advertising Agents,

South of East End of Machinery Hall.

ADVERTISEMENTS taken at this office for the Official Catalogue and all newspapers of the United States and Canadas. The principal papers of the country kept on file for inspection and use of exhibitors and visitors generally.

CENTENNIAL CATALOGUE CO.

S. W. Cor. Fourth and Library Sts., Philadelphia,

PUBLISHERS OF THE

OFFICIAL CATALOGUE

OF THE

INTERNATIONAL EXHIBITION OF 1876.

This Company owns the exclusive right to publish, sell, and distribute the "*Official Catalogue of the International Exhibition of 1876*," the work being printed under the direction of, and compiled from manuscript furnished by, the "U. S. Centennial Commission."

Advertisements taken on application to S. M. PETTENGILL & Co. Advertising Agents.

JOHN S. MORTON,
President.

MORDECAI D. EVANS,
Treasurer.

L. L. HYNEMAN,
Secretary.

S. HENRY NORRIS,
Solicitor.

JOHN R. NAGLE,
Publishing and Advertising Manager,
524 Market St., Philadelphia.

S. M. PETTENGILL & CO.,
Advertising Agents,
No. 701 Chestnut Street, Philadelphia,
No. 37 Park Row, New York,
No. 10 State Street, Boston,
Exhibition Grounds—South of East end of Machinery Hall, Building No. 41.

J. M. JOHNSON & SONS, Limited,
Sole European Agents,
No. 3 Castle St., Holborn, London.

DIRECTORS:

JOHN S. MORTON,
M. ROSENBACH,
GEORGE T. JONES,
WM. H. PENNELL,
STEPHEN F. WHITMAN,
JOHN R. NAGLE,
JOSEPH HEILBRUN.

Office of the Company on Exhibition Grounds, Building No. 41, South of East end of Machinery Hall.

MACHINERY HALL.

United States Centennial Commission.

INTERNATIONAL EXHIBITION.

1876

Official Catalogue.

PART III.

MACHINERY HALL, ANNEXES, AND SPECIAL BUILDINGS.

DEPARTMENT V.—MACHINERY.

SECOND AND REVISED EDITION.

PHILADELPHIA:
Published for the Centennial Catalogue Company
BY JOHN R. NAGLE AND COMPANY.
Printed at the Riverside Press, Cambridge, Mass.
1876.

CONTENTS.

NOTE.—The Alphabetical List of Exhibitors in the Department of Machinery and in Special Buildings is included in the General Index at the conclusion of Part IV. of the Official Catalogue.

BUILDINGS AND SPECIAL EXHIBITS WITHIN THE EXHIBITION GROUNDS.

[NOTE.—The buildings bear the numbers prefixed to them in this table, being the numbers adopted by the Centennial Guide Book Co. (Limited).]

BUILDINGS AND SPECIAL EXHIBITS WITHIN THE EXHIBITION GROUNDS.

[NOTE.—Descriptions of the Buildings will be found at the indicated part and page of the Official Catalogue.]

Buildings North of the Avenue of the Republic, and West of Belmont Av.

Buildings East of Belmont Avenue, and South of Fountain Avenue.

Buildings East of Belmont Avenue, and North of Fountain Avenue.

SUBJECT INDEX, NATIONAL EXHIBITS.

DEPARTMENT V.—MACHINERY.

NATIONS.	Machines, Tools, etc., of Mining, Chemistry, etc.	Machines and Tools for Working Metal, Wood, and Stone.	Machines and Implements of Spinning, Weaving, etc.	Machines, etc., used in Sewing, Making Clothing, etc.	Machines for Printing, Making Books, Paper-making.	Motors, Power Generators, etc.	Hydraulic and Pneumatic Apparatus.	Railway Plant, Rolling-Stock, etc.*	Machinery used in Preparing Agricultural Products.	Aërial, Pneumatic, and Water Transportation.	Machinery especially adapted to the Requirements of the Exhibition.	Shoe and Leather Exhibition.	Women's Work.	Special Buildings.
United States	17	19	28	30	32	34	40	45	48	50	52	105	87	117
Great Britain	54	54	54	55	55	55	55	56	56	56	...	116	98	130
Jamaica	...	...	...	...	...	...	...	...	...	...	...	.....	99	......
Canada	57	57	57	57	...	58	58	58	59	59	...	.....	99	130
Tasmania	...	...	...	...	...	...	...	...	...	...	...	.....	100	.....
France	60	60	60	60	60	60	61	61	61	61	...	.....	100	145
Germany	62	62	62	62	62	62	62	62	62	62	...	116	.....	144
Austria	63	...	63	...	...	63	...	63	63	...	...	.....	.....	......
Switzerland	...	...	...	...	...	63	...	63	...	...	...	.....	......	.....
Belgium	64	64	64	64	64	64	64	64	...	...	...	.....	100	......
Netherlands	...	65	...	65	...	...	65	...	....	...	...	.....	100	.....
Denmark	...	...	...	...	...	...	...	...	...	...	...	.....	100	.....
Sweden	65	65	...	66	66	66	66	66	...	66	...	....	100	144
Italy	67	...	67	...	67	67	67	...	67	67	...	.....	100	......
Tunis	...	...	...	...	...	...	...	...	....	...	...	.....	101	131
Japan	...	...	...	...	...	...	...	...	...	...	...	.....	......	144
Brazil	...	68	68	...	...	68	68	...	68	68	...	.....	101	145
Argentine Republic	...	...	69	...	69	...	...	69	....	69	...	.....	.....	.....
Chili	...	...	...	...	...	...	...	...	....	...	...	.....	.....	120
Spain	...	...	...	...	...	...	...	...	....	...	...	.....	.....	132
Portugal	...	...	...	...	...	...	...	...	....	...	...	.....	.....	148
Turkey	...	...	...	...	...	...	...	...	....	...	...	.....	.....	143
Russia	69	69	69	69	69	70	70	70	70	70	...	116	.....	......
U. S. Government	...	...	...	...	...	...	...	...	...	..	...	......	.....	72
Women's Centennial Executive Com.	...	...	...	...	...	...	...	...	....	...	...	.....	......	85

* Railway plant, cars, etc., are largely exhibited in the Annex (No. 106) to the Main Building, Catalogue, Part I., page 374.

Note.—The Machinery of the following countries is installed wholly or in part in the Main Building, and catalogued in Part I., viz.:

	Page		Page
New South Wales	340	Austria	211
Victoria	162	Denmark	224
Bermuda	174	Netherlands	361
Gold Coast	177	Norway	230
Queensland	179	Hawaii	251
Tasmania	182	Chili	262
India	186	Mexico	267
Canada	191		

No. 20. MACHINERY HALL.

Size, 360 by 1402 feet; annex, 208 by 210 feet.

Engineers and Architects, HENRY PETTIT, JOSEPH M. WILSON, *Philadelphia.*

Contractor, PHILIP QUIGLEY, *Wilmington, Del.*

Wrought and cast iron furnished by PUSEY, JONES, & CO., *Wilmington, Del.*

MACHINERY HALL is located west of the intersection of Belmont and Elm avenues, at a distance of 542 feet from the west front of the Main Exhibition Building, and 274 feet from the north side of Elm avenue. The north front of the building is upon the same line as that of the Main Exhibition Building, thus presenting a frontage of 3824 feet from the east to the west ends of the exhibition buildings upon the principle avenue within the grounds.

The principal portion of the structure is one story in height, showing the main cornice upon the outside at 40 feet from the ground, the interior height to the top of the ventilators in the avenues being 70 feet, and in the aisles 40 feet. To break the long lines upon the exterior, projections have been introduced upon the four sides, and the main entrances finished with facades, extending to 78 feet in height. The east entrance forms the principal approach from street-cars, from the Main Exhibition Building, and from the Pennsylvania Railroad depot. Along the south side are the boiler houses and other buildings for special kinds of machinery. The west entrance affords the most direct communication with George's Hill, which point affords the best view of the entire exhibition grounds.

The arrangement of the ground plan shows two main avenues 90 feet wide by 1360 feet long, with a central aisle between, and an aisle on either side. Each aisle is 60 feet in width; the two avenues and three aisles making the total width of 360 feet. At the centre of the building is a transept of 90 feet in width, which at the south end is prolonged beyond the Main Hall. This transept, beginning at 36 feet from the Main Hall and extending 268 feet, is flanked on either side by aisles of 60 feet in width, and forms the annex for hydraulic machines. The promenades in the avenues are 15 feet in width, in the transept 25 feet, and in the aisles 10 feet. All other walks extending across the building are 10 feet in width, and lead at either end to exit doors.

The foundations consist of piers of masonry. The superstructure consists of solid timber columns supporting roof trusses, constructed with straight wooden principals and wrought iron ties and struts. As a general rule, the columns are placed lengthwise of the building, at the uniform distance apart of 16 feet. The columns are 40 feet high to the heel block of the 90 feet span roof trusses over the avenues, and they support the heel of the 60 feet spans over the aisles at the height of 20 feet. The outer walls are built of masonry to a height of five feet, and above that are composed of glazed sash placed between the columns. Portions of the sash are movable for ventilation. Louvre ventilators are introduced in continuous lengths over both the avenues and the aisles. The building is lit entirely by side light.

The motive power is furnished by a Corliss engine of 1400 horse power. There are eight main lines of shafting, extending almost the entire length of the structure, and countershafts are introduced into the aisles where needed. The hangers are attached at the height of 20 feet from the floor.

The annex for hydraulic machines contains a tank 60 feet by 160 feet, with depth of water of 10 feet. In this hydraulic machinery is exhibited in full operation. At the south end of this tank is a waterfall 35 feet high by 40 feet wide, supplied from the tank by the pumps upon exhibition.

The contract in the erection of Machinery Hall was made January 27th, 1875, and the building was begun forthwith, and finished October 1st, 1875. The cost was $542,300. The exhibition area covers about 14 acres.

KEY TO THE NOTATION.

THE location of objects in the Machinery Building is shown by a letter and figure, indicating the nearest column of the building. The letters—A, B, C, to F—designate the successive ranges of columns, proceeding northward from the southern wall across the width of the building; the figures, the number of the column in each range, counting westwardly from the eastern wall, the entire length of the building, from 1 to 88. Thus C 5 is the column in the third range from the south, and the fifth from the eastern end of the building. The northwesternmost column is F 88.

The class of the classification (see page 13) to which each exhibit belongs is indicated by the small figures at the end of the line.

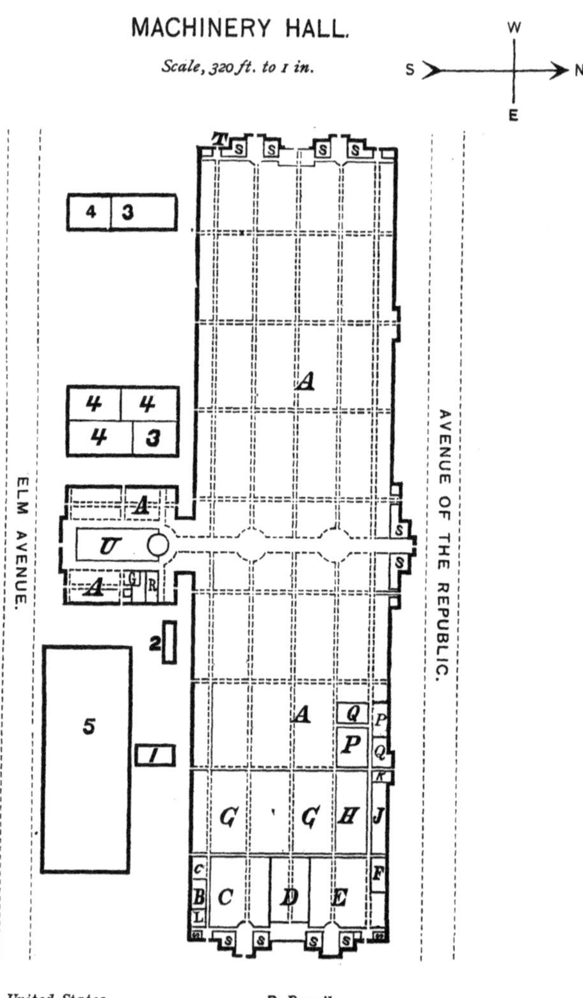

A *United States.*
B *Austria.*
C *German Empire.*
D *Canada.*
E *France.*
F *Spain.*
G *Great Britain.*
H *Belgium.*
J *Sweden.*
K *Denmark.*
L *Italy.*
P *Brazil.*
Q *Russia.*
R *Switzerland.*
S *Restaurants, etc.*
T *Ladies' Waiting-room.*
U *Tank.*
1. English Boiler-house.
2. Corliss Boiler-house.
3. Boiler-houses.
4. Machine Shop and Annex.
5. Shoe and Leather Shop.

Length, 1402 ft. Width, 360 ft. Height of Avenues, 70 ft. Height of Aisles, 40 ft.

SYNOPSIS OF THE CLASSIFICATION.

LOCATION.	DEPARTMENTS.	CLASSES.	GROUPS.
MAIN BUILDING.	I. MINING AND METALLURGY.	100—109	Minerals, Ores, Stone, Mining Products.
		110—119	Metallurgical Products.
		120—129	Mining Engineering.
	II. MANUFACTURES.	200—205	Chemical Manufactures.
		206—216	Ceramics, Pottery, Porcelain, Glass, etc.
		217—227	Furniture, etc.
		228—234	Yarns and Woven Goods of Vegetable or Mineral Materials.
		235—241	Woven and Felted Goods of Wool, etc.
		242—249	Silk and Silk Fabrics.
		250—257	Clothing, Jewelry, etc.
		258—264	Paper, Blank Books, Stationery.
		265—271	Weapons, etc.
		272—279	Medicine, Surgery, Prothesis.
		280—284	Hardware, Edge Tools, Cutlery, and Metallic Products.
		285—291	Fabrics of Vegetable, Animal, or Mineral Materials.
		292—296	Carriages, Vehicles, and Accessories.
	III. EDUCATION AND SCIENCE	300—309	Educational Systems, Methods, and Libraries.
		310—319	Institutions and Organizations.
		320—329	Scientific and Philosophical Instruments and Methods.
		330—339	Engineering, Architecture, Maps, etc.
		340—349	Physical, Social, and Moral Condition of Man.
ART GALLERY.	IV. ART.	400—409	Sculpture.
		410—419	Painting.
		420—429	Engraving and Lithography.
		430—439	Photography.
		440—449	Industrial and Architectural Designs, etc.
		450—459	Ceramic Decorations, Mosaics, etc.
MACHINERY BUILDING.	V. MACHINERY.	500—509	Machines, Tools, etc., of Mining, Chemistry, etc.
		510—519	Machines and Tools for working Metal, Wood, and Stone.
		520—529	Machines and Implements of Spinning, Weaving, etc.
		530—539	Machines, etc., used in Sewing, Making Clothing, etc.
		540—549	Machines for Printing, Making Books, Paper Working, etc.
		550—559	Motors, Power Generators, etc.
		560—569	Hydraulic and Pneumatic Apparatus.
		570—579	Railway Plant, Rolling Stock, etc.
		580—589	Machinery used in Preparing Agricultural Products.
		590—599	Aerial, Pneumatic, and Water Transportation.
			Machinery, and Apparatus, especially adapted to the requirements of the Exhibition.
AGRICULTURAL BUILDING.	VI. AGRICULTURE.	600—609	Arboriculture and Forest Products.
		610—619	Pomology.
		620—629	Agricultural Products.
		630—639	Land Animals.
		640—649	Marine Animals, Fish Culture, and Apparatus.
		650—662	Animal and Vegetable Products.
		665—669	Textile Substances of Vegetable or Animal origin.
		670—679	Machines, Implements, and Processes of Manufacture.
		680—689	Agricultural Engineering and Administration.
		690—699	Tillage and General Management.
HORTICULTURAL BUILDING.	VII. HORTICULTURE.	700—709	Ornamental Trees, Shrubs, and Flowers.
		710—719	Hot Houses, Conservatories, Graperies.
		720—729	Garden Tools, Accessories of Gardening.
		730—739	Garden Designing, Construction, and Management.

CLASSIFICATION.

DEPARTMENT V.—MACHINERY.

MACHINES, TOOLS, AND APPARATUS OF MINING, METALLURGY, CHEMISTRY, AND THE EXTRACTIVE ARTS.

CLASS 500.—Rock drilling.

CLASS 501.—Well and shaft boring.

CLASS 502.—Machines, apparatus, and implements for coal cutting.

CLASS 503.—Hoisting machinery and accessories.

CLASS 504.—Pumping, draining, and ventilating.

CLASS 505.—Crushing, grinding, sorting, and dressing. Breakers, stamps, mills, pans, screens, sieves, jigs, concentrators.

CLASS 506.—Furnaces, smelting apparatus, and accessories.

CLASS 507.—Machinery used in Bessemer process.

CLASS 508.—Chemical manufacturing machinery. Electroplating. Paint and powder mills. Blacking and soap-making machinery.

CLASS 509.—Gas machinery and apparatus.

MACHINES AND TOOLS FOR WORKING METAL, WOOD, AND STONE.

CLASS 510.—Planing, sawing, veneering, grooving, mortising, tonguing, cutting, moulding, stamping, carving, and cask-making machines, etc., cork-cutting machines.

CLASS 511.—Direct acting steam sawing machines, with gang saws. Bark mills.

CLASS 512.—Rolling mills, bloom squeezers, blowing fans. Rivet, nail, bolt, and tack making machinery.

CLASS 513.—Furnaces and apparatus for casting metals, with specimens of work.

CLASS 514.—Steam, trip, and other hammers, with specimens of work, anvils, forges, bellows.

CLASS 515.—Planing, drilling, slotting, turning, shaping, punching, stamping, cutting, and coining machines. Wheel cutting and dividing machines, emery wheels, drills, taps, gauges, dies, etc. Grindstones.

CLASS 516.—Stone-sawing and planing machines, dressing, shaping, and polishing, sand blasts, Tilghman's machines, glass-grinding machines, etc.

CLASS 517.—Brick, pottery, and tile machines. Machines for making artificial stone.

CLASS 518.—Furnaces, moulds, blowpipes, etc., for making glass and glassware.

CLASS 519.—Tools, implements, etc., for working metal, wood, and stone.

MACHINES AND IMPLEMENTS OF SPINNING, WEAVING, FELTING, AND PAPER MAKING.

CLASS 520.—Machines for the manufacture of silk goods.

CLASS 521.—Machines for the manufacture of cotton goods.

CLASS 522.—Machines for the manufacture of woolen goods, carpets, and tapestry.

CLASS 523.—Machines for the manufacture of linen goods.

CLASS 524.—Machines for the manufacture of rope and twine, and miscellaneous fibrous materials.
CLASS 525.—Machines for the manufacture of paper and felting.
CLASS 526.—Machines for the manufacture of india-rubber goods.
CLASS 527.—Machines for the manufacture of mixed fabrics.
CLASS 528.—Machines for the manufacture of wire cloth.

MACHINES, APPARATUS, AND IMPLEMENTS USED IN SEWING AND MAKING CLOTHING AND ORNAMENTAL OBJECTS.

CLASS 530.—Machines used in the manufacture of lace, floor-cloths, fancy embroidery, hair, ribbons, etc.
CLASS 531.—Sewing and knitting machines, clothes, corset, hat, and bonnet making machines.
CLASS 532.—Machines for preparing and working leather.
CLASS 533.—Machines for making boots and shoes.
CLASS 534.—Machines for ironing, drying, scouring, and cleaning.
CLASS 535.—Machines for making clocks and watches.
CLASS 536.—Machines for making jewelry.
CLASS 537.—Machines for making buttons, pins, needles, etc.
CLASS 538.—Pipes for smoking.

MACHINES AND APPARATUS FOR TYPESETTING, PRINTING, STAMPING, EMBOSSING, AND FOR MAKING BOOKS, AND PAPER WORKING.

CLASS 540.—Printing, stamping, embossing, and lithographing presses.
CLASS 541.—Typecasting machines, apparatus of stereotyping.
CLASS 542.—Types and typesetting machines. Type-writing machines.
CLASS 543.—Printers' furniture.
CLASS 544.—Bookbinding machines.
CLASS 545.—Paper-folding machines.
CLASS 546.—Paper and card cutting machines, paper box machines.
CLASS 547.—Envelope machines.

MOTORS AND APPARATUS FOR THE GENERATION AND TRANSMISSION OF POWER.

CLASS 550.—Boilers and all steam or gas generating apparatus for motive purposes.
CLASS 551.—Water-wheels, water engines, hydraulic rams, windmills.
CLASS 552.—Steam, air, or gas engines, electro-magnetic engines.
CLASS 553.—Apparatus for the transmission of power, shafting, belting, cables, transmission of power by compressed air, etc., gearing, cables.
CLASS 554.—Screw propellers, wheels for the propulsion of vessels, and other motors.
CLASS 555.—Implements and apparatus used in connection with motors, steam gauges, manometers, etc. Anti-friction metals.

HYDRAULIC AND PNEUMATIC APPARATUS, PUMPING, HOISTING, AND LIFTING.

CLASS 560.—Pumps and apparatus for lifting and moving liquids.
CLASS 561.—Pumps and apparatus for moving and compressing air or gas.
CLASS 562.—Pumps and blowing engines, blowers and ventilating apparatus.
CLASS 563.—Hydraulic jacks, presses, elevators, lifts, meters, cranes.
CLASS 564.—Fire engines, hand, steam, or chemical, and fire extinguishing apparatus, hose, ladders, and fire-escapes, etc.
CLASS 565.—Beer engines, soda-water machines, bottling apparatus, corking machines.
CLASS 566.—Stop valves, cocks, pipes, etc.
CLASS 567.—Diving apparatus and machinery.
CLASS 568.—Ice machines.

RAILWAY PLANT, ROLLING STOCK, AND APPARATUS.

CLASS 570.—Locomotives, models, drawings, plans, etc.
CLASS 571.—Carriages, wagons, trucks, cars, etc. Scales.

CLASS 572.—Brakes, buffers, couplings, and snow-plows.
CLASS 573.—Wheels, tires, axles, bearings, springs, etc.
CLASS 574.—Permanent ways, ties, chairs, switches, etc.
CLASS 575.—Station arrangements, signals, water-cranes, turn-tables.
CLASS 576.—Miscellaneous locomotive attachments.
CLASS 577.—Street railways and cars.

MACHINES USED IN PREPARING AGRICULTURAL PRODUCTS.

CLASS 580.—Flour mills.
CLASS 581.—Sugar refining machines.
CLASS 582.—Confectioners' machinery.
CLASS 583.—Oil-making machinery.
CLASS 584.—Tobacco manufacturing machines.
CLASS 585.—Mills for spices, coffee, etc.
CLASS 586.—Machines for preparing fancy goods.
CLASS 587.—Machines for preparing malt and spirituous liquors.

AERIAL, PNEUMATIC, AND WATER TRANSPORTATION.

CLASS 590.—Suspended cable railways.
CLASS 591.—Transporting cables.
CLASS 592.—Balloons, flying machines, etc.
CLASS 593.—Pneumatic railways, pneumatic dispatch.
CLASS 594.—Boats and sailing vessels. Sailing vessels used in commerce. Sailing vessels used in war. Yachts and pleasure boats. Rowing boats of all kinds. Life boats and salvage apparatus, with life rafts, belts, etc. Submarine armor, diving bells, etc. Ice boats. Models and drawings.
CLASS 595.—Steamships, steamboats, and all vessels propelled by steam.
CLASS 596.—Vessels for carrying telegraph cables and railway trains, also coal barges, water boats, and dredging machines, screw and floating docks, and for other special purposes.
CLASS 597.—Steam capstans, windlass, deck-winches, and steering apparatus, fans.

MACHINERY AND APPARATUS ESPECIALLY ADAPTED TO THE REQUIREMENTS OF THE EXHIBITION.

Boilers, engines, cranes, pumps, etc.

DEPT. V.—MACHINERY.

UNITED STATES.

Mining Machinery, Drills.

Machines, Tools, and Apparatus of Mining, Metallurgy, Chemistry, and the Extractive Arts.

1 **Waring Rock Drill Co., New York, N. Y.**—Mining, quarrying, and tunneling drills. A 54. 500

2 **Pennsylvania Diamond Drill Co., Pottsville, Pa.**—Prospecting drill, quarry drill, and samples of cores, continuous cylindrical sections of rock and mineral strata, bored out to any depth, and furnished; therefore, is a perfectly reliable method of proving mineral lands. Artesian wells bored of any size and depth. A 55. 500

2*a* **Beamisdarfer & Eby, Campbellstown, Pa.**—Rock-drilling machine. (*Annex 2.*) 500

2*b* **Union Rock Drill Co., New York, N. Y.**—Rock drills. A 6ɔ. 500

2*c* **American Diamond Rock Boring Co., Providence, R. I.**—Diamond-pointed rock drills. A 54. 500

3 **Gardiner Drill Co., New York, N. Y.**—Rock-drilling machines and appliances for operating in mines and quarries. A 55. 500

4 **Weaver, W., Phœnixville, Pa.**—The Victor rock drill. Two men with this machine will do the work of six by hand. It drills holes from half an inch to six inches in diameter to any depth and at any angle required. Price for machine driven by hand, $25ɔ; by steam, $750. A 55. 500

5 **Ingersoll Rock Drill Co., New York, N. Y.**—Steam or compressed air rock-drilling machine. A 60–61. 500

6 **Bolles, J. N., Baltimore, Md.**—Machinery for boring artesian wells, in operation. (*Outside of building.*) 501

6*a* **Mowbray, George M., North Adams, Mass.**—Electric batteries and exploders. A 59. 501

6*b* **Randolph, Theodore F., Morristown, N. J.**—Ditcher and excavator. C 77. 501

6*c* **Roberts, E. A. L., Titusville, Pa.**—Oil well torpedo. C 78. 501

6*d* **Robinson, John E., Boston, Mass.**—Sand and air chamber and artesian well. (*Annex 3.*) 501

7 **Bolles, Jesse N., Baltimore, Md.**—Boring machinery for artesian wells. A 56. 501

8 **Melvin & McMorris, Philadelphia, Pa.**—Artesian well, drilling and pumping. (*Outside of building.*) 501

9 **Pierce, Charles D., Peru, La Salle Co., Ill.**—Well boring and prospecting machine. One man and horse can bore 20 feet per hour. Bores any size or depth. Boulders, hard-pan, and quicksand easily handled. Has an established reputation in every State and Territory. $25 per day is made with one machine. Agents wanted in every county, also in foreign countries. Illustrated catalogue sent free on application. Address as above. (*Outside of building.*) 501

10 **Monitor Coal Cutter Co., Brazil, Ind.**—Compressed air coal-cutting machine. A 58. 502

11 **Hunt, Chas. W., New York, N. Y.**—Machinery for unloading vessels and storing cargoes. A 56. 503

12 **Sternbergh, James Hervey, Reading, Pa.**—Surface emery-grinding machine. B 37. 505

13 **Blake Crusher Co., New Haven, Conn.**—Machine for crushing ores, stones, etc. Extensively used for breaking stone for MacAdam roads, ballasting railroads, and for concrete. In mining operations, for the rapid and economical crushing of ores of all kinds, it has a world-wide reputation. A 58 *and* A 63. 505

14 **Fulton Foundry Co., Cleveland, O.**—Turn-table. A 58–59. 505

14*a* **Krom, S. R., New York, N. Y.**—Ore and laboratory separator; ore crushers. A 6ɔ. 505

15 **Kreider, Campbell, & Co., Philadelphia, Pa.**—E 50–51.

a Mineral mill. 505

b Paint mills, paint mixer. 508

16 **Coxe Bros. & Co., Jeddo, Pa.**—Working model of coal breaker. A 63. 505

17 **Baugh & Sons, Philadelphia, Pa.**—Mills for crushing and grinding minerals, bones, etc. A 61–62. 505

18 **State of Nevada, Gold Hill, Nevada.**—Quartz mill. (*South of Machinery Hall.*) 505

19 **Poole & Hunt, Baltimore, Md.**—Fertilizer and paint mixer. C 79. 505

20 **Bradford, H., Philadelphia, Pa.**—Coal and ore separator. This machine separates all solid substances that differ in specific gravity, and from the smallest particles to four inches in size. For sale by H. Bradford, room 26, Merchants' Exchange, corner Third and Walnut streets, Philadelphia. A 73. 505

21 **Albright & Stroh, Mauch Chunk, Pa.**—Coal jig for separating slate from coal, etc. B 19. 505

For classes of exhibits, indicated by numbers at end of entries, see Classification, pp. 13–15.

Mining, Chemical, Gas Machinery.

22 **Ball, Edwin P., Chicopee, Mass.**—Steam stamping machine for crushing ores and minerals. (*Annex 3.*) 505

23 **Bowron, William. M., Philadelphia, Pa.**—Waste house, fire grates, blast furnace, hot blast stoves. A 57. 506

24 **Koenigsberg, J., Lock Haven, Pa.**—Model of coke oven and discharging machine. A 57. 506

25 **Weimer, P. L., Lebanon, Pa.**—Charging apparatus for blast furnaces, blast furnace fixtures. B 69. 506

26 **Edgemoor Iron Co., Edgemoor, Del.**—Rotary puddler, hydraulic forged eye-bars, wrought and cast iron work for Main Exhibition Building. C 22. 506

26*a* **Caldwell & Mather, Philadelphia, Pa.**—Melting furnace. (*Annex 1.*) 506

26*b* **Manes, James, sr., New Haven, Conn.**—Revolving globe furnace for smelting gold and silver ores, etc. A 57–58. 506

26*c* **Baker, Charles H., Philadelphia, Pa.**—Self-gauging Bessemer tuyeres. (*Annex 2.*) 507

27 **Tully, John W., Industrial Paint, Varnish, and Filler Works,** Twentieth and Parrish streets, Philadelphia, Pa.—Paints and varnishes, scraper filling, Belgian varnish filler, American paint filling, Roman filler, iron priming and finishing paint, lubricating paste, wood filling, and French washing blue. A 67. 508

28 **Bryan & Snyder, Philadelphia, Pa.**—Manufacture of silver-plated ware. A 66. 508

29 **Zindgraf & Hohenadel, 215 Race** street, Philadelphia, Pa.—Machine for grinding and mixing paint. Manufacturers of machinery for grinding and mixing paint. Also mills for grinding drugs, spices, etc. Our mills are made with an improved stand for adjusting upper stone. A 66. 508

30 **Fichtenberg, Werner, New York, N. Y.**—Insect powder, exterminating powders and papers, powder bellows, bird lime. A 66. 508

31 **Reeves, John W., Philadelphia, Pa.**—Soap cutting machine. A 67. 508

31*a* **Condit, Hanson, & Van Winkle,** Newark, N. J.—Electro-plating machine. Condit, Hanson & Van Winkle, 236 Market street, corner Mulberry, Newark, N. J., exhibit the "Weston-Dynamo Electric Machine," doing electro, nickel, silver, gold, and copper plating. The machine is simple, easy to manage, requiring scarcely any attention. It is strong, durable, compact, reliable, powerful, and requires but little force to run it. It is a self-regulator, automatically adjusting the current to the amount of work done. From the great force obtained from a small amount of material, and the simplicity of its construction, the machines are sold at very low prices, $75 and upwards. The conversion of motion into electricity and its use for the electro deposition of the metals, etc., is of great importance, as it not only avoids the use of expensive materials and the deleterious and corrosive fumes produced by batteries, but saves a great deal of time, and the current is more uniform than can be obtained by the use of batteries. B 73. 508

32 **King, Wm. H., Philadelphia, Pa.**—Soap press. A 66. 508

33 **Hagner Drug Milling Co., Philadelphia, Pa.**—Double run flaxseed chasing mills. A 64. 508

34 **Mosser, W. F., & Co., Allentown, Pa.**—Bark mill, with independent grinding segments. A 48 *and Pump annex.* 508

35 **Carr Calvin, & Co., Cleveland, O.**—Galvanized iron circular cornice machinery. Owners of all circular machine and nearly all the brake and folding machine patents. See circular. B 68. 508

35*a* **Averill Chemical Paint Co., New York, N. Y.**—Paint, all colors, ready for use. (*Outside of building.*) 508

35*b* **Wyman, L. A., Boston, Mass.**—Ink and paint mill. A 66. 508

36 **Wallace & Sons, Ansonia, Conn.**—Magneto-electric machines, for deposition of metals and for electric light, proprietors of brass and copper rolling mills, Ansonia, Conn., office and warehouse 89 Chambers and 71 Reade streets, New York. Manufacturers of brass, rolled and in sheets, copper rivets and burs, brass and copper tubing, brass and copper wire, brass door rail, brass and iron jack chains, stair rods, copper tacks and nails, braziers, bolt and sheathing copper, etc., kerosene burners and trimmings. Price lists, with discount, furnished on application. A 67. 508

36*a* **Towsley, L. D., & Co., Philadelphia, Pa.**—Gas utilizer for manufacturing illuminating gas. A 65. 509

36*b* **Gilbert & Barker Manufacturing Co.,** Springfield, Mass.—Gas machine. A 77. 509

36*c* **Eichholt, John H., Greenpoint, L. I., N. Y.**—Gas generator. A 67. 509

36*d* **Patton, J. Desha, Norristown, Pa.**—Cylinder, governor, etc. C 27. 509

36*e* **McIlhenny, George A., Washington, D. C.**—Door for gas retorts. C 27. 509

36*f* **Hickman, Towsley, & Swan, St. Louis, Mo.**—Gas utilizer for manufacturing illuminating gas. A 65. 509

36*g* **Thomsen, Alexander, Worcester, Mass.**—Governor for gas. C 27. 509

36*h* **Day, George H., Haverhill, Mass.**—Lime hurdles and screens. C 27. 509

38 **Goodwin, Wm. W., & Co., 1016 Filbert** street, Philadelphia, Pa.—Gas meters of all descriptions, station meters, standard cubic foot measures and provers, photometers of all kinds, candle scales, pressure registers and gauges, pressure and vacuum registers, apparatus for determination of sulphur and ammonia in coal gas, density and specific gravity apparatus, etc. A 80. 509

38*a* **Walker, James H., Milwaukee, Wis.**—Model of gas works. C 27. 509

38*b* **Towsley, L. D., Cincinnati, O.**—Gas utilizer for manufacturing illuminating gas, and for saving one-half the coal-gas of cities. It is automatic, safe, durable, simple, and cheap. A 65. 509

39 **Morris, Tasker, & Co., Philadelphia, Pa.**—Gas-works machinery. A 70 *and* C 27. 509

40 **Harris, Griffin, & Co., Philadelphia, Pa.**—Gas meters, registers, gauges, photometers, provers, pumps, exhaust governors. A 78. 509

For location of objects, indicated by letter and figure, see Key to Notation, p. 10; ground plan, p. 11.

Gas Machines, Wood-working Machinery.

41 Mervine, Samuel P., jr., Philadelphia, Pa.—Gas regulator. A 73. 509

41*a* Automatic Gas Governor Co. of the U. S., Philadelphia, Pa.—Automatic gas governor. A 73. 509

41*b* Rand, A. W., Philadelphia, Pa.—Gas machine. A 71. 509

42 Rex & Bockius, Philadelphia, Pa.—Illuminating gas generator. C 69. 509

43 Excelsior Gas Machine Co., South Norwalk, Conn. — Gas machines. A 75. 509

44 Improved Steiner Gas Machine Co., Philadelphia, Pa.—Portable gas machines. A 75. 509

45 Walworth Manufacturing Co., Boston, Mass.—Gas machines for lighting country residences, public buildings, etc. A 76, E 75, *and* B 41. 509

46 Imperial Manufacturing Co., New York, N. Y.—Gas machines. A 73. 509

47 Tiffany, J. C., Boston, Mass.—Oil gas generator, dry gasometer, process for removing naphthaline in gas conduits, platinum appliance for combustion of coal in furnaces. (*Outside of building.*) 509

48 Vasquez, Chas. L., Philadelphia, Pa.—Automatic gas machine. A 73. 509

49 Starr, Jesse W., & Son, Camden, N. J.—Gas works, pipe. (*Outside of building.*) 509

50 Novelty Gas Machine Co., Baltimore, Md.—Carburetting gas machine. A 73 *and outside of building.* 509

51 Gruber, John P., Jersey City, N. J.—Gas works. A 53. 509

52 Bean, Joseph H., Cincinnati, O.—Automatic gas machine for residences, churches, etc. A 72. 509

53 American Meter Co., New York and Philadelphia.—Standard provers, meters, pressure registers, gauges, exhaust governors, bar and jet photometers; also analytical apparatus generally. A 69. 509

54 Burr, William H., Philadelphia, Pa.—Apparatus for making hydro-carbon gas. A 68. 509

55 Excelsior Gas Machine Co., South Norwalk, Conn.—Retort gas machine. A 75 *and outside of building.* 509

56 Daschbach, E. J., Pittsburg, Pa.—Gas machine, with automatic carburetter. A 72. 509

57 Ramsey, Robert H., Pottsville, Pa.—Bituminous coal gas machine, adapted to private residences, stores, and manufactories. Furnishes coal gas of largely increased illuminating power, at less than one dollar per thousand feet. Indorsed by insurance underwriters. A 72. 509

57*a* Rowland, T. F., Greenpoint, N. Y.—Specimens of forgings; model of steam stoker. A 69 *and* D 31. 509

Machines and Tools for Working Metal, Wood, and Stone.

58 Riehlé Bros., Philadelphia, Pa.—Mortising machines. E 54. 510

59 Douglass Manufacturing Co., Seymour, Conn.—Mechanics' edge tools and boring implements. A 43. 510

60 Lane & Bodley, Cincinnati, O.—Stroke power mortisers. A 50 *and saw-mill.* 510

60*a* Gerlach, Peter, & Co., Cleveland, O.—Stave-sawing machine. A 34. 510

60*b* Andrews, E., Williamsport, Pa.—Saw-sharpener, cross-cut saw handles, saws, gang-saw, hooks and stirrups, etc. B 78. 510

60*c* Palmer, Samuel R., Belfast, Me.—Stave-jointing machine. A 28. 510

60*d* Atkins, E. C., & Co., Indianapolis, Ind.—Saws. B 5 *and* A 5. 510

60*e* Knowlton, John L., Sharon Hill, Pa.—Saws, saw-sharpening and planer knife, and grinding machines. A 1 *and* B 1, *and saw-mill.* 510

60*f* Stranges Cylinder Saw & Machine Co., Taunton, Mass.—Cylinder-saw stave machine; foot lathe. B 74. 510

60*g* Curtis & Co., St. Louis, Mo.—Slotted circular saw. B 79. 510

60*h* Ames & Frost, Chicago, Ill.—Dovetailing machine. B 61. 510

61 Norris, W. R., Fort Ann, N. Y.—Diagonal planing and polishing machine. B 60. 510

62 Eureka Manufacturing Co., Boston, Mass.—Lathe, scroll saw, scroll saw attachment. B 36–37. 510

63 Havens, W. H., Paterson, N. J.—Iron circular saw tables. B 56. 510

64 Trump Bros., Wilmington, Del.—Foot-power scroll saws. B 57. 510

65 Burk, Wm. B., & Co., Philadelphia, Pa.—Cork-cutting machines, cork-tapering machine. B 60. 510

65*a* Dowling, T. W., Detroit, Mich.—Scroll saw. B 61. 510

65*b* Barnes, W. F. & John, Rockford, Ill.—Scroll and circular saws; lathes. B 57. 510

65*c* Russell, S. J., Chicago, Ill.—Wood lathes. B 56. 510

65*d* Providence Saw Works, Providence, R. I.—Jig-sawing machines. B 56. 510

66 Buss, Charles, & Sons, Marlboro', N. H.—Rotary bed, paneling, planers, band saw, lathes, slotter, slitter, cutting-up machines. B 49. 510

67 First & Pryibil, New York, N. Y.—Re-slitting band saw, carving machine, saws, planers, etc., for wood working. B 43. 510

68 Disston, Henry, & Sons, Philadelphia, Pa.—Saws and saw tools, trowels, carpenters' tools, files, knives, butt hinges, sheet steel. B 41–46. 510

68*a* Baxter, C. M., Lebanon, N. H.—Band saws; planer. B 64. 510

68*b* Forstner, Benjamin, Salem, Oregon.—Wood auger. D 68. 510

69 Walker Bros., Philadelphia, Pa.—Wood working machinery. B 53.

a No. 0. Scroll sawing machine, even tension spring, adjustable fastenings for saw blades and combined belt shifter and brake.

b No. 1. Scroll sawing machine-spring, has even tension, combined clamp fastening for saw blades; lower guides have parallel adjustment and the dust from saw is

For classes of exhibits, indicated by numbers at end of entries, see Classification, pp. 13–15.

Wood-working Machinery.

blown away from the slides by a fan blower attached.

c Power-feed panel raiser, for panels of any width or raise or thickness; has upright spindles and heads, swing table and, adjustable guards. 510

70 Wallace & Keller, Philadelphia, Pa. —Turning lathe. B 67. 510

71 Crossley, Harry A., Cleveland, O. —Stair jointer. B 67. 510

72 Silver & Deming Manufacturing Co., Salem, O.—Hub boxing machines, adjustable hollow auger, spoke tenoning machines. B 66 *and* F 54. 510

73 Graham, J. S., & Co., Rochester, N. Y.—Planing, tongueing, and grooving machines, circular re-sawing machine, moulding machine, matching heads, and cutters. B 44. 510

74 Moseley, Jerome S., Syracuse, N. Y. —Scroll saw machine, boring machine. In all of the wood-sawing machines on exhibition, the great principles involved in their mechanical construction are the many devices for starting, stopping, and controlling its speed without taking the attention of the operators from their work. The manner of holding the saw, and the manner of giving the saws more or less "rake or feed," have been the difficult problems to solve. Moseley's Patent Eureka Scroll Sawing Machine, with its improved apparatus, can be run at a speed from 800 to 1100 revolutions per minute, and will saw the lightest veneered work, such as piano or melodeon work, and is capable of running saws from one-sixteenth of an inch wide to any width that can be practically used in a scroll saw machine. The blower and self-adjusting blowpipe is a new feature, which adds greatly to the convenience of running and working this machine. It is attached in a simple manner to the upright shaft in which the saws are worked, and serves every purpose of blowing gently away from the work all sawdust that accumulates. The machine is admirably adapted for all kinds of scroll sawing, from the lightest to the heaviest, and does the work well. This machine received the first prize medal at the fair of the New York State Agricultural Society, held at Utica in the fall of 1870; also at Elmira, 1872; also at Albany, 1873, and at Rochester, 1874; also received a medal of special award at the Fair of the American Institute, held at New York city in 1872; and the first prize medal at the International Exhibition, Buffalo, N. Y., 1872. B 63. 510

75 Griffiths, John W., New York, N. Y. —Wood bending machines. B 74 *and* E 5. 510

76 Battle Creek Machinery Co., Battle Creek, Mich.—Carving, paneling, variety moulding, and dovetailing machine; moulders' solid steel cutters. B 55. 510

77 Lane Manufacturing Co., Montpelier, Vt.—Portable single circular saw mill, designed for common use as a portable saw mill, and also intended for use in fixed establishments of ordinary capacity. Sawyer sets the log, uprights both receded, and when desired, advanced, by power; dogging devices especially adapted for "live" or "through-and-through" sawing, and for holding frozen logs. Gauge roll (Fairbank's patent) in front of saw; tapering devices, elevated scale or rule. Over 2000 of these mills (Lane's patent) in use. Heavy double circular saw mill, intended for first-class establishments of the largest capacity; 72 inch lower saw and 40 inch upper saw, feed and jigging back works, operated from either front or back side of frame; saw-guide quickly removable; uprights advanced by both forward and backward motions of lever; setter rides on carriage; rolled-steel headblocks; improved dogs catch under and upper sides of logs, and swing away from saw when released; uprights receded or advanced by power. (*Saw Mill Building*); 24 inch traveling-bed or "Farrar," planing machine; 18 inch stationary bed or roll-feed planing machine; heavy matching, or tongueing and grooving machine; light matching, or tongueing and grooving machine. A 35. 510

78 Marston, J. M., 6 Taber St., Boston, Mass.—Combined hand and foot circular sawing, boring, and mitreing machines. E 77. 510

78*a* Holmes, James, Belfast, Me.—Machine for jointing staves. B 77. 510

78*b* Chesney, R. M., Philadelphia, Pa. —Scroll saw and wood-jointing machine; process shown. A 44–46. 510

78*c* Boynton, Eben B., New York, N.Y. —Saws, frames, sets, files, handles, etc. B 41. 510

79 Chase Turbine Manufacturing Co., Orange, Mass. (*Saw Mill annex.*)

a Machine for sawing staves, spool stock, box boards, etc. 510

b Leverset and circular saw mill. 511

80 Beach, Henry Lloyd, Montrose, Pa. —Scroll-sawing machines. There is no class of machinery on exhibition that attracts greater attention than the scroll sawing machines. Among the number that possess merits as to their mechanism are the two manufactured by Henry L. Beach, of Montrose, Pa. The No. 2, which is mostly of wrought iron, insuring great strength and durability, is especially noticeable; instead of the ordinary tight and loose pulley, the crank shaft carries a friction pulley, by which the saw is made to start and stop instantly without shifting the belt—a great saving of time on inside work. Both the Nos. 1 and 2 are provided with saw clamps, and very powerful and elastic spring, which give an even tension on the saw of from 10 to 75 lbs. No. 1 has a tilting table, which for pattern work is indispensable, and is used almost daily in any shop. Both the machines have air pumps, steel bearing for each saw, and are adjustable in every part to take up all lost tension. A 29. 510

81 Fay, J. A., & Co., Cincinnati, O.— Patent wood-cutting machinery. In the choice of machinery it is an object to select the best adapted to the work to be done. That a machine may be profitable, it must be so constructed as not likely to get out of order. In the display in Machinery Hall, section 8, columns 61, 62, and 63, by J. A. Fay & Co. of Cincinnati, of the several varieties of improved wood-cutting machines they manufacture, and the additions added to them during the past five years, it is claimed that the new features introduced place their machines

Wood-working Machinery.

in the front rank. The high reputation and character of this firm throughout this country and Europe, may be attributable—1st, to the high character, and excellence of their machines; 2d, to the improvements made upon them from year to year, increasing their labor-saving features; 3d, extensive facilities and abundant capital for manufacturing. Of the different machines for planing, matching, band sawing, boring, variety wood workers, combination edging and ripping-saw tables, carving, band re-sawing, and others for sash, doors, blinds, furniture, wheels, felloes, spokes, and agricultural implements, allusion here can only be made to the more important ones. The No. 2 patent variety wood-worker is peculiar and simple in its mechanical construction, and has capacity for great range and variety of work, being constructed in a substantial manner, and possesses many labor-saving qualities. Their patent band saw with elastic wheels embraces many new and valuable labor-saving features by which the breakage of saws is prevented. Their new carving and paneling machine is designed to meet the demands for an effective machine at low cost, and is adapted for any designs of panels in fine furniture, piano, and organ manufactures. The combination edging and ripping-saw table is built wholly of metal, and is quite novel, having a rising and falling saw, hand and power feed, and with a parallel movement of the gauge or fence for rapid and accurate work. It is also provided with planed iron table, and is in all respects admirably adapted for the purposes designed. The large six-roll double cylinder patent planing and matching machine seems to be perfect in all of its appointments. It is strong and powerful. It embraces many new and valuable improvements designed for the saving of labor, economy of lumber, and increasing the quantity of production. The patent band re-sawing machine embodies several novel features which have attracted much attention from visitors, not only of this country, but of Europe. It is simple, powerful, has a large range and capacity for work. The manner of connecting the two wheel shafts with an outside connection, the automatic friction feed, revolving frictionless guides, the perfect ease of adjustment, and ready manipulations by the operator, with many others which might be added, make it a very interesting exhibit for those interested in the reduction of lumber. B 62. 510

82 Clark Thread Co., Newark, N. J.—Self-acting spool-winding machine, spool-turning machine. C 33, *and* A 34. (*See also exhibit in Main Building*, A 76.) 510

83 Holmes, E. & B., Buffalo, N.Y.—Machines for making kegs, barrels, staves, and shooks. B 50–52. 510

84 Bush & Smith, West New Brighton, N. Y.—Wood-working machinery. B 77. 510

85 S. A. Woods Machine Co., Boston, Mass.—Planing, matching, moulding, surfacing, and other wood-working machinery. B 54. 510

86 Patterson, C. R., Pittston, Pa.—Pressure blocks independent, showing construction and same applied to J. C. Fay's planer. B 61. 510

87 Buckeye Engine Co., Salem, O.—Automatic shingle machine. B 70. 510

88 Richards, London, & Kelley, Philadelphia, Pa.—Wood-cutting machinery. A 44–46 *and Annex 1 and 2.* 510

89 Burt, C. S. & S., Dunleith, Ill.—Machines for sawing shingles, barrel-heads, etc. B 54. 510

90 Blaisdell, J. H., & Co., Philadelphia, Pa.—Wood-working machinery. B 75–76. 510

91 Warren, John, Detroit, Mich.—Paneling machine. B 78. 510

92 Bentel, Margedant, & Co., Hamilton, O.—Universal wood-working machines. Planing and matching, jointing, band and scroll saws, boring and shaping machines. Bentel, Margedant, & Co. have on exhibition twelve different machines, each of them presenting new features, which are improvements, and add greatly to their value and usefulness, and are all first-class in mechanical construction. The patent universal wood-workers for planing out of wind, jointing, squaring, smoothing, beveling, cornering, chamfering, tapering, mitreing, rabbeting, tenoning, halfing, panel-raising, tongueing, grooving, hand-matching, rolling-joints, gaining, plowing, serpentine and waved moulding, fluting, beading, ripping, splitting, cross-cut sawing, straight, circular, oval, and elliptical mouldings, dovetailing, etc. The patent band-sawing machine is, in its construction and improvements, new and highly valuable. This is a patent machine, the improvements on which are entirely new features. The mechanical cause of the breakage of band-saw blades unprecedentedly and successfully removed. The buckling, friction, heating, and crystallization of the saw-blades entirely overcome. Instantaneous starting and stopping of the motion of the saw-blade. The patent scroll saw machine with uniform tension is certain at all points of the stroke. The Hamilton patent surface planer for planing out of wind, jointing, squaring, smoothing, beveling, cornering, chamfering, mitreing, and tapering, is furnished with patent triangular shear-knife cutter-heads. It planes both smoothly and accurately. Sec. B 7, columns 51–52 *and* 53. 510

93 Ross, E. W., & Co., Fulton, N. Y.—Iron framed foot jointer for barrel staves. F 64, *and outside.* 510

94 Seymour & Whittock, Newark, N. J.—Sash dovetailing, mitre, wiring, borer, mortising machines, and sewing machine motors. A 39. 510

95 Smith, H. B., Smithville, N. J.—Iron framed wood-working machinery, with improvements. B 47. 510

96 Baggs, J. T., Bridgeport, O.—Sawing and grooving machine. B 60. 510

97 Rogers, C. B., & Co., Norwich, Conn.—Wood-working machinery. B 75–76. 500

98 Armstrong, Bro., & Co., Pittsburg, Pa.—Cork cutter and tapering machinery. A 5–39. 510

99 Greenlee, Bro., & Co., Chicago, Ill.—Sash, blind, and door clamping machines; sash, door and blind relishing and mortising machine. A 30. 510

100 Skidmore, A. F. & Geo. C., Grand Rapids, Mich.—Barrel hoop machines and coilers. A 49. 510

For classes of exhibits, indicated by numbers at end of entries, see Classification, pp. 13–15.

Wood and Metal-working Machinery.

101 **Houston, Smith, & Co., Montgomery, Pa.**—Outside bearing moulder, door tenoner, door mortiser. A 31. 510

102 **Goodall, Braun, & Waters, Philadelphia, Pa.**—Panel planer, planer and matcher, surfacer and matcher, band saw. B 77–78. 510

102*a* **Gould, Roscoe J., Newark, N. J.**—Dovetailing machine. A 33. 510

103 **Mussot, A., Cincinnati, O.**—General wood-working machinery. A 29. 510

104 **Greenwich Machine Works, Greenwich, N. Y.**—Weavers' wood-working machines, driven by hand, foot, or power. A 37. 510

105 **Knapp Dovetailing Machine Co., Northampton, Mass.**—Machines for cabinet dovetailing. A 35. 510

106 **Combined Power Co., New York, N. Y.**—Geared machinery for all powers. A 34. 510

107 **Colloday, Jos. O., & Bro., Philadelphia, Pa.**—Jointing machine, band saw machine, etc. B 56. 510

108 **Gleason, John, Philadelphia, Pa.**—Spoke and handle turning lathe, etc. B 64. 510

109 **Babbitt, F. S., Taunton, Mass.**—Combination foot lathe. B 61. 510

110 **Howard Manufacturing Co., Belfast, Me.**—Mitring machines, easily adjustable in all the different parts, cuts all angles, used by cabinet makers, carpenters, picture frame makers, car builders, etc. A 28. 510

111 **Earle, Benj. A., Philadelphia, Pa.**—Wool-oiling machine. D 48. 510

112 **Whitney, Baxter D., Winchendon, Mass.**—Wood-working machines. B 79–80. 510

113 **Benson, A. M., Cleveland, O.**—Stave machinery dresser and jointer. A 29. 510

114 **Goulding, Johnston, & Co., Louisville, Ky.**—Hoop and splint machine. B 66. 510

115 **Hart, Roswell, Rochester, N. Y.**—Machines for making half-round hoops for barrels, etc. B 46. 510

116 **Pope Manufacturing Co., Boston, Mass.**—Lathe scroll saw. Acme lathe $9.00; scroll saw, $5.00 and $7.00; darning machine, $10.00. C 64. 510

117 **Buck, Martin, Lebanon, N. H.**—Single, double, and triple tenoning machines, blind mortising and boring machine, slat planer, wedge and pin machine, band saws, etc. B 64. 510

118 **Bustin, Robert, St. Johns, N. B.**—Fire escape. Bustin's portable fire escape is one of the many new inventions that deserve special notice for its simplicity, cheapness, durability, and almost certain security to life. It is simple in its construction, easily adjusted, and can be carried in a small valise, thus insuring the traveler that, no matter how high in a hotel, he can in a moment rescue his own life, and if he has others in the room in the same perilous situation, save them at the same time. It can be used in many ways, as it is so ingeniously made that it is always ready for use. There is no machinery connected with it. It cannot get out of order. In case the lower part of the building is so enveloped in flames as to render a direct descent impossible, the parties can make a descent across the street. It is now on exhibition at the north end of Machinery Hall, where practical illustrations of its workings can be seen. The fire escapes, all complete, cost from $10.00 to $15.00. In every case you can save your apparatus. 564

119 **Lane & Bodley, Cincinnati, O.**—Stationary portable circular saw mill. (A 50, *Saw mill.*) 511

120 **Eureka Bark Mill Co., Lancaster, Pa.**—Bark mills. A 28. 511

121 **Harbert & Raymond, Philadelphia, Pa.**—Portable saw mill. (*Saw mill.*) 511

122 **Ross, E. W., & Co., Fulton, N. Y.**—Automatic circular saw mill. F 64 *and outside.* 511

122*a* **Scholfield, Socrates, Providence, R. I.**—Logging saw. (*Saw mill*, B 12.) 511

122*b* **Meiners, C., & Sons, Philadelphia, Pa.**—Band, saw mill and head blocks. B 13. 511

122*c* **Harvey, Easton, & Co., Lock Haven, Pa.**—Gang lathe mill. B 15. 511

122*d* **Stearns Manufacturing Co., Erie, Pa.**—Circular saw mill, double edging machine, log jacker, log turner, steam engine. (*Saw mill*, A 3, B 3.) 511

122*e* **Allis, Edward S., & Co., Milwaukee, Wis.**—Saw mill machinery. (*Saw mill*, A 10–11.) 511

123 **Flint, C. M., Fitchburg, Mass.**—Saw mill. B 13. (*Saw mill.*) 511

124 **Noyes, Frank G., Clinton, Iowa.**—Gang edger with four circular saws. B 12. (*Saw mill.*) 511

125 **Duncannon Iron Co., Philadelphia, Pa.**—Nail-cutting machines. B 25. 512

126 **Pennsylvania Tack Works, Norristown, Pa.**—Tack machines and their products. B 26. 512

127 **Garrison, A., & Co., Pittsburg, Pa.**—Chilled rolls for rolling metals. Manufacturers of chilled and sand rolls, ore and clay pulverizers, rotary squeezers, Haskin's patent double spiral pinions, and rolling mill castings of every description. B 27. 512

128 **Middleton, John W., Philadelphia, Pa.**—Cast and wrought iron, and steel ready for the planer. C 77. 512

128*a* **Lattimon, D. I., Philadelphia, Pa.**—Suction and blast fan. B 64. 512

128*b* **Hyslop, John, jr., Abington, Mass.**—Machine for making tacks and shoe nails. Hill, Clarke, & Co., selling agents, Boston, Mass. B 35. 512

128*c* **Morris, Wheeler, & Co., Philadelphia, Pa.**—Nail machine in operation, boiler and ship plates, nails, puddled bars, ores, etc. B 24. 513

129 **Flagg, Stanley G., & Co., Philadelphia, Pa.**—Malleable gray iron and steel castings. A 41. 513

130 **Midvale Steel Works, Philadelphia, Pa.**—Bar steel, steel forgings and castings. C 23. 513

(See also classification 573.)

For location of objects, indicated by letter and figure, see Key to Notation, p. 10; ground plan, p. 11.

Metal-working Machinery.

131 Dick, C. J. A., Philadelphia, Pa., Phosphor Bronze Smelting Works, 2038 Washington avenue.—Phosphor bronze ingots, axle bearings, castings, bells, wire, sheets, tubes, etc. A 6, 42. 513

132 Eames, Charles J., New York, N. Y.—Petroleum iron boiler plates, forge blooms, billets, jack plates, horseshoes, etc. (*Annex I.*) 513

132*a* Roberts, E. A. L., Titusville, Pa. —Compound metal. C 78. 513

133 Reed, S. G., Boston, Mass.—Apparatus for heating locomotive and carriage tires with gas; portable gas attachment for lighting streets. E 69. 513

134 Malleable Iron Fittings Co., Brawford, Conn.—Malleable iron steam and gas fittings and castings. A 4. 513

135 Lawrence, Frank, Philadelphia, Pa.—Cupola and trier. (*In building of C. Noble & Co.*) 513

135*a* Phosphor Bronze Smelting Works, C. J. A. Dick, Philadelphia, Pa. —See No. 131. 513

135*b* Harris, Samuel, Springfield, Mass.—Sifting machines. (*Adjoining Annex 2.*) 513

136 Keystone Portable Forge Co., 120 Exchange Place, Philadelphia, Pa.—Portable forges and pressure and exhaust blowers; forges, portable or stationary, for hand or power, forty-seven styles and sizes, for every class of work from lightest to heaviest, and patented and sold in all leading countries. English, French, and Belgian patents for sale. Also blowers for every purpose requiring either pressure or exhaust; all shown in operation. (*Annex No. 1, Machinery Hall.*) 514

137 Carnell, F. L. & D. R., 1844 Germantown avenue, Philadelphia, Pa.—Steam hammers. See illustrated catalogue. (*Annex* 1 *and* 3.) 514

137*a* Kacy, Robert F., Philadelphia, Pa.—Hand fan-blower. (*Adjoining Annex 2.*) 514

138 Forsaith, S. C., & Co., Manchester, N. H.—Abbe bolt forging machine, spring hammers. E 39 *and annex.* 514

139 Ferris & Miles, Philadelphia, Pa.—Machine tools and steam hammers. B 31 *and* 32. 514

140 Merrill, Chas., & Sons, New York, N. Y.—Drop hammer, parallel vises, differential blocks. C 4 *and Annex* 2. 514

141 Hammond, H., & Co., Hartford, Conn.—Cast steel hammer, anvil, and drop forgings. A 41. 514

142 Metz, George W., & Sons, Philadelphia, Pa.—Bellows. (*Annex* 1.) 514

143 Bayliss, John, New York, N. Y.—Hot blast water tuyere and forge, blacksmiths' bellows, portable forge and bellows. (*Annex* 1.) 514

144 Bradley Manufacturing Co., Syracuse, N. Y.—Cushioned helve hammers. B 29. 514

145 Tubular Barrow & Truck Manufacturing Co., New York, N.Y.—Self-acting steam hammer. (*Annex* 1.) 514

146 Empire Portable Forge Co., Troy, N. Y.—Portable fan-blowing forges. (*Annex* 1.) 514

147 Bullock, T. H., & Co., Cleveland, O.—Blacksmiths', moulders', hand, and coopers' bellows. (*Annex* 1.) 514

148 Hull & Belden Co., Danbury, Conn. —Power forging hammer, samples of drop forgings. C 72. 514

148*a* Mason, John L., Camden, N.J.—Tire shrinker, blacksmiths' tuyere and pinch bar. (*Annex* 1.) 514

148*b* Schierloh, H., Jersey City, N. J.—Heat welding compound, with samples of iron and steel welded. (*Annex* 1.) 514

148*c* Stiles & Barker Press Co., Middletown, Conn.—B 34, *and Annex* 1.
a Drop hammers. 514
b Sheet metal presses. 515

148*d* Pusey, Jones, & Co., Wilmington, Del.—D 33.
a Riveting machine. 514
b Sheet iron cleaner. 515

149 Howard, George C., 13½ S. Eighteenth street, Philadelphia, Pa.—Grindstone box, hacker, for truing and sharpening the stone, drill-press, boring and sapping machine. B 31. 515

150 Cooper, John H., Philadelphia, Pa. —Model of mechanical movement. C 31. 515

151 Mitchell, J. E., Philadelphia, Pa. Founded, 1810.—Column of 38 varieties of grindstones; two thousand tons in stock; seven sizes of machinists' grindstones in iron boxes. Send for descriptive pamphlet. B 28 *and* 29. 515

152 Sternbergh, J. H., Reading, Pa.—Surface-grinding machine, bolts, nuts, washers, rivets, wood screws, etc. B 37. 515

153 American Twist Drill Co., Woonsocket, R. I.—Automatic knife-grinders, emery wheels, and machinery. C 32. 515

154 Cooper, Jones, & Cadbury, Philadelphia, Pa.—Lathes. B 19. 515

155 Wattis, Edward, jr., Philadelphia, Pa.—Patent pocket flasks, with metallic collars secured without cement. B 34. 515

155*a* Laurence, Benjamin, Lowell, Mass.—Index and plain milling machine. B 29. 515

155*b* Sawyer, J. A., & Son, Worcester, Mass.—Combined hand and power iron planer, Hill, Clarke, & Co., selling agents, Boston, Mass. C 40. 515

155*c* Galligher, Bernard, Lynn, Mass. —Emery grinder; drills. C 39–40. 515

155*d* Weed & Co., Boston, Mass.—File cutting machine. G 30. 515

156 Stevens, W. X., East Brookfield, Mass.—Centre cutting shears for iron, to cut old steamboat shafts, rails, chain links, bolts, angle and merchant iron, cold; power unlimited. B 34. 515

157 Ferris & Miles, Philadelphia, Pa.—Planing, shaping, slotting, drilling, cut-off, turning, boring, punching, and shearing machines. B 31–32 *and Annex* 1. 515

158 Brown & Sharpe Manufacturing Co., Providence, R. I.—Machinery and tools. Manufacturers of universal and plain milling machines, grinding, screw, and tapping machines, screw finishing and

Metal-working Machinery.

polishing machines, reels, assorters, scales, and testers for roving and yarn, for cotton and woolen manufacturers' use, patent cutters for gear wheels, and for taps, beamers, twist drills, irregularly formed sewing machine and gun parts, milling and screw slotting cutters. B 38. 515

159 **Lobdell Car Wheel Co., Wilmington,** Del.—Solid die rivet machine. E 65. 515

159*a* **Richards, I. P., Providence, R. I.** —Punches for metal. A 42. 515

159*b* **Hendey Machine Co., Walcottville,** Conn.—Planer and shaper. D 35. 515

159*c* **Howard, William H., Philadelphia,** Pa.—Loom frame with automatic let-offs. B 31. 515

159*d* **Cosmopolitan Emery Wheel Co.,** Philadelphia, Pa.—Emery wheels for grinding saws, tools, etc. (*Annex* 1.) 515

160 **American Saw Co., Trenton, N. J.** —B 33.
- *a* Movable tooth circular, perforated, and solid saws. 510
- *b* Eccentric-geared power punching and shearing machines. 515

161 **Cornell University Machine Shop,** Ithaca, N. Y.—Foot lathe, magneto-electrical machine, measuring machine, tools, and gauges. B 68. 515

162 **Chase Manufacturing Co., New** York, N. Y.—Portable pipe and bolt cutting and threading machine. B 28. 515

163 **Smith, Oberlin, & Bro., Bridgeton,** N. J.—Upright or inclined foot and power presses, for cutting or drawing tinware, oil-can makers' tools, pipe tools, special drills, etc. C 27. 515

164 **Lovegrove & Co., Philadelphia, Pa.** —Pipe threading and cutting machine. B 75 *and Boiler House* 4. 515

165 **Thorne, De Haven, & Co., Philadelphia,** Pa.—Drilling machines. B 30. 515

166 **George & Du Laney, New York, N.** Y.—Screw machinery. C 55 *and* B 29. 515

166*a* **Clough & Williamson, Newark,** N. J.—Wire corkscrews and handles; machine for manufacturing same. B 38. 515

166*b* **Edwards, E. B., Columbia, Pa.**— Axle rolls. B 40. 515

166*c* **Cushing, N. B., Jersey City, N. J.** —Shears, and punching machines. B 26. 515

167 **Merriman, A. H., West Meriden,** Conn.—Power punching press. B 29. 515

168 **Jones, Lamson, & Co., Windsor, Vt.** —Engine lathes, screw machines, gang drills, etc. B 36. 515

170 **Sellers, William, & Co., Philadelphia,** Pa.—C 18 *to* 25 *and Annex* 1.
- *a* Steam hammers. 514
- *b* Machine tools, punching and shearing machines. 515

171 **Washburn Machine Shop, Worcester** Free Institute, Department Mechanical Engineering, Worcester, Mass.— Lathes with hardened steel bearings; grinding machines and drawing stands. C 38. 515

172 **Spiral Elliptic Spring Works, Cincinnati,** O.—Machinery for making upholstering springs. E 70. 515

173 **Worcester, E. J., & Co., Worcester,** Mass.—Vertical drills for metals, blacksmith's lathe. C 32. 515

174 **Schon, Mathias, Englishtown,** N. J.—Tire upsetting machine. (*Annex.*) 515

175 **Nichols, Pickering, & Co., Philadelphia,** Pa.—Portable rail punches. D 67. 515

176 **Prentice & Co., Worcester, Mass.** —Lathes, slide rests, drills. C 31. 515

177 **Van Hagen, C., & Co., Philadelphia,** Pa.—Rotary shapers, iron planers, drill sharpeners, drills, and boring tools. C 30. 515

177*a* **Vitrified Wheel and Emery Co.,** Ashland, Mass.—Emery and emery wheels. (*Annex.*) 515

177*b* **Long, Allstater, & Co., Hamilton,** O.—Punching and shearing machines. B 36. 515

177*c* **Broadbooks & Co., Batavia, N.Y.** —Folding chairs. C 43. 515

177*d* **Howard Iron Works, Buffalo,** N.Y.—Propeller wheel. C 29–30. 515

177*e* **Dudgeon, Richard, New York,** N.Y.—Punches. C 27. 515

177*f* **Temple, Edward B., Philadelphia,** Pa.—Planing machine for metals, etc. B 28. 515

177*g* **Old Colony Rivet Works, New** York, N.Y.—Iron planers, shears, cutters, punches, drilling machines, rivets, etc. B 28. 515

177*h* **Clark, John A., Newark, N. J.**— Drip pan for kerosene and other liquids. C 30. 515

178 **Miller's Falls Co., Miller's Falls,** Mass.—A 40.
- *a* Scroll saw. 510
- *b* Iron cutter, drilling machines. 515
- *c* Vises. 519

179 **Putnam Machine Co., Fitchburg,** Mass.—Machinists' tools, steam engines, Woodworth planers, water wheels, shafting, mill work, etc. C 28. 515

180 **Kreider, Campbell, & Co., Philadelphia,** Pa.—E 50.
- *a* Engine lathe. 515
- *b* Glassware grinding machine. 516

181 **American Watch Tool Co., Waltham,** Mass.—Lathes for watchmakers' use, and bench lathes for machinists. F 38–40. 515

182 **Coe, C. W., Fenton, Mich.—Hand** power drill press and screw cutter. B 29. 515

182*a* **Young, William, Easton, Pa.**— Young's patent water and gas main tapping machine. With this apparatus the main pipe is drilled and tapped, the service pipe screwed in, and connection made in one operation, without shutting off the water or changing tools. (*Pump annex* 7–5.) 514

183 **E. Horton & Son Co., Windsor** Locks, Conn.—Lathe and car-wheel chucks. B 30. 515

For location of objects, indicated by letter and figure, see Key to Notation, p. 10; ground plan, p. 11.

Metal and Stone-working Machinery.

184 Oneida Steam-Engine & Foundry Co., Oneida, N. Y.—Westcott's combination lathe chucks, works universally and independently, holds objects twenty-five per cent. larger than diameter of chuck, jaws all reversible. Little Giant drill chucks holds from o to one inch. B 30. 515

185 Whiton, David E., West Stafford, Conn.—Gear-cutting machines, machines for centering iron, lathe chucks, drill chucks, etc. C 31. 515

186 Wicaco Screw & Machine Works, Philadelphia, Pa.—Special machine screws, studs, rolls, punches, dies, drills, taps, reamers, mills, etc. B 37. 515

187 Bliss & Williams, Brooklyn, N. Y. —Presses for making tinware and articles of sheet metals. C 30. 515

188 Chase, Pliny E., Newark, N. J.— Back-geared, screw-cutting, conical-bearing foot lathes, slide rests, and fittings. B 36. 515

189 Northampton Emery Wheel Co., Leeds, Mass.—Solid emery wheels, and machinery for showing uses. B 37, *and Annex 1.* 515

190 Prouty, A. B., Worcester, Mass.— Chucks and jaws for iron planers. D 59. 515

191 Racine Hardware Manufacturing Co., Racine, Wis.—Jewelers' and dentists' polishing and turning lathes, power wheels, engraving blocks, and other tools. C 41. 515

192 Newbold, Richard S., & Son, Norristown, Pa.—Rotary shear for sheet and plate iron. B 33. 515

193 Watson, James, Philadelphia, Pa. —Non-changeable gap lathe. C 31. 515

194 Mitchell, J. H., Philadelphia, Pa.— Grindstone boxes. B 80. 515

195 Wharton, Wm., jr., Philadelphia, Pa.—Rail-bending machine. D 72. 515

196 Pratt & Whitney, Hartford, Conn. —Machinists' tools; gun and sewing machine machinery; drop forging, threading bolts, nuts, and pipe. C 23–26, *and Annex 1.* 515

197 Kennedy, De Lancy, New York, N. Y.—Shearing, punching, griping, and pressing tools and machinery; spiral punch and die. B 37. 515

198 Cummings, Geo. L., New York, N. Y.—Grindstone frames. B 34. 515

199 Flather & Co., Nashua, N. H.— Engine lathes, 17 and 14 inch swing, with hollow steel spindles, steel screws and shafts, wrought iron racks and case hardened nuts and handles. Self-reversing tapping machine, used in principal gun and sewing machine factories. Prices low. Hill, Clarke & Co., selling agents, 131 Milk street, Boston, Mass. C 38–40. 515

200 Doriot, Constant, 337 S. Seventh street, Philadelphia, Pa.—Foot-lathe, with slide rest; fine tool maker, and fine work of precision of all kinds. C 34. 515

201 Celluloid Emery Wheel Co., Newark, N. J.—Grinding and polishing wheels, made of emery or corundum, cemented into a mass with the new and remarkable material, celluloid. These wheels are all that can be required, as to strength and cutting qualities; they are perfectly even and homogeneous, and will not glaze under any circumstances. They may be used either wet or dry, as they never soften in water, oil, or any other lubricant. (*Annex 1.*) 515

202 Teal, C. A. & W. L., Philadelphia, Pa.—Boiler rolls, punching and shearing machines, hair-picking machine. C 25. 515

203 Scofield, Charles, Vineland, N. J.— Machine for straightening shafting in position. C 34. 515

204 Cox & Sons, Bridgeton, N. J.— Steam and gas-fitters' tools, supplies, etc. C 32. 515

205 Hamlin, G. A., Philadelphia, Pa.— Machinery for refitting valves. C 35. 515

206 Merritt, Daniel S., Bay City, Mich. —Machine for cutting heavy iron bars and plates; punch for all kinds of metal. B 36. 515

207 Fitchburg Machine Co., Fitchburg, Mass.—Engine lathes, drills, planer, and shaping machine. C 38. 515

208 Ames Manufacturing Co., Chicopee, Mass.—Engine lathes, planer, drills, edging machine, die-sinking machine. C 38 *to* 40. 515

208*a* Putnam & Estey, Fitchburg, Mass.—Emery wheels. (*Annex 1, 32.*) 515

208*b* Howard Iron Works, Buffalo, N. Y.—Automatic revolving die-bolt cutter and nut-tapping machines. C 29. 515

208*c* Reynolds, D. M., Port Deposit, Md.—Machine for cleaning and polishing sheet iron. C 36. 515

208*d* Cleveland Patent Manufacturing Co., Cleveland, O.—Bolt and pipe cutters; cutter heads. B 29. 515

209 Gray, J. Hammond, Philadelphia, Pa.—Screw machinery, for turning and threading screws, etc. B 27. 515

210 Hilles & Jones, Wilmington, Del.— Radial drills and slotting machine. B 37. 515

211 Hardy Machine Co., Biddeford, Me.—Hardy's improved traverse emery wheel card-grinders, for truing and grinding perfectly the teeth of cotton and wool cards. We warrant the "Hardy" card grinder, cloth-shear grinder, and planer knife grinder. B 35. 515

212 Stacy Stone Dressing Machine Co., New York, N. Y.—Stone-dressing machine. (*Annex 3.*) 516

213 Rogers, William A., Cambridge, Mass.—Automatic machine for grinding parallel surfaces on glass, etc. C 42. 516

214 Branch, Crookes, & Co., St. Louis, Mo.—Diamond circular saws and machinery for sawing stone. (*Saw mill.*) 516

215 Steam Stone Cutter Co., Rutland, Vt.—Stone channeling or quarrying machines; block of machine-cut marble. (*Annex 2.*) 516

216 Emerson Stone Saw Co., Pittsburg, Pa.—Diamond circular stone saw and machine. This machine, doing regular work, cuts in ordinary sandstone one hundred and fifty square feet per hour (counting both sides of the cut), and other stone in proportion, according to the

Stone, Brick, Glass-working Machinery.

relative hardness, leaving the stone perfectly in line, beautifully finished, ready to be placed into buildings, etc. This is more than can be accomplished by one hundred men in the same space of time, and at an expense not exceeding the cost of sharpening and wear of tools necessary to do the same amount of work. The highest honor (a gold medal) was awarded to this saw at the Cincinnati Exposition of 1874 and at the Pittsburg Industrial Exposition of 1875. (*Annex 2.*) 516

217 Batley, John, & Co., Philadelphia, Pa.—Shaping machine, for moulding, paneling, or carving on marble, etc. (*Annex 2.*) 516

218 Davis & Richmond, Detroit, Mich. —Hand machine for cutting and punching slate. (*Annex 2.*) 516

219 Ryan, James M., Cincinnati, O.—Silver-plated lathe, show cases, and process of cutting glass. D 38. 516

220 Ross, Thos., Rutland, Vt.—Stone-sawing machine. (*Annex 2.*) 516

221 Young, Hugh, New York, N. Y.—Reciprocating diamond stone-sawing machines. (*Saw mill.*) 516

222 Union Stone Co., Boston, Mass.—Solid emery wheels and machinery for grinding and polishing. Emery wheels, from one inch to six feet in diameter, and grinders for mounting them. Special machines for jointing plows, beveling boiler plates, gumming saws, etc. Patent automatic knife grinder, a decided success, for grinding planing machines, bookbinders', curriers', and long knives and shears of all kinds. Grinders' and polishers' supplies. B 37, *and Annex 1.* 515

223 Carnell, F. L. & D. R., 1844 Germantown avenue, Philadelphia, Pa.—Fire and red brick presses; working model of "Peerless" brick machine. The above firm manufacture brick machinery of every description, of which they have a fine illustrated catalogue, which will be mailed to any person sending them their address. (*Annex 1 and 3.*) 517

223*a* Aiken, Henry, Philadelphia, Pa.—Hydrostatic machine; stone-separating and clay-tempering machine. (*Annex 3.*) 517

223*b* Farr, George, New York, N. Y.—Working model of brick machine. (*Annex 3.*) 517

223*c* Maas, Albert W. M., Meridian, Miss.—Model and drawing of perpetual burning brick-kiln. (*Annex 3.*) 517

223*d* Whiteford, John, Detroit, Mich.—Brick moulding, off-bearing, and yard-leveling machine. (*Outside of building.*) 517

223*e* Miller, Samuel P., & Son, Philapelphia, Pa.—Hand brick pressing machines. (*Annex 3.*) 517

223*f* Wyatt, Charles B., Somerville, Mass.—Grate, bevel knife, and spring pressure for brickmakers' use. (*Annex 3.*) 517

224 Newkumet, Adam, Philadelphia, Pa.—Crucible and pottery ware machines, drying apparatus for glass-house pots, retorts, etc. (*Annex 3.*) 517

225 Miller, Samuel P., & Son, Philadelphia, Pa.—Hand brick press, model of clay-tempering machine, brickmakers' tools. (*Annex 3.*) 517

226 Carnell, Geo., Philadelphia, Pa.—Brick press and pug mill. (*Annex 3.*) 517

227 Morand, Augustus, Philadelphia, Pa.—Brick-making machine. (*Annex 3.*) 517

228 Garretson, I. H., Keokuk, Iowa.—Brick-moulding machine, ring fence. (*Annex 3.*) 517

229 Excelsior Brick & Stone Co., Philadelphia, Pa.—Model of brick machine, samples of brick and stone. (*Annex 3.*) 517

230 McLean & Bennor Brick Machine Co., Philadelphia, Pa.—Impact brick machine, making brick with a blow. (*Annex 3 and* C 59.) 517

231 Chambers, Bro., & Co., Philadelphia, Pa.—Archimedian brick machine. D 23. 517

232 Hotchkiss, James, Springfield, O.—Brick machine. (*Outside of building.*) 517

233 Gregg, Isaac, jr., & Co., Philadelphia, Pa.—Steam brick machine, one-faced front brick. (*Annex 3.*) 517

234 Hazlehurst, Samuel, St. Louis, Mo.—Hand brick-moulds. (*Annex 3.*) 517

235 Hoyt, Andrew J., Philadelphia, Pa. —Brick machine; steam hammer. (*Annex 3.*) 517

236 Gregg, Wm. L., Philadelphia, Pa. —Triple pressure brick machine for making and also re-pressing all kinds of brick; ceramic gas-kiln, for drying and burning red brick, fire brick, terra-cotta, china, lime, pottery, and drain pipe. (*Annex 3.*) 517

237 Great American Brick Machine Co., Croton, N. Y.—Brick machine and trucks. (*Annex 3.*) 517

238 Gregg Impact Brick Machine Co., Philadelphia, Pa.—Model of brick machine. (*Annex 3.*) 517

238*a* Stacy, George, New York, N. Y.—Fastening for stonecutters' use, etc. (*Annex 3.*) 517

239 Williams, S., & Son, Philadelphia, Pa.—Brickmakers' implements. (*Annex 3.*) 517

240 Stockwell, J. W., Portland, Me.—Cement pipe machinery, concrete mixing, sewer pipe tamper, moulds for drain pipe, samples of work. A. 55. 517

241 Martin, Henry, Lancaster, Pa.—Self-acting brick machine. (*Annex 3.*) 517

242 Lafler, J. A., Albion, N. Y.—Brick-making machine in operation, brick mould, bricks, and model of brick machine. (*Annex 3.*) 517

243 Hamilton, S. M., Baltimore, Md.—Perpetual brick kiln. (*Annex 3.*) 517

244 Mathieu, Charles, Colosse, N. Y.—Glass steam-engine, glass-blowing, knitting, spinning, and forming fancy glass ornaments. E 74. 517

245 Burgess, Warren S., Norristown, Pa.—Blowpipe, animal-clipping machine. E 75. 518

246 Holzer, William, Philadelphia, Pa. —Process of manufacture of druggists', chemists', perfumers', philosophical, and fancy glassware. B 32. 518

For location of objects, indicated by letter and figure, see Key to Notation, p. 10; ground plan, p. 11.

Glass and Metal-Working Machinery and Tools.

247 Brooke, Homer, New York, N. Y. —Glass manufacturers' moulds and presses, for making bottles, jars, lamps, lantern globes, and for all kinds of pressed and blown glass; also private moulds for patent medicine bottles. E 75. 518

248 Chase, B. F., E. Stroudsburg, Pa. —Glass-blowing machines. E 74. 518

249 Steele Bros., 209 South Eleventh street, below Walnut, Philadelphia, Pa.—Glass engraver at work. Decorated china and engraved glass. Dinner, dessert, and tea sets decorated, to order, in any color or design. Monograms, crests, initials engraved on glass. E 75. 518

249*a* Bevington & Winters, Philadelphia, Pa.—Glass furnace; china furnace; printing press and mineral cases, belonging to the art of porcelain printing. (*Annex 1.*) 519

250 McCaffrey & Bro., Philadelphia, Pa.—Hand-cut files and rasps. A 41. 519

251 Krumbhaar, Alexander, Philadelphia, Pa.—Hand-cut files and rasps. A 43. 519

252 Barnett, G. & H., Philadelphia, Pa. —Files and rasps. A 39-40. 519

253 Flagg, Stanley G., & Co., Philadelphia, Pa.—Carriage hardware. A 41. 519

253*a* Knight, Edward H., Philadelphia, Pa.—Monkey wrench. A 41. 519

253*b* Coe, A. G., & Co., Worcester, Mass.—Screw wrenches. B 41. 519

254 Hoopes & Townsend, Philadelphia, Pa.—Bolts, cold-punched nuts, washers, chain links, wood screws, rivets. C 32. 519

255 Stephens Patent Vise Co., New York, N. Y.—Parallel vise, with swivel, taper, table, woodworkers, and pipe attachment. B 6. 519

256 Billings & Spencer Co., Hartford, Conn.—Drop forgings for guns, pistols, sewing machines, and machinery generally; screw plates and dies, Packer ratchet drills, Barwick pipe wrenches, clamp, die, and common lathe dogs, marlinspikes, and calker's tools. B 40. 519

257 Brainard Milling Machine Co., Boston, Mass.—Standard, universal, index, and plain milling machines, for working metals in all shapes, cutting key seats, spur and bevel gears, twist drills, fluting taps and reamers, and making tools of all kinds. Are universally used in American establishments. C 38-40.

a Grinding machines for sharpening the milling cutters, without drawing the temper. 515

b Set screw machine, new design. 515

c Steel bar vises, combining strength with lightness and convenience. 519

258 Bedell, Otis T., New York, N. Y.—Screw wrench. B 40. 519

259 Monk, Chas., Brooklyn, N. Y.—Iron moulders' steel-finishing tools. B 40. 519

260 Silver & Deming Manufacturing Co., Salem, O.—Blacksmiths' post and table drills. F 54. 519

261 Morse Twist Drill and Machine Co., New Bedford, Mass. — Patent increase twist drills, beach chucks, machine relieved taps, screw plates, tap wrenches, adjustable dies, solid and split dies, pipe, solid, and shell reamers, adjustable and centre drill chucks, milling cutters, drill grinding machines, special tools. All tools to standard gauges. B 40. 519

262 Plumb, Burdict, & Barnard, Buffalo, N. Y.—Bolt-forging machines, with forge. (*Annex.*) 519

263 Clark Bros. & Co., Milldale, Conn.—Bolts, rivets, nuts, washers, etc. B 41. 519

264 Parker, Chas., Meriden, Conn.—Vises. B 41. 519

265 Fisher & Norris, Trenton, N. J.—Parallel double screw vises, hardened cast steel faced steam and drop hammer dies, steel faced ore stamp shoes, and all articles requiring hardened cast steel welded to cast iron. Warranted. B 41, *and Annex.* 519

266 Western File Co. (limited), Beaver Falls, Pa.—Machine-cut files. A 41. 519

267 Haase, John A., Philadelphia, Pa. —Floor and door clamps, ratchet drills. B 41. 519

268 Simonds Manufacturing Co., Fitchburg, Mass.—Knives and sickles for mowers and reapers, planing machine knives, circular saws. B 41. 519

268*a* Flanagin, W. J., & Co., Philadelphia, Pa.—Wrenches. B 41. 519

268*b* Bailey Wringing Machine Co., New York, N. Y.—Adjustable parallel vises. A 42. 519

268*c* Barnett, Oscar, Newark, N. J.—Malleable and gray iron castings, brass founders' flasks, etc. A 39. 519

268*d* Russell, Wm. C., New York, N. Y.—Adjustable wrench. D 73. 519

268*e* Cleveland Screw & Tape Co., Elyria, O.—Milled set and cap screws, taps and nuts. B 43. 519

269 Rutschmann Bros., Philadelphia, Pa. — Self-feeding hand drill. B 29. 519

270 Mudge Hook, Tooth, File, & Rasp Co., Brooklyn, N. Y.—Machine files and rasps. A 40. 519

271 Russell, Burdsall, & Ward, Port Chester, N. Y.—Bolts for manufacturers' use. A 40. 519

272 Clark Bros., Philadelphia, Pa.—Eccentric or cam rivet pipe tongs. B 40. 519

273 Pool, A. Alex., & Co., Newark, N. J. —Steel arbors for machinists and jewelers. B 40. 519

274 Wood, Geo. W., Philadelphia, Pa. —Self-adjusting flooring clamp and lifting jack. A 41. 519

275 Orum, Morris L., Philadelphia, Pa. —Flexible mandrels for bending metal pipe. B 40. 519

276 Eaton, Cole, & Burnham Co., 58 John street, New York, N. Y.—Brass and iron goods for steam, water, and gas; cast iron radiators, tools, etc. B 41. 519

277 Shaw, Thomas, Philadelphia, Pa. —Lathe tools. D 69. 519

278 Nicholson File Co., Providence, R. I.—Files, finished, ground, and forged; file steel. C 34. 519

For classes of exhibits, indicated by numbers at end of entries, see Classification, pp. 13-15.

Metal-Working Tools, Silk and Cotton-Working Machinery.

279 American File Co., Pawtucket, R. I.—Files, file-testing machine. C 34. 519

280 Hey, Henry T., Philadelphia, Pa. —Measuring gauge. A 41. 519

281 Spiral Tubing Co., Boston, Mass. —Machine for making spiral seam pipe. B 34. 519

282 Hewitt & Follensbee, Washington, D. C.—Machines for filing and setting saws. A 29. 515

283 Wilkinson, A. J., & Co., Boston, Mass.—Foot-power lathe, bench lathes, small-power planer, hand-planer. C 38–40. 519

284 Wyman, J. Dana, Boston, Mass.—Self-heating soldering iron. B 49. 519

285 Backus, Q. S., Winchendon, Mass. —Bit braces, ratchet braces, tack hammers, etc. A 40. 519

286 Johnson, Wm., Lambertville, N. J. —Universal lathe chuck. C 77. 519

Machines and Implements of Spinning, Weaving, Felting, and Paper Making.

287 Cutter, John D., & Co., New York, N. Y.—Jacquard silk loom in operation; mechanism for measuring silk while spooling it. D 31. 520

288 Knowles & Bro., Worcester, Mass. —D 51.
a Looms for silk dress goods, ribbons, webbings, etc. 520
b Looms for plain and fancy woolen goods. 522

290 Wrigley, John, Paterson, N. J.—Jacquard loom, changeable for power or hand. D 31. 520

291 Danforth Locomotive & Machine Co., Paterson, N. J.—Silk machinery. D 29. 520

292 Nonotuck Silk Co., Florence, Mass. —Machinery for throwing and finishing organzine, sewing silk, twist, and embroidery; machine for printing spools. D 41. 520

293 Holland Manufacturing Co., Willimantic, Conn.—Machines for winding, measuring, and testing the strength of sewing-silk and other threads. D 34. 520

294 Lawson, Peter, Lowell, Mass.—Drawing or roving can. B 58. 521

294*a* Sullivan Machine Co., Claremont, N. H.—Papier-maché roving cans. D 46. 521

294*b* Davis, Caleb S., Philadelphia, Pa. —Cotton goods finisher. D 46. 521

295 Avery, John G., Worcester, Mass. —Thread, twine, and cord machinery. D 54. 521

298 Butterworth, H. W., & Sons, Philadelphia, Pa.—Drying machines for muslins, prints, tickings, etc.; dyeing and sizing machines, calenders and finishing machinery of all kinds. Tinned sheet iron cotton cans, etc. D 44 *to* 48. 521

299 Willimantic Linen Co., Hartford, Conn.—Spool cotton thread-winding and ticketing machines; ring spinning frame. C 52, 53. 521

300 Clark Thread Co., Newark, N. J.—Self-acting spool-winding machine; show case. C 33 *and* A 34. 521

301 Dutcher Temple Co., Hopedale, Mass.—Dutcher's patent self-acting power loom temples. May be seen in operation upon the looms of Geo. Crompton, Esq., Messrs. J. & W. Lyall, and Messrs. L. J. Knowles & Bro., at the Centennial. C 37. 521

302 Kitson Machine Co., Lowell Mass.
a Cotton openers and lappers. 521
b Shoddy pickers and rag dusters. 522
c Leather needle-pointed card clothing, for carding hemp, flax, jute, and tow. C 4, 33 *and* 34. 527

303 Prouty, A. B., Worcester, Mass.—Card-setting machine. D 59. 521

305 Gibbs Loom Harness & Reed Co., Clinton, Mass.—Loom harness and reeds used for weaving. C 50. 521

305*a* Fales, Jenks, & Son, Pawtucket, R. I.—Combined fly frame and speeder; ring spinner frame. D 34–35. 521

305*b* Saco Water Power Machine Shop, Biddeford, Me.—Cotton machinery. C 35–37. 531

305*c* Long, Jas., Bro., & Co., Philadelphia, Pa.—Power looms. C 57. 521

305*d* Patent Forged Steel Spring Ring Co., Worcester, Mass.—Steel spring rings. C 34. 521

305*e* Wolfenden, Shore, & Co., Philadelphia, Pa.—Power loom. D 45. 521

305*f* Hertle & Thompson, New York, N. Y.—Wire heddles, for weaving woolens, cottons, etc. C 54. 521

306 Rockville Traverse Card Grinding Co., Rockville, Conn.—Traverse grinder for woolen and cotton cards and shears. C 50. 521

307 Poole, J. Morton, & Co., Wilmington, Del.—C 60.
a Glazing cylinder for finishing cotton goods. 521
b Chilled roll calenders, for paper-makers' use, ground chilled roll. 525

308 Hope & Co., Providence, R. I.—Pantograph engraving machine for calico-printers' plates. C 41. 521

309 Ingersoll & Balston, Greenpoint, N. Y.—Hand-power hay and cotton press. C 55. 521

310 Butler, Brown, & Co., Providence, R. I.—Ring travelers and belt hooks. C 34. 521

311 Ross, L. E., Providence, R. I.—Spring shuttle motion for looms, independent of speed; loom with motion attached. C 36. 521

312 Palmer European Patent Tentering & Finishing Machine Co., Norwich, Conn.—Machinery for stretching, tentering, and drying woven fabrics, laces, etc. C 56. 521

313 Providence Machine Co., Providence, R. I.—Roving machinery, card and spinning frame, built by Samuel Slater in 1790. D 36. 521

314 Hill, James, Providence, R. I.—Tin filling box, tin cotton can. D 35. 521

315 Wood, Thomas, 2106 Wood street, Philadelphia, Pa.—"Star loom" single box, five leaf; three box loom, 12 harness; four box loom-sliding cams; bobbin-winding machine; new style beaming machine; power hoisting machine; patent friction pulley; shafting, couplings, and pulleys; adjustable self-oiling hangers; self-oiling pillow blocks. C 54. 521

For location of objects, indicated by letter and figure, see Key to Notation, p. 10; ground plan, p. 11.

Cotton, Woolen, Paper-working Machinery.

315*a* Smith, J. A. V., Manchester, N. H. —Steel spreader flies. C 66. 521

315*b* Wolfendon, Shore & Co., Cardington, Pa.—Narrow loom. D 45. 521

316 Eaton & Ayer, Nashua, N. H.—Bobbins, spools, shuttles, skeivers, etc., for spinning and weaving textiles. C 60. 521

317 Leonard & Silliman, Bridgeport, Conn.—Mill spindle with driver, step and points. E 56. 521

318 Jenckes, E., & Co., Pawtucket, R. I.—Ring travelers, cotton binding belt holes, spinning rings, cotton and woolen mill supplies. C 35. 521

319 Foss & Pevey, Lowell, Mass.—Under-flat cotton card. C 38. 521

320 Cleveland Machine Works, Worcester, Mass.—Double-acting gig. D 47. 521

320*a* Corner & Cooper, Lowell, Mass.—Cotton stamps for cotton and woolen mills. D 50. 521

321 Howard, George C., 13¼ South Eighteenth street, Philadelphia, Pa.—Folding, rolling, and measuring, strength-testing, shearing, and brushing machines, for carpets or cloths. B 31. 522

322 Avery, John G., Worcester, Mass. —Continuous wool spinner. D 53. 522

323 Lyall, J. & W., New York, N. Y.—Positive motion looms, weaving various fabrics. C 46 *and* 49. 522

324 Smith, James, & Co., 137 Market street, Philadelphia, Pa.—Machinery for manufacturing fabrics; manufacturers' supplies. Manufacturers of card clothing, oak leather belting, Garnett machines, wool washers, barring machinery, etc.; also, dealers in manufacturers' supplies. Factory, corner of Race and Crown streets. D 62. 522

325 Furbush, M. A., & Son, Philadelphia, Pa.—Carding machines, self-acting spinning mule. D 52. 522

326 New England Co., Rockville, Conn. —Spooler, warp dresser, reel, beamer. D 46. 522

327 Thames River Worsted Co., Norwich, Conn.—Spinning frame with ring and transverse bar. D 48. 522

328 Parks & Woolson Machine Co., Springfield, Vt.—Cloth-shearing machine, cloth-brushing machine, etc. Manufacturers of cloth finishing machinery, consisting of improved shearing machines for shearing all kinds of broad and narrow woolen goods, carpet rugs, shawls, etc.; also, double-acting brushing machine and teasling gigs, etc., etc. D 60. 522

329 Naylor & Jeffries, Philadelphia, Pa. —Carpet rag looper; adjustable clamp. D 50. 522

329*a* Rhodes, Thomas, Philadelphia, Pa.—Yarn beam. D 49. 522

329*b* James, B., Worcester, Mass.—Leather head spools for silk, wool, and cotton manufacturers' use. D 50. 522

329*c* Dienelt & Eisenhardt, Philadelphia, Pa.—Carpet loom, bobbin-winder, and Jacquard machines. C 55. 522

330 Short, James, New Brunswick, N. J.—Positive motion loom for all kinds of carpets. This motion is a differential duplex motion, and is a mechanical motion not before known; all dead centres are obviated by the use of this motion; in looms twenty-five per cent. less power is required and a speed of twenty per cent. increase is gained. The motion is adaptable to all kinds of looms. D 47. 522

331 Crabb, William, Newark, N. J., branch, Twentieth and Filbert streets, Philadelphia, Pa.—Hackles, wood and leather card clothing, wool combs, picker teeth, comb pins. Manufacturer of wood and leather card clothing, hackles, gills, picker teeth, wool combs, and all kinds of hackle, gill comb and card pins, and general mill furnishing. C 58. 522

332 Butterworth, James, & Son, Philadelphia, Pa.—Rag, waste, and shoddy picker. D 58. 522

333 Dornan Bros. & Co., Philadelphia, Pa.—Power loom for weaving without shuttles. Dispensing with complicated "box or shuttle motion," and thereby making great saving in waste. Having almost unlimited capacity for shading colors into the fabric, by means of mails, controlled by the Jacquard machine, cheapness and simplicity of construction, diminished expense in running, by reason of lessened wear and tear, also saving in cost of production, inasmuch as two or more looms can be run by one attendant; lessened service required from loom fixer, and consequent reduction in expense of production, by reason of fixer giving attention to double the quantity of shuttle looms now in use. Cone bobbin-winder.—Winding direct from skein; can be adjusted to wind bobbin from one and a half to eight inches in diameter, having a compensating traveling rod and friction barrels, operating so as to give equal tension on the yarn at all times. Power loom shuttles.—So constructed that the bobbin is prevented from flying up and tearing the warp whilst in operation. Carpet fabric, original designs. D 46. 522

334 Silcott, Millikan, & Gold, Washington C. H., O.—Cloth-measuring and rolling machine. D 52. 522

336 Hillman, Lewis, Philadelphia, Pa. —Automatic measuring machine. D 43. 522

337 Draper, George, & Son, Hopedale, Mass.—Spinning frame, spooler, warper, and creel; twister, spinning rings. C 51. 522

338 Whitney, Baxter D., Winchendon, Mass.—Wool-spinning machine. D 53. 522

340 Atlas Manufacturing Co., Newark, N. J.—Burr picker, to extract foreign substances from wool; single and double burr machine. C 34, 35. 522

341 Crabb, William, Newark, N. J.—Rope-makers' pins, gills. C 63. 524

342 Kuh, Sol., Grand Junction, Iowa.—Straw-twister, etc. C 63. 524

343 Gavit Machine Works, Philadelphia, Pa.—Paper-making machine and adjuncts. F 65–73. 525

344 Lobdell Car Wheel Co., Wilmington, Del.—Chilled-iron callender rolls for paper. E 65. 525

345 Holyoke Machine Co., Holyoke, Mass.—Web callender; beating-rag engine. F 74. 525

For classes of exhibits, indicated by numbers at end of entries, see Classification, pp. 13–15.

Paper-working, Clothing-making, Sewing Machines.

346 Entrekin, William G., Philadelphia, Pa.—Enameler for burnishing photographs, paper, etc. C 41. 525

347 Ross, E. W., & Co., Fulton, N. Y.—Paper mill. F 64, *and outside.* 525

347*a* Pusey, Jones, & Co., Wilmington, Del.—Wire guides for paper machinery. D 33. 525

Machines, Apparatus, and Implements used in Sewing and Making Clothing and Ornamental Objects.

348 Butler Braider Co., Clinton, Mass.—Braiding machinery. C 42. 530

349 Wimpfheimer, Mrs. C., Philadelphia, Pa.—Loom for manufacture of hair-ribbon. C 42. 530

350 Suplee Needle Co., New York, N. Y.—Needles for hand and sewing machines. C 8. 530

351 Oppenheimer, J. D., Philadelphia, Pa.—Patent process for curling hair by steam or hot water. Manufacturer of real and imitation hair goods. C 43. 530

352 Howard, George C., 13¼ South Eighteenth street, Philadelphia, Pa.—Forming and pressing machines for straw, felt, leather, and buckram. We also make machines for drawing sheet metal. B 31. 531

353 American Buttonhole, Overseaming, & Sewing Machine Co., Philadelphia, Pa.—Sewing machines. C 61. 531

354 Franz & Pope Knitting Machine Co., Bucyrus, Ohio.—Automatic knitting machines, seamless hosiery knitting machines; samples of work. C 64. 531

355 Wheeler & Wilson Manufacturing Co., Bridgeport, Conn.—Sewing machines and attachments; samples of work. C 44. 531

356 Washburn Machine Shop, Worcester, Mass.—American drawing models, adjustable drawing tables. C 38. 531

357 Wensley, James, Philadelphia, Pa.—Improvement in buttonhole sewing machines. C 46. 531

358 Lamb Knitting Machine Manufacturing Co., Chicopee Falls, Mass.—C 64.
a Knitting machines. 531
b Egg beaters. 224

359 Howe Machine Co., Bridgeport, Conn.—Sewing machines and attachments; samples of work. C 52. 531

360 Rex & Bockius, Philadelphia, Pa.—Sewing machine. C 69. 531

361 Bartlett, Joseph W., New York, N. Y.—Reversible sewing machines. C 45. 531

362 Wilson Sewing Machine Co., Chicago, Ill.—Sewing machines. C 47. 531

363 Billings & Spencer Co., Hartford, Conn.—Sewing machine shuttles, drop-forged and cold-pressed, from bar steel. B 40. 531

364 Wilcox & Gibbs Sewing Machine Co., New York, N. Y.—Sewing machines with automatic tension, etc. C 50. 531

365 Warth, Albin, Stapleton, N. Y.—Cutting machines for clothing, notching implement for patterns, folding machine. C 70. 531

366 United States Corset Co., New York, N. Y.—Corset-weaving power loom. C 46. 531

367 DuLaney, G. L., & Co., New York, N. Y.—Sewing machine. C 55 *and* B 29. 531

368 Florence Sewing Machine Co., Florence, Mass.—Sewing machines. C 51. 531

369 Davis Sewing Machine Co., Watertown, N. Y.—Sewing machines. C 51. 531

369*a* Robinson, L. W., Champaign, Ill.—Treadle for sewing and other machines. B 77. 531

370 National Suspender Co., New York, N. Y.—Loom for manufacturing suspenders; process of weaving suspenders with the name in; samples of work. C 67–69. 531

371 St. John Sewing Machine Co., Springfield, O.—Sewing machines. C 54. 531

372 Beckwith Sewing Machine Co., New York, N. Y.—Sewing machines. C 55. 531

373 McLean & Bennor Machine Co., Philadelphia, Pa.—Sewing machines. C 60. 531

374 Johnson, Clark, & Co., Boston, Mass.—Sewing machines. Home, Shuttle, National, and Union sewing machines are furnished for domestic or export trade, at very low prices. The "Home" runs with treadle only; the others by hand or treadle. C 59. 531

375 Campbell & Clute, Cohoes, N. Y.—Double table knitting machine, yarn winder, turning-off machine. C 64. 531

376 Hart, Wm., jr., 127 North Fourth street, Philadelphia, Pa.—Apparatus for moulding, curving, or round-shaping, pasteboard, brass, and other flexible substances. Patented May 23, 1876. C 65. 531

377 Yule, George, Newark, N. J.—Wool forming machine, sizing, stiffening, body stretching, etc., for hatters' use. C 67. 531

378 Victor Sewing Machine Co., Middletown, Conn.—Sewing machines, adjustable drill chuck, compensating journal. C 58. 531

379 Wagener, Jeptha, Holtsville, N. Y.—Sewing machines, carriages, and attachments. The great advantages of this machine are its simplicity, general utility, velocity and perfection of work. It is mounted upon a carriage, which is easily thrown on or off the wheels by a child, and is as easily moved from room to room as a child's toy. It makes all the stitches of all the other well-known machines, and is easily changed from one stitch to another by the operator, and, by a new feed device, the ordinary fault of fulling the under layer in a seam is entirely obviated. The especial excellence and superiority of this machine are shown by even a brief inspection of its work. The Wagener has a manufacturing capital of $2,000,000. C 62. 531

380 Whitney Manufacturing Co., Paterson, N. J.—Sewing machines. C 58. 531

Clothing-making, Sewing, Washing Machines.

381 **Singer Manufacturing Co., Elizabethport, N. J.**—Sewing machines, samples of work, and case of machine twist. (*Special building.*) 531

382 **Home Knitter Co., Alliance, O.**—One-needle knitter for stockings. C 64. 531

382*a* **Decrow, A. W., Bangor, Me.**—Sewing machine treadle. E 69. 531

384 **New York Needle Co., Jersey City, N. J.**—Needles, shuttles, and sewing machine attachments. C 66. 531

385 **Shutt, Daniel, Philadelphia, Pa.**—Machine-needle threaders. C 64. 531

386 **Lathrop Anti-frictionate Co., New York, N. Y.**—Anti-frictionate sewing machine. D 68. 531

387 **Dyson Needle Co., New Britain, Conn.**—Spring-needles and points for knitting machines. C 63. 531

388 **Carpenter, Mrs. Mary P., New York, N. Y.**—Sewing machine. C 59. 531

389 **Haas, Joseph, Philadelphia, Pa.**—Ancient knitting machine. C 64. 531

390 **Hinkley, Jonas, Norwalk, O.**—Carpet and floor sweeper, knitting machines. C 62. 531

392 **Pearson, William, Philadelphia, Pa.**—Hosiery-seaming machine. C 62. 531

393 **Taft, J. C., Providence, R. I.**—Sewing machines. C 7. 531

394 **Hull & Belden Co., Danbury, Conn.**—Machine for forming fur hats. C 72, *and annex.* 531

395 **Domestic Sewing Machine Co., New York, N. Y.**—Sewing machines. C 57. 531

396 **Bickford, Dana, New York, N. Y.**—Automatic knitting machines. C 73. 531

397 **Willis, Charles E., Oyster Bay, N. Y.**—Sewing machine feed. C 65. 531

398 **Secor Sewing Machine Co., Bridgeport, Conn.**—Family sewing machines. C 59. 531

398*a* **Boles' Universal Feed-machine Co., New York, N. Y.**—Sewing machines and attachments. C 42. 531

399 **Wardwell Manufacturing Co., St. Louis, Mo.**—Family sewing machine. Makes a perfect lock-stitch, direct from two store spools; dispenses with the shuttle, bobbin, and tiresome rewinding of under-thread; its needle is self-setting and self-fastening; feeds in any direction; is noiseless, simple, light-running, always in order, and its use saves much valuable time and labor. Ladies should examine it before buying. C 67 *and* 68. 531

400 **National Hat-Pouncing Machine Co., New York, N. Y.**—Machinery to shear the surface of fur and wool hats. C 70. 531

401 **Eickmeyer Hat-Blocking Machine Co., New York, N. Y.**—Machinery to stretch, block, iron, and sew sweats into fur and wool hats. C 70. 531

402 **Cuming, M. A., New York, N. Y.**—Hand-power hydraulic hat press. C 62. 531

403 **Fish, Warren L., Newark, N. J.**—Sewing machines. C 46. 531

404 **McCloskey, John, Brooklyn, N. Y.**—Sewing machines. C 59. 531

404*a* **Hawley & Branson, Chicago, Ill.**—Knitting machines. C 66. 531

404*b* **Weed Sewing Machine Co., Hartford, Conn.**—Sewing machines and samples of work. C 45. 531

404*c* **Remington, E., & Sons, Ilion, N. Y.**—Sewing machines; samples of work. C 49. 531

404*d* **United States Sewing Machine Co., New York, N. Y.**—Sewing machines. C 62. 531

404*e* **Pusey, Jones, & Co., Wilmington, Del.**—Morocco glazing machine. D 33. 531

405 **Oakley & Keating, New York, N. Y.**—Washing machine. E 80. 534

406 **Buck, Isaiah D., Conshohocken, Pa.**—Suction washing machine. E 77. 534

407 **Woods, George, & Co., Cambridgeport, Mass.**—Drying process. E 78. 534

408 **Lewis, Rufus S., New Hampton, N. H.**—Ironer and polisher for laundry use. E 77. 534

409 **Sternberger, Leopold, Philadelphia, Pa.**—Steam starching, ironing, and polishing machines for laundries. Patent right of starching machine for sale. Address L. Sternberger, 503 Market street, Philadelphia. E 76. 534

410 **Calkins Champion Washer Co., Chicago, Ill.**—Washing machine. E 77. 534

410*a* **Barnard, A. B., West Fitchburg, Mass.**—Mangles. E 78. 534

410*b* **Howland, W. Penn, Auburn, N.Y.**—Mangles. E 78. 534

410*c* **Short, S., Cincinnati, O.**—Mangle and ironer; blanket washing machine. E 77. 534

410*d* **Pratt, Jas. W., Philadelphia, Pa.**—Laundry washer. E 78. 534

411 **York Manufacturing Co., York, Pa.**—Washing machine. D 78. 534

411*a* **Standard Laundry Machinery Co., Boston, Mass.**—Washing, starching and wringing machines. E 77. 534

412 **Bing, James, Philadelphia, Pa.**—Mangle. E 77. 534

413 **Walker, W. B., Boston, Mass.**—Machine for pressing garments; smoothing-iron and sad-irons. E 79. 534

414 **Briggs, Nicholas A., Shaker Village, N. H.**—Shaker washing machine. E 79. 534

415 **Burt & Putnam, Rockville, Conn.**—Washer for scouring cloth. E 78. 534

415*a* **Uhlinger, W. P., Philadelphia, Pa.**—Centrifugal hydro-extractor. (*Pump Annex 8–10.*) 534

416 **Felder, Charles, New York, N. Y.**—Plaiting, pinking, fluting, and crimping machines. C 62. 534

417 **Storrs, Levi B., Canton, N. Y.**—Pressing machines for tailors' use. E 79. 534

418 **American Watch Tool Co., Waltham, Mass.**—Watch lathes and attachments, with all modern improvements, as used in the best American watch factories; model and astronomical instrument mak-

Watch-making, Printing Machines.

ers' lathes. Hill, Clarke, & Co., agents, 131 Milk street, Boston, Mass. C 41 *and* D 40. 535

419 Hopkins, C., Waltham, Mass.—Machinery and tools for making and repairing watches. C 41. 535

420 Stilwell & Bierce, Newark, N. J.—Jewelers' lathes, foot-press for rolling-mill, gold ingot. D 80. 536

421 National Needle Co., Springfield, Mass.—Machine for making hand and sewing-machine needles. C 40. 537

422 Pyramid Pin Co., New Haven, Conn.—Machine for sticking pins in paper. Also the processes of rolling, boxing, and finishing, in a pyramidal form, the same number of pins (360) usually sold on papers. This company make no cheap pins, but manufacture exclusively from the best spring-tempered brass wire, thus offering to consumers fine pins, in compact and convenient form for toilet, office, and work-basket. C 42–43. 537

Machines and Apparatus for Type Setting, Printing, Stamping, Embossing, and for Making Books, and Paper Working.

424 Howard, George C., 13¼ South Eighteenth street, Philadelphia, Pa.—Plate press for steel, copper, or zinc plate burnishers; power machines, ink, wipe, polish, and print twelve per minute. Screw printing, embossing, punching, and cutting press. Perforating or cutting machines for stamps, checks, sheet metal. Rotary and direct acting, heavy punching, cutting, and bending machines for metal. B 31. 540

425 Kelsey, W. A., & Co., Meriden, Conn.—Portable printing presses. F 32. 540

426 Hickok, W. O., Harrisburg, Pa.—Paper-ruling machines, head-striking machine, book-binders' standing press, and board cutter. F 34. 540

427 Gordon, George P., New York, N. Y.—Printing presses. F 34–36. 540

428 Potter, C., jr., & Co., 12 and 14 Spruce street, New York, N. Y.—Builders of book, job, newspaper, printing, and lithographic presses. Warranted perfect in every respect, and with all the latest improvements of the age. F 28–29. 540

429 Rex & Bockius, Philadelphia, Pa.—Printing presses. C 69. 540

430 Hoover, H., & Co., Philadelphia, Pa.—Printing presses. E 45. 540

431 Lent, A. E., Philadelphia, Pa.—Press for printing steel and copper plates. E 27. 540

432 Degener & Weiler, New York, N. Y.—Printing machines. F 30. 540

433 Golding & Co., Boston, Mass.—Printing presses, printers' tools. E 31. 540

434 Rosenthal, Isador, New York, N. Y.—Apparatus for stamping patterns of ladies' garments. E 32. 540

435 Hammett, L. C., Philadelphia, Pa.—Printers' rollers and composition. E 40. 540

436 O'Shea, Andrew J., Jersey City, N. J.—Devices for registering printing. E 29. 540

437 Bagger, Louis, Washington, D. C.—Printing press using compound lithographic stones. E 31. 540

438 Gally, M., New York, N. Y.—Two printing presses. E 31. 540

439 Bullock Printing Press Co., Philadelphia, Pa.—Printing presses and stereotyping machinery. E 25. 540

440 Cottrell & Babcock, New York, N. Y.—Stop-cylinder press, roller-drum cylinder press, perfecting press for illustrated cut work. F 26–27. 540

440*a* Kneass, N. B., jr., Philadelphia, Pa.—Press, type, and plates for printing literature and music for the blind. Specimen work. E 32. 540

441 Child, C. C., Boston, Mass.—Printing presses. F 32. 540

442 Daughaday, J. W., & Co., Philadelphia, Pa.—Printing press, self-feeding attachment. E 31. 540

443 Woods, B. O., & Co., Boston, Mass.—Amateur printing presses, improved type cases. E 30. 540

444 Dickson, John, & Co., Philadelphia, Pa.—Engraving on vulcanized rubber for printing on letter-press. E 32. 540

445 Ferre, Samuel P., Philadelphia, Pa.—Chromotype cylinder printing press, prints five colors at once. E 32. 540

446 Rose & McDondald, Philadelphia, Pa.—Roller-combs and rollers. E 40. 540

447 Kurtz, H. I., Philadelphia, Pa.—Process of manufacturing lithographic pictures, with specimens. E 34. 540

448 Hoe, R. R., & Co., New York, N. Y.—Printing presses. E 30 *to* 37. 540

449 Maclachlan, Hopkins, & Co., New York, N. Y.—Paging and numbering machine. D 25. 540

450 Campbell Printing Press & Manufacturing Co., Brooklyn, N. Y.—Printing presses and auxiliaries, printers' material. E 28. 540

451 Parks, John A., New York, N. Y.—Hand and scraper pattern power lithographic printing presses. F 25. 540

452 Boston & Fairhaven Iron Works, Fairhaven, Mass.—Newspaper and job printing press. F 25. 540

453 Loag, Samuel, Philadelphia, Pa.—Designs and specimens of color printing from blocks and plates; plate engraved by acid process. E 30. 540

454 Howell & Bros., Philadelphia, Pa.—Cutting off and rolling machine, hanging up and hardening machines. F 55–80. 540

454*a* Waldron, J. E., New Brunswick, N. J.—Wall paper printing machine and turn-around racks. F 80. 540

455 Gorham, W. B., & Co., Boston, Mass.—Rotary, lever, and treadle presses. E 26, 28. 540

456 Mann, Wm. H., Philadelphia, Pa.—Steam paging and numbering machine. E 32. 540

457 Newbury, A., & B., Coxsackie, N. Y.—Printing press. F 33. 540

Printing, Book-making, Paper-working Machines.

457*a* Nelson, M., New York, N. Y.—Printing machine. E 31. 540

457*b* Johnson, Charles E., Philadelphia, Pa.—Automatic paper-feeding machine. E 35. 540

457*c* Pusey, Jones. & Co., Wilmington, Del.—Forming cylinder; calender rolls. D 33. 540

457*d* Burgess Proof Press Co., Belfast, Me.—Proof press. F 32. 540

457*e* Gally, Merritt, New York, N. Y.—Job printing press; magneto-mechanical perforator. E 28. 540

458 Globe Manufacturing Co., Palmyra, N. Y.—E 28.
a Printing presses. 540
b Paper cutters. 546

459 Mackellar, Smiths & Jordan, Philadelphia, Pa.—Type founding machinery for casting and finishing types, types and printing materials. E 28, 29–38. 541

460 Armstrong, John M., Philadelphia, Pa.—Electrotyped music plates; books and sheet music. E 40. 541

461 Grant, Geo. B., Boston, Mass.—Calculating machines. E 44. 542

462 Bain, John W., 532 Walnut street, Philadelphia, Pa.—Type-writer; supersedes the pen, faster, manifolds, keys like a piano; children, blind, and aged, print at once. C. O. D., $125. John W. Bain, general agent (to whom all orders must be sent). E 40. 542

463 Pratt, John, Centre, Ala.—Type-writing machine. E 40. 542

464 Standard Laundry Machinery Co., Boston, Mass.—Telegraph copying machine. E 77. 542

465 Page, Wm. H., & Co., Greenville, Conn.—Wood type, specimen books of wood type. E 40. 542

466 Bruce's, Geo. Son, & Co., New York, N. Y.—Book of printing types, and cases of samples of printing types. E 5. 542

467 Hoffman & Hoyt, New York, N. Y.—Copying presses. E 40. 542

468 Westcott, C. J., New York, N. Y.—Machine for casting, dressing, and setting type. E 29. 541

469 Brainard, Charles R., Boston, Mass.—"Bank" and copy distributor for printing office. E 40. 542

470 Novelty Paper Box Co., Philadelphia, Pa.—Book stitching and sewing machines. D 23. 544

471 Marshall, Son, & Co., Boston, Mass.—Bookbinders', printers', and paper-box manufacturers' shears and machinery. E 26–27. 544

472 Automatic Book-Sewing Machine Co., Milford, Conn.—Book-sewing, pamphlet wire-stitching, and magnetic lasting machines. F 33. 544

473 Standard Machinery Co., Mystic River, Conn.—Steam rounding and backing machine, automatic book trimmer, and power paper cutter. E 40. 544

474 Semple, Mary H., Lowell, Mass.—Steam cutter for bookbinders' use. F 33. 544

475 Wm. F. Murphy's Sons, Philadelphia, Pa.—F 34–36.
a Blank-book manufactory and printing office. 544
b Paper-cutting machine. 546

476 Francis & Loutrel, New York, N. Y.—Folding machine for blank-book makers and paper mills. F 34–36. 545

477 Forsaith, S. C., & Co., Manchester, N. H.—Newspaper folding machine. E 39, *and Annex 1.* 545

478 Chambers, Bro., & Co., Philadelphia, Pa.—Newspaper folder, paster, and trimmer; book-folder; periodical folder, paster, and coverer. D 23. 545

479 Clagne, Randall, & Co., Rochester, N. Y.—Machine for covering pamphlets. D 23. 545

480 Jaeger, Gustav L., 69, 71 Wooster street, New York, N. Y.—Machine for pasting and combining any kind of paper, pasteboards, or textile fabrics; finishes fifteen thousand sheets a day. Patent-rights for sale. D 24. 546

481 Brown & Carver, Philadelphia, Pa.—Card and paper cutters. E 26–27. 546

482 Beck, Charles, Philadelphia, Pa.—Machinery for making paper boxes and cutting paper. D 25. 546

482*a* Sanborn, Geo. H., New York, N. Y.—Paper cutters, knife grinder, embosser, stabbing, and backing machines. D 24. 546

483 Child, C. C., Boston, Mass.—Paper cutter. F 32. 546

484 Cleveland Paper Box Machine Co., Cleveland, O.—Sole manufacturers of machine for making paper boxes; also, cutting press, nicking machine for blanks, and box knives. This machine glues, folds, makes, dries, and discharges the box, having a capacity of fifteen thousand a day. D 25. 546

485 Riehl, M., & Sons, Philadelphia, Pa.—Self-clamping book-cutting machine and paper-cutting machine. D 25. 546

486 Kerr, Norman M., & Co., Philadelphia, Pa.—Manufacture of paper boxes. D 25. 546

487 Boomer & Boschert Press Co., Syracuse, N. Y.—Copying press, paper presses, glue press, leather-binding press, cloth-baling press. Packer's press for tank refuse—power, three hundred tons; standing and bookbinders' presses, Nos. 0, 1, 2, and 3—power, 30, 80, 120, and 200 tons. Cloth-baling press—power, 250 tons. Copying press for banks, freight, and post-offices—power 20 tons. (For presses for cider or lard, see *Agricultural Hall, S and T 12.*) E 39. 546

487*a* Bass, Joseph P., Bangor, Me.—Burnisher for polishing photographs. B 30. 546

488 Curtis & Mitchell, Boston, Mass.—Paper cutters, self-inking printing presses, card cutters, etc. D 24. 546

489 Sheridan, E. R. & T. W., New York, N. Y.—Paper cutters, book trimmer, shears, presses, sawing machine, etc. D 25. 546

490 Packer, Charles W., Philadelphia, Pa.—Machines for cutting card board. D 25. 546

For classes of exhibits, indicated by numbers at end of entries, see Classification, pp. 13–15.

Paper-working Machines, Engines, Boilers, etc.

491 **Vanhorn & Cranston, Brooklyn, N. Y.**—Paper-cutting machines. E 28. 546

492 **Lockwood, W. E. & E. D.,** 255 South Third street, Philadelphia, Pa.—Patent automatic envelope machine, which cuts, folds, gums, and counts 120 envelopes a minute. Automatic self-feeding envelope printing machine; capacity 6,000 an hour. Paper collar machine, which cuts, stamps, button-holes, and finishes 30,000 collars a day. Seed-bag envelope machines; envelope cutting press; small drug envelope machine. (*Section D 3, post 27, centre aisle.*) 547

493 **Hoole, John R., New York, N. Y.**—Perforating machine for checks, stamps, tickets, etc.; paging and numbering machine, for paging blank books and numbering bank notes, checks, coupons, tickets, etc. F 34–36. 547

494 **Cohen, Chas. J., Philadelphia, Pa.**—Machine for folding, gumming, and finishing self-sealing envelopes. D 26. 547

494*a* **Raynor, Samuel, & Co., New York, N. Y.**—Envelope machine. D 25. 547

Motors and Apparatus for the Generation and Transmission of Power.

495 **Williamson Bros., Philadelphia, Pa.**—Portable and stationary hoisting engines, with spur and frictional gearing. D 79, *and boiler house* 4. 550

496 **Tupper, Lorenzo B., New York, N. Y.**—Furnace grate bars. D 76. 550

497 **Connery, James W., Philadelphia, Pa.**—Concave calking for steam boilers, iron ships, and metallic vessels. D 76. 550

498 **Tupper, W. W., & Co., New York, N. Y.**—Grates for steam boiler furnaces, etc. D 78. 550

499 **Frick & Co., Waynesborough, Pa.**—Portable farm and stationary engines. D 75, *and boiler house 4.* 550

500 **Bigelow, H. B., & Co., New Haven, Conn.**—Combined and independent engines and boilers. D 71. 550

501 **Steam Generator Manufacturing Co. of Pennsylvania, Philadelphia, Pa.**—Sectional boiler. (*Boiler house 4.*) 550

502 **American Engine Co., Jersey City, N. J.**—Engines and thresher locomotive. D 75. 550

503 **Shaw, Thomas, 915 Ridge avenue, Philadelphia, Pa.**—Steam and vacuum gauges, test pumps, air chamber feeder, hydraulic valves and gauges. Cushion-seated valves, exhaust nozzles, planer bar. Gauge is free of springs, and measures by weight alone; has been adopted by United States Government and principal establishments as standard of pressure. Test pumps are of superior make and finish, adapted to pressure in small quantities, to every pressure desired. Air-chamber feeder, a useful invention; utilizes vibrations of water in pump to supply air-chambers with air. Hydraulic stop-valve; controls the highest pressure without leakage; has threaded seat. Cushion-seated valve; uses face of valve as dash-pot; prevents pounding. Exhaust nozzle absorbs noise of exhaust steam, and arrests sparks in locomotives. Planer bar, doubles the capacity, of iron planers; reaches through work. D 69. 550

504 **Reed, John A., New York, N. Y.**—Tapering corrugated sectional boilers. D 77. 550

505 **Steigert, Leopold, Cincinnati, O.**—Meat-chopping machines, with engine attachments, horizontal engine. D 78. 550

506 **Bent, Samuel S., New York, N. Y.**—Shaking grate bars for steam boilers, etc. E 75. 550

507 **Harrison Boiler Works, Philadelphia, Pa.**—Sectional safety steam boiler. First class bronze medal, London, 1862; first class bronze medal, New York, 1869; gold and silver Rumford medals, Boston, 1871; first class silver medal, Philadelphia 1874. *Section D 77, and boiler house No. 4.* 550

508 **Babcock & Wilcox, New York, N. Y.**—Sectional safety steam boiler. (*Boiler house 3.*) 550

509 **Meissner, Julius H., Philadelphia, Pa.**—Shelving grates and furnaces. E 76. 550

510 **Shore Bros., Philadelphia, Pa.**—Boiler feed, belt pumps, steam pump. E 75. 550

511 **Houghton, R. J., New York, N. Y.**—Boiler and tube compound for removing and preventing scale; specimens of scale. E 76. 550

512 **Snyder, Ward B., New York, N. Y.**—Steam engine. Snyder's Little Giant steam engine, one-horse power complete, with tubular boiler, $150; two-horse power, $200; three-horse power, $250. Send for circular. Factory, 84 Fulton street, N. Y. B 71. 550

513 **Howard Safety Boiler Manufacturing Co., Boston, Mass.**—Safety sectional wrought-iron nine-inch tube boiler. (*Boiler house 3.*) 550

514 **Ames Iron Works, Oswego, N. Y.**—Portable steam engines. B 74, *and boiler house.* 550

516 **Erie City Iron Works, Erie, Pa.**—Horizontal tubular boiler, portable engines, farm engine with vertical boiler and horizontal engine. C 76. 550

516*a* **Springfield Iron Works, Springfield, Mo.**—Turbine water wheel. D 80. 550

517 **Ryder Reciprocal Grate Association, Taunton, Mass.**—Reciprocal grates. Books on grates, combustion, and results of tests, sent free. D 68. 550

518 **Lowe & Watson, Bridgeport, Conn.**—Steam boiler. Lowe's patent steam boiler, made entirely of steel plates; proved by eight years' use, under all conditions, to be safe, durable, reliable, and very economical of fuel. Great and uniform steaming capacity. Process of combustion (smokeless with any fuel) obtained in construction and setting. (*Boiler house 3.*) 550

519 **Chalmers Spence Co., Philadelphia, Pa.**—Composition boiler and steam pipe covering; tube cleaner. D 78. 550

520 **Shuster, John T., Philadelphia, Pa.**—Boiler and pipe covering. D 78. 550

Engines, Boilers.

521 Murrill & Keizer, Baltimore, Md. —Automatic damper regulator for steam boilers. D 64, *and Pump annex*. 550

522 Baird & Huston, Philadelphia, Pa. —Horizontal tubular boiler. D 38 *to* 40. 550

523 Exeter Machine Works, 140 Congress street, Boston, Mass.—Sectional independent expansion and contraction boiler. Following is extract from report of the Franklin Institute, Philadelphia, Sept. 29, 1875, as to its safety qualities: "The Exeter Sectional Boiler" comes very near to it, if it does not solve that difficult problem of uniting small compartments composing a boiler of considerable size, and at the same time provide for the free escape of steam without lifting the water. Many sectional boilers are so constructed in combining their parts as to cause the steam generated in the lower portion of the apparatus to force its way in zig-zag courses through a whole neighborhood of narrow passages, or through a number of long, comparatively small and nearly horizontal tubes, into which it is quite impossible for the water to promptly follow, as it should do, in order to maintain perfect circulation and take up all the transmitted heat before effecting its escape. The water in the "Exeter" section exists in vertical masses about 3¼ inches square and 28 inches high, a form favorable to the ready liberation of the steam to and from the surface of the water, and securing at the same time prompt circulation and supply of water to the heated surfaces of the boiler. * * * We find, on careful and extended inquiry, that the "Exeter boiler," thus far in its existence and service, has an excellent record sufficient to justify us in making the assertion that it is equally as safe as any sectional boiler in the market known to us. We have not found any evidence, whether derived from the severest experimental tests to which a boiler can be subjected, or from long continued daily use, under the ordinary working conditions in the factory, which would prove it to be dangerous as a generator of steam. (*Boiler house* 3.) 550

524 Hoadley Co., J. C., Lawrence, Mass. — Portable steam engines, with or without wagons, various sizes, 9 to 100 horse power; automatic variable cut-off, giving uniform speed and great economy of fuel, requiring only 21 to 30 pounds of feed water, and 3 to 3¼ pounds of coal per horse power per hour. Cheap, light, compact, durable, safe, convenient, economical. D 80. 550

525 Kelley, Wm. E., New Brunswick, N. J.—Sectional safety boiler. (*Pump annex, and boiler house.*) 550

525*a* Smith, S. Decatur, Philadelphia, Pa.—Skeleton grate bar. E 77. 550

25*b* Potts Bros., Pottstown, Pa.—Flanged boiler iron, and boiler flue iron. B 24–25. 550

525*c* Wilson, Benj. F., Philadelphia, Pa.—Shuttle and stop valves. B 70. 550

525*d* Hoyt, J. B., New York, N. Y.—Steam generating furnace, for the perfect combustion of all the gases in bituminous coal, thereby preventing smoke. (*Boiler house* 6.) 550

525*e* O'Hara, Charles M., Boston, Mass. —Ash felting for steam pipes. B 69–71. 550

525*f* Winans, H. N., New York, N. Y. —Boiler powder, compounds and liquids; anti-incrustators; boiler cleaner. D 78. 550

526 Lovegrove & Co., Philadelphia, Pa. —Vertical tubular boilers. B 75, *and boiler house 4*. 550

527 Armstrong Heater Manufacturing Co., Toledo, O.—Improved heater, lime extractor, condenser, adjustable feed pump for steam boilers. D 74. 550

527*a* Hanmore, Jno. W., Newburgh, N. Y.—Comb felting, blast pipes, vacuum pans, etc. B 71. 550

527*b* McConn, John, Philadelphia, Pa. —Radiators, for steam or water, and boiler. E 76. 550

527*c* Miller, Charles B., Philadelphia, Pa.—Steam generator. (*Boiler house 4.*) 550

528 Firmenich, J., Buffalo, N. Y.— Steam boiler. (*Boiler house 4.*) 550

529 Ellis, Charles R., New York, N. Y. —Hot-water apparatus for heating buildings. D 75. 550

530 Haskins Steam Engine Co., John F. Haskins, Fitchburg, Mass.—Interchangeably-made vertical steam engines. C 10–74, *and boiler house 4*. 550

531 Kreider, Campbell, & Co., Philadelphia, Pa.—Horizontal steam engine. E 50. 550

532 American Road Steamer Co., Philadelphia, Pa.—Road steamer. E 80. 550

533 Hartford Steam Boiler Inspection & Insurance Co., Hartford, Conn.—Incrustation, scale, and defective iron from steam boilers, fragments of exploded boilers. D 76. 550

534 Colt's Patent Fire Arms Manufacturing Co., Hartford, Conn.—Steam engines, steam cylinder in boiler, interchangeable parts. D 74, *and boiler house 4, and quartz mill.* 550

535 Sample, McElroy, & Co., Keokuk, Iowa.—Semi-portable steam engine and boiler. This firm makes a specialty of manufacturing these engines, and are prepared to fill orders promptly, if addressed as above. D 77. 550

536 Payne, B. W., & Sons, Corning, N. Y. — Vertical engines with safety boilers; 3 to 4 horse power; impossible to explode; price, $250, complete, except smoke stack. (*Boiler house 4.*) 550

538 Vail, S. S., Keokuk, Iowa. — Reversible steam boiler, with automatic fuel feed. To remove scales, reverse ends. Convenient to clean or repair. Rights for sale. C 77. 550

539 Lynde, J. D., Philadelphia, Pa.— Safety boiler. B 71, *and boiler house 4*. 550

540 Peirce Rotary Tubular Boiler Co., New York, N. Y.—Rotary tubular steam boiler. (*Boiler house 5.*) 550

541 Smith, Charles D., Boston, Mass. —Steam tubular boiler, steam boiler furnace and setting grate bars; glass water gauge. C, *and boiler house 3*. 550

542 Gillis & Geoghegan, New York, N. Y.—Boiler feeder and steam trap. (*Boiler house 6.*) 550

Engines, Boilers, Water-Wheels.

543 Harrold, George W., Rochester, N. Y.—Automatic steam trap. D 64. 550

544 Johns, H. W., New York, N. Y.—F 64.
a Asbestos roofing, asbestos cement felting, lined hair felt. 228
b Asbestos steam packing. 555

545 Skinner & Wood, Erie, Pa.—C 78.
a Horizontal return flue boiler; variable grate surface for wood or coal. 550
b Portable engine, stop motion governor, self-oiling connecting rod, combined check, stop, and relief valve. 552

545*a* Starr, William M., Tyler, Texas.—D 78.
a Water wheel, car starter, glass cutter, etc. 581
b Road engine. 552

546 Sellers, William, & Co., Philadelphia, Pa.—C 18-25, *and Annex 1.*
a Injectors. 550
b Three cylinder engines. 552
c Shafting, hangers, couplings. 553

547 Haworth, James, Philadelphia, Pa.—Turbines, driven by hydrant-water power. D 73. 551

548 Lane Manufacturing Co., Montpelier, Vt.—Monitor turbine water-wheel. Sets in open flume or in a closed curb; perfectly balanced cylindrical gate; water applied upon the entire periphery of wheel. A 4, 35-36. 551

549 Grier, W. W., Hulton, Pa.—Hydraulic ram sentinel. D 79. 551

550 Stout, Mills, & Temple, Dayton, O.—Turbine water-wheels with and without flumes. Thousands of these wheels are in successful operation, driving all kinds of machinery. They have been introduced into nearly every civilized country in the world. They produce a very high percentage of power, are compact and durable. Call at Machinery Hall, and get descriptive catalogue, or address proprietors as above. D 80. 551

551 Stilwell & Bierce Manufacturing Co., Dayton, O.—Double turbine water-wheel, simple, durable, and powerful. D 80. 551

552 Dexter Spring Co., Hulton, Pa.—Carriage spring, in connection with fifth wheel. D 79. 551

553 Leffel, James, & Co., Springfield, O., and 109 Liberty street, New York.—Double turbine water-wheel. D 77. 551

554 Chase Turbine Manufacturing Co., Orange, Mass.—Turbine wheels. (*Pump annex.*) 551

555 Wolf, Abraham N., Allentown, Pa.—Turbine water-wheel and flume. (*Pump annex.*) 551

556 Buzby, Albert G., Philadelphia, Pa.—Water motor from hydrant pressure; model of centripetal railway. D 79. 551

557 Bodine Manufacturing Co., Mt. Morris, N. Y.—Brass turbine water-wheel. D 79. 551

558 Valentine, Wm. J., Fort Edward, N. Y.—Turbines, with and without register gates; hydraulic motor. D 79. 551

559 Wright & Rogers, Minneapolis, Minn.—Stationary, portable, locomotive, and marine steam engine. D 79. 551

560 Mosser, Wm. F., & Co., Allentown, Pa.—Turbine water-wheel. A 48, *and Pump annex.* 551

561 Wright, James, Minneapolis, Minn.—Cylinder meter motor. D 79. 551

562 Springfield Iron Works, Springfield, Mo.—Turbine wheel. D 80. 551

563 Bing, James, Philadelphia, Pa.—Turbine water-wheel. E 77. 551

564 Poole & Hunt, Baltimore, Md.—Turbine water-wheels and gearing. C 79. 551

565 Cox & Sons, Bridgeton, N. J.—Turbine water-wheels. C 32. 551

566 York Manufacturing Co., York, Pa.—Turbine water-wheels. D 78. 551

567 National Water-Wheel Co., Bristol, Conn.—Turbine water-wheels. D 77. 551

568 Barber & Son, Allentown, Pa.—Globe flume, with turbine wheel. D 77. 551

569 Brown, Son, & Co., Brookville, Pa.—Turbine water-wheels. D 78. 551

570 Cope, E. T., & Sons, West Chester, Pa.—Turbine water-wheel, with water-tight gates opening separately. (*Pump annex.*) 551

571 Bollinger, O. J., York, Pa.—Turbine water-wheel. (*Pump annex.*) 551

572 Risdon, T. H., & Co., Mount Holly, N. J.—Turbine water-wheel. Many sizes of this wheel, at tests by different engineers, and under different conditions, have given over 90 per cent. of the power of the water consumed. (*Pump annex.*) 551

573 Walton, Silas, Moorestown, N. J.—Turbine water-wheel. (*Pump annex.*) 551

574 Alcott, Thos. J., Mount Holly, N. J.—Turbine water-wheel. D 78. 551

575 Tait, Thomas, Rochester, N. Y.—Water-wheel. The guides form wedge-shaped openings under all degrees, cutting water off at periphery of wheel; counterpoising under any hydrostatic pressure. Surface joints prevent water escapement between curb and wheel. (*Pump annex.*) 551

576 Knowlton & Dolan, Logansport, Ind.—"Little Giant" turbine water-wheel, noted for economy in the use of water, and durability. (*Pump annex.*) 551

576*a* Howobin, W. T., Cohoes, N. Y.—Water-wheel governor; rollers. D 78. 551

576*b* Burnham, N. F., York, Pa.—Turbine water-wheel. (*Pump annex.*) 551

576*c* Capron Water-Wheel Manufacturing Co., Hudson, N. Y.—Water-wheels. D 77. 551

576*d* Rodney Machine Co., Orange, Mass.
a Double-acting turbine water-wheel. (*Pump annex.*) 551
b Rotary fulling mill. D 45. 552

577 Folsom, Andrew, Barrington, R. I.—Wheel constructed to operate in the direction of wind or water. (*Pump annex.*) 551

578 Peirce, Milton P., Wenonah, N. J.
a Turbine water-wheel. C 80. 551
b Portable steam engine. D 78. 552

For location of objects, indicated by letter and figure, see Key to Notation, p. 10; ground plan, p. 11.

Engines, Boilers.

579 **Abendroth & Root Manufacturing** Co., 96 Liberty street, New York, N. Y. —Wrought iron sectional safety boiler. These boilers were introduced to the public in 1867. There is now over forty-five thousand horse-power in use in all parts of the world. (*Boiler house 3.*) 552

580 **Fields, Wm., Wilmington, Del.** —Motor-power model-dumping coal wagon. B 79. 552

581 **Bolles, J. N., Baltimore, Md.**— Steam engine. (*Outside.*) 552

582 **Cobb, Z., & Sons, Wilmington, Del.** —Water engine for sewing machines, etc. E 68. 552

583 **Wetherill, Robt., & Co., Chester,** Pa.—Steam engine, with self-packing piston. B 69. 552

584 **Baird & Huston, Philadelphia, Pa.** —Steam engines. D 38–40. 552

585 **Lobdell Car Wheel Co., Wilmington,** Del.—Portable steam engine and boiler. E 65. 552

586 **Cornell University Machine Shop,** Ithaca, N. Y.—Steam engine. B 68. 552

587 **Rider, Wooster, & Co., Walden,** N. Y.—Compression engines, operating without valves, using compressed and heated air. B 80. 552

588 **Lovegrove & Co., Philadelphia,** Pa.—Steam engine. B 75, *and Boiler house 4.* 552

589 **Jerome, William R., Philadelphia,** Pa.—Electro-magnetic motor, for running sewing machines, etc. B 69. 552

590 **Dudgeon, Richard, New York,** N. Y.—Rotary engine. C 27. 552

590*a* **Murray Iron Works Co., Burlington,** Iowa.—Steam engine. E 60. 552

590*b* **Brayton, George B., Philadelphia,** Pa.—Hydro-carbon engine. A 71. 552

591 **Wardwell, George J., Rutland, Vt.** —Stationary and portable valveless steam engines. B 77. 552

592 **Moorhouse, R. O., & Co., Philadelphia,** Pa.—Steam engine, with gear for variable expansion adjusted by the governor. B 73. 552

593 **Hawley, Henry Q., Albany, N. Y.** —C 75.

a Water motors. 551

b Gas heating and cooking furnaces. 552

594 **Buckeye Engine Co., Salem, O.** —Automatic cut-off and throttling steam engines. B 70. 552

595 **Hussey, Charles A., New York,** N. Y.—Electro-magnetic engines. E 69. 552

596 **Gladwin, Charles P., Philadelphia,** Pa.—Plain-slide valve steam engines with governor and automatic stop and speeder. B 71, *and* C 77. 552

597 **Lidgerwood Manufacturing Co.,** New York, N. Y.—Hoisting and elevating engines. B 79, *and Annex 3.* 552

598 **Carlisle, Mason, & Co., Chicago,** Ill.—Chain elevating machinery. C 76. 552

599 **Shapley & Wells, Binghamton,** N. Y.—Steam engines. D 80, *and Boiler house 4.* 552

599*a* **Russell, William D., New York,** N. Y.—Engines. (*Outside of building.*) 552

599*b* **Butterworth, H. W., & Sons,** Philadelphia, Pa.—Sheet iron; tin cans. D 44 *to* 48. 552

599*c* **Baxter Steam Engine Co., New** York, N. Y.—Steam engines; in use in Gillinder & Sons' glass-house and in Nevada State building. 552

599*d* **Wisner & Strong, Pittston, Pa.**— Horizontal engine. B 71. 552

599*e* **Forbes, J. W., Chicago, Ill.**— Quartz battery for crushing quartz. A 73. 552

600 **Mitchell, J. H., Philadelphia, Pa.**— Steam engines. B 80. 552

600*a* **Hampson, Whitehill & Co., New** York, N. Y.—Stationary engine. B 73. 552

601 **New York Safety Steam Power Co.,** New York, N. Y.—Launch engines, stationary engine, combined engine and boiler. E 38–40. 552

602 **Lynde, J. D., Philadelphia, Pa.**— Duplex engine. B 71, *and Boiler house 4.* 552

603 **Naylor, Jacob, Philadelphia, Pa.**— Engines, horizontal and vertical boiler feed pump, and combined feed pump and heater. D 71–73. 552

604 **Roberts, E. A. L., Titusville, Pa.**— Exhaust engine; exhaust crank. C 78. 552

605 **Ervien, Charles W., & Bro.,** Philadelphia, Pa.—Steam engines. B 69, *and Pump annex.* 552

606 **McCutchen, John F., Philadelphia,** Pa.—Block for eccentric hooks of steam engine. B 77. 552

607 **Meeker, D. M., & Sons, Newark,** N. J.—Part of cylinder of the first steam engine used in America. B 76. 552

608 **Griffith & Wedge, Zanesville, O.**— Vertical portable engine, and centrifugal drying machine. C 74 *and* D 77. 552

609 **Klein, Chas. C., Philadelphia, Pa.** —Eccentric piston engine. C 79. 552

610 **Jeffery, Thos. B., Chicago, Ill.**— Rotary steam engines. B 77. 552

611 **Hartford Foundry & Machine** Co., Hartford, Conn.—Automatic and variable cut-off non-condensing steam engine. These engines, formerly known as the "Woodruff & Beach" iron works engine, have acquired a very wide reputation on account of their excellent performances. They are a type of steam motor, combining the prime essentials of solidity, durability, and great economy. There are now in daily use over three hundred, practically demonstrating their merits. (*Annex 1.*) 552

612 **Twiss, Nelson W., New Haven,** Conn.—Vertical engine, yacht engine. C 79. 552

613 **Blandy, H. & F., Zanesville, O.** —Portable, agricultural, and saw-mill engines, and stationary engine. B 68. 552

613*a* **Lewistown Brass & Engine Co.,** Lewistown, Pa.—Upright and horizontal engines. C 74. 552

For classes of exhibits, indicated by numbers at end of entries, see Classification, pp. 13–15.

Engines and Appliances, Belting, Shafting, etc.

613*b* Allis, Edward P. & Co., Milwaukee, Wis.—Steam engine. (*Saw mill. A* 10-11.) 552

614 Erie City Iron Works, Erie, Pa.—Stationary engine, horizontal engine. C 76. 552

615 Otis Bros. & Co., 348 Broadway, New York, N. Y.—Furnace engine for hoisting purposes. The blast furnace hoisting engine, is adapted for operating two platforms; store hoisting engines, small size, lifting power and gear combinations, lifting power with screw combinations, for use in factories, mills, etc., and safety platforms for freight purposes, with corner and side upright; tiercing truck for piling up heavy boxes or packages. B 38. 552

616 Bastet Magnetic Engine Co., Philadelphia, Pa.—Magnetic engines for sewing machines, organs, lathes, pumps, etc. B 75. 552

617 Wells Balance Engine Co., New York, N. Y.—Double piston engine. C 77. 552

618 Niagara Steam Pump Works, Brooklyn, N. Y.—Miniature engine. Direct acting piston, pressure, and fire pump, direct acting plunger mining pump, crank pump and engine; direct acting organ engine; direct acting agitator and oil pump; direct acting plunger, on boilers in saw mill, loaned Centennial Commission. (*Pump annex.*) 552

619 Brown, C. H., & Co., Fitchburg, Mass.—Automatic regulating cut-off steam engine. (*Saw mill.*) 552

620 Howard, George C., 13¼ South Eighteenth street, Philadelphia, Pa.—Patent belt gearing for operating machines of variable speed, sewing machines, etc. B 31. 553

621*a* Powers, W. P., La Crosse, Wis.—Belting. A *and* B, *Saw mill.* 553

621*b* Stow & Burnham, 500 North Fifteenth street, Philadelphia, Pa.—Flexible cable for transmitting power in any direction, also tools and machines operated therewith; drills workable wherever ratchet drill is used; flue cutter for removing locomotive flues. D 68. 553

621*c* Wahl, Albert, Philadelphia, Pa.—Health apparatus; back straightener and chest expander. E 75. 553

622 Eckfeldt & Richie, Philadelphia, Pa.—Oak-tanned leather butts, belting and fire hose. D 65. 553

623 Page Belting Co., Concord, N. H.—Leather belting and lace leather; driving belt (in use). D 64. 553

624 Roebling's Sons, John A., & Co., Trenton, N. J.—Wire rope, rigging, rope fastenings, bridge cables, rods, telegraph wire, etc. C 64. 553

625 AlexanderBros., 410 & 412 North Third street, Philadelphia, Pa.—Oak-tanned leather belting, and frame of specimen laps; also patent double belt-driving shaft No. 3, the construction of which greatly increases the effectiveness and durability of belts from 16 to 48 inches, or wider. Descriptive circulars furnished. D 64. 553

626 Cresson, Geo. V., Philadelphia, Pa.—Pulleys, hangers, couplings, wall boxes, pillow blocks, etc. C 71-73. 553

627 Heim, Anton, New York, N. Y.—Leather belting, hydraulic packing leather, tympan skins, lace leather, picker leather, elastic pulley; driving belt (in use). D 65. 553

628 Branch, Crookes, & Co., St. Louis, Mo.—Adjustable countershaft hanger and belt tightener, for intermediate motion without loose pulleys. (*Saw mill.*) 553

629 Rorer, Thomas I., Philadelphia, Pa.—Combined leather and canvas belting. D 65. 553

630 American Tubular Iron & Steel Association, Philadelphia, Pa.—Tubular iron and steel car axles, shafting, columns, bars. C 70-73. 553

631 Pennsylvania Combined Iron & Steel Association, Philadelphia, Pa.—Combined iron and steel rails, beams, girders, shafting plates, horse shoe and merchant bars. C 70-73. 553

632 Jones & Laughlins, American Iron Works, Pittsburg, Pa.—Bar, sheet, and plate iron, T-rails, shafting, hangers, pulleys, couplings. Manufacturers of bar, hoop, sheet, and plate iron; patent cold-rolled shafting; hangers, pulleys, couplings, T-rails, street rails, nails, and spikes. C 65 *and* 70. 553

633 Schieren, Charles A., New York, N. Y.—Oak-tanned leather belting; double belt (in use). D 64. 553

634 Charlton, John, Philadelphia, Pa.—Internal clamp coupling for shafting, main driving pulley, with internal clamp hub. C 71 *and* 73. 553

635 Hoyt, J. B., & Co., New York, N.Y.—Oak-tanned sole leather and belting. D 66. 553

636 Royer, H., San Francisco, Cal.—Fulled rawhide, belting, lacing, rope. D 66. 553

637 Chatfield, Underwood, & Co., New York, N. Y.—Angular belting. D 65. 553

638 Pusey, Jones, & Co., Wilmington, Del. C 74.

a Expanding pulleys. 553

b Temper cut-offs and governors for steam engines. 555

639 Jewell, P., & Sons, Hartford, Conn.—Leather belting, metallic-tipped belt lacings. D 67. 553

640 Mason, Volney W., & Co., Providence, R. I.—Friction clutches and pulleys, adjustable hangers; also, friction clutch pulleys, driving main lines of shafting in pump annex, and in Machinery Hall adjoining, near Corliss engine. D 66 *and Pump annex.* 553

641 Poole & Hunt, Baltimore, Md.—Shafting and appurtenances. C 79. 553

641*a* Eccles, James, Philadelphia, Pa.—Shaft coupling. D 60. 553

642 Gates, Josiah, & Sons, Lowell, Mass.—Leather belting, hose, lacing, and worsted apron leather and fire supplies. C 78. 553

643 Burgess & Son, Providence, R. I.—Leather belting, lace leather, picker leather, loom pickers. C 70. 553

644 Cook, A. B., & Co., Erie, Pa.—Adjustable dead pulleys, wooden belt pulleys, and taper sleeve pulleys. D 72. 553

For location of objects, indicated by letter and figure, see Key to Notation, p. 10; ground plan, p. 11.

Motors and Appliances.

645 **Fowler, F. G., Bridgeport, Conn.**—Propeller. B 72. 554

645*a* **Neafie & Levy, Philadelphia, Pa.**—Propeller wheels and blade. C 77. 554

645*b* **Lane Bros., Millbrook, N. Y.**—Motor for driving light machinery. C 77. 554

645*c* **Rhett, Roland, Baltimore, Md.**—Spring motor for sewing machines. C 71. 554

645*d* **Harper, William, jr., Philadelphia, Pa.**—Screw propeller. C 76. 554

646 **Brown, Edward, Philadelphia, Pa.**—Pyrometers for blast furnaces, bakers' ovens, tempering steel, etc.; revolution indicators. D 68. 555

647 **Woodruff, Joseph, Rahway, N. J.**—Balanced steam damper regulator. D 76. 555

648 **Wickersham & Bro., Philadelphia, Pa.**—Oil feeder, brass and glass oil cups. D 76. 555

649 **Pancoast & Maule, Philadelphia, Pa.**—Steam and hot water house heating apparatus, vertical tube radiators, pipe cutter. D 75. 550

650 **New York Belting & Packing Co., New York, N. Y.**—Rubber belting, packing, hose, tubing, car springs, vulcanite emery wheels, etc. D 75. 555

650*a* **Ashcroft, E. H., Boston, Mass.**—Steam and vacuum gauges; safety valves; oil testing machine. D 72–73. 555

650*b* **Allis, E. P., & Co., Milwaukee, Wis.**—Boiler feed regulator. (*On boiler in Campbell Press Building.*) 555

650*c* **Katzenstein, L., & Co., New York, N. Y.**—Metallic packing for piston rods and valve stems. E 40. 555

650*d* **Potter & Hoffman, Philadelphia, Pa.**—Steam packing. B 30. 555

651 **Parshall, C. H., Detroit, Mich.**—Lubricator. D 71. 555

652 **Belfield, H., & Co., Philadelphia, Pa.**—Brass and iron valves, cocks, steam gauges, whistles, gongs, steam heating apparatus, etc. D 74. 555

652*a* **Rue Manufacturing Co., Philadelphia, Pa.**—Boiler feeders; injectors. (*Boiler house 4, and Pump annex, Sec. 4, Col. 13.*)

653 **Allen's Sons, Josiah J., Philadelphia, Pa.**—Anti-lamina, for preventing and removing scale from boilers. D 76. 555

654 **Stilwell & Bierce Manufacturing Co., Dayton, O.**—Lime extracting heater and filter combined. Removes all impurities from feed-water for steam boilers; indispensable to an economical use of steam. D 80. 555

655 **Richards, Jackson, Philadelphia, Pa.**—Piston packing. D 69. 555

656 **Waters, C., & Co., Boston, Mass.**—Steam engine governors. D 74. 555

657 **Buffalo Steam Gauge & Lantern Co., Buffalo, N. Y.**—D 72.
a Steam gauges. 555
b Locomotive head light with patent burner, hand lantern. 576

658 **Lehman, B. E., Bethlehem, Pa.**—Gauge cocks, water gauges, oil cups, gate valves. D 70. 555

659 **American Oil Cabinet Co., Boston, Mass.**—Safety oil cabinets. D 72. 555

660*a* **Vulcanized Fibre Co., Wilmington, Del.**—Fish-bolt and carriage washers. D 65. 555

660*b* **Brown, Aug. P., New York, N. Y.**—Boiler fixture and engine governor. D 70. 555

660*c* **McShane, Henry, & Co., Baltimore, Md.**—Bells. (*Northeast tower.*) 555

660*d* **Christoffel, T. B., Williamsburg, N. Y.**—Tube cleaners and scrapers. D 66. 555

661 **Utica Steam Gauge Co., Utica, N. Y.**—Gauges, marine clocks, revolution counters, gauge testing apparatus. D 73. 555

662 **Cleveland Steam Gauge Co., Cleveland, O.**—Gauges, spring balances, test pump and gauge. D 72. 555

663 **Aultman, Miller, & Co., Akron, O.**—Self-registering dynamometer. D 68. 555

664 **Davis & DuBois, Philadelphia, Pa.**—Tallow cups for engines, etc. D 68. 555

665 **Lynde, J. D., Philadelphia, Pa.**—Governors, valves, feed water heaters, regulators and low water alarm combined. B 71, *and Boiler house 4.* 555

666 **Union Water Meter Co., Worcester, Mass.**—Water meters, steam gongs, governor valves, steam and water regulators. D 67. 555

667 **Kline, Aaron K., Sommerville, N. J.**—Governor for steam engines. D 69. 555

667*a* **Burnet, William, Washington, D. C.**—Lubricator. *Pump annex 8 and 9.* 555

667*b* **Hetzel, Herman V., Philadelphia, Pa.**—Speed indicator. B 73. 555

667*c* **Chard & Howe, New York, N. Y.**—Lubricating compound and cup. A 47. 555

667*d* **Canfield Manufacturing Co., Philadelphia, Pa.**—Steam and hydraulic stuffing-box packing, self-lubricating hempen fibre, gum core. D 68. 555

668 **Haurey, Henry F., Newark, N. J.**—Flue and tube brushes. D 69. 555

669 **Jenkins, Wm. H., & Co., Philadelphia, Pa.**—Boiler feeder, steam trap, damper regulator, low water alarm, safety valve, steam gauges. D 77. 555

670 **Bibb, B. C., & Son, Baltimore, Md.**—Fireplace heater. D 72. 555

671 **Post & Co., Cincinnati, O.**—Steam gauges. D 71. 555

672 **Greenwich Machine Works, Greenwich, N. Y.**—Horseshoe corking vise and bolt heading machine. A 37. 555

673 **Tracy, Eliashib, Philadelphia, Pa.**—Injector for boilers. D 68. 555

674 **Clark, Rufus F., Philadelphia, Pa.**—Cylinder oiler. E 69. 555

675 **Lathrop Anti-friction Co., New York, N. Y.**—Carbon composition machinery lubricator. D 68. 555

676 **Asbestos Patent Fibre Co. (limited), Philadelphia, Pa.**—Utilized fibre, paper, board; steam joints and packing, non-conducting pipe covering. D 69. 555

For classes of exhibits, indicated by numbers at end of entries, see Classification, pp. 13-15.

Motors and Appliances, Pumps.

677 Davis, J. B., Hartford, Conn.—Feed water heater and purifier. D 68. 555

678 Jasper, George F., Freeburg, Ill.—Heater and filter. D 78. 555

679 Brown, Fergus, & Co., Philadelphia, Pa.—Injector for steam boilers. (*In use in building.*) 555

680 Brown & Fergus, Philadelphia, Pa.—Steam injector for steam boilers. (*In building.*) D 68. 555

680*a* Metallic Art Works, Boston, Mass.—Plates and castings of bronze. C 71. 555

680*b* Jamison, Samuel S., Saltsburg, Pa.—Steam water-injector, car replacer, chimney top. B 64. 555

681 Le Van, W. Barnet, Philadelphia, Pa.—Steam engine governors, damper regulator, and furnace grate bars. D 70. 555

682 Willoughby, James D., Philadelphia, Pa.—Governor cut-off for steam engines. D 68 *and* 51, *and Pump annex.* 555

683 Woodruff, A. H., Lansing, Iowa.—Reverse and expansion gear for locomotives and propeller engines. D 69. 555

685 Newell, Wm. H., Philadelphia, Pa.—Injector valves. (*In building.*) 555

686 Allen, Stillman B., Boston, Mass.—Governor for steam engines. D 72. 555

686*a* Pickering, T. R., Portland, Conn.—Steam engine governors. C 74. 555

687 Osgood, Josiah A., Boston, Mass.—Crank pin oiler, metallic spring packing, etc. D 69. 555

688 McNab & Harlin Manufacturing Co., New York, N. Y.—Valves, cocks, whistles, water gauges, iron fittings, plumbers' materials. B 40. 555

689 Edson's Steam Recording Gauge Manufacturing Co., 91 Liberty street, New York, N. Y.—Gauges, electrical alarms, revolution counters. Sole makers of "Edson's Patent Recording Gauges" for steam or water, with or without the "time" attachment, or the "electrical alarm"; also "revolution counters," and "30-inch gauges." Reliable as "standards of pressure." Send for circulars. D 67. 555

690 Schutte & Goehring, Philadelphia, Pa.—Steam jet machinery, furnace blowers, ventilators, injectors, syphons, gas exhausters, condensers, etc. (*Pump annex.*) 555

690*a* Leonard, T. M., New York, N. Y.—Oil cup and dynamometer. B 52. 555

690*b* Miller, W. P., New York, N. Y.—Lubricant. D 52. 555

690*c* Pratt & Whitney Co., Hartford, Conn.—Automatic boiler-feeder and return steam trap. (*In use in Boiler houses.*) 555

690*d* Smith, Levi F., Philadelphia, Pa.—Low water indicators, lubricators, gauge, steam trap, blower, comb-wrench, car seat, etc. D 78. 555

691 Lonergan & McBride, Philadelphia, Pa.—Oil cups and lubricators. D 66. 555

692 Silver Lake Co., Boston, Mass.—Self-lubricating steam packing. D 68. 555

Hydraulic and Pneumatic Apparatus, Pumping, Hoisting, and Lifting.

693 Dart, Edward & Co., New York, N. Y.—Rotary pumps and engines, marine governors, cotton gins, presses, duplex plunger crank steam pump. (*Pump annex.*) 560

694 Cooper, Jones, & Cadbury, Philadelphia, Pa.—Pumps. B 19. 560

695 Silsby Manufacturing Co., Seneca Falls, N. Y.—Rotary steam pump. This firm also has two rotary steam fire engines and a hose cart on the Exhibition grounds, in charge of the Centennial fire brigade. Illustrated and descriptive circulars—English, Spanish, French, and German—may be had on application. A 4. 560

696 Valley Machine Co., Easthampton, Mass. — Bucket-plunger steam pumps. (*Pump annex.*) 560

697 Kelly, Wm. E., New Brunswick, N. J.—Steam pumps. (*Pump annex and Boiler house 3.*) 560

698 Aquometer Steam Pump Co., Philadelphia, Pa.—Steam pumps. (*Pump annex.*) 560

699 Hubbard & Aller, Brooklyn, N. Y.—Steam pumps. (*Pump annex.*) 560

700 Union Manufacturing Co., New Britain, Conn.—Iron and brass cistern; force, yard, drive well; garden engines, boiler, pumps, and rams. (*Pump annex.*) 560

700*a* Purvis, Edward, New York, N. Y.—Automatic steam valve. (*Pump annex 8–11.*) 560

700*b* Nichols, Harris & Walker, New London, Conn.—Acid pump and syphon. (*Pump annex 2–12.*) 560

700*c* Craig & Brevoort, New York, N. Y.—Condenser for steam pumps, steam engines, etc. (*Pump annex 2–12.*) 560

700*d* Hyneman, Isaac, Philadelphia, Pa.—Odorless excavating pump. (*Pump annex 1–5.*) 560

700*e* Le Page, W. N., Boston, Mass.—Force pumps. (*Pump annex 2–12.*) 560

700*f* Wood, Joseph, Red Bank, N. J.—Steam pump. E 69. 560

700*g* Hubbard, S. D., Pittsburg, Pa.—Steam pump. (*Boiler house 3.*) 560

700*h* Young, William, Easton, Pa.—Young's patent wrought iron, rubber-coated, brass cylinder lift and force pumps for deep wells and cisterns. Being made principally of wrought iron, are strong, light and durable. The cylinder and all the working parts are made of brass, works smooth, very durable, and will not rust the water as iron would. (*Pump annex 7–5.*) 560

701 Wiswall, H. M., Boston, Mass.—Rotary and oscillating pumps. (*Pump annex.*) 560

702 Norwalk Iron Works Co., South Norwalk, Conn.—Direct acting non-expansive steam pumps. C 76. 560

For location of objects, indicated by letter and figure, see Key to Notation, p. 10; ground plan, p. 11.

Pumps, Compressed-Air Engines.

703 La France Manufacturing Co., Elmira, N. Y.—P 11, *and Pump annex.*
a Rotary pumps and engine. 560
b Rotary steam fire engine. 564

704 Rumsey & Co. (limited), Seneca Falls, N. Y.—Pumps, hydraulic rams. B 45, *and Pump annex.* 560

705 Carr, Adam, New York, N. Y.—Direct action steam pumps; compound direct action pump; will save sixty per cent. in fuel and boilers; positive circulating steam radiators; noiseless friction hoisting engine; condensers for steam engines and pumps. (*Pump annex and Boiler house 4.*) 560

706 Douglas, W., & B., Middletown, Conn.—Pumps, hydraulic rams, pump chain, garden engines, curbs, chain pump fixtures; grindstone frame. (*Pump annex.*) 560

707 Vail & Wallace, Keokuk, Iowa.—Water elevator. (*Pump annex.*) 560

708 Mitchell, J. H., Philadelphia, Pa.—Deck pump for ship use. B 80. 560

709 Hooker, Wm. D., Dedham, Mass.—Direct acting steam pumps. (*Pump annex.*) 560

710 Chapman, Henry, Philadelphia, Pa.—Centrifugal hydro-extractor, for brewers' grains, etc. Kiln model. (*Pump annex 13.*) 560

710*a* Waring, J. B., Stamford, Conn.—Steam pump. (*Pump annex 12.*) 560

710*b* Toledo Pump Co., Toledo, O.—Wood pumps. (*Pump annex 5.*) 560

710*c* Hathorn, Davis, Campbell, & Davey, New York, N. Y.—Pump engine. C 3 *and* 4, *and Pump annex 27.* 560

710*d* Heold, Sisco & Co., Baldwinsville, N. Y.—Steam centrifugal pump and centrifugal pumps driven by belts. (*Pump annex.*) 560

711 Follensbee, Geo. S., Lewistown, Me.—Double propeller pump. (*Pump annex.*) 560

712 Grosvenor, J. A., Jersey City, N. J.—Pulsometer steam pump, operated by pressure of steam on surface of water. (*Pump annex.*) 560

713 Biggs, B. F., & Wells, La Fayette, Ind.—Wooden lifting and suction pump. (*Pump annex.*) 560

713*a* Ferrell & Jones, Philadelphia, Pa.—Combined steam pump and engine; centrifugal pump and yoke steam pump. (*Pump annex 8.*) 560

713*b* Matthewman & Johnson Pump Co., New Haven, Conn.—Excavating pump with deodorizing apparatus. (*Pump annex 12.*) 560

713*c* Blake, George F., Manufacturing Co., Boston, Mass.—Steam pump. (*Pump annex 8–9.*) 560

713*d* Eagle Odorless Excavating Co., Philadelphia, Pa.—Oderless excavator. (*Pump annex.*) 560

713*e* Roberts, E. A. L., Titusville, Pa.—Sand pump. C 78. 560

713*f* Crane Bros. Manufacturing Co., Chicago, Ill. (*Pump annex 7.*)
a Steam elevators and pumps. 560
b Hoisting engines and steam radiators. 563

714 King, Charles W., Boston, Mass.—Force pumps and house pumps with removable cylinders. (*Pump annex.*) 560

715 White, Clark, & Co., Baldwinsville, N. Y.—Centrifugal pump. (*Pump annex.*) 560

716 Poole & Hunt, Baltimore, Md.—Feed water heater and pump. C 79. 560

717 Willoughby, James D., Philadelphia, Pa.—Pulseless pulsometer. D 51 *and* 68, *and Pump annex.* 560

718 Bradley, J., & Co., Philadelphia, Pa. — Odorless excavating apparatus. (*Pump annex.*) 560

719 Gawthrop, A., & Son, Wilmington, Del.—Glass models of hydraulic rams with regulators, in operation. (*Pump annex.*) 560

720 Huffer, Abraham, Hagerstown, Md.—Automatic steam vacuum pump. (*Pump annex.*) 560

721 Pease, F. S., Buffalo, N. Y.—Pneumatic pump. (*Pump annex.*) 560

723 Bagley & Sewall, Watertown, N. Y.—Rotary metal force pump with self-packing joints, without stuffing-boxes or valves; pressure on working parts equalized; absolutely positive in action; volume of liquid discharged proportionate to power and speed applied. Specially adapted to use of paper makers, brewers, tanners, etc., and for fire protection. (*Pump annex.*) 560

724 Niagara Steam Pump Works, Brooklyn, N. Y.—Direct acting steam pump and crank pump. (*Pump annex.*) 560

725 Hydrostatic & Hydraulic Co., Philadelphia, Pa.—Shaw's compound propeller pumps for quarries, mines, etc. Propeller wheels secured to rotating shaft lifts from one thousand to one hundred thousand gallons per minute any height; has no valves, and is not liable to obstruction. Office, at Shaw's Engineering Depot, 915 Ridge avenue, Philadelphia, Pa. (*Pump annex.*) 560

726 Conde & Co., Philadelphia, Pa.—Steam pumping engine. (*Pump annex.*) 560

727 Nye, Gourlay, & Co., Chicago, Ill.—Steam vacuum pump. (*Pump annex.*) 560

730 Sluthour & Mintzer, Philadelphia, Pa.—(*Pump annex.*)
a Force and bilge hand pumps. 560
b Fire engines. 564

731 Albright & Stroh, Mauch Chunk, Pa.—B 19.
a Model of duplex steam pump. 560
b Fire-plugs. 566

732 Allison & Bannan, Port Carbon, Pa.—Improved air compressing engines. Correspondence and orders solicited. A 52. 561

732*a* Burleigh Rock Drill Co., Fitchburg, Mass.—Rock drilling machines, drill carriages, air compressor, tunelling and mining machines. A 51. 561

732*b* Taws & Hartman, Philadelphia, Pa.—Fittings for, and drawings of, blasting furnaces. B 20–21. 561

732*c* Union Rock Drill Co., New York, N. Y.—A 60.
a Air compressor. 561
b Hose couplings for rock drills. 564

733 Coffin & Woodward, Boston, Mass.—Main and bilge pump for vessels, force pump. D 39. 562

For classes of exhibits, indicated by numbers at end of entries, see Classification, pp. 13–15.

Hydraulic and Pneumatic Machines, Elevators.

734 Roots, P. H. & F. M., Connersville, Ind.—Rotary pressure blowers, hand blowers, gas exhauster. Patentees and manufacturers of positive blast rotary blowers, and gas exhausters, adapted to all purposes for which blast or exhaust are required; also of improved Bye passes and gas valves. (*Pump annex.*) 562

734*a* Patterson, C. R., Pittston, Pa.—Suction and blast fan. B 61. 562

734*b* Gould's Manufacturing Co., Seneca Falls, N. Y., New York office 15 Park Place.—Iron and brass force and lift pumps, rotary pumps, ship, railroad, mine, and quarry pumps, hydraulic rams, garden and fire engines. A very elaborate exhibit. (*Pump annex 8 and 10.*) 564

735 Ferris & Miles, Philadelphia, Pa. —Blowing engine, steam hammer, and steam drop. (*Annex 1.*) 562

736 Wilbraham, T., & Bros., Philadelphia, Pa.—Pressure blowers and steam engines, gas exhausters and steam engines. (*Pump annex.*) 562

737 Morris Co., I. P., Philadelphia, Pa. —Blowing engine—ten thousand seven hundred and forty cubic feet of air per minute. B 48. 562

738 Roddey, P. D., & Co., New York, N. Y.—Ship ventilator, fog alarm, bilge pump. (*Pump annex.*) 562

740 Murphy, Francis, Streator, Ill.—Ventilating apparatus for mines, tunnels, steamboats, etc. (*Pump annex.*) 562

741 Disston, Thomas S., Philadelphia, Pa.—Rotary pressure blower. (*Pump annex.*) 562

742 Sturtevant, B. F., Boston, Mass.—Pressure and fan blower. *Pump annex 10–9.* 562

743 Chase, F. D., Boston, Mass.—Patent ventilating ship deck irons, in brass composition, and galvanized iron; intended for vessel decks, steam car roofs, etc. Seven sizes; flues, from four to nine inches in diameter. Patented, June 23, 1863, improved 1875. (*Pump annex.*) 562

744 Wemner, P. L., Lebanon, Pa.—Blowing engine. B 69. 562

745 Exeter Machine Works, Boston, Mass.—Pressure blowers, fan blowers, and exhaust fans. (*Pump annex.*) 562

745*a* Boston Piston Meter Co., Boston, Mass.—Fluid meter. (*Pump annex 2–3.*) 563

746 Howard, George C., 13¼ South Eighteenth street, Philadelphia, Pa.—Hoisting machine; screw gear runs in a bath of oil; patent stop brake, belt shifter, pulleys self-oiling, on independent bearings, car for any location. Elevators made with double and single engines. B 31. 563

747 Gunpowder Pile Driver Co., Philadelphia, Pa.—Pile driver. (*Outside of building.*) 563

748 Ruoff, William, Philadelphia, Pa. —Double and single-geared jack screws, for moving and raising stone and all heavy weights. (*Pump annex.*) 563

749 Stewart, Ralph, & Co., Philadelphia, Pa.—Packing machines. D 23. 563

750 Eccles, James, Philadelphia, Pa.—Quadruple screw-power press, pivot centre for drawbridge, etc. D 60. 563

751 Sternberger, Leopold, Philadelphia, Pa.—Safety screw steam platform elevator. Patent right for sale. Address Jas. W. Rowley, 1511 North Twentieth street, Philadelphia. E 76. 563

751*a* Pennypacker, Matthias, Philadelphia, Pa.—Hand hoisting machine. (*Pump annex 1.*) 563

752 Harrison, W. H., Philadelphia, Pa. —Double-acting two-valve pump and hydraulic elevator. (*Pump annex.*) 563

753 Pneumatic Despatch Co., New York, N. Y.—Pneumatic tube. (*Outside of building.*) 563

754 Bolen, Crane, & Co., Newark, N. J. —Compound hydraulic press. (*Pump annex.*) 563

755 Eagle Meter Co., New York, N. Y. —Water meter. (*Pump annex.*) 563

756 Archbold, Samuel, 417 Walnut street, Philadelphia, Pa.—Marsland's liquid meter, for measuring water and other fluids. Of the turbine wheel form; has only one moving part, besides the register; is not at all affected by sand or silt passing through it; no friction, no wear—hence great durability; readily understood and easily operated. Manufactured by the American Meter Co., Philadelphia. (*Pump annex.*) 563

757 Dudgeon, Richard, New York, N. Y.—Hydraulic jacks, pullers, and expanders. C 27. 563

758 Taylor, John F., Charleston, S. C. —Steam and hydraulic cotton press. C 54–56. 563

759 National Meter Co., New York, N. Y.—Water meters. C 27. 563

759*a* Baily & Co., Faxcroft, Me.—Elevator for raising rocks, etc. (*Adjoining Annex 3.*) 563

759*b* United States Hoisting & Conveying Co., New York, N. Y.—Automatic machinery for hoisting, conveying, and depositing. (*Outside of Machinery Hall.*) 563

759*c* Higgins, H. Van, Chicago, Ill.—Water meter; oscillating piston meter. (*Pump annex 1.*) 663

759*d* Carlile & Elliott, Steubenville, O.—Safety lock for elevators. (*Pump annex 1.*) 563

760 Guerin, Thomas, San Francisco, Cal.—Instrument for measuring and regulating the flow of water from reservoir or canal. (*Pump annex 1–2.*) 563

761 Mason, Volney W., & Co., Providence, R. I.—Elevator hoisting machine and safety platform. Also, friction clutch pulleys, driving main line of shafting in pump annex and in Machinery Hall adjoining, near Corliss engine. D 66, *and Pump annex.* 563

762 Williams, S. S., & Co., Philadelphia, Pa.—Hod elevator. (*Pump annex.*) 563

763 Goldmark, Joseph, New York, N. Y.—Safety elevators for hotels, dwellings, and warehouses, operated by steam, water, or hand power. These elevators are absolutely safe, by virtue of the mechanical principles underlaying their construction; they, therefore, require no safety appliances whatsoever, beyond a common break. They are run in private resi-

Hydraulic Machines, Fire Engines and Appliances.

dences by water pressure, at an expense of less than half a cent for a round trip, and are used by women and children without requiring a special attendant. A 40. 563

763a Remington, E., & Sons, Ilion, N. Y.—Water meter. (*Pump annex 1.*) 563

764 Robertson, John, & Co., Brooklyn, N. Y.—Hydraulic pumps, hydraulic presses. (*Pump annex.*) 563

765 Ross, Thos., Rutland, Vt.—Steam crane. (*Annex 2.*) 563

766 Randall, Francis M., New York, N. Y.—Automatic steam and vacuum pump. (*Pump annex.*) 563

766a Maclay, J. W., New York, N. Y.—Water meter. (*Pump annex 1.*) 563

766b Ritter, J. R., Reading, Pa.—Model of hoisting apparatus. (*Pump annex 5.*) 563

767 Jones & Holmes, Providence, R. I.—Water elevators for open wells. (*Outside of building.*) 563

768 Bates, James, Baltimore, Md.—Hand elevator. (*Pump annex.*) 563

769 Yale Lock Manufacturing Co., Stamford, Conn.—Safety hoisting machinery, friction clutches and brakes, differential pulleys, drilling braces, stud end cutter. C 78. (*Outside.*) 563

770 Foulds, Thomas, jr., Trevorton, Pa.—Water elevator. (*Pump annex.*) 563

773 Otis Bros. & Co., 348 Broadway, New York, N. Y.—Passenger elevator, including engine, safety drum, etc. Manufacturers of brewery elevators, which are generally in use and with great satisfaction in many of the large breweries throughout the country. Their specialty in this line is the elevators, including independent hoisting engine, safety platform, with galvanized iron work, to prevent rust, with lifting ropes and safety ratchets, etc. B 38. 563

774 Leonard & Silliman, Bridgeport, Conn.—Grain elevator. E 56. 563

774a Sweetland, I. B., Pontiac, Mich.
a Brick and mortar elevator. (*Annex 3.*) 563
b Self-packing faucet, rubber packing. (*Annex 3.*) 566

775 Desper, W. E., & Co., Worcester, Mass.—Water meters. (*Pump annex.*) 563

776 Tatham & Bros., New York, N. Y.—B 21.
a Safety apparatus for hoisting machines. 563
b Drop and buck shot, lead and tin-lined lead pipe, tin-lined iron pipe, sheet lead. 566

777 Silsby Manufacturing Co., Seneca Falls, N. Y.—Rotary steam fire engines, horse hose carriage and hand hose reel. Also, in charge of the Centennial Fire Brigade, two rotary steam fire engines and horse hose cart. Illustrated and descriptive circulars, English, Spanish, French, and German, may be had on application. A 6. 564

778 Street, E. A., New York, N. Y.—Portable fire pump. B 45. 564

778a Halloway, Charles T., Baltimore, Md.—Chemical self-acting fire engine; portable fire extinguisher. A 40. 564

778b Birkinbine, H. P. M., Philadelphia, Pa.—Apparatus for operating hydraulic valves at a distance. B 46. 564

778c Fairbrother, H. L., & Co., Pawtucket, R. I.—Leather belting. D 9, 72. 564

778d Babson & Dwight, New York, N. Y.—Self-regulating fire-escapes. (*West end of Machinery Hall, opposite column 82.*) 564

778e Heywood, C. L., & Co., Boston, Mass.—Iron safety folding fire-escape ladder. B 68. 564

779 Straw, E. A., Manchester, N. H.—Steam fire engine. (*In use on grounds.*) 564

780 Schanz, C., Philadelphia, Pa.—Hook and ladder truck for firemen. B 54–56. 564

780a Falk, Louis, New York, N. Y.—Portable fire escape. A 5. 564

780b Wilson, W. H., New York, N. Y.—Firemen's hats and helmets. B 62. 564

781 Champion Fire Extinguishing Co., Louisville, Ky.—Chemical engines, with hook, ladder, and hose attachments, hand fire extinguishers. B 56. 564

782 Babcock Manufacturing Co., New York, N. Y.—Chemical engines, hook and ladder trucks, truck and engine combined, fire extinguishers. B 57–60. 564

783 Platt, Wm. K., & Co., Philadelphia, Pa.—Fire extinguishers. B 49. 564

784 Vose, Wm. T., Boston, Mass.—Hydropult, for extinguishing fires, washing and watering purposes. A 4. 564

784a Eureka Fire Hose Co., New York, N. Y.—Seamless cotton and linen fire hose. E 68. 564

784b Gutta-Percha & Rubber Manufacturing Co., New York, N. Y.—Rubber belting, hose, and packing. B 44. 564

785 Spawn, A. F., & Co., New York, N. Y.—Chemical fire engines, hose carriage, hook and ladder truck, firemen's supplies. B 64–66. 564

787 Nichols, B. S., & Co., Burlington, Vt.—Steam fire engine. (*Pump annex.*) 564

788 Gomersall, Alfred, Philadelphia, Pa.—Engines, pumps, model of hose carriage. C 79. 564

789 Greer, Samuel Y., Philadelphia, Pa.—Hand hose carriage, leather fire hose, leather fire buckets. B 50. 564

791 Rumsey & Co. (limited), Seneca Falls, N. Y.—Hand fire engine. B 45. 564

794 Dennisson, J. N., Newark, N. J.—Steam fire engine, portable waterworks. B 48. 564

795 Lamm, John, Port Deposit, Md.—Fire extinguisher. Permanent for dwellings, factories, etc.; useful to gardeners. Rights for sale by patentee. B 66. 564

796 Lindlaw, John E., New York, N. Y.—Fire escape. B 56. 564

797 Holmes, Horatio L., Providence, R. I.—Cap-bar and stand, combination tool post, with samples of work. (*Pump annex 1-5.*) 564

798 Daniels, T. E., Detroit, Mich.—Fire escape and ladder. (*Annex.*) 564

799 Wannalansett Manufacturing Co., Boston, Mass.—Linen fire hose, hose reels, pipes, couplings, etc. Ross Turner & Co., selling agents, 159 Devonshire street, Boston, Mass. A 41. 564

For classes of exhibits, indicated by numbers at end of entries, see Classification, pp. 13–15.

Hydraulic and Pneumatic Machines and Appliances.

800 **Clapp & Jones Manufacturing Co.,** Hudson, N. Y.—Piston steam fire engines. B 62. 564

801 **Button, L., & Son, Waterford, N.** Y.—Steam hand and fire engine. B 42-43. 564

802 **Zwietusch, Otto, Milwaukee, Wis.** —B 25.
a Chemical fire extinguisher. 564
b Soda-water apparatus, beer preserver, etc. 565

803 **Lippincott, Charles, & Co., Philadelphia, Pa.** —Apparatus for manufacturing and dispensing soda-water and other aerated beverages. A 27, D 3, *and* B 61. 565

804 **Bates, Benjamin, Baltimore, Md.** —Copper and silver carbonaters, with attachments. A 20. 565

806 **Matthews, John, New York, N. Y.** —Apparatus for making, bottling, and dispensing soda-water and aerated beverages. A 24. 565

807 **Puffer, A. D., Boston, Mass.—Beer** apparatus, soda, syrup and mineral-water apparatus. A 22. 565

808 **Postens, Edward, Philadelphia,** Pa.—Soda water and aerated beverages in bottles; apparatus and accessories. A 25. 565

809 **Tufts, James W., Boston, Mass.**— Soda water apparatus, generators, fountains, tumbler washers, etc. A 19 *and* B 23. 565

810 **Chapman & Co., Madison, Ind.**— Portable soda fountain. A 28. 565

811 **Fergus, James, & David, Philadelphia, Pa.**—Machine for bottling and corking liquors. A 22. 565

812 **Hey, Michael, Philadelphia, Pa.**— Beer pump, with bar fixtures, water pressure machine, beer cooler, air bung and regulator. Manufacturer of all kinds of beer pump bar fixtures, patent water pressure machine, patent beer coolers, patent air bung and patent air regulator, and all kinds of beer spigots and coupling, etc. E 68. 565

813 **Lalance & Grosjean Manufacturing** Co., New York, N. Y.—Seamless soda water fountains. A 21. 565

814 **Morris, Tasker, & Co., Philadelphia, Pa.**—Wrought iron tubes, tools, and brass work. A 70, *and* C 27. 566

815 **Kirk, Geo. R., Philadelphia, Pa.**— Patent regulating cylinder lubricator, with gauge showing contents, brass cocks, and valves. B 19–20. 566

815*a* **Carpenter, J. M., Pawtucket, R.** I.—Machinists' and blacksmiths' taps, pipe fitters' dies, and die stocks. Hill, Clarke & Co., selling agents, Boston, Mass. C 38-40. 566

815*b* **Birkinbine, John, Philadelphia,** Pa.—Fire hydrant and case. B 46. 566

815*c* **Powell, Wm., & Co., Cincinnati,** O.—Valves and lubricators. B 22. 566

815*d* **Talley, James, jr., Kansas City,** Mo.—Liquid faucet, automatic bung. B 29. 566

815*e* **Powell, Wm., & Co., Cincinnati,** O.—Regrinding globe valves; automatic lubricators, etc. B 22. 566

816 **Woodruff & Beaumont, Kankakee** City, Ill.—Stop valve. B 19. 566

817 **Flower, James, & Bro., Detroit,** Mich.—Stop valve, fire hydrant, machine for squaring nuts, oil cups. D 20. 566

818 **Evans, Dalzell, & Co., Pittsburg,** Pa.—Boiler, oil-well, radiator, artesian and hydraulic tubing; wrought iron pipe, coils, sockets, nipples, and fancy designs. B 25. 566

818*a* **Basshor, Thos. C., & Co., Baltimore, Md.**—Automatic relief valve for steam fire engines. A 6. 566.

818*b* **Porter, Charles E., Washington,** D. C.—Fountain nozzle—prevents clogging. B 19. 566

819 **Warren Foundry & Machine Co.,** Phillipsburg, N. J.—Gas and water pipe. (*Outside of Machinery Building.*) 566

820 **Mohawk & Hudson Manufacturing** Co., Waterford, N. Y.—Straightway valves, garden hydrants, fire hydrants. B 21. 566

822 **Bridgewater Iron Co., Bridgewater, Mass.**—Forgings, seamless copper and brass tubes, and bolts, chilled soft rolls, spikes, roll plates, metal sheathing, etc. B 22–23. 566

823 **Gloucester Iron Works, Philadelphia, Pa.**—Cast iron pipes, fire hydrants, stop valves, and lamp posts. B 26. 566

825 **National Tube Works Co., Boston,** Mass.—Iron boiler tubes, iron hydraulic, steam, gas, water, and sewage pipes, enameled pipe, injector. E 74, *and* D 10. 566

826 **Meyer, Henry C., & Co., New York,** N. Y.—Faucets, anti-freezing hydrants, street washers, combined hitch post and street washer. B 27. 566

827 **Crosby Steam Gauge & Valve** Co., Boston, Mass.—Steam gauges and safety valves, hydraulic and vacuum gauges, etc. D 67. 566

827*a* **Wood, R. D., & Co., Philadelphia,** Pa.—Hydrant. (*Pump annex 4-9.*) 566

827*b* **Shedd, J. Herbert, Providence, R.** I.—Hydrant box, taps, stops, gates, cover and valve. C 27, *and Pump annex 4.* 566

827*c* **Douglas, W. & B., Middletown,** Conn.—Pumps, hydraulic rams, garden engines, etc. (*Pump annex.*) 566

827*d* **American Tube Works, Boston,** Mass.—Brass and copper tubes. B 20-21. 566

828 **Cook & Pulver, New York, N. Y.**— Lubricating cups, and lubricating compound. D 69. 566

829 **Peet Valve Co., Boston, Mass.**— Brass and iron steam valves. B 22. 566

830 **Merrill & Keizer, Baltimore, Md.**— Gauge cocks for steam boilers. D 64. 566

831 **Wood, R. D., & Co., Philadelphia,** Pa.—Fire hydrants, cast iron pipe, Eddy valves, lamp posts, turbine wheels, duplex turbine. Cast iron pipe for gas and water from one and a half to seventy-two inches diameter. Fire hydrants; Mathew's patent anti-freezing sliding frost case; waste opened by positive motion, without springs, weights, or levers. All working parts removable from ground without dig-

Machinery Fittings, Valves, Tubes, etc., Locomotives.

ging. Valves; Eddy's patent straight way double gated gates, hung on universal joint; perfectly adjustable duplex turbine so arranged as to develop full power from variable quantities of water; lampposts; turbines; heavy machinery. B 18, *and Pump annex.* 566

832 Roots, P. H. & F. M., Connersville, Ind.—Tuyere irons and fire bed, bye pass, gas valves. Patentees and manufacturers of hand blowers for blacksmithing of all kinds; also, portable forges adapted to every variety of work; also, improved Tuyere iron and fire bed combined. (*Pump annex.*) 566

833 Allison, W. C., & Sons, Philadelphia, Pa.—Boiler tubes, oil-well tubing, steam pipe, rivets, bolts, nuts, washers, carriage bolts, forgings. B 24. 566

834 Cooper, Jones, & Cadbury, Philadelphia, Pa.—Supplies for plumbers, steam fitters, and machinists, etc. B 19. 566

835 Merchant & Co., Philadelphia, Pa. —Seamless brass and copper tubes, sheet and planished copper, brass wire and tubing, tin plates. B 19. 566

836 Patent Water & Gas Pipe Co., Jersey City, N. J.—Wrought iron asphaltee cement water pipe. B 22. 566

837 Flagg, Stanley G., & Co., Philadelphia, Pa.—Fittings for gas, steam, and water pipes. A 41. 566

838 Ludlow Valve Manufacturing Co., Troy, N. Y.—Sliding stop valves for water, gas, and steam, fire hydrants, etc. B 26. 566

839 Lunkenheimer, Fred., Cincinnati, O.—Automatic cylinder lubricators and glass oil-cups for steam engines; steam valves, with regrinding device; untrimmed brass castings. B 21 *and* 22. 566

840 Stileman, R. T. H., Philadelphia, Pa.—Water gates, fire hydrants, and station valves. B 19 *and* 20. 566

842 Lewistown Brass & Engine Co., Lewistown, Pa.—Brass goods. C 74. 566

843 Walworth Manufacturing Co., Boston, Mass.—Steam heating apparatus; steam and gas fitters' tools, etc.; laundry apparatus, etc.; pipe and fittings for steam, gas, and water. A 76, E 73 *and* B 41. 566

844 Radde, William, 548 Pearl street, New York, N. Y.—Patent glass-lined iron pipe; keeps water, chemicals, and all liquids perfectly pure; prevents poisoning by metallic water pipes; is a safe pipe for aquaria; resists frost, and gives full satisfaction. Patent underground telegraph system; secures perfectly reliable telegraphic connections, under all circumstances, and, thereby, life and property; is composed entirely of inorganic substances. Naked copper wires are drawn through very small glass tubes (3 to 18 and upwards), which are held in the required position in an iron pipe by paraffine wax. Both articles are cheap; need no repairs. B 3–20. 566

845 Chapman Valve Manufacturing Co., Boston, Mass.—Water, gas, and steam valves, with Babbitt metal seats. B 33-34. 566

846 Jarecki Manufacturing Co., Erie, Pa.—Brass work for steam, gas, water, oil, and iron fittings, adjustable pipe tongs. B 20–21. 566

847 Starr, Jesse W., & Son, Camden, N. J.—Castings for gas and water, lamp posts, fire hydrants, stop valves, etc. (*Outside of building.*) 566

848 Colwell Lead Co., New York, N. Y.—Lead pipe, sheet lead, block tin pipe, tin-lined lead pipe. B 22–23. 566

849 Long Dennis, & Co., Louisville, Ky.—Cast iron gas and water pipes. Have in operation three foundries, with melting and casting capacity of 200 tons daily; supply the gas and water mains for the principal cities and towns west, north, and south. B 20–21. 566

849*a* Warren Foundry & Machine Co., Phillipsburg, N. J.—Cast iron water pipe. (*In building near Machinery Hall.*) 566

849*b* Peck Bros., & Co., New Haven, Conn.—Brass-plated cocks, valves, and fittings for plumbers', gas and steam fitters' use. A 40. 566

850 Larlwig & Batten, New York, N. Y.—Champagne freezer. B 21. 566

851 O'Neill, Andrew, Ansonia, Conn.— Cast iron pipe; patent gas and water mains, jointing without hot lead, a saving of 50 per cent. over the old; O'Neill's patent-planished copper and brass, tinned or nickeled; nickeled sheet zinc and yellow metal couplings for soil or surface and telegraph pipes. B 3-22, *and outside.* 566

852 Mills, Thomas, & Bro., Philadelphia, Pa.—Vertical engine and ice cream freezer combined, ice cream freezers and freezing apparatus. E 65. 568

853 Knickerbocker Ice Co., Philadelphia, Pa.—Ice tools, elevators, wagons, and ice machinery. B 18. 568

Railway Plant, Rolling Stock, and Apparatus.

855 Burnham, Parry, Williams, & Co., Philadelphia, Pa.—Locomotives. E 41 -43, *and* E 45. 570

855*a* Rhode Island Locomotive Works, Providence, R. I.—Passenger locomotive engine; photographs of locomotives. E 46. 570

855*b* Brooks' Locomotive Works, Dunkirk, N. Y.—Narrow-gauge locomotive. (*West End Passenger R. R.*) 570

856 Pease, James H., Reading, Pa.— Historical chart of inventions and improvements of the locomotive and railway system. E 71. 570

857 Rogers Locomotive & Machine Works, Paterson, N. J.—Locomotive engine, and tender. D 41, 42, 43. 570

858 Danforth Locomotive & Machine Co., Paterson, N. J.—Locomotives. D 28 *and* 41. 570

859 Howe, Henry, Council Bluffs, Iowa.—Apparatus for supplying locomotives with water. D 68. 570

859*a* Dickson Manufacturing Co., Scranton, Pa.—Portion of the Stonebridge Lion locomotive. C 27. 570

For classes of exhibits, indicated by numbers at end of entries, see Classification, pp. 13–15.

Locomotives, Railway Plant, Scales.

859*b* Polytechnic College, Philadelphia, Pa.—Working model compressed locomotive with horizontal grip drivers for ascending planes. E 44. 570

859*c* Robinetz, James F., Petersburg, Va.—Model locomotive. (*Empire Transportation Co.'s building.*) 570

860 Rowand, John R., Philadelphia, Pa.—Locomotive-power brake. For the safety of life, in collisions, through the crushing of coal, in the ends of the platforms of locomotives. E 48. 570

861 Porter, Bell, & Co., Pittsburg, Pa. —Narrow-gauge passenger locomotive and tender. Exclusive specialty light locomotives. Catalogues sent on application. E 44-46. 570

863 Philadelphia & Reading Railroad Co., Philadelphia, Pa.—Locomotive and tender. D 44-47. 570

864 Dickson Manufacturing Co., Scranton, Pa.—Locomotive and mining machinery. E 49-53. 570

865 Pennsylvania Railroad Co., Altoona, Pa.—Locomotive built in 1831, baggage and passenger car combined (old style). (*Outside of building.*) 570

866 Mason Machine Works, Taunton, Mass.—Narrow gauge locomotive. (*In use on West End Railroad.*) 571

866*a* Johnson, Chas. E., & Co., Lansing, Iowa.—Self-coupling railway car. F 35. 571

866*b* Lebanon Manufacturing Co., Lebanon, Pa.—Coal cars. (*Outdoors, west of Machinery Hall.*) 571

867 Riehle Bros., Philadelphia, Pa.—Scales, testing machines, beams, rope-twisters, sand-sifters. E 54. 571

868 Fairbanks & Ewing, 715 Chestnut street, Philadelphia, Pa. (Manufacturers, E. & T. Fairbanks & Co., St. Johnsbury, Vt.)—Railroad track, weigh lock, hay, coal, platform, and counter scales of all descriptions; fine gold and druggists' scales; also improved testing machines for ascertaining the strength of metals, etc. Principal warehouses, Boston, New York, Philadelphia, Baltimore, New Orleans, San Francisco, St. Louis, Chicago, Louisville, Cincinnati, Cleveland, Buffalo, Pittsburg, Albany, Montreal, and London, England. E 56-60. 571

869 Brandon Manufacturing Co., Brandon, Vt.—Railroad, merchandise, post-office, and other scales, beams and trucks. E 61-63, *and* D 8. 571

870 Dell, John C., Philadelphia, Pa.—Scales and weights. D 62. 571

871 Buffalo Scale Co., Buffalo, N. Y.—Platform, counter, and combination beam scales. D 54. 571

872 Crossman, M., Marshall, Ill.—Hand car. (*Outside of Machinery Hall.*) 571

873 Becker & Sons, 232 E. 128th street, New York, N. Y.—Becker's construction of improved balances and weights of precision for druggists, chemists, assayers, and for all purposes where accuracy is required. D 51. 571

874 Meyers, F., Newark, N. J.—Scales. D 53. 571

875 Hitchcock, S. S., Des Moines, Iowa.—Scales. D 47. 571

877 Gilly, John L., Columbus, O.—Freight cars; car wheels. (*West of Machinery Hall.*) 571

878 Ball, C. A., & Co., Midland Park, N. J.—Trucks. C 9-71. 571

879 Willoughby, James D., Philadelphia, Pa.—Notifying scales, frictionless scales. D 8 *and* 51. 571

880 Chatillon, John, & Sons, New York, N. Y.—Spring balances, self-adjusting scales, counter scales, scale beams. D 50. 571

881 Harrisburg Car Manufacturing Co., Harrisburg, Pa.—Eight-wheeled box freight cars. B 1-9, *and* A 5-9. 571

883 Price, Lipsett, & Co., Philadelphia, Pa.—Railroad track scale, platform scales. E 76. 571

885 Robidoux, Joseph, & Sons, New York, N. Y.—Scale beams, frames, hooks, etc. D 49. 571

886 Steinway & Sons, New York, N. Y. —Metal frames for pianofortes, pianoforte actions. D 49. 571

887 Automatic Scale Co., Boston, Mass.—Automatic scales. D 51. 571

888 Reinhardt, Chas., Brooklyn, N. Y. —Druggists', gold, and diamond scales. D 62. 571

889 Henderson Hydraulic Car Brake Co., Philadelphia, Pa.—Car brake, by steam or hydraulic pressure. D 64-66. 572

889*a* Singer, Jacob, Harrisburg, Pa.—Automatic car coupler; brakeshoe. E 72. 572

889*b* Welch, Robert R., Frankford, Pa. —Automatic car coupler. E 74. 572

890 Lahaye, J. J., Reading, Pa.—Model cars with automatic couplings. In successful operation on the Philadelphia & Reading Railroad, by which company it was adopted after more than a year's trial. D 64. 572

891 Barton, C. S., Philadelphia, Pa.—Railway station indicator, operated from engine by compressed air or by hand. D 64. 572

892 Haase, John A., Philadelphia Pa.—Model of safety car-step. B 41. 572

892*a* Eames Vacuum Brake Co., Watertown, N. Y.—Injector, valve, vacuum, brake, etc. D 69. 572

892*b* Decrow, A. W., Bangor, Me.—Smoke conductor; railroad concussion brake. E 69. 572

894 Kline, Aaron K., Somerville, N. J. —Model of car coupling. D 69. 572

895 Nelson, Nels, Minneapolis, Minn. —Steam and air car brake, car coupler. D 65. 572

896 Bing, James, Philadelphia, Pa.—Brake shoe. E 76-77. 572

897 Westinghouse Air Brake Co., Pittsburg, Pa.—Automatic brakes, vacuum brakes, air compressors, speed indicators, engine governors, engine. D 67. 572

898 Cobb, Z., & Sons, Wilmington, Del. —Elliptic steel springs, for car seats and upholsterers, door springs. E 68. 573

For location of objects, indicated by letter and figure, see Key to Notation, p. 10; ground plan, p. 11.

Railway Plant, Wheels, Springs, Trucks, etc.

899 Cayuta Wheel & Foundry Co., Waverly, N. Y.—Chilled wheels for cars and engines; specimens and tests. E 64. 573

900 Lobdell Car Wheel Co., Wilmington, Del.—New and old railroad car wheels, tires, castings, etc. E 65. 573

901 Ramapo Wheel & Foundry Co., Ramapo, N. Y.—Railroad car and engine wheels. E 71. 573

902 Culmer Spring Co., Pittsburg, Pa. —Springs for railway purposes. Spiral draft, bolster, journal, equalizing bar, tender, brake release, switch, and valve springs. Spiral springs of all descriptions, made to order. E 69. 573

903 Bryant, George B., Pottsville, Pa. —Self-oiling car wheels, loose pulleys, cups, car journals; vehicle and carriage wheel hubs; independent car axles. E 66. 573

904 French, A., & Co., Pittsburg, Pa. —Elliptic springs for cars and locomotives. E 71. 573

905 Miltimore Car Axle Co., New York, N. Y.—Railroad car truck, with combined, stationary, and revolving axles, loose, independent wheels, and oscillating boxes. Six sets narrow gauge railroad car trucks, fitted with the Miltimore axles and wheels, are in use on the West End Passenger Railway. D 69–70. 573

906 Tryon, Geo. K., Son, & Co., Philadelphia, Pa.—Car and other bearings and articles of phosphor-bronze, composition, Babbitt, and type metal. E 71. 573

907 Davenport, Fairbairn, & Co., Erie, Pa.—Engine and car wheels. E 70. 573

908 Miles, W. A., Copake Iron Works, Copake, N. Y.—Car wheels. E 68. 573

909 Middleton, N. & A., & Co., Philadelphia, Pa.—Railroad car springs with section of trucks. E 66 *and* 70. 573

910 Barnum Richardson Co., Lime Rock, Conn.—Salisbury iron ore, charcoal pig iron, cast chilled car wheels. E 71. 573

910*a* Ewart Manufacturing Co., New York, N. Y.—Drive chains. E 62. 573

910*b* National Car Spring Co., New York, N. Y.—Elliptic, spiral, rubber, volute and rubber centre spiral car springs. E 68. 573

911 Standard Steel Works, Philadelphia, Pa.—Crucible steel locomotive and car wheel tires, castings, and forgings. E 72. 573

912 Midvale Steel Works.—Works and Office, Nicetown, Philadelphia, Pa. C 23.

a Cast steel tires, all sizes and sections; record of trial in hydraulic press of Baldwin locomotive works, April, 1876. 573

b Cast steel axles, guaranteed to stand five blows of seventeen hundred pounds' drop, falling twenty-five feet upon four-inch section, bearings three feet apart; axle reversed between blows. 573

c Same, bent, cold. 573

d Rails, twisted, cold. 574

e Solid cast steel forging, diameter thirteen inches: length, twelve feet. Tensile strength per square inch, 83,824 pounds; elastic limit, per square inch, 50,000 pounds; elongation under strain, 16.5 per cent. 513

f Solid steel castings; railroad crossing; planed anvil-face, weighing 3280 pounds. 513

g Miscellaneous ingots. 513

h Ingots of open-hearth steel, broken, showing solidity and characteristics of same. Elastic limit per square inch, 65,018 pounds; tensile strength, per square inch, 123,220 pounds; elongation under strain, 16.5 per cent. 513

i Tool, machinery, and spring steel, all shapes, with fractures and evidences of quality. 513

j Forgings. 514

913 Lang, Wm., Bailey, & Co., New York, N. Y.—Cast steel locomotive tires. F 70. 573

914 Whitney, A., & Sons, Philadelphia, Pa.—Car wheels and axles. E 72. 573

915 American Paper Car Wheel Manufacturing Co., Hudson, N. Y.—Coach, truck and car wheels, of paper, steel and iron combined. E 65. 573

916 Washburn Car Wheel Co., Hartford, Conn.—Steel-tired car wheels, cast iron centres. E 70. 573

916*a* White, Joseph J., Smithville, N. J. —Portable fare-box. D 64. 573

917 Sax & Kear, Pittston, Pa.—Steel-tired truck and car wheels, with cast iron centres. E 73. 573

918 Harrison, Samuel L., San Francisco, Cal.—Railroad car axle, with independent wheels. E 72. 573

919 Schoem, Wm. H., Wilmington, Del.—Locomotive, car, and wagon springs. E 67. 573

920 Nichols, Pickering, & Co., Philadelphia, Pa.—D 67.

a Railway elliptic, volute and spiral springs. 573

b Cast steel nut-lock washers. 574

921 Fields, Wm., Wilmington, Del.— Cast steel rails, made direct from iron ore. E 64. 573

922 McKee, Fuller, & Co., Catasauqua, Pa.—Railroad car wheels. D 65. 573

922*a* Baltimore Car Wheel Co., Baltimore, Md.—Chilled cast iron engine and car wheels; samples of iron. E 66. 573

922*b* Atwood Railway Wheel Co., New York, N. Y.—Railway wheels. E 69. 573

922*c* Vose, Dinsmore, & Co., New York, N. Y.—Elliptic, spiral, rubber, volute and rubber centre spiral car springs. E 68. 573

922*d* Roberts, A. & P., & Co., Philadelphia, Pa.—Hammered and rolled car axles. E 72. 573

922*e* Hopkins, D. A., Jersey City, N. J. —Car journal boxes. E 69. 573

922*f* Woodbury, James A., Boston, Mass.—Elastic steel tire car wheels. E 70. 573

922*g* Taylor Iron Works, High Bridge, N. J.—Passenger wheels on axle, narrow gauge wheels, sample wheels and sections; axles bent cold, etc. E 69. 573

923 Nashua Iron & Steel Co., Nashua, N. H.—Steel plates, tires, axles, shaftings, bars, and forgings; iron axles, bars, plates, car wheels, and forgings. E 66–67. 573

For classes of exhibits, indicated by numbers at end of entries, see Classification, pp. 13–15.

Railway Plant, Agricultural Machinery.

923*a* Eccles, James, Philadelphia, Pa. —Frictionless journal box for railroad car axles. D 60. 573

923*b* Columbia Car Spring Co., New York, N. Y.—Spiral and rubber car springs. E 69. 573

923*c* Jeffries, James, & Sons, Philadelphia, Pa.—Locomotive, tender, and elliptic car springs. E 69. 573

924 Hamilton Steeled Wheel Co., Philadelphia, Pa.—Car wheels and specimens of metal, process of manufacture. D 68. 573

925 Jersey City Wheel Foundry & Machine Works, Jersey City, N. J.—Elastic steel tired car wheels, chilled car wheels. D 68. 573

925*a* Potter & Hoffman, Philadelphia, Pa.—Railway construction tools. B 30. 573

925*b* Union Car Spring Co., Bridgeport, Conn.—Car springs, and steel. E 71. 573

926 Raddin, John, Lynn, Mass.—Elastic car and carriage wheels, automatic brakes, compensating wheels, bunters, elastic chains, etc. E 70. 573

927 Fisher & Norris, Trenton, N. J.— "Fisher" patent rail joints for broad and narrow gauge roads. B 6–41, *and Annex 1*. 574

928 Wharton Railroad Switch Co., Philadelphia, Pa.—Railroad switch, steel rail frogs, steel rail crossing. D 71–73. 574

930 Jersey City Iron Works, Jersey City, N. J.—Detachable steel rail frogs and crossings, safety switch stands, car replacer. D 71. 574

931*a* Cochrane, John, New York, N. Y. —Cleats to secure rails to the cross ties. E 48. 574

931*b* Wood, Joseph, Red Bank, N. J.— Adjustable spring, and stationary frogs. E 69. 574

931*c* Scheiner, J. H., Philadelphia, Pa. —Frogs for cars and signals. E 71. 574

931*d* Stillman, Wait J., Troy, N. Y.— Track guard. (*Outside of building.*) 574

931*e* Redding, W. E., New York, N. Y. —Railroad switches. (*Outside of building.*) 574

931*f* Mansfield Elastic Frog Co., New Haven, Conn.—Railroad frog. E 71. 574

931*g* Kasson, C. Vallette, Buffalo, N. Y. —Continuous rail, railway frog, and crossing. E 78. 574

931*h* Seely & Stevens, New York, N. Y. —Pellucidite,—architectural wood finish. (*Used on all wood work in Machinery Hall.*)

932 Pennsylvania Steel Co., Harrisburg, Pa.—Bessemer steel ingots, blooms, forgings, and rails, open hearth steel ingots and blooms, safety switch, steel rail crossing and frogs, car replacer. D 29, *and* E 62. 574

933 Diamond State Iron Co., Wilmington, Del.—Railway track fastenings and merchant bar iron. Manufacturers of railroad splice bars, all sizes; noted for fit, quality, and finish. Track bolts and spikes of superior iron; extra quality bar and horseshoe iron. E 62. 574

933*a* Lukens, J. H., Burlington, N. J.— Railway switch stand. D 71. 574

933*b* Barker, E. W., Portland, Me.— Car coupler. D 70. 574

933*c* Wood, Joseph, Red Bank, N. J.— Railroad frogs; switch stand. E 69. 574

933*d* Tuthill, Daniel S., Newburg, N. Y.—Railway tracks—to overcome contraction and expansion. E 72. 574

934 Pratt Manufacturing Co., New York, N. Y.—Elastic fish joints. E 62. 574

935 Bean, H. & B. F., Pawling, Pa.— Mail pouch holder and catcher for railroad cars while in motion, draw heads for cars. D 66. 575

936 Rousseau's Railway Signal Co., New York, N. Y.—Electric railway signals, office indicators, switch locks, circuit closer, etc. D 67. 575

937 Wharton, Wm., jr., Philadelphia, Pa.—D 72.

a Patent Bessemer steel street railway curves; cast iron street railway curves; cast iron street railway switches; cast iron street railway frogs; cast iron street railway crossing. 574

b Patent cast-iron street railway turntable. 575

938 Spahn, Emil P., Newark, N. J.— Models for automatic railroad crossings, gates, and signals. E 57. 575

939 Ridge, Elmer, Philadelphia, Pa.— Balance folding gates for railway crossings. D 65. 575

939*a* Lansing, H. S., Philadelphia, Pa. —Railroad crossing safety gate. (*Northeast of Machinery Hall.*) 575

939*b* Williams, Joseph S., Philadelphia, Pa.—Anti-frog tracks, rail switches, and crossings, rail supports, and car ventilator. P 72. 575

939*c* Heywood, C. L., & Co., Boston, Mass.—Railroad bridge guard, for the protection of train men, at bridges over railroads. E 41. 575

939*d* Hitchcock Lamp Co., Watertown, N. Y.—Lamps for fat oils and kerosene. D 40. 575

939*e* Post & Co., Cincinnati, O.—Railway passenger-car trimmings, locomotive head lights. D 71. 576

Machines used in preparing Agricultural Products.

940 Deal, M., & Co., Bucyrus, O.— Separator and smutter, brush smutter, warehouse separator, and mill machinery trucks, etc. E 57. 580

941 Bullock, C. K., Philadelphia, Pa.— Flour mill machinery. E 52. 580

942 Huntley, Halcomb, & Hine, Silver Creek, N. Y.—Purifier, bran dusters, bolting cloth. E 47. 580

944 Howes, Babcock, & Co., Silver Creek, N. Y.—Eureka smut and separating machine. Eureka brush polishing machine. The worst samples of smutty and foul wheat can be perfectly cleaned with these two machines. Grain separator, with patent zigzag arrangement for separating oats and all other seeds from wheat. Bolting cloth, elevator buckets, mill stone brush, pick handles. E 49. 580

944*a* Mungon Bros., Utica, N. Y.—Corn grinding mill, eye spindles, levers, etc. E 61-62. 580

Agricultural Machinery.

944*b* Cumbie & Donald, New York, N. Y. — Mechanical oven model. E 66, 67. 580

944*c* Stangeland, Elias, Rockdale, Minn. — Grain steaming machine. E 60. 580

944*d* Teter, W. L., Bristol, Tenn.—Self-regulating silent mill feed. E 63. 580

945 Noye, John T., & Son, Buffalo, N. Y.—Flour mill models, portable mills, millers' tools, middlings purifier, bran duster. E 47. 580

945*a* Gilbert, Calvin, Chambersburg, Pa.—Combined separating and scouring smut machine. E 57. 580

946 Ingraham & Beard, Chicago, Ill.—Grain scourer, smutter separator, grader, dustless malt and warehouse separator and grader. E 54. 580

947 Young, J., & S. Bernheisel, Green Park, Pa.—Flour bolt and middlings purifier combined, with bran separator and duster attached. E 57. 580

948 Harris, Clinton S., Elizabeth, N. J.—Smut and scouring machine, and suction fan for cleaning grain. E 58. 580

949 Richardson, D. M., Detroit, Mich.—Improved patent wheat scourer, polisher, and separator. The principles covered in this machine may be briefly stated as follows, viz.: It scours and polishes the wheat thoroughly, without breaking, cutting, scratching, wearing away, or impairing the bran fibre, thereby leaving the bran full strength. When the wheat goes upon the burrs, the bran comes off in large flakes or patches, and passes through without pulverizing and mixing with the flour; the blast can be adjusted to secure any desired separation. F 60. 580

950 Turner, Parks, & Co., Cuyahoga Falls, O.—Rolling screen separator, middlings purifier, malt scourer, garlic, rat-ball, and straw extractor. E 58. 580

952 Barnard & Leas Manufacturing Co., Moline, Ill.—Smutter, scourers, separator, flour packer, corn sheller, corn cleaner. E 48. 580

952*a* Conklin, N. A., Brooklyn, N. Y.—Corn chitting and hominy mill. F 48. 580

952*b* Roland, Francis, & Co., Reading, Pa.—Grain decorticator and separator; model of water wheel. E 61. 580

954 Woodward, Thos. B., Philadelphia, Pa.—Mill stones, mills, flour mill machinery. E 46. 580

955 Baltimore Pearl Hominy Co., Baltimore, Md.—Hominy mill or corn granulator. Manufacturers of breakfast hominy, samp, corn flour, pearl meal, etc. Sole owners and manufacturers Patent Buckeye Hominy Mill. F 59. 580

957 Griscom & Co., Pottsville, Pa.—Diamond mill stone dressing machines. (Will do as much work in one hour as can be done in a day with the pick.) Used by best mills. Thirty days' trial allowed. E 53. 580

958 Harrison, Edward, New Haven, Conn.—Vertical burr stone mills for grain, minerals, etc., and combined flouring mill and bolter. E 59. 580

959 Leonard & Silliman, Bridgeport, Conn.—Burr stone flour and grist mills. E 56. 580

959*a* United States Attrition Co., New York, N. Y.—Attrition mill for pulverizing ores, cereals, etc. F 49. 580

959*b* Allis, Edward P., & Co., Milwaukee, Wis.—Middlings purifier and duster, mill stones, cockle separator, and crushing rolls. E 56. 580

959*c* Hanna, C. T., Keokuk, Iowa.—Wheat steamer and dryer. E 57-58. 580

959*d* Macarthy, John, New York, N. Y.—Bran picker and duster. E 60. 580

959*e* Mecutchen, Jesse G., Philadelphia, Pa.—Smut machine, and mill stones. E 58-59. 580

959*f* Throops Grain Cleaner Co., Auburn, N. Y.—Grain scourer and separator; wheat brushing machine. E 68. 580

959*g* Kreider, Campbell, & Co., Philadelphia, Pa.—E 50.
a Grain mill. 580
b Spice mill. 585

960 Lafferty, H. W. & R., Gloucester, N. J.—Centrifugal sugar-draining machines, with mixer and elevator. E 46. 581

960*a* Schemedes, J. W. R., New York, N. Y.—Evaporator. E 57. 581

960*b* Colwell & Bro., New York, N. Y.—Vacuum pan and sugar refining apparatus. E 79. 581

960*c* Hepworth, S. S., New York, N. Y.—Centrifugal extractor. E 79-80. 581

961 Mills, Thomas, & Bro., 1301 and 1303 North Eighth street, Philadelphia, Pa.—Confectioners' tools, fruit-drop machine and rollers; flat stick, sour drop, and paper fringing machines. Patent candy slicer, cocoanut grater, cutters, egg beater, and toy machine. E 65. 582

962 Gardner, Mrs. John, Philadelphia, Pa.—Confectionery tools, candy machinery. F 48. 582

963 Croft, Wilbur, & Co., Philadelphia, Pa.—Revolving pans for making confections. E 64. 582

964 Mitchell, J. H., Philadelphia, Pa.—Cocoanut grater, candy slicer. B 80. 582

965 Anderson, J. P., Philadelphia, Pa. —Cocoanut graters, candy slicers. F 45. 582

966 Colburn, Levi J., Chicago, Ill.—Confectionery; process of manufacture. F 46. 582

967 Archer & Brownell, Richmond, Va.—Process of manufacturing plug and twist chewing and smoking tobacco, cigarettes. F 57. 584

967*b* Wulstein, Henry, New York, N. Y.—Tobacco granulator. F 55. 584

967*c* Tygh, James F., Philadelphia, Pa.—Tobacco stripping and booking machine; cigar moulds. F 60. 584

968 Cain, P. O., & Co., Philadelphia, Pa.—Cigar moulds. F 55. 584

969 Enterprise Manufacturing Co., Patented Hardware Manufacturers and Iron Founders, American and Dauphin streets, Philadelphia, Pa.—Coffee, drug, and spice mills, twenty sizes; measuring faucets, tobacco cutters, cheese knives, sad irons, bung-hole borers, sausage stuffers, fruit and jelly pressers. F 56. 585

970 Dell, John C., Philadelphia, Pa.—Coffee mills, scales. D 62. 585

Agricultural Machinery, Boats, Vessels, and Appliances.

971 Boyd, G., Philadelphia, Pa.—Coffee roaster, coffee cooler. (*Annex 1.*) 585

973 Weikel & Smith Spice Co., Philadelphia, Pa.—Coffee roasting and spice mill machinery. (*Annex 1.*) 585

974 Troemner, Henry, 710 Market street, Philadelphia, Pa.—Coffee mills; manufacturers of scales and balances in use at the U. S. Treasury, and all the U. S. Mints and Assay Offices. F 55. 585

975 McCollum, L. A., New York, N. Y. —Cracker machine, dough mixer, reversible dough brake, mechanical oven. E 66. 585

976 Silver & Deming Manufacturing Co., Salem, Ohio.—Meat choppers and meat stuffers. F 54. 586

976*a* Speihlman, Geo., Strasburg, Pa. —Meat chopper. F 55. 586

977 Ruger, J. W., & Co., Buffalo, N. Y. —Cracker, bread, and cake machinery and bakers' tools. F 62. 586

978 Murray Iron Works Co., Burlington, Iowa.—Meat choppers, lard presses, sausage stuffers, etc. This exhibit attracts special attention of butchers and sausage makers. The draw-cut movement of the knives (which is that of a knife used by hand), is the peculiar feature which is claimed, distinguishes these machines from all others, and secures to them a clean cut, without noise or pounding and with very little wear of the parts. Some of them have been in constant use for over four years, without repairs of any kind. Their beauty, and the smoothness and precision of their work, attracts very general attention from the many who are interested in this kind of machinery, they being the only "draw-cut" machines made. F 60. 586

979 Huber & McCarter, Lancaster, Pa. —Steam meat chopper. E 60. 586

979*a* Roberts, Carle, & Co., New York, N. Y.—Hand cutter. E 57. 586

979*b* Kenyon, J. H., Plainfield, N. J.— Hand and power meat choppers. F 61. 586

979*c* Nittinger, August, jr., Philadelphia, Pa.—Butchers' and packers' machinery. F 54. 586

980 Sauter, Charles, Reading, Pa.— Malt cleaning machine, cylinder-wheel malt chopper. E 69. 587

981 Reford, J. W., Philadelphia, Pa.— Grain-distilling and vapor-rectifying apparatus. E 69. 587

982 Boese, C., & Co., New York, N. Y. —Capping machines, for adjusting metallic capsules on bottles, jars, etc. E 68. 587

Aerial, Pneumatic, and Water Transportation.

982*a* Sewall, Day, & Co., Boston, Mass. —Shrouding, rope, etc. E 39. 590

983 Hartness, James, Detroit, Mich.— Section balloon, with life-boat attached. D 32. 592

984 Swarzmayer, John, Philadelphia, Pa.—Flying machine model. D 33. 592

985 Page, E. W., New York, N. Y.— Boat oars. D 32. 594

986 Bolles, J. N., Baltimore, Md.— Models for submarine work. A 56, *and outside.* 594

987 Fields, William, Wilmington, Del.—Models of armor-ship, and field-battery gun. E 64. 594

988 Chomel, I. A., Brooklyn, N. Y.— Swinging berths and platforms for prevention of sea-sickness. D 31. 594

989 Grinnell, Irving, New Hamburgh, N. Y.—Ice yacht. D 28–31. 594

989*a* Lyman, William, Middlefield, Conn.—Bow-facing rowing gear. D 31, *and on lake.* 594

990 Wilen, George C., Philadelphia, Pa.—Small boat. D 32. 594

991 Richards, H. J., West Troy, N. Y. —Ice yacht. D 34. 594

992 Walton, Lewis W., New York, N. Y.—Row-lock for boats. D 35. 594

993 Burr & Co., New York, N. Y.— Tackle blocks, etc. D 34. 594

993*a* Perry, E. L., New York, N. Y.— Life raft. D 37. 594

993*b* Whistler, Thos., Baltimore, Md. —Non-capsizable life boat. D 31. 594

993*c* Stoner, John B., New York, N. Y. —Floating lighthouse. D 35–36. 594

994 Desmond, Timothy, New York, N. Y.—Pair-oared gig. D 36. 594

994*a* Bird, John, Philadelphia, Pa.— Glass moulding press. (*Annex 3.*) 594

995 Adams, John & Co., Gloucester, N. J.—Life preserving mattress, self-righting life boat. D 33. 594

995*a* Lyman, W., Middlefield, Conn.— Rowing gear. D 31, *and on lake.* 594

995*b* Jackson, James L., New York, N. Y.—Steering apparatus; process and apparatus for making patterns. C 35–36. 594

996 Waters, E., & Sons, Troy, N. Y.— Paper boats, barrels, packages, cylinders, etc. D 35–36. 594

997 Bryant, John L., & Co., Philadelphia, Pa.—Double life boat. D 33. 594

998 Von Behren & Shaffer, Stryker, O.—Boat oar, handspike. D 38. 594

999 Smith, D. S., Philadelphia, Pa.— Canoe, "Dolphin," of Queenstown, Md. D 38. 594

1000 Jones, John McA., Philadelphia, Pa.—Boat-detaching apparatus. D 32. 594

1001 Begin, Peter N., Detroit, Mich.— Revolving head light for vessels. D 39. 594

1002 Hook, Gilman, West Harwich, Mass.—Toy yacht. D 32. 594

1003 Rider Life Raft Co., New York, N. Y.—Life rafts. D 40. 594

1004 Miles, Geo. W., Philadelphia, Pa. —Single scull shell. D 40. 594

1005 McGilvery, S. W., Belfast, Me. —Model for clipper ship. D 40. 594

1006 Powell, Richard, Washington, D. C.—Improvement in building iron vessels. D 39. 594

1006*a* Bradlee & Co., Philadelphia, Pa. —Cable and rigging chains. D 38. 594

1006*b* Fearon, Thomas, Yonkers, N. Y. —Shell boats, composite planking. E 40. 594

For location of objects, indicated by letter and figure, see Key to Notation, p. 10; ground plan, p. 11.

Boats, Vessels, and Appliances.

1006*c* Roach, John B., Chester, Pa.—Models of vessels, shaft and froggings. E 40. 594

1006*d* Glass, Wm., Philadelphia, Pa.—Race boat. D 36–37. 594

1006*e* Englis, John, & Son, Greenpoint, N. Y.—Steamship models. D 34. 594

1006*f* Flower, Wm., Bangor, Me.—Life saving apparatus, boat lowering, and detaching apparatus, etc. E 35. 564

1006*g* Goldie, George, Princeton, N. J.—Rowing machine. D 40. 594

1006*h* Pusey, Jones, & Co., Wilmington, Del.—Photographs and models of steamboats and steamships. C 74. 594

1006*i* Harrington, Charles B., Bath, Me.—Schooner yacht. D 32. 594

1006*j* Parcels, Thomas, Philadelphia, Pa.—Full-rigged schooner sailing yacht. D 49. 594

1006*k* Mallory, W. H., Bridgeport, Conn.—Steam yacht. *On Schuylkill river.* 594

1006*l* Cort, Mrs. C. A. van, New York, N. Y.—Torpedo boat. D 31. 594

1006*m* Francis, Frank, Philadelphia, Pa.—Model of bark. D 36. 594

1006*n* Johnson, Hilary C., Philadelphia, Pa.—Miniature model of a full rigged ship. D 40. 594

1006*o* Kahnweiler, David, New York, N. Y.—Cork jacket. D 40. 594

1006*p* Ormsbee, M., Brooklyn, New York.—Sleeve life preservers and collar rescuer. "The Sleeve Life Preservers" are used to great advantage in pleasure-swimming, and, as a teacher of the novice, learning the art. To skaters they afford comfort, keeping the arms warm and the body harmless from falling, besides saving life should the ice break, preventing cramp in the arms, however cold the weather. Cricketers also wear them. They make two excellent pillows for traveling on the cars, boats, etc. They can be placed side by side for a cushion, and are easily carried in the pocket, and can be put on very quickly. "The Collar Life Preserver" rescues persons from drowning; is used also as a cushion for the house, counting-room, or traveling in the cars or boats, and as a cabinet invalid chair cushion. It can be put on instantly for life saving, even by a child two years of age; is used as a seat in the parks to prevent colds and sickness from sitting upon the damp ground. Bathing-house proprietors can be furnished with life preservers at prices that must assure them a handsome income from their sale or rental, with bathing-dresses, and by keeping the Collar Life Preservers always ready, none of their patrons can possibly be drowned, as they can be rescued in less than a minute by any of the assistants. Either of the preservers costs $5; or $1, to hire for a trip to Europe, or elsewhere. For particulars, address Capt. M. Ormsbee, patentee and manufacturer, 52 Willow street, Brooklyn, New York. D 40. 594

1006*q* Tipton, John, Philadelphia, Pa.—Model of boat. D 36. 594

1006*r* Rowland, T. F., Greenpoint, N. Y.—Steam launch, metallic life boat. A 69 *and* D 31. 594

1006*s* Roach, John, & Son, New York.—Models, armor plate, and marine engine work. E 40. 594

1007 United States Bunting Co., Lowell, Mass.—Bunting and flags. F 40. 594

1008 Massachusetts State Commission, Leverett Saltonstall, Commissioner, N. E. Tower Main Building, Philadelphia, 18 Pemberton Square, Boston, Mass.—Water craft, old and new, and articles which take part in their construction and use,—being an historical exhibit of the growth of the marine interests of Massachusetts, from the earliest periods to the present time. F 38–40. 594

1009 American Life-Saving Suit Co., New York, N. Y.—Life-saving suit for ocean travel, surf belt for river travel. D 33. 594

1010 Wyatt, John L., Yonkers, N. Y.—Full-rigged clipper South Sea whale ship. E 38. 594

1011 Gildersleeve, S., & Sons, Gildersleeve's Landing, Conn.—Working models of wooden, steam, and sail vessels, for profitable freighting business. Largest carrying capacity on light draft with good sailing qualities. D 40. 594

1012 Poillon, C., & R., New York, N. Y.—Model of schooner yacht "Sappho" and pilot boats "Thomas S. Negus," of N. Y., and "E. C. Knight," of Philadelphia. E 39. 594

1013 Webb, Wm. W., New York, N. Y.—Models and plans of celebrated naval and other vessels. D 31. 594

1014 Cannon, John D., New Castle, Del.—Hooped skiff boat, without timbers or knees. D 31–32. 594

1015 Baird & Huston, Philadelphia, Pa.—Steam yacht. D 38–40. 595

1016 Harlan & Hollingsworth Co., Wilmington, Del.—Ships, models, drawings, and plans of vessels and machinery, paintings of ships and steamboats. D 29. 595

1017 Griffiths, John W., New York, N. Y.—Model of ocean steamship; "The Progressive Ship Builder." D 40. 595

1018 Zantzinger, Dan'l W., Washington, D. C.—Model and section of steamship, improvement in construction of iron vessels. The above improvement consists in providing small watertight compartments entirely surrounding the hull of the vessel. D 40. 595

1019 Grant, D. Conrad, Houghton, Mich.—Adjustable ice plow and naval ram, or submarine mortar, attached to miniature boat. D 40. 594

1020 New York Safety Steam Power Co., New York, N. Y.—Steam launch. E 38–40. 595

1021 Crowell, J. W., & Co., Cambridge, Md.—Models for steam and sail vessels. Builders of all classes of wooden vessels. Frames furnished of best quality of Chesapeake white oak. We invite inquiry as to our facilities. D 40. 595

1022 Thwait, Charles, Astoria, N. Y.—Model of steamship, with working machinery. D 35. 595

1022*a* Sulter, Frederick, Philadelphia, Pa.—Propeller screws, models and drawings of boiler, etc. D 78. 595

For classes of exhibits, indicated by numbers at end of entries, see Classification, pp. 13–15.

Vessels and Appliances, Machinery in Use.

1022*b* **American Steamship Co., Philadelphia, Pa.**—Models and paintings of the steamers of the company. C 41. 595

1023 **Pennsylvania Combined Iron & Steel Association, Philadelphia, Pa.**—Combined iron and steel armor plate, steel bore wrought iron guns. D 28-30. 594

1024 **American Dredging Co., 10 South Delaware avenue, Philadelphia, Pa.** — Improved grapple and dipper dredges, and machinery for river and harbor improvements. E 40. 596

1024*a* **Hawley, Abel, Washington, D. C.**—Rotary dredge. E 40. 596

1024*b* **Eau Claire Lumber Co., Eau Claire, Wis.** — Sheer rudder loom and pontoon bridge. (*Saw mill.*) 596

1025 **Cox, Frank, Philadelphia, Pa.**—Model for coffer dam for removing propellers from ships. E 39-40. 596

1026 **Coffin & Woodward, Boston, Mass.**—Capstans, chain-stopper, screw-steerer, and rudder-supporter, elastic-traveler, portable winch, windlasses, pumps, etc. Best modern improved articles. D 39. 597

1026*a* **Robinson, R. M., Philadelphia, Pa.**—Simple and compound anchor, with apparatus. D 5. 597

1027 **Sickles, F. E., Providence Steam Engine Co., Providence, R. I.**—Original models of some of exhibitor's early inventions, now in use in this country and abroad, viz.: Trip cut-off, patented 1842, and improvements thereon patented 1845; casting steam chest on cylinder, patented 1845; improvement on working exhaust valves, patented 1844; first machine made or used to apply power to the rudder of vessels (in operation), application filed 1849, patented in 1860, etc.; improved compound engine, patented 1875; also original models of improvement in sinking pneumatic piles; also other original models. D 38. 597

1028 **Getchett, John S., Washington, Me.**—Capstan. D 40. 597

1029 **American Ship Windlass Co., Providence, R. I.**—Capstans, windlass models. D 40. 597

1030 **Hutchinson, T. C., Philadelphia, Pa.**—Anchor. D 40. 597

1030*a* **Hamilton, S. M., Baltimore, Md.**—Hydraulic cement. (*Annex 3.*) 103

1031 **Hampton Emery Co., Chester, Mass.**—Emery in grains. B 37. 106

1032 **Potts Bros., Pottstown, Pa.**—Flanged boiler iron and boiler flue iron. B 24. 111

1032*a* **Potter & Hoffman, Philadelphia, Pa.**—Iron and steel; boiler plate; pig and bar iron. B 30. 111

1033 **Rittenhouse, E. W., & Bro., Baltimore, Md.**—Terra-cotta pipe. (*Outside of building.*) 206

Machinery and Apparatus Especially Adapted to the Requirements of the Exhibition.

1034 **Pease, F. S., Pease, Buffalo, N. Y.**—Furnishes all the oil used for the shafting in Machinery Hall. 201

1035 **Sellers, Wm., & Co., Philadelphia, Pa.**—Electric registers, showing number of admissions at gates throughout the day. 321

1036 **Ledgerwood Manufacturing Co., New York, N. Y.**—Ash-hoister. 503

1037 **American Twist Drill Co., Woonsocket, R. I.**—Emery grinding machine, used in the Centennial machine shop. 505

1038 **Stillwell & Bierce, Dayton, O.**—Heater used in boiler house No. 4. 506

1039 **McNeil, George, Philadelphia, Pa.**—Heater used in boiler house No. 4. 506

1040 **Sellers, Wm., & Co., Philadelphia, Pa.**—Lathes, used in the Centennial machine shop. 510

1041 **Prentice, A. F., & Co., Worcester, Mass.**—Lathe and drill, used in the Centennial machine shop. 510

1042 **Fitchburg Machine Co., Fitchburg, Mass.**—Lathe and drill for use in the Centennial machine shop. 510

1043 **Smith, H. B., Smithville, N. J.**—Full set of wood-working tools for Centennial carpenter shop. 510

1044 **Keystone Portable Forge Co., Philadelphia, Pa.**—Three 6 power forges 54 inches in diameter, for the Centennial machine shop. 514

1045 **Stephens Patent Vise Co., New York, N. Y.**—Vises, used in the Centennial machine shop. 514

1046 **Fisher & Norris, Trenton, N. J.**—Vises and anvils, used in the Centennial machine shop. 514

1047 **Mitchell, J. E., Philadelphia, Pa.**—Grindstones, used in the Centennial machine shop. 515

1048 **Andrews, W. D., New York, N. Y.**—50 horse power boiler and pumps; boiler for use, and pumps for supplying cataract. 550

1049 **Abendroth & Root, New York, N. Y.**—100 horse power boiler, supplying steam to steam pumps, etc. 550

1050 **Steam Generator Manufacturing Co., Philadelphia, Pa.**—100 horse power boiler, supplying steam to steam engines. 550

1051 **Babcock & Wilcox, New York, N. Y.**—150 horse power boiler, supplying steam to steam pumps, etc. 550

1052 **Harrison Boiler Works, Philadelphia, Pa.**—100 horse power boiler, supplying steam to steam engine. 550

1053 **Exeter Machine Works, Boston, Mass.**—7 horse power boiler, supplying steam to steam pumps, etc. 550

1054 **Kelly, W. E., New Brunswick, N. J.**—50 horse power boiler, supplying steam to steam pumps, etc. 550

1055 **Lynde, J. D., Philadelphia, Pa.**—50 horse power boiler, supplying steam to steam engines. 550

1056 **Miller, Charles B., Philadelphia, Pa.**—Boiler, used in boiler house No. 4. 550

1057 **Smith, C. D., Boston, Mass.**—Boiler, used in boiler house No. 3. 550

1058 **Lowe & Watson, Bridgeport, Conn.**—Boiler, used in boiler house No. 3. 550

Machinery in Use.

1059 Mast, P. P., & Co., Springfield, O.—Boiler, used in saw mill boiler house. 550

1060 Baxter Steam Engine Co., New York, N. Y.—Engine and boiler, used in Nevada quartz mill. 550

1061 Bowser, J. C., & Co., Fort Wayne, Ind.—Engine and boiler for use in shoe and leather building. 550

1062 Peirce Rotary Tubular Boiler Co., New York, N. Y.—Rotary boiler, for use in saw mill boiler house. 550

1063 Baxter Steam Engine Co., New York, N. Y.—Engine, used in the Women's Pavilion. 550

1064 Hoadley, J. C., Co., Lawrence, Mass.—80 horse power engine and boiler, for use in Machinery Hall. 550

1065 Williamson Bros., Philadelphia, Pa.—Portable hoisting engine, used while installing machinery. 552

1066 Gates, Josiah, Lowell, Mass.—One 30 inch double leather driving belt. 553

1067 Hoyt, J. B., New York, N. Y.—One 15 inch and one 20 inch belt, for driving shafts in Annex 1 and 2. 553

1068 Yale Lock Co., Stamford, Conn. —Three pulley blocks, for use in Machinery Hall. 553

1069 Fales, George S., Pawtucket, R. I.—One 30 inch double driving belt. 553

1070 Burgess & Son, Pawtucket, R. I. —One 30 inch double driving belt. 553

1071 Alexander Bros., Philadelphia, Pa.—One 30 inch double driving belt. 553

1072 Heims, Anton, New York, N. Y. —One 30 inch double driving belt. 553

1073 Schieren, C. A., New York, N. Y. —Belt for use in No. 4 shaft. 553

1074 Page, B. & P. Co., Concord, N. H. —One 30 inch double driving belt, in No. 2 shaft. 553

1075 Rorer, Thos. J., Philadelphia, Pa. —Belt for driving shaft in Annex 3. 553

1076 Goodyear Rubber Co., Philadelphia, Pa.—Belt for driving shaft in Pump annex. 553

1077 Jones & Laughlin, Pittsburg, Pa. —Shafting, pulleys and hangers, for driving Centennial machine shop tools. 553

1078 Fitts, B., Worcester, Mass.—Steam whistle, for use during exhibition. and 4. 555

1079 Woodruff, James, Rahway, N. J. —Dampers, used in boiler houses Nos. 3 and 4. 555

1080 Edson, M. B., New York, N. Y.—Steam gauges, for use in boiler houses Nos. 3 and 4. 555

1081 Nathan & Dreyfus, New York, N. Y.—Patent oil cups, for one line of shafting. 555

1082 Lawrence, W. H., Brooklyn, N. Y.—Safety oil cans, used in Machinery Hall. 555

1083 Barr, Robert J., Philadelphia, Pa. —Elliptic steam trap. 555

1084 Sluthour & Mitzner, Philadelphia, Pa.—Pump, for use in boiler house. 560

1085 Pratt, R. V., New York, N. Y.—Injector, used in boiler house No. 3. 555

1086 Caw, A., New York, N. Y.—Two steam pumps, in boiler house. 560

1086*a* Worthington, Henry P., New York, N. Y.—Duplex pumping engine, furnishing total supply of water for the Centennial Exhibition. (*On Schuylkill river, foot of Lansdowne valley.*) 560

1087 Niagara Pump Works, Brooklyn, N. Y.—Pump, for use in boiler house. 560

1088 Norwalk Iron Works, South Norwalk, Conn.—Five Earle pumps, for use in boiler house No. 6. 561

1089 Blake Manufacturing Co., New York, N. Y.—Pumps, for supplying boilers in boiler house No. 4. 561

1090 Knowles Steam Pump Works, New York, N. Y.—Pumps, for supplying boilers in boiler house No. 2. 561

1091 Philadelphia Hydraulic Works, Philadelphia, Pa.—Pump, for use in boiler house No. 2. 561

1092 Burton, S., & Son, Waterford, N. Y.—Fire engine, for use. 564

1092*a* Scott-Uda, Mrs. M., New York, N. Y.—Aerial ladder. (*In fire station 1.*) 564

1093 Amoskeag Manufacturing Co., Manchester, N. H.—Fire engine and hose carriage, for use. 564

1094 Silsby Manufacturing Co., Seneca Falls, N. Y.—Two engines and hose carriages, for use. 564

1095 Nichols, S. B., Burlington, Vt.—Fire engine and hose carriage, for use. 564

1096 Hoyt, J. B., New York, N. Y.—Three driving belts, for main driving pulley. 564

1098 Gutta-Percha Co., New York, N. Y.—Hose and two driving belts.

1099 Lansing, H. S., Philadelphia, Pa. —Safety railroad gate. 575

1100 Cook & Pulver, New York, N.Y.—Lubricators, for use in annexes. 576

1101 Hanmore, J. W., New York, N. Y.—Felting, covering steam pipe in Machinery Hall. 576

1102 O'Hara, O. M., Boston, Mass.—Felting, covering steam pipe in Machinery Hall. 576

1103 Johns, H. W., New York, N. Y.—Felting, covering steam pipe in Machinery Hall. 576

1104 Chalmers, Spence & Co., New York, N.Y.—Felting, covering steam pipe in Machinery Hall. 576

1105 Sleuster, John T., Philadelphia, Pa.—Felting, covering steam pipe in Machinery Hall. 576

1106 Snider, D. M., Philadelphia, Pa. —Felting, covering steam pipe in Machinery Hall. 576

For classes of exhibits, indicated by numbers at end of entries, see Classification, pp. 13–15.

GREAT BRITAIN.

(South of North Avenue, Columns 16 to 17 A to E; also in Pump Annex.)

Metal, Wood, Stone, Cloth, Paper-working Machinery.

Machines, Tools, and Apparatus of Mining, Metallurgy, Chemistry, and the Extractive Arts.

1 Holmes, Joseph E., Payton, Walter, & Taylor, Fenner B., London.
a Rock boring machine. 500
b Coal and rock cutting machine. 502

2 Baird, William, & Co., Gartsherrie Iron Works, Coatbridge, Scotland.—Coal-cutting machine. 502

3 Hurd, Frederick, & Co., Wakefield.—Coal-cutting machine; ratchet wedge shovel. 502

4 Macdermott, Martin, London.—Rock and coal perforators; machines for undercutting coal; screw wedge for breaking down coal. 502

5 Hardy Patent Pick Co. (limited), Sheffield.—Implements for coal, ironstone, gold, and silver mining, for quarrying and excavating; cast steel picks. 502

8 Pickering, Jonathan, Globe Works, Stockton-on-Tees.—Pulley blocks, hoists. 503

9 The Dunston Engine Works Co., Gateshead-on-Tyne, Durham.—Stone breaker; combined stone breaker and bone cutter. 505

10 Kimberley, Nathan Gold, London.—Centrifugal pulverizing mills. 505

11 Siemens, Charles William, London.—Models of furnaces for metallurgical operations, glass melting, etc. 506

12 Smith, Dillwyn, Liverpool.—Mechanical stokers and fire bars. 506

13 Sugg, William, Vincent Works, London.—Gas burners; a new illuminating power meter. 509

Machines and Tools for working Metal, Wood, and Stone.

14 Roberts, William, Bootle, near Liverpool.—Self-acting painting machine for venetian blinds, laths, hoop iron, etc. 510

15 Massey, B. & S., Openshaw, Manchester.
a Circular saw for cutting hot iron and steel. 511
b Steam hammers; steam stamps; models of steam hammers; samples of forgings. 514

16 Wright, Peter, & Sons, Constitution Hill Works, Dudley, Worcestershire.—Anvils; vises; tools of various kinds; hammers. 514

17 Brooks & Cooper, Mousehole Forge, Sheffield.—Anvils, vises, hammers, shear steel, etc. 514

17*a* Fairbairn, Kennedy & Naylor, Leeds.—Quadruple boring machine. 515

18 Beesley & Sons, Abbey Road Boiler Works, Barrow-in-Furness.—Punching, shearing, and angle-cropping machine for iron, steel, or other metals. 515

18*a* Greenwood & Batley, Albion Works, Leeds.—Bolt forging machines. 515

19 Heap, Joshua, & Co. (limited), Oldham.—Tools and machines, taps, hobs, pipe; bolt-screwing and nut-tapping machines. 515

21 Shearer, Hugh, London.—Machine for dressing stone. 516

22 Lavers, Alfred Hamilton, London.—Testing machine to show strength of cement. 517

Machines and Implements of Spinning, Weaving, Felting, and Paper Making.

23 Fleming, Thomas, & Son, West Grove Mill, Halifax.—Card clothing for carding machines, etc.; needle-point teeth. 520

24 Ambler, William, Bradford, Yorkshire.—Machine for making paper cop tubes used in spinning; machine for cleaning the teeth of wheel castings. 520

25 Mackenzie, Duncan, London.—Self-acting reader for the Jacquard loom. 520

26 Ingham, John, & Sons, Croft Head Works, Thornton, near Bradford.—Case of shuttles, etc., for weaving; tacking, shuttle pikes, stocks, and bowls for weaving. 520

27 Platt Bros., & Co. (limited), Hartford Works, Oldham, Lancashire.—Cotton gin. 521

28 Gadd, Thomas, Manchester.—Printing machine for large size garment rollers, angular engine; combined engraving and punching machine; setting-out table, with micrometer; combined varnishing and ruling machine; machine for setting out; ruling machine, cams, engravers' block, and lathe. 521

29 Lancaster, William, Willow Iron Works, Accrington, Lancashire.—Yarn-sizing dressing machine; self-stopping beaming machines; loom. 521

30 Booth, H., & Co., Preston, Lancashire.—Cotton-spinning machinery. 521

31 Carter, John, Halifax, Yorkshire.—Spinning frame. 521

31*a* Greenwood & Batley, Albion Works, Leeds.—Machine for tying in warps for looms. 521

32 Coats, J. & P., Ferguslie Thread Works, Paisley.—Spooling machine; thread-winding machine; machine for ticketing. 531

For classes of exhibits, indicated by numbers at end of entries, see Classification, pp. 13–15.

Cloth and Paper-working Machinery, Motors, Pumps.

35 Nussey & Leachman, Leeds.—Hydraulic cloth pressing and finishing machine. 522

36 Lawson, Samuel, & Sons, Hope Foundry, Leeds.—Machinery for carding, preparing, and spinning jute; cop-winding machine. 524

37 Fairbairn, Kennedy, & Naylor, Leeds.—Machinery for preparing and spinning jute, hemp, flax, tow, and similar fibres. Carding engine; drawing, roving, and spinning frames. 524

38 Marshall, T. J., & Co., Campbell Works, Kingsland.—Dandy rolls and wire cloth, for paper making, and pulp strainer. 525

Machines, Apparatus, and Implements used in Sewing and Making Clothing and Ornamental Objects.

39 Gimson & Coltman, Leicester.—Knitting machines; rip top and circular machines. 531

40 Wilson, Newton, & Co., London.—Sewing machines, their appliances and apparatus. 531

41 Kimball & Morton, Glasgow.—Sewing machines; machines for sewing sails and sacks over-edge. 531

43 Sanson, Robert Bell, London.—Spring arm endless band knife; cloth-cutting machine; parallel pressing machine for tailors' use. 531

44 Air Burning Co. (limited), Glasgow.—Ironing table. 534

45 Broadbent, Thomas, Chapel Hill, Huddersfield.—Hydro extractor, for extracting water from wool, cotton, etc. 534

Machines and Apparatus for Type-Setting, Printing, Stamping, Embossing, and for Making Books, and Paper Working.

46 Beatty, Francis S., Dublin.—Lithographers' manifold transfer machines, for the reproduction of printed matter of enlarged or reduced dimensions from that of the original. 540

46*a* Greenwood & Batley, Albion Works, Leeds.—Printing machine. 540

47 Lilly, John, & Co., London.—Perfecting and single cylinder printing presses. 540

48 Walter, John, London.—Printing press. 540

49 Shaw, William, London.—Logotypes and cases, shown in operation; printing press. 540

Motors and Apparatus for the Generation and Transmission of Power.

50 Green, Edward, & Son, Manchester.—Fuel economizer for heating the feed water for steam boilers. 550

51 Davey, Paxman, & Co., Colchester, Essex.
a Vertical boiler and water heater. 550
b Portable steam engine; vertical engine; steam corn dryer. 552

52 Galloway, W. & J., & Sons, Knott Mill Iron Works, Manchester.—Steel boilers, for use in the British section. 550

55 Wright, William, Vulcan Foundry, Coatbridge.—Hot water boilers for heating dwellings, conservatories, etc. 550

56 Moncrieff, John, North British Glass Works, Perth, Scotland.—Steam boiler water gauge glasses. 551

57 Wier, Marshall Arthur, London.—Pneumatic motor, water meter, hydrogyrometer, locomotive speed indicator, pneumatic gyrometer, reciprocating counter. 551

57*a* Holmes, Joseph E., Payton, Walter, & Taylor, Fenner B., London.—Cylinder engine; revolving steam engine and air compressor. 552

57*b* Hurd, Frederick, & Co., Wakefield.—High-speed air compressor. 552

57*c* Smith & Starley, Trafalgar Works, Coventry.—Electric motors. 552

58 Thermo-Electric Generator Co. (limited), London. — Thermo batteries worked by gas, charcoal, or coke, in nature approaching the appearance of a gas stove. 552

58*a* Moy, Thomas, London.—Small steam engines for tramways, etc. 552

58*b* King, F. L.—Steam engines. 552

59 Turner, Charles, Southampton.—Couplings for propeller shafts and other purposes. 554

60 Hewitt, William, Bristol.
a Model of improved screw propellers; model of an improved principle for driving machinery. 553
b Breech-loader gun; gun carriage. 266

61 Vansittart, Henrietta, Mrs., Twickenham.—Screw propeller. 554

62 Hicks, James Joseph, London.—Enamel water gauges for steam boilers. 555

63 Moncrieff, John, North British Glass Works, Perth.—Gauge glasses for indicating height of water in steam boilers. 555

Hydraulic and Pneumatic Apparatus, Pumping, Hoisting, and Lifting.

63*a* Pickering, Jonathan, Globe Works, Stockton-on-Tees.—Steam and water cylinders; steam pump. 560

64 Gwynne, John & Henry, Hammersmith Iron Works, London.—Model of compound surface-condensing engines with centrifugal pumps made to ⅛ scale. 560

64*a* Haynes, Thomas, & Sons, London.
a Platform pump; garden syringe. 560
b Water bringer, for overcoming friction caused by drawing water through long lengths of hose; self-acting hose coiler. 564

65 Gwynne & Co., London.
a Centrifugal pumps and engines. 560
b Gas exhauster and engine. 561

66 Ellis, William Irlam, Manchester.—Blower or exhauster for air or gas. 561

67 Appleby Bros., London.—Steam cranes. 563

68 Wallace & Tucker, Belfast.—Fire annihilator. 564

70 Needham & Kite, Phoenix Iron Works, London.—High pressure filter press. 565

For classes of exhibits, indicated by numbers at end of entries, see Classification, pp. 13–15.

Railway Plant, Agricultural Machinery, Vessels.

71 Lawrence & Co., London.—Refrigerators; mashing machines, spargers, etc. 565

72 Dennis, T. H. P., & Co., Anchor Iron Works, Clemsford.—High pressure valves for steam, hot or cold water, or gas. 566

Railway Plant, Rolling Stock, and Apparatus.

73 Welch, Alfred, London.—Railway cattle wagons. 571

74 Williams, Richard Price, London.—Continuous railway crossings; switches for doing away with facing points on railways. 574

75 Brierley, Sons, & Reynolds, London. —Railway signal model of railway junction. 574

76 Seaton, William, London.—Saddle rail and permanent way construction. 574

77 Saxby & Farmer, London.
a Models of railway switches; junction, with switches and signals. 574
b Railway signals, and level crossing gates. 575

Machines used in preparing Agricultural Products.

78 Sutcliffe, James S., Bacup, Lancashire.—Middlings flour separator. 580

79 Mirlees, Tait, & Watson, Glasgow.—Machinery in motion, consisting of sugar mills, valveless engine working an air pump for a vacuum pan, and driving centrifugal machines. 581

80 Collier, Luke, Rochdale.—Confectioners' machines. 582

81 Andrew, J. E. H., Stockport.—Machines for spinning tobacco; samples of twist tobacco from Europe. 584

Aerial, Pneumatic, and Water Transportation.

82 Siebe & Gorman, London.—Diving apparatus for two divers; figure of diver in diving suit, with the helmet and speaking apparatus. 594

82*a* Wallace & Tucker, Belfast.—Model of turret system of life preservation, in case of shipwreck. 594

83 Cruickshank, A. B., Dundee, Scotland.—Self-acting safety cleats for boats and yachts. 594

84 Logan, John Maxwell, Cambridge.—Model of four-oared racing boat, to take to pieces for convenience in traveling. 594

85 Inman Steamship Co. (limited), Liverpool.—Full rigged model and oil painting of the steamer "City of Berlin." 594

86 Hill & Clark, London.—Boat disengaging hooks. 594

86*a* Bradford, William Henry, Great Saughall, near Chester.
a Model of life boats, lateen rig, life or salvage boat. 594
b Model of a ship's course indicator. 597

87 Clark, Standfield, & Co., London.—Models of floating and gridiron depositing docks. 596

88 Roby, George, Wigan.—Hydro-pneumatic and other vessels for the storage of gunpowder, etc. 596

90 Wood, John William, Harwich, Essex.—Iron self-adjusting shot hole, rivet hole, and leak stopper. 597

91 Martin, Claude, London.—Self-canting anchors; chain cables; model of H. M.'s turret ram "Alexandra." 597

92 Gümpel, Charles Godfrey, London.—Ship's rudder. 597

92*a* Cooke, Joseph, & Co., Midland Davy Lamp Works, Birmingham.—Miners' safety lamps. 120

92*b* Bainbridge, Emerson, Duke of Norfolk's Collieries, Sheffield.—Miners' safety lamp. 120

(N.B.—Certain exhibits of machinery from Great Britain are installed in the Main Building, and catalogued in Part I.

For classes of exhibits, indicated by numbers at end of entries, see Classification, pp. 13–15.

CANADA.

(*Central Aisle, Columns 1 to 7.*)

Metal, Wood, Stone, Cloth, Clothing-working Machinery.

Machines, Tools, and Apparatus of Mining, Metallurgy, Chemistry, and the Extractive Arts.

1 Hannahan, Joseph, Ottawa, Ont.—Rock-drilling bits. 500

3 Symonds, W. S., & Co., Halifax, N.S.—Gold quartz crushing machine. 505

4 Freeland, R., Toronto, Ont.—Soap-making machinery. 508

Machines and Tools for Working Metal, Wood, and Stone.

9 Kennedy, W., & Son, Owen Sound, Ont.—Facing and jointing planer. 510

11 Machine Co., Bowmanville, Ont.
a Turning lathe for wood, moulding machine, planing and notching machine. 510
b Metal turning lathe, planing machine. 515

14 Waterous Engine Works Co., Brantford, Ontario, Canada. — Twenty-horse power portable saw mill: capacity, six to ten thousand feet per day; shipping weight, eight tons. A strictly portable saw mill, practical, efficient, economical, and durable; obtained first medal and diploma at Exposition Santiago Chili, South America, September, 1875. 510

15 Mitchell & Teeple, Harriston, Ont. Wood-sawing machine. 510

18 McKecknie & Bertram, Dundas, Ont.—Wood-moulding machine. 510

20 Harris, James, & Co., St. John, N. B.
a Shingle machine. 510
b Register grates. 513

21 Lordly, Howe, & Co., St. John, N. B.—Turning lathe. 510

22 Nelson, Thomas, & Co., Dundas, Ont.—Cast iron water pipe. 513

23 Campbell, George, Toronto, Ont.—Portable saw forges. 514

24 Mitchell, R., & Co., Montreal, Q.—Lead tube bending machine. 515

26 McKecknie & Bertrand, Dundas, Ont.—Iron turning lathes, radial drill, slotting and iron shaping machines. 515

27 Tool Co., Hamilton, Ont.—Engine lathe, bolt cutter, drilling machine, portable radial drill, steam hammer. 515

29 Stephenson, M., Stratford, Ont.—Hand-drilling machine, for drilling both the fish holes in railroad iron at the same time in their exact position and without measuring, effecting a great saving in labor. 515

30 Smark, J., Brockville, Ont.—Drilling machines. 515

31 Fisher, J., & Co., Kincardine, Ont.—Clipping boiler plate machine. 515

32 Mitchell, R., & Co., Montreal, Q.—Lead tube bending machine. 515

33 Dunn, P., Cote St. Paul, Q.—Wire nail machine. 515

34 McFarlane, Thum, & Co., Fredericton, N. B.—Vertical power drill. 515

35 Coore, E. R. N., & Co., St. John, N. B.—Nail machine. 515

37 Bulmer & Sheppard, Montreal, Q.—Brick machine. 517

37*a* Tiffany, Geo. S., London, Ont.—Tile and brick machine. 517

Machines and Implements of Spinning, Weaving, Felting, and Paper Making.

38 Powers, S. H., Woodstock, N. B.—Self-acting hand loom. 521

39 Becker, A., Montreal, Q.—Sample of card clothing. 522

40 Boeck, Chs., Toronto, Ont.—Combing machines for brush makers. 524

Machines, Apparatus, and Implements used in Sewing and Making Clothing and Ornamental Objects.

44 Wilkie & Osborne, Guelph, Ont.—Sewing machines. 531

45 Wanzer & Co., Hamilton, Ont.—Sewing machines. 531

48 St. Amand, O., Quebec, Q.—Sewing machine. 531

49 Lawlor, J. D., Montreal, Q.—Sewing machines. 531

51 Williams, C. W., Manufacturing Co., Montreal, Q.—Sewing machines. 531

52 Harris, Th., Montreal, Q.—Sewing machine needle sharpener. 531

55 Popham, James & Ebenezer, Montreal, Ca. — Popham steam peg breaker — now being patented both in Canada and the United States—will cut off and entirely remove the peg-ends that have so long troubled manufacturers and dealers in boots and shoes, and leaves the inside of the sole as free from peg-points and nails as the outside. Attached to the machine will be found samples of the work done, a close inspection of which will conclusively demonstrate the reality of the improvement. 533

56 Clarke, R., St. John, N. B.—Lasts. 533

For classes of exhibits, indicated by numbers at end of entries, see Classification, pp. 13–15.

Engines, Boilers, Pumps, Railway Plant and Appliances.

Motors and Apparatus for the Generation and Transmission of Power.

62 **Tandy, G. J., Kingston, Ont.**—Steam boiler. 550

63 **McKay, Adam, Dartmouth, N. S.**—Model steam boiler. 550

64 **Kennedy, Wm., & Sons, Owen Sound, Ont.**—Water-wheel. 551

65 **Tuerk, F. W., Berlin, Ont.**—Working model water-wheel. 551

66 **Barber & Harris, Meaford, Ont.**—Water-wheel. 551

67 **Goldie & McCulloch, Galt, Ont.**
a Turbine water-wheel. 551
b Steam engine. 552

69 **Harris, J., & Co., St. John, N. B.**—Water-wheel. 551

70 **Fleck, A., Ottawa, Ont.**—Oscillating steam engine. 552

71 **Thomson Williams' Manufacturing Co., Stratford, Ont.**—Stationary engine. 552

72 **Martin, Chs., Belleville, Ont.**—Vertical steam engine. 552

75 **Piper, Thos., Hamilton, Ont.**—Model four-cylinder engine. 552

77 **Brush, Geo., Eagle Foundry, Montreal, Ca.**—Portable steam hoisting engine, for use on wharves, in mines, quarries, coal yards, etc., and erection of buildings; is very compact and easily handled; all levers and working parts being within easy reach of the driver, without moving from his post. 552

83 **Fleming, Geo., & Sons, St. John, N. B.**—Oscillating engine. 552

85 **Smith, J. G., Dartmouth, N.S.**—Miniature steam engine. 552

86 **Dixon, Smith, & Co., Toronto, Ont.**—Belting. 553

87 **Sandall, John, Moncton, N.B.**—Valve link motion. 553

91 **McKeough, J. W., Chatham, Ont.**—Brass dome. 555

92 **Morrison, James, Toronto, Ont.**—Steam, vacuum, hydraulic gauges. 555

93 **Piper, Thos., Hamilton, Ont.**—Steam boiler detector gauge. 555

94 **Myers, S., & Son, St. John, N. B.**—Governor. 555

Hydraulic and Pneumatic Apparatus, Pumping, Hoisting, and Lifting.

95 **Patrick, Rob., Galt, Ont.**—Rotary pump. 560

96 **Cox, H. W., Peterborough, Ont.**—Rotary force pumps. 560

97 **Oakville Manufacturing Co., Oakville, Ont.**—John Dayer, Andrew J. Bounsall, and George C. Bounsal, foundry and iron pump manufactory; force, well, and cistern pumps. 560

100 **Bowes, E., & Son, Stratford, Ont.**—Force pumps. 560

101 **Webster, Stephen, St. Catherines, Ont.**—Oil-storing tank. 560

102 **Smart, J., Brockville, Ont.**
a Cistern, well, and force pump. 560
b Jack screws. 563

105 **Barnes, C. C., St. John, N. B.**—Rotary pump. 560

106 **Jones, C. C., Fredericton, N. B.**—Barrel pump. 560

107 **Wilson, Clarke, & Co., Yarmouth, N. S.**—Ship pump. 560

111 **Small & Fisher, Woodstock, N. B.**—Barrel lifter. 563

112 **Dailey, M. E., Ottawa, Ont.**—Telescope trestle. 563

113 **Ronald, John D., Chatham, Ont.**—Steam fire engine, hose cart and hose. 564

117 **Murphy & Harle, Montreal, Q.**—Pneumatic fire extinguisher. 564

118 **Bustin, Robert, St. John, N. B.**—Fire escape. 564

119 **Smith, H. F., Toronto, Ont.**—Soda water fountain. 565

120 **Sells, H., Vienna, Ont.**—Cider mill and press. 565

121 **Brazil, P., Barrie, Ont.**—Cider mill and press. 565

122 **Date, John, Montreal, Q.**—Diving apparatus. 567

123 **Pitts, D. H., Halifax, N. S.**—Submarine armor. 567

Railway Plant, Rolling Stock, and Apparatus.

124 **Meyer, F. W. A., Montreal, Q.**—Drawing of engine and tender. 570

127 **Knolt, Kennard, Petersville, L., Ont.**—Cattle car and refrigerating tender. 571

128 **Brydon, Robert, Newberg, Ont.**
a Grain car. 571
b Grain car door fastener. 573

129 **Muir, Thomas, London, Ont.**—Rail joint protector and car-coupler. 572

130 **McNabb, M.**—Car coupler. 572

131 **Chrisholm, R. K., Oakville, Ont.**—Car coupler. 572

132 **Chisholm, R. N., Oakville, Ont.**—Car coupling. 572

132*a* **Griffin, J. K., Toronto, Ont.**—Model of car coupler. 572

133 **Richard, E. O., & Bro., St. Roch, Q.**—Car brakes and coupling. 572

134 **Car Wheel Co., Toronto, Ont.**—Car wheels and axles. 573

136 **Harris, J., & Co., St. John, N. B.**—Railroad car wheels and axles. 573

136*a* **Osborne, Henry, St. Andrews, Q.**—Model of car axle. 573

137 **Von Staden, W. G., Strathroy, Ont.**—Bent posts and rafters for railroad cars. 574

140 **Nunn, W. C., Belleville, Ont.**—Railway telegraph signals, with revolving and fixed lamps, and electric gong. 575

143 **Miller, Flanges Co., Fredericton, N.B.**—Locomotive flanges. 576

144 **Ramsay, R. H., Cobourg, Ont.**—Ramsey's car truck shifting apparatus, patented March 14, 1876. The power required to run a car on the level track is sufficient to remove the trucks, and replace them again. Expense reduced from twelve thousand dollars to one hundred. Correspondence with railroad companies invited. 576

147 **Colford, Henry, Halifax, N. S.**—Spark arresters for house, factory, and locomotive. 576

Machines used in Preparing Agricultural Products.

148 **Rochelle, L. N. & A. H., St. Anselme, Ont.**—Magnetic separator and dryer. 580

148*a* **Wilson, J. P., Montreal, Q.**—Vacuum pan. 581

149 **Copping, G. H., Toronto, Ont.**—Lozenge machine. 582

151 **Scales, Rob., Toronto, Ont.**—Evaporator and tobacco lump machine. 584

152 **Adams, J. L., Montreal, Q.**—Tobacco cutter. 584

153 **Marengo, J. & A., Montreal, Q.**—Cigarette machine. 584

Aerial, Pneumatic, and Water Transportation.

155 **Herald, D., Gore's Landing, Ont.**—Canoes. 594

156 **English, W., Peterborough, Ont.**—Hunting canoe. 594

159 **Power, W., & Co., Kingston, Ont.**—Ship models. 594

160 **Lapierre, Zephirin, Isle of Orleans, Q.**—Sailing boat rigged, rowing boat, winter canoe. 594

163 **Baldwin, P., St. Roch, Quebec, Q.**—Ship model. 594

164 **Dunn & Samson, Levis, Q.**—Ship models. 594

165 **Rose, N., Levis, Q.**—Ship models. 594

166 **Dinning, H., Quebec, Q.**—Ship models. 594

167 **Marquis, F. H., Levis, Q.**—Ship models. 594

168 **Auger, E., Quebec, Q.**—Ship models. 594

169 **Cotman, W., Quebec, Q.**—Ship models. 594

170 **Samson & Co., Quebec, Q.**—Ship models. 594

171 **Gingras, E., Quebec, Q.**—Ship models. 594

172 **Oliver, J., Quebec, Q.**—Ship models. 594

173 **Oliver, F. H., Quebec, Q.**—Ship models. 594

174 **Quebec Advisory Board, Quebec, Q.**—Ship models. 594

175 **Sewell, E. W., Levis, Q.**
a Winter canoe, drawings of safety ship, ship and yacht models. 594
b Drawing of steamship for Canadian trade. 595

176 **Robitaille, Th., Quebec, Q.**—Complete cod-fishing boat; "Micmac" bark canoe. 594

177 **Charland, W., Levis, Q.**—Ship model. 594

178 **Grenier, Frs., Isle of Orleans, Q.**—Pilot boat. 594

179 **Girard, A., Murray Bay, Q.**—Poplar canoe. 594

182 **Ross, Elizah, Portland, N. B.**—Single scull racing boat, spoon-set oars, set single scull oars, set oars, life boat model. 594

183 **Barrill, Jos., Yarmouth, N. S.**—Ship model, improved gear for reefing sail. 594

184 **Moreley, E., Darmouth, N. S.**—Ship models. 594

185 **Garmount, Wm.**—Ship model. 594

186 **Dailey, M. E., Ottawa, Ont.**—Model ocean ship. 595

187 **Merritt, Abel, Chatham, Ont.**—Propeller boat. 595

188 **Richelieu & Ontario Navigation Co., Montreal, Q.**—Steamboat models. 595

189 **Wildgoose, F. H., Montreal, Q.**—Steamboat model. 595

190 **Meyer, F. W. A., Montreal, Q.**—Drawing longitudinal section steamboat. 595

192 **Beautey, H., Quebec, Q.**—Dragging or grappling apparatus. 596

193 **Carroll, S., Widden, Ont.**—Marine compass, automatic ship trimmer. 597

194 **Pitts, D. H., Halifax, Ont.**—Ship windlass and cable brake. 597

195 **Mosler, Geo. J., Maitland Island, N. B.**—Ship wheel. 597

196 **Harris, James, & Co., St. John, N. B.**—Capstan. 597

197 **Pitts, D. H., Halifax, N. S.**—Mast hoop clamp, cable brake, metal jib hank. 597

198 **Couvrette & Frigon, Montreal, Q.**—Stern of ship (model). 597

198*a* **Harris, James, & Co., St. John, N. B.**—Ships' iron knees, straps. 284

198*b* **Coldbrook Rolling Mills Co., St. John, N. B.**—Cut and clinch nails, spikes and knees. 284

198*c* **Weddleton, J. B., Yarmouth, Ont.**—Head earrings for ships. 284

For classes of exhibits, indicated by numbers at end of entries, see Classification, pp. 13–15.

FRANCE.

(*North of Central Aisle, Columns 1 to 7.*)

Metal, Wood, Stone, Cloth-working Machinery, Motors.

Machines, Tools, and Apparatus of Mining, Metallurgy, Chemistry, and the Extractive Arts.

1 Fleury, Jules Martin, Paris.—Grinding mill. 505

2 David Bros., Charleville (Ardennes). —Portable forges. 506

3 Perret, Michel, Paris.—Apparatus for combustion. 506

4 Goyard, F., Paris.—Crucibles and furnaces. 506

6 Enfer, Ernest, Paris.—Portable forges; forges for the laboratory; gas pressure bellows apparatus; bellows. 506

7 Chenaillier, Paris.—Universal evaporator. 506

8 Faure & Kessler, Clermont-Ferrand. —Apparatus for the concentration of sulphuric acid. 508

9 Desmoutis, Quennessen, & Le Brun, Paris.—Platina apparatus. 508

10 Pelouze, E., & Audouin P., Paris.—Condenser for gas works. 509

11 Lascole, A., Paris.—Gas apparatus. 509

Machines and Tools for Working Metal, Wood, and Stone.

12 Arbey, F., Paris.—Wood-working machinery. 510

13 Branche, H., Paris.—Machines and tools. 510

14 Rous, Edmond, Paris.—Tools of precision. 510

15 Dugoujon, sr., Paris.—Saws. 510

17 Limet-Lapareille & Co., Paris.—Files. 515

18 La Quintinie, A., & Co., Paris.—Machines and tools for goldsmiths; designs of machines for soap, confectionery, and matches. 515

20 Durand, F., & Marais, Paris.—Brick machines. 517

Machines and Implements of Spinning, Weaving, Felting, and Paper Making.

21 Guinet, Ant., & Co., Lyons.—Silk-weaving looms. 520

22 Richard, J. S., Paris.—Machines and looms for textiles. 521

23 Pierron & Dehaitre, Paris.—Weaving machine. 522

24 Couture, Paris.—Breaking machine for textile fabrics. 523

25 Maigrou, F. A., Paris.—Rope machine. 524

26 Deny, Louis, Paris.—Open copper cylinder and refiner for paper manufacture. 525

27 Thomine, F., Paris.—Machine for the manufacture of fishing nets. 527

Machines, Apparatus, and Implements used in Sewing and Making Clothing and Ornamental Objects.

28 Legat, D., Paris.—Machine for sewing straw hats. 531

29 Cornely, E., Paris.—Embroidering machines. 531

Machines and Apparatus for Type Setting, Printing, Stamping, Embossing, and for Making Books, and Paper Working.

29*a* Alauzet, Paris.—Printing machines. 540

30 Coblence, Paris.—Electrotypes. 541

31 Derriey, Ch., Paris.—Typography, engraving, and electrotypes. 542

31*b* Derriey, Ch., Paris.—Printing type. 542

32 Tucker, Paris.—Types and cuts. 542

33 Lecerf, L., Paris.—Printing materials. 543

34 Vital, A., Paris.—Rollers for lithographic presses. 543

Motors, and Apparatus for the Generation and Transmission of Power.

35 Leroy, François, Marseilles.—Models of marine boilers. 550

36 Fontaine, Hippolyte, Paris.—Steam engines. 552

37 Electro-Magnetic Machine Manufacturing Co., Paris.—Gas machines, galvano-plastic machine, machine to transmit power. 552

38 Mignon & Rouart, Paris.—Noiseless gas motors. 552

39 Chauveau, Paris.—Steam engines. 552

40 Breguet, Paris.—Electro-magnetic machines. 552

41 Rous, Edmond, Paris.—Hermetic clasps for oil cups, etc. 553

For classes of exhibits, indicated by numbers at end of entries, see Classification, pp. 13–15.

Motors, Hydraulic Apparatus, Railway Plant, Agricultural Machinery.

42 Welby, Rouen.—Belting. 553

43 Jacob, Ch. Moise, Paris.—Oiling cushions. 553

44 Domange, Lemierre, & Co., Paris.— Belting. 553

45 Perreaux, L. G., Paris.—Screw pro-peller. 554

45*a* Bourdin, Paris.—Motor for sewing machines. 554

46 Dechamp, C., Lyons.—Safety boiler apparatus. 555

47 Cazaubon, Dominique, Paris.—Cocks for steam, water, and gas pumps, and water closets. 555

48 Lion & Guichard, Paris.—Metallic manometer. 555

49 Macabies, Paris.—Automatic feeder. 555

50 Rigollot, Paris.—Cocks for water, steam, and gas. 555

50*a* Serrin, Paris.—Regulator for elec-tric light. 555

51 Cuau, Paris.—Boiler injector. 555

52 Coux-des Roseaux, Asnieres, near Paris.—Automatic oil cups for steam machines; fire-proof insulator for steam pipes. 555

Hydraulic and Pneumatic Apparatus, Pumping, Hoisting, and Lifting.

53 Neut, L., & Dumont, L., Paris.—Cen-trifugal pumps. 560

54 Garlaudat, Paris.—Refrigerating ap-paratus. 562

55 Enfer, A., jr., Paris.—Portable forges and bellows. 562

56 David Bros., Charleville (Ardennes). —Portable forges. 562

57 Enfer, Ernest, Paris.—Portable forges, bellows, gas apparatus. 562

58 Morane, jr., Paris.—Hydraulic press for candle manufacture. 563

59 Chrétien, J., Paris.—Automatic ap-paratus for unloading coal. 563

60 Rous, Edmond, Paris.—Pulleys and tackles. 563

61 Mégy, Echeverria, & Bazan, Paris. —Elevators, regulators, etc. 563

62 Gaussart, Epernay (Marne).—Ma-chines for charging wines with gas. 564

63 Constant, Port-a-Binson (Marne).— Wine press. 565

64 Appert-Mandart, Reims (Marne).— Hooks and clasps for champagne. 565

65 Lejeune, Epernay (Marne).—Ma-chine for charging wines with gas. 565

66 Renard, Epernay (Marne).—Wires and strings for champagne. 565

67 Paillet & Co., Epernay (Marne).— Corks. 565

68 Cazaubon, D., Paris.—Soda water machines; siphons. 565

69 Freal, Epernay (Marne).—Bottling machines. 565

70 Gervais, E., Bordeaux.—Bottling machines. 565

71 Guéret Bros., Paris.—Soda water machine. 565

72 Logette, Ay (Marne).—Clasps for bottles and machines for applying. 565

73 Maldine, H., Paris.—Soda water machines, siphons. 565

74 Maurice, Widow, & Guenin, Eper-nay (Marne).—Bottling machines. 565

75 Michelot, jr., Epernay (Marne).— Stands and cases for wines. 565

76 Thessier, Fevre, Paris.—Table ap-paratus for Seltzer water. 565

77 Tricourt, A., Reims (Marne).—Wine-making machines. 565

78 Mestre, A. de, Bordeaux.—Bottling machines. 565

79 Mondollot, A., Paris.—Soda water machine, siphons. 565

80 Cicile-Larbre, Reims (Marne).— Bottle cleaners. 565

81 Durafort, Paris.—Soda water ma-chine. 565

82 Fisse-Thirion, & Co., Reims.—Bot-tling machine. 565

83 Rigollot, Paris.—Cocks for water, steam, and gas. 566

84 Perreaux, L. G., Paris.—Rubber valves. 566

85 Giffard & Berger, Paris.—Ice ma-chines. 568

86 Carrè, E., Paris.—Ice machine. 568

Railway Plant, Rolling Stock, and Apparatus.

87 Edoux, Leon, Paris.—Special sys-tem for mountain railroads. 570

88 Joliot, S., Vincennes.—Car brakes. 572

89 Le Bas, Paris.—Automatic clutch. 572

90 Arbel Lucien, Rive-de-Gier (Loire). —Forged iron wheels for locomotives and cars. 573

91 Brunon Bros., Rive-de-Gier (Loire). —Wheels manufactured by hydraulic pressure. 573

Machines used in Preparing Agricultural Products.

92 Aubin & Baron, Paris.—Bolting mill. 580

93 Durrschmidt, Lyons.—Emery mill-stones. 580

93*a* Deplanque, Son, sr., Maison-Al-font (Seine).—Emery millstones. 580

94 Beyer Bros., Paris.—Soap and choco-late machines. 582

95 Hermann, G., Paris.—Chocolate ma-chines. 582

96 Durvie, Ivry-la-Bataille (Eure).— Mechanic kneading machine. 582

97 Beyer Bros., Paris.—Soap and choco-late machines. 585

Aerial, Pneumatic, and Water Transportation.

98 General Transatlantic Co., Paris. —Model of the steamship "Pereire." 595

For classes of exhibits, indicated by numbers at end of entries, see Classification, pp. 13–15.

GERMANY.

(*South of Central Aisle, Columns 1 to 7, and Pump Annex.*)

Metal, Wood, Stone, Cloth, Paper-working Machinery, Pumps, etc.

Machines, Tools, etc., of Mining, Chemistry, etc.

1 Sparre, Julius von, Dortmund.—Model of a drill. 500

2 Wünschmann, Reinh., Leipsic.—Candle-making machine. 508

Machines and Tools for Working Metal, Wood, and Stone.

3 Kahlke & Detlefsen, Hamburg.—Cutting machine and apparatus for cleaning boiler tubes. 515

3*a* Schäffer & Budenberg, Buckau.—Polishing machines. 516

4 Schlickeysen, C., Berlin.—Brick, turf, cement, and clay machines. 517

5 Loeff, Paul, Berlin. — Model of a kiln for bricks, etc. 517

Machines and Implements of Spinning, Weaving, etc.

6 Windmüller & Meynen, Zwischenahn, Oldenburg.—Wooden spools. 520

8 Grothe, H., Berlin.—Models. 521

9 Bodemer, Georg, Zschopau.—Apparatus for spinning. 521

10 Beuthner Bros., Berlin.—Carders. 522

11 Mechanical Card Factory, Mittweida.—Cards. 522

Machines, etc., used in Sewing, Making Clothing, etc.

12 Huhn, Heinr., & Co., Aix-la-Chapelle.—Needles. 530

13 Lammertz, Leo., Aix-la-Chapelle.—Needles. 530

14 Bellé, R., Aix-la-Chapelle.—Needles. 530

15 Pastor, Ph. H., Sons, Burtscheid, near Aix-la-Chapelle.—Needles. 530

16 Zimmermann, Jos., Aix-la-Chapelle.—Needles. 530

17 German Sewing Machine Factory, Frankfort-on-Main.—Sewing machines. 531

18 Müller, Cl., Dresden.—Sewing machines. 531

19 Kiehle, R., Leipsic.—Sewing machines. 531

20 Hamburg-American Sewing Machine Factory Joint Stock Co.—Sewing machines, etc. 531

21 Schmalz, F. G., Altenburg.—Machines for making gloves. 532

22 Hemmer, L. Ph., Aix-la-Chapelle.—Fulling and washing machine. 534

23 Dausch, J. G., Munich.—Instruments and apparatus for watchmakers. 535

Machines for Printing, Making Books, Paper Working, etc.

26 Traiser, Carl, Darmstadt. — Ruling machine. 541

27 Lotz, Ferd., Offenbach-on-Main.—Lithographic machinery. 543

Motors, Power Generators, etc.

29 Schilling, F. A., Bremerhaven.—Steam engines. 552

30 Gas Motor Factory, Deutz. — Gas motors. 552

31 Blancke, C.W. J., & Co., Merseburg.—Pyrometer, steam gauges, vacuum meters, etc. 555

32 Bodemer, Georg, Zschopau, near Chemnitz.—Regulators. 555

33 Schäffer & Budenberg, Buckau, near Magdeburg.—Steam gauges, pyrometers, lubricators, etc. 555

34 Blanke, Em. A. R., Frankfort-on-Oder.—Steam packing, etc. 555

35 Gehrckens, C. Otto, Hamburg.—Stuffing boxes, steam packing. 555

36 Wertheim, Louis, Bornheim, near Frankfort-on-Main.—Steam packing. 555

Hydraulic and Pneumatic Apparatus.

37 Alléoud, Emanuel, Metz.
a Siphon pumps. 560
b Mechanical lever. 563

38 Weyhe, Wilh., Bremen. — Rotary pumps. 560

39 Royal Saxon Fire Extinguisher Co., Leipzig. — Fire extinguishing apparatus. 564

40 Schultz, Ernst, Aschaffenburg.—Atmospheric apparatus for firemen, miners, etc. 564

Railway Plant, Rolling Stock, etc.

42 Glöeckner Bros., Tschirndorf, near Halbau.—Blocks for brakes. 572

43 Camozzi & Schlösser, Frankfort-on-the-Main.—Railway switch. 574

43*a* Schäffer & Budenberg, Buckau.—Spark catchers. 576

Machines used in Preparing Agricultural Products.

43*b* Israel Bros., Dresden.—Mill and grind stones. 580

43*c* Osenbruck & Co., Hemelingen, near Bremen.—Cigar moulds. 584

Aerial, Pneumatic, and Water Transportation.

44 Dücker, Baron F. F. von, Bückeburg.—Drawing of a wire-rope railway. 590

46 Hamburg-American Steamship Co., Hamburg.—Model of a mail steamship. 595

For classes of exhibits, indicated by numbers at end of entries, see Classification, pp. 13–15.

AUSTRIA.

(*South of South Aisle, Columns 1 to 5.*)

Mining, Weaving, Agricultural Machinery, Motors.

Machines, Tools, etc., of Mining, Chemistry, etc.

1 Rosenegger, Josef, Oberalm, near Hallein, Salzburg.—Model of a glass-melting furnace, cylinder furnace. 506

Machines and Implements of Spinning, Weaving, etc.

3 Schram, Willibald, Vienna.—Jacquard looms. 521

4 Surber, J. Jacques, Vienna.—Weavers' reeds and heddles. 527

Motors, Power Generators, etc.

5 Hock & Co., Julius, Vienna.—Petroleum motor with pump. 550

6 Popper, Joseph & David, Vienna.—Patent boiler incrustation preserver, boiler fittings. 550

Railway Plant, Rolling Stock, etc.

7 Tagleicht, Karl, Vienna.—Locomotive spark catcher and flue. 576

Machinery used in Preparing Agricultural Products.

8 Vojtěchovsky & Reznicek, Prague.—Machines for candy production. 582

SWITZERLAND.

(*Section 1, Pump Annex.*)

Railway Appliances.

Motors, Power Generators, etc.

1 Sulzer Bros., Winterthur, Canton Zurich.—Model of a new system of reversing gear for valve engines. (*Pump annex.*) 555

1*a* Pictet, Raoul, & Co., Geneva.—Machine for producing ice with the aid of anhydrous sulphurous acid. 568

Railway Plant, Rolling Stock, etc.

2 Swiss Manufacturing Co., Neuhausen, near Schaffhausen.—Model of an apparatus for heating railway carriages. (*Pump annex.*) 571

Machines pertaining to watchmaking are exhibited in Swiss section, Main Building, and catalogued in that volume.

For classes of exhibits, indicated by numbers at end of entries, see Classification, pp. 13–15.

BELGIUM.

(*North of North Aisle, Columns 7 to 18.*)

Metal, Cloth, Paper-working Machinery, Motors.

Machines, Tools, and Apparatus of Mining, Metallurgy, Chemistry, and the Extractive Arts.

1 Dubois, Wm. & François Joseph, Seraing, near Liége.—Drilling machine for mines, tunnels, etc. 500

2 Chaudron, Joseph, Brussels.—Apparatus for boring and tubing mining shafts. 501

3 Libotte, Nicholas, Gilly, near Charleroi.—Cages with system of parachute. 502

4 Muller & Co., Clermont, near Liége. —Safety fuse for miners. 502

5 Souheur, Arnold, Seraing, near Liége.—Safety lamps for coal mines. 502

6 Van Haecht, Emile, Haeren, near Brussels.—Models of fat-rendering works, with samples of stearine and oleine. 508

Machines and Tools for Working Metal, Wood, and Stone.

7 De Tombay, Auguste, Marcinelle, near Charleroi.
a Model of a trip-hammer. 514
b Model of steam shears. 515

8 Jullien & Jennar, Bomereé, near Charleroi.—Tuyere and axle. 514

9 Nicaise, Ch., & Co., and Gobert, Aug., La Louvière.—Machinery for making bolts. 516

Machines and Implements of Spinning, Weaving, and Paper Making.

10 Bède & Co., Verviers.—Wool cleaning machine. 522

11 Delrez, Felix, Verviers.—Cards. 522

12 Dethiou, Gilles, & Co., Verviers.—Cards. 522

13 Horstmans Bros., Liége.—Cards. 522

14 Martin, Célestin, Verviers.—Looms, mechanical winder, cards. 522

15 Martin, Th. J., Pisseroule-Dison, near Verviers.—Cards. 522

Machines, Apparatus, and Implements used in Sewing and Making Clothing and Ornamental Objects.

16 Turner, B. B., & Co., Brussels.—
a Festooning and embroidering machines. 530
b Sewing machines for gloves, straw hats, buttonholes, etc. 531

17 Joint Stock Society for the Manufacture of Machines and Tools of Precision, Saint Josse-ten-Noode.—Sewing and knitting machines. 531

Machines and Apparatus for Type-setting, Printing, Stamping, Embossing, and for Making Books, and Paper Working.

18 Derkx-Schlopfer, I. F., Anderlecht, near Brussels.—Wooden printing types. 542

Motors, Power Generators, etc.

19 Van den Kerchove, P., Ghent.—Corliss and Rider engines. 552

20 Dolne, L., & Co., Verviers.—Belting. 553

21 Horstmans Bros., Liége.—Belting. 553

22 Versé-Spelmans, Brichot, Ant., & Co., Brussels.—Belting. 553

23 Dervaux, Alfred, Brussels.—Feeding apparatus for boilers. 555

Hydraulic and Pneumatic Apparatus.

24 Moreau, Léon, Brussels.—Rotary pumps. 560

24*a* Banolas, R., & Co.—Fire extinguishers. 564

Railway Plant, Rolling Stock, etc.

25 Durieux & Co., Louvain.—Wheels for cars, carriages, etc. 573

26 Mabille, Valère, Mariemont.—Railway plant. 573

27 Legrand, Achille, Hyon, near Mons. —Sleepers and cushions for mining railways. 573

28 Léonard, F. L. J., Fayt, near Seneffe. —Railway brake, signals, and gates. 575

For classes of exhibits, indicated by numbers at end of entries, see Classification, pp. 13–15.

NETHERLANDS.

[*The Machinery Exhibit of the Netherlands is installed in the Main Building, and catalogued in Part I.*]

SWEDEN.

(*North of North Aisle, Columns 7 to 16.*)

Stone, Metal, Wood, Cloth, Paper-working Machines, Motors.

Machines, Tools, and Apparatus of Mining, Metallurgy, Chemistry, and the Extractive Arts.

1 **Nilson, G., Eskilstuna.**—Jacks. 503

1*a* **Wiklund, W., Stockholm.**—Centrifugal pump. 504

2 **Alsing, J. R., Stockholm.**—Model of cylinder for crushing hard materials. 505

6 **Soderqvist, R., Goteborg.**—Gas apparatus. 509

Machines and Tools for Working Metal, Wood, and Stone.

7 **Bergström, J. W., Stockholm.**—Screw-cutting machine. 510

8 **Bolinders, J. & C. G., Machine Manufacturing Stock Co., Stockholm.**
a Sawing machines. 510
b Machines for making metal cartridges; emery wheels. 515

9 **Von Essen, H. H., Baron, Tidaholm.**—Iron for turning veneer. 510

10 **Stridsberg & Biork, Thorsträlla.**—Blades for frame, circular, timber, wood, and pit saws; machine knives, trowels, ship scrapers, plane irons, etc. 510

11 **Fagersta Manufacturing Co., Westanfors.**—Saw blades. 510

12 **Sandvikens Iron Works (limited), Sandviken.**—Piston rod for steam hammer. 514

14 **Brehmer, E. F. A., Stockholm.**—Drilling machine. 515

15 **Köping Mechanical Works Co. (limited), Köping.**—Turning machine. 515

15*a* **Samuelson, S. H., Foskefors, Rada.**—Machine for making hollow peat bricks. 517

Machines, Apparatus, and Implements used in Sewing and Making Clothing and Ornamental Objects.

16 **Hedlund, Joh., Eskilstuna.**—Sewing machines. 531

17 **Husquarna Arms Manufacturing Co. (limited), Jönköping.**—Sewing machines. 531

Machines for Printing, Making Books, Paper Working, etc.

19 **Brehmer, E. F. A., Stockholm.**
a Paging and ticket counting machines, date stamps, etc. 542
b Paper-cutting machine. 546

Motors, Power Generators, etc.

20 **Atterberg, A. J., Hagforsen, Rada.**—
a Drawings of turbines. 551
b Drawing of blast engine. 552

21 **Wenström, W., Orebro.**—Drawing of a turbine. 551

22 **Kristinehamn Machine Manufacturing Co., Kristinehamn.**—Marine steam engine, tank engine. 552

24 **Köping Mechanical Works (limited), Köping.**—Cast iron cylinders for a sixty-horse power propeller steam engine. 552

27 **Motala Iron & Steel Co., Motala.**—Compound marine engine. 552

27*a* **Runqvist, C. R., Stockholm.**—Oscillating steam engine governors. 555

28 **Kockum Machine Manufacturing Co. (limited), Malmo.**—Steam engines. 552

29 **Sandvikens Iron Works Co. (limited), Sandviken.**—Axles for propellers. 553

For classes of exhibits, indicated by numbers at end of entries, see Classification, pp. 13–15.

Motors, Railway Plant, Models of Vessels.

Hydraulic and Pneumatic Apparatus.

29a Wiklund, W., Stockholm.—Centrifugal pump. 560

31 Atterberg, A. J., Hagforsen, Rada.—Drawing of blowing engine. 562

Railway Plant, Rolling Stock, etc.

34 Bjorkman, C. R., Kristinehamn.—Drawing of a narrow-gauge locomotive. 570

34a Kristinehamn Machine Manufacturing Co. (limited), Kristinehamn.
a Locomotive. 570
b Railway car wheels. 573

37 Sandvikens Iron Works Co. (limited), Sandviken.—Railway wheels and axles. 573

38 Adelskold, C., Stockholm.—Model of an axle box for railway cars. 573

39 Arboga Foundry & Machine Manufacturing Co., Arboga.—Railway wheels, tires and axles. 573

41 Ekman, Carl, Finspang.—Railway wheels. 573

42 Fagersta Iron & Steel Works, Westanfors.—Railway axles and springs. 573

43 Köpings Machine Manufacturing Co. (Limited), Koping.—Axles. 573

45 Ankarsrums Works, Ankarsrum.—Railway switches. 574

46 Ostrand, Herrman, Helsingborg.—Drawing of a railway switch. 574

Aerial, Pneumatic, and Water Transportation.

47 Lesjofors Iron & Steel Co. (limited), Langbanshyttan.—Wire cables. 591

49 Royal Swedish Commission.—Models of fishing boats. 594

51 Kockum Machine Manufacturing Co., Malmo.—Models of steamers, and torpedo boat. 594

For classes of exhibits, indicated by numbers at end of entries, see Classification, pp. 13-15.

NORWAY.

[*The Machinery Exhibit of Norway is installed in the Main Building, and catalogued in Part I.*)

ITALY.

(*North of North Aisle, Columns 16 to 19.*)

Metal, Cloth, Paper-working, Agricultural Machinery, Motors.

Machines, Tools, and Apparatus of Mining, Metallurgy, Chemistry, and the Extractive Arts.

1 Paresi, E. Giuseppe, Parma.—Furnace for lime. 506

2 Agrarian Committee of Chiavari.—Sulphur machine. 508

Machines and Implements of Spinning, Weaving, and Paper Making.

3 Ferrari, Bartolomeo, Parma.—Apparatus for silkworms. 520

Machines for Printing, Making Books, Paper Working, etc.

4 Perisi, Achille, & Son, Naples.—Pianografo-voltacarte, mechanical invention. 545

Motors, Power Generators, etc.

5 Zanini, Pasquale, Rome.—Steam machine. 550

Hydraulic and Pneumatic Apparatus.

6 Gasparini, Giacomo, Rome.—Hydraulic machine. 563

Agricultural Engineering and Administration.

7 Bertea, Stefano, Alessandria.—Lozenge machine. 582

Aerial, Pneumatic, and Water Transportation.

8 D'Allessandro, Benedetto, Benvenuto, Rome.—Life-preserver. 594

9 Villa, Cav. Ignazio, Milan.—Drawings of nautical machinery and architecture. 594

10 Origone, Paolo, Genoa.—Design for an iron steamer, and model in relief. 595

11 Zaffarini, Cav. Cesare, Ferrara.—Nautical machine. 597

For classes of exhibits, indicated by numbers at end of entries, see Classification, pp. 13–15.

BRAZIL.

(*North of North Aisle, Columns 16 to 21.*)

Machinery, Weapons, Hardware, Motors, Vessels and Appliances.

Chemical Manufactures.

1 Souza, Fausto de.—Metal fuses for artillery. 204

2 Pyrotechnical Laboratory, Rio de Janeiro.
a Fuses for artillery. 204
b Apparatus for guiding signal rockets. 205

3 Military Archives of Rio de Janeiro. —Pyrotechnical maps. 205

Weapons, etc.

4 Army Arsenal, Rio de Janeiro.
a Breech-loading rifle, and sword bayonet; revolver. 265
b Model of rifled brass field gun, with accessories. 266
c Mounted rifled gun and casemate; brass rifled gun and accessories; brass mortars; shot and shell, canister and grape for heavy ordnance; apparatus for guiding rockets, used as a projectile. 267
d Spears. 268

5 Arsenal at Bahia.—Drum used by the Brazilian army. 265

6 Arsenal in the Province of Rio Grande do Sul.—Weapons and articles used by the Brazilian army. 265

7 Navy Arsenal, Rio de Janeiro.
a Leather buckets for artillery service. 266
b Leather cartridge boxes for heavy ordnance. 267

Hardware, Edge Tools, Cutlery, and Metallic Products.

8 Silvino, Tripo di.—Hand tools. 280

9 Province of Minas Geraes.—Hand tools and instruments. 280

10 Arsenal of the Province of Bahia.
a Hand tools. 280
b Locks for naval and ships' stores. 284

11 Ipanema Iron Works.
a Hand tools. 280
b Imperial crown and cross of cast iron; samples of cast iron. 283

12 Army Arsenal, Rio de Janeiro.—Cast iron ventilator, and samples of cast iron. 283

13 Santos, Cauto dos.—Imperial crown of cast iron; samples of cast iron. 283

14 Bieunemback & Bro.—Chair of cast iron; samples of iron grates. 283

15 Slichal, Fabiano.—Horse shoes of different shapes. 284

Engineering, Architecture, Maps, etc.

16 Navy Yard at Rio de Janeiro.—Models of dry docks cut into the rock. 330

Machines and Tools for Working Metal, Wood, and Stone.

17 National Mint, Rio de Janeiro.— Stamping machine, edging machine, hand tools and instruments. 510

Machines and Implements of Spinning, Weaving, Felting, and Paper Making.

18 Rezende, Luiz de, Rio de Janeiro.— Machine for reeling and skeining silk, apparatus for counting the twist, samples of silk and cocoons. 520

Motors, Power Generators, etc.

19 Navy Arsenal, Rio de Janeiro.
a Models of engines for small monitors and mortar ships; steam engine to be used as motor at the pyrotechnical laboratory at Rio de Janeiro. 552
b Pulleys, pulley stand shafts, and flying wheels. 553

20 Army Arsenal at Rio de Janeiro.
a Iron drums and chairs for transmitting motion. 553
b Iron screw propeller and its cog wheel. 554

Hydraulic and Pneumatic Apparatus.

21 Cósta, T. C. da.
a Pumps. 561
b Hydraulic ram. 563
c Nozzle fire plug. 564

22 Neves, F. Candido das, Rio de Janeiro.—Stop cocks. 566

23 Russell, B. G., Rio de Janeiro.—Lead pipes and hydraulic syphons, copper valve box. 566

Machines used in Preparing Agricultural Products.

24 Birrenback & Bros., Iron Works, Province of S. Paulo.—Hand mill. 585

Aerial, Pneumatic, and Water Transportation.

25 Navy Arsenal, Rio de Janeiro.—Models of iron clads, casemate and monitor ships, men of war and steam launches; models of corvettes and launches, designed by Trajano de Carvalho. 595

Arboriculture and Forest Products.

26 Navy Arsenal, Rio de Janeiro.—Samples of wood used for ship building. 600

For classes of exhibits, indicated by numbers at end of entries, see Classification, pp. 13-15.

ARGENTINE REPUBLIC.

(*North of North Aisle, Columns 21 to 23.*)

Cloth and Paper-working Machines, Vessels.

Machines and Implements of Spinning, Weaving, and Paper Making.

1 **Provincial Commission, Province of** Santiago del Estero.—Weaving loom. 522

Machines for Printing, Making Books, Paper Working, etc.

2 **Estrada, Angel, Prov. of Buenos** Ayres.—Samples of printing, types, electrotypes, corners, etc. 542

3 **Cañarte, Bernardo R., Province of** Buenos Ayres.—Album of typographic works. 542

Railway Plant, Rolling Stock, etc.

4 **Gardella, Luis, Province of Buenos** Ayres.—Plan of a rotary machine with boiler. 570

Aerial, Pneumatic, and Water Transportation.

5 **Provincial Commission, Province of** Corrientes.—Oars. 594

6 **Office of the Harbor Master, Prov**ince of Buenos Ayres.—Model of mixed frigate, with wooden hull and auxiliary machine; models of steam lighter, pleasure steam yacht, and whaler. 595

7 **Roibon, Federico, Province of Corri**entes.—Model of rafts for crossing the "Paso de la Patria" during the war with Paraguay, in 1866. 596

RUSSIA.

(*North of North Aisle, Columns 22 to 25.*)

Metal, Stone, Cloth, Paper-working Machines.

Machines, Tools, etc., of Mining, Chemistry, etc.

1 **Yevleff, Andrew, Moscow.—Gold**beater's skins and sample of leaf gold. 505

2 **Administration of the Mining Dis**trict in Western Poland.—Plan of gas smelting furnace. 506

3 **Admiralty Electroplate Establish**ment, Cronstadt.—Specimens of metallic layers by electrotyping. 508

Machines and Tools for Working Metal, Wood, and Stone.

4 **Lessner, Gustavus, St. Petersburg.** —Planing, drilling, and turning machine. 515

5 **Popoff, Basil, St. Petersburg.—** Workbench. 515

6 **Practical Technological Institute,** St. Petersburg.—Lathes, planing, shaping, and drilling machines. 515

7 **Smithery of the Port of St. Peters**burg.—Apparatus for stamping bolts with threads; specimen of bolts, for armor plates and stamped row locks. 515

Machines and Implements of Spinning, Weaving, Paper Making, etc.

8 **Tilzoff, John, Moscow.—Weaving** slays. 520

Machines, etc., used in Sewing, Making Clothing, etc.

9 **Rauer, Augustus, Warsaw.—Album** of reduced patterns for tailors. 531

Machines for Printing, Making Books, Paper Working, etc.

10 **Alissoff, Michael, St. Petersburg.—** Type-writing machine, and new photo-lithographic process of music printing. 542

For classes of exhibits, indicated by numbers at end of entries, see Classification, pp. 13-15.

Machinery, Motors, Railway Plant, Vessels.

11 Goldberg, Isidor, St. Petersburg.—
a Printing types and electrotypes, stereotypes. 542
b Pasteboard cutter. 546

12 Lorchetes, Alfred, Liban.—Steganographic apparatus. 542

13 Wolf, Morris, St. Petersburg.—Sample book of typographical types. 542

Motors, Power Generators, etc.

15 Lesser, Gustavus, St. Petersburg.—Section of a steam cylinder with steam distributing apparatus. 550

16 Steam Engine Works, Port of Cronstadt.—Steam engine and boiler for a barge. 550

17 Lilpop, Rau, & Lovenstein, Warsaw.—Portable steam engine, ten horse power. 552

18 Pootilof Iron Works Co., St. Petersburg.—Steam engine. 552

18*a* Imperial Technical School, Moscow.—Model of a steam engine with parallel motion and regulator. 552

19 Admiralty Tyova Works, near St. Petersburg.—Chains and moving tackle. 553

20 Herezinesk, W., Warsaw.—Cordage transmission straps. 553

21 Hofmark, Bruno, St. Petersburg.—Wire transmission belt. 553

22 Miiek, William, Warsaw.—Cordage transmission straps. 553

23 Tember, K., & Schovede, L., Warsaw.—Leather transmission belts. 553

24 Cohnfeld, S., St. Petersburg.—Automatic feeding apparatus. 555

Hydraulic and Pneumatic Apparatus.

26 Admiralty Tyova Works, near St. Petersburg.
a Dawnton's ship pump and fire pump. 560
b Diving apparatus. 567

27 Friedland, Michael, St. Petersburg.—Pumps, rotary system. 560

28 Liarsky, Nicolas, Smolensk.—Load roller. 563

29 Tretzer, Adolphus, Warsaw.—Fire engine. 564

30 Lange & Co., Moscow.—Fire engine hose. 564

31 Mick, William, Warsaw.—Fire engine hose. 564

32 Hesse, Charles, Riga.—Metal capsules. 565

Railway Plant, Rolling Stock, etc.

34 Lilpop, Rau, & Loevenstein, Warsaw.
a Bolts, screws, and other railway and car fittings. 571
b Buffer spring and coupling appliance; wheel and spring for railway carriages. 572

35 Shiloff, L. P., Moscow.
a Patent railway car lock. 571
b Railway signals. 575

37 Pootilof Iron Works Co., St. Petersburg.—Railway ties, axles, and wheels. 573

38 Abookoff Steel Foundry, near St. Petersburg.—Railway wheels, ties, and axles. 573

39 Russian Rail Manufacturing Co., Government of Riazan, District of Pronsk.—Railway ties, chairs, nails, bolts and nuts. 574

Machinery used in Preparing Agricultural Products.

41 Yosefow Sugar Manufacturing Co., Government of Warsaw.—Metallic sugar loaf form. 581

Aerial, Pneumatic, and Water Transportation.

42 St. Petersburg River Yacht Club.—Rowing boats. 594

43 Alexandroosky, ——, St. Petersburg.—Air bags for raising sunken vessels. 594

44 Makaroff, T. R. N., St. Petersburg.—Patent safety mats for instantly stopping leakage in ship bottoms. 594

45 Modeling Workshop in the Naval Museum, St. Petersburg.—Models of ships, yachts, and circular iron clads. 595

46 Russian Steamboat & Trade Co., Odessa.—Model of steam schooner for the coal trade. 595

47 Naval Museum, St. Petersburg.
a Models of a floating dock and graving dock in Cronstadt. 596
b Model of steering apparatus. 597

48 Engineers' Shop of the Port of St. Petersburg.—Apparatus for lowering boats and boat furniture. 597

49 Steam Engine Works, Port of Cronstadt.—Admiral's caboose. 597

51 Mast Maker's Shop, Port of Cronstadt.—Models of masts, etc. 597

For classes of exhibits, indicated by numbers at end of entries, see Classification, pp. 13–15.

THE UNITED STATES GOVERNMENT BUILDING.

Scale, 150 ft. to 1 in.

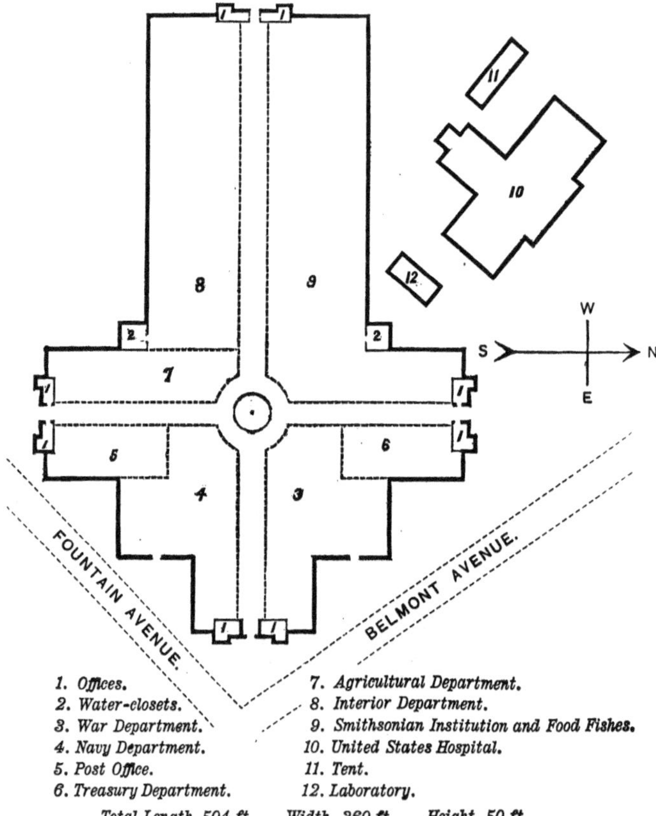

1. Offices.
2. Water-closets.
3. War Department.
4. Navy Department.
5. Post Office.
6. Treasury Department.
7. Agricultural Department.
8. Interior Department.
9. Smithsonian Institution and Food Fishes.
10. United States Hospital.
11. Tent.
12. Laboratory.

Total Length, 504 ft. Width, 360 ft. Height, 50 ft.

SPECIAL BUILDINGS.

EXHIBITION MADE BY THE UNITED STATES GOVERNMENT.

CONTRIBUTING DEPARTMENTS.

WAR DEPARTMENT.—Hon. J. DONALD CAMERON, Secretary of War.

NAVY DEPARTMENT.—Hon. GEORGE M. ROBESON, Secretary of the Navy.

TREASURY DEPARTMENT.—Hon. LOT M. MORRILL, Secretary of the Treasury.

INTERIOR DEPARTMENT.—Hon. Z. CHANDLER, Secretary of the Interior.

POST-OFFICE DEPARTMENT.—Hon. JAMES M. TYNER, Postmaster-General.

AGRICULTURAL DEPARTMENT.—Hon. FREDERICK WATTS, Commissioner of Agriculture.

SMITHSONIAN INSTITUTION.—Prof. JOSEPH HENRY, Director of Smithsonian Institution.

COMMISSION OF AMERICAN FOOD FISHES.—Prof. S. F. BAIRD, Commissioner.

BOARD ON BEHALF OF U. S. EXECUTIVE DEPARTMENTS AT THE INTERNATIONAL EXHIBITION OF 1876.

Col. S. C. LYFORD, Ordnance Corps, U. S. Army, Chairman of the Board, and Representative of the War Department at the Exhibition.

Rear Admiral THORNTON A. JENKINS, U. S. Navy, Representative of Navy Department.

Hon. R. W. TAYLER, First Comptroller Treasury, Representative of Treasury Department.

Hon. JOHN EATON, Commissioner of Education, Representative of Interior Department.

Dr. C. F. MACDONALD, Superintendent Money Order Bureau, Representative of Post-Office Department.

WILLIAM SAUNDERS, Superintendent Propagating Garden, Representative of Agricultural Department.

Prof. S. F. BAIRD, Assistant Secretary Smithsonian Institution, Representative of Smithsonian Institution, and Commissioner of American Food Fishes.

WM. A. DE CAINDRY, Secretary of the Board.

UNITED STATES GOVERNMENT BUILDINGS.

MAIN BUILDING, No. 51.

Architect, JAMES H. WINDRIM.—Size, Floor Area, 102,840 square feet.

This structure is situated at the intersection of Belmont and Fountain Avenues, is built in the form of a Latin cross, and is of framed white pine, unplaned, with two tiers of windows. It contains for exhibition contributions from the different Executive Departments of the United States Government.

ORDNANCE LABORATORY BUILDING, No. 54.

Architect, Col. T. T. S. LAIDLEY, Ordnance Corps, U. S. A.—Size, 53 feet by 23 feet.

This building is located north of Main Building, and is built of wrought iron, rivetted, covered with a light casing of wood. It is designed with the view of preventing the great loss of life that usually results from the demolition of a building of ordinary construction, by the explosion of even a small amount of powder. In the event of an explosion in this building, the roof and sides fall at once, and the iron frame is left standing, in order to shield the inmates from being crushed beneath the ruins. The building, as well as its contents, is on exhibition.

UNITED STATES ARMY POST HOSPITAL, No. 52.

Size, 35 feet by 39 feet, and Addition of 40 feet by 14 feet.

This Hospital is situated north of the Main Building, is two stories in height, and is intended to hold twenty-four beds. It is built of wood, and contains medical appliances of all kinds, including medicines, instruments, hospital stores, clothing, books, and furniture, models of hospitals, cars, boats, ambulances, etc., microscopical and other specimens. The construction of the building and its contents are on exhibition.

TRANSIT OF VENUS BUILDINGS.

This structure is situated southwest of Government Building, consisting of,—

1. Transit House.—Dimensions, 10 feet by 8 feet.
2. Photographic House.—Dimensions, 12 feet by 10 fect.
3. Equatorial House.—Dimensions, 11 feet in diameter.

All the instruments employed in observing and recording the phenomena of the late transit of Venus are so placed on exhibition that the various processes will be exemplified by practical workings.

WAR DEPARTMENT.

Signal Section.

SIGNAL SECTION.

The instruments exhibited in the Signal Service Section of the United States Army are all of American manufacture, and only such as have been devised for the signal service of the army by officers or enlisted men of the corps.

METEOROLOGICAL INSTRUMENTS.

The display of self-recording instruments consists of barographs, anemographs, thermographs, rain-gauges, and evaporator. Some of these are worked by electrical batteries, others by mechanical means. Those recording the velocity and direction of the wind, the amount of rainfall and changes of temperature, are connected with their respective wind-cups, wind-vanes, rain-receivers, and thermometers, exposed upon an artificial glass roof, beneath which the recording apparatus is placed, each electrical instrument having its own battery. Artificial currents of air and water are used to obtain uninterrupted working.

UNITED STATES SIGNAL STATION.

This department consists of a model United States signal service station, similar to those established in different sections of the United States. Here are exhibited the meteorological instruments used on station; the manner of taking, recording, and transmitting to the central office at Washington the observations upon which the weather reports, storm warnings, etc., are based; the method of publishing and distributing the predictions forwarded from the office of the Chief Signal Officer of the army, as well as the various means adopted to furnish at the earliest practicable moment all weather information which would be of benefit to commerce and agriculture. Specimens of the publications, charts, and maps of the office of the Chief Signal Officer are also exhibited.

PRINTING DEPARTMENT.

Here are exhibited in detail the printing of "weather maps" and "farmers' bulletins."

FIELD WORK.

This portion of the exhibition comprises a complete United States field-telegraph train, with capacity to erect 50 miles or more of portable telegraph line; portable signal tower 75 feet high, with its wagon; semaphore, signal flags, torches, rockets, bombs, and mortars, colored lights, heliographs (for communicating by means of sun flashing), and international flags, and other apparatus used in communicating with troops in the field or with vessels.

Quartermaster, Medical, Engineer Sections.

MODEL DEPARTMENT.

The model department comprises models of the different instruments used in field signaling, models of station meteorological instruments and portable instrument shelter, and a new electrical instrument for transmitting by telegraph the isobarometric and isothermal lines of the Signal Service weather maps.

QUARTERMASTER SECTION.

Uniforms.—Revolutionary uniforms, and those of succeeding years; present uniforms of the army.

Camp and Garrison Equipage.—Tents, flags, cooking utensils and tools; field music—drums, bugles, etc.; bunks, blankets, and bedsacks.

Means of Transportation.—Wagon and harness; ambulance and harness; aparajo; pack saddle; historic wagon; portable and traveling forges.

Machines.—For cutting out clothing; for brass screwing shoes; for testing fabrics.

Farriers' and Saddlers' Tools.

Standard Horse Shoes.

Veterinary Chest.

Kiernan's System of Horse Shoeing.

MEDICAL SECTION.

This display represents the character of the work of the medical staff of the United States army in peace and war. Four classes of objects are exhibited by the objects themselves, by models, or by photographs.

1. Hospitals for Sick and Wounded Soldiers.

a Post hospital of 24 beds of full size.

b Four full-sized hospital tents, with furniture representing the tent ward which served as the unit of the "tent field hospital" used during the civil war of 1861–65.

c Models of the barrack "General Hospitals" used during the war of 1861–65, viz.: a model of the form of barrack ward for 60 beds, on the scale of half an inch to the foot; and four ground-plan models showing combinations of such wards in general hospitals.

2. Medical and Hospital Supplies.

Samples of articles on the medical supply table of the army; medicines; hospital stores; surgical instruments and dressings; hospital furniture, bedding, clothing, and appliances; books, blank forms for reports, and stationery; medical panniers and medicine wagons, and samples of the artificial arms, legs, trusses, and other apparatus issued by the medical department to disabled soldiers.

3. Transportation of Sick and Wounded.

Stretchers, litters, and ambulances, full size and models; models of hospital railroad cars, hospital steamboat, and hospital ocean steamship, illustrating mode of transporting sick and wounded during the late war.

4. Treatment of Diseases and Injuries of Soldiers.

Army medical museum, represented by medical, surgical, anatomical, and microscopical specimens, photographs of specimens, and catalogue of museum; catalogue of Surgeon-General's office; photographed title pages of rare books on military medicine and surgery, etc.; medical and surgical publications of Surgeon-General's office.

The Post Hospital, for twenty-four beds, constructed from plans approved by the War Department, contains the greater part of the display of the Medical Department, as follows:

Room 1, 45x25, a ward with twelve beds, furniture, bedding, clothing, etc.

Room 2 (the other ward, same size), models of hospitals, ambulances, hospital cars, boats, and ships, specimens from museum, etc.

Room 3, the dispensary, samples of medical supplies.

Room 4, the office, samples of surgical instruments, medical and surgical books, blanks, etc.

Room 5, dining room, table ware, mess furniture.

Room 6, kitchen, cooking apparatus.

Room 7, office of officer in charge of the display.

Rooms on second floor, stretchers, litters, medicine chests, and panniers; artificial legs and arms, trusses for rupture, and other apparatus.

Tent ward, full-sized hospital tents, pitched in the rear of the post hospital.

Ambulances, medicine wagons, and carts, full-sized, parked near the tent ward.

ENGINEER SECTION.

Maps and Drawings.

Map of the United States, showing work done by corps of engineers, 1776–1876.

Drawing of Rock Island bridge.

Map of canal and locks, Des Moines rapids.

Map of Mississippi river, from Le Claire, Iowa, to Rock Island, Illinois.

Drawings of improvements of Mississippi river between mouths of the Illinois and Ohio.

Plans of improvements on Hudson river, near Albany.

Drawing of iron landing pier, Delaware breakwater harbor.

Drawing of foundation of Fort Delaware.

Drawing of dynamometer for determining force required to screw down iron piles of Lewes pier.

Drawing of Delaware breakwater, with details of breakwater and ice barrier.

Map of shore of Delaware harbor, including Cape Henlopen.

Chart of Schuylkill river, from mouth to Chestnut Street bridge, showing improvements made by United States in its navigation from 1870 to 1875.

Drawing of dredge-boat "Henry Burden."

Drawing of mortar mill and concrete mixer.

Map of flood plain of Minnesota and Mississippi rivers, showing connection with basin of Red river and Lake Winnepeg.

Drawings of snag boat.

Chart of Galveston entrance.

Detailed drawings and photographs, illustrating experimental works at Galveston entrance.

Chart of Indianola harbor.

Detail drawings of end dock.

Charts of Lake Survey.

Lighthouse drawings, Eleventh district.

Drawing of river and harbor works.

Plans of cribs and pile pier at Chicago.

Maps and hydrographs of Ohio, Monongahela, and Great Kanawha rivers.

Drawings of crib work for piers on Lake Ontario.

Special map of region west of Mississippi river.

Special triangulation map of region west of Mississippi river.

Detailed topographical sheets of above region.

Specimen copies of photolithographic atlas,

Engineer, Ordnance Sections.

crayon topographical atlas, and geological atlas.

Models of Harbor Improvements.

Work at Hallet's Point, N. Y. (Hellgate.)

Northern extremity of Cape Cod.

Section of iron landing pier of Delaware breakwater harbor.

Iron ice barrier proposed for Horse Shoe of Delaware river.

Breakwater at Dunkirk, N. Y.

Crib and lighthouse on Spectacle reef, Lake Huron.

Angle crib and lighthouse at Harbor of Refuge, Lake Huron.

Model showing shore lines and breakwater at Harbor of Refuge, Lake Huron.

Crib and pier at Chicago, Illinois.

Crib work for piers on Lake Ontario.

"Mattress" or "apron" used in improvements of harbor at mouth of Cape Fear river, N. C.

Models of Machinery and Appliances.

Steam drilling scow.

Capstan-head and machinery for screwing down iron piles at Delaware breakwater landing pier.

Derrick for landing shafts.

Eccentric clamp or "nipper" for sustaining piles.

Snag boat, showing hull.

Dredge-boat "McAlester."

Large grapple.

Photographs.

Views of Hallet's Point, N. Y.; snag boat; Red river; cribs and piers at Chicago, Ill.; country west of Mississippi river (Wheeler expedition).

Materials, Specimens, and Samples.

Specimens of borings at site of landing pier of Delaware breakwater; of iron used in construction of landing pier; of timber piles taken from between tides at Reedy Island; ice barrier; of building stone, concrete, and woods, collected from various parts of the United States; of fossil trees; of large cypress stump, taken from mouth of Cape Fear river, N. C.

Miscellaneous.

United States bridge equipage, pontoon wagons, loaded; tool wagon; forge; model of bridge train, wagons, and loads; reserve and advance guard bridges; siege and mining tools; field photographic outfit; reconnoissance instruments; bridge model; models of torpedoes; models of apparatus for measuring subaqueous explosions, in glass tank; torpedoes, full size, models, 1874–'75; ground mine; cable stop; junction boxes; torpedo cables, multiple and single; operating box; electrical apparatus used with torpedoes; iron plate from torpedo target, showing effects of thirty pounds of dynamite exploded under water at thirty feet distance; models of King, De Russy, and Hunt self-depressing gun carriages; models of mortar carriage and muzzle-pivoting gun carriage; surveying, astronomical, and barometrical instruments for field work; publications of the engineer bureau.

ORDNANCE SECTION.

Sea Coast Guns.

20 in. Rodman gun, on carriage and chassis, with hydraulic buffer, on platform; implements.

12 in. Thompson b. l. rifle, experimental, under Laidley's gun lift.

9 in. Sutcliffe b. l. rifle, experimental, on carriage and chassis, with Sinclair's friction-brake, mounted on platform; implements.

10 in. Woodbridge gun, experimental; in slings, under Laidley sling cart.

8 in. m. l. converted rifle, experimental, on 10 in. casemate carriage and chassis, with pneumatic buffers, mounted on platform in model of casemate; implements.

Mann's 8 in. b. l. rifle, wrought iron, experimental, mounted on top carriage and chassis.

8 in. siege howitzer, mounted on wooden siege carriage.

Siege Guns.

4.5 in. siege rifle gun, mounted on Benton's experimental iron siege carriage, with limber; implements.

Field Guns.

Light 12 pdr. gun, 4.62 in. wooden carriage, with limber; implements.

Sutcliffe 3.9 in. b. l. rifle, experimental.

Hotchkiss 3.9 in. b. l. rifle, experimental.

Moffat 3.15 in. b. l. rifle, experimental.

Mann's 3 in. b. l. rifle, experimental.

3 in. wrought iron, m. l. rifle, mounted on Benton's experimental iron 12 pdr. field carriage, with limber and caisson; implements; model horse harnessed to limber, with mounted driver.

10 pdr. Parrot rifle, mounted on Watervliet arsenal experimental iron field carriage, with limber.

3 in. Whitworth field piece, on carriage.

2.5 in. Woodbridge gun, experimental; fired 1327 times.

Hotchkiss field cannon, experimental.

Rebel b. l. pieces, field and boat, experimental skids.

Lyman's multicharge rifle, cal. 6 in., experimental skids.

Bomford and Wade perforated gun, experimental; used to determine experimentally exterior lines of heavy cannon, by means of pressure at different points of bore.

Mountain howitzer, mounted on carriage.

Mountain howitzer battery, on stands.

Volley and Repeating Guns.

Gatling gun, short barrel, cal. 45, on cavalry carriage; model horse in harness.

Hotchkiss revolving cannon, on carriage, experimental.

Union repeating (coffee-mill) gun, on carriage, experimental.

Regua battery, on carriage, experimental.

Guthrie & Lee gun, on carriage, experimental.

Vandenburgh volley gun, on carriage, experimental.

Revolutionary Guns.

6 pdr. French guns, bronze, presented by Lafayette; forming enclosure around models of modern gun plant.

12 pdr. siege gun, bronze, mounted on wooden carriage, with limber.

8 in. howitzer, bronze, mercer.

24 pdr. howitzers, Byer's; cast in Philadelphia.

Anthony Wayne howitzers, intended to be used on horseback; cast in Germantown, Philadelphia, by D. King.

Mortars.

13 in. sea-coast mortars, on bed, with centres, pintles, chassis mounted, on platform; implements.

24 pdr. Coehorn mortars, on beds.

Carriages.

New cavalry forge cart.

Projectiles.

Shot, shells, grape, canister, etc., for various weapons and calibres; smooth-bored and rifled; fired and unfired; hand-grenades,

War and Navy Departments, Ordnance and Appliances.

bombs, rockets, torpedoes, etc. Experimental projectiles from West Point.

Small Arms.

Historical collection of muzzle-loaders, wall-pieces, muskets, musketoons, rifles, pistols, flintlocks, percussion, breech-loaders, fixed and movable chambers, revolvers, tip-up barrels, needle guns, cylindered, magazine, chassepot, repeating, coffee-mill, drop-lever, slap-over guns, American and foreign.

Bayonets, blades, knives, swords and scabbards, lances, pikes, halberds, cleaning appliances, etc.

Accoutrement.

Sets of infantry, cavalry, and artillery equipments; cartridge boxes, canteens, metal work on scabbards, etc.; powder horns and flasks, cartridges, and cases of various materials and calibres; primers, locks, fuses; cartridge-making machinery.

Models.

Minute man.

Rifle private, full dress, Hall breech-loading rifle, 1818.

Private, mounted rifles, Mexican War, 1845.

Infantry private, 1858–1866, regulation equipment.

Cavalry private, 1865, Spencer, Mann's equipment.

Infantry man, full dress, 1876.

Infantry man, marching outfit, 1876.

Cavalry man, present, full dress, 1876.

Light-artillery man, full dress, 1876.

Horse, carved in wood, for cavalry equipment.

Horse, carton pièrre, for artillery harness.

Horse, stuffed, for Gatling cart.

Rock Island Arsenal, Illinois, in photo-relief.

Hitchcock gun-plant, with gun in sections, with set test specimen Hitchcock gun material, showing tensile and torsional strength; sample forging-disk; Dank's iron bloom; Graff, Bennett, & Co., Hitchcock's gun materials; long turnings H.G. material; and thin turnings H.G. material.

Rodman gun-plant, with specimen, showing tensile compression and torsional strength of the American cast-iron used in Rodman gun.

Woodbridge gun, with set specimens, showing tensile strength of Woodbridge gun construction; reel-wire for Woodbridge gun; and half-ring, bronzed, Woodbridge gun.

Cast of bore in gutta-percha of 8 in. m. l. converted rifles, with centres for same on trestles.

Glass-case specimens, containing small models, relics, etc.

Tree, cut in two by musketry at the battle of the Wilderness, Va.

Boards of component parts of small arms, and progressive work on scabbards.

Rodman guns, mounted in barbette and in casemate.

Mortar, mounted on bed with centre pintle chassis.

Table with models, field and siege carriages.

Lead bullets, joined together by collision in mid-air at the battle of Petersburg, Va.

Machines.

Casemate gin; Baxter engines.

Cartridge Machinery.

Portable gas furnace for annealing cartridge shells; double-action press; drawing presses; case and cup anvil trimmers; header; primer; cup venting, and impression machines; bullet, ball-trimming, and greasing, tapering, and loading machines; cup anvil press; rotary fan; packing tables and work boxes.

Gun-making Machinery.

Drop hammer; forge; trimming jumper; barrel-boring lathe, for nut boring and quick boring; barrel-turning lathe; straightening stand; polishing stand; vises, with machine for bending swivels; trimming press; drill press; rifling, brush, and profiling machines; milling and screw machines; clamp milling machine; machine for bending swivels; grindstone; engine lathe; emery mill grinder; second drilling receiver; first turning stock; lock-bedding with post and spare pulley; air pump and reservoir; bench for assembling guns.

Instruments.

Laidley laboratory, showing principles of construction, and illustrating experiments in ballistics; models pressure; pendulum eprouvette; camera lucida for representation with model of Frankford target; Shultz chronoscope, with Russel's interrupter; vignotti machine; Le Boulangé chronograph; Benton thread, and electro-ballistic machines; target for electro-ballistic machines; recoil dynamometer; mercurial densimeter; scales for mercurial densimeter; stereometer; collection of inspecting instruments for cannon and projectiles for 3 in. rifle and 15 in. gun; iron tube for firing through with safety; firing stand.

Miscellaneous.

Boards showing rifle practice.

Publications from ordnance office and artillery school.

Medal, army target practice; stadia, silver (1 cavalry, 1 infantry); telemetres (1 battery, 1 infantry, and 1 field).

Corrugated iron powder barrels; copper powder barrel.

NAVY DEPARTMENT.

ORDNANCE BRANCH.

Rifled and Smooth Bore Guns.—15 in. guns on Ericssen's and Edes's steam carriages.

[These two guns are mounted on a circular platform and inclosed in a wooden turret, representing in size and form a monitor's iron turret.]

Pieces of heavy ordnance, muzzle and breech loading, of antiquated styles and manufacture.

Guns from 11 in. to 3 in. calibre, and 100 pdrs. to 12 pdrs., variously mounted.

Torpedoes.—Automatic, stationary, and movable; electric batteries, wires, fuses, etc.; illustrating progress made by the torpedo school.

Small Arms.—Muskets, rifle and smooth bore, breech- and muzzle-loading; pistols, swords, cutlasses, bowie knives, battle axes, tomahawks, boarding helmets, etc.

Ordnance publications.

Samples of gunpowder.

Inspecting instruments for heavy guns; implements for gauging and inspecting shot and shell.

Fuse presses; machines for making percussion caps; metallic cartridges; solid head metallic musket and pistol cartridge now used in the navy, showing the different stages of manufacture; other musket cartridges and cartridge inventions in possession of the navy.

Rifle projectiles for heavy guns; inventions of Dahlgren, Holroyd, Dana, Parrot, Hotchkiss, James, Brooks, and other inventors.

Sub-calibre and elongated projectiles for smooth bore guns; solid shot, shell, incendiary shell, grape, canister, shrapnel, as used at present, and as previously used or proposed.

Projectiles which have been fired at iron targets; models of projectiles; model gun-carriages; war rockets, hand grenades; leather work of navy ordnance; sponges, rammers, and scrapers of different styles and inventions; fuses, cannon primers, and caps, cannon locks, night signals, impressions from guns, vent impressions; gun sights; breech, reinforce, and trunnion.

Figures of sailors, showing the dress and arms at different periods.

Miscellaneous articles and naval relics.

NAVIGATION BRANCH.

Navy bunting and navy flags, illustrating the present state of the bunting manufacture in the United States, as shown in the bunting made for the navy and known as "navy bunting," and also the mode of making flags by dyeing in pattern.

Bunting testing machine.

Navy sounding machines and auxiliary apparatus, showing the improvements in Sir William Thomson's sounding machine, and the various devices for detaching sinkers, and bringing up specimens of bottom, water, etc.

Navy signal apparatus, showing the colored lights (Coston's), with specimens.

Navy compasses and compass-testing instruments, showing specimens of the navy compass, azimuth circle, tell-tale, boat, and monitor compasses.

Portable compass-testing instrument, with specimens to illustrate development of the liquid compass.

Specimens of the old dry or air compass of American makers, illustrating the progress of improvement.

Adjustable binnacle.

NAVAL OBSERVATORY.

Publications.

Photographs of astronomical and other objects.

Chronometers.

Objects illustrative of American Arctic explorations.

Buildings and instruments used in the observations of the transit of Venus, December 8, 9, 1874.

HYDROGRAPHIC OFFICE.

Nautical charts, books, etc., published by the Hydrographic Office.

NAUTICAL ALMANAC OFFICE.

Publications of the office.

YARDS AND DOCKS BRANCH.

Plans of navy yards at Portsmouth, N. H.; Boston, Mass.; New York, N. Y.; Washington, D. C.; Norfolk, Va.; Pensacola, Fla., and Mare Island, Cal.

Plans of machinery at Boston navy yard; plans of dry docks at Boston, Mass., and Norfolk, Va.

Photographs of buildings, etc., at Portsmouth, N. H.; New York, N. Y.; Norfolk, Va.; League Island, Pa.; Boston, Mass., and Mare Island, Cal.

Models of dry docks at Boston, Mass.; New York, N. Y.; Norfolk, Va., and Mare Island, Cal.

Pyramid of blocks of wood taken from naval vessels.

STEAM ENGINEERING BRANCH.

Machinery of the "Nipsic."

The machinery of the various sizes of steam launches.

The engines of the "Epervier."

Part of the original machinery of the torpedo boat "Spuyten Duyvel," a steam launch, with the first torpedo machinery used in the United States Navy.

Detail drawings of compound engines.

Photographs of machine shops, foundries, etc., showing improved tools used in the manufacture and construction of steam machinery.

Two compound boilers.

Baird's distiller, illustrating the method of making fresh water on board ship at sea.

EQUIPMENT AND RECRUITING BRANCH.

Young's ship's galley, with utensils for cooking for 500 men.

Hemp, manila, and wire rope; cable, blocks, chain cables, etc.

CONSTRUCTION AND REPAIR BRANCH.

Models of the "Constitution;" "Mississippi;" "Jamestown;" "St. Mary's;" "Portsmouth;" "Constellation;" "Niagara;" "Merrimac;" "New Ironsides;" "Hartford;" "Monitor;" "Kearsage;" "Vandalia;" "Constitution;" "President;" "Ohio;" "Enterprise;" "Washington," and "Fulton."

Full-rigged model.

MEDICAL AND SURGICAL BRANCH.

Medicines and Hospital Stores used in the Navy.

Surgical instruments and appliances usually supplied in the service; additional case of surgical instruments occasionally supplied in lieu of the standard operation case.

Cots and stretchers for transportation of wounded in action.

Model of a sick bay; the part of the ship usually allotted for hospital accommodation.

Model of hospital ship.

Fan for ventilating the hold of a ship in hot climates.

Starting funnel arrangement for aerating distilled water.

Set of record and account books for a naval hospital.

Fracture bedstead, for elevating the patient and changing position.

Bed with woven wire mattress.

Photographs and plans of naval hospitals.

PAY, PROVISION, AND CLOTHING BRANCH.

Articles and materials of clothing issued in the navy.

Package, showing the manner of packing clothing for sea.

Navy rations in glass jars, and packages of the same as prepared for sea.

"Small stores," articles for mess use: pans,

spoons, knives, etc., tobacco, soap, needles, thread, and other small articles.

Packages of tobacco and soap as packed for sea use.

Paymasters' books and blanks for a ship with complement of 200 men; paymasters' stationery; stewards' stores, scales, and tools used in issuing provisions.

Iron safe; locks used on paymasters' store-rooms, three in number.

Specimen of candles.

TREASURY DEPARTMENT.

(Owing to want of sufficient appropriation by Congress for defraying the expense of the participation in the Exhibition by the Treasury Department, no definite arrangements have yet been made for contributions from it.—March 31, 1876.)

INTERIOR DEPARTMENT.

PATENT OFFICE.

Publications.—Annual reports; official gazette; indexes to patents, general and yearly; volumes of patents, monthly and weekly; decisions of Commissioner of Patents; mechanical dictionary; official classification.

Drawings of Models.—Selected series (60,000), intended to serve in the illustration of the Patent Office work, from the classes given below.

Models.—Selected series (5000), intended to serve in the illustration of the Patent Office work, from the following classes: agriculture; harvesters; mills and presses; architecture; civil engineering; railways; navigation; metallurgy; metal working; wood working; steam; hydraulics; pneumatics; mechanical movements; hoisting; horse powers; journals and bearings; vehicles; fire arms; textile; printing and stationery; stone; clay; glass; leather; light; heat; electricity; household; chemistry; gas; ice, and fine arts.

Miscellaneous Collections of Interest.—The original Declaration of Independence; Gen. Washington's commission from the Continental Congress; personal effects of Gen. Washington, such as furniture, porcelain, clothing, cane, sword, traveling escritoire, surveying compass, camp equipage, including tent, mess-kit, money-chest, etc.

Weapons of historical interest, such as bayonets from General Braddock's line of march; muskets presented by the Emperor of Morocco to Mr. Jefferson; war saddle of Baron De Kalb; sabres of honor presented to United States officers by sovereigns and beys; model of invention by President Lincoln.

PENSION OFFICE.

Publications.—Annual reports; graphic illustrations; wall maps; wall charts; portfolios of diagrams, etc.; collections of historical interest; selections from the archives of the office relative to the Revolutionary war.

GENERAL LAND OFFICE.

Publications.—Annual reports; digests, and other documents.

Graphic Illustrations.—Maps, charts, and atlas of surveys; miscellaneous collections; instruments and processes employed in the land survey.

INDIAN OFFICE.

Publications.—Reports and other publications.

Illustrations.—Portraits, photographs, maps of reservations, etc.

Models.—Wigwams, communal houses, canoes, etc.

Miscellaneous Collection of Interest.—Costumes, male and female, adult and others; weapons of war and the chase; tents, wigwams, canoes, etc.; domestic utensils; specimens of food; toys, games, and festivals; arts and manufactures of the tribes; ethnological collections, etc.

EDUCATION OFFICE.

Publications by the Office.—Annual and special reports, and circulars of information.

Publications by other Offices or Persons.—Foreign reports on American education; foreign educational reports and documents; treatises on pedagogy; and educational journals.

Graphic Representations.—Wall maps and charts; portfolios of engravings, drawings, and photographs; busts; paintings, and other portraits.

Models of Educational Buildings.—The primitive log school-house; country school-house of to-day; city graded school-house; college buildings; details as to dormitories, ventilative apparatus, school-rooms, etc.; models of adobe and sod school-houses.

Specimens of School Furniture, Apparatus, and text-books.—Historic collection, showing progress in text-books; specimens and models of school desks, seats, black boards, school maps, charts, etc.; specimens of modern slates, globes, natural history cabinets, chemical and philosophical apparatus, chemical appliances, etc.

Miscellaneous Collections of Interest.—Selected volumes of state and city educational reports; catalogues of private schools, academies, seminaries, colleges, and professional schools, selected series; catalogues and reports of orphan, reformatory, and charitable schools for the young, etc.; catalogues and reports of institutions for the deaf mute, blind, etc.; catalogues and reports of libraries; catalogues and reports of museums of art, of science, and of natural history.

These miscellaneous collections, some bound and others in their original condition, will be exhibited as showing specimens of the materials for the study of education, which are published by the systems and corporations themselves.

Volumes of manuscript returns made to the Bureau of Education by educators and school officials of every grade, and used in the preparation of its annual and special reports.

CENSUS OFFICE.

Publications.—Decennial censuses; statistical atlas, 1870.

Graphic Illustrations.—Maps, charts, and diagrams.

Miscellaneous Articles of Interest.—Original schedules of the census of 1790; selected volumes of schedules of subsequent censuses.

GEOLOGICAL AND GEOGRAPHICAL SURVEY OF THE TERRITORIES.

1st Division.

Publications.—Reports, bulletins, etc.

Graphic Illustrations.—Topographical and geological atlases; wall maps and charts; panoramic photographs; stereoscopic views; photographic portfolios; photographic transparencies; paintings, landscapes, portraits, etc.

Models and Reliefs.—Topographical and geographical relief maps; relief sections; models of displacement; models of ancient ruined cliff habitations; models of same restored.

Collections of Interest.—Geological and mineralogical cabinets; pottery, costumes, weapons, implements, toys, etc.

2d Division.

Publications.—Reports; bulletins; monographs, etc.

Graphic Illustrations.—Topographical and geological atlases; wall maps and charts; panoramic and stereoscopic views; portfolios, albums, and transparent photographs.

Models and Reliefs.—Topographical and geological relief maps; geological structural sections; models of displacement.

Miscellaneous Collections.—Geological and mineralogical specimens; arms, clothing, etc.

POST-OFFICE DEPARTMENT.

The exhibition of this Department is classed under the following general heads:

A MODEL WORKING POST-OFFICE.

This is a branch office or station of the Philadelphia office, and shows the practical workings of the following divisions of this Department, viz.: Box and general delivery system; system of carrier delivery and collections; registered letter system; money-order system; foreign mail system, etc.

RAILWAY MAIL SERVICE DIVISION.

Two railway post-offices or postal cars, equipped with mail-bag catchers, and all other first-class appointments of that service, under charge of railway post-office clerks, by whom the mailing and distribution of outgoing mails is performed. Several models of mail catchers are also exhibited under this head.

Model mail cars,—small size,—exhibiting the practical working of the mail-bag catcher upon a miniature truck inside the building.

STAMPS, STAMPED ENVELOPE, AND POSTAL CARD DIVISION.

Machine in operation manufacturing stamped envelopes; machine in operation manufacturing postal cards; specimens of all stamps, stamped envelopes, and postal cards; specimens of registered-letter envelopes and post-office official envelopes; specimens of all United States post-office stamps and stamped envelopes, formerly used and now out of date.

MAIL EQUIPMENT DIVISION.

Leather pouches for letter mails; canvas bags for printed and miscellaneous matter; also registered-letter mail bags; mail locks, now in use; mail locks, out of use.

TOPOGRAPHICAL DIVISION.

Railway and general postal-route maps, and money-order office maps.

DIVISION OF BOOKS AND BLANKS.

Specimens of all books, blanks, etc., used by the Department; letter scales; marking and rating stamps.

AGRICULTURAL DEPARTMENT.

The exhibit from the Agricultural Department embraces as follows:

BOTANICAL DIVISION.

A collection of all the timber trees of the United States, in sections, showing interior and exterior surfaces; specimens of flowers, leaves, and fruits; herbarium specimens of grasses and other specialties.

STATISTICAL DIVISION.

Large outline maps of the United States, showing forest areas, extent, and value of farming lands, and amount of production, by counties; arrangement of charts and diagrams detailing amount of special products, by sections; statistics of farm animals, and illustrated statistics of industrial education; statistical album of miscellaneous details, with charts, diagrams, etc.

ENTOMOLOGICAL DIVISION.

Collections of fruit and vegetable models; birds beneficial and injurious to farmers and orchardists; poultry types, illustrated by stuffed specimens; collection of grains and cereals; collection of textile fibres of the United States, with specimens of their manufacture; specimens of tobacco, from different tobacco-producing sections of the United States; mounted collection of beneficial and injurious insects.

MICROSCOPICAL DIVISION.

Series of water-color drawings illustrating typical genera of microscopic fungi; preparations illustrating the characteristics of poisonous and edible mushrooms common to the United States; illustrations displaying the varied character of the starch granules of plants; drawings and illustrations explaining method of distinguishing vegetable and animal fibres, their kind and quality; drawings displaying vegetable and animal cellulose and starches, and illustrating methods of detecting them in organizations.

CHEMICAL DIVISION.

Fertilizers.—Mineral—including phosphates, apatite, coprolites, and all minerals and materials yielding potash, etc.; vegetable —muck, peat, sea-weed, and other products of vegetable decomposition; animal—including guanos, bones, refuse from abattoirs, fisheries, oil manufactures, cancerine, etc.; agricultural products and materials obtained by chemical processes from flour, meal, bran, hominy; methods of preserving, etc., with special products of manufacture, viz.: starch, dextrine, sago, sugars, gums, glucose; products obtained by fermentation: wine, beer, ale, etc.; products of acetous fermentations; tanning materials of the United States: barks, leaves; tanning solutions, with modes of manufacture; dyes of the United States; resins and products of distillation of resinous materials; oils, vegetable, fixed, and others; products of milk, classified according to methods of production.

HORTICULTURAL DIVISION.

Specimens of economic and utilizable plants, showing methods of growth, culture, etc., grapes, cotton, tobacco, flax, broom corn, jute, corn, sorghum, yucca fibres, etc.

SMITHSONIAN INSTITUTION, AND COMMISSION ON AMERICAN FOOD FISHES.

The Smithsonian Institution makes the following exhibits:

Publications of the Institution.

Smithsonian contributions to knowledge; miscellaneous collections; annual reports, and other publications.

Meteorological work of the Institution: Charts showing the mean temperature, rainfall, and barometric pressure of the United States.

International exchanges; statistics of number of correspondents; extent of distribution by exchange.

General condition; financial statement.

COLLECTION TO ILLUSTRATE THE ANIMAL RESOURCES OF THE UNITED STATES.

IN CHARGE OF G. BROWNE GOODE.

Animals Beneficial or Injurious to Man—Mammals; birds; reptiles; amphibians; fishes; elasmobranchiates; marsipobranchiates; leptocardians; insects; arachneans; crustaceans; worms; mollusks; radiates; protozoans and marine products not of animal nature.

Means of Pursuit and Capture.—Hand-implements; implements for seizure of objects; missiles; baited hooks; angling tackle; nets, and traps.

Apparatus for Wholesale Destruction.—Hunting animals; decoys and disguises; pursuit—its methods and appliances.

Means of Utilization.—Preparation and preservation of foods; manufacture of textile fabrics, felts and stuffings; preparation of the skin and its appendages; the hard materials; oils, glues, drugs, perfumes, chemical products, fertilizers and lime; preservation of the animal for scientific uses.

Animal Products and their Applications.—Food; clothing; materials employed in the arts and manufactures.

Protection and Culture of Useful Animals.—Investigation; protection, and propagation.

COLLECTION TO ILLUSTRATE THE FISHERY RESOURCES OF THE UNITED STATES.

This is covered to a considerable extent by the preceding group, in connection with which it is arranged. The special features will embrace the following:

Fishing vessels, boats, etc., life size and models.

The apparatus and dories used in the whale fisheries.

Nets, traps, and pounds.

Hooks, lines, baits, etc.

Casts, photographs, and drawings of fish and other aquatic animals.

Prepared or living specimens of aquatic animals.

Products of the waters.

Economical applications of the above products.

E.—COLLECTION TO ILLUSTRATE THE ETHNOLOGY OF THE UNITED STATES.

IN CHARGE OF DR. CHARLES RAW.

(*This exhibition is made conjointly with the Indian Bureau of the Interior Department.*)

Objects of Stone.

Flaked and chipped stone; raw material (pieces of flint, etc.); flakes and cores of flint, obsidian, etc.; rude or unfinished implements; arrow and spear heads; perforators and scrapers; cutting and sawing implements; dagger-shaped implements; leaf-shaped implements; digging implements, and wedge or celt-shaped implements.

Pecked, ground, and polished stone; wedges or celts; chisels; gouges; adzes; grooved axes; hammers; ceremonial weapons; cutting tools; scraper and spade-like implements; pendants and sinkers; discordal stones, etc.; pierced tablets and boat-shaped objects; grinding and polishing stones; stone vessels; mortars; pestles; tubes; pipes; ornaments, and sculptures.

Objects of Copper.

Implements and ornaments.

Objects of Bone.

Implements, weapons, and ornaments.

Objects of Shell.

Utensils, implements, and ornaments.

Objects of Clay.

Mound pottery and terra-cottas.

Objects of Wood.

Fragmentary objects and carvings of an early date.

Ethnological Series.

Man.—Skulls, mummies, etc.

Culture.—Aliments, food (mineral and vegetable), drinks, narcotics, and medicines.

Habitations.—Models of houses, tents, etc., and appurtenances.

Furniture.—Cradle boards, mats, etc.

Vessels and other utensils of household use.—Earthenware; carved horn and wooden ware; stone ware; wicker work; bladders and boxes.

Utensils for smoking, etc.—Pipes; tobacco pouches; snuff apparatus, etc.

Receptacles used as means of transportation.—Pouches, bags, raw-hide cases, burden-nets, etc.

Clothing.—Raw material; complete suits; head, body, hand, leg, and foot clothing; parts of dress.

Personal adornment.—Skin ornamentation; head, neck, breast, body, and limb ornaments; toilet articles.

Implements of general use of war and the chase, and of special crafts.—Implements for cutting, drilling, etc.; lances, bows and arrows, clubs, tomahawks, etc.; shields, body armor, etc.; implements for fire-making, arrow-making, pottery, for procuring and manufacturing food; agricultural implements; implements used in spinning, weaving, sewing, and embroidery.

Means of locomotion and transportation.—Snow shoes, ice creepers, etc.; balsas, dugouts, bark canoes, hide boats, etc.; saddles, bridles, halters, harness, etc.; sleighs, etc.

Games and pastimes.—Gambling implements; masks, etc., used in dancing; rackets, balls, etc.; toys.

Music.—Drums, rattles, whistles, flutes, etc.

Art.—Pictorial representations and carvings.

Superstition.—Charms, mythological figures, etc.

COLLECTION TO ILLUSTRATE THE MINERAL RESOURCES OF THE UNITED STATES.

In charge of W. P. Blake.

The principal objects of this collection of the useful ores and minerals of the country have been to illustrate: 1st. The nature and variety of the mineral resources of the United States; 2d. The geographical distribution and geological associations of the minerals; 3d. The extent to which they have been utilized; 4th. The mechanical, metallurgical, and chemical processes by which they are extracted or converted into useful products; 5th. The inherent and comparative qualities of the extractive products. A portion of the collection is arranged according to the nature of the objects, irrespective of locality, but the bulk of the Exhibition is grouped geographically by States. There is also a section devoted to models and drawings, and one to geological maps and graphic charts. This collection occupies the northeast portion of the Government Building, upon the right of the main aisle.

I. SYSTEMATIC SERIES, GROUPED IRRESPECTIVE OF LOCALITY, IN THE FOLLOWING ORDER:

a Crystalline minerals, chiefly for scientific and educational purposes.

b Fuels and petroleum.

c Ores, metals, and their immediate derivatives.

d Ornamental stones and gems.

e Building stones; marbles, etc.

f Artificial stones; lime; mortars; cement.

g Fictile materials and direct products, including refractory materials, etc.

h Pigments; colors; detergents.

i Grinding, abrading, and polishing substances.

k Fertilizing substances.

l Sulphur, salts, and minerals chiefly used in chemical manufactures.

II. ORES, MINERALS, AND METALLURGICAL PRODUCTS, GROUPED BY STATES.

Maine.—Iron ores, limestone and pig iron; granite for buildings and monuments.

New Hampshire.—Granitic and metamorphosed rocks; granite; geological map of the State.

Vermont.—Marble; slate of various colors; roofing slate, etc.; iron ores and limonite; chilling pig iron; spiegeleisen; kaolin and fire brick; sand for glass making; copper ores, copper, and metallurgical products; scythe stones.

Massachusetts.—Iron ore, siderite; magnetic iron ore, and steel produced from it; iron and steel wire; emery, massive and associate; corundum, corundophylite, diaspore, red oxide of titanium, and ilmenite; argentiferous lead ore, galenite; copper ore; syenite and porphyry; porphyry, a series of polished specimens; granite; sand for glass making; glass, cut and pressed; pearl ash and red lead; kaolin; potters' clay, brick clay, etc.; potters', paper, and alum clay; marble and limestone; geological map of the State.

Rhode Island.—Granite, for building and monumental purposes; magnetite; anthracite and graphitic coal, in large mass and in lumps.

Connecticut.—Granite and building stone; marble and limestone; serpentine marble, verd antique; barytes (sulphate of barytes); kaolin, brick clay, and products; iron ores, limonite, etc.; pig iron; iron ore, spathic and associates; cement steel; mining picks and hammers; copper and alloys, nickel silver, etc.; feldspar, silex, etc., for pottery puposes; geological map of the State.

New York.—Magnetic iron ores, building stones, etc.; fluxes, fuels, and iron; Bessemer steel; hematite, magnetite, etc.; malleable cast iron; puddled iron and muck bar; limestone and lime; hydraulic limestone, hydraulic cement, and cement drain-pipe; kaolin, crude and washed; "incombustible mineral wool," or nitrous fibre "slag felting;" lead and tin foil; fire clay and fire clay goods, refractory materials, etc.

New Jersey.—Magnetic iron ores; iron ore; massive and granular willemite; zinc ores and franklinite; zinc; spiegel iron, "franklinite iron"; calamine (silicate of zinc); potters' and brick clay and iron-stone china ware; refractory furnace materials, fire brick, etc.; fire-brick clay and fire brick, etc.

Pennsylvania.—Iron ore, flux, and fuel; coal and coke; kaolin; limestone; iron ores, limonite, specular iron, etc.; copper ores; copper and copper products; petroleum and petroleum products; glass, and materials for its manufacture; window glass and materials; pig iron and ores; nickel and cobalt ores and products; cast steel; sheet iron; chromite.

Maryland.—Iron ore, flux, and fuel.

Virginia.—Zinc ores, calamine; lead ores, galena, cerussite, etc.; gypsum; barytes; kaolin; iron ores, magnetite, hematite, limonite, and fossil ore; coal and coke; copper ores; salt brine, fossil salt, and prepared salt; gold-bearing quartz; manganese; granite.

West Virginia.—Bituminous coal; coke; iron ores, black band, brown hematite, and fossil ores.

North Carolina.—Gold and silver ores; copper ores; marble; corundum and the associate minerals; iron ores and iron; muscovite (mica); geological map of North Carolina.

South Carolina.—Phosphatic fossils, mineral fertilizers, etc.; minerals and ores.

Alabama.—Ores and coal; spiegeleisen and ores; geological map of Alabama.

Minerals, Geological Maps and Publications

Tennessee.—Iron ores, coal and mineral products; copper pyrites and vein stone; refined copper; geological map of Tennessee.

Georgia.—Auriferous gravel; gold-bearing quartz, etc.

Kentucky.—A series of specimens illustrating the mineral resources of the State.

Louisiana.—Rock salt; sulphur.

Ohio.—Open hearth steel; iron ores, flux and fuel; pig iron; potters' clay and pottery; crude and manufactured plaster; building stone.

Indiana.—Specimens of block coal, and iron ores; potters' clay; "Indianite."

Missouri.—Lead ores, galena, cerussite, etc.; pig lead; zinc ores; barytes, associated with lead ores; marble, limestone, and granite; iron ores, magnetite, specular iron, hematite; pig iron; copper ore; coal and coke; fossil plants, etc.; porphyry.

Michigan.—Iron ores, flux, and Bessemer pig iron; specular and magnetic; native copper, crystallized; mass and stamp work, with silver and associate minerals, and in amygdaloid and "ash bed;" building stone; native silver; copper and "copper conglomerate."

Colorado.—Gold and silver ores; gold, and ores containing tellurium; silver and copper ore.

Utah.—Silver ores.

Idaho.—Gold and silver ores.

Montana.—Silver ores; argentiferous galena.

Arizona.—Copper ores; gold quartz, and other minerals.

Nevada.—Silver and gold ores.

California.—Gold and silver ores; auriferous gravel, "cement" with gold; quicksilver ores, cinnabar and native quicksilver; copper ores; tin ores and tin.

III. MODELS AND DRAWINGS.

IV. GEOLOGICAL MAPS AND GRAPHIC CHARTS.

Geological Map of the United States and Territories.

Geological and other Maps of the State of New Hampshire.

Geological Reports and Publications.

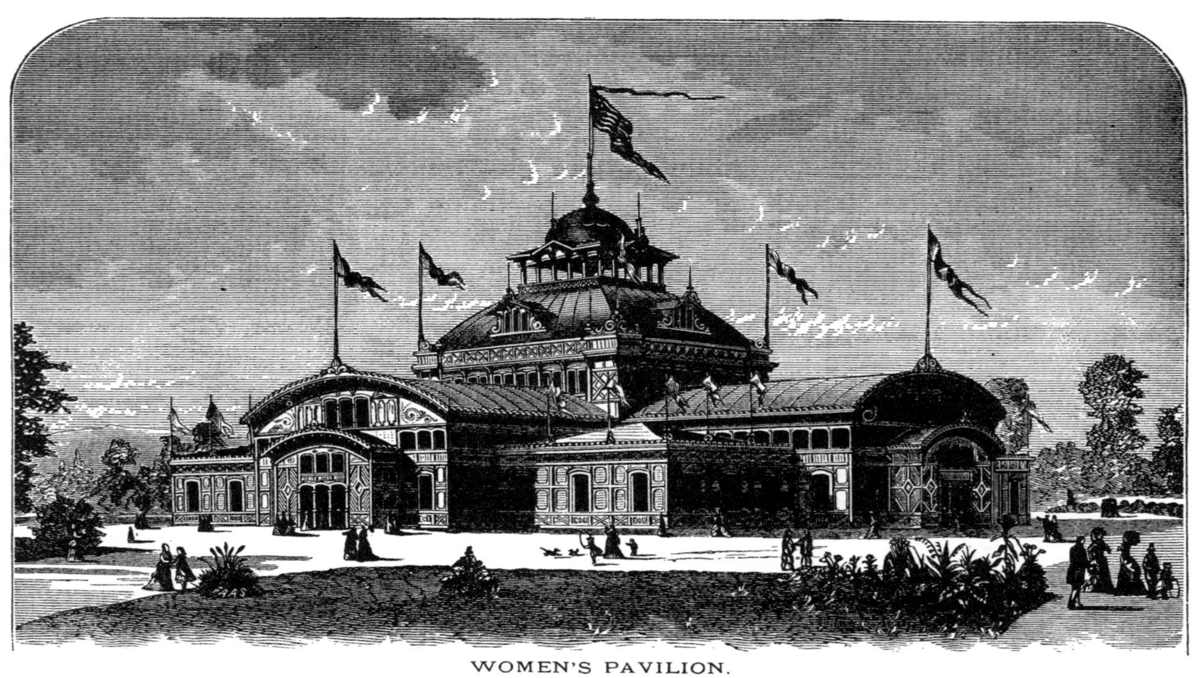

WOMEN'S PAVILION.

WOMEN'S PAVILION.

Scale, 80 ft. to 1 in.

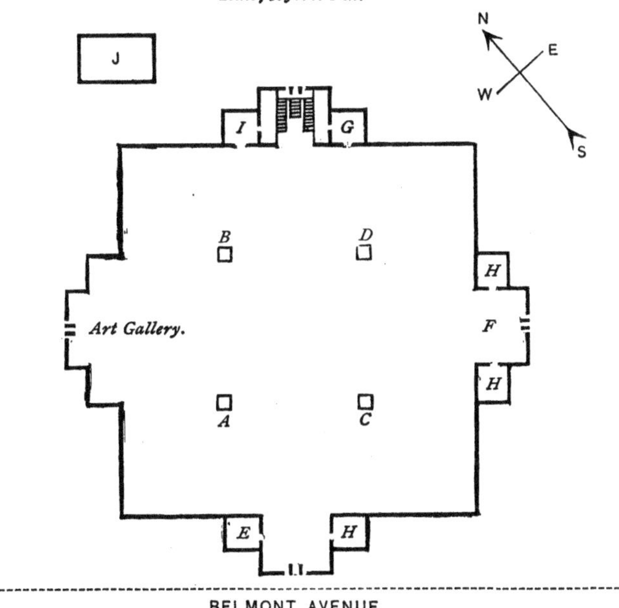

Section A.—*Art, Industrial Art, Educatiou.*
" B.—*Manufactures, etc.*
" C.—*Foreign Exhibits—Great Britain, Canada, Brazil, Norway, Sweden, Japan, France, Egypt, Tunis, Italy, Spain, Netherlands.*
" D.—*Needlework, inventions, patents, etc.*
E.—*Library.*
F.—*Benevolent Institutions.*
G.—*Editorial Office of "The New Century for Women."*
H —*Committee Rooms.*
I.—*Dressing Room.*
J.—*Kindergarten.*

Total Length, 208 ft. Width, 208 ft. Height of Nave, 41 ft. Height of Dome, 67 ft.

No. 153. WOMEN'S PAVILION.

Architect, H. J. SCHWARZMANN.—Size, 26,368 square feet.

THIS pavilion was erected by money raised through the exertions of the women of the United States, and is devoted exclusively to the results of women's labor. It is built of wood, and is situated on Belmont avenue, adjacent to the Horticultural grounds.

OFFICERS AND MEMBERS OF THE WOMEN'S CENTENNIAL EXECUTIVE COMMITTEE.

President, MRS. E. D. GILLESPIE, Philadelphia.

Vice-President, MRS. JOHN SANDERS, Philadelphia.

Secretary, MRS. RICHARD P. WHITE, Philadelphia.

Treasurer, MRS. FRANK M. ETTING, Philadelphia.

Members.

MRS. JOHN W. FORNEY, Philadelphia.
MRS. RICHARD P. WHITE, Philadelphia.
MRS. HENRY COHEN, Philadelphia.
MRS. AUBREY H. SMITH, Philadelphia.
MRS. MATTHEW SIMPSON, Philadelphia.
MRS. EMILY R. BUCKMAN, Philadelphia.
MRS. A. H. FRANCISCUS, Philadelphia.
MISS ELIZABETH GRATZ, Philadelphia.
MISS MCHENRY, Philadelphia.
MRS. CRAWFORD ARNOLD, Philada.
MRS. H. C. TOWNSEND, Philadelphia.
MRS. JOHN PENN BROCK, Philadelphia.
MRS. THEODORE CUYLER, Philadelphia.
MRS. ROBERT K. WRIGHT, Philadelphia.
MRS. L. C. HUGHES, Arizona.
MRS. FRED. MACCRELLISH, California.
MRS. M. E. P. BOULIGNY, Dist. of Col.
MRS. J. M. WASHBURN, Dakotah.
MRS. ELLEN CALL LONG, Florida.
MRS. F. R. WEST, Iowa.
MRS. W. S. RAND, Kentucky.
MRS. F. W. CROWELL, Kansas.
MRS. M. C. LUDELING, Louisiana.
MRS. BION BRADBURY, Maine.
MRS. JAMES T. FIELDS, Massachusetts.
MRS. K. S. MINOR, Mississippi.
MRS. S. B. BOWEN, Montana.
MRS. W. L. DAYTON, New Jersey.
MRS. EDWARD F. NOYES, Ohio.
MRS. F. W. GODDARD, Rhode Island.
MRS. M. J. YOUNG, Texas.
MRS. C. J. FAULKNER, West Virginia.
MRS. J. B. THORP, Wisconsin.
MRS. WORTHINGTON HOOKER, Conn.
MRS. W. O. ROCKWOOD, Indiana.
MRS. WM. GEO. REED, Maryland.
MISS E. S. STEVENS, New Hampshire.
MRS. GEN. G. W. CULLUM, New York.
MRS. J. GREGORY SMITH, Vermont.
MRS. J. M. HECK, North Carolina.
MRS. AARON V. BROWN, Tennessee.
MISS ELIZA R. SNOW, Utah.

MRS. GOV. BEVERIDGE, Illinois.

CHAIRMEN OF WARDS

IN THE

CITY OF PHILADELPHIA.

WARD.	
Second,	Mrs. C. M. PETERSON.
Third,	Mrs. B. MORTON.
Fifth,	Miss FORNEY.
Sixth,	Miss BOMEISLER.
Seventh,	Mrs. R. L. ASHHURST.
Eighth,	Mrs. TUNIS.
Ninth,	Miss LOUISA E. CLAGHORN.
Tenth,	Miss MAGEE.
Eleventh,	Mrs. ALEX. H. NEWITT.
Twelfth,	Mrs. WILLIAM CONN.
Thirteenth,	Mrs. T. W. BAILY.
Fourteenth,	Mrs. I. HYNEMAN.
Fifteenth,	Mrs. A. W. RAND.
Sixteenth,	Mrs. DR. KNORR.
Eighteenth,	Mrs. DR. CLARIDGE.
Nineteenth,	Mrs. T. W. SWAIN.
Twentieth,	Mrs. ABNER LINCOLN.
Twenty-first,	Mrs. W. B. STEPHENS.
Twenty-second,	Miss ZELL.
Twenty-fourth,	Mrs. E. F. HARDIE.
Twenty-fifth,	Mrs. ROBERT KENNEDY.
Twenty-sixth,	Miss CARR.
Twenty-seventh,	Mrs. C. MCILVAINE.
Twenty-eighth,	Mrs. T. J. DAVIS.
Twenty-ninth,	Mrs. W. B. MANN.
Thirty-first,	Mrs. E. H. RYAN.

Furniture, Laundry Appliances, Woven Goods.

Ceramics—Pottery, Porcelain, Glass, etc.

1 **Hoopes, Ellen C., Soho Pottery,** Pittsburg, Pa.—Ironstone china toilet set. Sec. B. 210

Furniture and Objects of General Use in Construction and in Dwellings.

2 **Olson, Christine, Chicago, Ill.**—Organ and table made of three thousand pieces of wood. Sec. D. 217

3 **Stiles, Mrs. E. W., Philadelphia, Pa.** —Combination desk and book paper file. Sec. D. 217

4 **Chapman, Miss Laura M., Friendship,** N. Y.—Lap table. Sec. D. 217

5 **Spofford, Mrs. Jennie H., Philadelphia,** Pa.—Mattress supporter, mosquito bar. Sec. D. 217

7 **James, Mary I., Cambridge, Mass.**—Holly wood chess table. Sec. A. 217

8 **Page, Mrs. Elizabeth M., Philadelphia,** Pa.—Dirt catcher. Sec. D. 217

9 **Steele, Mrs. M. W., Woodbury, N. J.** —Toy set, quill furniture. Sec. B. 217

10 **Dickerson, Mrs. Y. G., Belfast,** Me.—Embroidered camp chair, foot rest, and sofa pillow. Sec. D. 217

11 **Mountain, Mrs. H. B., New York,** N. Y.—Life-preserving mattress. Sec. D. 217

12 **Cowen, Mrs. S. J., Hartford, Conn.**—Book case. Sec. D. 217

13 **Williams, Mrs. G. A., Baltimore,** Md.—Leather table with checker board. Sec. D. 217

14 **Phillips, Mrs. Richmund L., New** York, N. Y.—Table painted in water colors. Sec. D. 217

15 **Ladd, Miss Gertie, North Hero, Vt.** —Student's book-frame. Sec. D. 217

16 **Allen, Mary W., Cambridge, Mass.** —Chess table, with pen and ink sketches. Sec. D. 217

17 **Story, Miss Mary, Cambridge, Mass.** —Chess table, with etchings. Sec. D. 247

18 **Women's Executive Committee of** Wisconsin.—Easel. Sec. D. 217

19 **French, Julie Blanche, Boston,** Mass.—Bedsteads containing drawers, interior safe, etc. Sec. D. 217

20 **Davey, Mrs. Israel, Brandon, Vt.**—Slate stand tops and panels. Sec. A. 217

21 **Mitchell, Mrs. Carrie, Normal, Ill.**—Combined bureau, table, cupboard, and sink. Sec. D. 217

22 **Bulfinch, Miss Ellen S., Cambridge,** Mass.—Book rack, with pen and ink etchings. Sec. A. 220

23 **Smith, Mrs. O., Chicago, Ill.—Range.** Sec. D. 222

24 **Sherwood, Amanda S., Philadelphia,** Pa.—Griddle greaser. Sec. D. 224

25 **Fox, Jane Ann, Stamford, N. Y.**—Dish drainer. Sec. D. 224

26 **Whitman, Mrs. E. J., Oakland, Cal.** —Kettle and pan scraper. An indispensable article for kitchen use. State rights for sale. Sec. D. 224

27 **Boynton, Mrs. E. E., Evanston, Ill.** —Tea kettle one hundred years old. Sec. D. 224

28 **Kelsey, Phœbe M., Philadelphia,** Pa.—Meat tenderer. Sec. D. 224

29 **Steiger, Mrs. Hannah, Laurel, Md.** —Lock barrel cover. Sec. D. 224

30 **Hunkins, Mrs. D. Grace, Allegheny,** Pa.—Rolling pin, containing ten articles used in cooking. Sec. D. 224

31 **Sterling, Mrs. Charlotte, Gambia,** O.—Dish washer. Sec. D. 224

32 **Wells, Miss Glory Anna, Luzerne,** Pa.—Dish washer. Sec. D. 224

33 **Inesly, Susan V., New York, N. Y.**—Reversible sad iron stand. Sec. D. 225

34 **Short, Mrs, S., Cincinnati, O.**—Blanket washer, mangle, ironer, paint cleaner, and stretcher for drying curtains, etc. Sec. D. 225

35 **Ball, Mrs. S. P., Philadelphia, Pa.**—Gas smoothing iron. Sec. D. 225

36 **Tremper, Miss Marietta, New York,** N. Y.—Window-washing machine. Sec. D. 225

37 **Colvin, Margaret P., Battle Creek,** Mich.—Triumph rotary washing machine, combining three principles: 1st, forcing steam through the goods—a powerful detergent; 2d, revolving in hot suds, with a constant change of position; 3d, the alternate elevation and falling of the goods is equivalent to light pounding. This machine is the successful result of years of experiment by a practical woman, to accomplish the perfect cleansing of all fabrics, from carpets to laces, without rubbing. With this machine, a child of twelve years can do more work, and do it better, than two women by ordinary methods. Sec. D.

38 **Bancroft, Sarah H., Media, Pa.**—Bathing chair. Sec. D. 226

39 **Griswold, Mrs. Ellen D., Hagerstown,** Md.—Sash fixture. Sec. D. 227

40 **Reibert, Babetta, Montgomery, S.C.** —Bell pulls. Sec. D. 227

41 **Anderson, Miss Ellen D., Frederick,** Md.—Shutter fastener. Sec. D. 227

Yarns and Woven Goods of Vegetable or Mineral Materials.

42 **Collignon Bros., New York, N. Y.**—Cane-seat work, made by women. Sec. D. 229

Woven and Felted Goods of Wool, etc.

43 **Wilkinson, Mrs. James A., Providence,** R. I.—Yarn from the hair of an Esquimaux dog. Sec. D. 235

44 **Bates, Mrs. Edward, Newport, R. I.** —Hand-spinning and carding of wool and flax. Sec. D. 235

45 **Shapleigh, Mrs. E. B., Philadelphia,** Pa.—Hand-made rug. Sec. D. 239

46 **Ham, Miss Amanda S., Rochester,** N. Y.—Rag rug, Sec. D. 239

47 **Wingate, Mrs. J. F., Hampton, N. H.** —Rag rugs. Sec. D. 239

Clothing, Jewelry, and Ornaments; Traveling Equipments.

48 **Drury, Mrs. L., Springfield, O.**—Dress cutting system. Sec. D. 250

For location of objects, see ground plan, p. 83.

Clothing, Embroideries, Laces, Fancy Articles.

49 Brooks, C. S., Philadelphia, Pa. —System for cutting clothing. Sec. D. 250

50 Union Benevolent Society, Philadelphia, Pa.—Infants' clothing. Sec. D. 250

51 Jones, Mrs. M. A., Philadelphia, Pa. —Children's clothing, dress-cutting system. Sec. D. 250

52 Tardy, Mrs. C., Paterson, N. J.—Infants' exercising corset. Sec. D. 250

53 Brosse, Madame S. C., San Francisco, Cal.—Models for self-measurement. Sec. D. 250

54 Keyser, Mrs. E., Philadelphia, Pa.—Misses' clothing and infants' outfits. Sec. D. 250

55 Harman, Mrs. E. F., New York, N. Y.—Dress and pattern designer. Sec. D. 250

56 Cornwell, Mrs. Elmira, Philadelphia, Pa.—Self-fitting chart, and patterns for cutting ladies' and children's clothing. Sec. D. 250

57 Overend, Rebecca C., Fairlee, Md.—Tippet and muff from pod of wild cotton. Sec. B. 250

58 Livingston, L. M., New York.—Garment cutting, tailors' system. Sec. D. 250

59 Flynt, Mrs. Olivia P., Boston, Mass. —Weather protector, linen duster, skirts, and under garments. Sec. D. 250

60 Stearns, Mrs. A. B., Woburn, Mass. —Diagrams for cutting dresses and shirts. Sec. D. 250

62 Dyer, Miss Fannie E., Providence, R. I.—Child's apron. Sec. D. 250

63 Merritt, Mrs. Jane E., Brooklyn, N. Y.—Cape made from the silk of the milk weed pod. Sec. B. 250

64 Gardiner, Miss Mary Jane, Warwick, R. I.—Trimming cutter. Sec. D. 250

65 Blauvelt, Mrs. Mary, New York, N. Y.—Marking and cutting gauge for tailors and dressmakers. Sec. D. 250

66 Kellogg, Mrs. D. G. M., Keokuk, Ia.—Hosiery. Sec. B. 250

67 Forsyth, Mrs. S. M., Manchester, Ia.—Hosiery. Sec. B. 250

68 Champney, Mary H., Billerica, Mass.—Stockings knit at ninety-eight years of age. Sec. D. 250

69 Lovering, Mrs. Abigail F., Oxford, Me.—Mittens knit at the age of one hundred years and four months. Sec. D. 250

70 Women's Centennial Committee of Lowell, Mass.—Lowell hosiery. Sec. D. 250

71 Robbins, L. E., Boston, Mass.—Diagram for cutting dresses. Sec. D. 250

72 Employment Society, Providence, R. I.—Sec. D.
a Infant's shirt, child's skirt, and afghan. 250
b Embroidered flannel skirt. 252

73 Bonney, Sarah E., Sterling, Mass.—Sec. B.
a Muff, boa, and cap. 250
b Feather fans. 254

74 Shaw, Mrs. James, jr., Providence, R. I.—Infant's socks. Sec. D. 251

75 Summer, Mrs. Sallie O., Providence, R. I.—Mittens. Sec. D. 251

75*a* Conant, Mrs. Orpha, Dwight, Ill.—Hat of common grass, gathered, bleached, and sewed in her eighty-fourth year. Sec. D. 251

76 Todd, Miss Lizzie, Columbus, O.—Embroidery. Sec. D. 252

77 Marsh, Mrs. Charles P., Woodstock, Vt.—Embroidery for camp chair. Sec. D. 252

78 Bach, Jennie & Flora, Philadelphia, Pa.—Embroidered table cover. Sec. D. 252

79 Lucas, Mrs. Mary, Charlotte, N. C. —Lace trimmed and embroidered handkerchief. Sec. D. 252

80 Paul, Mrs. C. F., Saratoga Springs, N. Y.—Honiton collar and lace. Sec. D. 252

81 Beach, Edith, West Hartford, Conn. —Child's rug. Sec. D. 252

82 Brush, Miss Jennie, New York, N. Y.—Embroidered lambroquins. Sec. D. 252

83 Todd, Miss Lizzie, Columbus, O.—Embroidered shawls and sacque. Sec. D. 252

84 Ladies of Immanuel Church, Bellows Falls, Vt. — Needlework. Sec. D. 252

85 St. John's Guild, New Haven, Conn. —Ecclesiastical embroidery. Sec. D. 252

86 Burton, Susie, Laurel, Md.—Tapestry picture: Joseph presenting his Father to Pharaoh. Sec. D. 252

87 Jones, Anna S., Worcester, Mass.—Tatted cushion cover. Sec. D. 252

88 Luce, Miss Caroline, Washington, D. C.—Honiton lace. Sec. D. 252

89 Weld, Mrs. William G., Boston, Mass.—Embroidered panels; imitation of antique lace. Sec. D. 252

90 Skuse, M. J. & F. A., Boston, Mass. —Irish point lace. Sec. D. 252

91 Shepherd, Mrs. Emeline, Northampton, Mass. — Embroidered handkerchief. Sec. D. 252

92 Jones, Miss Anna, Worcester, Mass. —Cushion cover. Sec. D. 252

93 Leonard, Miss Louise, New Bedford, Mass.—Lace ends for necktie. Sec. D. 252

94 Fay, Sarah R., Lancaster, Mass.—Embroidered blanket. Sec. D. 252

95 Hathaway, Mrs. Mary, New Bedford, Mass.—Embroidered scarf. Sec. D. 252

96 Nye, Mrs. Clement D., New Bedford, Mass.—Lace necktie. 252

97 Women's Executive Committee of Wisconsin.—Seal of Beloit College, embroidered on white satin. Sec. D. 252

98 Brown, Nettie, Keokuk, Ia.—English point guipure. Sec. D. 252

99 Leigerot, Mrs. Marie, Keokuk, Ia. —Thread lace. Sec. D. 252

100 Clothier, Miss Minnie J., Nevada, Ia.—Honiton point. Sec. D. 252

101 Scott, Mrs. T. R., Burlington, Ia.—Point lace bertha; handkerchief of Honiton point. Sec. D. 252

102 Scott, Mrs. John, Keokuk, Ia.—Guipure barb. Sec. D. 25

For location of objects, see ground plan, p. 83.

Embroideries, Laces, Fancy Articles.

103 Young Ladies' Society, Grinnell, Pa.—Baby blanket; Bible cushion. Sec. D. 252

104 Little, Miss, Hagerstown, Md.—Old Spanish lace. Sec. D. 252

105 Larkum, Mrs. Edward, Providence, R. I.—Crochet tidy. Sec. D. 252

106 Arnold, Mrs. John H., Pawtucket, R. I.—Pincushion cover and tidies in antique lace. Sec. D. 252

107 Bradley, Mrs. N. M., Providence, R. I.—Embroidered suspenders. Sec. D. 252

108 Kelley, Miss Lina, Providence, R. I.—Pincushion cover in antique lace. Sec. D. 252

109 Torrey, Miss, Baltimore, Md.—Guipure lace tidies. Sec. D. 252

110 Whitehead, Mrs. C. E., New York, N. Y.—White lace. Sec. D. 252

111 Reynolds, Mrs. W. H., Providence, R. I.—Embroidered flannel skirt. Sec. D. 252

112 Jessop, Mrs. Henry, Brooklyn, N. Y.—Honiton lace; English and Irish point lace. Sec. D. 252

113 Hassam, Miss Harriet A., Frederick, Md.—Embroidered ribbon. Sec. D. 252

114 Mordecai, Miss Rosa, Philadelphia, Pa.—Parasol cover, tatted to imitate Irish lace. Sec. D. 225

115 Taylor, Miss, Baltimore, Md.—Darning on cloth. Sec. D. 252

116 Ralston, Miss Florence, Providence, R. I.—Tatted tidy. Sec. D. 252

117 Hoard, Mrs. John W., Providence, R. I.—Netted tidy. Sec. D. 252

118 Congdon, Miss C. A., Providence, R. I.—Children's afghans. Sec. D. 252

119 Carroll, Mrs. Andrew J., Providence, R. I.—Netted shawl, afghan, and embroidered handkerchief. Sec. D. 252

120 Walker, Mrs. Victoria, Providence, R. I.—Embroidered carriage robe and child's skirt. Sec. D. 252

121 Whittemore, Miss Jennie, Charleston, S. C.—Worsted picture of General Washington. Sec. D. 252

122 Cheeny, Miss Daisy, East Greenwich, R. I.—Tatted tidy. Sec. D. 252

123 Wiggin, Mrs. Abby N., Providence, R. I.—Button holes in silk. Sec. D. 252

124 Brown, Miss Fanny G., Providence, R. I.—Embroidered sofa pillow. Sec. D. 252

125 Fuchs, Helene, St. Louis, Mo.—Embroidered lace dress. Sec. D. 252

126 States, Mrs. E. J., Boston, Mass.—Embroideries and infants' dresses. Sec. D. 252

127 Bravo, Miss Sofia, St. Augustine, Fla.—Pincushion cover and Spanish needle work. Sec. B. 252

128 King, Mrs. Henry, Georgetown, D.C.—Embroidered cashmere shawl. Sec. D. 252

129 Weiller, Julia, Philadelphia, Pa.—Embroidered picture. Sec. D. 252

130 Noot, L., New York, N. Y.—Hand-made laces. Sec. C. 252

131 Whitesides, Mrs. E. G., Philadelphia, Pa.—Braiding and embroidery. Sec. D. 252

132 McCarthy, Miss Eva, Washington, D. C.—Piano cover. Sec. D. 252

133 American Button Hole, Overseaming, & Sewing Machine Co., Philadelphia, Pa.—Sewing machine work. Sec. D. 252

134 Anthony, Mrs. Sarah E., Smyrna, Del.—Embroidered picture. Sec. D. 252

135 Smyth, Mrs. M. H., Philadelphia, Pa.—Embroidery and lace mending. Sec. D. 252

136 Auerbach, Mrs. Annie T., Troy, Ala.—Embroidered white satin spread. Sec. D. 252

137 Stansbury, Mrs. J. C., Jersey City, N. J.—Thread lace. Sec. D. 252

138 Shepherd, Mrs. E. M., Northampton, Mass.—Embroidery and lace. Sec. D. 252

139 Heubel, Miss Melanie, Philadelphia, Pa.—Embroidered picture. Sec. D. 252

140 Huston, Mrs. A. B., Cincinnati, O.—Embroidered motto. Sec. A. 252

141 Purkis, Miss E. W., Providence, R. I.—Sec. B.
a Tatting in thread and silk. 252
b Cross in spatter work. 254

142 Palmer, Mrs. John S., Providence, R. I.—Sec. D.
a Tidy and barb in tatting. 252
b Tidy in spatter work; cross made from pith of Japan rose. 254

143 Welsh, Mrs. A. S., Ames, Ia.—Embroidered dressing gown, fire screen, and toilet cushion. Sec. D. 252

144 Plaisted, Miss Anna D., Dubuque, Ia.—Sachet and needlework. Sec. D. 252

145 Toole, Mrs. J. C., Dubuque, Ia.—Embroidered table cover. Sec. D. 252

146 Sheffield, Mrs. S. K., Dubuque, Ia.—Embroidered footstool. Sec. D. 252

147 Smythe, Miss Dora A., Dubuque, Ia.—Embroidered pin cushion. Sec. D. 252

148 Parrott, Mrs. Natt, Waterloo, Ia.—Pillow shams. Sec. D. 252

149 Guilbert, Mrs., Waterloo, Ia.—Hand sewing, Sec. D. 252

150 Gray, Mrs. John H.—Chenille work. Sec. D. 252

151 Lovejoy, Mrs. Perley R., Mt. Washington, Md.—Sec. D.
a Handkerchief, transferred work. 252
b Sachet and wild flowers embroidered on satin. 255

153 Davey, Mrs. Israel, Brandon, Vt.—Sec. A.
a Jewelry. 253
b Paper weights. 254

154 Walcott, Eloise B., Boston, Mass.—Indian basket work. Sec. D. 254

155 Nye, Miss Mary, New Bedford, Mass.—Mats for finger bowls. Sec. D. 253

156 Abbe, Mrs., New Bedford, Mass.—Toilet cushions and mats. Sec. D. 254

For location of objects, see ground plan, p. 83.

Fancy Articles, Stationery, Medicine.

157 **Kesiah, Margaret, Saratoga, N. Y.** —Indian work. Sec. B. 254

158 **Scott, Miss S., Nevada, Ia.**—Toilet box. Sec. D. 254

159 **Dodge, Mrs. A. C., Dubuque, Ia.**—Counterpane with India ink designs. Sec. D. 254

160 **Sisters of the Visitation, Ottawa, Ia.**—Chenille flowers and toilet cushion in fish scale work. Sec. D. 254

161 **Burdie, Mrs. A. S., Des Moines, Ia.**—Moss roses. Sec. D. 254

162 **Iowa College for the Blind.**—Fancy work by pupils. Sec. D. 254

163 **Ward, Hetta L. H., Newark, N. J.** —Violet pin and ear rings. Sec. B. 254

164 **Jacquemin, Mrs. Eliza F., St. Louis, Mo.**—Artificial flowers. Sec. B. 254

165 **Kohn, Miss Annetta, New York, N. Y.**—Autograph album. Sec. B. 254

166 **Candee, Mrs. Charles T., New Haven, Conn.** — Pansies in wool. Sec. D. 254

167 **Vogel, A. C., Washington, D. C.**—Crimping and curling pin. Sec. D. 254

168 **Vanderpool, Mrs. Emily N., New York, N. Y.**—Fan in Japanese style. Sec. D. 254

169 **Wilhelm, Mrs. A. C., Philadelphia, Pa.**—Screw button for shoes, gloves, etc. Sec. D. 254

170 **Parkhill, Miss Harriet R., Jacksonville, Fla.** — Ornaments and flowers made of fish scales. Sec. D. 254

171 **West, Miss Julia M., Bristol, R. I.** —Cross in spatter work. Sec. B. 254

172 **Atwater, Miss Carrie A., New Haven, Conn.**—Paper cut with scissors in imitation of lace. Sec. B. 254

173 **Bailey, H. F., Walworth, Wis.**—Ornamental paper cuttings. Sec. B. 254

174 **Schmidt, Josephine, Baltimore, Md.**—Satin tidy, painted in oil. Sec. A. 254

175 **Dunning, Miss, Canaan, Conn.**—Wooden tray, decorated. Sec. A. 254

176 **Pierce, Mrs. Mary R., Philadelphia, Pa.** — Thread and needle bank. Sec. C. 254

177 **Requa, Emma M., New York, N. Y.**— Miniature Independence Bell. Sec. B. 254

178 **Bacon, Mrs. L. C., Boston, Mass.**—Decorated lamp shades. Sec. B. 254

179 **Jenkins, Mrs. R. E., Bordentown, N. J.**—Dolls' shoes. Sec. B. 254

180 **Martin, Mrs. J. H., Philadelphia, Pa.**—Feather flowers. Sec. B. 254

181 **Harley, Elizabeth G., Haddonfield, N. J.**—Complete darner. Sec. D. 254

182 **Yohe, Mrs. Daniel, Philadelphia, Pa.**—Lamp mat. Sec. D. 254

183 **Schmitt, Madam Katherine, Philadelphia, Pa.**—Hair jewelry. Prize medals of 1854 and 1874. Sec. B. 254

184 **Whitman, Mrs. E. J., Oakland, Cal.** —Buttons that require no needle or thread. Sec. D. 254

185 **Newberry, Miss Rose, New York, N. Y.**—Silk scent bags, painted in water colors. Sec. D. 254

186 **Brush, Miss J., New York, N. Y.**—Satin lambroquins. Sec. D. 254

187 **Tremper, Miss Marietta, New York City.**—Shawl strap and bag combination. Sec. D. 255

188 **Laumonier, Mrs. Celine, New York, N. Y.**— Combined traveling bag and chair. Sec. D. 255

189 **Merckell, Mrs. J. H., Chicago, Ill.** —Faded mink, sable, and seal furs restored to original color. Sec. B. 256

Paper, Blank Books, and Stationery.

190 **Stiles, Mrs. E. W., Philadelphia, Pa.**—Revolving ink stand. Sec. D. 258

191 **McNair, Linda H., Oakland, Cal.**—Book marker, pencil holder, and paper cutter combined. Sec. D. 258

192 **Jay, Miss Elizabeth C., New York, N. Y.**—Postage stamp moistener. Sec. D. 258

193 **Miller, Harriet G., Springfield, Mass.**—Specimens of job printing. Sec. D. 261

Medicine, Surgery, Prothesis.

194 **Marshall, Clara, Women's Medical College of Pennsylvania.**—Materia medica cabinet and pharmaceutical preparations. Sec. C. 272

195 **Blake, Mary J. S., Boston, Mass.**—Surgical instrument. Sec. C. 276

196 **Treadwell, Mrs. F. C., Philadelphia, Pa.**—Dental work. Sec. B. 277

197 **Ramborger, Annie D., Philadelphia, Pa.**—Dental work. Sec. B. 277

Hardware, Edge Tools, Cutlery, and Metallic Products.

198 **School of Design, Cincinnati, O.**—Original metal work; hinges, lockplates, handle plates, etc. Sec. A. 284

199 **Goldsborough, Mrs. G. R., Queenstown, Md.**—Lock. Sec. A. 284

Carriages, Vehicles, and Accessories.

200 **Spofford, Mrs. Jennie H., Philadelphia, Pa.**—Spring saddle. Sec. D. 296

201 **Ruth, Mrs. Sarah, Philadelphia, Pa.**—Sunshade for horses. Sec. D. 296

202 **Jones, Mrs. D. S., Washington, D. C.**—Carriage afghan. Sec. D. 296

Educational Systems, Methods, and Libraries.

203 **Fitts, Ellen E., Boston, Mass.** — Geographical globes. Sec. D. 300

204 **Covell, Miss Adelia C., New York, N. Y.** — Perspective outline models for schools. Sec. D. 300

205 **Bradley, Miss Anna J., Boston, Mass.** — The thirteen primary forms of crystallization, made of mica. Sec. A. 301

206 **Ladd, Miss Gertie, North Hero, Vt.** —Music. 302

207 **Woman's Art School, Cooper Union, New York, N. Y.**—Normal School Work. Sec. A. 302

For location of objects, see ground plan, p. 83.

Education, Science, Sculpture.

208 **Sill, Miss Anna P., Rockford, Ill.**—History, catalogues, programmes, and magazine, of Rockford Seminary. Sec. E. 304

209 **Women's Centennial Committee,** Providence, R. I.—Volume of Herald of the Centennial. Sec. E. 304

210 **Ladd, Miss Marion, North Hero,** Vt.—Manuscript tale and poem. Sec. E 306

211 **Willard, Mrs. Harriet J., Chicago,** Ill.—Books and pamphlets written by Chicago ladies. Sec. E. 306

212 **Cowen, Mrs. S. J., Hartford, Conn.**—Mrs. H. B. Stowe's works. Sec. E. 306

213 **Larned, Ellen D., Thompson, Conn.**—History of Wyndham county, Conn., from 1600 to 1760. Sec. E. 306

214 **Caulkins, Frances M., New London,** Conn.—Histories of Norwich and New London; Literary remains of Martha Day. Sec. E. 306

215 **Barrett, Elizabeth G. B., New Haven,** Conn.—Poems. Sec. E. 306

216 **Hillhouse, Mary, New Haven,** Conn.—German Songs in English Rhyme; Hymns from the Latin. Sec. E. 306

217 **Porter, Rose, New Haven, Conn.**—Miscellaneous literature. Sec. E. 306

218 **Smith, Julia E., Glastenbury, Conn.**—Translation of the Bible. Sec. C. 306

219 **Harbert, Elizabeth B., Evanston,** Ill.—Books. Sec. C. 306

220 **Women's Centennial Committee of** Massachusetts.—Books edited, compiled, and translated by Massachusetts women. Sec. C. 306

221 **Hale, Sarah Josepha, Philadelphia,** Pa.—Books. Sec. C. 306

222 **Stone, Lucy, Boston, Mass.**—"Women's Journal" and pamphlets. Sec. C. 306

223 **Brotherson, Mrs. H. B. M., Peoria,** Ill.—A poem. Sec. C. 306

224 **Beach, Mrs. John S., New Haven,** Conn.—The Spirit of Seventy-Six. Sec. C. 306

225 **James, Mrs. T. P., Cambridge, Mass.**—The Potts Memorial. Sec. C. 306

Institutions and Organizations.

226 **Richards, Margaret C., Philadelphia,** Pa.—Work of Indian women. Sec. C. 312

227 **Janvier, Mary R., Northam, India.**—Curiosities from India. Sec. B. 312

Scientific and Philosophical Instruments and Methods.

228 **Whitner, Mrs. Mary A. E., Philadelphia,** Pa.—Multiscope. Sec. D. 324

229 **French, Elizabeth J., Philadelphia,** Pa.—Electro-magnetic appliances. Sec. D. 325

230 **Tuckerman, Mrs. Lucius, New** York, N. Y.—Descriptive tablet of New York Infirmary and Medical College for Women. Sec. E. 346

231 **Women's Centennial Committee of** Massachusetts.—Photographs of New England Hospital, New Bedford Orphans' Home, New Bedford Mariners' Home, Lowell Old Ladies' Home. Sec. A. 346

Sculpture.

232 **Guild, Mrs. Emma C., Waltham,** Mass.—Sketch in plaster. Sec. A. 400

233 **Nevin, Blanche, Philadelphia, Pa.**—Plaster models: Eve; Cinderella. Sec. A. 400

234 **Whitney, Anne, Belmont, Mass.**—Bronze bust. Sec. A. 400

235 **Massachusetts State Normal Art** School.—Casts: historical ornaments, flowers in relief, medallion portraits, bas-relief of antique figure. 400

236 **Freeborne, Sarah M., New York,** N. Y.—Sec. A.

a Sculpture, Vision of St. Christopher. 400
b Bas-reliefs in silver. 401

237 **Ward, Emily Winthrop, New** York, N. Y.—Bas-relief in plaster, Gates of Life. Sec. A. 401

238 **Perkins, Mrs. E. W., Boston, Mass.**—Sec. A.

a Bas-relief on stone jug. 401
b Carved cabinet and footstool. 405

239 **Wilsey, Mrs. A. W., Syracuse, N.** Y.—Little old folks and chair, cut with a penknife. Sec. A. 405

240 **Hewett, Mrs. Milwaukee, Wis.**—Carved ebony book form. Sec. E. 405

241 **Patterson, Mrs. S. C., Baltimore,** Md.—Wall clock, cut with a penknife; salad fork and spoon. Sec. A. 405

242 **Cutler, Misses N. M. & M. A.,** Providence, R. I.—Carved wall pocket, glove box, hanging cross, and frame. Sec. A. 405

243 **Herrick, Lizzie A., Tilton, N. H.**—Carved Easter eggs. Sec. A. 405

244 **Women's State Centennial Committee,** Wisconsin.—Memorial shrine of carved ebony. Sec. A. 405

245 **Schools of Drawing and Design,** Lowell, Mass.—Carved frame. 405

246 **Brainard, Miss M. M., Worcester,** Mass.—Wood carving. Sec. A. 405

Collective Exhibit of Carved Work, Painting, etc., from Ladies of the Cincinnati School of Design, Cincinnati, O. (*Sec. A.*)

247 **McLaughlin, Miss M. Louise.**—Bust of female head: The Pleasing Thought. 400

248 **Banks, Miss Fannie M.**—Carved Estey organ. 405

249 **Pitman, Miss Agnes.**—Carved piano. 405

250 **Pitman, Mrs. & Miss.**—Carved oak door, ebony inlaid and black walnut door. 405

251 **Johnson, Misses H. & M.**—Carved black walnut bedstead, ebony inlaid. 504

252 **Huston, Mrs. A. B.**—Carved dining-room mantel. 405

For location of objects, see ground plan, p. 83.

Wood Carvings.

253 **Pitman, Mrs. & Miss.**—Carved dining-room shelves. 405

254 **Barrett, Mrs. T. M.**—Carved cabinet. 405

255 **Pitman, Mrs. Agnes.**—Carved hanging cabinet, ebony inlaid. 405

256 **Tidball, Miss Flora.**—Child's carved bedstead. 405

257 **Pitman, Miss Agnes.**—Carved chest of drawers, and mantel bracket, ebony inlaid. 405

258 **Pack, Miss Mary L.**—Carved oak secretary cabinet. 405

259 **White, Mrs. A.**—Carved dressing bureau. 405

260 **Caldwell, Miss Hattie D.**—Carved altar cross. 405

261 **Johnson, Misses Hattie & Mary.**—Carved hanging cabinet, picture frames, wall pocket. 405

262 **Cooper, Miss Alice.**—Carved "*prie-dieu*" and stool. 405

263 **Jordan, Miss Laura B.**—Carved mahogany hanging cabinet. 405

264 **Abbott, Mrs. E. F.**—Carved dressing stand. 405

265 **Rice, Miss Julia H.**—Carved parlor table. 405

266 **Laws, Miss Lizzie T.**—Carved gothic flower stand. 405

267 **Gurley, Miss Clara.**—Carved writing desk. 405

268 **Collord, Miss Helen.**—Carved ebony prayer book covers. 405

270 **Hirst, Miss Claude R.**—Carved parlor easel and jewel casket. 405

271 **Banks, Miss Fanny M.**—Carved flower stand. 405

272 **De Pilgrom, Miss V.**—Carved black walnut bedstead. 405

273 **Barrett, Mrs. S. M.**—Carved chess table and picture frame. 405

274 **Pitman, Miss Agnes.**—Carved hanging secretary, walnut and ebony. 405

275 **White, Mrs. A.**—Carved picture frame. 405

276 **Collard, Miss Isora.**—Carved book racks and casket. 405

278 **McDowell, Miss W. H.**—Carved gothic stand. 405

279 **Huston, Mrs. A. B.**—Carved dog kennel frame. 405

280 **Dominick, Mrs. G.**—Carved cherry wall pocket and casket. 405

281 **Tidball, Miss Flora J.**—Carved flower stand. 405

282 **Collard, Miss Helen.**—Carved picture frame. 405

283 **Vallandingham, Miss N.**—Gentleman's carved dressing stand. 405

284 **Collier, Miss Lizzie M.**—Carved tea pot rest. 405

285 **Hesser, Mrs. C. F.**—Carved flower stand. 405

286 **Huston, Mrs. A. B.**—Carved bread plate. 405

287 **Stern, Miss Jessie.**—Carved wall pocket and card receiver. 405

288 **Donnelly, Miss A.**—Carved flower stand and picture frame. 405

289 **Drake, Miss Ada P.**—Carved jardinière. 405

290 **Swift, Miss Mary P.**—Carved writing desk. 405

291 **McCloskey, Miss Lizzie.**—Carved wall pocket and photograph frame. 405

292 **Collard, Miss H. A.**—Carved trencher, picture frame, and flower stand. 405

293 **Pitman, Miss A.**—Carved fruit plate and card receiver, library stool, lamp stand, and picture frame. 405

294 **Dunlap, Miss Sarah.**—Carved wall pocket. 405

295 **Hollingshead, Miss H.**—Carved casket and picture frame. 405

296 **Kidd, Mrs. N. R.**—Carved flower stand. 405

297 **Metcalf, Miss Flora.**—Carved shield. 405

298 **Newell, Miss Emma.**—Carved fruit plate. 405

299 **Caldwell, Miss Hattie D.**—Carved picture frame. 405

300 **Dodd, Mrs. William.**—Carved casket. 405

301 **Rice, Miss M.**—Carved picture frame. 405

302 **Menzies, Miss R. N.**—Carved corner bracket. 405

303 **Brashear, Miss Lillie.**—Carved parlor easel. 405

304 **Scudder, Miss Tillie.**—Carved medicine cupboard. 405

305 **Doherty, Miss Clara.**—Carved fruit plate. 405

306 **Tazzer, Miss Augusta.**—Carved rocking chair. 405

307 **Moore, Miss A. G.**—Carved flower stand. 405

308 **Kemper, Mrs. Theodore.**—Carved tray. 405

309 **Shaler, Miss Minnie.**—Carved chess board and picture frame. 405

310 **Merrill, Miss Susie.**—Carved flower stand and carved and painted bracket. 405

311 **Temple, Mrs. O. H.**—Carved picture frame and wall bracket. 405

312 **Brashear, Miss Lillie.**—Carved flower stand. 405

313 **Stribley, Miss May.**—Carved picture frame and casket. 405

314 **Tatum, Miss Lizzie.**—Carved flower stand. 405

315 **Huston, Mrs. A. B.**—Painted slate panels. 410

316 **Barrett, Mrs. S. M.**—Silver bronze panels and oil painting. 410

317 **Hirst, Miss Claude R.**—Oil painting. 410

318 **Drake, Miss Ada P.**—Painted tiles. 410

319 **Dominick, Mrs. G.**—Illumination and medieval lettering. 411

For location of objects, see ground plan, p. 83.

Paintings.

320 Ladies' Centennial Committee, Worcester, Mass.—Wood carvings. Sec. A. 405

321 Force, Mrs. F. H., Cincinnati, O.—Carved black walnut corner cabinet. Sec. A. 405

322 Dodd, Mrs. Wm., Cincinnati, O. —Carved boudoir table and parlor easel. Sec. A. 405

323 Williams, Mrs. E., Cincinnati, O.—Child's carved mahogany bedstead. Sec. A. 405

324 McLaughlin, Miss M. Louise, Cincinnati, O.—Carved hanging cabinet, walnut and ebony, and jardinière. Sec. A. 405

Painting.

325 Way, Agnes C., Pittsburg, Pa.—Oil painting. Sec. A. 410

326 Sartain, Emily, Philadelphia, Pa.—Oil paintings. Sec. A. 410

327 Linderman, Mrs. Sophia, Philadelphia, Pa.—Oil paintings: A Turkish Lady; The Laplander's Evening Call; Princess Dornroschen. Sec. A. 410

328 Ferguson, Mrs. Mary L., Philadelphia, Pa.—Oil paintings: Natural Bridge, Virginia; Sunset over the Blue Ridge. Sec. A. 410

329 Natt, Phebe Davis, Philadelphia, Pa.—Oil painting: "There was an Old Woman who Lived in a Shoe." Sec. A. 410

330 Caller, Alice, Salem, Mass.—Painted panel. Sec. A. 410

331 Taneyhill, Flora, Alliance, O.—Oil painting. Sec. A. 410

332 Gilbert, Lucia M., Pittsford, Vt.—Oil painting on slate: Copy of Gustav Richter's Neapolitan Boy. Sec. A. 410

333 McLaughlin, Miss M. Louise, Cincinnati, O.—Painted slate panels. Sec. A. 410

334 Webster, Mrs. Elizabeth S., Hartford, Conn.— Partridges hanging, and game on table. Sec. A. 410

335 Bell, Lucy A., Exeter, N. H.—Portrait of Governor Bell. Sec. A. 410

336 Weeks, Caroline, Greenland, N. H. —Portrait of Governor Bartlett. 410

337 Stevens, M. Elizabeth, Jamaica, L. I.—Field daisies on red medallion. Sec. A. 410

338 Webster, Mrs. S. A., New York, N. Y.—Panels: Wild Roses and Daisies; Clematis and Woodbine. Sec. A. 410

339 Maxim, Nellie, Plainfield, N. J.—Panel, Daisies. Sec. A. 410

340 Henry, Mrs. Annie M., Boston, Mass. — Oil paintings: Wild Flowers; Horned Owl. Sec. A. 410

341 Field, Miss E. C., New York, N. Y. —Panel: Apple Blossoms. Sec. A. 410

342 Woodward, Laura, New York, N. Y.—Oil painting: Autumn in the Adirondack Mountains. Sec. A. 410

343 Greatorex, Eliza, New York, N. Y. —Oil paintings on panels: The Old Porch; The Old Bloomingdale Church; The Somerindyke House. Sec. A. 410

344 Schmidt, Josephine, Baltimore, Md.—Landscapes in oil. 410

345 Culver, Mrs. J. O., Madison, Wis. —Art cabinet, with painted panels and medallion. Sec. A. 410

346 Clarke, Kate W., Hyde Park, Ill.—Zononia, Mrs. Swisshelm's rustic home; Pine Woods in Autumn. Sec. A. 410

347 Warner, Miss Naidine, New York, N.Y.—Painting: Mackerel. Sec. A. 410

348 Remington, Elizabeth H., New York, N.Y.—Oil painting: The Two Kings, Corn and Cotton. Sec. A. 410

349 Cook, Miss H. M., Providence, R.I.—Painting: Snow Scene. Sec. A. 410

350 Burt, Miss Helen, New York, N.Y. —Oil paintings: Quiet Ruminations. Sec. A. 410

351 Rose, Adelaide, Port Jervis, N.Y. —Oil painting: The Wreath's Daybreak. Sec. A. 410

352 Paul, Miss Kate, Providence, R. I. —Beethoven and Quartette, copied in oil from an engraving. Sec. A. 410

353 Keep, Mrs. John R., Hartford, Conn. —Painting: Ear of Corn. Sec. A. 410

354 Rafter, Susan L. Johnson, Brooklyn, N.Y.— Painting: Fruit; decorated table top: Wreath of Nasturtiums. Sec. A. 410

355 Fraley, Miss Mollie E., Marshall, Texas.—Oil painting: Flowers. Sec. A. 410

356 Fraley, Miss Mary E., Marshall, Texas.—Oil paintings: Jephtha; The Murder of the Innocents. Sec. A. 410

357 Conant, Miss C. W., New York, N.Y.—Oil painting: The Charity Scholar. Sec. A. 410

358 Twombly, Mrs. John H., Madison, Wis.—Oil painting: The White Mountains, from the Conway valley. Sec. A. 410

359 Talbot, Miss Eleanor W., Providence, R. I.—Oil painting: Children at Play. Sec. A. 410

360 Martin, Mrs. S. L., Rupert, Vt. —Panels, paper weights, rulers, etc., painted in oil on slate, and enameled. Sec. A. 410

361 Holbrook, Harriet Jane, New York, N.Y.—Panels: Snowballs; Cactus; fruit-piece in oil, and portraits of Lady and Gentleman. Sec. A. 410

362 Hine, Franc E., Saratoga Springs, N.Y.—Flowers on slate panel. Sec. A. 410

363 Donaldson, Lucy, Baltimore, Md. —Panels: Wild Flowers; Roses. Sec. A. 410

364 Williams, Mary E., Salem, Mass. —Oil paintings: Roman Beggar; An Alchemist; Autumn Wild Flowers of New England. Sec. A. 410

365 Anthony, Miss Margaret M., Providence, R.I.—Oil painting: Fruit. Sec. A. 410

366 Studley, Mrs. Thos. E., Providence, R. I.—Child's portrait, in oil. Sec. A. 410

367 Stephens, Miss Maud, New York, N.Y.—Oil paintings: Autumn Leaves; A Picture within a Picture. Sec. A. 410

368 Porter, Miss Rebecca T., New Haven, Conn.—Oil painting: Absorbed. Sec. A. 410

For location of objects, see ground plan, p. 83.

Paintings.

369 Knowlton, Helen M., Boston, Mass. —Oil painting: Paper Mills at Newton Lower Falls. Sec. A. 410

371 Wadsworth, Miss A. E., Boston, Mass.—Oil painting: Woman Washing. Sec. A. 410

372 Adams, Miss Elizabeth, Boston, Mass.—Oil painting. Sec. A. 410

373 Osborn, Miss H. Frances, Peabody, Mass.—Oil painting on panel: Apple Blossoms. Sec. A. 410

374 Caller, Miss Alice, Salem, Mass. —Oil painting on panel: Violets. Sec. A. 410

375 Lane, Miss S. M., Boston, Mass. —Oil painting: Flowers. Sec. A. 410

376 Graves, Miss L., New Haven, Conn.—Panels in oil: Pond Lilies; Fuchsias. Sec. A. 410

377 Odenheimer, Mrs. B., New York, N.Y.—Oil painting: Guinevere. Sec. A. 410

378 Tolles, Sophie M., New York, N.Y. —Portraits of Linda Gilbert and P. T. Quinn. Sec. A. 410

378*a* Joes, Mrs. Arthur C., Brooklyn, N.Y.—Miniature portraits. Sec. A. 410

379 Boyd, Mrs. Kate, Canastota, N. Y. —Oil paintings: Portland Light, Maine; Old Orchard Beach; Don; Brook Trout. Sec. A. 410

380 Morris, Mary Hay, Baltimore, Md. —Oil paintings: Violin, Music, and Books; Fruit. Sec. A. 410

381 Nicholson, Martha A., Baltimore, Md.—Panels: Autumn Leaves; Bird. Sec. A. 410

382 Herrick, Caroline K., Orange, N.J. —Panel: Fringed Gentians. Sec. A. 410

383 Ricketts, Miss, Baltimore, Md.—Oil painting: White Grapes. Sec. A. 410

384 Pollock, Miss, Baltimore, Md.—Portrait of Samuel M. Janney. Sec. A. 410

385 Kay, Helena de, New York, N.Y. —Oil painting: Withered Golden Rod; panel: Sun Flowers. Sec. A. 410

386 Porter, Mrs. Susan C., Hartford, Conn.—Study of an Italian Girl. Sec. A. 410

387 Monks, Mary E., New York, N.Y. —Oil paintings: Calla Lilies; Water Lilies. Sec. A. 410

388 Farnham, Mrs. Sarah A., Hartford, Conn.—Oil painting: Camp in the Adirondacks. Sec. A. 410

389 Dixon, Maria R., New York, N.Y. —Oil painting: Catch me if you can. Sec. A. 410

390 Ackerman, Mary, Brooklyn, N.Y. —Oil painting: Hagar and Ishmael. Sec. A. 410

391 Palmer, Addie C., Concord, N.H.—Ebony panels: Roses, Azaleas. Sec. A. 410

392 Scott, Mrs. E. M., Chicago, Ill.—Oil painting: Roman Boy; panel: Roses. Sec. A. 410

393 Perry, Laura C., Poultney, Vt.—Slate panels. Sec. A. 410

394 Thomas, Mrs. Annie N., New York, N.Y.—Oil paintings: Morning Glories and Fuchsias. Sec. A. 410

395 Perkins, Fanny, New York, N.Y. —Portrait of a young Girl and Water Lilies. Sec. A. 410

396 Brounscombe, Jennie, New York, N.Y.—Painting: Elsie Venner. Sec. A. 410

EXHIBIT FROM SCHOOL OF DESIGN FOR WOMEN, PITTSBURG, PA.—SEC. A.

397 Murtland, Mary M.—Oil paintings: Hanging Basket, Flowers. 410

398 Reed, Annie.—Oil painting, Hanging basket. 410

399 Holmes, C.—Oil painting: Flowers. 410

399*a* Loomis, Eurilda.—Oil painting: Flowers. 410

400 Henderson, Annie W.—Water color paintings: Mullein, Roses. 410

401 Kerfoot, Annie.—Water color paintings: Bread and Wine: Florence. 411

402 Spring, Mary.—Water color landscapes. 411

403 Ferguson, Edith.—Water color painting: Peaches. 411

404 Hazlewood, M.—Water color painting: Wild Grapes. 411

---

405 Darrah, Sophia T., Boston, Mass. —Sec. A.

a Oil painting: Stranded Sloop. 410
b Water color painting: Woods in Autumn. 411

406 Wood, Miss Martha J., Pittsford, Vt.—Sec. A.

a Oil paintings: Roman Peasant; Monk; German Interior. 410
b Painting on enameled slate: Magdalen. 413

407 Sauerwein, Loulie C., Mt. Washington, Ind.—Sec. A.

a Oil paintings, Indian sketches. 410
b Water color sketches. 411

408 McLaughlin, Miss M. Louise, Cincinnati, O.—Sec. A.

a Painted panels. 410
b Painted plates, cups, teapot, stands, etc. 413

409 Voster, Sarah H., Portsmouth, N. H.—Sec. A.

a Oil painting. 410
b Water color painting. 411
c Painted plates. 413

410 Nourse, Mrs., Georgetown, D. C.—Water color painting of flowers. Sec. A. 411

411 Dowe, Florence A., Ithaca, N. Y.—Flowers in water colors: Spring Wild Flowers and June Garden Pets. Sec. A. 411

412 Stewart, Alice, Chicago, Ill.—Orchids and ferns in water colors. Sec. A. 411

413 Burt, Martha, New York, N. Y.—Water color painting: Homely Flowers. Sec. A. 411

414 Northam, C. Gussie, Brooklyn, N. Y.—Water color figure: Amateur Theatricals. Sec. A. 411

415 Bliss, Mrs. Lydia S., Attleboro', Mass.—Panel: Cactus in Blossom. Sec. A. 411

415*a* Nourse, Mrs. J. E., Washington, D. C.—Miniature in ivory. Sec. A. 411

For location of objects, see ground plan, page 83.

Paintings, Engravings, Photographs.

416 **Badger, Mrs. C. M., Madison,** Conn.—Water color paintings: Night-Blooming Cereus and Apple Blossoms. Sec. A. 411

417 **Grout, Miss S. A., Uxbridge, Mass.** —Water color painting: Flowers. Sec. A. 411

418 **Chaplin, Miss Christine, Boston,** Mass.—Water color painting, illustrating a poem. Sec. A. 411

419 **Bullard, Miss, Worcester, Mass.**—Water color painting: Newport Grasses. Sec. A. 411

420 **Washburn, Mrs. H. B., East River,** Conn.—Water color painting: Apples. Sec. A. 411

421 **Hooper, Mrs. G. W., New Haven,** Conn.—Water color design. Sec. A. 411

422 **Lockwood, Minnie S., New Haven,** Conn.—Water color painting: Grasses and Cardinal Flowers. Sec. A. 411

423 **Davenport, Elizabeth W., New** Haven, Conn.—Water color painting: Cardinal Flowers and Clematis. Sec. A. 411

424 **Ward, Hetta L. H., Newark, N. J.** —Water color painting: From the Swamp. Sec. A. 411

425 **Olmsted, Mrs. Anna M., Hartford,** Conn.—Water color paintings: Dead Duck, Snow Bird, Flowers. Sec. A. 411

426 **Olmsted, Miss Mamie, Hartford,** Conn.—Water color painting: Dead Duck. Sec. A. 411

427 **Barney, Mrs. Sarah E., Farmington,** Conn.—Water color paintings: Hollyhocks and Fleur de Lis. Sec. A. 411

428 **Davis, Georgie A., New York, N.** Y.—Water color study: At the Prison Window. Sec. A. 411

429 **Bradford, Anne H., West Winsted,** Conn.—Water color painting: First Chickens of the Season. Sec. A. 411

430 **Lyman, Miss Abby, New Haven,** Conn.—Water color drawings: Blackberry Blossoms, Apple Blossoms, Daisies, Crab-apples, Rocks and Ferns. Sec. A. 411

431 **Burton, Mrs. Mary H., Hartford,** Conn.—Water color drawing: Autumn Field Flowers. Sec. A. 411

432 **Dunning, Miss M., Canaan, Conn.** —Tile painted on wood. Sec. A. 411

433 **Franklin, Mrs. Anna L., Hartford,** Conn.—Water color copy: Turin. Sec. A. 411

434 **Donlevy, Alice, New York, N. Y.**—Illumination: "Light! More Light!" Sec. A. 411

435 **Porter, Miss Sarah, Farmington,** Conn.—Tiles painted on wood. Sec. A. 411

436 **Burton, Mrs. Mary H., Hartford,** Conn.—Water color copies: Italian Peasants. Sec. A. 411

437 **Warner, Mrs. George, Hartford,** Conn.—Water color painting: Daisies. Sec. A. 411

438 **Klippart, Josephine, Columbus,** O.—Water color painting. Sec. A. 411

439 **Ladies' Centennial Committee,** Worcester, Mass.—Paintings. Sec. A. 411

440 **Blakemore, Mrs. J. W., Philadelphia,** Pa.—Water color painting. Sec. A. 411

441 **Gordon, Margaret S. G., Philadelphia,** Pa.—Water color paintings. Sec. A. 411

442 **Robbins, Miss Ellen, Boston, Mass.** —Decorated china. Sec. A. 413

443 **Marquand, Miss Laura M., Boston,** Mass.—Decorated china. Sec. A. 413

444 **Shippen, Mrs. R. R., Boston, Mass.** —Decorated porcelain table top. Sec. A. 413

445 **James, Mary I., Cambridge, Mass.** —Painting on porcelain. Sec. A. 413

446 **Homans, Miss S. E., Boston, Mass.** —Painted porcelain. Sec. A. 413

447 **McLaughlin, Miss M. Louise, Cincinnati,** O.—Decorated egg cups, original design. Sec. A. 413

448 **Meredith, Mrs. L. P., Cincinnati,** O.—Decorated plates, flowers. Sec. A. 413

449 **Russell, Helen A., New York, N.** Y.—Decorated china. Sec. A. 411

450 **Cunningham, Alice H., Boston,** Mass.—Decorated china. Sec. A. 411

Engraving and Lithography.

451 **Mitchell, Mrs. Nellie D., Philadelphia,** Pa.—Pastel painting. Sec. A. 420

452 **Hopkins, Florence J., Washington,** D. C.—Ferns in ink. Sec. A. 420

453 **James, Mary I., Cambridge, Mass.** —Pen and ink etchings. Sec. A. 420

454 **West, Elizabeth J., Philadelphia,** Pa.—Marking with indelible ink. Sec. D. 420

455 **Hubbard, Mabel G., Cambridge,** Mass.—Charcoal sketch. Sec. A. 420

456 **Bell, Mrs., Philadelphia, Pa.**—Colored crayons. Sec. A. 420

457 **Landis, Mrs. D. C., Philadelphia,** Pa.—Pastel painting. Sec. A. 420

458 **Phillips, E. B., Philadelphia, Pa.**—Marking in indelible ink. Sec. D. 420

459 **Smyth, Mrs. M. H., Philadelphia,** Pa.—Indelible ink marking. Sec. D. 420

460 **Torrey, Martha A., Philadelphia,** Pa.—Indelible ink marking. Sec. D. 420

461 **Kay, Helena de, New York, N. Y.** —Decorative drawings on wood. Sec. A. 420

462 **Davis, Georgie A., New York, N.** Y.—Pen and ink study: Edwin Booth as Iago; drawing on wood: Bridge of Sighs. Sec. A. 420

463 **Burt, Martha, New York, N. Y.**—Crayon portrait of Sothern. Sec. A. 420

464 **Stone, Mary L., New York, N. Y.** —Illustration of Hans Andersen's Snow Queen, on wood; block drawing of Italian Girl. Sec. A. 420

465 **Curtis, Jessie, New York, N. Y.**—Pen and ink drawings: Puck; Sunday Morning; Negro Reading; proofs of drawings on wood. Sec. A. 420

For location of objects, see ground plan, page 83.

Drawings, Photographs.

466 Harrison, Mrs. Margarita W., Jersey City, N. J.—Pen and ink sketch: Santa Claus; drawings on wood: Sunset; The Listeners. Sec. A. 420

467 Nourse, Mrs. Cora S., New York, N. Y.—Humming birds drawn on wood. Sec. A. 420

468 Davis, Mrs. J. A., Providence, R. I.—Marking in indelible ink. Sec. A. 420

469 Wilson, Miss Mary, Bellows Falls, Vt.—Penciling: Horses' Heads. Sec. A.

470 Barton, Isabelle, New York, N. Y. —Crayon picture: Little Wide-Awake. Sec. A. 420

471 Gay, Miss Alice, West Randolph, Vt.—Crayon picture: Pharaoh's Horses. Sec. A. 420

472 Wilson, Mrs. Robert, Easton, Md. —Crayon drawing: Olympia. Sec. A. 420

473 Atkinson, Lizzie H., Baltimore, Md.—Crayon portrait. Sec. A. 420

474 Phelps, S. Louise, East Orange, N. J.—Crayon portrait. Sec. A. 420

EXHIBIT FROM SCHOOL OF DESIGN FOR WOMEN, PITTSBURG, PA.—SEC. A.

475 Murtland, Mary M.—Crayon drawings: Discobulus, Venus of Milo, Minerva, Cupid. 420

476 Loomis, Eurilda.—Crayon drawing: Apollo; anatomical drawings; original drawings by pupils. 420

---

477 Leavitt, Miss H. J., Boston, Mass. —Crayon portrait of Mrs. Bancroft. Sec. A. 420

478 Humphreys, Miss L. B., New York, N. Y.—Drawing on wood: "My Son's Fair Wife, Elizabeth." Sec. A. 420

479 Willets, Margarita, New York, N. Y.—Proof of drawing on glass. Sec. A. 420

480 Coman, Mrs. C. B., New York, N. Y.—Charcoal sketch: In the North Woods. Sec. A. 420

481 Tuthill, Sarah S., Farmington, Conn.—Pencil drawing: Venus of Milo. Sec. A. 420

482 Lounds, Carrie A., New York, N. Y.—Crayon: My Brother's Portrait. Sec. A. 420

483 Wilson, Linnie R., Philadelphia, Pa.—Crayon head: Romulus. Sec. A. 420

484 Bryant, Miss, New York, N. Y.— Drawing on stone: Morning Glory. Sec. A. 420

485 Clinton, Lucille, New York, N. Y. —Crayon head of E. W. Stoughton. Sec. A. 420

486 Peck, Emma A., Hartford, Conn.— Crayon portraits: A Child; A Lady in Old Fashioned Costume. Sec. A. 420

487 Messick, Mrs., Providence, R. I.— Ornamental writing: Washington's Farewell Address; Declaration of Independence. Sec. B. 420

488 Wallace, Mrs. Mary W., New York, N. Y.—Drawings on wood: The Broken Doll, Flower Gathering. Sec. A. 420

489 Chamberlain, Mrs. Agnes H., New York, N. Y.—Drawing on stone: Pitcher Plant; botanical drawings. Sec. A. 420

490 Greatorex, Eliza, New York, N. Y. —Pen and ink sketches: Homes of Oberammergau; Old New York—from the Battery to Bloomingdale. Sec. A. 420

491 Commonwealth of Massachusetts, Department of Education.— Primary, grammar, high, and free evening industrial schools: drawings of pupils; Massachusetts State Normal Art School: flowers and fruit. 420

492 Schools of Drawing & Design, Lowell, Mass.—Crayon portraits of Mozart, Longfellow, and Lady Moon; Child's Head, Storks. 420

493 Bache, Miss Jennie, Brooklyn, N. Y.—Crayon picture. 420

493*a* Woman's Art School, Cooper Union, New York, N. Y.—Sec. A.
- *a* Drawings from casts, photo-crayons. 420
- *b* Work of engraving by pupils. 421
- *c* Work of normal teachers' class. 421

494 Earls, Rebecca H. C., Philadelphia, Pa.—Crayon portrait of Brahmin Narayan Shesshadri; crayon study: Giraffe. Sec. A. 420

495 Burt, Miss Helen, New York, N.Y. —Drawing on wood: Little Lone Bird House. Sec. A. 420

496 Bondi, Bianca, New York, N. Y. —Sec. A.
- *a* Drawing on stone: Two Shoes. 420
- *b* Wood engravings. 422

497 Wormley, Mrs. Annie E., Columbus, O.—Microscopic illustrations on steel. Sec. A.

498 Sartain, Emily, Philadelphia, Pa.— Steel engravings: portrait of R. W. Emerson; Christ Walking on the Sea; Raising of Jairus's Daughter. Sec. A. 421

499 Liggett, Miss C. S., Saratoga Springs, N. Y.—Engraved cards, and general engravings. Sec. A. 421

500 Crane, Abby T., New York, N. Y. —Wood engravings. Sec. A. 422

501 Donlevy, Alice, New York, N. Y.—Wood engraving, The Lord's Prayer, proofs of decorative designs, book and newspaper illustrations. Sec. A. 422

502 Zoble, Mrs. Sophia G., New York, N. Y.—Wood engravings. Sec. A. 422

503 Hallock, Mary, New York, N. Y.— Wood engravings, book and newspaper illustrations. Sec. A. 422

504 Sherman, Miss F. M., New Haven, Conn.—Lithograph: Madonna and Child. Sec. A. 423

505 Clapp, Mrs. F. W., Framingham, Mass.—Photograph: Views of Framingham. Sec. A. 430

506 Hunt, Mrs. Chas. S., Weymouth, Mass. — Photographs of distinguished Massachusetts women. Sec. A. 430

507 Dayton, Miss M. G., Washington, D. C.—Enameled photographs. Sec. A. 430

508 Luther, Miss M. M., Warren, R. I. —Painted photograph: An Interior. Sec. A. 430

For location of objects, see ground plan, p. 83.

Designs, Decorations.

509 Tryatt, Miss Fanny, New York, N. Y.—Photographs from life. Sec. A. 430

510 Chapin, Miss, Providence, R. I.—Colored photograph of Commodore Whipple. Sec. A. 430

511 Hare, Miss E. A., Suffolk, Va.—Crystal photograph: Dom Pedro. Sec. A. 430

512 Schools of Drawing & Design, Lowell, Mass.—Photographs. Sec. A. 430

Industrial and Architectural Designs, etc.

513 Lowell School of Design of the Massachusetts Institute of Technology, Boston, Mass.—Designs by pupils for laces, silks, Brussels carpeting, oil cloths, printed robes, and calico. Sec. A. 440

514 Schools of Drawing & Design, Lowell, Mass.—Designs by pupils, for carpets, wall papers, handkerchiefs, etc. Sec. A. 440

515 Donlevy, Alice, New York, N. Y.—Design for book covers, drawn on wood, for printing in colors. Sec. D. 440

516 Boyd, Mrs. Kate, Canastota, N. Y.—Designs for wall paper. Sec. D. 440

517 Brownscombe, Jennie, New York, N. Y.—Designs for newspaper illustrations. Sec. D. 440

518 Stigale, Mrs. E. M., Philadelphia, Pa.—Model of cemetery enclosure. Sec. D. 441

Ceramic Decorations, Mosaics, etc.

519 Drown, Mrs. C. L., New York, N. Y.—Illuminated glass signs. Sec. D. 453

520 Vanderpool, Mrs. Emily N., New York, N. Y.—Monograms. Sec. B. 454

521 Collins, Miss Carrie L., Hartford, Conn.—Case for shaving papers, with pen and ink sketch on cover. Sec. B. 454

522 Hewett, Mrs., Milwaukee, Wis.—Illustrated poem. Sec. E. 454

523 Nourse, Mrs. Cora S., New York, N. Y.—Frame with designs in engraved proof, pencil, and water colors. Sec. B. 454

524 Davenport, Elizabeth W., New Haven, Conn.—Water color painting in silk. Sec. B. 454

525 Sterling, Mrs. E. J., Brooklyn, N. Y.—Decorated tiles. Sec. A. 454

526 Sweet, Mrs. John E., Ithaca, N. Y.—Wax flowers. Sec. B. 454

527 Ward, Susan Hayes, Newark, N. J.—Fireplace tiles, illustrating British ballads. Sec. A. 454

528 Hinds, Mrs. F. B., Providence, R. I.—Hair wreath. Sec. B. 454

529 Sahler, Miss Elizabeth, Kingston City, N. Y.—Spring and summer flowers, and autumn leaves, in wax. Sec. B. 454

530 Shellman, Miss Mary B., Westminster, Ind.—Moss and stone picture of church and graveyard. Sec. B. 454

531 Roberts, Jennie M., Chicago, Ill.—Hair wreath, flowers and fruit. Sec. B. 454

532 Greatorex, Eliza, New York, N. Y.—Illustrated books and albums. Sec. A. 454

533 Whitney, Annie H. & Alice G. Chandler, Lancaster, Mass.—Carved wooden fireplaces with painted tiles, pottery and china on the shelves, and paintings above. Sec. A. 454

534 Macdaniel, Miss Fanny L., New York, N. Y.—Illustrated hymn in pressed flowers, frame of pressed flowers. Sec. A. 454

535 Brothers, Mrs. H., 80 West Seventh street, Cincinnati, O.—Wax flowers and materials for making them. Manufacturer of excelsior sheet wax, wax flowers, and materials for making them. Artist of wax work, in all its branches. Sec. B. 454

536 Jeremias, Triny, Philadelphia, Pa.—Tissue-paper flowers. Sec. B. 454

537 Dickeson, Anna Mary, Philadelphia, Pa.—Shell work. Sec. B. 454

538 Holcomb, Sallie N., Philadelphia, Pa.—Hair work. Sec. B. 454

539 Bickerton, Mrs. Anna B., Philadelphia, Pa.—Preserved and wax flowers. Sec. B. 454

540 McPherren, Hattie E., Millersville, Pa.—Wax cross. Sec. B. 454

541 Kampmann, Mrs. Louise, Philadelphia, Pa.—Hair work. Sec. B. 454

542 Goodwin, Alice H., Hartford, Conn.—Climbing ferns and autumn leaves. Sec. C. 454

543 Springer, Mrs. L. R., Boston, Mass.—Wax work, preserved flowers. Sec. B. 454

544 Heubel, Miss Melanie, Philadelphia, Pa.—Wax work. Sec. C. 454

545 Whittington, Fannie L., New York, N. Y.—Basket of wax flowers. Sec. B. 454

546 Wilson, Mrs. Henry C., Philadelphia, Pa.—Phantom bouquet. Sec. B. 454

547 Martin, Mrs. Edna, Cambridge, Mass.—Oil painting on porcelain and wood panel. Sec. A. 454

548 Judkins, Miss Eliza M., Cambridge, Mass.—Paintings on mica. Sec. A. 454

549 Cook, Miss H. M., Providence, R. I.—Book, with illustrations in birch bark. Sec. A. 454

550 Yoster, Sarah H., Portsmouth, N. H.—Frames of paper cuttings. Sec. A. 454

551 Bradford, Anne H., West Winsted, Conn.—Shells containing marine views. Sec. A. 454

552 Terry, Miss Jennie, Hartford, Conn.—Fans painted in water colors. Sec. A. 454

553 Gittings, Mrs. James, Baltimore, Md.—Illuminated poem. Sec. A. 454

554 Alexander, Miss E., Baltimore, Md.—Latin psalm illuminated. Sec. A. 454

555 Smith, Emily A., Baltimore, Md. Fire screen, painted in water colors. Sec. A. 454

For location of objects, see ground plan, p. 83.

Fancy Articles, Machines, Needlework.

556 Crichton, Antoinette K., Baltimore, Md.—Illuminated books: Daybreak, The Falling Rain, A Maiden's Toilette, The Maryland Coat of Arms. Sec. E. 454

557 Denroche, Sarah B., New York, N. Y.—Illuminated maps, for photographs; portfolio and lantern. Sec. D. 454

558 Schools of Drawing & Design, Lowell, Mass.—Decorated cups and saucers, and tiles. 454

559 Whittier, Miss H. A., Lowell, Mass.—Decorated box and tiles. 454

560 Hales, Florence, Ridgewood, N. J. —Autumn leaves, in wax. Sec. B. 454

561 Proell, Mrs. Gustave, Gastein, Austria.—Pressed flowers, with pictures of Alpine scenery. Sec. B. 454

562 Goddard, Miss Lucy, Boston, Mass.—Glass screen, with pressed ferns. Sec. B. 454

563 Clark, Miss A. F., Worcester, Mass.—Fire screen. Sec. B. 454

564 Upton, Mrs. E. W., Peabody, Mass. —Jewel case, butterfly, and needle book, painted in water colors. Sec. B. 454

565 Graves, Miss L., New Haven, Conn. —Painted candles. Sec. B. 454

566 Lockwood, Minnie S., New Haven, Conn.—Text with illuminated border. Sec. B. 454

567 Robbins, Miss Ellen, Boston, Mass. —Illuminated mirror. Sec. B. 454

568 Hooper, Alice S., Boston, Mass.— Portfolio, box, and tray, with pen and ink sketches. Sec. B. 454

569 Hollowell, Anna D., Medford, Mass.—Illuminated mirror. Sec. B. 454

570 Hendry & Bartholomew, Ansonia, Conn.—Bird cages made by women. Sec. B. 454

Machines used in Sewing, etc.

571 Compton, Geo., Worcester, Mass. —Cotton loom for dress goods. Sec. B. 521

572 Bromley, John, & Sons, Philadelphia, Pa.—The manufacture of ingrain carpets. Sec. D. 530

573 Townsend, Mrs. G. L., Philadelphia, Pa.—Vertical handle attachment to sewing machines. Sec. D. 531

574 White, Mrs. L. S., Philadelphia, Pa.—The manufacture of confectionery. Sec. B. 582

Aerial, Pneumatic, and Water Transportation.

575 Edson, Temperance P., Dedham, Mass.—Self-inflating life preserver. Sec. 594

Land Animals.

576 Bonney, Sarah E., Sterling, Mass. —Stuffed birds. Sec. B. 635

577 Janvier, Mrs. Mary R., Sabathu, India.—Lammergeir, or bearded vulture. Sec. B. 635

Hothouses, Conservatories, Graperies.

578 Lovejoy, Mrs. Carrie P., Columbus, O.—Preserved fern leaves. Sec. B. 709

579 Ware, Mrs. M. L., Philadelphia, Pa.—Preserved flowers. Sec. B. 709

580 Davey, Mrs. Israel, Brandon, Vt.— Trailing arbutus, poppies, leaves, etc. Sec. A. 709

581 Watson, Jane, Massillon, O.— North American mosses. Sec. C. 709

582 Shaw, Miss Emma, Elmwood, R. I.—Pressed ferns. Sec. B. 709

583 Luther, Mrs. B. J., Providence, R. I.—Mosses from Narragansett Bay. Sec. B. 709

584 Parkhill, Miss Harriet R., Jacksonville, Fla.—Florida sea-weeds. Sec. B. 709

585 Bray, Maria H., Gloucester, Mass. —Marine algæ. Sec. B. 709

586 Hathaway, Mrs. P. V., Stevenson, Ill.—Native flora of Illinois. Sec. B. 709

Garden Tools, Accessories of Gardening.

587 Pierce, Mrs. Mary R., Philadelphia, Pa.—Flower stands. Sec. C. 721

588 Williams, Mrs. Jeff., St. Josephs, Missouri.—Terra-cotta hanging basket. Sec. C. 721

589 Slocum, Mrs. Martha E., New York.—Plant protector. Sec. D. 721

GREAT BRITAIN.

590 Rooke, Mrs. Henry A., London.— Couvrette of macramé lace. 252

591 Rooke, Miss E. E., Hertfordshire. —Macramé lace. 252

592 Greene, Miss, London.—Needlework. 252

593 Palmer, Miss H. M., London.— Point-lace parasol cover. 252

594 Hudson, Mrs. M. A., Buckingham. —Point lace. 252

595 Harding, Miss Caroline, Norfolk.— Embroideries. 252

596 Paget, Miss Nina, London.— Needlework. 252

597 Parker, Miss M. E., Dundee.— Lace shawl; embroidered screen. 252

598 Royal School of Art Needlework, London.—Artistic needlework and embroideries in appliqué, crewels, and silk. 252

599 Preble, Miss Mary, London.— Oil paintings. 410

600 Wilkinson, Miss G., London.— Water color paintings. 411

601 Frere, Miss Catherine F., London. —Water color paintings, and silk fan, with water color designs. 411

Articles contributed by Her Majesty The Queen.

602 Two table napkins spun by Her Majesty. Etchings by H.M. the Queen. A table cloth embroidered and made by

For location of objects, see ground plan, p. 83.

Needlework, Laces, Paintings.

H.R.H. Princess Louis of Hesse, and H.R.H. Princess Christian of Schleswig Holstein. A banner screen embroidered by H.R.H. the Princess Beatrice. Drawings of flowers by H.R.H. the Princess Louise.

JAMAICA.

603 **Nash, Mrs. Francilla, Kingston.**—Dagger plant ornaments. 254

CANADA.

604 **Abbey, Loretto, Toronto.**—Vestments. 250

604*a* **Beverly, Mrs., Oshawa.**—Knitted shawl. 250

605 **Grant, Mrs. Joseph, Aberfoyle.**—Mitts and gauntlets. 251

606 **Webster, Mrs. R. A., Ottawa.**—Point lace. 252

607 **Scales, Mrs., Toronto.**—Berlin wool work. 252

608 **Gemmel, Miss A., Toronto.**—Embroidered piano cover. 252

609 **Zimmerman, Mrs. D., Toronto.**—Bead work. 252

610 **Hammond, Mrs., Hamilton.**—Needlework. 252

611 **Park, Miss, Waterdown.**—Tatting and knitting. 252

612 **Robertson, Mrs., Stratford.**—Berlin wool work. 252

613 **Convent of St. Joseph, Toronto.**—Berlin wool work and sofa cushion. 252

614 **Geddes, Mrs., Montreal.**—Tapestry. 252

614*a* **Roberts, Mrs. James S., Charleston, S. C.**—Needlework: Scene from Shakspeare. 252

615 **McDonald, Mrs. de B., Montreal.**—Gobelin tapestry. 252

616 **Carrier, Miss, Montreal.**—Lace work. 252

617 **Fairbanks, Miss Isabella, Halifax.**—Lace. 252

618 **Conner, Miss Edith, Halifax.**—Lace. 252

719 **Sutcliffe, Mrs., Halifax.**—Needlework. 252

620 **Pierce, Miss C., Halifax.**—Needlework. 252

621 **Rutterford, Miss I., Halifax.**—Lace work. 252

621*a* **Perley, Miss H. A., Fredericton, N. B.**—Point lace. 252

622 **Romans, Misses, Halifax.**—Crotchet work. 252

623 **Viell, Miss, Halifax.**—Lace. 252

624 **Farrell, Misses, Halifax.**—Lace. 252

625 **Renni, Mrs. C. E., Halifax.**—Lace. 625

626 **Pryor, Mrs. H., Halifax.**—Fancy work. 252

627 **Farrell, Mrs. K., Toronto.**—Worsted work. 252

628 **Crawford, Miss, Toronto.**—Tatting flounce. 252

629 **Nunn, Mrs., Belleville.**—Point lace. 252

630 **Cramer, Miss, Toronto.**—Embroidery. 252

631 **Brown, Miss, Brampton.**—Needle work. 252

632 **Strickland, Misses, Oshawa.**—Embroidery. 252

633 **Vean, Miss M., Oshawa.**—Embroideries. 252

634 **Hooper, Miss Ellen, Oshawa.**—Lace work. 252

635 **West, Mrs., Ottawa.**—Berlin wool work. 252

636 **Heslop, Mrs., Toronto.**—Fancy wool work. 252

637 **Barclay, Mrs., Toronto.**—Berlin wool work. 252

638 **Norman, Miss, Hamilton.**—Lace work. 252

639 **Abbey, Loretta, Toronto.**—Silk embroidery. 262

639*a* **Jardine, Miss E., Richibucto, N. B.**—Point and net lace. 252

640 **Elleson, Annie, Toronto.**—Fancy work. 254

641 **Epouse, Miss L., Halifax.**—Fancy work. 254

642 **Hartshorne, Mrs., Halifax.**—Fancy work. 252

643 **Gilpin, Mrs., Halifax.**—Fancy work. 254

645 **Neville, Mrs., Ottawa.**—Leather work. 255

646 **Constant, Mrs., Halifax.**—Leather work. 255

647 **Mitchell, Miss M. A., Toronto.**—Leather work. 255

648 **Convent of the Sacred Heart, Province of Quebec.**—Plan of the institution. 300

649 **Convent of Lachine, Province of Quebec.**—Plan of the institution. 300

650 **Convent of Joliet, Province of Quebec.**—Plan of the institution. 300

651 **Convent of Good Shepherd, Province of Quebec.**—Plan of the institution. 300

652 **Convent of Jesus Maria, Province of Quebec.**—Plan of the institution. 300

653 **Convent of Hochlaya, Province of Quebec.**—Plan of the institution. 300

654 **Congregation of Notre Dame, Province of Quebec.**—Plan of the institution. 300

655 **Convent of St. Hyacinthe, Province of Quebec.**—Plan of the institution. 300

656 **Asile de la Providence, Montreal.**—Plans of buildings. 300

657 **Glassford, Mrs., Morrisburg.**—Oil paintings. 410

658 **Smelan, Mrs., Toronto.**—Oil paintings. 410

658*a* **James, Mrs. J. A., Richibucto, N. B.**—Paintings. 410

658*b* **Mazen, Mrs. E. M., Frederickton, N. B.**
a Oil painting. 410
b Water color painting. 411

659 **Chamberlain, Mrs., Ottawa.**—Water color paintings. 411

For location of objects, see ground plan, p. 83.

Paintings, Fancy Articles, Embroideries.

660 **Whitney, Miss, Montreal.**—Pictures. 411

661 **Harrison, Mrs., Montreal.**—Pictures. 411

662 **Bourne, Miss Bessie, Halifax.**—Paintings. 411

663 **Kent, Miss, Toronto.**—Painting. 411

664 **Morrison, Mrs., Opera House.**—Photographs of buildings. 430

664*a* **Stephenson, Mrs. E. J., St. John, N. B.**
a Inlaid table. 452
b Hair pictures. 454

665 **Farquhassen, Miss, Whitby.**—Painting in velvet. 454

666 **French, Mrs. B., Prescott.**—Canadian autumn leaves. 454

667 **Tully, Mrs. K., Toronto.**—Moss picture. 454

668 **Baird, Mrs. A. G., Toronto.**—Moss picture. 454

669 **Comens, Loretta, Toronto.**—Wax flowers. 454

669*a* **Warren, Mrs. E. J., St John, N. B.**—Bark pictures. 454

TASMANIA.

670 **Meredith, Hon. Mrs., Orford.**—Oil painting, Tasmanian fish. 410

671 **Hull, Mrs. Hugh M., Hobart Town.**—Avoca, in Tasmania, by Moonlight. 420

672 **Meredith, Hon. Mrs., Orford.**—Table top with flowers. 45

673 **Graves, Mrs. John, Woodcock.**—Table top with Tasmanian ferns. 454

674 **Hope, Miss Mary, Hobart Town.**—Table top with Tasmanian flowers. 454

675 **Blyth, Miss, Hobart Town.**—Table top with Tasmanian flowers. 454

676 **Mitchell, Mrs., Swansea.**—Gum from oyster bay pine tree. 603

677 **Thompson, Mrs. John, Cormiston.**—Native bread. 621

FRANCE.

678 **Talhouet, Roy, Mrs., Paris.**—Silk embroideries. 225

679 **Menon, Mrs. Marie, Directress of** the Levallois-Perret School for Drawing and Painting, Paris.—Pupils' work. 300

680 **Chateau de Villiers, Young Ladies'** Institute, Paris.—Pupils' work. 300

681 **Rougier, Miss Jeanne, Paris.**—Oil painting: The Animal Merchant. 410

BELGIUM.

682 **Everaert, Julie, & Sisters, Brussels.**—Laces. 252

NETHERLANDS.

683 **Diest, E. van, Arnhem.**—Silk bed cover, with mosaic work on border. 252

684 **Loke, Mrs. C.**—Footstool, cushion, and embroidered kerchief. 252

685 **Suermoudt, Mrs., Amersfoort.**—Embroidered cover and counterpane. 252

686 **Oldenborgh, Mrs. M. J., Dordrecht,**—Imitation tiger skin and wax roses. 254

687 **Amersfoordt, Mrs. H. M., Badhoeve.**—Oratorio—"God's Ubiquity." 302

DENMARK.

688 **Tscherning, Miss, Copenhagen.**—Oil painting of flowers. 410

689 **Rousholdt, Miss, Copenhagen.**—Flower painting on terra-cotta vases. 454

SWEDEN.

690 **Rappe, Eugenie, Baroness, Skälsnäs, Tjureda.**—Pasteboard frames. 220

691 **Soderberg, Maria, Stockholm.**—Mantle. 250

692 **Andersdotter, Margreta, Lällarp, Torscuna.**—Embroidery. 252

693 **Bagge, Charlotte, Kramfors, Hemösaad.**—Embroidery and frames. 252

694 **Ehrenpohl, Charlotte, Enslöf, Halmslad.**—Embroideries. 252

695 **Fürst, Batty, Upsala.**—Needlework. 252

696 **Pählman, S., Ulexio.**—Embroidery. 252

697 **Segebader, Herminia, Trimethon.**—Embroideries. 252

698 **Jönsfon, Helena, Stockholm.**—Fancy articles, ornamented with moss. 254

699 **Klinghammar, Tersa, Landskrona.**—Flowers and ornaments made from fish scales. 254

700 **Ehrenpohl, Charlotte, Enslöf, Halmslad.**—Inkstand of burned clay. 258

701 **Bianchini, Emerentia, Stockholm.**—Carvings in cork. 405

702 **Andersson, Amanda, Stockholm.**—Oil paintings. 410

703 **Ehrenpohl, Charlotte, Enslöf, Halmslad.**—Oil painting. 410

704 **Ramsay, Ebba, Tobsborg.**—Water color painting of flowers. 411

705 **Ramsay, Ebba, Tobsborg.**—Herbarium. 709

ITALY.

706 **Carson, Mrs. Caroline A., Rome.**—Easel. Sec. D. 217

707 **Romani, G., Rome.**—Embroideries. Sec. D. 252

708 **Regina, B., Rome.**—Embroideries. Sec. D. 252

709 **Gerosa, Adele, Rome.**—Embroidery. Sec. D. 252

710 **Pozzi, Vittoria, Rome.**—Pearl and coral jewelry. Sec. B. 253

711 **Crotta, Giamina, Rome.**—Music. Sec. D. 302

712 **Beceari, Adelaide G., Rome.**—"La Donne," a newspaper, edited and written by women. Sec. D. 306

713 **Maraini, Madame Adelaide, Rome.**—Sec. A.
a Marble busts: Sandalphon, Marble Faun, Cupid and Psyche, Innocence. 400
b Bas-reliefs: Angels before and after the resurrection. 401

For location of objects, see ground plan, p. 83.

Sculpture, Paintings, Embroideries.

714 Freeman, Miss Florence, Rome.—Sec. A.
a Marble bust. 400
b Bronze vase. 401

715 Hosmer, Miss Harriet, Rome.—Sec. A.
a The African Sibyl. 400
b Lord Brownlow's Gates. 401

716 Foley, Miss M. F., Rome.—Bas reliefs: Charles Sumner, Joshua. Sec. 401. 401

717 Fauchinetti, Adelaide, Rome.—Landscape in oil. Sec. A. 410

718 Walker, Miss W., Rome.—Oil paintings. Sec. A. 410

719 Penniman, Miss Ellen A., Rome.—Oil paintings. Sec. A. 410

720 Clark, Miss Sarah A., Rome.—Sec. A.
a Oil paintings. 410
b The Dante Album. 411

721 Borzina, Leopoldina, Rome.—Water color paintings. Sec. A. 411

722 Wratislau, Miss Matilda, Rome.—Water color painting: Peasant's Head. Sec. A. 411

723 Conolly, Mrs. Isabella, Rome.—Illuminations. Sec. A. 411

724 Carson, Mrs. Caroline, Rome.—Painted banner. Sec. A. 411

725 Work of Roman women, exhibited by Mrs. Augustus Hemenway, Boston, Mass.—Sec. B.
a Scafati rugs. 239
b Contadina apron. 250
c Roman pearls. 253
d Ornament palm branches. 254
e Oil painting: Temple of Esneh, Egypt. 410
f Water color painting: Peasant Spinning Silk. 411

TUNIS.

726 Raschid, Lilla.—Embroidered shoes. 252

727 Houssein Bey, Mrs.—Embroidered shashea cover and jacket, embroidered by a Moorish princess. 252

728 Jewish & Moorish costumes worn in Tunis. 256

BRAZIL.

729 Oliveira, Maria de, Province of Rio de Janeiro.—Crotchet shawl. 250

730 Immaculate Conception, School of the, Rio de Janeiro.—Embroidered stole for priest. 250

731 Pereira, F. C., Province of Ceará.—Embroidered and trimmed chemise. 250

732 Hegreville, Paulina, Province of Parana.—Knit woolen shawl. 250

733 Silva, Zulmira Cinitea de, Rio de Janeiro.—Robe de frivolité, for child. 250

734 Mangin, F. H., Province of Paranà.
a Child's dress. 250
b Crochet shawl. 252

735 Netto, Maria Pinto, Province of Rio de Janeiro.
a Robe de chambre, embroidered. 250
b Linen embroideries. 252

736 Orphans' School of Sancta Thereza, Rio de Janeiro.
a Stole for priest. 250
b Embroidered cushions. 252

736*a* Matta, Carolina A. da, Rio de Janeiro.—Cushion in tapestry work. 252

738 Neves, Isabel S. das, Rio de Janeiro.—Cushion in tapestry work. 252

739 Municipal School of St. Sebasteao, Rio de Janeiro.—Tapestry work by pupils. 252

740 Municipal School of San José.—Tapestry work by pupils. 252

741 Leao, Maria de, Province of Paraná.—Interlacings, and collar of linen thread. 252

742 Costa, M. E. da, Province of Paraná.—Collar of linen thread. 252

743 Miró, Osminda, Province of Paraná.—Crochet lace for towels. 252

744 Almeida, Anardina B. d', Rio de Janeiro.—Crochet counterpane. 252

745 Assumpçaó, M. M., Province of raná.—Crochet handkerchief. 352

746 Ribas, J. S. G., Province of Paranà.—Crochet handkerchief. 252

747 Huy, Luiza M., Province of Paraná.—Interlacings in crochet; embroidered handkerchief and towel; lace. 252

748 Municipal School of St. Sebasteao, Rio de Janeiro.—Embroideries. 252

749 A. C. C., S. Salvador da Bahia.—Embroidered cushion. 252

750 Dias, H. J., Bahia.—Embroidered cushion. 252

751 Society Amante da Instrucçao, Orphan girls of, Rio de Janeiro.—Embroideries on velvet and silk. 252

752 Misericordia School, Orphan Girls of, Rio de Janeiro.—Embroidered cushions. 252

753 Luz, F. F. da, Province of Paranà.—Embroidered slippers. 252

754 Leáo, M. M. de, Rio de Janeiro.—Embroideries. 252

755 Chaves, M. G. M., Rio de Janeiro.—Embroidered cushions. 252

756 Boa Viagem, Baroness da, Rio de Janeiro.—Embroidered pillow shams, towels, etc. 252

757 Pirapitinga, Baroness de, Province of Rio de Janeiro.—Embroidered towels and underwear. 252

758 Gama, D. Eulalia de Salvanha da, Rio de Janeiro.—Towels and pillow shams in labyrinth lace. 252

759 Commission General for the National Exhibitions, Rio de Janeiro.—Handkerchiefs in labyrinth lace, and laces for borders, by women of the province of Rio Grande do Nórte; laces, handkerchiefs, pillow shams, seives, etc., by women of the Provinces of Parahyba, Alagôas, and Goyaz. 252

760 Rozario, G. M. da, Province of Paraná.—Lace made of linen thread. 252

761 Lopez, J. F., Province of Paraná.—Embroidered handkerchief. 252

762 Kelim, Clara, Province of Paranà.—Embroidered handkerchiefs. 252

763 Aranjo, G. M. d', Province of Paraná.—Embroidered handkerchief. 252

764 Leáo, A. C. de, Rio de Janeiro.—Pillow shams in sieve lace. 252

For location of objects, see ground plan, p. 83.

Embroideries, Laces, Fancy Articles.

765 Alagoàs, Province of.—Towel for toilet table, in embrodiery and sieve lace. 252

766 Jacobina, Theresa D., Rio de Janeiro.—Tapestry work. 252

767 Oliveira, Alzira H. d', Rio de Janeiro.—Cushion in tapestry work. 252

768 Nunes, Henriqueta M., Rio de Janeiro.—Cushion in tapestry work. 252

769 Ferreira, Maria, Province of Cearà.—Crochet case. 254

770 Director of the Colony of Paranà.—Fringes of linen thread, made by an Indian girl of the colony. 254

771 Alves, M. R., Province of Paranà.—Toilet covers. 254

772 Itamaraty, Viscountess de, Rio de Janeiro.—Embroidered pin case. 254

773 Silva, M. M., Province of Paranà.—Embroidered watch case. 254

774 Faria, Maria D. de, Rio de Janeiro.—Cushion of silk remnants. 254

775 Vianna, B. R., Province of Paranà.—Embroidered watch case. 254

776 Province of Cearà, Ladies of.—Feather flowers. 254

777 Province of Bahia, Ladies of.—Feather flowers. 254

778 Silveira de Souza, Sisters, Province of Sancta Catharina.—Artificial flowers of fish scales, egg-skin, sea shells, etc. 254

779 Sancta Catharina, Province of.—Flowers of fish scales. 254

780 Nattė, Mille, Rio de Janeiro.—Feather flowers, fans, coiffures, ornaments, etc.; ornaments made of bugs. 254

781 Province of Paranà, Ladies of.—Bouquet of fish scale flowers, and stand of alum. 254

782 Commission General for the National Exhibition.—Feather flowers, made by the orphans of the school of the Immaculate Conception. 254

783 Convent das Merces, San Paulo.—Branch made of the pith of the fig-tree. 254

784 Serzidillo, D. Anna M., Parà.—Frame made of cork. 254

785 Lopez, Emilia, Rio de Janeiro.—Flower stand of leather. 255

786 Leme, Rosalina Paes, Rio de Janeiro.—Leather flowers 255

For location of objects, see ground plan, p. 83.

SHOE AND LEATHER BUILDING.

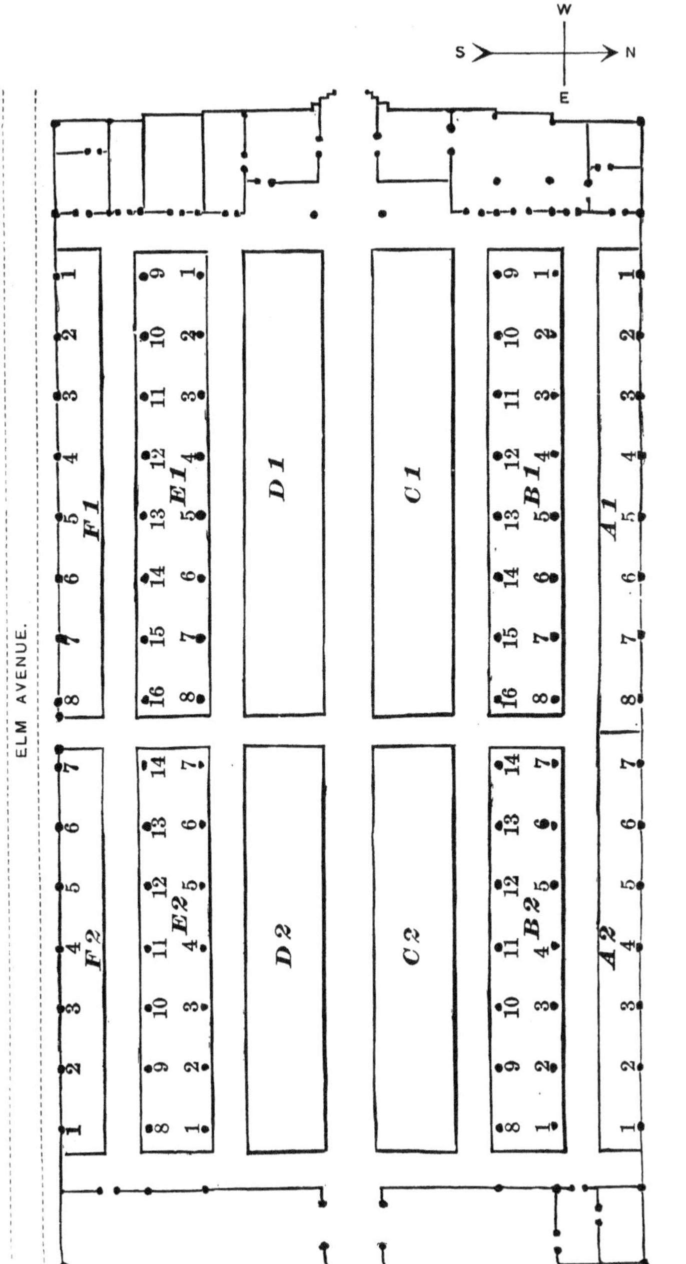

SHOE AND LEATHER BUILDING.—GROUND PLAN.

SHOE AND LEATHER BUILDING. No. 7.

Architect, A. B. BARRY.—Size, 314 feet by 160 feet.

The building is constructed of wood, two stories high, and is situated on Elm Avenue, south of Machinery Hall. Its name indicates its purpose.

KEY TO THE NOTATION.

THE location of objects in the Shoe and Leather Building is shown by a letter and two figures, indicating the nearest column of the building. The letter and first figure designate the section of the building, the second figure the column within that section. The system of numbering is shown on the annexed ground plan.

The class of the classification (See Part I., pages 27–45) to which each exhibit belongs is indicated by the small figures at the end of the line.

Oils, Leather Dressing.

Oils and Leather Dressing.

1 **Dodd, A. W., & Co., Gloucester,** Mass.—Oils for tanners' use. F 1-3. 201

1*a* **Hyde Bros., & Swift, New York,** N. Y.—Tanners' oils. A 2-1. 201

1*b* **Brown, B. F. & Co., Boston, Mass.** —Shoe blacking, leather dressing and bronzes. F 1-3. 202

1*c* **Cole, W. D., Ashland, Mass.**—Belt and hose stuffing. A 2-3. 202

2 **Miller, Frank, Son, & Co., New York,** N. Y.—F 1-4.
a Harness oils. 201
b Shoe blacking, leather dressings, etc. 202

2*a* **Stump, F., & Co., Philadelphia,** Pa.—Blacking, polishing and burnishing inks. A 2-1. 202

2*b* **Boyer, W. P., & Co., Philadelphia,** Pa.—Shoe blacking. F 1-2. 202

2*c* **Hausler, John, Philadelphia, Pa.**—Shoe blacking. F 1-2. 202

2*d* **Fletcher & Dwyer, Lynn, Mass.**—Burnishers for finishing edges and heels of boots and shoes. D 1-6. 202

2*e* **Bartlett, H. A., & Co., Philadelphia, Pa.**—Shoe blacking. F 1-1. 202

3 **Levi & Berg, Philadelphia, Pa.**—Shoe blacking and ladies' shoe dressing. F 1-3. 202

4 **Annear, John, Philadelphia, Pa.**—Shoe blacking and stove polish. F 1-2. 202

5 **Mason, Jas. S., & Co., Philadelphia,** Pa.—Shoe blacking. F 1-5. 202

7 **Bixby, S. M., & Co., New York, N. Y.**—Shoe blacking and leather dressing. F 1-4. 202

8 **Restrorff & Bettmann, New York,** N. Y.—Leather polish for boots, shoes, traveling bags, etc. B 2-2. 202

9 **Sawyer, H., Boston, Mass.**—Crystal blue. F 1-3. 202

10 **Reed, Geo. H., & Sons, Boston,** Mass.—Dressings, inks, varnishes, and stains for leather. F 1-3. 202

11 **Hauthaway, C. L., & Sons, Boston,** Mass.—Leather dressings, blackings, stains, and varnishes. These goods are favorably known throughout the United States, Canadas, and Europe, and were awarded medals at Boston and Vienna. Visitors at the Shoe and Leather Building will see upon the various exhibits of boots, shoes, harness, and horse collars, specimens of the high finish derived by the use of our dressings, as many of the best goods there are finished with our articles. They are considered indispensable in all manufactories using leather. Our exhibit consists of twenty-one different articles adapted to leather, all of our own invention and production. House established in 1854. E 1-11. 202

11*a* **Connihan, E., & Co., Charlestown,** Mass.—Water proof leather preservative. F 1-3. 202

For classes of exhibits, numbered at end of entries, see Classification, Part I., pp. 27-45.

Boots and Shoes.

Boots and Shoes.

12 Johnson, N. M., St. Louis, Mo.—Boots and shoes. C 2-11. 251

13 Wells, M. D., & Co., Chicago, Ill.—Boots and shoes. C -14. 251

14 Fargo, C. H., & Co., Chicago, Ill.—Women's, misses', and children's shoes; men's boots. C 2-11. 251

15 Falley, L., & Co., Lafayette, Ind.—Men's, boys', and women's calf and kip boots and shoes. C 1-15. 251

16 Knees, Chas., Frederick, Md.—Cordovan leather patterns. for boots and shoes. D 1-8. 251

17 Semenetz, Rudolf, Cleveland, O.—English top boots. D 2-4. 251

18 Stribley & Co., Cincinnati, O.—Ladies', misses', and children's shoes. C 2-12. 251

18*a* Davis, Whitcomb, & Co., Boston, Mass.—Seamless felt shoes. D 1-4. 251

18*b* Graves, Ball, & Co., Albany, N. Y.—Shoe lasts. D 2-7. 251

18*c* Ransom, W. A., & Co., New York, N. Y.—Men's, women's, misses', and children's sewed, nailed, and pegged shoes and gaiters. D 2-5. 251

18*d* Keene Bros., Lynn, Mass.—Women's, misses', and children's boots and shoes. D 1-7-8. 251

18*e* Valpey & Anthony, Lynn, Mass.—Women's, misses', and children's boots and shoes. D 1-7-8. 251

18*f* Bartlett & Doak, Lynn, Mass.—Women's, misses', and children's boots and shoes. D 1-7-8. 251

18*g* Boynton & Bancroft, Lynn, Mass.—Women's, misses', and children's soles. D 1-7-8. 251

18*h* Mower, E. W. & C. F., Lynn, Mass.—Women's, misses', and children's boots and shoes. D 1-7-8. 251

18*i* Bubier, S. M., & Sons, Lynn, Mass.—Women's, misses', and children's boots and shoes. D 1-7-8. 251

18*j* Bacheller, C. H., & Co., Lynn, Mass.—Women's, misses', and children's boots and shoes. D 1-7-8. 251

19 Hocker, Geo., Cincinnati, O.—Ladies' and gentlemen's boots and shoes. C 2-13. 251

20 Kilsheimer, F., Cincinnati, O.—Men's boots, shoes, and gaiters. C 2-13. 251

21 Prichard, Smith, & Co., Cincinnati, O.—Boots and shoes. C 2-12. 251

22 Alter, Frank & Co., Cincinnati, O.—Boots and shoes. C 2-12. 251

23 Cincinnati Shoe Manufacturing Co., Cincinnati, O.—Ladies', misses', and children's boots and shoes. C 2-11. 251

24 Feary, Thos., & Sons, Albany, N. Y.—Ladies', misses', children's, and infants' shoes. C 2-11. 251

25 East New York Boot, Shoe, & Leather Manufacturing Co., Albany, N. Y.—Women's, misses', and children's shoes. C 2-13. 251

26 Newcomb & Walker, Elmira, N. Y.—Men's, boys', youths', women's, misses', and children's shoes. C 1-14. 251

27 Burt, Edwin C., New York, N. Y.—Ladies' shoes. C 2-14. 251

28 Burt & Mears, New York, N. Y.—Men's boots and shoes. C 2-14. 251

28*a* Dress Reform Co., Boston, Mass.—Designs for ladies' shoes. D 1-6. 251

29 Bay State Shoe & Leather Co., New York, N. Y.—Boots and shoes. C 2-14. 251

30 Thierry, Ernest J., New York, N. Y.—Gentlemen's gaiters, shoes, and slippers. C 2-14. 251

31 Brooks, Edwin A., New York, N. Y.—Cork-sole boots and shoes. C 2-13. 251

32 Creed, Eugene, New York, N. Y.—Boot, shoe, and gaiter uppers. C 1-15. 251

33 Kenny & McPartland, New York, N. Y.—Ladies', misses', and children's shoes. D 1-5. 251

34 Leh, H., & Co., Allentown, Pa.—Boots and shoes. D 2-4. 251

35 Adler & Clement, Baltimore, Md.—Ladies', misses', and children's shoes; leather tips formed from the sole. D 1-4. 251

36 Dixon, W. T., & Bro., Baltimore, Md.—Ladies,' misses', and children's shoes. D 1-2. 251

37 Banister & Tichenor, Newark, N. J.—Men's and boys' boots, shoes, and slippers. Finest class hand and machine-sewed. Any of the goods on exhibition duplicated on orders. D 2-4. 251

38 Canfield, M. B. & I., Newark, N. J.—Gentlemen's boots and shoes. D 2-5. 251

39 Miller, McCullogh, & Ober, Newark, N. J.—Gents' boots and shoes. D 2-4. 251

40 Brown, Alex. P., & Co., Philadelphia, Pa.—Ladies', misses', children's, and infants' boots and shoes. C 1-15. 251

41 Evans, Thos. R., 28 South Fourth street, Philadelphia, Pa.—"Evans's American gaiter," and graduated expanding boots and shoes. Patented. D 2-5. 251

42 Jenkins Bros. & Co., South Abington, Mass.—Steel shanks for boots and shoes. C 1-15. 251

43 Erskine, M. A., & Co., Philadelphia, Pa.—Ladies' shoes. C 1-12. 251

44 Graf, L., & Bro., Newark, N. J.—Boots and shoes. C 1-13. 251

45 West Bros., Philadelphia, Pa.—Ladies', misses', children's, and infants' shoes. C 1-13. 251

45*a* Moore, Wm. B., Camden, N. J.—Metal tips for shoes, corsets, etc. D 1-4. 251

45*b* Barrows & Boyd, New York, N. Y.—Ladies' and children's fine shoes. D 2-5. 251

45*c* Shaw, Chas. A., Boston, Mass.—Improved shoe lasts. D 1-5. 251

45*d* Prouty, Isaac, & Co., Spencer, Mass.—Men's, boys', and youths' boots. D 1-3. 251

45*e* Kent, Edward E., & Co., Spencer, Mass.—Men's, boys', and youths' boots. D 2-7. 251

45*f* Cooper, R., Ithaca, N. Y.—Centennial shoe. D 1-5. 251

For location of objects, indicated by letter and figure, see Notation, p. 105; ground plan, p. 103.

Boots and Shoes.

46 **Gates, Allen, & Bro., 413 Dillwyn** streets, Philadelphia, Pa.—Ladies' machine-sewed turn boots, shoes, and slippers. Warranted equal in quality and workmanship to hand-made shoes. C 1-14. 251

47 **Sollers, S. D., & Co., Philadelphia,** Pa.—Infants' and children's shoes and slippers. C 1–14. 251

48 **Richelderfer, J. H., Philadelphia, Pa.** —Over gaiters and leggings. C 1–13. 251

49 **Kelley & Moore, Philadelphia, Pa.**— Ladies' shoes. C 1–12. 251

50 **Targett, John, Philadelphia, Pa.**— Boot, shoe, and gaiter patterns. C 1-12. 251

50*a* **Claflin, Waldo M., Philadelphia,** Pa.—Men's and boys' boots and shoes, with Estabrook, Wires, & Co. screws. C 1–12. 251

50*b* **Pratt, Henry J., Abington, Mass.**— Last-block fastening. D 1–6. 251

50*c* **Butterfield, Wm., & Co., New** York, N. Y.—Button fastener, and plate-lace hook. D 1–6. 251

50*d* **Phinney, S. C. & J. G., Stoughton,** Mass.—Boot and shoe counters, made of sole leather. D 2–4. 251

51 **Schmid, Jacob, Philadelphia, Pa.**— Ladies' boots and shoes. C 1–12. 251

52 **Benkert, C., & Son, Philadelphia,** Pa.—Gentlemen's boots and shoes. C 1–16. 251

53 **Zaun, Jacob, & Son, Philadelphia,** Pa.—Men's boots and shoes. C 1–13. 251

54 **Dreisbach, Wm., & Co., Philadelphia,** Pa.—Shoe bows and wooden heels. C 1–15. 251

55 **Heulings, Abram, American Hotel,** Chestnut street, opposite Independence Hall, Philadelphia, Pa.—Ice creepers which can be attached to any lady's or gentleman's boot or shoe, and worn alike in the parlor or on icy sidewalks. C 1-15. 251

56 **Meyer, C. Adolph, Philadelphia, Pa.** —French calf boots, shoes, and gaiters. C 1–12. 251

57 **Helweg & Co., Philadelphia, Pa.**— Boots and shoes. C 1–16. 251

59 **Mayer & Stern, Philadelphia, Pa.**— Ladies', children's, and infants' shoes. C 1–12. 251

60 **Dalsheimer Bros., Philadelphia, Pa.** —Ladies', misses', children's, and infants' shoes. C 1–15. 251

61 **Sausser, Dangler, & Co., Philadelphia,** Pa.—Women's, misses', and children's shoes. C 1–13. 251

62 **Ziegler Bros., Philadelphia, Pa.**— Ladies', misses', children's, and infants' shoes. C 1–14. 251

63 **Laird, Schober, & Mitchell, Philadelphia,** Pa.—Boots and shoes. C 1-15. 251

64 **Schiff, W. L., Philadelphia, Pa.**— Children's shoes, and ladies' white kid boots and slippers. C 1–15. 251

64*a* **Claflin, Aaron, & Co., New York,** N. Y.—Wax, grain, split, kip, and calf boots, brogans, etc. D 1–2. 251

64*b* **Gittens, J. K., Brooklyn, N. Y.**— Cork and wool insoles. C 2–13. 251

64*c* **Saller, Lewin, & Co., Philadelphia,** Pa.—Men's, boys', women's, and misses' boots and shoes. C 1–13. 251

64*d* **De Haven, A. R., & Son, Philadelphia,** Pa.—Ladies' hand-sewed boots and shoes. C 1–12. 251

64*e* **Fontyn, George, Philadelphia, Pa.** —Men's boots, shoes, and gaiters. C 1-13. 251

64*f* **Reimel, Louis, Philadelphia, Pa.**— Shoe uppers. C 1–14. 251

64*g* **Gray Bros., Syracuse, N. Y.**— Ladies' and misses' fine shoes. D 1-4. 251

65 **Simonds, N. J., Woburn, Mass.**— Bevel and moulded heel stiffenings from leather and leather boards. D 2–6. 251

66 **Walker, J. H. & G. M., Worcester,** Mass.—Boots. D 1–8. 251

67 **Hamilton Web Co., Wickford, R. I.** —Boot and gaiter webs. D 1–3. 251

68 **Lilly, Young, Pratt, & Brackett,** Boston, Mass.—Men's, boys', and youths' boots and shoes. D 1–3. 251

69 **Connolly & Power, Boston, Mass.**— Gentlemen's boots, shoes, and gaiters. D 2–6. 251

70 **Haskell, B. C., & Dickerman, Boston,** Mass.—Shoe findings, buckles, buttons, laces, button hooks, over gaiters, shoe trimmings, and tools. D 2–7. 521

70*a* **Cushman, Ara, & Co., Auburn,** Me.—Men's boots and shoes. D 2–7. 251

70*b* **Henderson, C. M., Chicago, Ill.**— Men's boots and shoes. D 2–4. 251

70*c* **Krippendorf & Hart, Cincinnati, O.** —Ladies', misses', and children's shoes. C 2–12. 251

70*d* **American Novelty Shoe Co., Meadville,** Pa.—Wooden shoes. D 2–4. 251

71 **Jones, Frederick, & Co., Boston,** Mass.—Boots and shoes. D 1–2. 251

72 **Batcheller, E. & A. H., & Co., Boston,** Mass.—Men's, boys', youths', women's, and misses' boots, shoes, and brogans. D 1–1. 251

72*a* **De Waru, Laurens E., Philadelphia,** Pa.—Boots and shoes showing the Gordian seam. D 1–3. 251

73 **Henshaw, Ed., Boston, Mass.—Shoe** findings, tools, store supplies, etc. D 2–7. 251

74 **Aub, Hackenburg, & Co., Philadelphia,** Pa.—Machine silk for leather work. D 1–5. 251

75 **Jenkins, Lane & Sons, Boston,** Mass.—Boots, shoes, and brogans. D 1–1. 251

76 **Fogg, Houghton, & Coolidge, Boston,** Mass.—Men's, boys', youths', women's, and children's boots and shoes. D 1–1. 251

77 **Dane, J. F., Grinnell, & Co., Boston,** Mass.—Men's boots, brogans, etc. D 1–3. 251

78 **Robbins & Kelloggs, Boston, Mass.** —Women's, misses', and children's shoes. D 1–3. 251

For classes of exhibits, numbered at end of entries, see Classification, Part I., pp. 27–45.

Boots, Shoes, Trunks.

79 Emerson's, Thomas, Sons, Boston, Mass.—Men's, boys', and youths' shoes. Manufacturers of hand and machine fine sewed and nailed work; owners of the patent for the celebrated "Hersome Gaiter." D 1-1. 251

80 Sears & Warner, Boston, Mass.—Shoe manufacturers' goods, lastings, and serges. D 1-8. 251

81 Peckert, Charles D., & Co., Lynn, Mass.—Ladies' and misses' boots and shoes. D 1-7. 251

82 Ventilating Waterproof Shoe Co., Lynn, Mass.—Ladies' and misses' boots. D 1-7. 251

83 The Moulded Heel Stiffening Co., Lynn, Mass.—Moulded rubber counters for boots and shoes. D 1-7. 251

83*a* Wood, W. D., & Co., Haverhill, Mass.—Boot and shoe trimmings. D 1-6. 251

83*b* Emerson, R. W., & Co., Boston, Mass.—Women's, misses', and children's pegged boots and shoes. D 1-1. 251

83*c* Mawhinney, H. H., & Co., Boston, Mass.—Boots and shoes. D 1-4. 251

83*d* Shaw, John, 2d, & Bro., Lynn, Mass.—Women's boots and shoes. D 1-7. 251

84 Tebbetts, Charles B., Lynn, Mass.—Ladies' and gents' boots, shoes, slippers, and fancy ties. D 1-7. 251

85 Woolredge, A. M., Lynn, Mass.—Ladies' shoes. D 1-7. 251

86 Bancroft, E. F., & Co., Lynn, Mass.—Ladies' and misses' boots and shoes, and ladies' and gents' fancy and plain slippers. D 1-7. 251

87 Mower & Bro., Lynn, Mass.—Ladies' and misses' boots and buskins. D 1-7. 251

88 Sweetzer, C. S., & Co., Lynn, Mass.—Ladies' and misses' boots. D 1-7. 251

89 Breed, W. F., Dole, & Co., Lynn, Mass.—Ladies' and misses' boots. D 1-7. 251

90 Breed, F. W., Lynn, Mass.—Ladies' boots and shoes. D 1-7. 251

91 Breed, A. F., Lynn, Mass.—Men's, ladies', and misses' boots and shoes. D 1-7. 251

92 Coffin, C. A., & Co., Lynn, Mass.—Men's boots and shoes. D 1-7. 251

93 Mudge, W. R., Lynn, Mass.—Leather, straw, and pattern boards, paper soles, stiffenings, etc. D 1-6. 251

94 Sutherland, I. G., Lynn, Mass.—Boot and shoe patterns, and sample boots and shoes. D 1-6. 251

95 Buffum, Charles, Lynn, Mass.—Ladies' and misses' boots. D 1-7. 251

95*a* Rogers, Evan T., San Josè, Cal.—Seamless gaiters and shoes. D 1-5. 251

95*b* Boynton & Bancroft, Lynn, Mass.—Shoe soles, sole leather and roundings. D 1-7. 251

95*c* Dawley & Derby, New York, N.Y.—Shoe lasts, boot trees, crimps, clamps, toe stretchers. D 2-4. 251

95*d* Reutzel, P. J., New York, N.Y.—Boot, shoe, and gaiter uppers. D 1-4. 251

95*e* National Boot & Shoe Tip Co., Boston, Mass.—Colored rawhide tips and toe protectors. D 1-2. 251

95*f* Dalsheimer, Leon, & Bro., Camden, N. J.—Boots and shoes. C-13

96 Mower, F. B., Lynn, Mass.—Ladies', misses', and children's boots. D 1-7. 251

97 Ordway & Clark, Haverhill, Mass.—Ladies' and gents' walking boots and slippers. D 1-6. 251

98 How, Moses, Haverhill, Mass.—Ladies' and misses' shoes and slippers. D 1-5. 251

98*a* Oliver, Stephen, jr., Lynn, Mass.—Women's boots and shoes. D 1-7. 251

98*b* Morgan & Dore, Lynn, Mass.—Ladies' boots and shoes. D 1-7. 251

98*c* Hawkins, Thos. H., Vineland, N. J.—Ladies', misses', and children's boots and shoes. D 1-5. 251

98*d* Turnbull & Samuels, Philadelphia, Pa.—Composition heel. D 2-5. 251

98*e* Justh, E. L., Washington, D. C.—Improved shoes. C 1-15. 251

99 Goodrich & Whitehouse, Haverhill, Mass.—Misses', children's, and infants' boots and shoes. D 1-6. 251

100 Goodrich & Porter, Haverhill, Mass.—Ladies' and misses' boots and shoes. D 1-5. 251

101 How, George C., Haverhill, Mass.—Kid slippers and ties. D 1-6. 251

102 Gardner Bros., Haverhill, Mass.—Ladies' and misses' boots and shoes. D 1-5. 251

103 Farrar, John B., Haverhill, Mass.—Gents' boots and opera and low-cut shoes. D 1-6. 251

104 Johnson, L., & Co., Haverhill, Mass.—Ladies' and gentlemen's shoes and slippers. D 1-6. 251

105 Nichols, George H., & Co., Haverhill, Mass.—Men's boots and shoes. D 1-6. 251

106 Goodrich, J., jr., Haverhill, Mass.—Ladies' boots. D 1-6. 251

106*a* Parker, Charles F., & Co., Boston, Mass.—Boots and shoes. D 1-4. 251

106*b* Dohle, Henry, Omaha, Neb.—Boots and shoes. D 2-3. 251

106*c* American Wooden Shoe Co., Chicago, Ill.—Wooden shoes and slippers. 251

106*d* Estabrook, Wires, & Co., Milford, Mass.—Clinching screws for boots and shoes. E 1-14. 251

106*e* Foster & Quiggle, Milford, Mass.—Shoes made with Estabrook's clinching screws. E 1-14. 251

Trunks, Valises, etc.

107 Simon, Edward, & Bro., New York, N. Y.—Trunks, bags, bag frames and trimmings, and fancy brass goods. G 2. 255

For location of objects, indicated by letter and figure, see Notation, p. 105; ground plan, p. 103.

Traveling Equipments, Harness, Rubber Goods.

108 **Lagowitz, J., & Co., New York, N. Y.**—Trunks, traveling bags, and satchels. G 2. 255

109 **Hacker, J. C., & Co., New York, N. Y.**—Pocket books, bill books, card and cigar cases, etc. G 2. 255

110 **Lambert, P. W., & Co., New York, N. Y.**—Pocket books, belts, toys, and Russia leather goods. C 1-16. 255

111 **Gillmore, J. C., & Co., New York, N. Y.**—Fine trunks, traveling cases and bags. G 1. 255

112 **Thorne, John W., New York, N. Y.**—Saratoga trunk and trunk clamp. G 1. 255

112*a* **Peddie, T. B., & Co., Newark, N.J.**—Trunks, valises, traveling bags, and ladies' satchels. G 2. 255

112*b* **Roemer, William, Newark, N. J.**—Trunks, bags, and shawl straps. G 1. 255

112*c* **Rowen, John, Philadelphia, Pa.**—Trunks, satchels, and pocketbooks. G 1. 255

112*d* **Doughty, S. H., New York, N.Y.**—Ladies' belts. D 1-5. 255

113 **Crouch & Fitzgerald, New York, N. Y.**—Trunks, valises, shawl straps, and leather goods. G 2. 255

115 **Simpson, J. F., Philadelphia, Pa.**—Trunk closer, lock, strap, and socket. G 1. 255

116 **Watt, F. H., Philadelphia, Pa.**—Trunks, traveling bags, and fancy leather goods. G 2. 255

117 **Unruh, John, & Sons, Philadelphia, Pa.**—Leather trunks and valises. G 1. 255

118 **Waas, H. A., Philadelphia, Pa.**—Trunk. G 1. 255

119 **Palmer, Lt. George H., Nashville, Tenn.**—Army, sportsmen's, travelers', and miners' equipments, adopted by the United States Army. Part proprietorship in foreign patents for sale. Foreign orders solicited. G 1. 255

Saddlery, Hardware.

120 **Albright, Andrew, Newark, N. J.**—Hard rubber-coated harness and carriage trimmings. D 2-2. 284

121 **Celluloid Harness Trimming Co., Newark, N. J.**—Celluloid martingale rings and harness mountings. D 2-1. 284

121*a* **Osborn, H. F., Newark, N. J.**—Saddlers' and harness-makers' tools and machinery. D 2-2. 284

122 **Kuenhold, F. B., Newark, N. J.**—Saddlery and coach hardware. D 2-2. 284

123 **Crane & Co., Newark, N. J.**—Flexible rubber bits, wrought hand-forged bits. D 2-2. 284

124 **Theiberath, Charles M., & Bro.,** 10 and 12 Ward street, Newark, N. J.—Manufacturers of gold, silver, nickel-plated and leather covered harness mountings. D 2-3. 284

125 **Manning, Robert, Newark, N. J.**—Winkers and winker plates. D 2-1. 284

126 **Buerman, August, Newark, N. J.**—Saddlery and harness hardware, bits, spurs, etc. D 2-1. 284

127 **Wiener & Co., Newark, N. J.**—Saddlery, hardware, and trimmings. D 2-1. 284

128 **Tompkins, Samuel E., & Co., Newark, N. J.**—Tompkins' patent gig trees; coach pads and gig saddles; hames, bits, etc.; coach and saddlery hardware in silver, gold, or nickel. D 2-1. 284

129 **Waldron, J. V., & Bro., New York, N. Y.**—Crests, coats of arms, monograms, bits, bosses, rosettes, etc., for harness. D 2-1. 284

130 **Reynolds, Samuel, & Co., Pittsburg, Pa.**—Fine XC plate, silver plate, gold and japanned post bits, snaffle, ring bits and stirrups, iron gig and coach hames, all styles buckles, rings, loops, etc.; malleable iron castings for agricultural machinery. D 2-2. 284

131 **Jenks, A. S., Philadelphia, Pa.**—Driving bits. D 2-3. 284

131*a* **Whelen, Richard P., New York, N. Y.**—Bridle bits. D 2-3. 284

Fabrics of Vegetable, Animal, or Mineral Materials.

132 **Davidson Rubber Co., 30 Franklin street, Boston, Mass.**—Rubber goods, used in druggist, surgical, stationery, and fine rubber work. We use nothing but the finest stock, and make superiority in finish and quality our aim. C 2-8. 285

133 **Gossamer Rubber Co., Boston, Mass.**—Gossamer water-proof cloaks, coats, and overcoats, hats, caps, and umbrellas. C 2-11. 285

134 **Taylor, W. B. S., 365 Broadway, New York, N. Y.**—Gas tight flexible tubing, for portable light and gas stoves, and gas-proof cloth for gasometers. C 2-9 *and* 10. 285

135 **Goodyear Rubber Co., New York, N. Y.**—Rubber goods, enameled and table oil cloths. C 2-9 *and* 10. 285

136 **National Rubber Co., Providence, R. I.**—Rubber boots, shoes, clothing, cloths, stationers' and druggists' articles, mats, belting, hose, cushions, beds, pillows, etc. C 2-9 *and* 10. 285

137 **New Brunswick Rubber Co., New Brunswick, N. J.**—Rubber boots and shoes. C 2-11. 285

138 **Vulcanized Fibre Co., Wilmington, Del.**—Hard and flexible goods of vulcanized fibre. G 1. 285

139 **Chadeayne & Christian, Yonkers, N. Y.**—Rubber boots. G 1. 285

139*a* **Star Rubber Co., Trenton, N. J.**—India-rubber goods for mechanical purposes. G 1. 285

Carriages, Vehicles, and Accessories.

140 **Peters Calhoun Co., Newark, N. J.**—Harness, saddles, and bridles. E 1-12. 296

For classes of exhibits, numbered at end of entries, see Classification, Part I., pp. 27-45.

Harness, Leather-Working Machinery.

142 Kessler & Bro., Philadelphia, Pa.—Wooden and plated hames. E 1-5. 296

142*a* Karr, Wm., Karrsville, N. J.—Draft harness. E 1-1. 296

142*b* Crittenden, L. S., Cuba, N. Y.—Combination horse blanket and fly protector. E 1-12. 296

142*c* Hallett, Hervey H., Rockland, Mass.—Harness saddle. E 1-13. 296

142*d* Ries, Anton, Philadelphia, Pa.—Harness. E 1-4. 296

142*e* Taylor, Marshall B., Ludlow, Vt.—Whip lashes. E 1-5. 296

142*f* Hamly, Wm., Ripon, Wis.—Wire stitched horse collars. E 1-4. 296

142*g* Rosenthal, Henry, New York, N. Y.—Leather back horse brushes. F 1-1. 296

142*h* Heydecke, Wm., Newark, N. J.—Wood hames. E 1-13. 296

143 Haedrick, Henry G., & Sons, Philadelphia, Pa.—Harness and saddlery; preparation for polishing and dressing harness. E 1-10. 296

143*a* Burns & Degnan, St. Louis, Mo.—Ventilated side saddle. E 1-11. 296

144 Moyer, E. P., & Bros., Philadelphia, Pa.—Harness, saddlery, and trunks. E 1-3. 296

145 Hansell, W. S., & Sons, Philadelphia, Pa.—Harness and saddlery, and horse clothing. E 1-4. 296

146 Lynch, Anthony, Philadelphia, Pa.—Gold-mounted double and single harness. E 1-10. 296

147 Sallada & Pearson, Philadelphia, Pa.—Ladies' and gentlemen's riding and driving whips. E 1-13. 296

148 McFadden, Patrick, Philadelphia, Pa.—Single harness and saddlery. F 1-1. 296

149 Yeager, Daniel A., Media, Pa.—Double and single harness, riding saddles and bridles. E 1-2. 296

150 Wilson, R. F., Milton, Pa.—Fly nets. E 1-4. 296

150*a* Wrigglesworth, W. J., Darlington, Wis.—Horse collar, collar, cap, and pad. E 1. 296

150*b* Phillips, Samuel R., Philadelphia, Pa.—Harness, saddles, whips, etc. E 1-2. 296

150*c* Golcher Bros., Philadelphia, Pa.—Bridle winkers. F 1-1. 296

151 Weaver & Bardall, Western Penitentiary, Pittsburg, Pa.—Leather whips. E 1-13. 296

152 Moseman, C. M., & Bro., New York, N. Y.—Single and double harness and saddlery. E 1-1 *and* 9. 296

153 Korne & Currie, New York, N. Y.—Single and double harness. E 1-5. 296

154 Moore, Thomas, New York, N. Y.—Plain and fancy horse collars. E 1-2. 296

155 Manheim, William, New York, N. Y.—Harness loops and back curtain loops. F 1-2. 296

156 American Whip Co., Westfield, Mass.—Driving and riding and leather whips and lashes. F 1-1. 296

157 Wilder, J. Lyman, Hartford, Conn.—Patent leather harness work, rosettes, etc. E 1-5. 296

158 Hill, James R., & Co., Concord, N. H.—Single and double harness and collars. "The Concord harness" is made in all styles and of every description, from the lightest, finest, and most elegant in use, to the heaviest and strongest required for any kind of work. Are remarkable for style, workmanship, strength, and durability. Correspondence solicited. Circulars furnished on application. E 1-1 *and* 9. 296

159 Gale, A. D., Pittsfield, Mass.—Double coach harness and paper trunk. E 1-6. 296

160 Motts, George, Washington, D. C.—Gold mounted buggy harness. E 1-4. 296

161 Lighthouse, J. C., Rochester, N. Y.—Horse collars and pads. E 1-5. 296

162 Stewart, John P., Rochester, N. Y.—Carriage and draft horse collars. E 1-13. 296

162*a* Spencer, Robert, Brooklyn, N. Y.—Saddle cloths. E 1-13. 296

Leather Machinery.

163 Pusey, Jones, & Co., Wilmington, Del.—Tanning apparatus and glazing machine for morocco factory. E 2-3 *and* 10. 532

163*a* Mitchell, J. E., Philadelphia, Pa.—Curriers' blocks, clearing and scouring stones. A 2-2. 532

163*b* Smith, Wm. M., Philadelphia, Pa.—Device for regulating sewing machines. E 2-2. 532

163*c* Stoddard & Fifield, North Brookfield, Mass.—Skiving machines. F 2-1. 532

163*d* Carl, Frederick, Somerville, Mass.—Model of stuffing mill for leather. E 2-9. 532

163*e* Lewis, Rufus E., New Hampton, N. H.—Machine for currying leather. F 2-3. 532

163*f* Bowser, J. C., Fort Wayne, Ind.—Stationary engine, boiler, and fixtures. E 2-1. 532

163*g* Newton, E. P., Gloversville, N. Y.—Glove, mitten, and leather cutting machines. F 2-4. 532

164 Walters, G. C., Philadelphia, Pa.—Wet-skin sewing machine. E 2-2 *and* 9. 532

166 Horn, W. H., & Bro., Philadelphia, Pa.—Tanners', curriers', and shoemakers' tools and machinery. D 2-3. 532

167 Osborne, C. S., & Co., 96 Mechanic street, Newark, N. J.—Saddlers' and harness makers' tools. Manufacturers of saddlers' and harness makers' tools of superior quality and finish. Established 1826. Send for catalogue. E 2-4 *and* 11. 532

For location of objects, indicated by letter and figure, see Notation, p. 105; ground plan, p. 103.

Leather-Working Machinery and Tools.

168 **Knox, David, Lynn, Mass.**—Pebbling and polishing machine; sole-cutting machine. F 2-4. 532

168a **McLaughlin, Grover, & Lloyd,** New York, N. Y.—Machine knives, leather, cloth, and paper dies or cutters. D 2-5. 532

168b **Sturtevant, Benjamin F., Boston,** Mass.—Hot blast apparatus for tanneries and curriers' shops. F 2-1 *and* 2. 532

169 **Coogan, Owen, Pittsfield, Mass.**—Boarding and graining machine. E 2-9. 532

170 **Reed, Harvey, Vineland, N. J.**—Combination tannery. F 2-5. 532

171 **Lockwood, Frederick A., Fall** River, Mass.—Automatic leather-scouring machine. E 2-12. 532

172 **Baker, George W., Wilmington,** Del.—Skin-sewing machine. E 2-9 *and* 2. 532

173 **Fisk, Joseph E., Salem, Mass.**—Leather-whitening and buffing machine. E 2-10. 532

174 **Lampert, Henry, Rochester, N. Y.**—Round beam hide worker. E 2-9. 532

175 **Rosensteel, W. H., Johnstown,** Pa.—Model of leather-dressing machine. F 2-5. 532

176 **Thompson & Nowell, Boston,** Mass.—New patent bark-cutting and rossing machine. Tanners are respectfully invited to examine the machine and obtain circulars of information. E 2-3. 532

177 **Swain, Fuller, & Co., Lynn, Mass.**—Beating-out, moulding, and buffing machines. E 1-6 *and* 14. 532

178 **Plummer, W. E., Boston, Mass.**—Leather, buffing, whitening, and skiving machine; rotary tan press; round leach for leaching bark. E 2-5 *and* 11. 532

179 **Gibson, F. N., New Ipswich, N. H.**—Raising, creasing, and waving machine for harness makers, etc. F 2-6. 532

179a **Harkinson, Robert, Philadelphia,** Pa.—Hooks for tanners' use. A 2-3. 532

Shoe Machinery.

180 **Tapley Heel Burnishing Machine** Association, Boston, Mass.—Heel-burnishing machine. E 1-7 *and* 15. 533

180a **Stowe, A. F., Worcester, Mass.**—Splitting, rolling, boot shaping, and side welt machines. F 2-1. 533

180b **Morse, Eddy, & Co., Boston, Mass.**—Wax thread, tripp sewing, burnishing, leveling, and sole cutting machines. F 2-1. 533

180c **Union Edge Setter Co., Lynn,** Mass.—Edge burnisher for boots. E 1-15. 533

180d **Hall, M. H., Philadelphia, Pa.**—Cutting machine for boots and shoes. F 2-4. 533

180e **Domestic Sewing Machine Co.,** New York, N. Y.—Boot and shoe sewing machines. E 2-9. 533

181 **Tubular Rivet Co., Boston, Mass.**—Rivets for boots, shoes, harness, belting, etc. F 2-6. 533

182 **American Shoe Tip Co., Boston,** Mass.—Boots and shoes with wire-quilted soles and toe protection. F 2-7. 553

183 **Roney, James B., Philadelphia, Pa.**—Shoe trimming and edge setting machine. E 1-10 *and* 14. 533

184 **Howe Machine Co., Bridgeport,** Conn.—Boot and shoe sewing machines. F 2-3. 533

185 **Buzzell, J. G., & Co., Lynn, Mass.**—Buffing and heel securing machines. F 2-3 *and* 6. 533

186 **Carver Cotton Gin Co., East Bridgewater,** Mass.—Leveling, counter skiver, and welt cutter, and shank machines. F 2-5. 533

187 **McKay Sewing Machine Association,** Boston, Mass.—Shoe sewing and riveting machines and out-sole tacker. The McKay Sewing Machine is in use for sewing soles to boots and shoes; will sew nine hundred pairs per day; thirty-five million pairs are annually sewed on it in the United States. The riveting machines are for riveting soles to boots and shoes. The rivets are corrugated, automatically cut to the proper length, and firmly clinched on the insole. Three hundred pairs per day can be riveted, either in a channel or on the surface. The outsole tackers are for laying out soles. The nails clinch, are thoroughly buried in the insole, and always hold the sole. E 1-15. 533

188 **May, Withey, & Drake, Lynn,** Mass.—Shoe drying machine. F 2-6. 533

189 **Stimpson, Edwin B., New York,** N. Y.—Shoe machinery. E 1-6 *and* 14. 533

190 **Hanan & Dewees, New York, N.** Y.—Cutting dies and punches, shoe patterns, and lasts. D 2-7. 533

191 **Hautin Sewing Machine Co., New** York, N. Y.—Shoe sewing machine. E 2-11. 533

191a **Saurbier, H., & Sons, Newark, N.** J.—Saddlers', tanners', and shoemakers' tools. F 1-2. 533

191b **Barnett, G. & H., Philadelphia,** Pa.—Shoe rasps and files. D 2-2. 533

191c **American Cable Screw Wire Co.,** Boston, Mass.—Screw, cable screw wire, and tacking machines. E 2-10. 533

191d **Sturtevant, B. F., Boston, Mass.**—Steam blowers and peg machine. F 2-1-2. 533

191e **Whittemore, D., Boston, Mass.**—Shoe and harness machines. F 1-5, 6, *and* 7. 533

191f **Heaton, David, Providence, R. I.**—Button fastener. E 2-3. 533

192 **S. W. Jamison Boot & Shoe** Crimping Machine Co., New York, N. Y.—Steam boot and shoe crimping machine. E 2-6 *and* 13. 533

192a **Wheeler & Wilson Manufacturing** Co., Bridgeport, Conn.—Shoe sewing machines. E 2-4 *and* 11. 533

192b **Smith, W. M., Philadelphia, Pa.**—Device for driving sewing machines. E 2-2. 533

192c **Stephens, W. A., Philadelphia,** Pa.—Sole screwing machine. E 2-13. 533

For classes of exhibits, numbered at end of entries, see Classification, Part I., pp. 27-45.

Leather-Working Machinery and Tools, Leather.

192*d* **Kafer & De Lacy, Trenton, N. J.**—Steam burnishing iron heater. E 2-7. 533

193 **Goodyear & McKay Sewing Machine Association, Boston, Mass.**—Shoe sewing machines. E 1-8 *and* 16. 533

194 **Graves, L. S., Rochester, N. Y.**—Machines for stripping, splitting, rolling and moulding, and heel pressing. E 2-7 *and* 14. 533

196 **Cutlan Shoe Sewing Machine Co., Philadelphia, Pa.**—Turned shoe sewing machine, channeler and edge turner. F 1-8. 533

197 **Redifer, S. S., Philadelphia, Pa.**—Shoe lasts, patterns for dies. D 2-5. 533

198 **Miller, Thomas L., Philadelphia, Pa.**—Beveling, channeling, moulding, and sewing machines for shoes. F 1-8. 533

200 **Cushman, C. S., Philadelphia, Pa.**—Leather and shoe stitching attachment. E 1-12. 533

201 **Evans, Thomas R., Philadelphia, Pa.**—Boot and shoe tree, lengthener, stretcher, and lasts. D 2-5. 533

202 **Smith, J. Barton, & Co., Philadelphia, Pa.**—Rasps and files for shoemakers and manufacturers. E 2-13. 533

203 **Graf, Leopold, Newark, N. J.**—Shoe burnishing and polishing machine. F 2-4. 533

203*a* **Tuck, S. V., Brockton, Mass.**—Shoe knives and tools. D 2-6. 533

203*b* **Tingley, John, Philadelphia, Pa.**—Rotating detachable shoe heel, and machine for attaching. D 1-5. 533

Animal and Vegetable Products.

204 **Wedekind, Hallenburg, & Bro., Louisville, Ky.**—Oak sole leather. B 2-3 *and* 10. 652

205 **Trautwein, C., & Co., Louisville, Ky.**—Chestnut oak sole leather. B 2-3 *and* 10. 652

206 **Stoll, J. B., & Co., Louisville, Ky.**—Oak skirting leather. B 2-3 *to* 10. 652

207 **Ohio Falls Oak Leather Co., Louisville, Ky.**—Oak harness, bridle, and belting leather. B 2-3 *and* 10. 652

208 **Conrad, Fabel, & Mooney, Louisville, Ky.**—Oak sole leather. B 2-3 *to* 10. 652

209 **Schellberg, B. F., Germania P. O., Ala.**—Rough leather. A 2-7. 652

210 **Burt, F. H., & Son, Mannington, W. Va.**—Oak sole leather. A 1-6. 652

211 **Wisconsin Leather Co., Milwaukee, Wis.**—Sole, upper, and harness leather. A 1-5, B 2-5. 652

212 **Hidden, E. S., Milburn, N. J.**—Leather boards for shanking insoles and counters by improved process; also, patent excelsior carriage washers from compressed leather fibre. A 2-1. 652

213 **Hurkamp, J. G., Fredericksburg, Va.**—Virginia sumac. A 2-3. 652

213*a* **Baer, A. P., & Co., Baltimore, Md.**—Chestnut oak extract; quercitron and chestnut oak bark. A 1-5. 652

214 **Leas & McVitty, Philadelphia, Pa.**—Oak sole leather. A 2-6. 652

215 **Keen & Coates, Philadelphia, Pa.**—Oak-tanned sole leather for finest boot and shoe work. A 2-7. 652

216 **Williams', Chas. B., Sons, Philadelphia, Pa.**—Oak-tanned slaughter sole leather. A 2-6. 652

217 **Horton, Crary, & Co., Sheffield, Pa.**—Hemlock sole leather. A 1-5. 652

218 **Shriver, A. K., & Sons, Union Mills, Md.**—Oak sole leather. A 1-5. 652

219 **Sommerville, Jas. N., Bellefonte, Pa.**—Oak sole and belt leather. A 1-6. 652

220 **Downing & Price, Wilmington, Del.**—Oak sole and belt leather. A 1-6. 652

221 **DeLong Bros., Philadelphia, Pa.**—Oak rough slaughter leather. A 2-7. 652

222 **Spanogle & Pennabaker, Philadelphia, Pa.**—Oak sole leather. A 2-6. 652

223 **Hibernia Tannery, Blaine, Pa.**—Buenos Ayres sole leather. A 2-5 *and* 6. 652

224 **Hench, Geo., Centre, Pa.**—Oak sole leather. A 2-5 *and* 6. 652

225 **Hench, A. L., Alum Banks, Pa.**—Hemlock sole leather. A 2-5 *and* 6. 652

226 **McNeal & Black, Man's Choice, Pa.**—Slaughter sole. A 2-5 *and* 6. 652

227 **Mapleton Tannery, Mapleton, Pa.**—Texas sole. A 2-5 *and* 6. 652

228 **Rife, Henry J., Philadelphia, Pa.**—Sole and harness leather, and finished calfskins. A 2-5. 652

229 **Forepaugh, W. F., & Bro., Philadelphia, Pa.**—Oak-tanned whole hides. A 1-4. 652

230 **Leas, Wm. B. Shirley, Tannery, Philadelphia, Pa.**—Oak sole leather. A 1-4. 652

231 **Hoffman, Jacob, Philadelphia, Pa.**—Oak sole leather. A 2-5. 652

232 **Rosensteel, W. H., Johnstown, Pa.**—Union crop leather. A 1-7. 652

233 **Hardenburgh, Hartwell, & Co., English Centre, Pa.**—Sole leather. A 1-5. 652

234 **Howard, J. W. & A. P., & Co., Corry, Pa.**—Hemlock sole leather. A 1-5. 652

235 **Greenawalt, J. & J. K., Harrisburg, Pa.**—Oak sole, harness, wax upper, kip, and calf leather. A 2-6. 652

236 **Wilkinson, J. P., & Bro., Unionville, Pa.**—Oak sole and harness leather. A 2-7. 652

237 **Underhill & Noble, Athens, Pa.**—Hemlock sole leather. A 1-7. 652

238 **Ray, Daniel P., Tyrone, Pa.**—Union crop sole leather. A 2-7. 652

239 **Webb, Wm. B., Frankford, Pa.**—Leather aprons for worsted machinery, picker, band, and lace leather. A 2-7. 652

For location of objects, indicated by letter and figure, see Notation, p. 105; ground plan, p. 103.

Leather.

240 Bechtel, John A., & Son, Newport, Pa.—Oak sole leather. A 2–6. 652

241 Mosser & Keck, Allentown, Pa.—Union crop backs. A 2–7. 652

242 Genseman, Miller, & Co., Pinegrove, Pa.—Oak slaughter sole leather. A 2–7. 652

243 Rippman, C. A., Newport, Pa.—Slaughter sole and rough skirting leather. A 2–7. 652

244 Kerper, Henry, Reading, Pa.—Oak rough leather. A 2–7. 652

244*a* Spaulding, Edward, Boston, Mass.—Hemlock sole leather. A 1–5. 652

244*b* Chatfield, Underwood, & Co., New York, N. Y.—Oak sole and rough leather. A 2–4. 652

244*c* Thorne, McFarland, & Co., New York, N. Y.—Hemlock sole leather, from Thorndale, Laporte, and Torvanda tanneries. A 1–7. 652

244*d* Faust, Alvin, D., & Son, Upper Dublin, Pa.—Oak sole and rough leather. A 2–7. 652

244*e* Corbin, A., & Co., New Milford, Pa.—Hemlock sole leather. A 1–7. 652

245 Bare, John, Mt. Union, Pa.—Union crop sole leather. A 2–7. 652

246 Baer, Arthur P., & Co., hide & leather dealers, Nos. 7 & 9 Cheapside, Baltimore, Md., proprietors of Schlosser Tannery.—Slaughter oak sole leather. Vienna medal. A 1–4. 652

247 Deford & Co., First National & Battle Run Tanneries, Baltimore, Md.—Slaughter sole leather. A 2–4. 652

248 Appold, Geo., & Sons, Baltimore, Md.—Slaughter oak sole leather. A 2–4. 652

249 Jenkins, Staylor, & Co., Baltimore, Md.—Oak sole leather, from the Baltimore Star, Mt. Vernon, Swift-Run, and Prospect tanneries. A 2. 652

249*a* Halsey, Saml., & Son, Newark, N. J.—Patent and enameled leather. B 1–5. 652

249*b* Buck, C., Fleming, Pa.—Oak sole leather. A 2–7. 652

249*c* Maynard, Ely & Roso, Baltimore, Md.—Calf and kip skins. D 2. 652

249*d* Lapham, Smibert, & Co., Chicago, Ill.—Sole leather. A 1–6. 652

249*e* Robertson & Hoople, New York, N. Y.—Hemlock sole leather. A 1–7. 652

249*f* Frantz, D., & Son, Louisville, Ky.—Oak sole leather. A 2–3. 652

250 Decker, David, Wellsburg, N. Y.—Union back sole leather. A 2–4. 652

251 Palmer & Decker, Elmira, N. Y.—Union back sole leather. A 2–4. 652

252 Kinley, Adam, Breesport, N. Y.—Union crop sole leather. A 2–5. 652

252*a* Shultz, Southinck, & Co., New York, N. Y.—Hemlock and Union crop sole leather. A 1–8. 652

253 Osterhout, W. H., Ridgway, Pa.—Hemlock sole leather. A 1–8. 652

254 Wilcox Tanning Co., Wilcox, Pa.—Hemlock sole leather. A 1–8. 652

255 Innes, Adam, Granville Centre, Pa.—Union slaughter backs sole leather. A 1–8. 652

256 Innes, Adam, Grovers, Pa.—Crop sole leather. A 1–8. 652

257 Childs & Bloomer, Nicholson, Pa.—Slaughter crop sole leather. A 1–8. 652

258 McKinstry & Childs, Schultzville, Pa.—Slaughter crop leather. A 1–8. 652

259 Hoyt, J. B., & Co., New York, N. Y.—Oak-tanned leather belting. A 1–4. 652

260 Hoyt Bros., New York, N. Y.—Hemlock sole leather. A 2–3. 652

261 Brown, E. T., & Co., 82 Gold street, New York, N. Y.; Luzerne Tannery, James Davis & Co., Pittston, Pa.—Union crop sole leather; very solid, fair color. A 2–4. 652

262 Lee, W. Creighton, Salladaybush & Tioga Tanneries, New York, N. Y.—Hemlock sole leather. A 1–7. 652

263 Hubbard & North, Oswego, New York, N. Y.—Hemlock sole leather. A 1–6. 652

264 Wells, Henry F., Germania Tannery, Ludleytown, N. Y.—California hemlock sole leather. A 1–6. 652

265 Kenyon, J. A., & Co., Trout Creek Tannery, Cannonville, N. Y.—Texas hemlock sole leather. A 1–6. 652

266 Bulkley, J. E., & Sons, New York, N. Y.—Hemlock sole leather. A 1–8. 652

267 Horton, G. B., & Co., New York, N. Y.—Hemlock sole leather. A 1–7. 652

268 Lapham, H. G., Tunkhannock Tannery, Tunkhannock, Pa.—Union back sole leather. A 2–4. 652

269 Rockwell Bros., Clarendon Tannery, Warren, Pa.—Hemlock sole leather. A 1–7. 652

270 Costello, P. & P., Camden Tannery, Camden, N. Y.—Hemlock sole leather. A 1–7. 652

271 Beach & Dodge, Harrisville, Lewis Co., N. Y.—Hemlock sole leather. A 2–7. 652

271*a* Prichett & Baugh, Philadelphia, Pa.—Oak sole leather from Strasburg, Path, and Franklin tanneries. A 2–3. 652

271*b* Kirkpatrick, Kinzey & Co., Philadelphia, Pa.—Union sole leather. A 2–4. 652

271*c* Howell, Joseph & Co., Philadelphia, Pa.—Oak sole leather. A 2–3. 652

271*d* Hersey, Washburn, & Co., Boston, Mass.—Hemlock sole leather. A 1–3. 652

271*e* Steinwand, Chas., Philadelphia, Pa.—Calf and kip skins. B 2–13. 652

272 Adams & Shaler, New York, N. Y.—Sole leather. A 1–8. 652

273 Thomas Extract Co., Elmira, N. Y.—Sole leather and belting leather, tanned with Thomas's clarified extract of hemlock bark exclusively, and with other tanning materials, in various percentages. A 2–5. 652

For classes of exhibits, numbered at end of entries, see Classification, Part I., pp. 27–45.

Leather.

274 Perry, F. H., & Co., Limestone, N. Y.—Hemlock sole leather. A 1-7. 652

275 Lampert, Henry, Rochester, N. Y. —Sole and upper leather. E 2-9. 652

276 Devereaux, A., & Son, Deposit, N. Y.—Hemlock sole leather. A 1-5. 652

277 Spaulding, Edward, Boston, Mass. —Hemlock sole leather. A 1-5. 652

279 Proctor, Thos. E., Boston, Mass. —Hemlock sole leather, curried leather, and splits. A 1-5. 652

280 Fairbrother, H. L., & Co., Pawtucket, R. I.—Belting lace and hame string leather. A 1-4. 652

281 Jewett & Keating, Buffalo, N. Y.—Hemlock sole leather. A 1-6. 652

282 Williams, C. H., & G. L., Buffalo, N. Y.—Hemlock sole leather. A 1-6. 652

283 Rumsey, A., & Co., Buffalo, N. Y. —Hemlock sole leather. A 1-6. 652

284 Gardner, N. H., & Co., Buffalo, N. Y.—Hemlock sole leather. A 1-6. 652

285 Schoellkopf, J. F., & Son, Buffalo, N. Y.—Hemlock sole leather. A 1-6. 652

286 Rose, Adolf, Buffalo, N. Y.—Hemlock sole leather. A 1-6. 652

287 Bush & Howard, Buffalo, N. Y.—Hemlock sole leather. A 1-6. 652

288 Nepper, E. & D., Cincinnati, O. —Oak sole leather. A 2-5. 652

289 Elasas & Pritz, Cincinnati, O.—Oak sole leather. A 2-5. 652

290 Ballauf, Louis, Cincinnati, O.—Oak sole leather. A 2-5. 652

291 Steigler, A., & Co., Cincinnati, O.—Oak sole, harness, and skirting leather. B 2-11. 652

292 Kessler, Henry, Cincinnati, O. —Oak sole and harness leather. A 2-5. 652

293 Lang & Wanner, Cincinnati, O. —Oak sole and harness leather. A 2-5. 652

294 Bardes, Louis C., Cincinnati, O. —Harness leather. B 2-4. 652

295 Lawrence, John H., Cincinnati, O.—Skirting, calf, seating, and bridle leather. B 2-11. 652

296 Martin & Riedle, Cincinnati, O. —Russet leather. B 2-11. 652

297 Freiberg, Henry, Cincinnati, O. —Harness leather. B 2-11. 652

298 Lappe & Hax, Pittsburg, Pa.—Oak butts and rough skirting leather. A 2-4. 652

Harness, Kip, and Calf.

299 Groetzinger, A. & J., Alleghany City, Pa.—Oak sole leather. A 2-4. 652

300 Alexander, E. H., Alleghany City, Pa.—Imitation French calf and kip skins. B 2-13. 652

300*a* Wunderlich, Reinhard, New Albany, Ind.—Harness leather. B 2-3-10. 652

300*b* Day, Theodore, New Albany, Ind. —Wax leather. B 2-8-10. 652

300*c* Schuman, John W., Louisville, Ky.—Oak harness leather. B 2-3-10. 652

300*d* Rockenback, H., New Albany, Ind.—Harness leather. 2-3-10. 652

301 Woelfel, Fred'k, Alleghany City, Pa.—Harness leather. B 2-12. 652

301*a* Halsey, Samuel, & Son, Newark, N. J.—Patent and enameled leather. B 1-5. 652

301*b* Hahn, H., & Stumpf, East Newark, N. J.—Wax calfskins. B 2-11. 652

301*c* Wetzlar, Albert, New York, N. Y. —Calf, kip, wax upper and split leather. B 2-5. 652

301*d* Steinmand, Charles, Philadelphia, Pa.—Calf and kip skins. B 2-13. 652

301*e* Straus, M., Newark, N. J.—Leather. B 2-9. 652

301*f* Baltimore Calfskin Association, Baltimore, Md.—Calfskins rough, finished, and in the hair. B 2-6. 652

301*g* Loeb & Bros., Philadelphia, Pa.—Waxed calfskins. B 2-11. 652

301*h* Maynard, Ely, & Rose, Baltimore, Md.—Finished calf and kip skins. B 2-11. 652

302 Kiefer, Stiefel, & Co., Alleghany City, Pa.—Harness leather. B 2-12. 652

303 Holstein, A., Alleghany City, Pa.—Harness leather. B 2-5. 652

304 Lappe & Hax, Alleghany City, Pa. —Harness leather. B 2-5. 652

305 Lappe, J. C., Alleghany City, Pa.—Harness leather. B 2-5. 652

306 Callery, Jas., & Co., Pittsburg, Pa. —Harness and saddlers' leather. B 2-5. 652

307 Braun, Frederick, Philadelphia, Pa.—Calf and kip skins. B 2-13. 652

308 Ludy, C., & Sons, Philadelphia, Pa.—Finished oak calfskins. B 2-11. 652

309 Wensley, Jas., Philadelphia, Pa.—Shoe uppers. B 2-13. 652

310 Schuman, F., & Son, Philadelphia, Pa.—Calf and kid leather. B 1-6. 652

311 Chambers, Edwin, West Chester, Pa.—Finished calfskins. B 2-6. 652

312 Mardorf, C., Freeport, Pa.—Harness, calf, veal kip, and upper leather. B 2-13. 652

313 Hollinger, Amos, Lancaster, Pa.—Oak harness leather. B 1-4. 652

314 New York Manufacturing Leather Co., New York, N. Y.—Leather cloth for upholstering and carriages. B 2-5. 652

315 Moffat, David, & Co., New York, N. Y.—Oak-tanned harness leather. B 2-7. 652

316 Michel, A. M., New York, N. Y.—Buff, grain, and calf skins; harness leather; boots and shoes. B 2-5. 652

317 Brown, Elijah T., & Co., 82 Gold street, New York, N. Y.—Cromwell's finished calfskins, sold in this market twenty years; have a high reputation in foreign markets. B 2-12. 652

318 Shattuck & Binger, New York, N. Y.—Tanned alligator skins, black and colored. B 2-12. 652

For location of objects, indicated by letter and figure, see Notation, p. 105; ground plan, p. 103.

Leather.

319 Studwell, Sanger, & Co., New York, N. Y.—Imitation goat, splits and buff; finished calf, russet and union backs. B 2–12 *and* A 2–6. 652

320 Haubner & Heller, New York, N. Y.—Finished calf and kip skins. A 2–3. 652

321 Thomas Extract Co., Elmira, N. Y. —All kinds of light leather tanned with Thomas's clarified extract of hemlock bark exclusively, and with other tanning materials in various percentages. Thomas's bark granulating mill. B 2–12. 652

322 Weed, J. B. & F. M., & Co., Binghamton, N. Y.—Imitation goat, split, kip, and harness leather. B 2–12. 652

323 Miller, J. & J., & Co., Boston, Mass. —Hemlock extract and leather tanned by same. B 2–2. 652

324 Osborne, F., jr., & Co., Boston, Mass.—New Orleans kip leather, plain and buffed. B 2–2. 652

325 Butler, Dunn, & Co., Boston, Mass. —Buff leather made from slaughter hides. B 2–1. 652

326 Thompson, B. F., & Co., Boston, Mass.—Buff and split leather; also, imitations of goat, kid, and morocco insides, of grain leather. B 1–1. 652

326*a* Scofield & Stevenson, New York, N. Y.—Calfskins, harness, wax upper, grain and welt leather. B 2–5. 652

326*b* Beiser, A. & J., New York, N. Y. —Cordovan leather. A 2–2. 652

326*c* Karrer, Joseph & Aaron, Detroit, Mich.—Calf and kip leather. B 2–12. 652

326*d* Herring, W. P., & Co., Governeur, N. Y.—Rough hemlock calfskins. B 2–7. 652

326*e* Schaff, Wm., & Co., Louisville, Ky.—Harness leather. B 2–3–10. 652

326*f* England & Bryan, Philadelphia, Pa.—Finished shoes kirting, waxed upper and split leather. A 2–1. 652

327 Cummings, John, & Co., Boston, Mass.—Imitation goat, polish grain, calf, split, and buff leather. B 2–2. 652

327*a* Stengel, George, Newark, N. J.— Patent leather. B 1. 652

327*b* Spanogle, Samuel, Nassville, Pa. —Rough kip and calf leather. B 2. 652

327*c* Barth, A., & Co., Louisville, Ky.— Harness, skirting, and wax leather. B 2, 3–10. 652

327*d* Mooney, W. W. & J. E., Columbus, Ind.—Sole, harness, skirting, and belt leather. B 2, 3–10. 652

328 Guild, Josiah F., Boston, Mass.— Pebble grain, imitation goat, buff, and split leather. B 2–9. 652

329 Proctor, Thomas E., Boston, Mass. —Curried leather and splits. B 2–8. 652

330 Way, John S., & Co., Bridgeport, Conn.—Leather, buffalo robes. A 2–1. 652

331 Zipp, Philip C., Baltimore, Md.— Calf, kip, and grain leather. B 2–6. 652

332 Appold, George, & Sons, Baltimore, Md.—Chestnut, oak-tanned calf skins. B 2–4. 652

333 Sharp, Tudor, & Co., Baltimore, Md.—Oak buff upper leather, and rough skirting. A 2–2. 652

334 Cunningham & Co., Nashville, Tenn.—Oak harness and rough leather. B 2–1. 652

336 Wisconsin Leather Co., Milwaukee, Wis.—Harness, wax upper, and split leather. B 2–5. 652

337 National Leather Co., Detroit, Mich.—Whip, lace, and upper leather, calfskins and robes. A 2–2. 652

338 Weil, J., & Bros., Chicago, Ill.— Upper, harness, kip, and calf leather. B 2–8. 652

339 Walker, Oakley, & Co., Chicago, Ill.—Wax calf union tannage, imitation goat grains, wax upper, card leather. B 2–8. 652

Morocco and Sheep.

340 Foster, A. J., & Co., Boston, Mass. —Grain leather, goat and sheep skins. B 2–14. 652

341 Ely, Henry G., & Co., New York, N. Y.—Imitation goat pebbled leather, finished wax-split leather. B 2–14. 652

342 Rockwell, J. S., & Co., New York, N. Y.—Sheep leather. Manufacturers of colored and russet linings; pebbled sheep in all colors; white and colored skivers for shoe manufacturers; hatters' skivers; trunk and bag leather and linings; bookbinders' and pocket-book makers' leather of every kind; suspender and organ leather; sumac and alum roans and skivers. This exhibit is entirely of sheep leather. B 1–16. 652

343 Guion, Geo. G.—New York, N. Y.— Morocco leather. B 1–7. 652

344 Howell, T. P., & Co., Newark, N. J. —Harness, patent, Russia, and pocketbook leather, sheepskin mats, and roans. B 1–8. 652

345 Meyer, Richard, New Durham, N. J.—Superior buck skins, for pianoforte, shoe, glovemakers, and others. B 1–14. 652

346 Pusey, Scott, & Co., Wilmington, Del.—Kid, straight-grain pebbled, and French morocco. B 2–7. 652

347 Jones, W., & Co., Wilmington, Del. —Morocco leather. B 2–14. 652

348 Bush, Wm., & Co., Wilmington, Del.—Morocco leather. B 1–8. 652

349 Larrabee, E., & Sons, Baltimore, Md.—Colored roans and linings, buff splits and wax uppers. B 1–15. 652

350 Wentz & Clark, Philadelphia, Pa. —Morocco leather. B 1–14. 652

351 Bockius, Geo., Philadelphia, Pa.— Morocco leather. B 1–5, *and* G 1. 652

352 Wood, Geo., Philadelphia, Pa.— Morocco and sheep leather. B 1–13. 652

353 Schollenberger, Wm., & Sons, Philadelphia, Pa.—Calf, kid, sheep alum, and roan leather; satchels, pocket books, and fancy leather goods. B 1–12. 652

354 Amer, Wm., & Co., Philadelphia, Pa.—Morocco leather. B 1–4. 652

355 O'Callaghan, Francis O., Philadelphia, Pa.—Skivers and sheep skins. B 1–13. 652

356 Hummel, G. W., & Co., Philadelphia, Pa.—Morocco leather. B 1–12. 652

For classes of exhibits, numbered at end of entries, see Classification, Part I., pp. 27–45.

Leather, Saddlery, Furs.

357 McNeely & Co., Philadelphia, Pa. —Morocco leather, sheepskins, and skivers. B 1-4. 652

358 Adams & Keen, Philadelphia, Pa. —Morocco and kid leather. B 1-14. 652

359 Bronx Wool & Leather Co., New York, N. Y.—Morocco and sheep leather. B 1-15. 652

360 Locher & Atkinson, Baltimore, Md. —Morocco. B 1-6. 652

361 Martin, A. B., & Co., Lynn, Mass. —Kid and goat morocco leather. B 1-6. 652

362 Block, A., & Co., Philadelphia, Pa. —Colored sheepskins. B 1-6. 652

363 Seavey, Foster, & Bowman, Philadelphia, Pa.—Machine silk twist. D 1-6. 652

GREAT BRITAIN.

West of Centre Aisle, Sect. C., Col. 3 to 4.

1 Brookes, W., & Sons, Walsall, England.—Saddlery. 296

2 Wilson, Walker, & Co., Leeds, England.—Colored skivers, calf, roans, moroccos, and kids, in every style of finish and for all purposes. 652

3 Edinburgh Western Tanning Co., Edinburgh, Scotland.—Hog skins for saddlery. 652

4 Hooper, Cleve, jr., London, Eng.—Colored skivers and basils, materials for tanning and making glue. 652

5 Hooper, C. W., & Sons, London, Eng.—Materials for tanning and making glue. 652

6 Angus, George, & Co., Liverpool, Eng.—Oak sole leather. (*In U. S. section.*) A 2-3. 652

GERMANY.

West of Centre Aisle, Sect. C, Col. 2 to 3.

1 Wolf, S., Mainz.—Shoes. 251

2 Spicharz, P. J., Offenbach.—Calf, glove, and French kid. 652

3 Simon, C., & Son, Kirn.—Colored and black moroccos, and calfskins. 652

4 Meyer, E., Berlin.—Colored glove kid. 652

5 Bruning, H. W., Neumunster.— Smooth and grained calf, kid and upper leather. 652

6 Schaller, G., Laher Baden.—Colored and black moroccos. 652

7 Kaumanus, F. H., Ehrenbreitstein, B. A.—Sole leather, rheinish oak slaughter sole. 652

RUSSIA.

West of Centre Aisle, Sect. C, Col. 1 to 3.

1 Bauerfeind, Adolphus, Warsaw.— Russian and calf leather. 652

2 Panisheff, John, Mournshkine, Gov-ernment of Nijnii Novgorod, district of Makarief.—Sheepskins, dressed and half dressed. 652

3 Alafoozoff & Alexandroff, Kazan.— Russian leather. 652

4 Mikhailoff, Alexis, Moscow.—Furs, sable, ermine, Korsard fox, Siberian squirrel. 652

5 Grunwald, Morice, Riga.—Furs, and stuffed fur animals. 652

6 Komaroff, Nicetas, Moscow.—Sheep and lamb skins, dressed. 652

7 Solin Bros., Nijnii Novgorod.— Seal grease. 652

8 Ossipoff, Michael, Kieff.—Tallow. 652

9 Zinovieff, Alexander, St. Petersburg. —Boot legs and vamps. 652

10 Tembler, K., & Schwede, L., War-saw.—Manufactured leather. 652

11 Tehernish, E., Shartash Village, Government of Perm, district of Ekaterinburg.—Manufactured leather. 652

12 Sorakin, Tihlon, Moscow.—Colt leather. 652

13 Sevebreunikoff, Simon, Mourashkin-agon, Nijnii Novgorod, district of Makarieff.—Horse leather. 652

14 Savin, Theodore, Ostashkoff, Gov-ernment of Tver.—Russian leather and blacked boot legs. 652

15 Rene, John, St. Petersburg.—Sole leather, boot legs, and vamps. 652

16 Pervoff, Stephen, Poshekhonze, Government of Faraslow.—Calf leather and boot legs. 652

17 Ostrom Bros., Uleaborg, Fin-land.—Sole leather. 652

18 Muller, Edward, St. Petersburg.— Boot legs and vamps. 652

19 Long, Frederick, St. Petersburg.— Calf leather, boot legs, and vamps. 652

20 Koorikoff, P., St. Petersburg.— Leather. 652

21 Hufner, Rudolph, St. Petersburg.— Boot and Russian leather. 652

22 Emelianoff, Alexander, St. Peters-burg.—Boot legs. 652

23 Efinoff, —— St. Petersburg.—Boot legs and vamps. 652

24 Company of the Wladimir Tannery, St. Petersburg.—Sole leather. 652

25 Broosnitzine, Nicolas, & Sons, St. Petersburg.—Sole and boot leather and boot legs. 652

26 Bensenson, John, St. Petersburg.— Boot legs. 652

For location of objects, indicated by letter and figure, see Notation, p. 105; ground plan, p. 103.

DESCRIPTION OF BUILDINGS AND SPECIAL EXHIBITS.

No. 1. MAIN BUILDING.

See Part I., page 23.

No. 2. MACHINERY HALL.

See Part III., page 9.

No. 3. STOKES & PARRISH MACHINE SHOP, etc.

Size, 112 feet by 60 feet.
STOKES & PARRISH, Philadelphia.

Constitutes a part of Annex No. 2 to Machinery Hall, and is intended to execute repairs and machine work for the exhibitors. It is located south of Machinery Hall.

No. 4. AMERICAN BOILER HOUSE.

Is situated south of Machinery Hall, near the Hydraulic Annex, and furnishes steam for the American Section.

No. 5. CORLISS BOILER HOUSE.

Architects, PETTIT & WILSON, Philadelphia.—Size, 40 feet by 80 feet.
CORLISS STEAM ENGINE COMPANY, Providence, R. I.

Is built of composite stone and wood, and furnishes steam for the Corliss engine in Machinery Hall from twenty vertical tubular boilers, aggregating 1400 horse-power. It is situated south of Machinery Hall.

No. 6. ENGLISH BOILER HOUSE.

Size, 24 feet by 71 feet.

A composite wood and stone building, furnishing steam to English and other foreign exhibitors in Machinery Hall, and situated to the south of it.

No. 7. SHOE AND LEATHER EXHIBITION BUILDING.

See Part III., page 105.

No. 8. CENTENNIAL BOARD OF FINANCE OFFICE.

Architect, H. J. SCHWARZMANN.—Size, 140 feet by 212 feet.

A one-story frame building, situated on the left hand side of the main entrance to the Exhibition grounds, and occupied by the Board of Finance for the transaction of daily business.

No. 9. U. S. CENTENNIAL COMMISSION OFFICE.

Architect, H. J. SCHWARZMANN.—Size, 192 feet by 140 feet.

Located on the right hand side of the main entrance to the Exhibition grounds. It is built of wood, one story high, and is used as a business office by the Centennial Commission.

No. 10. CENTENNIAL NATIONAL BANK.

Architects, H. J. SCHWARZMANN, HUGH KAFKA.—Size, 72 feet by 40 feet.
E. A. ROLLINS, President.

Situated at the northwest corner of the Main Exhibition Building, and east of the Centennial Commission Office. It is one story high, built of wood, and is the medium for transacting the financial affairs of the Exhibition.

No. 11. WEIMER'S MACHINE WORKS, LEBANON, PA.

This outdoor exhibit is located south of Machinery Hall, between the Shoe and Leather Building, and Stokes & Parrish Machine Shop, and consists of bells, car dumps, carts for coal, iron bars, and steel coil tuyere.

No. 12. BARTHOLDI'S FOUNTAIN.

See Part II., page 146.

Architect, BARTHOLDI, of Paris.—Size, basin, 26 feet in diameter; height, 30 feet, statue, 11 feet.

Situated in the Esplanade in front of the main entrance to the grounds.

No. 13. CATHOLIC TOTAL ABSTINENCE FOUNTAIN.

See Part II., page 146.

Architect, HERMAN KIRN, Philadelphia.

Situated at the junction of Fountain Avenue and the Avenue of the Republic, at the northwestern corner of Machinery Hall. In design it is a circular platform, with four arms projecting at right angles, terminating in four smaller circular platforms. From the centre of the large circle rises a marble rockwork sixteen feet high, with a diameter of eighteen feet at base, on which stands a statue of Moses smiting the rock. The water descends from numerous fissures into a basin forty feet in diameter. On each of the circular platforms is a drinking fountain, twelve feet in height and eight feet eight inches in diameter, surrounded with statues nine feet high, representing Father Mathew, Charles Carroll, Archbishop John Carroll, and Commodore John Barry. It has been erected by contributions made by the numerous societies forming the Catholic Total Abstinence Union of America.

No. 14. FULLER, WARREN, & CO.'S STOVE BUILDING.

Size, 60 feet by 45 feet.

FULLER, WARREN, & CO., New York city, Chicago, Ill., Cleveland, O., and Troy, N.Y.

Located at the east end of Machinery Hall, and facing the Fountain of the Catholic Total Abstinence Society. It contains samples of stoves, heaters, and ranges in operation; is built of wood, one story high, surmounted by a cupola.

No. 15. GILLENDER & SONS' GLASSWARE BUILDING.

Architect, JAMES H. WINDRIM.—Size, 60 feet by 90 feet.

GILLENDER & SONS, Philadelphia.

A one-story frame house, situated west of Machinery Hall, on the walk to the Fifty-second Street entrance, where glass in process of manufacture is shown.

No. 16. CAMP OF WEST POINT CADETS.

Located on the eastern slope of George's Hill, at the western end of Fountain Avenue. The tents accommodate 300 cadets, with officers and band.

No. 17. IRON PIPE.

ANDREW O'NEILL, Ansonia, Conn.

This is an outdoor exhibit, situated south of Machinery Hall, and consists of water and gas pipes, showing patent process of jointing.

No. 18. LIBERTY STOVE WORKS.

Architect, C. C. PHILLIPS.—Size, 45 feet by 34 feet.

CHARLES NOBLE & CO., Philadelphia.

A one-story frame building, located west of Machinery Hall, and south of the Catholic Total Abstinence Fountain, on Fountain Avenue; containing different varieties of heaters, stoves, and ranges manufactured by Noble & Co.

No. 19. SAWMILL ANNEX.

Size, 276 feet by 80 feet, and

No. 20. BOILER HOUSE.

Architects, PETTIT & WILSON, Philadelphia.
Size, 48 feet by 30 feet.

UNITED STATES CENTENNIAL COMMISSIONERS.

Exhibit direct-acting steam saw machines and gang saws. Are on Fountain Avenue, west of Machinery Hall, and consist of a one-story frame open building, and a boiler house attached.

No. 21. RAILROAD ENGINE HOUSE.

This building is used for storing and repairing the engines of the Narrow-Gauge Railroad Company, and is located west of Machinery Hall.

No. 22. ST. CECILIAN ORGANS.

T. C. KNAUFF, Philadelphia, Pa.

This exhibit consists of miniature organs, and some clocks made in 1676, 1776, and 1876. The building is frame, one story high, and in design resembles an organ. It is situated south of Mineral Annex, No. 1, near eastern entrance to Main Building.

No. 23. AUTOMATIC RAILROAD.

Size, 20 feet by 150 feet.

CHARLES W. HUNT, New York.

Illustrations of the mode of unloading vessels by means of a railroad worked by a self-acting apparatus. Is situated west of Machinery Hall.

No. 24. MONUMENT—THE AMERICAN SOLDIER.

NEW ENGLAND CO., Hartford, Conn.

This is a colossal monument situated between the Main Building and Art Gallery, on Avenue of the Republic. It is made of Westerly granite, is 21 feet 6 inches high, weighs 30 tons, and is the largest statue of modern times.

No. 25. GUNPOWDER PILE DRIVER.

Size, 35 feet by 12 feet.

GUNPOWDER PILE-DRIVING CO., Philadelphia.

Is built in the open air to exhibit the operation of pile-driving by means of gunpowder. It is situated southwest of Machinery Hall, between it and the barrier.

No. 26. STARR'S IRON WORKS.

JESSE W. STARR & SON, Camden, N. J.

The space allotted to Messrs. Starr & Son is occupied with gas works, pipes, special castings, stop-valves, lamp-posts, and fire hydrants. It is located southwest of Machinery Hall, close to the barrier.

No. 27. WEST END RAILWAY OFFICE.

This is a two-story frame building, situated west of Machinery Hall and north of Railroad engine house, on line of narrow-gauge road, and designed for the transaction of the Company's business.

No. 28. PNEUMATIC TUBES.

A. BRISBANE.

These tubes are placed on a platform, showing the process of transmitting messages and packages by this method. The exhibit is situated west of the gas machine, near fence on Elm Avenue.

No. 29. EXHIBIT OF NEW ENGLAND GRANITE CO., HARTFORD, CONN.

Situated in front of Board of Finance office, and consists of a Corinthian monument, 46 feet high, crowned with the statue of Hope. A canopy, 40 feet high, surmounted by spire and cross, under canopy a figure indicative of Memory. A Gothic monument with four polished columns at corners of die; a model of statue representing soldier of 1776 (life size); an individual memorial crowned with cross; a Gothic column, surmounted by spire and turrets; a Scotch granite polished monument, 16 feet high, with circular dome terminating in a finial; an individual memorial; a small monument, terminating in an urn; and a rustic monument, with ivy-circled column surmounted with cross.

No. 30. PATENT RAILROAD CROSSING.

This exhibit is located on line of narrow-gauge road near Elm Avenue, and west of Machinery Hall. It is designed to keep dirt from accumulating between the rails and planks of crossing.

No. 31. NEVADA QUARTZ MILL.

Size, 60 feet by 43 feet.

STATE OF NEVADA.

Exhibits the process of manipulating ores and precious metals. It is a one-story frame building, situated south of Machinery Hall.

No. 32. STORE HOUSE.

A one-story brick building, 10 feet by 10, used for the storage of oil for the machinery department. It is between the Nevada quartz mill and the barrier.

No. 33. FRICTION DRUM.

I. S. MUNDY, Newark, N. J.

Situated west of gas machine, near Elm Avenue, and consists of an improved portable friction drum.

No. 34. U. S. HOISTING MACHINE.

STOKES & PARRISH.

This exhibit adjoins the machine shop of Stokes & Parrish, south of Machinery Hall, and consists of a derrick with engine and boiler attachment.

No. 35. CHILIAN AMALGAMATING MACHINERY.

COMMISSION FOR CHILI.

Contains working models of amalgamating machinery used in working ores, and has a boiler house with small cylinder boilers. Is situated west of Machinery Hall.

No. 36. CAMPBELL PRINTING PRESS BUILDING.

Architect, ALEXANDER B. BARY.—Size, 88 feet by 144 feet.

CAMPBELL PRINTING PRESS AND MANUFACTURING CO., Brooklyn, N. Y.

The various printing presses manufactured by this company are exhibited in operation; the power is furnished by a thirty (30) horse-power engine and boiler. Specimens of type printing from the date of the invention, and of sunlight printing, are shown, and a complete printing office, of the fashion of 1776, is also in operation.

No. 37. OLD LOCOMOTIVE AND CARS.

EXHIBITED BY PENNSYLVANIA RAILROAD CO.

This exhibit is situated on line of Narrow-Gauge Railroad, west of Machinery Hall, and consists of the engine "John Bull," with tender and two passenger cars, standing upon the rails and stone sleepers of the first piece of track laid for the Camden & Amboy Railroad, in 1831; also, the first iron prow used on ships in crossing the Atlantic Ocean.

No. 38. CAR HOUSE.

Size, 140 feet by 44 feet.

Situated west of Machinery Hall, on line of Narrow-Gauge Railroad; designed for the exhibition of cars.

No. 39. POLICE STATION.

This building is situated southwest of Glass Factory, and is used by the Centennial Guard for quarters, etc.

No. 40. AVERILL CHEMICAL PAINT CO.

Size, 36 feet by 42 feet.

Contains exhibits of the Averill Chemical Paint ready for use, and applied. The building is constructed on the Rogers patent, has no frame work, and is put together with bolts and iron tongues. It is west of the Liberty Stove Works, on Fountain Avenue.

No. 41. OFFICIAL CATALOGUE AND NEWSPAPER ADVERTISING OFFICE.

Size, 20 feet by 30 feet.

CENTENNIAL CATALOGUE COMPANY—S. M. PETTENGILL & CO., New York, Philadelphia, and Boston.

A one-story building, occupied jointly by the Centennial Catalogue Company, and S. M. Pettengill & Co., Newspaper Advertising Agents. Contains bound volumes and files of the principal newspapers of the country, specimen numbers of old newspapers, photographs of editors and publishers, etc. Situated south of the east end of Machinery Hall.

S. M. Pettengill & Co., established 1849, are agents for all the newspapers of the United States and Canada, which are received and filed at their spacious and conveniently located offices, 37 Park Row, New York; 701 Chestnut Street, Philadelphia; 10 State Street, Boston, and upon the Centennial grounds. They have built up a large business by faithful attention to the interests of their customers, for whom they save time, trouble, and expense. Their long experience and large facilities are put at the service of those who consult them respecting the best methods of advertising.

No. 42. STOKES & PARRISH BOILER HOUSE.

Size, 10 feet by 12 feet.

Contains a boiler and engines; situated east of the southern central entrance of the Main Building.

No. 43. EHRET'S WATER-PROOF ROOFING.

M. EHRET, JR., Philadelphia, Pa.

A circular pavilion, showing fire and water-proof roofing. It is located to the east of the central southern entrance of the Main Building.

No. 44. TOMBSTONES.

This exhibit is situated south of the Main Building, near central entrance, and consists of tombstones, inclosed by ornamental iron fence.

No. 45. TERRA-COTTA PIPES.

Exhibited by E. W. Rittenhouse & Bro., Baltimore, Md. Comprises drain pipes of different sizes, elbows, angles, etc. Southwest of Machinery Hall, and adjoining the Gas Machine.

No. 46. MINERAL ANNEX, 1 and 2.

An extension of the Main Building, to the east of its south central entrance. It contains the greater part of the American exhibits in Department I. (Mining and Metallurgy), which are catalogued in Part I., pages 47 to 60.

No. 47. FIRE-PROOF VENTILATED BUILDING.

Architect and Builder, ROBERT IRWEST.—Size, 13 feet by 13 feet.

This is a one-story building composed of hollow bricks, peculiar in construction. Located south of Main Building and Annex No. 2.

No. 48. HEWITT & BRENNAN'S SWINGS.

These swings are known as aerial chairs, and are operated by means of a treadle with foot-pressure, leaving the hand entirely free. They number six, and are situated on Agricultural Avenue, immediately south of the American Restaurant, and south of Main Building, where the exhibit is known as aerial chairs.

No. 49. ORNAMENTAL STONE WORK.

An exhibit of brown stone, representing a double entrance to dwelling, elaborately carved, with rough dressed trimmings. Located south of St. Cecilian Organ and Main Building Annex No. 1.

No. 51. UNITED STATES GOVERNMENT BUILDING.

See Part III., page 72.

No. 51½. BARTHOLDI ELECTRIC LIGHT.

Is situated immediately west of Cook, Son & Jenkins' Pavilion, on border of lake, and consists of arm of statue to be erected in New York harbor.

No. 52. UNITED STATES ARMY POST HOSPITAL.

See Part III., page 73.

No. 52½. HOWE MONUMENT.

This monument was erected by the Howe Machine Co., to the memory of Elias Howe, Jr., the first inventor of sewing machines in this country. It was designed by Mr. Ellis, and cast by Wood Bros., of Philadelphia, and is situated at the western end of the lake, opposite northern central entrance to Machinery Hall.

No. 53. UNITED STATES HOSPITAL TENT.

See Part III., page 73.

No. 53½. JERUSALEM BAZAAR.

Situated on south side of Fountain Avenue, and due north of Turkish Bazaar. Designed for sale of olive wood.

No. 54. UNITED STATES LABORATORY.

See Part III., page 73.

No. 54½. PHILADELPHIA "TIMES" PAVILION.

Architects, WILSON BROS. & Co., Philadelphia.—Size, 28 feet by 17 feet.
A. K. McCLURE, Editor.

The Centennial business office of the "Times," a daily paper, issued morning and evening, and printed on a Hoe perfecting press in Machinery Hall. It is a one-story frame building, located on Belmont Avenue, opposite and east of the lake.

No. 55. PENNSYLVANIA STATE BUILDING.

Architects, H. J. SCHWARZMANN, HUGH KAFKA.—Size, 97 feet by 55 feet.

A two-story frame building, with a tower, of Gothic style. It faces the lake, between Fountain Avenue and the Avenue of the Republic; contains reception-rooms and offices for the use of the State Commissioners and visitors.

No. 55½. HUNGARIAN WINE PAVILION.

Architect, H. J. SCHWARZMANN.

JACOB KOHN, Manager.

This structure is circular in form, situated on State Avenue, north of the Japanese and Mississippi buildings, and devoted to the sale of Hungarian wines exclusively.

No. 56. OHIO STATE BUILDING.

Architects, HEARD & SONS, Cleveland, O.—Size, 45 feet by 44 feet, and Annex, 60 feet by 40 feet.

A two-story stone pavilion, located at the junction of State and Belmont Avenues. It supplies accommodation for the State Commissioners.

1 **Hoffman, A. O., Thompson, Wm.,** and others, Springfield, O.—Springfield limestone, course No. 16. 102

2 **Mc Nally, Wm. G., Cleveland, O.**—Coat of arms of Ohio, carved from Berea stone. 102

3 **Berea Stone Co., Berea, O.**—Berea sandstone, course Nos. 1 and 2. 102

4 **Hurst, J. R., Cleveland, O.**—Independence sandstone, course No. 4. 102

5 **Ford, O. D., Cleveland, O.**—Euclid sandstone, course No. 3. 102

6 **Halderman, L., & Son, Cleveland, O.**—Amherst stone, course No. 5 and window No. 4. 102

7 **Wagner, John, Cleveland, O.**—Independence sandstone, course No. 6. 102

8 **Amherst Stone Co., Cleveland, O.**—Amherst stone, course No. 7. 102

9 **Black River Stone Co., Cleveland, O.**—Stone from Grafton, Ohio, course No. 8 and window No. 10. 102

10 **Paul, John, & Co., Massillon, O.**—White sandstone from Massillon, Ohio, course No. 9. 102

11 **Wilson & Hughes Stone Co., Cleveland, O.**—Amherst stone, course No. 10 and window No. 9, and Independence stone, course No. 19. 102

12 **Clough Stone Co., Amherst, O.**—Amherst stone, course No. 11, and one-half front entrance. 102

13 **Worthington & Sons, Amherst, O.**—Amherst stone, course No. 12, and one-half front entrance. 102

14 **Ohio Stone Co., Cleveland, O.**—Amherst stone, course No. 13. 102

15 **McDermott, J., & Co., Cleveland, O.**—Berea stone, course No. 14 and window No. 8. 102

16 **Coshocton Stone Co., Coshocton, O.**—Sandstone, course No. 15 and window No. 2. 102

17 **Stitt, Price, & Co., Columbus, O.**—Columbus limestone, course No. 16. 102

18 **Finnegan, M., Cincinnati, O.**—Cincinnati stone, window No. 3. 102

19 **Finnegan, J. H., Cincinnati, O.**—Cincinnati stone, course No. 18. 102

20 **Montgomery, R. M., Youngstown, O.**—Sandstone, part of course No. 20. 102

21 **Caldwell & Tod, Youngstown, O.**—Stone from Tod quarry, part of course No. 20. 102

22 **Byers & McIlhainy, Youngstown, O.**—Stone from Youngstown, part of course No. 20. 102

23 **Mauser & Haid, Youngstown, O.**—Stone from Youngstown, part of course No. 20. 102

24 **Hamilton, Homer, Youngstown, O.**—Stone from Youngstown, part of course No. 20. 102

25 **Warthorst & Co., Massillon, O.**—Stone from Massillon, course No. 21. 102

26 **Stocking, Z. S., Mansfield, O.**—Red sandstone from Mansfield, two vestibule windows. 102

27 **Bosler, Marcus, Dayton, O.**—Dayton limestone, part of gable end and three windows. 102

28 **Huffman, Wm., Dayton, O.—Dayton** limestone, part of front gable and three windows. 102

29 **Diamond Glass Co., Ravenna, O.—** Double-thick glass, from ground white sandstone, in windows. 214

30 **American Inlaid Wood Co., Cleveland, O.—**Inlaid wood floor, ladies' parlor. 227

31 **Garry Iron Roofing Co., Cleveland, O.—**Sections of corrugated iron roof. 227

32 **American Sheet & Boiler Plate Co., Cleveland, O.—**Section iron roofing tile. 227

33 **House & Davidson, Cleveland, O.—** Pair front doors. 227

34 **Champion Fence Co., Kenton, O.—** —Wrought and malleable iron fence and gate. 283

35 **Buringer Bros., Dayton, O.—** Ohio coat of arms of galvanized iron, in gable. 291

36 **Heard & Sons, Cleveland, O.—** Architectural design of building. 441

No. 56½. CENTENNIAL POLICE STATION.

This building is situated immediately north of State Avenue and Hungarian Wine Pavilion, and is used as quarters, etc, of Centennial Guards.

No. 57. INDIANA STATE BUILDING.

Size, 50 feet by 42 feet.

A two-story frame building, on State Avenue, opposite the United States Government buildings, containing accommodations for the State Commissioners and for visitors from Indiana.

The exhibit consists of a chair made of one hundred different kinds of wood from one county. Specimens of block and coking and cannel coal; flag from natural bed of limestone; black walnut; model of Bailey gun, and a painting by Cox, of the Sierra Valley. The walls are occupied with panels, presenting in brief form the growth and industries of representative counties and cities. In the reading-room is a large map showing railroad system, with margin presenting agricultural and manufacturing statistics.

No. 57½. SPONGE FISHERS OF TURKEY.

This building contains an exhibit of sponge and fruit, situated on south side of Fountain Avenue, and north of Vermont State building and Turkish Café.

No. 58. ILLINOIS STATE BUILDING.

Architects, WHEELOCK & THOMAS.—Size, 60 feet by 40 feet.

Situated on State Avenue, north of the United States Government Buildings; the headquarters of the Illinois Commissioners.

No. 58½. BETHLEHEM BAZAAR.

Located on Fountain Avenue, adjoining Jerusalem Bazaar, and intended for sale of olive wood.

No. 59. WISCONSIN STATE BUILDING.

Size, 50 feet by 40 feet.

For the accommodation of the State Commissioners. Located on State Avenue, north of the United States Government Exhibition Buildings.

No. 59½. SCREW FOG-HORN AND BELL.

Situated at northwest corner of Belmont and State Avenues. Exhibit consists of one caloric engine, which pumps air for fog-horn; tank for air; and stationary engine.

No. 60. MICHIGAN STATE BUILDING.

Size, 48 feet by 53 feet.

On State Avenue; built of native woods and stone; interior with raised panel work; marble wainscoting; parquette floors, all highly finished. Contains reception, Commissioners', dressing, parcel, three reserve rooms, and ladies' parlor.

No. 61. NEW HAMPSHIRE STATE BUILDING.

Size, 30 feet by 40 feet; two projections, 9 feet by 15 feet each.

In the style of an Italian villa, two stories in height, and containing ten rooms, the roof protected by an awning and used for an outlook. This exhibit consists of views of White Mountains scenery, and home of General John Stark, the hero of Bennington.

No. 62. CONNECTICUT STATE BUILDING.

Architect, D. R. BROWN, from a design by DONALD G. MITCHELL.—Size, 30 feet by 40 feet.

This cottage is erected in the old Colonial style, somewhat modified, and is designed for the use of the citizens and exhibitors of the State of Connecticut. It is situated on State Avenue, not far distant from the United States Government Exhibition Buildings. Exhibit consists of the Royal Arms, which, before the revolution, hung above the Speaker's chair in the House of Representatives, at Hartford, painted in 1724. Rustic chess stand, ham, nutmegs, frames, etc., made from the wood of the Charter Oak. Ancient furniture, clock, tile, settee, etc., etc.

No. 63. MASSACHUSETTS STATE BUILDING.

Size, 85 feet by 56 feet.

Situated on State Avenue, opposite the New York State Building; is built of wood, two stories high, and contains offices and rooms for Commissioners and visitors.

No. 64. DELAWARE STATE BUILDING.

Size, 54 feet by 34 feet.

Built in the Swiss-Gothic style, from native woods of the State. It is occupied by the State Commissioners, the first floor being used for reception-rooms, while the second floor is devoted to business purposes. Is situated on State Avenue, north of the British Commission, opposite the New York State Commission.

No. 65. MARYLAND STATE BUILDING.

Size, 92 feet by 60 feet.

For the use of the State Commissioners and visitors. Situated on State Avenue, north of the British Government buildings, and is built of wood, two stories high. This exhibit consists of minerals, woods, building stone, specimens of art by pupils of Maryland Institute and School of Art and Design, portraits of Governors, three engines by Baltimore & Ohio Railroad, models of fish-house and hatching-house.

No. 67. JAPANESE DWELLING.

Architect, MATSUO-EHE, Tokio.—Size, 102 feet by 48 feet.

This building, usually called the Japanese Government Building, is intended as a dwelling-house for Japanese workmen. The wood and other articles that enter into its composition, and also the vases and flowers in the surrounding garden, were imported from Japan, and all the work has been done by Japanese artisans. It is situated south of the British buildings.

No. 68. WEST VIRGINIA STATE BUILDING.

Size, 115 feet by 40 feet.

Northwest of the Catholic Total Abstinence Fountain, built of wood, two stories high. Headquarters for State Commissioners and visitors from West Virginia. The exhibit consists of twenty pyramids of coal, mineral waters, ores, agricultural products, oils, tobacco, building stone, veneers, salt, glass, and a memorial shield made of seventy-eight varieties of wood, viz.:

Minerals, Ores, Stone, Mining Products.

1 Central Virginia Copper Mine, Virginia.—Copper ores, iron pyrites, and collection of minerals found on line of Chesapeake & Ohio Railroad. 100

2 Stack, I. I., Virginia.—Hematite ore. 100

3 Lancaster Furnace & Mining Co., Taylor county, West Va.—Carbonate of iron. 100

4 McCreery, W., Raleigh county, West Va.—Hematite ore. 100

5 Harvey, R. T., Putnam county, West Va.—Iron ore. 100

6 Dickinson, H., Pendleton county, West Va.—Hematite ore. 100

7 Miller, George, Pendleton county, West Va.—Hematite ores. 100

8 Boggs, J. C., Pendleton county, West Va.—Hematite ore. 100

9 Davis, Madam, Deneza, Pendleton county, West Va.—Hematite ores. 100

10 Garloe, A. E., Marion county, West Va.—Carbonate of iron. 100

11 Brown, T. L., Kanawha county, West Va.—Black band iron ore. 100

12 Hamilton, Jas., Jefferson county, West Va.—Barytes. 100

13 Melville, A. W., Jackson county, West Va.—Iron ore. 100

14 Bond, E., Harrison county, West Va.—Iron ore. 100

15 McMechen, S. A., Hardy county, West Va.—Iron ores. 100

16 Alexander, W. A., Greenbrier county, West Va.—Calc spar. 100

17 Lewis, F., & Co., Grant county, West Va.—Calc spar and iron ores. 100

18 Hill, Wm., Fayette county, West Va.—Iron ore. 100

19 Wilson, Lewis, Barbour county, West Va.—Carbonate of iron. 100

20 Stout, H. L., Phillippi, West Va.—Carbonate of iron. 100

21 Nickell, G. W., Greenbrier county, West Va.
- *a* Iron ore. 100
- *b* Coal. 100

22 Hovey, W. M., Kanawha county, West Va.
- *a* Iron ores. 100
- *b* Coals. 101

23 McLean, J. L., Putnam county, West Va.
- *a* Carbonate of iron. 100
- *b* Bituminous coal. 101

24 Great Western Mining & Manufacturing Co., Ky.
- *a* Iron ore. 100
- *b* Coal. 101

25 Boteler, A. R., Jefferson county, West Va.
- *a* Hematite ore. 100
- *b* Marble. 102

26 Ruffner, L., & Lewis, J. D., Kanawha county, West Va.
- *a* Black flint. 100
- *b* Building sandstone. 102

27 Armstrong, A., Taylor county, West Va.
- *a* Carbonate of iron. 100
- *b* Building sandstone. 102

28 Capon Iron Works, Hardy county, West Va.
- *a* Iron ores. 100
- *b* Limestone. 103

29 White, C. S., Hampshire county, West Va.
- *a* Iron ores. 100
- *b* White glass and sand. 104

30 Bloomery Iron Works, Hampshire county, West Va.
- *a* Iron ores. 100
- *b* Fire clay. 104

31 Shimp, Jas., Hardy county, West Va.
- *a* Iron ores. 100
- *b* Potters' clay. 104

32 Muenchmeyer, H. & L., Wood county, West Va.
- *a* Iron ore. 100
- *b* Potters' clay. 104

33 Cantley, R. K., Greenbrier county, Va.
- *a* Flint. 100
- *b* Semi-bituminous coal. 102
- *c* Limestone and silicious coral. 103

34 Kingwood Gas, Coal, & Iron Co., Preston county, West Va.
- *a* Carbonate of iron. 100
- *b* Coal. 101
- *c* Fire clay. 104

35 Clay, Cecil, Greenbrier county, West Va.
- *a* Iron ore. 100
- *b* Building sandstones. 102
- *c* Clay. 104
- *d* Mineral waters. 101

36 Elk River Iron & Coal Co., Braxton county, West Va.
- *a* Iron ore. 100
- *b* Limestone. 103
- *c* Sandstone for furnaces. 104

37 Mendenhall, U., Morgan county, West Va.
- *a* Hematite ore. 100
- *b* Limestone. 103
- *c* White glass sand. 104

38 Willey, W. T., Monongahela county, West Va.
- *a* Iron ores. 100
- *b* Coals. 101
- *c* Building sandstone. 102
- *d* Limestone. 103
- *e* Fire clay. 104

39 Peterkin, G. G., Greenbrier county, West Va.
- *a* Iron ores and black oxide of manganese. 100
- *b* Mineral waters. 107

40 Johnson, J. F., Pendleton county, West Va.
- *a* Hematite ores. 100
- *b* Mineral water. 107

41 Dulin, C., Wirt county, West Va.—Petroleum. 101

42 Volcano Oil & Coal Co., Wood county, West Va.—Bituminous coal. 101

43 Hale & Porter, Wirt county, West Va.—Petroleum. 101

44 Aspenwall & Low, Wayne county, West Va.—Cannel coal. 101

45 Ferguson, Waye, Wayne county, West Va.—Bituminous and cannel coal. 101

46 Barnes, J. H., Taylor county, West Va.—Bituminous coal. 101

47 McGreggor, Dr., Ritchie county, West Va.—Petroleum and Ritchie mineral. 101

48 Beckley, A., Raleigh county, West Va.—Bituminous coal. 101

49 Prince, G. H., Raleigh county, West Va.—Bituminous coal. 101

50 Raymond Coal Co., Putnam county, West Va.—Bituminous coal. 101

51 Austen Coal Co., Preston county, West Va.—Coal and coke. 101

52 Hill, M. L, Ohio county, West Va.— Bituminous coal. 101

53 Virginia Coal Co., Mineral county, West Va.—Semi-bituminous coal. 101

54 Hartford City Coal & Salt Co., Mason county, West Va.—Bituminous coal. 101

55 Gaston Coal Mines, Marion county, West Va.—Gas coal. 101

56 Aspinwall & Low, Lincoln county, West Va.—Coal. 101

57 Falling Rock Coal Co., Kanawha county, West Va.—Cannel coal. 101

58 Lewis, J. D., Kanawha county, West Va.—Coal. 101

59 Enterprise Coal Co., Kanawha county, West Va.—Splint coal. 101

60 Kanawha Semi-Cannel Coal Co., West Va.—Coal. 101

61 Mill Creek Cannel Coal Co., Kanawha county, West Va.—Cannel coal. 101

62 Lewiston Coal Co., Kanawha county, West Va.—Coal. 101

63 Monongahela Gas Coal Co., Harrison county, West Va.—Gas coal. 101

64 Despard Gas Coal Co., Harrison county, West Va.—Gas coal. 101

65 Murphy's Run Coal Mine, Harrison county, West Va.—Gas coal. 101

66 Letterman, W. H., Fayette county, West Va.—Bituminous coal. 101

67 Cole, B., Fayette county, West Va.— Bituminous coal. 101

68 Coal Valley Coal Co., Fayette county, West Va.—Gas coal. 101

69 Gauley, ——, Kanawha Coal Co., Fayette county, West Va.—Coal and coke. 101

70 Longdale Coal & Iron Co., Fayette county, West Va.—Coal and coke. 101

71 Nuttallberg Coal Co., Fayette county, West Va.—Coal and coke. 101

72 Stanton Rock Coal Co., Brooke county, West Va.—Bituminous coal. 101

73 Brown, T. L., Boone county, West Va.—Cannel coal. 101

74 Peytona Cannel Coal Co., Boone county, West Va.—Cannel coal. 101

75 Ball, A., Boone county, West Va.— Cannel coal. 101

76 Corrathers, L., Taylor county, West Va.

a Cannel coal. 101
b Fire clay. 104

77 Radcliff, R. S., Marion county, West Va.

a Bituminous coal. 101
b Limestone. 103

78 Hall, W. W., Pleasants county, West Va.

a Petroleum. 101
b Brine. 107

79 Boggs Run Mining Co., Ohio county, West Va.

a Bituminous coal. 101
b Building sandstone. 102
c Limestones. 103

80 Hudson, J. & D., Hancock county, West Va.

a Bituminous coal. 101
b Building sandstone. 102
c Limestone. 103

81 Browse, R. H., Pleasants county, West Va.—Building sandstone. 102

82 Waddle, J. & M., Ohio county, West Va.—Building sandstone. 102

83 Osborne, J., Monroe county, West Va.—Marble. 102

84 Camden, P. B., Lewis county, West Va.—Building sandstone. 102

85 Rall, R., Jefferson county, West Va. —White marble. 102

86 Strider, S. W., Jefferson county, West Va.—Black marble. 102

87 Strider, J. S., Jefferson county, West Va.—Black and white marble. 102

88 Withrow, Jas., Greenbrier county, West Va.—Marbles. 102

89 Miller, J. H., Fayette county, West Va.—Building sandstone. 102

90 Lanham, Gabriel, Taylor county, West Va.

a Building sandstone. 102
b Limestone. 103

91 Laidley, J. B., Cabell county, West Va.

a Building sandstone. 102
b Brine. 107

92 Lanham, Zadock, Taylor county, West Va.—Limestone. 103

93 Gwinn, M., Summers county, West Va.—Hydraulic limestone. 103

94 Lang, A. J., Ohio county, West Va. —Hydraulic limestone and cement. 103

95 Thompson, O. D., Ohio county, West Va.—Hydraulic limestone. 103

96 Wells, J., Ohio county, West Va. —Limestone. 103

97 Potomac Cement Mills, Jefferson county, West Va. — Hydraulic limestone and cement. 103

98 Mann, M., Greenbrier county, West Va.—Limestone. 103

99 Donnaghe, A. P., Wood county, West Va.—Potters' clay. 104

100 Pickering, N. A., Wirt county, West Va.—Potters' clay. 104

101 Johnson, D. D., Tyler county, West Va.—Fire clay. 104

102 Glade Fire Brick Co., Marion county, West Va.—Fire clay. 104

103 Wolfe, A., Hardy county, West Va. —White glass sand. 104

104 Wells, N., Brooke county, West Va.—Potters' clay. 104

105 Williamson, J. R., Barbour county, West Va.—White sand for glass. 104

106 Seatt, J., Raleigh county, West Va. —Millstone rock. 106

107 Sawtall, G., Ohio county, West Va. —Whetstones. 106

108 Simpson, I. E., Wood county, West Va.—Mineral water. 107

109 Sweet Chalybeate Springs county, West Va.—Mineral water. 107

110 Kanawha Salt Co., Kanawha county, West Va.—Brines and bitterns. 107

111 Alexander, E. S. & M. S., Hardy county, West Va.—White sulphur water. 107

112 **Duffy, J. W., Hardy county, West** Va.—Sulpho-chalybeate water. 107

113 **Parrow, N. D., Hardy county,** West Va.—Mineral waters. 107

114 **Peyton, G. L., & Co., Greenbrier** county, West Va.—Mineral water. 107

115 **Humphreys, A. R., Greenbrier** county, West Va.—White sulphur water. 107

116 **McPherson, Joel, Greenbrier** county, West Va.—Mineral water. 107

117 **Williams, J. V., Grant county,** West Va.—Calcareous marl. 107

Metallurgical Products.

118 **Capon Iron Works, Hardy county,** West Va.—Slag, bloom, wrought iron and cold blast charcoal iron. 111

119 **Bloomery Iron Works, Hampshire** county, West Va.—Cold blast charcoal iron. 111

120 **Elk River Iron & Coal Co., Braxton** county, West Va.—Slag and cold blast charcoal iron. 111

Chemical Manufactures.

121 **Kanawha Salt Co., Kanawha** county, West Va.—Salt. 200

122 **Sharp & Staples, Wood county,** West Va.—Lubricating and refined oils. 201

123 **Camden Consolidated Oil Co.,** Wood county, West Va.—Oils. 201

124 **Lerner, H., Mason county, West** Va.—Bromine. 201

125 **Hale, E. W., Wirt county, West** Va.—Parmenter oil. 201

126 **Smith, P. P., Lewis county, West** Va.—Yellow ochre. 202

127 **Boteler, A. R., Jefferson county,** West Va.—Yellow ochre. 202

128 **Scott, H., Hardy county, West** Va.—Yellow ochre. 202

129 **Fisher, W., Hardy county, West** Va.—Yellow ochre. 202

130 **Wood, A. M., Hardy county, West** Va.—Yellow ochre. 202

131 **Peters, W. L., Cabell county, West** Va.—Mineral paint. 202

Ceramics—Pottery, Porcelain, Glass.

132 **Glade Fire-brick Co., Marion** county, West Va.—Fire brick. 207

133 **Donnaghe, A. P., Wood county,** West Va.—Crockery. 210

Furniture and Objects of General Use in Construction and in Dwellings.

134 **Schafer B., Wood county, West** Va.—Patent office desks. 217

Fabrics of Vegetable, Animal, or Mineral Materials.

135 **Robson, Mary E., Fayette county,** West Va.—Basket. 289

Educational Systems, Methods, and Libraries.

136 **Gray, W., Marshall county, West** Va.—Schoolwork of Bunwood Public School, Marshall county, West Va. 300

137 **Young, J., Mason county, West** Va.—Schoolwork of Mason county public schools. 300

138 **McGreggor, Dr., Ritchie county,** West Va.—Schoolwork of Ritchie county public schools. 300

139 **Staley, T. J., Tyler county, West** Va.—Work from Buckhannon public school. 300

140 **Radcliff, R. S., Marion county,** West Va.—Schoolwork of Fairmount public schools, Marion county. 300

141 **Ruffner, L., & Lewis, J. D., Kanawha** county, West Va.—Schoolwork of public schools, Charleston, Kanawha county. 300

Engineering, Architecture, Maps, etc.

142 **Johnson, H. H., Hampshire county,** West Va.—Embossed maps of the United States and West Virginia, for use of the blind. 335

Sculpture.

143 **Crawford, G. B., Brooke county,** West Va.—Ornamental bracket of native woods. 405

144 **Doddridge Music & Art School,** Wheeling, West Va.—Oil paintings. 410

145 **Henderson, D. E., Jefferson** county, West Va.—Oil painting. 410

Photography.

146 **Donnaghe, A. P., Wood county,** West Va.—Photograph of Burning Spring school. 430

147 **Pickering, N. A., Wirt county,** West Va.—Photograph of Elizabeth High School. 430

148 **City of Wheeling, West Va.**—Photographic views of free schools. 430

149 **Lerner, H., Mason county, West** Va.—Photograph of Clifton public school. 430

150 **Kanawha Salt Co., Kanawha** county, West Va.—Photograph of Union public school, Charleston, Kanawha county. 430

151 **Turner, G. H., Jefferson county,** West Va.—Photograph of Shepperd College, Jefferson county. 430

152 **Bloomery Iron Works, Hampshire** county, West Va.—Photograph of Deaf, Dumb, and Blind Asylum, Hampshire county. 430

153 **Peters, W. L., Cabell county, West** Va.—Photograph of Marshall College. 430

154 **Wells, N., Brooke county, West** Va.—Photograph of public schools. 430

Aerial, Pneumatic, and Water Transportation.

155 **Young, J., Mason county, West** Va.—Model of steamboat. 595

Arboriculture and Forest Products.

156 **Kyle, Henry, Wetzel county, West** Va.—Sections of woods. 600

157 **Peterson, W. F., Wetzell county,** West Va.—Sections of wood. 600

158 **Johnson, D. D., Tyler county, West** Va.—Timber. 600

159 **Armstrong, A., Taylor county,** West Va.—Timber. 600

160 McCreery, W., Raleigh county, West Va.—Samples of timber. 600

161 Beckley, A., Raleigh county, West Va.—Cross sections of timber. 600

162 Prince, G. H., Raleigh county, West Va.—Woods. 600

163 Dall & Callaway, Putnam county, West Va.—Stakes and hoop poles. 600

164 Browse, R. H., Pleasants county, West Va.—Specimens of woods. 500

165 Banjoy, N. I., Pendleton county, West Va.—Laurel wreath and vine. 600

166 Hammer, B., Pendleton county, West Va.—Section of locust wood. 600

167 Hammer, Jacob, Pendleton county, West Va.—Sections of wild cherry and yellow pine. 600

168 Johnson, J. F., Pendleton county, West Va.—Sections of various woods. 600

169 Mestrezall, W., Monongahela county, West Va.—Walnut board. 600

170 Fairchild, Lawhead, & Co., Monongahela county, West Va. — Woods used in wagon building. 600

171 Ruffner, L., & Lewis, J. D., Kanawha county, West Va. — Cross sections of twenty-one varieties of timber. 600

172 McKnight & Rohrer, Jefferson county, West Va.—Axe handles and felloes. 600

173 Clay, Cecil, Greenbrier county, West Va.—Specimens of woods. 600

174 Letterman, W. H., Fayette county, West Va.—Samples of woods. 600

175 Heald, D., Fayette county, West Va.—Molasses hogshead shook. 600

176 Guard, Jas., Fayette county, West Va.—White oak stave. 600

177 Abbott, J. M., Fayette county, West Va.—Holly. 600

178 Cassady, R. B., Fayette county, West Va.—Maple. 600

179 Miller, J. H., Fayette county, West Va.—Woods. 600

180 Sinsel, J. B., Fayette county, West Va.—Samples of ash. 600

181 Elk River Iron & Coal Co., Braxton county, West Va.—Charcoal. 600

182 Brown, S. H., Fayette county, West Va.—Veneers. 601

183 Peters, W. L., Cabell county, West Va.—Poplar boards, polished. 601

Agricultural Products.

184 Leigh, Wm., Berkeley county, West Va.—Corn. 620

185 Downer, J. E., Cabell county, West Va.—Corn on stalk. 620

186 Settle, J. G., Fayette county, West Va.

a Wheat, buckwheat, and corn. 620
b Tobacco. 623

187 Marrs, John, Fayette county, West Va.—Oats. 620

188 Robson, H. A., Fayette county, West Va.—Corn. 620

189 Blake, L., Fayette county, West Va.—Corn. 620

190 Dickinson, M., Fayette county, West Va.—Corn. 620

191 Rice, J. P., Harrison county, West Va.—Wheat. 620

192 Bartlett, P. W., Harrison county, West Va.—Wheat. 620

193 Rider, B. D., Harrison county, West Va.—Corn, wheat, oats and buckwheat. 620

194 Bartlett & Riley, Harrison county, West Va.—Wheat. 620

195 Green, R. H., Harrison county, West Va.—Wheat. 620

196 Waters, G., Harrison county, West Va.—Corn. 620

197 Hickman, J., Harrison county, West Va.—Corn. 620

198 Bassett, D., Harrison county, West Va.—Wheat and corn. 620

199 Morrison, D., Harrison county, West Va.—Corn. 620

200 Sayre, J., Jackson county, West Va.—Corn. 620

201 Hopkins, A. D., Jackson county, West Va.—Wheat. 620

202 Fisher, J. W., Gilmer county, West Va.—Corn. 620

203 Wilson, H., Hardy county, West Va.—Oats. 620

204 Bean, Peter, Hardy county, West Va.—Buckwheat. 620

205 McNeal, R., Hardy county, West Va.—Corn. 620

206 Maslin, Thos., Hardy county, West Va.—Corn. 620

207 Williams, G. P., Hardy county, West Va.—Wheat. 620

208 Bean, J., Hardy county, West Va.—Oats and wheat. 620

209 Handley, H., Greenbrier county, West Va.—Oats, corn, timothy, orchard grass, and orchard grass seed. 620

210 Alexander, W. A., Greenbrier county, West Va.—Wheat. 620

211 Koontz, G., Jefferson county, West Va.—Corn. 620

212 Turner, G. H., Jefferson county, West Va.—Wheat. 620

213 Flemming, R. E., Marion county, West Va.—Corn and wheat. 620

214 Gray, W., Marshall county, West Va.—Corn on stalk. 620

215 Waddle, J. & M., Ohio county, West Va.—Corn. 620

216 Wilson, G. W., Ohio county, West Va.—Corn. 620

217 Dyer, J. P., Pendleton county, West Va.—Corn. 620

218 Cunningham, S., Pendleton county, West Va.—Corn. 620

219 Millar, Wm. C., Pendleton county, West Va.—Wheat. 620

220 Harris, T. M., Ritchie county, West Va.—Corn. 620

221 Browse, R. H., Pleasants county, West Va.—Corn and wheat. 620

222 Williams, J. S., Taylor county, West Va.—Corn and wheat. 620

223 Riley, John, Taylor county, West Va.—Wheat. 620

224 Sheppard, L., Wirt county, West Va.—Corn. 220

225 Settle, W., Fayette county, West Va.

a Corn. 620
b Tobacco. 623

226 Dempsey, J. E., Fayette county, West Va.
a Wheat, corn, oats, and timothy. 620
b Tobacco. 623

227 Harvey, William T., Fayette county, West Va.
a Rye, wheat, and corn. 620
b Tobacco. 623

228 Hashbarger, A. P., Fayette county, West Va.
a Oats. 620
b Tobacco. 623

229 Sinclair, G. W., Taylor county, West Va.—Beans. 621

230 Keesey, I. B., Fayette county, West Va.—Laurel root. 622

231 O'Neal, Cheuvront, & Co., Doddridge county, West Va.—Tobacco. 623

232 Crager, Joe, Fayette county, West Va.—Tobacco. 623

233 Cassady, R. B., Fayette county, West Va.—Tobacco. 623

234 Nugen, J., Fayette county, West Va.—Tobacco. 623

235 Braughan, J. J., Fayette county, West Va.—Tobacco. 623

236 Carter, W., Fayette county, West Va.—Tobacco. 623

237 Dempsey, J. A., Fayette county, West Va.—Tobacco. 623

238 Ballard, G. W., Lewis county, West Va.—Tobacco. 623

239 Johnson, D. D., Taylor county, West Va.—Tobacco. 623

240 Staley, T. J., Tyler county, West Va.—Tobacco. 623

241 Seamon, H., Wheeling, West Va.—Tobacco and cigars. 623

Animal and Vegetable Products.

242 Oschbacher, John, & Son, Wood county, West Va.—Grape wine. 660

243 Muenchmeyer, H. & L., Wood county, West Va.—Grape wine. 660

Textile Substances of Vegetable or Animal Origin.

244 Browse, R. H., Pleasants county, West Va.—Flax. 666

245 Settle, J. G., Fayette county, West Va.—Flax. 666

No. 69. CANADIAN LOG HOUSE.

Size, 75 feet by 56 feet.

CANADIAN COMMISSION.

See Part IV., page 134.

Is one story high, constructed of logs, and located close by the British Government buildings. It constitutes an exhibit of the timbers of Canada.

No. 70. MISSOURI STATE BUILDING.

Architect, L. C. MILLER, St. Louis.—Size, 58 feet by 48 feet, with tower.

Location, State Avenue, George's Hill. Headquarters of Board of State Centennial Managers, organized by State Legislature; President, Thomas Allen; Secretary, J. L. Tracy. Exhibits in Main Hall, Education Department, Mineral Annex, Agricultural Hall.

Nos. 71, 72, 73. BRITISH GOVERNMENT BUILDINGS.

Architect, THOMAS HARRIS, of London.—Size, No. 1, 5000 sup. feet; No. 2, 1200 sup. feet.

These edifices have been erected for the use of the members of the Royal Commission. The large one is the residence of the Commissioners and delegates, while the smaller furnishes accommodations for the members of the staff. They are built in a picturesque, half-timbered style, essentially English, and are located north of Machinery Hall. A bake-house and laundry are also attached to the above.

No. 74. NEW YORK STATE BUILDING.

Architects, CROFF & CAMP.—Size, 60 feet by 34 feet.

The Commissioners of the State of New York have offices in this building. It is a two-story structure, surrounded by about half an acre of ground. It is situated on State Avenue, north of the British buildings.

No. 75. COLONEL LIENARD'S GEORAMA.

Designer, COL. LIENARD, Paris.—Size, area 1250 square feet.

An open-air exhibit, models of the cities of Paris and Jerusalem, in gypsum. The contour of the ground is shown, and the streets appear fully delineated. It is in the centre of Fountain Avenue, at the head of the lake.

No. 76. POP-CORN BUILDINGS.

Architects, H. J. SCHWARZMANN, HUGH KAFKA.—Size, 41 feet by 32 feet each.
J. A. BAKER, Dayton, Ohio.

One of these buildings is situated on Fountain Avenue opposite the northern extremity of the lake; the other is on Agricultural Avenue, east of and opposite the New England Farmers' Home and Modern Kitchen. They are devoted exclusively to the sale of pop-corn, and are built of wood, one story high.

No. 77. CIGAR STANDS.

The stands are located at various points north of the Avenue of the Republic, and west of Belmont Avenue.

No. 78. SODA WATER STANDS.

These stands are situated at various points north of the Avenue of the Republic, and west of Belmont Avenue.

No. 79. TUNISIAN CAFÉ AND BAZAAR.

A decorated pavilion with stained glass windows, designed for the display of Tunisian products. Situated on Fountain Avenue, north of Pennsylvania State building.

No. 80. CHRISTOPHER COLUMBUS MONUMENT.

Located at corner of Belmont and Fountain Avenues. It was erected by the Columbus Monument Association. It is of colossal size, and represents the Genoese navigator in a standing posture, with the right hand resting on a globe, and the left holding a chart; an anchor and rope indicating his occupation.

No. 81. DRINKING FOUNTAIN.

Size, 25 feet in diameter.
Erected by the SONS OF TEMPERANCE of Pennsylvania.

This fountain is built of wood, the structure inclosing it being circular in form, and it is situated at the junction of Fountain and Belmont Avenues. The Singer & Talcott drinking fountain is a marble fountain situated between the Bethlehem Bazaar and Tunisian Café.

No. 82. "TROIS FRÈRES PROVENÇAUX" RESTAURANT.

Architect, LEHMAN, of Paris.—Size, 177 feet by 110 feet.
LOUIS GOYARD, Proprietor.

A two-story frame structure, situated on the corner of Belmont and Fountain Avenues. It has large garden surroundings, and is a duplicate of the restaurant of the same name in Paris as regards its management.

No. 83. NEW YORK "TRIBUNE" BUILDING.

Architect, E. E. RATH.—Size, 30 feet by 21 feet.
NEW YORK TRIBUNE, New York.

A small octagonal wooden building, with verandas and a high tower-like roof. It is located close to the French Restaurant and the lake, and is used as an office for the correspondents and reporters of "The Tribune."

No. 84. WORLD'S TICKET OFFICE.

Architect, H. J. SCHWARZMANN.—Size, 60 feet square.
COOK, SON & JENKINS, London, New York, and Philadelphia.

Situated immediately north of the eastern end of Machinery Hall. It is hexagonal in form, and contains a main hall and four private offices. Tickets to all parts of the world are offered for sale, and ornamental articles manufactured in Palestine are exhibited.

No. 85. PRESSED FUEL COMPANY'S BUILDING.

Polygon, 24 feet in diameter.

E. F. LOISEAU, Philadelphia.

Constructed of iron and situated in a garden plot on the Avenue of the Republic, west of the lake and opposite to Machinery Hall. It exhibits the fuel in a state of combustion, to demonstrate its economy and adaptability.

No. 86. SPANISH GOVERNMENT BUILDING.

Decagonal, 50 feet in diameter.

A one-story frame building, situated on the Avenue of the Republic, west of the Catholic Total Abstinence Fountain. Intended as headquarters of the Spanish soldiers.

86½. SPANISH EXHIBITION BUILDING.

Architect, ALEXANDER B. BARY.—Size, 80 feet by 100 feet.

Constructed of wood, in a style similar to Machinery Hall; adjacent to Spanish Engineers' Pavilion.

Educational Systems, Methods, and Libraries.

1 **Goig & Co., Jaime, Alcira, Province of Valencia.**—Books for primary instruction. 300

2 **Rodriguez Mañanes, Pedro, Zamora.**—Explanation of engravings and patterns for cutting garments. 300

3 **Fábregas y Bru, José, Havana, Island of Cuba.**—Writing desk. 300

4 **Superior Normal School, Salamanca.**—Programme for children's schools. 300

5 **Illera y Marúz, Manuel, Salamanca.**—Rational programme for lectures in normal school. 300

6 **Rodriguez Martin, Vicente, Sequeros, Province of Salamanca.**—Lineal designs. 300

7 **Sanchez, Pilar, Sevilla.—Objects for** the instruction of children. 300

8 **Board of Primary Instruction, Vitoria, Province of Alava.**—Treatise on primary instruction. 300

9 **Azpiazu, José Antonio de, Vitoria,** Province of Alava.—Method of penmanship. 300

10 **Solano y Viton, Pablo, Valencia.**—Books for primary instruction. 300

11 **Aguilar, Simon, Valencia.—Books** for primary instruction. 300

12 **Solis, Prudencio, Valencia.—Books** for primary instruction. 300

13 **Perales, Baltasar, Valencia.—Books** for primary instruction. 300

14 **Montells y Nadal, Jacinto, Sevilla.**—Books for primary instruction. 300

15 **Gazapo y Loma, Juan Manuel, Madrid.**—Syllable book. 300

16 **Collado, Cayetano, Madrid.—Intuitive** instruction. 300

17 **Borja y Alarcon, Pedro, Madrid.**—Geographical stick. 300

18 **Ladies' Seminary, Madrid.—Work** by pupils, and writing by the professors. 300

19 **Molinero, Enrique, Madrid.—Alphabets.** 300

20 **Gonzalez y Luna, Ildefonso, Jaen.**—Specimen of penmanship. 300

21 **Diaz y Martinez, Manuel, Jerez de la** Frontera, Province of Cádiz.—Apparatus for primary instruction. 300

22 **College of Messrs. Peffort, Barcelona.**—Work done by pupils. 300

23 **National Institute for the Deaf and** Dumb, and Blind, Madrid.—Method of instruction. 303

24 **Nebreda y Lopez, Cárlos, Madrid.**—Works for the instruction of the deaf and dumb, and blind. 302

25 **Institute for the Deaf and Dumb,** and Blind, Sevilla.—Documents of the college. 302

26 **Campillo y Correa, Narciso, Madrid.**—Rhetoric and poetry. 306

27 **Cornellas y Grau, Clemente, Madrid.**—French grammar, etc. 306

28 **Escolapios of San Antonio, Madrid.**—Books. 306

29 **García Ayuso, Francisco, Madrid.**—Arabian grammar, study of philology, etc. 306

30 **Garriga Marrill, Pedro, Madrid.**—Tachigraphy. 306

31 **Giol y Soldevilla, Isidro, Madrid.**—Course of photography 306

32 **Galdo, Manuel María José de, Madrid.**—Manual of natural history. 306

33 **Institute of Secondary Instruction** of San Isidro, Madrid.—Memoirs. 306

34 **Martinez Cubells, Enrique, Madrid.**—Lessons in geometry. 306

35 **Montero Montero, Antonio, Madrid.**—Programmes, catalogues, etc., of the polytechnic school. 306

36 **Monreal y Ascaso, Bernardo, Madrid.**—Course of geography, and history of Spain. 306

37 **Moya, Ambrosio, Madrid.—Lessons** in arithmetic. 306

38 **National Library, Madrid.—Books** published, and awarded works. 306

39 **Institute of Secondary Instruction** of the Noviciate, Madrid.—Complete collection of memoirs. 306

40 **Pereda y Martinez, Sandalio de, Madrid.**—Programme of natural history. 306

41 **Puerta, Gabriel de la, Madrid.**—Treatise on chemistry, medicine, etc. 306

42 Ramos Lafuente, Madrid.—Text-book for instruction in natural and physico-chemical sciences. 306

43 Salvador y Aznar, Felipe, Madrid.—Manual of book-keeping, etc. 306

44 Suaña y Castellet, Emeterio, Madrid.—Course of Latin. 306

45 Sanchez Casado, Félix, Madrid.—Bachelor's guide. 306

46 Fernandez Cardin, Joaquin María, Madrid.—Elements of mathematics. 306

47 Vallin y Bustillo, Acisclo F., Madrid.—Text-books of secondary instruction. 306

48 Vicuña, Gumersindo, Madrid.—Facultative works. 306

49 Institute of Secondary Instruction, Pamplona, Province of Navarra.—Memoirs, catalogues, plans, etc. 306

50 Literary University, Oviedo.—Books. 306

51 Institute of Secondary Instruction, Palencia.—Memoirs and treatises. 306

52 Literary University, Salamanca.—Memoirs, catalogues, discourses, etc. 306

53 Institute, Santander.—Books, speeches, catalogues, and photographs. 306

54 Menendez & Pintado, Marcelino, Santander.—Geometrical album. 306

55 Institute, Segovia.—Text-books. 306

56 Literary University, Sevilla.—Opening speeches. 306

57 Loscos, Francisco, Castelseras, Province of Teruel.—Herbarium for the study of botany. 306

58 Respaldiza, Domingo, Valladolid.—Books. 306

59 García Arboleya, José, Havana, Island of Cuba.—Logarithm tables. 306

60 Cerero, Rafael, Havana, Island of Cuba.—Treatise on the science of engineering. 306

61 Nautical School, Barcelona.—Text-books of the Director. 306

62 Fine Art School, Barcelona.—Programmes of instruction. 306

63 School of Industrial Engineers, Barcelona.—Tables and projects. 306

64 Cornet y Mas, Cayetano, Barcelona.—Compendium of Spanish tachigraphy. 306

65 Briz, Francisco Pelayo, Barcelona.—Collection of popular songs. 306

66 Miralles & Peris, Manuel, Barcelona.—Plan of studies in a mercantile college. 306

67 Veterinary School, Leon.—Memoirs dedicated to the Exhibition at Philadelphia. 306

68 Faculty of Medicine, Madrid.—Works. 306

69 Mata y Fontanet, Pedro, Madrid.—Medical works and treatises. 306

70 Cabello y Aso, Luis, Madrid.—Architectural essays and works. 306

71 Grande, José María, Madrid.—Works on singing. 306

72 Master of San Juan, Aureliano, Madrid.—Treatise on general anatomy. 306

73 Busto y Lopez, Andrés, Madrid.—Chirurgical pathology. 306

74 Quijano, Lopez, Cárlos, Madrid.—Treatise on chirurgical operations. 306

75 Cortejarena & Aldebó, Francisco de, Madrid.—Manual of obstetrics. 306

76 Sanchez y Merino, Ramon, Madrid,—General treatise on fevers. 306

77 Santero y Moreno, Tomás, Madrid.—Medical clinic. 306

78 Fernandez de Figares, Manuel, Granada.—Manual of experimental physics. 306

79 Local Institute of Secondary Instruction, Baeza, Province of Jaen.—Photographs of its interior and exterior. 306

80 Mingote, Policarpo, Leon.—Course of geography. 306

81 Ruiz de la Peña, Francisco, Leon.—Latin translation, grammatical system, etc. 306

82 Prieto, Anastasio, Logroño.—Regulation for the Normal School. 306

83 Saenz Navarrete, José, Logrono.—Documents referring to the foundation and progress of his college. 306

84 Royal Academy, Madrid.—Collection of its works. 306

85 Carreras, Mariano, Madrid.—Political economy. 306

86 Fernandez de Castro, Manuel, Madrid.—Treatise on electricity, metallurgy, etc. 306

87 Cortázar, Daniel, Madrid.—Treatise on mathematics. 306

88 Comeleran, Francisco A., Madrid.—Treatise on the Latin language. 306

89 Chamorro, Rafael, Madrid.—System of explaining heat, light, electricity, etc. 306

90 Page, Eugenio Roman, Badajoz.—Register of property. 306

91 Graells, Francisco, Barcelona.—Geometric books. 306

92 Magza y Jaime, Juan, Barcelona.—Elementary treatise on physiology. 306

93 Superior Normal School of Masters, Barcelona.—Books. 306

94 Fernandez Fontecha, Francisco, Cádiz.—Course of astronomy and navigation. 306

95 Foly y Velasco, Federico, Cádiz.—Text-books. 306

96 Oferrall, Javier, Cádiz.—French selections. 306

97 Moreno y Espinosa, Alfonso, Cádiz.—Compendium of universal history. 306

98 Rubio y Diaz, Vicente, Cádiz.—Elements of mathematics. 306

99 Literary University, Santiago, Province of La Coruña.—Books. 306

100 Pimentel y Donaire, Miguel, Madrid.—Legislative collection on primary instruction. 306

101 Vilella y Font, Sebastian, Madrid.—Fables of Fedro. 306

102 Saco y Arce, Juan A., Orense.—Grammar. 306

103 Lasala Martinez, Atanasio, Orense.—Elements of arithmetic and algebra. 306

104 Gaité Nuñez, Joaquin, Orense.—Elements of arithmetic and geography. 306

105 Luciro Gonzalez, Juan, Orense.—Works on philosophy. 306

106 Antiguedad, Celestino, Palencia.—Books on primary instruction. 306

107 Normal School, Palencia.—Books on primary instruction. 306

108 Flores Arrate, Leon, Palencia.—Writing books. 306

109 School of Music & Recitation, Madrid.—Memoirs. 306

110 Direction of Customs, Madrid.—Statistics. 306

111 Romero y Andia, Antonio, Madrid.—Musical instruction. 306

112 Lopez Almagro, Antonio, Madrid.—Method of playing the harmonium. 306

113 Gil y Justo Moné, Juan, Madrid.—Method of melodies. 306

114 Marzo y Feo, Enrique, Madrid.—Method of playing the hoboe. 306

115 Mata, Manuel de la, Madrid.—Method of playing the piano. 306

116 Nuñez Robres, Lázaro, Madrid.—The music of the people. 306

117 Ayllon, Rafael, Madrid.—Musical works. 306

118 Borrell, Mariano, Madrid.—Arts and industry. 306

119 Rebolledo, José A., Madrid.—Treatise on construction of houses, etc. 306

120 Novoa y Lopez, Angel, Pontevedra.—The pontifical infallibility. 306

121 Barrios, Cándido, Madrid.—Works on artillery. 306

122 School of Engineers of Highways, Canals, & Ports, Madrid.—Works. 306

123 School of Mountain Engineers, San Lorenza del Escorial, Province of Madrid.—Memoirs of the school. 306

124 Corps of Engineers, Madrid.—Books, memoirs, and projects. 306

125 School of Mining Engineers, Madrid.—Books. 306

126 Veterinary School, Madrid.—Books and pictures. 306

127 High School of Architecture, Madrid.—Books, catalogues, and designs. 306

128 Conservatory of Arts, School of Commerce, etc., Madrid.—Memoirs, books, designs, studies, etc. 306

129 Gonzalez Hidalgo, Joaquin, Madrid.—Scientific works on natural history. 306

130 Llorente y Lázaro, Ramon, Madrid.—Compendium of the bibliography of Spanish veterinary system. 306

131 Ramirez, Concepçion, Madrid.—Treatise on the penal code. 306

132 Magaz, Juan, Madrid.—Elementary treatise on human physiology. 306

133 Seco Baldor, José, Madrid.—Study of the cholera of past centuries. 306

134 Calleja Sanchez, Julian, Madrid.—Scientific anatomy. 306

135 Bailly Baillière, Cárlos, Madrid.—Catalogues of the museums and laboratories of the medical faculty. 306

136 Gastaldo, José, Madrid.—Cataract and its treatment. 306

137 Jareño de Alarcon, Francisco, Madrid.—Models and plans of the principal schools. 306

138 Calvo y Pereyra, Mariano, Madrid.—Architectural works. 306

139 Elizalde, José Antonio, Madrid.—Course of descriptive geometry. 306

140 Vallin y Bustillo, Acisclo, F., Madrid.—Theory of unknown quantities. 306

141 Rodriguez, Eduardo, Madrid.—Manual of general physics. 306

142 Maldonado Macanaz, Joaquin, Madrid.—General principles of the art of colonization. 306

143 Gonzalez Marti, Manuel, Madrid.—Manual of the infantry service. 306

144 Arsenal, Madrid.—Military works. 306

145 Mechanics'Athenæum, Tarragona.—Rules. 306

146 Society "Centra de Lecturo," Reus, Province of Tarragona.—Memoirs and rules. 306

147 Gonzalez Hidalgo, Joaquin, Madrid.—Works on the mollusks of Spain, Portugal, and the Pacific. 306

148 García Maceira, Antonio, Zamora.—Treatise on the sugar cane. 306

149 Literary University, Granada.—Anatomical treatise. 306

150 Board of Agriculture, Industry, & Commerce, Oviedo.—Memoirs of the Asturian exhibition, 1863. 305

151 Gonzalez Domingo, Cecilio, Salamanca.—Invitations for the Exhibition at Philadelphia. 306

152 Cuevas, José Alfonso, Játiva, Province of Valencia.—Synoptic table of the history of Spain. 306

153 Normal School, Toledo.—Works on teaching. 306

154 Normal School, Valencia.—Works on teaching. 306

155 Casan Alegre, Joaquin, Valencia.—Universal history. 306

156 Ollero, Andrés F., Valencia.—Descriptive geography and domestic economy. 306

157 Hernandez, Agapito, Madrid.—Books on primary education. 306

158 Fraile y Valles, Gumersindo, Sevilla.—Arithmetics. 306

159 Bastida, Puyals de la, Vicente, Madrid.—Books on primary instruction. 306

160 Villegas, Enrique, Córdoba.—Books for primary instruction. 306

161 Ollero, Andrés F., Cuenca.—Treatise on education. 306

162 Normal School, Guadalajara.—School memoirs. 306

163 Diego, Pedro de, Madrid.—History of Spain. 306

164 Besson, Eduardo Augusto, Búrgos.—Books for elementary instruction. 306

165 Normal School, Cádiz.—Text-books. 306

166 Aguilar Mayor, Mariano, Lérida.—Books for primary instruction. 306

167 García, Nicanor, Villalba, Province of Lugo.—Books for primary instruction. 306

168 Central Normal School, Madrid.—Books for primary instruction. 306

169 Vallin y Bustillo, Acisclo, Madrid.—Books for primary instruction. 306

170 Carderera, Mariano, Madrid.—Books on primary instruction. 306

171 Cuenca, Hermenegildo, Cádiz.—Reading books for schools. 306

172 Normal School, Avila.—Books. 306

173 Normal High School, Barcelona.—Books. 306

174 Tranque y Cassi, Lorenzo, Barcelona.—Book on instruction. 306

175 Araño y Majó, Miguel, Barcelona.—Books on primary instruction. 306

176 Rodriguez, Eduardo, Lopez, Barcelona.—Method to reform writing. 306

177 Tubert y Carrera, Juan, San Martin de Provençals, Province of Barcelona.—Synopsis. 306

178 Economical Society of Friends of the Country, Sevilla.—Catalogue and memoirs. 306

179 Society for the Protection of Animals and Plants, Cádiz.—Publications. 306

180 Royal Academy of History, Madrid.—Books. 306

181 Royal Academy of Fine Arts, Madrid.—Books. 306

182 Academy of Physical & Moral Sciences, Madrid.—Publications. 306

183 Academy of Medicine, Madrid.—Spanish Pharmacopœia. 306

184 Special School for Painting, Sculpture, and Engraving, Madrid.—Memoirs, programmes, and statistics. 306

185 Astronomical & Meteorological Observatory, Madrid.—Annual and meteorological observations. 306

186 Spanish Society of Natural History, Madrid.—Annals. 306

187 Mineral Society, Salamanca.—Memoir. 306

188 Mercantile Athenæum, Madrid.—Books, rules, and periodicals. 306

189 Spanish Society of Professors of Sciences, Madrid.—Rules and reviews. 306

190 Economical Society, Madrid.—Copies of the pamphlet "El Centenario" and of the Review. 306

191 Association for the Protection of Young Artisans, Madrid.—Memoirs. 306

192 Academy of Sciences, Havana, Island of Cuba.—Documents and works. 306

193 Royal Academy of Sciences & Arts, Barcelona.—Books and dissertations. 306

194 Athenæum of Barcelona.—Reports. 306

195 Society of Industrial Engineers, Barcelona.—Publications. 306

196 Royo, Mariano, Zaragoza.—Treatise on irrigation. 306

197 Castelví, Bartolomé, Zaragoza.—Books. 306

198 Chao, Alejandro, Havana, Island of Cuba.—Life of Lord Byron. 306

199 Royal Academy of Sciences & Arts, Barcelona.—Rules and memoirs. 306

200 Catalanian Agricultural Institute of San Isidro, Barcelona.—Rules and reviews. 306

201 Economical Society of Friends of the Country, Barcelona.—Papers. 306

202 Society of Barcelona of Friends of Instruction, Barcelona.—Rules, memoirs, and documents. 306

203 Academy of Tachigraphy.—Documents. 306

204 Society of Patrons of National Production.—Documents. 306

205 Geographical & Statistical Institute.—Publications. 306

206 Reynal, Lorenzo, Tarragona.—Synopsis of the English language. 306

207 Cuchí, Tomás, Tarragona.—Special treatises. 306

208 Ford y Cusido, widow of, Tarragona.—Commercial Review. 306

209 Gil Sumbiela, Luis, Valencia.—Treatise on stenography. 306

210 Perez M. Miguel, Mariano, Medina del Campo, Province of Valladolid.—Almanacs. 306

211 Borao, Gerónimo, Zaragoza.—Dictionary. 306

212 Cuesta, Pedro, Zaragoza.—Works on medicine and pharmacy. 306

213 Sainz, Juan Antonio, Zaragoza.—Works on medicine and pharmacy. 306

214 Mondria, Mariano, Zaragoza.—Works on medicine and pharmacy. 306

215 Martinez Anguiano, Pedro, Zaragoza.—Works on medicine and pharmacy. 306

216 Robert y Serrat, José, Zaragoza.—Elements of general anatomy. 306

217 Torres y García, Roman, Zaragoza.—Books for primary and superior instruction. 306

218 Villar García, Martin, Zaragoza.—History of Latin literature. 306

219 Puente Villancio, José, Zaragoza.—Manual of the history of the middle ages. 306

220 Juncal, Benito, Pontevedra.—Treatise on education. 306

221 Gonzalez-Regueral, Severiano, Pontevedra.—"La Reforma," periodical. 306

222 Somoza Piñeiro, Ramon, Menza, Province of Pontevedra.—Treatise on syphons applied for the irrigation of pastures. 306

223 Angel Crehuet, widow of, Salamanca.—Prolegomena of law. 306

224 Navarro Izquierdo, Luciano, Salamanca.—Treatise on geometry. 306

225 Oscariz y Lasaga, Victor, Santander.—Pamphlets of literary studies. 306

226 Royal Academy of Seville.—Speeches, catalogues, and poetry. 306

227 Society of Andalusian Bibliophilists.—Books. 306

228 Gironès & Orduña, Seville.—Poetry. 306

229 Valdaraque, Rafael, Seville.—Poetry. 306

230 Asensio y Toledo, José María, Seville.—Literary works. 306

231 Sanchez, Pilar, Seville.—"Ernestina," geographical novel. 306

232 Meseguer, Manuel, Amposta, Province of Tarragona.—Text-books. 306

233 Alvarez, Romualdo, Tortosa, Province of Tarragona.—Works on instruction. 306

234 Avela, Eduardo, Madrid.—Farmers' almanacs. 306

235 Florez, José María, Madrid.—Books and maps. 306

236 Yeves, Cárlos, Madrid.—Books and periodicals. 306

237 **Maffei, Eugenio, Madrid.**—Mineral bibliography. 306

238 **Fuente, Vicente de la, Madrid.**—Life of Santa Teresa de Jesús. 306

239 **Santamaría de Paredes, Vicente,** Madrid.—The defense of right of property. 306

240 **García Ayuso, Francisco, Madrid.**—Historical and dramatical works. 306

241 **Gaya y Marzal, Cárlos María,** Madrid.—Treatise on tachigraphy. 306

242 **Ruiz de Salazar, Emilio, Madrid.**—"El Magisterio Español," periodical, and "La Familia," review. 306

243 **Massat, Alfredo, Cartagena, Province of Múrcia.**—Description of metaliferous soil. 306

244 **Pereiro Rey, Manuel, Orense.**—Application of sulphur. 306

245 **Perez, Joaquin, Orense.**—Descriptive pamphlet of the steeple of the cathedral. 306

246 **Alvarez Gimenez, Emilio, Pontevedra.**—Studies on dramas and comedies. 306

247 **Pimentel, Antonio, Pontevedra.**—Pamphlets. 306

248 **His Majesty the King of Spain,** Madrid.—Catalogues. 306

249 **Cárlos, A. de, & Son, Madrid.**—Literary works and "La Illustracion," periodical. 306

250 **Direction General of Cavalry,** Madrid.—Work on breeding horses. 306

251 **Direction of Public Instruction,** Madrid.—Books. 306

252 **Direction of Hydrography, Madrid.**—Books. 306

253 **Medina & Navarro, Madrid.**—Periodicals and books. 306

254 **Cámara, Miguel, H. de, Madrid.**—"La Guirnalda," periodical. 306

255 **Monasterio, Mariano, Madrid.**—Work on construction. 306

256 **Vergara, Mariano, Madrid.**—"El Averiguador," periodical. 306

257 **Frontáura, Cárlos, Madrid.**—"Los Niños," review. 306

258 **Galdós & Cámara, Madrid.**—National episodes. 306

259 **Utor, Luís María, Madrid.**—Modern agriculture. 306

260 **Crespo y Pozas, Leonardo, Madrid.**—Studies. 306

261 **Llacayo, Augusto, Madrid.**—Books on medicine and military surgery. 306

262 **Almirante, José, Madrid.**—Dictionaries. 306

263 **Perojo, José del, Madrid.**—"Contemporary Review." 306

264 **Eguilaz Yanguas, Leopoldo, Madrid.**—Study on the value of Arabic letters in the Spanish alphabet. 306

265 **Carderera, Mariano, Madrid.**—Dictionary of education. 306

266 **Murillo, Mariano, Madrid.**—Bulletin of the library. 306

267 **Fernandez de Castro, Manuel, Madrid.**—Electricity and railroads. 306

268 **Fernandez Peña, Pedro, Madrid.**—Geographical atlas. 306

269 **García Blanco, Antonio M.**—Madrid.—Text works. 306

270 **Codera, Francisco, Madrid.**—Work on numismatic errors. 306

271 **Rada y Delgado, Juan de Dios de la, Madrid.**—Work on "Vertu and Antiquities." 306

272 **Aldama, Lúcas de, Madrid.**—Treatise on industry and mines. 306

273 **Pascual, Manuel Joaquin, Madrid.**—Scientific works. 306

274 **Mata y Fontanet, Pedro, Madrid.**—Scientific and literary works. 306

275 **Suarez, Victoriano, Madrid.**—Scientific and literary works. 306

276 **Aguileta y Martinez, Eusebio,** Nalda, Province of Logroño.—School books and special treatises. 306

277 **Gomez Ayazza, Nicolás, Logroño.**—Text-books, and "El Riojano," periodical. 306

278 **Martinez Aleson, Tiburcio, Logroño.**—Work on teaching children. 306

279 **Soto Freire, Manuel, Lugo.**—History of Galicia and introductory manual. 306

280 **Panero Martinez, Manuel, Lugo.**—"The Heart of Childhood." 306

281 **Perez Villamil, Ramon Antonio,** Lugo.—Pamphlet on weights and measures. 306

282 **Rodriguez Villa, Antonio, Madrid.**—Etiquette of the house of Austria. 306

283 **Marichalar, Amalio, y Manrique,** Cayetano, Madrid.—History of the legislation of Spain. 306

284 **Cortés y Morales, Balbino, Madrid.**—Dictionary of legislation and jurisprudence. 306

285 **Bailly Baillière, Cárlos, Madrid.**—Books. 306

286 **Cruz Ruiz, Ciriaco, Madrid.**—Greek grammar. 306

287 **Leguina, Enrique, Madrid.**—Book, "Illustrious Sons of Santander." 306

288 **Conceiro, Gregorio María, Madrid.**—Philosophy of the creation. 306

289 **Martinez Acubillla, Indalecio,** Madrid.—Moral guide of youth. 306

290 **Palacios, Patricio, Córdoba.**—Universal history and elements of geography. 306

291 **Rey y Gorrindo, Pedro, Córdoba.**—Theory of unknown quantities. 306

292 **Surós, Antonio, Gerona.**—Text and school books. 306

293 **Obradors y Font, Sebastian, Gerona.**—Treatise on Latin roots. 306

294 **Lozano de Vilches, Enriqueta,** Granada.—Literary works. 306

295 **University, Granada.**—Works, speeches, and memoirs. 306

296 **Ribot, Estéban & Bros., Granada.**—Memoir. 306

297 **Vidal Domingo, Antonio, Huesca.**—History and geography. 306

298 **Serra y Navarro, Mariano, Jaen.**—Report on the condition of agriculture in Jaen. 306

299 **Board of Public Instruction, Lérida.**—Books. 306

300 **Prieto, Atanasio, Logroño.**—Treatise on arithmetic. 306

301 **Corral y Pastor, Anicéto, Alesanco,** Province of Logroño.—Compendium of Castilian grammar. 306

302 Diez, Domingo, Logroño.—Key to moral theology, etc. 306

303 Frovincial Institute, Búrgos.—Statistics, memoirs, etc. 306

304 Beson, Eduardo Augusto de, Búrgos.—Scientific works. 306

305 Dupuy, L., Santiago, Cádiz.—Books on silk industry. 306

306 Astronomical Observatory, San Fernando, Province of Cádiz.—Annals and almanacs. 306

307 Miró, Juan, Jarez de la Frontera, Province of Cádiz.—Books for instruction. 306

308 Vallarino, Baltasar, Cádiz.—Book, "The Anchor Weighed." 306

309 Leon Mainez, Ramon, Cádiz.—"Cronica de los Cervantistas," review. 306

310 Gonzalez, Manuel, Gran Canaria, Canary Islands.—Natural history. 306

311 Berthelot, Sabino, Canary Islands.—Plans, designs, and books on natural history. 306

312 Torres y Gonzales, Bernardino, Tomelloso, Province of Ciudad-Real.—Treatment of intestinal strangulation. 306

313 Torres y Fernandez, Santos, Tomelloso, Province of Ciudad-Real.—Treatment of inguinal ruptures. 306

314 Puente y Rocha, Juan de Dios de la, Córdoba.—Memoir on birds, useful or destructive to agriculture. 306

315 Massa y Sanguineti, José, Córdoba.—Elementary lessons in physics and chemistry. 306

316 Loma y Corradi, Blas de, Alicante.—Review of public instruction. 306

317 Herreros Berenguer, Mariano, Alicante.—On the decimal system. 306

318 Chastron, Leon, Alicante.—Works of D. Leon Chastron. 306

319 Carratalá & Gadea, Alicante.—Typographical album. 306

320 Garcia Arias y Usano, Benito, Avila.—Biblical pictures. 306

321 Pou, Luis, Palma, Balearic Islands.—Book, "La Sal." 306

322 Vidal y Roger, Andrés, Barcelona.—Weekly periodical. 306

323 Jover y Puig, Antonio, Barcelona.—Books on tachigraphy. 306

324 Bastinos, Antonio J., Barcelona.—Books on labor, instruction, and education. 306

325 Rius, Antonio, Barcelona.—Italian grammar. 306

326 Pasaráns y Viñals de Pujol, Elisa, Barcelona.—Books. 306

327 Maspons y Labrós, Francisco, Barcelona.—Popular Catalonian tales. 306

328 Pelayo Briz, Francisco, Barcelona.—Catalonian works. 306

329 Lopez Fabra, Francisco, Barcelona.—"Don Quixote de la Mancha." 306

330 Paula Folch, Francisco, Barcelona.—Medical books. 306

331 Tolrá, José, & Co., Barcelona.—Pamphlets. 306

332 Porcar y Tió, Jaime, Barcelona.—Works on education and morals. 306

333 Llerens Bros., Barcelona.—Dictionaries. 306

334 Lladós y Rius, Magin, Barcelona.—"El Porvenir de la Industria" (periodical). 306

335 Moreno y Roig, Barcelona.—History of the Church, etc. 306

336 Matallana, Mariano, Barcelona.—Manual for conversation on railroads. 306

337 Casals, Miguel, Barcelona.—Monthly publications. 306

338 Milá y Fontanal, Manuel, Barcelona.—Poetry. 306

339 Horticultural Society, Barcelona.—Horticultural Review. 306

340 Trilla & Serra, Barcelona.—"La Madeja" (periodical). 306

341 Alvarez Carretero, Antonio, Búrgos.—Books. 306

342 Hernandez Martin, Antonio, Búrgos.—Works on the instruction of the deaf and dumb. 306

343 Avila, Calixto, Búrgos.—Guide of Búrgos and Jura de Santa Gadea. 306

344 Archillas y Lopez, Ricardo, Baeza, Province of Jaen.—Paper read at the opening of the Baeza Institute. 306

345 Ginez de los Rios, Hermenegildo, Baeza, Province of Jaen.—Memoirs and projects. 306

346 Serra y Navarro, Mariano, Jaen.—Memoir on the condition of agriculture in the province. 306

347 Torres y Puig, Alejandro, Baeza, Province of Jaen.—Memoir. 306

348 Direction of Customs, Madrid.—Ordinances, models, and documents. 306

349 Alvarez de Araujo y Cuéllar, Angel, Madrid.—Books. 306

350 Gaspar, Editors, Madrid.—Collection of books from the Universal Museum. 306

351 High Normal School of Masters, Salamanca.—Memoir. 306

352 Guichot, Joaquin, Seville.—History of the town of Seville, etc. 306

353 Gozart y Seva, Printers, Alicante.—Catholic seminary. 306

354 Camilo Jover, Nicasio, Alicante.—"El Constitucional" (Liberal daily paper). 306

355 Suso, Manuel, Alicante.—"La Revelacion" (spiritual periodical). 306

356 Corporation of Barcelona.—Reports of public schools. 306

357 Provincial Institute for Secondary Instruction, Palma.—Memoirs. 306

358 Sanchez Almonacid, Mariano, Cuenca.—Memoirs of the Institute. 306

359 Ballester, Guillermo, Madrid.—Memoirs and regulations of the Hispano-Roman College. 306

360 Director of the Institute for Secondary Instruction, Pontevedra.—Memoirs. 306

361 Institute for Secondary Instruction, Seville.—Books, catalogues, and reports. 306

362 Alará, Mariano, Vilarrodona, Province of Tarragona.—Statistical data. 306

363 Provincial Institute, Tarragona.—Memoirs. 306

364 Institute for Secondary Instruction, Toledó.—Memoirs. 306

365 Navarro Reverter, Juan, Valencia.—"From the Turia to the Danube," memoirs of the Vienna Exhibition. 306

366 **Institute for Secondary Instruction, Zamora.**—Memoirs. 306

367 **Naranjo y Garza, Félipe, Madrid.**—Works on mineralogy. 306

368 **National Archæological Museum, Madrid.**—Historical descriptive information. 306

369 **Colmeiro, Manuel, Madrid.**—History of political economy in Spain. 306

370 **Commission of Naturalists of the Pacific, Madrid.**—Works on natural history. 306

371 **Gascon, Domingo, Madrid.**—"Guia del Peluquero" (periodical). 306

372 **Tuero, José Maria, Madrid.**—Book, "Hur icanes." 306

373 **Borja y Alarcon, Pedro, Madrid.**—Studies on the application of photography to topography. 306

374 **High Normal School of Masters of the Province, Salamanca.**—Books, models, plans, designs, etc. 306

375 **Normal School of Masters, Seville.**—Memoirs. 306

376 **Solís, Prudencio, Valencia.**—Atlas of lineal designs. 306

377 **Moreno Villena, Pedro, Valencia.**—Treatise on political economy. 306

378 **Calleja Sanchez, Julian, Valladolid.**—Works on anatomy. 306

379 **School of Fine Arts, Valladolid.**—Works by pupils. 306

380 **Veterinary School, Zaragoza.**—Historical relation and statistical dates. 306

Institutions and Organizations.

381 **Diaz Acevedo, Cleto, Havana, Island of Cuba.**—Procedure for the preservation of objects of natural history; zoological objects. 311

382 **His Majesty the King of Spain, Madrid.**—Sacred music. 313

383 **Romero Andía, Antonio, Madrid.**—Operatic music. 313

384 **Inzenga, José, Madrid.**—"Echoes from Spain" (popular songs). 313

385 **Ocon, Eduardo, Málaga.**—Popular Spanish songs. 313

386 **Iñiguez, Buenaventura, Seville.**—Musical methods for singing. 313

Scientific and Philosophical Instruments and Methods.

387 **Gallardo Bastant, Luis, Barcelona.**—Equinoctiometer. 320

388 **Astronomical Observatory of San Fernando, Cádiz.**—Instruments. 320

389 **Coello y Quesada, Francisco, Madrid.**—Maps of Spain and its possessions. 320

390 **Collantes de Teran, Francisco, Seville.**—System of classification of autonomous medals. 320

391 **Foulon, José, Las Corts de Sarriá, Province of Barcelona.**—Electric indicator. 320

392 **Lamana y Gonzalez, Saturnino, Logroño.**—Metric decimal indicator. 321

393 **Bartolomé & Agustin Castelvi, Zaragoza.**—Grain measures. 322

394 **Onís, Juan de, Masnou, Province of Barcelona.**—Chronometer. 323

395 **Flonis y Pujól, Juan, Masnou, Province of Barcelona.**—Nautical chronometer. 323

396 **Aguirre, Francisco, Soria.**—Clock. 323

397 **Gallardo Bastant, Luis, Barcelona.**—Electric piles. 325

398 **Aguirre, Francisco, Soria.**—Electric piles. 325

399 **Echen ique y Torres, Florencio Zaragoza.**—Portable telegraphic apparatus for campaigns. 326

400 **Jorba, José, Barcelona.**—Piano attachment. 327

401 **Guarro, Mariano, Barcelona.**—Piano. 327

402 **Sancho Velasco, Agapito, Búrgos.**—Music boxes. 327

403 **Arias, Vicente, Ciudad-Real.**—Guitars. 327

404 **Flores Laguna, José, Madrid.**—Music boxes. 327

405 **Romero y Andiá, Antonio, Madrid.**—Clarionet and system. 327

Engineering, Architecture, Maps, etc.

406 **Garriga y Roca, Miguel, Barcelona.**—Architecture. 330

407 **Isabella II. Canal, Madrid.**—Photographs of works. 330

408 **Gonzalez del Valle, Manuel, Segovia.**—Model of a bridge. 330

409 **Alvear y Lara, Francisco, Havana, Island of Cuba.**—Project for the supply of potable water. 330

410 **Revenga, Antonio, Valencia.**—Design of brakes. 332

411 **Corps of Military Engineers, Madrid.**—Books, plans, models. 333

412 **Bernaldez, Emilio, Madrid.**—Military books. 333

413 **Heriz, Enrique, Barcelona.**—Models of barks, with pamphlet. 334

414 **Tranque y Cassi, Lorenzo, Barcelona.**—Map of physical geography. 335

415 **Paz Mosquera, Manuel de la, Jaen.**—Topographical map of the province. 335

416 **Provincial Deputation, Lugo.**—Geometrical map of the Galician provinces. 335

417 **War Depository, Madrid.**—Maps and plans. 335

418 **Direction of Hydrography, Madrid.**—Hydrographic atlas. 335

419 **Gonzalez del Valle, Manuel, Segovia.**—Plan of provincial high roads. 335

420 **Observatory of the Royal College of Belen, Havana, Island of Cuba.**—Meteorological observations. 335

Physical, Social, and Moral Condition of Man.

421 **Lopez y Gomèz, Salvador, Seville.**—Work on gymnasiums. 340

422 **Mutual Aid Society, Orense.**—Rules. 343

423 **Feu, P., & Sons, Madrid.**—Collection of medals. 344

424 **National Mint, Madrid.**—Antique and modern coins. 344

425 **Cervera, Valerio, Madrid.**—"The Permanent Suffrage" (pamphlet). 345

426 Typographical Establishment of Oliva, Salamanca. 345

427 Provincial Hospitality, Seville.—Rules of the building, pictures, etc. 346

428 Provincial Board of Agriculture, Industry, and Commerce, Santander.—Memoirs, catalogues, and programmes. 349

Painting.

429 Bibilioni, José, Barcelona.—Design in Indian ink. 411

430 Sanchez, Pedro, Cádiz.—Aquarelles. 411

431 Guisasola, Federico, Pontevedra.—Aquarelles. 411

Engraving and Lithography.

432 Provincial Academy of Fine Arts, Cadiz.—Drawings by the pupils. 420

433 Provincial Deputation, Cádiz.—Calligraphic picture. 420

434 Lopez Valdemoro Ortiz de Lazcano, Madrid.—Crayon drawing. 420

435 Aramburu, Ricardo, Seville.—Crayon picture. 420

436 Reynoso, Emilio, Havana, Island of Cuba.—Calligraphic works. 420

437 Gelabert, R., & Bro., Barcelona.—Engravings. 421

438 Lemus, Eugenio, Madrid.—"Danæ," engraved on copper. 421

439 Maura, Bartolomé, Madrid.—"Surrender of Breda," engraved on copper. 421

440 Martinez Espinosa, Juan, Madrid.—Engravings. 421

441 Salcedo, Pedro, Morata, Province of Madrid.—Plan of the Escorial. 421

442 Arnanz, José, Havana, Island of Cuba.—Stone engraving. 421

443 Vidal y Roger, Andrés, Barcelona.—Music, engraved and printed. 422

444 National Calcography, Madrid.—Cuts. 422

445 Solá y Roca, Ramon, Barcelona.—Cuts. 423

446 Mencha y Rodriguez, Faustino, Logroño.—Lithographed figure. 423

447 Carderera y Solano, Valentin, Madrid.—Spanish iconography. 423

448 Fortanet, T., Madrid.—Printed books. 423

448*a* Museum of Artillery, Madrid.—Collection of plates.

449 Ariza y Campano, José, Seville.—Typographic picture. 423

449*a* Gonzalez y Montblanch, Modesto, Barcelona.—Lithography. 423

450 Mateu, José Maria, Madrid.—Chromo-lithographic plates. 424

451 Arnanz, José, Havana, Island of Cuba. — Chromo-lithographs and oleographs. 424

451*a* Blasquez, E.—Album of chromos. 424

Photography.

452 Mariezcurrena, Heribert, Barcelona.—Photographs. 430

453 Nobas, Narciso, Barcelona.—Photographs. 430

454 Moragas, Manuel, Gracia, Province of Barcelona.—Photograph of astronomical clock. 430

455 Casiñol, Leopoldo, Jerez de la Frontera, Province of Cádiz.—Heliochromo. 436

456 Napoleon, A. F., & Son, Barcelona.—Photographs. 430

457 Provincial Commission, Lugo.—Photographic reproductions of buildings. 430

458 Rodriguez Cortes, César, Lugo.—Photographic reproduction of engravings. 430

459 Spreafico, José, Málaga.—Album, with views. 430

460 Alviach & Co., Madrid.—Photographs. 430

461 Juliá y Garcia, Eusebio, Madrid.—Photographs. 430

462 Laurent, J., & Co., Madrid.—Photographs. 430

463 Diaz Otero, Eduardo, Madrid.—Photographs. 430

464 National Mint, Madrid.—Photographs. 430

465 Institute of Secondary Instruction, Seville.—Photographic view. 430

466 Sebastia Vila, Pedro, Seville.—Photographs. 430

467 Arce, Inocencio, Barcelona.—Photograph. 430

468 Economical Society of Friends of the Country, Seville.—Photographs. 430

469 Arce, Inocencio, Barcelona.—Photo lithographic reproductions. 432

470 Almela y Vinet, Francisco, Seville.—Application of varnish to photographs. 432

Industrial and Architectural Designs, Models, and Decorations.

471 Mestres, José O., Barcelona.—Architectural monuments. 441

472 Soler, Federico, Barcelona.—Commemorative project. 441

473 Guastavin, Rafael, Barcelona.—Architectural plans. 441

474 Garriga y Roca, Miguel, Barcelona.—Architectural plans and designs. 441

475 Tenas, Ramon, Barcelona.—Project of a church. 441

476 Rovira y Rabassa, Antonio, Barcelona.—Project of a monument. 441

477 Alonso, Arsenio, Madrid.—Project of a triumphal arch. 441

478 Duque, Eugenio, Madrid.—Projects of monuments. 441

479 Marin Baldo, José, Madrid.—Project of a monument at Colon. 441

Decoration with Ceramic and Vitreous Materials, Mosaic and Inlaid Work.

480 Bustamente & Gallo, Madrid.—Mosaic in wood. 450

481 Rodriguez, Desiderio, Cienfuegos, Cuba.—Inlaid table. 452

482 Cuevas, Fernandez, Pascual, Bribiesca, Province of Búrgos.—Pictures of birds, made with their feathers. 454

483 Ruiz, Manuel, Cádiz.—Picture of human hair, and picture made of wafers. 454

484 Lozano y Villarejo, Mateo, Madrid.—Album. 454

485 Serrano y Arenas, Purificacion, Havana, Island of Cuba.—Fancy work. 454

486 Camacho de Diaz, Soledad, Havana, Island of Cuba.—Paper work made by means of scissors. 445

Arboriculture and Forest Products.

487 Forest District of Avila.—Collection of woods. 600

488 Medinaceli, Duchess, widow of, Las Navas y Valdemaqueda, Province of Madrid.—Trunk of pine tree. 600

489 Clarós, José Maria, La Calera, Province of Badajoz.—Cork. 600

490 Moiano, Pedro, Badajos.—Cork. 600

491 Carrion, Barcarrota, Province of Badajoz.—Cork. 600

492 Castellanos, Eduardo, Burguillos, Province of Badajoz.—Cork. 600

493 Tos, José, Badajoz.—Corks. 600

494 Garriga Francisco, Domingo, San Quirse de Besora, Province of Barcelona.—Arboriculture. 600

495 Corps of Forest Engineers, of various towns of the Province of Búrgos.—Collection of woods. 600

496 Provincial Commission of Búrgos.—Pine hoops. 600

497 Santa Marta, Marquis of, Cáceres.—Cork and manufactures. 600

498 Montenegro, Pedro L., Cáceres.—Cork and manufactures. 600

499 Torrevias Tunels, Martin, Mesas de Ibor, Province of Cáceres.—Cork and manufactures. 600

500 Diaz Agero, José, Malladas y Fresno, Province of Cáceres.—Corks. 600

501 Torre Diaz, Count of, Jerez de la Frontera, Province of Cádiz.—Cork. 600

502 Castro Chirino, Alonzo, Isle of Hierro, Canary Islands.—Wood. 600

503 Dominguez Mendez, Benigno, Isle of Hierro, Canary Islands.—Wood. 600

504 Delgado, Francisco, Isle of Gran Canaria, Canary Islands.—Wood. 600

505 Melian, Juan, Isle of Gran Canaria, Canary Islands.—Wood. 600

506 Gonzalez, Manuel, Isle of Gran Canaria, Canary Islands.—Pine wood. 600

507 Provincial Board of Agriculture, Castellon.—Cork. 600

508 San Bernardo, Count of, Hornachuelos, Province of Córdoba.—Cork. 600

509 Lopez Seoane, Victor, Coruña.—Collection of woods. 600

510 Güito y Vall-llovera, José, Romaña, Province of Gerona.—Cork. 600

511 Institute of Secondary Instruction, Province of Huelva.—Woods. 600

512 Martin Carnes, Eulogio, Aracena, Province of Huelva.—Woods. 600

513 King, Guillermo, & Co., Higuera de Aracena, Province of Huelva.—Cork. 600

514 Corporation of Bollullos del Condado, Province of Huelva.—Cork. 600

515 Chief Engineer of Woods & Forests, Province of Jaen.—Wood. 600

516 Tuñon de Lara, Mateo, Carolina, Province of Jean.—Natural and prepared cork. 600

517 Provincial Institute, Province of Lugo.—Woods. 600

518 Corps of Forest Engineers, Madrid.—Woods, ashes, coal, and barks. 600

519 Iscar, Fernando, Tèrmino de Cabaco, Province of Salamanca.—Cork. 600

520 Catáneo, Francisco, Segovia.—Woods. 600

521 Gonzalez de Salcedo, F., Constantina, Province of Seville.—Cork. 600

522 Corporation of Poveda, Province of Soria.—Yew wood. 600

523 Corporation of Gallinero, Province of Soria.—Beech wood. 600

524 Corporation of Villaciervos, Province of Soria.—Juniper wood. 600

525 Corporation of Talvaila, Province of Soria.—Pine wood. 600

526 Corporation of Cortos, Province of Soria.—Oak wood. 600

527 Corporation of Navaleno, Province of Soria.—Pine wood. 600

528 Corporation of Molinos del Duero, Province of Soria.—Pine and poplar wood. 600

529 Campos, Manuel Maria, Havana, Island of Cuba.—Construction woods. 600

530 Inspection General of Woods & Forests, Havana, Island of Cuba.—Construction woods. 600

531 Uria & Pinilla, Navia de Luarca, Province of Oviedo.—Charcoal linget. 600

532 Inspection of Woods & Forests, San Juan, Puerto Rico.—Woods. 600

533 Gonzalez, Manuel, Aquadilla, Puerto Rico.—Ornamental woods. 601

534 Quiroga Lopez, Benigno, Province of Lugo.—Construction and ornamental woods. 601

535 Inspection General of Woods & Forests, Havana, Island of Cuba.—Ornamental woods. 601

536 Verdú Perez, Joaquin, Monóvar, Province of Alicante.—Bastard saffron. 602

537 Monroig, daughter and heir of Ramon, Barcelona.—Dye-stuffs. 602

538 Sande Olivares, Jerónimo, Garrovillas, Province of Cáceres.—Dyers' weed. 602

539 Aguilera, Francisco, Priego, Province of Córdoba.—Sumac. 602

540 Lozano y Escobar, Romualdo, Buenache, Province of Cuenca.—Sumac. 602

541 Gallego, Domingo, Buenache, Province of Cuenca.—Sumac powder. 602

542 Corporation of Romancos, Province of Guadalajara.—Sumac. 602

543 Ayuso de las Heras, Angel, Valdearenas, Province of Guadalajara.—Madder root. 602

544 Acero, Antonio, Jaen.—Sumac. 602

545 Guerra M. de Soto, Anacleto, Portillo, Province of Valladolid.—Madder root. 602

546 Velicia, Félix, Traspinedo, Province of Valladolid.—Sumac. 602

547 Inspection General of Woods & Forests, Havana, Island of Cuba.—Dye woods. 602

548 Medinaceli, Duchess, widow of, Madrid.—Resinous products. 603

549 Gonzalez, Manuel, Las Palmas, Canary Islands.—Resins. 603

550 Avilés y Merino, Francisco, Córdoba.—Fennel resin. 603

551 Corps of Forest Engineers, Salas, Province of Búrgos.—Resinous products. 603

552 Corporation of Armallanes, Province of Guadalajara.—Pitch. 603

553 Corporation of Mountain Engineers, Madrid.—Resins. 603

554 Ferrandiz, Juan, San Vicente, Province of Alicante.—Salt wort. 604

555 Gonzalez Conde, Diego, Mahora, Province of Albacete.—Saffron. 602

556 Delgado, José, Tarazona, Province of Albacete.—Dried saffron. 602

557 Perez, Albert, & Co., Monóvar, Province of Alicante.—Anis. 602

558 Gonzalez, Manuel, Gran Canaria, Canary Islands.—Seeds. 602

559 Castro y Chirino, Alonzo de, Isle of Hierro, Canary Islands.—Seeds. 602

560 Cabezuelas, Count of, Campo de Criptana, Province of Ciudad-Real.—Saffron. 602

561 Rodriguez, Antonio, Manzanares, Province of Ciudad-Real.—Saffron. 602

562 Rodriguez, Luis, Manzanares, Province of Ciudad-Real.—Saffron. 602

563 Gonzalez y Rubio, Máximo, Ciudad-Real.—Saffron. 602

564 Muñoz Mendez, Eugenio, Humanes, Province of Guadalajara.—Apricot seed. 605

565 Barnuevo, Manuel, Múrcia.—Pine seed. 605

566 Onís, Federico, Cantalapiedra, Province of Salamanca.—Flax seed. 605

567 Fernandez, Manuel, Tembleque, Province of Toledo.—Saffron. 605

568 Corporation of Baños, Province of Cáceres.—Chestnut burrs. 605

569 Sanz Pasalodos, Julian, Portillo, Province of Valladolid.—Pine tree cones. 605

570 Sanz, Mariano, Pedrajaz de San Estéban, Province of Valladolid.—Pine seed. 605

571 Tablares, Félipe, Megues de Iscar, Province of Valladolid.—Pine seed. 605

PHILIPPINE ISLANDS.

Educational Systems, Methods, and Libraries.

572 Municipal School for Girls, Province of Manila.—Programme, etc., and pupils' work. 300

573 College of St. Tomas, Province of Manila.—Tables, designs, etc. 300

574 College of San José, Province of Manila.—Books and drawings. 300

575 Municipal Athenæum for Children, Province of Manila.—Album, programme of instruction, and books. 300

576 Jordana y Morera, Ramon, Inspector-General of Woods & Forests, Province of Manila.—Work on the production of the public forests of the Philippine Islands. 306

577 Vidal & Soler, Sebastian, Chief-Engineer of Woods & Forests, Province of Manila.—Books on forestal, woods, and climate of the Philippine Islands. 306

578 Inspection-General of Woods & Forests.—Books on arboriculture. 306

579 Loyzaga & Co., Province of Manila.—"El Comercio" (evening paper), "Revista Mercantil" (semi-monthly paper). 306

580 Ramirez & Girandier, Province of Manila.—"El Diario de Manila" (daily periodical). 306

581 Gonzalez & Moreno, Province of Manila.—"Manual del Viajeró" (The Travelers' Manual). 306

582 The Future of the Philippines, Province of Manila.—"El Porvenir Filipino" (periodical). 306

583 Ramirez & Girandier, Province of Manila.—"La Ilustracion" (semi-monthly paper). 306

584 Gimenez & Preysler, Province of Manila.—"El Oriente" (semi-monthly illustrated paper). 306

Institutions and Organizations.

585 Prieto, Federico, Tabaco, Province of Albay.—Human skulls. 312

586 Sales, Juan, Province of Manila.—Models of negroes, Spanish mestizos, Philippine Indians, etc. 312

Engineering, Architecture, Maps, etc.

587 Inspection-General of Public Works, Manila, Province of Manila.—Plans of public works. 330

588 Municipal Athenæum, Province of Manila.—Meteorological observations. 335

Physical, Social, and Moral Condition of Man.

589 Nueva Cáceres, Bishop of, Province of Nueva Cáceres.—Books on religious instruction. 348

Aerial, Pneumatic, and Water Transportation.

590 Inspection-General of Woods & Forests.—Models of boats and vessels. 594

591 Jackson, Eduard, Province of Manila.—Model of lorcha and life-boat. 594

592 Arsenal of Cavite, Province of Cavite.—Models of boats and vessels. 594

No. 87. UNITED STATES SIGNAL OFFICE.

This exhibit consists of a field telegraph train, with battery, wire wagons, lance trucks, a portable signal tower, and other signaling appliances. It is situated on State Avenue, opposite the English Government buildings.

No. 88. TENNESSEE STATE HEADQUARTERS.

A circular tent, containing specimens of minerals, also a portable charcoal stove patented and exhibited by Rice Moore, of Nashville, Tennessee. Situated on State Avenue, between the Maryland and Iowa buildings.

No. 89. MISSISSIPPI STATE BUILDING.

Size, 42 feet by 25 feet.

Situated on State Avenue, opposite and west of the Japanese Dwelling. The wood used in this structure is from the State of Mississippi, and numbers some hundred varieties in all.

No. 90. GEORGE'S HILL RESTAURANT.

Architects, H. J. SCHWARZMANN, HUGH KAFKA.—Size, 112 feet by 72 feet.
TALMAN & KOHN, Philadelphia.

Located in the western portion of the grounds, on George's Hill, in the vicinity of the State buildings. It is a one-story structure, built of wood, and is also called the Hebrew Restaurant.

No. 91. BISHOP RICHARD ALLEN'S MONUMENT.

Size, base 6 feet by 6 feet; height, 16 feet.

Erected in memory of the Rev. Richard Allen, founder and first bishop of the African Methodist Episcopal Church; situated between Fountain and State Avenues, west of the United States Government Buildings.

No. 92. BOSTON "DAILY ADVERTISER," AND BOSTON "HERALD."

Size, 29 feet by 16 feet.

A one-story frame building, situated on Fountain Avenue opposite northwest corner of Machinery Hall; used as the headquarters of the correspondents and attaches of the newspapers erecting it.

No. 93. AMERICAN NEWSPAPER EXHIBITION.

Architect, M. J. MORILL, Brooklyn, N. Y.—Size, 70 feet by 46 feet.
GEO. P. ROWELL & CO., New York City.

A two-story frame structure of Swiss architecture, on Fountain Avenue, near the lake. It contains a large hall, and a reading-room supplied with newspapers from all parts of the United States. In April, 1876, the United States published regularly 8129 newspapers, a number which exceeds the combined issues of all the other nations of the earth. Regular files of most of these newspapers, and sample copies of all, are alphabetically arranged for exhibition, and a printed catalogue of the whole may be obtained for twenty-five cents. Messrs. George P. Rowell & Co. conduct an agency for the reception of advertisements for all American newspapers, at their office, No. 41 Park Row, New York.

No. 94. CALIFORNIA STATE BUILDING.

Size, 55 feet by 105 feet.

A two-story frame building, situated on State Avenue, opposite the British Government buildings. It contains accommodations for the State Commissioners and visitors, also a large hall for the purpose of exhibiting specimens of the agricultural productions of California.

No. 95. CENTENNIAL FIRE PATROL, No. 1.

This building is situated at the corner of Belmont and State Avenues, and contains two steam fire engines and one truck.

No. 96. TURKISH CAFÉ.

Architect, PIERRE MONTANI.—Size, 51 feet by 65 feet.
TURKISH COMMISSION.

An octagonal frame building, with a coffee-room, parlors, and bazaars, situated on a walk between Fountain Avenue and the Avenue of the Republic, near their junction north of Machinery Hall.

No. 97. FRANK LESLIE'S PAVILION.

This building is situated at eastern end of lake, on Belmont Avenue, adjoining the office of Cook, Son, & Jenkins. It is octagonal in shape, Moorish in design, and highly ornamented. It is used as an office of Frank Leslie's publications.

No. 98. IOWA STATE BUILDING.

Size, 40 feet by 53 feet.

This is a two-story frame building, with portico in front and bay windows on both sides, located on State Avenue between the Missouri and Tennessee buildings, and used as a headquarters for Commissioners from this State.

No. 99. RHODE ISLAND STATE BUILDING.

Architects, WM. R. WALKER and T. J. GOLD, Providence, R. I.

A building of combined Swiss and Gothic architecture, situated on State Avenue, north of the Mississippi State building.

No. 100. VERMONT STATE BUILDING.

Architect, LAMOS, Ticonderoga, Vt.

A building of Doric architecture, northwest of Machinery Hall, and near Fountain Avenue. It contains an Estey organ, from Brattleboro', Vt., and files of Vermont newspapers.

No. 101. MEMORIAL HALL (ART GALLERY).

See Part II., page 9.

No. 102. ART ANNEX.

See Part II., page 10.

No. 103. THE B'NAI B'RITH MONUMENT.

Erected by the Israelites to religious liberty, and situated between the Art Gallery and its annex.

No. 104. PHOTOGRAPHIC EXHIBITION BUILDING.

See Part II., page 137.

No. 105. VIENNA BAKERY, OR COMPRESSED YEAST BUILDING.

Architects, H. J. SCHWARZMANN, HUGH KAFKA.—Size, 146 feet by 105 feet.
GAFF, FLEISCHMANN, & CO., Blissville, Long Island, N. Y.

Designed to exhibit the advantages of using compound yeast in baking. It also contains a coffee house.

No. 106. ANNEX TO MAIN BUILDING (CARRIAGES, STOVES, etc.).

See Part I., page 374.

No. 107. SWEDISH SCHOOL-HOUSE AND METEOROGRAPH.

Architects, ISÆUS & JACOBSSON.—Size, 40 feet by 50 feet.

Situated in the Swedish Government grounds, north of the Main Exhibition Building. A one-story frame house, containing school-rooms and the interior arrangements of a Swedish school-house. The framework for the building was imported from Sweden, and is on exhibition by G. O. Wengstion, of Stockholm.

METEOROGRAPH.—A one-story latticed structure east of Swedish school-house, surmounted by semi-globular cups, connected with apparatus in the interior, showing the velocity of the wind.

No. 108. JAPANESE BAZAAR.

This building is situated on Lansdowne drive, immediately north of Department of Public Comfort, and is designed for sale of Japanese wares.

No. 109. JUDGES' HALL.

Architects, H. J. SCHWARZMANN, HUGH KAFKA.—Size, 152 feet by 113 feet.

A two-story frame building, situated north of the Main Exhibition Building, containing ten committee rooms and four private rooms for the judges; also one large hall in the centre, and a smaller hall in the rear. It is intended for the accommodation of the International Board of Judges. The President of the Centennial Commission and the Chief of the Bureau of Awards have offices in this building.

No. 110. CENTENNIAL PHOTOGRAPHIC ASSOCIATION BUILDING.

Architects, H. J. SCHWARZMANN, HUGH KAFKA.—Size, 150 feet by 30 feet.

The Photographic Association have erected a one-story frame building, located north of the Main Exhibition Building on the east side of Belmont Avenue. It contains one room for the exhibition of photographs, and three rooms for photographers for working purposes.

No. 111. SHEET METAL PAVILION.

Size, 22 feet by 40 feet.
Architect, E. C. RYER.

Situated on Lansdowne drive and Belmont Avenue, opposite lake. Marshall Bros. & Co., Girard Avenue below Front Street, Philadelphia, Pa., exhibit the utilization of galvanized and leaded sheets in the construction of this building. American polished, cleaned, and refined sheets, galvanized cemetery and house work, and corrugated iron. The building itself is a specimen of the workmanship of the Kittredge Cornice and Ornament Co., Salem, O., and illustrates the application of sheet metal to architectural purposes.

No. 112. GERMAN EMPIRE PAVILION.

Architects, H. J. SCHWARZMANN, HUGH KAFKA.—Size, 83 feet by 33 feet.

Constructed of stone, one story high, furnishing accommodations for the Imperial Commissioners as well as German visitors. It is located on Lansdowne drive, between Belmont and Agricultural Avenues.

No. 113. PENNSYLVANIA RAILROAD OFFICE.

Architect, J. M. WILSON, Engineer of Bridges and Buildings, Pennsylvania Railroad Co.—Octagon, 75 feet in diameter.

A two-story frame building, situated on the northeast corner of Belmont Avenue and the Avenue of the Republic, adjoining the Judges' Hall. It is designed for the general ticket office of the four great trunk lines, viz.: New York Central, Erie, Baltimore & Ohio, and Pennsylvania Railroads. Tickets are sold to all points, and information is furnished regarding routes of travel.

No. 114. OFFICE U. S. CENTENNIAL COMMISSION.

The western wing of the Public Comfort Building. It contains offices and committee rooms, and conveniences for newspaper correspondents.

No. 115. BRAZILIAN EMPIRE PAVILION.

This structure is of wood, situated on Lansdowne drive, adjoining the German Government building, and intended for use of the Brazilian Commission.

No. 116. THE DAIRY ASSOCIATION BUILDING.

Architects, H. J. SCHWARZMANN, HUGH KAFKA.—Size, 76 feet by 25 feet; pavilion, 80 feet by 30 feet.

Situated on the north side of Lansdowne Valley, southwest of Horticultural Hall. It is a two-story rustic building, and the surrounding grounds are laid out as a garden in which is a pavilion for the additional accommodation of visitors.

No. 117. RESTAURANT LAFAYETTE.

Architect, H. J. SCHWARZMANN.—Size, 130 feet by 30 feet.

This is a two-story wooden building, located northwest of the Art Gallery, between Lansdowne drive and the brook. It is conducted on the French plan.

No. 118. DEPARTMENT OF PUBLIC COMFORT.

Architects, BALDERSTON & HUTTON, Philadelphia.—Size, 264 feet by 112 feet.

DEPARTMENT OF PUBLIC COMFORT COMPANY, Limited.

W. MARSH KASSON, Chairman, Philadelphia.

Located on the corner of the Avenue of the Republic and Agricultural Avenue, opposite the northwestern corner of the Main Exhibition Building, and fronting the Esplanade. It is a two-story frame building, containing a reception room and ladies' parlor, free to all, barber shop, coat and baggage room, lunch counter, and lavatories. Tickets for places of amusement are on sale, and a daily register of all visitors is kept. The western section of the building is occupied by the President of the Centennial Commission. Office desk room is afforded to exhibitors. The centre portion of the building is surmounted with an open-air gallery, giving a view of the grounds.

No. 119. EMPIRE TRANSPORTATION COMPANY'S BUILDING.

Architects, WILSON BROS. & CO., Philadelphia.—Size, 70 feet by 60 feet.

EMPIRE TRANSPORTATION CO., Philadelphia.

This structure is located north of the eastern end of the Main Exhibition Building, and exhibits by models the method of transportation used by the Empire Transportation Company and its auxiliaries in the United States.

No. 120. FRENCH GOVERNMENT PAVILION.

Architect, DE DARTEIN, France.—Size, 100 feet by 50 feet.

DEPARTMENT OF PUBLIC WORKS, France.

Is constructed of brick and iron, and exhibits models in relief and designs of all the public works of France executed during the last few years; also a collection of books and publications relative thereto. It is situated west of the Art Gallery, on Lansdowne drive.

No. 121. CENTENNIAL FIRE PATROL.

Architect, H. J. SCHWARZMANN.—Size: (1.) 60 feet by 58 feet. (2.) 84 feet by 74 feet.

The Fire Patrol is accommodated in two buildings, built of wood, one story high, containing halls for the engines, stalls for the horses, and dormitories for the firemen. The smaller house is at the northeast corner of the Main Exhibition Building, and the larger at the intersection of Lansdowne drive and Belmont Avenue. They are supplied with steam fire engines, hose trucks, ladders, and patent fire extinguishers.

No. 122. THE PENNSYLVANIA EDUCATIONAL HALL.

Architects, PETERS & BURGER.—Size, 148 feet by 100 feet.

The object of this Hall is the exhibition of the educational interests of the State of Pennsylvania. It is situated north of the Art Gallery, fronting on the Lansdowne drive. The building is octagonal in shape, and contains thirty-two alcoves for the display, a large assembly room, and a reception room. The following summary represents the exhibits:

1 **Representations of kindergarten,** primary, grammar, and high schools, with their appropriate furniture, fittings, text-books, apparatus, and work.

Systems of graded schools, with views and models of buildings, charts of statistics, specimens of apparatus, and volumes of scholars' work.

Schools of counties, with county and township maps of school-houses, photographs of buildings, charts of statistics, and scholars' work; plans of school buildings, with systems of heating, lighting, and ventilating, and designs.

Department of Public Instruction charts, showing statistics and outline of public school system, reports, forms, certificates, and laws.

Text-books, school furniture and merchandise, school apparatus and philosophical apparatus; school ornamentation, consisting of a fountain, a series of Rogers' groups, vases, hanging baskets, statues, engravings, etc. 300

2 **Academies and Seminaries,** with pictures of buildings, specimens of apparatus, cabinet collections, drawings, and paintings.

Universities and colleges, with pictures of buildings, maps of grounds, views of interior rooms, charts of history and statistics, courses of study, text-books, and productions of professors and alumni.

Technical schools and departments, with drawings, casts, models of bridges, specimens of apparatus, etc. 301

3 **Normal Schools.—Views of buildings** and grounds, models, courses and methods of study, catalogues and reports, charts of statistics, and students' work.

Schools of Design.—Drawings, models, etc.

Commercial Schools.—Specimens of penmanship, etc. 302

4 **Institution for the Blind.—Apparatus** for teaching, intellectual and industrial work done by the blind.

Institution for the Deaf and Dumb.—Apparatus and methods of teaching. 303

5 **Orphan Schools.—Views of build-**ings, scholars' intellectual and industrial work, books of record, forms and charts.

School for the Feeble-minded.—Textbooks, apparatus, methods, etc. 346

6 **Sunday-schools.—Collections of** Sunday-school material, incentives, maps, charts, forms, and models. 348

7 **Peirce's Union Business College,** 39 South Tenth street, Philadelphia, Pa. Thomas May Peirce, M.A., Principal and Proprietor; Rev. John Thompson, Business Manager, Residence, 2002 Brandywine street.

BRIEF DESCRIPTION OF THE OBJECTS ON EXHIBITION. *I. Penmanship:* (A.) Seven (7) sets of resolutions engrossed by order of the Philadelphia Board of Public Education, at different times during the past five years, and borrowed from the owners for the purpose of showing the high order of talent employed by the college. (B.) The improvement in writing of fourteen hundred (1400) pupils of the college, showing the success of the penman as a teacher. (C.) A "reward of merit" engrossed by the penman, the like of which is given once a month to the pupil who makes the most improvement in writing during the month. (D.) A large piece of "Specimens of Spencerian Penmanship," and a set of resolutions, complimentary of the Principal, written by the penman, and a "deceiving picture" made with pen, brush, and pencil, by the professor of drawing, each illustrating the power and ability of the executor. (E.) A piece of ornamental penmanship with a bouquet in the centre drawn with the pen, which with the drawings in the work done for the Board of Education, show the penman's skill in pen-drawing. *II. Book-keeping:* (A.) A case of samples of merchandise used by the pupils of the college in the transaction of business among themselves in the Actual Business Department, thus furnishing each pupil with an original and independent set of transactions for his books. (B.) Samples of college currency used in the payment of bills, together with copies of the various business papers used by the students. *III. Course of Instruction:* (A.) A small piece of lettering naming the subjects taught. (B.) A diploma setting forth the subjects of examination for graduation. *IV. Objects of Institution and Classes who patronize it:* A large piece of penmanship setting forth the same in detail.

PARTICULAR MERIT WHICH THE EXHIBITOR CLAIMS FOR HIS EXHIBIT.—I. The highest order of talent in the penman in all the departments of work done with the pen. II. Superior plans for the improvement of the writing of pupils in addition to the excellence of the teacher. III. Ingenious and successful plans for teaching book-keeping and imparting a sound, practical, and economical preparation of young men for business life. 343

No. 123. TELEGRAPHIC BUILDING.

Architects, BALDERSTON & HUTTON, Philadelphia.—Size, 80 feet by 75 feet.

DEPARTMENT OF PUBLIC COMFORT COMPANY, Limited.

W. MARSH KASSON, Chairman, Philadelphia.

The reception room of the Public Comfort building opens from the east into the telegraphic department, which furnishes communication with every portion of the world. Is a one-story frame building opposite the northwest corner of the Main Exhibition Building, fronting the Esplanade. All of the instruments and appliances of the latest design are on exhibition and in use.

1 **Philips, Wm. J., Philadelphia, Pa.**—Printing telegraph instrument, combining the bell, dial, and printing telegraph in one instrument.

2 **Phillips, Eugene F., Providence, R. I.**—Covered wire for telegraphic purposes.

3 **Gray, Elisha, Chicago, Ill.**—Electro-harmonic telegraph, including apparatus for transmitting tunes and eight or more messages simultaneously.

4 **Atlantic & Pacific Telegraph Co.,** Philadelphia, Pa.—Automatic and duplex telegraph apparatus.

5 **Gray & Barton, Western Electric** Telegraph Co., Chicago, Ill.—Printing telegraph instrument, with unison attachment.

6 **Frost & Hanline, Philadelphia, Pa.**—Automatic thermostat for fire-alarm telegraph.

7 **Brooks, David, Philadelphia, Pa.**—Underground cables for telegraph wires.

8 **Gamewell, J. N., & Co., New York,** N. Y.—American fire-alarm telegraph, with non-interference repeaters and signal-boxes, and mechanical gong apparatus.

9 **American District Telegraph Co.,** Philadelphia, Pa.—District telegraph signal-boxes, with self-starting registers for messengers, guides, and interpreters.

10 **Philadelphia, Reading, & Potts-**ville Telegraph Co., Philadelphia.—Duplex and Morse telegraph apparatus.

No. 124. AMERICAN FUSEE COMPANY'S BUILDING.

Size, 14 feet by 14 feet.

W. R. DAVENPORT, New York.

Situated on Lansdowne drive, north of the Judges' building.

No. 125. GLASS MAGAZINE.

Architect, H. J. SCHWARZMANN.—Size, 40 feet by 40 feet.

KLAUTSHECK, THOMAS, & STUART, Philadelphia.

This magazine is erected adjoining the Photographic Association Building, opposite the lake. It is constructed mainly of glass from the factories of the above firm, and contains a full assortment of plate and window glass, and glass shades for the accommodation of exhibitors; is two stories high, and is connected by a bridge with Belmont Avenue.

No. 126. MOORISH VILLA.

Constructed in Morocco by native workmen; exhibited by Dr. Max Schmidl, for the display of native products and fancy articles; conducted by Abd el Kader ben Katib. It is situated on Lansdowne drive, opposite Sheet Metal Pavilion.

No. 127. AMERICAN BIBLE SOCIETY PAVILION.

Architect, I. C. SIDNEY.—Size, 17 feet by 23 feet.

Located near Lansdowne Valley, south of Horticultural Hall, close to the bridge; oval in shape, and surmounted by a carved roof with a projecting cornice. It bears the inscription, "The Bible without note or comment." In front is an open Bible, and over it the text from Jeremiah xxii. 29: "O earth, earth, earth, hear the word of the Lord." Only Bibles and Testaments are sold.

No. 128. HUNTERS' CAMP.

"FOREST AND STREAM" PUBLISHING CO., N. Y., WM. C. HARRIS, Manager.

This camp illustrates sportsmen's life in the backwoods, and contains what is known as a permanent camp, built of logs and bark, with all the appurtenances of hunting and fishing, including portable boats, sporting firearms, rods and fishing tackle ready for use, portable cooking apparatus, specimens of game birds, a kennel of sporting dogs, etc., etc. An additional feature is a lake or pond stocked with game fish, and a running stream containing brook trout. It is located in the ravine south of Horticultural Hall.

No. 129. OFFICE WATER DEPARTMENT.

A frame building situated on Belmont Avenue, next to the Glass Magazine.

No. 130. SODA WATER STANDS.

These are located at various points east of Belmont Avenue and south of Fountain Avenue.

No. 131. CIGAR STANDS.

These are situated at various points east of Belmont Avenue and south of Fountain Avenue.

No. 132. SINGER SEWING MACHINE BUILDING.

Architect, JAMES VAN DYKE, Elizabeth.—Size, 81 feet by 56 feet.
SINGER MANUFACTURING CO., New York City.

Contains an exhibit of every style of machine manufactured by the Singer Manufacturing Company, and samples of work. It is constructed of wood, and is located on Lansdowne drive, north of the Art Gallery.

No. 133. MEDICAL DEPARTMENT.

Architect, H. J. SCHWARZMANN.—Size, 65 feet by 32 feet 6 inches.

This department is instituted for the immediate gratuitous relief of accidents and sudden cases of illness occurring within the Exhibition grounds. It is located in Lansdowne ravine, equidistant from the Main Building and Horticultural Hall, and contains two wards, of three beds each, for male and female patients. An ambulance is provided for the removal of patients to their homes or to city hospitals.

Officers.

WILLIAM PEPPER, M.D., Medical Director.
THEODORE HERBERTE, M.D., Secretary and Resident Physician.
JACOB ROBERTS, M.D., Member of Staff.
S. W. GROSS, M.D., Member of Staff.
H. C. WOOD, M.D., Member of Staff.
R. G. CURTIN, M.D., Member of Staff.
HAMILTON OSGOOD, M.D., Member of Staff.
DE FORREST WILLARD, M.D., Member of Staff.

No. 134. PORTUGUESE GOVERNMENT BUILDING.

Architects, H. J. SCHWARZMANN, HUGH KAFKA.—Size, 55 feet by 51 feet.

A one-story wooden structure, with cupola, located on the northeast corner of Agricultural Avenue and Lansdowne drive, and used to accommodate Commissioners and visitors from Portugal.

No. 135. BANKERS' EXHIBIT.

Architect, JAMES H. WINDRIM, Philadelphia.—Size, 69 feet by 41 feet.

Erected by the banks, bank officers, and bankers of the country for the exhibition of coins and currency. It is located east of the Art Gallery, and between the Photographic Gallery and the Vienna Bakery.

No. 136. FRENCH GLASS EXHIBIT.

R. DE BERGNE.

This building is constructed entirely of glass, and situated on Lansdowne drive, adjoining Moorish Villa. Is designed to show window glass, tiles, marble, onyx, etc.

No. 137. KINDERGARTEN.

Located north of Carriage Annex on Lansdowne drive, designed to show object teaching. Is a wooden structure, one story high.

No. 138. CENTENNIAL POLICE STATION.

Situated at northeast corner of Main Building, designed for accommodation of police, with cells for prisoners.

No. 139. PHILADELPHIA PAVILION.

Architects, H. J. SCHWARZMANN, HUGH KAFKA.—Size, 88 feet by 66 feet.

For the accommodation of the municipal government of the city of Philadelphia. It contains a hall and parlors, and a room devoted to the use of the Park Commission. It is a one-story frame building, situated on Lansdowne drive, east of Horticultural Hall.

No. 140. MUSIC PAVILION.

Pavilion with ornamented dome, situated in Lansdowne Ravine, near the bridge. For use of bands.

No. 141. BURIAL CASKET BUILDING.

Architect, N. B. GLEASON, Rochester, N. Y.—Size, 42 feet by 22 feet.

SCHUYLER & ARMSTRONG and S. STEIN, Proprietors.

The exhibit consists of various designs of funeral caskets, shrouds, etc. It is a one-story frame house with turrets, and is situated on Lansdowne drive near the bridge, and north of Art Gallery Annex.

No. 142. PERFORATED METALS.

This is a one-story brick building with skylight, located between the Carriage Annex and Lansdowne drive, and designed to show the practicability of using perforated window blinds in dwellings.

No. 143. RUBBER ROOFING.

This building is situated on Lansdowne drive, between the Carriage Annex and Pennsylvania Educational Hall. It is octagonal in shape, and surmounted by a tower ten feet high. The exhibit consists of rubber roofing.

No. 144. OFFICE OF CUBAN ACCLIMATION GARDEN.

See Part IV., page 134.

Architect and Manager, JULES LACHAUME.—Size, 12 feet by 25 feet.

This structure is designed to show tropical produce, seeds, vegetable physiology, and rustic work, and is situated directly south of Horticultural Hall.

No. 145. NAVAL GROUP.

This bronze statue is situated on the plaza immediately west of Art Gallery.

No. 146. DYING LIONESS.

This bronze work of art is in the plaza due east of Art Gallery.

No. 151. HORTICULTURAL HALL.

See Part IV., page 147.

No. 152. AGRICULTURAL HALL.

See Part IV., page 9.

No. 153. WOMEN'S PAVILION.

See Part III., page 85.

No. 154. FROBEL'S KINDERGARTEN.

Architect, JAMES P. SIMS.—Size, 45 feet by 18 feet.

Situated northeast of the Women's Pavilion. Contains specimens of school work, and illustrates the operation of kindergarten teaching.

No. 155. NEW JERSEY STATE BUILDING.

Architect, CARL PFEIFFER, New York.—Size, 56 feet by 82 feet.

A two-story wooden building erected for the accommodation of the New Jersey State Commissioners, containing offices and private rooms. It is situated on Belmont Avenue, adjacent to the Women's Pavilion. Messrs. Hall & Son, of Perth Amboy, N. J., furnished the brick in the chimney, and Messrs. Maurer & Brevier, of Perth Amboy, the tiles used in the roofing of the building.

No. 156. THE "SOUTH" RESTAURANT.

Architects, H. J. SCHWARZMANN.—Size, 182 feet by 92 feet.
E. MERCER, Atlanta, Ga.

Situated on the northwest corner of State and Belmont Avenues, and is a one-story frame building.

No. 157. KANSAS AND COLORADO STATE BUILDING.

Architect, E. F. KARR.—Size, 132 feet square.

This structure is intended for the accommodation of the Commissioners from the States of Kansas and Colorado, and also for exhibition purposes. It is a two-story wooden building, containing an exhibition hall, private rooms and offices, and is situated east of the Southern Restaurant. The Kansas exhibit consists of agricultural products, minerals, silk cocoons, building stone, cotton, plaster of Paris, birds and animals.

The Colorado exhibit embraces mineral, geological, and ornithological specimens, petrifactions, views of Colorado scenery, the Maxwell cabinets of minerals, birds and animals of the Rocky Mountains, etc.

No. 158. NEW ENGLAND FARMER'S HOME AND MODERN KITCHEN.

Size, 49 feet by 35 feet.
MISS E. B. SOUTHWICK, Boston.

A representation of a New England farmer's home 100 years ago, combined with a modern kitchen, thus illustrating 1776 and 1876. It is one story high, and situated on the corner of State and Agricultural Avenues.

No. 159. THE AMERICAN RESTAURANT.

Architects, H. J. SCHWARZMANN, HUGH KAFKA.—Size, 300 feet by 200 feet.
TOBIASON & HEILBRUN, Philadelphia.

Situated between Agricultural and Horticultural Halls. The seating capacity is five thousand. The banquet room accommodates six hundred guests. The waiters speak various languages. There is a pavilion devoted to ice cream, etc. A bill of fare will be served either *à la carte* or *table d'hôte.*

No. 160. GERMAN RESTAURANT.

Architect, H. J. SCHWARZMANN.—Size, 200 feet by 150 feet.
PHILIP J. LAUBER, Philadelphia.

Contains three acres for garden arrangements, and is situated north of Horticultural Hall, on Lansdowne drive.

No. 161. TEA AND COFFEE PRESS EXTRACT BUILDING.

Architects, HAYES & MCIVOR, Elmira, N. Y.—Size, 100 feet by 45 feet.

A two-story frame building, composed of four observatories connected by verandas. Located opposite the southeast corner of the Agricultural Building, and devoted to the exhibition of the process of making coffee, tea, and other extracts, by means of pressure caused by the expansion of the materials used.

No. 162. BUTTER AND CHEESE FACTORY.

Size, 100 feet by 116 feet.

A model factory, three stories high, built of wood, and situated east of the Agricultural Building, between it and Lansdowne drive.

No. 163. SODA WATER STANDS.

These structures are located at various points east of Belmont and north of Fountain Avenues.

No. 164. CIGAR STANDS.

These stands are found at various points east of Belmont and north of Fountain Avenues.

No. 165. FARM WAGON ANNEX.

See Part IV., page 135.

No. 166. POMOLOGICAL ANNEX.

See Part IV., page 135.

No. 167. BREWERS' BUILDING.

See Part IV., page 136.

No. 168. APIARY.

See Part IV., page 140.

No. 169. PACIFIC GUANO COMPANY'S PAVILION.

MR. JOHN M. GLIDDON, Manager.

This is, in style, similar to a Moorish kiosk. The exhibit consists of various products of the soil, guano in its various processes of manufacture, models of company's works at Wood's Hole and Chisolius Island, fossil remains, etc., while several acres of ground, in close proximity to their pavilion, are planted in cotton, cane, tobacco, etc., to demonstrate the efficacy of their manufacture. The building is situated on Fountain Avenue, east of Women's Pavilion.

No. 170. ANNEX TO HORTICULTURAL HALL, OR SPECIAL FLOWER PAVILION.

This building is made of glass and iron, located immediately north of Horticultural Hall, and is intended for the display of specialties in flowers.

No. 171. WIND MILLS.

See Part IV., page 140.

No. 172. "PRACTICAL FARMER" (NEWSPAPER OFFICE).

See Part IV., page 140.

No. 173. HAY PRESS.

One Dedrich portable engine, six horse-power, for running hay presses. The presses take in loose hay, baling and banding 20 tons to the hour, or 280 bales.

No. 174. CENTENNIAL POLICE STATION.

A frame building situated east of Hay Press and Agricultural Hall, intended for accommodation of Centennial Guards.

No. 175. SAFETY ELEVATED RAILWAY.

ROY STONE, Proprietor.

This railroad is situated over Belmont Ravine, north of Horticultural Hall. It was designed by Roy Stone, and first erected at Phœnixville, Pa. Examined and fully approved by eminent engineers. Brought here as an exhibit and for conveyance of passengers under the concession to West End Railroad Co. Intended for rapid transit in cities, or for very cheap country railroad for passengers and freight.

No. 176. BOILER HOUSE.

Situated east of Agricultural Hall, and furnishes steam for engine in that building.

No. 177. VIRGINIA STATE BUILDING.

A frame structure one story high, with veranda all around, situated on State Avenue east of the Kansas and Colorado building, facing Horticultural grounds.

No. 178. THE PROTECTIVE FIRE APPARATUS COMPANY OF NEW YORK.

Size, 8 feet by 10 feet.

This is a one-story wooden building, situated on Agricultural Avenue, west of Agricultural Hall, and is designed to display fire extinguishers.

No. 179. POP-CORN STAND.

Situated at corner of Agricultural Avenue, near station of Narrow-Gauge Railroad.

No. 180. FOUNTAIN OF THE JORDAN L. MOTT IRON WORKS OF NEW YORK.

Located east of Horticultural Hall. This is an iron fountain 45 feet in diameter and 26 feet high. There are four figures at the base, and the top is surmounted by the design of "Venus Rising from the Sea."

In the interior of the different buildings are located several fountains of varied designs.

INDEX OF EXHIBITORS.

DEPARTMENT V. AND SPECIAL BUILDINGS.

A.

B.

C.

D.

E.

F.

G.

H.

I.

J.

K.

L.

N.

O.

P.

Q.

R.

S.

V.

W.

Y.

BUILDING No. 41,

OCCUPIED JOINTLY BY THE

CENTENNIAL CATALOGUE COMPANY,

AND

S. M. Pettengill & Co., Newspaper Advertising Agents,

South of East End of Machinery Hall.

ADVERTISEMENTS taken at this office for the Official Catalogue and all newspapers of the United States and Canadas. The principal papers of the country kept on file for inspection and use of exhibitors and visitors generally.

CENTENNIAL CATALOGUE CO.

S. W. Cor. Fourth and Library Sts., Philadelphia,

PUBLISHERS OF THE

OFFICIAL CATALOGUE

OF THE

INTERNATIONAL EXHIBITION OF 1876.

This Company owns the exclusive right to publish, sell, and distribute the "*Official Catalogue of the International Exhibition of 1876*," the work being printed under the direction of, and compiled from manuscript furnished by, the "U. S. Centennial Commission."

Advertisements taken on application to S. M. PETTENGILL & Co., Advertising Agents.

JOHN S. MORTON,
President.

MORDECAI D. EVANS,
Treasurer.

L. L. HYNEMAN,
Secretary.

S. HENRY NORRIS,
Solicitor.

JOHN R. NAGLE,
Publishing and Advertising Manager,
524 Market St., Philadelphia.

S. M. PETTENGILL & CO.,
Advertising Agents,
No. 701 Chestnut Street, Philadelphia,
No. 37 Park Row, New York,
No. 10 State Street, Boston,
Exhibition Grounds—South of East end of Machinery Hall, Building No. 41.

J. M. JOHNSON & SONS, Limited,
Sole European Agents,
No. 3 Castle St., Holborn, London.

DIRECTORS:

JOHN S. MORTON, WM. H. PENNELL,
M. ROSENBACH, STEPHEN F. WHITMAN,
GEORGE T. JONES, JOHN R. NAGLE,
JOSEPH HEILBRUN.

Office of the Company on Exhibition Grounds, Building No. 41, South of East end of Machinery Hall.

AGRICULTURAL BUILDING.

United States Centennial Commission.

INTERNATIONAL EXHIBITION.

1876

Official Catalogue.

PART IV.

AGRICULTURAL AND HORTICULTURAL HALLS AND ANNEXES.

DEPARTMENT VI.—AGRICULTURE.
DEPARTMENT VII.—HORTICULTURE.

SECOND AND REVISED EDITION.

PHILADELPHIA:
Published for the Centennial Catalogue Company
BY JOHN R. NAGLE AND COMPANY.
Printed at the Riverside Press, Cambridge, Mass.
1876.

CONTENTS.

BUILDINGS AND SPECIAL EXHIBITS WITHIN THE EXHIBITION GROUNDS.

[Note.—The buildings bear the numbers prefixed to them in this table, being the numbers adopted by the Centennial Guide Book Co. (Limited).]

Buildings South of the Avenue of the Republic.

1. Main Exhibition Building.
2. Machinery Hall.
3. Machine Shop.
4. American Boiler House.
5. Corliss Boiler House.
6. British Boiler House.
7. Shoe and Leather Exhibition Building.
8. Office Centennial Board of Finance.
9. Office U. S. Centennial Commission.
10. Centennial National Bank.
11. Weimer Machine Works.
12. Bartholdi Fountain.
13. Catholic Total Abstinence Union Fountain.
14. Fuller, Warren, & Co., Heating Apparatus.
15. Gillender & Sons, Glassware Manufactory.
16. Camp of West Point Cadets.
17. Iron Pipe.
18. Liberty Stove Works.
19. Annex, Saw Mill.
20. Boiler House.
21. Railway Engine House.
22. St. Cecilia Organs.
23. Automatic Railway.
24. Monument—American Soldier.
25. Gunpowder Pile-Driver.
26. Jesse Star & Son, Iron Works.
27. West End Railway Offices.
28. Pneumatic Tubes.
29. New England Granite Co.'s Exhibit.
30. Railroad Crossings.
31. State of Nevada Quartz Mill.
32. Store House.
33. Friction Drum.
34. Stokes & Parrish, U. S. Hoisting Machine.
35. Chilean Amalgamating Machinery.
36. Campbell Printing Press.
37. Old Locomotive and Car.
38. Car House.
39. Police Station.
40. Averill Paint Co.
41. Centennial Catalogue Co.
42. Stokes & Parrish, Boiler House.
43. Ehret's Waterproof Roofing.
44. Tombstones.
45. Terra Cotta Pipe.
46. Mineral Annex, 1 and 2.
47. Fireproof Ventilated Building.
48. Swings.
49. Ornamental Stone Work.

Buildings North of the Avenue of the Republic, and West of Belmont Av.

51. United States Government Building.
51½. Bartholdi Electric Light.
52. United States Hospital.
52½. Howe Monument.
53. United States Hospital Tent.
53½. Jerusalem Bazaar.
54. United States Laboratory.
54½. Office Philadelphia "Times."
55. Pennsylvania State Building.
55½. Hungarian Wine Pavilion.
56. Ohio State Building.
56½. Police Station.
57. Indiana State Building.
57½. Sponge Fishers of Turkey.
58. Illinois State Building.
58½. Bethlehem Bazaar.
59. Wisconsin State Building.
59½. Fog Horn and Bell.
60. Michigan State Building.
61. New Hampshire State Building.
62. Connecticut State Building.
63. Massachusetts State Building.
64. Delaware State Building.
65. Maryland State Building.
66. Arkansas State Building.
67. Japanese Dwelling.
68. West Virginia State Building.
69. Canadian Log House.
70. Missouri State Building.
71. British Government Building.
72. British Government Building.
73. British Government Building.
74. New York State Building.
75. Liènard's Relief Plans, Paris, Jerusalem, Italy, etc.
76. Pop-corn Stand.
77. Cigar Stand.
78. Soda Water Stand.
79. Tunisian Café and Bazaar.
80. Columbus Monument.
81. Drinking Fountains.
82. Restaurant "Trois Frères Provençaux."
83. Office New York "Tribune."
84. World's Ticket Office, Cook, Son, & Jenkins.
85. Loiseau's Pressed Fuel Company.
86. Spanish Government Buildings.
87. United States Signal Office.
88. Tennessee State Building.
89. Mississippi State Building.
90. George's Hill Restaurant.
91. Bishop Allen Monument.
92. Office of the Boston "Advertiser" and Boston "Herald."
93. Rowell's Newspaper Exhibition B'ld'g.
94. California State Building.
95. Centennial Fire Patrol, No. 1.
96. Turkish Café.
97. Office Frank Leslie's Publications.
98. Iowa State Building.
99. Rhode Island State Building.
100. Vermont State Building.

BUILDINGS AND SPECIAL EXHIBITS WITHIN THE EXHIBITION GROUNDS.

Buildings East of Belmont Avenue, and South of Fountain Avenue.

101. Art Gallery.
102. Art Gallery Annex.
103. B'nai B'rith Monument of Religious Liberty.
104. Photographic Art Building.
105. Vienna Bakery and Coffee House.
106. Principal Annex to Main Exhibition Building.
107. Swedish Government Building.
108. Japanese Bazaar.
109. The Judges' Hall.
110. Centennial Photographic Company.
111. Sheet-metal Pavilion.
112. German Government Building.
113. Railroad Ticket Office.
114. Office United States Centennial Commission.
115. Brazilian Government Building.
116. The Dairy.
117. Restaurant "La Fayette."
118. House of Public Comfort.
119. Empire Transportation Company.
120. French Government Building.
121. Centennial Fire Patrol, No. 2.
122. Pennsylvania Educational Building
123. Telegraph Office.
124. American Fusee Company.
125. Klautscheck, Thomas, & Stewart's Glass Magazine.
126. Moorish Villa.
127. American Bible Society.
128. Hunter's Camp.
129. Office Water Department.
130. Soda Water Stands.
131. Cigar Stands.
132. Singer's Sewing Machines.
133. Centennial Medical Department.
134. Portugal Government Building.
135. Bankers' Building.
136. French Glass Exhibit.
137. Kindergarten.
138. Centennial Police Station.
139. Philadelphia City Building.
140. Music Pavilion.
141. Burial Caskets.
142. Perforated Metal Building.
143. Rubber Roofing.
144. Cuban Acclimation Office.
145. Naval Group.
146. The Dying Lioness.

Buildings East of Belmont Avenue, and North of Fountain Avenue.

151. Horticultural Hall.
152. Agricultural Hall.
153. The Women's Pavilion.
154. The Women's School House.
155. New Jersey State Building.
156. Restaurant of the South.
157. Kansas and Colorado State Building.
158. New England Farmer's Home 100 years ago, and Modern Kitchen.
159. Great American Restaurant.
160. German Restaurant.
161. Tea and Coffee Press.
162. Butter and Cheese Factory.
163. Soda Water Stand.
164. Cigar Stand.
165. Farm Wagon Building.
166. Pomological Building.
167. Brewers' Building.
168. Model House Apiary.
169. Guano Company.
170. Special Flower Exhibit Building.
171. Wind Mills.
172. Office "Ohio Farmer."
173. Hay Press.
174. Police Station.
175. Elevated Railroad.
176. Boiler House.
177. Virginia State Building.
178. Protective Fire Apparatus.
179. Pop-corn Stands.
180. J. L. Mott Co. Fountain.

SUBJECT INDEX, NATIONAL EXHIBITS.

NATIONS.	DEPARTMENT VI. AGRICULTURE.										DEPT. VII. HORTICULTURE.					
	Arboriculture and Forest Products.	Pomology.	Agricultural Products.	Land Animals.	Water Animals, Fish Culture, and Apparatus.	Animal and Vegetable Products.	Textile Substances of Vegetable or Animal Origin.	Machines, Implements, and Processes of Manufacture.	Agricultural Engineering and Administration.	Tillage and General Management.	Ornamental Trees, Shrubs, and Flowers.	Hot-houses, Conservatories, Graperies.	Garden Tools, Accessories of Gardening.	Garden Designing, Construction and Management.	Statistics of Exhibiting Countries.	Commissioners to the Exhibition.
United States.	15 135	15	15 136	18	18	19 136	24	25 135 137	35 135 138	38	151 153	152	152 154	153 154	163	...
Great Britain..	40	...	40	...	...	139	41.	41	139	...	156	...	156	...	169	173
‡New Zealand..	...	...	42	...	...	...	42	...	...	...	156	...	...	...	174	177
‡New S. Wales.	...	...	...	...	...	42	...	...	...	...	...	...	...	...	178	179
‡Victoria.........	...	...	...	...	...	...	...	...	...	...	...	...	...	...	181	182
‡S. Australia....	...	...	...	...	...	...	...	43	...	...	...	...	...	...	183	184
‡Cape of Good Hope..........	...	...	43	...	...	43	43	...	...	...	...	...	...	...	185	186
‡Jamaica.........	...	43	...	...	...	...	...	...	...	...	...	156	...	...	187	187
‡Bahamas	...	...	...	...	...	...	...	...	...	...	...	...	...	...	188	188
‡Bermudas	...	...	...	...	...	...	...	...	...	...	...	...	...	...	189	190
‡British Guiana	...	...	...	...	...	...	...	...	...	...	...	...	...	...	190	191
‡Ceylon	...	...	...	...	...	...	...	...	...	...	...	...	...	...	191	...
‡Straights Settlements......	...	...	...	..	...	...	...	...	...	...	...	...	...	...	192	...
‡Gold Coast..	...	...	...	...	...	...	...	...	...	...	...	...	...	...	192	...
‡Mauritius.......	...	...	...	...	...	...	...	...	...	...	...	...	...	...	193	...
‡Queensland	...	...	...	...	...	...	...	...	...	...	...	...	...	...	194	195
‡Seychelles Archipelago	...	...	...	...	..	...	...	...	...	...	...	...	...	...	196	...
‡Tasmania	...	...	...	...	...	...	...	...	...	...	...	...	...	...	196	198
‡Trinidad........	...	...	...	...	...	...	...	...	...	...	...	...	...	...	198	...
‡India..............	...	...	...	...	...	...	...	...	...	...	...	...	...	...	199	...
Canada..........	44 134	44	44	44	44	44 139	45	46	46	...	...	...	157	...	202	204
*France	48	48	48	...	48	49	51	51	51	...	157	157	157	157	205	209
Germany	53	...	53 139	...	...	53	54	54	54	...	...	...	...	158	210	215
Austria..........	55	55	55	...	55	55	56	56	56	...	...	...	...	158	216	221
‡Switzerland....	...	...	...	...	...	...	...	...	...	...	...	...	...	...	222	225
Belgium.........	...	...	...	...	...	...	...	...	...	...	...	...	...	...	226	228
Netherlands...	57	...	57	...	57	57	...	...	...	..	158	...	158	...	230	234
Denmark	...	...	...	...	...	...	...	...	...	...	...	...	...	...	235	236
Sweden..........	59	...	59	...	59	59	...	60	60	...	...	..	...	...	237	240
Norway.........	61	...	61	61	61	61	...	62	62	...	...	...	...	...	241	243
Italy	63	63	63	...	63	63	66	67	67	...	...	...	159	...	244	249
‡Egypt	...	...	...	...	...	...	...	...	...	...	...	...	...	...	250	252
Tunis	...	...	...	...	...	...	...	...	...	...	...	...	...	...	253	253
‡Orange Free State..........	...	...	...	...	...	...	..	...	...	...	...	...	...	...	254	255
‡Luxemburg....	...	...	...	...	...	...	...	...	...	...	159	...	...	...	256	...
‡China............	...	...	...	...	...	...	...	...	...	...	...	...	...	...	256	257
Japan...	128	...	128	...	128	129	129	...	129	...	129	...	129	129	258	259
‡Hawaii	...	...	...	...	...	...	...	...	...	...	159	...	...	...	260	261
‡Brazil	...	...	...	...	...	...	...	...	...	...	...	...	...	...	262	263
Argentine Republic.........	76	...	77	81	81	81	86	...	88	...	159	...	...	159	264	265
‡Chili	...	...	...	...	...	...	...	...	...	...	...	...	...	...	266	267
‡Peru	...	...	...	...	...	...	...	...	...	...	...	...	...	...	268	270
‡Mexico..........	...	...	...	...	...	...	...	...	...	...	...	...	...	...	271	274
†Liberia	...	...	88	...	...	88	88	...	...	...	...	...	...	...	275	...
Spain	...	...	...	...	...	...	...	...	...	...	160	160	...	160	277	280
Philippine Islands	130	130	130	131	131	131	132	133	...	...	160	...	...	...	...	...
Portugal........	89	90	92	...	99	99	120	...	122	...	...	...	...	...	281	284
‡Turkey..........	...	...	..	...	...	...	...	...	...	...	...	...	...	...	286	288
Russia...........	123	123	123	...	124	124	126	127	127	...	...	...	...	...	289	294

* Metallurgical exhibit of France, page 48.
† Metallurgical exhibit of Liberia, page 88.
‡ Countries marked thus have Agricultural exhibits which are installed in the Main Building, and catalogued in Part I.

No. 152. AGRICULTURAL HALL.

Size, parallelogram, 820 by 540 feet.

Architect, JAMES H. WINDRIM, *Philadelphia*.

Contractor, PHILIP QUIGLEY, *Wilmington, Del.*

Wrought iron furnished by ALLISON & SONS, *Philadelphia*.

Erectors, BELL BROTHERS.

THE Agricultural Exhibition Building stands north of Horticultural Hall, on the eastern side of Belmont avenue. A novel combination of materials is illustrated in its construction. It consists of a long nave crossed by three transepts, all composed of Howe truss arches of Gothic form. The four courts inclosed between the nave and transepts, as also the four spaces at the corners of the building, having the nave and transepts for their sides, are roofed in and form spaces for exhibits. The building covers an area of above ten acres. Stock yards for the exhibition of horses, cattle, sheep, swine, poultry, etc., are in the vicinity of the exhibition grounds.

The contract was made July 26th, 1875, and the building was begun in September 1875, and finished in April, 1876. It cost $260,000.

KEY TO THE NOTATION.

THE location of objects in the Agricultural Building is shown by a letter and figure, indicating the nearest column of the building. The letters—A, B, C, to T—designate the successive ranges of columns, proceeding eastward from the western wall across the width of the building; the figures, the number of the column in each range, counting northwardly from the southern wall, the entire length of the building, from 1 to 28. Thus C 5 is the column in the third range from the west, and the fifth from the southern end of the building. The northeasternmost column is T 28.

The class of the classification (see pages 12–14) to which each exhibit belongs is indicated by the small figures at the end of the line.

AGRICULTURAL HALL.

Scale, 225 ft. to 1 in.

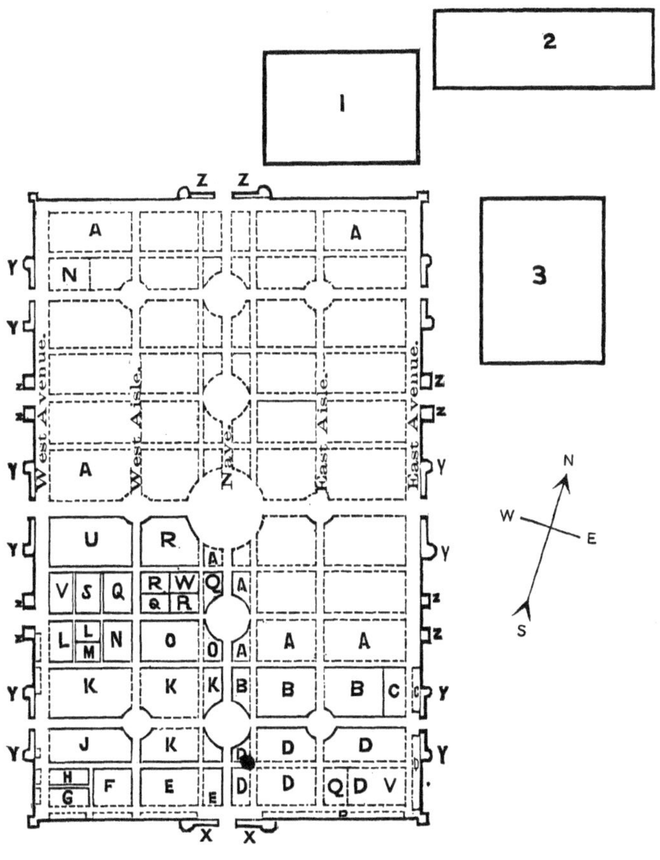

A *United States.*
B *Canada.*
C *Liberia.*
D *England.*
E *Germany.*
F *Austria.*
G *Japan.*
H *Venezuela.*
J *Netherlands.*
K *France.*
L *Sweden.*
M *Denmark.*
N *Norway.*
O *Brazil.*
P *Belgium.*
Q *Portugal.*
R *Spain and Phil. Islands.*
S *Argentine Republic.*
U *Russia.*
V *Italy.*
W *Mexico.*
X *Dept. of Public Comfort.*
Y *Water-closets.*
Z *Offices.*
1. Wagon Building.
2. Brewers' Building.
3. Pomological Building.

Total Length, 540 ft. Width, 820 ft. Height, 75 ft.

SYNOPSIS OF THE CLASSIFICATION.

LOCATION.	DEPARTMENTS.	CLASSES.	GROUPS.
MAIN BUILDING.	I. MINING AND METALLURGY.	100—109	Minerals, Ores, Stone, Mining Products.
		110—119	Metallurgical Products.
		120—129	Mining Engineering.
	II. MANUFACTURES.	200—205	Chemical Manufactures.
		206—216	Ceramics, Pottery, Porcelain, Glass, etc.
		217—227	Furniture, etc.
		228—234	Yarns and Woven Goods of Vegetable or Mineral Materials.
		235—241	Woven and Felted Goods of Wool, etc.
		242—249	Silk and Silk Fabrics.
		250—257	Clothing, Jewelry, etc.
		258—264	Paper, Blank Books, Stationery.
		265—271	Weapons, etc.
		272—279	Medicine, Surgery, Prothesis.
		280—284	Hardware, Edge Tools, Cutlery, and Metallic Products.
		285—291	Fabrics of Vegetable, Animal, or Mineral Materials.
		292—296	Carriages, Vehicles, and Accessories.
	III. EDUCATION AND SCIENCE	300—309	Educational Systems, Methods, and Libraries.
		310—319	Institutions and Organizations.
		320—329	Scientific and Philosophical Instruments and Methods.
		330—339	Engineering, Architecture, Maps, etc.
		340—349	Physical, Social, and Moral Condition of Man.
ART GALLERY.	IV. ART.	400—409	Sculpture.
		410—419	Painting.
		420—429	Engraving and Lithography.
		430—439	Photography.
		440—449	Industrial and Architectural Designs, etc.
		450—459	Ceramic Decorations, Mosaics, etc.
MACHINERY BUILDING.	V. MACHINERY.	500—509	Machines, Tools, etc., of Mining, Chemistry, etc.
		510—519	Machines and Tools for working Metal, Wood, and Stone.
		520—529	Machines and Implements of Spinning, Weaving, etc.
		530—539	Machines, etc., used in Sewing, Making Clothing, etc.
		540—549	Machines for Printing, Making Books, Paper Working, etc.
		550—559	Motors, Power Generators, etc.
		560—569	Hydraulic and Pneumatic Apparatus.
		570—579	Railway Plant, Rolling Stock, etc.
		580—589	Machinery used in Preparing Agricultural Products.
		590—599	Aerial, Pneumatic, and Water Transportation.
			Machinery, and Apparatus, especially adapted to the requirements of the Exhibition.
AGRICULTURAL BUILDING.	VI. AGRICULTURE.	600—609	Arboriculture and Forest Products.
		610—619	Pomology.
		620—629	Agricultural Products.
		630—639	Land Animals.
		640—649	Marine Animals, Fish Culture, and Apparatus.
		650—662	Animal and Vegetable Products.
		665—669	Textile Substances of Vegetable or Animal origin.
		670—679	Machines, Implements, and Processes of Manufacture.
		680—689	Agricultural Engineering and Administration.
		690—699	Tillage and General Management.
HORTICULTURAL BUILDING.	VII. HORTICULTURE.	700—709	Ornamental Trees, Shrubs, and Flowers.
		710—719	Hot Houses, Conservatories, Graperies.
		720—729	Garden Tools, Accessories of Gardening.
		730—739	Garden Designing, Construction, and Management.

CLASSIFICATION.

DEPARTMENT VI.—AGRICULTURE.

ARBORICULTURE AND FOREST PRODUCTS.

CLASS 600.—Timber and trunks of trees, entire or in transverse or truncated sections, with specimens of barks, leaves, flowers, seed vessels, and seed.

Masts, spars, knees, longitudinal sections of trees, railway ties, ship timber, lumber roughly sawn; as planks, shingles, lath, and staves.

Timber and lumber prepared in various ways to resist decay and combustion; as by injection of salts of copper and zinc.

CLASS 601.—Ornamental woods used in decorating and for furniture; as veneers of mahogany, rosewood, ebony, walnut, maple, and madrona.

CLASS 602.—Dyewoods, barks, and galls for coloring and tanning.

CLASS 603.—Gums, resins, caoutchouc, gutta percha, vegetable wax.

CLASS 604.—Lichens, mosses, fungi, pulu, ferns.

CLASS 605.—Seeds, nuts, etc., for food and ornamental purposes.

CLASS 606.—Forestry.—Illustrations of the art of planting, managing, and protecting forests. Statistics.

CLASS 607.—Fruit trees and shrubs.

POMOLOGY.

CLASS 610.—Fruits of temperate and semi-tropical regions; as apples, pears, quinces, peaches, nectarines, apricots, plums, grapes, cherries, strawberries, and melons.

CLASS 611.—Tropical fruits and nuts, oranges, bananas, plantains, lemons, pineapples, pomegranates, figs, cocoanuts.

AGRICULTURAL PRODUCTS.

CLASS 620.—Cereals, grasses, and forage plants.

CLASS 621.—Leguminous plants and esculent vegetables.

CLASS 622.—Roots and tubers.

CLASS 623.—Tobacco, hops, tea, coffee, spices, condiments, herbs.

CLASS 624.—Seeds and seed vessels.

LAND ANIMALS.

CLASS 630.—Horses, asses, mules.

CLASS 631.—Horned cattle.

CLASS 632.—Sheep.

CLASS 633.—Goats, alpaca, llama, camel.

CLASS 634.—Swine.

CLASS 635.—Poultry and birds.

CLASS 636.—Dogs and cats.

CLASS 637.—Wild animals.

CLASS 638.—Insects, useful and injurious. Honey bees, cochineal, silk-worms.

MARINE ANIMALS, FISH CULTURE, AND APPARATUS.

CLASS 640.—Marine mammals.—Seals, cetaceans, etc., specimens living in aquaria, or stuffed, salted, preserved in alcohol, or otherwise.
CLASS 641.—Fishes, living or preserved.
CLASS 642.—Pickled fish, and parts of fish used for food.
CLASS 643.—Crustaceans, echinoderms, beche de mer.
CLASS 644.—Mollusks, oysters, clams, etc., used for food.
CLASS 645.—Shells, corals, and pearls.
CLASS 646.—Whalebone, shagreen, fish-glue, isinglass, sounds, fish-oil.
CLASS 647.—Instruments and apparatus of fishing.—Nets, baskets, hooks, and other apparatus used in catching fish.
CLASS 648.—Fish culture.—Aquaria, hatching pools, vessels for transporting roe and spawn, and other apparatus used in fish breeding, culture, or preservation.

ANIMAL AND VEGETABLE PRODUCTS.

(Used as food or as materials.)

CLASS 650.—Sponges, seaweed, and other growths used for food or in the arts.
CLASS 651.—The dairy.—Milk, cream, butter, cheese.
CLASS 652.—Hides, furs, and leather, tallow, oil, and lard, ivory, bone, horn, glue.
CLASS 653.—Eggs, feathers, down.
CLASS 654.—Honey and wax.
CLASS 655.—Animal perfumes; as musk, civet, ambergris.
CLASS 656.—Preserved meats, vegetables, and fruits. Dried, or in cans or jars. Meat and vegetable extracts.
CLASS 657.—Flour; crushed and ground cereals, decorticated grains.
CLASS 658.—Starch and similar products.
CLASS 659.—Sugar and syrups.
CLASS 660.—Wines, alcohol, and malt liquors.
CLASS 661.—Bread, biscuits, crackers, cakes, confectionery, cocoa, chocolate, etc.
CLASS 662.—Vegetable oils, oil cake.

TEXTILE SUBSTANCES OF VEGETABLE OR ANIMAL ORIGIN.

CLASS 665.—Cotton on the stem, in the boll, ginned, and baled.
CLASS 666.—Hemp, flax, jute, ramie, etc., in primitive forms and in all stages of preparation for spinning.
CLASS 667.—Wool in the fleece, carded, and in bales.
CLASS 668.—Silk in the cocoon and reeled.
CLASS 669.—Hair, bristles.

MACHINES, IMPLEMENTS, AND PROCESSES OF MANUFACTURE.

CLASS 670.—Tillage.—Manual implements, spades, hoes, rakes. Animal power machinery, plows, cultivators, horse-hoes, clod-crushers, rollers, harrows. Steam power machinery, plows, breakers, harrows, cultivators.
CLASS 671.—Planting.—Manual implements, corn-planters and hand-drills. Animal power machinery, grain and manure drills, corn and cotton planters. Steam power machinery, grain and manure drills.
CLASS 672.—Harvesting.—Manual implements; grain-cradles, sickles, reaping-hooks. Animal power machinery, reapers and headers. Mowers, tedders, rakes, hay elevators, and hay loaders.
Potato diggers.
CLASS 673.—Preparatory to marketing.—Thrashers, clover-hullers, corn-shellers, winnowers, hay, cotton, flax, jute, ramie, wine, oil, and sugar making apparatus. Cleaners and smutters. Horse powers.

CLASS 674.—Applicable to farm economy.—Portable and stationary engines, chaffers, hay and feed cutters, slicers, pulpers, corn mills, farm boilers and steamers, incubators, edged tools, mills, meat choppers.

CLASS 675.—Dairy fittings and appliances.—Churns for hand and power, butter-workers, cans and pails, cheese-presses, vats, and apparatus, ice-cream freezers, cedar-ware.

AGRICULTURAL ENGINEERING AND ADMINISTRATION.

CLASS 680.—Laying out and improving farms.—Clearing (stump extractors), construction of roads, draining, irrigating, models of fences, gates, drains, out-falls, dams, embankments, irrigating machinery, stack building and thatching.

CLASS 681.—Commercial fertilizers, phosphatic, ammoniacal, calcareous, etc.

CLASS 682.—Transportation.—Wagons, carts, sleds, harness, yokes, traction engines, and apparatus for road making and excavating.

CLASS 683.—Farm buildings.—Models and drawings of farm houses and tenements, barns, stables, hop-houses, fruit-driers, ice-houses, windmills, granaries, barracks, apiaries, cocooneries, aviaries, abattoirs, and dairies.

TILLAGE AND GENERAL MANAGEMENT.

CLASS 690.—Systems of planting and cultivation.

CLASS 691.—Systems of draining and application of manures.

CLASS 692.—Systems of breeding and stock feeding, training.

CLASS 693.—Veterinary surgery and appliances.

UNITED STATES.

Forest Products, Pomology, Agricultural Products.

Arboriculture and Forest Products.

1 Begg, Jonathan, Gilroy, Cal.—Collection of coniferæ of the Pacific Coast. E 25. 600

2 Peirce, Milton P., Wenonah, N. J.—Native wood. E 26. 600

3 Western North Carolina Land Company, Charlotte, N. C.; branch office, 32 S. Third st., Philada.—Lands heavily wooded, rich in minerals, and well-adapted to grazing and agricultural purposes. Hard and soft woods in variety, and of gigantic growth; medicinal herbs, magnetic and hematite iron ores, manganese, gold, mica, etc. E 19. 600

4 State of Indiana.—**Timber, all kinds** found in the State. G 20. 600

4*a* Norcross, Kent, & Co., Philadelphia, Pa.—Shingles and logs. F 26. 600

5 State Board of Iowa (collective exhibit), Fairfield, Iowa.—Woods, native and cultivated; wood seeds, soils. C 15. 600

5*a* Rowand, Hillman, & Son, Kirkwood, N. J.—Charcoal. E 26. 600

6 Graham, Dorsett, & Co., New York, N. Y.—Cabinet woods. F 28. 600

6*a* State of New Jersey. — Native woods. E 17–18. 600

6*b* State of Wisconsin.—Forest products. F 20–21. 600

6*c* New Hampshire State Centennial Board.—Native woods. E 20–21. 600

6*d* Land Department Central Pacific R. R. Co.—Woods. B 15 *to* 19. 600

7 Woods, Perry, & Co., Cleveland, Ohio.—White pine lumber. F 25. 600

8 State of Oregon, Portland, Oregon. —Native woods, medicine roots, and bark; shingles. E 22. 600

9 Eastern Burnettizing Co., Boston, Mass.—Burnettized lumber for bridges, wharves, railroads, and all positions where wood is liable to decay. F 26. 600

10 State of Delaware (collective exhibit), Dover, Del.—Timber in the rough and dressed. F 17. 600

11 Albemarle Swamp Land Co., North Carolina.—Cedar and cypress shingles, staves, etc. F 26. 600

12 Davis, Wire, & Co., North Carolina. —Ribbed cedar and cypress shingles. F 28. 600

13 State of West Virginia (collective exhibit).—Forest products. F 19. 600

14 Gove, E., Bath, Maine.—Basswood panels. F 28. 601

14*a* Cross & Mehling, Grand Rapids, Mich.—Imitation of walnut burl, etc. E 26. 601

14*b* Macatee & Bro., Front Royal, Va. —Ground sumac. F 28. 602

14*c* Williams, R. H., Milford, Del.—Quercitron bark. F 26. 602

15 Burk, William B., & Co., Philadelphia, Pa.—Corks and sponges. E 25. 603

16 Smythe, Earle, & Co., New York, N. Y.—Crude elastic gums, with botanical specimens of same. E 28. 603

16*a* Day, Austin G., Seymour, Conn.—India-rubber producing plants, from tropical countries; crude India-rubber; crude kerite, or substitute for rubber. H 27–28. 603

17 Butz, Alfred L., Philadelphia, Pa.—Machine and hand-cut corks. E 25. 603

17*a* Delta Moss Co., New Orleans, La. —Southern moss. E 25. 604

18 Michigan State Agricultural College (collective exhibit).—Forestry. E 25. 606

Pomology.

19 Atlantic Co. for the Culture of Cranberries, Weymouth, N. J.—Cranberries, natural and preserved. J 28. 610

20 State Board of Iowa, Fairfield, Iowa. —Apples and pears in wax models. C 15. 610

20*a* Bannihe, John H., Egg Harbor City, N. J.—Strawberries and plants; grapes. K 14. 610

21 Collings, E. Z., Waterford, N. J.—Cranberries in jars, showing different varieties. C 20. 610

21*a* West Jersey Land & Cranberry Co., Atco, N. J.—Cranberries and vines. C 20. 610

21*b* Michigan Pomological Society, Detroit, Mich.—Apples. (*Nave of Agricultural Building.*) 610

21*c* Bonzano, H., New Orleans, La.—Pecan nuts. H 28. 611

Agricultural Products.

22 State Board of Iowa, Fairfield, Iowa. —Corn, small grains, grass seeds, vegetable seeds, etc. C 15. 620

23 Branson, David H., Guthrieville, Pa. —Indian corn. N 10–11. 620

24 Beeson, Jacob, & Co., Detroit, Mich. —Samples of grain. J 17. 620

25 State of Massachusetts (collective exhibit), Boston, Mass.—Agricultural products. E *and* F 23. 620

26 Possiponti, Angola, Harrisburg, Pa. —Straw for the manufacture of straw-goods. E 15. 620

For classes of exhibits, indicated by numbers at end of entries, see Classification, pp. 12–14.

Agricultural Products.

27 Thompson, C. B., Chillicothe, Ohio. —Broom corn. F 15. 620

27*a* Schaffer, William L., Philadelphia, Pa.—Maize and sheaf. E 16. 620

27*b* Western Washington Industrial Association, Philadelphia, Pa.—Grains. D 20. 620

27*c* Seneca County Agricultural Society, Geneva, N. Y.—Grains, grass, seeds, etc. F 16. 620

27*d* New Hampshire State Centennial Board. E 20–21.
- *a* Corn, wheat, barley, rye, oats, buckwheat, peas, beans, grasses, etc. 620
- *b* Potatoes, vegetables. 622

27*e* State of Wisconsin.—Agricultural products. F 20–21. 620

28 U. S. Hullers Oat Co., Williamsport, Pa.—Oats without hull, oat-flour, and feed. H 15. 620

28*a* Culbertson, J., Brandon, Miss.— Rice and corn. F 15. 620

28*b* Schoonmaker, Henry, Cedar Hill, N. Y.—Cereals. H 15. 620

28*c* Hornly, Alex., Craigville, N. Y.— Cereals. G 26. 620

28*d* Land Department Central Pacific R. R. Co.—Grain. B 15–19. 620

28*e* Talmadge, Dan., Sons, New York, N. Y.—Carolina rice. G 16. 620

28*f* Lachicotte, P. R., & Sons, Georgetown, S. C.—Carolina rice. H 16. 620

28*g* Smith, J. C., Chicago, Ill.—Variety of grains raised in the State. G 22. 620

28*h* Mohawk & Hudson Manufacturing Co., Hartford, N. Y.—Pressed hay. S 8. 620

28*i* Montana Territory, Montana.—Cereals. G 15. 620

29 State of Indiana (collective exhibit). G 20.
- *a* White, red, and amber wheat, oats, rye, barley, Indian corn, grass-seed, etc. 620
- *b* Cloverseed, white and colored, butter-beans. 624

30 Landreth, D., & Sons, Philadelphia, Pa. H 15.
- *a* Cereals, grasses, and tobacco. 620
- *b* Field and garden seeds. 624

The full and entire exhibit the production of their own seed-farms in Pennsylvania, New Jersey, Virginia, and Wisconsin.

31 State Michigan Agricultural College. H *and* I 20 *to* 21.
- *a* Farm products. 620
- *b* Seeds of forest trees. 624

32 State of Oregon, Portland, Oregon. E 22.
- *a* Native grasses, cultivated grasses, grain in the sheaf. 620
- *b* Grain in the sack; cultivated grass-seed. 624

33 State of Delaware, Dover, Del. F 17.
- *a* Cereals. 620
- *b* Seeds. 624

34 Ohio State Centennial Board (collective exhibit), Cleveland, Ohio. D *and* E 16.
- *a* Grains, grasses. 620
- *b* Seeds. 624

35 State of West Virginia (collective exhibit). F 19.
- *a* Grasses and agricultural products. 620
- *b* Tobacco. 623
- *c* Wheat, corn, oats, barley, and rye. 624

35*a* Felten, A. L., Philadelphia, Pa.— Vegetables. (*Centre of nave.*) 621

35*b* McNaughton & Co., Philadelphia, Pa.—Bermuda vegetables. J *and* K 17 621

36 Bliss, B. K., & Sons, seedsmen, 34 Barclay street, New York, N. Y.—Potatoes. H 15. 622

Collection of two hundred varieties potatoes. Seed potatoes a specialty. The following well-known varieties were first sent out by this firm: "Early Rose," "Late Rose," "King of the Earlies," "Bresee's Prolific," "Peerless," "Climax," "Extra Early Vermont," "Compton's Surprise," "Brownell's Beauty," "Snowflake," "Eureka," "Alpha," and "Ruby."

37 Murdoch, Aug., New York, N. Y.— American mustard. I 28. 623

38 Bourgeois, Edmund, New Orleans, La.—Perique tobacco, sole agent for Grand Point, St. James, La Perique tobacco and Ledoux's Perique cigarettes. G 25. 623

39 Weikel & Smith Spice Co., Philadelphia, Pa.—Mustard, spices, celery-salt, blacking. K 14. 623

40 Kinney, Francis S., New York, N. Y. —Cigarettes and tobacco. G 25. 623

41 Frishmuth Bros. & Co., Philadelphia, Pa.—Leaf tobacco; fine-cut and smoking tobacco. I 24. 623

42 Swank, M. J., Philadelphia, Pa.— Cigars. G 25. 623

43 Fell, C. J., & Bro., Philadelphia, Pa. —Spices, mustards, crude and manufactured. J 21. 623

44 Stewart, Ralph, & Co., Philadelphia, Pa.—Scotch snuff. G 26. 623

45 Holbrook, Edward, Louisville, Ky. —Manufactured tobacco. H 25. 623

45*a* Sorver, Cook, & Co., Philadelphia, Pa.—Tobacco. F 25. 623

45*b* Pearson, J. R., & Co., Danville, Va.— Tobacco. N 25. 623

46 Israel, J. N., 1338 South St., Philadelphia, Pa.—Cigars. Cigar manufacturer and wholesale dealer in leaf, chewing, and smoking tobacco. G 26. 623

47 Boyd, G., & Co., Philadelphia, Pa.— Coffee, green and roasted. C 22. 623

48 Wardle, George F., Philadelphia, Pa.—Plug chewing tobacco. G 24. 623

49 Blackwell, W. J., & Co., Durham, N. C.—Plug, leaf, and smoking tobacco. H 23. 623

50 Batchelor Brothers, Philadelphia, Pa.—Cigars, tobacco-plants. G 23. 623

50*a* Harrauff & Engle, Elizabethtown, Pa.—Tobacco. G 24. 623

50*b* Goetze, F. A., & Bro., New York, N. Y.—Snuff. F 25. 623

50*c* Rieders, M. H., New York, N. Y.— Cigarettes. G 24. 623

51 Trowbridge, W. H., Danville, Va.— Chewing and smoking tobacco. G 24. 623

52 Shelton Tobacco Curing Co., Asheville, N. C.—Tobacco-hanger. G 24. 623

For locations of objects, indicated by letter and figure, see Key to Notation, p. 9; ground plan, p. 10.

Agricultural Products.

53 Wilkens, H., & Co., Baltimore, Md.—Smoking tobacco and snuff. Manufacturers of the well-known brands:—"Commodore," Sweet Eighteen, Golden Eagle, "Dairy Queen," "Seal of Virginia," Always Ahead, Queen of North Carolina and Bullhead; "Excelsior," bright and extra Cavendish; Oriental Turkish and "German Imperial;" "Strassburger Snuff," and coarse French Rappee. H 24. 623

54 Cills, Wm., Philadelphia, Pa.—Tobacco packing-box. I 26. 623

55 V. Martinez Ybor & Co., Key West, Fla.—Cigars. I 24. 623

56 Western North Carolina Land Co., Philadelphia, Pa.—Cereals, fruits, cotton, and tobacco. E 19. 623

57 Marburg Bros., Baltimore, Md.—Smoking and leaf tobacco. G 26. 623

58 Volinia Farmers' Club, Volinia, Mich.—General farm products, cereals, etc. K 15. 623

59 Seidenberg & Co., 84 and 86 Reade st., New York, N. Y. Factory, Key West, Fla.—Key West and Havana cigars. I 23. 623

60 Shuck, Samuel, Bedford, Pa.—Anti-nervous cigars. I 26. 623

60*a* Stewart, Isaac T., Philadelphia, Pa.—Tobacco. F 25. 623

60*b* Richey, Henry A., New York, N. Y.—Plug tobacco, etc. H 24. 623

60*c* Hart, R. T., McComb City, Miss.—Manufactured tobacco. J 25. 623

60*d* Cusick, Linn, & Co., Philadelphia, Pa.—Tea boxes. I 26. 623

60*e* Pickering, Thomas R., Portland, Conn.—Connecticut-seed leaf tobacco. H 25. 623

61 Watkins, W. M. & C., Milton, N. C.—Plug and fine leaf tobacco. I 25. 623

61*a* Consolidated Tobacco Co., San Francisco, Cal.—Tobacco. I 24. 623

61*b* Grant, L. J., & Co., Richmond, Va.—Manufactured tobacco. F 25. 623

61*c* Jacoby, S., & Co., New York, N. Y.—Cigars. G *and* H 24. 623

61*d* Landis, Israel L., Lancaster, Pa.—Tobacco. B 22. 623

61*e* Cochran & Gillespie, Philadelphia, Pa.—Leaf tobacco. H 26. 623

62 Bailey, Samuel M., Richmond, Va.—Plug tobacco. I 25. 623

62*a* Hancock, Salmon, & Co., Richmond, Va.—Manufactured tobacco, and labels. J 26. 623

62*b* Lovett, Joseph L., Emilie, Pa.—Tobacco. H 24. 623

62*c* Lottier, Lawrence, Richmond, Va.—Manufactured tobacco. H *and* I 25. 623

63 Mayo, P. H., & Brother, Richmond, Va.—Plug tobacco. H 25. 623

64 Holbrook, Harry C., Louisville, Ky.—Plug tobacco. G 25. 623

65 Turpin & Brother, Richmond, Va.—Plug tobacco. H 25. 623

66 Suehnel, Emil J., Philadelphia, Pa.—Cigars. G 24. 623

67 Cohen, John B., Philadelphia, Pa.—Cigars. G 24. 623

68 Gulden, Charles, New York, N. Y.—German and French mustards. J 19. 623

69 Lorillard, P., & Co., New York, N. Y.—Plug and fine-cut chewing tobacco, smoking tobacco and snuffs. F 24. 623

70 Lovell & Buffington, Covington, Ky.—Fine-cut chewing tobacco. G 25. 623

71 Kimball, Wm. S., & Co., Rochester, N. Y.—Chewing and smoking tobacco, and cigarettes. E 25. 623

72 Felgner, F. W., & Son, Baltimore, Md.—Smoking tobacco. Manufacturers of all kinds of smoking tobacco. H 26. 623

72*a* Williams, Thomas C., & Co., Richmond, Va.—Plug tobacco. F 25. 623

72*b* Carroll, John W., Lynchburg, Va.—Chewing and smoking tobacco. H 25. 623

73 Gail & Ax, Baltimore, Md.—Smoking and fine-cut chewing tobacco; snuffs. I 26. 623

74 Kerbs & Spiess, New York, N. Y.—Cigars. G 26. 623

75 Armistead, Louis L., Lynchburg, Va.—Granulated smoking tobacco. I 24. 623

76 Mellen, L. F., West Springfield, Mass.—Connecticut-seed leaf tobacco. I 26. 623

77 Brito, Joseph Z., & Co., New York, N. Y.—Cigarettes. H 25. 623

78 Alces, George, New York, N. Y.—Cigars. H 24. 623

78*a* Haya, Sanchez, & Co., New York, N. Y.—Cigars. I 24. 623

79 Sullivan & Burk, Detroit, Mich.—Cigars of home manufacture. H 26. 623

80 Gumpert Bros., Philadelphia, Pa.—Cigars. G 28. 623

81 Colburn, A., & Co., Philadelphia, Pa.—Mustard, spices, and washing-blue. G 28. 623

82 Bonnett, Schenck, & Earle, New York, N. Y.—Spices and mustard. G 28. 623

83 Allen, J. F., & Co., Richmond, Va.—Granulated plug and cut smoking tobacco, plug tobacco, cigarettes. H *and* I 25. 623

84 Dean, William G., New York, N. Y.—Mustard. I 28. 623

85 Ledoux, C. Z., St. James Parish, La.—Cigarettes. G 25. 623

86 Bamberger, H., & Co., Philadelphia, Pa.—Tea caddies and teas. H 28. 623

86*a* Dunn, T. J., & Co., Philadelphia, Pa.—Seed and Havana seed cigars. G 25. 623

87 Kühn, von, & Silberman, Philada., Pa.—Tobacco pipes. H 25. 623

88 Tobacco-Growers of Penn's Manor, Morrisville, Pa.—Unsweated tobacco. This tobacco (known as Duck Island) is grown in Bucks Co., Pa., and adjoining islands. We believe it equal in texture, quality, and flavor to any grown in the United States, except that produced from Havana seed. See circular, to be had at case. I 24. 623

89 Buist, Robert, jr., Philadelphia, Pa.—Seeds. G 15. 624

For classes of exhibits, indicated by numbers at end of entries, see Classification, pp. 12–14.

Land and Water Animals, Animal and Vegetable Products.

90 Fulton, Joseph W., Libertyville, Iowa.—Corn, grains, grass, and field seeds, vegetable seeds, etc. C 15. 624

91 Meehan, Thomas, Philadelphia, Pa. —Seeds of native hardy trees and shrubs. G 16. 624

91*a* Commercial Exchange Association, Philadelphia, Pa.—Flour, grain, seeds, etc. H 15. 624

91*b* State of New Jersey.—Wheat, rye, oats, corn, buckwheat, clover, and grass seeds. E 17–18. 624

91*c* Van Vranken, J. B., Marcellus, N. Y. —Teasels set in frame. H 15. 624

91*d* Claussen, Charles A., New York, N. Y.—Clover seed. G 15. 624

91*e* Johnson, Robbins, & Co., Wethersfield, Conn. Garden seed. G 15. 624

92 Thurlow, H., Skaneateles, N. Y.— Teasels. H 15. 624

93 Rogers, C. B., Philadelphia, Pa.— Field and garden seeds. I 16. 624

94 Red Wing Mills, Red Wing, Minn. —Fife-wheat. I 26. 624

95 McLaughlin, J. M., & Son, Skaneateles, N. Y.—Teasels. H 15. 624

96 Thorburn, J. M., & Co., New York, N. Y.—Garden, flower, field, and tree seeds. I 16. 624

97 Henderson, Peter, & Co., New York, N. Y.—Field and garden seeds. I 16. 624

98 Illinois State Board of Agriculture (collective exhibit), Springfield, Ill.—Samples illustrating the agricultural, horticultural, geological, and other resources of the State. G 22. 600–624

98*a* Myers, Ephraim, Creagerstown, Md.—Tree, shrub, and flower seeds. C 15. 624

Land Animals.

99 Michigan State Agricultural College, Lansing, Mich. E 25.
a Birds, useful and injurious. 635
b Insects, useful and injurious. 638

99*a* Barrett, J. O., Glen Beulah, Wis.— "Old Abe," the live war-eagle,—carried for three years during the war of the rebellion by the 8th Regt. Wis. Vols. J 17. 635

99*b* Axe, Edwin C., Philadelphia, Pa. —Stuffed birds. A 23. 635

99*c* McIlvaine, John H., Philadelphia, Pa.—Birds. E 26. 635

100 Beath, J. R., Philadelphia, Pa.— Stuffed birds. K 23. 635

100*a* Land Dept. Central Pacific R. R. Co.—Birds. B 15–19. 635

101 Aldrich, P. W., Readville, Mass.— Stuffed birds. K 23. 635

102 Howlett, C. K., Hudson, Ohio.— Stuffed birds of America. K 23. 635

103 Brown, Clark D. W., Taxidermist and naturalist, Aurora, Ills.—Stuffed birds artistically arranged, representing the gathering of nations to the Centennial. Orders for groups, artistic or scientific, promptly filled and safely packed. K 24. 635

104 Crenshaw, George, Philadelphia, Pa.—Stuffed Hamburg fowls, with their young. K 24. 635

104*a* Hartley, Richard, Philadelphia, Pa. E 28.
a Birds. 635
b Insects. 638

105 Academy of Natural Sciences, Allentown, Pa. K 23.
a Birds with their nests and eggs. 635
b Quadrupeds. 637

106 Rosenbaum, F., Watertown, Wis.
a Wisconsin birds. K 23. 635
b Animals of Wisconsin. 637

107 Forster, Christian, Hamilton, Ohio. K 24.
a Mounted birds of North America. 635
b Mounted animals of North America. 637

108 Wallace, John, New York, N. Y.— Stuffed animals. K 24. 635

108*a* Zimmerman, Henry O. R., Georgetown, Del.—Insects. K 24. 638

108*b* Brown, Miss Nellie, Philadelphia, Pa.—Process of hatching and rearing silkworms without mulberries. A 24. 638

[*Special displays of Live-Stock are arranged to be held during September, October, and November.*]

Water Animals, Fish Culture, and Apparatus.

109 Ward, Henry A., Rochester, N. Y. —Casts of fossils, zoological specimens, mammals, birds, reptiles, fishes, batrachians, etc., stuffed and mounted. K 26–27. 640

109*a* Crenshaw, George, Philadelphia, Pa.—Stuffed fish. A 23. 641

109*b* Cuvier Club, Cincinnati, Ohio.— Fish. A 18. 641

109*c* Gates, H. C., Wilkesbarre, Pa.— Eels and other live fish. A 22. 641

110 Seher, H. L., Philadelphia, Pa.— American and imported leeches. A 22. 642

111 Hapgood & Co., San Francisco, Cal. —Preserved salmon. A 19. 642

112 Goodale, S. L., Saco, Maine.—Food extract from the juices of fish. J 23. 642

113 Rogers, John S., Gloucester, Mass. —Gelatine, isinglass, and glue made from salt-fish skins. A 22. 646

114 Norwood, C., & Son, Ipswich, Mass. —Isinglass. A 22. 646

114*a* Wahl Brothers, Chicago, Ill.— Glue. K 22. 646

115 Müller, Gustave, Chicago, Ill.— Russian isinglass. A 22. 646

116 Norwood, C., & Son, Ipswich, Mass.—Isinglass. A 22. 646

117 Fox, George, Jr., Philadelphia, Pa. —Split and glued bamboo trout fly rods. A 27. 647

118 Shipley, A. B., & Son, Philadelphia, Pa.—Fishing tackle. A 15. 647

119 Terrell, J. A., Bloomfield, Ky.— Angler's transparent float. A 26. 647

120 Mansfield, G. H., & Co., Canton, Mass.—Braided fishing lines. Manufacturers of braided fishing lines. Waterproof silk lines in all sizes and lengths suitable for fly fishing; oiled, raw, and fancy silk lines; linen and cotton lines, various sizes. We give personal attention to the business, and guarantee full lengths and best quality. Trade-mark on every line. A 26. 647

Fish Culture and Apparatus, Animal and Vegetable Products.

120*a* **Cook, L. C., Philadelphia, Pa.**—Trout rod and case. A 27. 647

121 **Conroy, Bissett, & Malleson, New York, N. Y.**—Fishing rods, reels, lines, flies, and fishing tackle. A 28. 647

121*a* **McBride, Miss Sarah J., Mumford, Pa.**—Artificial flies for fishing. A 19. 647

122 **City of Gloucester, Essex co., Mass.**—Exhibit of her progress, development, and industries as the largest fishing port in the United States. A *and* B 20 *and* 21. 647

123 **Slack, Mrs. J. H., Bloomsbury, N. J.**—Flight of coste trays, combination hatching box. A 24. 648

124 **Murphy & Broom, Philadelphia, Pa.**—Aquarium tanks. C 26. 648

125 **Clarke, N. W., Northville, Mich.**—Fish-hatching apparatus. A 24. 648

126 **Taxis, E. W., Philadelphia, Pa.**—Aquarium tank. A 21. 648

126*a* **Pacific Guano Co., Boston, Mass.**—Aquarium with living fish. A *and* B 28. 648

126*b* **Craig, Daniel, Philadelphia, Pa.**—Parlor aquarium. A 21. 648

Animal and Vegetable Products.

127 **Crawford & Walton, Philadelphia, Pa.**—Bleached sponge. F 26. 650

128 **American Condensed Milk Co., New York, N. Y.**—Condensed milk. J 21. 651

128*a* **Sensenberger, Wm., Philadelphia, Pa.**—Rennet. K 17. 651

128*b* **American Condensed Milk Co., New York, N. Y.**—Preserved milk. J 21. 651

129 **Napheys, George C., & Son, Philadelphia, Pa.**—Refined leaf lard. K 20. 652

130 **Chalmers, James, & Sons, Williamsville, N. Y.**—Gelatine. K 22. 652

131 **Wilcox, W. J., & Co., New York.**—Refined leaf-lard, lard stearine, and lard oil. K 21. 652

132 **Stein, Hirsh, & Co., Chicago, Ill.**—Egg albumen, blood albumen, casein and dried blood. J 22. 652

133 **Brown, William H., Peabody, Mass.**—Prepared sizing, glue. K 20. 652

134 **Franklin Glue Works, Pittsburg, Pa.**—Glue, neats-foot oil. K 20. 652

135 **Upton, George, Boston, Mass.**—Glue in sheets, broken, ground, and powdered. K 20. 652

136 **Peter Cooper's Glue Factory, New York, N. Y.**—Glue, gelatine, neats-foot oil. K 22. 652

137 **Lister Brothers, Newark, N. J.**—Glue, tallow, etc. C 25. 652

138 **Cassard Bros. & Co., Baltimore, Md.**—Refined lard. K 21. 652

138*a* **Wahl Brothers, Chicago, Ill.**—Gelatine, neats-foot oil, horns, hoofs, and bones. K 22. 652

138*b* **Butchers' Slaughtering & Melting Association, Brighton, Mass.**—Steamed bones, horns, hoofs, etc. K 22. 652

138*c* **Holcomb, E., Grand Rapids, Mich.**—Deer-skin lace leather. K 24. 652

138*d* **Ward, N., & Co., Boston, Mass.**—Cattle bones, tallow, grease, hoofs, neats-foot oil, etc. A 26. 652

138*e* **Upton, Elijah W., Peabody, Mass.**—Glue. K 19. 652

139 **Meriam Packing Co., Boston, Mass.** J 20.
a Hides, tallow, etc. 652
b Mess beef, concentrated roast beef, and canned turtle. 656

140 **State of Oregon (collective exhibit,** Portland, Oregon. E 22.
a Glue, condensed cider. 652
b Dried fruit. 656
c Farina, flour, and oatmeal. 657

140*a* **Milligan & Higgins Glue Co., N.Y.**—Glue. K 19. 652

140*b* **Stearne, P., Adams, N. Y.**—Deer-heads. E 28. 652

141 **Mellen & Co., New York, N. Y.**—Renovated live-geese feathers. H 17. 653

142 **Harbison, W. C., New Castle, Pa.**—White Mountain honey. J 23. 654

142*a* **Hurd, Lewis, Kewanee, Ill.**—Fruit honey. J 24. 654

143 **Fritsch, Joseph, Carlstadt, N. J.**—Sunbleached wax, and candles. J 23. 654

144 **Lewis, W. K., & Brothers, Boston, Mass.**—Preserves, pickles, catsups, condensed milk, canned fruits, meats, and vegetables. J 22. 656

145 **Portland Packing Co., Portland, Maine.**—Canned vegetables, fruits, meats, poultry, and shell-fish. J 23. 656

146 **Warner, Rhodes, & Co., Philadelphia, Pa.**—Canned fruits and vegetables, fresh and preserved. J 24. 656

147 **Atmore & Son, Philadelphia, Pa.**—Mincemeat and English plum-pudding. J 24. 656

148 **Slocum, W. H., & Bro., Philadelphia, Pa.**—Mincemeat canned goods. J 23. 656

150 **Anderson & Campbell, Camden, N. J.**—Canned fruits, vegetables, fruit-butter, and mincemeat. J 24. 656

150*a* **Bigelow, Jona, Boston, Mass.**—Labeling machine. J 22. 656

150*b* **Macfarlane, N. H., & Co., New York, N. Y.**—Refined lard. K 19. 656

150*c* **Ashbourne, Alex. P., Philadelphia, Pa.** K 17.
a Pulverized cocoanut. 656
b Cocoanut vinegar. 661

150*d* **Armstrong, Herran M., & Co., Louisville, Ky.**—Pork products. K 22. 656

151 **Boyd, G., & Co., Philadelphia, Pa.**—Dried grain and fruit. C 22. 656

153 **Reeves, Parvin, & Co., Philadelphia, Pa.**—Canned vegetables. J 23. 656

154 **Wright, Joshua, & Son, Philadelphia, Pa.**—Minced meat. J 24. 656

155 **Wilson Packing Co., Chicago, Ill.**—Hermetically sealed cooked meats; corned beef, ham, tongue, and fresh beef. J 23. 656

156 **Norris, J. W., & Co., New York, N. Y.**—Aromatic hams, white-sugar cured and delicately flavored. J 20. 656

Animal and Vegetable Products.

157 Githens & Rexsamer, Philadelphia, Pa.—Canned fruits and vegetables. J 23. 656

158 Du Vivier & Co., New York, N. Y. —Pickles and delicacies. J 20. 656

159 Haller, Ella G., New York, N. Y.— Choice fruits. J 21. 656

160 Gordon & Dilworth, New York, N. Y.—Preserved domestic and foreign fruits, jellies, canned goods, sauces, syrups, and general table delicacies. J 23. 656

161 Chambers, Jos. M., Dover, Dela-ware.—Canned goods; dessert fruits a specialty. Strawberries, raspberries, cherries, pineapples, peaches, Bartlett pears, tomatoes, etc.

The location (Dover, Delaware) of this canning house gives the all-important advantages which are essential to ensure the superior quality and flavor of canned goods.

The fruit is allowed to fully mature on the trees before being picked, thereby securing a richness of flavor. As the fruit ripens it is carefully picked, pared by hand, and each piece carefully placed in the cans, filling them as full as possible not to mash or bruise the fruit, after which the cans are filled with heavy syrup made from the best granulated sugar.

No deleterious substances or patent preserving-powders used. All lovers of good desserts send for circular. I 24 *and* J 22. 656

162 Snedeker, David, New York, N. Y. —Preserved fruit, vegetables, meat, etc. I 24. 656

163 McMurray, L., & Co., Baltimore, Md.—Canned vegetables, fruits, and oysters. J 24. 656

163*a* Ritter, Philip J., Philadelphia, Pa. —Butter. J 21. 656

163*b* Annapolis Canning Co., Annapolis, Md.—Canned goods. J 25. 656

164 Richardson & Robbins, Dover, Del. —Canned and preserved fruits, potted meats, etc. J 24. 656

165 Fruit-Growers' Trade Co. of New Jersey, New York, N. Y.—Cranberries, natural and preserved, canned tomatoes, etc. D 24. 656

166 Clarkson, F. M., & Son, Bridgeville, Del.—Evaporated and conserved fruits and vegetables. J 42. 656

167 Borden, John G., Brewsters, N. Y. —Condensed milk, coffee, and cocoa, extract of beef, etc. J 22. 656

167*a* Hazard, E., & Co., New York, N. Y. —Canned fruits. J 22. 656

167*b* Turner, J., M'f'g Co., New York, N. Y.—Sauce. K 9. 656

167*c* Greenfield, Nelson, New York, N. Y.—Flavors and coloring for confectionery. K 27. 656

167*d* Archdeacon, W., Chicago, Ill.— Pickles, preserves, jellies, sauces, and canned goods. J 22. 656

167*e* Provost, Stephen H., New York, N. Y.—Tomato, walnut, and mushroom sauce. J 24. 656

167*f* Selser & Brother, Philadelphia, Pa.—Canned fruits and vegetables; catsups. J 25. 656

167*g* Farmers' Fruit Preserving Co. of Kent co., Del., Lebanon, Del.—Canned fruits and vegetables. J 24. 656

167*h* Smith, Wright, St. Louis, Mo.— Table sauce. J 22. 656

168 American Desiccating Co., Phila-delphia, Pa.—Crystallized cocoanut. J 24. 656

168*a* Knight, C. P., & Bro., Philadel-phia, Pa.—Fruit jellies. J 25. 656

169 Flood, Wm. M., Philadelphia, Pa. —Mutton in alcohol. A 27. 656

170 Gulden, Charles, New York, N. Y. —Tomato catsup, capers, and olives. J 19. 656

171 New York Desiccating Co., New York, N. Y.—Prepared cocoanut for pies, cakes, etc. I 24. 656

172 Libby, McNeal, & Libby, Philadel-phia, Pa.—Canned cooked meats. J 24. 656

172*a* Schepp, Leopold, New York, N. Y. —Desiccated cocoanut. K 28. 656

172*b* Cook, J. W. & V., Portland, Ore-gon.—Canned salmon. J 25. 656

173 Reckhow Preserving Co., Paterson, N. J. Office 138 Chambers street, New York, N. Y. Trade mark "Monticello."— Pickles, canned goods, salad cream, table sauces, olives, capers manufactured from the best material. Quality guaranteed as represented. J 22. 665

174 New York Hop Extract Co., New York, N. Y.—Hop extract. K 17. 656

175 Little Creek Canning Co., Little Creek, Del.—Canned fruits and vegetables. J 23. 656

176 Jones, John Winslow, Portland, Maine.—Canned green corn, lobster, mackerel, salmon, and beef. B 24. 656

177 Cassard, Geo., Baltimore, Md.— Pepper hams. K 21. 656

178 Zane, Norny, & Co., Philadelphia, Pa.—Fruit-preserving powder. J 23. 656

179 Annear, John, & Co., Philadelphia, Pa.—Pennsylvania sauce. J 21. 656

180 La Croix, James, East Medway, Mass.—Canned vegetables, apples, etc. J 23. 656

181 Brooks, C. D., Boston, Mass.— Pickles, preserves, canned goods, etc. J 21. 656

182 MacGowan, John K., Philadelphia, Pa.—Table sauce. J 21. 656

182*a* King, William, Brooklyn, N. Y.— Table sauce. J 20. 656

182*b* Bechstein & Co., New York, N. Y. —Sugar-cured hams, breakfast bacon, and beef tongues. J 20. 656

182*c* Black & Krebs, Baltimore, Md.— Sugar-cured hams, refined lard. K 21. 656

183 Underwood, W., & Co., Boston, Mass.—Canned meats, fish, fruits, vegetables, etc.; pickles, catsups, sauces, etc. J 24. 656

184 Cowdrey, E. T., & Co., Boston, Mass.—Canned vegetables, meats, and fruits, pickles, preserves, and jellies. J 21. 656

185 Burnham & Morrill, Portland, Maine.—Canned meats, soups, fish, and vegetables. J 23. 656

For locations of objects, indicated by letter and figure, see Key to Notation, p. 6; ground plan, p. 10.

Animal and Vegetable Products.

186 Harris, Milo, Jamestown, N. Y.—Dried fruits. D 23. 656

187 Dingee, Squire, Chicago, Ill.—Pickles, chow-chow, and sauces. J 21. 656

188 Holgate, Geo., & Co., Oshkosh, Wis.—Preserved fruits and vegetables; preserved meats in joint. J 23. 656

189 Williams, John, South Haven, Mich.—Evaporated fruits and vegetables. D 24. 656

190 George, P. T., & Co., Baltimore, Md.—Hams, lard, and lard oil. Pork packers and curers of the Maryland hams, and manufacturers of refined lard and lard-oil. Lard prepared for the Brazil and West India markets a specialty. K 21. 656

190*a* Evans Bros., Cincinnati, Ohio.—Hams, shoulders, etc. J 15-16. 656

190*b* Erie Preserving Company, Brant, Erie co., N. Y., and New York city.—Canned fruits and vegetables. K 18 & 19.

These "fruits" and "vegetables" are prepared practically in the field where grown. Only fully ripe and carefully-assorted fruits are packed. The tins are uniformly filled full of fruit; the interstices are then filled with spring-water and refined white sugar, which, mingling in the juices of the fruit, forms a heavy, rich syrup.

"Vegetables." The preserving-houses are located directly in the midst of a rich, fertile agricultural country, upon the shores of Lake Erie, where sweet corn, sweet peas, tomatoes, etc., are grown in great abundance and perfection, the tempering lake breezes exercising a highly beneficial climatic influence. The peculiar delicacy of flavor these vegetables possess is owing to this favored location and their being perfectly fresh, not allowed to wilt or pass through any heating or sweating process; are invariably packed the same day they are picked, usually within two hours after. "Erie sweet corn" is packed, young and tender, solidly in the cans, in its own milk. Nothing goes into the can save the sweet tender corn. It will always be found the same. 656

190*c* Hemp, Day, & Co., New York, N. Y.—Canned fruits, meats, fish, etc. J 25. 656

190*d* Perry, F. H., Providence, R. I.—Canned fruits. J 21. 656

191 Jacob, Chas., jr., & Co., Cincinnati, Ohio.—Hams, shoulders, breakfast bacon, mess pork, mess and dried beef, beef tongues, etc. J 15-16. 656

192 Keck, J. L., & Bros., Cincinnati, Ohio.—Pickled meats, lard, etc. J 15-16. 656

193 Kahn & Forbes, Cincinnati, Ohio.—Hams, breakfast bacon, and family mess pork. J 15-16. 656

194 Evans, Lippincott, & Cunningham, Cincinnati, Ohio.—Bacon, hams, mess pork, lard, and breakfast bacon. J 15-16. 656

195 Davis, S., jr., & Co., Cincinnati, Ohio.—Smoked hams, breakfast bacon, bacon sides, shoulders, and mess pork. J 15-16. 656

196 Morrison, James, & Co., Cincinnati, Ohio.—Hams, bacon, mess pork, lard, English meats, etc. J 15-16. 656

197 Fell, C. J., & Bro., Philadelphia, Pa. J 21.

a Gelatine. 656

b Self-raising flour. 657

198 Cereals Manufacturing Co., New York, N. Y.—Crushed wheat, flour, meal, etc. J 28. 657

199 Lagomarsino & Cuneo, Philadelphia, Pa.—Macaroni, vermicelli, fancy paste, farina, etc. J 26. 657

200 Outcalt, John, Spotswood, N. J.—Hominy, samp, corn flour from corn grown on Monmouth and Princeton battle-fields, Graham flour, wheaten grits, etc. J 26. 657

200*a* Pillsbury, Charles A., & Co., Minneapolis, Minn.—Flour. J 26. 657

200*b* Gambrill, C. A., & Co., Baltimore, Md.—Flour. J 25. 657

201 Tyrrell, J. F., & Co., New York, N. Y.—Oatmeal. J 27. 657

202 Schumacher, Ferd., Akron, Ohio.—Oatmeal, barley, farina, cracked wheat, flour, hominy, meal, feed, and grain. J 26. 657

203 Hecker, George V., & Co. (Croton Mills, Cherry st.), New York, N. Y.—Self-raising flour, buckwheat, griddle-cake flour, farina, and cracked wheat.

Heckers' Superlative family flours, which received the First Premium at the World's Fair, London; and the World's Fair, New York. Very popular with those desiring "fine bread and biscuit as can be produced."

Heckers' Self-raising Flour, for Bread, Biscuit, Puddings, Cakes, etc., by adding only cold water or milk. This valuable improvement, introduced in 1850, by Hecker & Brother, was awarded the only Gold Medal given for Self-Raising Flour.

Heckers' Griddle Cake Self-Raising Flour. For Griddle Cakes, Muffins, Fritters, Waffles, Doughnuts, and for any use where a batter is required.

Acid used in making Heckers' Self-Raising Flour.

Heckers' Farina, a delicate and appropriate food for all seasons.

Heckers' Wheaten Grits, invaluable to dyspeptic and sedentary persons. J 25. 657

204 Red Wing Mills, Red Wing, Minn.—Flour. J 26. 657

205 Baltimore Pearl Hominy Co., Baltimore, Md.—Breakfast hominy, meal, flour, samp, etc. J 28. 657

205*a* Deener, Cissel, & Welsh, Georgetown, D. C.—Flour. I 25. 657

205*b* Pollock, James, Vincennes, Ind.—Flour. J 24. 657

205*c* Prentzel, Samuel F., Philadelphia, Pa.—Oatmeal and oatina. J 25.

206 Jewell Brothers, Brooklyn, N. Y.—Plain and self-raising flour, babies' cereal food. J 28. 657

206*a* Heaton, Edward, New Haven, Conn.—Granum. I *and* J 15. 657

206*b* Taylor, A. A., Toledo, Ohio.—Flour. J 24. 657

For classes of exhibits, indicated by numbers at end of entries, see Classification, pp. 12-14.

Animal and Vegetable Products.

206*c* Baldwin, Homer, Youngstown, Ohio.—Flour. J 25. 657

206*d* Bedell & Conklin, Brooklyn, N. Y. —Meal, flour, hominy, etc. J 25. 657

206*e* Christian, J. A., & Co. Minneapolis, Minn.—Flour. J 25. 657

206*f* Porter & Mowbray, Winona, Minn. —Flour. J 24. 657

206*g* Eisenmayer & Co., St. Louis, Mo. —Flour. J 25.

206*h* Thilenius, G. C., Cape Girardeau, Mo.—Flour. K 23. 657

206*i* Oswego Milling Co., Oswego, N. Y.—Flour. J 25. 657

207 Miller, Charles L., Colon, Mich.— Pumpkin flour. J 28. 657

208 Stuart & Douglas, Cedar Rapids, Iowa.—Oatmeal. J 22. 657

209 Duryea's Glen Cove Starch Co., Glen Cove, N. Y.—Laundry starch, corn starch, and maizena. J 15–16. 658

210 Kingsford, T., & Son, Oswego, N. Y.—Laundry starch, corn starch, etc. J 13–14. 658

211 Wood, Julius J., & Co., Columbus, Ohio.—Laundry starch, corn starch for food. J 21. 658

212 Erkenbrecher, Andrew, Cincinnati, Ohio.—Starch, plain, perfumed, and flavored, St. Bernhard pure, refined pearl, wheaten, pulverized, "cornena" (copyrighted), corn flour for culinary purposes, "gloss sateena" (copyrighted) for laundry use. Manufacturer of perfumed and flavored starch. J 17, 18, 19. 658

213 Barnett, William, Philadelphia, Pa.—Wheat starch. J 21. 658

213*a* Fox, George, Cincinnati, Ohio.— Starch. J 22. 658

213*b* Stone & Co., Chicago, Ill.—Zoline, starch gloss. K 17. 658

214 Miller, H. J., & Co., West Liberty, Ohio.—Maple sugar and molasses. J 25. 659

214*a* Hutter, Robert, Philadelphia, Pa. —Grape sugar, etc. D 24. 659

215 Post, C. C., Burlington, Vt.—Maple sugar and syrup. C 24. 659

216 Murdock, Albert L., Boston, Mass. E 25.
a Beet sugar. 659
b Peat. 660

216*a* McDonald, M. C., Philadelphia, Pa.—Crystal drips syrup. J 25. 659

216*b* New Hampshire State Centennial Board.—Sugar. E 20–21. 659

217 Nennich, Henry, Philadelphia, Pa. —Vinegar. G 28. 660

217*a* Agnew, Eisenbeis, & Co., Allegheny, Pa.—Table, pickling, and aromatic vinegars. H 28. 660

217*b* Boden, H. W., & Co., Milwaukee, Wis.—Vinegar. H 28. 660

217*c* Hexamer, F. M., New Castle, N. Y. Russet cider. K 13. 660

218 Chalvin, H. A., New York, N. Y.— Cordials, syrups, and extracts. K 18. 660

219 Hincke, Julius, Egg Harbor City, N. J.—Domestic wines. American grape wines, from Hincke's vineyards, all vintages since 1868, highly recommended for table use, as well as for invalids. K 12. 660

219*a* Boden, A. F. W., & Co. (A. F. W. Boden, Henry Riedeburg), 298 Milwaukee st., Milwaukee, Wis.—Vinegar. Manufacturers of cider and white wine vinegar. H 28. 660

220 Urbana Wine Co., Hammondsport, N. Y.—Champagne, still wines, and brandy from native grapes. K 12. 660

221 Johnson, T. H., Bricksburg, N. J.— Unfermented wines. J 23. 660

222 Mills, William H., Sandusky, Ohio. —Still and sparkling domestic wines. K 14. 660

223 American Champagne Co., New York, N. Y.—Still and sparkling wines. K 13. 660

224 Sattler & Co., Baltimore, Md.— Whisky. K 18. 660

224*a* Speer, Alfred, Passaic, N. J.—Native wines. K 29. 660

224*b* Cooley, John E., & Co., Sing Sing, N. Y.—Native wines. K 16. 660

224*c* Shafer, J. Calvin, New York, N. Y. —Fruit syrups, juices, brandy, and cordial. K 16. 660

224*d* Brecht, C. F., Philadelphia, Pa.— Wines and brandies. K 12. 660

224*e* Smith, Isaac, Centre Island, N. Y. —Apple wine. K 7. 660

224*f* White Elk Vineyards, Keokuk, Iowa.—Wines. K 16. 660

225 United Wine-Growers, Egg Harbor, N. J.—Native grape wines. K 8. 660

226 American Wine Co., St. Louis, Mo. —Sparkling and still wines. K 14. 660

227 Dreyfus, B., & Co., San Francisco, Cal.—California wines and brandies. K 14. 660

228 Poeschel, M., & Scherer, Hermann, Mo.—Native wines. K 13. 660

229 Kohler & Frohling, San Francisco, Cal.—California wines and brandies. K 10–11. 660

230 Keller, J. S., Orwigsburg, Pa.— Wine and whisky. K 13. 660

231 Wehr, C. Werk, & Son, Middle Bass Island, Ohio.—Native wines. K 8. 660

232 Buena Vista Vinicultural Society, San Francisco, Cal.—Wines and brandy. K 11. 660

233 Keller, M., Los Angelos, Cal.— Wines and brandies. K 7. 660

234 Pleasant Valley Wine Co., Hammondsport, N. Y.—Champagne, still wines, and brandies. K 14. 660

235 Middleton, G. W., & Co., Philadelphia, Pa.—Alcohol, rectified, French, and Cologne spirits; double rectifier. K 16. 660

236 Landsberger, J., & Co., San Francisco, Cal.—Champagnes and brandies. J *and* K 8. 660

237 Beller, Jacob, Detroit, Mich.—Native grape wines, currant and elderberry wines. K 7. 660

238 Hathaway, Vincent, & Co., Boston, Mass.—Boston ginger ale. K 17. 660

239 Hannis Distillery Co., Philadelphia, Pa.—Whisky. K 15. 660

240 Hughes, H. R. & M., Pittston, Pa. —Stock ale. K 16 *and Brewers' Building.* 660

For locations of objects, indicated by letter and figure, see Key to Notation, p. 6; ground plan, p. 10.

Animal and Vegetable Products.

241 Pierce, S. S., & Co., Boston, Mass. —Champagne cider. J 23. 660

242 Naglee, H. M., San José, Cal.—Brandy. K 10. 660

243 Trommer Extract of Malt Co., Fremont, Ohio.—Extract of barley malt. K 18. 660

244 Landauer Bros., Philadelphia, Pa. —Rye whisky. K 16. 660

245 Levy, James, & Bro., 27 and 33 Sycamore street, Cincinnati, Ohio.—Bourbon and rye whiskies; specialty, Kentucky whiskies, both in bond and tax paid. K 16. 660

245*a* Lawrence, Daniel, & Sons, Boston, Mass.—Rum. K 13. 660

245*b* Le Franc, Charles, San José, Cal. —Wine and brandies. K 14. 660

246 Pointe aux Peaux Wine Co., Monroe, Mich.—Native wines. H *and* J 20. 660

247 Goetze, F. A., Jersey City, N. J.—Native wines. K 13. 660

248 Huck, John A., Chicago, Ill.—Wines. K 12. 660

249 Mahé, Gustave, San Francisco, Cal. —Golden wine. Extract from the report of the Committee of Industrial Exhibition of the Mechanics' Institute, San Francisco, California: "Mr. Mahé's wine is made from what is called the Mission Grape, without any admixture of foreign grapes. It is singularly light and pure, and has obtained the First Premium and only Medal awarded to the California Wine, at the Tenth Industrial Exhibition of the Mechanics' Institute, San Francisco. Mr. Mahé's property consists of about one hundred acres, forty-five of which are planted with vines. Of the seventy thousand feet of vineyard, twelve thousand are in vines nine years old, eight thousand five years old, thirty-five thousand in their fourth year, and the remaining fifteen thousand are three years old. Mr. Mahé estimates that when all these vines are in full bearing (which will be in two or three years' time), they will yield an average of from thirty to thirty-five thousand gallons of wine. In 1874 eighteen thousand feet in bearing yielded eight thousand five hundred gallons. The whole vineyard is planted with the grape known as the California Mission. The cellars, which are two and three floors deep, have a capacity of a hundred thousand gallons in casks and bottles together. The wine is to be kept in the cellar at least three years, that length of time being necessary to give it the greatest part of its valuable qualities, and Mr. Mahé intends to give it to the consumer in glass only, that he may be satisfied it cannot be used in any but its naturally pure state.

"At the vintage, which is always in October, from the 15th to the 30th, the grapes, as soon as they have been gathered and brought to the press, are stripped from the stems. The stems are carefully thrown aside, and the grapes fall from the stripping machine into a mill, which breaks the grape without crushing the seeds. From this mill the broken grapes fall on the press, from which the juice passes directly through India-rubber pipes into the casks, arranged on the lowest floor to receive it. There the juice ferments, and is drawn off three times the first year, twice the second year, and once only the third year; and always in January. The third year the wine is bottled in the month of February, and is not offered for use till six months later, about September.

"The pulp and solid part of the grapes left in the press are subjected to the action of a hydraulic press of sixty thousand pounds' force worked easily by one man. The distillation of the Golden Wine showed the following per centage of alcohol: vintage of 1869, 12 per cent.; vintage of 1870, 11 per cent; vintage of 1871, 11¼ per cent. It contains, therefore, the same proportion of alcohol as the wines of Bordeaux."

In order to enable the visitors to the Exhibition to appreciate the qualities of the wine of California, we have established in Agricultural Hall, near our exhibit, at the north entrance, a buffet, where an excellent lunch, including a half bottle of Golden Wine, will be daily served up, at the price of one dollar. Our fellow-citizens and our foreign friends are respectfully invited to honor us with a call. L. PONTON DE ARCE, *Manager*. K 14. 660

250 Steuben County Vineyard Association, Bath, N. Y.—Native grape wines and brandy. K 12. 660

251 Criqui, Joseph, Newark, N. J.—Wine. K 9. 660

252 Kelley's Island Wine Co., Kelley's Island, Ohio.—Champagnes and claret wines, etc.; Catawba brandy. K 11. 660

253 Perkins, Stern, & Co., New York, N. Y.—California wines and brandies. K 8. 660

254 Whitman, Stephen F., & Son, Philadelphia, Pa.—Variety of manufactures in confectionery and chocolate. K 25. 661

254*a* Richardson, J. J., & Co., Philadelphia, Pa.—Confectionery. K 28. 661

254*b* Miller, George, & Sons, Philadelphia, Pa.—Confectionery. K 25. 661

255 Baker, Walter, & Co., Boston, Mass. —Chocolate and cocoa preparations. K 25. 661

256 Rumford Chemical Works, Providence, R. I.—Yeast powder, cream tartar, acid phosphate, and bread preparation. K 21. 661

257 Wilson, Walter G., & Co., Philadelphia, Pa.—Crackers and biscuit. K 23 *and* 24. 661

258 Larrabee, E. J., & Co., Albany, N. Y. —Biscuit, crackers, etc. K 22. 661

259 Croft, Wilbur, & Co., Philadelphia, Pa.—Confectionery, lozenges, glace fruit, etc. K 26. 661

260 Morse, G. Byron, Philadelphia, Pa. —Plain and fancy cakes, milk and cream biscuits, rolls, buns, pastry, etc. K 26. 661

261 Chase & Co., Boston, Mass.—Confectionery. K 28. 661

262 Hartman, John, Philadelphia, Pa. —Crackers, cakes, and biscuits. K 24. 661

263 Weaver, J. R., Philadelphia, Pa.—Confectionery. K 27. 661

264 Schall & Co., New York, N. Y.—Ornamental confectionery. K 25. 661

For classes of exhibits, indicated by numbers at end of entries, see Classification, pp. 12–14.

Animal and Vegetable Products, Textile Substances.

265 Mockridge, E., & Co., Philadelphia, Pa.—Azumea, bread, cakes, pastry, etc. K 21. 661

266 Greenfried & Strauss, Confectioners, 63 Barclay street, New York, N. Y. —Manufacturers of all kinds of confectionery, such as lozenges, pipe, gumdrops, pan-work, creams, extra imperials, fine almonds, medicated lozenges, chocolates, and pistache goods. Special attention given to the export trade. Goods packed for the South American market in glass and tins. Importers of and dealers in oils and materials for manufacturing confectionery. Manufacturers of XXX powdered sugar. Listas de precis en la lengua castillana à haber en la officina à Nueva York. K 26. 661

267 Dexter, E. M., & Co., Philadelphia, Pa.—Ornamental confectionery. K 27. 661

268 Laurent, F., N. W. cor. Arch and Sixth sts., Philadelphia, Pa. — Confectionery and decorative ornaments for cakes. Manufacturer of fine confectionery and ornaments for decorating cakes, such as bride's, centre-pieces, flowers, roses, gum-paste leaves, etc. K 28. 661

269 Henry Maillard, New York, N. Y. —Bonbons, chocolate, ornamental confectionery. K 25. 661

270 Thorn & Brother, Trenton, N. J.— Crackers, butter, oyster, wine, and scroll biscuit. K 24. 661

271 Geilfuss, H., Philadelphia, Pa.— Ornamental confectionery. K 28. 661

272 Heide & Wirtz, New York, N. Y.— Almond paste. K 23. 661

272*a* Page, D. L., Philadelphia, Pa.— Candies. K 26. 661

272*b* Palmer Baking-Powder Co., Philadelphia, Pa.—Baking powder. K 24. 661

273 Carrick, David, & Co., Philadelphia, Pa.—Crackers, cakes, ship-bread, etc. K 23. 661

274 Exton, Adam, & Co., Trenton, N. J. —Butter, oyster, and wine crackers. K 23. 661

275 Runkel, H., & Co., Clifton, N. Y.— Chocolate goods and cocoa for confectioners. K 28. 661

276 Snider Bros. & Co., Cincinnati, Ohio.—Cream biscuit. K 23. 661

277 National Yeast Company, Seneca Falls, N. Y.—Dry-hop yeast cakes. K 17. 661

278 Smith's Homeopathic Pharmacy, New York, N. Y.—Alkethrepta, soluble chocolate, and chocolate confections. K 27. 661

279 Thurston, Hall, & Co., Cambridgeport, Mass.—Boston crackers. K 21. 661

280 Schall & Co., New York, N. Y.— Ornamental confectionery, representing the history of the United States. K 25. 661

Textile Substances of Vegetable or Animal Origin.

281 Murdock, Albert L., Boston, Mass. —Cotton from all countries. E 25. 665

281*a* Mohawk & Hudson Manufacturing Co., Waterford, N. Y.—Pressed cotton. S 8. 665

281*b* Tayler, D. M., Helena, Ark.—Raw cotton. D 25. 665

281*c* Pritchard, A., Galveston, Texas. —Raw cotton. E 24. 665

282 Claghorn, Herring, & Co., Philadelphia, Pa.—The cottons of the world. G 18 *and* 19. 665

282*a* Cheasham, John T., Bethany, Ga. —Cotton plants. F 24. 665

282*b* Campbell, George, Westminster, Vt.—Wool. E 14. 665

282*c* Maxwell, Edward, Delta, La.— Cotton. E 24. 665

282*d* Cotton Exchange, Memphis, Tenn. —Raw cotton. E 24. 665

282*e* Kellogg, Adam, Kellogg's Landing, La.—Bale of cotton. E 24. 665

282*f* McGaughy, B. R., Verona, Miss. —Cotton. E 24. 665

282*g* Gurney, Wm., Charleston, S. C.— Cotton and cotton plant. J 17. 665

282*h* Maxwell & Goodman, Delta, La. —Raw cotton. H 17. 665

282*i* Levy, Edward S., New Orleans, La.—Raw cotton. J 20. 665

282*j* Sledge, McKay, & Co., Memphis, Tenn.—Raw cotton. E 24. 665

282*k* St. Louis Cotton Exchange, St. Louis, Mo.—Raw cotton. D 24. 665

282*l* New Orleans Cotton Exchange, New Orleans, La.—Raw cotton. 665

283 State of West Virginia (collective exhibit).—Hemp and flax. F 19. 666

284 George Stratford, Jersey City, N. J. —Oakum. I 17. 666

285 Davey, W. O., & Sons, Jersey City, N. J.—Oakum. H 17. 666

286 Mills', B., Sons, Jersey City, N. J. —Oakum. H 17. 666

287 Collyer, Robert H., Chicago, Ills.— China grass. S 10. 666

288 State of Oregon, Portland, Oregon. —Wool and woolen fabrics. E 22. 667

289 Bond, George W., Boston, Mass.— Commercial wools. I 19. 667

290 Northern Ohio Woollen Mills, Cleveland, Ohio.—All-wool shoddies. I 18. 667

290*a* New Hampshire State Centennial Board.—Wool. E 20–21. 667

290*b* Hiatt, E. J., & Brothers, Chester Hill, Ohio.—Merino wool in fleece. F 24. 667

291 Wilkens, Theodore, New York, N. Y.—Hair moss for upholstering. E 26. 669

292 Mellen & Co., New York, N. Y.— Curled horse-hair tickings. H 17. 669

293 Herzog, J., & Co., San Francisco, Cal.—"Eureka hair" (patented), good and clean substitute for curled hair. "Will not harbor moths or other vermin," cool and healthy material for mattrasses and upholstery. H 17. 669

294 Franklin Glue Works, Pittsburg, Pa.—Curled hair. K 20. 669

295 Wilkens, William, & Co., Baltimore, Md.—Bristles, horse-hair, fibre, curled hair, etc. H 17. 669

For locations of objects, indicated by letter and figure, see Key to Notation, p. 6; ground plan, p. 10.

Machines, Implements, and Processes of Manufacture.

296 **Collins & Co., Hartford, Conn.**—Axes, hatchets, adzes, machetes, railway and mining tools, plows, etc. N 24. 670

297 **Myers & Ervien, Office, 13 North** Fifth st., Philadelphia, Pa.—Hay-forks, etc.; potato-drags. Manufacturers of hay, manure, spading, coke, charcoal, spall, barley, sluice, tanners', turnip, and oyster forks, potato and manure drags, etc. S 25. 670

297*a* **Gibs & Lee, New York, N. Y.**—Steam spader. M 24. 670

297*b* **Hopkins, A. P., Bentleysville, Pa.**—Road-scraper. C 21. 670

297*c* **Kelsey, John, Yardleyville, Pa.**—Harrow and scraper. L 26. 670

297*d* **Maxwell, Rowland, & Co., Holmesburg, Pa.**—Shovels, spades, and scoops. T 26. 670

297*e* **Estes, William A., South Boston, Mass.**—Plow, harrow, and stone truck. L 26. 670

298 **Holland, Edward, Atlanta, Ga.**—Buggy-plow and cultivator. K 24. 670

299 **Harper, Smith, Philadelphia, Pa.**—Steel hoes, rakes, etc. T 26. 670

300 **Bean, H. & B. F., Pawling, Pa.**—Corn-marker, cultivator, grain and seed sower. N 19. 670

301 **Bateman, E. S. & F., Spring Mills, N. J.**—Field and garden cultivators. N 23. 670

302 **Peppler, Thomas, Hightstown, N. J.**—Plow and cultivator. M 24. 670

303 **Kissell, Blount, & Co., Springfield, Ohio.**—Corn cultivator. N 24. 670

304 **Bucher, Gibbs, & Co., Canton, Ohio.**—Plows on revolving tables representing "1776 and 1876." L 24. 670

305 **Decker, P. H., Chicago, Ill.**—Hollow tooth harrow, and roller mold-board plow. P 26. 670

306 **Ward, Samuel B., Locust Mount, Va.**—Plow, rake, etc. L 24. 670

307 **Cooke & Foulke, Shelbyville, Ill.**—Cultivator. M 19. 670

308 **Park, H. & H., Mt. Victory, Ohio.**—Fork, hoe, and broom handles. T 25. 670

309 **Stuart & Kirkland, Jackson, Miss.**—Plows. N 24. 670

309*a* **Michigan Double Stave Barrel Co., Charlotte, Mich.**—Barrels, etc. R 28. 670

309*b* **Holland, Ed., Atlanta, Ga.**—Buggy-plow. K 24. 670

310 **Deere & Co., Moline, Ill.**—Steel plows, gang and sulky plows, walking corn-cultivators. Q 24. 670

311 **Morrison Brothers, Fort Madison, Iowa.**—Self-cleaning iron and wood beam plow. L 24. 670

312 **Sheble & Fisher, Philadelphia, Pa.**—Hay and manure forks, rakes, potato-hooks, and manure-drags. S 25. 670

313 **Wallace, Samuel J., Keokuk, Iowa.**—Straddle-row cultivator. L 26. 670

314 **Miller & Wallace, Keokuk, Iowa.**—Texas plow. L 26. 670

315 **Isaacs, Fred. H., Newark, N. J.**—Sulky gang-plow. M 25. 670

316 **Cotton, A. C., Vineland, N. J.**—Reversible scuffle-hoe. D 17. 670

317 **Heydrick, W. H. H., Philadelphia, Pa.**—Steam plow, and farm engine. L 23. 670

318 **Myer, B., Newark, N. J.**—Plows. N 25. 670

319 **New York Manufacturing Co., New York, N. Y.** P 17.
- *a* Plow, cultivator, etc. 670
- *b* Corn-sheller, root-cutter, etc. 674

320 **Brewster, Dodge, & Huse, Peru, Ill.**—Wheel corn-cultivator, steel plows for old ground and for breaking prairie-sod. Q 26. 670

321 **Greenwich Machine Works, Greenwich, N. Y.**—Cultivator and shovel plow. M 26. 670

322 **Richmond Plow Works, Richmond, Ind.**—Steel plows. L 25. 670

323 **Moline Plow Co., Moline, Ill.**—Wood-beam plows, steel-beam plows, and cultivators. Q 26–28. 670

324 **Laurence & Chapin, Kalamazoo, Mich.**—Plows. M 24. 670

325 **Muschert, B. F., Morrisville, Pa.**—Cultivator plow. M 23. 670

325*a* **Strombeck, Charles W., Syracuse, N. Y.**—Harrow. L 27. 670

325*b* **Bidwell, J. C., Pittsburg, Pa.**—Plows, and steel castings. S 28. 670

325*c* **Ellis, Minot, Greenfield, Mass.**—Swivel plows. L 24. 670

325*d* **Feenders, Harm., Charles City, Iowa.**—Clod-crusher. Q 12. 670

325*e* **Causland, McCoy, & Causland, Philadelphia, Pa.**—Pick-axe. M 26. 670

325*f* **Lamborn, Lewis, Hamorton, Pa.**—Cultivator with attachment for eradicating potato bugs. N 28. 670

325*g* **Cagwin & Young, Joliet, Ill.**—Spading-plow. M 23. 670

325*h* **Auburn M'f'g Co., Auburn, N. Y.**—Agricultural hand implements. Intersection of aisle N and main transept. 670

326 **Rogers, C. B., Philadelphia, Pa.**—Cultivators, berry and fruit baskets. M 26. 670

326*a* **Kroh, C. & P. G., Kroghville, Wis.**—Cultivator. M 24. 670

326*b* **Deats, L. M., & Co., Pittstown, N. J.** N 23.
- *a* Plows. 670
- *b* Power corn-shellers. 674

327 **Benson, B. S., Baltimore, Md.**—Steam plow. N 9. 670

328 **Speer, Alexander, & Sons, Pittsburg, Pa.**—Iron and steel plows. M and L 28. 670

329 **South Bend Iron Works, South Bend, Ind.**—Chilled plows and attachments, specimens of chilled metal. P 26. 670

330 **Hull, David H., Syracuse, N. Y.**—Machine for stripping and booking tobacco. M 22. 670

331 **Brous, T. Miles, Philadelphia, Pa.**—Plows. M 24. 670

For classes of exhibits, indicated by numbers at end of entries, see Classification, pp. 12–14.

Machines, Implements, and Processes of Manufacture.

332 Buford, B. D., & Co., Rock Island, Ill.—Plows and cultivators. O 28. 670

333 Wyckoff & McDonald, Hightstown, N. J.—Two-horse gang-plow. M 16. 670

334 Binder & Schweibing, Mauch Chunk, Pa.—Adjustable corn-plow. L 23. 670

335 Estes, William A., Boston, Mass. —Anti-friction plow. N 26. 670

336 Travis, A. B., Brandon, Mich. L 22.
- *a* Horse wheat-hoe. 670
- *b* Seed-drill. 671

337 Root, D., Son & Co., Mount Joy, Pa.—Steel and iron plows, cultivators, and agricultural steels. L 28. 670

338 Reynolds, E. D. & O. B., Brockton, Mass. N 25.
- *a* Gang plows and attachments, cultivators, harrows, and horse-hoes. 670
- *b* Seed-drills, planters, etc. 671

339 Allen, R. H., & Co., New York, N. Y. Q and R 25.
- *a* Plows, cultivators, harrows, and horse-hoes. 670
- *b* Seed-sowers. 671
- *c* Corn-sheller and separator. 673
- *d* Horizontal and vertical burr-stones, brick-machines, seed-hullers. 674

340 Chicago Plow Co., Chicago, Ill.— Plows and cultivators. P 28. 670

342 Avery, B. F., & Sons, Louisville, Ky.—Plows, cultivators, etc. N 28. 670

343 Walker, James R., Detroit, Mich.— Iron plow. K 28. 670

344 Harnish, Edward P., Felton, Del. L 22.
- *a* Cultivator. 670
- *b* Corn-planter. 671

345 Gregg & Co., Trumansburg, N. Y. R 20.
- *a* Sulky-plow. 670
- *b* Mowing-machine. 672

346 Hutchinson, Samuel, Griggsville, Ill.—Adjustable harrow. P 28. 670

348 Gifford, Johnson, & Co., Hudson, N. Y.—Pulverizing-cultivators, corn-cultivators, and hilling-plows. O 26. 670

349 Carr & Hobson, New York, N. Y. —N, O, *and* P 28.
- *a* Plows and other agricultural implements. 670
- *b* Hay-cutters, corn-shellers, mills, presses, etc. 674
- *c* Churns. 675

350 Ames, Oliver, & Sons, North Easton, Mass.—Shovels, spades, scoops, and drainage tools. S 26. 670

351 Griffiths, George, Philadelphia, Pa. —Shovels, spades, handles, coal-hods, and pans. These goods are as produced at factory. We exhibit a spade used by Washington's army at Valley Forge. It was dug up by the late Rev. Dr. Brainerd. The handle replaced by one of style used at that date. T 27. 670

351*a* Fisher, Samuel, Philadelphia, Pa. —Gang-plow and cultivator-comb. O 26. 670

351*b* Orchard City Agricultural Works, Burlington, Iowa. P 28.
- *a* Plows. 670
- *b* Rakes. 672

351*c* Wayne Agricultural Company, Richmond, Ind. S 25.
- *a* Cultivators. 670
- *b* Drills. 671
- *c* Mowers and reapers. 672

351*d* Bowers & Stitzer, Hackettstown, N. J. L 11.
- *a* Beam-plow. 670
- *b* Churn worked by a dog. 675

352 Bergstresser, E. L., Hublersburg, Pa.—Corn-planter. K 18. 671

353 Rowland, T., & Sons, Philadelphia, Pa.—Shovels and spades. T 17. 670

354 Walton, Silas, Moorestown, N. J. —Garden and field cultivator. L 25. 670

355 Rue, J. Chalmers, Englishtown, N. J.—Gang-plow. L 25. 670

356 Smith, Peter E., Scotland Neck, N. C. M 24.
- *a* Sulky-plow. 670
- *b* Cotton-seed planter. 671

357 Bayliss, Edwin, Massillon, Ohio. O 17–18.
- *a* Wheel-harrow, iron cultivator, and shovel-plow. 670
- *b* Harvester. 672

358 Ward's Fertilizer Co., Boston, Mass. M 26.
- *a* Harrows. 670
- *b* Potato-planter and digger. 671

359 Brown, Hinman & Co., Columbus, Ohio. T 25.
- *a* Weeding-hoes, garden-rakes, manure and spading forks. 670
- *b* Scythe-snaths, grain-cradles, hay-forks, etc. 672

360 Mabbett, Truman, Vineland, N. J. O 26.
- *a* Hand and horse cultivators. 670
- *b* Berry-crates. 674

361 Withington, Cooley, & Co., Jackson, Mich. T 25.
- *a* Cast-steel hoes, rakes, and potato-hooks. 670
- *b* Hay and manure forks, scythe-snaths, etc. 672

362 Morrison & Fay, Bryan, Ohio. M 25.
- *a* Plow. 670
- *b* Corn-sheller. 674

364 Brownback, P. N., Limerick Station, Pa. N 16.
- *a* Threshing-machine, dust-conveyer, and plows. 670
- *b* Self-acting hay-rake, mower, and reaper. 672
- *c* Sausage-cutter, stuffer, etc. 674

366 Higganum Manufacturing Co., Higganum, Conn. L 25.
- *a* Plows and agricultural implements. 670
- *b* Corn-shellers, hay-spreaders, etc. 674
- *c* Cider-mills, meat-cutters, etc. 673

367 Remington, E., & Sons, Ilion, N. Y. O 19.
- *a* Plows, cultivators, hoes, shovels. 670
- *b* Mower, horse and hand rakes. 672
- *c* Cotton-gin. 673
- *d* Milk-cooler. 675

368 Pennsylvania Agricultural Works, York, Pa. O *and* P 24.
- *a* Plows, cultivators, and tools for cultivation. 670
- *b* Seed-planter. 671
- *c* Threshing-machines, horse-powers. 673
- *d* Cotton-gins, steam-engines, and agricultural steels. 674

Machines, Implements, and Processes of Manufacture.

369 New York Plow Co., New York, N. Y. N 21.
a Plows, harrows, rollers, clod-crushers, etc. 670
b Hay-rakes. 672
c Corn-shellers. 673
d Cider and wine mills. 674

370 Hillborn, Buckman, & Co., New-town, Pa. Q 16.
a Plows. 670
b Mower, horse-rake, etc. 672
c Corn-sheller. 673
d Fodder-cutter. 674

371 Wheeler & Melick Co., Albany, N. Y. Q 7.
a Ithaca or American wheel horse-rake. 670
b Centennial self-acting wheel horse-rake. 672
c Saratoga or New York wheel horse-rake. 672
d Clover-huller, thresher and cleaner, thresher and shaker, straw-preserving thresher, one and two horse and lever powers. 673
e Feed-mill, cutter, wood-sawing machine, horse pitchforks, etc. 674
f Dog, calf, or donkey power, for churning, etc. 675

372 Allen, S. L., & Co., No. 119 South Fourth st., Philadelphia, Pa.—Farm and garden tools. Manufacturers of the Planet, Jr., hand seed-drills and wheel-hoes. Also of improved horse-hoes and cultivators, insect fumigators, etc. M 20. 671

373 Farmers' Friend Manufacturing Co., Dayton, Ohio.—Grain-drill and grass-seed sower, grain-drill and broad-cast seed sower combined, grain-drill and fertilizer combined. N 17. 671

374 Mast, P. P., & Co., Springfield, Ohio.—Grain-drills and seed-sowers, broadcast seeder and cultivator, riding or walking cultivator, and plow-sulky. M 17. 671

375 McSherry, D. E., & Co., Dayton, Ohio.—Grain and seed drills. We claim a positive force-feed, constructed in such a manner as not to allow any grain to pass that is not carried out by the spiral wheel working inside of a cap or case underneath the hopper; provided with a patent washer, which prevents the grain from being broken, and causing a regular flow of seed. It is regulated by the change of cog-wheels, which is simple, durable, and making positive quantities. The quantities per acre are not raised by the roughness of the ground or the box being full or nearly empty. It has also been used successfully in drilling corn, beans, peas, etc. It is provided with a grass-seed box, which can be used either in front or rear of machine. An iron lift-bar is attached, which is strong, neat, and durable, by means of which the hoes are raised out of the ground, and at the same time throwing the whole machine out of gear. To the drill is attached a long hoe, iron drag-bars which can be changed from single to double rake, or vice versa; added to this is an iron shaft-bar, which is held permanent by bolts, therefore not detracting from the strength of the frame. There is a light, strong frame, constructed with six pieces of timber and an iron axle running the whole width of it. It has a surveyor-chart, that measures the ground actually sown. It has high wheels, broad tread. We also have a spring hoe, known as the Willoughby patent. Weight of drill about 525 pounds.

The Rice drill has a positive force-feed, constructed with a spiral wheel, provided with two washers or disks, one at each end of feed-wheel, working inside of cap or case underneath the hopper, causing a regular flow of seed. The quantity is regulated by change of cog-wheels, making positive quantities. The frame is constructed of six pieces of timber, making it strong and durable. It is provided with a pair of shafts for one horse only. Has an iron axle running whole width of frame. It has high wheels, broad tread, and weighs about 400 pounds.

Broad-cast seeders. This is a positive force-feed, constructed with a spiral wheel and flange, working inside cap, thereby causing a regular flow of seed, and only allows such grain to pass out as is carried by the wheel. The washers at the side of the wheel protect the grain from being broken or injured. The quantity is regulated by changing cog-wheels, making a positive quantity sown. The roughness of the ground or the box being full or nearly empty has no effect on the discharge of seed. It has six iron spouts for the grain to pass through and scatter in front of the hoes. Has twelve hoes, six inches apart. The points are steel and are reversible; can be regulated to the depth desired. Has iron drag-bars, to which the hoes are attached. These being all under the main frame, with a lift-bar attached to raise them out of the ground. It has a grass and flax seed attachment, and has an iron axle running the whole width of the frame. Has high wheels, broad tread, and weighs about 450 pounds. M 18. 671

376 Campbell, J. & J. A., Harrison, Ohio.—Drill. M 23. 671

377 Buist, David, Philadelphia, Pa.—Seed-sower. K 19. 671

380 Clarridge, John, Mt. Sterling, Ohio.—Corn and cotton-seed planter. M 17. 671

381 S. J. Waite Manufacturing Co., Worcester, Mass. N 22.
a Breast-drill, corner-brace, saw-sett, and lathe. 671
b Apple-parer. 674

382 Nash & Brother, New York, N. Y.—Potato-planter. N 19. 671

383 Selby, James, & Co., Peoria, Ill.—Corn-planter. M 22. 671

383*a* Beatty, Matthew O., Concord, N. C.—Cotton-planter, guano-distributor, and cultivator combined. M 23. 671

384 Bickford & Huffman, Macedon, N. Y.—Grain-drill and attachments. L 18. 671

Last fall Bickford & Huffman were invited by chief of Centennial bureau to perform seeding of grain for the field trial to take place this year at Philadelphia. Seeding accomplished with following results: Actual measurement of ground 45$\frac{53}{100}$ acres. Field to be sown with wheat 5 pecks to the acre. Quantity required 56 bushels 54½ pounds; quantity sown, 57 bushels 27½ pounds—an excess of only 33 pounds upon entire field of 45$\frac{53}{100}$ acres, or less than ⅔ pound excess per acre. To account for which, if it need

For classes of exhibits, indicated by numbers at end of entries, see Classification, pp. 12–14.

Machines, Implements, and Processes of Manufacture.

be accounted for, three headlands, upon which were lapped three tubes, were sown. This result was considered very satisfactory, and demonstrates the accuracy of the quantity-wheel. The fertilizer attachment, which has been transferred to the rear, is an improvement, and makes the distribution even and uniform. The machine is nicely balanced, and the weight removed from the horse's neck.

385 Hall, H. L., Chicago, Ill.—Combined seed-sower and cultivator. L 19. 671

386 Vandiver Corn-Planter Co., Quincy, Ill.—Corn-planter. M 19. 671

387 Stokes, F. N., Urbana, Ohio.—Planter, fertilizer, and pulverizer. K 18 *and* 19. 671

387*a* Cooper, Mark, Union, S. C.—Combined fertilizer, refiner, and seed-planter. M 22. 671

387*b* Brown, H. L. & C. P., Shortsville, N. Y.—Grain-drill, with and without attachments. M 21. 671

388 Hoosier Drill Co., Milton, Ind.—Wheat-drill with grass-seed attachment, corn-drill. K 15. 671

388*a* Screw Mower and Reaper Co., Philipsburg, N. J.—R, S, *and* T 15.
a Grain drills. 671
b Mowing and reaping machines. 672
c Hay and stalk cutters. 674

390 Johnson & Gere, Owego, N. Y.—Grain-drill and attachments, fertilizer-sower. L 19. 671

390*a* Gibbs & Lee, Brooklyn, N. Y.—Steam spader. M 24. 671

390*b* Rothchild, Joseph, Shelbyville, Ky.—Corn-planter. K 18. 671

391 Eagle Manufacturing Co., Davenport, Iowa. M 26.
a Walking cultivator. 671
b Sulky rake. 672

392 Asay & Wood, Philadelphia, Pa.—Combined corn-planter, fertilizer-distributor, and deflecting cultivator. N 22. 671

392*a* Bliss, B. K., & Sons, seedsmen, 34 Barclay St., New York, N. Y. Randolph's hand seed-sower, for sowing all kinds of garden-seeds with accuracy and despatch; can be easily operated by a lady or child. Highly recommended by experienced gardeners and farmers. Its cost is trifling, compared with the advantages resulting from its use. The saving in time and seeds will undoubtedly repay the outlay in the planting of a single week. $1.25 each. Sent by mail, postpaid, to any address in the U. S. upon receipt of $1.50.

Randolph's fertilizer distributor, for distributing all kinds of concentrated fertilizers, as phosphates, guano, ashes, plaster, or chemical manures, without touching the material with the hands, a matter of some importance when caustic substances are used. One man can do the work of three by the ordinary method. Price, $5. B 28. 671

393 Crowell, J. B., & Co., Green Castle, Pa.—Grain, guano, and grass-seed drills. L 12. 671

394 Willoughby, James D., Philadelphia, Pa.—Grain-drill, with and without fertilizer attachment. L 22. 671

395 Sweeney, Hugh M., Worcester, Mass.—Liquid fertilizing machine. L 21. 671

396 Springfield Manufacturing Co., Springfield, Ill.—Climax corn-planter. L 19. 671

An excellent two-horse check row corn-planter; six chamber rotary drop; universal wrought-iron coupling; broad steel runners; woven wire open heel; simple in construction; certain in operation. Send for illustrated circular.

398 Rentchler, D. & H., Belleville, Ill.—Grain and seed drills. M 19. 671

399 Heamer, Andrew J., Pittsfield, Ill.—Hedge-trimmer. M 14. 671

400 Seymour, John B., Philadelphia, Pa.—Box-hoe seed-planter. T 8. 671

401 Rutschman Bros., Philadelphia, Pa. S 24.
a Self-feeding hand-drill. 671
b Meat-chopper. 674

402 Keystone Manufacturing Co., Sterling, Ill. L 19.
a Corn-planter. 671
b Corn-sheller, cider mill and press. 673

403 Esterly, George, & Son, Whitewater, Wis. P 20 *and* 21.
a Cultivator and seeder combined. 671
b Harvester, self-raking reaper. 672

404 Brown, George W., Galesburg, Ill.—N 15.
a Corn-planter. 671
b Field corn-stalk cutter. 672

405 Goodell Co., Antrim, N. H. T 14.
a Broadcast seed-sower. 671
b Apple-parers, peach-parers, cherry-stoners, etc. 674

406 Hagerstown Agricultural Implement Manufacturing Co., Hagerstown, Md. R *and* S 26.
a Grain, seed, and fertilizing drills. 671
b Clover huller and cleaner. 673
c Feed-cutter. 674

407 Williams Bros., Ithaca, N. Y. P 12.
a Fertilizer and grain-sower. 671
b Horse hay-rake. 672
c Portable engine. 674

408 Adriance, Platt, & Co., New York, N. Y.—Self-raking reapers and mowers. T 15. 672

408*a* Rank, Amos, & Co., Canton, Ohio.—Mowers, reapers, etc. K 13. 672

408*b* Perry, John G., Kingston, R. I.—Mowers. P 22. 672

408*c* Johnston, Samuel, Brockport, N.Y.—Automatic harvesters and binders. B 13–14. 672

409 Eagle Mowing & Reaping Machine Co., Albany, N. Y.—Mowing and reaping machines. T 18. 672

410 Osborne, D. M., & Co., Auburn, N. Y.—Mowing and reaping machines. O 13 *and* 14. 672

411 Wood, Walter A., Hoosac Falls, N. Y. S *and* T 13–14.
a Droppers. 671
b Mowers, reapers, harvesters, etc. 672

412 Warder, Mitchell, & Co., Springfield, Ohio.—Reapers and mowers. P 15. 672

413 Thomas, John H., & Sons, Springfield, Ohio.—Sulky-spring tooth hay-rake. L 15. 672

Machines, Implements, and Processes of Manufacture.

413*a* Kelly, William E., New Brunswick, N. J.—Reciprocating screw mowing-machine. R 17. 672

413*b* Chaplin, C. H., Tecumseh, Mich.—Rake. L 14. 672

413*c* Schenck, P. C., jr., Neshanic, N. J.—Mower and reaper. K 15. 672

413*d* Wells, French, & Co., Chicago, Ill.—Potato-digger. R 24. 672

413*e* Whiton, David E., West Stafford, Conn.—Mowing-machine. R 14. 672

413*f* Mills, Peck, & Co., Otsego, Mich.—Field and garden hoes. R 28. 672

414 Whiteley, Fassler, & Kelly, Springfield, Ohio.—Reapers and mowers. O 15 *and* 16. 726

415 Prout, H. N., Westfield, Mass.—Adjustable hoeing-machine. Q 28. 672

416 Ohmer, Augustus J., Hamilton, Ohio. — Hand mowing-machines. M 13. 672

417 Dodds, John, Dayton, Ohio.—Sulky horse hay-rakes. M 15. 672

418 Barnes, George, & Co., Syracuse, N. Y.—Mower-knives, reaper-sickles, spring keys, and cotters. M 15. 672

419 Taylor, B. C., Dayton, Ohio.—Wheel horse hay and grain rake. L 14. 672

420 Coates, A. W., Alliance, Ohio.—Lock-lever horse hay-rake. L 15. 672

421 Whittemore Bros., Boston, Mass.—Hay-rake and feed-cutter. L 20. 672

422 Chadborn & Coldwell, Newburgh, N.Y.—Lawn-mower; smoked-beef cutter. N 13. 672

423 Wisner, J. E., Friendship, N. Y.—Self-discharging rake. M 14. 672

424 Converse, Bolivar C., Springfield, Ohio.—Reaping-machine. R 16. 672

425 Eagle Company, Riverton, Conn.—Grain, grass, and bush scythes, grass-hooks, corn and hay knives. T 25. 672

426 Huber Manufacturing Co., Marion, Ohio.—Revolving hay-rake. L 16. 672

427 Dutton, R., Yonkers, N. Y.—Reaping and mowing machine. R 25. 672

428 Rochester Agricultural Works, Rochester, N. Y.—Reapers and mowers. T 14. 672

429 Seiberling, J. F., Akron, Ohio.—Mower and attachments. Q 14. 672

430 Whitman & Miles Manufacturing Co., Akron, Ohio.—Mowing and reaping machine knives, sickles, and sections. T 18. 672

431 Aultman, Miller, & Co., Akron, Ohio.—Mower with table-rake reaper. Q 15. 672

431*a* Royce, John S., Cuylerville, N. Y.—Reapers. Q 25. 672

431*b* Gordon, James F., Rochester, N.Y.—Self-binding harvester. P 17. 672

432 Spink, James L., & Co., Minneapolis, Minn. — Mowers and reapers. Q 14. 672

433 Bellaire Manufacturing Co., Bellaire, Ohio. — Mower and reaper. P 14. 672

434 Russell, C., & Co., Canton, Ohio.—Self-raker, reaper, and mower combined, single mower. R 14. 672

435 Tschop, Albert, Harrisburg, Pa.—Self-dumping wheel hay-rake. L 15. 672

436 Hewit, John C., Pennsgrove, N. J.—Potato-digger. M 16. 672

437 New London Scythe Co., New London, N. H.—Scythes. Q 28. 672

437*a* Haynes, W. H., North Sudbury, Mass.—Hay-elevator. M 21. 672

438 Graham, Emlen, & Passmore, Philadelphia, Pa.—Lawn-mower. L 13 *and* 14. 672

439 Nellis, A. J., Pittsburg, Pa.—Harpoon horse hay-fork. Nellis' O. H. H. H. fork and patent method for mowing and stacking hay or straw. Will save the farmer its cost every season. Also manufacturers of agricultural steels, and Nellis' patent cotton-tie steel-tempered by Nellis' process to suit all kinds of soil. Samples free. Address A. J. Nellis & Co., Pittsburg, Pa. S 17. 672

440 Field & Carpenter, Port Chester, N. Y. — Self-discharging hay-rake. L 15. 672

440*a* Ball, Samuel, Cogan's Station, Pa.—Grain-cradle. L 22. 672

440*b* Strait, H., Troy, N. Y.—Potato-digger. O 26. 672

440*c* Long, Allstatter, & Co., Hamilton, Ohio. L 14.

a Rake, knives, sickles, mower, etc. 672
b Fodder-cutter. 674

441 Clegg, Wood, & Co., Dayton, Ohio.—Self-discharging hay-rake. L 15. 672

442 Hills' Archimedean Lawn-Mower Co., Hartford, Conn.—Lawn-mowers. N 13. 672

443 Norton, James, Hightstown, N. J.—Potato-digger, and Rigg's patent gang-plow, for cultivating corn, cotton, potatoes, etc., manufactured by Wyckoff & McDonald, Hightstown, N. J. M 16. 672

444 Fisher, Henry, Canton, Ohio, U. S. A.—Patent prairie-mower knife-grinders, for sharpening harvester-knives; patent farm and plantation bells; patent ladles, hay-knives, harvester-knives, sections, etc. Illustrated descriptive circulars sent free upon application. T 24. 672

445 Gibbs & Sterrett Manufacturing Co., Corry, Pa.—Mower and attachments, hay-conveyer. Q 17 *and* 18. 672

446 The Johnston Harvester Co., Brockport, N.Y.—Self-raking reaper, harvester, mower, and automatic grain-binder. O 20 *and* 21. 672

447 Pennock Manufacturing Co., Kennett Square, Pa.—Corn-sheller and hay-fork. Q 12. 672

448 Wright, James W., Minneapolis, Minn.—Grain-harvester and binder. N 22. 672

449 Superior Mower & Reaper Works, A. J. Sweeney & Son, Proprietors, Wheeling, W. Va. — Mowing-machine without cog-wheels or shafts; a worm-wheel on the axle drives a double-threaded steel screw, which directly operates the knife. P 16. 672

450 Bradley Manufacturing Co., Syracuse, N. Y. — Self-dumping hay-rake, mower, and self-raking harvester. Q 14. 672

For classes of exhibits, indicated by numbers at end of entries, see Classification, pp. 12–14.

Machines, Implements, and Processes of Manufacture.

451 Norwalk Lawn-Mower Co., Norwalk, Conn.—Lawn-mowers. M 14. 672

452 Chapman Binder Co., Rochester, Minn.—Reaper and binder. T 17. 672

453 Towanda Eureka Mower Co., Towanda, Pa. — Mower and reaper. Q 19. 672

454 Bartram Sewing-Machine Co., Danbury, Conn.—Revolving cutter lawn-mowers. M 14. 672

455 Perry, Stuart, Newport, N. Y.—Hay-tedder. M 15. 672

457 Hand, S. A., Philadelphia, Pa.—Lawn-mower. M 13. 672

458 Mayo, M. C., Boston, Mass.—Mowing-machine. T 19. 672

459 Nye, S. R., Winchendon, Mass.—Horse-rake. The peculiarities of the S. R. Nye and Improved Bay State Rake are: 1st. The peculiar shape of the teeth, those at each end being brought forward of those in the centre, which prevents the hay from scattering or roping out. This is particularly advantageous when working on a side, hill, or gleaning. 2d. Also the manner of holding each tooth in its proper position laterally by what is called the guide, which prevents them from flopping about. 3d. Each tooth is independent of all others, thereby enabling it to pass over an obstruction twenty inches high without in the least affecting the teeth next by the side of it. 4th. The dumping arrangement, whereby any boy or girl who can drive a horse can rake as well as a man, as it is dumped entirely by the power of the horse. 5th. This rake has been submitted to some of of the best mechanical talent in the country, who have pronounced it, with these improvements, to be simple and durable, having the unqualified approbation of farmers everywhere. 4000 of these rakes will be manufactured for the harvest of 1876. L 15. 672

460 Treman, Valentine, & Green, Ithaca, N. Y.—Corn sheller and hoe. L 27. 672

461 Maule, James S., Lewisburg, Pa.—Mower and automatic reaper. S 17. 672

462 Ithaca Agricultural Works, Ithaca, N. Y.—Wheel-rake and attachments. N 15. 672

463 Holt, Hiram, & Co., East Wilton, Me.—Grass and bush scythes, hay-knives, etc. T 25. 672

464 Read, C. A., Bridgeport, Conn.—Lawn-mower. M 14. 672

465 Morgan, D. S., & Co., Brookport, N. Y.—Reaping and mowing machines. P 18. 672

466 Goodwin, William F., Stelton, N. J.—Mowing and reaping machine. Q 13. 672

467 Kenyon Brothers, Carbondale, Pa. —Potato-digger. M 15. 672

468 Mann, H. F., Pittsburg, Pa.—Harvesting and mowing machine. S *and* T 19. 672

469 Gammon & Deering, Chicago, Ill.—Harvester, automatic binder, wind-mill. No class of farm machinery has undergone so many valuable changes by way of improvements during the past forty-three years as the reapers, mowers, and harvesters. This reaper is protected by the patent secured by C. W. & W. W. Marsh in 1858, which saves the labor and annoyance of three men in binding the grain as it comes from the machine. In the Western and Middle States, where the grain is grown most extensively, the Marsh harvester is sold in great numbers. The Marsh harvester, which is popularly known in the West as the King of the Harvest Field, combines the essential features of simplicity, utility, durability, and lightness of draft. As it is the original of the harvester class, which has so completely revolutionized the trade in nearly all classes of these machines, it is but fair to say that the proprietors, who have made this machine such a wonderful success, have spared neither pains nor money in adding from year to year the many improvements so well known in its mechanism and general appearance. The Marsh harvester is a light machine, only weighing 800 pounds. It is made of the best material, all the timber used being seasoned at least three years, every part liable to breakage being especially well and carefully made. It cuts the grain clean, with little waste, takes up, down, and crinkled grain, and draws easily with two horses. The farmer who purchases a Marsh harvester is sure to get a thoroughly tried and popular machine. The Plano Gordon self-binding harvester and automatic wire-binder, which the inventors have been for several years in perfecting, is acknowledged by experienced mechanics a good and highly valuable addition. While the inventors do not claim for the automatic binder perfection, they do claim that the present one works very satisfactorily. A large number are in use in the West and Southwest; and from the numerous testimonials from farmers and local committees appointed to test their merits, there can be no question that the binder is very valuable and fast becoming in general use. The harvester, together with the automatic binder, is in all respects first class, as it works almost to perfection, binds the bundles tight, and does not leave the straw unbound upon the field. It reduces the labor of harvesting to the very minimum, shortens the time in completing the work, is in no way complicated, is not likely to get out of order, and one trial commends it to those desiring to purchase a first-class machine. It is labor-saving, manifestly popular, does clean, economical work, has been fully tested, embodies the improvements of many years, and its work will pay for it in a short time, reducing as it does the cost of harvesting to the farmer. O 20 *and* 21. 672

470 Handy Horse Hay-Fork Co., Conneautsville, Pa.—Hand horse hay-fork. L 22. 652

471 Otis Brothers & Co., New York, N. Y.—Mowing-machine.
The hay-maker is noiseless, light-draft, very strong, and of great cutting power. The knife is actuated by a new mechanical movement consisting of but two pieces. S 22. 672

472 Harrison Manufacturing Co., Lansing, Mich.—Rubber-lined knife-head for reapers and mowers. T 17. 672

For locations of objects, indicated by letter and figure, see Key to Notation, p. 6; ground plan, p. 10.

Machines, Implements, and Processes of Manufacture.

473 Champion Machine Co., Springfield, Ohio.—Reapers, mowers, rakers, and droppers. Q 15. 672

474 Hanes, John, Moorestown, N. J.—Corn-sheller. T 23. 672

475 Lewis, James H., Detroit, Mich.—Potato-digger. N 15. 672

476 Richardson Manufacturing Co., Worcester, Mass.—Combined mower and reaper, hay-tedder, etc. M 14. 672

478 Collyer, Robert H., Chicago, Ill.—Flax machinery. S 10. 672

479 Lee, James, jr., Stonersville, Berks Co., Pa.—Hay-tedder with or without rake. Merit: superior manner in which it turns the hay. L 15. 672

480 Westfall, D. B., Lyons, N. Y.—Potato-digger. L 16. 672

481 Gulick, Edwin, New Brunswick, N. J.—Safety-seat for harvesters and mowers. T 8. 672

483 Vermont Farm Machine Co., Bel-lows Falls, Vt.—Gleaner, horse, hay, and grain rake. K 15. 672

484 Dunn Edge Tool Co., West Water-ville, Me.—Scythes, axes, grass-hooks, hay, straw, and corn knives. R 24. 672

485 Riggs, M. B., Palmyra, N. Y.—Potato-digger. L 26. 672

486 Stevens, Ansel, Gorham, Maine.—Mower. T 21. 672

487 McMentry, John, Lexington, Ky.—Reaper and mower. P 17. 672

488 McPherson, D., Caledonia, N. Y.—Automatic grain-binder. R 17. 672

489 Patrons' Manufacturing Associa-tion, Indianapolis, Ind.—Direct draft mower. L 25. 672

490 Aultman, C., & Co., Canton, Ohio. Q *and* R 22.

a "New" Buckeye mower. 672
b Improved Buckeye mower. 672
c Improved Buckeye mower and dropper. 672
d Improved Buckeye mower and table-rake reaper. 673

491 Stratton & Cullum, Meadville, Pa.—Hay-loading machines. S 25. 673

492 Sandwich Manufacturing Co., Sandwich, Ill.

a Harvester. 672
b Self-feeding corn-sheller. 674

The Adams and French harvester differs from other riding and binding machines in not using canvas or belts, and cuts and elevates grain, wet, green, or dry. There are many good reasons why this harvester is considered by experienced mechanics and farmers to possess many excellences, which have been recently added in the various improvements, some of them being entirely new, giving it very decided advantages. First, it uses no canvas or belts; the vibrating rakes carry the grain uniformly, evenly, and with great accuracy. Second, the raking apparatus is peculiarly constructed, so that it cannot be affected by weeds or dampness; and this feature the farmer will recognize. Third, it has capacity for three binders when time presses; this capacity is of very great importance, as time is money, especially in the Western States, where this machine is mostly sold. It is manufactured in Sandwich, Ill., and principally sold in Kansas, Nebraska, Illinois, Missouri, Iowa, and Oregon. The Adams patent self-feeding power corn-sheller, known as picker-wheel machine, is a strictly automatic corn-shelling machine. The corn is shelled from the cob in much the same way it would be done by hand, and without subjecting the ears to undue pressure, in consequence of which the cobs are not broken and mixed with the grain and the kernels are not cracked and ground. The annual product of corn is immense; and to properly and expeditiously prepare it for our market is a herculean task, but, aided by these thorough and cleaning shellers, the corn is rapidly made ready, and is in the best possible condition, the quality of the work being above just criticism. To this is added the adaptability of the machines to all qualities of corn, frosted, sound, or soft, and performing a great amount of work in a given time, with a given power, leaving the cob whole, suitable for fuel when needed, and the corn perfectly clean. The self-feeding is a saving of much labor and considerable expense, and commends the machine wherever introduced. The farmers' sheller is a compact little machine, but cannot take the place of the self-feeders, being designed for individual use, avoiding the delays of making use of self-feeders, often owned by a number, who are compelled to wait one on another. S *and* T 20–21.

493 Rue, George W., Hamilton, Ohio. N 15.

a Garden-cultivator. 670
b Potato-digger. 672

494 Pritz, A., & Sons, Dayton, Ohio. S 16.

a Grain-drill. 670
b Field-roller. 671
c Self-raking reaper and mower. 672

The Centennial Dorsey self-raking reaper and mower, combined with controllable rake. A. Pritz & Sons, manufacturers, have added to this reaper a perfect controllable self-rake, and one that can be operated by the driver to rake off at will, or the sheaf can be held as long as desired.

The "Centennial Dorsey" will be made with five rakes, either of which can be made to rake the sheaf or act as a reel, as the driver may see fit. The reaper, when left alone, will make one sheaf every revolution of the rakes, but the driver can instantly and very easily make any rake make a sheaf. In heavy grain a sheaf can be made of any size, from one to five sheaves in every sixteen feet of ground gone over, and in light grain the rakes can be held until the proper amount of grain may be on the platform. The Centennial Dorsey rake being under the control of the driver, any size sheaf can be made. This reaper is strong and durable; has no side draught; has the weight on the rakes and drive-wheel; is easily managed, being entirely automatic and under the control of the driver.

495 Harbert & Raymond, Philadelphia, Pa. P 10.

a Mower and hay-rakes. 672
b Threshing-machine and clover-mill. 673
c Portable steam-engine, portable saw-mill, and hay-cutters. 674

For classes of exhibits, indicated by numbers at end of entries, see Classification, pp. 12–14.

Machines, Implements, and Processes of Manufacture.

496 Burt, Hildreth, & Co., Harvard, Mass. N 14.
a Burt's Union horse-power. The pivots and axles are all hardened and durable. Large truck wheels, and runs easy and at low elevation.
Lawn mower, recent invention. 672
b Rocking saw-table, pendulum-balanced, rapid and safe, for sawing cord-wood.
Wood-splitter, cheap, simple, and efficient. 674

497 Cohu, A. B., New York, N. Y. P 28.
a Rake. 672
b Corn-sheller, stalk-cutter, hand-saw-mill. 674
c Churn. 675

498 Richardson, William H., Philadelphia, Pa.—Corn-husking machine, machine for cutting standing corn and husking. T 22. 673

499 Pitts, H. A., Sons, Manufacturing Co., Chicago, Ill.—Thresher, separator, and cleaner, horse-power. S 19. 673

500 New Era Manufacturing Co., Elm-wood, Ill.—Grain-grader, grain-separator, smut ball extractor, scourer, and wheat-brush machine. R 23. 673

500*a* Hall's Self-Feeding Cotton-Gin Co., Sing Sing, N. Y.—Self-feeding cotton-gin and condenser. K 11. 673

500*b* Keller, Henry, Sank Centre, Minn. —Farm mills. T 25. 673

500*c* Kibler, N., Pittsfield, Ill.—Farm mills. M 25. 673

500*d* Freeman & Clark, Racine, Wis.—Farm mill; grain and seed separator. F 28. 673

500*e* Birdsell Manufacturing Co., South Bend, Ind.—Thresher, cleaner, huller, etc. L 18. 673

500*f* Ellis, Hoffman, & Co., Pottstown, Pa.—Endless chain horse-power thresher and cleaner. L 11–12. 673

500*g* Lidy, Geo. F., & Co., Waynesboro', Pa.—Fanning-mill, grain and seed separator. T 26. 673

501 Albion Coffee-Huller Co., New York, N. Y.—Coffee hulling, polishing, and separating machine. O 22. 673

502 Brayley, James, Buffalo, N. Y.—Threshing-machine and double pinion horse-power. T 7 and 8. 673

503 Shreiner, J. H., Mechanicsburg, Pa. T 26.
a Grain-drill and shovels. 671
b Grain-fan and seed-separator. 673

504 Case, J. I., & Co., Racine, Wis.—Threshing-machine. T 9. 673

505 Tubbs, Hoyt, Osceola, Pa.—Grain separator and cleaner, separator and fanning-mill. S 8. 673

505*a* Pierpont, Wm., Salem, N. J.—Threshing-machine with grain and seed separator. S 7. 673

505*b* Stone, Sarah M., & Porter, Samuel G., Lancaster, Pa.—Grain-fan. T 27. 673

505*c* Hulshizer & Larzelere, Doyles-town, Pa. P 9.
a Horse-power, thresher and cleaner, thresher and shaker, cutting boxes. 673
b Corn-shellers. 674

505*d* New York Manufacturing Co., New York, N. Y.—Wine press. P 17. 673

506 Heebner & Sons, Lansdale, Pa.—Horse-powers, threshers, separators, and cleaners. O 7. 673

507 Cartrite, Barnard, Norwalk, Ohio. —Fanning-mill, box of grain and fixtures. T 28. 673

508 Kenosha Fanning-Mill Co., Ken-osha, Wis.—Fanning-mill. S 28. 673

509 Miller, A. S., Republic, Ohio.—Fruit-ladder. T 23. 673

510 Fay, C. J., Camden, N. J.—Portable hay and cotton press. R 11. 673

511 Spence, L., Martin's Ferry, Ohio.—Thresher and cleaner, double cleaner, horse-power, etc. O 8. 673

512 Brown Cotton Gin Co., New Lon-don, Conn.—Cotton-gin with feeder and condenser; presses. P 21 *and* Q 12. 673

513 Nichols, Shepard, & Co., Battle Creek, Mich.—Grain-thresher, separator, and cleaner. R 7 *and* 8. 673

514 Kenyon, Silas R., Newark, N. J.—Corn-husking machine. S 26. 673

514*a* Hafner, John A., Pittsburg, Pa.—Threshing-machine gear and coil springs. K 12. 673

514*b* Cockle Separator Manufacturing Co., Milwaukee, Wis.—Separating machines. Q 11. 673

515 Hagerstown Steam Engine and Machine Co., Hagerstown, Md.—Grain threshing, separating, cleaning, and bagging machine. R 26. 673

516 Harder, Minard, Cobleskill, N. Y. —Railway horse-power, thresher and cleaner, model of railway horse-power. M *and* N 7. 673

The two Grand Gold Medals were awarded Harders' two-horse power, and thresher and cleaner, at the great National Implement Trial, Auburn, N. Y., for "slow and easy movement of the horses, fifteen rods less than one and one-half miles' travel per hour; thorough and conscientious workmanship and material in every place; nothing slighted; mechanical execution of the very best kind," as shown by official report of Judges, distributed at column M 7, Agricultural Hall, International Exhibition.

517 New Hampshire State Centennial Board. E 20–21.
a Agricultural implements. 673
b Freezers. 675

518 Read, Calvin D., & Ellis D., Ayer, Mass.—Corn-sheller. N 22. 673

518*a* Wakeman, R., Port Deposit, Md. —Hay or cotton press. M 10 *and* 11. 673

518*b* Scattergood, H. V., Philadelphia, Pa.—Cotton-gin and feeder. L 14. 673

518*c* Basset, Nathan, Philadelphia, Pa. —Sifting-machines. T 23. 673

518*d* Brown Cotton-Gin Co., New London, Conn.—Cotton-gins. Q 12. 673

518*e* New York Cotton-Gin Co., New York, N. Y.—Hand-gin. S 7. 673

518*f* Cardwell, J. W., & Co., Richmond, Va.—Rice-thresher. K 7. 673

518*g* Jones, John A., Mt. Pleasant, Del. —Potato-assorter. L 27. 673

519 Sheeler, Buckwater, & Co., Roy-ers Ford, Pa.—Horse-power and threshing-machine. K 10–11. 673

520 Kahnweiler, David, New York, N. Y.—Cotton-seed huller. S 11. 673

Machines, Implements, and Processes of Manufacture.

521 Judkins, Mark D., Osakio, Minn.—Self-sacking grain-separator. T 8. 673

522 Shields & Bro., Philadelphia, Pa.—Corn-huskers. B 24. 673

523 Westinghouse, G., & Co., Schenectady, N. Y.—Grain-threshing machine. T 25. 673
The exhibitor claims these advantages: a complete cylinder and concave, no loosening of teeth, unusual separating capacity, and perfect cleaning apparatus.

524 Pumphrey, W. F., Fairfield, Iowa.—Seed-mill and grain-separator. S 7. 673

525 Wood, O. K., & Co., West Chazy, N. Y.—Grain and seed separator and fanning-mill combined. T 28, *wall.* 673

526 Silver & Deming Manufacturing Co., Salem, Ohio. Q 23.
a Endless chain, two horse-power, for general purposes. 673
b Drag sawing-machine, feed-cutters, etc. 674

527 Gaar, Scott, & Co., Richmond, Ind. O 9.
a Grain thresher, separator, and cleaner. 673
b Portable farm-engine. 674

528 Manley, Almond D., Washington, Mich. R *and* Q 9. 674
Mounted railway tread-power and circular wood-saw. Notable features of power, centre balance, elevation easily varied when running, wrought chain, no cogs, centre roller drive, motion controlled by governor, runs steady with belt off, least traverse wheels, remarkable durability, greatest power at given elevation, never removed from trucks. 674

529 Blymyer Manufacturing Co., Cincinnati, Ohio. M *and* N 8. 673
a Thresher and cleaner, corn-cob crushers, etc. 673
b Cane-mills, steam-engine, sugar-evaporator, etc. 674

529*a* Wagoner, Elijah, Westminster, Md.—Feed-cutter and masticator. S 7. 673

530 Evans & Baird, West Chester, Pa. T 7 *and* 8.
a Horse-railway power and thresher. 673
b Dairy churn and power. 675

531 Rankin Manufacturing Co., Allegheny, Pa.—Hand and power meat-choppers, sausage-stuffers, portable engine, etc. L 12. 674

532 Post, C. C., Burlington, Vt.—Implements for making maple sugar. C 24. 674

533 Slocum, W. H., & Bro., Philadelphia, Pa.—Apple-parer and corer, meat-cutter, raisin and currant cleaner. T 23. 674

533*a* Hughes, H. D., Radnor, Pa.—Flour barrel. A 22. 674

533*b* Evans, Wm. P., Malvern, Pa.—Wheat-feeder, oscillating engine, etc. J 25. 674

533*c* Mosher, A. J., Portland, Me.—Bag-holder. A 27. 674

533*d* Best, John, Lancaster, Pa.—Agricultural engines. K 8. 674

533*e* Branden Manufacturing Co., Branden, Vt.—Howe scales. P 13. 674

533*f* Frederick, L. W., Hall, Ind.—Wagon. S 23. 674

533*g* Fairbanks & Ewing, 715 Chestnut st., Philadelphia, Pa.—Scales (manufacturers, E. and T. Fairbanks & Co., St. Johnsbury, Vermont), railroad track, weigh-lock, hay, coal, platform, and counter scales of all descriptions, fine gold and druggists' scales; also improved testing-machines for ascertaining the strength of metals, etc. Principal warehouses: Boston, New York, Philadelphia, Baltimore, New Orleans, San Francisco, St. Louis, Chicago, Louisville, Cincinnati, Cleveland, Buffalo, Pittsburg, Albany, Montreal, and London, England. L 24. 674

533*h* Day, S. A., & Co., Baltimore, Md.—Automatic incubator for hatching eggs. B 23. 674

533*i* Cooper, J. G., Scranton, Pa.—Wagon-spring brace. S 28. 674

533*j* Donner & Suhl, San Francisco, Cal.—Hay and stalk cutter. M 23. 674

533*k* Skinner & Wood, Erie, Pa.—Boiler and engine. K 8. 674

533*l* Chandler & Taylor, Indianapolis, Ind.—Farm-engine and saw-mill. R 11 *and* 12. 674

534 Boyer, Wm. L., & Bro., Philadelphia, Pa.—Farm grist-mills, railway horse-power, feed-cutter, lawn-mowers, saw-table, broom-winder. R 24. 674

535 Nittinger, A., jr., & Son, Philadelphia, Pa.—Butchers' machinery, tools, and supplies. T 24. 674

536 J. C. Hoadley Co., Lawrence, Mass.—Portable steam-engines. L 7. 674

537 Empire Portable Forge Co., Troy, N. Y.—Portable fan-blowing forges for farms. T 22. 674

537*a* Lee, E. S., & Co., Rochester, N.Y.—Tree pruner. Q *and* R 25. 674

537*b* West Grove Manufacturing Co., West Grove, Pa.—Liquid atomizer. N 10. 674

537*c* Wharry, John R., Moundsville, West Va.—Vegetable and fruit slicer. N 21. 674

538 Ross, John, Williamsburg, N. Y.—Grain-mills, paint and drug mills, etc. R 23. 674

539 Hotsenpiller & Co., Springfield, Ohio.—Hominy-mill. M 21. 674

540 Corbett, A., Hicksville, N. Y.—Poultry incubator. C 24. 674

540*a* Bergner, George, & Co., Washington, Ill.—Apple and peach parer, apple corer and slicer. R 28. 674

540*b* Smith, John M., & Sons, Philadelphia, Pa.—Cedar water-tank, Scotch mashing-machine, valve for brewers and malt-houses. M 12. 674

541 Vanderbilt, Henry S., Washington, D. C.—Lifting-jack. I 17. 674

541*a* Stoddart, J. C., Lockport, N. Y.—Steam calliope. (*East end of Main Transept.*) 674

542 Dederick, P. K., & Co., Albany, N. Y.—Hay and cotton presses, bale-tie machines, coal-tubs, dumping-car, brick and tile machine, etc. Q 10. 674

For classes of exhibits, indicated by numbers at end of entries, see Classification, pp. 12-14.

Machines, Implements, and Processes of Manufacture.

544 Furst & Bradley Manufacturing Co., Chicago, Ill.—Plows, harrows, hay-rakes, etc. Breaking and old-ground plows, sulky or riding plows, gang-plows, corn-cultivators, sulky hay-rakes, etc. O 25. 674

545 Garst, David W., Washington, D. C.—Dried-beef chopper. S 23. 674

546 Munson Brothers, Utica, N. Y.—Wheat-flouring and corn-grinding portable mill, millstone eye, spindles, and oil-tight bush. R 24. 674

547 Conrad, E. C., Philadelphia, Pa.—Coffee-machine. D 25. 674

548 Sandusky Machine & Agricultural Works, Sandusky, Ohio.—Cylinder corn-sheller. M 16. 674

549 Lombard, Daniel, Boston, Mass.—Rice and coffee cleaning mortars, coffee-shelling machine. P 23. 674

550 Dickey, A. P., Racine, Wis.—Fanning-mills, for cleaning all kinds of grain, perfectly separating all foul substances; also grades the grain, putting best out at the side of the fan, and balance in front; also cleans and separates all kinds of seeds. Will pay for itself in one season's use. Send for catalogue and prices. T 27. 674

550*a* Munsel & Dexter, Elizabeth, N. J.—Lifting-jack. I 28. 674

551 Toll, Chas. H., Schenectady, N.Y.—Brooms. H 15. 674

552 Mansfield Machine Works, Mansfield, Ohio.—Mounted portable steam-engine. P 8. 674

553 Mitchell, J. E., Philadelphia, Pa.—Farmers' grindstones, mounted, mower, knife-grinders, scythe and whetstones; grindstone of 1776. N 20. 674

554 Hazard, Thomas, Wilmington, Ohio.—Straw-cutters. O 22. 674

556 Bruner, M., jr., Fremont, Ohio.—Hay-press. R 11 *and* 12. 674

557 Bailey Wringing-Machine Co., 99 Chambers st., New York, N. Y., Ameriican meat and vegetable choppers, for use of families, hotels, and butchers. More than 60,000 now in use. S 24. 674

558 Bushfield, W. H., Jersey City, N.J.—Dried-beef cutter. S 23. 674

559 Whitemore, D. H., Worcester, Mass.—Apple parer and slicer, meat-cutter, etc. N 22. 674

560 Foster, Calvin A., Fitchburg, Mass.—Meat-chopper and apple-parer. S 23. 674

560*a* Nevins, Wm., Titusville, Pa.—Combined machine for marking, ridging, planting, etc.; potato-digger. L 22. 674

561 Pierpont, C., & Co., New Haven, Conn.—Fodder-cutter. P 22. 674

562 Fitzhugh, J. R., Philadelphia, Pa.—Hay-elevator. P 19. 674

563 Hall's Self-feeding Cotton-Gin Co., New London, Conn.—Self-feeding cotton-gin. T 12. 674

564 Bates, Hyde, & Co., Bridgewater, Mass.—Power and hand cotton-gins. R 10. 674

566 Bradford, W. A., & Co., Chicago, Ill.—Cider-mill. T 13. 674

566*a* Wakeman, R., Port Deposit, Md.—Power-press. Q 11. 674

566*b* Emery, Horace L., Albany, N. Y.—Cotton-gin, lint-cleaner. Q 11. 674

566*c* Wilson Brothers & Co., Harrisburg, Pa.—Fodder-cutter. O 22. 674

566*d* Lee, George W., Homeworth, Ohio.—Fodder-cutter. T 25 *and* A 25.

566*e* Ross, John, Williamsburgh, N.Y.—Flour-mills, farm-mills, paint-mills, and mixers. R 23. 674

566*f* Esmond & Dunham, New York, N. Y.—Press and compress combined. S 24. 674

566*g* Cousland & Cousland, Philadelphia, Pa.—Adjustable picks, with movable bits. M 26. 674

566*h* Cooper, I. G., Scranton, Pa.—Hay and straw cutter. J 7. 674

566*i* Scharf, Louis, Philadelphia, Pa.—Combined water cooler and filter. F 19. 674

566*j* Baugh & Sons, Philadelphia, Pa.—Mills for crushing and grinding bones, minerals, woods, etc. K 25. 674

567 Dernell, H. F., & Co., Athens, N. Y.—Tools for cutting and storing ice. N 24. 674

567*a* Belcher & Taylor Agricultural Tool Co., Chicopee Falls, Mass.—Hay-cutters, vegetable-cutters, corn-sheller, and bag-holder. T 21. 674

567*b* Skinner, E. W., Sioux City, Iowa.—Adjustable sugar-cane crusher. T 12. 674

567*c* Deas, R. M. H., New York, N. Y.—Drinking-fountain. K 14. 674

567*d* Purdy, Hiram, Burlington, Iowa.—Cyclone heater, car-door, odorating apparatus. I 28. 674

567*e* Barrows, Savery, & Co., Philadelphia, Pa.—Steamer for cooking food. L 8. 674

567*f* Aldrich, Isaiah, Philadelphia, Pa.—Can soldering and capping machine. M 24. 674

567*g* Morse, Dudley, Norwich, N. Y.—Hay-fork and wagon-jack. H 23. 674

567*h* Smith, J. G., Fauburg, Ill.—Boiler for cooking. C 24. 674

568 Chesley, Plumer, Chelsea, Mass.—Meat-chopper. R 24. 674

569 Hanck, S., & Bro., Lebanon, Pa.—Vegetable-cutters. M 22. 674

570 Longaker, Thomas F., Philadelphia, Pa.—Stable-hook. C 20. 674

571 Schenck, Marcus P., Fulton, N. Y.—Fruit-press, apple and horseradish grater. P 11. 674

572 Peabody, George H., Brooklyn, N. Y.—Rice huller and polisher. L 16. 674

573 Boomer & Boschert Press Co., Syracuse, N. Y. S *and* T 12.

a Power cider-press (double platform), 200 tons capacity, sixty barrels in ten hours. Hand cider-press, power 125 tons. Wine-press, power 60 tons, Nos. 1, 2, and 3. Lard or tanking presses, power 80–120 and 200 tons. 673

b Apple-grater. 674

"For presses" for paper, cloth, etc., see Machinery Hall, E 39.

Machines, Implements, and Processes of Manufacture.

574 **Ross, E. W., & Co., Fulton, N. Y.** P 22.
a Feed-cutter, straw-cutter for paper-mills. 674
b Crank paddle-churn. 673

575 **Treat, J. A., Cleveland, Ohio.**—L 12.
a Washing boiler, and automatic blind governor. 674
b Factory churn. 675

576 **Speakman, Miles, & Co., West Chester, Pa.** M 13.
a Corn-sheller, insect-destroyer, pruning-shears, etc. 674
b Butter-worker and butter-printing table. 675

577 **Pilling, Geo. P., Philadelphia, Pa.**—Milking-tubes. M 12. 675
Silver patent tubes for milking cows without using the hands. No stripping required, saving time and labor. Set of four sent postpaid on receipt of two dollars. Also, capon and veterinary instruments.

578 **Packer, Charles W., Philadelphia, Pa.**—Ice-cream freezers. O 12. 675

578*a* **Simmons & Sons, Bloomington, Ill.**—Ice-cream freezer. M 10. 675

578*b* **Buckhardt, W. H., & Co., Philadelphia, Pa.**—Tank and casks. H 24. 675

578*c* **Olmstel, John W., Northport, N. Y.**—Ice-cream freezer. M 10. 675

578*d* **Weinhagen, H., New York, N. Y.**—Cream gauges, grape-sugar test, wine-testing apparatus, and dairy fixtures. M 12. 675

578*e* **Conver, W. H., Agnew Mills, Pa.**—Churns. M 11. 675

579 **Koehler, J. G., Philadelphia, Pa.**—Cedar-ware, churns, measures, etc. M 10. 675

580 **Clement & Dunbar, Philadelphia, Pa.**—Cedar-ware, churns, and ice-cream freezers. O 11. 675

581 **Blatchley, C. G., Philadelphia, Pa.**—Horizontal ice-cream freezer, cucumber-wood pumps. O 11. 675

582 **Carter, Henry C., New York, N. Y.**—Butter-pail. M 10. 675

583 **Markham, H. C. & D. C., Lyons Falls, N. Y.**—Curd-sink. M 12. 675

584 **Hollister, King, & Young, Factory Point, Vt.**—Shipping boxes. M 12. 675

585 **Moos, Joseph, Philadelphia, Pa.**—Ice-cream refrigerator and ice-cream shipping-apparatus. O 12. 675

585*a* **Fisher, J. H., Chicago, Ill.**—Refrigerator. K 11. 675

586 **Chick, W. H., & Co., St. Louis, Mo.**—Churns, egg-beater, and ice-cream freezers. M 11. 675

587 **Keen & Hagerty, Baltimore, Md.**—Ice-cream freezers, cake-mixer, and egg-beater. O 10. 675

588 **Emmert, William P., Freeport, Ill.**—Butter-churns, tread-power, etc. M 12. 675

589 **Elliget, James, Cleveland, Ohio.**—Bottles, kegs, mugs, and pitchers. M 10. 675

590 **Reid, A. H., Philadelphia, Pa.**—Butter-worker. L 11. 675

591 **Rogers, Francis P., Philadelphia, Pa.**—Milk-cans, pans, buckets, strainers, butter-kettles, etc. L 11. 675

591*a* **Anchor Manufacturing Co., Philadelphia, Pa.**—Barrels and kegs. I 26. 675

591*b* **Judge, Owen, Scranton, Pa.**—Barrel-heads. J 28. 675

591*c* **Dibble, Andrew J., Franklin, N.Y.**—Churns, milk-pans. L 8. 675

591*d* **Downs, W. H., East Newport, Maine.**—Churns. L 11. 675

591*e* **Hollister, King, & Young, Factory Point, N.Y.**—Butter package. M 12. 675

591*f* **White Mountain Freezer Co., Laconia, N. H.**—Ice-cream freezer, ice-crusher. M 4. 675

592 **Ellsworth, John T., Barre, Mass.**—Oscillating churn. M 11. 675

592*a* **Finnegan, A. J., Minneapolis, Minn.**—Butter-package. M 10. 675

592*b* **Burkhardt, Geo. J., & Co., Philadelphia, Pa.**—Cedar reservoir and dye-tub. M 17. 675

592*c* **Le Valley, Darius A., Pawtucket, R. I.**—Revolving milking-stool. K 17. 675

592*d* **Bettle, Harbert, Philadelphia, Pa.**—Ice cream can holder. L 12. 675

592*e* **Seed, Frederick, Cincinnati, Ohio.**—Churn. L 11. 675

593 **Guernsey, Daniel, Watertown, N. Y.**—Gilt-edge milk-pans and cooler. L 10. 675

594 **Shaw, Philander, Scituate, Mass.**—Butter-working machine, butter-mould, and stamp. M 12. 675

595 **Cornish & Curtis, Fort Atkinson, Wis.**—Rectangular churn and butter-worker; without floats or agitators of any kind; durable, and easy to work. Endorsed by prominent dairymen everywhere. M 11. 675

596 **Murdock, Albert L., Boston, Mass.**—Dairies of the different breeds of cattle. H 17. 675

597 **Justice, L. B., Philadelphia, Pa.**—Machine for making ice cream, water ices, frozen fruits, etc. O 10. 675

598 **Porter Blanchard's Sons, Concord, N. H.**—Churns. N 12. 675
The celebrated "Blanchard Churn" has been proved and im-proved and approved for over a quarter of a century, and over a hundred thousand of them are now in successful operation. It is simple, durable, effective, and cheap. Send to the manufacturers for churns, agencies, or descriptive circulars. "Get the best."

599 **Thompson, S. W., jr., Detroit, Mich.**—Barrel-shooks. C 20. 675

600 **Hardin, L. S., Louisville, Ky.**—New method of setting milk for making butter. M. 12. 675

601 **Bartlerond, John W., Churchville, Pa.**—Churn, butter-worker, and cream-regulator. M 11. 675

602 **Smith, Hamilton E., New York, N. Y.**—Iron enameled churns. K 11. 675

For classes of exhibits, indicated by numbers at end of entries, see Classification, pp. 12–14.

Agricultural Engineering and Administration.

603 **Ashley, H. A., Springfield, Ohio.**—Ditching-machine. D 19. 680

603a **Bean, H. & B. F., Pawling, Pa.**—Picket fence. D 24. 680

603b **Ripley, Theodore, Hallowell, Maine.**—Shovel scraper. C 20. 680

604 **Pressey, G. W., Hammonton, N. J.**—Stump-puller and rock-lifter. C 17. 680

605 **Murdock, John, & Son, Poseyville, Ind.**—Wheat ricker. M 15. 680

606 **Bowen, C. M., Maine Avenue, N. J.**—Stump, grub, and rock extractor. D 17. 680

607 **Randolph, Theodore F., Morristown, N. J.** Ditcher and excavator. C 18. 680

608 **Fay, C. J., Camden, N. J.**—Stump and rock lifter. R 11. 680

609 **Hall, S. W., Elmira, N. Y.**—Fencing-machine, machine-made worm-fence, bracket, and wire fences. O 23. 680

610 **Patterson, William, Salem, N. J.**—Wrought-iron road-scraper. D 18. 680

611 **Cotton, A. C., Vineland, N. J.**—Stone and stump extractor. D 17. 680

612 **Drake & Parmley, Painesville, Ohio.**—Fence-post base. D 18. 680

613 **Rhodes & Waters, Elyria, Ohio.**—Post-hole digger. C 19. 680

614 **Starbuck, Nathan, Wilmington, Ohio.**—Mounted ditcher. C 17. 680

615 **Thompson, Woodard, Gardiner, Me.**—Self-loading and unloading hod-road scraper, model of scraper, and model of railway joint. C 19. 680

616 **Leatherbarrows, John, Philadelphia, Pa.**—Wrought-iron and wire fencings. D 17. 680

617 **Pioneer Iron Works, Brooklyn, N. Y.**—Portable iron railroad and steam road-roller. D 22. 680

617a **Landis, Israel L., Lancaster, Pa.**—Fence and gate models, step-ladder. B 22. 680

617b **Frey, Abram, Philadelphia, Pa.**—Portable fence. B 23. 680

617c **Speakman, Thomas, Philadelphia, Pa.**—Models of fences. B 23. 680

617d **Treat, J. A., Cleveland, Ohio.**—Carriage gate. (*Outside of Agricultural Building.*) 680

618 **Chicago Scraper and Ditcher Co., Chicago, Ill.**—Scraper and ditcher for roadmaking, repairing, and excavating. C 20. 680

619 **Potts, William W., Swedeland, Pa.**—Iron-post portable fence. Simple, durable, economical, and storm-proof. Saves time and money. D 23. 680

620 **Rumford Chemical Works, Providence, R. I.**—Fertilizers, bone charcoal, etc. K 21. 681

621 **Josiah J. Allen's Sons, Philadelphia, Pa.**—Guano, bone, and other fertilizers. D 28 681

621a **Fisher, W. A., Bryn Mawr, Pa.**—Fertilizers. D 26. 681

622 **Bradley Fertilizer Co., Boston, Mass.**—Fertilizers. H 28. 681

622a **Jarvis & Hooper, Detroit, Mich.**—Fertilizers. B 26. 681

623 **Ward's Fertilizer Co., Boston, Mass.**—Odorless fertilizers. D 28. 681

624 **United States Fertilizing & Chemical Co.**, 104 Chestnut street, Philadelphia, Pa.—Phosphatic salts, bone, and fertilizers. Sole owners of Pratt's patent "acid grinding" process, by which the greatest percentage of available bone phosphate of lime is obtained. The "national soluble bone" manufactured under this process is guaranteed to contain not less than from 28 to 33 per cent. of available bone phosphate of lime. Also manufacturers of agricultural chemicals generally. C 28. 681

625 **Baugh & Sons, Philadelphia, Pa.**—Raw bone superphosphate, ground raw bones; nitrogen. C 28. 681

626 **Matheys, Charles F., Philadelphia, Pa.**—Nitro-phosphate and ground bone. E 26. 681

627 **Ames, Manning, & Ames, Hagerstown, Md.**—Buffalo-bone meal for agricultural purposes. C 26. 681

628 **Crocker, L. L., Buffalo, N. Y.**—Fertilizers for grain, tobacco, cotton, etc., plant-food for plants and flowers. C 26. 681

629 **Peck Brothers, Northfield, Conn.**—Bone-dust. D 28. 681

630 **Franklin Glue Works, Pittsburg, Pa.**—Bone-dust, etc. K 20. 681

631 **White, Geo. E.**, 159 Front Street, New York, N. Y.—Superphosphates, acid bone-black, raw materials for fertilizers, and agricultural chemicals. This house furnished all the fertilizers purchased by the Centennial Commission for its farms where the mowers and reapers are tested. D 28. 681

632 **Swift & White, New York, N. Y.**—Superphosphate of lime, ground bone, dried ground meat, and refined poudrette. C 25. 681

633 **Pacific Guano Co., Boston, Mass.**—Commercial fertilizers. A and B 28. 681

633a **Mapes, Charles V., New York, N. Y.**—Guano, bone, phosphate, etc. E 28. 681

634 **Lister Brothers, Newark, N. J.**—Superphosphate of lime, guano, ground bone, bone charcoal, sulphate of ammonia, agricultural salts, and other fertilizers. C 25. 681

635 **Tygert, J. E., & Co., Philadelphia, Pa.**—Bone phosphate and ground bone. C 25. 681

636 **Atkinson, Empson, Woodstown, N. J.**—Machine for cutting and setting up corn, road-scraper. S 28. 681

637 **Harrisburg Fertilizer Co., Harrisburg, Pa.**—Flour of bone, ground bone, superphosphate, animal compost, and lubricators. B 25. 681

638 **Walton, Whann, & Co., Wilmington, Del.**—Artificial fertilizers, bone-meal, and ground bone. C 25. 681

639 **Kyser, James, & Son, Cleveland, Ohio.**—Whiffletree, check, and neck-yoke fastenings. M 10. 682

For locations of objects, indicated by letter and figure, see Key to Notation, p. 6; ground plan, p. 10.

Agricultural Engineering and Administration.

640 **Remington, E., & Sons, Ilion, N. Y.**—Carriage gearing. P 20. 682

640*a* **Drown, W. A., Philadelphia, Pa.** Umbrellas for wagons, carriages, and mowers. R 17. 682

640*b* **Tibbles, George N., Jersey City Heights, N. J.**—Power or speed traction engines. C 17. 682

640*c* **Bradbury, Henry, Philadelphia, Pa.**—Packing boxes. I 26. 682

641 **Higganum Manufacturing Co., Higganum, Conn.**—Trucks. L 25. 682

642 **Allen, R. H., & Co., New York, N. Y.**—Farm cart, water barrel, garden barrows, etc. Q *and* R 25. 682

642*a* **Tubular Barrow & Truck Co., Jersey City, N. J.**—Barrow and trucks, coaling tubs. R 26–28. 682

642*b* **Fitch, Homer W., & Co., Lithgow, N. Y.**—Hay-conveyer. M 25. 682

643 **Mount, Joseph K., & Co., Hightstown, N. J.**—Model hay-conveyer. C 24. 682

644 **Beecher, C. T., Waterbury, Conn.**—Whiffletree gear. N 22. 682

645 **Cohu, A. B., New York, N. Y.**—Wagon-jack. P 28. 682

646 **State of Massachusetts, Boston, Mass.**—Maps and plans of farm buildings. E *and* F 23. 683

646*a* **Jewett, Solomon W., Rutland, Vt.**—Architectural models. D 24. 683

647 **Osborne Manufacturing Co., New York, N. Y.**—Bird and animal cages. D 25. 683

648 **Bost, Caleb E., Davidson College, N. C.**—Beehive. J 28. 683

648*a* **Goldsmith, Francis J., Painesville, Ohio.**—Invertible troughs. B 22. 683

648*b* **Losee, Alfred, New York, N. Y.**—Folding coop. C 19. 683

648*c* **Isham, Charles R., Peoria, N. Y.**—Glass honey-boxes. A 27. 683

649 **Gay & Bryant, Dresden, Ohio.**—Post-hole digger. C 19. 683

650 **Shields & Bro., Philadelphia, Pa.**—Tanned hog's head, hog-rings and holders. B 24. 683

651 **Collings, E. Z., Waterford, N. J.**—Cranberry-plants growing, representing cranberry-bog. C 20. 683

652 **Boyd, G., & Co., Philadelphia, Pa.**—Fruit and grain-dryer. C 22. 683

653 **Lockwood, James L., & Co., Stamford, Conn.**—Portable fruit-drier. C 24. 683

654 **Leonard, Henry, Basil, Ohio.**—Revolving buckeye-ball on pedestal and college building. C 24. 683

655 **Murphy, R. R., Fulton, Ill.**—Honey extractor, for removing honey from the comb. C 24. 683

656 **Gunther, G., New York, N. Y.**—Brass, silver-plated, and japanned bird-cages. C 25. 683

656*a* **Halderman, Frank, Mahanoy City, Pa.**—Bird cage. K 7. 683

657 **Murphy & Broom, Philadelphia, Pa.**—Bird-cages, wire garden-furniture, rustic work, etc. C 26. 683

658 **Wimpfheimer, David, Philadelphia, Pa.**—Automatic vinegar apparatus. D 23. 683

659 **Harris, Milo, Jamestown, N. Y.**—Domestic fruit-dryer, model of lumber-kiln and of coal-oil still. D 23. 683

660 **Ryder, B. L., Chambersburg, Pa.**—American drier or pneumatic evaporator. D 24. 683

661 **Tiffany, O. F., San Francisco, Cal.**—Fruit-dryer. C 21. 683

661*a* **Jones Fruit Evaporating Co., Chicago, Ill.**—Pneumatic evaporator. C 23. 683

661*b* **Ellsbury & Hayward, Winona, Minn.**—Minnesota fruit and illustrations. C 24. 683

661*c* **Cowder & Jones, Norristown, Pa.**—Wind-mill with water-wheel. (*Outside of building.*) 683

661*d* **Chapman, Frank W., Morrison, Ill.**—Honey-extractor. A 27. 683

661*e* **Millett, D. Caldwell, Holmesburg, Pa.**—Hive and bees. C 25. 683

661*f* **Reynolds, A. J., & Co., Washington, D. C.**—Fruit-evaporators. C 22. 683

661*g* **Chapman, John Winslow, Hyannis, Mass.**—Barrel-heading, etc. A 22. 683

661*h* **Bradford, H., Philadelphia, Pa.**—Cotton-bale ties. H 17. 683

661*i* **Bouscaven, G., Cincinnati, Ohio.**—Model of apparatus to extract saccharine juices of plants by diffusion. T 22. 683

661*j* **Deitz, George A., Chico, Cal.**—California fruit-dryer. C 18. 683

661*k* **Ellis, Charles R., New York, N. Y.**—Glass and marble tank. A 20. 683

662 **Lindermann, O., & Co., New York, N. Y.**—Bird and animal cages. D 25. 683

663 **Williams, John, South Haven, Mich.**—Model of evaporator. D 24. 683

664 **Goodrich, C. C. & F. W., Portland, Conn.**—Tobacco-hook with wilting-frame and builders' horse. Harvest your tobacco without laying it on the ground. D 25. 683

665 **Kappe, W. J. H., Quincy, Ill.**—Transportation coop for live poultry. D 25. 683

666 **Hendryx & Bartholomew, Ansonia, Conn.**—Bird cages and trimmings. D 25. 683

667 **Conrad, E. C., Philadelphia, Pa.**—Bird cage. D 25. 683

668 **O'Neill, Wm. C., & Co., Philadelphia, Pa.**—Kegs and barrels made with single staves. F 28. 683

669 **Elphee, Edmund, Montezuma, N. Y.**—Grain-seed wreath-picture, representing the harvest of 1875. H 15. 683

669*a* **Scantlin, Thos., & Sons, Evansville, Ind.**—Sugar-evaporator, self-measuring oil-tank. C 23. 683

669*b* **Kennard, Amos, Clearfield, Pa.**—Cant-hook for rolling logs in saw-mill. M 14. 683

670 **Foot, Scovill D., New York, N. Y.**—Portable fruit-preserver. I 23. 683

671 **Vermont Farm-Machine Co., Bellows Falls, Vt.**—Sugar-evaporator, and fixtures for making sugar. K 15. 683

For classes of exhibits, indicated by numbers at end of entries, see Classification, pp. 12–14.

Agricultural Engineering, Administration, Management.

672 Wood, Robert, & Co., 1136 Ridge avenue, Philadelphia, Pa.—Ornamental iron and bronze works. Fountains, vases, verandas, stairs, lampposts, improved stable-fittings and furniture, wire-work of every description, wrought and cast iron railings. Also "statuary bronzes"—colossal, heroic, or life-size—in the highest style of art. L 10. 683

673 Shaw, Philander, Scituate, Mass. —Beehive, with comb and hive of bees. M 12. 683

674 Dana, C. H., West Lebanon, N. H. —Automatic label-machine, labels, punches, and registers for marking live-stock. N 12. 683

This machine is simple in its construction. With it labels of any description can be made with great rapidity for attaching to the animal's ear.

Four thousand labels can be made per hour. They are made of iron-wire rolled flat and washed with tin, and stamped with numbers from one to one thousand, and with any name ordered. Mr. Dana is offering the label machine for foreign countries, and good-will of business.

674*a* Rose, W. L., Wadesboro', N. C— Iron cotton-tie. D 24. 683

674*b* Worrall, E. Penn, West Chester, Pa.—Beehive, showing bees at work. B 19. 683

674*c* Jackson, James L., New York, N. Y.—Stable fixtures. T 10 *and* 11. 683

675 Deardorff, Isaac N., Canal Dover, Ohio.—Smoke-house stove. It saves fuel, increases volume of smoke, with easy regulation of production and distribution. Removes all danger from fire. N 21. 683

676 Betts, Albert C., Troy, N. Y.—Machine for making wire fencing, with samples. P 23. 683

677 U. S. Wind-Engine & Pump Co., Batavia, Ill.—Windmills for pumping water, etc. Q 23. 683

678 State of Michigan.—Soils. H *and* I 20 *to* 21. 690

678*a* State of New Jersey.—Soils, subsoils, greensand marls, calcareous marls, mineral phosphates, fish guano, cancerine, lime, superphosphates, etc. E 17–18. 690

678*b* Rider, A. J., Atsion, N. J.—Cranberry bog and basket with cranberries. F 26. 690

Tillage and General Management.

679 Hirner, C. G., Allentown, Pa.—Farmers' Union Cattle-Powder, an artificial food for fattening stock and to increase the quantity and quality of milk and butter. B 28. 692

679*a* Rynal, P. H., Jackson, Mich.— Horse and cattle food. R 27. 692

680 Phillips, J. B., Philadelphia, Pa.— Devices for training and educating horses. B 26. 692

680*a* May, David T., & Co., New York, N. Y.—Artificial leg of horse, with perforated stocking. B 21. 692

681 Miller, Frederick A., Philadelphia, Pa.—Condition powder for live-stock. B 26. 692

682 Hoeptner, Martin, 311 Columbia av., Philadelphia, Pa.—Prepared food for cage-birds. Natural food for mocking-birds, thrushes, blackbirds, nightingales, robins, starlings, skylarks, and all soft-billed birds. B 28. 692

683 Greenough, J. J., Syracuse, N. Y. —Machine for cleaning animals. B. 22. 692

684 Long, J. C., jr., Philadelphia, Pa. —Prepared food for mocking-birds; grains and seeds for birds, pigeons, and poultry; bird invigorator; drinking fountains, etc. B 26. 692

685 Kirk, Charles H., & Co., Philadelphia, Pa.—Prepared food for horses and cattle. B 26. 693

686 Ausable Horse Nail Co., New York, N. Y.—Horseshoe nails. B 24. 693

687 Caryl, A. H., & Son, Forge Village, Mass.—Horseshoe nails pointed and finished, also not pointed. These nails are made by hammers from hot rods, and of the best Norway iron. B 24. 693

688 Burden, H., & Sons, Troy, N. Y.— Working model of horseshoe machine, samples of horse-shoes, boiler rivets, and merchant iron. A 23. 693

689 Tallman, G. W., New York, N. Y. —Elastic hose stocking. B 23. 693

690 American Shearer Manufacturing Co., Nashua, N. H.—Shearing and clipping machines. B 22. 693

691 Putnam, S. S., & Co., Neponset, Mass.—"Government standard" forged and hammer-pointed horseshoe nails. These nails are made from the best Norway iron, are drawn out under hammers when nearly at a welding heat, whereby they are enabled to produce a nail that is tough and stiff, and perfectly reliable in all respects, ready for the blacksmith to drive. B 24. 693

692 Lhernault, Auguste, New York, N. Y.—Machine for clipping horses. B 21. 693

692*a* Russell, William, Cincinnati, Ohio.—Hand and machine made horse-shoes, etc. B 23. 693

692*b* Hull, Theodore, Newark, N. J.— Horseshoes. B 24. 693

692*c* Davis, H. S., Camden, N. J.— Horseshoes. B 24. 693

692*d* New Hampshire State Centennial Board.—Agricultural literature. E 20–21. 693

692*e* Campbell, C. A. J., Philadelphia, Pa.—American trotting-horse shoes. B 23. 693

692*f* Baker, Joseph P., Melrose, Mass. —Horseshoes, etc. B 24. 693

693 Smith, Aaron W., Manchester, N. H.—Jointed horseshoes. B 24. 693

694 Atkins, J. L., Nashville, Tenn.— Horseshoes and plates. B 24. 693

695 Rhode Island Horseshoe Co., Providence, R. I.—Machine-hammered horseshoes. B 23. 693

696 Ward, Henry A., Rochester, N. Y. —Stuffed Bactrian camel and Shetland pony. K 26 *and* 27. 693

697 Gadsden, John W., Philadelphia, Pa.—Veterinary anatomical specimens. A 28. 693

For locations of objects, indicated by letter and figure, see Key to Notation, p. 6; ground plan, p. 10.

Veterinary Appliances.

698 National Horse Nail Co., Vergennes, Vt.—Horseshoe nails. B 24. 693

699 Gornes, John M., St. Louis, Mo.—Horseshoes. B 24. 693

700 Carroll, William, Philadelphia, Pa.—Horseshoes. B 24. 693

701 Day, Austin G., Seymour, Conn.—H 27–28.
a Vulcanized bituminous concrete paving-blocks. 103
b Kerite manufactured articles; hard-rubber goods. 285

701*a* McElroy & Co., Philadelphia, Pa.—Clay pipes. H *and* I 25. 254

701*b* Ashbourne & Co., Philadelphia, Pa.
a Cocoanut-cream oil and soap. 201
b Ink from cocoanut shell. 202
c Cocoanut tooth-powder, cosmetic. 203

702 Tower, L. C., Chester, Pa.—Thermometers. A 16. 320

703 Collison, H. C., Dover, Del.—Syrup drip for measuring-vessels. S 25. 320

704 Wheelock, Jerome, Worcester, Mass.—High-pressure steam engine. *Engine house,* T 16. 552

705 Neafie & Levy, Philadelphia, Pa.—High-pressure engine. Engine rooms, T 13. 552

705*a* Canby, George, & Co., Philadelphia, Pa.—Pumps for supplying aquariums with water. A 24. 560

705*b* Knowlton, E. J., Ann Arbor, Mich.—Bathing apparatus. K 7. 594

706 Protective Fire Apparatus Co., New York, N. Y.—Apparatus for extinguishing fires. (*South side of Agricultural Hall.*) 594
Agricultural Hall is protected by this apparatus.

The Protective Fire Apparatus consists of four systems:

System 1. Injecting into burning buildings or compartments of vessels pure carbonic acid gas.

System 2. Impregnating water with carbonic acid gas as it flows through the main water-pipe or fire-plugs, thereby throwing through the hose upon the fire a continuous stream of carbonic acid gas.

System 3. Throwing by hose-attachment impregnated water from the apparatus itself.

System 4. Injecting beneath the surface of oil or fluids carbonic acid gas.

All for the purpose of extinguishing fire.

706*a* Murtfeldt, Miss, Kirkwood, Mo.—Botanical specimens of Missouri. I 22. 709

707 Janes & Kirtland, New York, N.Y.—Ornamental fountain. (*Intersection of nave and main transept.*) 722

For classes of exhibits, indicated by numbers at end of entries, see Classification, pp. 12–14.

GREAT BRITAIN.

(*South of South Transept, east of Nave.*)

Agricultural, Animal, and Vegetable Products.

Arboriculture and Forest Products.

1 Nicoll, Donald, London.—Starch and compounds rendering fabrics and timber uninflammable; carbon combined with caoutchouc, for the preservation of wood and iron. 600

Agricultural Products.

2 Delf, W., Colchester.—Wheat. 620

3 Field, W., Liverpool.—Oats. 620

Animal and Vegetable Products.

5 Chapman, Edwin, & Co., London.— Koumiss, a beverage prepared from cow's milk; koumiss extract, for converting milk into koumiss. 651

6 Evans & Stafford, Leicester.—Stilton cheese. 651

7 Hooker, J., London.—A large tin of milk which has been exposed to the air for five years; also desiccated milk, condensed milk, and other preparations made with milk. 651

9 Green, John, London.—Gelatine for cigar-boxes, printers, engravers, and artificial-flower makers. 652

14 Lovey, Edward, Ponsnooth, Cornwall.—Beehives, with samples of honey and wax. 654

15 Schneider, Edward Albert, London. —Liquid essence of beef. 656

16 Nicoll, Donald, London.—Tea and coffee combined with milk and sugar, contained in soluble capsules for distribution in single cups; aërated beverages in vessels to allow rapid distribution in single draughts; preserved food. 656

17 Geyelin & Co., London.—Concentrated animal and vegetable food. 656

18 Goodall, Backhouse, & Co., Leeds.
a Yorkshire relish sauce. 656
b Orange quinine wine. 660

19 Keen, Robinson, Bellville, & Co., London.—Preparations from mustard, barley, oats, etc. 656

20 Pratt, James, London.—Sauce. 656

21 Smith, T. & H., & Co., Edinburgh.
a Essences of coffee and coffee with chicory. 656
b Aërated waters. 660
c Chemical products. 200
d Flavoring extracts. 203

22 Jaap, J., Glasgow.—Curry powders. 656

23 Menier, Emile, London.—Chocolates and cocoas. 656

23*a* Yuille, Andrew, Glasgow.
a Essences of coffee and chocolate, coffee and milk, condensed milk. 656
b Vinegar. 660

23*b* Mellin, Gustav, London.—Non-farinaceous food for infants and invalids. 656

25 Mackay, John, Edinburgh.—Fluid flavoring quintessences and articles of diet for table use. 656

26 Ledger, H., & Co., London.—Pure extract of meat. 656

27 Ball, James, London.—Sauce. 656

28 Lea & Perrins, Worcester.—Sauce. 656

37 Crosse & Blackwell, London.—Pickles, sauces, vinegars, jams, jellies, marmalades; potted and preserved meats; preserved fruits, soups, and fish; oils for salads, etc.; preserved provisions, sausages, vegetables, etc. 656

38 Field, W., Liverpool.—Oatmeal. 657

38*a* Richards & Co., London.—Self-raising flour. 657

39 Hunter, John, & Son, Woodhall Mills, Juniper Green, near Edinburgh.—Oatmeal and pot barley. 657

40 Plunkett, John, & Co., Portland Works, Dublin.—Malt for brewing and distilling, and roasted malt for coloring and flavoring porter and ale. 657

41 McCann, John, Beamond Mills, Drogheda.—Oatmeal and groats. 657

42 Maw, Thomas, Leeds.—
a Pickles and sauces. 656
b Syrups. 659
c Vinegar. 660
d Lozenges, baking powder. 661

42*a* Campbell, Thomas, Allentown, Pa. —Malt and whisky. 660

42*b* Haig, J., & Co., Scotland.—Whisky. 660

43 Corry, William, & Co., Belfast, Ireland.
a Aërated waters from Cromac Springs, Belfast. 660
b Non-metallic valves, plungers, connections, taps, and cylinder-linings. 565

44 Burke, Edward & John, Dublin.— English ales, Dublin stout, Irish and Scotch whiskies. 660

44*a* Grant, Thomas, The Distillery, Maidstone.—Cherry brandy. 660

44*b* Cork Distillery Co., Cork.—Whisky. 660

45 Wright, Herbert, & Co., Diamond Brewery, Dover.—Pale ale and stout. 660

46 Ind, Coope, & Co., Burton-on-Trent, Staffordshire.—Ale. 660

46*a* Inman Brothers, Huddersfield, Yorkshire.—Aërated waters. 660

46*b* Bewley & Draper, Dublin.—Aerated waters. 660

For classes of exhibits, indicated by numbers at end of entries, see Classification, pp. 12–14.

Machines, Implements, Engineering, and Administration.

47 Bindley & Co., Burton-on-Trent.—Ales. 660

47*a* Tennent, J. & R., Glasgow.—Bottled ales. 660

48 Mott & Co., Leicester.—Cowslip wine. 660

49 Muir, Jas., & Son, Calton Hill Brew-ery, Edinburgh.—Ales. 660

49*a* Cantrell & Cochrane, Dublin.—Gin-ger ale, aërated beverages, etc. 660

50 Johnson & Co., Canterbury.—Pale ale. 660

50*a* Murree Brewery Co., Punjab, East India.—Bottled ales. 660

51 Pendock Brothers, Bristol.—Cider and perry. 660

52 Richardson, Earp, & Slater.—Trent and Northgate Brewery, Newark-upon-Trent.—Ale. 660

53 Stevens, Thomas, Wrexham, North Wales.—Ornamental confectionery, birthday and christening cake, meringues, medallions, ornamental sugar-stand; rich cake. 661

53*a* Fry, Joseph Storrs, & Sons, Bristol. —Chocolate and cocoa, and specimens illustrative of the process of manufacture. 661

54 Gissing, Anthony S., & Sons, Eye, Suffolk.—Fancy biscuits, baking powder. 661

54*a* Allen, Frederick, & Sons, London. —Confectionery and medicated confectionery. 661

54*b* Smith, Thomas, & Co., London.— Wedding-cakes, ornaments, novelties for parties. 661

Textile Substances of Vegetable or Animal Origin.

56 The Mill Hill Wool and Rag Ex-tracting Co. (limited), Mill Hill Works, Huddersfield.—Wools made from old rags, etc. 667

57 Bowes, John L., & Bro., Liverpool. —Raw materials used in the woollen and worsted trade. 667

58 Smith, David, & Co. (limited), Ken-sington Works, Halifax, Yorkshire.— Cleaned wools and wools extracted from waste products. 667

Machines, Implements, and Processes of Manufacture.

60 Wills, Arthur Winkler, Park Mills, Birmingham.—Hoes, axes, etc. 670

62 Fison, J. P., Teversham Works, Cambridge.—Agricultural machinery: vertical steam engine and boiler, chaff cutter, centrifugal pump, steam threshing-machine and chain harrow, models of portable steam engine, movable hut, centrifugal pump, and furrow plows. 670

63 Fussell, James, Sons, & Co., Mell's Iron Works, near Frome, Somersetshire. —Edge tools used in agriculture. 670

64 Wilkinson, William, & Sons, Spring Works, Sheffield.—Sheep and garden shears. 672

64*a* Greening, N., & Sons, Warrington. —Woven wire for rice, flour, and other mills. 673

64*b* Brown, J. B., & Co., London.—Gal-vanized wire netting, etc. 673

66 Lloyd, T., & Sons, London.—Flour mills, dressing machines, grinding mill, and coffee mills. 673

66*a* Cheavin, G., Boston, Lincolnshire. —Filters. 673

66*b* Barnard, Bishop, & Barnards, Nor-wich.—Galvanized wire netting. 673

66*c* Needham & Kite, London.—Filter press for clarifying liquids. 673

67 Crook, Graham, & Co., Halifax.— Boilers. 674

67*a* Kay & Hilton, Liverpool.—French burr millstones for wheat grinding. 674

68 Clark & Dunham, London.

a Mill stones and lubricators. 674

b Chrondometers for measuring and weighing grain. 322

68*a* Wellock, J., & Co., Bradford.— Waterproof material for cart and wagon covers. 682

69 Aveling & Porter, Rochester, Kent. —Agricultural locomotive engine, locomotive crane engine, steam road roller, wagons for road locomotive engines. 682

70 Neighbour, G., & Sons, London.— Beehives and bee furniture. 683

71 Barnard, Bishop, & Barnards, Nor-wich.—Stable fittings. 683

72 Lovey, Edward, Cornwall.—Bee-hives. 683

---

73 Colthurst, Symons, & Co., Bridge-water.—Scouring bricks. 106

74 Star Plate Universal Polishing Powder Co., London.—Polishing powder. 106

75 Jaap, J., Glasgow.—Artificial yeast. 200

76 Higgin, T., & Co., Northwich.—Salt. 200

77 Harper, Twelvetras, & Co., London. —Soap powder. 201

78 Rawlins & Son, Prescot.—Ultra-marine, smalts, etc. 202

79 Eastwood & Co., London.—Red terra cotta chimney shafts. 206

80 Phillips, J., & Co., Devonshire.— Terra cotta bricks and drain pipes. 206

81 Johnson & Co., Sussex.—Terra cotta. 206

82 Edwards, J., & Son, Burslem.— Ironstone white ware and fancy decorated goods. 210

83 Edwards, J., Fenton.—Porcelain and ironstone china. 213

For classes of exhibits, indicated by numbers at end of entries, see Classification, pp. 12–14.

NEW ZEALAND.

(*East Aisle, Columns 1 to 5.*)

Agricultural Products, Textile Substances.

Agricultural Products.

1 **Banks, E. H., Christchurch.** — Oats and other cereals. 620

2 **Wood, W. D., Christchurch.**—Wheat. 620

3 **Cunningham, P., & Co., Christchurch.** —Wheat grown in Canterbury. 620

4 **Ruddenklan, J. G., Addington, Canterbury.**—Wheat. 620

5 **Wilkins, Robert, Christchurch.**—Perennial rye grass and cocksfoot seed. 624

Textile Substances of Vegetable or Animal Origin.

6 **Peter, W. S., Anama, Ashburton, Canterbury.**—Merino wool. 667

7 **Bealey, Samuel, Canterbury.**—Merino and Romney Marsh wool. 667

8 **Rutherford, A. W., Amuri, Nelson.** —Merino wool. 667

9 **Anstey, G. A., Amuri, Nelson.**—Merino wool. 667

10 **Wason, J. Cathcart, South Rakaia, Canterbury.**—Wools. 667

11 **Hall, John, Hororata, Canterbury.**— Merino wool. 667

12 **Rickman, F. M., Rangiora, Canterbury.**—Romney Marsh wool. 667

13 **Braithwaite, Arthur, Hutt, Wellington.**—Romney Marsh wool. 667

NEW SOUTH WALES.

(*East Aisle, Columns 1 to 5.*)

Animal and Vegetable Products.

Animal and Vegetable Products.

1 **Fallon, James T., Albury.**—Wines. 660

2 **Munro, A., Bebeah, Singleton.**— Wines. 660

3 **Carmichael, G. L. & J. B., Porphyry, Williams River.**—Wines. 660

4 **Brecht, Carl J. P., Rosemount, Denman.**—Wines. 660

5 **Powell, Edward, Richmond.**— Wines. 660

6 **Parnell, Montague, West Maitland, Hunter River.**—Wines. 660

7 **Wyndham, Wadham, Bukkulla, Inverell.**—Wines. 660

8 **Wyndham, George, Branxton, Hunter River.**—Wines. 660

9 **Doyle, J. F., Kaludah, Lochinvar.** —Wines. 660

For classes of exhibits, indicated by numbers at end of entries, see Classification, pp. 12–14.

SOUTH AUSTRALIA.

(*East Aisle, Columns 1 to 5.*)

Machines, Implements, and Accessories of Manufacture.

Machines, Implements, and Accessories of Manufacture.

1 **South Australian Commissioners,** Adelaide.—Reaping Machine. 672

2 **South Australian Commissioners,** Adelaide.—Castings from South Australian iron ores. 111

3 **Saunders, Robert,** Manager of the Burra Burra Copper Mine, near Adelaide. —Model of improved ore dresser. 505

4 **Hancock, H. R.,** Moonta Copper Mines, near Adelaide.—Jigging machine. 505

CAPE OF GOOD HOPE.

(*South of South Transept, east of Nave.*)

Agricultural, Animal, and Vegetable Products, Textile Substances.

Agricultural Products.

1 **Letterstedt & Co., Cape Town.**—Wheat. 620

2 **Clear, E., Cape Town.—Wheat.** 620

Animal and Vegetable Products.

3 **Dier & Dietz, Port Elizabeth.**—Skins. 652

4 **Barry, Arnold, & Co., Cape Town.**—Wheat flour. 657

Textile Substances of Vegetable or Animal Origin.

5 **Grewar, John W., Uitenhage.**—Scoured wool. 667

6 **Priest, W., Graff Reinet.—Fleece** wool. 667

7 **Rubidge, C., Graff Reinet.—Grease** wool. 667

8 **Stewart, A. C., & Co., Port Elizabeth.**
a Grease and scoured wool. 667
b Angora hair. 669

9 **Court, P. W., Port Elizabeth.—" Fidus,"** snow-white, and grease wool. 667

10 **Barry & Nephews, Cape Town.**—Washed and scoured wool. 667

11 **Barry, Arnold, & Co., Cape Town.**—Washed and grease wool. 667

12 **Dier & Dietz, Port Elizabeth.**—Wool. 667

13 **Barry & Newpews, Mossel Bay.**—Aloes. 272

JAMAICA.

(*South of South Transept, east of Nave.*)

Pomology.

Pomology.

1 **Thompson, Robert, Jamaica.**—A succession of fruit by each steamer during the season, including oranges, limes, lemons, citrons, shaddocks, forbidden fruit, ripley pines, sugar-loaf pines, black pines, bananas, mangoes, yams, cocoanuts, bread-fruit, etc. 610

For classes of exhibits, indicated by numbers at end of entries, see Classification, pp. 12-14.

CANADA.

(East Aisle, Columns 4 to 7.)

Pomology, Agricultural Products, Land and Water Animals.

Arboriculture and Forest Products.

1 **Munro, D. R., St. Johns, N. B., Canada.**—Collection of forest woods, shrubs, etc., evergreen and deciduous, indigenous to the province of New Brunswick, used for shipbuilding, constructional, cabinet, and ornamental purposes, polished, etc. Sixty-seven specimens, accompanied with foliage and cone, interesting and instructive to the student of nature. Collected and prepared by D. R. Munro. 600

2 **Alder, M., Victoria, B. C.—Charcoal.** 600

3 **Miller, J. & J., New Mills, Restigouche, N. B.**—Extract of hemlock bark. 602

Pomology.

9 **Fisher, M., Victoria, B. C.—Cranberries.** 610

10 **Loggie, A., & Co., New Westminster, B. C.**—Cranberries. 610

Agricultural Products.

11 **Rennie, Wm., Toronto, Ont.**
a Grains. 620
b Seeds. 624

12 **Murton, H., Guelph, Ont.—Oatmeal.** 620

13 **Wilson, Jas., Fergus, Ont.—Oatmeal.** 620

14 **Martin & Sons, Mount Forrest, Ont.**—Oatmeal. 620

15 **Aspden & Pritchard, London, Ont.**—Oatmeal and oats. 620

16 **Scott & Co., Highgate, Ont.—Oatmeal.** 620

17 **McKay, Thomas, & Co., Ottawa, Ont.**—Oatmeal. 620

18 **Corn Exchange Association, Toronto, Ont.**—Grain and oatmeal. 620

19 **Weatherston, N., & Co., Toronto, Ont.**—Grain. 620

20 **Charlesworth, M., & Son, Egmondville, Ont.**—Bran and shorts. 620

21 **Morton, Geo., & Son, Knipton, Ont.**—Malt. 620

22 **Osborne, Wm., Hamilton, Ont.**—Malt. 620

23 **Slater, R. P., Galt, Ont.—Malt.** 620

24 **Northwood, Howard, Chatham, Ont.**—Malt. 620

25 **Kerr, J. R., Victoria, B. C.—Grass,** oats, and wheat. 620

26 **Tolmie, Dr., Victoria, B. C.—Wheat** in the stalk. 620

27 **Boyd, J., Victoria, B. C.—Grass and** cereals. 620

28 **Council of Agriculture, Montreal,** Quebec.—Cereals. 620

29 **Brodie & Harvey, Montreal, Quebec.**—Corn, oatmeal, and buckwheat. 620

30 **Advisory Board of P. E. Island,** Charlottetown.—Cereals. 620

31 **Canadian Commission.**
a Corn-wheat grown by Indians of British Columbia, and cereals from Manitoba. 620
b Indian or wild tea and wild hops from Manitoba. 623

32 **Advisory Board of Nova Scotia.**
a Cereals. 623
b Seeds. 624

33 **Ontario Advisory Board, Toronto,** Ont.—Cereals from counties of York, Perth, Simcoe, Bruel, Huron, Wellington, Peterboro', Cardwell, Durham, Essex, Hastings, Lincoln, Lanark, Middlesex, Victoria, Russell, Peel, Frontenac, Lennox, Kent, Renfrew, Wentworth, Northumberland, Lambton, Carleton, Prince Edward, Addington, Waterloo, Halton, Brant, Grey, Oxford, and Ontario. 620

34 **Muirhead & Gray, London, Ont.**
a Barley and oatmeal. 620
b Peas. 621

35 **Girdlestone, C. H., & Co., Windsor,** Ont.—Tobacco and cigars. 623

36 **Downie, W., Saainch, B. C.—Hops.** 623

37 **Moses, D. D., Saainch, B. C.—Hops.** 623

38 **Wain, N., Saainch, B. C.—Hops.** 623

39 **Cook, Isaac, Saainch, B. C.—Hops.** 623

40 **Mann, J. W., Simcoe, Ont.—Grass** and turnip seed. 624

41 **Fuller, S. S., Stratford, Ont.—Flaxseed.** 624

Land Animals.

42 **Carnell, J. H., St. John, N. B.**
a Stuffed birds and ducks. 635
b Fur-bearing animals, etc. 637

43 **Egan, Thomas J., Halifax, Nova** Scotia.
a Six cases Canadian birds. 635
b One pair caribou.
c Two caribou heads.
d Two moose heads.
e One black bear. 637

44 **Norvell, G. F., Hamilton, Ont.**—Stuffed birds. 635

44*a* **Foley, C., Lindsay, Ont.—Stuffed** birds. 635

Water Animals, Fish-Culture, and Apparatus.

45 **Loggie, A., & Co., New Westminster,** B. C.—Salmon and trout. 641

46 **Advisory Board of Nova Scotia.**—Fishes. 641

For classes of exhibits, indicated by numbers at end of entries, see Classification, pp. 12–14.

Animal and Vegetable Products, Textile Substances.

47 **Crowe, A. H., Halifax, N. S.**—Fishes. 641

47a **McLeod, R.**—Medusa head, star fish. 641

48 **O'Leary, H., Richibucto, N. B.**
a Salmon. 641
b Lobsters. 643

49 **Mack, J. N., Halifax, N. S.**—Smoked alewives. 642

50 **Barber, J., Halifax, N. S.**
a Canned mackerel. 642
b Canned lobsters. 643

51 **Deas, J. S., Fraser River, B. C.**—Canned salmon. 642

52 **Noble, R. B., Richibucto, N. B.**
a Mackerel, etc. 642
b Lobster. 643

53 **Bain, J. D., Restigouche, N. B.**
a Mackerel. 642
b Lobsters. 643

54 **Holbrook & Cummington, New Westminster, B. C.**—Canned salmon. 642

56 **Christian, P., Halifax, N. S.**—Canned lobsters. 643

57 **Geological Survey, British Columbia.**—Clam-shells used by Indians. 645

58 **Erwin & Wise, British Columbia.**—Isinglass. 646

59 **Pitts, D. H., Halifax, N. S.**—Reel for cod-fishing. 647

Animal and Vegetable Products.

60 **Sharp, J. S., St. John, N. B.**—Butter. 651

61 **McLeod, R. E., & Co.**—Cheeses. 651

62 **Harvey, J., & Co., Hamilton, Ont.**—Sheep-skins. 652

63 **Crowe, A. H., Halifax, N. S.**—Fish oils. 652

64 **Netz, Christian.**
a Lard. 652
b Pork and sausages. 656

65 **Hatheway, F. A., St. John, N. B.**—Moose and caribou heads. 652

66 **Barnhill, B. B., St. John, N. B.**—Moosehead. 652

67 **Langley & Co., Victoria, B. C.**—Oil. 652

68 **Loggie, A., & Co., New Westminster, B. C.**—Oolachan or pure oil. 652

69 **Doel, W. H., Toronto, Ont.**—Hen's nest. 653

70 **Walsh, B., Halifax, N. S.**—Pork. 656

71 **Woodrell, W., Halifax, N. S.**—Beef. 656

72 **Belcher, J. W., Halifax, N. S.**—Fruits in sugar. 656

73 **Canadian Meat & Produce Co., Sherbrook, Quebec.**—Canned meats. 656

74 **Bain, J. D., Restigouche, N. B.**—Beef and soups. 656

75 **Graham, John, Sussex, N. B.**—Spiced rolled bacon. 656

76 **Canadian Commission.**
a Dried Indian berries. 656
b Indian bread. 661

76a **Guthrie & Hevenor, St. John, N. B.**
a Fruit preserves. 656
b Raspberry vinegar. 660

77 **Mewhort, Jos., Montreal, Quebec.**—Self-raising flour. 657

78 **Parkyn, Jas., Montreal, Quebec.**—Flour. 657

79 **McDougall, John, Bowmanville, Ont.**—Flour. 657

80 **Wadsworth, J. P., Meaford, Ont.**—Flour. 657

81 **King, Joseph G., Port Hope, Ont.**—Three samples gilt-edged, patent process flour; three samples gilt-edged flour; three samples patent process flour; three samples flour. 657

82 **Corn Exchange Association, Toronto, Ont.**—Flour. 657

83 **Weatherston, N., & Co., Toronto, Ont.**—Flour and meal. 657

84 **Charlesworth, M., & Son, Egmondville, Ont.**—Flour. 657

85 **Brodie & Harvie, Montreal, Quebec.**—Self-raising flour. 657

86 **Catelli Bros., Montreal, Quebec.**—Vermicelli and macaroni. 658

87 **Spinnelli, M. R., Montreal, Quebec.**—Macaroni and vermicelli. 658

88 **Troop, O. V., & Co., Mammoth Vinegar Works, St. John, New Brunswick.**—Vinegar. The various grades of vinegars from this factory are readily sold for medicinal, pickling, and culinary purposes in the maritime provinces. 660

89 **Febur, Michel Le, Montreal, Quebec.**—Vinegar. 660

90 **McLeod, McNaughton, & Co.**—Ales and porter. 660

91 **Blackwood, R., & Co., Montreal, Quebec.**—Champagne, cider, etc. 660

92 **Croskill, G. H., Halifax, N. S.**—Cordials. 660

93 **Costin, P., Halifax, N. S.**—Champagne cider. 660

94 **Knight, J., Halifax, N. S.**—Liquors. 660

95 **Smith, R., & Co., Brantford, Ont.**—Bottled wines. 660

96 **Canada Wine-growers Association, Toronto, Ont.**—Wines and brandies. 660

97 **Hastings, James, Toronto, Ont.**—Wines. 660

98 **Farrell, A. P., Cayuga, Ont.**—Wine. 660

99 **Wilson, Charles, Toronto, Ont.**—Ginger ales. 660

100 **Waterhouse, Joseph, Chatham, Ont.**—Ales and porter. 660

101 **Labatt, John, London, Ont.**—Ales and porter. 660

102 **Davis, Thos., & Bro., Toronto, Ont.**—Ales and porter. 660

103 **Birely & Co., Hamilton, Ont.**—Vinegar. 660

104 **Casci, V., Toronto, Ont.**
a Wines. 660
b Plaster work. 400

Textile Substances of Vegetable or Animal Origin.

105 **Nicol Bros., Belmont, Ont.**—Flax. 666

106 **Stahlschmidt & Co., Victoria, B. C.**—Wool. 667

For classes of exhibits, indicated by numbers at end of entries, see Classification, pp. 12–14.

Machines, Implements, Engineering and Administration.

107 Canadian Commission. — Indian wool from British Columbia. 667

108 Harvey, J., & Co., Hamilton, Ont.—Wool. 667

Machines, Implements, and Processes of Manufacture.

109 Richardson, Thos., Fergus, Ont.—Plow. 670

110 Acton Plow Co., Acton, Ont.—Plow. 670

111 Ross, George, Chatham, Ont.—Plows. 670

112 Monroe & Hogan, Seaforth, Ont —Plow. 670

113 Duperon, Chas., Stratford, Ont.—Harrow. 670

114 Gillis, George, Gananoque, Ont.—Harrow, cultivator, and harrow and cultivator combined. 670

115 Bell, Charles, Parkhill, Ont.—Plow. 670

116 Wilson & Piper, Strathroy, Ont.—Combined sulky-harrow and hay-rake. 670

117 Wilkinson, George, Aurora, Ont.—Furrow plows, wrought frame and iron plows. 670

118 McDonald, A. S., Osgoode, Ont.—Cylinder cultivator. 670

119 McLaurin, Edmund, Trafalgar, Ont.—Plow. 670

120 Yeandle, Thomas, Stratford, Ont.—Plows. 670

121 Grant, Peter, Clinton, Ont.—Horse-power pitchfork. 670

122 Connell Bros., Woodstock, N. B.—Plow. 670

123 Dennis, Rowland, London, Ont.
a Plow. 670
b Potato-digger. 672

124 Dow, John, Gananoque, Ont.—Harrow and cultivator. 670

125 Harris, J., & Co., St. John, N. B.
a Plows. 670
b Mower, hay-rake, and potato-diggers. 672
c Thresher. 673
d Hay-cutter. 674

126 Watson, John, Ayr, Ont.
a Plows, roller. 670
b Horse-power grain-drill, turnip-drill. 671
c Grain-choppers, corn-sheller. 673
d Straw-cutters, root-cutter and pulper. 674

127 Vessot, J. & S., Joliette, Quebec.—Combined sower, harrow, and roller. 671

128 Mann, James W., Simcoe, Ont.—Turnip-drill. 671

129 Martin, Stephen, Osgoode, Ont.—Potato-digger. 672

130 Gray, A. G., St. John, N. B.—Mower. 672

131 McKenzie, Wm., Charlottetown, P. E. I.—Potato-digger. 672

132 Harris, A., Son, & Co., Brantford, Ont.—Mower, reaper, and rake. 672

133 Sawyer, L. D., & Co., Hamilton, Ont.—Mower, reaper. 672

134 Green Bros., Waterford, Ont.—Single reaper. 672

135 Bawtenheimer, P. M., Hamilton, Ont.—Potato-digger. 672

136 Head, Thos., Dundas, Ont.—Potato-digger. 672

137 Elliott, Thos., Peterboro', Ont.—Combined hay-rake and loader. 672

138 Forsyth & Co., Dundas, Ont.—Combined mower and reaper, single reaper. 672

139 Sharmon & Foster, Stratford, Ont.
a Mower and reaper combined. 672
b Thresher and separator. 673

140 Massey Mfg. Co., Newcastle, Ont.
a Mowing-machine and horse-rake. 672
b Grain-crusher. 673

141 Sells, Hugh, Vienna, Ont.—Cider-mills and presses. 673

142 Armstrong, E. F., Goderich, Ont.—Fanning-mill. 673

143 Haggert Bros., Brampton, Ont.—Horse-power separator. 673

144 Bricker, Jac., Berlin, Ont.—Threshing-separator. 673

145 Champion, A., Arkona, Ont.—Thresher and boiler. 673

146 Wilson, Thos., Richmond Hill, Ont.—Fanning-mill. 673

147 Gerolamy, Wm. A., Owen Sound, Ont.—Fanning-mill. 673

148 Abell, John, Woodbridge, Ont.
a Separator with carriers. 673
b Portable engine. 674

149 Anderson, Alex., London, Ont.—Straw-cutters and hay-knives. 674

150 Luke & Tolton Bros., Guelph, Ont.—Straw-cutter, etc. 674

151 Maxwell, David, Paris, Ont.—Power and hand straw-cutters, root-cutters, and pulpers. 674

151*a* James, Jos., Forest, Ont.—Bag-holder. 674

152 Ashley & Smith, Belleville, Ontario.—Manufacturers and sole assignees for the dominion of Canada of Fraser's patent improved cheese-hoops and gang-press. From five to fifteen cheeses may be pressed with one screw, each cheese receiving its full power; and one man can put ten cheeses to press after the hoops are filled as quickly as one man with the old press can put two cheeses to press. 675

153 Pitts, D. H., Halifax, N. S.—Horizontal churn. 675

Agricultural Engineering and Administration.

154 Strong, J. E., Newtonbrook, Ont.—Farm gate. 680

155 Marcon, W. H., Guelph, Ont.—Crushed bones. 681

156 Attwood, A. C., London, Ont.—Bee-hive, etc. 683

---

157 Purdy & Green, Portland, N. B.—Lime. 103

158 Canadian Commission.
a Tripoli earth from British Columbia. 104
b Head of a Wauptee Indian, Manitoba. 312

159 Borthwick, W., Ottawa, Ont.—Mineral waters. 107

160 Gray, Young, & Sparling, Seaforth, Ont.—Salt. 200

Agricultural Engineering and Administration.

161 **International Salt Co., Goderich,** Ont.—Salt. 200

162 **Coleman & Gowinlock, Seaforth,** Ont.—Salt. 200

163 **Harrison & Evans, Goderich, Ont.** —Salt. 200

164 **Rigg, Ben., Stratford, Ont.**—Soap. 201

165 **McKelvey, Jas., St. Catharines.**— Refrigerators. 224

166 **Canadian Commission.**
a Indian yarn from B. C. 235
b Indian blankets from B. C. 237

167 **Anderson, Alex., London, Ont.,** Canada.—Bread-knives. 281

168 **Stephen, Alex., & Son, Halifax,** N. S.
a Brooms. 286
b Pails. 289

169 **Brazil, Peter B., Barrie, Ont.**
a Sleigh. 295
b Snow-plow. 572

170 **Bruce, Robt., St. Catharines, Ont.** —Tree-pruner. 720

For classes of exhibits, indicated by numbers at end of entries, see Classification, pp. 12–14.

FRANCE.

West of Nave, Columns 3 to 7.)

Metallurgy, Mining Engineering, Agricultural Products.

Minerals, Ores, Stone, Mining Products.

1 Laroche, A., Saulxures, Vosges.—Coal. 101

2 Asphalt Mining Co., Pyrimont-Seyssel, Ain.—Asphaltum. 101

3 Biron & Son, Paris.—Stone staircase and samples of colored Echaillon stone. 102

4 Cornu, Eugéne, & Co., Paris.—Marble and Algerian onyx. 102

5 Marga, Eugene, Paris.—Samples of marble. 102

6 Parfonry & Lemaire, Paris.—Marble for furniture. 102

7 Pont-Ollion, Nicolet, Grenoble, Isere.—Cements. 103

8 Thorrand & Co., Grenoble.—Cement. 103

9 Soullier & Brunot, Teil, Ardèche.—Hydraulic lime. 103

10 Lime, Cement, & Plaster Manufacturing Co., Paris.—Limes, cements, plasters, and bricks. 103

11 Hydraulic Lime Stock Co., Montèlimar, Drôme.—Lime, cement, and artificial paving blocks. 103

12 Holl, Samuel J., Dieppe, Seine-Inferieure.—Chalk. 103

13 Pinson, Paris.—Shell, ivory, mother of pearl, and artificial stone. 103

14 Pavin de la Farge, L. & E., Viviers, Ardèche.—Hydraulic lime and Portland cement. 103

15 Louquéty & Co., Boulogne-sur-Mer.—Cements. 103

16 Lauzun & Co., Bourg St. Andeol, Ardèche.—Artificial stone pavement, mosaics, granite, and artificial marble. 103

17 Mailfert & Mathelin, Chatillon-sur-Seine, Côte d'Or.—Moulding sand for foundries. 104

18 Deplanque, jr., Maisons, Alfort, Seine.—Emery in grains and powder. 106

19 Roger, Son, & Co., La Ferté-sous-Jouarre, Seine and Marne.—Millstones. 106

20 Fauqueux, A., La Ferté-sous-Jouarre, Seine and Marne.—Millstones. 106

21 Lithographic Stone Quarry Co., Paris.—Lithographic stone. 106

22 Clément, Clément, & Co., Paris.—Diamonds. 106

23 Durrschmidt, Lyons.—Emery in grains and powdered. 106

24 Bertrand, Jules, & Co., La Ferté-sous-Jouarre, Seine and Marne.—Millstones. 106

25 Bailly & Co., La Ferté-sous-Jouarre, Seine and Marne.—Millstones. 106

26 Weyl & Co., Paris.—**Mineral waters** from Aulus Springs. 107

Metallurgical Products.

27 Desmoutis, Quennessen, & Le Brun, Paris.—Platinum. 110

28 Chappée, A., Mans, Sarthe.—**Iron** pipes for water and gas. 111

29 Durenne, A., Paris.—**Monumental** fountain. 111

30 Martin, Pierre Emile, Sireuil, Charente.—Iron and steel. 111

31 Terrenoire, La Voulte, & Besseges, Lyons.—Iron and steel castings. 111

32 Marseilles Gas Co., Marseilles.—Spiegeleisen iron. 111

33 Marquise Foundry and Construction Works, Paris.—Iron pipes and chandeliers. 111

34 Secrétan, É., Paris.—**Copper.** 112

Mining Engineering.

36 Davey, Bickford, Watson, & Co., Rouen.—Safety fuse for mines. 120

37 Cosset, Dubrulle, Lille, Nord.—Safety lamps for miners. 120

38 Galibert, A., Paris.—**Apparatus for** breathing amid suffocating gases. 120

Arboriculture and Forest Products.

1 Delmas, Augustin, Toulouse.—**Nat**ural woods. 600

2 Gouturon, Mezin, Lot-and-Garonne.—Corks. 602

Pomology.

3 Charozé Bros., La Pyramide, Maine-and-Loire.—Fruits. 610

Agricultural Products.

4 Barthe, G., Paris.—**Corn.** 620

5 Dumoutier, Ch., Claville, Eure.—Agricultural products. 620

6 Thoreau, E., & Son, Chateau de la Chèze, Maine-and-Loire.—Barley. 620

7 Gutmann & Bloch, Paris.
a Barley. 620
b Hops and malt. 623

8 Fos, Miss J., Paris.—**Medicated** cigarettes. 623

Water Animals, Fish Culture, and Apparatus.

9 Colin, jr., Nantes.—**Preserved fish.** 641

For classes of exhibits, indicated by numbers at end of entries, see Classification, pp. 12–14.

Animal and Vegetable Products.

10 Dupland, E., Ville-en-Bois, Loire-Inferieure.—Preserved sardines. 641

11 Jacquier & Saupiquet, Nantes.—Sardines in oil. 641

12 Maille & Tandeau, Paris.—Anchovies in oil. 641

13 Maré, C., Nantes.—Sardines. 641

14 Peltier & Paillard, Paris.—Sardines in oil. 641

15 Philippe & Co., Nantes.—Sardines in oil. 641

16 Terrien, Palais, Belle-Ile-en-Mer.—Sardines in oil. 641

17 Caillebotte & Dumagnou, Paris.—Sardines and pickled fish. 642

18 Dufour, A., & Co., Bordeaux.—Sardines. 642

19 Peltier & Paillard, Paris.—Sardines in oil. 642

20 Clement & Co., Paris.—Pearls. 645

Animal and Vegetable Products.

21 Coupiac, E., Roquefort Cheese-Factory, Roquefort, Aveyron.—Cheese. 651

22 Bageau, H., Paris.—Waterproof glue for leather. 652

23 Corbel, Eug., & Co., Nantes.—Leather. 652

24 Clavé, Bertrand, Coulommiers, Seine-and-Marne.—Leather. 652

25 Burel, J., Paris.—Peltry; kid-skins. 652

26 Bayvet Bros., Paris.—Morocco, sheep, calf, goat, and kid skins. 652

27 Basset & Co., Paris.—Kid for shoes. 652

28 Allain, Jules, Paris.—Kid for shoes. 652

29 Leven, M., senior & junior, Paris.—Calf-skin. 652

30 Fortier, Beaulieu, Paris.—Leather for furniture. 652

31 Tréfousse & Co., Chaumont, Haute-Marne.—Leather and dyes for leather. 652

32 Sueur, F., jr., Paris.—Leather. 652

33 Sorro Bros., Millan, Aveyron.—Calf-skin. 652

34 COLLECTIVE EXHIBIT OF THE LEATHER MANUFACTURERS OF SAINT-SAEMS, SEINE INFERIEURE.—LEATHER. 652

- Lefebvre, Felix.
- Lecourtois, Arthur.
- Lemonnier, Jules.
- Sergent, Edmond.
- Fache-Havé & Brother.
- Frigot, Emile.
- Lefebvre, Florentin.
- Binet, Hippolyte.
- Lenormand, Emile.
- Morisset, Mrs.
- Blot, Eugène.
- Dumesnil, Paul.

35 Revillon Bros., Paris.—Peltries. 652

36 Daubin & Co., Paris.—Lard. 652

37 Duchesne Bros., Paris.—Morocco leather. 652

38 Peltier & Paillard, Paris.—Preserved meats. 656

39 Passion, Marc, Paris.—Preserved food. 656

40 Ségur & Obier, Périgueux, Dordogne.—Preserved food and paté de foie gras. 656

41 Vicat, J. H., Paris.—Mustard and pickles. 656

42 Terrien, senior, Palais, Belle-Ile-en-Mer.—Preserved food. 656

43 Maré, C., Nantes.—Green peas. 656

44 Lenoir, A., Paris.—Preserved game, poultry, etc.; patés. 656

45 Lecourt, Francois, Paris.—Preserved food. 656

46 Landrin, Augustin, Paris.—Preserved fruits and vegetables. 656

47 Lamarche & Veillon, Paris.—Preserved game and patés de foie gras. 656

48 Jacquier & Saupiquet, Nantes.—Preserved food. 656

49 Henry, Louis, Paris.—Patés de foie gras. 656

50 Groult, jr., Paris.—Conserves. 656

51 Tivollier, Auguste, Toulouse.—Paté de fois gras. 656

52 Fau, J., Bordeaux.—Prunes. 656

53 Escoffier, J., Nice.—Preserved fruits. 656

55 Dronne, L. F., Paris.—Paté de foie gras and preserved meats. 656

56 Dione, A. C., Paris.—Preserved food. 656

57 Lamarche & Veillon, Paris.—Paté de foie gras. 656

58 Deriviere, Julien, Paris.—Preserved food. 656

59 Dardelle & Co., Paris.—Preserved and dried vegetables. 656

60 Cormier & Véron, Paris.—Preserved food. 656

61 Colin, Joseph, Nantes.—Preserved food. 656

62 Chevallier, Appert, Paris.—Preserved food. 656

63 Caillebotte & Dumagnou, Paris.—Preserves. 656

64 Boyer, P., & Co., Gignac, Hérault.—Truffles, capers, and olives. 656

65 Bornibus, Alexandre, Paris.—Mustard and pickles. 656

66 Bonfils Bros. & Co., Paris.—Preserved truffles. 656

67 Philippe & Co., Nantes.—Preserved food. 656

68 Fiton & Nouvialle, Bordeaux.
a Preserved food and fruits. 656
b Liquors. 660

68*a* Barthe, G., Paris.—Flour. 657

69 Ecorcheville & Legrand, Paris.
a Preserved fruits. 656
b Confectionery. 661

70 Dufour, A., & Co., Bordeaux.
a Prunes. 656
b Wines. 660

For classes of exhibits, indicated by numbers at end of entries, see Classification, pp. 12–14.

Vegetable Products, Wines, Liquors.

71 **Dandicolle & Gaudin, Bordeaux.**
a Preserved food. 656
b Wines and liquors. 660

72 **Rousseau Bros., Paris.**
a Preserved fruits. 656
b Liquors. 660

73 **Maille & Tandeau, Paris.**
a Mustard, pickles, and anchovies in oil. 656
b Vinegar. 660

74 **Lesage & Paignard, Paris.**
a Preserves. 656
b Confectionery. 661

75 **Louit Bros. & Co., Bordeaux.**
a Preserves and mustard. 656
b Vinegar. 660
c Chocolates. 661

76 **Mauprivez, A., Paris.—Tapioca.** 658

77 **Say, C., Paris.—Refined Sugar.** 659

78 **Déjardin, E., Paris.—Orange** syrup. 659

79 **Antheaume & Sons, Bourget-les-**Paris, Seine.
a Glucose. 659
b Caramels. 661

80 **Lefèvre & Rémondet, Savigny-les-**Beaune, Côte d'Or.—Sparkling wines. 660

81 **Combier, J., Saumur, Maine-and-**Loire.—Liquors. 660

82 **Chenu, Laffitte, & Co., Bordeaux.—** Wines. 660

83 **Brizard & Roger, Bordeaux.—** Liquors. 660

84 **Passier, A., Sautenary, Cote d'Or.—** Wines. 660

85 **Otard, Dupuy, & Co., Cognac.—** Brandies. 660

86 **Pinet, Castillon, & Co., Cognac.—** Brandies. 660

87 **Perrier, J., & Co., Chalons-sur-**Marne.—Champagne wines. 660

88 **Montigny, de, & Co., Reims.—** Champagne wines. 660

89 **Montheuil, Franc, senior, Bordeaux.** —Wines. 660

90 **Montebello, Alfred de, & Co.,** Mareuil-sur-Ay, Marne. — Champagne wines. 660

91 **Meukow, A. C., Cognac.—Bran-**dies. 660

92 **Merman, G., Bordeaux.—** Wines. 660

93 **Merman & Maitre, Bordeaux.—** Wines. 660

94 **Merman, Jules, & Co., Bordeaux.—** Wines. 660

95 **Mayer, Albert, Paris.—Liquors.** 660

96 **Mercier, Eug., Epernay.—Cham-**pagne wines. 660

97 **Reignard, Paris.—Wines.** 660

98 **Promis, Justin, Bordeaux.—Wines** and brandies. 660

99 **Poligny Society of Agriculture,** Science, & Art, Poligny, Jura.—Wines. 660

100 **Poitevin, Ch., & Co., Bordeaux.—** Wines. 660

101 **Roullé, E., Bordeaux.—Wines.** 660

102 **Rojat, Jules, Nimes, Gard.—White** wine vinegar. 660

103 **Roederer, Théophile, & Co., Reims.** —Champagne wines. 660

104 **Rivière, Gardrat, & Co., Cognac.—** Brandies. 660

105 **Ricaumont, de, & Co., Libourne.—** Wines. 660

106 **Sabatier-Granier & Son, Manduel,** Gard.—Wines and brandies. 660

107 **Rouyer, Guillet, & Co., Saintes,** Charente Inferieur.—Brandies. 660

108 **Roussillon, J., & Co., Epernay,** Marne.—Champagne wines. 660

109 **Fontaine, Sarget de la, Bordeaux.** —Wines. 660

110 **Soudée, Paris.—Wines and bran-**dies. 660

111 **Tarbouriech, Louis, Cette, Hérault.** —Wines. 660

112 **Marchand Bros., Paris. — Liq-**uors. 660

113 **Lossy & Co., Reims.—Champagne** wines. 660

114 **Lentilhac, de, Ballargeaux, St.** Aulaye.—Wines. 660

115 **Launay, de, & Co., Paris.—Cham-**pagne wines. 660

116 **Larronde Brothers, Bordeaux.—** Wines and brandies. 660

117 **Lamart, A., Beaumetz-les-Loges,** Pas-de-Calais.—Liquors. 660

118 **Labrunie, P. A., Bordeaux.—** Wines. 660

119 **Javerzac, Viremondoy, & Co., Pont-**de-Bordes, Lot-and-Garonne.—Wines and brandies. 660

120 **Irroy, Ernest, & Co., Reims.—** Champagne wines. 660

121 **Guilhou, A., senior, Bordeaux.—** Wines. 660

122 **Guichard-Potheret & Son, Chalon-**sur-Saone.—Wines. 660

123 **Hivert, Pellevoisin, & Godet, La** Rochelle.—Brandies. 660

124 **Anthoine, Paris.—Wines.** 660

124*a* **Benoit, Charles, Reims.—Cham-**pagne wines. 660

125 **Barral, J. L., Paris.—Wines.** 660

126 **Beaucourt, Fortuné, Margaux-**Medoc, Gironde.—Wines. 660

127 **Bellot, Jules, & Co., Cognac, Cha-**rente.—Brandy. 660

128 **Beuverand, de, & Poligny, de,** Chassagne, Côte d'Or.—Wines. 660

129 **Bollinger, J., Ay-Champagne,** Marne.—Champagne wine. 660

130 **Bontou, jr., Bordeaux.—Wines.** 660

131 **Boulle, E., Bordeaux.—Wines.** 660

132 **Bourgoin-Jamain, jr., Beaune,** Côte d'Or.—Wines. 660

133 **Boutelleau & Co., Barbezieux near** Cognac.—Brandies. 660

134 **Brugalieres, Etienne, Floressas,** Lot.—Wines. 660

135 **Chaboseau & Payen, Levallois-**Perret, Seine.—Liquor. 660

136 **Chateau d'Issan, Roy, G., Mar-**gaux, Gironde.—Wines. 660

For classes of exhibits, indicated by numbers at end of entries, see Classification, pp. 12–14.

Wines, Liquors, Vegetable Products, Agricultural Machines.

137 **Chiapella, Jérome, Bordeaux.**—Wines. 660

138 **Clavelle, Jules, Bordeaux.** — Wines. 660

139 **Clerc, J. B., Bordeaux.—Wines.** 660

140 **Collin, Ad., Chalons-sur-Marne.**—Champagne wines. 660

141 **Coudert, G., & Son, Limoges,** Haute-Vienne.—Brandies. 660

142 **Cunliffe, Dobson, & Co., Bordeaux.** —Wines. 660

143 **Curlier Bros. & Co., Paris.**—Brandies. 660

144 **Cusenier, E., & Co., Ornans, near** Pontarlier.—Liquors. 660

145 **Delizy & Doistau, jr., Pantin,** Seine.—Liquors. 660

146 **Thoreau, E., & Son, Chateau de la** Chèze, near Saumur.—Champagne and red wines. 660

147 **Tivet, B., Bordeaux.—Liquors and** bitters. 660

148 **Agricultural Union, Chateau-neuf,** Charente.—Brandies. 660

149 **Gourry & Co., Cognac.—Brandies.** 660

150 **Goerg, I., & Co., Chalons-sur-**Marne.—Champagne wines. 660

151 **Giojuzza & Giobertini, Paris.**—Wines. 660

152 **Gerin, E., Saint Jean d'Angéley,** Charente.—Brandy. 660

153 **Garros, J. L., Bordeaux.—Wines.** 660

154 **Garnier, P., Noyon, Oise.**—Liquors. 660

155 **Gadrad, D. G., & Co., Cognac.**—Brandies. 660

156 **Frois, Leo, & Co., Bordeaux.**—Wines. 660

157 **Fournier, Jules, Epernay, Marne.** —Champagne wines. 660

158 **Fournier, A., Chateau de Figeac,** Gironde.—Wines. 660

159 **Fouchez, L., & Co., Cognac.**—Brandies and liquors. 660

160 **Dessandier, F., & Co., Jarnac-Cog-**nac.—Brandies. 660

161 **Detrie-Grandjean, Saint Loup-sur-**Semouse, Haute Saone.—Kirschwasser. 660

162 **Ditely, E., Paris.—Wines.** 660

163 **Dolin, Mrs., Chambéry, Haute** Savoy.—Vermouth. 660

164 **Druelle, Reims.—Champagne** wines. 660

165 **Dubois, E., & Co., Saint Jean** d'Angéley, near Cognac.—Brandies. 660

166 **Duquénel, Paris.—Wines and bran-**dies. 660

167 **Duret, Jules, & Co., Cognac.**—Brandies. 660

168 **Durozier, M., & Co., Cognac.**—Liquors. 660

169 **Laplante, Edard de, Guyotville,** near Algeria.—Wines. 660

170 **Faure, J., & Co., Cognac.—Brandies.** 660

171 **Faurie, J., sr., Narbonne.—Wines.** 660

172 **Ferret, Bros., & Co., Macon.**—Wines. 660

173 **Fil, Francois, Narbonne, Ande.**—Wines. 660

174 **Fisse, Thirion, & Co., Reims.**—Champagne wines. 660

175 **Seignouret Bros.—Bordeaux.**
a Wines and brandies. 660
b Olive oil. 662

176 **Mestrezat & Co., Bordeaux.**
a Wines and brandies. 660
b Olive oil. 662

177 **Reinhardt, L., & Co., Paris.—Bon-**bons. 661

178 **Biardot, Alphonse, Paris.—Confec-**tionery. 661

179 **Chenu, P., Paris. — Confection-**ery. 661

180 **Combet, Joseph, Paris. — Confec-**tionery. 661

181 **Ménier, Paris.—Chocolates.** 661

182 **Nègre, Joseph, Grasse, Alpes Mari-**times.—Confectionery. 661

183 **Lombart, Paris.—Chocolates.** 661

184 **Marge, jr., Lyons.—Patés.** 661

185 **Mottet, J., & Co., Marseilles.—Olive** oil. 662

185*a* **Chudaca, Léon, Alger.—Oil.** 662

186 **Plagniol, James de, Marseilles.** — Olive oil. 662

Textile Substances of Vegetable or Animal Origin.

187 **Chabert, J., & Co., Chomérac, Ar-**dèche.—Raw silk. 668

188 **Boudon, Louis, St. Jean-du-Gard,** Gard.—Raw silk. 668

189 **Arlès, Dufour, Lyons.—Raw** silk. 668

190 **Thomas, F., Pont des Charettes,** Gard.—Cocoons and raw silk. 668

191 **Pellet, A. P., St. Jean-du-Gard,** Gard.—Raw silk. 668

Machines, Implements, and Processes of Manufacture.

192 **Rabache, A., Clunay-sur-Odon,** Calvados.—Double plow. 670

193 **Couture, Paris. — Stripping ma-**chines for textiles. 673

194 **Druelle, Reims.—Corking appara-**tus for champagne wines. 673

195 **Deny, Louis, Paris. — Cylinder** press for sugar. 673

196 **Maurice & Guenin, Epernay.** — Corking machines. 673

197 **Mabille Bros., Amboise, Indre and** Loire.—Wine and oil presses. 673

198 **Logette, Ay, Marne. — Clasps for** bottles, and machines for using them. 673

199 **Gervais, E., Bordeaux. — Corking** machines. 673

200 **Fréal, Epernay, Marne.—Machines** for filling bottles. 673

200*a* **Dubois, Emile, St. Jean d'Angéley.** Bottling machine. 673

201 **Fisse, Thirion, & Co., Reims.—Iron** clasps and bottling apparatus. 673

For classes of exhibits, indicated by numbers at end of entries, see Classification, pp. 12–14.

Agricultural Machines, Engineering.

202 **Mercier, Eug., Epernay.—Apparatus** for vine-culture and for the manufacture of sparkling wines. 673

203 **Malligand, Ed., jr., Paris.—Alcohol** tester. 673

204 **Pernollet, Jh., Paris.—Sieves, sort-**ers, and root knives. 673

205 **Tricourt, A., Reims.—Wine manu-**facturing machines. 673

206 **Chenaillier, Paris.—Evaporator.** 673

207 **Cicile, Larbre, Reims, Marne.—** Machines for cleaning bottles. 673

208 **Dornon, L., Lyons.—Gauzes for** bolting-rooms and sieves. 674

209 **Perard, V., Paris.—Sheep-shear-**ing machine. 674

210 **Fauqueux, A., La Ferté-Sous-**Jouarre, Seine and Marne.—Millstones. 674

211 **Durvie, Ivry-la-Bataille, Eure.—** Mechanical kneading-trough. 674

212 **Scheidecker, Ch., Paris.—Shearing** machines. 674

213 **Roger, jr., & Co., La Ferté-Sous-**Jouarre, Seine and Marne. — Millstones. 674

214 **Sensfelder, Arcueil, Seine.—Shear-**ing machines. 674

215 **Aubin & Baron, Paris.—Mill-**stones. 674

216 **Bailly & Co., La Ferté-Sous-Jou-**arre, Seine and Marne.—Millstones. 674

217 **Bertrand, J., & Co., La Ferté-Sous-**Jouarre.—Millstones. 674

Agricultural, Engineering, and Administration.

218 **Coignet, senior & junior, & Co.,** Paris.—Manure. 681

219 **Midi Phosphate Manufacturing** Co., Paris.—Phosphate of lime. 681

220 **Jacquand, senior & junior, Lyons.—** Animal charcoal, phosphates, etc. 681

221 **Solfatare de Pozzuoli Manufactur-**ing Co., Paris.—Artificial manure. 681

222 **Sensfelder, Arcueil, Seine.—Arti-**ficial manure. 681

223 **Tancrede Bros., Paris.—Animal** charcoal. 681

224 **Desfeux, Ph., Paris.—Models of** agricultural sheds. 683

---

225 **Brot, Leopold, Paris.**

a Furniture and mirrors with double shutters and triple front. 217

b Mirrors with gilt frames. 219

For classes of exhibits, indicated by numbers at end of entries, see Classification, pp. 12–14.

GERMANY.

(West of Nave, Columns 1 to 4.)

Forest, Agricultural, Vegetable, Animal Products.

Arboriculture and Forest Products.

1 Köerper & Co., Mannheim.—Resinous products in a manufactured state. 603

Agricultural Products.

1*a* Aly, August, Hamburg.—Barley, oats, grits, buckwheat, etc. 620

2 Noll, Joh. Balth., Giessen.—Cigars. 623

3 Grosskopf, L., Koenigsberg.—Cigarettes. 623

4 Eckstein, A. M., & Sons, Göttingen.—Tobacco and cigarettes. 623

5 Gaus, August, Baden-Baden.—Tobacco and cigarettes. 623

6 Landfried, P. J., Rauenburg.—Cigars. 623

7 Scherzinger, W., Stollhofen.—Tobacco and cigarettes. 623

8 Lotzbeck Bros., Lahr.—Snuff and tobacco. 623

9 Naumann, L., Dresden.—Spices. 623

10 Muller, A., Dresden.—Cigarettes. 623

Animal and Vegetable Products.

13 Köerper & Co., Mannheim.—Grease and oil. 652

16 Dessauer, A., Aschaffenburg.—Parchment glue. 652

17 Winter, Fr., Offenbach-on-Main.—Glue. 652

21 Leipsic Malt Factory, Schkeuditz, near Leipsic.—Malt. 656

22 Moskopf, Th., Fahr, near Neuwied.—Mustard. 656

24 Naumann, L., Dresden.—Extracts, essences, etc. 656

28 Schörke, A., Gorlitz.—Grape sugar, assorted syrups. 659

COLLECTIVE EXHIBIT OF GERMAN WINES. 660

29 Altenkirch, F., Lorch.
30 Dahlen, J. F. J., Lorch.
31 Germersheimer, Jac., Lorch.
32 Dahlen, F. K., Lorch.
33 Travers, Franz, Lorch.
34 Wittemann, Peter, Lorch.
35 Fendel, H. J., Lorch.
36 Jung, Joh. Ant., Assmanshausen.
37 Brück, Erwin, Assmanshausen.
38 Grün, Wilh., Assmanshausen.
39 Kerber, Pet. Jos., Assmanshausen.
40 Aumüller, Jac., Rüdesheim.
41 Brandmüller, J. B., Rüdesheim.
43 Dietrich & Co., Rüdesheim.
44 Dilthey, Sahl, & Co., Rüdesheim.
45 Ehrhardt, C., Rüdesheim.
46 Ehrhardt, J., Rüdesheim.
48 Jung, J. J., Rüdesheim.
49 Jung & Co., Rüdesheim.
50 Krass, J. A., Rüdesheim.
51 Meuschel, J. W., sr., Rüdesheim.
52 Schulz & Reuter, Rüdesheim.
53 Winkel & Rothenbach, Rüdesheim.
54 Burgeff, N., Geisenheim.
55 Höhl Bros., Geisenheim.
56 Lade, Fritz, Geisenheim.
57 Quitman, A., Geisenheim.
58 Rothe & Thorndike, Geisenheim.
59 Metternich, Prince von, Johannisberg.
60 Forst, J., Johannisberg.
61 Klein, Joh., Johannisberg.
61*a* Germont, L. F., Winkel.
62 Müller, Gottl., Winkel.
63 Cunibert, Baron von, Oestrich.
64 Peez, Ernst, Oestrich.
65 Rasch, Oestrich.
66 Steinheimer, C. J. B., Oestrich.
68 Lauer & Krämer, Eltville.
69 Nilkens, A., Eltville.
70 Preusel & Bachmann, Eltville.
72 Schmidt & Kett, Eltville.
73 Kindlinger, V., Neudorf.
74 König, J. B., Rauenthal.
75 Siegfried, Rauenthal.
76 Rosenstein, B., Wiesbaden.
77 Zais, Wilhelm, Wiesbaden.
78 Diener, H., Hochheim.
80 Feist Bros. & Sons, Frankfort-on-Main.
81 Kehrmann, Fr., Coblentz.
82 Buhl, F. P., Deidesheim.
82*a* Jordan, L. A., Deidesheim.
82*b* Schellhorn, Walbillich.
83 Feis, Louis, Deidesheim.
84 Eckel Bros., Deidesheim.
85 Seyler, Fr., Deidesheim.
86 Frölich, F. A., Edenkoben.
87 Vornberger, J. M., Würzburg.
87*a* Labroise Bros., Neustadt-on-Hardt.
88 Lang, F. J., Würzburg.
89 Oppmann, J., Würzburg.
91 Valckenberg, P. J., Worms.
92 Langenbach, J., & Sons, Worms.
93 Bach, A. H., Mayence.
95 Dreydelsohn & Co., Mayence.

For classes of exhibits, indicated by numbers at end of entries, see Classification, pp. 12–14.

Wines, Textile Substances, Machines, Implements.

95*a* Saarbach, E., & Co., Mayence.

96 Jäger & Son, Rüdesheim.

97 Meyer & Coblenz, Bingen.

98 Orb & Weiss, Westhofen.

99 Herbster, J., Sulzburg.

100 Durlacher, S., & Sons, Kippenheim.

101 Schütt, A., Bühl.

102 Rössler, A., Neuweier.

103 Brogsitter, P. F., Ahrweiler.

103*a* Kessler, C. E., & Co., Esslingen.

---

104 Häusler, C. S., Hirschberg, Silesia.—Wine and cider. 660

105 Rhenish Sparkling Wine Co., Schierstein.—Wine. 660

106 Henkell & Co., Mayence.—Wine. 660

107 Lindecke, A. G., Magdeburg.—Wines. 660

107*a* Wetterhahn, G., Mayence.—Wines. 660

108 Bäcker & Fier, Treves.—Liqueurs and brandies. 660

109 Behrensen, Th., Kiel.—Wines and brandies. 660

110 Boyens, P. W., Tönning.—Liqueurs and spirits. 660

111 Brumby, G., Luckau.—Bitters. 660

112 Dammann, L., & Cordes, Thorn.—Spirits, bitters, essences, etc. 660

113 Hoffmann, M. & J., Pfalzburg.—Liqueurs. 660

114 Kadach, J., Berlin.—Bitters and cherry-juice. 660

115 Keiler, J. S., Dantzic.—Liqueurs. 660

116 Landauer & Macholl, Heilbronn.—Liqueurs. 660

117 Stein, G. & L., Offenburg.—Liqueurs. 660

118 Stibbè, H., Cologne.—Liqueurs and essences. 660

119 Underberg-Albrecht, H., Rheinberg.—Bitters. 660

120 Drouven, Jac., & Co., Coblentz.—Liqueurs, arrack punch-syrup. 660

121 Gilka, J. A., Berlin.—Liqueurs and spirits. 660

122 Lehment, Fr. & C., Kiel.—Liqueurs and spirits. 660

123 Köpp, Th., & Son, Wesel.—Spirit of vinegar and extracts. 660

124 Ulex, G. F., successors, Neuhaus-on-the-Oste.—Bitters. 660

125 Kantorowicz, H., Posen.—Liqueurs and fruit juices. 660

126 Lazar Brothers, Königsberg, Prussia.—Fruit juices. 660

127 Naumann, Fr., Delitzsch.—Liqueurs and fruit juices. 660

128 Bernhardt, A., Breslau.—Essences and liquors. 660

129 Schneider & Schorn, Magdeburg.—Essence of Jamaica rum. 660

130 Buck Bros., Lübeck.—Vinegar. 660

131 Stengel, W., Leipzig.—Potato brandy. 660

132 Meyer, Edward, Stadthagen.—Herb-bitters. 660

133 Ackermann, Louis, Berlin.—Liqueurs. 660

133*a* Kirchner, A., & Co., Deedesdorf.—Liquors. 660

134 Wiedenbrug, H. T., Barmbeck.—Liqueurs. 660

COLLECTIVE EXHIBIT OF BAVARIAN HOPS, BEER, AND LITERATURE RELATING THERETO. 660

135 Dreifuss & Binswanger, Nuremberg.

136 Sahlmann Bros., Fürth.

137 City Council of Spalt.

138 Carl, J., Nuremberg.

139 Homann, C., Nuremberg.

140 Bottinger, H. F., Würzburg.

141 Böutteville, Baron von Mering.

142 Geisel, L., Neustadt-on-the-Hardt.

143 Pschorr Brewery, Munich.

144 Baron von Thüngen Brewery, Weissenbach.

145 Weltz, H., Speier.

---

146 Bavarian Joint-Stock Brewery, Aschaffenburg.—Beer. 660

146*a* Sick, Chr., Speier.—Beer. 660

147 Dortmund Brewery, Aix-la-Chapelle.—Beer. 660

148 Friedrichshöhe Joint-stock Brewery, Berlin.—Beer. 660

149 Hildebrand, J., Pfungstadt.—Beer. 660

150 Overbeck, Peter, Dortmund.—Beer. 660

152 Berlin Brewing Co., Tivoli, Berlin.—Beer. 660

152*a* Roeper, J. F., Neuwied.—Macaroni, vermicelli, tapioca, etc. 661

152*b* Stollwerk Bros., Cologne.—Chocolates, etc. 661

Textile Substances of Vegetable or Animal Origin.

154 Mens, R. von, Carlsdorf, Silesia.—Merino wool. 667

155 Stein, H., & Co., Frankfort-on-Main.—Spun horse-hair. 669

Machines, Implements and Processes of Manufacture.

156 Mayer & Co., Kalk, near Cologne.—Winnowing and sorting machine. 672

157 Royal Wurtemberg Furnaces, Friedrichsthal.—Scythes, choppers, etc. 674

158 Joacks & Behrns, Lubeck.—Model of a set of millstones. 674

Agriculture Engineering and Administration.

161 Raumer, C. von, Kunnersdorf, Silesia.—Works and models relating to drainage and irrigation. 681

For classes of exhibits, indicated by numbers at end of entries, see Classification, pp. 12–14.

AUSTRIA.

(*West of West Aisle, Columns 1 to 4.*)

Forest, Agricultural, Animal and Vegetable Products.

Arboriculture and Forest Products.

1 Weissmann, David, Adlersberg, & Isaac Leib, Perehinsko, Gallicia.—Sounding-board wood. 600

2 Frankl, I. G. & L., Vienna.—Austrian timber for furniture manufacturers. 600

Pomology.

4 Zierotin, Countess Gabriel von, Charles Pohl, chief gardener, Blauda, Moravia.—Gooseberry and currant bushes, two different fruits growing on the same stem. 610

6 Markó & Weyden, Budapest.—Turkish prunes. 611

Agricultural Products.

7 Lyka, Demeter, Pázmánd, Hungary. —Wheat. 620

8 Solnitzky & Mittler, Brunn.
a Malt and barley. 620
b Pulses. 621

9 Gogl, Dr., jr., Zeno, Krems.—Mustard. 623

10 Chleborad, Franz, Ladislav, Mraiditz.—Hops. 623

12 Tanzer Bros., Prague.—Hops. 623

13 Schwarz & Sons, Benjamin, Auscha, Bohemia.—Hops. 623

14 Schary, Johann Michael, Prague.—Hops. 623

Water Animals, Fish Culture and Apparatus.

18 Topich, Antonio, Lissa, Dalmatia.—Preserved fish. 641

Animal and Vegetable Products.

19 Kreitner & Sons, David, Hohenbruck, Bohemia.—Leather. 652

20 Ieleinek, Adolph, Lieben, Bohemia. —Glove leather. 652

22 Ianesch, Edward, Klagenfurt, Karnthen.—Leather. 652

23 Hoffman, I. and S., Klagenfurt, Karnthen.—Leather. 652

24 Foges, I., Gaudenzdorf, near Vienna. —Leather, calf and goat skins. 652

25 Eckstein, H. M., Lieben.—Kid leather. 652

26 Cernstein, Anton V., Pardubitz, Bohemia.—Cow leather and calf skin. 652

27 Breuer, Miromil, Elbeteintz, Bohemia.—Patent leather. 652

30 Suess, A. H., & Sons, Vienna.—Leather. 652

31 Schmitt, Franz, Rehberg, near Krems.—Leather. 652

32 Schmalzl, George, Gaudenzdorf, near Vienna.—Leather, skins. 652

33 Neuner, Christof, Klagenfurt and Trieste.—Leather. 652

34 Mehlshmidt, Franz, Prague.—Kid leather. 652

34*a* Nachtmann, Jacob, Tannwald.
a Honey. 654
b Raspberry syrup. 659
c Wine and liquors. 660

36 Tschurtschenthaler, Alois, Botzen. —Conserved and dried fruits. 656

37 Sandpichler, Leopold, Gorz.—Candied fruit. 656

37*a* Gfall, Josef Anton, Innsbruck.—Condensed meat and milk. 656

38 Kaufmann, M., Brunn.—Moravian malt. 657

39 Solnitzky & Mittler, Brunn.
a Barley. 657
b Malt. 660

41 Rosenthal, I., Vienna.—Wheat, wheaten flour. 657

42 Chiozza, Luigi, Cervignano, near Trieste.—Maize products. 658

43 Frizzi, Luigi, Trient.—Wine. 660

45 Auchmann, F., Marburg, Styria.—Champagne. 660

46 Archleb, Josef, The Farms, Kvasnei. —Liquor. 660

47 Abeles, Heinrich, Vienna.—Wine. 660

48 Magazzin, Matteo, Zara.—Liquors. 660

49 Luxardo, Girolamo, Zara, Dalmatia. —Liquors. 660

51 Lord & Co., F., Vienna.—Liquor. 660

53 Siebenbürger Wine Association, Klausenburg.—Wines. 660

54 Cosmacendi, Anton, Zara.—Liquors. 660

55 Mumelter, Alois, Bozen.—Tyrol wines. 660

56 Kriehuber, Alois Edler von, Marburg, Styria.—Wine. 660

57 Königstädtler Bros., Neusatz, Hungary.—Spirit alcohol. 660

58 Ganz, Joseph, Dornberg, near Gorz. —Wine. 660

59 Fischer, Johann, jr., & Franz Hubert, Presburg, Hungary.—Champagne. 660

60 Dreher, Anton, Kleinschwechat, near Vienna.—Beer. 660

61 Dalbello, Antonio, Spalato, Dalmatia.—Liquor. 660

62 Brewery Administration, Budweis, Bohemia.—Beer. 660

For classes of exhibits, indicated by numbers at end of entries, see Classification, pp. 12–14.

Animal and Vegetable Products, Textiles, Implements.

64 **Borhegyi Bros., Gaya, Moravia.**—Wine. 660

65 **Wretzl, Michael, Marburg, Styria.**—Wine. 660

66 **A. Schwartzer's Successors,** Edward & Emmerich Grossinger, Vienna.—Wine. 660

67 **Sessler, Moritz & Leopold, Tyrnau,** Hungary.—Malt. 660

68 **Schnabel, Julius, Orávitzá, Hungary.**—Slivovitz brandy. 660

69 **Schenkel, August, Gut Lukaufzen,** near Luttenberg.—Wine. 660

70 **Scarizza Giovanni, Spalato, Dalmatia.**—Liquors. 660

70*a* **Stampalia, Tommaso, Zard.—Maraschino.** 660

71 **Romer & Son, I., Vienna.—Wine.** 660

72 **Reiser, Dr. Othmar, Vienna.**—Wine. 660

74 **Prima Societa Enologica Dalmatia,** Spalato, Dalmatia.—Wine. 660

75 **Pokorny, Franz, Agram, Croatia.**—Fruit distillery, wine. 660

76 **Perko, Francis, Marburg, Styria.**—Wine. 660

77 **Noziczka, L. C., & W. Umgelter,** Brunn.—Malt. 660

78 **Mittler & Co., Brunn.—Malt.** 660

79 **Strakosch, Ignaz, Gross Seelovitz,** Moravia.—Liquor essences. 660

80 **Neuman & Sons, Emanuel, Waitzen, Hungary.**—Vinegar essences. 660

81 **Spreng, Fridolin, Graz.—Biscuits.** 661

82 **Brichta, Jacob, Trencsin, Hungary.**—Juniper berries and oil. 662

Textile Substances of Vegetable or Animal Origin.

83 **Russ & Co., M. H., Prague.**—Hops. 666

83*a* **Zeschks, L., Agram.—Rags.** 666

84 **Land & Forest Economy District** Union, Neustadtl, Moravia.—Flax. 666

85 **Narbuth, Johann, Palanka, Hungary.**—Hemp. 666

86 **Károlyi, Count Alois, Stampfen,** Hungary.—Sheep wool in fleeces and rolls. 667

87 **Hunyady, Count Emerich, Uermenyi,** Hungary.—Wool fleeces. 667

88 **Sheep-wool Washing Co., Budapest.**—Cleaned wool. 667

Machines, Implements, and Processes of Manufacture.

89 **Auer, Josef, Senftenberg, near** Krems.—Vine shears, gardeners' and insect scissors, pruning saw, and sheep shears. 670

91 **Austrian Commission, Vienna.**—Scythes and sickles. 672

92 **Mosdorfer, Balthasar, Weiz, Styria.**—Sickles. 672

93 **Reibstein, Ignaz, Bubenc, Bohemia.**—Beehives and utensils. 674

Agricultural Engineering and Administration.

94 **Wärmer, Sigmund, Vienna.—Drain** pipes. 680

95 **Konnstein, Gottfried, Prague.**—Ether and essences. 681

96 **Sheep-wool Washing Co., Budapest.**—Potash. 681

97 **Haas & Rosenfeld, Gaya.—Ether.** 681

For classes of exhibits, indicated by numbers at end of entries, see Classification, pp. 12–14.

(N. B.—Other Austrian Exhibits in this Department are installed in the Main Building, and catalogued in that volume.)

SWITZERLAND.

(NOTE.—*The Agricultural Exhibit of Switzerland is installed in the Main Building, and catalogued in that volume.*)

BELGIUM.

(NOTE.—*The Agricultural Exhibit of Belgium is installed in the Main Building, and catalogued in that volume.*)

NETHERLANDS.

(*West of West Aisle, Columns 3 to 5.*)

Agricultural, Animal, Vegetable Products.

Arboriculture and Forest Products.

1 **Thyssen, C. J. F.**—Sieve frames. 600

2 **Kleintjes, J., Rotterdam.**—Plant 100 years old. 601

3 **Hulskamp, F. A., Amsterdam.**—Cork. 604

Agricultural Products.

4 **Dutch Agricultural Society** (collective exhibit.—Agriculture, horticulture, arboriculture. 620

5 **Agricultural Association** (collective exhibit), Geldrian.—Agricultural products. 620

6 **Zeeland Association for Encouragement** of Agriculture & Cattle-Breeding (collective exhibit), Middleburg.—Seeds, dye-woods, plants, and photographs of cattle. 620

7 **Bouma, N. G. & J. G., Sneek.**—Buckwheat. 620

8 **Poel, Cz. P. van der, Brielle.**
a Wheat, barley, oats. 620
b Cabbage. 621
c Seeds. 624

9 **Post, C. G. van der, Gouda.**—Cigars. 623

10 **Bleckmann, A. & B. C., & Van der Poel, H., Arnhem.**—Cigars. 623

11 **Mignot, A. J., & de Block, A. A. M., Eindhoven.**—Cigars. 623

12 **Jagt, P. G. van der, & Francois, J., Utrecht.**—Cigars. 623

13 **Koppen, H. T., & Son, Leerdam.**—Cigars. 623

Water Animals, Fish Culture and Apparatus.

14 **Maas, A. E., Scheveningen.**—Boats, nets, hooks, etc. 647

Animal and Vegetable Products.

15 **Heil, L. W., Haarlem.**—Edam cheese. 651

16 **Goede, D., Alkmaar.**—Cheese. 651

17 **Vliet, A. van, Bergambacht.**—Cheese and butter. 651

18 **Jong, de, M. & K., Hoorn.**—Edam cheese. 651

21 **Draisma van Valkenburg, S., Leeuwarden.**—Liver-oil containing iodine and iron. 652

22 **Heijnsbergen, P. van, Zaandam.**—Liver-oil containing iron. 652

23 **Klütgen, J. H., Rotterdam.**—Bed-feathers. 653

24 **Visser, J., Amersfoort.**—Brown and white wax. 654

25 **Surie, Widow J. W., & Son, & Co., Rotterdam.**—Preserved eatables. 656

26 **Nieuwenhuijs, J. H., jr., & Co., Amsterdam.**—Conserved eatables in tins, boxes, and bottles. 656

28 **Hoogenstraaten, D. A. J., Leiden.**—Vegetables and fruit in cans and boxes. 656

29 **Wolff, M. B., Amersfoort.**—Flour, ground and unground. 657

30 **Schober, J. H. S., Utrecht.**—Flour. 657

For classes of exhibits, indicated by numbers at end of entries, see Classification, pp. 12–14.

Animal and Vegetable Products.

31 Van Marken, J. C., jr., Delft.
a Corn. 657
b Alcohol. 660
c Corn cakes. 661
d Oil. 662

32 Grootes, Pz. M., Westzaan.—Cacao, chocolate, and chocolatine. 658

33 Driessen, C. A., J. P., & H. T., Rotterdam. — Cacao, chocolate, and cacao-butter. 658

34 Haagen, R. C. van, Utrecht.—Cacao, cacao-butter, and chocolate. 658

35 Egberts, B. H., Dalfsen.—Succory. 658

36 Duijvis, J., Koog-aan-de-Zaan.— Starch. 658

37 Veenhoven, Schuringa, & Co., Wil-dervank.—Potato-flour. 658

38 Sloet van Marxveld, G., Baron, Vol-lenhoven.—Syrup in bottles. 659

39 Verweij, N., & Co., Tiel.—Sugar of grape and potato-meal. 659

40 De Bont, M. J., Amsterdam.—Con-fectionery and chocolate, in forms and moulds. 659

41 Visser, J., Amersfoort.—Brown and white mead. 660

42 Pollen, L. P. M., Rotterdam.—Liq-uors. 660

43 Schade van Westrum, J. C., Schie-dam.—Gin. 660

44 Kiderlen, E., Delfshaven.—Alcohol and potash. 660

45 Bal, J. J., Middelburg.—Red currant wine. 660

46 Catz, S., Pekel, A.—Bitters and liq-uors. 660

47 Groen, Gz. J. B., Amsterdam.—Bit-ters and wine. 660

48 Stibbe, Lz. G., Kampen.—Fine liq-uors and bitters. 660

49 Nolet, J. J. G., Schiedam.—Gin and spirits. 660

50 Bootz, Erven Wed, F. A., Amster-dam.—Liquors. 660

51 Blankenheijm, J. J. M., & Lede, C. A. E. van, Rotterdam.—Gin. 660

52 Hoppe, P., Amsterdam.—Gin, liq-uors, and distillations. 660

53 Bols, de Erven Lucas, Amsterdam. —Fine liquors. 660

54 Oostra, G. Wildervank, Groningen. —Liquor and elixir. 660

55 Hofman, A. J. T., Woerden.—Liq-uors, bitters, extracts, and spirits. 660

56 Wynand, Fockink, Amsterdam.— Fine liquors. 660

57 Houtman, A., & Co., Schiedam.— Gin. 660

58 Valk, J. van der, & Co., Delfshaven. —Gin made of grain double distilled. 660

59 Zuijlekom, van Levert, & Co., Am-sterdam—Fine liquors, bitters, gin, brandy, etc. 660

60 Meder, J. J., Schiedam.—Swan gin. 660

61 Levert & Co., Amsterdam.—Liq-uors. 660

62 Rademakers, A. C., Delfshaven.— Gin. 660

63 Smits, F. H. M., Breda.—Strong beer. 660

64 Van Dulken, Weiland, & Co., Rotter-dam.—Gin, brandy, and alcohol. 660

65 Lensvelt, G., Gravenhage.—Table-biscuit, cake, ship-bread. 661

66 Ulrich, W. D., Rotterdam.—Ship-biscuit. 661

67 De Jongh, Wz. D., Dordrecht.— Vegetable oils and seed cakes. 662

68 Kruijsmulder, Cz. D., Amsterdam.— Vegetable oils. 662

69 Dutch Association for Encourage-ment of Flax Industry, Rotterdam.—Flax and linseed. 666

70 Gorter Brothers, Dokkum.— Flax. 666

71 Van Casteel, A. F., Rotterdam.— Holland, Freeland, and Iceland flax. 666

---

72 Mulder, L., Arnhem.—Agricultural newspaper. 306

For classes of exhibits, indicated by numbers at end of entries, see Classification, pp. 12–14.

DENMARK.

(NOTE.—*The Agricultural Exhibit of Denmark is installed in the Main Building, and catalogued in that volume.*)

SWEDEN.

(West Avenue, Columns 6 to 10.)

Forest, Agricultural, Animal, and Vegetable Products.

Agriculture, Arboriculture, and Forest Products.

1 **New Gellivara Co. (limited), Lulea.**—Fir timber grown at the latitude of 67° N.; specimens of lumber. 600

Agricultural Products.

3 **Fogelmark, Sixten, Ava, Lulea.**—Cereals. 620

4 **Hagendahl, C. A., Orebro.**
a Cereals. 620
b Seeds. 624

5 **Hofmeister, Ch., Ingelstad, Kristianstad.**—Cereals. 620

6 **Hultenberg, C. A., Borgholm.**—Barley. 620

6*a* **New Gellivara Co. (limited), Lulea.**—Agricultural products. 620

7 **Kalmar Agricultural Society, Westervik.**—Cereals. 620

8 **Norbotten Agricultural Society, Lulea.**—Agricultural products. 620

10 **Platen, Count Carl von, Örbyhus.**—
a Cereals. 624
b Seeds of forage plants. 620

12 **Scheële, G. von, Kilanda, Göteborg.**
a Cereals. 620
b Grass seeds. 624

14 **Stenström, O. E., Gardsjö, Karlstad.**—Cereals. 620

15 **Upsala Agricultural Society, Upsala.**
a Cereals. 620
b Seeds. 624

16 **Westerbottens Agricultural Society, Umea.**—Cereals. 620

17 **Westmanlands Agricultural Society, Stenby, Strömsholm.**
a Cereals. 620
b Seeds. 624

19 **Orebro Agricultural Society, Orebro, Nora.**—Cereals. 620

21 **Berggren, D. & J., Stockholm.**—Tobacco. 623

22 **Dahl, P., Carlshamn.**—Snuff. 623

23 **Hennig & Papenhagen, Kalmar.**—Chicory. 623

Water Animals, Fish Culture, and Apparatus.

27 **Amundson, Mrs. C. M., Uddevalla.**—Oyster anchovy. 642

28 **Andersson, Gustaf, Fjellbacka.**—Anchovy and sardines. 642

29 **Bergström, H. C., Lysekil.**—Anchovy and herrings. 642

30 **Ericsson, N. O., Tangen, Lysekil.**—Anchovies and herrings. 642

31 **Hallgren, J. J., Gullholmen, Oroust.**—Anchovies and herrings. 642

32 **Royal Swedish Commission, Stockholm.**
a Pickled fish. 642
b Instruments and apparatus for fishing. 647

33 **Lundgren, P. W., Stockholm.**—Preserved fish. 642

34 **Lysell, Aug., Lysekil.**—Anchovies. 642

35 **Nilsson, Edv., Grebbestad.**—Preserved mackerel. 642

Animal and Vegetable Products.

38 **Wästfelt, Carl C., Kölingsholm, Mullsjö.**—Rennet. 651

40 **Ericsson, Anders, Stockholm.**—Calfskins. 652

41 **Johannesson, C. S., Stockholm.**—Leather. 652

44 **Frommel, C. J., Göteborg.**
a Preserved fruits. 656
b Confections. 661

45 **Wikström, Zacharias, Stockholm.**—Preserved vegetables. 656

46 **French Steam Flour Mills, Landskrona.**—Flour and grit. 657

47 **Scheële, G. von, Kilanda, Göteborg.**—Flour and other products of grinding. 657

48 **French Steam Flour-Mills, Ystad.**—Flour and other products of grinding. 657

52 **Berg, C. G., Karlshamn.**—Punch and whisky. 660

53 **Bergen, J. N. von, & Son, Karlshamn.**—Punch. 660

54 **Broddelius & Akerman, Göteborg.**—Punch. 660

55 **Cederlund's, J., Sons, Stockholm.**—Punch. 660

56 **Creutz, A., Mariefred.**—Punch. 660

57 **Dahlheim & Engström, Stockholm.**—Punch. 660

59 **Högstedt & Co., Stockholm.**—Punch. 660

60 **Moboda Manufacturing Co., Moboda.**—Spirits made from lichens. 660

61 **Tulldahl, A. H., Landskrona.**—Pale ale. 660

62 **Petterson, Otto, Stockholm.**—Punch. 660

63 **Platin, C. G., & Co., Göteborg.**—Punch. 660

64 **Thalin, Waldemar, Nyköping.**—Punch. 660

For classes of exhibits, indicated by numbers at end of entries, see Classification, pp. 12–14.

Machines, Implements, Engineering, and Administration.

65 Wallis, A. B., Dybeck, Ystad.—Ale. 661

65a Ullander, A., Upsala.—Punch. 660

66 Feith, H. J., & Son, Upsala.—Biscuits. 661

67 Royal Swedish Commission, Stockholm.—Dried bread. 661

Machines, Implements, and Processes of Manufacture.

69 Eklundh, L. P., Ulricehamn.—Plows. 670

70 Göteborg Machine Co. (limited), Göteborg.—Plows. 670

72 Petterson, C. E., Elfdalen.—Scythes. 672

73 Andersson, J., Orebro.—Cow and sheep bells. 675

74 Atterling, C., Orebro.—Dairy apparatus. 675

75 Kallinge Iron Works, Malmö.—Dairy utensils of iron and pewter. 675

76 Rehnström, W., Köping.—Drawing of dairy-houses and utensils. 675

Agricultural Engineering and Administration.

79 Friestedt, A. W., Stockholm.—Commercial fertilizers. 681

80 Betou, P. D. in de, Stockholm.—Artificial manures. 681

81 Superphosphate Manufacturing Co., Stockholm.—Fertilizers. 681

84 Löfvenskiöld, Ch., Mariestad.—Drawings of farm-houses. 683

For classes of exhibits, indicated by numbers at end of entries, see Classification, pp. 12–14.

NORWAY.

(*West of West Aisle, Columns 6 to 10.*)

Forest, Agricultural, Animal, and Vegetable Products, Fish Culture.

Arboriculture and Forest Products.

1 **Holst, Chr., Ladegaardsöen, Christiania.**—Samples of Norwegian wood. 600

4 **Holmen's Sawing & Planing Mills,** Drammen.—Grooved and tongued flooring boards and mouldings. 600

5 **Koldfossen's Bobbin Works, near** Bergen.—Blocks and bobbins of birch and alder, condenser props, etc. 600

6 **Thams & Co., M., Orkedal.**—Trunks of trees, planks, battens, staves, cornices, cases, etc. 600

Agricultural Products.

7 **Schirod, Chr., Aker.**—Wheat, rye, corn, and barley. 620

8 **Holst, Chr., Ladegaardsöen, Christiania.**—Cereals in ear and seeds. 620

9 **Agricultural School, Aas near Christiania.**
a Oats, rye, and barley. 620
b Seeds. 624

10 **Rosenkrone, Baron, Rosendal.**—Grain. 620

11 **Stend Agricultural School.**
a Corn. 620
b Potatoes. 622

11*a* **Brovold, T.**—Grain. 620

11*b* **Torkildsen, J.**—Grain. 620

11*c* **Svanoe, Chr.**—Grain. 620

Land Animals.

12 **Holst, Chr., Ladegaardsöen, Christiania.**—Photographs of Telmark cows and description of the race. 631

Marine Animals, Fish Culture and Apparatus.

13 **Museum of Bergen, Bergen.**
a Mammals. 640
b Fishes. 641
c Crustaceans. 643
d Mollusks, oysters, etc., stuffed and in alcohol. 644

15 **Bergens Rögeri, Bergen.**—Red herrings. 642

16 **Board of Commerce, Bergen.**
a Herrings, cods, lings, saithes, tusks, haddocks, etc., pickled and dried. 642
b Fish-oil, fish-roes. 646

17 **Board of Commerce, Alesund.**
a Dried and salted fish. 642
b Collection of fishing tackle. 647

18 **Hjul & Platou, Christiania.**—Anchovies. 642

19 **Johnsen, Chr., Christiansund.**—Salted and dried cod. 642

21 **Mohn, Peter, Bergen.**—White herrings. 642

22 **Nordrock, Wm., Christiania.**—Anchovies. 642

23 **Tellefsen, Mrs. Rina, Christiania.**—Anchovies. 642

24 **Smith, Mrs. Gina, Christiania.**—Anchovies. 642

25 **Soyland, L. B., Flekkefjord.**—Preserved fish. 642

26 **Dons, Henrik, Christiania.**—Fish and anchovies. 642

27 **Helgesen, H. A., Aalesund.**—Preserved salmon, lobsters, etc. 642

28 **Ronneberg, Carl A., Aalesund.**—Salt fish. 642

29 **Hjorth, Fr., Fredrikstad.**—Anchovies. 642

30 **Lund, Georg, Christiania.**—Anchovies. 642

31 **Thorne, Chr. Aug., Moss.**—Anchovies. 642

32 **Egidius, Peter, Bergen.**—Herring and anchovies. 642

33 **Bordewich & Co., Lyngvær.**—Fish-meal, fish-glue, caviar, fish-oil. 646

34 **Dahl, Jens. O., Havöen.**—Cod and herring nets, cod-lines. 647

35 **Erichsen, Thomas, Bergen.**—Fish-hooks. 647

36 **Fagerheim Net Company, Bergen.**—Salmon and herring seines, cod, mackerel, and herring nets. 647

37 **Kraasby Brothers, Aalesund.**—Bait for cod-lines. 647

38 **Falck, Ytter, Christiania.**—Norwegian fishing sled with implements. 647

39 **Bergen Glass Works, Bergen.**—Buoys and floats for fishing nets and lines. 647

Animal and Vegetable Products.

40 **Rosing's, A., widow, Christiania.**
a Condensed milk. 651
b Crackers of fishmeal. 661

40*a* **Stend Agricultural School.**—Butter. 651

41 **Lund, Georg, Christiania.**—Preserved old cheese. 651

42 **Klem, Hansen, & Co., Trondhjem.**—Leather and belting. 652

43 **Meyer, Samuel B., Bergen.**—Leather. 652

44 **Hallen, J. P., Christiania.**—Leather. 652

45 **Fossen's Tannery, Flekkefjord.**—Leather. 652

For classes of exhibits, indicated by numbers at end of entries, see Classification, pp. 12–14.

Animal and Vegetable Products, Implements, Engineering.

46 Dalen's Tannery, Flekkefjord.—Leather. 652

48 Haar & Wesnaes, Stavanger.—Preserved meats, etc. 656

49 Helgesen, H. A., Aalesund.—Preserved meats, etc. 656

50 Stavanger Preserving Company, Stavanger.—Preserved meats, beef, fowls, fish, milk, cream, etc. 656

51 Dons, Henrik, Christiania.—Preserved meats, game, poultry, soups. 656

52 Tellefsen, Mrs. Rina, Christiania.—Preserved game. 656

53 Norwegian Condensed Milk Company, Christiania.—Condensed milk. 656

54 Thorne, Chr. Aug., Moss.—Preserved meat and vegetables. 656

55 Norwegian Preserving Co., Mandal.—Preserved meats and vegetables. 656

56 Christiania Brewery, Christiania.—Pale ale. 660

57 Dahl, E. C., Trondhjem.—Pale ale. 660

58 Forseth, O. N., & Co., Christiania.—Pale ale. 660

59 Frydenlund Brewery, Christiania.—Pale ale. 660

60 Hamar Brewery, Hamar.—Pale ale. 660

61 Kongsberg Brewery, Kongsberg.—Pale ale. 660

63 Lysholm, Jorgen B., Trondhjem.—Norwegian brandy and punch. 660

64 Poulsen, H., & Co., Christiania.—Arrack punch. 660

65 Ruud, J. A., Christiania.—Pale ale from Moss brewery, Norwegian corn brandy. 660

66 Aass, P. L., Drammen.—Beer. 660

68 Wriedt, Chr., Drammen.—Beer. 660

69 Tandberg, Frants, Drammen.—Norwegian cordials. 660

70 Salicath, Oscar, Christiania.—Sugar-drops and punch. 660

71 Anisdahl, R. O., Skien.—Drops and peppermint. 662

Machines, Implements, and Processes of Manufacture.

72 Cathrineholm's Foundry, Fredrickshald.—Agricultural implements. 670

72*a* Stend Agricultural School.—Plows. 670

73 Rosing, Ulrik, Christiania.—Mask for killing cattle. 674

Agricultural Engineering and Administration.

74 Norwegian Fish Guano Company, Christiania.—Fish guano. 681

75 Bordewich & Co., Lyngvær.—Fish guano. 681

76 Foyn, Sven, Tonsberg.—Fish guano. 681

77 Holst, Chr., Ladegaardsöen, Christiania.—Norwegian artificial manure. 681

77*a* Foyn, Sven, Tonsberg.—Whale oil, stearine. (*See Department II., Main Building.*) 201

77*b* Board of Commerce, Aalesund.—Models of fishing boats. 594

77*c* Museum of Bergen, Bergen.—Models of fishing boats; fisherman's hut and ice store. 594

For classes of exhibits, indicated by numbers at end of entries, see Classification, pp. 12–14.

ITALY.

(*West of East Avenue, Columns 1 to 4.*)

Fruits, Agricultural, Animal, Vegetable Products.

Arboriculture and Forest Products.

1 Favare, Marquis Delle, Palermo.—Sumac leaves. 602

2 Romano, Gaetano, Palermo.—Sumac. 602

3 Cernigliano, Vizzi Carmelo, Trapani.—Sumac leaves. 602

4 Castorina & Parlato, Catania.—Sumac. 602

5 Scala, Baron Sciacca della, Palermo.—Sumac. 602

6 Aula, Domenico, & Co., Trapani.—Sumac. 602

7 Special Committee of Salerno, Salerno.—Manna. 603

8 Chamber of Commerce and Arts, of Bari.—Sweet almonds, mustard seed. 605

9 Parlato, Luigi, Syracuse, Sicily.—Almonds. 605

10 Niceforo, Nicola, Catania.—Hazel nuts. 605

11 Elia, Antonino, & Sons, Catania.—Pistachio almonds, flax seed, hazel nuts, mustard seed. 605

12 Agricultural Committee of Palermo.—Collection of seeds. 605

13 Mazzullo, Cav. Luigi, Messina.—Dried nuts. 605

14 Council of Polizzi, Generosa, Palermo.—Avellane nuts. 605

Pomology.

15 Rossi, Cav. Cesard Leopardi, Comiso, Syracuse.—Olives. 611

16 Crispo, Monceada Carlo, Catania.—Lemons, oranges. 611

17 Chamber of Commerce and Arts, of Bari.—Olives. 611

18 Lanzara, Raffaele, Salerno.—Lemons, oranges. 611

Agricultural Products.

19 Ciaccio, F. Paul, Palermo.—Various grains. 620

20 Agrarian Colony of S. Martino, Palermo.—Grains. 620

21 Grande Latino, Baron Corrado, & Bros., Avola, Palermo.—Grain products. 620

22 Porcari, Baron Angiolo, Palermo.—Grain products. 620

23 Fornasa, Vincenzo, Cologna Veneta, Verona.—Various cereals. 620

24 Ferrarini Bros. & Co., Formigine, Modena.—Rice. 620

25 Malinverni, Secondo, Vercelli, Novara.—Rice. 620

26 Scocchiolini, Adone, Rome.—Mustard. 623

Water Animals, Fish Culture and Apparatus.

27 Avellino, Antonio, Leghorn.—Sardines in oil. 642

28 Stiassi, Filippo, Bologna.—Eels. 642

Animal and Vegetable Products.

29 Agrarian Committee of Chiavari.
a Cheese. 651
b Fruits. 656
c Wine and vinegar. 660

30 Guscetti, E., Milan.
a Parmesan and Gorgonzola cheese. 651
b Sausages. 656

31 Baldini, Agostino, & Co., Pescia, Lucca.—Sole leather. 652

32 Aste, D. Stefano, Public Slaughter House, Florence.—Albumen. 652

33 Casarino, Mariellus, St. Gottard, Genoa.—Leather. 652

34 Fornari, Antonio J. Batta, Fabriano, Ancona.—Leather. 652

35 Mercurelli, Pietro, Fabriano, Ancona.—Sole and colored leather. 652

36 Baluffi, Nicola, & Co., Ancona.—Dressed hides, leather for saddlery. 652

37 Varale, Antonio, Biella, Turin.—Dressed hides. 652

38 Banfi, Giuseppe Flavio, Milan.—Glue. 652

39 Fibbi, Raffaele, Fabriano, Ancona.—Glue and size. 652

40 Fino, Luigi, & Co., Turin.—Albumen. 653

41 Tramontani, D., Bologna.—Honey. 654

42 Brolo, Duke Federigo Lancia di, Palermo.—Honey of orange flower. 654

43 Scala, Baron Sciacca della, Palermo.—Honey and wax. 654

44 Morandi, Pietro, Milan.
a Wax. 654
b Liquors. 660

45 Reali, Giuseppe & Gavazzi, Ercole, Venice.—Wax. 654

46 Bartolucci-Godolini Brothers, Rome.—Honey. 654

47 Acclimatization and Agricultural Society of Palermo.
a Honey. 654
b Fruits in alcohol. 656

For classes of exhibits, indicated by numbers at end of entries, see Classification, pp. 12–14.

Animal and Vegetable Products, Wines.

48 **Giannelli, Raffaello, Sienna.**
a Honey. 654
b Juniper berries. 656

49 **Massardo, Nicolo, Sampierdarena,** Genoa.—Preserves. 656

50 **Figatner, Enrico, Milan.—Dried** meat. 656

51 **Troia, Alfri, Syracuse.—Paste for** soup. 656

52 **Contessini, Gerini & Co., Leghorn.** —Candied fruits. 656

53 **Curry, Giacomo, Leghorn.—Pre-**serves. 656

54 **Bougleuse Bros. & Co., Leghorn.—** Paste for soup. 656

55 **Klein, Enrico, Leghorn.—Candied** fruits. 656

56 **Samoggia, Gaet. & Brothers, Bo-**logna. — Bologna sausages and salted meats. 656

57 **Lanzarini Brothers, Bologna.—Sau-**sages and salted meats. 656

58 **Colombini, Ulisse, Bologna.—Sau-**sages and salted meats. 656

59 **Serrazanetti, Giovanni Anzola, Bo-**logna.—Tomato sauce and preserved tomatoes. 656

60 **Nenzioni Brothers, Bologna.—Pre-**served tomatoes. 656

61 **Zappoli Brothers, Bologna.—Bolog-**na sausages and salted meats. 656

62 **Grillini, Nanni & Co., Bologna.—** Sausages and salted meats. 656

63 **Zanetti, Guido, Bologna.—Sausages** and salted meats. 656

64 **Bordoni, Natale & Co., Bologna.—** Sausages and salted meats. 656

65 **Bassi, Medando, & Ugo Brothers,** Bologna.—Sausages and salted meats. 656

66 **Tacconi, Paolo, Bologna. —Sausa-**ges and salted meats. 656

67 **Orsi, Raphael, Bologna.—Sausages** and salted meats. 656

68 **Frigieri, Giuseppe, Modena.—** Hams, bologna sausages, etc. 656

69 **Bellantani, Giuseppe, Modena.—** Bologna sausages and salted meats. 656

70 **Zironi, Giovanni, Fiorano, Mode-**nese.—Salted meats. 656

71 **Forni, Alessandro, Bologna.—** Sausages and salted meats. 656

72 **Molinari Brothers, Modena.—Bo-**logna sausages. 656

73 **Special Committee of Salerno.—** Paste for soup. 656

74 **Napoli, Francesco, Salerno.—Pre-**served tomatoes. 656

75 **Peracchi, Enrico, Parma.—Tomato** sauce. 656

76 **Domenici, Annibale, Pontasserchio,** Pisa.—Pork, meat, and bologna. 656

77 **Frosini, Edoardo, & Brother, Pon-**sana, Pisa.—Paste for soup. 656

78 **Gentili, Ferdinando, Pontasserchio,** Pisa.—Paste for soup. 656

79 **Carulli, David, Cremona.—Bologna** and salted meats. 656

80 **Castino, G. B., & E. Scotto, Turin.—** Paste for soup. 656

81 **Stiassi, Filippo, Bologna.—Morta-**delle and other bologna sausages, eels. 656

82 **Pinardi, Pietro, Gottolengo, Bres-**cia.—Mustard and preserves. 656

83 **Gardenghi, Enrico, Modena.—** Sausages, meats, zamponi. 656

84 **Greco, Marco, Bologna.—Liq-**uors. 656

85 **Tosi, Bellucci, Giacomo, Modena.** —Preserves. 656

86 **Luca, de, Francesco, Termini, Pa-**lermo.—Paste for soup. 656

87 **Russo, Biagio, Termini, Palermo.—** Paste for soup. 656

88 **Cammarato, Carmelo, Palermo.—** Paste for soup. 656

89 **Bruno, Giuseppe, Palermo.—Pre-**serves. 656

90 **Verdone & Patera, Palermo.—** Sauces and conserves. 656

91 **Merlo, Vincenzo, Baron, Palermo.—** Dried figs. 656

92 **Sciacca della Scala, Baron, Palermo.** —Dried figs. 656

93 **Guli, Salvatore, Cav., Palermo.—** Candied fruits. 656

94 **Ferrari, Sebastiano, Rome.—Paste** for soup. 656

95 **Palazzo, Duke del, Catania.—Paste** for soup. 656

96 **Amato Brothers, Catania.—Candied** fruits. 656

97 **Caliri, Salvatore, Messina.**
a Candied fruits. 656
b Liquors. 660

98 **Botti, Alessandro, Chiavari, Genoa.**
a Dried fruits. 656
b Wine. 660

99 **Bornia Brothers, Treviso.**
a Pickles. 656
b Vinegar. 660

100 **Guglielmini, Andrea, Salerno.**
a Dried fruits. 656
b Wine. 660

101 **Rinaldo, Raffaele, Salerno.**
a Dried fruit. 656
b Wine. 660

102 **Agosti Brothers, Bagnoria, Rome.**
a Dried prunes. 656
b Vermouth, wines, liquors. 660

103 **Viscardi, Geremia, Bologna.**
a Preserved fruits. 656
b Small biscuits. 661

104 **Chamber of Commerce & Arts,** Bari.
a Dried figs. 656
b Wine. 660
c Chocolate. 661

105 **Simone, Raffaele, de Torre An-**nunziata, Naples.—Best flour paste. 657

106 **Lazzaro, Salvatore, Messina.—** Liquors. 660

107 **Marzi Brothers, Poggibonsi, Sien-**na.—Wines. 660

108 **Castiglioni, Domenico, Parma.—** Wines. 660

109 **Calegari, Giuseppe, Piacenza.—** Wines and liquors. 660

110 **Ghizzoni, Luigi, Piacenza.—Liq-**uors. 660

For classes of exhibits, indicated by numbers at end of entries, see Classification, pp. 12–14.

Wines and Liquors.

111 Clerici, Costantino, Milan.—Vermouth. 660

112 Torelli, Lenaf Luigi, Count, Milan. —Wines. 660

113 Italian Enological Committee, Turin.—Wesin and vermouth. 660

114 Ricci, Emiliano, Sienna.—Liquors. 660

115 Torricelli, Andrea, Florence.—Various liquors. 660

116 Minutillo, Giovanni, Palermo.—Liquors. 660

117 Guli, Salvatore Luigi di, Palermo. —Wines. 660

118 Giacone, Pietro, Palermo.—Marsala wines. 660

119 Martillaro, Mar. Carlo, Palermo.—Wines. 660

120 Catanzaro, Giuseppe, Termini, Palermo.—Wines. 660

121 Florio, Ignazio, & Vincenzo, Palermo.—Marsala wines. 660

122 De Nava, Giuseppe di P., Reggio, Calabria.—Wines. 660

123 Gabaldoni, Andrea Carlo, Varese Ligure, Sestri Levante.—Wines. 660

124 Enological Society of Scandiano. —Wine. 660

125 Malatesti, Augusto, Modena. —Wine. 660

126 Enological Society of Savigliano. —Wine. 660

127 Buton, G., & Co., Bologna.—Liquors. 660

128 Rossi, Leopardi Cav. Cesard, Comiso, Syracuse.—Wine. 660

129 Maltese, Felice, Mayor of Vittorio Scoglitti, Sicily.—Wines. 660

130 Greco-Cassia, Cav. Luigi, Syracuse.—Wine. 660

131 Vitale, Tommaso, Palermo.—Nespole liquor. 660

132 Albiate, Edward, Duke, Palermo.—Casks of duca. 660

133 Zeni, Niccolo, Ferrara, Rosolio.—Cordial made from cocoa. 660

134 Caretti Brothers, Rome.—Vermouth and liquors. 660

135 Strutt, Arthur I., Rome.—Wine. 660

136 Bisco, Luigi, & Co., Brescia.—Liquors. 660

137 Tarussi, Luigi, & Brothers, Leghorn.—Vermouth, wine. 660

138 Vitiello & Torrese, Torre del Greco, Naples.—Wines. 660

139 Anselmi & Marassi, Naples.—Alcohol. 660

140 Del Bono, Enrico, Syracuse.—Wine. 660

141 Giordano, Gio. Batta, Vittorio, Sicily.—Wine. 660

142 Terranova Commillesi, G. B., Vittorio, Sicily.—Wine. 660

143 Maltese, Allessandrello, Vittorio, Sicily.—Wine. 660

144 Targia, Arezzo della, Syracuse.—Liquors, curacoa. 660

145 Mezio, Calcedonio, Syracuse.—Wine. 660

146 Scuderi, Giuseppe, Catania.—Wine. 660

147 Mancini, Antonino, Catania.—Wine. 660

148 Euplio, Reina, Catania.—Wine. 660

149 Paterno, Castello di Bisiari Giuseppe, Catania.—Wine. 660

150 Contarella, Franco, Baron, Catania.—Wine. 660

151 Romeo, Michele, Catania.—Wine. 660

152 Rossi, Tedeschi Francesco, Catania.—Wine. 660

153 Mannino, Francesco, Baron, Catania.—Wine. 660

154 Crispo, Moncada Carlo, Catania.—Wine. 660

155 Grasso, Carmelo, Catania.—Liquors. 660

156 Carpanetti, Luciano, Bologna.—Liquors. 660

157 Paci, Cesare, Florence.—Wine. 660

158 Liccioli, Filippo, Florence.—Wine. 660

159 Agrarian Committee for Thirty Exhibitors, Florence.—Wine. 660

160 Ottaviani Brothers, Messina.—Wines. 660

161 Salvo, Salvatore di, Giarre Moscali, Messina.—Wines. 660

162 Salvo, Salvatore de, Messina.—Wines. 660

163 Pasali, Gaetano, Fermo, & Cottignano, Ascoli Piceno.—Liquors. 660

164 Solinas, Arras Giuseppe, Sassari. —Wines. 660

165 Giacobini, Coriolano, Fano, Pesaro.—Liquors. 660

166 Leno, de Coronei, Nicolo, S. Demetrio, Corone, Calabria Citra.—Wine. 660

167 Agostini, Della Seta, Count Alfredo, Pisa.—Wine. 660

168 Lullato, G. Batta, Como.—Liquors. 660

169 Bonei Cassuccini Ottavio, Sienna. —Wine. 660

170 Zigliani, Cammillo, Bergamo.—Vinegar and essence of vinegar. 660

171 Magnaghi, Girolamo, Alexandria. —Vermouth. 660

172 Rossi, Vittorio, Asti, Alexandria. —Vermouth. 660

173 Bertea, Stefano, Alexandria.—Elixirs, wines, liquors. 660

174 Borelli, Luigi, Asti, Alexandria.—Eau-de-vie. 660

175 Metzger Brothers, Asti, Alexandria.—Beer. 660

176 Boschiero, Cav. Giovanni, Asti, Alexandria.—Wines. 660

177 Mossone, Antonio, Andorne, Turin.—Liquors. 660

178 Martini, Sola, & Co., Turin.—Vermouth. 660

179 Genta, Giovanni, Turin.—Vermouth. 660

180 Poglione, Widow, & Sons, Brà, Cuneo.—Wine. 660

For classes of exhibits, indicated by numbers at end of entries, see Classification, pp. 12–14.

Wines, Vegetable Products, Agricultural Implements.

181 Cavallone, Giovanni, Crescentino, Novara.—Vermouth. 660

182 Bellardi, Dom., & Co., Turin.—Vermouth and liquors. 660

183 Cinzano, Franco, & Co., Turin.—Vermouth. 660

184 Casoni, Giuseppe, Finale, Emilia.—Liquors. 660

185 Napoli, Giuseppe, Baronissi, Salerno.—Wine. 660

186 Palmieri, Benedetto of Gius., Salerno.—Wine. 660

187 Lanzara, Raffaello, Salerno.—Wine. 660

188 Murino, Nicola, Salerno.—Wine. 660

189 Agnini, Tommaso, Finale, Emilia.—Liquors. 660

190 Bellosi, Gio. Batto, Scandiano, Emilia.—Liquors. 660

191 Musi, Luigi, Bologna.—Liquors. 660

192 Savorini, Francesco, S. John Pasiato, Bologna.—Liquors. 660

193 Ronzani, Camillo, Bologna.—Beer. 660

194 Tucci, Savo Benedetto, Rome.—Wine. 660

195 Jacobini Brothers, Rome.—Wine. 660

196 Rospigliosi, Clemente, Prince, Rome.—Wine. 660

197 Stella, Cav. Musio, Syracuse.—Wine. 660

198 Reggio, Arangio Francesco, Augusta, Sicily.—Liquors. 660

199 Salibra, Antonino, Syracuse.—Wine and liquors. 660

200 Bonanno, Michele, Baron, Syracuse.—Wine. 660

201 Maltese, Felice, Vittorio, Sicily.—Wine. 660

202 Cassale Brothers, Syracuse.—Wine and liquors. 660

203 Melfi, G. B., S. Antonino, Baron, Chiaramonte, Syracuse.—Wine. 660

204 Lanza, Cav. Salvatore, Syracuse.—Wine. 660

205 Adorno Puma, Cav. Gaet., Syracuse.—Wine. 660

206 Bruschetti, C. Vincenso, Camerino, Maurata.—Wine. 660

207 Piombino, Prince of, Foligno, Umbria.—Wine. 660

208 Farinola, M. Paolo, Florence.—Wine. 660

209 Albergotti, Geo., & Agostino Bros., Arezzo.—Wine. 660

210 Uffredugi, Giacomo, Perugia, Umbria.—Wine. 660

211 Rospigliosi, Clemente, Prince, Lampovecchio, Florence.—Wine. 660

212 Galimberti, Giuseppe, Milan.—Liquors and vermouth. 660

213 Marini & Poggi, Milan.—Liquors, stomachic and febrifuge elixirs. 660

214 Zannini & Galliani, Milan.—Liquors and extract of tamarind. 660

215 Isolatelli & Co., Milan.—Vermouth and liquors. 660

216 Cordini, Gaetano, & Brivio, Busto Arsizio, Milan.—Vermouth and liquors. 660

217 Branca Brothers & Co., Milan.—Vermouth, liquors, alcohol. 660

218 Facheris, Enrico, Lodi, Milan.—Wines and vinegar. 660

219 Vittone, Domenico, Milan.—Vermouth and liquors. 660

220 Ricasoli, Bettino, Baron, Florence.—Wines. 660

221 Montini, Pasquale, Fabriano, Ancona.—Vermouth and liquors. 660

222 Brenna, Santo, Como.—Liquors. 660

223 Nistri, Ferdinando, Florence.—Liquors. 660

224 Mostardini, Adolfo, Florence.—Liquors. 660

225 Cita, Francesco, & Co., Naples.—Liquors. 660

226 Marini, Ambrogio, Milan.—Liquors. 660

227 Scala, Giuseppe, Naples.—Wines. 660

228 Galloni, Luigi, Rome.—Wines. 660

229 Evoli, Ma. Giovanni, Rome.—Liquor. 660

230 Scala Pasquale, Naples.—Wine. 660

231 Francica Brothers, Naples.—Wine. 660

232 Barra, Luigi, Naples.—Wine. 660

233 Patalano, Orazio, Ischia Island, Naples.—Wine. 660

234 Masetti, Piero Pompeo, Count, Florence.—Wine. 660

235 Siccoli, Guido, Florence.—Wine. 660

236 Fantozzi, Cesare, Foligno, Umbria.—Liquors. 660

237 Burchi, Serafino, Pisa.
a Liquors. 660
b Candies. 661

238 Viliani, Dante, Pistoga.
a Liquors. 660
b Cakes, small biscuits. 661

239 Tamburini, Gaetano, Bologna.—Torrone and candies. 661

240 Cantelli, Giuseppe, Casapulla, Caserta.—Torrone. 661

241 Cerri, Luigi, Cremona.—Torrone with almonds. 661

242 Pirrone, Antonino, Messina.—Sea biscuits. 661

243 Andronico, Giuseppe, Nice, Messina.—Biscuits and paste for sea. 661

244 Loreti, Gioacchimo, Rome.—Candy, cakes, and chocolate. 661

245 Moriondo & Gariglio, Turin.—Chocolate and confectionery. 661

246 Pagni, Faustino, & Co., Pontedera, Pisa.—Biscuits, English style. 661

Textile Substances of Vegetable or Animal Origin.

247 Facchini, Pietro F., & Co., Bologna.—Raw and combed hemp. 666

247*a* Kluftinger, L., Bologna.—Raw and combed hemp. 666

For classes of exhibits, indicated by numbers at end of entries, see Classification, pp. 12–14.

Agricultural Implements and Engineering.

Machines, Implements, and Processes of Manufacture.

248 Cagliesi, Raffaele, Ancona.—Plow. 607

249 Tomaselli, Giacomo, Cremona.—Plows. 670

250 Toroiatti, Luigi di Gio., Venice.—Harrow. 670

251 Porri, Luigi, Pisa.—Plow-share. 670

252 Rossi, Ercole, Parma.—Plow. 670

253 Calzoni, Alessandro, Bologna.—Agricultural machine. 670

254 Gattola, Nicola, Bari.—Plow. 670

255 Biggi, Giovanni, & Co., Piacenza.—Hand reaping machine. 672

256 Uliengo, Giovanni, Biella, Novara.—Butter machine. 675

Agricultural Engineering and Administration.

257 Filopanti, Quirico, Bologna.—Plan of General Garibaldi's system of irrigation relating to the River Tiber. 680

258 Tramontani, D., Bologna.—Bee-hive. 683

Collective Exhibit.

259 Special Committee of Messina.—Samples of Sicilian products for exportation.

For classes of exhibits, indicated by numbers at end of entries, see Classification, pp. 12–14.

BRAZIL.

West of Nave, Columns 6 to 10.

Forest and Agricultural Products.

Arboriculture and Forest Products.

1 Leao, Hermelino de.—Coal obtained from pine heart. 600

2 Muricy, Dr.—Pine heart. 600

3 Araujo & Silva.—Samples of woods. 600

4 Juparana, Baron of.—Samples of woods. 600

5 Faria, Souza.—Samples of woods. 600

6 Villa-Franca, Baron of.—Samples of woods. 600

7 Provincial Commission of S. Paulo.—Samples of woods. 600

8 Cavalcanti.—Samples of woods from Alagoas. 600

9 Province of Rio de Janeiro.—Samples of woods. 600

10 Castro, Borja.—Samples of woods used at the custom-house dock works, Rio de Janeiro. 600

11 Penitentiary, Rio de Janeiro.—Show-cases made of Brazilian woods. 600

12 Couceiro. — Samples of woods in mosaic. 600

13 Barbósa, F.—Samples of woods. 600

14 Muricy & Leao, Drs.—Samples of woods from Parana. 600

16 Province of Bahia. — Samples of woods and medicinal leaves. 600

17 Leite, Severino.—Ticus leaves. 600

18 Silva, Domingos.—Samples of woods from Macahé. 600

19 Province of Parana.—Lumber and timber. 600

20 Bueno, Pimenta.—Samples of woods from Para. 600

21 Rocha, Ignacio da. — Pine lumber from Parana. 600

22 Province of Goyaz.
a Paparo or paper tree and samples of wood. 600
b Resins. 603

23 Colony Itajahy.—Samples of woods for construction and furniture. 600

24 Barbósa, J. F.—Samples of woods. 600

25 Gama, Azarias.—Cipó-pão (wood). 601

26 Municipality of S. Francisco.—Ornamental woods. 601

27 Municipality of S. José.—Ornamental woods. 601

28 Oliveira, P. M. de.—Cumaté (dyeing wood). 602

29 Province of Ceará.
a Dyeing wood. 602
b Resins and gum. 603
c Berries of mamona. 605

30 Perdigao.—Resins. 603

31 Province of Para.
a Resins and caoutchouc. 603
b Nuts. 605

32 Province of St. Catharina.
a Samples of woods. 600
b Resins. 603

33 Province of Amazonas.
a Samples of woods. 600
b Samples of indigo. 602
c Isca-de-tracoa, made by ants, and caoutchouc. 603
d Seeds. 605

34 Province of Alagoas.
a Samples of woods. 600
b Gums and resins. 603

35 Province of Ceara. — Resins and caoutchouc. 603

36 Costa, Gaudencio da.—Caoutchouc from Para. 603

37 Province of Pernambuco.
a Woods. 600
b Dyeing wood. 602
c Gums. 603
d Nuts. 605

38 Province of Rio-Grande-do-Norte.—Wax-dust, resins, gum, and caoutchouc. 603

39 Province of Minas-Geraes.—Resins. 603

40 Araujo, Castro. — Wax on the branch. 603

41 Sarafana, Felix. — Wax on the branch. 603

42 Rebello, Dr.—Dyeing barks. 603

43 Andrade, Ildefonso de.—Barks. 603

44 Martins, J. A.—Barks and leaves of the Eucalyptus giganteus. 603

45 Sardinha.—Resins. 603

46 Silva, T. R. da.—Resins. 603

47 District of Principe.—Resins. 603

48 Portugal, F. P. d'Azevedo.—Balsams. 603

49 District of Quebranguelo.—Resins. 603

50 Commission for Acari.—Resins. 603

51 Paes-Leme, Rosalina.—Linseed. 605

Agricultural Products.

52 Scheffer, Melchior.—Barley in ear and threshed. 620

53 Martins, Ant.—Barley. 620

54 Schamalake.—Barley. 620

55 Richter, Frederico.
a Cereals. 620
b Mustards and tobacco. 623

For classes of exhibits, indicated by numbers at end of entries, see Classification, pp. 12–14.

Agricultural Products.

56 Leao, Hermelino de.
a Rye, wheat, oats, linseed, and maize. 620
b Beans. 621
c Seeds. 624

57 N——. N——.
a Maize on the cob; carnauba straw. 620
b Tea from S. Paulo; coffee from Bahia. 623

58 Province of Parana.
a Wheat and rye. 620
b Medicinal plants. 621
c Manioc tubers. 622
d Matte, a substitute for tea; coffee, tobacco, cigarettes. 623

59 District of Lages.—Cereals. 620

60 Colony Santa-Maria da Soledade.
a Rye, oats, and barley. 620
b Seeds and linseed. 624

61 Commission General for the National Exhibitions.
a Rice, corn, and barley. 620
b Medicinal plants. 621
c Spices, coffee, matté. 623
d Seeds. 624

62 Sampaio. J. M. Leite.—Unhulled rice. 620

63 Gomes, Cordeiro.—Unhulled rice. 620

64 Mello, J. C. de.—Rice. 620

65 Mendes, Olinte.—Corn. 620

66 Carvalho, B. Rocha.—Rice. 620

67 Souza, Bento de.—Wheat. 620

68 Valle, R. J. Ferreira.—Unhulled rice. 620

69 Municipality of Lage.—Wheat. 620

70 District of Quebranguelo.—Beans and guandu. 621

71 District of Votuverava.—Medicinal plants. 621

72 Correa, Laurenço.—Medicinal plants. 621

73 Freitas, G. de Sz.—Medicinal plants. 621

74 Araujo, A. J. Roiz d'.—Medicinal plants. 621

75 Araujo, J. P. de Souza.—Medicinal plants. 621

76 Piratininga, L. Tebiriçá.—Medicinal plants. 621

77 Foggia, Z. M.—Medicinal plants. 621

78 Barbósa, Norbérto.—Medicinal plants. 621

79 Guimarães, J. F.—Medicinal plants. 621

80 Dias, C. Falcao.—Medicinal plants. 621

81 Barros, Dr. J. J. d'Albuquerque.— Medicinal plants. 621

82 Athayde, M. E. de Sz.—Almacega (Icica-Icicariba). 621

83 Philippe, A.—Tears of the Virgin (medicinal plant). 621

84 Perdigao.
a Mediurinal plants. 621
b Bacury seeds. 624

85 Province of Ceara.
a Medicinal plants and beans. 621
b Coffee. 623

86 Province of Goyaz.
a Medicinal plants. 621
b Tobacco. 623

87 Muricy & Leao.
a Beans. 621
b Seeds. 624

88 Leao, Ermelindo de.
a Beans. 621
b Ginger and snuff. 624

89 Province of Para.
a Barley. 620
b Cocoa, ginger, and tobacco. 623

90 Province of Alagoas.
a Medicinal plants. 621
b Vanilla and other seeds. 624

91 Province of S. Paulo.
a Medicinal roots. 621
b Chocolate. 623

92 Araujo, Rodrigues de.—Medicinal plants. 622

93 Moura, Ferreira de.—Potatoes. 622

94 Dr. Muricy.
a Sweet flag. 622
b Spices and tobacco. 623
c Seeds. 624

95 Brant, J. F. d'Andrade.—Manioc roots. 622

96 Heredia, Sa, Dr.—Heredia root. 622

97 Municipality of Cametá.—Cocoa. 623

98 Triste, J. M. d'Araujo.—Cloves of India. 623

99 Portella, F. Fernandes.—Vanilla. 623

100 Guimaraes, M. A., & Pedrozo, H. —Vanilla aromatica. 623

101 Padua, A. de.—Vanilla.

102 Silva & Sons.—Cocoa. 623

103 Pinho, L. F. do.—Chocolate. 623

104 Lima, Dias.—Chocolate. 623

105 Ribeiro, J. A. F.—Chocolate. 623

106 Liborio & Ferreira.—Chocolate. 623

108 Province of Sergipe.—Coffee. 623

109 Province of Parahyba do Nórte.— Coffee. 623

110 Presidency of Sancta Catharina.— Coffee. 623

111 Falcao, J. J. Franco.—Coffee. 623

112 Albuquerque, A. de Sa.—Coffee. 623

113 Lacerda, A. F. de.—Coffee. 623

114 Breves, J. J. de Sz.—Coffee. 623

115 Cósta, P. M.—Coffee. 623

116 Silva, C. J., & Sons.—Coffee. 623

117 Carrao, Councillor.—Coffee and tea. 623

118 Montenegro, Commander.—Coffee from Nova-Louzan. 623

119 Atibaia, Baron of.—Coffee. 623

120 Tavares, J. Pinto—Coffee from Par-ahyba-do-Sul. 623

121 Monteiro, P. J.—Coffee from Rio de Janeiro. 623

122 Portella, J. T. M.—Coffee from Mu-ribéca. 623

123 Bornaud, L.—Coffee from Caravel-las. 623

124 Magalhaes, F. L. d'Almeida.—Cof-fee from Triumpho. 623

125 Fernandez, C. J.—Coffee from Mar-agogipe. 623

For classes of exhibits, indicated by numbers at end of entries, see Classification, pp. 12–14.

Agricultural Products.

126 Belens, J. L.—Coffee. 623

127 Reines, N. A., Claudio.—Coffee from Monte Vernon. 623

128 Cunha, J. J., Alves da.—Coffee from Rio de Janeiro. 623

129 Valein, M. d'Aguiar.—Coffee from Bananal. 623

130 Vergueiro, J.—Coffee from Ibicaba. 623

131 Siqueira, M. B. de.—Coffee and tobacco from Goyaz. 623

132 Nogueira, Dr. P. R.—Coffee from S. Paulo. 623

133 Barros. L. A. de Sz.—Coffee from S. Paulo. 623

134 Krull, Frederika.—Coffee from S. Paulo. 623

135 Province of Goyaz.—Tobacco and cigarettes. 623

136 Colony of Assunguy.—Tobacco leaves. 623

137 Presidency of the Province of Bahia.—Cigars. 623

138 Pereira & Braga, Cigar Manufactory.—Cigars. 623

139 Paes-Leme, Rosalina V.
a Cigars and tobacco from the Colony Blumenau. 623
b Matte from St. Catharina. 623

140 S. Joao de Nictheray, Manufactory of.—Cigars and cigarettes. 623

141 Moreira, Dr. d'Assis C.—Tobacco from Codó. 623

142 Queiróz & Sons.—Tobacco from S. Paulo. 623

143 Levy, Salamon.—Snuff from Teffé. 623

144 Schild, Joao.—Cigars from the Colony Sancta-Cruz. 623

145 Herbst, Augusto.—Twist tobacco from the Colony Blumenau. 623

146 Rosenstock, G.—Tobacco from the Colony Joinville. 624

147 Kopsch, Ch.—Tobacco from the Colony Blumenau. 623

148 Merck, Maxim.—Tobacco from the Colony Blumenau. 623

149 Vander-Berg.—Tobacco leaves from the ex-Colony Sancta-Cruz. 623

150 Seidler, C.—Leaf tobacco. 623

151 Kalden, Baron of.—Leaf tobacco from the Colony Sancto-Angelo. 623

152 Ketterman, V.—Leaf tobacco from the Colony Sancto-Angelo. 623

153 Dietrich, A.—Leaf tobacco from the Colony Joinville. 623

154 Faria, B. de.—Tobacco from Bahia. 623

155 Grava, Fr. L. Sa.—Tobacco from Cachocira. 628

156 Aranha, J. D.—Tobacco and cigarettes. 623

157 Ferreira, E. A.—Cigarettes. 623

158 Ferreira, Candido J.—Cigars from Cachocira. 623

159 Paraiso, D. V.—Carolina tobacco. 623

160 Cerqueira & Co.—Snuff, cigars, and cigarettes. 623

161 Mendouca, M. J.—Tobacco from Goyaz. 623

162 Pinheiro, J. E.—Tobacco from Pará. 623

163 Jardim, J. R. de Moraes.—Tobacco from Goyaz. 623

164 Menezes, Rev. M. de.—Tobacco. 623

165 Nascimento, Rev. A. F.—Tobacco. 623

166 Panitz, J. C.—Tobacco from S. Leopoldo. 623

167 Senna, N. B. de.—Tobacco from Mucury. 623

168 Santos, M. A. dos.—Tobacco. 623

169 Silva, A. Ignacio da.—Rolled tobacco. 623

170 Constantino, J.—Tobacco from Balpuedy. 623

171 Souza, M. L. de.—Cigarettes from Parana. 623

172 Ribas, J. L. Sá.—Twist tobacco. 623

173 Cokin, E.—Twist tobacco. 623

174 Gonsalves, J. P.—Cigars. 623

175 Gama, T. J. de Sz.—Cigars. 623

176 Abreu, J. Monteiro d'.—Cigars. 623

177 Borba, N. M.—Cigarettes. 623

178 Miranda, J. B. de.—Cigarettes. 623

179 Perneta, F. D.—Cigarettes. 623

180 Ribas, A. L. d'Andrade.—Cigarettes and matte. 623

181 Ramos, L. F.—Cigarettes. 623

182 Lepage, J.
a Cigarettes. 623
b Seeds. 624

183 Miranda-Russo, F. A.—Tea from S. Paulo. 623

184 Rego-Freitas, A. P. de.—Tea from S. Paulo. 623

185 Neves, J. Ribeiro.—Tea from S. Paulo. 623

186 França, F. A. Galvao da.—Tea from S. Paulo. 623

187 Xavier, J. Ribeiro.—Tea from S. Paulo. 623

188 Mosqueira, A. L. M.—Tea from Minas-Geraes. 623

189 Correa, Ildelfonso.—Matte. 623

190 Province of Minas-Geraes.—Matte. 623

191 Leao, Major V. F. de.—Matte in leaves, dried, and powdered. 623

192 Pacheco, D. dos Santos.—Matte leaves. 623

193 Braga, J. M. da Silva.—Matte leaves. 623

194 Torres, G. d'A.—Matte. 623

195 Bley, J.—Matte. 623

196 Xavier, A. de Paula.—Matte. 623

197 Torres, M. d'A.—Matte. 623

198 Cercal, M. d'Oliveira.—Matte in leaves. 623

199 Portugal, P. P. d'Azevedo.—Matte. 623

200 Sepper, H.—Matte. 623

201 Cortez, P. de Siqueira.—Matte. 623

For classes of exhibits, indicated by numbers at end of entries, see Classification, pp. 12-14.

Agricultural Products, Land Animals.

202 Macedo, Tiburcio de.—Matte. 623
203 Diarson, J.—Matte. 623
204 Souza, Bento de.—Matte. 623
205 Constanca, Maria, & Sons.—Coffee and cocoa. 623
206 Correa, Pereira.—Matte. 623
207 Luz, Ferreira de.—Matte. 623
208 Camargos, Baron de.—Tea and coffee. 623
209 Province of Sancta Catharina.—Coffee. 623
210 Guimaraes, Ant.—Coffee from La Guayrá. 623
211 Friburgo & Sons.—Coffee. 623
212 Nobrega, J.—Coffee from Boa Esperanca. 623
213 Munhoz, Caetano.—Matte. 623
214 Ayrosa, M. A.—Coffee. 623
215 Rocha-Leao, M. da.—Coffee. 623
216 Costa-Pereira, A. B. da.—Coffee from Piedade. 623
217 Gama, P. N. Nogueira da.—Coffee from Concordia. 623
218 Juparana, Baron of.—Coffee from Sta. Monica. 623
219 Rio-Novo, Viscountess of.—Coffee from Uniao. 623
220 Pripodi, Silvino.—Coffee. 623
221 Jardien, Gomes de.—Coffee. 623
222 Bella-Vista, Baron of.—Coffee. 623
223 Machado, Marcondes.—Coffee. 623
224 Vieira, Ant.—Coffee. 623
225 Magalhaes, Almeida.—Coffee. 623
226 Barros, Teixeira da.—Coffee. 623
227 Lima, Freitas.—Coffee. 623
228 Jordao, Miranda.—Coffee. 623
229 Costa, Maria da.—Coffee. 623
230 Camargo, Pompen de.—Coffee from Campinas. 623
231 Nogueira, Almeida.—Coffee from Campinas. 623
232 Jordao, R.—Coffee. 623
233 Vergueiro & Co.—Coffee. 623
234 Barros, Souza.—Coffee from S. Paulo. 623
235 Camargo, Santos.—Coffee and tobacco. 623
236 Amaral, Thereza do.—Coffee from Campinas. 623
237 Amaral, Francisco do.—Coffee from Campinas. 623
238 Nogueira, Ramos.—Coffee from S. Paulo. 623
239 Gaviao, Bernardo.—Coffee from S. Paulo. 623
240 Souza, Paula.—Coffee from S. Paulo. 623
241 Barros, Raphael de.—Coffee from S. Paulo. 623
242 C——, A. M.—Coffee from Iguape. 623
243 Jordao, Silverio.—Coffee. 623
244 Araraguara, Baron de.—Coffee. 623
245 Tavares, Pinto.—Coffee. 623
246 Souza-Gueiroz, Baron de.—Coffee from S, Paulo. 623
247 Commission for the Province of St. Catharina.—Coffee. 623
248 Santos, Cornelio dos.—Coffees. 623
249 Prados, Viscount of.—Coffee from Minas-Geraes. 623
250 Assiz, Ferreira d'.—Coffee from Minas-Geraes. 623
251 Ribeiro, Silva.—Coffee from Minas-Geraes. 623
252 Alves, Assiz.—Coffee from Minas-Geraes. 623
253 Freire, Manuel.—Coffee from S. Paulo. 623
254 Carvalho, Zacharias de.—Coffee from Sergipe. 623
255 Freire & Bros.—Coffee. 623
256 Breve, Souza.—Coffee. 623
257 Jaguary, Viscount of.
a Coffee. 623
b Seeds. 624
258 Rocha-Ferreira, D. da.—Tobacco. 623
259 Parana, D. V.—Tobacco. 623
260 Commission for the Province of Maranhao.—Coffee and tobacco. 623
261 Colony of Blumenau.—Tobacco and cigars. 623
262 Colony of Itajahy.—Twisted tobacco and mate. 623
263 Figueredo, Pinto de.—Twisted tobacco. 623
264 Province of Amazonas.
a Medicinal plants. 621
b Cloves and tobacco. 623
265 Veiga.—Tobacco from Rio de Janeiro. 623
266 Oliveira, Coelho d'.—Tobacco from Minas-Geraes. 623
267 Province of Matto Grosso.—Tobacco and cigars. 623
268 Province of Rio-Grande-do-Sul.—Tobacco in leaf, and mate dust. 623
269 Pinto & Bro.—Leaf tobacco. 623
270 Testa, Umbellino.—Tobacco and coffee from Bahia. 623
271 Souza, Vasconcellos de.—Tobacco from Bahia. 623
272 Viotti.—Cigarettes. 623
273 Paulo Cordeiro, J.—Snuff. 623
275 Rocha, Correa da.—Snuff. 623
276 Novaes, Sonza.—Cigarettes. 623
277 Province of Bahia.—Cigars. 623
278 Agner, Luiz.—Matte. 623
279 Martins, Luiz.—Tea. 623
280 Rodovalho, P.—Matte. 623
281 Fluminense Agriculture Institute.—Tea made from coffee-leaves. 623
282 Central Exportation Co.—Matte. 623

Land Animals.

284 Moreira, Dr. Nicolâu J.—Butterfly, "Porta Espelhos" (*Attacus aurota Lepidopterous*).
285 Rezende, Luiz de.—Silkworms and moths.
286 Wirmond, Ernesto E.—Collection of insects.

Animal and Vegetable Products.

Water Animals, Fish Culture, and Apparatus.

287 Province of Parana.—Isinglass. 646

Animal and Vegetable Products.

288 Province of Matto-Grosso.
a Quinine. 650
b Hides and furs. 652

289 Agricultural Institute.
a Sage. 650
b Flour. 657
c Arrowroot. 658

290 Province of Allagoas.
a Indigo-plant and vegetable dyes; caroba, quinine, etc. 650
b Hides and furs. 652
c Vegetable milk. 656

291 Province of S. Paulo.
a Camomile. 650
b Hides and leather. 652
c Liquors, aguardente, etc. 660
d Chocolate. 661

292 Commission General for the International Exhibitions, Rio de Janeiro.
a Turtle butter and cheese. 651
b Skins, hides, and leather. 652
c Wax. 654
d Preserved beef and tongues. 656
e Sugar. 659
f Wines and liquors. 660
g Vegetable oils. 662

293 Juliano, Fr.—Cheese. 651

294 Carneiro, B. Rodriguez.—Cheese. 651

295 Ubatuba, Dr.
a Condensed milk. 651
b Extract of mint. 656

296 Cabral, J. F. D.—Milk of Mangabeira. 651

297 Moraes Rozeira, M. G. de.—Cheese. 651

298 Leao, Dr. A. E.—Cheese. 651

299 Director of Paranápanema.—Butter. 651

299*a* Oliveira, Ignacio de.—Glue. 652

300 District of Principe.
a Skins and hides. 652
b Wax. 654

301 Andrade, J. C. Paes de.—Glue. 652

302 Ubatuba, D. M. P. S.—Tallow, lard, and oil. 652

303 Maciel, D. F.—Steer skins. 652

304 Cortez, P.—Steer hide. 652

305 Botelho, A. C. A.—Skin of a Boa aquatica. 652

306 Athayde, M. E. S.—Skins. 652

307 Feydel Son, I.—Tanned and raw hides. 652

308 Andrade, I. J.—Hides and skins. 652

309 Costa Eymoel & Co.—Hides, leather, and soles. 652

310 Klippel & Brother.—Hides and soles. 652

311 Perneta.—Stag-horns. 652

312 Colony of Blumenau.—Various products. 652

313 Province of Amazonas.—Hides and furs. 652

314 Province of Goyaz.—Hides, furs, and leather. 652

315 Province of Ceara.
a Hides and furs. 652
b Dried beef. 656
c Confectionery. 661

316 Province of Rio Grande do Sul.
a Leather. 652
b Preserved tongue and beef. 656

317 Province of Rio Grande do Norte.
a Oil and tallow. 652
b Powdered honey-wax. 654

318 Province of Parana.
a Hides, furs, and ox-horns. 652
b Wax. 654
c Manioc flour and fecula. 657
d Aguardente from sugar-cane, and liquor from maté herb and quince. 660

319 Long & Co.—Wax. 654

320 Miro, D. Maria.—Wax. 654

321 Safarana, A. T.—Beeswax and wax candles. 654

322 Province of Goyaz.—Beeswax. 654

323 Araujo, J. Pereira de Sz.—Yellow wax. 654

324 Araujo, J. A. Vieira.—Honey. 654

325 Xavier, A. de Paula.—Honey. 654

326 Xavier, D. Leocadia de P.—Wax. 654

327 Mendes, J. Olinto.—Honey and wax. 654

328 Macedo & Azeredo.—Wax. 654

329 Province of Ceará.—Sun-dried beef and confectionery. 656

330 Canoza, Rosalina R. Botelha.—Preserved vegetables. 656

331 Vasconcellos, F. P. de.—Preserved vegetables. 656

332 Castro, M. José de.—Sweetmeats. 656

333 Silva, Leal, & Santos.—Preserves. 656

334 Guttier & Wagner.—Preserved fruits. 656

335 Province of Para.—Preserved meats. 656

336 Santos & Ferreira.—Preserved vegetables, marmalade, and fruit-butter. 656

337 Province of Maranhao.
a Rice. 656
b Vegetable oils. 662

338 Province of Pernambuco.
a Dried fruits. 656
b Manioc and arrow-root flour. 657
c Sugar. 559
d Aguardente from sugar-cane. 660
e Cocoa oil. 662

339 Tamancao Factory.—Crushed rice. 657

340 Schimmelpfung, A.—Rye flour. 657

341 Dezincourt.—Arrowroot flour. 657

342 Alvarenga, Dr.
a Flour. 657
b Tapioca. 658

343 Leao, Hermelindo de.—Rice. 657

344 Murucy, Dr.—Maize and rye-flour. 657

345 Directory Board of the Colony of Angelina.—Corn-flour from the colony. 657

346 Silva, Carneiro da.—Manioc-flour. 657

347 Tripodi, Silvino.—Rice. 657

For classes of exhibits, indicated by numbers at end of entries, see Classification, pp. 12–14.

Animal and Vegetable Products.

348 Cordeiro, jr.—Rice on the branch. 657

349 Tarranbae, J.—Arrowroot flour. 657

350 Carvalho, Lima.—Manioc and orris-root flour. 657

351 Province of Sancta Catharina.—Flour, rice, and arrowroot flour. 657

352 Guimaraes, Antonio.
a Rice. 657
b Aguardente from sugar-cane, orange, etc. 660

353 N—— N——.
a Rice. 657
b Farinas. 658
c Vinegar. 660

354 Silva, M. C., & Sons.—Tapioca. 657

355 Pereira, J. J.—Farina of manioc. 657

356 Colony of Angelina.—Wheat flour. 657

357 Silva, J. J. Correa da.—Farina of manioc and tapioca. 657

358 Province of Parana.
a Feculas. 657
b Matté liquor. 660

359 Province of Pernambuco.—Manioc and arrowroot flour. 657

360 Leao & Alves Grist Mill.—Wheat flour. 657

361 Pirapitinga, Baron of.—Polvilho (a starch). 658

362 Province of Sancta Catharina.—Polvilho (a starch). 658

363 Fleminense Agricultural Institute.—Polvilho (a starch). 658

364 Pirapitinga, Baron of.—Tapioca and orris-root. 658

365 Constanca, Maria, & Sons.—Tapioca and orris-root. 658

366 Pinheiro, Thomaz.—Sugar. 659

367 Carvalho & Oliveira.—Syrup of ipecac. 659

368 Diaz, Isidoro.—Sugar and syrup. 659

369 Maua, Viscount of.—Refined sugar. 659

370 Dezincourt.—Crystallized sugar. 659

371 Barros, Bernardino de.—Brown and white sugar. 659

372 Barros, Fernandes de.—Sugar. 659

373 Costa & Co.—Refined sugar. 659

374 Costa, Ribeiro de.—Sugar. 659

375 Souza, Alves de.—Sugar. 659

376 Vianna, Paula.—Sugar. 559

377 Boa-Viagem, Baron of.—Sugar. 659

378 Wanderley, Barros.—Sugar. 659

379 Villa-Franca, Baron de.—Sugar. 659

380 Leao, Souza.—Sugar. 659

381 Virgens, Bernardo da.—Sugar. 659

382 Bastos, Rodriguez.—Sugar. 659

383 Braga & Co.
a Syrups. 659
b Liquors; aguardente, cognac, etc. 660

384 Province of Bahia.
a Refined sugar. 659
b Chocolate of musgo. 661

385 Barroso, Paula.
a Sugar. 659
b Aguardente from sugar-cane. 660

386 Castro, Ribeiro de.
a Sugar. 659
b Brandy from sugar-cane. 660

387 Virgens, M. B. das.—Sugar. 659

388 Mansell, Carré, & Co.—Sugar. 659

389 Braga & Co.—Syrups. 659

390 Colony of Iatahy.—Sugar-cane brandy. 660

391 Braga & Brother.—Brandy, liquors, and alcohol. 660

392 Vellez Perdigao, D.—Alcoholic drinks and pineapple vinegar. 660

393 Freyung, Otto.—Liquors. 660

394 Belache.—Liquors. 660

395 Bella Vista, Baron of.—Sugar-cane brandy and orange liquor. 660

396 Amaral Raposó, J. do.—Liquors. 660

397 Carreira, F. L.—Wines and brandies. 660

398 Carneiro, F. Lucas.—Pao wine. 660

399 Bastos & Camacho.—Liquors and cordials. 660

400 Teixeira, A. de A.—Tonic liquors. 660

401 Boully, José.—Pao wine. 660

402 Votuvera Commission.—Pao wine. 660

403 Silva, J. H. da.—Brandy and wines. 660

404 Falcao, Paulino P.—Sugar-cane brandy. 660

405 Souza, M. I. M. de.—Brandy and Laranginha. 660

406 Mendes, J. Olinto.—Liquor. 660

407 Menezes, B. A. de.—Quince liquor. 660

408 Xavier, A. P.—Honey wine, alcohol, and brandy. 660

409 Castelnuova, T.—Absinthe. 660

410 Moraes Rozeira, M. G. de.—Wines. 660

411 Vasconcellos, Francisco P. de.—Orange wine and alcoholic drinks. 660

412 Marizon, F. M. Celli de.—Laraginha. 660

413 Araujo, Ignacio de.—Liquors. 660

414 Oliveira, Roiz de.—Liquors. 660

415 Carvalho, Leitao de.—Laranginha and gin. 600

416 Falcao, Piris.—Aguardente. 660

417 Raposo, Amaral.—Wines and liquors. 600

418 Pinto, Oliveira.—Aguardente from sugar-cane and caju wine. 660

419 Azevedo, Pereira de.—Aguardente. 660

420 Carvalho, M. de.—Gin. 660

421 Jeremoabo, T.—Aguardente from honey. 660

422 Schulmann & Co.—Wine and vinegar from sugar-cane. 660

423 Pimenta, Mattos.—Hesperidina-Yaguarembo'. 660

424 Oliveira, C., & Sons.—Wine and aguardente from sugar-cane; vinegar from pine apple. 660

425 Frey, Otto.—Liquors. 660

For classes of exhibits, indicated by numbers at end of entries, see Classification, pp. 12–14.

Animal and Vegetable Products, Textile Substances.

426 Vasconcellos, P. de.—Orange wine. 660
427 Cattermolle, Erdman.—Wines and liquors. 660
428 Alves & Co.—Liquors. 660
429 Barroso, Carvallo.—Alcohol. 660
430 Silveira, N.—Aguardente. 660
431 Pinheiro, Thomaz.—Laranginha. 660
432 Caipora, Guimaraes.—Laranginha. 660
433 Bella-Vista, Baron of.—Aguardente. 660
434 Province of Para.—Guarana. 660
435 Pereira, Estevao.—Laranginha, aguardente from sugar-cane. 660
436 Itabapoana, Baron de.—Laranginha. 660
437 Silva, Carneiro da.—Laranginha. 660
438 Rebello, Silva.—Liquor from coffee and other plants. 660
439 Mamede.—Caju wine for medicinal purposes. 660
440 Macedo, J. de.—Liquors. 660
441 Le Page.—Wines and Vinegar. 660
442 Viotti.—Peach liquor. 660
443 Vianna, Oliveira.—Aguardente. 660
444 Biagem, Boa, Baron da.—Aguardente. 660
445 Sardinha.—Wine. 660
446 Pinho, Francisco do.—Chocolate. 661
447 Leao, Hermelino de.—Farina biscuit. 661
448 Murici, Dr. Leao, Ermelindo de.—Tapioca biscuits. 661
449 Silva, Leal, & Santos.—Vermicelli. 661
450 Province of Bahia.—Musgo chocolate. 6.6
451 Pinho, Francisco do.—Chocolate. 6.6
452 Dias, J. D.—Vegetable oils. 662
453 Cohin, Eliezer.—Oil of copahiba. 662
454 Cavalcante, J. B.—Oil of andiroba. 662
455 Barbósa, J. E. C.—Oil of batiputa. 662
456 Braga, J. F. C.—Oil of copahiba. 662
457 Veiga, J. A. da.—Oil of togo. 662
458 Silva, T. R. da.—Cocoanut oil. 662
459 Jorge, M. F. A.—Cocoanut oil. 662
460 Stechel, Frederico.—Oils. 662
461 Barreto, Jr.—Oils of copahiba, andiroba, etc. 662
462 Falcao, Dias C.—Oils. 662
463 Ferreira Valle, R. J.—Cocoanut oil. 662
464 Vyeira, M. L.—Cocoanut oil. 662
465 Vyeira, S. A.—Andiroba oil. 662
466 Province of Maranhao.—Oil of anaja. 662
467 District of Paulo Affonso.—Cajunut oil. 662
468 Province of Ceará.—Oils. 662
469 Presidency of the Province of Bahia.—Ricinus and cocoanut oil. 662
470 Perdigao.—Vegetable oils. 662

Textile Substances of Vegetable or Animal Origin.

471 Mello, Correio de.—Brown cotton. 665
472 Hayer, Martin.—Cotton. 665
473 Moreira, Collares.—Cotton from Maranhao. 665
474 Province of Ceara.—Cotton. 665
475 Province of Matto Grosso.—Guinea cotton. 665
476 Province of Parahyba.—Cotton. 665
477 Province of Rio Grande do Norte.—Cotton. 665
478 C——, J. T. A.—Cotton from S. Paulo. 665
479 Barros, Souza.—Cotton from S. Paulo. 665
480 Maylasky.—Cotton from Soracaba. 665
481 B——, A. A.—Cotton from S. Paulo. 665
482 A——, J. C.—Cotton from S. Paulo. 665
483 Province of Alagoas.—Vegetable wool. 665
484 Province of Pernambuco.
a Russian cotton. 665
b Tow. 666
c Bristles. 669
485 Province of Parana.
a Cotton. 665
b Flax. 666
c Wool. 667
d Animal hair. 669
486 Province of Maranhao.—Ginned cotton. 665
487 Municipality of Quebranguelo.—Cotton in the boll and twisted. 665
488 Province of San Paulo.—Cotton. 665
489 Miranda, M. M. de.—Ginned cotton. 665
490 Athayde, M. E. Souza.—Cotton on the stem. 665
491 G. B. T., Rio de Janeiro.—Cotton on the stem. 665
492 Soares, O. J.—Cotton. 665
493 Merch, Maximiliano.—Cotton. 665
494 Paes Leme, Rosalina.—Cotton. 665
495 Silva, F. J. Xavier da.—Cotton. 665
496 Colony Itajahy.—Cotton. 665
497 Mello, J. Correira de.—Cotton, called creoulo. 665
498 Brava, Fray Luiz da.—Cotton. 665
499 Colony of Sancta Maria de Soledade.—Cotton. 665
500 Colony Blumenau.—Cotton. 665
501 Decker, Isaac.—Cotton. 665
502 Valle, Raymundo J. F.—Cotton on the stem. 665
503 Commission for Carnaru.—Grey cotton. 665

For classes of exhibits, indicated by numbers at end of entries, see Classification, pp. 12–14.

Textile Substances, Machinery, Engineering, Administration.

504 **Barros, Diogo A. de.—Cotton in** skeins. 665

505 **J. C. A., Limeira.—Cotton.** 665

506 **Commission General for the National Exhibitions**, Rio de Janeiro.
a Hemp and other vegetable fibres. 666
b Horse-hair and other hair. 669

507 **Province of Pernambuco.**
a Vegetable fibres. 666
b Bristles. 669

508 **Province of Sancta Catharina.**—Tucum thread and paina. 666

509 **Commission for Votureava.—Isca** de Roceira. 666

510 **Province of Amazonas.—Piassaba** fibres. 666

511 **Barros, L. Gomes de.—Cipo matta** gente for withes. 666

512 **Muricy, Dr.—Cipo florao.** 666

513 **Leao, Rego Barros S.—White embira.** 666

514 **Palma, Ant. J. da.—Red embira.** 666

515 **Lacerda, A. F. de.—Piattaba fibres.** 666

516 **Bley, J.—Fibres of the Urtica speciosa.** 666

517 **Barros, A. Aguiar de.—Vegetable** fibres. 666

518 **Guimaraes, M. A.—Betas and fibres** of tucum. 666

519 **Oliveira, P. M. de.—Tapuru.** 666

520 **Taborda Ribas, M.—Isca of Urupe.** 666

521 **Bofim, F. Theodoro do.—Fibres of** the Anona silvatica. 666

522 **Killian, J. E.—Vegetable fibres.** 666

523 **Ferreira, S. P., & Negrao, J. de S.**—Fibres of the Cecropia pellata. 666

524 **Leao, Agostinho de.—Paina.** 666

525 **Cruz, B. A. da, & Bomfun, Florindo** T.—Fibres of bombax and of the Copaifera officinalis. 666

526 **Portella, Felix F.—Vegetable hair.** 666

527 **Ferreira & Co., Gasper P.—Fibres** of the umbauba tree. 666

528 **Bomfin, F. Theodoro do, and** others.—Vegetable fibres. 666

529 **Paes Leme, Rosalina.—Flax.** 666

530 **Keller, Philippe.—Flax.** 666

531 **Kalden, Baron of.—Prepared flax.** 666

532 **Ackermann, Carlos, & Bladern, G.** —Prepared flax. 666

533 **Barros, F. Fernandes de.—Fibres** of tucum. 666

534 **Leao, E. de.—Flax.** 666

535 **Almeida, A. Rufino de.—Vegetable** fibres. 666

536 **Province of Ceará.—Fibres of tu-**cum and paina. 666

537 **Steele, J.—Jute.** 666

538 **Leite, Severino.—Vegetable hair** and wool. 666

539 **Lang & Co.—Hemp and flax.** 666

540 **Province of Para.—Jute.** 666

541 **Province of Bahia.—Vegetable** hair. 666

542 **Province of S. Paulo.—Paina.** 666

543 **Villa-Franca, Baron of.—Paina.** 666

544 **Agricultural Institute.—Wool.** 667

545 **Schimmelpfeng, A.—Wool.** 667

546 **Wirmond, Ernesto.—Wool.** 667

547 **Province of Paraná.**
a Wool. 667
b Hair. 669

548 **Province of Alagoas.—Vegetable** wool. 667

549 **Santos Reis & Co., Pedro A. dos.**—Reeled silk. 668

550 **Mello Netto, Franc de Paula.**—Cocoons. 668

551 **Schrazer, Paulo.—Cocoons.** 668

552 **Eugenia & T.—White silk.** 668

553 **Morvira, Nicolau J.—Cocoons.** 668

554 **Moreira, Nicolau.—Silk-worms.** 668

555 **Reis, Luciano.—Silk in the cocoon** and reeled. 668

556 **Resende, Luiz de.—Silk-worms,** cocoons, reeled silk, and apparatus for reeling silk. 668

Machines, Implements, and Processes of Manufacture.

557 **Bierremback & Brother.—Plows.** 670

558 **Antunes, J. A.—Machine for pre-**paring coffee. 674

559 **Blanchet, J.—Small plows.** 670

560 **Province of S. Paulo.—Plows.** 670

561 **Province of Parana.—Plows.** 670

Agricultural Engineering and Administration.

562 **Province of Amazonas.—Guano.** 681

563 **Muricy & Leao.—Guano.** 681

Chemicals.

564 **Yeiga, F. Aprigio da.—Pharma-**ceutical products. 200

565 **Lepage, F. J.—Pharmaceutical** products. 200

566 **Dias, Duarte.—Drugs.** 200

567 **Province of Ceara.—Medicinal oils.** 200

568 **Alves, Leao.—Pharmaceutical** preparations. 200

569 **Dias, C. Falcon.—Pharmaceutical** preparations. 200

570 **Braga, jr.—Pharmaceutical prepa-**rations. 200

571 **Military Hospital of Rio de Janeiro.** —Pharmaceutical preparations. 200

Fabrics of Vegetable, Animal, or Mineral Materials.

572 **Province of Amazonas.**
a Brooms. 286
b Cordage of rattan. 287

ARGENTINE REPUBLIC.

(West of West Aisle, Columns 9 to 13.)

Arboriculture and Forest Products.

Arboriculture and Forest Products.

1 Commission of the Chaco Argentine Territory.
a Collection of natural and polished woods. 600
b Indigo plant and curupai bark. 602

2 Gallegos, Miguel, Chaco Argentine Territory.—A cane; samples of wood. 600

3 Aguilar, Francisco D., Province of San Juan.—Flowers made from carob tree wood; chica wood; collection of woods to be presented to the National Department of Agriculture. 600

4 Laugan, Juan, Province of San Juan.—Collection of woods. 600

5 Provincial Commission, Province of Santa Fé.
a Collection of woods, polished lignum-vitæ. 600
b Laurel bark and tanning materials. 602

6 Echevarria, Cecilio, Province of Santa Fé.
a Collection of woods; polished samples. 600
b Dyes. 602

7 Provincial Commission, Province of Cordoba.
a Collection of woods; polished samples. 600
b White carob tree and molle seed. 605

8 Cornejo, John, Province of Salta.
a Cherimoya seed. 600
b Palo Santo resin. 603

10 Provincial Commission, Province of Salta.
a Collection of seeds and woods. 600
b Dyeing and tanning materials. 602

11 Villar, Salvador, Province of Jujui.
a Collection of woods. 600
b Socondo and pastilla bark. 602
c Palm, lignum-vitæ, quina-quina and pacara seeds, etc. 605

12 Provincial Commission, Province of Catamarca.
a Collection of woods. 600
b Dyeing and tanning materials. 602
c Visco and lignumvitæ seeds, etc. 605

13 Provincial Commission, Province of La Rioja.
a Collection of woods. 600
b Tar, carob resin, and Lata incense. 603
c Yareta plant, containing much resin. 604
d Collection of seeds. 605

14 Cecenarro, Vicente, Province of Catamarca.—Viscote wood. 600

15 Lafone, Quevedo, Samuel Province of Catamarca.—Black carob wood. 600

16 Andalgala Commission, Province of Catamarca.
a Cactus. 600
b Dyeing and tanning products. 602

17 Provincial Commission, Province of Tucuman.
a Samples of wood in logs, partly polished. 600
b Cebil bark for tanning, Socondo. 602

18 Provincial Commission, Province of Mendoza.
a Samples of wood in logs. 600
b Chanar bark for cleaning cloth and Retortuno for tanning. 602
c Gums and resins. 603

19 Videla, Victor, Province of San Luis.
a Collection of woods; polished samples. 600
b Barks for tanning. 602

20 Provincial Commission, Province of Corrientes.—
a Collection of polished and unpolished woods. 600
b Bark of black laurel and curupay tree, used for tanning, etc. 602
c Peanuts, and creeping plant called curuhay guazu. 605

21 Roibon, Enrique, Province of Corrientes.—Caroba wood. 600

22 Resoagli, Luis, Province of Corrientes.—Collection of woods; boxes. 600

22*a* River Bermejo Navigation Co., Chaco, Argentine Territory.—Palo santo wood. 600

23 Bella Vista Sub-Commission, Province of Corrientes.
a Collection of woods. 600
b Orange seed, chichita, suspiros, peanuts. 605

24 Ferrér, Vicente, Province of Corrientes.—Sticks of different woods. 600

25 National Department of Agriculture, Province of Corrientes.—Samples of Urunday wood. 600

26 Justice of the Peace of Ensenada, Province of Buenos Ayres.—Collection of woods. 600

27 Valdes, Emiliano, & Cipriano, Province of Buenos Ayres.
a Collection of curromamuel and other woods. 600
b Mushrooms grown on willow bark. 604

28 Agricultural School of Santa Catalina, Province of Buenos Ayres.—Beehives made of black acacia. 600

29 Roibon, Federico, Province of Corrientes.—Pictures of trees in water-colors. 600

30 Boero, José, & Poletti, Antonio, Province of Buenos Ayres.—A rack made of twenty-five kinds of wood. 600

31 Iniguez, Manuel, Province of Buenos Ayres.—Specimens of woods. 600

For classes of exhibits, indicated by numbers at end of entries, see Classification, pp. 12–14.

Arboriculture, Forest, and Agricultural Products.

32 Provincial Commission, Province of Santiago del Estero.
a Collection of woods in logs. 600
b Collection of dyeing woods, etc. 602

33 Provincial Commission, Province of Entre-Rios.—Samples of polished woods. 600

34 Elola, P., Province of Entre-Rios.—Collection of woods. 600

35 Berdue, Martin, Province of Entre-Rios.—Box made of different woods. 600

36 Parana Commission, Province of Entre-Rios.
a Collection of woods. 600
b Roots and barks; cochineal and dyeing materials. 602
c Turpentine. 603

37 Roman, José, Province of Buenos Ayres.—Carob and mandubay wood. 600

38 Garrigos, J. M., Province of Buenos Ayres.—Collection of woods. 600

39 Gallino, J. A., Province of Entre-Rios.—Collection of woods. 600

40 Echebehere, Pedro, Province of Buenos Ayres.—Collection of woods. 600

41 Fontes, Vicente, & Neyra, Sisto, Province of Buenos Ayres.—Collection of woods. 600

42 Calderon, Pedro, Province of Buenos Ayres.—Collection of woods. 600

43 Gonzalez, Meliton, Province of Buenos Ayres.—Collection of woods. 600

45 Provincial Commission, Province of San Luis.
a Dyeing and tanning products. 602
b Gum and resin. 603

46 Medina, Luis R., Province of Catamarca.
a Visco and coco woods. 600
b Cocoanut bark. 602

47 Hurley, Tomas, Province of Catamarca.—Dyeing products. 602

47*a* Vidal, M. A., Province of San Juan.—Quillo and retortuno for dyeing. 602

47*b* Caecedo, A., Province of San Juan.—Retortuno for dyeing. 602

47*c* Correa, B., Province of San Juan.—Retortuno root for dyeing. 602

47*d* Roderiguez, V., Province of San Juan.—Retortuno root for dyeing. 602

47*e* Poblete, F., Province of San Juan.—Romerrillo. 602

48 Sievert, Max, Province of Salta.
a Silk and wool dyed with the product of the lapacho tree; other dyeing products. 602
b Peat. 604

49 Gonzales, Joaquin, Province of La Rioja.
a Sacanza and roots for dyeing. 602
b Guano, etc. 603

50 Wurffbain, Gustavo, Province of La Rioja.
a Roots for tanning and dyeing, cleansing substances replacing soap, jume for making soap. 602
b Cotton-seed. 605

51 Gelos, Martin, Province of La Rioja.—Dyeing and tanning products. 602

52 Fava, Carlos, Province of Corrientes.—Cochineal and indigo-plant. 602

53 Lopez, Feliciano, Province of Corrientes.—Mbui plant, for dyeing silk and wool. 602

54 Pujol, Eliza, Province of Corrientes.—Root of isypoyu, for dyeing; coloring-roots. 602

55 Poisson, J. T., Province of Corrientes.—Urucu-seed, for dyeing. 602

56 Ritsch, Felipe, Province of Mendoza.—Roots for tanning. 602

57 Ocampo & Acosta, Province of Cordoba.—Bark, seed, and other products for tanning. 602

59 Ubach de Colon, José, Province of Entre-Rios.—Sarsaparilla, carob-bark, and other tanning and dyeing products. 602

60 Sub-commission of the Department of Diamante, Province of Entre-Rios.—Cochineal, carob-bark, and other dyeing and tanning materials. 602

61 Soler, Ventura, Province of Entre-Rios.—Laurel and carob-bark and other dyeing and tanning materials. 602

62 Rodriguez, Severo, Province of San Juan.
a Resins of chilca, etc. 603
b Carob and myrrh seed. 605

63 Balban, Nonasca, Province of Catamarca.—Carob-resin and black resin. 603

64 Flores, Nicanor, Province of Salta.—Tar. 603

65 Sollá, Juan, Province of Salta.—Yareta, a resinous plant. 603

66 Riso, Petrona, Province of Catamarca.—Cherimolia seed. 605

66*a* Flemming, Miguel, Province of Salta.—Tipa and tarco seed. 605

67 Machado, Ruben, Province of Catamarca.—Mistol and carob tree seed. 605

67*a* Goyri, Bernardo, Province of Entre-Rios.—Samples of seeds. 605

68 Ponce, Isidora, Province of Catamarca.—Molle seed. 605

69 Esparsa, José, Province of Catamarca.—Seed of acacia aroma, for dyeing and medicinal purposes. 605

70 Miranda, José, Province of Catamarca.—Acacia for feed, and for hedges. 605

71 Albarez, Francisco, Province of La Rioja.—Walnuts. 605

72 Larrahona, Pedro, Province of La Rioja.—Malingasta nuts. 605

73 Chaves, Crisologo, Province of La Rioja.—Tusca seeds. 605

74 Peluffo, Vicente, & Co., Province of Buenos Ayres.—Collection of seeds. 605

Agricultural Products.

75 Imaz Bros., Province of Buenos Ayres.—Wheat. 620

76 Unzué, Saturnino, Province of Buenos Ayres.—Wheat and corn. 620

77 Grego, A., Province of Buenos Ayres.—Wheat. 620

78 Diaz, Eugenio, Province of Buenos Ayres.—Wheat. 620

79 Traverso, Juan, Province of Buenos Ayres.—Wheat. 620

For classes of exhibits, indicated by numbers at end of entries, see Classification, pp. 12–14.

Agricultural Products.

80 **Bruno, Domingo, Province of Buenos Ayres.**—Wheat. 620

80*a* **Vidal, Augustin, Province of Buenos Ayres.**—Wheat. 620

81 **Alonso, Manuel, Province of Buenos Ayres.**—Wheat. 620

82 **Ibarra, Venero, Province of Buenos Ayres.**—Wheat. 620

83 **Provincial Commission, Province of Buenos Ayres.**—Wheat. 620

83*a* **Cornejo, John, Province of Salta.**—Sugar cane. 620

84 **Bertolate, G., Province of Buenos Ayres.**—Wheat. 620

85 **Buffa, Agustin, Province of Buenos Ayres.**—Wheat. 620

86 **Lanzon, N., Province of Buenos Ayres.**—Wheat. 620

87 **Malvichini, N., Province of Buenos Ayres.**—Wheat. 620

88 **Costa, Bartolo, Province of Buenos Ayres.**—Wheat. 620

89 **Justice of the Peace of Juarez, Province of Buenos Ayres.**—Wheat. 620

90 **Justice of the Peace of Patagones, Province of Buenos Ayres.**—Wheat, barley, and corn. 620

91 **Guerin, N., Province of Buenos Ayres.**—Wheat. 620

92 **Mildred, Juan, Province of Buenos Ayres.**
- *a* Wheat and barley. 620
- *b* Lucern seed. 624

93 **Justice of the Peace of Bahia Blanca, Province of Buenos Ayres.**—Wheat, barley, and corn. 620

94 **Burgos, R., Province of Buenos Ayres.**—Wheat. 620

95 **Acuña, Francisco, Province of Buenos Ayres.**—Barley and corn. 620

96 **Peluffo, Angel, Province of Buenos Ayres.**
- *a* Barley. 620
- *b* Lima beans. 621
- *c* Seeds; hemp and flax, lucern, lentils, palmacristi, etc. 624

97 **Agricultural School of Santa Catalina, Province of Buenos Ayres.**—Corn and grasses. 620

98 **Arce, Invencio, Province of Buenos Ayres.**—Corn. 620

99 **Justice of the Peace of Zarate, Province of Buenos Ayres.**—Corn. 620

100 **Martinez, Hercules, Province of Buenos Ayres.**—Corn. 620

102 **Valdez, Emiliano, Province of Buenos Ayres.**—Corn. 620

104 **Agricultural School of Santa Catalina, Province of Buenos Ayres.**—Fresh beans; lentils. 620

105 **Valdes, Emiliano & Cipriano, Province of Buenos Ayres.**
- *a* Barley, sugar-cane, straw, etc. 620
- *b* Garlic. 621

106 **Galarani, Carlos, Province of Buenos Ayres.**
- *a* Flax, barley, corn, wheat, maize, and cattle-feed. 620
- *b* Beans. 621

107 **Government of the Province of San Juan.**—Grasses, straw, maté herb, etc. 620

108 **Rodriguez, Victor, Province of San Juan.**—Junquille grass. 620

109 **Sarmiento, Juan L., Province of San Juan.**—Yellow and white corn; wheat. 620

110 **Correa, Benidicto, Province of San Juan.**—Corn and wheat. 620

111 **Mazo, Julian, Province of San Juan.**
- *a* White and red corn. 620
- *b* Lima beans. 621

112 **Amafil, Benigno, Province of San Juan.**—Yellow corn. 620

113 **Frias, Salvador, Province of San Juan.**—White corn, barley, wheat. 620

114 **Vidal, Marco A., Province of San Juan.**—Red corn, white wheat. 620

115 **Jones, Fabian, Province of San Juan.**—Red corn; wheat. 620

116 **Aguilar, Juan M., Province of San Juan.**—Red corn; wheat. 620

117 **Ruiz, Clemente, Province of San Juan.**
- *a* Red corn, wheat. 620
- *b* Beans. 621
- *c* Lucern seed. 624

118 **Jofré, Roman, Province of San Juan.**—Red corn. 620

119 **Rufino, Geronimo C., Province of San Juan.**
- *a* White corn. 620
- *b* Beans and peas. 621

120 **Figueroa, Tomas, Province of San Juan.**—White corn. 620

121 **Ruiz, G., Province of San Juan.**—White corn. 620

122 **Balaguer, Tristan, Province of San Juan.**—Corn. 620

123 **Rosa, Rosauro de la, Province of San Juan.**
- *a* Corn. 620
- *b* Lucern seed. 624

124 **Baca, John, Province of San Juan.**—Corn, wheat. 620

125 **Lloveras, Lisandro, Province of San Juan.**—White corn. 620

126 **Cordero, Pedro J., Province of San Juan.**
- *a* White corn. 620
- *b* Peas, barley, and wheat. 621
- *c* Lucern seed. 624

127 **Castro, Pedro, Province of San Juan.**—White corn. 620

128 **Bates, Benjamin, Province of San Juan.**
- *a* Wheat. 620
- *b* Canary seed. 624

133 **Bodarata, Juan, Province of San Juan.**—Barley. 620

134 **Ramirez & Co., Province of San Juan.**
- *a* Barley, white corn. 620
- *b* Lima beans, peas, etc. 621

137 **Day, Frederica, Province of San Juan.**—Wheat. 620

138 **Muñoz, Brancisco, Province of San Juan.**—Wheat. 620

139 **Ledesma, H., Province of San Juan.**—Wheat. 620

For classes of exhibits, indicated by numbers at end of entries, see Classification, pp. 12–14.

Agricultural Products.

140 Provincial Commission, Province of Salta.
a Corn, peanuts, barley, wheat, melons, sugar-cane, etc. 620
b Tobacco. 623
c Onion and lucern seed. 624

141 Flemming, Miguel, Province of Salta.
a Wheat and corn. 620
b Potatoes. 622

142 Toro, Ignacio, Province of Salta.— Wheat, barley, corn, and lucern seed. 620

143 Gonzalez, Joaquin, Province of La Rioja.—Corn for flowers, and also for flour, wheat, lucern seed. 620

144 Davila, Guillermo, Province of La Rioja.
a White corn, sugar corn, wheat. 620
b Lima beans. 621

145 Larrohona, Pedro, Province of La Rioja.
a Corn, wheat, and barley. 620
b Lima beans. 621

146 Villafane, Nicolasa, Province of La Rioja.
a Corn. 620
b Lima beans. 621

147 Illaños, José Manuel, Province of La Rioja.—White corn, barley, wheat. 620

148 Provincial Commission, Province of La Rioja.
a Corn, wheat, barley. 620
b Lima beans. 621
c Onion seed. 624

149 Gonzalez, Ventura, Province of La Rioja.—Wheat. 620

152 Alvarez, Francisco, Province of La Rioja.
a Wheat in stalks. 620
b Lima beans. 621

153 Muro, Froilan, Province of Cata-marca.
a Corn. 620
b Beans and peas. 621

154 Diaz, Ramon, Province of Cata-marca.
a Wheat. 620
b Lima beans. 621

155 Artaza, Santiago, Province of Cata-marca.
a Wheat. 620
b Beans and peas. 621

156 Provincial Commission, Province of Catamarca.
a Corn, wheat, barley, and grasses. 620
b Lima beans. 621
c Indian pepper, tobacco, cigars, etc. 623

157 Molina, José, Province of Catamarca.
a Corn, wheat. 620
b Beans. 621

158 Vega, G., Province of Catamarca. —White corn. 620

159 Artasa, Manuel, Province of Cata-marca.—Corn, etc. 620

160 Miranda, José A., Province of Cata-marca.—White corn. 620

161 Sub-commission of the Department of Ancasti, Province of Catamarca.
a Corn. 620
b Lima beans, etc. 621

162 Sub-commission of the Department of Alto, Province of Catamarca.—White corn. 620

163 Alvarez, S., Province of Catamarca. —Wheat. 620

164 Ahamada, B., Province of Cata-marca.—Wheat. 620

165 Riso, Ventura, Province of Cata-marca.—Geneva wheat. 620

166 Herrera, Miguel, Province of Cata-marca.—Wheat. 620

167 Aguilar, Olegaria, Province of Cat-amarca.—Wheat. 620

168 Tula, Nabor, Province of Cat-amarca.—Wheat, lucern seed. 620

169 Sub-commission of Belen, Prov-ince of Catamarca.
a Corn, wheat. 620
b Beans. 621

170 Sub-commission of the Depart-ment of Pachin, Province of Catamarca.
a Small corn, wheat, Geneva seed, white and yellow corn. 620
b Lima beans. 621

171 Sub-commission of the Depart-ment of Santa Maria, Province of Catamarca.—Corn and wheat. 620

172 Alric, Antonio, Province of San Luis.—Corn, wheat, and barley 620

173 Provincial Commission, Prov-ince of San Luis.
a Corn, wheat, barley, and cattle feed. 620
b Beans. 621

174 Arrondo, Agustin, Province of Entre-Rios.—Wheat. 620

175 Paraña Commission, Province of Entre-Rios.
a Corn, etc. 620
b Beans and peas. 621
c Potatoes. 622
d Tobacco. 623

176 Gualeguaychu Sub-commission, Province of Entre-Rios.—Wheat, corn, etc. 620

177 Goyri, B., Province of Entre-Rios. —Corn. 620

178 Balugera, Domingo, Province of Entre-Rios.—Rice and corn. 620

179 Crespo, Manuel, Province of Entre-Rios.—Paraná wheat. 620

180 Uruguay and Paraná Commission, Province of Entre-Rios.
a Collection of seeds and cereals. 620
b Collection of seeds. 624

181 Meyer, Edmundo, Province of Santa Fé.—Wheat and barley. 620

182 Ceretti, L., Province of Santa Fé.— Wheat. 620

183 Lubary, T., Province of Santa Fé.— Wheat. 620

184 Colonia San Carlos Sub-commis-sion, Province of Santa Fé.—Barley. 620

185 Nickisch, Manuel, Province of Santa Fé.
a Corn. 620
b Lima beans, etc. 621

186 Iturrapse Co., Province of Santa Fé.—Wheat. 620

187 Bergeré, Dr., Province of Santa Fé. —Peanuts. 620

188 Blanchaud, Miguel, Province of Santa Fé.
a Peanuts, corn, and wheat. 620
b Chick-peas. 621
c Leaf tobacco. 623

189 Beken, Federico, Province of San-ta Fé.—Wheat. 620

190 Schuling, German, Province of Santa Fé.—Corn. 620

For classes of exhibits, indicated by numbers at end of entries, see Classification, pp. 12-14.

Agricultural Products.

191 **Pillier, N., Province of Santa Fé.**—Wheat. 620

192 **Carignano Bros., Province of Santa Fé.**—Wheat. 620

193 **Vaivas, Carlos, Province of Santa Fé.**—Wheat. 620

194 **Provincial Commission, Province of Santa Fé.**—Dry lucern, corn. 620

195 **Frischi, Cristino, Province of Santa Fé.**—Wheat. 620

196 **Arminchiardi, Juan, Province of Mendoza.**—Wheat. 620

197 **Fourcade, Pedro, Province of Mendoza.**—Wheat. 620

198 **De la Cruz Videla, Juan, Province of Mendoza.**—Wheat. 620

199 **Roman, Medardo, Province of Mendoza.**
a Wheat. 620
b Lima beans. 621

200 **Sanchez, Modesto, Province of Mendoza.**—White Lima beans. 621

201 **Provincial Commission, Province of Mendoza.**—Corn. 620

202 **Agricultural Villa of Mendoza, Province of Mendoza.**
a Corn and wheat. 620
b Lima beans and peas. 621

203 **Provincial Commission, Province of Jujui.**
a Rice, corn, and wheat. 620
b Indian pepper, tobacco. 623

204 **Provincial Commission, Province of Tucuman.**
a Corn, rice, wheat. 620
b Sweet potatoes, etc. 622
c Tobacco, cigars, etc. 623

205 **Commission of the Chaco Argentine Territory.**
a Corn, sugar-cane, espartillo grass. 620
b Tapoyua, used as a food; mandioca, for making starch and chipa bread, etc. 622
c Flowers made of saffron; tobacco. 623

206 **Harbor-master, Chaco Argentine Territory.**—Sugar-cane plant, espartillo grass, etc. 620

207 **Ferré, Vicente, Province of Corrientes.**—Sugar-canes. 620

208 **Commission of the Province of Corrientes.**
a Sugar-cane. 620
b Mandioca. 622
c Tobacco, maté herbs, etc. 623

209 **Bella Vista Sub-commission, Province of Corrientes.**
a Corn. 620
b Popi from mandioca. 622
c Tobacco. 623

210 **Appleyard, Juan B., Province of Corrientes.**
a Rice. 620
b Maté herbs. 623

211 **Provincial Commission, Province of Santiago del Estero.**
a Wheat. 620
b Sweet potatoes. 622

212 **Michelond, Miguel, Province of Santa Fé.**—Peach sugar-cane. 620

213 **Provincial Commission, Province of Cordoba.**
a Wheat. 620
b Peas and beans. 621
c Sweet potatoes. 622
d Cigars, pepper, tobacco, mustard, etc. 623

214 **Ferrando, Juan, Province of Entre-Rios.**—Lima beans and peas. 621

214*a* **Aubone, Daniel, Province of San Juan.**—Beans. 621

215 **Escobar, Juan de Dios, Province of San Luis.**—Lima beans. 621

215*a* **Farias, José A., Province of San Juan.**—Beans, peas, etc. 621

216 **Pouyet, Miguel, Province of Mendoza.**—Collection of garden-seeds, beans, peas, etc. 621

216*a* **Davila, Bonifacio, Province of La Rioja.**—Beans. 621

217 **Denner, Santiago, Province of Santa Fé.**
a Lima beans. 621
b Tobacco seed. 624

217*a* **Bascuñan, Francisco, Province of La Rioja.**
a Beans. 621
b Lucern seed. 624

218 **Cordoba, Demetrio, Province of Catamarca.**—Lima beans. 621

219 **Sans, N. Roca, Province of Mendoza.**—Potatoes. 622

220 **Audielo, M., Province of Buenos Ayres.**—Potatoes. 622

221 **Polá, Juan, Province of Salta.**—Potatoes, red and sweet oca oxalis. 622

222 **Delgado, Daniel, Lamincha, Province of Catamarca.**—Potatoes. 622

223 **Maxit, José, Province of Entre-Rios.**—Potatoes. 622

224 **Pfeiffer, Pedro, Province of Santa Fé.**—Potatoes. 622

225 **Rizo, Isidoro, Province of Catamarca.**—Coffee. 623

226 **Bustamante, O., Province of Catamarca.**—Tobacco and cut maize leaves for cigarettes. 623

226*a* **Appleyard, T. B., Province of Corrientes.**—Tobacco. 623

227 **Barros, Sebastian, Province of Catamarca.**—Cumin and anise. 623

227*a* **Coudert, A., Province of Buenos Ayres.**—Cigarettes. 623

228 **Augier, Uladislao, Province of Catamarca.**—Cumin seed. 623

229 **Alvarez, Cruz, Province of Catamarca.**—Cumin seed. 623

230 **Arrillaga, Javier, Province of Corrientes.**—Maté herb packed in tapir skin. 623

230*a* **Esquivel, Peter A., Province of Corrientes.**—Cigars. 623

231 **Vera, Matilde, Province of Corrientes.**—Pigeons stuffed with maté; herbs packed in wolf skins. 623

232 **Alegre, John, Province of Corrientes.**—Maté. 623

233 **Beita, Valentin, & Co., Province of Santa Fé.**—Tobacco, coffee, pepper, cinnamon, cumin, cloves, chocolate. 623

234 **Silva, F., Province of Santa Fé.**—Arazá (a spice). 623

234*a* **Cobo, L., Province of Tucuman.**—Tobacco. 623

235 **Aragon, S., Province of Santa Fé.**—Tobacco. 623

237 **Invernice, Pedro, Province of Santa Fé.**—Spurge. 623

For classes of exhibits, indicated by numbers at end of entries, see Classification, pp. 12–14.

Animals, Animal and Vegetable Products.

238 Granada, Salvador, Province of Cordoba.—Chocolate. 623

239 Villar, Salvador, Province of Jujui.
a Coffee. 623
b Castor beans, etc. 624

240 Carrillos, Pablo, Province of Jujui. —Tobacco. 623

241 Baigorra, José, Province of Jujui.— Wild cocoa, etc. 623

242 Burela, Serapio, Province of Salta. —Tobacco. 623

243 Davalos, Benjamin, Province of Salta.—Tobacco leaves. 623

244 Waile, S., Province of Salta.—Cigarettes. 623

245 Zolezi, Nicolas, Province of Buenos Ayres.—Snuff and cigars. 623

246 Lago & Son, Antonio, Province of Buenos Ayres.—Cigarettes. 623

247 Andes, Mendez M. de, Province of Buenos Ayres.—Cigarettes. 623

248 Daumas, J., & Co., Province of Buenos Ayres.—Cigarettes and tobacco. 623

249 Coll, Vitoria, & Co., Province of Buenos Ayres.—Cigarettes. 623

250 Schroeder, Nicolas, Province of Buenos Ayres.—Leaf tobacco and cigars. 623

251 Lista, Manuel,& Schröder,T.,Province of Buenos Ayres.—Leaf tobacco. 623

252 Casanco, Juan, Province of Santa Fé.—Flax and spurge seed. 624

253 Peluffo, Vicente, & Co., Province of Buenos Ayres.—Seeds. 624

255 Arenales, A. M. Alvarez de, Province of Buenos Ayres.—Jerusalem artichoke seed. 624

Land Animals.

258 Provincial Commission, Province of Mendoza.—Collection of birds. 635

259 Lemos, Abraham, Province of Mendoza.
a Hawk, woodpecker, wild sandpiper. 635
b Lynx, stuffed mataco, etc. 637
c Lizard, scorpions, insects, etc. 638

260 Nuñez, Santos, Province of Catamarca.—Humming-bird. 635

261 Franco, Luis A., Province of Catamarca.—Humming-bird. 635

262 Poblete, Tiburcio, Province of San Juan.—Ostrich skin. 635

263 Provincial Commission, Province of San Juan.—Prepared skins of terntern, partridge, chimango, craw birds, etc. 635

264 Dominguez, José, Province of San Juan.—Prepared skins of banduria. 635

265 Rosario Tala, Sub-commission, Province of Entre-Rios.—Stuffed gull and quail. 635

267 Provincial Commission, Province de San Luis.
a Nest of hornero. 635
b Lizard skin. 638

268 Provincial Commission, Province de Catamarco.
a Mataco and quirquincho shells. 635
b Wasp's nest. 638

269 Echevets, Gabriel, Province of Buenos Ayres.—A stuffed wildcat of Balcarce. 637

269*a* Goyena, John, Province of Buenos Ayres.—Stuffed toad and rabbit. 637

269*b* Rio, T. R. del, Province of Buenos Ayres.—Toads. 637

269*c* Fuente, D. G. de la, Province of Buenos Ayres.—Toads. 637

270 Gonzalez, Juan, Province of Buenos Ayres.—Polecat and small fox, stuffed. 637

271 Valdés, Emiliano & Cipriano, Province of Buenos Ayres.—Stuffed rat. 637

272 Rosario Tala, Sub-commission, Province of Entre-Rios.—Stuffed polecat. 637

274 Echavarria, Cecilio, Province of Santa Fé.—Vipers. 638

275 Commission of the Chaco Argentino Territory.—Rattlesnake and coral viper. 638

276 Provincial Commission, Province of Corrientes.—Curiyú viper's skin. 638

277 Fernandez, Severo, Province of Corrientes.—Viper skins. 638

278 Fava, Carlos, Province of Corrientes.—Viper skins. 638

279 Poisson, Juan T., Province of Corrientes.—Viper's skin. 638

280 Bella Vista Sub-commission, Province of Corrientes.—Spiders and their silk in cocoons, snakes. 638

281 Gonzalez, Pedro J., Province of Corrientes.—Dissected guana (South American lizard). 638

282 Diaz, Eulogia, Province of Corrientes.—Stuffed viper. 638

283 Jurado, G. Doraliza de, Province of San Luis.—Black wasp's comb. 638

284 Escobar, Juan de D., Province of San Luis.—Snake skin. 638

286 Laborda, Franklin, Province of San Luis.—Insects, snake, and lizard. 638

287 Day, Edmund, Province of Mendoza.—Viper. 638

288 Sanchez, Modesta, Province of Mendoza.—Viper. 638

289 Iñiguez, M. A., Province of Buenos Ayres.—Vipers in alcohol. 638

Water Animals, Fish Culture and Apparatus.

290 Provincial Commission, Province of Corrientes.—Shells. 645

291 Arteaga, Amancio, Province of Santa Fé.—Shells. 645

292 Provincial Commission, Province of San Juan.—Baskets. 647

293 Machado, Ruben, Province of Catamarca.—Basket of aibé straw. 647

294 Provincial Commission, Province of Salta.—Fishing-lines, etc. 647

Animal and Vegetable Products.

295 Parana Commission, Province of Entre-Rios.
a Sponges. 650
b Colt-grease, shad-oil, leather, skins, etc. 652
c Ostrich feathers. 653
d Sausage, jelly. 656
e Domestic beer, lemonade, and wine. 660

For classes of exhibits, indicated by numbers at end of entries, see Classification, pp. 12–14.

Animal and Vegetable Products.

296 Provincial Commission, Province of Salta.
a Cheese. 651
b Viper, vicugna, lion, chinchilla, and other skins; soles. 652
c Honey and wax. 654
d Dried peaches and nuts. 656
e Wheat flour. 657
f Mandioca and wheat starch. 658
g Querosilla and sugar-cane syrups and sugar. 659
h Aguardente brandy. 660

297 Dubois, B. B., Province of Entre- Rios.—Cheese. 651

298 Vasquez, Lucrecio, Province of Cordoba.—Achala cheese. 651

299 Vaillard, Hipolito, Province of Santa Fé.—Cheese. 651

299*a* Elia, Eveguiel, Province of Buenos Ayres.—Cheese. 651

300 Provincial Commission, Province of San Luis.
a Butter. 651
b Lion, hare, fox, buck, otter, and heron skins. 652
c Eggs, condor and ostrich feathers. 653
d Palpa and honey syrups. 659

301 Sola, Juan, Province of Salta.
a Cheese. 651
b Paisarana, fruit of the Indian fig. 656

302 Linares, Calisto, Province of Salta. —Cheese. 651

303 Arias, Francisco, Province of Bue- nos Ayres.—Sheepskin. 652

303*a* Oliden, T., Province of Buenos Ayres.—Marrow oil. 652

304 Justice of the Peace of Patagones, Province of Buenos Ayres.
a Sheepskins. 652
b Ostrich feathers. 653
c Cherry liqueur and Chacoli wine. 660

305 Balcarce, German, Province of Buenos Ayres.—Sheep, goat, wild boar, otter, deer, weasel, wolf, and wild cat skins, etc. 652

305*a* Silges & Ferrando, Province of Buenos Ayres.—Hides and tallow. 652

306 Martinez, Luiz, Province of Buenos Ayres.—Hides. 652

306*a* Costa, Angel, Province of Buenos Ayres.—Charcoal. 652

307 Fragueiro, G., Province of Buenos Ayres.—Otter and sheepskins. 652

307*a* Ergueta, Manuel, Province of San Luis.—Guaraco's skin. 652

307*b* Ledesma Bros., Province of Cor- doba.
a Goat skins. 652
b Wheat flour. 657

308 Provincial Commission, Province of Buenos Ayres.—Sea-lion skin, ox and colt hide. 652

309 Valdez, Emiliano, Province of Buenos Ayres.—Lion-skin, colt, and ox-hides. 652

310 Fuente, Diego G. de la, Province of Buenos Ayres.—Aguara skin. 652

311 Barrotaran, Juan, Province of Bue- nos Ayres.—Lamb skins. 652

312 Dugan, Tomas, Province of Buenos Ayres.—Sheepskins. 652

313 Gomez, Lorenzo, Province of Buenos Ayres.—Flamingo skin from La Laguna de los Padres (Balcarce). 652

314 Mora, J., Province of Buenos Ayres. —Sheepskin. 652

315 Acuña, P. Garcia, Province of Buenos Ayres.—Cow tripes prepared for export. 652

316 Battini, Angel Petro, Province of Buenos Ayres.—Leather. 652

317 Duportal, Emilio, Province of Buenos Ayres.—Skins. 652

318 Arnault, Augusto, Province of Buenos Ayres.—Domestic cat-skins for the cure of rheumatism. 652

319 Escalada & Co., Buenos Ayres.— Tanned and colored kid skins for gloves. 652

320 Bernard, Joaquin, Province of Buenos Ayres.—Sheep and lamb skins. 652

321 Bellocq Bros., Province of Buenos Ayres.—Calf skins. 652

322 Iniguez, A. Manuel, Province of Buenos Ayres.—Charcoal of curumanuel wood. 652

323 Jacquemard, Victor, Province of Buenos Ayres.—Animal charcoal. 652

324 Mujica, E. S., Province of Buenos Ayres.—Prepared blood for refining sugar and clarifying syrups. 652

325 Gauther, Adolfo, Province of Buenos Ayres.—Tallow. 652

326 Santillan Bros. & Co., Province of Santiago del Estero.—Leather for boots and lizard leather for gaiters: skins, etc. 652

327 Gelos, Martin, Province of La Rioja. —Wild-boar skins. 652

328 Gonzalez, Joaquin, Province of La Rioja.—Lion, vicugna, and ai-ai skins. 652

329 Provincial Commission, Province of La Rioja.
a Leather, lion, goat, vicugna, and other skins, etc. 652
b Dried peaches, raisins, and pressed olives. 656
c Starch. 658
d Nonogasta syrup. 659
e Wine and brandy. 660

330 Commission of the Chaco Argen- tine Territory.
a Tiger, wolf, deer, cat, and lion skins, etc. 652
b Mandioca starch for making chipa bread. 653
c Guaviranú liquors, sugar cane and orange juices. 660

331 Provincial Commission, Province of Catamarca.
a Skins, leather, etc. 652
b Lime and orange sweetmeats. 656
c Flour. 657

332 Andalgalá Sub-commission, Prov- ince of Catamarca.—Vicugna, alpaca, gray fox, lamb skins, leather, etc. 652

333 Vergara, Altillo, Province of Cata- marca.—Swan skin. 652

334 Tinogasta Sub-commission, Prov- ince of Catamarca.—Lion, chinchilla, fox, wild-cat, ferret, and wild-boar skins. 652

335 Medina, J., Province of Catamarca. —Ampalagua and otter skins. 652

336 Santa Maria Sub-commission, Province of Catamarca.—Vicugna, chinchilla, and fox skins. 652

For classes of exhibits, indicated by numbers at end of entries, see Classification, pp. 12–14.

Animal and Vegetable Products.

337 Pachin Sub-commission, Province of Catamarca.—Wildcat, ferret, guana skins, etc. 652

338 Belen Sub-commission, Province of Catamarca.
a Alpaca and vicugna skins. 652
b White wine. 660

339 Provincial Commission, Province of Tucuman.
a Skins and leather. 652
b Wheat starch. 658
c Sugar. 659
d Biscuits. 661

340 Provincial Commission, Province of Entre-Rios.—Swan and deer skins. 652

341 Victoria Sub-commission, Province of Entre-Rios.—Chajá skin. 652

342 Benites, A., & Co., Province of Entre-Rios.
a Tallow. 652
b Wax and honey. 654
c Preserved meats, beef extracts, etc. 656

343 Allurralde, Punte y Carril, Province of Entre-Rios.—Horse hide. 652

344 Darcher, Amadeo, Province of Entre-Rios.—Sea-wolf, fox, wildcat, and otter skins, etc. 652

345 Barcos, Pedro B., Province of Entre-Rios.—Skins. 652

346 Rosario Sub-commission, Province of Entre-Rios.—Buck, otter, ferret, coati, lion, fox, weasel, wildcat skins, etc. 652

347 Victoria Sub-commission, Province of Entre-Rios.—Skins. 652

348 Alurralde, Rodolfo, Province of Entre-Rios.—Wildcat skin. 652

349 Fuento, Gregorio T. de la, & Del Carril, Pedro A., Province of Entre-Rios.—Sea-wolf, horse, deer skins, etc. 652

350 Provincial Commission, Province of Entre-Rios.—Wildcat, fox, otter skins, etc. 652

351 Fontes, Vicente M., & Neygra, Sixto, Province of Entre-Rios.—Tiger, lion, wolf, fox, ferret, otter, rabbit, wildcat, and weasel skins. 652

352 Goyri, Bernardo, Province of Entre-Rios.—Fox and weasel skins. 652

353 Maglioni, Francisco, Province of Entre-Rios. — Carpincho and deer skins. 652

354 Ceballos, Desiderio, Province of Salta. — Soles, black and morocco leather. 652

354*a* Garcia, Domingo, Province of Rioja.
a Glue. 652
b Grape syrup. 659

355 Saenz, Victoriano, Province of Salta.—Tiger skin. 652

356 Zorilla, Benjamin, Province of Salta.—Llama skin. 652

357 Correras, Segundo, Province of Mendoza.—Lion skin. 652

358 Provincial Commission, Province of Mendoza.
a Fox skins. 652
b Ostrich feathers. 653
c Dried peaches, sweatmeats, preserved lemons, etc. 656

359 Gomez, Cecilio, Province of Mendoza.—Chancho wild-boar skin.

360 Ribero, Jacinto, Province of San Luis.—Wildcat skins. 652

361 Sierra, Ramon de la, Province of San Luis.—Aguará purse and occiput of an ostrich. 652

362 Lahiton, Pedro, Province of San Luis.—Tanned hides, morocco, etc. 652

363 Ladies' Commission, Province of San Luis.
a Peach preserve, plum, melon, peach, lemon, water-melon, and quince sweetmeats, etc. 656
b Lemon and orange liquors. 660

364 Rodriguez, Severo, Province of San Juan.
a Tanned hide. 652
b Musk and peeled raisins. 656
c Wines. 660

365 Vidart, Juan A., Province of San Juan.—Lina hides. 652

366 Ruiz, Clemente, Province of San Juan.—Merino metis skin. 652

367 Moreno, Federico, Province of San Juan.—Ox hide. 652

368 Provincial Commission, Province of San Juan.
a Horns and fox skins. 652
b Raisins, preserved fruits. 656

369 Rodriguez, Victor, Province of San Juan.
a Horn combs. 652
b Raisins, etc. 656
c Wheat starch. 658
d Wines. 660

370 Provincial Commission, Province of Cordoba.
a Horn flasks and combs; lion, wild cat, and goat skins. 652
b Flava wax and honey. 654
c Sweetmeats. 656
d Flour, bran, etc. 657
e Indian fig-syrup. 659

371 Iriarte, Cárlos, Province of Cordoba. —Tanned goat skins. 652

372 Ocampo & Acosta, Province of Cordoba.—Tanned hides. 652

373 Provincial Commission, Province of Jujui.
a Vicugna, llama, tiger, and other skins. 652
b Wax and wild honey. 654
c Dried peaches. 656
d Corn and wheat flour. 657
e Sugar. 659
f Querosilla mead. 660

374 Dagorret, Modesta, Province of Corrientes.—Tanned viper skin, sole leather, hides, etc. 652

375 Provincal Commission, Province of Corrientes.
a Otter skins. 652
b Ostrich feathers. 653
c Wax. 654
d Citron, peanut, lime, and other sweetmeats; cocoanuts. 656

376 Bella Vista Sub-commission, Province of Corrientes.—Otter skins. 652

377 Echevarria, Cecilio, Province of Santa Fé.
a Wolf, lion, tiger, fox, ostrich, and other skins. 652
b Wax. 654
c Wild fruit, preserved. 656
d Sugar-cane brandy. 660

For classes of exhibits, indicated by numbers at end of entries, see Classification, pp. 12-14.

Animal and Vegetable Products.

378 Provincial Commission, Province of Santa Fé.
a Wolf, lion, goat, otter, hare, fox, deer skins, etc. 652
b Sweetmeats. 661

379 Martinez, Jonas, Province of Catamarca.—Ostrich feathers. 653

380 Suarez, R., Province of Santa Fé.—Ostrich feathers. 653

381 Soler, Ventura, Province of Entre-Rios.—Ostrich feathers. 653

382 Mavit, José, Province of Entre-Rios.—Honey. 654

383 Invernizzo, J., & Toschini, J., Province of Entre-Rios.—Wax and honey. 654

384 Otero, José, Province of Buenos Ayres.—Honey and wax. 654

385 Barraquero, Carmen, Province of Mendoza.
a Wax and honey. 654
b Preserves. 656
c Grape, quince, and cherry syrups. 659
d White wine. 660

386 Pouyet, Miguel, Province of Mendoza.
a Honey. 654
b Nuts, almonds, and fruits. 656
c Cognac and wines. 660

387 Aragon, J. M., Province of Santa Fé.—Honey. 654

388 Iramon, Juan, Province of Santa Fé.—Honey and wax. 654

389 Jurado, Doraliza, G. de, Province of San Luis.—Honey. 654

390 Albarracin, Saturnino, Province of San Juan.—Wax. 654

391 Cortinez, Domitilio, Province of San Juan.—Honey. 654

392 Piñero, Aurelio, Province of Cordoba.—Wax. 654

393 Passel, Teodoro, Province of Cordoba.—Wax. 654

394 Cespedes, José, Province of Mendoza.—Dried apples and figs. 656

394*a* Biraben, A., Province of Entre-Rios.—Preserved meats. 656

395 Godoy, Nicolas, Province of Mendoza.—Preserved citrons. 656

395*a* Vignolles, Henry, Province of Santa Fé.—Preserved meats and patés. 656

396 Sanchez, Modesto, Province of Mendoza.—Preserved grapes. 656

397 Chaves, Rosaura, Province of Mendoza.—Olives. 656

398 Campos, Enrique, Province of Mendoza.
a Milk-extract. 656
b Orange-wine, anisette. 660

399 Rufino, Gerónimo C., Province of San Juan.—Musk-grape raisins. 656

400 Ramirez & Co., Province of San Juan.—Raisins. 656

401 Sarmiento, J. L., Province of San Juan.
a Raisins. 656
b Brandy. 660

402 Bates, Benjamin, Province of San Juan.
a Almonds and raisins. 656
b Flour and bran. 657

403 Herrera, P. J., Province of San Juan.—Nuts. 656

404 Mazo, Julian, Province of San Juan.—Raisins and figs. 656

405 Herrera, José, Province of San Juan.—Almonds. 656

406 Tacheret, Cárlos, Province of San Juan.—Figs. 656

407 Tacheret, Emilio, Province of San Juan.—Figs. 656

408 Jones, Fabian, Province of San Juan.—Figs. 656

409 Jofré, Ramon, Province of San Juan.
a Figs. 656
b Wines and vinegar. 660

410 Frias, Salvador, Province of San Juan.—Musk raisins. 656

411 Ruiz, Clemente S., Province of San Juan.—Nuts. 656

412 Aguilar, J. M., Province of San Juan.—Carob paste. 656

413 Governor of the Province, Province of Jujui.—Nuts. 656

414 Bascuñan, Francisco, Province of La Rioja.—Dried figs. 656

415 Olivera, Bernardo, Province of La Rioja.—Dried figs. 656

416 Gonzales, Ventura, Province of La Rioja.
a Raisins and dried figs. 656
b Nonogasta syrup. 659
c Wine. 660

417 Larrohona, Pedro, Province of La Rioja.—Raisins. 656

418 Garcia, Domingo, Province of La Rioja.
a Raisins. 656
b Nonogasta syrup. 659
c Wine, brandy, and anisette. 660

419 Dávila, Carmen T. de, Province of La Rioja.—Preserved olives, lime and peach preserves, and cayote sweetmeat. 656

420 Bustos, Sophia G., Province of La Rioja.—Quince preserve. 656

421 Treloar, Guillermo A., Province of La Rioja.
a Carob paste. 656
b Wines. 660

422 Moujon, Mercedes I., Province of Catamarca.—Raisins. 656

423 Santa Coloma, Isaac, Province of Catamarca.—Raisins, preserves, etc. 656

424 Herrera, Ramon, Province of Catamarca.—Musk-raisins. 656

425 Delgado, Manuel, Province of Catamarca.—Dried figs. 656

426 Medina, Luis R., Province of Catamarca.—Nuts. 656

427 Aguero, Patricia, Province of Catamarca.—Musk raisins. 650

428 Franco, Luis A., Province of Catamarca.—Candied quinces. 656

429 Acosta, Maria E. de, Province of Catamarca.—Candied quinces. 656

430 Colodrero, A., Province of Corrientes.—Yatay palm cocoanuts. 656

431 Videla, Victor, Province of San Luis.
a White carob and carob paste. 650
b Syrup, etc. 657

For classes of exhibits, indicated by numbers at end of entries, see Classification, pp. 12-14

Animal and Vegetable Products.

432 **Escobar, Juan D., Province of San Luis.**
a Dried figs and peaches. 656
b Wine and carob mead. 660

433 **Ronchetti, Valentin, Province of Santa Fé.**—Pickled partridges. 656

434 **Nikisch, Manuel, Province of Santa Fé.**—Pickled tongues. 656

435 **Garvino, Signor, Province of Entre-Rios.**—Salt meat and tongues; gelatine. 656

436 **Valdes, Emiliano and Cipriano,** Province of Buenos Ayres.—Salt tongues and beef, etc. 656

437 **Olidon, Tomas, Province of Buenos Ayres.**
a Sheep tongue, dried mutton and beef. 656
b Cognac bitters. 660

438 **Beriso, Juan, & Co., Province of Buenos Ayres.**—Dried tongues. 656

439 **Cambaceres, Antonio, Province of Buenos Ayres.**—Jerked beef and salt tongues. 656

440 **Roverano Bros., Province of Buenos Ayres.**—Sweetmeats in syrup. 656

442 **Colla, Juan, Province of Entre-Rios.**—Flour. 657

443 **Cabilla, A., Province of Entre-Rios.**—Grits. 657

444 **Buada, F., Province of Entre-Rios.**—Flour. 657

445 **Dubois, José B., Province of Entre-Rios.**—Flour. 657

446 **Berizo, Domingo, Province of Entre-Rios.**—Flour. 657

448 **Pillier, N., Province of Santa Fé.**—Flour. 657

449 **Iturraspe & Co., Province of Santa Fé.**—Bran, flour. 657

450 **Wart, Carlos de, Province of Santa Fé.**—Flour. 657

451 **Quelet, Enrique, Province of Santa Fé.**—Wheat flour. 657

452 **Bauer, G., Province of Santa Fé.**—Flour. 657

453 **Lubary, Tomas, Province of Santa Fé.**—Flour. 657

454 **Frank & Lami, Province of Santa Fé.**—Flour. 657

455 **Fristchi, Celestino, Province of Santa Fé.**—Wheat flour. 657

456 **Gallo, B., Province of San Juan.**—Flour and bran. 657

457 **Frias, Salvador, Province of San Juan.**—Flour and Chingo flour. 657

458 **Appleyard, T. B., Province of Corrientes.**
a Mandioca flour. 657
b Mandioca starch. 658

459 **Fourcade, Pedro, Province of Mendoza.**—Flour and bran. 657

460 **Casas, Molino de, Province of Mendoza.**—Flour. 657

461 **Armenchiardi, Juan, Province of Mendoza.**
a Corn meal and flour. 657
b Macaroni, vermicelli. 658

462 **Tillar, Cárlos, Province of Jujui.**—Flour. 657

463 **Alric, Antonio, Province of San Luis,**—Flour and bran. 657

464 **Provincial Commission, Province** of Santiago del Estero.—Flour. 657

466 **Navarro, Cornelio, Province of** Mendoza.—Wheat starch. 658

467 **Gazzo, Luis, Province of Santa Fé.**—Vermicelli. 658

468 **Dávila, Nicolasa, Province of La Rioja.**—Nonogasta syrup. 659

468*a* **Mendevil, Fidel, Province of Tucuman.**—Sugar. 659

469 **Dávila, Guillermo, Province of La Rioja.**—Nonogasta syrup. 659

470 **Gordillo, Alcibiades, Province of La Rioja.**—Nonogasta syrup. 659

471 **Dominguez, José D., Province of San Juan.**—Syrup. 659

472 **Ovejero, Sisto, Province of Salta.**
a Sugar. 659
b White wine. 660

473 **Figueroa, José E., Province of Catamarca.**—Syrup. 659

473*a* **Garcia, S., Province of Tucuman.**—Sugar. 659

474 **Brisuela, Primitivo, Province of Catamarca.**—Grape syrup. 659

475 **Araob, Adelaida, Province of Catamarca.**—Grape syrup. 659

476 **Castello, Guadalupe, Province of Catamarca.**—Grape syrup. 659

477 **Leri, Petrona de, Province of Catamarca.**—Grape syrup. 659

478 **Aguero, Patricia, Province of Catamarca.**—Grape syrup. 659

478*a* **Mendez & Keller, Province of Tucuman.**
a Sugar. 659
b Wines. 660

479 **Aybar, J. R., Province of Catamarca.**—Grape syrup. 659

479*a* **Arguellos & Oliver, Province of Tucuman.**—Loaf sugar. 659

479*b* **Garcia, Fidel, Bros., Province of Tucuman.**—Sugars. 659

480 **Laborda, Franklin, Province of San Luis.**—Orange, lemon, currant, banana, and peach syrup. 659

481 **Bagley, M. S., Province of Buenos Ayres.**—Bitters. 660

482 **Pizzona, Miguel, Province of Buenos Ayres.**—White and red wines. 660

483 **Plá, José, & Co., Province of Buenos Ayres.**—Anisette brandy. 660

484 **Loy, José, Province of Buenos Ayres.**—Hesperidina bitters. 660

485 **Nuttall, Enrique, Province of Buenos Ayres.**—Hesperidina bitters. 660

486 **Calatroni, Pedro, Province of Buenos Ayres.**—Banana balm, bittersweet tonic, and liquors. 660

487 **German Brewery, Province of** Buenos Ayres.—Chivilcoy beer. 660

488 **Hanot, Jorge, Province of Buenos Ayres.**—Orange-flower water, Chartreuse and Kerman liquor. 660

489 **Dominguez, José, Province of San Juan.**—Vinegar. 660

490 **Terramola, Delfin, Province of San Juan.**—Wine and vinegar. 660

491 **Zavalla, Pedro J., Province of San Juan.**—Wine. 660

For classes of exhibits, indicated by numbers at end of entries, see Classification, pp. 12–14.

Animal and Vegetable Products, Textile Substances.

492 **Quiroga, Isidro, Province of San** Juan.—White wine. 660

493 **Quiroga, Abraham, Province of** San Juan.—Wine. 660

494 **Balaguer, Juan E., Province of San** Juan.—White and red wine. 660

495 **Coll, Francisco M., Province of San** Juan.—Bordeaux wine. 660

496 **Doncel, Rosauro, Province of San** Juan.—Wine. 660

497 **Doncel, José E., Province of San** Juan.—Trinidad wine. 660

498 **Carraffa, Vicente, Province of San** Juan.—Wines and brandy. 660

499 **Herrera, Pedro, Province of San** Juan.—Brandy. 660

500 **Baca, Vicente, Province of San** Juan.—Brandy. 660

501 **Castro, Saturnino, Province of San** Juan.—Brandy. 660

502 **Espada, Tadeo, Province of San** Juan.—Wine. 660

503 **Dejorti, Eusebio, Province of San** Juan.—Wine. 660

504 **Lemaistre, Hilario, Province of** Mendoza.—Wines, quince, gin, ratafia, and cherry liquors. 660

505 **Blanco, Eusebio, Province of Men**doza.—Wines. 660

506 **Guerin, Eugenio, Province of Men**doza.—Wines. 660

507 **Michel, Salvador, Province of** Salta.—Wines. 660

508 **Flemming, M., Province of Salta.**—Wine. 660

509 **Dávalos, Asuncion, Province of** Salta.—Wine. 660

510 **Morales, Emilio, Province of Salta.** —Bitters; cumin, orange and vanilla liquors, cocoa extract, banana balm, cognac, etc. 660

511 **Flores, Nicanor, Province of Salta.** —Wines. 660

513 **Lopez, Filipe, Province of Salta.**—Wines. 660

514 **Velez, Amadeo, Province of Salta.** —Wine. 660

515 **Alvarez, Francisco, Province of** La Rioja.—White wines. 660

516 **Dávila, Bonifacio, Province of** La Rioja.—Wines and anise brandy. 660

517 **Dávila, Domingo, Province of** La Rioja.—Wines. 660

518 **Gordillo, Alcibiades, Province of** La Rioja.—Wines. 660

519 **Dávila, Guillermo, Province of La** Rioja.—Wines. 660

520 **Chaves, Crisologo, Province of La** Rioja.—Wines and anise brandy. 660

521 **Dávila, Nicolasa V. de, Province** of La Rioja.—Wines. 660

522 **Gonzalez, Zoraida Dávila de,** Province of La Rioja.—Mint, coffee, orange, cocoa, and Peruvian bark, liquors. 660

523 **Muro, Froilan, Province of Cata**marca.—Wine. 660

524 **Augier, Uladislao, Province of** Catamarca.—Wine. 660

525 **Lafone Queveda, Samuel A., Prov**ince of La Rioja.—Wines, cognac, and liquors. 660

526 **Franco, Luis A., Province of Cat**amarca.—Wines. 660

527 **Figueroa, Molas, & Co., Province of** Catamarca.—Wine. 660

528 **Narvaez, Dermidio, Province of** Catamarca.—Wines and brandies. 660

529 **Miranda, José A., Province of Cat**amarca.—Wine and brandy. 660

530 **Figueroa, Manuel, Province of** Catamarca.—Wine. 660

531 **Cisnero, Juan B., Province of** Catamarca.—Wine and brandy. 660

532 **Teferina, Daniel, Province of Cat**amarca.—Wines. 660

533 **Molina, Mardoqueo, Province of** Catamarca.—Wine. 660

534 **Ageret, H., Province of Corrientes.** —Lime and orange liquors. 660

535 **Villa, Luis, Province of Corrientes.** —Sugar-cane juice. 660

536 **Alzric, Antonio, Province of San** Luis.—Soda water and lemonade. 660

537 **Billar, Salvador, Province of Jupui.** —Sugar-cane brandy. 660

538 **Gibelli, S., Province of Entre-Rios.** —Wine. 660

539 **Clavarino, S., Province of Entre-**Rios.—Wine. 660

540 **Campora, A., Province of Entre-**Rios.—Wine. 660

541 **Conte Gran, Anselmo, Province of** Entre-Rios.—Vermouth wine and elixir. 660

542 **Costa, Luis, Province of Santa Fé.** —Cognac, vermouth wine, and liquors. 660

543 **Defagot, Cipriano, Province of** Entre-Rios.—Peach liquor. 660

544 **Magdelin, Fernando, Province of** Santa Fé.—Beer. 660

545 **Fontam, Luis T., Province of Santa** Fé.—Anise liquor. 660

546 **Bagley, M. S., & Co., Province of** Buenos Ayres.—Biscuits and crackers. 661

546*a* **Konig, Richard, & Co., Province** of Buenos Ayres.—Sweetmeats. 661

547 **Bromvers, Enrique, Province of** Buenos Ayres.—Crackers and biscuits. 661

548 **Masset, Gustavo, Province of** Buenos Ayres.—Crackers. 661

Textile Substances of Vegetable or Animal Origin.

550 **Rizo, Isidoro, Province of Cata**marca.—Palo borracho cotton. 665

551 **Provincial Commission, Province** of Catamarca.—Cotton and raw palo borracho cotton. 665

551*a* **Silva, Florentius, Province of** Santa Fé.—Cotton. 665

552 **Colina, J. N., Province of Rioja.**—Cotton grown in Vinchina. 665

553 **Dávila, Guillermo, Province of La** Rioja.—Cotton. 665

For classes of exhibits, indicated by numbers at end of entries, see Classification, pp. 12–14.

Textile Substances.

553a Ledesma, Dr., Province of Tucuman.
a Cotton. 665
b Goat's hair. 669

554 Alvarez, Francisco, Province of La Rioja.—Cotton. 665

555 Wurffbain, Gustavo, Province of La Rioja.—Cotton. 665

556 Molina, Mardoqueo, Province of La Rioja.—Cotton and cotton pods. 665

557 Provincial Commission, Province of Salta.
a Cotton. 665
b Chaguar thread and bark, yuchan fibre. 666
c Bristle rope and fabrics for sieves. 669

557a Echevarria, Cecilio, Province of Santa Fé.
a Cotton. 665
b Angora wool. 667

558 Fava, Carlos, Province of Corrientes.—Cotton. 665

559 Bella Vista Sub-commission, Province of Corrientes.
a Raw cotton. 665
b Wool. 667

560 Commission of the Chaco Argentine Territory.—Cotton. 665

561 Provincial Commission, Province of San Luis.
a Cotton. 665
b Wool. 667

562 Invernizzo, John, & Toschini, J., Province of Entre-Rios.
a Cotton. 665
b Cocoons and spun silk. 668

563 Parana Commission, Province of Entre-Rios.
a Fibres and rope. 666
b Wild silk cocoons. 668

564 Provincial Commission, Province of Corrientes.—Ropes made of caraguatá fibre. 666

564a Posadas, G., Province of Buenos Ayres.—Fibre ropes, and lines. 666

655 Torres, Esteban N., Province of Corrientes.—Caraguatá fibres. 666

566 Gelabert, Miguel, Province of Corrientes.—Caraguatá fibre cord. 666

567 Roibon, Enrique, Province of Corrientes.—Caraguatá cord. 666

568 Lescano, José D., Province of Corrientes.—Caraguatá leaves. 666

569 Gelos, Martin, Province of La Rioja.—Feather-grass. 666

570 Carreras, Rosaura C., Province of Mendoza.—Chard thread. 666

571 Provincial Commission, Province of Mendoza.—Hemp and ropes. 666

572 Commission of the Province of Santiago del Estero.—Prepared chaguar fibre. 666

573 Billar, Salvador, Province of Jujui.—Chaguar and yuchan ropes. 666

574 Galarani, Carlos, Province of Buenos Ayres.—Spun flax and flax-straw. 666

575 Meyer, E., Province of Santa Fé.—Hemp. 666

576 Cataneo, Juan, Province of Santa Fé.—Raw flax. 666

577 Stegman, Jorge, Province of Buenos Ayres.—Wool. 667

577a Fortunny, Louis, Province of Buenos Ayres.—Wool. 667

578 Morgan, N., Province of Buenos Ayres.—Wool. 667

579 Peredieu & Bradley, Province of Buenos Ayres.—Wool. 667

579a Provincial Commission, Province of San Luis.—Wool. 667

580 Martinez & Laplaceta, Province of Buenos Ayres.—Wool. 667

581 Molina, Juan C., Province of Buenos Ayres.—Alpaca wool. 667

582 Guevara, Edelmira L. de, Province of Buenos Ayres.—Fleece of Angora goat. 667

583 Guerrero, Carlos T., Province of Buenos Ayres.—Wool. 667

584 Duportal, Emilio, Province of Buenos Ayres.—Wool. 667

585 Chas, Francisco, Province of Buenos Ayres.—Fleece of Negretti lamb. 667

586 Nazar & Co., Romulo, Province of Buenos Ayres.—Wool. 667

587 Latham, Wilfren, Province of Buenos Ayres.—Merino wool, etc. 667

588 Movas, José, Province of Buenos Ayres.—Wool. 667

589 Durand, Augusto, Province of Buenos Ayres.—Wool. 667

590 Castes, Mariano Artayeta, Province of Buenos Ayres.—Wool. 667

591 Unsué, Mariano, Province of Buenos Ayres.—Wool. 667

592 Classen, Enrique, Province of Buenos Ayres.—Wool. 667

593 Tucker, T. E. C., Province of Buenos Ayres.—Wool. 667

594 Iraizo, Geronimo, Province of Buenos Ayres.—Wool. 667

595 Frers, German, Province of Buenos Ayres.—Wool. 667

596 Justice of the Peace of Patagones, Province of Buenos Ayres.—Wool. 667

597 Clarke, Cárlos, Province of Buenos Ayres.—Wool. 667

598 Huergo, Aureliano, Province of Buenos Ayres.—Wool. 667

599 Valdes, Emiliano & Cipriano, Province of Buenos Ayres.—Wool. 667

600 Zubiaurre, Ovidio, Province of Buenos Ayres.—Wool. 667

601 Gutierrez, Gervasio, Province of Buenos Ayres.—Wool. 667

602 Perez, Enrique, Province of Buenos Ayres.—Wool. 667

603 Corrales, I. W., Province of Buenos Ayres.—Wool. 667

604 Gregoire, N., Province of Buenos Ayres.—Wool. 667

605 Provincial Commission of the Province of Buenos Ayres.—Wool. 667

606 Camblond, M., Province of Buenos Ayres.—Wool. 667

607 Bonnement, I. B., Province of Buenos Ayres.—Wool. 667

608 Bernard, Joaquin, Province of Buenos Ayres.—Wool. 667

For classes of exhibits, indicated by numbers at end of entries, see Classification, pp. 12–14.

Textile Substances, Engineering and Administration.

609 **Schweikart, Andrés, Province of** Buenos Ayres.—Wool. 667

610 **McClymont, Guillermo, Province** of Buenos Ayres.—Wool. 667

611 **Hale, Samuel B., Province of Bue-**nos Ayres.—Wool. 667

612 **Galarani, Carlos, Province of** Buenos Ayres.—Wool. 667

613 **Vazquez, Lucrecio, Province of** Cordoba.—Wool. 667

614 **Gomez, Fecundino, Province of** Mendoza.—Wool. 667

615 **Gonzalez, Daniel, Province of Men-**doza.—Wool. 667

616 **Davila, Bonifacio, Province of La** Rioja.—Wool. 667

617 **Gavino, Domingo, Province of** Entre-Rios.—Wool. 667

618 **Dennis, Francis Antonio, Province** of Entre-Rios.—Wool. 667

619 **Fuente, Gregorio F. de la, Prov-**ince of Entre-Rios.—Wool. 667

620 **Correa, Benito, Province of San** Juan.—Wool. 667

621 **Rodriguez, Estanislao, Province of** San Juan.—Alpaca wool. 667

622 **Zavalla, Lorenzo, Province of San** Juan.—Angora wool. 667

624 **Newton, Ricardo, Province of Bue-**nos Ayres.—Silk, spun and in cocoons. 668

625 **Peluffo, Angel, Province of Buenos** Ayres.—Silk in cocoons. 668

625*a* **Victorica, Henry, Province of** Buenos Ayres.—Cocoons. 668

625*b* **Massuchi, Martin, Province of** Buenos Ayres.—Spun silk. 668

625*c* **Sub-commission of San Carlos,** Province of Santa Fé.—Spun silk. 668

625*d* **Bequer, T., Province of Buenos** Ayres.—Silk cocoons. 668

625*e* **Pouyet, Miguel, Province of Men-**doza.—Silk cocoons. 668

626 **Justice of the Peace of San Vicente,** Province of Buenos Ayres. — Horse-hair. 669

627 **Provincial Commission, Province** of Buenos Ayres.—Cow-hair. 669

628 **Lagraña, Cipriano, Province of** Buenos Ayres.—Angora hair. 669

Agricultural Engineering and Administration.

629 **Carenon, E., & J. Lacroze, Prov-**ince of Buenos Ayres. — Model of a pump. 680

630 **Silveyra, Agustin, Province of Bue-**nos Ayres.—Artificial manure. 681

631 **Jacquemard, Victor, Province of** Buenos Ayres.—Artificial manure. 681

632 **Mujica, E. S., Province of San Juan.** —Artificial manure from boiled and dried blood. 681

632*a* **Provincial Commission, Province** of Salta.
a Hair sieves. 224
b Horse-hair rope. 287

LIBERIA.

(*East Avenue, Columns 4 to 7.*)

COLLECTIVE EXHIBIT.

Minerals, Animal and Agricultural Products.

Morris, Edward S., & Co., St. Paul's River & Philadelphia, Pa.
a Iron ore. 100
b Fresh and sweet palm-oil hermetically sealed in glass jars, for medical and family use; palm-oil in casks; palm kernel oil; soap made of fresh and sweet palm-oil. 201
c Indigo. 202
d African curiosities. 312
e Coffee-hulling machinery. 585
f Cam-wood, hardwoods. 600
g Gums. 603
h Coffee, green and roasted; cocoa, ginger, and spices. 623
i Palm kernels. 624
j Ivory. 652
k Palm kernel meal. 657
l Arrow-root. 658
m Sugar. 659
n Cotton. 665
o Flax from the Island of St. Helena, ramie. 666

For classes of exhibits, indicated by numbers at end of entries, see Classification, pp. 12–14.

SPAIN.

(*Nave, South of Main Transept, Columns 13, 14.*)

Pomology.

Pomology.

1 **Jover, Francisco, Alhama, Province** of Almeria.—Grapes. 610

2 **Daza y Ruiz, Francisco, Purchena,** Province of Almeria.—Grapes. 610

3 **Romero, Manuel Carbonero, Purchena,** Province of Almeria.—Grapes. 610

4 **Sanchez Bros. & Granados,** Ochanes, Province of Almeria.—Grapes. 610

5 **Ibañez, Luis Gallego, Cazorla, Province** of Jaen.—Pears. 610

6 **Economical Society of Friends of** the Country, Valencia.—Paintings of grapes. 610

7 **Bernabeu y Diego, Juan B., Jabea,** Province of Alicante.—Almonds. 611

8 **Scals, José, Jijona, Province of Alicante.**—Almonds. 611

9 **Piña, Juan Bautista, Monforte,** Province of Alicante.—Almonds. 611

10 **Soriano, Isidro Martinez, Monóvar,** Province of Alicante.—Almonds. 611

11 **Verdu y Perez, Joaquin, Monóvar,** Province of Alicante.—Almonds. 611

12 **Perez, Albert, & Co., Monóvar,** Province of Alicante.—Almonds. 611

13 **Feliú y Rodriguez, José, Benisa,** Province of Alicante.—Almonds. 611

14 **Linares, José Ramon, Albanchez,** Province of Almeria.—Almonds. 611

15 **Trell y Chacon, Miguel del, Berja,** Province of Almeria.—Almonds. 611

16 **Martin, Francisco Regaña, Cabeza,** de Vaca, Province of Bajadoz.—Walnuts. 611

17 **Feliú, Juan, Palma, Balearic** Islands.—Almonds. 611

18 **Wallés, Edmundo, Ibiza, Balearic** Islands.—Almonds. 611

19 **Fuster, Francisco, Palma, Balearic** Islands.—Almonds. 611

20 **Fuster, Miguel, Palma, Balearic** Islands.—Almonds. 611

21 **Mulet, Antonio, Palma, Balearic** Islands.—Almonds. 611

22 **Melian y Artiles, Matias, Las Palmas,** Canary Islands.—Almonds. 611

23 **Provincial Board of Agriculture,** Castellon.—Walnuts and acorns. 611

24 **Berruezo, José Antonio, Villarel,** Province of Castellon.—Almonds. 611

25 **Garcés, Vicente, Castellon.**—Almonds. 611

26 **Soldevilla, Tomás Moragrega, Castellon.**—Pomegranates. 611

27 **Lara, Rafael J. de, Cordoba.**—Oranges, lemons, and citrons. 611

28 **Veja de Armijo, Marquis of, Cordoba.**—Oranges and lemons. 611

29 **Corporation of Palma del Rio,** Province of Cordoba.—Walnuts. 611

30 **Cabezas y Saravia, José, Cordoba.** —Hazelnuts. 611

31 **Cruz Durán, Juan de la, Aracena,** Province of Huelva.—Walnuts and chestnuts. 611

32 **Sala, Emilio de, Huelva.**—Almonds. 611

33 **Montemayor, María, Moguer, Province** of Huelva.—Almonds. 611

34 **Cueva, Fernando de la, Huelva.**—Almonds. 611

35 **Carnes, Eulogio Martin, Aracena.** Province of Huelva.—Walnuts. 611

36 **Caras, Serafin, Huesca.**—Walnuts. 611

37 **Moreno, Rufino, Cazorla, Province** of Jaen.—Walnuts. 611

38 **Bulnes, Francisco de Paula, Cazorla,** Province of Jaen.—Walnuts. 611

39 **Corporation of Ponferrada, Province** of Leon.—Walnuts and chestnuts. 611

40 **Corporation of Congosto, Province** of Leon.—Chestnuts. 611

41 **Fernandez, Tomás, Armunia, Province** of Leon.—Walnuts. 611

42 **Prado, Maximo Alonso, Leon.**—Walnuts, chestnuts, and hazelnuts. 611

43 **Agelét, Ramon, Lérida.**—Walnuts. 611

44 **Jover, Luisa de, Province of Lerida.**—Almonds. 611

45 **Ignes, Pedro, Cervera, Province** of Lerida.—Hazelnuts. 611

46 **Corporation of Lorenzano, Province** of Lugo.—Walnuts. 611

47 **Quiroga Vasquez, Quiroga, Province** of Lugo.—Chestnuts. 611

48 **Huelin, Guillermo, & Son, Málaga.** —Almonds. 611

49 **Provincial Deputation, Múrcia.**—Almonds. 611

50 **Roca Bros., Múrcia.**—Pomegranates. 611

51 **Yañez, Francisco Vila, Viana, Province** of Orense.—Chestnuts and walnuts. 611

52 **Vaamonde, Ramon María, Puirgin,** Province of Orense.—Chestnuts and walnuts. 611

53 **Rey, Manuel Pereiro, Orense.**—Hazelnuts. 611

54 **Candedo, Manuel, Coles, Province** of Orense.—Hazelnuts. 611

Pomology.

55 Diaz, Francisco, Trandeiras, Province of Orense.—Walnuts. 611

56 Rodriguez, Manuel Iglesias, Celanova, Province of Orense.—Fruits. 611

57 Provincial Board of Agriculture, Industry and Commerce, Oviedo.—Chestnuts, walnuts, and hazelnuts. 611

58 Rios, Eugenio Montero, Pontevedra.—Oranges, lemons, and citrons. 611

59 Brabo, Bernardo, Fregeneda, Province of Salamanca.—Almonds. 611

60 Paulino, Felipe Perez, Fregeneda, Province of Salamanca.—Almonds. 611

61 Hortal, Ignacio, Fregeneda, Province of Salamanca.—Almonds. 611

62 Garcia, José Sanchez, Fregeneda, Province of Salamanca.—Almonds. 611

63 Corbalan, Juan, Sancelle, Province of Salamanca.—Almonds. 611

64 Viesca, Marquis of, Fregeneda, Province of Salamanca.—Almonds. 611

65 Miguel, Ramon, Hinojosa, Province of Salamanca.—Almonds. 611

66 Rivero, Tomás, Hinojosa, Province of Salamanca.—Almonds. 611

67 Garrido, Juan, Valero, Province of Salamanca.—Walnuts. 611

68 Martin, Lorenzo Calvo, Mogarraz, Province of Salamanca.—Walnuts. 611

69 Bellido, Narciso, Zorita, Province of Salamanca.—Walnuts. 611

70 Sanchez, Antonio Capita, Mairena, Province of Sevilla.—Oranges. 611

71 Viñas, Antonio, Reus, Province of Tarragona.—Almonds. 611

72 Magriña, Antonio, Gandesa, Province of Tarragona.—Almonds. 611

73 Peira y Mach, Agustin, Scala Dei, Province of Tarragona.—Almonds, walnuts, and hazelnuts. 611

74 Franch & Segriá, Uldemolins, Province of Tarragona.—Hazelnuts. 611

75 Escoda, Antonio, Vilaseca, Province of Tarragona.—Hazelnuts. 611

76 Bufill, B., Reus, Province of Tarragona.—Almonds. 611

77 Gasull, Bartolomé, Province of Tarragona.—Almonds and hazelnuts. 611

78 Consul & Virgili, Tarragona.—Hazelnuts. 611

79 Domingo, Dimas, Reus, Province of Tarragona.—Almonds and raisins. 611

80 Prieto, Eusebio, Reus, Province of Tarragona.—Walnuts. 611

81 Gil, Francisco, Reus, Province of Tarragona.—Almonds and hazelnuts. 611

82 Pellicer, Francisco, Porrera, Province of Tarragona.—Almonds and hazelnuts. 611

83 Sostres, Francisco Reus, Province of Tarragona.—Hazelnuts. 611

84 Vigueres y Monlló, Francisco, Uldemolins, Province of Tarragona.—Almonds. 611

85 Montaña, Francisco Roca, Cambrils, Province of Tarragona.—Almonds. 611

86 Margales, Francisco Escoda, Vandellós, Province of Tarragona.—Almonds. 611

87 Puigcercós y Anglès, Francisco, Ulldemolins, Province of Tarragona.—Almonds. 611

88 Llurba, Francisco, Uldemolins, Province of Tarragona.—Almonds. 611

89 Fumaña Bros., Reus, Province of Tarragona.—Almonds and hazelnuts. 611

90 Prius, Francisco, Reus, Province of Tarragona.—Hazelnuts. 611

91 Comas, Francisco, Reus, Province of Tarragona.—Hazelnuts. 611

92 Pfeiffer, Herman, Reus, Province of Tarragona.—Hazelnuts. 611

93 Coll, José, Valls, Province of Tarragona.—Walnuts. 611

94 Miret y Segriá, José, Uldemolins, Province of Tarragona.—Walnuts. 611

95 Domenech y Monte, José, Vilaseca, Province of Tarragona.—Almonds 611

96 Grau y Vilanova, José, Maria, Maspujols, Province of Tarragona.—Hazelnuts. 611

97 Anlestia, José, Ciurana, Dosaiguas, Province of Tarragona.—Hazelnuts. 611

98 Illas, José Montagut, Reus, Province of Tarragona.—Hazelnuts. 611

99 Forasté y Ferré, Juan, Vilaseca, Province of Tarragona.—Almonds. 611

100 Magriña, Luis, Falset, Province of Tarragona.—Hazelnuts. 611

101 Magriña, Manuel Serrano, Tibisa, Province of Tarragona.—Hazelnuts. 611

102 Artells, Miguel, Reus, Province of Tarragona.—Almonds and hazelnuts. 611

103 Bassedas y Andreu, Miguel, Reus, Province of Tarragona.—Hazelnuts. 611

104 Magriña, Mariano, La Selva, Province of Tarragona.—Hazelnuts. 611

105 Salvadó, Mateo, Tarragona.—Hazelnuts. 611

106 Abelló y Boada, Pablo, Barbara, Province of Tarragona.—Almonds, hazelnuts, walnuts, and pine-nuts. 611

107 Fausá, Pablo, La Canonja, Province of Tarragona.—Almonds and hazelnuts. 611

108 Sirvent y Oliver, Pedro, Reus, Province of Tarragona.—Almonds and hazelnuts. 611

109 Montoliu, Plácido Maria de, Tarragona.—Hazelnuts. 611

110 Anguera y Anglès, Falset, Province of Tarragona.—Hazelnuts and almonds. 611

111 Escolá y Franch, Ramon, Reus, Province of Tarragona.—Hazelnuts and almonds. 611

112 Monlleó, Ramon, Uldemolins, Province of Tarragona.—Almonds. 611

113 Siscar, Ramon, La Canonja, Province of Tarragona.—Hazelnuts. 611

114 Roy, Ponseti & Co., Tarragona.—Hazelnuts and almonds. 611

115 Soberano & Co., Reus, Province of Tarragona.—Hazelnuts and almonds. 611

116 Salvadó, Salvador, Riudoms, Province of Tarragona.—Hazelnuts. 611

117 Freixá, Sebastian, Reus, Province of Tarragona.—Hazelnuts. 611

Pomology, Agricultural Products.

118 **Robres, Sebastian Garcia de, Scala** Dei, Province of Tarragona.—Almonds. 611

119 **Barcuys, Tomás, Maspujols, Province** of Tarragona.—Hazelnuts. 611

120 **Esteve, A., Widow & Son of, Reus,** Province of Tarragona.—Hazelnuts, almonds, and walnuts. 611

121 **Society of Agriculture, Valencia.** —Walnuts and acorns. 611

122 **Lassala y Palomares, Vicente,** Masia de la mar.—Province of Valencia. —Almonds. 611

123 **Fernandez, Tomás Vicente, Fuentesauco,** Province of Zamora.—Walnuts. 611

124 **Poey, Juan, Habana, Cuba.**—Oranges. 611

Agricultural Products.

125 **School of Agriculture, Vitoria, Province** of Alava.—Cereals. 620

126 **Maroni, José, Hellin, Province of** Albacete.—Wheat. 620

127 **Guerrero, José, Hellin, Province of** Albacete.—Summer wheat. 620

128 **Espinosa, Juan, Hellin, Province of** Albacete.—Wheat. 620

129 **Dios Aguado y Alarcon, Juan de,** Corral Rubio, Province of Albacete.—Cereals. 620

130 **Guevara, Vicente Ladron de, Tobara,** Province of Albacete.—Wheat. 620

131 **Ramos, Juan Bautista, Alicante.**—Summer wheat. 620

132 **Sellés, Joaquin, Elche, Province of** Alicante.—Maize. 620

133 **Gimenez, Fco Sanchez, Alicante.**—Wheat. 620

134 **Perez, Joaquin Verdú, Monóvar,** Province of Alicante.—Wheat, barley, and maize. 620

135 **Sanchez, José, Alicante.—Barley.** 620

136 **Gil, Joaquin, Alicante.—Wheat.** 620

137 **Scals, José, Gijona, Province of** Alicante.—Wheat. 620

138 **Linares, José Ramon, Albanchez,** Province of Almeria.—Maize and wheat. 620

139 **Daza, Francisco, Purchena, Province** of Almeria.—Cereals. 620

140 **Perez, Mariano Valverde, Fontiveros,** Province of Avila.—Summer wheat. 620

141 **Rodriguez, Francisco Mariano,** Fontiveros, Province of Avila.—Barley. 620

142 **Sainz, Matias, Donvidas, Province** of Avila.—Summer wheat. 620

143 **Coca, Juan de, Langa, Province of** Avila.—Summer wheat and barley. 620

144 **Sacristan, Tomás, Sinlabajos, Province** of Avila.—Summer wheat. 620

145 **Diaz, Gaspar, Cabezas del Pozo,** Province of Avila.—Summer wheat. 620

146 **Guerra, Blas, Cabezas del Pozo,** Province of Avila.—Summer wheat. 620

147 **Paradinas, José, Cabezas del Pozo,** Province of Avila.—Summer wheat. 620

148 **Rodriguez, Bernardo Nava, Langa,** Province of Avila.—Summer wheat. 620

149 **Paradinas, Gregorio, Bernuy Zapardiel,** Province of Avila.—Winter barley. 620

150 **Astorga, Pedro Gonzalez, Gutierrez Muñoz,** Province of Avila.—Winter barley. 620

151 **Astorga, Agapito Gonzalez, Gutierrez Muñoz,** Province of Avila.—Summer wheat. 620

152 **Rodriguez, Roberto, Villamayor,** Province of Avila.—Summer wheat. 620

153 **Garcia, Isidro Sanchez, Horcajo de** las Torres, Province of Avila.—Summer wheat. 620

154 **Calafate, Antolin Fernandez, Horcajo** de las Torres, Province of Avila.—Summer wheat. 620

155 **Lambas, Manuel, Palacios de Goda,** Province of Avila.—Summer wheat. 620

156 **Saiz, Cleto Lopez, Palacios de Goda,** Province of Avila.—Summer wheat. 620

157 **Castro, Eusebio Ramiro, Arévalo,** Province of Avila.—Summer wheat. 620

158 **Navajas, Felipe Saenz, Arévalo,** Province of Avila.—Summer wheat. 620

159 **Moreno, Cayetano, Villalba de los** Barros, Province of Badajoz.—Wheat and barley. 620

160 **Rebollo, Demetrio, Cabeza de Vaca,** Province of Badajoz.—White wheat. 620

161 **Molano, Pedro, Badajoz.—Wheat** and barley. 620

162 **Gregori, Tomás, Badajoz.—Wheat** and barley. 620

163 **Venegas, Juan, Valle de Matamoras,** Province of Badajoz.—Wheat. 620

164 **Lopo, Casimiro, Badajoz.—Wheat** and barley. 620

165 **Lopo, Felix, Badajoz.—Wheat and** barley. 620

166 **Amador, Alfonse, Guareña, Province** of Badajoz.—Red wheat. 620

167 **Sanchez, María Romero, Cabeza de** Vaca, Province of Badajoz.—Lammas wheat and barley. 620

168 **Ortiz, Eugenio, Villagarcia, Province** of Badajoz.—Wheat, barley, and oats. 620

169 **Moreno, José Salvador, Cabeza de** Vaca, Province of Badajoz.—Oats. 620

170 **Borrallo, María, Cabeza de Vaca,** Province of Badajoz.—Rye. 620

171 **Soler y Siguier, José, Mahon, Balearic** Islands.—Summer wheat. 620

172 **Detlós, Gertrudis de, Ripoll, Province** of Barcelona.—Maize. 620

173 **Vila, Juan, Martorell, Province of** Barcelona.—Wheat. 620

174 **Bosh y Gausa, Luis, Barcelona.**—Wheat. 620

175 **Subirach, Mariano, Vich, Province** of Barcelona.—Barley. 620

176 **Gariga, Francisco Domingo, San** Quirse de Basora, Province of Barcelona. —Cereals. 620

Agricultural Products.

177 Dodero y Ponte, Josè, Pomar de Badalona, Province of Barcelona.—Carrobs. 621

178 Gordojueta, Remigio, Miranda de Ebro, Province of Burgós.—Red wheat. 620

179 Abad, Gregorio, Aranda de Duero, Province of Burgós.—White wheat. 620

180 Villanueva, Felipe de, Carcedo de Burgós, Province of Burgós.—Wheat. 620

181 Moral, Santiago, & Bros., Burgós. —Lammas wheat. 620

182 Mate, Antonio, Burgós.—Wheat. 620

183 Gonzalez, Dionisio, La Molina, Province of Burgós.—Wheat. 620

184 Horcajo, Marcos, Lerma, Province of Burgós.—Wheat and rye. 620

185 Quintana y Ruiz, Fidel, Burgós. —Cereals. 620

186 Fernandez, Primitivo, Burgós.—Winter barley. 620

187 Alonso, Julian, Lerma, Province of Burgós.—Common barley. 620

188 Provincial Deputation, Burgós.—Oats. 620

189 Corporation of Miranda de Ebro, Province of Burgós.—Maize. 620

190 Beson, Eduardo A. de, Burgós.—White maize. 620

191 Provincial Commission of Miranda de Ebro, Burgós.—Red and summer maize. 620

192 Roman, Simon, Cáceres.—Cereals. 620

193 Lubian, Saturnino, Plasenzuela, Province of Cáceres.—Wheat and barley. 620

194 Perez y Romero, Francisco Garcia, Jerez de la Frontera, Province of Cadiz. —Canary seed, St. Peter's corn, and maize. 620

195 Pley y Bondigue, Francisco, Puerto-Real, Province of Cadiz.—Maize. 620

196 Corporation of Chiclana, Province of Cadiz.—Wheat, barley, and maize. 620

197 Corporation of Tarifa, Province of Cadiz.—Wheat, barley, and canary seed. 620

198 Vega Grande, Count of, Las Palmas, Canary Islands.—Maize. 620

199 Society of Friends of the Country, Las Palmas, Canary Islands.—Maize. 620

200 Ponce de Leon, Juan, Las Palmas, Canary Islands.—Cereals. 620

201 Provincial Commission of Tenerife, Canary Islands.—Cereals. 620

202 Escribano, José, Vinaróz, Province of Castellon.—Carrobs. 621

203 Provincial Board of Agriculture, Castellon.—Cereals. 620

204 Rubisco, Cayetano Clemente, Ciudad-Real.—Wheat and barley. 620

205 Cabezuelas, Count of, Campo de Criptana, Province of Ciudad-Real.—Cereals. 620

206 Loro, Francisco, Daimiel, Province of Ciudad-Real.—Maize. 620

207 Sanchez, Sotero, Daimiel, Province of Ciudad-Real.—Panic-grass. 620

208 Criado, José Gomez, Villa del Rio, Province of Córdoba.—Wheat. 620

209 Corporation of Cabra, Province of Córdoba.—Wheat. 620

210 Valverde, Francisco, Aguilera, Priego, Province of Córdoba.—Wheat. 620

211 Priego, Rafael Molina, Province of Córdoba.—Wheat. 620

212 Sarmiento, Antonio Alba, Priego, Province of Córdoba.—Wheat. 620

213 Serrano, Tomás, Priego, Province of Córdoba.—Wheat. 620

214 Vallejo, Rafael, Córdoba.—Wheat. 620

215 Corporation of Bujalance, Province of Córdoba.—Black wheat. 620

216 Escribano, Luis, Pozoblanco, Province of Córdoba.—Wheat. 620

217 Prieto, Sabastian, Encinas-Reales, Province of Córdoba.—Wheat. 620

218 Ariza y Ariza, José, Baena, Province of Córdoba.—Wheat. 620

219 Gimenez, José Maria, Baena, Province of Córdoba.—Wheat. 620

220 Navarro, Rafael, Córdoba.—Barley and wheat. 620

221 Hoces, Ana de, Córdoba. — Black wheat. 620

222 Galan, Alfonso Blanco, Dos Torres, Province of Córdoba.—Wheat. 620

223 Matilla, Carlos, Córdoba.—Wheat. 620

224 Conde, Juan, Córdoba. — Canary-seed, wheat, and barley. 620

225 Corporation of Lucena, Province of Córdoba.—Wheat. 620

226 Cabanar y Blanco, Rafael, Córdoba. —Barley. 620

227 Estrada, Ramon, Córdoba.—Wheat and barley. 620

228 Puentes y Roldan, Felipe, Córdoba. —Barley. 620

229 Santaló, Estéban, Córdoba.—Wheat. 620

230 Fernandez, Antonio, Córdoba. — Wheat. 620

231 Barbudo, Francisco de P., Córdoba. —Barley and wheat. 620

232 Barrionueva, Fernando, Córdoba. —Black wheat and barley. 620

233 Sisternes, Manuel, Córdoba.—Black wheat. 620

234 Carmona, Salvador, Montemayor, Province of Córdoba.—Wheat. 620

235 Fernandez, Gumersindo, Hinojosa, Province of Córdoba.—Red wheat. 620

236 Sanchez, Manuel, Belmez, Province of Córdoba.—Wheat. 620

237 Aurea y Rivera, Antonio, Belmez, Province of Córdoba.—Wheat. 620

238 Pacheco, Rafael Granados, Benameji, Province of Córdoba.—Barley. 620

239 Velasco, Bernardo Dominguez, Benameji, Province of Córdoba.—Wheat. 620

240 Corporation of Hornachuelos, Province of Córdoba.—Wheat. 620

241 Malgarejo, María Josefa, San Clemente, Province of Córdoba.—Wheat. 620

Agricultural Products.

242 Plaza y Garrejo, Felipe, Villarejo de Fuentes, Province of Cuenca.—Wheat. 620

243 Redondo, Peregrin, Valverde de Júcar, Province of Cuenca.—Wheat. 620

244 Bautista, Mariano, Olmedilla de Alarcon, Province of Cuenca.—Wheat. 620

245 Torre, Pablo de la, Tarancon, Province of Cuenca.—Summer wheat. 620

246 Salazar y Cuebas, Pio, Santa Maria de los Llanos, Province of Cuenca.—Summer wheat. 620

247 Melgarejo, Manuel, San Clemente, Province of Cuenca.—Summer wheat. 620

248 Hellin, Desiderio, San Clemente, Province of Cuenca.—Summer wheat. 620

249 Bruse, José Maria, Cuenca.—Common barley. 620

250 Massó y Soler, Félix, Blanes, Province of Gerona.—Wheat and maize. 620

251 Marti, Diego García, Guadalajara.—Wheat. 620

252 Muñoz, Marcelino, Sigüenza, Province of Guadalajara.—Wheat and barley. 620

253 Medrano, Félix, Guadalajara.—Barley. 620

254 Reyes y Rich, Juan A., Guadalajara.—Barley. 620

255 Lopez, José María, Huelva.—Wheat and white maize. 620

256 Riera y Fernandez, José, Huelva.—Wheat. 620

257 Soldán, Antonio, La Palma, Province of Huelva.—Wheat and barley. 620

258 Carrasco, José María, Bonares, Province of Huelva.—Wheat. 620

259 Cerero y Barreda, Emilio, Trigueros, Province of Huelva.—Wheat. 620

260 Orta, Pedro de, Cartaya, Province of Huelva.—White maize. 620

261 Vargas, José Rafael, Escacena del Campo, Province of Huelva.—Wheat. 620

262 Lanzas, Juan Antonio, Alcubierre, Province of Huesca.—Red wheat. 620

263 Gabarres, Mariano, Alcubierre, Province of Huesca.—Red wheat. 620

264 Gabarres, José, Alcubierre, Province of Huesca.—Red wheat. 620

265 Lapiedra, Joaquin, Sariñena, Province of Huesca.—Red wheat. 620

266 Lasierra, Francisco, Pallazueia, Province of Huesca.—Red wheat. 620

267 Lasierra, Joaquin, Pallazuela, Province of Huesca.—Summer wheat. 620

268 Otal, José María, Castillo de Carbino, Province of Huesca.—Wheat, maize, and barley. 620

269 Nasarre, Voto, Lupiñen, Province of Huesca.—Red wheat. 620

270 Altemir, José, Sariñena, Province of Huesca.—Red wheat. 620

271 Oliver, D. L., Huesca.—Hard wheat, black oats, and barley. 620

272 Villalta y Uribe, Antonio Fernandez, Torre, Don Gimeno, Province of Jaen.—Wheat. 620

273 Herreros, Juan Ignacio, Iznatoraf, Province of Jaen.—Wheat. 620

274 Abolafia, Antonio Diaz, Jaen.—Yellow maize. 620

275 Anievas, Justo María, Jaen.—White maize. 620

276 Jontoja, Manuel, Jaen.—Wheat. 620

277 Prado, Maximo Alonso, Leon.—Cereals. 620

278 Nuñez, Lino, Sahagun, Province of Leon.—Lammas wheat. 620

279 Santos, Pablo, Fuentes de los Oteros, Province of Leon.—Summer and lammas wheat. 620

280 Corporation of Pajares de Oteros, Province of Leon.—Barley and rye. 620

281 Corporation of Valdefresno, Province of Leon.—Wheat, barley, and rye. 620

282 Corporation of Valverde del Camino, Province of Leon.—Wheat, barley, and rye. 620

283 Corporation of Vega de Infanzones, Province of Leon.—Barley and rye. 620

284 Corporation of Arganza, Province of Leon.—Wheat, barley, and rye. 620

285 Corporation of Mansilla Mayor, Province of Len.—Wheat, barley, and rye. 620

286 Corporation of Mansilla de las Mulas, Province of Leon.—Wheat, barley, and rye. 620

287 Corporation of Congosto, Province of Leon.—Wheat, barley, and rye. 620

288 Corporation of Ponferrada, Province of Leon.—Wheat, barley, and rye. 620

289 Fernandez, Tomás, Armunia, Province of Leon.—Wheat, barley, and rye. 620

290 Corporation of Páramo del Sil, Province of Leon.—Maize. 620

291 Corporation of Encinedo, Province of Leon.—Rye. 620

292 Corporation of Magaz, Province of Leon.—Rye. 620

293 Corporation of Omaña, Province of Leon.—Wheat. 620

294 Alós, Francisco, Balaguer, Province of Lérida.—Wheat. 620

295 Oliveres, Mauricio, Torreserona, Province of Lérida.—Wheat. 620

296 Lafont, Andrés, Borjar, Province of Lérida.—Wheat. 620

297 Lopez, Manuel, Puigvert, Province of Lérida.—Barley. 620

298 Ball, José, Agramunt, Province of Lérida.—Barley and wheat. 620

299 Ron, Ramon, Vinaixa, Province of Lérida.—Wheat. 620

300 Viela, Ramon Terez de, Tórrega, Province of Lérida.—Barley. 620

301 Andreu, Roque, Tórrega, Province of Lérida.—Wheat. 620

302 Jover, Luisa de, Tórrega, Province of Lérida.—Wheat. 620

303 Corporation of Agramunt, Province of Lérida.—Wheat and barley. 620

304 Corporation of Puigvert, Province of Lérida.—Barley. 620

305 Corporation of Vinaixa, Province of Lérida.—Wheat. 620

Agricultural Products.

306 Corporation of Las Borjas, Province of Lérida.—Wheat. 620

307 Pinós, José Maria, Malpartida, Province of Lérida.—Common wheat. 620

308 Paradela, Domingo, Castroverde, Province of Lugo.—Barley and rye. 620

309 Laje, Domingo Antonio, Corgo, Province of Lugo.—Rye. 620

310 Vasquez, José Leoncio, Mondoñedo, Province of Lugo.—Husked maize. 620

311 Freire, Manuel Soto, Panton, Province of Lugo.—Maize. 620

312 Ferreiro y Hermida, Antonio, Alfox, Province of Lugo.—Yellow maize. 620

313 Armesto, Ramon, Puebla del Brollon, Province of Lugo.—Wheat. 620

314 Corporation of Lorenzana, Province of Lugo.—Yellow maize. 620

315 Legaspi, Juan, Villalba, Province of Lugo.—Rye. 620

316 Pallares, Count of, Villalba, Province of Lugo.—Wheat. 620

317 Montenegro, Manuel Pardo, Fox, Province of Lugo.—Yellow maize. 620

318 Pillado, Eliseo Martinez, Fox, Province of Lugo.—Wheat and early maize. 620

319 Martinez, Ramon Antonio, Sarria, Province of Lugo.—Yellow maize, wheat, and barley. 620

320 Mendez, José Perez, Sober, Province of Lugo.—Barley and wheat. 620

321 Calatrava, Francisco Garcia, Alcobendas, Province of Madrid.—Wheat, barley, and oats. 620

322 Gago, Juan Borrego, Ronda, Province of Malaga.—Wheat. 620

323 Romero, Joaquin Perez, Santa Maria de la Rabida, Province of Orense.—Cereals. 620

324 Rodriguez, Manuel Iglesias, Celanova, Province of Orense.—Cereals. 620

325 Rey, Manuel Pereiro, Province of Orense.—Cereals. 620

326 Diaz, Francisco, Trandeiras, Province of Orense.—Rye. 620

327 Vila, Francisco, Viana del Bollo, Province of Orense.—Rye. 620

328 Vaamonde, Ramon Maria, Pungin, Province of Orense.—Maize. 620

329 Romero y Romero, José, Ginzo de Limia, Province of Orense.—Rye. 620

330 Anta, Ignacio, Orense.—Rye and maize. 620

331 Iglesias, Ramon, Beiro, Province of Orense.—Rye and maize. 620

332 Board of Agriculture, Industry, and Commerce, Oviedo.—Wheat and maize. 620

333 Durango, Manuel Martinez, Palencia.—Barley. 620

334 Gregorio, Sotero, Palencia.—Wheat and barley. 620

335 Gutierrez, Juan Francisco, Palencia,—Wheat and barley. 620

336 Dominguez, Miguel, Palencia.—Barley. 620

337 Sevilla, José, Fuentes de Nava, Province of Palencia.—Wheat. 620

338 Rodriguez, Tomás, Fuentes de Nava, Province of Palencia.—Wheat. 620

339 Pombo, Pedro, Fuentes de Nava, Province of Palencia.—Wheat 620

340 Solorzano, Juan, Baltanas, Province of Palencia.—Oats. 620

341 Gutierrez, Simon, Monzon, Province of Palencia.—Rye. 620

342 Tabarés, Federico Rodriguez, Torremormojon, Province of Palencia.—Wheat. 620

343 Escudero, Felipe, Cisneros, Province of Palencia.—Wheat. 620

344 Herrero, Agustin, Mazariegos, Province of Palencia.—Wheat. 620

345 Herrero, Pedro Romero, Amuscol, Province of Palencia.—Wheat. 620

346 Prieto, Basilio, Herrero, Herrera de Valdecañas, Province of Palencia.—Wheat. 620

347 Monedero, Joaquin, Cevico de la Torre, Province of Palencia.—Wheat. 620

348 Palacin, Deogracias, Palenzuela, Province of Palencia.—Wheat. 620

349 Piñeiro, Ramon Somoza, Merza, Province of Pontevedra.—Cereals. 620

350 Onis, Federico, Cantalapiedra, Province of Salamanca.—Cereals. 620

351 Peña, Josefa Gonzalez de la, Mancera de Abajo, Province of Salamanca.—Wheat. 620

352 Cabrera, Victoriano, Cantalapiedra, Province of Salamanca.—Wheat. 620

353 Bellido, Narciso, Zorita de la Frontera, Province of Salamanca.—Wheat. 620

354 Blazquez, Agustin, Tordillos, Province of Salamanca.—Wheat. 620

355 Rodriguez, Zacarias, Cantalapiedra, Province of Salamanca.—Wheat, barley, and rye. 620

356 Merino, Miguel, Cordobilla, Province of Salamanca.—Wheat. 620

357 Pineda, Eduardo de, Los Huelmos, Province of Salamanca.—Wheat and barley. 620

358 Fuentes, José, La Pinilla, Province of Salamanca.—Wheat and rye. 620

359 Rodriguez, Julian, Doñinos, Province of Salamanca.—Wheat and barley. 620

360 Sanchez, Francisco, Las Torres, Province of Salamanca.—Wheat. 620

361 Martin, Saturnino, Cilleros el Hondo, Province of Salamanca.—Wheat. 620

362 Hernando y Nieto, Francisco, Bóveda del Rio al Mar, Province of Salamanca.—Wheat. 620

363 Paradinas, Acacio, Cantalapiedra, Province of Salamanca.—Wheat and barley. 620

364 Mulas, Sinforiano, Villar de Gallimazo, Province of Salamanca.—Wheat. 620

365 Martin, Santiago, Tarazona, Province of Salamanca.—Wheat. 620

366 Perez, Domingo, Aldeatejada, Province of Salamanca.—Wheat. 620

367 Andrés, Leon, Tarazona, Province of Salamanca.—Wheat. 620

Agricultural Products.

368 **Mayoral, Andrés, Los Huelmos,** Province of Salamanca.—Wheat. 620

369 **Garcia, Rafael, Cantalapiedra, Province** of Salamanca.—Summer wheat and barley. 620

370 **Toribio, Antonio Martin, Villares** de la Reina, Province of Salamanca.—Summer wheat and barley. 620

371 **Corporation of Vetigudino, Province** of Salamanca.—Wheat. 620

372 **Mozas, Antonio Alfonso de las,** Province of Salamanca.—Summer wheat. 620

373 **Poveda, Paulino, Pedroso, Province** of Salamanca.—Lammas wheat, barley, and rye. 620

374 **Delgado, Miguel Gonzalez, Ragama,** Province of Salamanca.—Summer wheat. 620

375 **Terreros, Santiago Juanes, Villares** de la Reina, Province of Salamanca.—Summer wheat. 620

376 **Diaz, Gaspar, Villaflores, Province** of Salamanca.—Summer wheat. 620

377 **Liaño, Martin Gomez de, Peñaranda** de Bracamonte, Province of Salamanca.—Summer wheat. 620

378 **Hernandez, Antonio, Malpartida,** Province of Salamanca.—Summer wheat. 620

379 **Escribano, Francisco, Dehesa de** Terrados, Province of Salamanca.—Summer wheat. 620

380 **Marcos, Estéban, Parada de Rubiales,** Province of Salamanca.—Summer wheat. 620

381 **Carbayo, Luis, San Cristobal de la** Cuesta, Province of Salamanca.—Summer wheat. 620

382 **Samaniego, Manuel Garcia, Salamanca.**—Summer wheat. 620

383 **Sanchez, Felipe Perez, Fregenada,** Province of Salamanca.—Summer wheat. 620

384 **Paulino, Diego Perez, Fregenada,** Province of Salamanca.—Wheat. 620

385 **Garcia, Angel, Cantalapiedra, Province** of Salamanca.—Barley. 620

386 **Torre Ajero, Mariano & Cipriano** de la, Arollo de Cuellar, Province of Segovia.—Wheat, rye, and barley. 620

387 **Gonzalez, Ezequiel, Segovia.**—White wheat. 620

388 **Lopez, Mariano, Balisa, Province** of Segovia.—Wheat and barley. 620

389 **Satnyen, Pedro, Riaza, Province of** Segovia.—Cereals. 620

390 **Hernandez, Juan, Villacastin,** Province of Segovia.—Lammas wheat. 620

391 **Gordo, Feliciano, Villacastin, Province** of Segovia.—Summer wheat. 620

392 **Palatin y Moreno, Fernando, Sevilla.**—Maize. 620

393 **Andrade, Manuel Zayas, Arahal,** Province of Sevilla.—Wheat. 620

394 **Gonzalez, Rafael, Sevilla.—Maize.** 620

395 **Miura y Fernandez, Bentonto, Sevilla.**—Seed wheat. 620

396 **Pantion, Manuel Fernandez, Sevilla.**—Maize. 620

397 **Ojeda y Gomez, Juan, Sevilla.**—Maize. 620

398 **Maza, Juan Gomez de la, Olivares,** Province of Sevilla.—Barley. 620

399 **Silva y Perez, José, Olivares, Province** of Sevilla.—Maize. 620

400 **Perez, José, Olivares, Province of** Sevilla.—Barley. 620

401 **Ojeda, Juan Maria Rodriguez, Olivares,** Province of Sevilla.—Wheat. 620

402 **Cotan y Muñoz, Manuel, Olivares,** Province of Sevilla.—Wheat. 620

403 **Cotan, Antonio Garcia, Olivares.** Province of Sevilla.—Wheat. 620

404 **Estrada y Lasarte, Manuel, Osuna,** Province of Sevilla.—Barley. 620

405 **Ramirez, Manuel Tamayo, Osuna,** Province of Sevilla.—Barley. 620

406 **Castro y Torres, Francisco, Osuna,** Province of Sevilla.—Wheat. 620

407 **Morillas, Ramon Farfán, Cantillana,** Province of Sevilla.—Wheat. 620

408 **Rivas y Morillas, Antonio, Cantillana,** Province of Sevilla.—Barley. 620

409 **Teruel, Pedro, & Bro., Cantillana,** Province of Sevilla.—Wheat. 620

410 **Sanchez, Benito Navarro, Mairena** del Alcor, Province of Sevilla.—Wheat. 620

411 **Lozano, Manuel Seda, Mairena de** Alcor, Province of Sevilla.—Barley. 620

412 **Mendez, Antonio, Mairena del** Alcor, Province of Sevilla.—Seed wheat. 620

413 **Puente, Salvador & Alejandro Linares,** Burguillos, Province of Sevilla.—Wheat. 620

414 **Martinez Sainz Bros., Sevilla.**—Wheat. 620

415 **Caso-Galindo, Count of, Carmona,** Province of Sevilla.—Wheat. 620

416 **Dos Fuentes, Viscount of, Carmona,** Province of Sevilla.—Wheat. 620

417 **Vallejo, José, Mairena del Alcor,** Province of Sevilla.—Canary seed. 620

418 **Rosa y Silva, José de la, Villamanrique,** Province of Sevilla.—Maize. 620

419 **Puig, Juan, La Rinconada, Province** of Sevilla.—Seed wheat. 620

420 **Alba, Diego Sanchez, Lebrija, Province** of Sevilla.—Summer wheat. 620

421 **Vasquez y Rodriguez, Ignacio, Aznalácazar,** Province of Sevilla.—Barley and wheat. 620

422 **Mendez, Felipe, Mairena del Alcor,** Province of Sevilla.—Wheat and barley. 620

423 **Auñon y Leon, Antonio, Moron,** Province of Sevilla.—Wheat and barley. 620

424 **Villalón y Torres, Andrés, Moron,** Province of Sevilla.—Barley and canary seed. 620

425 **Amores, Manuel, Salteras y Olivares,** Province of Sevilla.—Barley and St. Peter's corn. 620

426 **Serrano, Miguel Perez, Olivares,** Province of Sevilla.—Wheat. 620

427 **Leon, Manuel Gimenez, Carmona,** Province of Sevilla.—Wheat. 620

428 **Orejuela, Joaquin de, Utrera, Province** of Sevilla.—Wheat, barley, and maize. 620

Agricultural Products.

429 **Búrgos, Felipe de, Utrera, Province** of Sevilla.—Wheat, barley, and maize. 620

430 **Rivas, Pedro, Utrera, Province of** Sevilla.—Wheat. 620

431 **Cuadra, Enrique de la, Utrera, Province** of Sevilla.—Cereals. 620

432 **Cuéllar, José Antonio, Utrera, Province** of Sevilla.—Wheat, barley, and maize. 620

433 **Riarola, Rafael, Utrera, Province** of Sevilla.—Wheat and barley. 620

434 **Crespo, Rafael, Utrera, Province of** Sevilla.—Wheat and barley. 620

435 **Saavedra, Francisco, Utrera, Province** of Sevilla.—Wheat. 620

436 **Dominguez, Pedro, Utrera, Province** of Sevilla.—Maize. 620

437 **Royo, Damian, Soria.**—Wheat. 620

438 **Corporation of Villar de Maya,** Province of Soria.—Wheat, barley, and oats. 620

439 **Corporation of Almanzan, Province** of Soria.—Wheat, rye, and barley. 620

440 **Gimenez, Justo, Valderrodilla, Province** of Soria.—Wheat. 620

441 **Corporation of Rioseco, Province** of Soria.—Wheat. 620

442 **Corporation of Baraona, Province** of Soria.—Wheat and barley. 620

443 **Carretero, Pedro, Utrilla, Province** of Soria.—Wheat. 620

444 **Ballano, Faustino, Aguaviva, Province** of Soria.—Wheat. 620

445 **Velasco, Francisco, Aguaviva, Province** of Soria.—Lammas wheat. 620

446 **Flour Association of Reus, Province** of Tarragona.—Wheat. 620

447 **Virgili, Pablo, Tarragona.**—Urgel wheat, maize, barley, oats, and millet. 620

448 **Plana, Antonio, & Bro., Reus, Province** of Tarragona.—Wheat. 620

449 **Sedo, Juan Vilanova, Reus, Province** of Tarragona.—Wheat. 620

450 **Avila & Marti, Reus, Province of** Tarragona.—Wheat. 620

451 **Saperas, Francisco, Reus, Province** of Tarragona.—Wheat. 620

452 **Marti, Bornas & Co., Reus, Province** of Tarragona.—Wheat. 620

453 **Forasté y Ferré, Juan, Villaseca,** Province of Tarragona.—Wheat. 620

454 **Jausa, Pablo, La Canonja, Province** of Tarragona.—Maize. 620

455 **Domingo, Dimas, Reus, Province** of Tarragona.—Maize and barley. 620

456 **Gatell y Folch, Juan, Altafulla,** Province of Tarragona.—Maize. 620

457 **Mas Blanch, Julio C. de Esteve de,** Amposta, Province of Tarragona.—Rice. 620

458 **Corporation of Amposta, Province** of Tarragona.—Rice. 620

459 **Bignell, Jaime, San Carlos de la** Rapita, Province of Tarragona.—Rice. 620

460 **Soxias y Domenech, Juan, Villaseca,** Province of Tarragona.—Maize. 620

461 **Oller, Pedro, Reus, Province of** Tarragona.—Maize. 620

462 **Montaner, Amalio, Reus, Province** of Tarragona.—Panic grass. 620

463 **Margenat, Antonio Báges, Reus,** Province of Tarragona.—Millet. 620

464 **Barenys y Magriñá, Juan Bautista,** Villaseca, Province of Tarragona.—Barley, 620

465 **Fonts, Mariano, Reus, Province of** Tarragona.—Barley. 610

466 **Moreno, Manuel Ortiz, Ocaña, Province** of Toledo.—Wheat, barley, and oats. 620

467 **Fernandez, Manuel, Tembleque,** Province of Toledo.—Wheat. 620

468 **Pasaran, Isidoro, Olías del Rey,** Province of Toledo.—Wheat. 620

469 **Esteban, Francisco, Toledo.**—Summer wheat. 620

470 **Negrete, Acisclo Fernandez, Villatobas,** Province of Toledo.—Wheat and barley. 620

471 **Serrano y Fernandez, Federico,** Madridejoz, Province of Toledo.—Summer wheat. 620

472 **Mejia, Isaac, Ocaña, Province of** Toledo.—Summer wheat and barley. 620

473 **Redondo, Juan Bautista, Carmena,** Province of Toledo.—Wheat and barley. 620

474 **Indo, Valentin Martinez, Arges,** Province of Toledo.—Summer wheat. 620

475 **Campo, Victoriano Martin del,** Madridejos, Province of Toledo.—Summer wheat. 620

476 **Diego, Fabian de, Guadamur, Province** of Toledo.—Summer wheat. 620

477 **Ortiz, Rufo Moreno, Escalonilla,** Province of Toledo.—Summer wheat. 620

478 **Perez, Luis, Toledo.**—Summer wheat. 620

479 **Huelbes y Ortiz, Emilio de, Ocaña,** Province of Toledo.—Summer wheat and oats. 620

480 **Arrue, Miguel, Benaguacil, Province** of Valencia.—Wheat. 620

481 **Reig y Garcia, Fernando, Puebla** de Vallbona, Province of Valencia.—Wheat and maize. 620

482 **Lasala y Palomares, Vicente, Masia** de la Mar, Province of Valencia.—Wheat and yellow maize. 620

483 **Agricultural Society of Valencia,** Valencia.—Rice, maize, barley, and oats. 620

484 **Valdovi, Rafael Gonzalez, Torrente,** Province of Valencia.—Maize. 620

485 **Ferrandis y Soler, José, Onteniente,** Province of Valencia.—Maize. 620

486 **Montealegre, Widow & Son of, Medina** del Campo, Province of Valladolid.—Common wheat. 620

487 **Corporation of Medina del Campo,** Province of Valladolid.—Common red wheat. 620

488 **Rico, Antonio Ceinos, Fontihoyuelo,** Province of Valladolid.—Common red wheat. 620

489 **Monedero, Eusebio, Valoria la** Buena, Province of Valladolid.—Wheat. 620

Agricultural Products.

490 Monedero, Ventura, Valoria la Buena, Province of Valladolid.—Summer wheat. 620

491 Lozano, Juan, Molacillo, Province of Zamora.—Summer wheat. 620

492 Silva, Genaro, Montamarta, Province of Zamora.—Wheat. 620

493 Falcon, Felipe, Benavente, Province of Zamora.—Wheat. 620

494 Alejano, Salvador Fernandez, Fuentesauco, Province of Zamora.—Summer wheat. 620

495 Temprano, José, Vardemarban, Province of Zamora.—Summer wheat. 620

496 Marron, José Victor, Alcañices, Province of Zamora.—Wheat. 620

497 Rodriguez y Rodriguez, Fernando, Villamayor, Province of Zamora.—Wheat. 620

498 Vecinos, Isidoro, Molacillos, Province of Zamora.—Wheat and barley. 620

499 Garcia, Miguel, Fuentes Pradas, Province of Zamora.—Summer wheat and common barley. 620

500 Angas, Francisco, Candasnos, Province of Zaragoza.—Wheat. 620

501 Sasót, Joaquin, Candasnos, Province of Zaragoza.—Wheat. 620

502 Grós, José Avio, Candasnos, Province of Zaragoza.—Wheat. 620

503 Claver, Marianó, Peñalba, Province of Zaragoza.—Wheat. 620

504 Rosas, Manuel, Bujaraloz, Province of Zaragoza.—Summer and acclimated wheat and rye. 620

505 Rozas, Eusebio, La Almolda, Province of Zaragoza.—Wheat. 620

506 Sampér, Joaquin, Bujaraloz, Province of Zaragoza.—Wheat. 620

507 Grós, Mariano, Bujaraloz, Province of Zaragoza.—Wheat. 620

508 Peisen, José J., Balfarta, Province of Zaragoza.—Wheat. 620

509 Pállas, José, Bujaraloz, Province of Zaragoza.—Wheat. 620

510 Escamilla, Segundo, Bujaraloz, Province of Zaragoza.—Wheat. 620

511 Buil, José, Castejon de Monegros, Province of Zaragoza.—Wheat. 620

512 La Viñaza, Count of, Epila, Province of Zaragoza.—Wheat. 620

513 Loring Bros., Malaga.—Wheat. 620

514 School of Agriculture, Vitoria, Province of Alava.—Leguminous plants and esculent vegetables. 621

515 Aguado, Juan de Dios, Corral Rubio, Province of Albacete.—Lentils and blue vetch. 621

516 Ruiz, Santiago, Hellin, Province of Albacete.—Rice. 621

517 Verdu y Perez, Joaquin, Monóvar, Province of Alicante.—Esculent vegetables. 621

518 Daza y Ruiz, Francisco, Purchena, Province of Almeria.—Kidney beans. 621

519 Linares, José Ramon, Albanchez, Province of Almeria.—Chick-peas. 621

520 Perez, Mariano Valverde, Fontiveros, Province of Avila.—Chick-peas. 621

521 Rodriguez Francisco Mariano, Fontiveros, Province of Avila.—Chick-peas. 621

522 Sainz, Matias, Donvidas, Province of Avila.—Chick-peas. 621

523 Lambas y Gutierrez, Gregorio, Palacios de Goda, Province of Avila.—Chick-peas. 621

524 Gonzalez, Manuel, Barco de Avila, Province of Avila.—French peas. 621

525 Soto, José Diaz, Cabeza de Vaca, Province of Badajoz.—Chick-peas. 621

526 Moreno, Cayetano, Villalba de los Barros, Province of Badajoz.—Chick-peas. 621

527 Paredes, Cárlos, Guareña, Province of Badajoz.—Beans. 621

528 Venegas, Juan, Valle de Matamoros, Province of Badajoz.—Kidney beans. 621

529 Tortades, José de, Vich, Province of Barcelona.—Kidney beans. 621

530 Fontordera, Juan de, Vich, Province of Barcelona.—Kidney beans. 621

531 Mascaró, José, Vich, Province of Barcelona.—Spanish peas. 621

532 Picó, Mariano de, Vich, Province of Barcelona.—Leguminous plants and esculent vegetables. 621

533 Prat, José., Vich, Province of Barcelona.—Lupine. 621

534 Lerda y Daniel, José, Vich, Province of Barcelona.—Spanish peas. 621

535 Soler y Stussa, Valentin, Barcelona.—Esculent vegetables. 621

536 Garriga, Francisco Domingo, San Quirse de Besora, Province of Barcelona.—Esculent vegetables. 621

537 Provincial Deputation of Búrgos.—Pipirigallo (Hedysarum onobrythis) and galgana (lathyrus cicera). 621

538 Commission of the Province of Búrgos.—Esculent vegetables. 621

539 Arribas, Indalecio Anton, Lerma, Province of Búrgos.—True bitter vetch. 621

540 Garcia y Garcia, Francisco, Miranda de Ebro, Province of Búrgos.—Kidney beans. 621

541 Morales, Luis, Miranda de Ebro, Province of Búrgos.—Lentils. 621

542 Garcia, Antonio Gimenez, Guijo de Santa Barbara, Province of Cáceres.—Chick-peas and kidney beans. 621

543 Sande Olivares, Jerónimo de, Garrovillas de Alconetar, Province of Cáceres.—Chick-peas. 621

544 Martin, Ramon, Olvera, Province of Cádiz.—Chick-peas. 621

545 Perez, Francisco Garciá, Jerez de la Frontera, Province of Cádiz.—Chick-peas, beans and Spanish peas. 621

546 Corporation of Tarifa, Province of Cádiz.—Beans. 621

547 Provincial Commission, Isle of Tenerife, Canary Islands.—Chick-peas. 621

548 Leon, Juan Ponce de, Isle of Gran Canaria, Canary Islands.—Kidney beans and chick-peas. 621

549 Quevedo, José C., Isle of Gran Canaria, Canary Islands.—Kidney beans and chick-peas. 261

Agricultural Products.

550 **Vega Grande, Count of, Isle of Gran** Canaria, Canary Islands.—Kidney beans. 621

551 **Provincial Board of Agriculture,** Castellon.—Esculent vegetables. 621

552 **Rubisco, Cayetano Clemente, Ciu**dad Real.—Beans. 621

553 **Las Cabezuelas, Count of, Campo** de Criptana, Province of Ciudad-Real.—Beans. 621

554 **Cabanas y Blanco, Rafael, Córdoba.** —Esculent vegetables. 621

555 **Matilla, Cárlos, Córdoba.—Lupine** and Spanish peas. 621

556 **Prieto, Sebastian, Encinas Reales.** —Chick-peas and beans. 621

557 **Corporation of Cabra, Province of** Córdoba.—Esculent vegetables. 621

558 **Gimenez, José Maria, Baena, Prov**ince of Córdoba.—Beans and chick-peas. 621

559 **Barrionuevo, Fernando, Córdoba.** —Moorish beans. 621

560 **San Bernardo, Count of, Córdoba.** —Moorish beans. 621

561 **Vallejo, Rafael, Córdoba.—Moorish** beans. 621

562 **Pacheco, Rafael Granados, Bena**mejo, Province of Córdoba.—Beans. 621

563 **Poyato, Manuel, Zuheros, Prov**ince of Córdoba.—Chick-peas. 621

564 **Escribano, Luis, Pozoblanco, Prov**ince of Córdoba.—Chick-peas. 621

565 **Blanco, Alfonso, Dos-Torres, Prov**ince of Córdoba.—Chick-peas. 621

566 **Torrico, Manuel, Hinojosa, Prov**ince of Córdoba.—Chick-peas. 621

567 **Sanz y Calatañazor, Jerónimo Cór**doba.—Chick-peas. 621

568 **Conde, Juan, Córdoba.—True bitter** vetch. 621

569 **Carrillo, Librado, Priego, Province** of Córdoba.—White kidney beans. 621

570 **Massó y Soler, Felix, Blanes, Prov**ince of Gerona.—Esculent vegetables. 621

571 **Sanchez, Juan Francisco, Siguenza,** Province of Guadalajara.—Flesh-colored kidney beans. 621

572 **Gil, Santiago, Siguenza, Province** of Guadalajara.—White kidney beans. 621

573 **Heras, Angel Ayuso de las, Valde**arenas, Province of Guadalajara.—Kidney beans. 621

574 **Reyes y Rich, Juan, Guadalajara.** —Beans. 621

575 **Soldan, Antonio, La Palma, Prov**ince of Huelva.—Esculent vegetables. 621

576 **Riera y Fernandez, José, Huelva.**—Esculent vegetables. 621

577 **Carrasco, José Maria, Bonares, Prov**ince of Huelva.—Beans. 621

578 **Otal, José Maria, Castillo de Cara**bineros, Province of Huesca.—Chick-peas and beans. 621

579 **Paula Bulnes, Francisco de, Cazorla,** Province of Jaen.—Chick-peas. 621

580 **Vasquez, Francisco, Cazorla, Prov**ince of Jaen.—Chick-peas. 621

581 **Quesada y Salazar, Pedro de, Val**depeñas, Province of Jaen.—Chick-peas. 621

582 **Quesada, Cárlos Garcia de, Valde**peñas, Province of Jaen.—Chick-peas. 621

583 **Estéban y Balen, Andrés, Navas** de San Juan, Province of Jaen.—Chick-peas. 621

584 **Herreros, Juan Ignacio, Iznatorof,** Province of Jaen.—Chick-peas. 621

585 **Higueras, José, Los Villares, Prov**ince of Jaen.—Lentils. 621

586 **Prado, Máximo Alonso de, Leon.**—Esculent vegetables. 621

587 **Corporation of Vega de Infanzones,** Leon.—Kidney beans. 621

588 **Corporation of Valdefresno, Prov**ince of Leon.—Chick-peas and kidney beans. 621

589 **Corporation of Arganza, Province** of Leon.—Chick-peas and kidney beans. 621

590 **Corporation of Congosto, Province** of Leon.—Chick-peas and kidney beans. 621

591 **Corporation of Mansilla Mayor,** Province of Leon.—Chick-peas and kidney beans. 621

592 **Corporation of Villaturriel, Prov**ince of Leon.—Chick-peas and kidney beans. 621

593 **Corporation of Valverde del Ca**mino, Province of Leon.—Chick-peas and kidney beans. 621

594 **Corporation of Mansilla de las** Mulas, Province of Leon.—Chick-peas and kidney beans. 621

595 **Corporation of Ponferrada, Prov**ince of Leon.—Chick-peas and kidney beans. 621

596 **Corporation of Encinado, Province** of Leon.—Kidney beans. 621

597 **Corporation of Pajares de los Ote**ros, Province of Leon.—Chick-peas. 621

598 **Corporation of Magaz, Province of** Leon.—Kidney beans. 621

599 **Corporation of Omaña, Province** of Leon.—Kidney beans. 621

600 **Fernandez, Tomás, Armunia, Prov**ince of Leon.—Kidney beans and chick-peas. 621

601 **Nuñez, Lino, Sahagun, Province** of Leon.—Kidney beans. 621

602 **Santos, Pablo, Fuentes de los Ote**ros, Province of Leon.—Kidney beans. 621

603 **Oliveres, Mauricio, Torreserona,** Province of Lérida.—Kidney beans on the vine. 621

604 **Bó, Ambrosio, Albesa, Province of** Lérida.—Kidney beans. 621

605 **Jovér, Luisa de, Tárrega, Province** of Lérida.—Kidney beans. 621

606 **Ignés, Pedro, Cervera, Province of** Lérida.—Blue vetch. 621

607 **Freire, Manuel Soto, Panton, Prov**ince of Lugo.—Chick-peas and beans. 621

608 **Pillado, Eliséo Martinez, Foz, Prov**ince of Lugo.—Beans. 621

609 **Martinez, Ramon Antonio, Sarriá,** Province of Lugo.—Kidney beans. 621

Agricultural Products.

610 Moreno, Ramon Armesto, Puebla del Brollon, Province of Lugo.—Colored kidney beans. 621

611 Valcárcel, Teresa Pardo, Sariñao, Province of Lugo.—Chick-peas. 621

612 Corporation of Puebla de Brollon, Province of Lugo.—Beans. 621

613 Mendez, Alejo Perez, Monforte, Province of Lugo.—Chick-peas. 621

614 Calatrava, Francisco García, Alco- bendas, Province of Madrid.—Chick-peas. 621

615 Pascual, Elías, Alfarnate, Province of Málaga.—Chick-peas. 621

616 Marin, Juan F. García, Caravaca, Province of Múrcia.—Kidney beans. 621

617 Anta, Ignacio, Orense.—Beans. 621

618 Rodriguez, Manuel Iglesias, Cela- nova, Province of Orense. — Esculent vegetables. 621

619 Rodriguez y Gomez, Camilo, Ginzo de Limia, Province of Orense.—Chick-peas. 621

620 Rey, Manuel Pereiro, Rivela, Prov- ince of Orense.—Kidney beans. 621

621 Iglesias, Ramon, Canedo y Veiro, Province of Orense.—Kidney beans. 621

622 Provincial Board of Agriculture, Oviedo.—Kidney beans and peas. 621

623 Llanos, Andrés, Saldaña, Province of Palencia.—Chick-peas and French peas. 621

624 Carrasco, Antolin Galan, Carrion, Province of Palencia.—Chick-peas. 621

625 Carande, Isidoro, Nogal de las Huertas, Province of Palencia.—Chick-peas. 621

626 García, Ignacio, Herrera del Rio Pisuerga, Province of Palencia.—White French peas. 621

627 Gallego, Felix, Cevico de la Torre, Province of Palencia. — White French peas. 621

628 Gutierrez, Juan Francisco, Palencia. —White French peas. 621

629 Monedero, Juan, Quintana del Pu- ente, Province of Palencia.—Carrobs. 621

630 Ortega, Demetrio, Palenia.—Beans. 621

631 Gutierrez, Calisto, Palencia.— Beans. 621

632 Rivas, Galo Ruiz, Province of Pa- lencia.—Peas. 621

633 Colambres, Genaro, Perales, Prov- ince of Palencia.—True bitter vetch. 621

634 Onís, Federico, Cantalapiedra, Province of Salamanca.—Esculent vegetables. 621

635 Toribio, Antonio Martin, Villares de la Reina.—Chick peas, lentils, and beans. 621

636 Carbayo, Luis, San Cristobal de la Cuesta, Province of Salamanca.—Lentils and chick-peas. 621

637 Nieto, Francisco Hernandez, Bó- veda del Rio Almar, Province of Salamanca.—Chick-peas. 621

638 Garcia, Rafael, Cantalapiedra, Province of Salamanca.—Chick-peas. 621

639 Ronco, Gregorio, Ragama, Prov- ince of Salamanca.—Chick-peas. 621

640 Terrero, Santiago Juanes, Villares, Province of Salamanca.—Chick-peas. 621

641 Salvadios, Gaspar Diaz, Villaflores, Province of Salamanca.—Chick-peas. 621

642 Mayoral, Andrés, Los Huelmos, Province of Salamanca.—Chick-peas. 621

643 Poveda, Paulino, Pedroso, Province of Salamanca.—Chick-peas. 621

644 Garcia, Angel, Cantalapiedra, Province of Salamanca.—Peas. 621

645 Rodriguez, Zacarías, Cantalapiedra, Province of Salamanca.—Carrobs. 621

646 Fuentes, José, La Pinilla, Province of Salamanca.—Black peas. 621

647 Hernandez, Vicente, Cantalapiedra, Province of Salamanca.—Peas. 621

648 Iglesias, Angel, Monterrubio de Armuña, Province of Salamanca.—Lentils. 621

649 Hernandez, Baldomero, Parada de Rubides, Province of Salamanca.—Beans. 621

650 Gomez, Miguel Martin, Baliso, Province of Segovia.—Chick-peas. 621

651 Gimenez Isidro, Villacastin, Prov- ince of Segovia.—Chick-peas. 621

652 Linares, Salvador & Alejandro, Burgillos & Alcalá del Rio, Province of Sevilla.—Beans and Spanish peas. 621

653 Velasco, Ramon, Carmona, Prov- ince of Sevilla.—Chick-peas. 621

654 Olivares, Manuel Garcia, Olivares, Province of Sevilla.—Chick-peas. 621

655 Ojeda, Manuel, Sevilla.—Chick- peas. 621

656 Leon, Manuel Gimenez, Viso del Alcor, Province of Sevilla.—Chick-peas. 621

657 Terán, Francisco Collantes de, Al- calá de Guadaira, Province of Sevilla.—Chick-peas. 621

658 Puig, Juan, Sevilla.—Chick-peas. 621

659 Ojeda y Gomez, Juan, Sevilla.— Chick peas. 621

660 Orejuela, Joaquin de, Utrera, Prov- ince of Sevilla.—Chick-peas and Spanish peas. 621

661 Cuadra, Enrique de la, Utrera, Province of Sevilla.—Esculent vegetables. 621

662 Amores, Manuel, Salteres y Oli- vares, Province of Sevilla. — Esculent vegetables. 621

663 Perez y Serrano, Miguel, Olivares, Province of Sevilla. — Chick-peas and Spanish peas. 621

664 Muñoz y Leon, Antonio, Moran, Province of Sevilla.—Chick-peas. 621

665 Mendez, Felipe, Mairena del Alcor, Province of Sevilla.—Chick-peas. 621

666 Saavedra, Francisco, Utrera, Prov- ince of Sevilla.—Chick-peas. 621

667 Lavado, Antonio, Fernandez, Agua- dulce, Province of Sevilla.—Beans. 621

668 Alcaraz, Manuel de, Osuna, Prov- ince of Sevilla.—Beans. 621

669 Rivas, Pedro de, Utrera, Province of Sevilla.—Beans. 621

670 Gonzales, Rafael, Sevilla.—Beans. 621

Agricultural Products.

671 Mayorga, Ramon Diaz, Moron, Province of Sevilla.—Beans. 621

672 Saavedra, José Maria, Mairena del Alcor, Province of Sevilla.—Beans. 621

673 Torres, Andrés Villalon, Moron, Province of Sevilla.—Beans and Spanish peas. 621

674 Viñaz, José Maria Gimenez, Mairena del Alcor, Province of Sevilla.—Spanish peas. 621

675 Burgós, Felipe de, Utrera, Province of Sevilla.—Spanish peas. 621

676 Cuéllar, José Antonio, Utrera, Province of Sevilla.—Esculent vegetables. 621

677 Royo, Damian, Soria.—Blue vetch. 621

678 Lenguas, Pablo, Soria.—Blue vetch. 621

679 Barenys y Mariné, José, Vilaseca, Province of Tarragona.—Beans and peas. 621

680 Fausa, Pablo, La Canonja, Prov-ince of Tarragona.—Blue vetch, lentils, and Lima beans. 621

681 Virgili, Pablo, Tarragona.—Kidney beans, Lima beans, and blue vetch. 621

682 Gil, Francisco, Reus, Province of Tarragona.—Beans. 621

683 Prieto, Eusebio, Reus, Province of Tarragona.—Spanish peas and blue vetch. 621

684 Ollér, Pedro, Reus, Province of Tarragona.—Peas, beans, and true bitter vetch. 621

685 Grau y Plá, José, Reus, Province of Tarragona.—Peas, beans, and true bitter vetch. 621

686 Montaner, Amalio, Reus, Province of Tarragona.—Beans. 621

687 Sorias y Domenech, Juan, Vilaseca, Province of Tarragona.—Kidney beans. 621

688 Monner, Juan, La Riera, Province of Tarragona.—Kidney beans. 621

689 Pullés, Antonio Morera, & Son, Tar-ragona.—Chick-peas. 621

690 Llurba, Juan Bautista, Ulldemolins, Province of Tarragona.—Chick-peas. 621

691 Vidal y Bas, Benito, Province of Tarragona.—Beans. 621

692 Fonts, Mariano, Reus, Province of Tarragona.—Beans. 621

693 Margenas, Antonio Bages Reus, Province of Tarragona.—Kidney beans. 621

694 Perez, Lino, Toledo.—Kidney beans and chick-peas. 621

695 Basarán, Isidoro, Olías del Rey, Province of Toledo.—Blue vetch. 621

696 Society of Agriculture, Valencia.— Esculent vegetables. 621

697 Palomares, Vicente Lassala, Masia de la Mar, Province of Valencia.—Beans and carrobs. 621

698 Lassala y Camp, Vicente, Albo-raya, Province of Valencia.—Beans. 621

699 Alborts y Alborts, Cárlos, Picasent, Province of Valencia.—Carrobs. 621

700 Ferrandis y Soler, Onteniente, Province of Valencia.—Carrobs. 621

701 Casta, Joaquin Pardo de la, Ta-bernes, Province of Valencia.—Carrobs. 621

702 Baldoví, Rafael Gonzalez, Torrente, Province of Valencia.—Carrobs. 621

703 Arrue, Miguel, Benguacil, Prov-ince of Valencia.—Kidney beans. 621

704 Vaca, Francisco Cabeza de, Puente Duero, Province of Valladolid.—Chick-peas. 621

705 Lecanda, Eloy, Valbueno de Duero, Province of Valladolid.—Chick-peas. 621

706 Cocho, Tiburcio, Santovenia, Prov-ince of Valladolid—Blue vetch and lentils. 621

707 Corporation of Fuentesauco, Prov-ince of Zamora.—Chick-peas. 621

708 Mateos, Facundo Martin, Fuente-sauco, Province of Zamora.—Chick-peas. 621

709 Bausela, Estéban Garcia, Castro-verde, Province of Zamora.—Chick-peas. 621

710 Poey, Juan, Habana, Cuba.—Vege-tables of the country. 621

711 Sereiz, Eduardo Campos, Alicante. —Carrobs. 621

712 Llampallas, Antonio, Masnou, Province of Barcelona.—Carrobs. 621

713 Escoda y Teixido, Antonio, Villa-seca, Province of Tarragona.—Carrobs. 621

714 Freixa, Sebastian, Reus, Province of Tarragona.—Carrobs. 621

715 Salvado, Salvador, Rindoms, Prov-ince of Tarragona.—Carrobs. 621

716 Monserrat y Cavallé, José, San Carlos de la Rápita, Province of Tarragona.—Carrobs. 621

717 Ibern y Rovira, José, Torredem-barra, Province of Tarragona.—Carrobs. 621

718 Montaña, Francisco Roca, Cam-brils, Province of Tarragona.—Carrobs. 621

719 Corporation of Amposta, Province of Tarragona.—Carrobs. 621

720 Bassedos y Andreu, Miguel, Reus, Province of Tarragona.—Carrobs. 621

721 Zaforta, Juan Burguez, Palma, Balearic Islands.—Carrobs. 621

722 Diego, Francisco Polop, Jativa, Province of Valencia.—Carrobs and photograph of the carrob tree. 621

723 Diego y Carsi, Ignacio & José, Jativa, Province of Valencia.—Carrobs. 621

724 Llandes, Mariano Ontonedo, Jativa, Province of Valencia.—Carrobs. 621

725 Practical School of Agriculture, Alava.—Beet-roots. 622

726 Gonzalez, Manuel, Barco de Avila, Province of Avila.—Onions. 622

727 Provincial Deputation of Búrgos. —Beet-roots and potatoes. 622

728 Board of Agriculture of the Prov-ince of Castellon.—Garlic. 622

729 Montoya, Vicente Llopis, Castellon. —Peanuts. 622

Agricultural Products.

730 Lara, Mateo Tuñon de, Andújar y Menjivar, Province of Jaen.—Licorice-root. 622

731 Asensio, Ramon, Caravaca, Province of Múrcia.—Potatoes. 622

732 Vila, Francisco, Viana del Bollo, Province of Orense.—Potatoes. 622

733 Rodriguez, Manuel Iglesias, Celanova, Province of Orense.—Tubers. 622

734 Rey, Manuel Pereiro, Orense.—Onions. 622

735 Carraura, Ramon, Cantalapiedra, Province of Salamanca.—Beet-roots. 622

736 Torre Ajero, Mariano & Cipriano de la, Arroyo de Cuéllar, Province of Segovia.—Madder-root. 622

737 Moreno, Santiago Merino, Berlanga de Duero, Province of Soria.—Onions, garlic, and potatoes. 622

738 Fonts, Mariano, Reus, Province of Tarragona.—Garlic. 622

739 Redondo, Juan Bautista, Carmena, Province of Toledo.—Potatoes. 622

740 Society of Agriculture of Valencia. Licorice-root, peanuts, edible cyperus, and garlic. 622

741 Lassala y Camps, Vicente, Alboraya, Province of Valencia.—Edible cyperus. 622

742 Dios Quemada, Juan de, & Sons, Vilovia, Province of Valladolid.—Madder-root. 622

743 National Manufactory of Tobacco, Alicante.—Tobacco. 623

744 Corral, Luis Marrin del, La Laguna, Canary Islands.—Tobacco. 623

745 Mendez, Benigno Dominguez, Valverde, Canary Islands.—Tobacco. 623

746 Garcia, Domingo, Orotava, Canary Islands.—Tobacco. 623

747 Lugo, Luis Benitez de, Orotava, Canary Islands.—Tobacco. 623

748 Society "El Porvenir Agricola," Isle of Gran Canaria, Canary Islands.—Leaf-tobacco and cigars. 623

749 Olivares, José del Castillo, Telde, Canary Islands.—Coffee. 623

750 Armas, Antonio, Valle de Agaete, Canary Islands.—Coffee. 623

751 Barrenengoa, Dámaso, Ciudad-Real. —Coffee. 623

752 Ortiz, Juan, Almodóvar del Pinar, Province of Cuenca.—Saffron. 623

753 Chillaron, Silvestre, Villarejo de Fuentes, Province of Cuenca.—Saffron. 623

754 Redondo, Peregrin, Valverde de Fúcar, Province of Cuenca.—Saffron. 623

755 Corporation of Liñola, Province of Lérida.—Chamomile flowers. 623

756 Liné y Canes, José, Liñola, Province of Lérida.—Chamomile flowers. 623

757 Mar, Ramon, Lérida.—Chamomile flowers. 623

758 National Manufactory of Tobacco, Madrid.—Tobacco. 623

759 Meric & Co., Colonial Company, Madrid.—Ground coffee. 623

760 Menchero, Eduardo, Cartagena, Province of Múrcia.—Spanish opium. 623

761 National Manufactory of Tobacco, Sevilla.—Tobacco. 623

762 Corporation of La Pueblía de Eca, Province of Soria.—Saffron. 623

763 Corporation of Valtueña, Province of Soria.—Saffron. 623

764 National Manufactory of Tobacco, Valencia.—Tobacco. 623

765 Leon, José, Rocafort, Province of Valencia.—Tobacco. 623

766 Masiá, Francisco, Requena, Province of Valencia.—Saffron. 623

767 Gomez, Bernardo, Requena, Province of Valencia.—Saffron. 623

768 Piñango, Norberto, Reguena, Province of Valencia.—Saffron. 623

769 Central Commission of the Island of Cuba, Habana, Cuba.—Leaf-tobacco. 623

770 Bock & Co., Habana, Cuba.—Tobacco. 623

771 Allones, Ramon, Habana, Cuba.—Tobacco. 623

772 Arrigunaga, Fernando, Hàbana, Cuba.—Tobacco. 623

773 Genér, José, Habana, Cuba.—Tobacco. 623

774 Upmann, H. & Co., Habana, Cuba. —Tobacco. 623

775 Romero, Juan, Bernabé, Habana, Cuba.—Tobacco. 623

776 Morales, José, Habana, Cuba.—Tobacco. 623

777 Jané, Manuel, Habana, Cuba.—Tobacco. 623

778 Valle, Suarez & Co., Habana, Cuba. —Tobacco. 623

779 Tolosa, Enrique, & Bro., Habana, Cuba.—Tobacco. 623

780 Asay, Celestino, Habana, Cuba.—Tobacco. 623

781 Diaz, Bances & Co., Habana, Cuba.—Tobacco. 623

782 Alvarez, Julian, Habana, Cuba.—Tobacco. 623

783 Murias, Pedro, & Co., Habana, Cuba.—Tobacco. 623

784 Rio, J. P. del, & Co., Habana, Cuba. —Tobacco. 623

785 Camino, Cuesta, & Co., Habana, Cuba.—Cigarettes. 623

786 Ortiz, Isidoro, Habana, Cuba.—Cigarettes. 623

787 Poey, Juan,, Habana, Cuba.—Coffee. 623

788 Brotons, Bros., Orihuela, Province of Alicante.—Ground pepper. 623

789 Velasco, Cayetano Sabater, Múrcia.—Ground pepper. 623

790 Laorden, Juan Bernabé, Múrcia.—Ground pepper. 623

791 Báguena, Joaquin, Múrcia.—Ground pepper. 623

792 Arjona y Gomez, Jesús, Jaraiz de la Vera, Province of Cáceres.—Ground pepper. 623

793 Parrales, Valentin, Jaraiz de la Vera, Province of Cáceres.—Ground pepper. 623

Agricultural Products, Animals, etc.

794 **Guerra, Felipe Leon, Gata, Province of Cáceres.**—Ground pepper. 623

795 **Enciso, Angel Morales, Jaraiz de la Vera,** Province of Cáceres.—Ground pepper. 623

796 **Jabon, Blas., Jaraiz de la Vera,** Province of Cáceres.—Ground pepper. 623

797 **Brotons, Carlos, Alicante.**—Flax-seed. 624

798 **Soria, Francisco Fuster, Monforte,** Province of Alicante.—Carrob seed. 624

799 **Verdu, Joaquin, Monóvar,** Province of Alicante.—Anise and Cumin seed. 624

800 **Riscal, de Alègre, Marquis of, Alia,** Province of Cáceres.—Seeds. 624

801 **Provincial Board of Agriculture,** Castellon.—Lucern seed, flax seed, and carrob seed. 624

802 **Sanchez, Sotero, Daimiel,** Province of Ciudad-Real.—Anise-seed. 624

803 **Peñalver, José Diaz, Membrilla,** Province of Ciudad-Real. — Anise-seed. 624

804 **Lara, Antonio Crespo, Benameji,** Province of Córdoba.—Anise-seed. 624

805 **Prieto, Sebastian, Encinas Reales,** Province of Córdoba.—Anise-seed. 624

806 **Conde, Juan, Córdoba.**—Flax seed and beneseed. 624

807 **Avilèz y Merino, Francisco, Córdoba.**—Fleawort and mustard seed. 624

808 **Chillaron, Silvestre, Villarejo de** Fuentes, Province of Cuenca.—Anise-seed. 624

809 **Hidalgo, Valeriano, Los Hinojosos,** Province of Cuenca.—Anise-seed. 624

810 **Fernandez de Villalta, Antonio,** Torre Don Jimeno, Province of Jaen.—Anise and lavender seed. 624

811 **Corporation of Pozo Alcon,** Province of Jaen.—Cumin-seed. 624

812 **Ferreiro, Antonio, Mondoñedo,** Province of Lugo.—Furze-seed. 624

813 **Paradela, Domingo, Castroverde,** Province of Lugo.—Linseed. 624

814 **Provincial Deputation, Múrcia.**—Seeds. 624

815 **Fuentes y Ponte, Javier, Múrcia.**—White sorghum seed. 624

816 **Onis, Federico de, Cantalapiedra,** Province of Salamanca.—Carthamus seed. 624

817 **Virgili, Pablo, Tarragona.**—Flax-seed and linseed. 624

818 **Grau, José, Reus, Province of Tarragona.**—Linseed. 624

819 **Gatell y Folch, Juan, Altafulla,** Province of Tarragona.—Beans. 624

820 **Margenat, Antonion Bagès, Reus,** Province of Tarragona.—Flax-seed. 624

821 **Negrete, Acisclo Fernandez, Vilatobas,** Province of Toledo.—Anise-seed. 624

822 **Huelbes y Ortiz, Emilio, Ocaña,** Province of Toledo.—Anise and cumin seed. 624

823 **Valencian Society of Agriculture,** Valencia.—Seeds. 624

824 **Llandes, Mariano Ontoneda, Manuel,** Province of Valencia.—Peanut-seed. 624

825 **Aspiroz, Rafael Vives, Villa Oliva,** Province of Valencia.—Peanut-seed. 624

826 **Ordunna, Salvador Navarro, Villa** Oliva, Province of Valencia.—Beans. 624

827 **La Viñaza, Count of, Epila, Province of Zaragoza.**—Linseed and flax seed. 624

828 **Ramirez, Antonio, Alicante.**—Linseed. 624

829 **Sirvent, Antonio, San Vicente,** Province of Alicante.—Canary-seed. 624

830 **Calabuig, Bartolomé, Bañeras,** Province of Alicante.—Pine seed. 624

831 **Molano, Manuel, Badajoz.**—Acorns. 624

832 **Carretero, Agustin, Salvaleon,** Province of Badajoz.—Acorns. 624

833 **Gomez, Antonio Enrique, Montero.**—Province of Córdoba.—Acorns. 624

834 **Corporation of Añora, Province of** Córdoba.—Acorns. 624

835 **Escribano, Luis, Pozoblanco, Province of Córdoba.**—Acorns. 624

836 **Galan, Alfonso Blanco, Dos-Torres,** Province of Córdoba.—Acorns. 620

837 **Desttos, Gertrudis de, San Feliú** de Codina, Province of Barcelona.—Pine cone seed. 624

838 **Corporation of Cartaya, Province** of Huelva.—Pine cone seed. 624

839 **Serrano, José Lorenzo, Zalamea,** Province of Huelva.—Acorns. 624

Land Animals.

840 **Bayla, Juan de la, Santander.**
a Rabbit and birds. 635
b Domestic and Angora cats. 636
c Boar. 637

841 **Riscal de Alegre, Marquis of, Alia,** Province of Cáceres.—Eggs, chrysalis and butterfly of the silk worm. 638

842 **Argona, Jesus, Jaraiz, Province of** Cáceres.—Cocoons. 638

843 **Quevedo, José C., Isle of Gran Canaria,** Canary Islands.—Cochineal. 638

844 **Davidson, Guillermo, & Co., Villa** de la Orotova, Canary Islands.—Cochineal. 638

845 **Torre, Rafael de la, Las Palmas,** Canary Islands.—Cochineal. 638

846 **Corps of Engineers of Woods &** Forests, Madrid.—Anatomical pictures of various insects. 638

847 **Vidaur, Aurelio Lopez, Santander.**—Collection of beetles. 638

Marine Animals, Fish Culture, and Apparatus.

848 **Roca, Bartolomé, Palma de Mallorca,** Balearic Islands.—Anchovies in oil. 641

849 **García & Piñon, Coruña.**—Preserved Fish. 641

850 **Cotrofe, Miguel, Coruña, Preserved** fish. 641

851 **Codes, Tomás Lopez de, Isla Cristina,** Province of Huelva.—Salt and pressed sardines. 641

852 **Provincial Commission, Lugo.**—Cured eels. 641

Marine Animals, etc., Animal and Vegetable Products.

853 Riego, Vicente, Vivero, Province of Lugo.—Pressed and preserved sardines. 641

854 Vicente, Pascual, & Co., Vivero, Province of Lugo.—Pressed and preserved sardines. 641

855 Arzadum & Co., Villagarcia, Province of Pontevedra.—Preserved fish. 641

856 Martinez, Joaquin, Pontevedra.—Preserved fish. 641

857 Otero, Francisco, Grove, Province of Pontevedra.—Pressed sardines. 641

858 Mandado, Nicolas, & Sons, Aldán, Province of Pontevedra.—Pressed sardines. 641

859 Larravide, Bráulio de, Laredo, Province of Santander.—Preserved fish. 641

860 Codes, Tomás Lopez de, Isla Cristina, Province of Huelva.—Salt tunny-fish. 642

861 Arzadum & Co., Villagarcia, Province of Pontevedra.—Shell-fish, cockles, and sea-sleeves. 644

862 Martinez, Joaquin, Pontevedra.—Cockles, mediterranean scallop, and other shell-fish. 644

863 Codes, Tomás Lopez de, Isla Cristina, Province of Huelva.—Sardine oil. 646

864 Vicente, Pascual, & Co., Vivero, Province of Lugo.—Sardine oil. 646

865 Riego, Vicente, Vivero, Province of Lugo.—Sardine oil. 646

866 Lopez, Francisco Ramon, Vivero, Province of Lugo.—Sardine oil. 646

Animal and Vegetable Products.

867 Provincial Deputation, Múrcia.—Spunk. 650

868 Riudavets y Femenias, Francisco, Mahon, Balearic Islands.—Condensed milk, and coffee and milk. 651

869 Fábreques, Guillermo, Mahon, Balearic Islands.—Condensed milk, and coffee and milk. 651

870 Visa, Agustin B., Mahon, Balearic Islands.—Coffee and condensed milk. 651

871 Clemente, Manuel Martin, Torrejoncillo, Province of Cáceres.—Cheese from sheep's milk. 651

872 Provincial Board of Agriculture, Morella, Province of Castellon.—Cheese from sheep's milk. 651

873 Coca, José, Maria, Daimiel, Province of Ciudad-Real.—Cheese from sheep's milk. 651

874 Villahermosa, Manuel, Manzanares, Province of Ciudad-Real.—Cheese from sheep's milk. 651

875 Camacho, Miguel Gonzalez, Manzanares, Province of Ciudad-Real.--Cheese from sheep's milk. 651

876 Pozoblanco, Luis Escribano, Province of Córdoba.—Cheese. 651

877 Falero y Fajardo, Plácido, Fuente de Pedro Naharro, Province of Cuenca.—Cheese. 651

878 Melgarejo, Maria Josefa, San Clemente, Province of Cuenca.—Cheese. 651

879 Moron, José Garcia, Cabezas Rubias, Province of Huelva.—Cheese. 651

880 Callejon, Francisco Gimenez, Jaen.—Cheese. 651

881 Rodriguez, Vicente, Becerreá, Province of Lugo.—Butter. 651

882 Vega, Manuel Pardo de la, Rabado, Province of Lugo.—Salt butter. 651

883 Novoa, Juan Caraballo & Son, Lobaces, Province of Orense.—Imitation butter. 651

884 Board of Agriculture, Industry and Commerce, Oviedo.—Cheese. 651

885 Peña, Justo Estévez, Hinojosa del Duero, Province of Salamanca.—Cheese. 651

886 Basarán, Isidoro, Olias del Rey, Province of Toledo.—Cheese. 651

887 Quiros' Widow & Sons, San Bartolomé de Pinares, Province of Avila.—Hides. 652

888 Provincial Commission, Búrgos.—Hides. 652

889 Martin, Francisco Cazador, Castellon.—Hides. 652

890 Barrera, Angel, Lugo.—Hides. 652

891 Provincial Deputation, Múrcia.—Hides. 652

892 Conde, Juan Manuel, Valverde, Province of Orense.—Hides. 652

893 Antonio, Manuel de, Salamanca.—Common glue. 652

894 Medrano, Segundo Bartolomé, Valdeavellano, Province of Soria.—Sheep skins. 652

895 Sotorra, Antonio Cort, Reus, Province of Tarragona.—Hides. 652

896 Sans, Jaime, Widow of, Reus, Province of Tarragona.—Catalanian sole-leather. 652

897 Rocamora, Jerónimo, Reus, Province of Tarragona.—Catalanian sole-leather. 652

898 Allustante, Manuel, Zaragoza.—Calf-skins and dressed skins. 652

899 Molano, Pedro, Badajoz.—Honey. 654

900 Fábregues, Guillermo, Mahon, Balearic Islands.—Nougat of honey and almonds. 654

901 Olives, Bernardo José de, Ciudadela, Balearic Islands.—Honey. 654

902 Salvadó, José, Barcelona.—Objects of wax. 654

903 Domingo, Gregorio de, Santibañez del Val, Province of Búrgos.—Honey. 654

904 Cepeda, Julian, Yeste, Province of Cáceres.—Honey. 654

905 Dominguez, Benigno, Pinar, Canary Islands.—Honey. 654

906 Provincial Board of Agriculture, Morella, Province of Castellon.—Honey. 654

907 Llausola, Vicente, Castellon.—Wax. 654

908 Rubisco, Cayetano, Clemente, Moral de Calatrava, Province of Ciudad-Real.—Wax and honey. 654

909 Corporation of Palma del Rio, Province of Córdoba.—Honey. 654

910 Mayordomo, Manuel, Fresneda de la Sierra, Province of Cuenca.—Honey. 654

Animal and Vegetable Products.

911 **Herraiz, Eustasio, Cardenete, Province** of Cuenca.—Honey. 654

912 **Torralba, José, Cardenete, Province** of Cuenca.—Honey. 654

913 **Corporation of Berninches, Province** of Guadalajara.—Honey. 654

914 **Cepeda, Ignacio, Almonte, Province** of Huelva.—Honey. 654

915 **Castillo, Juan Herrera, Cartaya,** Province of Huelva.—Honey. 654

916 **Alvarez, José Maria, Cartaya, Province** of Huelva.—Honey. 654

917 **Fernandez, Francisco, Cartaya,** Province of Huelva.—Honey. 654

918 **Vazquez, Bartolomé, Villanueva** de los Castillejos, Province of Huelva.—Honey. 654

919 **Serrano, José Lorenzo, Zalamea la** Real, Province of Huelva.—Wax. 654

920 **Miñon, Pedro Alonso, Leon.**—Honey. 654

921 **Martinez, Juan Panero, Astorga,** Province of Leon.—Wax. 654

922 **Monforte, Andrés Andrade, Province** of Lugo.—Honey. 654

923 **Lopez, Manuel Gonzalez, Incio,** Province of Lugo.—Honey. 654

924 **Corporation of Valle de Oro, Province** of Lugo.—Wax. 654

925 **Tato, Manuel, Lugo.—Wax.** 654

926 **Portillo, Serafin Rodriguez, Madrid.**—Ornamental wax candles. 654

927 **Provincial Deputation, Múrcia.**—Honey. 654

928 **Velasco, Manuel, Verin, Province** of Orense.—Honey. 654

929 **Robo, Modesto Perez, Verin, Province** of Orense.—Wax. 654

930 **Caramés, José Garcia, Forcarey,** Province of Pontevedra.—Wax. 654

931 **Corbalán, Juan, Saucelle, Province** of Salamanca.—Honey. 654

932 **Sanchez, Rosa Hernandez, La** Hinojosa, Province of Salamanca.—Honey. 654

933 **Garcia, José Sanchez, Fregeneda,** Province of Salamanca.—Honey. 654

934 **Gascon, Andrés Sanchez, Cepeda,** Province of Salamanca.—Wax. 654

935 **Roman, José Palacios, Coronil,** Province of Sevilla.—Honey. 654

936 **Ramos, Eustaquio, Soria.—Honey** and wax. 654

937 **Aguirre, Simon, Soria.—Honey.** 654

938 **Perez, Vicente Antonio, Talavera** de la Reina, Province of Toledo.—Wax candles and wax. 654

939 **Lecanda, Eloy, Valbuena de Duero,** Province of Valladolid.—Honey. 654

940 **Domec, Gregorio, Zuera, Province** of Zaragoza.—Honey. 654

941 **Izquierdo, Nicolás, Zuera, Province** of Zaragoza.—Honey. 654

842 **Poey, Juan, Habana, Cuba.-Honey.** 654

943 **Vegüer y Naguer, Juan, Habana,** Cuba.—Honey. 654

944 **Central Commission, Habana,** Cuba.—Honey. 654

945 **Carratalá, Francisco, San Juan,** Province of Alicante.—Olives. 656

946 **Girones, Manuela, Agost, Province** of Alicante.—Olives. 656

947 **Samper, Ramon, Muchamiel, Province** of Alicante.—Olives. 656

948 **Espinós, Joaquin, & Co., Ondara y** Beniarbeig, Province of Alicante.—Muscatel raisins. 656

949 **Almodóvar, Antonio Sanchez, Alicante.**—Preserves. 656

950 **Bernabeu y Diego, Juan B., Jabea,** Province of Alicante.—Raisins. 656

951 **Verdú y Perez, Joaquin, Monóvar,** Province of Alicante.—Dried figs. 656

952 **Lèrin, Eduardo Campos, Alicante,** Dried figs. 656

953 **Miralles, Clemente, Alicante.**—Vegetable preserves. 656

954 **Garcia, Manuel, Elche, Province** of Alicante.—Fig bread and dates. 656

955 **Benito, Juan Bautista Pina, Monforte,** Province of Alicante.—Figs. 656

956 **Meson, José, Arenas de San Pedro,** Province of Avila.—Olives. 656

957 **Vaca, José, Badajoz.—Ham.** 656

958 **Terron, Jacinto, Badajoz.—Pork** sausages and black pudding. 656

959 **Maria, Juan Martinez Santa, Burguillos,** Province of Badajoz.—Dried beef and sausages. 656

960 **Sanabria, José, Badajoz.—Sausages.** 656

961 **Visa, Agustin, Mahon, Balearic** Islands.—Sausages. 656

962 **Roca, Bartolomé, Palma, Balearic** Islands.—Vegetable preserves. 656

963 **Arrom, Lorenzo, Llubi, Balearic** Islands.—Vegetable preserves. 656

964 **Puig & Llagostera, Barcelona.**—Preserved olives. 656

965 **Trias y Travesa, José, Masnou,** Barcelona.—Dessicated vegetables. 656

966 **Vernis, Jaime, Vich, Province of** Barcelona.—Preserved meats. 656

967 **Luna, José, La Rambla, Province** of Barcelona.—Preserved fruits, vegetables, etc. 656

968 **Parent Bros., Barcelona.—Fruits** in liquors and sweetmeats. 656

969 **Castell, Joaquin Pedrosa de, Esparraguera,** Province of Barcelona.—Olives. 656

970 **Provincial Commission, Miranda** de Ebro, Province of Búrgos.—Preserved fruits. 656

971 **Olivares, Jeronimo de Sande, Garrovillas** de Alconetar, Province of Cáceres.—Pork sausages. 656

972 **Garcia, Antonio Gimenez, Guijo de** Santa Barbara, Province of Cáceres.—Preserved fruits. 656

973 **Cuevas, Joaquin de las, Puerto** Real, Province of Cadiz.—Sausages. 656

974 **Provincial Board of Agriculture,** Castellon.—Dried figs. 656

975 **Aguila y Aguila, Santiago, Villarrubia** de los Ojos, Province of Ciudad-Real.—Olives. 656

976 **Puzini Bros., Córdoba.—Fruits in** syrup. 656

977 **Lara, Rafael J. de, Córdoba.**—Olives. 656

Animal and Vegetable Products.

978 San Bernardo, Count of, Córdoba. —Olives. 656

979 Cabezas y Sarabia, José, Córdoba. —Olives. 656

980 Albear y Ward, Francisco, Montilla, Province of Córdoba.—Prunes. 656

981 Plaza, Juan Antonio, Montoro, Province of Córdoba.—Olives. 656

982 Alvarez, Rafael Ceballos, Adamúz, Province of Córdoba.—Olives. 656

983 Blanco, José Maria, Santiago, Province of La Coruña.—Quince marmelade. 656

984 Cotrofe, Miguel, Coruña.—Preserved meats and birds. 656

985 Garcia & Piñon, Coruña.—Preserved meats and birds. 656

986 Romero & Ferrin, Coruña.—Alimentary preserves. 656

987 Gomez y Gomez, Enrique, Lepe, Province of Huelva.—Figs. 656

988 Cruz, Rafael Trianes de la, Huelva. —Figs. 656

989 Corporation of Cartaya, Province of Huelva.—Figs. 656

990 Vasquez, Bartolomé, Villanueva, de los Castillejos, Province of Huelva.—Figs. 656

991 Mesa, Francisco Carrion, Huelva. —Fruits in brandy. 656

992 Carnes, Eulogio Martin, Aracena, Province of Huelva.—Hams. 656

993 Moreno, Maria, Cazorla, Province of Jaen.—Figs. 656

994 Barrutia, Elías, Cazorla, Province of Jaen.—Figs. 656

995 Romerotoro, Marquis of, Alcaudete, Province of Jaen.—Dried apples and prunes. 656

996 Elvira, José, Logroño.—Peach jam. 656

997 Moreno, Juan Miguel, Calahorra, Province of Logroño.—Vegetable preserves. 656

998 Ocon, Miguel, Calahorra, Province of Logroño.—Vegetable preserves. 656

999 Muro, Paulino, Calahorra, Province of Logroño.—Vegetable preserves. 656

1000 Provincial Commission, Jover, Province of Lugo.—Ham. 656

1001 Gimenez, Lucio Chapresto, Marbella, Province of Málaga.—Figs. 656

1002 Gomez, Antonio J., Málaga.—Muscatel raisins. 656

1003 Kreisler, Juan, Málaga.—Raisins. 656

1004 Gros, Federico, & Co., Málaga.—Raisins. 656

1005 Huelin, Guillermo, & Son, Málaga.—Muscatel raisins. 656

1006 Provincial Deputation, Múrcia.—Olives. 656

1007 Fuentes y Ponte, Javier, Múrcia. —Olives. 656

1008 Abarca, Gerónimo Vidal, Alhama, Province of Múrcia.—Fig bread 656

1009 Escudero, Tomás, Corella, Province of Navarra.—Preserved capsicum and tomatoes. 656

1010 Gayoso, Tomás Ramon, Rante, Province of Orense.—Peeled and dried chestnuts. 656

1011 Rey, Manuel Pereiro, Orense.—Olives. 656

1012 Santamarina, José, Verin, Province of Orense.—Olives. 656

1013 Anta, Ignacio, Orense.—Peeled and dried chestnuts. 656

1014 Romero, Joaquin Perez, Santa Cruz de la Rabeda, Province of Orense. —Peeled and dried chestnuts. 656

1015 Provincial Board of Agriculture, Industry, and Commerce, Cangas de Tineo, Province of Oviedo.—Ham. 656

1016 Diaz, Juan, Oviedo.—Sweetmeats. 656

1017 Arcadun & Co., Villagarcia, Province of Pontevedra.—Preserved partridge and veal. 656

1018 Martinez, Joaquin, Pontevedra.—Vegetable preserves. 656

1019 Onís, Federico de, Cantalapiedra, Province of Salamanca.—Fruit syrup. 656

1020 Martin, Lorenzo Calvo, Mogarraz, Province of Salamanca.—Figs. 656

1021 Paulino, Cipriano Perez, Fregeneda, Province of Salamanca.—Prunes. 656

1022 Molina's Widow & Son, Sevilla. —Olives. 656

1023 Carmona, Manuel, Sevilla.—Olives. 656

1024 Orihuela, Pedro, Sevilla.—Olives. 656

1025 Fernandez, Joaquin, Sevilla.—Olives. 656

1026 Garcia, Sebastian, Scala Dei, Province of Tarragona.—Dried fruits. 656

1027 Gatell y Folch, Juan, Altafulla, Province of Tarragona.—Olives. 656

1028 Fonts, Mariano, Reus, Province of Tarragona.—Olives and pimenton (ground fruit of the pepper plant). 656

1029 Serra, Olegario, Reus, Province of Tarragona.—Fruits in syrup. 656

1030 Esteve, D. A., Widow & Son of, Reus, Province of Tarragona.—Olives. 656

1031 Montaner, Amalio, Reus, Province of Tarragona.—Olives. 656

1032 Grau y Fló, José, Reus, Province of Tarragona.—Olives. 656

1033 Roca Vinardell, Tortosa, Province of Tarragona.—Preserved fruits. 656

1034 Pellicer, Francisco, Porrera, Province of Tarragona.—Figs. 656

1035 Coll, José, Valls, Province of Tarragona.—Muscatel raisins. 656

1036 Basarán, Isidoro, Olias del Rey, Province of Toledo.—Prunes. 656

1037 Capsir, José Damian, Puebla de Rugat, Province of Valencia.—Preserved fruits. 656

1038 Estellés, Gerardo, Játiva, Province of Valencia.—Muscatel raisins. 656

1039 Stárico y Ruiz, Ricardo, Ribarroja, Province of Valencia.—Fig bread. 656

Animal and Vegetable Products.

1040 **Lassala y Palomares, Vicente,** Masía de la Mar, Province of Valencia.—Figs. 656

1041 **Cañamás, Blas Antonio, Province** of Valencia.—Muscatel raisins. 656

1042 **Artigues, Serapio, Játiva, Province** of Valencia.—Muscatel raisins. 656

1043 **Fabiá, Manuel Andrés, Torrente,** Province of Valencia.—Grape syrup. 656

1044 **Martí, Enrique, Alcira, Province** of Valencia.—Vegetable preserves. 656

1045 **Espinós, Joaquin, & Co., Godella,** Province of Valencia.—Muscatel raisins. 656

1046 **Vives y Aspiroz, Rafael, Villa de** Oliva, Province of Valencia.—Muscatel raisins. 656

1047 **Calabuig, Bartolomé, Bocairente,** Province of Valencia.—Muscatel raisins. 656

1048 **Valencian Society of Agriculture,** Valencia.—Dried fruits. 656

1049 **Garcia, Miguel, Zamora.—Fruits** in syrup. 656

1050 **Perez, Bàrbara, Zamora.—Hams** and pork sausages. 656

1051 **Gasca y Beltran, Joaquin, Zaragoza.**—Preserved fruits. 656

1052 **Royo, Mariano, Zaragoza.—Preserved** strawberries. 656

1053 **Costa & Co., Habana, Cuba.—Preserved** fruits. 656

1054 **Bosehi, Juan, & Co., Habana,** Cuba.—Preserved fruits. 656

1055 **Casado, F. N., Malaga.—Raisins.** 656

1056 **Mark, Joah A., Malaga.—Raisins.** 656

1057 **Catala, Antonio, Jabea, Province** of Alicante.—Muscatel raisins. 656

1058 **Bolufer, Cristobal, Jabea, Province** of Alicante.—Muscatel raisins. 656

1059 **Girones y Domenech, Manuel,** Alicante.—Sugared almonds. 656

1060 **Ruidavets y Femenias, Francisco,** Mahon, Balearic Islands.—Nougat. 656

1061 **Visa, Agustin B., Mahon, Balearic** Islands.—Nougat. 656

1062 **Fàbregues, Guillermo, Mahon,** Balearic Islands.—Nougat. 656

1063 **Estapé y Cardona, José, Habana,** Cuba.—Guava paste. 656

1064 **Echarrieta, Santiago, San Josè de** las Lajas, Cuba.—Guava paste. 656

1065 **Gomez, J., & Co., Habana, Cuba.**—Confectionery. 656

1066 **Usano, Martin, Toledo.—Marchpane.** 656

1067 **Martin y Valverde, Laureano,** Toledo.—Marchpane. 656

1068 **Labrador, Cipriano, Toledo.**—Marchpane. 656

1069 **Perez, Abdon Atienza, Tarazona** de la Mancha, Province of Albacete.—Wheat flour. 657

1070 **Sellés, José, Alicante.—Wheat** flour. 657

1071 **Benito, Isidro, Avila.—Wheat** flour. 657

1072 **Lagarza, Eduardo, Badajoz.**—Flour. 657

1073 **Gil Bros. & Rico, Aranda de** Duero, Province of Búrgos.—Flour. 657

1074 **Conde & Bros., Cabia, Province of** Búrgos.—Flour. 657

1075 **Toval, Antonio, Búrgos.—Grits.** 657

1076 **Arqueaga, Rodrigo, Búrgos.**—Grits. 657

1077 **Vega Grande, Count of, Isle of** Gran Canaria, Canary Islands.—Maize flour. 657

1078 **Gordo, Julian, Luzaga, Province** of Guadalajara.—Flour and bran. 657

1079 **Fontoya, Manuel, Jaen.—Flour** and bran. 657

1080 **Martos, Juan Francisco, Jaen.**—Flour and bran. 657

1081 **Prado, Maximo Alonso de, Leon.**—Flour. 657

1082 **Provincial Deputation, Múrcia.**—Maize flour and rice. 657

1083 **Pombo, Pedro, Abarca, Province** of Palencia.—Wheat flour. 657

1084 **Mora, Celestino Merino de la,** Grijota, Province of Palencia.—Flour. 657

1085 **Vega, Lucas Ortiz, Grijota, Province** of Palencia.—Flour 657

1086 **Barrios, Marcelo, Grijota, Province** of Palencia.—Flour. 657

1087 **Ascoitia, Higinio de, Grijota,** Province of Palencia.—Flour. 657

1088 **Barrios, Rios & Co., Palencia.**—Flour. 657

1089 **Durango, Manuel Martinez,** Husillos, Province of Palencia.—Flour. 657

1090 **Dulce y Alvarez, Blas, Herrera** de Valdecañas, Province of Palencia.—Flour. 657

1091 **Sanchez, Basilio Igea, Peñaranda** de Bracamonte, Province of Salamanca.—Flour. 657

1092 **Villa Alcazar, Marquis of, Tejares,** Province of Salamanca.—Flour. 657

1093 **Carretero, E., Widow of, Segovia.**—Flour. 657

1094 **Carretero, Martin, Segovia.**—Flour. 657

1095 **Riber, Villa & Puerta, Segovia.**—Flour. 657

1096 **Saperas, Francisco, Reus, Province** of Tarragona.—Flour and bran. 657

1097 **Industrial Flour Mill of Reus,** Province of Tarragona.—Flour and bran. 657

1098 **Gatell y Folch, Juan, Altafulla.**—Province of Tarragona —Maize flour. 657

1099 **Estéban, Francisco, Toledo.**—Wheat flour. 657

1100 **Huelbes y Ortis, Emilio, Ocaña,** Province of Toledo.—Vetch flour. 657

1101 **Martinez, Gomez & Co., Sueca,** Province of Valencia.—Decorticated rice. 657

1102 **Society "La Edetana," Province** of Valencia.—Rice. 657

1103 **Quemada, Juan de Dios, & Sons,** Viloria, Providence of Valladolid.—Wheat flour. 657

1104 **Hornedo y Velasco, Pedro, Valladolid.**—Wheat flour. 657

Animal and Vegetable Products.

1105 Pardo, R. & P., Corcos, Province of Valladolid.—Wheat flour. 657

1106 La Patilla, Count of, Benavente, Province of Zamora.—Wheat flour. 657

1107 Palomar, Nasciso, Zaragoza.—Flour. 657

1108 Higuera, Tomàs, Zaragoza.—Flour. 657

1109 Segura, Josė, Sevilla.—Grits. 657

1110 Ribera, Guarner & Bros., Alicante.—Vermicelli and fine pastes. 658

1111 Esteve, Juan M., Alicante.—Starch. 658

1112 Ponseti y Gomila, José, Mahon, Balearic Islands.—Soup paste. 658

1113 Batlló Bros., Barcelona.—Starch. 658

1114 Draper y Frecios, Salvador, San Martin de Provensals, Province of Barcelona.—Starch. 658

1115 Provincial Board of Agriculture, Castellon.—Starch. 658

1116 Provincial Deputation, Múrcia.—Soup pastes. 658

1117 Rey, Manuel Pereiro, Orense.—Fæcula of potatoes. 658

1118 Barrera, Pedro Garcia, Ciudad-Rodrigo, Province of Salamanca.—Starch. 658

1119 Carnero & Colsa, Salamanca.—Starch. 658

1120 Moro, José, Salamanca.—Starch. 658

1121 Mirat & Son, Salamanca.—Starch. 658

1122 Jarrin, Bernardo, Salamanca.—Soup pastes. 658

1123 Martinez Sainz Bros., Sevilla.—Soup pastes and starch. 658

1124 Gil, Gregorio, Valladolid.—Starch. 658

1125 Cuevas & García, Valladolid.—Vermicelli. 658

1126 Castañeda, Romualdo Ruiz, Torralba de Calatrava, Province de Ciudad-Real.—Arrope (a kind of syrup). 659

1127 Rey, Luis Jouva, Granada.—Sugar and molasses. 659

1128 Torrent, Francisco, Almuñecar, Province of Granada.—Sugar. 659

1129 Huelin, Guillermo & Son, Málaga.—Unrefined sugar. 659

1130 Provincial Deputation. Múrcia.—Jelly and syrup. 659

1131 Roca Bros., Mürcia.—Pomegranate syrup. 659

1132 Mallet, Ildefonso, Zaragoza.—Oriental nectar. 659

1133 Central Commission of the Island of Cuba, Habana.—Sugar. 659

1134 Iznaga, Natividad, Habana, Cuba.—Sugar. 659

1135 Veguer y Nagüer, Juan, Habana, Cuba.—Sugar. 659

1136 Poey, Juan, Habana, Cuba.—Sugar and Guarapo (fermented sugar cane liquor). 659

1137 Girart, Nicolas, Regla, Cuba.—Sap of the sugar-cane. 659

1138 Capsir, José Damian, Puebla de Rugat, Province of Valencia.—Grape syrup. 659

1139 Gasco y Beltran, Joaquin, Zaragoza.—Raspberry syrup. 659

1140 García Muñoz, Emilia Samá de, Habana, Cuba.—Sugar. 659

1141 Skiret Bros., San Juan de Puerto Rico.—Sugar. 659

1142 Balanzátegui, Canuto, El Ciego, Province of Alava.—Red wine. 660

1143 Riscal de Alegre, Marquis of, El Ciego, Province of Alava.—Red wine. 660

1144 Tortosa, Joaquin, Hellin, Province of Albacete.—Brandy. 660

1145 Gil, Eloy, Hellin, Province of Albacete.—Wine. 660

1146 Lopez, Celestino, Tarazona de la Mancha, Province of Albacete.—Brandy. 660

1147 Aroca, José, Tarazora de la Mancha, Province of Albacete.—White wine. 660

1148 Lopez, Alonso, Tarazona de la Mancha, Province of Albacete.—Brandy. 660

1149 Sanchez, José Acacio, Tarazona de la Mancha, Province of Albacete.—Red wine. 660

1150 Pedraja, Bernardo Gomez, Tarazona de la Mancha, Province of Albacete.—Red wine. 660

1151 Fernandez, Antonio, Tarazona de la Mancha, Province of Albacete.—Red wine. 660

1152 Simarro, Miguel, Tarazona de la Mancha, Province of Albacete.—Red wine. 660

1153 Lara, Celestino Picazo, Tarazona de la Mancha, Province of Albacete.—Red wine. 660

1154 Tendero, Gerónimó, Tarazona de la Mancha, Province of Albacete.—Red wine. 660

1155 Picazo, Pedro Bautista, Tarazona de la Mancha, Province of Albacete.—Red wine. 660

1156 Serrano, María Rosa, Tarazona de la Mancha, Province of Albacete.—Red wine. 660

1157 Dénia, Rafael, Tarazona de la Mancha, Province of Albacete.—Red wine. 660

1158 Albi y Ginėr, Antonio, Jabea, Province of Alicante.—Muscatel vinegar. 660

1159 Ferriz y Martinez, Cristóbal, Campo de Mirra, Province of Alicante.—Wine. 660

1160 Rojas Aguado, José, Agres, Province of Alicante.—Wine. 660

1161 Gumiel y García, Luis, Aspe, Province of Alicante.—Anise-seed cordial. 660

1162 Romany, Vicente, & Sons, Déina, Province of Alicante.—White wine. 660

1163 Albert, Antoliano Perez, Monóvar, Province of Alicante.—Wines and brandies. 660

1164 Campos, Eduardo, Alicante.—Wine. 660

1165 Alsina, José, Partido de Campello, Province of Alicante.—White and red wine. 660

Animal and Vegetable Products.

1166 **Alenda, Antonio, & Son, Novelda,** Province of Alicante.—Brandy. 660

1167 **Almodóvar, Antonio Sanchez,** Alicante.—Wines. 660

1168 **Prast, Queremon Alfonso, Monóvar,** Province of Alicante.—Brandy. 660

1169 **Vidal, Joaquin Calpena, Monóvar,** Province of Alicante.—Red wine. 660

1170 **Muñoz, Lorenzo Fernandez, San** Juan, Province of Alicante.—Wine. 660

1171 **Ortuño y Maestre, Juan Francisco,** Salinas, Province of Alicante.—Wine. 660

1172 **Verdú y Perez, Joaquin, Monóvar,** Province of Alicante.—Wines. 660

1173 **Leach, Giró & Co., Alicante.**—White wines. 660

1174 **Novelda, Tomás Escolano, Province** of Alicante.—Brandy. 660

1175 **Berenguer, Raimundo, Monóvar,** Province of Alicante.—Sweet brandy. 660

1176 **Cerdá, Enrique, Monóvar, Province** of Alicante.—Vinegar. 660

1177 **Verdú y Rico, Monóvar, Province** of Alicante.—Vinegar. 660

1178 **Perez Verdú Brothers, Monóvar,** Province of Alicante.—Vinegar and wines. 660

1179 **Paya, Ciro Perez, Monóvar, Province** of Alicante —Wines. 660

1180 **Verdú, Marcial, Monóvar, Province** of Alicante.—Red wine. 660

1181 **Verdú y Cortés, Vedasto, Monóvar,** Province of Alicante.—Vinegar. 660

1182 **Verdu y Perez, Luis, Monóvar,** Province of Alicante.—Wines. 660

1183 **Rico, Antonio Perez, Monóvar,** Province of Alicante.—Wines. 660

1184 **Rico y Albert, Alejandro, Monóvar,** Province of Alicante.—Wines. 660

1185 **Verdú, Remedios Perez, Monóvar,** Province of Alicante.—Vinegar and wines. 660

1186 **Albert, Perez, & Co., Province of** Alicante.—Vinegar and wines. 660

1187 **Gisbert y Marco, Francisco, Ibi,** Province of Alicante.—Red wine. 660

1188 **Boculini, Juan Baeza, Alicante.**—Red wine. 660

1189 **Ferrer, Jaime, Alicante.—Vinegar.** 660

1190 **Faes Bros. & Co., Sax, Province** of Alicante.—Anise-seed cordial and spirits of wine. 660

1191 **Coquillat y Sempere, José, Elche,** Province of Alicante.—Muscatel wine. 660

1192 **Amorós, Juan Esteve, Monforte,** Province of Alicante.—Wine. 660

1193 **Garcia, Luis Gumiel, Aspe, Province** of Alicante.—Brandies. 660

1194 **Agulló, Francisco Fuentes, & Bros.,** Elche, Province of Alicante.—Wines, vinegar, alcohol, and pomegranate wine. 660

1195 **Pina, Juan Bautista, Monforte,** Province of Alicante.—Mistela (national drink). 660

1196 **Benito, Juan Pina, Monforte, Province** of Alicante.—Wine. 660

1197 **Scals, José, Jijona, Province of** Alicante.—Wine. 660

1198 **Somoza, Ramon Maria Nava,** Moraleja Matacabras, Province of Avila. —White wine. 660

1199 **Soria, Mariano, Nava del Rey,** Province of Avila.—Vinegar. 660

1200 **Davernat & Co., Velez-Rubio,** Province of Almeria.—Fig-brandy. 660

1201 **Abadia, Nicolas, Bros., Velez-**Rubia, Province of Almeria.—Wines. 660

1202 **Vilches & Jover, Alhama, Province** of Almeria.—Wines and brandies. 660

1203 **Trell y Chacon, Miguel del, Berja,** Province of Almeria.—Wines. 660

1204 **Daza y Ruiz, Francisco, Pur-**chena, Province of Almeria.—Wines. 660

1205 **Romero, Manuel Carbonero, Pur-**chena.—Province of Almeria.—Wine. 660

1206 **Roca, Bartolomé, Palma, Balearic** Islands.—Brandies and wines. 660

1207 **Viza, Agustin, Mahon, Balearic** Islands.—Refined vinegar. 660

1208 **Prohens, Damian, Félanitx, Ba-**learic Islands.—Anise-seed cordial. 660

1209 **Jaime, Miguel, Santa Maria, Ba-**learic Islands.—Anise-seed cordial. 660

1210 **Bisellach, Guillermo, Benisalen.** Balearic Islands.—Wines. 660

1211 **Munar, Gabriel, Benisalen, Ba-**learic Islands.—Wines. 660

1212 **Mulet, Antonio, Beñalbufar, Ba-**learic Islands.—Malmsey wine. 660

1213 **La Cenia, Marquis of, Beñalbufar,** Balearic Islands.—Muscatel wine. 660

1214 **Humbert, Nicasio, Llummayor,** Balearic Islands.—Wines. 660

1215 **Ferrant, Manuel, Barcelona.**—Vinegar. 660

1216 **Soler y Stussa, Valentin, Barce-**lona —Wines and vinegars. 660

1217 **Society Burchers, Pedro Miret,** San Juan de Vilasar, Province of Barcelona.—Liquors. 660

1218 **Ballester y de Torres, Laureano,** Mediona, Province of Barcelona.—Wines. 660

1219 **Castells de Mas, Joaquin Pedrosa** de, Esparraguera, Province of Barcelona. —Wines. 660

1220 **Valls, Pedro, & Viñas, Gospar,** Esparraguera, Province of Barcelona.—Wines and liquors. 660

1221 **Llampallas, Antonio, Masnou,** Province of Barcelona.—Wines. 660

1222 **Ventura y Sampere, Amado, Mas-**nou, Province of Barcelona.—Liquors and anise.seed cordial. 660

1223 **Pascual, Miguel, Masnou, Province** of Barcelona.—Wines. 660

1224 **Golar y Sirasol, José, Villanueva** y Geltrú, Province of Barcelona.—Red wine. 660

1225 **Cusi y Ferret, Federico, Villa-**nueva y Geltrú, Province of Barcelona.—Hygienic wine. 660

1226 **Juandó y Rafecas, Juan, Villa-**nueva y Geltrú, Province of Barcelona.—Wines. 660

1227 **Marqués, Jerónimo, Villanueva** y Geltrú, Province of Barcelona.—Wines. 660

Animal and Vegetable Products.

1228 **Alegret, Francisco, Villanueva** y Geltrú, Province of Barcelona.—Mistela (national drink). 660

1229 **Solà, Félix, Villanueva y Geltrú,** Province of Barcelona.—Red wine. 660

1230 **Baro y Gibert, Josè, Villanueva** y Geltrú, Province of Barcelona.—Virgin wine. 660

1231 **Roig y Serra, Juan, Villanueva y** Geltrú, Province of Barcelona.—Wines. 660

1232 **Creux, Teodoro, Villanueva y** Geltrú, Province of Barcelona.—Wines. 660

1233 **Dodero y Ponte, Josè Oriol, Pomar** de Badalona, Province of Barcelona. —Wines. 660

1234 **Valenti, Joaquin, Cabrera de Ma**taró, Province of Barcelona.—Wine. 660

1235 **Sivilla y Martorell, Narciso, Vil**lafranca de Panadés, Province of Barcelona.—Anise-seed wine. 660

1236 **Girona, Silvestre, Villafranca de** Panadés, Province of Barcelona.—Anise-seed cordial. 660

1237 **Olivella, Cristóbal, Villafranca** de Panadés, Province of Barcelona.—Imitation wines. 660

1238 **Mullol, Buenaventura Rius, Villa**franca de Panadés, Province of Barcelona.—Wines. 660

1239 **Escofet Nello, Margarita, Widow** of, Province of Barcelona.—Macon wine and imitations. 660

1240 **Font, Salvador, Mataró, Province** of Barcelona.—Liquors. 660

1241 **Palau, Joaquin de, Mataró, Prov**ince of Barcelona.—Wines. 660

1242 **Monte, Pedro Prat del, Barcelona.** —Florentine vermouth. 660

1243 **Fontanals, José Teresa, Barce**lona.—Beer. 660

1244 **Sallés, Salvador, Barcelona.**—Wine. 660

1245 **Plá y Vila, Pedro, Barcelona.**—Brandy. 660

1246 **Oliver Bros., Barcelona.**—Wines. 660

1247 **Codina y Riu, Ramon, San Boy de** Llobregat, Province of Barcelona.—Wine. 660

1248 **Duràn, Eduardo, San Vicente,** Province of Barcelona.—Wine. 660

1249 **Gerona, Manuel, Villa de Cabals,** Province of Barcelona.—Wine. 660

1250 **Santacana, José, La Granada,** Province of Barcelona.—Mistela wine. 660

1251 **Deu, José, & Co., Masqueja y** Martorell, Province of Barcelona.—Wine. 660

1252 **Fornell y Batllaura, Juan, Abella,** Province of Barcelona.—Wine. 660

1253 **Oliver y Coll, Francisco, Papiol,** Province of Barcelona.—Wine, liquors, and vinegar. 660

1254 **Beltran y Rosell, Manuel, Igua**lada, Province of Barcelona.—Wine. 660

1255 **Robira y Grau, Jose, San Martin** de Sarroca, Province of Barcelona.—Wines and imitations. 660

1256 **Barrera, Gabriel, Tayà, Province** of Barcelona.—Wine. 660

1257 **Bosch y Grau, José, Badalona,** Province of Barcelona.—Brandy. 660

1258 **Amèll y Carbonell, José, Sitges,** Province of Barcelona.—Wine. 660

1259 **Puig, José Buenaventura, Sitges,** Province of Barcelona.—Muscatel and Malmsey wine. 660

1260 **Ventallò y Llobateras, Domingo,** Tarrasa, Province of Barcelona.—Wines. 660

1261 **Castelét, Buenaventura, Tarrasa,** Province of Barcelona.—Wines. 660

1262 **Galí, Antonio, Tarrasa, Province** of Barcelona.—Wines. 660

1263 **Pons, Antonio Castells de, Espar**raguera, Province of Barcelona.—Wines. 660

1264 **Castell de Mas, Joaquin Pedrosa** de, Esparraguerra, Province of Barcelona.—Wine. 660

1265 **Camprubí, Juan, Barcelona.**—Liquor and anise-seed cordial. 660

1266 **Puig & Llagosteras Bros., Barce**lona.—Vinegar. 660

1267 **Llobet, Antonio Maria, Barce**lona.—Wine. 660

1268 **Patiño, José Maria, Cabeza de** Vaca, Province of Badajoz.—Wine. 660

1269 **Carrasco, Alfonso, Guareña.** Province of Badajoz.—Wine. 660

1270 **Sifredi, Juan Bautista, Almen**dralejo, Province of Badajoz.—Brandy and wine. 660

1271 **Paredes, Carlos, Guareña, Prov**ince of Badajoz.—Muscatel wine. 660

1272 **Cortés, José Inocente, Guareña,** Province of Badajoz.—Pedro Jimenez wine. 660

1273 **Lopez, Aureliano, Badajoz.**—Red and white wine. 660

1274 **Benito y Reoyo, Genaro, Búrgos.** —Brandy. 660

1275 **Regulez, Dionisio, Miranda de** Ebro, Province of Búrgos.—Wine. 660

1276 **San Roman, Agustin Lopez de,** Valle de Mena, Province of Búrgos.—Red and white wine. 660

1277 **Goya y Lopez, Marcelino, Búr**gos.—Vinegar. 660

1278 **Franco, Ramon Santivañez,** Casar de Palomero, Province of Cáceres. —Wine. 660

1279 **Olivares, Jeronimo Sande, Garro**villas, Province of Cáceres.—Wine. 660

1280 **Bustamante, Bernardino, Villa**miel, Province of Cáceres.—Wine. 660

1281 **Bacas y Estévez, Ignacio, Cilleros,** Province of Cáceres.—Wine. 660

1282 **Herran & Co., Jerez de la Fron**tera, Province of Cadiz.—Wine. 660

1283 **Troya, Ildefonso, Prado del Rey,** Province of Cadiz.—Wine. 660

1284 **Hontoria y Tezanos, Joaquin,** Sanlúcar, Province of Cadiz.—Wine. 660

1285 **Hidalgo y Verjano, Eduardo,** Sanlúcar, Province of Cadiz.—Wines and vinegar. 660

1286 **Blanco, Antonio, Prado del Rey,** Province of Cadiz.—Wine. 660

1287 **Argüeso y Argüeso, Leon de,** Sanlúcar, Province of Cadiz.—Wine. 660

Animal and Vegetable Products.

1288 Martinez, Antonio, Sanlúcar, Province of Cadiz.—Wine. 660

1289 Linares y Obeso, Diego, Sanlúcar, Province of Cadiz.—Wine. 660

1290 Urmeneta, Fermin de, Chiclana, Province of Cadiz.—Brandy. 660

1291 Sanchez, Antonio, Chiclana, Province of Cadiz.—Wine. 660

1292 Rivas, Francisco Martinez de, Chiclana, Province of Cadiz.—Wine. 660

1293 Hugues, Guillermo H., Puerto de Santa Maria, Province of Cadiz.—Wine. 660

1294 Alvarez, Serafin, Puerto de Santa Maria, Province of Cadiz.—Wine. 660

1295 Segundo, Federico, Puerto de Santa Maria, Province of Cadiz.—Wine. 660

1296 Rudolph, Federico, Puerto de Santa Maria, Province of Cadiz.—Wine. 660

1297 Carli, Ramon, Puerto de Santa Maria, Province of Cadiz.—Wine. 660

1298 Pico, José Maria, Puerto de Santa Maria, Province of Cadiz.—Wine. 660

1299 Pró, José Maria, Puerto de Santa Maria, Province of Cadiz.—Wine. 660

1300 Parilla, José de Puentes, Jerez de la Frontera, Province of Cadiz.—Wine. 660

1301 Gonzalez, Biass & Co., Jerez de la Frontera, Province of Cadiz.—Wines. 660

1302 Santarelli Bros., Jerez de la Frontera, Province of Cadiz.—Wines. 660

1303 Lopez, Juan Antonio, Widow of, Jerez de la Frontera, Province of Cadiz.—Wines. 660

1304 Lebrun & Co., La Orotava, Canary Islands.—Wines. 660

1305 Davison, Guillermo, & Co., La Orotava, Canary Islands.—Wines. 660

1306 Carpinter & Co., La Orotava, Canary Islands.—Wines. 660

1307 Bruce, Hamilton, & Co., La Orotava, Canary Islands.—Wines. 660

1308 Monteverde, Antonio, La Orotava, Canary Islands.—Wine. 660

1309 Tolosa, Fernando, La Orotava, Canary Islands.—Wine. 660

1310 Lopez, Juan José Barriuso, La Victoria, Canary Islands.—Wines and brandies. 660

1311 Diego, Wood & Co., Las Palmas, Canary Islands.—Wines. 660

1312 Castello y Olivares, José del, Las Palmas, Canary Islands.—Wines. 660

1313 Vega Grande, Count of, Las Palmas, Canary Islands.—Wine. 660

1314 Avilés, Nicolás, Las Palmas, Canary Islands.—Wine. 660

1315 Quevedo y Perez, José C., Isle of Gran Canaria, Canary Islands.—Wines. 660

1316 Gourié, Alfonso, Las Palmas, Canary Islands.—Wines. 660

1317 Quintana, Juan de, Las Palmas, Canary Islands.—Wine. 660

1318 Massieu, Domingo, Balsequillo, Canary Islands.—Wine. 660

1319 Peraza, Alejandro, Granadilla, Canary Islands.—Wine. 660

1320 Llovera y Llovet, Vicente, Masia de Cucalon, Province of Castellon.—Wine. 660

1321 Villores, Marquis of, Torreblanco, Province of Castellon.—Wines. 660

1322 Vilanova y Piera, Pascual, Alcalá de Chisvert, Province of Castellon.—Wines. 660

1323 Provincial Board of Agriculture, Borriol, Province of Castellon.—Vinegar and wines. 660

1324 Ripolles y Perez, Manuel, Castellon.—Brandies. 660

1325 Gascó, F. B., Castellon.—Brandy. 660

1326 Climent, Vicente, Castellon.—Wines. 660

1327 Cloramunt, Hilarion, Vinaroz, Province of Castellon.—Wines. 660

1328 Mazorra, Mateo, & Son, Valdepeñas, Province of Ciudad-Real.—Wine. 660

1329 Mazarron, Miguel, Valdepeñas, Province of Ciudad-Real.—Wines. 660

1330 Mudela, Marquis of, Valdepeñas, Province of Ciudad-Real.—Wines. 660

1331 Fraile, Maria de la Asuncion, Valdepeñas, Province of Ciudad-Real.—Wines. 660

1332 Peinado y Lasa, Tiburcio, Tomesollo, Province of Ciudad-Real.—Brandy. 660

1333 Villena y Parra, Sinforiano, Tomesollo, Province of Ciudad-Real.—Brandy and spirits of wine. 660

1334 Ramirez, Primo, Tomesollo, Province of Ciudad-Real.—Brandy and spirits of wine. 660

1335 Gijon, Trinidad, Torralba, Province of Ciudad-Real.—Wine. 660

1336 Delgado y Palacios, Juan, Ciudad-Real.—Alcohol and anise-seed cordial. 660

1337 Ruiz, Romualdo, Torralba, Province of Ciudad-Real.—Wines. 660

1338 Medraño, José, Ciudad-Real.—Wine. 660

1339 Soria, Marciano de, Valdepeñas, Province of Ciudad-Real.—Wine. 660

1340 Avansay, Hipólito, & Son, Valdepeños, Province of Ciudad-Real.—Wine. 660

1341 Blanco y Alcalde, Rafael, Cabra, Province of Córdoba.—Wine. 660

1342 Carretero, Pedro, Córdoba.—Wine. 660

1343 Molina, Isidro, Rute, Province of Córdoba.—Wine. 660

1344 Perez, Diego Ecija, Rute, Province of Córdoba.—Brandy. 660

1345 Ruiz, Francisco Moreno, Doña Mencia, Province of Córdoba.—Brandy. 660

1346 Calvo, José María, Cabra, Province of Córdoba.—Brandies. 660

1347 Rubio, José Calvo, Aguilar, Province of Córdoba.—Montilla wine. 660

1348 Várgas, Sebastian, Villaviciosa, Province of Córdoba.—Wines. 660

1349 Infante, José Escobar, Villaviciosa, Province of Córdoba.—Wine. 660

1350 Arribas, Antonio Escobar, Villaviciosa, Province of Córdoba.—Wine. 660

Animal and Vegetable Products.

1351 Módenes, Juan, R., Baena, Province of Córdoba.—Wines. 660

1352 Neges, Francisco de Paula, Baena, Province of Córdoba.—Wine. 660

1353 Fernandez, Francisco, Baena, Province of Córdoba.—Wine. 660

1354 Salas, Francisco Solano, Montilla, Province of Córdoba.—Montilla wine. 660

1355 Jurado, José, Montilla, Province of Córdoba.—Montilla wine. 660

1356 Raigon, Antonio, Montilla, Province of Córdoba.—Montilla wine. 660

1357 Navarro, Antonio José, Montilla, Province of Córdoba.—Montilla wine. 660

1358 Alvear, Carlos, Montilla, Province of Córdoba.—Montilla wine. 660

1359 Alvear y Ward, Francisco, Montilla, Province of Córdoba. — Montilla wine. 660

1360 Polo, Bartolomé, Montilla, Province of Córdoba.—Montilla wine. 660

1361 Canela, José, Lucena, Province of Córdoba.—Montilla wine. 660

1361*a* Canela, Antonio, Lucena, Province of Córdoba.—Montilla wine. 660

1362 Sotomayor, Eduardo Alvarez, Lucena, Province of Córdoba.—Wine. 660

1363 Valle, José Muñoz, Lucena, Province of Córdoba.—Wine. 660

1364 Valenzuela, Josè Valle, Lucena, Province of Córdoba.—Wine. 660

1365 Algar, José Ruiz de, Lucena, Province of Córdoba.—Wine. 660

1366 Gallardo, José, Montilla, Province of Córdoba.—Wines. 660

1367 Villalba y Sotomayor, Manuel, Montilla, Province of Córdoba.—Montilla wine. 660

1368 La Corte, Marquis of, Cabra, Province of Córdoba.—Wines. 660

1369 López, Pedro, Córdoba.—Wine. 660

1370 Neyralores, Gerardo, Fao, Province of La Coruña.—White wine. 660

1371 Bustindui, José Antonio, San Clemente, Province of Cuenca.—Wines. 660

1372 Moreno, Domingo, Tarancon, Province of Cuenca.—Wine. 660

1373 Retamoso, Count of, Tarancon, Province of Cuenca.—Wine and brandy. 660

1374 Torre y Salto, Antonio de la, Tarancon, Province of Cuenca. — Red wine. 660

1375 Valera, Julian Martinez, Chilaron, Province of Cuenca.—Red wine. 660

1376 Carné, José, Tarancon, Province of Cuenca.—Red wine. 660

1377 Escobar y del Campo, Francisco, Rubielos Bajos, Province of Cuenca.—Red wine. 660

1378 Vilaret, Agustin, Blanes, Province of Gerona.—Malmsey wine. 660

1379 Descals, Francisco Puig, Rozar, Province of Gerona.—Wine. 660

1380 Vega y Tejada, Ezequiel de la, Guadalajara.—Wines. 660

1381 Martinez, Gregorio Garcia, Guadalaiara.—Wine. 660

1382 Reyes, Juan A., Guadalajara.—Wine. 660

1383 Muñoz y Mendez, Eugenio, Humanes, Province of Guadalajara.—Wine. 660

1384 Martí, Diego Garcia, Guadalajara.—Wines. 660

1385 Iñiguez, José, Gibraleon, Province of Huelva.—Wine and brandy. 660

1386 Cepeda, Ignacio de, Almonte, Province of Huelva.—Wine and vinegar. 660

1387 Roldan, Manuel Moreno, Almonte, Province of Huelva.—Wine. 660

1388 Acebedo, Francisco, Almonte, Province of Huelva.—Manzanilla wine. 660

1389 Lagarú, Francisco, Almonte, Province of Huelva.—White wine. 660

1390 Gonzalez, Nicolás Gomez, Huelva.—Wines and brandy. 660

1391 Cueva, Fernando de la, Huelva.—Wines and brandy. 660

1392 Diaz y Gomez, Eduardo, Huelva.—Wines. 660

1393 Mesa, Francisco Carrion, Huelva.—Brandy and anise-seed cordial. 660

1394 Martın & Colombo, Huelva. — Alcohol and brandy. 660

1395 Lopez, Luis Maria, Huelva. — White wine. 660

1396 Quintero, Juan García, Huelva.—Vinegar. 660

1397 Torre y Figueroa, Antonio de la, Huelva.—Red wine. 660

1398 Penillos, García & Co., Bollullos, Province of Huelva.—Wines. 660

1399 Society "Palma y Quesada," Aguilar, Province of Córdoba.—Wines. 660

1400 García y Ruiz, Pedro, Bollullos, Province of Huelva.—Wines. 660

1401 Neble, José Maria, Bollullos, Province of Huelva.—Wines. 660

1402 Garcia, Pedro, Bollullos, Province of Huelva.—Wines. 660

1403 Dominguez, Francisco, Bollullos, Province of Huelva.—Brandies. 660

1404 Molina, Federico, Rociana, Province of Huelva.—Wine, vinegar, and arrope (national drink). 660

1405 Carrasco, José Maria, Donares, Province of Huelva.—Wine and vinegar. 660

1406 Pinzon, Luis H., Moguer, Province of Huelva.—Wine and brandy. 660

1407 Gimenez de Tejada Bros., Moguer, Province of Huelva.—Wines and vinegar. 660

1408 Gimenez de Tejada, Servando, Moguer, Province of Huelva.—Wines and vinegar. 660

1409 Flores, Antonio, Moguer, Province of Huelva.—Wines and brandy. 660

1410 Ramirez, Francisco Perez, Moguer, Province of Huelva.—Wines. 660

1411 Carmona, Josè Gomez, Moguer, Province of Huelva.—Wines and alcohol. 660

1412 Iñiguez, Rafael, Moguer, Province of Huelva.—Wines. 660

Animal and Vegetable Products.

1413 Thorices, Basilio, Moguer, Province of Huelva.—Wines and vinegar 660

1414 Thorices, Francisco R., Moguer, Province of Huelva.—Wines and vinegar. 660

1415 Gonzalez, Manuel, Moguer, Province of Huelva.—Wine and vinegar. 660

1416 Soldan, Antonio, La Palma, Province of Huelva.—Wines and brandy. 660

1417 Martinez, Eduardo, La Palma, Province of Huelva.—Wines. 660

1418 Cepeda, Manuel, La Palma, Province of Huelva.—Wines. 660

1419 Cueva, Manuel de la, La Palma, Province of Huelva —Anise-seed cordial and brandy. 660

1420 Pinzon, Rafael Iñiguez, Manzanilla, Province of Huelva.—Wines. 660

1421 Marquez, Rufino José, Manzanilla, Province of Huelva.—Wines. 660

1422 Estrado, Diego P., Manzanilla, Province of Huelva.—Wine. 660

1423 Rivera, Antonio Marquez, Manzanilla, Province of Huelva.—Wines. 660

1424 Mercado, Manuel, Manzanilla, Province of Huelva.—Wines. 660

1425 Rodriguez, José Trigueros, Province of Huelva.—Wines. 660

1426 Cecero y Barreda, Emilio, Trigueros, Province of Huelva.—Wine. 660

1427 Montiel, Eliezer, Trigueros, Province of Huelva.—Wines. 660

1428 Zambrano, José Antonio, Villalba del Alcor, Province of Huelva.—Wines and vinegar. 660

1429 Espina, José Maria, Villalba del Alcor, Province of Huelva.—Vinegar. 660

1430 Oliver, D. L., Huesca.--Wines. 660

1431 Arnal, Dionisio, Castelflorite, Province of Huesca.—Claret. 660

1432 Beótegui, Fernando, Sena, Province of Huesca.—Claret. 660

1433 Salinas, Francisco, Castelflorite, Province of Huesca.—Wine. 660

1434 Laguna, Alejandro, Grañen, Province of Huesca.—Wines and claret. 660

1435 Budios, Leon, Sariñena, Province of Huesca.—Wine. 660

1436 Sampietra, Antonio, Sariñena, Province of Huesca.—Wine. 660

1437 Bastarás, Antonio, Lanaja, Province of Huesca.—Wine. 660

1438 Lasheras, Manuel, Alcubierre, Province of Huesca.—Claret. 660

1439 Lacruz, Francisco, Alcubierre, Province of Huesca.—Wine and claret. 660

1440 Adrid, Antonio, Alcubierre, Province of Huesca.—Claret. 660

1441 Calvo, Antonio, Poleñino, Province of Huesca.—Claret. 660

1442 Lasierra, Joaquin, Pallazuela, Province of Huesca.—Claret. 660

1443 Lasierra, Francisco, Pallazuela, Province of Huesca.—Claret. 660

1444 Lacruz, Antonio, Alcubierre, Province of Huesca.—Red wine. 660

1445 Ruata, Juan, Alcubierre, Province of Huesca.—Claret. 660

1446 Casamayor, Manuel, Alcubierre, Province of Huesca.—Red wine. 660

1447 Vasquez, Francisco, Cazorla. Province of Jaen.—Red wine. 660

1448 Marin, José, Cazorla, Province of Jaen.—Red wine. 660

1449 Almagro, Sebastian Cañada, Jaen. —San Vicente wine, brandy, and ratafia. 660

1450 Las Almenas, Count of, Espeluy, Province of Jaen.—White wine. 660

1451 Corporation of Arganza, Province of Leon.—Wines. 660

1452 Fernandez, José, Sahagan, Province of Leon.—Wines. 660

1453 Martinez, Lúcas Prado, Galleguillos, Province of Leon.—Wine. 660

1454 Isla, Pedro, Benazolbe, Province of Leon.—Wine. 660

1455 Corporation of Valdefresno, Provvince of Leon.—Red wine. 660

1456 Corporation of Armunia, Province of Leon.—Red wine. 660

1457 Corporation of Valverde del Camino, Province of Leon.—Red wine. 660

1458 Corporation of Villaturiel, Province of Leon.—Red wine. 660

1459 Corporation of Valdemimbre, Province of Leon.—Red wine. 660

1460 Corporation of Pajares de los Oteros, Province of Leon.—Red wine. 660

1461 Corporation of Ponferrada, Province of Leon.—White wine. 660

1462 Corporation of Congosto, Province of Leon.—White wine. 660

1463 Bustamente, Angel Maria, Astorga, Province of Leon. —Anise-seed cordial. 660

1464 Bon, Ramon, Vinaixa, Province of Lérida.—Wine. 660

1465 Alós, Francisco, Balaguer, Province of Lérida.—Wine. 660

1466 Codina, Ramon, Belloch, Province of Lérida.—Wine. 660

1467 Reixados, Antonio, Lérida.—Wine. 660

1468 Corporation of Vinaixa, Lérida.—Wine. 660

1469 Rubea, Miguel, Barbens, Province of Lérida. 660

1470 Lamolla Bros., Lérida. — Anise-seed cordial. 660

1471 Ochoa & Bro., Cervera del Rio Alhama, Province of Logroña. — Claret. 660

1472 Poves y Quintano, Galo de, Allauri, Province of Logroño. — Red wine. 660

1473 Caballero, Andrés, Cenicero, Province of Logroño.—Wine. 660

1474 Pascual y Caballero, Pedro, Cenicero, Province of Logroño.—Wine. 660

1475 Artacho, Juan Bautista, Cenicero, Province of Logroño.—Wine. 660

1476 Bobadilla, Natalio, Fernandez, Cenicero, Province of Logroño. — Wine. 660

1477 Bujanda, Pablo, Cenicero, Province of Logroño.—Wine. 660

1478 Sotes, Angel, Cenicero, Province of Logroño.—Wine. 660

1479 Nalda, Pedro García, Cenicero, Province of Logroña.—Wine. 660

Animal and Vegetable Products.

1480 **Olavarrieta, Manuel Saenz,** Cenicero, Province of Logroño.—Wine. 660

1481 **Bazan, V. Celestino,** Cenicero, Province of Logroño.—Wine. 660

1482 **Mata, Trinidad de la,** Alfaro, Province of Logroño.—Anise-seed cordial, liquors, and gin. 660

1483 **Estéfani, Joaquin Gonzalez,** Cuzcurrita, Province of Logroño.—Champagne. 660

1484 **Cirat y Villafranqueza, Count of,** Haro, Province of Logroño.—Medoc. 660

1485 **Ozalla, Tomás, & Barona, Felix,** Treviana, Province of Logroño.—Claret. 660

1486 **Zubia, Ildefonso,** Logroño.—Sherry. 660

1487 **Andrade, Andrés,** Velacha, Province of Lugo.—Red wine. 660

1488 **Varela, Manuel Diaz,** Monforte, Province of Lugo—Wine. 660

1489 **Guitian, José,** Amandi, Province of Lugo.—Wine. 660

1490 **Pascual, Widow & Sons of,** Madrid.—Champagne and liquors. 660

1491 **Garcia y Garcia, Manuel,** Arganda del Rey, Madrid.—Wine and brandy. 660

1492 **Cortés, Balbino,** Madrid.—Wines. 660

1493 **San Roman, Agustin Lopez de,** Navalcarnero, Province of Madrid.—Red wine and brandy. 660

1494 **Calatrava, Francisco Garcia,** Alcobendas, Province of Madrid.—Muscatel wine and vinegar. 660

1495 **Navas, Manuel Garcia,** Málaga.—Brandy. 660

1496 **Pino y Gomez, Julio del,** Málaga.—Brandy. 660

1497 **Bueno, Joaquin, & Co.,** Málaga.—Brandy, wine and liquors. 660

1498 **Romero, Ramon Garcia,** Málaga.—Wine. 660

1499 **Morales, Pedro, & Co.,** Ojen, Province of Málaga.—Brandy. 660

1500 **Muñoz, Atenodoro,** Chapera, Province of Málaga.—Wines. 660

1501 **Saenz, I.,** Ronda, Province of Málaga.—Wines. 660

1502 **Menchero, Eduardo,** Cartagena, Province of Múrcia.—Orange wine. 660

1503 **Ferro, Bartolomé,** Cartagena, Province of Múrcia.—Wine. 660

1504 **Gil, Antonio Marsilla,** Bullas.—Province of Múrcia.—Anise-seed milk and brandy. 660

1505 **Roca Bros.,** Múrcia.—Wines. 660

1506 **Spottorno, Bartolomé,** Cartagena, Province of Múrcia.—Wine. 660

1507 **Castilla, Camilo,** Corella, Province of Navarra.—Wines. 660

1508 **Gimenez, Babil,** Tafalla, Province of Navarra.—Wine and brandy. 660

1509 **Orduña, Calisto,** Cascante, Province of Navarra.—Wines. 660

1510 **Leizaur y Rodriguez, Gabino,** Peralta, Province of Navarra.—Wine. 660

1511 **Anta y Temes, Federico,** Orense.—Wines. 660

1512 **Bobo, Feliciano Perez,** Orense.—Wines. 660

1513 **Amor, Bernardo,** Orense.—Wines. 660

1514 **Romero, Javier,** Orense.—Vinegar and brandy. 660

1515 **Vasquez, José,** Orense.—Wine, vinegar, and brandy. 660

1516 **Leis, Widow of the Marquis of,** Orense.—Wines. 660

1517 **Montenegro, Antonio,** Orense.—Wine. 660

1518 **Mayo, Ignacio Anta,** Orense.—Wine and brandy. 660

1519 **Diaz, Laureano Balbis,** San Ciprian de Viñas, Province of Orense.—Wine. 660

1520 **Muñoz, Federico Rodriguez,** San Ciprian de Viñas, Province of Orense.—Wine. 660

1521 **Rapela, Laureano Diaz,** San Ciprian de Viñas, Province of Orense.—Wine. 660

1522 **Gogueira y Diaz, Manuel,** San Ciprian de Viñas, Province of Orense.—Wines. 660

1523 **Diaz, Camila,** San Ciprian de Viñas, Province of Orense.—Wine. 660

1524 **Fernandez y Conde, Pedro,** San Ciprian de Viñas, Province of Orense.—Wine. 660

1525 **Novoa, Manual Ramiro,** San Ciprian de Viñas, Province of Orense.—Wine. 660

1526 **Rapela, Manuel,** San Ciprian de Viñas, Province of Orense.—Wine. 660

1527 **Mosquera, Antonio,** Coles, Province of Orense.—Wine. 660

1528 **Mendez, Urbano Moreno,** Verin, Province of Orense.—Wine. 660

1529 **Garcia, Jacobo André,** Verin, Province of Orense.—Wine. 660

1530 **Moreno, Ramon Sanchez,** Verin, Province of Orense.—Wine. 660

1531 **Velasco, Manuel de,** Verin, Province of Orense.—Wine. 660

1532 **Salgado, Pedro Antonio,** Barco de Valdeorras, Province of Orense.—Wine. 660

1533 **Salgado, Cárlos,** Barco de Valdeorras, Province of Orense.—Wine. 660

1534 **Salgado, Joaquin Maria, Widow of,** Barco de Valdeorras, Province of Orense.—Wine. 660

1535 **Alba, Telesforo,** Barco, de Valdeorras, Province of Orense.—Wine. 660

1536 **Rivera, Ramon,** Sejalbo, Province of Orense.—Wine. 660

1537 **Gonzalez, Antonio,** Sejalbo, Province of Orense.—Wine. 660

1538 **Riobóo, José Fernandez,** Sejalbo, Province of Orense.—Wine. 660

1539 **Bastos, Manuel Fernandez,** Rivadavia, Province of Orense.—Wine. 660

1540 **Estévez, José Vila,** Rua de Valdeorras, Province of Orense.—Wine. 660

1541 **Mouré, Manuel,** Rua de Valdeorras, Province of Orense.—Wines. 660

1542 **Losada, Maria Josefa,** Rua de Valdeorras, Province of Orense.—Wine. 660

Animal and Vegetable Products.

1543 Rey, Manuel Pereyro, Canedo, Province of Orense.—Wine. 660

1544 Labarta, Miguel, Canedo, Province of Orense.—Wines and vinegar. 660

1545 Vila, Francisco, Viana del Bollo, Province of Orense.—Wine. 660

1546 Bahamonde, Antonio Varela G., Castrelo de Miño, Province of Orense.—Wines. 660

1547 Gonzalez, Francisco, Petin, Province of Orense.—Wines. 660

1548 Diz, Manuel Fernandez, San Ciprian de Viñas, Province of Orense.—Wine. 660

1549 Board of Agriculture, Oviedo.—Cider. 660

1550 Zarracina, Tomás, Gijon, Province of Oviedo.—Cider. 660

1551 Dominguez, Miguel, Palencia.—Wine. 660

1552 Herrero, Pedro Romero, Palencia.—Wine. 660

1553 Cachurro, Modesto, & Bro., Dueñas, Province of Palencia.—Wines. 660

1554 Gutierrez, Juan Francisco, Palencia.—Wine. 660

1555 Balbas, José, Torquemada, Province of Palencia.—Wine. 660

1556 Palomino, Toribio, Torquemada, Province of Palencia.—Wine. 660

1557 Mora, José Manuel, Melogar de Yuso, Province of Palencia.—Wines. 660

1558 Monedero, Joaquin, Cevico de la Torre, Province of Palencia.—Wine. 660

1559 Martin, Francisco Garcia, Dueñas, Province of Palencia.—Wines. 660

1560 Sutelo & Veiga, Redondela, Province of Pontevedra.—Wines. 660

1561 Almansa, Eulogio Troncoso de, Puenteáreas, Province of Pontevedra.—Wines. 660

1562 Blanco, Joaquin A. Piñeiro, Mourente, Province of Pontevedra.—Wines and vinegar. 660

1563 Onís, Federico, Cantalapiedra, Province of Salamanca.—Wines. 660

1564 Sierra, Viesca de la, Marquis of, Fregeneda, Province of Salamanca.—Port wine. 660

1565 Hortal, Ignacio, Fregeneda, Province of Salamanca.—Sweet wines. 660

1566 Corbalan, Juan, Saucelle, Province of Salamanca.—Wine. 660

1567 Martin, Lorenzo Calvo, Mogarraz, Province of Salamanca.—Wine. 660

1568 Hernandez, Ramon, Salamanca.—Rum and liquors. 660

1569 Gutierrez, Vicente, Reinosa, Province of Santander.—Gin. 660

1570 Cortines, Celis, Santander.—Liquors. 660

1571 Rasilla, José, Los Corrales, Province of Santander.—Liquors and wines. 660

1572 Ibarra, J. M., & Sons, Sevilla.—Wines. 660

1573 Penillos, García & Co., Sevilla.—Wines. 660

1574 Valencia, Josè, Sevilla.—Wines. 660

1575 Olmedo, Juan, Sevilla.—Wine, liquor, and vinegar. 660

1576 Bordallo, Rodrigo, Sevilla.—Wine, liquors, and brandy. 660

1577 Huerta, Constantino de la, Sevilla.—Wine and vinegar. 660

1578 La Motilla, Marquis of, Sevilla.—White wine. 660

1579 Galindo, Widow of, Valencia, Province of Sevilla.—Wine and liquors. 660

1580 Silva & Arcos, Espartinas, Province of Sevilla.—Wines. 660

1581 Mayorga, Ramon Diaz, Moron, Province of Sevilla.—White wine and vinegar. 660

1582 Alvarez, José, Constantina, Province of Sevilla.—Wine and brandy. 660

1583 Rosa y Silva, José de la, Villamanrique, Province of Sevilla.—Wine and brandy. 660

1584 Romero, Enrique, Constantina, Province of Sevilla.—Brandy. 660

1585 Olmo, Sebastian del, Constantina, Province of Sevilla.—Brandy. 660

1586 Salcedo, José J. Gonzalez de, Constantina, Province of Sevilla.—Wine. 660

1587 Torres, Juan Lainez, Arahal, Province of Sevilla.—Wine. 660

1588 Capdevila, José Diaz, Arahal, Province of Sevilla.—Wine. 660

1589 Reina, Manuel Arias, Arahal, Province of Sevilla.—Wine. 660

1590 Zerpa, José, Villanueva del Ariscal, Province of Sevilla.—Wine. 660

1591 Amores, Manuel, Villanueva del Ariscal, Province of Sevilla.—Wine and vinegar. 660

1592 Lucena, Nicolás, Osuna, Province of Sevilla.—Wine. 660

1593 Celis, José G. de, Salteras, Province of Sevilla.—Wine. 660

1594 Arenas, Antonio Rivas, Cantillana, Province of Sevilla.—Brandy. 660

1595 Valle y Villar, Luis del, Lebrija, Province of Sevilla.—Wine. 660

1596 Rabio, Juan Miguel, Dos-Hermanos, Province of Sevilla.—Wine. 660

1597 Olivencia Bros., Olivares, Province of Sevilla.—Wine. 660

1598 Liendo, Manuel, Gines, Province of Sevilla.—Wine. 660

1599 Cotan, Antonio García, Olivares, Province of Sevilla.—Vinegar. 660

1600 Siscar, Ramon, La Canonja, Province of Tarragona.—Wine. 660

1601 Robers, Sebastian García de, Scala Dei, Province of Tarragona.—Wine. 660

1602 Peira y Mach, Agustin, Scala Dei, Province of Tarragona.—Wine. 660

1603 Gotell y Folch, Juan, Altafulla, Province of Tarragona.—Wine and vinegar. 660

1604 Grás, Pedro, Reus, Province of Tarragona.—Wine. 660

1605 Boulé, José, Reus, Province of Tarragona.—Wine and garnacha (national drink). 660

1606 Soberano & Co., Reus, Province of Tarragona.—Wine. 660

Animal and Vegetable Products.

1607 **Fumaña Bros., Reus, Province of** Tarragona.—Wine. 660

1608 **Abelló & Son, Reus, Province of** Tarragona.—Wine. 660

1609 **Gil, Francisco, Reus, Province of** Tarragona.—Wine. 660

1610 **Marti y Badia, Ramon, Reus,** Province of Tarragona.—Mistela (national drink) and spirits of wine. 660

1611 **Plá, Francisco, Reus, Province of** Tarragona.—Spirits of wine and anise-seed cordial. 660

1612 **Pujol y Salvat, Francisco, Reus,** Province of Tarragona.—Garnacha (national drink) and muscatel wine. 660

1613 **Esteve, A., Widow & Son of,** Reus, Province of Tarragona.—Vinegar and alcohol. 660

1614 **Sirvent y Oliver, Pedro, Reus,** Province of Tarragona.—Wine and spirits of wine. 660

1615 **Clariano, Rafael, Reus, Province** of Tarragona.—Wine. 660

1616 **Montagut, José, Reus, Province** of Tarragona.—Wine and vinegar. 660

1617 **Fonts, Mariano, Reus, Province** of Tarragona.—Wine. 660

1618 **Avelló y Boada, Pablo, Reus,** Province of Tarragona.—Wine. 660

1619 **Pujol, José Odena, Reus, Province** of Tarragona.—Muscatel wine. 660

1620 **Valero, Francisco, Reus, Prov-**ince of Tarragona.—Port wine. 660

1621 **Rocamora, Pablo, Reus, Province** of Tarragona.—Anise-seed brandy. 660

1622 **Domingo, Tomás, Reus, Province** of Tarragona.—Brandy and wine. 660

1623 **Potan y Mico, Antonio, Vimbodi,** Province of Tarragona.—Wine. 660

1624 **Estradé y Alsamora, José, Vim-**bodi, Province of Tarragona.—Wine. 660

1625 **Plassa y Alfonso, José, Vimbodi,** Province of Tarragona.—Mistela (national drink). 660

1626 **Roig y Sancho, Isidro, Vimbodi,** Province of Tarragona.—Mistela (national drink). 660

1627 **Aragonés, Ramon Zamora, Pobo-**leda, Province of Tarragona.—Garnacha (national drink) and wine. 660

1628 **Figuerolo, Juan, Tarragona.—** Wine. 660

1629 **Morera y Pulles, A., & Son, Tar-**ragona.—Wine and imitations, anise-seed cordial, and garnacha (national drink). 660

1630 **Carey Bros. & Co., Tarragona.** —Wine and imitations. 660

1631 **Montoliu, Placido Maria de, Mo-**rell, Province of Tarragona.—Wine. 660

1632 **Sardá, Pablo, Tarragona.—Wine.** 660

1633 **Consul & Virgili, Tarragona.—** Wine. 660

1634 **Nogues, Romeu & Co., Tarra-**gona.—Wine and brandy. 660

1635 **Oliva, Gregorio, Tarragona.—** Spirits of wine and brandy. 660

1636 **Roig, Ponseti & Co., Tarragona.** —Wine. 660

1637 **Compte, Jaime, Torraja, Province** of Tarragona.—Wines. 660

1638 **Bella, Juan, Valls, Province of** Tarragona.—Garnacha wine. 660

1639 **Coll, José, Valls, Province of Tar-**ragona.—Muscatel wine. 660

1640 **Roca y Murtra, Ramon, Valls,** Province of Tarragona.—Spirits of wine and anise-seed cordial. 660

1641 **Anglés y Font, José, Ulldemolins,** Province of Tarragona.—Red wine. 660

1642 **Montlleo y Mor, José, Ulldemo-**lins, Province of Tarragona.—Mistela (national drink). 660

1643 **Figuerola, Antonio, Porrera, Prov-**vince of Tarragona.—Wine. 660

1644 **Compte, José Amorós, Porrera,** Province of Tarragona.—Wine. 660

1645 **Amorós, Vicente, Porrera, Prov-**ince of Tarragona.—Wine. 660

1646 **Montlleo, Jaime, Porrera, Prov-**ince of Tarragona.—Garnacha wine. 660

1647 **Pellicier, Francisco, Porrera,** Province of Tarragona.—Garnacha wine. 660

1648 **Simó, Pio, Porrera, Province of** Tarragona.—Wines. 660

1649 **Simó, José Maria, Porrera, Prov-**ince of Tarragona.—Garnacha wine. 660

1650 **Llaberia, Joaquin Sabatér, Por-**rera, Province of Tarragona.—Wine. 660

1651 **Capdevila é Ibern, José, Torre-**dembarra, Province of Tarragona.—Wine. 660

1652 **Sanroma y Boada, Domingo, Tor-**redembarra, Province of Tarragona.—Mistela (national drink). 660

1653 **Llorat y Fontanillas, José, Torre-**dembarra, Province of Tarragona.—Wine. 660

1654 **Castellarnau, Joaquin de, Pera-**fort, Province of Tarragona.—Wine. 660

1655 **Mirét, Juan, Vilaseca, Province** of Tarragona.—Mistela (national drink). 660

1656 **March, Juan de, Vilaseca, Prov-**ince of Tarragona.—Mistela (national drink) and wine. 660

1657 **Dalmau y Amat, Domingo de,** Montbrio de Tarragona, Province of Tarragona. — Wine and mistela (national drink). 660

1658 **Porqueras, Juan, Vilella Alta,** Province of Tarragona.—Malmsey wine. 660

1659 **Boulé, José, Reus, Province of** Tarragona.—Wines. 660

1660 **Viñas y Pamies, José, Poboleda,** Province of Tarragona.—Wine. 660

1661 **Montaner y Rincon, José, Reus,** Province of Tarragona.—Wine. 660

1662 **Caselles, Pedro, & Co., Reus, Prov-**ince of Tarragona.—Wine. 660

1663 **Borras, S. S., & Lassalle, Reus,** Province of Tarragona.—Wines and imitations. 660

1664 **Ferratges, Josè Vidiella, Reus,** Province of Tarragona.—Wine. 660

1665 **Salvadó, Mateó, Riudoms, Prov-**ince of Tarragona.—Wine. 660

1666 **Sarro y Salat, Antonio, Bárbara,** Province of Tarragona.—Brandy. 660

1667 **Aragonés, Tomás, Cornudella,** Province of Tarragona.—Wines. 660

Animal and Vegetable Products.

1668 Folch, Joaquin Brú, Cambrils, Province of Tarragona.—Wine. 660

1669 Gallisa, Juan Aragonés, Dosaiguas, Province of Tarragona.—Wine. 660

1670 Crusat, Bartolomé Llebaria, Dosaiguas, Province of Tarragona.—Wine. 660

1671 Cabré, José Nolla, Dosaiguas, Province of Tarragona.—Wine. 660

1672 Anlestia, José Ciurana, Dosaiguas, Province of Tarragona.—Wine. 660

1673 Aragonés, Juan Sangenis, Dosaiguas, Province of Tarragona.—Wine. 660

1674 Magriña, Luis de, Falset, Province of Tarragona.—Wines. 660

1675 Anguerá y Angles, Ramon, Falset, Province of Tarragona.—Mistela (national drink) and wine. 660

1676 Ortiz, Emilio, Huelbes, Ocaña, Province of Toledo.—Wine. 660

1677 Gurrido, Valentin, Ocaña, Province of Toledo.—Wine and brandy. 660

1678 Caballero y Cabello, Martin, Ocaña, Province of Toledo.—Wine. 660

1679 Basarán, Isidoro, Olias del Rey, Province of Toledo.—Wine. 660

1680 Lázaro, Olallo, Talavera de la Reina, Province of Toledo.—Anise-seed cordial. 660

1681 Perera & Sons, Sagunto, Province of Valencia.—Wine. 660

1682 Requena, Manuel, & Sons, Játiva, Province of Valencia.—Wine. 660

1683 Suñer, Enrique, Masanasa, Province of Valencia.—Dr. Suñer's liquor. 660

1684 Caruana Bros., Bétera, Province of Valencia.—Wine. 660

1685 Comas y Delgado, Rafael, Onteniente, Province of Valencia.—Wine. 660

1686 Villar, Manuel, Sagunto, Province of Valencia.—Wine. 660

1687 Lluch, Francisco, Sagunto, Province of Valencia.—Wine. 660

1688 Valero, Juan, Requena, Province of Valencia.—Wine. 660

1689 Piñango, Norberto, Requena, Province of Valencia.—Wine. 660

1690 Omlin, Juan, Requena, Province of Valencia.—Wine. 660

1691 Moron, Francisco de P., & Co., Albaida, Province of Valencia.—Brandy. 660

1692 Pujol, José Maria, Valencia.—Wine. 660

1693 Gisbert, Mariano, Torrente, Province of Valencia.—Wine. 660

1694 Iranzo, Jaime, Turis, Province of Valencia.—Wine. 660

1695 Navarro, Eduardo, Turis, Province of Valencia.—Wine. 660

1696 Latorre, Federico, Turis, Province of Valencia.—Wine. 660

1697 Artigues, Serapio, Játiva, Province of Valencia.—Wine. 660

1698 Olías, Vicente, Chiva, Province of Valencia.—Wine. 660

1699 Torner, Juan, Carcagente, Province of Valencia.—Orange wine. 660

1700 Ferrandis y Soler, José, Onteniente, Province of Valencia.—Wine. 660

1701 Lorenzo Puig Bros., Monsenat, Province of Valencia.—Wine. 660

1702 Pieza, Honorato, Monsenat, Province of Valencia.—Wine. 660

1703 Pardo, Joaquin, Valencia.—Orange wine. 660

1704 Reig y Garcia, Fernando, Puebla, de Vallbona, Province of Valencia.—Wine. 660

1705 Albors, Cárlos, Picasent, Province of Valencia.—Wine. 660

1706 Bodi, Salvador, Carcagente, Province of Valencia.—Orange wine. 660

1707 Lassala, Vicente, Llano de Cuarte, Province of Valencia.—Wine. 660

1708 Ricart y Sanz, Salvador, Rafelbuñol, Province of Valencia.—Wine. 660

1709 Starico y Ruiz, Ricardo, Ribarroja, Province of Valencia.—Wine. 660

1710 Bosca y Pascual, Blas, Puebla de Rugat, Province of Valencia.—Wine. 660

1711 Calabuyg, Bartolomé, Valencia.—Wine. 660

1712 Cañamás, José Damian Capsir, Puebla de Rugat, Province of Valencia.—Wine. 660

1713 Domenech, Angel, Valencia.—Wine and orange wine. 660

1714 Lavarias, Antonio, Cheste, Province of Valencia.—Red wine. 660

1715 Guillen, Valero Navarro, Cheste, Province of Valencia.—Red wine. 660

1716 Campos, Vicente, Cheste, Province of Valencia.—Red wine. 660

1717 García, Francisco, Cheste, Province of Valencia.—Red wine. 660

1718 Tarin, German, Cheste, Province of Valencia.—Red wine. 660

1719 Luay, Leoncio, Cheste, Province of Valencia.—Red wine. 660

1720 Martí, Salvador, Cheste, Province of Valencia.—Red wine. 660

1721 Jordan, Vicente, Cheste, Province of Valencia.—Wine. 660

1722 Tamarit, Eulogio, Cheste, Province of Valencia.—Wine. 660

1723 Garcia, Pascual, Cheste, Province of Valencia.—Wine. 660

1724 Jordan, Manuel, Cheste, Province of Valencia.—Wine. 660

1725 Garcia, Luis Campos, Cheste, Province of Valencia.—Wine. 660

1726 Ortega, Vicente, Valencia.—Liquors. 660

1727 Costa, José Plá, Olleria, Province of Valencia.—Wine. 660

1728 Diego, Francisco Polop, Játiva, Province of Valencia.—Brandy, mistela, and wine. 660

1729 Nager y Juan, Pedro J., Olleria, Province of Valencia.—Wine. 660

1730 Calvo, Francisco, Valencia.—Orange wine. 660

1731 Herrera, José, Nava del Rey, Province of Valladolid.—Wine. 660

1732 Sañudo, Ramon Trueba, Nava del Rey, Province of Valladolid.—Wine. 660

1733 Pimentel, Pedro Antonio, Rueda, Province of Valladolid.—Vinegar. 660

Animal and Vegetable Products.

1734 Villalva, Benigno, Corrales de Duero, Province of Valladolid.—Wine. 660

1735 Alonso, Bernardo Real, Peñaflor, Province of Valladolid.—Wine. 660

1736 Prasencio, Mariano, Tudela de Duero, Province of Valladolid—Wine. 660

1737 Zunzúnegui, Angel, Cabezon, Province of Valladolid.—Wine. 660

1738 Malfaz, Agustin, Cabezon, Province of Valladolid.—Wine. 660

1739 Revila, Antonio, Cabezon, Province of Valladolid.—Wine. 660

1740 Ganzalez, Benito, Cabezon, Province of Valladolid.—Wine. 660

1741 Villaverde, Rafael, Cabezon, Province of Valladolid.—Wine. 660

1742 Sotillo, Manuel, Valladolid.—Wine. 660

1743 Redondo Bros., Valladolid.—Wine. 660

1744 Zurbano, José, Cabezon, Province of Valladolid.—Wine. 660

1745 Red, Baltasar de la, Cabezon, Province of Valladolid.—Wine. 660

1746 Pimentel, Casilda Arévalo de, Rueda, Province of Valladolid.—Wine. 660

1747 Vaca, Francisco Cabeza de, Puente Duero, Province of Valladolid.—Wine. 660

1748 Caballero, Marquis of, Nava del Rey, Province of Valladolid.—Wine. 660

1749 Eyries, Agustin, Valladolid.—Wine. 660

1450 Diaz, Juan, Valladolid.—Liquors. 660

1751 Mesones, Mariano Bayon, Rueda, Province of Valladolid.—Wine. 660

1752 Corporation of Medina de Campo, Province of Valladolid.—Wine. 660

1753 Diez, Crispulo Paredes, Valladolid.—Liquors. 660

1754 Gimeno, Mariano, Rueda, Province of Valladolid.—Wine. 660

1755 Board of Agriculture, Valbuena de Duero, Province of Valladolid.—Wine and brandy. 660

1756 Cosio y Cuenca, Eloy, Valladolid.—Liquors. 660

1757 Diez y Diez, Luis, Valladolid.—Wine. 660

1758 Montero, Ramon Bayon, Rueda, Province of Valladolid.—Wine. 660

1759 Arias, Francisco Galan, Fuentesauco, Province of Zamora.—Wine. 660

1760 Serrano, Manuel, Formoselle, Province of Zamora.—Wine. 660

1761 Puga, Sons of, Zamora.—Liquors. 660

1762 Requejo, Miguel, Zamora.—Wine. 660

1763 Furitero, Leonardo, Toro, Province of Zamora.—Wine. 660

1764 Villaboa, Victoriano, Zamora.—Wine. 660

1765 Weches, Santiago, Coreses, Province of Zamora.—Wine. 660

1766 Temprano, José, Verdemarban, Province of Zamora.—Wine. 660

1767 Pernia, Nicasio, Castro Verde, Province of Zamora.—Wine. 660

1768 Dieguez, Manuel, Zamora.—Anise-seed cordial. 660

1769 Royo, Mariano, Zamora.—Alcohol. 660

1770 Porta, Mariano, Zaragoza.—Anise-seed cordial and prepared anise-seed used for its manufacture. 660

1771 Pórtoles, Miguel, Zaragoza.—Anise-seed cordial. 660

1772 Lichtenstein, Julio, Cariñena, Province of Zaragoza.—Wine. 660

1773 Lahoz, Victorio, Escatron, Province of Zaragoza.—Anise-seed cordial. 660

1774 Ariño, Antonio, Escatron, Province of Zaragoza.—Anise-seed cordial. 660

1775 Lacaze, Juan Pablo, Zaragoza.—Wine. 660

1776 Figueras, Iñigo, Zaragoza.—Wine. 660

1777 Perez, Mariano, Zaragoza.—Wine. 660

1778 Vallier, José, Zaragoza.—Wine. 660

1779 Bailo, Angel, Habana, Cuba.—Liquors. 660

1780 Zulueta, Julian, Habana, Cuba.—Brandies. 660

1781 Soler, L., & Co., Cárdenas, Cuba.—Brandies. 660

1782 Central Commission of the Island, Habana, Cuba.—Sherry. 660

1783 Domech, Pedro, Jerez.—Sherry. 660

1784 Duff, Gordon & Co., Jerez.—Sherry. 660

1785 Loring Bros., Málaga.—Málaga and Montilla wine. 660

1786 Schoki, Málaga.—Málaga. 660

1787 Vintro y Vila, Agustin, Barcelona.—Preserved yeast. 661

1788 Cano, Antonio, Carrion de Calatrava, Province of Ciudad-Real.—Crackers. 661

1789 Rivera Guarner, Alicante.—Chocolate. 661

1790 Barrengoa, Dámaso de, Ciudad-Real.—Chocolate. 661

1791 Blanco, José Maria, Santiago, Province of La Coruña.—Chocolate. 661

1792 Leal, Francisco, Coruña.—Chocolate. 661

1793 Castro, Enrique Calvo de, Ferrol, Province of La Coruña.—Chocolate. 661

1794 Palá, Juan, Huesca.—Chocolate. 661

1795 Prado, Máximo Alonzo de, Leon.—Chocolate. 661

1796 Alonso, Pedro Antonio, Mansilla de las Mulas, Province of Leon.—Chocolate. 661

1797 Fernandez, José, Sahagun, Province of Leon.—Chocolate. 661

1798 Alonso, Blas, Widow of, Leon.—Chocolate. 661

1799 Silva, Tomás Rubio, Astorga, Province of Leon.—Chocolate. 661

Animal and Vegetable Products.

1800 Panero y Martinez, Juan, Astorga, Province of Leon.—Chocolate. 661

1801 Garcia, Manuel, Lérida.—Chocolate. 661

1802 Reixades, Antonio, Lérida.—Chocolate. 661

1803 Ruiz, Francisco Enciso de, Munilla, Province of Logroño.—Chocolate. 661

1804 Fernandez, Francisco, & Bro., Lugo.—Chocolate. 661

1805 Meric & Co., Madrid.—Chocolate. 661

1806 Lopez, Matias, Madrid.—Chocolate. 661

1807 Lopez & Vaquez, Madrid.—Chocolate. 661

1808 Dubois, L., Widow of, Múrcia.—Chocolate. 661

1809 Bobo, Francisco Perez, Orense.—Chocolate. 661

1810 Anta y Temes, Federico, Orense.—Chocolate. 661

1811 Fernandez, Antonio Maria, Oviedo.—Chocolate. 661

1812 Acebal y Menendez, Benito, Oviedo.—Chocolate. 661

1813 Ortiz, Tadeo, & Sons, Palencia.—Chocolate. 661

1814 Garcia, Benito, Pontevedra.—Chocolate. 661

1815 Crespo, José Sanchez.—Chocolate. 661

1816 Pies, Federico Sanchez, Salamanca.—Chocolate. 661

1817 Nácar, Juan Prieto; Salamanca.—Chocolate. 661

1818 Ramos, Eustaquio, Soria.—Chocolate. 661

1819 Macaya, Juan, Reus, Province of Tarragona.—Chocolate. 661

1820 Gonzalez, José Maria, Talavera, Province of Toledo.—Chocolate. 661

1821 Lázaro, Olallo, Talavera, Province of Toledo.—Chocolate. 661

1822 Cuevas & Garcia, Valladolid.—Chocolate. 661

1823 Escarda, Salustiano Mariño, Benovente, Province of Zamora.—Chocolate. 661

1824 Escudero, Dionisio, & Son, Tarazona, Province of Zaragoza.—Chocolate. 661

1825 Ascaso, Domingo, Zaragoza.—Chocolate. 661

1826 Iriarte, José Maria, Habana, Cuba.—Chocolate. 661

1827 Fernandez, José, Matanzas, Cuba.—Chocolate. 661

1828 Plana & Co., Habana, Cuba.—Chocolate. 661

1829 Amores, Julian, Elche de la Sierra, Province of Alcabete.—Olive oil. 662

1830 Maroni, José, Hellin, Province of Alcabete.—Olive oil. 662

1831 Sandoval, José Joaquin, Jacarilla, Province of Alicante.—Olive oil. 662

1832 Payas, Ciro Perez, Monóvar, Province of Alicante.—Olive oil. 662

1833 Rico, Antonio Perez, Monóvar, Province of Alicante.—Oil. 662

1834 Verdú, Remedios Perez, Monóvar, Province of Alicante.—Olive oil. 662

1835 Albert, L. Perez, & Co., Monóvar, Province of Alicante.—Olive oil. 662

1836 Alegret, Emilio Perez, Ibi, Province of Alicante.—Olive oil. 662

1837 Pina, Juan Bautista, Monforté, Province of Alicante.—Olive oil. 662

1838 Verdú y Perez, Joaquin, Monóvar, Province of Alicante.—Olive oil. 662

1839 Moreno, Pedro Contreras, Velez-Rubio, Province of Almeria.—Olive oil. 662

1840 Trell, Miguel del, Berja, Province of Almeria.—Natural olive oil. 662

1841 Meson, José, Arenas de San Pedro, Province of Avila.—Olive oil. 662

1842 Patiño, José Maria, Cabeza de Vaca, Province of Badajoz.—Olive oil. 662

1843 Cáceres, Damian, Guareña, Province of Badajoz.—Olive oil. 662

1844 Fernandez, Secundino, Zafra, Province of Badajoz.—Olive oil. 662

1845 Delgado, Francisco Gomez, Badajoz.—Olive oil. 662

1846 Fluxá y Palet, Miguel, Selva, Balearic Islands.—Oils. 662

1847 Zaforteza, Juan Burguez, Buñolas, Balearic Islands.—Oils. 662

1848 Puig & Llagostera Bros., Barcelona.—Olive oil. 662

1849 Porcar y Tió, Manuel, Barcelona.—Olive oil. 662

1850 Fornell, Ramon, & Co., Barcelona.—Olive oil. 662

1851 Oliver y Coll, Francisco, Ripoll, Province of Barcelona.—Olive oil. 662

1852 Pons, Antonio Castell de, Esparraguera, Province of Barcelona.—Olive oil. 662

1853 Ferran, Manuel, Barcelona.—Olive oil. 662

1854 Soler y Stussa, Valentin, Barcelona.—Oil. 662

1855 Castell de Mas, Joaquin Pedrosa de, Esparraguera, Province of Barcelona.—Olive oil. 662

1856 Villegas, Vicente Villarroel, Alcántara, Province of Cáceres.—Olive oil. 662

1857 Ayaz, José Diaz, Plasencia, Province of Cáceres.—Olive oil. 662

1858 Santivañez, Pedro José, Casar de Palomero, Province of Cáceres.—Olive oil. 662

1859 Arjona, Manuel, Jaraiz, Province of Cáceres.—Olive oil. 662

1860 Gomez, Juan Crisóstomo Gomez, Villamiel, Province of Cáceres.—Olive oil. 662

1861 Botejana, Juan Vicente, Villas Buenas, Province of Cáceres.—Olive oil. 662

1862 Hernandez, Juan, Gata, Province of Cáceres.—Natural olive oil. 662

1863 Casillas, Ramon, Acebo, Province of Cáceres.—Olive oil. 662

1864 Bacás y Estevez, Ignacio, Cilleros, Province of Cáceres.—Olive oil. 662

Animal and Vegetable Products.

1865 Guerra, Felipe Leon, Gata, Province of Cáceres.—Olive oil. 662

1866 Cepeda, Julian, Jerte, Province of Cáceres.—Oil. 662

1867 Valmorisco, Pedro Navas, Guadalupe, Province of Cáceres.—Olive oil. 662

1868 Valiente, Eusebio, Hoyos, Province of Cáceres.—Olive oil. 662

1869 Luguiz y Lopez, Francisco, Puerto de Santa Maria, Province of Cadiz.—Olive oil. 662

1870 Artiles, Matias Helian, Las Palmas, Canary Islands.—Olive oil. 662

1871 Girona y Mato, Ramon, Alcora, Province of Castellon de la Plana.—Olive oil. 662

1872 Mascaró, José, Alcora, Province of Castellon de la Plana.—Olive oil. 662

1873 Grangell, Pascual, Alcora, Province of Castellon de la Plana.—Olive oil. 662

1874 García y Moreno, Julian, Altura, Province of Castellon de la Plana.—Virgin olive oil. 662

1875 Escribano, José, Vinaróz, Province of Castellon de la Plana.—Olive oil. 662

1876 Arnau & Tomás, Segorbe, Province of Castellon de la Plana.—Olive oil. 662

1877 Ricart, Juan Martinez, Segorbe, Province of Castellon de la Plana.—Oil. 662

1878 Aguila y Aguila, Santiago del, Villarubia de los Ojos, Province of Ciudad-Real.—Olive oil. 662

1879 Medrano, José, Ciudad-Real.—Olive oil. 662

1880 Milla, Manuel, Montoro, Province of Córdoba.—Olive oil. 662

1881 Infante, Juan de Dios, Villaviciosa, Province of Córdoba.—Olive oil. 662

1882 Cantual y Lopez, Josè, Córdoba.—Olive oil. 662

1883 Estrada, Eduardo, Aguilar, Province of Córdoba.—Olive oil. 662

1884 Santaló, Estéban, Córdoba.—Olive oil. 662

1885 San Bernardo, Count of, Córdoba.—Olive oil. 662

1886 Alvarez, Rafael Ceballos, Adamion, Province of Córdoba.—Olive oil. 662

1887 Alguacil, Miguel Pineda, Espejo, Province of Córdoba.—Olive oil. 662

1888 Lopez, Espejo, Province of Córdoba.—Olive oil. 662

1889 Casado, Francisco, Espejo, Province of Córdoba.—Olive oil. 662

1890 Vega y Lopez, Luis, Espejo, Province of Córdoba.—Olive oil. 662

1891 Pineda, José Ramirez, Espejo, Province of Córdoba.—Olive oil. 662

1892 Medinaceli, Duchess, Widow of, Espejo, Province of Córdoba.—Olive oil. 662

1893 Fuente el Salce, Count of, Montoro, Province of Córdoba.—Olive oil. 662

1894 Rodriguez, José, Montemayor, Province of Córdoba.—Olive oil. 662

1895 Moreno, Sebastian, Montemayor, Province of Córdoba.—Olive oil. 662

1896 Uruburu, José, Montemayor, Province of Córdoba.—Olive oil. 662

1897 Moreno, José Maria, Montemayor, Province of Córdoba.—Olive oil. 662

1898 Corporation of Bujalance, Province of Córdoba.—Olive oil. 662

1899 Prieto, Sebastian, Encinas-Reales, Province of Córdoba.—Olive oil. 662

1900 Pavon, Pablo, Baena, Province of Córdoba.—Olive oil. 662

1901 Bastida, Martin, Montoro, Province of Córdoba.—Olive oil. 662

1902 Cabezas y Sarabia, José, Montoro, Province of Córdoba.—Olive oil. 662

1903 Piédrola, Rafael, Montoro.—Province of Córdoba.—Olive oil. 662

1904 Lara y Pineda, Rafael J. de, Montoro, Province of Córdoba.—Olive oil. 662

1905 Saenz, Eusebio, Lucena, Province of Córdoba.—Olive oil. 662

1906 Carmona, Joaquina, Lucena, Province of Córdoba.—Olive oil. 662

1907 Algár, Francisco, Lucena, Province of Córdoba.—Olive oil. 662

1908 Valdecañas, Count of, Lucena, Province of Córdoba.—Olive oil. 662

1909 Medinaceli, Duke of, Lucena, Province of Córdoba.—Olive oil. 662

1910 Gomez, Antonio Enrique, Montoro, Province of Córdoba.—Olive oil. 662

1911 Escribano, Luis, Pozoblanco, Province of Córdoba.—Olive oil. 662

1912 Galan, Alfonso Blanco, Dos-Torres, Province of Córdoba.—Olive oil. 662

1913 Castillejo, Pedro, Fuente-Ovejuna, Province of Córdoba.—Olive oil. 662

1914 Cabello, José Garcia, Santa-Ella, Province of Córdoba.—Olive oil. 662

1915 Criado, Dolores, Villa del Rio, Province of Córdoba.—Olive oil. 662

1916 Zamora, Pedro Alcalá, Priego, Province of Córdoba.—Olive oil. 662

1917 Valverde, Francisco Aguilera, Priego, Province of Córdoba.—Olive oil. 662

1918 Castilla, José Eugenio, Priego, Province of Córdoba.—Olive oil. 662

1919 Roldan, Manuel, Montoro, Province of Córdoba.—Olive oil. 662

1920 Cano, Rafael, Adamúz, Province of Córdoba.—Olive oil. 662

1921 Cano, Juan, Adamúz, Province of Córdoba.—Olive oil. 662

1922 Estrado y Perjano, Ramon, Adamúz, Province of Córdoba.—Olive oil. 662

1923 Lara, Antonio Crespo, Benameji, Province of Córdoba.—Olive oil. 662

1924 Rio, Pedro del, Castro del Rio, Province of Córdoba.—Olive oil. 662

1925 Sepúlveda, V. Muñoz de, Córdoba.—Olive oil. 662

1926 Campo, Francisco Escobar, Rubielos Bajos, Province of Cuenca.—Olive oil. 662

1927 Cid, Julian, Tarancon, Province of Cuenca.—Olive oil. 662

Animal and Vegetable Products.

1928 Torres, Mariano L., Barchin del Hoyo, Province of Cuenca.—Olive oil. 662

1929 Baillo, José Maria, Barchin del Hoyo, Province of Cuenca.—Olive oil. 662

1930 Reyes y Rich, Juan A., Guadalajara.—Olive oil. 662

1931 Molina, Federico, Rociana, Provvince of Huelva.—Olive oil. 662

1932 Soldán, Antonio, La Palma, Provvince of Huelva.—Olive oil. 662

1933 Carrasco, José Maria, Bonares, Province of Huelva—Olive oil. 662

1934 Zambrano, José A., Villalba del Alcor, Province of Huelva.—Olive oil. 662

1935 Iñiguez, José, Gibraleon, Province of Huelva—Olive oil. 662

1936 Iñiguez, Encarnacion, Gibraleon, Province of Huelva.—Olive oil. 662

1937 Morales, Teresa, San Juan del Puerto, Province of Huelva.—Olive oil. 662

1938 Santa, Martin Maria, San Juan del Puerto, Province of Huelva.—Olive oil. 662

1939 Marquez, Rufino J., Manzanilla, Province of Huelva.—Olive oil. 662

1940 Velarde, José Eduardo, Manzanillas, Province of Huelva.—Olive oil. 662

1941 Cerero, Luis, Trigueros, Province of Huelva.—Olive oil. 662

1942 Montiel, Eliecer, Trigueros, Province of Huelva.—Virgin olive oil. 662

1943 Ortá, Manuel de, Trigueros, Provvince of Huelva.—Olive oil. 662

1944 Rodriguez, José Rodriguez, Trigueros, Province of Huelva.—Olive oil. 662

1945 Escolar, Angel, Almonte, Province of Huelva.—Olive oil. 662

1946 Cepeda, Ignacio de, Almonte, Province of Huelva.—Olive oil. 662

1947 Lagares, Francisco, Almonte, Province of Huelva.—Olive oil. 662

1948 Pineda, Nicanor Infante, Aracena, Province of Huelva.—Olive oil. 662

1949 Oliva, Juan Martin de, Aracena, Province of Huelva.—Olive oil. 662

1950 Carnes, Eulogio Martin, Aracena, Province of Huelva.—Olive oil. 662

1951 Ramirez, Ignacio Nagales, Aracena, Province of Huelva. 662

1952 Barrera, Joaquin Moya, Aracena, Province of Huelva.—Olive oil. 662

1953 Cruz, Rivero, Rafael Trianes de la, Huelva.—Olive oil. 662

1954 Las Cuebas, Fernando de, Huelva, —Olive oil. 662

1955 Mora, Antonio de, Huelva.—Olive oil. 662

1956 Figueroa, Eduardo, Huelva.—Olive oil. 662

1957 Arnal, Dionisio, Castelflorite, Province of Huesca.—Olive oil. 662

1958 Nasarre, Voto, Albalate de Cinca, Province of Huesca.—Olive oil. 662

1959 Laguna, Celeste, Sariñena, Province of Huesca.—Olive oil. 662

1960 Lapiedra, Joaquin, Sariñena, Province of Huesca.—Olive oil. 662

1961 Las Almenas, Count of, Espeluy, Province of Jaen.—Olive oil. 662

1962 Campos, Antonio Lopez, Ubeda, Province of Jaen.—Olive oil. 662

1963 Ibañez, Luis Gallego, Cazorla, Province of Jaen.—Olive oil. 662

1964 Acapulco, Marquis of, Torre Don Jimeno, Province of Jaen.—Olive oil. 662

1965 Villalva, Antonio Fernandez, Torre Don Jimeno, Province of Jaen.—Olive oil. 662

1966 Manjon, Juan A., Iznatoraf, Province of Jaen.—Olive oil. 662

1967 Salcedo y Gamez, Miguel, Jimena, Province of Jaen.—Olive oil. 662

1968 Torres, Manuel Alfonso, Jimena, Province of Jaen.—Olive oil. 662

1969 Oliveres, Mauricio, Torreserona, Province of Lérida.—Olive oil. 662

1970 Teréz, Ignacio, Tárrega, Province of Lérida.—Olive oil. 662

1971 Corporation of Agramunt, Province of Lérida.—Olive oil. 662

1972 Corporation of Puigvert, Province of Lérida.—Olive oil. 662

1973 Corporation of Las Borjas, Province of Lérida.—Olive oil. 662

1974 Corporation of Vinaixa, Province of Lérida.—Olive oil. 662

1975 Alos, Francisco, Balaguer, Province of Lérida.—Olive oil. 662

1976 Pinós, José Maria, Lérida.—Olive oil. 662

1977 Lafont, Andrés, Borjas, Province of Lérida.—Oil. 662

1978 Lopez, Manuel, Puigvert, Province of Lérida.—Oil. 662

1979 Ball, José, Agramunt, Province of Lérida.—Olive oil. 662

1980 Ron, Ramon, Vinaixa, Province of Lérida.—Oil. 662

1981 Zubia, Ildefonso, Logroño.—Olive oil. 662

1982 Lazan, Marquis of, Cuzcurrita de Rio Tiron, Province of Logroño.—Olive oil. 662

1983 Alcalde, Javier, Logroño.—Olive oil. 662

1984 Pascual, Elías, Alfarnate, Province of Málaga.—Olive oil. 662

1985 Corporation of Teba, Province of Málaga.—Olive oil. 662

1986 Garcia, Dolores, Widow of Estor, Múrcia.—Olive oil. 662

1987 Lopez, José Maria, Caravaca, Province of Múrcia.—Oil. 662

1988 Coracèr Agustin Mascareñas, Verin, Province of Orense.—Olive oil. 662

1989 Velasco, Manuel, Verin, Province of Orense.—Oil. 662

1990 Ullan, Romualdo, Masueco, Province of Salamanca.—Olive oil. 662

1991 Martin, Lorenzo Calvo, Mogarraz, Province of Salamanca.—Olive oil. 662

1992 García, José Sanchez, Fregeneda, Province of Salamanca.—Olive oil. 662

1993 La Viesca, Marquis of, Fregeneda, Province of Salamanca.—Olive oil. 662

1994 Bullon, Agustin, Miranda del Castañar, Province of Salamanca.—Olive oil. 662

1995 Corbalan, Juan, Sancelle, Province of Salamanca.—Olive oil. 662

Animal and Vegetable Products.

1996 Villaranea, Ramon Miguel, Hinojosa de Duero, Province of Salamanca.—Olive oil. 662

1997 Ortál, Ignacio, Fregeneda, Province of Salamanca.—Olive oil. 662

1998 Villaranda, Joaquin Romo, Hinojosa de Duero, Province of Salamanca.—Olive oil. 662

1999 Gascon, Andrés Sanchez, Cepeda, Province of Salamanca.—Olive oil. 662

2000 Paulino, Diego Perez, Fregeneda, Province of Salamanca.—Olive oil. 662

2001 Herrero, Julian, Lumbrales, Province of Salamanca.—Olive oil. 662

2002 Paulino, Cipriano Perez, Fregeneda, Province of Salamanca.—Olive oil. 662

2003 Mendoza, Ignacio Halcon, Lebrija, Province of Sevilla.—Olive oil. 662

2004 Cisneros, Honorio de, Constantina, Province of Sevilla.—Olive oil. 662

2005 Morejon, Manuel Solis, Cantillana, Province of Sevilla.—Olive oil. 662

2006 Arenas, Antonio Rivas, Cantillana, Province of Sevilla.—Olive oil. 662

2007 Teruel, Pedro, & Bros., Cantillana, Province of Sevilla.—Olive oil. 662

2008 Reina, Cláudio Gimenez de, Arahal, Province of Sevilla.—Olive oil. 662

2009 Quintanilla, Antonio Torres, Arahal, Province of Sevilla.—Olive oil. 662

2010 Zallas y Trigueros, Miguel, Sevilla.—Olive oil. 662

2011 Piñar, Enrique, & Bros., Arahal, Province of Sevilla.—Olive oil. 662

2012 Benjumea y Jiló, Eduardo, Arahal, Province of Sevilla.—Olive oil. 662

2013 Andrade, Manuel Zayas, Arahal, Province of Sevilla.—Olive oil. 662

2014 Puig, Juan, Sevilla.—Olive oil. 662

2015 Garcia, Pedro Leanis, Sevilla.—Olive oil. 662

2016 Leygonier, Cayetano, Sevilla.—Olive oil. 662

2017 Puerta Zayas, Aniceto de la, Sevilla.—Olive oil. 662

2018 Serrano, Miguel Perez, Olivares, Province of Sevilla.—Olive oil. 662

2019 Masa, Juan Gomez de la, Olivares, Province of Sevilla.—Olive oil. 662

2020 Daoiz, Count of, Moron, Province of Sevilla.—Olive oil. 662

2021 Daoiz, José, Moron, Province of Sevilla.—Olive oil. 662

2022 Angulo, José, Moron, Province of Sevilla.—Olive oil. 662

2023 Mendez, Felipe, Mairena del Alcor, Province of Sevilla.—Olive oil. 662

2024 La Hasta, Lorenzo Dominguez de, Carmona, Province of Sevilla.—Olive oil. 662

2025 Velasco, Ramon, Carmona, Province of Sevilla.—Olive oil. 662

2026 Reina, José Martinez de, Dos-Hermanas, Province of Sevilla.—Olive oil. 662

2027 Ibarra, J. M., & Sons, Dos-Hermanas, Province of Sevilla.—Olive oil. 662

2028 Sanchez, José Arcos, Coronil, Province of Sevilla.—Olive oil. 662

2029 Rosa y Silva, José de la, Villamanrique, Province of Sevilla.—Olive oil. 662

2030 La Motilla, Marquis of, Pilas, Province of Sevilla.—Olive oil. 662

2031 Martinez, Joaquin, Bros., Utrera, Province of Sevilla.—Olive oil and pressed olives. 662

2032 Martinez, Casimiro Carro, Utrera, Province of Sevilla.—Olive oil and pressed olives. 662

2033 Orejuela, Francisco de, Utrera, Province of Sevilla.—Olive oil and pressed olives. 662

2034 Dominguez, Pedro, Utrera, Province of Sevilla.—Olive oil and pressed olives. 662

2035 Bascon, Antonio, Utrera, Province of Sevilla.—Olive oil and pressed olives. 662

2036 Peña, José Gonzalez de la, Utrera, Province of Sevilla.—Olive oil and pressed olives. 662

2037 Cuadra, Enrique de la, Utrera, Province of Sevilla.—Olive oil and pressed olives. 662

2038 Calero, Juan, Utrera, Province of Sevilla.—Olive oil and pressed olives. 662

2039 Giraldez, Vicente, Utrera, Province of Sevilla.—Olive oil and pressed olives. 662

2040 Riarola, Rafael, Utrera, Province of Sevilla.—Olive oil and pressed olives. 662

2041 Franquet y Dara, José, Gandesa, Province of Tarragona.—Olive oil. 662

2042 Grau, José Maria de, Mas-Pujols, Province of Tarragona.—Olive oil. 662

2043 Sanz y Salvá, Francisco, Mas-Pujols, Province of Tarragona.—Olive oil. 662

2044 Llausádo y Pamies, José, Mas-Pujols, Province of Tarragona.—Olive oil. 662

2045 Pamies y Ortoneda, Juan, Mas-Pujols, Province of Tarragona.—Olive oil. 662

2046 Orovio, Manuel de, Riudoms, Province of Tarragona.—Olive oil. 662

2047 Salvadó, Salvador, Riudoms, Province of Tarragona.—Olive oil. 662

2048 Salvadó, Mateo, Riudoms, Province of Tarragona.—Olive oil. 662

2049 Miret, Juan, Constanti, Province of Tarragona.—Olive oil. 662

2050 Domingo, Tomás, Constanti, Province of Tarragona.—Olive oil. 662

2051 Montoliù, Plácido María de, Morell, Province of Tarragona.—Olive oil. 662

2052 Consul & Virgili, Tarragona.—Olive oil. 662

2053 Magriña y Suñer, Antonio, Gandesa, Province of Tarragona.—Olive oil. 662

2054 March, Juan de, Vilaseca, Province of Tarragona.—Olive oil. 662

2055 Corporation of Amposta, Province of Tarragona.—Olive oil. 662

2056 Bufill, B., Reus, Province of Tarragona.—Olive oil. 662

Animal and Vegetable Products, Textile Substances.

2057 **Montagut, José, Illa, Province of** Tarragona.—Olive oil. 662

2058 **Pellicér, José, Reus, Province of** Tarragona.—Olive oil. 662

2059 **Fumaña Bros., Reus, Province** of Tarragona.—Olive oil. 662

2060 **Odena y Pujol, José, Reus, Prov-**ince of Tarragona.—Olive oil. 662

2061 **Avello, A., & Son, Reus, Province** of Tarragona.—Olive oil. 662

2062 **Gasull, Bartolomé, Reus, Prov-**ince of Tarragona.—Olive oil. 662

2063 **Gil, Francisco, Reus, Province** of Tarragona.—Olive oil. 662

2064 **Morlius, José Maria, Reus, Prov-**ince of Tarragona.—Olive oil. 662

2065 **Rincon, José Montaner, Reus,** Province of Tarragona.—Olive oil. 662

2066 **Sirvent y Oliver, Pedro, Reus,** Province of Tarragona.—Olive oil. 662

2067 **Carol, Antonio, & Co., Reus, Prov-**ince of Tarragona.—Olive oil. 662

2068 **Esteve, D. A., Widow & Son of,** Reus, Province of Tarragona.—Olive oil. 662

2069 **Basseda y Andreu, Miguel, Reus,** Province of Tarragona.—Olive oil. 662

2070 **Zamora, Francisco, Reus, Prov-**ince of Tarragona.—Olive oil. 662

2071 **Peña y Mach, Agustin, Scala-**Dei, Province of Tarragona.—Olive oil. 662

2072 **Garcia, Sebastian, Scala-Dei,** Province of Tarragona.—Olive oil. 662

2073 **Robles, Sebastian Garcia de,** Scala-Dei, Province of Tarragona.—Olive oil. 662

2074 **Gatell y Folchs, Juan, Altafulla,** Province of Tarragona.—Oil. 662

2075 **Siscar, Ramon, La Canonja, Prov-**ince of Tarragona.—Oil. 662

2076 **Indo, Valentin Martinez, Argis,** Province of Toledo.—Olive oil. 662

2077 **Redondo, Juan Bautista, Carmena,** Province of Toledo.—Oils. 662

2078 **Basaran, Isidoro, Olias del Rey,** Province of Toledo.—Olive oil. 662

2079 **Moreno, Manuel, Ortiz, Ocaña,** Province of Toledo.—Olive oil. 662

2080 **Diego, Francisco Polop, Játiva,** Province of Valencia.—Olive oil. 662

2081 **Diego y Carsi, Ignacio & José,** Játiva, Province of Valencia.—Oil. 662

2082 **Calabuyg, Bartolomé, Bocayrente,** Province of Valencia.—Olive oil. 662

2083 **Lasalla y Palomares, Vicente,** Masia de la Mar, Province of Valencia.—Olive oil. 662

2084 **Cañamas, Blas Antonio, Olisa,** Province of Valencia.—Olive oil. 662

2085 **Albors y Albors, Cárlos, Picasent,** Province of Valencia.—Olive oil. 662

2086 **Valdobi, Rafael Gonzalez, Tor-**rente, Province of Valencia.—Olive oil. 662

2087 **Reig y Garcia, Fernando, Puebla** de Valbona, Province of Valencia.—Olive oil. 662

2088 **Olias, Vicente, Chiva, Province** of Valencia.—Olive oil. 662

2089 **Bremont, Manuel Sanz, Bemfayo** de Espioca, Province of Valencia.—Olive oil. 662

2090 **Latorre, Federico, Turis, Prov-**ince of Valencia.—Olive oil. 662

2091 **Carceller, Saturnino, Valencia.**—Peanut oil. 662

2092 **Caruana & Bros., Betera, Prov-**ince of Valencia.—Olive oil. 662

2093 **Flores, P. Manuel Serrano, Fer-**moselle, Province of Zamora.—Olive oil. 662

2094 **Val, Miguel Hipólito del, Gallur,** Province of Zaragoza.—Olive oil. 662

2095 **La Linde, Baron of, Zaragoza.**—Olive oil. 662

2096 **Bureta, Countess of, Alagon,** Province of Zaragoza.—Olive oil. 662

2097 **Vallier, José, Zaragoza.**—Olive oil. 662

2098 **Baerla, Mariano Perez, Zaragoza.**—Olive oil. 662

2099 **Lopez y Pastor, Luis, Velilla de** Ebro.—Olive oil. 662

2100 **Mendoza, Francisco Estéban,** Zaragoza.—Olive oil. 662

2101 **Arpal, Manuel Vicente, Caspe,** Province of Zaragoza.—Olive oil. 662

Textile Substances of Vegetable or Animal Origin.

2102 **Morand, Pedro, Hellin, Province** of Albacete.—Esparto grass. 666

2103 **Bañon, Francisco Prast, Hellin,** Province of Albacete.—Esparto grass. 666

2104 **Lopez, Benito, Hellin, Province** of Albacete.—Esparto grass. 666

2105 **Guevara, Vicente Ladron de,** Tobarra, Province of Albacete.—Hemp. 666

2106 **Alvarez, Francisco Rodriguez,** Province of Albacete.—Esparto grass. 666

2107 **Leon, Romualdo, Albacete.**—Esparto grass. 666

2108 **Amores, Julian, Elche de la** Sierra, Province of Albacete.—Hemp. 666

2109 **Parras, Enrique, Lietor, Province** of Albacete.—Esparto grass. 666

2110 **Bushnell, Enrique, Hellin, Prov-**ince of Albacete.—Esparto grass. 666

2111 **Lopez, José Beltran, Elche, Prov-**ince of Albacete.—Hemp ropes. 666

2112 **Campoamor, Ramon de, Alicante**—Esparto grass. 666

2113 **Brotons Bros., Orihuela, Province** of Alicante.—Hemp. 666

2114 **Lledo y Gomis, Vicente, Cam-**pello, Province of Alicante.—Twisted Esparto grass. 666

2115 **Sandoval, José Joaquin, Jacarilla,** Province of Alicante.—Hemp. 666

2116 **Alhorque & Barkes, Alicante.**—Esparto grass. 666

2117 **Beltran y Lopez, José, Elche,** Province of Alicante.—Hemp. 666

2118 **Spencer & Roda, Enis, Province** of Almeria.—Esparto grass. 666

2119 **Linares, Clemente, Albanchez,** Province of Almeria.—Hemp. 666

Textile Substances.

2120 Daza y Ruiz, Francisco, Purchena, Province of Almeria.—Flax and hemp. 666

2121 Trell, Miguel del, Berja, Province of Almeria.—Esparto grass. 666

2122 Calvache, Diego, Carboneras, Province of Almeria.—Palmetto leaves. 666

2123 Forestal District, Enis, Province of Almeria.—Esparto grass. 666

2124 Molina, Manuel Martinez, Oria, Province of Almeria.—Tow. 666

2125 Gonzalez, Manuel, Barco de Avila, Province of Almeria.—Flax. 666

2126 Garriga, Luis, Barcelona.—Rigging and cordage. 666

2127 Marquez, Cavalit & Co., Hospitalet, Province of Barcelona.—Hemp thread. 666

2128 Provincial Commission, Province of Búrgos.—Hemp and flax. 666

2129 Corporation of Briviesca, Province of Búrgos.—Flax. 666

2130 La Cruz, Valentin de, Carrascalejo, Province of Cáceres.—Flax. 666

2131 Muñoz, José Diaz, Puerto de Santa Cruz, Province of Cáceres.—Flax. 666

2132 Sande, Olivares, Jeroñimo de, Garrovillas de Alconetar.—Cyperus. 666

2133 Riscal de Alegre, Marquis of, Alia, Province of Cáceres.—Nettle. 666

2134 Dabner, Guillermo H., La Laguna, Canary Islands.—Agave. 666

2135 Society of Friends of the Country, Las Palmas, Canary Islands.—Agave and ropes of agave. 666

2136 Provincial Board of Agriculture, Castellon.—Cordage of hemp, flax, and esparto grass. 666

2137 Safon, Antonio, Castellon.—Vegetable hair. 666

2138 Armengod, Joaquin, Castellon.—Hempen ropes. 666

2139 Aguila y Aguila, Santiago del, Villarrubia, Province of Ciudad-Real.—Hemp. 666

2140 Melgarejo, Maria Josefa, San Clemente, Province of Cuenca.—Esparto grass 666

2141 Ribot, Esteban, & Bros., Granada.—Hemp, tow, and ropes. 666

2142 Salcedo, Antonio Puche, Guadix, Province of Granada.—Esparto grass. 666

2143 Corporation of Almonacid de Zorita, Province of Guadalajara.—Hemp. 666

2144 Castillo y Mesquita, Francisco del, Huelva.—Palmetto leaves, rush mats, ropes, and vegetable hair. 666

2145 Oliver, D., Huesca.—Esparto grass. 666

2146 Otal, José Maria, Huesca.—Esparto grass. 666

2147 Arnal, Dionisio, Castelflorite, Province of Huesca.—White esparto grass. 666

2148 Berrio y Torrero, Vicente, Beas de Segura, Province of Jaen.—Hemp and flax. 666

2149 Corporation of Huesco, Province of Jaen.—Esparto grass. 666

2150 Corporation of Cabra del Santo Cristo, Province of Jaen.—Esparto grass. 666

2151 Corporation of Congosto, Province of Leon.—Flax. 666

2152 Corporation of Vega de Infanzones, Province of Leon.—Flax. 666

2153 Corporation of Omaña, Province of Leon.—Flax. 666

2154 Corporation of Armunia, Province of Leon.—Flax. 666

2155 Corporation of Villaturiel, Province of Leon.—Flax. 666

2156 Corporation of Páramo del Sil, Province of Leon.—Flax. 666

2157 Corporation of Encinedo, Province of Leon.—Flax. 666

2158 Dorado, Manuel, Láncara, Province of Lugo.—Flax. 666

2159 Paseiro, Bonifacia, Castroverde, Province of Lugo.—Flax. 666

2160 Corps of Engineers of Woods and Forests, Madrid.—Esparto grass. 666

2161 Diaz, Antonio, Málaga.—Objects made of hemp. 666

2162 Romero, Rafael Escalante, Teba, Province of Málaga.—Esparto ropes. 666

2163 Economical Society of Múrcia.—Agave. 666

2164 Pulgar, Joaquin Perez del, Caravaca, Province of Múrcia.—Esparto grass. 666

2165 Gonzalez, Tomás Dacal, Frires, Province of Orense.—Flax. 666

2166 Rodriguez, Manuel Iglesias, Celanova, Province of Orense.—Flax. 666

2167 Romero y Romero, José, Guinzo de Limia, Province of Orense.—Flax. 666

2168 Calvo, Lorenzo, Salamanca.—Flax. 666

2169 Casado y Febrero, Francisco, Sevilla.—Hempen ropes. 666

2170 Igualada, Francisco, Sevilla.—Cordage and sandals of hemp. 666

2171 Monner, Juan, La Riera, Province of Tarragona.—Hemp. 666

2172 Batllé y Marca, Pedro, Province of Tarragona.—Ropes. 666

2173 Valencian Society of Agriculture, Valencia.—Esparto grass, hemp, nettle, and agave. 666

2174 Philadelphia Commission of Valencia.—Objects made of hemp. 666

2175 Villalva, Benigno, Corrales de Duero, Province of Valladolid.—Hemp. 666

2176 Borbujo, Juan, Benavente, Province of Zamora.—Flax. 666

2177 Marron, José Victor, Alcañices, Province of Zamora.—Flax. 666

2178 La Viñaza, Count of, Epila, Province of Zaragoza.—Flax and hemp. 666

2179 Loring Bros., Málaga.—Esparto grass. 666

2179*a* Corps of Engineers of Woods and Forests, Madrid.—Esparto grass. 666

2180 Robles, Vicente, Badajoz.—Pelt. 667

2181 Moreno, Cayetano, Villalba de los Barros, Province of Badajoz.—Merino wool. 667

Textile Substances, Machines, Engineering, etc.

2182 **Arenzana, Son of, & Co., Badajoz.**—Merino wool. 667

2183 **Carrasco, Alfonso, Guareña,** Province of Badajoz.—Merino wool. 667

2184 **Espinosa, Fernando Montero de,** Badajoz.—Merino wool. 667

2185 **Patiño, José Maria, Cabeza de** Vaca, Province of Badajoz.—Merino wool. 667

2186 **Provincial Commission, Burjos.**—Coarse and fine wool. 667

2187 **Hernaiz, Francisco, Huerta de** Abajo, Province of Búrgos.—Merino wool. 667

2188 **Agero, José Diaz, Moraleja, Prov**ince of Cáceres.—Wool. 667

2189 **Santa Marta, Marquis of, Cáceres.**—Wool. 667

2190 **Montoya, Vicente Llopis, Bojas,** Province of Castellon.—Wool. 667

2191 **Guimera, Giner, Morella, Prov**ince of Castellon.—Wool. 667

2192 **Provincial Board of Agriculture,** Morella, Province of Castellon.—Wool. 667

2193 **Valdeavellano, J. Garcia, Espiel,** Province of Córdoba.—Wool. 667

2194 **Conde, Juan M., Córdoba.**—Wool. 667

2195 **Lozano, Juan Antonio, Belmez,** Province of Córdoba.—Wool. 667

2196 **Cortés y Velarde, Enrique,** Fuente Ovejuna, Province of Córdoba.—Wool. 667

2197 **Torrico, Manuel, Hinojosa, Prov**ince of Córdoba.—Wool. 667

2198 **Yaniz, Ambrosio, Cuenca.**—Wool. 667

2199 **Hernandez, Pedro, Moguer,** Province of Huelva.—Wool. 667

2200 **Soldan, Antonio, La Palma, Prov**ince of Huelva.—Wool. 667

2201 **Otal, José Maria, Almudevar,** Province of Huelva.—Wool. 667

2202 **Gimenez, Francisco, Jaen.**—Wool. 667

2203 **Freires, Manuel Soto, Panton,** Province of Lugo.—Wool. 667

2204 **Cruz Gomez, Juan de la, Caravaca,** Province of Múrcia.—Shoddy. 667

2205 **Garcia y Garcia, Manuel, Sala**manca.—Wool. 667

2206 **Garcia, Mariano, Salvatierra de** Tórmes, Province of Salamanca.—Wool. 667

2207 **Diaz, Cándido, Villaflores, Prov**ince of Salamanca.—Wool. 667

2208 **Torroja, Ricardo, Zaratan, Prov**ince of Salamanca.—Wool. 667

2209 **Cabrera, Victoriano, Cantala**piedra, Province of Salamanca.—Wool. 667

2210 **Onis, Federico de, Cantalapiedra,** Province of Salamanca.—Wool. 667

2211 **Lozoya, Marquis of, Segovia.**—Wool. 667

2212 **Tomé, Gabino, Segovia.**—Wool. 667

2213 **Quintanilla, Antonio, Carmona,** Province of Sevilla.—Wool. 667

2214 **Rosa, José de la, Villamanrique,** Province of Sevilla.—Wool. 667

2215 **Zayas y Trigueros, Miguel, Ara**hal, Province of Sevilla.—Wool. 667

2216 **Vasquez, Juan, Sevilla.**—Wool. 667

2217 **Cuadra, Enrique de la, Utrera,** Province of Sevilla.—Wool. 667

2218 **Gonzalez, Ramon, Quintana Re**donda, Province of Soria.—Wool. 667

2219 **Delgado, Manuel, Tejarejo, Prov**ince of Soria.—Wool. 667

2220 **Romero, Angel, Soria.**—Wool. 667

2221 **Perez, Lino, Toledo.**—Wool. 667

2222 **Corporation of Medina del Campo,** Province of Valladolid.—Wool. 667

2223 **Salarich, Joaquin, Vich, Province** of Barcelona.—Silk in the cocoon and reeled. 668

2224 **Riscal de Alegre, Marquis of,** Alia, Province of Cáceres.—Cocoons. 668

2225 **La Viesca, Marquis of, Fregeneda,** Province of Salamanca.—Spun silk. 668

2226 **Paulino, Cipriano Perez, Fre**geneda, Province of Salamanca.—Spun silk. 668

2227 **Villalta y Uribe, Antonio, Jaen.**—Cocoons. 668

2228 **Gonzalez, Pedro, Eutaimo, Prov**ince of Orense.—Cocoons. 668

Machines, Implements, and Processes of Manufacture.

2229 **Albornoz, Juan Gil., Avila.**—Plows. 670

2230 **Cruz, Rafael Trianes de la, Huel**va.—Models of harrows. 670

2231 **Corps of Engineers of Woods** and Forests, Madrid.—Manual implements. 670

2232 **Philadelphia Commission of Va**lencia.—Agricultural instruments. 670

2233 **Perez, Felipe, Habana, Cuba.**—Cultivator. 670

2234 **Serrano, Juan, Castellon.**—Implements for tillage. 670

Agricultural Engineering and Administration.

2235 **Barnosell, Pedro, Vallecas, Prov**ince of Madrid.—Guano. 681

2236 **Provincial Deputation, Múrcia.**—Barrilla for fertilizing. 681

2237 **Muñoz, Bruno, Peñaranda, Prov**ince of Salamanca.—Girth. 682

2238 **Provincial Commission of Valen**cia.—Harness appendages. 682

2239 **Villar, Francisco Maria del,** Barcelona.—Projects of rural constructions. 683

2240 **Garriga, Francisco Domingo, San** Quirse de Besora, Province of Barcelona.—Model of feeding-trough. 683

2241 **Cruz, Rivero, Rafael Trianes de** la, Huelva.—Plan of country house. 683

Tillage and General Management.

2242 **Garriga, Francisco Domingo, San** Quirse de Besora, Province of Barcelona.—Systems of rotation and calculations for agricultural products. 690

2243 **Corps of Engineers of Woods and** Forests, Madrid.—Plan of the special school, and technical designs made by the pupils; books on forestry, and models of implements used for the proper cultivation of forests. 690

PORTUGAL.

(*South of South Avenue, Columns 13 to 17.*)

Arboriculture and Forest Products.

Arboriculture and Forest Products.

1 Menezes, Jose de Vasconcellos Carneiro, Marco de Canavezes, Oporto.—Woods, corkwood. 600

2 Archer, Jacintho F., Setubal, Lisbon.—Corks and corkwood. 600

2a Almeida, Jacintho Pacheco, Ponta Delgada.—Samples of wood. 600

3 Almeida, Antonio Joaquim de, Villa Nova de Ourem, Santarem.—Timber. 600

3a Bettencourt, Francisco, Ponta Delgada.—Samples of wood. 600

4 Administrative Council of Castro Daire, Castro Daire, Viseu.—Timber. 600

5 Administrative Council of Penacova, Penacova, Coimbra.—Corkwood. 600

6 Admistrative Council of Penalva, Penalva, Viseu.—Timber. 600

6a Salles, Jose Joaquim Pereira, Mirandella, Braganca.—Corkwood. 600

7 Albergaria, Thomas Antonio Pinto Soases, Villa Cha Averi.—Corkwood and oak bark. 600

8 Administrative Council of Vourella, Vourella, Viseu.—Timber. 600

9 Gago, Joao Henriques Nunes, Galveas, Portalegre.—Corkwood. 600

10 Goulao, Joao Pereira Pestana Pina, Niza, Portalegre.—Corkwood. 600

11 Vaz Preto, Geraldes, Manuel Louza, Castello Branco.—Corkwood. 600

12 Joaquim Guilherme de Vascomellos & Sons, Elvas, Portalegre.—Corkwood. 600

13 Herdeiros de Roberto & Hunter Reynolds, Estremoz, Evora.—Corks. 600

14 Almeida, Francisco Aleas, Miranda do Douro, Braganca.—Corkwood. 600

15 Rebocha, Francisco Freire, Constanca, Santarem.—Timber. 600

16 Ventura, Jose Goncalves da Costa, Quinta do Mosteiro, Oporto.—Corkwood. 600

17 Agricultural Society of Oporto, Oporto.—Woods. 600

19 Fernandes, Joaquim, Mogao, Santarem.—Cork. 600

19a Castro, Joao Vaz, Pacheco, Ponta Delgada.—Samples of wood. 600

20 Queiroz, Jose de Sequeira Pinto, S. Sebastiao do Duque, Vianna do Castello.
a Corkwood and barks. 600
b Walnuts and chestnuts. 605

21 Ramalho, Jose Maria, Evora.—Corkwood and corks. 600

22 Frausto, Antonio Joaquim, Montalvao, Portalegre.—Corkwood. 600

22a Rocha, Francisco Coelhovda, Feira. —Corks. 600

23 Faria, Manuel Simplicio, Niza, Port Legre.—Corkwood. 600

24 Falcao, Joao Carlos da Costa, Fundao.—Chestnut staves, and rods for making hoops. 600

26 Guerra, Jose Manuel, Miranda do Douro, Braganca.—Corkwood. 600

27 Murta, Ramiro Cesar, Castello de Vide.—Corkwood. 600

28 Mesquita, Pedro Jose de, Sinde, Coimbra.—Corkwood. 600

29 Ororio, Manuel de Arevedo Ferraz, Monforte, Castello Branco.—Corkwood. 600

30 Murteira, Joaquim Antonio, Campo Maior, Portalegre.—Timber. 600

31 Maria, Angelica, Montargil, Portalegre.—Corkwood. 600

32 Netto, Joao Mascarenhas, Silves, Faro.—Corks and corkwood. 600

33 Nunes & Co., Grandola, Lisbon.—Corks and corkwood. 600

34 Ratto, Antonio Gonsalves, Barquinha, Santarem.—Corkwood. 600

35 Souza, Joze Saldanha Oliveira e, Lisbon.—Corkwood. 600

36 Salgado, Julio Bivar d'Azevedo, Sardoal, Santarem.—Corkwood. 600

37 Souza, Pedro Augusto Pereira Abreu e, Santa Marinha, Villa Real.—Corkwood. 600

38 Lagrifa, Juan, Grandola, Lisbon.—Corks. 600

39 Lacerda, Jose de Aragao Costa, Aldea Nova do Cabo, Castello Branco.—Chestnut rods, staves. 600

40 Orb, J. Augusto de, Portalegre.—Corkwood. 600

41 Marcal, Joao Lopes, Evora.—Corkwood. 600

42 Peres, Roure, & Co., S. Thrago de Cacem, Lisbon.—Corkwood. 600

43 Margiochi, jr., Francisco Simoes, Lisbon.—Corkwood. 600

44 Ribeiro, J. Lopes, Anciaes, Braganca.—Corkwood. 600

45 Ribeiro, Serafim Garcia, Oliveira do Hospital.—Corkwood. 600

46 Rodrigues, Manuel Antonio, Ferradosa, Braganca.—Corkwood. 600

47 Moraes, Antonio, S. Thiago, Lisbon. —Corks and corkwood. 600

48 Mendonca, Manuel F. de, Lisbon.—Corkwood. 600

49 Rankin, William, & Sons, Almada, Lisbon.—Corkwood. 600

50 Ventura, Jose Goncalves da Costa, Quinta do Mosteiro, Oporto.—Corkwood. 600

For classes of exhibits, indicated by numbers at end of entries, see Classification, pp. 12–14.

Arboriculture and Forest Products, Pomology.

51 Valente, Jose Justiniano d'Oliveira, Aveiro.—Pine kernels. 600

52 Vilarinho & Nephew, Silves, Faro. —Corks and corkwood. 600

53 Proenca, Francisco Tavares d'Almeida, Castello Branco.—Corkwood. 600

54 Silva, Antonio Jose de Sousa e Vallongo, Oporto.—Cherry tree. 600

55 Peres, Joaquim Manuel de Mattos, Evora.—Corkwood. 600

56 Moreno, P., & Sons, Portalegre.— Corks and corkwood. 600

57 Cordeiro, Caetano Manuel, Evora.— Cork. 600

58 Menezes, C., & Co., Oporto.—Cork and manufactures. 600

59 Direction of the Works of the River Mondego and Figueira bar, Coimbra.— Timber woods and barks. 600

60 Ferreira, Manuel Felix, Villa Cha, Braganca.—Corkwood. 600

61 Vasconcellos, Catharina Mousinho Almadamin, Nisa, Portalegre.—Corkwood. 600

62 Vaz, Eduardo Augusto da Cruz, Castello Branco.—Corkwood. 600

63 Vargas, Antonio Alexandre, Alcacer do Sal, Lisbon.—Corkwood. 600

64 Outeiro Fundao, Viscount of, Castello Branco.—Corkwood. 600

65 Vasconcellos, Joaquim Guilherme de, Elvas, Portalegre.—Woods. 600

66 Saramago, Francisco Ferreira, Reguengo, Evora.—Corkwood. 600

67 Silva, Manuel Joaquim da, Redondo, Evora.—Oak-galls. 600

68 Andrade, Antonio Garcia de, Elvas, Portalegre.—Scarlet oak-bark and corkwood. 600

69 Almeida, Augusto de Asevedo Pinto de, Feira, Aveiro.—Corks. 600

70 Beca, Agostinho da Rocha, Penafiel, Porto.—Corkwood, pine tree, and oakbark. 600

71 Coelho, Manuel Diogo, Castello de, Vide, Portalegre.—Timber. 600

72 Carreira, Jose Ivo, Peniche, Leiria. —Juniper-wood. 600

73 Calca e Pina, Antonio, Souzel, Portalegre.—Corkwood. 600

74 Robinson, George, Portalegre.— Corkwood. 600

75 Ramalho, Jose Maria, Evora.—Corkwood. 600

76 Salema Mattos, & Co., S. Thiaigo do Cacem.—Corks. 600

77 Pinheiro, Francisco Rodrigues, Marvao, Portalegre.—Corkwood. 600

78 Pereira, Francisco Jose.—Cork and corkwood. 600

79 Souza, Antonio Joaquim, Lanudos, Oporto.—Corkwood. 600

80 Administrator of the Conselho of Mangualde, Mangualde, Viseu.—Timber. 600

81 Almeida, Joaquim Ribeiro, Campanha, Oporto.—Corkwood. 600

82 Camello, Joaquim Augusto da Silveira, Penafiel, Oporto.—Corks. 600

83 Board of Public Forests, Lisbon.— Shipbuilding timber and construction, corks and corkwood. 600

85 Carlos Brandao & Son, Oporto.— Corkwood and cork. 600

86 Casa Nova, Manuel Gonsalves, Beires, Oporto.—Corkwood. 600

87 Biester Campos, & Co., Lisbon.— Corkwood, prepared. 600

88 Zagallo, Antonio Carlos, Elvas, Portalegre.—Corkwood. 600

89 Machado, Joao Jose de Souza, Paredes, Oporto.—Timber. 600

89*a* Costa Basto & Co., Oporto.—Mahogany woods. 601

90 Corte Real, Antonio Freire, Valle de Prazeres, Castello Branco.—Dyewood. 602

91 Cassola, Antonio Joaquim, Portalegre.—Oak tree and cork tree barks. 602

92 Veiga, Jose Mendes, Covilha, Castello Branco.—Wood dyes. 602

93 Nogueira, Henrique de Sa, Portalegre.—Cork tree bark, oak tree bark, middle layer. 602

94 Cardoso, Francisco de Paula, Alpedrinha, Castello Branco.—Sumac. 602

95 Chaves & Brother, Lisbon.—Saffron-flower. 602

96 Poiares, Antonio Jose da Silva, Cantanhede, Coimbra.—Pitch. 603

97 Gago, Joao Henriques Nunes, Galveas, Portalegre.—Acorns. 605

98 Saraiva, Francisco Martins, Belmonte, Castello Branco.—Dried chestnuts. 605

99 Souza, Manuel Lopes de, Guarda.— Walnuts and chestnuts. 605

100 Silva, Joaquin Nunes da, Elvas, Portalegre.—Acorns. 605

101 Rego, Antonio Profirio Gomes do, Covilha, Castello Branco.—Chestnuts. 605

102 Souto, Antonio Duarte da Cunha, Freixinho, Viseu.—Dried chestnuts. 605

103 Oliveira Soares, M. E. de, Evora.— Acorns. 605

104 Company of Lezirias do Tagus & Sado, Lisbon.—Corkwood. 606

Pomology.

105 Martins, Jeronymo, & Son, Lisbon. —Nuts. 611

106 Margalhaes, Luis Antonio, Aldea, Nova do Cabo, Castello Branco.—Chestnuts. 611

107 Morao, Maria Emilia d'Almeida, Penamacor, Castello Branco.—Olives. 611

108 Mesquita, Pedro Jose de, Sinde, Coimbra.—Dried chestnuts. 611

109 Pereira, Pedro Maria Dantas, Torres Vedras, Santarem.—Almonds. 611

110 Pinto, Clemencia, Villa Boim, Portalegre.—Acorns. 611

111 Oliveira, Verissimo Ferreira A. de, Montalvao, Santarem.—Olives. 611

112 Pessoa, Luis Manuel da Costa, Alfandega da Fé, Braganca.—Olives. 611

113 Ornellas & Lister, Lisbon.—Olives. 611

For classes of exhibits, indicated by numbers at end of entries, see Classification, pp. 12–14.

Pomology.

114 Botilheiro, Jose Fernandes, Marvao, Portalegre.—Walnuts. 611

115 Burguete, Miguel Serrao, Sardoal, Santarem.—Walnuts and hazelnuts. 611

116 Silveira, Manuel Jose da, Arganil, Coimbra.—Walnuts. 611

117 Costa, Joao Carlos, Elvas, Portalegre.—Acorns. 611

118 Peres, Joaquim Manuel de Mattos, Evora.—Acorns. 611

119 Santos, Ascencio Jose dos, Valenca, Vianna do Castello.—Chestnuts, filberts, and almonds. 611

120 Pimenta, Jose Maria Dantas, Torres Novas, Santarem.—Walnuts and almonds. 611

121 Coelho, Manuel Diogo, Castello de Vide, Portalegre.—Walnuts and chestnuts. 611

122 Figueira, Manuel Duarte, Castello Branco.—Olives. 611

123 Gomes, Francisco Antonio.—Moncorvo, Braganca.—Olives. 611

124 Gomes, Francisco Antonio.—Olives. 611

125 Garfias, M. J. de L., Villa Nova de, Portimao, Faro.—Almonds. 611

126 Guerra, Joaquim Jose da, Elvas, Portalegre.—Olives. 611

127 Guedes, Francisco Domingues, Castello Branco.—Olives. 611

127*a* Abrancalha Abrantes, Viscount da, Santarem.—Olives. 611

128 Grillo, Manuel Francisco, Ribeiro de Niza, Portalegre.—Walnuts and hazelnuts. 611

130 Jose, Joaquim das, Neves & Sons, Lisbon.—Almonds. 611

132 Peixoto, Jose Nunes de Soura, Penafiel, Oporto.—Acorns. 611

133 Coelho, Jose Justino, Villa de Tamega, Villa Real.—Walnuts. 611

134 Correa, Joaquin, Penacova, Coimbra.—Walnuts. 611

135 Menezes, Manuel Antonio Horta da Vitlarica, Braganca.—Figs. 611

136 Castel Branco, Manuel de Barros, Portalegre.—Chestnuts. 611

137 Direction of Works of the River Mondego and the Figueira bar, Coimbra. —Olives. 611

138 Transto, Leandro Pinto, Maroao, Portalegre.—Walnuts and chestnuts. 611

139 Guerra, Jose da Conceicao, Elvas, Portalegre.—Grapes, olives. 611

140 Castro, Luis Bernardo Lampairo M., Amedo, Braganca.—Walnuts. 611

141 Coutinho, Luis C. de Lucena Araiyo, Vilha da Fonte, Viseu.—Dried chestnuts. 611

142 Camara, Municipal of Penafiel, Penafiel, Oporto.—Walnuts, chestnuts, and filberts. 611

143 Coelho, Antonio Jose, Villela do Tamega, Villa Real.—Dried chestnuts. 611

144 Campos, Antonio Carlos de, Moncorvo, Braganca.—Almonds. 611

145 Miranda, Joaquim Lobo de, Lagos, Faro.—Almonds. 611

146 Nunes, Guilhermes Francisco Pereira, Oliveira do Hospital, Coimbra.—Olives. 611

147 Neves, Adelino, & Son, St. Antonio dos Olivaes, Coimbra.—Filberts. 611

148 Lourinho, Antonio Jose, Monte Carvalho, Portalegre.—Walnuts, chestnuts, and hazelnuts. 611

149 Lanhoso, Jose, Regoa.—Walnuts and almonds. 611

150 Lecocq, Joao Jose, Castello de Vide, Portalegre.—Almonds and walnuts. 611

151 Lopes, Jose Martins Thomar, Santarem.—Figs. 611

152 Lobo, Jose Maria, Guarda.—Walnuts. 611

153 Murteira, Manuel Maria, Campo Maior, Portalegre.—Olives. 611

154 Mattos, Manuel Antonio de, Campo Maior, Portalegre.—Olives. 611

155 Mendes, Casemiro Esteves, Aviz, Portalegre.—Walnuts. 611

153 Martel, Joaquin Trigueras, Pestana, Castello Branco.—Olives. 611

157 Martins, Antonio Joaquin da Silva, Elvas, Portalegre.—Olives. 611

158 Miranda, Manuel Patricio de, Povoa de Meadas, Portalegre.—Olives. 611

159 Miranda, Antonio Augusto Lobo de, Lagos, Faro.—Almonds. 611

159*a* Ribas, Limas, Guarda.—Olives. 611

160 Mira, Jose Paulo de, Evora.—Olives. 611

161 Nogueira, Henrique de Sa, Portalegre.—Chestnuts. 611

162 Margarido, Luis Jose Ferreira, Villa Nova de Foscoa, Guarda.—Almonds. 611

163 Moraes, Antonio da Silva, Sardoal, Santarem.—Almonds. 611

164 Matta, Anacleto da Fonseca, Sardoal, Santarem.—Chestnuts. 611

165 Vasconcellas, Manuel S., Quaresma, Cardeisa, Coimbra.—Walnuts. 611

166 Veiga, Francisco Antonio, Goes, Coimbra.—Dried chestnuts. 611

167 Vinva, Jorge, & Sons, Pereiras, Santarem.—Almonds. 611

168 Visetto, Jose Bernardo, Tavira, Faro.—Almonds. 611

169 Veiga, Jose Mendes, Covilha, Castello Branco.—Almonds. 611

170 Saramago, Francisco Ferreira, Reguengo, Evora.—Almonds. 611

171 Saraiva, Francisco Martins, Belmonte, Castello Branco.—Leguminous fruits. 611

172 Antonio, Eduardo Montalvas de, Franca, Portalegre.—Acorns. 611

174 Inchado, Jose Antonio Dias, Mourao, Portalegre.—Walnuts. 611

176 Jara, Loulé, Faro.—Almonds. 611

177 Neves, Jose Joaquin dos, & Bros., Lisbon.—Almonds. 611

178 Trincao, Romao Antunes, Lapas, Santarem.—Walnuts. 611

179 Tavares, Antonio Jose, Covilha, Castello Branco.—Nuts, almonds, etc. 611

180 Trigo, Antonio Manuel de Sousa, Moncorvo, Braganca.—Almonds. 611

For classes of exhibits, indicated by numbers at end of entries, see Classification, pp. 12–14.

Pomology, Agricultural Products.

181 Themuda, Engracia, Narcisca, Barellos.—Oranges. 611

182 Teixeira, Manuel Joaquin Xavier Eiro, Villa Real.—Dried chestnuts. 611

183 Taborda, Joao Manuel Correa Freixo Espada a'Cinta, Braganca.—Almonds. 611

184 Teixeira, Francisco Loureiro Campello, Oporto.—Chestnuts. 611

185 Manuel, Antonio, Mangual de, Viseu.—Walnuts and filberts. 611

186 Mello Faro, Joaquin Carvalho d'Azevedo Resende, Viseu.—Walnuts, filberts, almonds, and chestnuts. 611

187 Magalhaes, Antonio de Barros Sattam, Viseu.—Dried chestnuts. 611

Agricultural Products.

188 Baptista & Co., Lisbon.—Wheat. 620

189 Albergaria, Thomas Antonio Pinto Soares, Villa Cha, Aveiro.—Husks, rye, and Indian corn. 620

190 Almeida, Antonio Mendes Alcacer do Sal, Lisbon.—Wheat. 620

191 Calisto & Dias, S. Thomé de Mira, Coimbra.—Rice. 620

192 Camara, Municipal of Penafiel, Penafiel, Oporto.—Grasses and serradella. 620

193 Souza, Jose d'Andrade e, Portalegre.—Indian corn. 620

194 Souza, Jose Saldanha Oliveira e. —Wheat and rye. 620

195 Santa Clara, Francisco de Paula, Elvas, Portalegre.—Wheat and barley. 620

196 Rosa, Jose da Graca Pereira, Niza, Portalegre.—Rye, Indian corn, and millet. 620

197 Reis, Antonio Nunes dos, Turcifal, Lisbon.—Wheat. 620

198 Rego, Antonio Profirio Gomes do, Covilha, Castello Branco.—Indian corn. 620

199 Ramos, Manuel Nogueira, Goes, Coimbra.—Wheat. 620

200 Almeida, Antonio Joaquim de, Villa Nova de Ourem, Santarem.—Indian corn. 620

201 Cruz, Joao Maria, Setubal, Lisbon. —Spartum. 620

202 Castro, Joao Lopes de, Montargil, Portalegre.—Wheat. 620

203 Corinho, Jose Maria, Montargil, Portalegre.—Indian corn and wheat. 620

204 Corado, Vicente Joaquim, Arronches, Portalegre.—Wheat. 620

205 Cunha Ozorio, Joaquim Felizardo da, Arronches, Portalegre.—Wheat. 620

206 Calca e Pina, Augusto, Souzel, Portalegre.—Wheat. 620

207 Cervantes, Pedro, Peniche, Leiria. —Orchilla weed. 620

208 Calça e Pina, Antonio, Souzel, Portalegre.—Cereals. 620

209 Pinto, Jose Clemente, St. Cruz, Coimbra.—Wheat. 620

210 Gago, Joao Henriques Nunes, Galveas, Portalegre.—Wheat and rice. 620

211 Antao, Manuel Antonio, Miranda do Douro, Bragança—Wheat. 620

212 Araujo, Bernardo, Bretiande, Viseu.—Indian corn. 620

213 Almeida, Joaquim Ribeiro de, Campanha de Vaixo, Oporto.—Indian corn. 620

214 Contada, Jose Domingues, Carapecos, Braga.—Indian corn. 620

215 Britto, Joao de, Lisbon.—Wheat. 620

216 Gouvea, Jose dos Santos, Constanca, Santarem.
a Cereals. 620
b Leguminous plants. 621

217 Mello e Faro, Joaquim Carvalho d'Azevedo, Resende, Viseu.
a Indian corn and wheat. 620
b Pannick grass. 624

218 Yosso, Joas Jose da Matta, Serpa, Beza.
a Oats. 620
b Chick-peas. 621

219 Tavares, Antonio Jose, Covilha, Castello Branco.
a Cereals. 620
b Leguminous fruits. 621

220 Teixeira, Carlos Augusto, Grandola, Lisbon.
a Rice. 620
b Beans. 621

221 Guerreiro, Antonio Manuel, Villa Nova da Cerveira, Vianna do Castello.
a Wheat, rye, Indian corn. 620
b Beans. 621
c Linseed. 624

222 Gomes, Antonio Luis, Valença, Vianna do Castello.
a Indian corn. 620
b Beans. 621
c Linseed. 624

223 Miranda, Antonio Augusto Lobo de, Lagos, Faro.
a Indian corn and wheat. 620
b Peas, carob beans, lupines. 621
c Linseed. 624

224 Magalhaes, Luis Antonio, Aldea Nova do Cabo, Castello Branco.
a Rye. 620
b Beans, kidney beans. 621
c Potatoes. 622

225 Rapozo, Luis, Miranda do Douro, Braganca.—Rye. 620

226 Ribeiro, Jose Rodrigues, Miranda do Douro, Braganca.—Barley. 620

227 Rua, Manuel Ribeiro, Magueija, Viseu.—Wheat. 620

228 Rosette, Jose, Palancoulo, Braganca.—Wheat. 620

229 Velho, Jose Bernardino Bringel, Beja.—Wheat. 620

230 Vieira, Francisco de Lemos Cunha, Evora.—Wheat, rye, and barley. 620

231 Machado, Pedro Xavier, Portalegre.—Wheat and rye. 620

232 Moraes, Jose Bazilio de, Arronches, Portalegre.—Wheat. 620

233 Murteira, Antonio Maria, Campo Maior, Portalegre.—Wheat. 620

234 Lobao Francisco Rasquilha, jr., S. Bartholomeo, Portalegre. — Wheat and rye. 620

For classes of exhibits, indicated by numbers at end of entries, see Classification, pp. 12–14.

Agricultural Products.

235 Lobo, Jose Maria, Guarda.—Trefoil, ray-grass. 620

236 Lemos, Francisco Antonio Pereira, Villarelhos, Braganca.—Wheat. 620

237 Neves, Francisco Xavier, Azinhoza, Braganca.—Wheat. 620

238 Nogueira, Manuel Martins, Goes, Coimbra.—Indian corn. 620

239 Nunes, Guilherme Francisco Pereira, Oliveira do Hospital, Coimbra.—Wheat. 620

240 Pera, Francisco Marcos, Miranda do Douro, Braganca.—Wheat. 620

241 Lopes, Jacintho, Elvas, Portalegre.—Wheat. 620

242 Lima, Antonio Joaquim Fernandes, Villa Nova da Cerveira, Vianna do Castello.—Wheat and Indian corn. 620

243 Lemos, Joao Gonsalves de, Louza, Coimbra.—Indian corn. 620

244 Mechanical Bakery of the Poorhouse, Lisbon.—Wheat. 620

245 Pessoa, Antonio Jose dos Reis, S. Bartholomeo, Coimbra.—Indian corn and wheat. 620

246 Pinheiro, Jose Henrique, Sta. Maria, Braganca.—Wheat. 620

247 Pinto, Jose, Penude, Viseu.—Indian corn. 620

248 Pinto, Joao de Azevedo, Campello, Oporto.—Indian corn. 620

249 Pamperio, Ricardo de Souza, Vallongo, Oporto.—Cereals. 620

250 Margalhaes, Francisco T., Sinde, Coimbra.—Indian corn. 620

251 Leite, Antonio Bernardo d'Oliveira, Cabeceiras de Basto, Braga.—Indian corn and wheat. 620

252 Lobo, Bartholomeo Jose, Oliveira do Hospital, Coimbra.—Indian corn. 620

253 Madeira, Joaquim Anastasio, Monforte, Portalegre.—Wheat. 620

254 Mendes, Bernardo, Portalegre.—Indian corn. 620

255 Marmello, Jose, Portalegre.—Indian corn. 620

256 Nunes, Antonio, Elvas, Portalegre.—Wheat. 620

257 Ortega, Maria Luisa, Miranda do Douro, Braganca.—Wheat. 620

258 Oliveira, Claudino Augusto Mocorvo, Bragança.—Indian corn. 620

259 Valente, Antonio Joaquim, Torre do Cabedal, Portalegre.—Wheat. 620

260 Vargas, Antonio Alexandre, Alcacer do Sal, Lisbon.—Wheat. 620

261 Viscount of Alcacer do Sal, Alcacer do Sal, Lisbon.—Wheat. 620

262 Valdez, Antonio de Campos, Alcacer do Sal, Lisbon.—Wheat and rice. 620

263 Vasconcellos, Ezequiel Augusto de, Elvas, Portalagere.—Wheat. 620

264 Silva Carvalho, Jose Leonardo da, Vianna, Evora.—Wheat and barley. 620

265 Silva, Manuel Joaquim da, Redondo, Evora.—Wheat. 620

266 Sardinha, Joao Maria da Silva, Monforte, Portalegre.—Wheat, rye, barley, and oats. 620

267 Lacerda, Jose de Aragao Costa, Aldea Nova do Cabo, Castello Branco.—Trefoil. 620

268 Andrade, Adriano Pequito Seixas de, Gaviao, Portalegre.—Rice. 620

269 Acciole, Joao da Fonseca, Portalegre.—Oats. 620

271 Bastos, Manuel Jose Teixeira, S. Miguel de Refoyos, Braga.—Indian corn. 620.

272 Brandao, Francisco Antonio, Reboreda, Vianna.—Indian corn. 620

273 Peres, Joaquim Manuel de Mattos, Evora.—Wheat. 620

274 Pimentel, Antonio Augusto de Moraes, Castello Branco, Braganca.—Rye and wheat. 620

275 Pinto, Antonio Rodrigues, Coimbra.—Cereals. 620

276 Silveira, Manuel Jose da, Arganil, Coimbra.—Indian corn. 620

277 Poiares, Antonio Jose Silva, Cantanhede, Coimbra.—Indian corn, wheat, rice. 620

278 Silva, Antonio Lopes da, Balazar, Oporto.—Indian corn. 620

279 Penedo, Francisco Antonio, Beja.—Wheat. 620

280 Picao, Amaro Jose de Bastos, Aventosa, Portalegre.—Wheat. 620

281 Peireira, Henrique Augusto, Setubal, Lisbon.—Rice. 620

282 Pinto, Luis Marques, Elvas, Portalegre.—Wheat. 620

283 Souza, Augusto Pereira d'Abreu, Sta. Marinha, Villa Real.—Indian corn. 620

284 Souza, Victorino Alves, Oporto.—Wheat. 620

285 Silva, Joaquim Medas da, Ribeiro das Avessas, Porto.—Indian corn. 620

286 Lousa, Jose Luis Rodrigues, Verdoejo, Vianna do Castello.—Indian corn and rye. 620

287 Salgueiro, Jose Avelino Affonso, Segandoes, Vianna do Castello.—Indian corn. 620

288 Salgueiro, Jose Avelino Affonso, Segandoes, Vianna Castello.—Indian corn, and rye. 620

289 Santos, Antonio Ferreira dos, Rio Tinto, Oporto.—Wheat and barley. 620

290 Carneiro, Jose Antonio, Sta. Eulalia, Portalegre.—Wheat and rye. 620

291 Coelho, Jose Fialho, Moura, Beja.—Wheat and barley. 620

292 Campanhia das Lezirias do, Tejo e Sado, Lisbon.—Wheat and barley. 620

293 Pinheiro, Jose de Moura, Idanha a Nova, Castello Branco.—Wheat. 620

294 Queiroz, Sebastiao Machado Botelho, S. Pedro, Villa Real.—Indian corn. 620

295 Ruivo, Joao Lopes, Vianna do Alemtejo.—Wheat, rye, and barley. 620

296 Carvalho, Joao Antonio de, Porto de Moz, Leiria.—Wheat. 620

297 Chaves & Brother, Lisbon.—Wheat. 620

298 Dornas, Luis Cazemiro Pinto dos, Bigorne, Viseu.—Rye. 620

For classes of exhibits, indicated by numbers at end of entries, see Classification, pp. 12-14.

Agricultural Products.

299 **Diogo, Paulo Joao, Miranda do** Douro, Bragança.—Rye. 620

300 **Duro, Francisco dos Santos, Vianna** do Alemtejo.—Wheat, barley, and maize. 620

301 **Figueiredo, Augusto de Sa, Mar-**ques e, Barrelas, Viseu.—Wheat. 620

302 **Freitas, Joao Alves Pinto de, S.** Joao d'Ovil, Oporto.—Indian corn and wheat. 620

303 **Ferreira, Joao Dias, Vallongo,** Oporto.—Wheat and Indian corn. 620

304 **Filippe, Jose Antonio, Cepoes, Vi-**seu.—Indian corn. 620

305 **Franco, Jose da Costa, Beja.**—Wheat. 620

306 **Franco, Eduardo, Fronteira, Por-**talegre.—Wheat. 620

307 **Ferreira, Jose, Montargil, Porta-**legre.—Wheat. 620

308 **Fonseca Santos, Antonio Germano** da, Redondo, Evora.—Wheat. 620

309 **Ferro, Martinho Luiz, Beringel,** Beja.—Wheat. 620

310 **Fonseca, Francisco da Costa Ra-**mos Pinto da, Fronteira.—Wheat. 620

311 **Gomes, Jose da Costa, Balazar,** Oporto.—Wheat. 620

312 **Guimaraes, Jose Fernandes, Serpa,** Beja.—Wheat. 620

313 **Lapa, Joaquim Pereira, Sernacelho,** Viseu.—Wheat and rye. 620

314 **Lima, Lino, Anciaes, Bragança.**—Rye and wheat. 620

315 **Caetano, Joaquim Antonio, Mon-**targil, Portalegre.—Indian corn. 620

316 **Leao, Antonio Moreira, Guilhufe,** Oporto.—Wheat and rye. 620

321 **Moreira, Joao Baptista, Rates,** Oporto.—Wheat. 620

322 **Valente, Jose Justiniano d'Oliveira,** Estarreja, Aveiro.—Barley and oats. 620

323 **Trigo, Jose Antonio Horta da Vil-**lanica, Braganca.—Wheat. 620

324 **Tavares, Jose da Costa Andrade,** Alpedrinha, Castello Branco.—Wheat. 620

325 **Vieira, Manuel Pinto da Silva, S.** Thiago de Custoias, Oporto.—Wheat and barley. 620

326 **Teixra, Manuel Joaquim Xavier,** Ciro, Villa Real.—Barley. 620

327 **Teixeira, Francisco Loureiro,** Campello, Oporto.—Wheat. 620

328 **Xavier, Francisco de Paulo, Bena-**vente, Santarem.—Wheat. 620

329 **Monteiro, Jose de Sousa, Viseu.**—Rye and Indian corn. 620

330 **Manuel Luis, Gondivae, Oporto.**—Indian corn. 620

331 **Moutinho, Joaquim Thome, Rio** Tinto, Oporto.—Indian corn and rye. 620

332 **Mousa, Joao Carlos, Marques de, &** Gomes, Francisco, S. Salvador, Aveiro.—Indian corn, wheat, rye, barley, and rice. 620

333 **Martins, Anselmo Jose, Eiro, Villa** Real.—Rye. 620

334 **Mourao, Victorino Teixeira Correia,** Lordello, Viseu.—Indian corn. 620

335 **Macias, Francisco de Pera, Mi-**randa do Douro, Braganca.—Wheat. 620

336 **Mostardinha, Jose Marques, Oli-**veirinha, Aveiro.—Wheat. 620

337 **Malta, Affonso Bernardino Ochoa,** Braganca.—Wheat. 620

338 **Mirandella, Pedro Aleixo de, Mi-**randella, Braganca.—Wheat. 620

339 **Malheiro, Manuel Joao Barrellas,** Viseu.—Indian corn. 620

340 **Menezes, Jose de Vasconcellos Car-**neiro, Soalhaes, Mario de Canavezes.—Indian corn, wheat, barley, rye. 620

341 **Magalhaes, Antonio de Barros,** Sattam, Viseu.—Wheat. 620

342 **Carvalho, Luis Candido, Valle** Passos, Villa Real.
a Indian corn and rye. 620
b Beans. 621

343 **Coelho, Luis Pires Sardoal, San-**tarem.
a Cereals. 620
b Chick-peas and kidney beans. 621

344 **Correa, Joaquim, Penacova, Coim-**bra.
a Indian corn, rye, wheat, and barley. 620
b Beans and peas. 621

345 **Carvalho, Joaquim Augusto da Sil-**veira, Penafiel, Oporto.
a Rice and maize. 620
b Beans and peas. 621

346 **Costa, Manuel Jorge da, Valongo,** Oporto.
a Barley. 620
b Beans. 621

347 **Barbosa, Manuel Carneiro, Va-**longo, Oporto.
a Indian corn. 620
b Beans. 621

348 **Bastos, Pedro Jose da Silva, Mi-**randa do Corvo, Coimbra.
a Indian corn. 620
b Beans. 621

349 **Alvarrao, Joao do Bomsucesso,** Elvas, Portalegre.
a Canary-seed. 620
b Chick-peas. 622

350 **Alvim, Joao Cordoso de Souza,** Alter do Chao, Portalegre:
a Cereals. 620
b Spices. 623
c Linseed. 624

351 **Beca, Agostinho da Rocha, Pena-**fiel, Oporto.
a Millet-seed. 620
b Beans. 621

352 **Callado Senior, Joao da Costa,** Alter do Chao, Portalegre.
a Wheat. 620
b Chick-peas, kidney beans, and lupines. 621

353 **Chichorro, Andre Guilherme, Mon-**forte, Portalegre.—Wheat. 620

354 **Almeida, Joaquim Ribeiro, Cam-**panha, Oporto.
a Indian corn. 620
b Beans. 621

355 **Administrative Council of Monte-**mor o Velho, Coimbra.
a Indian corn, wheat, and rice. 620
b Beans and peas. 621

For classes of exhibits, indicated by numbers at end of entries, see Classification, pp. 12–14.

Agricultural Products.

356 **Administrative Council of Guimaraes**, Braga.—Wheat, rye, Indian corn, pannick. 620

357 **Annes, Antonio Joaquim**, Eiro, Villa Real.
a Indian corn. 620
b Beans. 621

358 **Administrative Council of Poiares**, Poiares, Coimbra.
a Lupines. 620
b Beans. 621

359 **Araujo & Brother**, Lisbon.
a Rice flour. 620
b Leguminous flour. 621

360 **Asevedo, Jose Rodrigues de**, Benavente, Santarem.
a Indian corn. 620
b Kidney beans and lentiles. 621

361 **Pereira, Jose Agostinho Mancio**, S. Thiago, Lisbon.
a Rice. 620
b Kidney beans. 621

362 **Silva, Antonio Jose de Sousa e**, Vallongo, Oporto.
a Wheat. 620
b Linseed. 624

363 **Palmeiro, Xavier Rosado**, Alter do Chao, Portalegre.
a Barley, wheat, oats, rye, Indian corn. 620
b Beans. 621

364 **Pinto da Fonseca, Francisco Ramos**, Fronteira, Portalegre.
a Wheat. 620
b Chick-peas. 621

365 **Ribas, Simao**, Guarda.
a Wheat and Indian corn. 620
b Chick-peas, potatoes, onions, and garlic. 621

366 **Silva, Antonio Jose da**, Leca do Balio, Oporto.
a Rye. 620
b Beans. 621

367 **Bogalho, Joao Joaquim**, Villa Boim.
a Wheat. 620
b Beans. 621

368 **Calça e Pina, Antonio**, Souzel, Portalegre.
a Cereals. 620
b Leguminous articles. 621

369 **Coutto, Joaquim Lucio do**, Elvas, Portalagre.
a Wheat. 620
b Chick-peas. 621

370 **Figueiredo, Jose Paulo Teixeira de** Matheus, Villa Real.
a Indian corn. 620
b Potatoes. 622

371 **Direction of Works of the River** Mondego and the Figueira bar, Coimbra.
a Indian corn, rye, and oats. 620
b Seeds. 624

372 **Cordes, Balthazar**, Barcarena, Lisbon.
a Wheat. 620
b Beans. 621

373 **Cardozo, Antonio Augusto Correa** da Silva, Cellorico, Guarda.
a Rye, wheat, and barley. 620
b Kidney beans, and chick-peas. 621

374 **Gomes, Antonio Xavier Correa**, Sattam, Viseu.
a Pannick and rye. 620
b Beans. 621

375 **Fernandes, Manuel Ignacio**, Telloes, Villa Real.
a Rye, Indian corn. 620
b Beans. 621

376 **Fernandes, Antonio Vicente d'Almeida**, Benavente, Santarem.
a Indian corn. 620
b Kidney beans and chick-peas. 621

377 **Formosinho, Jose Maria Gomes**, Serpa, Beja.
a Barley and rye. 620
b Beans. 621

378 **Fragozo**, S. Thiago, Lisbon.
a Rice. 620
b Kidney beans. 621

379 **Fernandes, Joaquim Filippe**, Beja.
a Wheat. 620
b Leguminous plants. 621

380 **Fiuza, Domingos Antonio**, Evora.
a Wheat, rye, and barley. 620
b Beans. 621

381 **Guerra, Joaquim Jose da**, Elvas, Portalegre.
a Wheat. 620
b Leguminous fruits. 621

382 **Vaz Preto Geraldes, Manuel Louza**, Castello Branco.
a Wheat. 620
b Beans and peas. 621

383 **Egreja, Manuel Antonio**, Torroso, Oporto.
a Indian corn. 620
b Beans. 621

384 **Inchado, Jose Antonio Dias**, Mourao, Portalegre.
a Cereals. 620
b Kidney beans. 621

385 **Marreco, Miguel Antunes**, Miranda do Corvo, Coimbra.
a Indian corn. 620
b Beans. 621

386 **Leas, Manuel da Cunha**, Sobreira, Oporto.—Wheat, 620

387 **Egreja, Jose Francisco de Serra**, Novaes, Oporto.
a Wheat and Indian corn. 620
b Beans. 621

390 **Saraiva, Francisco Martins**, Belmonte, Castello Branco.
a Cereals. 620
b Onions. 621

391 **Sobrinho, Rafael Baptista**, Alvito, Beja.
a Wheat. 620
b Beans. 621

392 **Souza e Mello, Antonio Machado** de, S. Sebastiao, Ponta Delgada.
a Barley and corn. 620
b Kidney beans. 621

393 **Souza, Manuel Lopes de**, Guarda.
a Cereals. 620
b Kidney beans and chick-peas. 621
c Potatoes. 622

394 **Matto, Antonio Mendes de**, Alpedrinha, Castello Branco.
a Cereals. 620
b Leguminous fruits. 621

395 **Vaz, Eduardo Augusto da Cruz**, Castello Branco.
a Wheat. 620
b Chickpeas and beans. 621

396 **Vasella, Jose jr., Gomes**, Serpa, Beja.
a Wheat. 620
b Beans. 621

For classes of exhibits, indicated by numbers at end of entries, see Classification, pp. 12–14.

Agricultural Products.

397 **Abrancalha, Viscount of, Abrantes,** Santarem.
a Wheat, barley, rice, Indian corn. 620
b Butter. 651

398 **Boa, Viscount of, Vista, Beja.**—Wheat. 620

399 **Villas, Manuel Pereira, Torroso,** Oporto.
a Barley, corn, wheat, Indian corn. 620
b Beans. 621

400 **Veiga, Francisco Antonio, Goes,** Coimbra.
a Indian corn. 620
b Beans. 621

401 **Valente, Jose Justiniano d'Oliveira,** Estarreija, Aveiro.
a Oats and barley. 620
b Seed. 624

402 **Montoso, Andre de Brito Monforte,** Portalegre.
a Indian corn. 620
b Beans. 621

403 **Mira, Jose Paula de, Evora.**
a Wheat, barley, Indian corn. 620
b Kidney-beans, lupines. 621

404 **Novaes, Antonio Jose Cabeceiras** de Basto, Braga.
a Indian corn. 620
b Beans. 621

405 **Oliveira, Manuel Rodrigues, Fraguas,** Viseu.—Indian corn, wheat. 620

406 **Mendes, Luis Antonio Soares, Castello** Branco.
a Wheat. 620
b Chick-peas and kidney beans. 621

407 **Moniz, Antonio Bernardino da** Fonseca, Baracal, Guarda.
a Indian corn, rye, wheat. 620
b Kidney beans. 621
c Millet-seed. 624

408 **Oliveira, Verissimo, Ferreira A. de,** Montalvo, Santarem.
a Cereals. 620
b Beans. 621

409 **Lacerda, Jose de Aragao Costa,** Aldea Nova do Cabo, Castello Branco.
a Indian corn, wheat. 620
b Beans, chick-peas. 621

410 **Pedroza, Maria Jose Lopes, Lavos,** Coimbra.
a Cereals. 620
b Beans, chick-peas, lupines. 621
c Linseed. 624

411 **Mourato, Mathias, Alpalhao, Portalegre.**
a Cereals. 620
b Kidney beans. 621

412 **Viuva Marques & Sons, Lisbon.**
a Indian corn and wheat. 620
b Beans. 621

413 **Morgado, Joaô Alves, Constanca,** Santarem.
a Cereals. 620
b Leguminous fruits. 621

414 **Queiroz, Jose de Sequeira Pinto,** S. Sabastiao do Duque, Vianna do Castello.
a Cereals and husks. 620
b Beans. 621
c Seeds and pine kernels. 624

415 **Rangel, Manuel de Souza, Guilhufe,** Oporto.
a Corn. 620
b Beans. 621

416 **Ribeiro, J. Lopes, Anciaes, Braganca.**
a Corn. 620
b Beans. 621

417 **Roquete, Jose Ferreira, Salvaterra,** Santarem.
a Cereals. 620
b Kidney beans. 621

418 **Rijo, Filippe de Jesus, Elvas, Portalegre.**
a Wheat. 620
b Chick-peas. 621

419 **Risques, Augusto, Aviz, Portalegre.**
a Cereals. 620
b Beans. 621
c Potatoes. 622

420 **Souza, Manuel Paulo de, Miranda** do Douro, Braganca.
a Wheat and rye. 620
b Chick-peas. 621

421 **Sa, Antonio Alves do Conto e, Germunde,** Oporto.
a Wheat and Indian corn. 620
b Beans. 621

422 **Souto, Antonio Duarte da Cunha,** Freixinho, Viseu.
a Indian corn. 620
b Beans. 620

423 **Silva, Joaquim Ribeiro da, Valongo,** Oporto.
a Wheat. 620
b Beans. 621

424 **Salgado, Julio Bivar d'Azavedo e,** Sardoal, Santarem.
a Cereals. 620
b Beans. 621

425 **Silva, Antonio Jose da, Salvaterra,** Santarem.
a Wheat. 620
b Chick-peas. 621

426 **Silva, Joaquim Tavares da Cruz,** Aldei da Matta, Portalegre.
a Millet. 620
b Beans. 621

427 **Coelho, Luis Pires, Sardoal, Santarem.**
a Cereals. 620
b Chick-peas and kidney beans. 621

428 **Pimentel, Jose Reis, Castello de** Vide, Portalegre.
a Cereals. 620
b Chick-peas. 621

429 **Coelho, Manuel Diogo, Castello de** Vide, Portalegre.
a Cereals. 620
b Beans. 621

430 **Casqueiro, Jose Maria, Crato, Portalegre.**
a Cereals. 620
b Beans. 621

431 **Caldeira, Miguel Joaquim, Elvas,** Portalegre.
a Wheat. 620
b Chick-peas. 621

432 **Coutinho, Fernando Alffonso d'Almeida,** Sepins, Coimbra.
a Wheat and Indian corn. 620
b Beans. 621

For classes of exhibits, indicated by numbers at end of entries, see Classification, pp. 12-14.

Agricultural Products.

433 Casa Nova, Manuel Gonsalves, Beires, Oporto.—Wheat, corn, Indian corn, barley. 620

434 Christina, Manuel Lopes, Alhaes, Viseu.—Wheat. 620

435 Carvalho, Luis Xavier do Amaral, Rio de Moinhos, Viseu.—Wheat and Indian corn. 620

436 Calcado, Antonio Jose, S. Pedro, Villa Real.—Indian corn. 620

437 Cadaval, Francisco de Sousa, Villa Nova da Cerveira, Vianna do Castello.—Wheat and Indian corn. 620

438 Coelho, Antonio Jose, Villa do Tamega, Villa Real.—Rye. 620

439 Coelho, Joao dos Santos, Villa Nova de Souto de El Rei, Viseu.—Indian corn and wheat. 620

440 Azevedo, Joao Rodrigues de, Bena-vente, Santarem.
a Wheat. 620
b Chick-pea. 621

441 Peixoto, Jose Nunes de Sousa, Penafiel, Oporto.
a Indian corn. 620
b Vegetable seed. 624

442 Cadaval, Francisco de Sousa, Villa Nova da Cerveira, Vianna do Castello.—Beans. 621

443 Corte Real, Antonio Freire, Valle de Prazeres, Castello Branco.—Kidney beans. 621

445 Abreu, Francisco Rodrigues de, Abrantes, Santarem.—Kidney beans. 621

446 Alcantara, Francisco Augusto Mendes de, Lagares, Coimbra.—Beans. 621

447 Alves, Jose Martins, Novaes, Opor-to.—Beans. 621

448 Administrative Council of Coim-bra.—Leguminous fruits. 621

449 Grillo, Manuel Francisco, Ribeiro de Niza, Portalegre.
a Kidney beans. 621
b Potatoes. 622

450 Ramires, Jose Peres, S. Thiago, Lisbon.
a Kidney beans. 621
b Linseed. 624

451 Leao, Jose Maria Carneiro, Figuei-ra, Oporto.
a Pannick grass. 620
b Beans. 621
c Millet-seed. 624

452 Veiga, Jose Mendes, Covilha, Cas-tello Branco.
a Pumpkins, leguminous fruits, and potatoes. 621
b Seeds. 624

453 Rosa de Jesus, Maria Angelica, Porto.—Turnips, radishes, etc. 621

454 Monteiro, Julio Pereira, Villa Fer-nando, Guarda.—Potatoes. 622

455 Vasconcellos, Duarte, Loureiro, Vi-seu.—Hops. 623

456 Alvim, Joao Cardoso de Souza, Al-ter do Chao, Portalegre.—Mustard. 623

457 Calcada, Antonio da Costa, S. Pedro, Villa Real.—Beans. 621

458 Castro, Miguel Ozorio, Cabral de Santa Clara, Coimbra.—Beans and peas. 621

459 Carvalho, Antonio Jose de, Elvas, Portalegre.—Chick-pea. 621

460 Coelho, Jose Justino, Villa do Tamega, Villa Real.—Beans and chick-peas. 621

461 Andrade, Francisco B. d'Almeida, Celorico Guarda.
a French and other beans. 621
b Potatoes. 622

462 Alvarrao, Joao de, Bom Successo, Elvas, Portalegre.
a Chick-pea. 621
b Canary-seed. 624

463 Pimenta, Isidoro E. O. C. Marques, Villa Boim, Portalegre.—Chick-peas and kidney beans. 621

464 Pygnatelli, Jose da Cunha, Guarda.
a Kidney beans. 621
b Linseed. 624

465 Freire, Joao Pereira, Penafiel, Opor-to.
a Beans. 621
b Pine kernels and seeds. 624

466 Santos, Ascencio Jose dos, Valenca, Vianna do Castello.—Beans and peas. 621

467 Pereira, Jose Geraldode Sa, Tran-coso, Guarda.—Kidney beans. 621

468 Botilheiro, Jose Fernandes, Mar-vao, Portalegre.—Kidney beans. 621

469 Condessa d'Anadia, Santa Clara, Coimbra.—Beans. 621

470 Carvalho, Jose Fernandes Antunes de, Goes, Coimbra.—Beans. 621

471 Cruz, Jose Bento, Armamar, Viseu. —Bean. 621

472 Castro, Jose d'Almeida Siloa e, Mi-randa do Corvo, Coimbra.—Beans. 621

473 Costa, Antonio Ferreira da, Villa Cha de Cangueiros, Viseu.
a Beans. 621
b Potatoes. 622

474 Asevedo, Jose de, Alter do Chaos, Portalegre.—Kidney beans. 621

475 Braga, Luiz Barbosa, Penafiel, Oporto.—Beans. 621

476 Barjona, Pedro Simoes Affonso, S. Thomé de Misa, Coimbra.—Beans. 621

477 Poiares, Antonio Jose da Silva, Cantanhede, Coimbra.—Beans. 621

478 Souza, Jose Luis Rodrigues de, Va-lenca, Vianna do Castello.—Beans. 621

479 Silva, Antonio Jose de Sousa e, Vallongo, Oporto.—Beans and onions. 621

480 Pinto, Antonio Rodrigues, S. Bar-tholomeu, Coimbra.—Beans, chick-peas, and lupines. 621

481 Pinto, Luis Marques, Elvas, Por-talegre.—Beans. 621

482 Pinto, Antonio Mascarade, Villa Boim, Portalegre.—Chick-peas. 621

483 Pinto, Augusto Leal de Gouvea, Miranda do Corvo, Coimbra.—Beans. 621

484 Mello, Bento de Castro Coelho e, S. Thiago, Coimbra.—Beans. 621

485 Martins, Joaquim, Boucas, Oporto. —Beans. 621

486 Joaquim Guilherme de Vasconcel-los & Sons, Elvas, Portalegre.—Leguminous plants. 621

Agricultural Products.

487 Jara, Loule, Faro.—Carob beans. 621

488 Guimaraes, Victorino Barbosa, Penafiel, Oporto.—Beans. 621

489 Gomes, J. Carlos, & Moura, F. A., Margues de, S. Salvador, Aveiro.—Peas, lupines, lentils. 621

490 Torres, Bernardo Jose, Novaes, Oporto.—Garlic. 621

491 Tenorio, Matheus Rodrigues, Alter do Chao, Portalegre.—Kidney beans. 621

492 Gomes, Jose Libanio, Villa Nova de Portimao, Faro.—Carob. 621

493 Martins, Jeronymo, & Son, Lisbon. —Beans. 621

496 Moreira, Luis Jose, Lanudos, Oporto.—Beans. 621

497 Martins jr., Manuel Jose, Amorim, Oporto.—Beans. 621

498 Mattos, Manuel Henriques de, Goes, Coimbra.—Beans. 621

499 Moutinho, Joaquim Thomé, Gondomar, Oporto.—Beans. 621

500 Faro, Joaquim de Carvalho Azevedo, Reizende, Viseu.—Beans. 621

501 Fernandes, Jose Antonio, Valenca, Vianna do Castello.—Beans. 621

502 Ferreira, Joao Dias, Valongo, Oporto.—Beans. 621

503 Falcao, Maria Miquelina, Miranda do Corvo, Coimbra.—Beans. 621

504 Ferreira, Manuel da Costa, Marvao, Portalegre.—Kidney beans. 621

505 Fernandes, Joaquim Pinto, Campello, Oporto.—Beans. 621

506 Freire, Amancio Antonio de Sequeira, Alemquer, Lisbon.—Kidney beans. 621

507 Gomes, Joao Carlos, Ilhavo, Aveiro. —Beans. 621

508 Vieira, Venancio Dias de Figueiredo, Eiro, Aveiro.—Beans. 621

509 Visetto, Francisco Manuel, Tavira, Faro.—Carob. 621

510 Santos, Antonio Joaquin, Vianna. —Beans. 621

512 Soares, Jose B., Celorico, Guarda. —Kidney beans and chick-peas. 621

513 Sampaio, Alexandre Tavares de Mello, Guarda.—Kidney beans and chick-peas. 621

514 Silva, Jose Nunes da, Elvas, Portalegre.—Beans. 621

515 Dias, Luis Antonio, Miranda do Corvo, Coimbra.—Beans. 621

516 Meira, Matthias, Ribeira de Niza, Portalegre.—Kidney beans and chick-peas. 621

517 Neves, Adelino, Santo Antonio dos Olivaes, Coimbra.—Beans. 621

518 Neves, Francisco Xavier, Azinhosa, Braganca.—Chick-peas. 621

519 Neves, Jose Marquesdas, Vallongo, Oporto.—Beans. 621

520 Negrao, Joaquim d'Almeida, Portimao, Faro.—Carob. 621

521 Oliveira, Fortunato Antonio, Goes, Coimbra.—Beans. 621

522 Ozorio, Alvaro de Azevedo, Tarouca, Viseu.—Beans. 621

523 Vasconcellos, Manuel S. Quaresma, Candeixa, Coimbra.—Chick-peas. 621

524 Magalhaes, Francisco F. Sinde, Coimbra.—Beans. 621

525 Pinto, Clemencia, Villa Boim, Portalegre.—Chick-peas. 621

526 Pimentel, Antonio Augusto de Moraes, Castello Branco, Braganca.—Chick-peas, lupines. 621

527 Martins, Anselmo Jose, Ciro, Villa Real.—Beans. 621

528 Lapa, Joaquim Pereira, Sernacelhe, Viseu.—Beans. 621

529 Leite, Antonio Bernardo d'Oliveira, Cabeceiras de Basto, Braga.—Beans. 621

530 Lessa, Antonio dos Santos, Boucas, Oporto.—Beans. 621

531 Monteiro, Francisco Vaz, Ponte de Sor, Portalegre.—Kidney beans. 621

532 Oliveira Soares, M. E. de, Evora.
a Cereal. 620
b Leguminous fruits. 621

533 Moran, Jose Antonio Martins, Vianna do Alemtejo.—Windsor beans. 621

534 Lemos, Joao Gonsalves de Souza, Coimbra.—Beans. 621

535 Ozorio, Manuel de Azevedo Ferrao, Monforte, Castello Branco.—Kidney beans. 621

536 Macedo Pinto, Joaquim Ferreira de, Taboaco, Viseu.—Beans. 621

537 Lopes, Jose Ramos, Airo, Braga.—Beans. 621

538 Mourao, Victorino F. C., Lordello, Villa Real.—Beans. 621

539 Motta, Abel Maria, Rabacal, Coimbra.—Chick-peas. 621

540 Lobo, Jose Maria, Guarda.—Kidney beans. 621

541 Lopes, Jacintho, Elvas, Portalegre. —Beans and chick-peas. 621

542 Miranda, Joaquim Lobo de, Lagos, Faro.—Beans. 621

543 Menezes, Jose Vasconcellos Carneiro, Marco de Canavezes, Oporto.—Beans. 621

544 Loureiro, Antonio Lopes, Amorim, Oporto.—Beans. 621

545 Leite, Joao Baptista de Araujo, Mirandella, Braganza.—Chick-peas. 621

546 Leite, Joaquim Maria Felgueiras, Mogadouro, Braganca.—Chick-peas. 621

547 Lima, Antonio Joaquim Fernandes, Villa Nova da Cerveira, Vianna do Castello.—Beans. 621

548 Macedo jr., Ventura Luis de, Lisbon.—Kidney beans, chick-peas. 621

549 Mattos, Manuel Antonio de, Campo Maior, Portalegre.—Chick-peas. 621

550 Mendes, Casemiro Esteves, Aviz, Portalegre.—Kidney beans. 621

551 Moreira, Domingos, jr., Boucas, Oporto.—Beans. 621

552 Maia, Manuel de Arevedo, Villa do Conde, Oporto.—Beans. 621

553 Maia, Jose Gomes, Amorim, Oporto. —Garlic. 621

555 Leitao, Alberto, Penacova, Coimbra.—Chick-peas and beans. 621

For classes of exhibits, indicated by numbers at end of entries, see Classification, pp. 12-14.

Agricultural, Animal, and Vegetable Products.

556 Salgado, Marianno Roza, Lanudos, Oporto.—Beans. 621

557 Santos, Joaquim Ferreira, S. Martinho do Campo, Oporto.—Beans. 621

558 Souza, Pedro Augusto Pereira Abreu e, Santa Marinha, Villa Real.—Beans. 621

559 Rodrigues, Francisco Pedro, Grandola, Lisbon.—Beans. 621

560 Reis, Antonio Simoes dos, Condeixa, Coimbra.—Beans. 621

561 Rebello Valente & Allen, Oporto.—Beans. 621

562 Matta, Anacleto da Fonseca, Sardoal, Santarem.—Kidney beans. 621

563 Mendes, Raymundo Jose Soares, Abrantes, Santarem.—Chick-peas, kidney beans. 621

564 Guedes, Viscount de, Evora.—Beans. 621

565 Carreira, Jose Ivo, Peniche, Leiria.—Castor-oil beans. 621

566 Albergaria, Thomaz Antonio Pinto Soares, Villa Cha, Aveiro.—Beans. 621

567 Coelho, Jose Justino, Villa do Tamega, Villa Real.—Beans. 621

568 Carvalho, Luis Xavier do Amaral, Rio de Moinhos, Viseu.—Beans. 621

569 Seixas, Jose Maria Ayres de, Gaviao, Portalegre.- Beans. 621

570 Silva, Marcellino Ferreira da, Lisbon.—Chick-peas and kidney-beans. 621

571 Silva, Jeronymo Jose Alves da, Elvas, Portalegre.—Chick-peas. 621

572 Silva, Antonio Jose da, Boucas, Oporto.—Beans. 621

573 Factory of Tobacco, Lealdade, Oporto.—Cut leaf, cigars, cigarettes, and snuff. 623

574 Factory of Miguel Augusto da Silva Pereira, Oporto.—Tobacco. 621

575 Factory of Tobacco, Liberdade, Oporto.—Cut tobacco, cigars, and cigarettes. 623

576 Lisbon Tobacco Co., Lisbon.—Cigars and snuff. 623

578 Ferreira & Co., Lisbon.—Chocolate. 623

579 Vasconcellos, Duarte, Loureiro, Viseu.—Hops. 623

580 Cunha, Antonio Jose, Paredes de Coura, Vianna do Castelho.—Millet seed. 624

581 Coutinho, Luis C. de Lucena, Araujo, Villa da Fonte, Viseu.—Millet seed. 624

582 Camello, Joaquim Augusto da Silveira, Penafiel, Oporto.—Seeds. 624

583 Administrative Council of Cantanhede, Coimbra.—Seeds. 624

584 Albergaria, Thomaz Antonio Pinto Soares, Villa Cha, Aveiro.—Grape seed. 624

585 Mesquita, Pedro Jose de, Sinde, Coimbra.—Linseed. 624

586 Margarido, Luis Jose Ferreira, Villa Nova de Foscoa, Guarda.—Sumach. 624

587 Alvim, Joao Cardoso de Souza, Alterido do Chao, Portalegre.—Linseed. 624

588 Sousa, Jose Luis Rodrigues, Verduejo, Vianna do Castello.—Linseed. 624

589 Castel-Branco, Manuel de Barros, Portalegre.—Acorns. 624

590 Fernandes, Joaquim Filippe, Beja.—Acorns and seeds. 624

591 Valente, Jose Justiniano d'Oliveira, Estarreja, Aveiro.—Seeds, pine kernels. 624

592 Guerreiro, Antonio Manuel, Villa Nova da Cerveira, Vianna do Castello.—Linseed. 624

Marine Animals, Fish Culture, and Apparatus.

593 Neto, Manuel Jose Setubal, Lisbon.—Preserved fish. 641

594 Ornellas & Linder, Lisbon.—Preserved fish. 641

595 Fabrica Povoense, Povoa de Varsim.—Preserved fish. 641

596 Freitas, Joao S., jr., Setubal, Lisbon.—Preserved sardines. 641

597 Direction of the Works of Mondego River and Figueira bar, Coimbra.—Preserved fish. 641

598 Romao, Joanna Balbina, Aveiro.—Preserved fishes. 641

599 Leite & Co., Francisco, Alcantarilha, Faro.—Salt tunny-fish. 642

599*a* Pilao e Luxes, A. d'O., e J. G. L., Ovar.—Models of fishing nets. 647

599*b* Oliveira, Gaspar Jose, Oporto.—Fishing nets. 647

Animal and Vegetable Products.

600 Gomes, J. Carlos, & Moura, F. A., Marques de S. Salvador, Aveiro.
a Seaweeds. 650
b Olive oils. 662

601 Queiroz, Jose de Sequeira Pinto, S. Sebastiao do Duque, Vianna do Castello.
a Seaweeds. 650
b Wine and brandy. 660

602 Morgado, Francisco Xavier Annes, Miranda do Douro, Braganca.—Cheese. 651

603 Formosinho, Jose Maria Gomes, Serpa, Beja.—Cheese. 651

604 Franco, Jose da Costa, Beja.—Cheese. 651

605 Coelho, Antonio, Gouvea, Guarda.—Cheese. 651

606 Lobo, Jose Maria, Guarda.—Cheese. 651

607 Saraiva, Francisco Martins, Belmonte, Castello Branco.—Cheese. 651

608 Sobrinho, Jose Guerreiro de L., Ferreira, Beja.—Cheese. 651

609 Callado, Joao da Costa, jr., Alter do Chao, Portalegre.—Cheese. 651

610 Pereira, Jose Francisco, Castello de Vide, Portalegre.—Cheese. 651

611 Penedo, Francisco Antonio, Beja.—Cheese. 651

612 Valladares, Pedro d'Ordaz, Castello Branco.
a Cheese. 651
b Olives. 656
c Wine. 660
d Olive oil. 662

Animal and Vegetable Products.

613 **Viegas, Agostinho Thomas dos** Santos, Cea, Guarda.
a Cheese. 651
b White wine. 660
c Olive oil. 662

614 **Vicondessa d'Oleiros, Castello** Branco.
a Cheese. 651
b Olives. 656
c Olive oil. 662

615 **Calca e Pina, Antonio, Souzel, Portalegre.**
a Cheese. 651
b Honey. 654
c Preserved meats. 656
d Olive oil. 662

616 **Pimentel, Jose Reis, Castello de** Vide, Portalegre.
a Cheese. 651
b Honey. 654

617 **Aboim, Joao Cardoso de Souza, Al**ter do Chao, Portalegre.
a Cheese. 651
b Preserved meats. 656
c Wines and vinegar. 660

618 **Abrunhosa, Joao Caetano de, Cas**tello Branco.
a Cheese. 651
b Olives and preserved meat. 656
c Olive oil. 662

619 **Alvim, Joao Cardoso de Souza, Al**ter do Chao, Portalegre.
a Cheese. 651
b Preserved meat. 656
c Wine and vinegar. 660

621 **Coelho, Manuel Diogo, Castello de** Vide, Portalegre.
a Cheese. 651
b Preserved meats and olives. 656

622 **Alcantara, Francisco Augusto** Mendes de, Lagares, Coimbra.
a Cheese. 651
b Wine and brandy. 660

623 **Cazal, Eliziario, Cea, Guarda.**
a Cheese. 651
b Red wine. 660
c Vegetable oils. 662

623*a* **Pimenta, Isidora, E. O. C. Mar**gues, Villa Boim, Portalegre.
a Cheese. 651
b Honey. 654
c Preserved meat. 656
d Brandy. 660

624 **Fernandes, Joaquim Filippe, Beja.**
a Cheese. 651
b Olive oil. 662

624*a* **Boa, Viscount da, Vista, Beja.**
a Cheese. 651
b Olive oil. 652

625 **Gago, Joao Henriques Nunes, Gal**veas, Portalegre.
a Cheese. 651
b Olive oil. 662

626 **Vaz Preto, Geraldes, Manuel Lou**sa, Castello Branco.
a Cheese. 651
b Honey. 654
c Wine. 660
d Olive oil. 662

627 **Tenreiro, Manuel Guerra, Freixo** d'Espada á Cinta, Braganca.
a Cheese. 651
b Honey. 654
c Olives. 656
d Olive oil. 662

628 **Taborda, Joao Manuel Correa, Frei**xo d'Espada á Cinta, Braganca.
a Cheese. 651
b Olives. 656
c Olive oil. 662

629 **Goncalves, Jose Joaquim, Elvas,** Portalegre.
a Cheese. 651
b Honey. 654

630 **Martel, Joaquim Trigueiros Pesta**na, Castello Branco.
a Cheese. 651
b Olive oil. 662

631 **Oliveira Soares, M. E. de, Evora.**
a Cheese. 651
b Honey. 654
c Vinegar. 660
d Olive oil. 662

632 **Oliveira, Jose Miguel de, Moura,** Beja.
a Cheese. 651
b Preserved meat. 656

633 **Lobo, Bartholomeo Jose, Oliveira** do Hospital, Coimbra.
a Cheese. 651
b Red wine. 660
c Olive oil. 662

634 **Veiga, Jose Mendes, Covilha, Cas**tello Branco.
a Cheese. 651
b Dried fruits and olives. 656
c Vinegar. 660
d Olive oil. 662

635 **Cavalleri, P., & Co., Lisbon.**
a Butter and cheese and milk. 651
b Olives, gums, preserved meat and fruits. 656

636 **Raposo, Joao, do Carmo, Moura.**
a Cheese. 651
b Olives. 656
c Olive oil. 662

637 **Pinto, Luis Marques, Elvas, Port**alegre.
a Cheese. 651
b Preserved meat. 656

638 **Pinto, Joaquim Pereira da Costa,** Sousel, Portalegre.
a Cheese. 651
b Olive oil. 662

639 **Moraes, Rodrigo Antonio Leite de,** Oporto.—Hides. 652

640 **Viuva Chaves & Son, Guimaraes.**—Leather and skins. 652

641 **Alcantara & Bros., Joao Antonio,** Lisbon.—Leather and skins. 652

642 **Godinho, Francisco Ferreira, Cruz,** Quebrada.—Leather and skins. 652

643 **Jose Maria d'Andrade, & Bros.,** Valenca.—Leather and calfskin. 652

643*a* **Lamos, Jose, & Co., Lisbon.**—Belting and cables for machinery. 652

644 **Santos, Narcizo Jose dos, Evora.**—Animal charcoal. 652

645 **Lamas & Co., Jose, Lisbon.**—Leather. 652

645*a* **Ramos, Joaquim Antonio, Beja.**—Goatskins. 652

646 **Ferreira, Camillo P. da C., Oliveira** d'Azemeis.—Leather. 652

647 **Joao Antonio Alcantara & Sons,** Lisbon.—Leather and skins. 652

For classes of exhibits, indicated by numbers at end of entries, see Classification, pp. 12-14.

Animal and Vegetable Products.

648 Gama, Antonio Domingos d'Oliveira, Oporto.—Hides. 652

649 Ferreira, Antonio Cyprianno, Lisbon.—Leather and skins. 652

650 Fernandes, Lucas, Macao, Santarem.—Skins. 652

651 Ferreira & Bro., Casaes dos Gallegos, Santarem.—Kidskins. 652

652 Cassola, Antonio Joaquim, Portalegre.—Leather and skins. 652

653 President of the Municipal Chamber of Lisbon.—Tallow. 652

654 Jeronymo, Francisco Manuel, Coicas, Braganca.—Skins, hides. 652

655 Jose Maria d'Andrade & Bros., Valenca.—Leather, calfskin. 652

656 Oliveira, Custodio de, Adufe, Braga.—Glue. 652

657 Viuva, Machado, & Sons, Alcanena.—Hides. 652

658 Cerqueira, Lima, & Co., Vianna do Castello.—Leather, hides, skins, and glue shavings. 652

659 Smidt, Joao Luis, Oporto.—Skins. 652

660 Martins, Andre, Sobrado, Oporto.—Wax. 654

661 Veira, Manuel, Meires, Oporto.—Honey. 654

661*a* Mello, Antonio Jose Teixeira, Lisbon.—Wax. 654

662 Tenorio, Matheus Rodrigues, Alter do Chao, Portalegre.—Honey. 654

662*a* Silva, Diogo Monteiro, Lisbon.—Manufactured wax. 654

663 Torregon, Antonio Joaquim, Redondo, Evora.—Honey. 654

664 Juzarte, Jose Francisco, Monforte, Portalegre.—Honey. 654

665 Garcia, Jose Camillo, Almodovar, Beja.—Wax. 654

666 Espada, J. C., Vallejo, Portalegre.—Honey. 654

670 Garcao, Jose Maria, Elvas, Portalegre.—Honey and wax. 654

671 Figueiredo, Joaquim de, Aviz, Portalegre.—Honey. 654

672 Contreiras, Jose da Silva, Almodovar, Beja.—Honey-comb and honey. 654

673 Bussaco, Jose Rodrigues, Grandala, Lisbon.—Honey. 654

674 Boucinha, Manuel da Costa, Balthasar, Oporto.—Honey and honey-comb. 654

675 Braga, Joas Jose de Sousa, Oporto.—Honey. 654

676 Mello, Antonio Jose, Ferreira, Lisbon.—Honey and wax. 654

677 Moraes, Jose, Basilio deArronches, Portalegre.—Honey. 654

678 Atlen Rebello Volente, Oporto.
a Honey. 654
b Wines. 660
c Olive oil. 662

679 Pessoa, Luis Manuel da Costa, Alfandega da Fé, Bragança.—Honey. 654

680 Loureiro, Bento Maria, Aldeia Nova, Beja.—Honey. 654

681 Saramago, Francisco Ferreira, Reguengo, Evora.—Honey. 654

682 Sena, Joao Pereira, Montargil, Portalegre.—Honey. 654

683 Vinva de Manuel, Pedro do, Alter do Chao, Portalegre.—Wax. 654

684 Vassallo, Jose Baptista, Alcanena, Santarem.—Bleached wax. 654

685 Vieia, Francisco de Semas, Cunha, Evora.—Honey. 654

686 Vieira, Jose Augusto, Evora Cidade, Evora.—Honey, white and yellow wax. 654

687 Miranda, Joaquin Antonio de Reguengo, Portalegre.—Honey and honeycomb. 654

688 Moreira, David Martins, Castello de Vide, Portalegre.—Bleached wax. 654

689 Moita, Jose Francisco, Aldeia Nova, Beja.—Honey. 654

690 Raposa, Vicente Narcizo, Castello de Vide, Portalegre.—Honey. 654

691 Silva, Joao Miguel, Santa Eulalia, Portalegre.—Honey. 654

692 Costa da Mendiga, Jose da, Mendiga, Leisia.—Honey. 654

693 Santos, Luis Marcelino dos, Freiro, Braganca.—Honey. 654

694 Silva, Antonio Mendes da, Linhares, Braganca.—Honey. 654

695 Pereira, Jeronymo, Serpa, Beja.—Honey. 654

696 Pinheiro, Jose de Sousa Idanha a, Nova Castello, Braganca.—Honey. 654

697 Carvalho, Jose Fernandes Antonio de, Goes, Coimbra.—Honey. 654

698 Abreu, Jose Martins de, Aloens, Viseu.—Honey. 654

699 Albergaria, Thomas Antonio Pinto, Loases, Villa Cha Avero.—Honey and wax. 654

700 Almeida, Francisco de Mattos, Penafiel, Porto.—Wax. 654

701 Adelino, Joao Manuel Joaquim, Elvas, Portalegre.—Honey. 654

702 Almida, Joaquin S. Momao, Castello de Vide, Portalegre.—Honey. 654

703 Perez, Roure, & Co., S. Thiago do Cacem, Lisbon.
a Honey and wax. 654
b Rice. 657
c Wine. 660
d Olive oil. 662

704 Lemos, Francisco Antonio Pereira, Villarelhos, Braganca.
a Honey. 654
b Red wine. 660

705 Falcao, Jeronymo Fernandes, Lamas, Coimbra.
a Honey. 654
b Wine. 660

706 Bello, Manuel Guei fao, Marcas, Santarem.
a Honey. 654
b Wines. 669
c Olive oil. 662

For classes of exhibits, indicated by numbers at end of entries, see Classification, pp. 12–14.

Animal and Vegetable Products.

707 Pimentel, Antonio Augusto de Moraes, Castello Branco, Bragança.
a Honey. 654
b Olives. 656
c Olive oil. 662

708 Baptista, Jose Antonio, Mirandella, Bragança.
a Honey. 654
b Brandy. 660

709 Baptista, Jose Ignacio de Macedo, Mirandella, Bragança.
a Honey. 654
b Brandy. 660

710 Allen Rebello Volente, Oporto.
a Honey. 654
b Port and muscadine wine. 660
c Olive oil. 662

711 Administrador do Concelho de Poiares, Poiares, Coimbra.
a Wax. 654
b Olive oil. 662

712 Pinto, Clemencia, Villa Boim, Portalegre.
a Honey. 654
b Brandy. 660

713 Andrade, Antonio Pequito, Leiras de Gavias, Portalegre.
a Honey. 654
b Dried grapes. 656

714 Calca e Pina, Augusto, Sourel, Portalegre.
a Honey. 654
b Olive oil. 662

715 Figueiredo, Jose Cereira de, Sattam, Visen.
a Honey. 654
b Wine. 660

716 Coelho, Jose Fialho, Mousa, Beja.
a Honey. 654
b Preserved meat. 656

717 Fernandes, Manuel Ignacio, Telloes, Villa Real.
a Honey. 654
b Dried chestnuts. 656

718 Fonseca Santos, Antonio Germano da, Redondo, Evora.
a Honey. 654
b Vinegar. 660
c Olive oil. 662

719 Gouvea, Jose dos Santos, Constanca, Santarem.
a Honey. 654
b Wine. 660

720 Fernandes, Jose Manuel, Redondo.
a Honey. 654
b Vinegar. 660

721 Magalhaes, Jose Joaquim do Silva, Villa Nova da Gaia, Oporto.
a Wax. 654
b Olive oil. 662

722 Tocha, Jose Rodrigues, Estremos, Coova.
a Honey. 654
b Olives. 656
c Wine and vinegar. 660
d Olive oil. 662

723 Monte, Jose Manuel do, Redondo, Evora.
a Wax and honey. 654
b Brandy and vinegar. 660
c Olive oil. 662

724 Nunes, Antonio Candido, Elvas, Portalegre.
a Honey. 654
b Vinegar. 660

725 Miranda, Antonio Augusto Lobo de, Lagos, Faro.
a Honey. 654
b Wine, brandy, vinegar. 660
c Olive oil. 662

726 Lemos, Antonio da Cunha d'Azevedo, S. Joao da Pesqueira, Viseu.
a Honey. 654
b Wine and brandy. 660

727 Menezes, Jose de Vasconcellos, Canavezes, Porto.
a Honey. 654
b Wine, vinegar. 660
c Olive oil. 662

728 Margiochi, Francisco, jr., Simoes, Lisbon.
a Honey. 654
b Wine. 660
c Olive oil. 662

729 Marcal, Joao Lopes, Evora.
a Honey. 654
b Olive oil. 662

730 Pinto Basto, Augusto Ferreira, Oliveira do Bairro, Aveiro.
a Honey. 654
b Olive oil. 662

731 Silva, Joaquim Nunes da, Elvas, Portalegre.
a Honey. 654
b Olive oil. 662

732 Sobrinho, Rafael Baptista, Alvito, Beja.
a Honey. 654
b Wines. 660

733 Vasconcellos, Catharina Mousinho Almadaminus, Nisa, Portalegre.
a Honey. 654
b White wine. 660

734 Viscount of Guedes, Evora.
a Honey. 654
b Wine. 660
c Olive oil. 662

735 Mattos, Manuel Antonio de, Campo Maior, Portalegre.
a Honey. 654
b Dried grapes. 656
c Brandy, wines, vinegar. 660
d Olive oil. 662

736 Mira, Jose Paulo de, Evora.
a Honey. 654
b Vinegar. 660
c Olive oil. 662

737 Montoia, Diogo Lopes, Castello Branco.
a Honey. 654
b Olive oil. 662

738 Morgado, Joas Aloes, Constanca, Santarem.
a Honey. 654
b Brandy, red and white wine, vinegar. 660
c Olive oil. 662

739 Matta, Antonio Nunes, Grandola, Lisbon.
a Honey. 654
b Wine. 660

740 Queimado, Isidoro Maria, Redondo, Evora.
a Honey. 654
b Brandy, white wine, and vinegar. 660

741 Rosa, Jose da Graca Pereira, Nisa, Portalegre.
a Honey. 654
b Preserved meat. 656
c White wine, brandy, and vinegar. 660
d Olive oil. 662

For classes of exhibits, indicated by numbers at end of entries, see Classification, pp. 12-14.

Animal and Vegetable Products.

742 **Rosa, Joaquim Matheus Vieira,** Villa Nova de Ourem, Santarem.
a Honey. 654
b Olive oil. 662

743 **Rodrigues, Francisco Pedro, Grandola,** Lisbon.
a Wax and honey. 654
b Wine. 660
c Olive oil. 662

744 **Sa, Antonio Aloes do Conto e, Germunde,** Oporto.
a Honey. 654
b Olive oil. 662

745 **Santos, Joaquim Ferreira, S. Martinho** do Campo, Oporto.
a Honey. 654
b Wine. 660

746 **Serra, Joaquim, Valle Formoso,** Santarem.
a Honey. 654
b Olive oil. 662

747 **Sa, Sabino Barros de, Pouco de** Soudo, Santarem.
a Honey. 654
b Olive oil. 662

748 **Santos, Ascencio Jose dos, Valenca,** Vianna do Castello.
a Wax. 654
b Sweetmeats. 656
c Wine. 660

749 **Pereira, Joao M., Constania, Santarem.**
a Honey. 654
b Olive oil. 662

750 **Pedroso, Henrique Caldeira, Castello** Branco.
a Honey. 654
b Olives. 656
c White wine. 660
d Olive oil. 662

751 **Bertao, Ladislau Xavier, Torrao,** Beja.
a Honey. 654
b Olive oil. 662

752 **Rosado, Joao Antonio Margues,** Redondo, Evora.
a Honey. 654
b Red and white wine, and brandy. 660
c Olive oil. 662

753 **Rosado, Antonio Joaquim da Silva,** Zambujeiro, Evora.
a Honey. 654
b Red wine. 660

754 **Pinheiro, Candido Alberto A., Monxique,** Faro.
a Honey. 654
b Olives. 656
c Olive oil. 662

755 **Mascarenhas, S., Faro.**—Dried fruits. 656

756 **Moura, Francisco Antonio Margues,** Ilhavo, Aveiro.—Olives. 656

757 **Menezes, Jose Correa, Lamego, Viseu.**—Dried fruits. 656

758 **Mattos, Maria do Livramento,** Oporto.—Preserved fruit. 656

759 **Maria do, Gloria, & Co., Oporto,**—Preserved fruits. 656

760 **Leal, Costa, & Co., Lisbon.**—Preserved meats, fish, and fruits. 656

761 **Torres, Rodrigo Bravo, Novellos,** Penafiel.—Olives and pickled pepperpods. 656

762 **Trigo, Antonio Manuel de Sousa,** Moncorvo, Bragança.—Sweetmeats. 656

763 **Themuda, Engracia Narcisa, Barcellos.**—Sweetmeats. 656

764 **Teixeira, Francisco de Sa, Salsedas,** Viseu.—Dried figs. 656

765 **Victorino, Jose, Braganca.**—**Ham.** 656

766 **Varsea & Coelho, Oporto.**—Preserved meats, fish, olives, etc. 656

767 **Tapadinha, Jose Joaquim, Portalegre.**—Preserved meats. 656

768 **Trindade, Alfredo, Faro.**—**Figs.** 656

769 **Themudo, Jose Vicente, Castello de** Vide, Portalegre.—Preserved meats. 656

771 **Sanhoso, Jose Regoa.**—**Elderberries,** raisins, and dried figs. 656

773 **Oliveira & Co., Jose Antonio de.**—Preserved meats, fish, fruits, vegetables, and sweetmeats. 656

774 **Jose Joaquim dos Neves & Sons,** Lisbon.—Dried figs. 656

775 **Lehmann, J. W., Gustav, Oporto.**—Sweetmeats. 656

777 **Guimaraes, Antonio, Faro.**—**Dried** figs. 656

778 **Gomes, Jose Libanio, Villa Nova** de Portimao, Faro.—Dried figs. 656

779 **Gouvea, Jose Bernardino d'Abren,** Sande, Viseu.—Preserved fruits. 656

780 **Rodrigues & Nephew, Fernando,** Lisbon.—Preserved meat, vegetables, and fruits. 656

781 **Franco, Joaquim, Portimao, Faro.**—Dried figs. 656

782 **Ferreira Convent, Ferreira d'Aves,** Viseu.—Dried plums. 656

783 **Dantas Pimenta, Jose Maria, Torres** Novas, Santarem.—Dried fruit. 656

784 **Castanheiro, Balthazar Rodrigues,** Lisbon.—Sweet fruits. 656

785 **Barros, Jose Xavier Pereira, Villa** Real, Tras-os-Montes.—Sweetmeats. 656

786 **Leitao, Alberto, Penacova, Coimbra.**—Dried damsons. 656

787 **Pimenta, Anna Augusta de Souza,** S. Joao de Lobrigos, Viseu.—Dried fruits. 656

788 **Ornellas & Lisher, Lisbon.**—Preserved fruits and vegetables, sweetmeats and fruits. 656

789 **Le Cocq, Joao Jose, Castello de** Vide, Portalegre.—Olives. 656

790 **Silva, Domingos da, Elvas, Portalegre.**—Olives. 656

791 **Valentim, Jose, Arraiollos, Evora.**—Preserved meats. 656

792 **Mendes, Augusto Alexandre Esteves,** Aviz, Portalegre.—Preserved meat. 656

793 **Mascarenhas, Luis de, Portimao,** Faro.—Dried figs. 656

794 **Rodrigues, Antonio Manuel, Vinhaes,** Braganca.—Sausages. 656

795 **Romao, Joanna Balbina, Aveiro.**—Sweetmeat. 656

796 **Mello, Luis de Mendonca e, Tavira,** Faro.—Dried figs. 656

797 **Miranda, Joao Eduardo Lobo de,** Faro.—Dried figs. 656

For classes of exhibits, indicated by numbers at end of entries, see Classification, pp. 12–14.

Animal and Vegetable Products.

798 Roza, Julia Pimenta Cobral, Setubal, Lisbon.—Preserved orange. 656

799 Rijo, Joaquin Antonio, Elvas, Portalegre.—Olives. 656

800 Regallo, Jose Maria da Fonseca, Campo Maior, Portalegre.—Olives. 656

801 Serzedello, Joao Pereira, Elvas, Portalegre.—Preserved asparagus and olives. 656

802 Souza, Jose Saldanha Oliveira e.—Olives. 656

803 President of the Commission of Vianna, Vianna do Castelho.—Preserved fish. 656

804 Mina, S. Thome de, Coimbra.—Preserved fish. 656

805 Vidamrel, J. J. da, Trinidad Dias, Coimbra.—Preserved fish. 656

806 Callisto, Manuel M. Pimentel, Coimbra.—Preserved fish. 659

807 Carvalho, Albino Justinianno, Condeixa, Coimbra.—Dried figs. 656

808 Campello, Evaristo Jose Ferraz de Moraes, Anciaes, Braganca.—Raisins. 656

809 Carvalho, Antonio Miguel de, Sattam, Viseu.—Olives. 656

810 Correa, Antonio de Sousa, Oporto.—Olives. 656

811 Cellas Convent, Santo Antonio do Olivaes.—Preserved fruits. 656

812 Carmo, Bazilia Maria do, Arronches, Portalegre.—Preserved meat. 656

813 Conceicao, Joas Nunes da, Elvas, Portalegre.—Dried fruit, olives, and pickles. 656

814 Belem, Silvestre Polycarpo Correa, Lisbon.—Preserved fruits, preserved fish, and vegetables. 656

815 Campos, Luis Jose de, S. Pedro de Miragaia, Oporto.—Olives. 656

816 Castro, Joaquim Caetano de, Oporto.—Hams. 656

817 Piteira, Fernandez Joaquim Filippe, Reguengo, Evora.—Pork meat. 656

818 Proenca, Vasconcellos, Faro.—Figs. 656

819 S. Bento d'Ave Maria Convent, Oporto.—Sweetmeat. 656

820 Semide Convent, Semide, Coimbra.—Preserved turnips. 656

821 Silva, Francisco Ferreira da, Oporto.—Sausages. 656

822 Sta. Clara Convent, Guimaraes.—Sweetmeats. 656

823 Souza, Conceicao Margues, Alves, Oporto.—Preserved fruits. 656

824 Sta. Rosa de Lima Convent, Guimaraes.—Preserved fruits. 656

825 Santa Clara Convent, Santa Clara, Coimbra.—Sweetmeat. 656

826 Rocha, Feliciano Antonio da, Setubal, Lisbon.—Preserved fish. 656

827 Passos, Jose Francisco Rodriguez, Fuzeta, Faro.—Dried figs. 656

828 Peixto, Augusto Gavia, Serpa, Beja.—Olives. 656

829 Botelho, Antonio C., Fayal, Azores.—Sausages. 656

830 Carvalho, Rosa Guilhermina de, Cancella Velha, Porto.—Chocolate. 656

831 Cid, Jose Ignacio, Mirandella, Braganca.—Olives, murt. 656

832 Cruz, Jose Bento, Armamamar, Viseu.—Honey. 656

833 Angelica, Rosa de Jesus Maria, Oporto.—Preserved fruits. 656

834 Barros, Rita Candida de, Castello de Vide, Portalegre.—Olives. 656

834*a* Pereira, Pedro Maria Dantas, Torres Vedras, Santarem.
a Dried grapes. 656
b Olive oil. 660

835 Larcher, Emilia Adelaide, Portalegre.
a Preserved fruits. 656
b Syrups of groseille. 659

836 Miranda, Joaquim, Lobo de, Lagos, Faro.
a Dried figs. 656
b Red wine and vinegar. 660

837 Martins, Isidoro, Borba, Evora.
a Dried fruits. 656
b Wines. 660
c Olive oil. 662

838 Negrao, Joaquim d'Almeida, Portimao, Faro.
a Dried figs. 656
b Wine. 660

839 Gallope, Fernando dos Santos, Portalegre.
a Currant syrup. 656
b Wine. 660

840 Bentes, Antonio Joaquim, Serpa, Beja.
a Olives. 656
b Olive oil. 662

841 Andrada, Antonia Garcia de, Elvas, Portalegre.
a Preserved meat. 656
b Olive oil. 662

842 Castello Branco, Joao da Silva Ferrao, Santa Iria, Lisbon.
a Pickles, preserved fruits, and sardines in oil. 656
b Olive oil. 662

843 Cunha, Joaquim Guilherme da, Castello Branco.
a Olives. 656
b Wines. 660
c Olive oil. 662

844 Castel-Branco, Antonio Mendo, Caldeira, Alter do Chao, Portalegre.
a Preserved meat. 656
b Vinegar. 660
c Olive oil. 662

845 Atalya, Count of, Santarem.
a Honey. 656
b Wine. 660
c Olive oil. 662

846 Guerra, Jose da Conceicao, Elvas, Portalegre.
a Dried fruits. 656
b Wine and liquor. 660

847 Theotonio, Joaquim Manuel, Serpa, Beja.
a Olives. 656
b White wine. 660
c Olive oil. 662

848 Taborda, Antonio Theodoro Ferreira, Penamacor, Castello Branco.
a Olives. 656
b Red wine. 660
c Olive oil. 662

For classes of exhibits, indicated by numbers at end of entries, see Classification, pp. 12–14.

Animal and Vegetable Products.

849 Trinoao, Roman Antunes, Lapas, Santarem.
a Dried figs and grapes. 656
b Wines and brandy. 660

850 Administrative Council of Lausado, Lausado, Oporto.
a Sweet fruit. 656
b Red wine. 660

852 Almeida, Bernardo Caieiro de, Serpa, Beja.
a Olives. 656
b Olive oil. 662

853 Barboza, Paulo da Silva, Oporto.
a Sweetmeats. 656
b Biscuits. 661

854 Burguete, Miguel Serrao, Sardoal, Santarem.
a Olives, dried fruit. 656
b Vinegar. 660

855 Costa Falcao, Antonio Ozorio d'Azevedo da, Alpedrinha, Castello Branco.
a Olives. 656
b White wine. 660
c Olive oil. 662

856 Figueiredo, Antonio Jose de, Carrazeda d'Anciaes, Braganca.
a Olives. 656
b Wine. 660
c Olive oil. 662

857 Ferreira, Antonio Manuel, Torres Novas, Santarem.
a Dried fruits. 656
b Wine and brandy. 660

858 Feria, Jose Maria de la, Serpa, Beja.
a Olives. 656
b Wine and brandy. 660

859 Figueira, Gaspar Augusto, Evora.
a Sugared almonds. 656
b Wines and brandy. 660

860 Ferreira & Co., Lisbon.
a Candy. 656
b Syrups. 659
c Lemonade. 660

861 Martins, Jeronymo, & Son, Lisbon.
a Dried fruits. 656
b Wines. 660
c Olive oil. 662

862 Guedes, Francisco Domingues, Castello Branco.
a Sausages. 656
b Olive oil. 662

863 Magalhaes, Luis Antonio, Aldea Nova do Cabo, Castello Branco.—Timber, corkwood, sweet fruits.
a Dried fruits. 656
b Wine. 660
c Olive oil. 662

864 Mendes, Luis Antonio Soares, Castello Branco.
a Dried chestnuts. 656
b Vinegar. 660

865 Macedo Pinto, Joaquim Ferreira de, Toboaco, Viseu.
a Preserved fruits, elderberries. 656
b Wines. 660
c Olive oil. 662

866 Lemos, Antonio Maria Tovar de Moura, Beja.
a Olives. 656
b Vinegar. 660
c Olive oil. 662

867 Lacerda, Jose de Aragao Costa, Aldea Nova do Cabo, Castello Branco.
a Olives, potatoes. 656
b Wine, vinegar. 660

868 Nunes, Guilherme, Francisco Pereira, Oliveira do Hospital, Coimbra.
a Dried fruits. 656
b Wheat flour. 657
c White wine and vinegar. 660

869 Lima, Honorio Fiel, Portalegre.
a Preserved fruits. 656
b Wine. 660
c Olive oil. 662

870 Larcher Marcal, Maria Adelaide, Portalegre.
a Preserved fruits, truffles. 656
b Syrups. 659

871 Souza, Manuel Alves de, Castello Branco.
a Olives. 656
b Olive oil. 662

872 Souza Pinto, Francisco de Gamboa, Castello Novo, Castello Branco.
a Olives. 656
b Olive oil. 662

873 Vaz, Eduardo Augusto da Cruz, Castello Branco.
a Preserved meat, olives. 656
b Red wine. 660
c Olive oil. 662

875 Santa Anna, Jose Candido de, Elvas.
a Olives. 656
b Olive oil. 662

876 Salgado, Julio Bivar d'Azevedo, Sardoal, Santarem.
a Dried pears. 656
b Wines. 660
c Olive oil. 662

877 Pinto, Francisco Xavier de Moraes, Mirandella, Braganca.
a Raisins. 656
b Red wine. 660

878 Perdigao, Miguel Salvado R., S. Miguel de Machede, Evora.
a Preserved fruit. 656
b Wine. 660

879 Pinto, Antonio Joaquim Nogueira, Villa Real.
a Red wine. 656
b Raisins. 660

880 Pires, Antonio Joaquim, Lisbon.
a Sweet fruits and meats. 656
b Liquors. 660

881 Ramos, Joao Joaquim, Redondo, Evora.
a Preserved grapes. 656
b Starch. 658
c Red and white wine, brandy. 660

882 Pimenta, Jose Maria Dantas, Torres Novas, Santarem.
a Dried figs. 656
b Wine and brandy. 660

883 Costa, Jose Rodrigues da, Penamacor, Castello Branco.
a Olives. 656
b Olive oil. 662

884 Antonio, Eduardo, Montalvao, Portalegre.
a Preserved meat and frnits. 656
b Olives and olive oil. 662

885 Teixeira, Francisco Loureiro, Campello, Oporto.—Wheat flour. 657

886 Veiga, Maria Christina de Napoles Figueiredo, Goes, Coimbra. — Potato flour. 657

887 Lopes, Alvaro Pereira de Bettencourt, Ponta Delgada.—Flour. 657

888 Lima, Lino, Anciaes, Braganca.—Wheat and rye flour. 657

For classes of exhibits, indicated by numbers at end of entries, see Classification, pp. 12–14.

Animal and Vegetable Products.

889 Leao, Antonio Moreira, Guilhufe, Oporto.—Wheat and rye flour. 657

890 Egreja, Manuel Antonio, Torroso, Oporto.—Corn flour. 657

891 Egreja, Jose Francisco de Serra, Novaes, Oporto.—Wheat and corn flour. 657

892 Moreira, Joas Baptista, Rates, Oporto.—Wheat flour. 657

897 Gomes, Jose da Costa, Balazar, Oporto.—Wheat flour. 657

898 Ferreira, Januario da Silva, Elvas, Portalegre.—Corn flour. 657

899 Costa & Brother, Portalegre.—Corn flour. 657

901 Acacio Manuel Pereira, & Augusto Risques, Alter do Chao, Portalegre.—Corn, wheat, and rye flour. 657

902 Nunes, Vicente Ferreira, Lisbon, Lisbon.—Rice. 657

903 Pinto, Joao de Arevedo, Campello, Oporto.—Corn flour. 657

904 Villar, Manuel Pereira, Torroso, Oporto.—Barley flour. 657

905 Moreno, Jose Joaquim, S. Thiago, Lisbon.—Rice. 657

906 President of the Municipality of Peñafiel, Oporto.—Corn flour. 657

907 Costa, Antonio Ignacio da, Elvas, Portalegre.—Corn flour. 657

908 Silva, Antonio de Sousa e Vallongo, Oporto.—Corn flour. 657

909 Silva, Antonio Manuel, Vimioso, Braganca.—Wheat flour. 657

910 Souza, Victorino Alves, Oporto.—Wheat flour. 657

911 Pereira, Henrique Augusto, Setubal, Lisbon.—Wheat flour. 657

912 Pinto, Antonio Rodrigues, Coimbra.—Wheat flour. 657

913 Casa Nova, Manuel Gonsalves, Beires, Oporto.—Barley flour. 657

914 Carvalho, Jose Joaquim de, Ermida, Villa Real.—Wheat flour. 657

915 Pullido, Manuel, Marvao, Portalegre.—Wheat flour. 657

916 Silva, Antonio Lopes da, Balasar, Oporto.—Corn flour. 657

917 Conceicao, Jose dos Santos, Leca de Bailio, Oporto.—Indian corn flour. 657

918 Camara, Hermelinda Gago da, Ponta Delgada, Azores.
a Potato flour. 657
b Macaroni. 658

919 Camara, D. H. Gagoda, Ponta Delgada, Azores.
a Arrowroot flour, potato. 657
b Macaroni. 658

920 Baptista & Co., Lisbon.
a Wheat flour. 657
b Macaroni. 658

921 Chaves & Brother, Lisbon.
a Semolino. 657
b Macaroni. 658

922 Pamperio, Ricardo de Souza, Vallongo, Oporto.
a Wheat flour. 657
b Biscuits. 661

923 Pamperio, Antonio di Sousa Motta, Vallongo, Oporto.
a Wheat flour. 657
b Biscuits. 661

924 Alves & Bros., Lisbon.—Macaroni. 658

924*a* Mendonca, Thomaz Antunes de, Lisbon.—Starch and rice powder. 658

925 Sobrinho, Felix Fernandes Torres, Oporto.—Macaroni. 658

926 Rodrigues, Jose Galhardo, Oporto.—Macaroni. 658

928 Lemos, Francisco Ferreira de, Oporto.
a Macaroni. 658
b Refined sugar. 659

929 Manso, Jose Marques, S. Bartholomeu, Coimbra.—Orgeat syrup. 659

930 Madeira Sugar Manufacturing Co., Funchal, Madeira.
a Sugar. 659
b Molasses brandy. 660

931 Silva, Francisco da, Chamusca, Santarem.—Red wine. 660

931*a* Nascimento, Manuel Antonio, Ponta Delgada.—Samples of liquors. 660

932 Amaral, Antonio da Costa Correa, Santa Comba Dao, Viseu.—Red wine. 660

933 Araujo, Joaquim Cardoso de, Oliveira de Bairro.—Red wine. 660

934 Affonso, Domingos, Arialva, Lisbon.—Wines and vinegar. 660

935 Almeida, Francisco Manuel de, Serpa, Beja.—White wine. 660

936 Aguilar, jr., Bernardo Teixeira de, Lisbon.—Red and white wine. 660

938 Joao Bento, Valle Passos, Villa Real.—Red wine. 660

939 Allen, George, & Co., Lisbon.—Port wine. 660

940 Gama, Manuel Telles da, Lisbon.—Wines. 660

941 Hunt, Roope, Teage, & Co., Oporto.—Port wine. 660

942 Eca, Jose Ferreira de, Vallongo, Oporto.—Brandy. 660

942*a* Ramalho, Jose Maria, Evora.
a Red wine. 660
b Olive oil. 662

943 Fialho, Jacintho Maria, & Son, Ferreira, Beja.—Red wine. 660

944 Rodrigues Leitao, J. J., & Sons, Funchal, Madeira.—Madeira wine and white grape juice. 660

945 Vasconcellos, Adelino d'Almeida, Nellas, Viseu.—White wine. 660

946 Freire, Bernardo Xavier, Guarda.—White wine. 660

947 Freire, Amancio Antonio de Sequeira, Alemquer, Lisbon.—Wine. 660

948 Gomes, Joao Carlos, Ilhavo, Aveiro.—Brandy. 660

949 Garcia, Antonio Joaquim, Samil, Braganca.—Wine. 660

951 Galvao, Jose Augusto Ferreira Peixoto, Montemor-o-Velho, Coimbra.—Brandy. 660

For classes of exhibits, indicated by numbers at end of entries, see Classification, pp. 12–14.

Animal and Vegetable Products.

952 Guisado, Joao Baptista Ribeiro, Peniche, Leiria.—Wine and vinegar. 660

953 Galvao, Sabino Jose M. dos Anjos, Azueira, Lisbon.—Wine. 660

954 Galhardo, Francisco Ferreira, Penamacor, Castello Branco.—Red wine. 660

955 Guedes, Antonio Pinto de Carvalho, Nogueira, Villa Real.—Red wine. 660

956 Iglesias, Manuel, Lisbon.—Wine. 660

957 Janes, Jose Alonso, Requengo, Evora.—Red wine. 660

958 Mello, Bento de Castro Coelho e, S. Thiago, Coimbra.—Red wine. 660

959 Monteiro, Manuel F., Portalegre. —Vinegar. 660

961 Esteves, Manuel de Miranda, Celorico, Guarda.—Red wine. 660

962 Infante, Joao Maria de Magalhaes, Cantanhede, Coimbra. — White wine, brandy, and vinegar. 660

963 Esteves, Joao Manuel, Gondomil, Vianna do Castello.—Wine. 660

964 Kebe, E., & Co., Oporto.—Port wine. 660

965 Drach, Jose Ribeiro Guimaraes, Abrantes, Santarem.—White wine. 660

966 Franqueira, Romao, Fontelonga, Braganca.—Brandy. 660

967 Ferro, Narcizo Teixeira Martins, Oporto.—Wine. 660

968 Ferreira & Dourado, Oporto.—Port wine. 660

969 Cabral, Paes F., & Sons, Sernache, Viseu.—Wine. 660

970 Ferreira, Antonia Adelaide, Godim, Villa Real.—Wine. 660

971 Fortes, Jose Maria, Santar, Viseu. —Wines. 660

972 Faria, M. A. P. Ramos, Colorico de Basto, Braganca.—Wine. 660

973 Freitas, Domingos Antonio de, Ameias, Coimbra.—Wine. 660

974 Fonseca, Joaquim Apolinario, Christello Couvo, Vianna de Castello.—Wine. 660

975 Ferreira, Jose Joaquim Gomes, Castanheiro, Braganca.—Wine. 660

976 Ferreira, Jose Mendes, Lamego, Viseu.—Wine. 660

977 Feijo, Anselmo Guilherme Borges, Godim, Villa Real.—Wine. 660

978 Ribas, Limas, Guarda.—White and red wines. 660

979 Fonseca, Bernardo da Silveira Pinto da, Varzea de Abrunhaes, Viseu.—Wine. 660

980 Fonseca, Themudo de Magelhaes da, Lamego.—Wine. 660

981 Fragozo, Jose Maria, Chamusca, Santarem.—Wine. 660

982 Fialho, Francisco Antonio, Aldeia do Mato, Evora.—Red wine. 660

983 Figueiredo, Antonio Joaquim Marques, Villa Nova de Reguengo, Evora.—Red wine. 660

984 Falcao, Jose Maria Fernandez, Cadafais, Lisbon.—Wine. 660

985 Fonseca, Jose Maria da, Lisbon.—Wine and cognac. 660

986 Franco, Manuel Antunes, Cortegana, Lisbon.—Red wine. 660

987 Ferrari, Gustavo, Lisbon.—Wine. 660

988 Falcao, Francisco Paes de Mattos, Bringel, Beja.—Wine and vinegar. 660

989 Ferreira, Joaquim Ignacio, Lisbon. —Wine. 660

998 Duarte, Julio Cesario Ferreira, Arcos, Aveiro.—Wine. 660

999 Dias, Jose da Fonseca, Oliveira do Bairro, Aveiro.—White wine. 660

1000 Deus, Joao Rodrigues de, Torres Novas, Santarem.—Wine. 660

1001 Dias, Daniel Jose Ferreira, Torres Novas, Santarem.—Wine. 660

1002 Duarte, Jose Baptista, Castello de Vide, Portalegre.—Wine. 660

1003 Doria, Jose, Beja.—Wine. 660

1004 Doria, B., Covilha, Castello Branco.—Wine. 660

1005 Dejante & Co., Bom Successo, Lisbon.—Wine. 660

1006 Coelho, jr., Antonio Ferraz, Caldas da Rainha, Leiria.—White wine. 660

1007 Cardoso, Manuel Pedro, Sobral de Monte Agraco, Lisbon.—Wine. 660

1008 Campos, Antonio Joaquim Potes, Evora.—Red wine. 660

1009 Castilho, Antonio de, Villa Soeiro, Guarda.—Red wine. 660

1010 Costa, Francisco, Collares, Lisbon.—Wine. 660

1011 Dias, Manuel Ignacio, Goes, Coimbra.—Vinegar. 660

1012 Duraes, Luis Antonio, Parada, Viseu.—Wine. 660

1013 Dow & Co., Oporto.—Port wine. 660

1014 Frexedas, Joao Felix de Faria, Castello de Vide, Portalegre.—Wine. 660

1015 Fernandes, Antonio Vicente d'Almeida, Benavente, Santarem.—Wines. 660

1016 Figueira, Jose Ricardo de Carvalho, Peniche, Leiria.—Wine. 660

1017 Fernandes, Joao Salvino d'Almeida, Benavente, Santarem.—Wine. 660

1018 Ferraz & Choque, Lisbon.—Wine. 660

1019 Faria, Simao Paes de, Torres Novas, Santarem.—Wine and brandy. 660

1020 Falcao, Joao de Souza, Alpiarca, Santarem.—Wine and brandy. 660

1021 Ferreira, Francisco de Souza, Rio Maior, Santarem.—White wine. 660

1022 Climaco, jr., Joao, Matacaes, Lisbon.—Red wine. 660

1023 Costa, Joao Victorino Pereira da, Torres Vedras, Lisbon.—White wine. 660

1024 Torre Novas, Count of, Lisbon.—Wine. 660

1025 Carneiro, Antonio Soares, Lagoa, Faro.—Red wine. 660

1026 Caldeira, Ricardo Jose, Alegrete, Portalegre.—Wine. 660

For classes of exhibits, indicated by numbers at end of entries, see Classification, pp. 12–14.

Animal and Vegetable Products.

1027 Camara, Jose Maria Figueiredo Cabral da, Otta, Lisbon.—Wine. 660

1028 Alcacovas, Count of, Paco d'Arcos, Lisbon.—Wine. 660

1029 Cunha, Gregorio da, Olhalvo, Lisbon.—Wine. 660

1030 Garcia, Pedro de Souza, Estremoz, Evora.—Wine and brandy. 660

1031 Gomes, Jose.—Brandy. 660

1032 Guapo, Jose Daniel, Portalegre.—Wines. 660

1033 Godinho, Francisco, Reguengo, Evora.—Wines. 660

1034 Jansen, J. H., & Co., Lisbon.—Beer, and ginger beer. 660

1035 Kopke & Co., Massarellos, Oporto.—Wines. 660

1036 Rodrigues, J. J. Leitao, & Sons, Funchal, Madeira.—Madeira wine. 660

1037 Jacintho Maria Fialho & Son, Ferreira, Beja.—Red wine. 660

1039 Coelho, Luis Pires, Sardoal, Santarem. 660

1040 Cortez, Benedicto, Celorico, Guarda.—Red wine. 660

1041 Calleya, Cypriano Ribeiro, Lisbon.—Wine. 660

1042 Costa, Agostinho N. d'Oliveira, Villa Franca de Xira, Lisbon.—Wine. 660

1043 Castello, Lucas da Silva Cardozo, Campo Grande, Lisbon.—Wine. 660

1044 Costa, Joao Cezario, Evora.—Red wine. 660

1045 Castello Branco, D. Joaquina Ferrao, Lisbon.—Wine. 660

1046 Carvalho, Jose Avelino N. de Carvalho, Torres Vedras, Lisbon.—Red wine. 660

1047 Brito, Augusto Pereira, Torres Novas, Santarem.—Red and white wine and brandy. 660

1048 Bexiga, Antonio Soares, Torres Novas, Santarem.—Brandy. 660

1049 Bivar, Jeronymo d'Almeida Coelho de, Portimao, Faro.—Red wine. 660

1050 Bivar, Jeronymo, Faro.—Red and white wine. 660

1051 Borges, Jose, Corroados, Santarem.—Red and white wine. 660

1052 Bello, Francisco Serrianno Carvilho, Castello de Vide, Portalegre.—White and red wine. 660

1053 Baracho, Jose de Sousa, Torres Novas, Santarem.—Red wine. 660

1054 Cordes, Balthasar, Barcarena, Lisbon.—Red and white wine. 660

1055 Carvalho, Joaquim Freire de, Villa de Frades, Beja.—Red and white wine. 660

1056 Aragao, Francisco de Pina, Linhares, Guarda.—White and red wine. 660

1057 Abreu, Antonio de, Olhalvo, Lisbon.—Wine. 660

1058 Abreu, Francisco Antonio Maxino, Azambuja.—Wine. 660

1059 Azevedo, Manuel Rodrigues de, Benavente, Lisbon.—Wine. 660

1060 Branco, Joao Vicente, Massarellos, Oporto.—Gin. 660

1061 Barros, Antonio Manuel Ferreira, Ucanha, Viseu.—Brandy. 660

1062 Barao de Nellas, Nellas, Viseu.—Wine. 660

1063 Borga, Francisco Maximino, Villa Nova de Ourem, Santarem.—Red and white wine. 660

1064 Batalhos, Jose dos, Prazeres, Cartaxo, Santarem.—Red and white wine. 660

1065 Pereira, Manuel Augusto, Lisbon.—Red and white wine. 660

1066 Peixoto, Antonio Jose da Cunha A., Ohallo, Lisbon.—Wine. 660

1067 Rocha, Jose Alexandre da, Valle de Prazeres, Castello Branco.—Red wine. 660

1068 Pinheiro, Joaquim Garcia, Villa Nova, Reguengo, Evora.—Red wine. 660

1069 Prego, Ezequiel de Paula Sa, Alemquer, Lisbon.—White and red wine. 660

1070 Affonso, Joao Hilario, Redondo, Evora.—Wine and brandy. 660

1072 Alvares, Sabastido, Borba, Evora.—Red wine. 660

1073 Azeveda, Manuel Rodrigues de, Bucellas, Lisbon.—White wine. 660

1074 Assis, Domingos Francisco de, Alhandra, Lisbon.—Red wine. 660

1075 Barbosa, Manuel Paes Ferrao, Povoa de Midoes, Coimbra.—Red wine. 660

1076 Baiza, Miguel de Sousa, Sanfins, Villa Real.—Wine, muscadine wine. 660

1077 Ramalho, Esteves Goncalves, Villa Nova de Reguengo, Evora.—Red wine. 660

1078 Reixo, Jose Antonio Nunes, Villacosa.—White wine. 660

1079 Silva & Cosens, Oporto.—Port wine. 660

1080 Soares, Antonio, Carrazede d'Anciaes, Braganca.—Vinegar. 660

1081 Sousa, Bernardino Jose de Mello, Penafiel, Oporto.—Vinegar. 660

1082 Pimenta, Jose Maria, Dantas, Torres Novas.—Wine. 660

1083 Pereira, Candido Manuel, Lavradio, Lisbon.—Wine. 660

1084 Ramalho, Antonio Jose, Reguengo, Evora.—White wine. 660

1085 Pinheiro, Jose, Azambujo, Lisbon.—Red and white wine. 660

1086 Ferreira, Jose Henriques, Lisbon.—Red wine. 660

1087 Fragoso, jr., Luis Antonio, Ferreira, Cuba.—Wine. 660

1088 Figueira, Boaventura da Piedade, Cuba, Beja.—White wine. 660

1089 Fialho, Francisco d'Abreu, Portimao, Faro.—Red wine. 660

1090 Gonsalves, Jose dos Santos, Taboa, Coimbra.—Red wine. 660

1091 Fragoso, Manuel Figueira Sonto Mayor, Vidigueira, Beja.—Wines. 660

1092 Guerra, Jose Ignacio Pinto, Miranda do Douro, Braganca.—Wine. 660

1093 Guerra, Francisco Aranches do Amaral, Coimbra.—Wine and vinegar. 660

For classes of exhibits, indicated by numbers at end of entries, see Classification, pp. 12-14.

Animal and Vegetable Products.

1094 Fora, Jose Augusto dos Santos, Figueira da Foz, Coimbra.—Wine. 660

1095 Faria, Francisca Albertina de, Rates, Oporto.—Wine. 660

1096 Fonseca, Manuel Coelho da, Oliveira do Hospital, Coimbra.—Wine. 660

1097 Fonsecca, Francisco Maximo da, Sontello, Viseu.—Wine. 660

1098 Figueiredo, Manuel, Gonsalves, Aveiro.—Wine. 660

1099 Ferreira, Adriano Baptista, Vaccarica, Aveiro.—White wine. 660

1100 Freire, Joao Pereira, Penafiel, Oporto.—Wine. 660

1101 Falcao, Maria Miguelma, Miranda do Corvo, Coimbra.—Brandy. 660

1102 Bassoa, Jose Luis de, S. Momcede, Vianna do Castello.—Wine and brandy. 660

1103 Brandao, Francisco Antonio, Reboreda, Vianna.—White wine. 660

1104 Brito, J. F. L. Costa, Parada, Viseu.—White wine. 660

1105 Barreira, Antonio, jr., Alfandega da Fe, Braganca.—Red wine. 660

1106 Boto, Joao de Sousa Dounas, Ervedosa, Viseu.—Red wine. 660

1107 Brandao, Augusto Ferreira, Vaccarica, Aveiro.—White wine. 660

1108 Bernardo Augusto Lopes & Co., Figueira da Fox, Coimbra.—Red wine. 660

1109 Barao do Calvario, Penafiel, Oporto.—Wines. 660

1110 Barao, Jose Correa de, Sabrosa, Villa Real.—Red wine. 660

1111 Lopes, Jacintho, Elvas, Portalegre.—Red and white wine. 660

1112 Lima, Carlos Joas Ribeiro, Melgaco, Vianna do Castello.—Wine. 660

1113 Lima, Joao Jose Xavier de, Vill' Alva, Beja.—White wine. 660

1114 Lisbao, Antonio da Silva, Penafiel, Oporto.—Wine. 660

1115 Laranja, Manuel Duarte, Coruche, Santarem.—White wine. 660

1116 Leite, Francisco de Paula, Alcacer do Sal, Lisbon.—Wines. 660

1117 Leal, Francisco da Costa, Arneiro, Lisbon.—Red wine. 660

1118 Oliveira Soares, Eduardo, Evora.—Red wine. 660

1119 Bintrago, Jose Carniero d'Almeida de, Tuscifal, Lisbon.—Red wine. 660

1120 Silva, Daniel Pereira da, Celorico, Guarda.—Wines. 660

1121 Silveira, Joao Vicente da, Abrigada, Lisbon.—Wines. 660

1122 Silva, Jose Gomes da, Collares, Lisbon.—Wine. 660

1123 Souza, Joao Candido de Castro e, Beja.—White wine. 660

1124 Souza, Jose Maximo Coelho J., Guarda.—Red wine. 660

1125 Silva, Antonio Martins da, Redondo, Evora.—Red wine. 660

1126 Sereto, Domingos Francisco, Villa Nova de Reguengos, Evora.—Red wine. 660

1127 Silva, A. Augusto da, Lisbon.—Wine. 660

1128 Salgado, Antonio Lopes Vidigal, Coruche, Santarem.—Red wine. 660

1129 Simoes, Francisco, Villa Soeiro, Guarda.—Red wine. 660

1130 Sa, Antonio Manuel da Cunha e, Torre de Ervedal, Leiria.—Wine. 660

1131 Souza, Joaquim da Silva, Ribeira de Baixo, Leiria.—Brandy. 660

1132 Silva, Francisco Jose de Bastos e, Torres Vedras, Lisbon.—Wines. 660

1133 Santos, Joao Bernardo dos, Lagoa, Faro.—Wine. 660

1134 Souza, Francisco Jose de, Labrugeira, Lisbon.—Red wine. 660

1135 Silva, Ernesto de Mendonca e, Abrigada, Lisbon.—Wines. 660

1136 Silva, Antonio Pires da, Villa Franca de Xira, Lisbon.—Wines. 660

1137 Ozorio, Jose Augusto de Sa Pereira, Bretiande, Viseu.—Red wine. 660

1138 Ozorio, Antonio Perfeito Pereira Pinto, Cambres, Viseu.—Wine. 660

1139 Oliveira, Domingos Carneiro de, Agrella, Porto.—Wine. 660

1140 Nunes, Jose Cabrita, Lagoa, Faro.—Red wine. 660

1141 Outeiro, Viscount of, Fundo, Castello Branco.—Red wine. 660

1142 Vasconcellos, Joaquim Guilherme de, Elvas, Portalegre.—Red and white wine. 660

1143 Silva, Francisco Candido da, Torres Novas.—Wine. 660

1144 Silveira, Joao Vicente da, Abrigada, Lisbon.—Wine. 660

1146 Vasconcellos, Antonio de, Villa Nova, Vidgueira, Beja.—White wine. 660

1147 Vilhena, Agostinho de, S. Thiago, Lisbon.—Red wine. 660

1148 Esperanca, Viscount of, Cuba, Beja.—Red and white wine and vinegar. 660

1149 Nogueira, Henrique de Sa, Portalegre.—Red wine. 660

1150 Nascimento, Manuel Antonio do, Ponta Delgada, Azores.—Liquors, brandy, cognac. 660

1151 Oliveira, Jose Bernardo de, Mondim de Basto, Villa Real.—Brandy. 660

1152 Oliveira, Antonio Simoes de, Moluido, Viseu.—Wine. 660

1153 Offley, Cramp, & Forresters, Oporto.—Wine. 660

1154 Vasconcellos, Adelino d'Almeida, Nellas, Viseu.—White wine. 660

1155 Serrado, Viscount of, Viseu.—Wine. 660

1156 Villafanha, Antonio de, Tondella, Viseu.—Red and white wine. 660

1157 Valle, Jose de Seixas do, Bassar, Viseu.—Wine. 660

1158 Veiga, Ricardo Antonio da, Povoa de Midoes, Coimbra.—Red wine. 660

1159 S. Thome, Viscount of, Soure, Coimbra.—Red wine. 660

1160 Valle, Manuel de Sousa Dias, Oporto.—Wine. 660

1161 Vieira, Venancio Dias de Figueiredo, Eiro, Aveiro.—Wine. 660

For classes of exhibits, indicated by numbers at end of entries, see Classification, pp. 12–14.

Animal and Vegetable Products.

1162 Moidnenta da Beira, Viscount of, Viseu.—Red wine. 660

1163 Viuva Pinto, & Son, Lisbon.—Red and white wine. 660

1164 Viuva, Pevelin, & Sons, Torres Vedras, Lisbon.—Red and white wine. 660

1165 Welsh Brothers, Funchal, Madeira.—Madeira wines, grape juice, etc. 660

1166 Abrigada, Viscount of, Lisbon.—Muscatel and other wines. 660

1167 Mossamedes, Viscount of, Bemfica, Lisbon.—Wine. 660

1168 Carnide, Viscount of, Carnide, Lisbon.—Red and white wine. 660

1169 Velloso, Antonio Guedes, Cambres, Setubal, Lisbon.—Red wine. 660

1170 Vilhena, Barbosa Arthur Peres de, Cartaxo, Guarda.—Red wine. 660

1171 Sagiosa, Viscountess of, Sagiosa, Guarda.—White wine. 660

1172 Nunes, Jose Jacintho, Grandola, Lisbon.—Wine. 660

1173 Nobre, Manuel de Barros, Tavora, Viseu.—Red wine. 660

1174 Neves, Fortunato Vieira das, Taboa, Coimbra.—White wine. 660

1175 Vas Freire, Jose Sebastiao Torres, Evora.—Red and white wine. 660

1176 Pereira, Widow Theotonio, & Sons, Lisbon.—White and red wine. 660

1177 Velho, Francisco da Rosa, Evora.—Red and white wine. 660

1178 Formosinho, Widow of Joao Martins, Lagoa, Faro.—Wine. 660

1179 Velles, Luis Nunes de, Portalegre.—Brandy. 660

1180 Judice, A. J., Widow of, Mexilhoeira, Faro.—Wine. 660

1181 Menezes, Jose Maria da Silveira, Borba.—White wine. 660

1182 Mazziotti, Antonio Maria Dias P. Chaves, Collares, Lisbon.—White and red wine. 660

1183 Machado, Pedro Xavier, Portalegre.—White wine. 660

1184 Martins, Miguel Castro, Montargil, Portalegre.—Wines. 660

1185 Mattos, Bento F. M., Mondim de Basto, Villa Real.—Wine. 660

1186 Lisboa, Luis Emilio, Vieira.—Wine. 660

1187 Neves, Jose Eloy das, Cadaval, Lisbon.—White and red wine, and brandy. 660

1188 Natividade, Jose Gonzalves, Constanca, Santarem.—White wine. 660

1189 Lobo, Francisco Teixeira, Sabrosa, Villa Real.—Muscadine wine. 660

1190 Lima, Jose Duarte, Cartaxo, Santarem.—Red and white wine, brandy. 660

1191 Mello, Hygino Otto de Queiros, Laniego, Viseu.—Red wine. 660

1192 Lebre, Manuel Ferreira, Anadia, Aveiro.—Red wine. 660

1193 Lemos, Alexandre Maria de, Lamego, Viseu.—Red wine. 660

1194 Montes, Jose Nunes Moraes, Castello Branco.—Red wine. 660

1195 Martins, Benedicto Matheus, Elvas, Portalegre.—Wine. 660

1196 Macedo, Luis A. d'A. Estremos, Evora.—Red wine. 660

1197 Macedo, Camillo de jr., Peso da Regoa, Villa Real.—Wines and brandy. 660

1198 Magalhaes, Luis Francisco da Silva, Villarinho de S. Romao, Villa Real.—Red wine. 660

1199 Leitao, Alipio, Penacova, Coimbra.—Red wine and vinegar. 660

1200 Meirelles, Antonio de Chaves, Povoa de Midoes, Coimbra.—Red wine. 660

1201 Lima, Jose Duarte, Cartaxo, Lisbon.—Wine. 660

1202 Moraes, Jose Alves de, Vinhaes, Braganza.—Wine. 660

1203 Madeira, Jose, Povoa de Midoes, Coimbra.—Red wine. 660

1204 Leite, Francisco de Moraes, Villa Flor, Braganza.—Wine and vinegar. 660

1205 Leite, Guilherme da Costa, Santo Thirso, Porto.—Wine. 660

1206 Oliveira, Augusto Jose de, Lisbon.—Red wine. 660

1207 Oliveira, Jose Vaz Rato de, Alter do Chao, Portalegre.—Brandy and vinegar. 660

1208 Ornellas, A. de, Funchal, Madeira.—Madeira wine. 660

1209 Magalhaes, Joao Guedes de.—Red wine. 660

1210 Moraes, Joaquim Claudino de, Regoa, Villa Real.—Red wine. 660

1211 Monteiro, Joaquim Soares, Mesquinhata, Oporto.—Wine. 660

1212 Magalhaes, Roberto Augusto Pinto de, Valle de Mendis, Villa Real.—Red wine. 660

1213 Motta, Luiz Antonio, Ferreira da Andraes, Villa Real.—Wines. 660

1214 Mourao, Luis Teixeira, Cazal de Loivos, Villa Real.—Red wine. 660

1215 Marques, Joao Antonio de Meirelles, Villa Real.—Red wine. 660

1216 Monteiro, Jose Justino Teixeira, Covas do Douro, Villa Real.—Red wine. 660

1217 Mello, Joao, C. da Rosa Malheiro, Candedo, Villa Real.—White wine, brandy. 660

1218 Matheus, Jose Paulino, S. Miguel de Lobirgo, Villa Real.—Wine. 660

1219 Lobo, Nicolau Joaquim Salles, Evora.—Red wine, vinegar. 660

1220 Lopes, Jose Ramos, Airo, Braga.—Wine. 660

1221 Meirelles, Antonio Nunes de Chaves, Povoa de Midoes, Coimbra.—Red wine. 660

1222 Miranda, Jose Victorino de, Matacaes, Lisbon.—Red wine. 660

1223 Pinto, Joao Adriano, Alfandega da Fé, Braganza.—Brandy. 660

1224 Pascoal, Otero, Oporto.—Beer. 660

1225 Macedo, Antonio Luis de, Arruda dos Vinhos, Lisbon.—Red wine. 660

1226 Martins, Luis Antonio, Torres Vedras, Lisbon.—Wine. 660

For classes of exhibits, indicated by numbers at end of entries, see Classification, pp. 12–14.

Animal and Vegetable Products.

1227 Moniz, Antonio Bernardino da Fonseca, Barocal, Guarda.—Wine. 660

1228 Madeira, Alexandre Jose, Candedo, Villa Real.—Wine. 660

1229 Monteiro, Abilio Affonso da Silva, Ventosa do Bairro, Aveiro.—Red wine. 660

1230 Mello, Antonio Maria de, Miranda do Corvo, Coimbra.—Red wine. 660

1231 Marques Estevao Jose, Aldeia de Mato, Evora.—White and red wine. 660

1232 Marques Maria Jose Perpetua, Redondo, Evora.—Red wine. 660

1233 Pavao, Antonio Augusto Gonsalves, Villa Real.—Wine. 660

1234 Pinheiro, Custodio Jose, Valverde, Villa Real.—Wine. 660

1235 Moura, Christiano Augusto da Silva, Midoes, Coimbra.—Red wine. 660

1236 Moraes & Mouro, Figueira, Coimbra.—Wine. 660

1237 Lima, Antonio Joaquim Fernandes, Villa Nova da Cerveira, Vianna do Castello.—Wine. 660

1238 Marques, Estevao Jose, Evora.—Brandy. 660

1239 Miranda, Felix Honorio Gomes de, Torres Vedras, Lisbon.—Red and white wine. 660

1240 Lima, Jose Duarte de, Cartaxo, Santarem.—Wine, vinegar. 660

1241 Leito, Manuel Pinto, Fontes, Villa Real.—Wine. 660

1242 Lago, Francisco d'Assis Pereira do, Arcos, Braganca.—Red wine. 660

1243 Mattos, Joao Chrisostomo de Carvalho, Villarouco, Viseu.—Red wine. 660

1244 Levita, Joaquim Fortunato, Portalegre.—Brandy. 660

1245 Lopes, Manuel Joao, Fuseta, Faro.—Red wine. 660

1246 Negreiros, Bento Antonio, Trigo de Mirandella, Braganca.—Red wine. 660

1247 Napoles, Miguel Tudella de Souza, Castelloes, Viseu.—White wine. 660

1248 Lima, Antonio dos Santos, Pavoa de Midoes, Coimbra.—Brandy. 660

1249 Leitao, A. Baptista Covilha, Castello Branco.—Red wine. 660

1250 Lopes, Antonio Camillo da Silva, Coruche, Santarem.—Wine. 660

1251 Lopes, Jose Olaia, Castello Branco.—Wines. 660

1252 Lobo, Bernardino Vas, Celorico de Basto, Braga.—Wine. 660

1253 Lopes, Joao da Cunha, Silvares, Viseu.—Wine. 660

1254 Lobo, Jose Nogueira Pereira, Ranhudos, Viseu.—Wine. 660

1255 Leao, Manuel da Cunha, Sobreira, Oporto.—Corkwood and corks. 600

1256 Lima, Joao Ferreira, Braganza.—Wine. 660

1257 Magalhaes, Francisco Jose, Portalegre.—Red wine. 660

1258 Motta, Ranulfo Antonio, Portimao, Faro.—Red and white wine. 660

1259 Mello, Miguel Antonio de Sousa, Villa Franca de Xira, Lisbon.—Red wine. 660

1260 Moita, Antonio F. da Silva, Torres Novas, Santarem.—Wines. 660

1261 Jansen, J. H., & Co., Lisbon.—Beer and ginger beer. 660

1262 Kopke & Co., Massarellos, Oporto.—Port wine and muscadine wine. 660

1263 Leacock & Co., Funchal, Madeira.—Wine. 660

1264 Morte Certa, Antonio Pedro Cardoso, Alcacer do Sal, Lisbon.—Wine. 660

1265 Louro, Francisco Rico, Aldeia de Matto, Evora.—Red wine. 660

1266 Mello, Jose de, Thomar, Santarem.—Red and white wine. 660

1267 Moraes, Jose Correa Pinto de, Constanca, Santarem.—Red and white wine. 660

1268 Martins, Jose Maria, Setubal, Lisbon.—Wines. 660

1269 Martins, Joao Pedro, Setubal, Lisbon.—Wines. 660

1270 Martel, Joao Campello Trigueiros, Sacavem, Lisbon.—Red and white wine. 660

1271 Mesquita, Antonio da Silva, Cartaxo, Santarem.—Red and white wine. 660

1272 Machado, Thomaz Jose, Lisbon.—Wines. 660

1273 Monteiro, Antonio Manuel, Vill-Alba, Beja.—Red wine. 660

1274 Marquez de Pombal, Oeiras, Lisbon.—White and red wine. 660

1275 Machado, Honorato Jose Torres, Azambuja, Lisbon.—Brandy, wine, and vinegar. 660

1276 Ribeiro, Francisco Maria, Couto de Cima, Viseu.—Wine. 660

1277 Ribeiro, Serafim Garcia, Oliveira do Hospital.—Brandy. 660

1278 Rodrigues, Antonio Caetano, Oporto.—Port wine. 660

1279 Ribeiro, Manuel, Penafiel, Oporto.—Brandy. 660

1280 Rodrigues, Antonio, Eiro, Braganca.—Brandy. 660

1281 Magalhaes, Vicente Xavier, Tavira, Faro.—Red wine. 660

1282 Mendonca, Manuel Marcal, Oelhao, Faro.—Red wine. 660

1283 Mira, Jose Maria de, Vidigueira, Beja.—White wine. 660

1284 Motta, Anacleto da Fonseca, Sardoal, Santarem.—Wine. 660

1285 Moreno, Jose Joaquim, S. Thiago, Lisbon.—Wine. 660

1286 Ribeiro, Jose Joaquim, S. Joao da Pesqueira, Viseu.—Red wine. 660

1287 Rego, Manuel Diogo, Moncorvo, Braganca.—Red wine. 660

1288 Camacho, Henrique Jose Maria, Funchal, Madeira.—Superior reserve wines, and other qualities. 660

1289 Creswell & Co., Lisbon.—Red wine. 660

1290 Coutinho, Joaquim Jose, Alpiarca, Santarem.—Red and white wine and brandy. 660

1291 Carneiro, Joao Bento Gil, Azambuja.—Red wine. 660

For classes of exhibits, indicated by numbers at end of entries, see Classification, pp. 12–14.

Animal and Vegetable Products.

1292 **Corte Real, Antonio Freire, Valle** de Prazeres, Castello Branco.—Red wine and brandy. 660

1293 **Rego, Francisco Maia do, Alfandega** da Fé, Braganca.—Red wine. 660

1294 **Roma, J. M. Goncalves, Troviscoso**, Vianna.—Wine. 660

1295 **Robollo, Domingos Jose, Castello** Branco.—Red wine. 660

1296 **Roquette, Jose Ferreira, Salvaterra**, Santarem.—Wines. 660

1297 **Ramires, Balthazar Peres, Evora.** —Wine and vinegar.

1298 **Ramalho, Antonio Pinheiro, Reguengo**, Evora.—White wine. 660

1299 **Ramos, Antonio Pedro de Carvalho**, Rio Maior, Santarem.—White wine. 660

1300 **Rosa, Jose Maria, Rio Maior**, Santarem.—White wine. 660

1301 **Rapozo, Joaquim Nunes Vieira**, Coruche, Santarem.—Red wine. 660

1302 **Ribeiro, Joaquim Antonio, Alcacer** do Sal, Lisbon.—Red wine. 660

1303 **Rodrigues, Manuel Antonio, Sobreira**, Villa Real.—White wine. 660

1304 **Chaves, Jose Luciano Pereira**, Carrica, Viseu.—Wine. 660

1305 **Borges de Sousa, Asambuja, Lisbon**.—White wine. 660

1306 **Costa, Jose da, Abravezes, Viseu.** —Wine. 660

1307 **Bernardo, Vasco, Coruche, Santarem**.—Red wine. 660

1308 **Cossart, Gordon, & Co., Madeira.** —Madeira wine. 660

1309 **Carvalho, Jose Raymundo Lopes** de, Torres Novas, Santarem.—Red wine. 660

1310 **Carnelho, Victorino Antonio do** Reis, Anca, Constanhede.—Vinegar. 660

1311 **Carvalho, Francisco Garcia de**, Arganil, Coimbra.—Vinegar. 660

1312 **Soeiro, Balthazar Rodrigues, jr.**, Campo Maior, Portalegre.—Brandy. 660

1313 **Sobrinho, Jose Martins Leitao**, Villa de Frades, Beja.—Red wine. 660

1314 **Silva, Antonio Jose da, Salvaterra**, Santarem.—Red wine. 660

1315 **Sauvage, C., Vendas Novas, Evora**.—Brandy. 660

1316 **Sequeira e Sa, Francisco Theodorico**, Vidigueira, Beja.—White wine. 660

1317 **Soure, Joaquim Manuel Soares** de, Ferreira, Beja.—Red wine. 660

1318 **Santos, Jose Fogaco de C. e, Aljubere**, Lisbon.—Wine. 660

1319 **Silva, Joaquim Jose de Freitas e**, Cartaxo, Santarem.—Wines. 660

1320 **Santos, Antonio Vicente dos**, Aphandra, Lisbon.—Wines. 660

1321 **Silva, Jose Maria da, Elvas, Portalegre**.—Brandy and red wine. 660

1323 **Canto e Castro, Miguel do, Lisbon.** —White wine. 660

1324 **Calasons, Jose Dias de S., Gaviao**, Portalegre.—Red wine. 660

1325 **Coutinho, Luis da Silva, Cascaes**, Lisbon.—White and red wine. 660

1326 **Costa, Antonio Jacome da, Gaviao**, Portalegre.—Brandy. 660

1327 **Silva, Jose Gonsalves da, Portalegre**.—Red wine and brandy. 660

1328 **Soares, Jose Severino, Ribeira de** Santarem.—Wines and alcohol. 660

1329 **Carvalho, Jose Joaquim de, Eremida**, Villa Real.—Wine. 660

1330 **Couraca, Jose de Gouveia, Faia**, Viseu.—Wine. 660

1331 **Castello Branco, Fernando d'Almeida** Loureiro, S. Miguel do Outeiro, Viseu.—Wine. 660

1332 **Carinho, Bartholomeu, Montargil**, Portalegre.—Red and white wine. 660

1333 **Caldas, Manuel Duarte Silva, S.** Joao Baptista, Santarem.—Red wine. 660

1334 **Couto, Antonio Severino do**, Pragança, Lisbon.—Wine. 660

1335 **Castro, Jose d'Almeida Silva e**, Miranda do Corvo, Coimbra.—Vinegar. 660

1336 **Carvalho, Ananias Cardoso de**, S. Thiago, Viseu.—Wine. 660

1337 **Cabral, Constantino do Valle** Coelho, Oporto.—Port wine. 660

1338 **Cabral, Antonio Paes, Senhorim**, Viseu.—Wine. 660

1339 **Carvalho, Alonso Pinto Teixeira** de Santa Martha de, Penaguiao, Villa Real.—Wine. 660

1340 **Cabrita, Joao Carlos, Cuba, Beja.** —Wine. 660

1341 **Cabreira, Antonio, Evora.**—Red and white wine and brandy. 660

1342 **Carvalhosa, Jose Felix de Almeida**, Ordisqueira, Lisbon.—White wine. 660

1343 **Costa Cabral, Joao Rebello da**, Lisbon.—Red and white wine. 660

1344 **Pereira, Antonio d'Almeida, S.** Pedro de Franca, Viseu.—Wine. 660

1345 **Pecanha, Jose Pereira de Castro**, Vianna do Castello.—Wine. 660

1346 **Carvalho, Antonio Marques de**, Chamusca, Santarem.—White and red wine and brandy. 660

1347 **Caravalho, Joao Affonso de, Villa** Franca de Xira, Lisbon.—Red and white wine. 660

1348 **Cunha, Joao Augusto da, S. Joas** da Ribeira, Santarem.—Red and white wine. 660

1349 **Cardoso, jr., Setubal, Lisbon.**—Wines and liquors. 660

1350 **Carvalho, Francisco Jose de, Faro.** —Anisette brandy. 660

1351 **Capello, Manuel Joaquim da Silva**, Vill' Alva, Beja.—Red wine. 660

1352 **Costa, Joao Maria da, Alhandra**, Lisbon.—Red wine. 660

1353 **Costa, Domingos Antonio da**, Elvas, Portalegre.—Red and white wine. 660

1354 **Condessa Geraz de Lima, Lisbon.** —Wine. 660

1355 **Camara, Tristao Prestrello da**, Funchal, Madeira.—Dry Madeira wine. 660

1356 **Claro, Francisco Germano, Lisbon**.—Red and white wine. 660

For classes of exhibits, indicated by numbers at end of entries, see Classification, pp. 12–14.

Animal and Vegetable Products.

1357 **Campos, Francisco Ferreira,** Rio Maior, Santarem.—Red wine. 660

1358 **Cruz, Manuel Mendes da,** Lagares, Coimbra.—Wine. 660

1359 **Carneiro, Custadio Gil dos Reis,** Refojos, Oporto.—Wine. 660

1361 **Borges, Candido Marcelino,** Torres Novas, Santarem.—Red and white wine. 660

1362 **Blanco, Joao Diago,** Alvito, Beja.—Red and white wine. 660

1363 **Blandy, Carlos R.,** Funchal.—Madeira wine. 660

1364 **Carvalho, Dionisio Antonio N. de,** Leniche, Peiria.—Wine and vinegar. 660

1365 **Cunha, Alexandre de Sena,** Coruche, Santarem.—Red wine. 660

1366 **Cabrita, Joao Carlos,** Cuba, Beja.—Wines and liquors. 660

1367 **Botelho, Antonio da Costa,** Santarem.—Wine. 660

1368 **Barcellos, Francisco Maria,** Torres Vedras, Lisbon.—Red and white wine. 660

1369 **Salgueiro, Baroness of,** Leiria.—Red wine. 660

1370 **Barao de Viamonte,** Leiria.—Red wine. 660

1371 **Barros e Cunha, Jose de,** Torres Vedras, Lisbon.—Wine. 660

1373 **Brito, Jose Maria de Barros Carvalhaes,** Nisa, Portalegre.—Red wine and brandy. 660

1374 **Biker, Antonio Pedro,** Faro.—Red wine. 660

1375 **Cerveira, Jose Rodrigues,** Anadia, Aveiro.—Red and white wine. 660

1376 **Castro, Damiao Martins,** S. Pedro da Cova, Porto.—Red wine. 660

1377 **Coutinho, Fernando Affonso** d'Almeida, Cantanhede, Coimbra.—Red and muscadine wine. 660

1378 **Canella, Agostinho,** Arcos, Aveiro.—Red and white wine. 660

1379 **Campos, Antonio de Freitas,** Arcos, Aveiro.—Red wine. 660

1380 **Costa Pereira & Co.,** Figueira, Coimbra.—Red and white wine. 660

1381 **Castanheira, Jose Rodrigues Mendes,** Azere, Coimbra.—Wine. 660

1382 **Caceres, Francisco Albuquerque** Mello Pereira, Pereira, Oporto.—White and red wine. 660

1383 **Chaves, Antonio Joaquim,** Sta. Martha de Penaguiao, Villa Real.—Wine. 660

1384 **Coutinho, Jose Maria d'Almeida,** Cidadelhe, Villa Real.—Wine. 660

1385 **Castro, Luis de,** Valle de Passos, Villa Real.—Red wine. 660

1386 **Cruz, Joaquim Rodrigues,** Mesao Frio, Villa Real.—White wine. 660

1387 **Cancella, Francisco,** Arcos, Aveiro.—Red and white wine. 660

1388 **Cunha, Antonio Duarte da,** Freixinho, Viseu.—Red wine. 660

1389 **Costa, Victorino Alves da,** Arumamar, Viseu.—Wine. 660

1390 **Cardoso, Joaquim Maria do Amaral,** Tamega, Aveiro.—Red and white wine. 660

1391 **Correa, Jose Augusto,** Santa Comba Dao, Viseu.—Red wine. 660

1392 **Cardozo, Antonio,** Abreiro, Braganca.—Red wine. 660

1393 **Castro, Ayres de S. Mariz e,** Carraseda d'Anciaes, Braganca.—Wine. 660

1394 **Castro, Jose de,** Braganca.—Muscadine and other wines. 660

1395 **Commenda, Elias Rebeiro,** Villa Flor, Braganca.—Red wine. 660

1396 **Cunha, Bernardino Alves Teixeira,** Celorico de Basto, Braga.—Wine. 660

1397 **Cunto, Manuel d'Aguino Alves do,** Nogueira, Villa Real.—Wine. 660

1398 **Castro, Antonio Augusto d'Almeida,** Mesao, Villa Real.—Wine. 660

1399 **Bairrada Commercial Wine Co.,** Vaccarica, Aveiro.—Red and white wine. 660

1400 **Camello, Joaquim Augusto da Silveira,** Penafiel, Oporto.—Wine and cider. 660

1401 **Coutinho, Antonio Joaquim de** Moura, Onteiro, Braga.—Wine. 660

1402 **Casa de Pasos,** Barcellos.—Wine. 660

1403 **Carvalho, Jose Velloso Pinto de,** Lamego, Viseu.—White wine. 660

1404 **Cruz, Jose Lopes da,** Nogueira, Villa Real.—Red wine. 660

1405 **Costa, Jose Joaquim Pinto da,** Nogueira, Villa Real.—Red wine. 660

1406 **Cordeiro, Antonio Montes,** Godim, Villa Real.—Red wine. 660

1407 **Champalimaud, Antonio Montes,** Godim, Villa Real.—Red wine. 660

1408 **Chaves, Manuel Jose da Cunha,** Valle Passos, Villa Real.—Wine. 660

1409 **Asevedo, Jose Ferreira da Silva,** Rates, Oporto.—Red wine. 660

1410 **Alexandre, Joaquim Peres de,** Taboa, Coimbra.—Red wine. 660

1411 **Alexandre, Manuel,** Taboa, Coimbra.—Red wine. 660

1412 **Abreu, Francisco Jose de,** Lamego, Viseu.—Red wine. 660

1413 **Costa, Francisco Bento da,** Gomiei, Viseu.—Wine. 660

1414 **Contada, Jose Domingues,** Carapecos, Braga.—Wine. 660

1415 **Carvalho, Jose Teixeira da,** Cavez, Braga.—Wine. 660

1416 **Castello Branco, Manuel Antonio** Pereira, Abraveses, Viseu.—Wine. 660

1417 **Aragao, Alexandre de,** Villa Flor, Braganca.—White and red wine. 660

1418 **Abreiro, Joao Vaz de,** Mirandella, Braganca.—Wine. 660

1419 **Almeida, Ignacio Bernardino de,** Alfondega da Fé, Braganca.—White wine. 660

1420 **Asevedo, Jose de,** Villa Flor, Braganca.—White wine. 660

1421 **Andrade, Basilio Augusto Xavier de,** Coimbra.—Red and white wines. 660

1422 **Almeida, Manuel Lourenco,** Oporto.—Muscadine wine. 660

For classes of exhibits, indicated by numbers at end of entries, see Classification, pp. 12-14.

Animal and Vegetable Products.

1424 Administrative Council of Montenior-o-o-Velhò, Montenior-o-Velho, Coimbra.—Vinegar. 660

1425 Alcoforado, Maria H. S., Barcellos, Braga.—Wine. 660

1426 Amaral, Antonio Gomes Silva do, Cima de Villa, Viseu.—Wine. 660

1427 Andrade, Bernardo Antonio da Silva, Cima de Villa, Viseu.—Wine. 660

1428 Almeida, Jose Bernardo de, Lordosa, Viseu.—Wine. 660

1429 Amaral, Leonor Carvalho Fonseca, Mangualde, Viseu.—Wine. 660

1430 Amaral, Bernardo Rodrigues do, Espinho, Viseu.—Wine. 660

1431 Avelino, Joaquim Cumieira, Villa Real.—Bastardo and muscadine wine. 660

1432 Azevedo, Antonio Lopes de Nogueira, Villa Real.—Red and white wine. 660

1433 Pereira, Joaquim J. Peral, Lisbon. —Wines. 660

1434 Aragao, Alexandre A. de Mattos Mascarenhas Vasconcellos, Sebal Grande, Coimbra.—Vinegar. 660

1435 Antonio Nicolau d'Almeida jr., & Bro., Oporto.—Wine, port wine, and brandy. 660

1436 Amaral, Pedro d'Albuquerque Silva, Mangualde, Viseu.—White and red wines. 660

1437 Andressen, J. H., Oporto.—Port wine. 660

1438 Rodrigues, Antonio Caetano, & Co., Oporto.—Wines. 660

1439 Alves, Francisco, Passacos, Villa Real.—Wine. 660

1440 Moura, Antonio Gomes de, & Co., Oporto.—Wine and port wine. 660

1442 Sarmento, Bernardo Figueiredo Sepulveda, Santa Justa, Braganca.—Red and white wine. 660

1443 Souza, Joaquim Jose de, Ferreira, Vianna do Castello.—Wine. 660

1444 Silva, Antonio Xavier Torres e, Villa de Caminha.—Wine. 660

1445 Santos, Antonio dos, Povoa de, Lusiannes, Viseu.—Wine. 660

1446 Sampaio, Jose da Cunha, Villa Nova de Famalicao, Braga.—Wines. 660

1447 Souto Maior, Lourenco da Cunha, S. Martinho de Dunna, Braga.—Wine. 660

1448 Sousa, Jose Henriques Coelho de, Refoyos, Braga.—Wine. 660

1449 Paes, Antonio da Silva, Parada, Viseu.—White and red wine. 660

1450 Poiares, Antonio Jose da Silva, Contanhede, Coimbra.—Red wine. 660

1451 Pereira de Mello, Antonio Leite, Peral, Lisbon.—Wines. 660

1452 Silva, Antonio Ferreira da, Sabrosa, Villa Real.—White wine. 660

1453 Silva, Antonio da, Nogueira, Villa Real.—Red wine. 660

1454 Sequeira, Luis Clemente de, Ervedosa, Viseu.—Red wine. 660

1455 Souza, Hector de Lemos e, Sangemil, Viseu.—Wine. 660

1456 Soares, Joao Baptista Ribeiro, Lamego, Viseu.—Red and white wine. 660

1457 Sousa, Manuel Jose, Coimbra.—Red wine. 660

1458 Sousa, Julio Cesar, Paradolinho, Villa Real.—Red and white wine. 660

1459 Serodio, Jose Antonio Gonçalves, Passos, Villa Real.—Wine and brandy. 660

1461 Sandeman & Co., Oporto.—Port wine. 660

1462 Agricultural Society of Oporto, Oporto.—White and red wine. 660

1463 Portella, jr., Jose Ferreira, Anadia, Aveiro.—Red wine. 660

1464 Pinto, Antonio Peixoto, Sabrosa, Villa Real.—Wine. 660

1465 Pinto, Manuel Feireira, Cambres, Viseu.—Red wine. 660

1466 Silva, Francisco Pereira da, Carrasede d'Anciaes, Braganca.—Wine. 660

1467 Simoes, Antonio Augusto da Costa, Vaccarica, Aveiro.—White wine. 660

1468 Sarmento, Antonio Ferreira, Vinhaes, Braganca.—Wine. 660

1469 Seabra, Alexandre de, Arcos, Aveiro.—White and red wine. 660

1470 Sobral, Jose Joaquim, Soutello, Viseu.—Muscadine and white wines. 660

1471 Sousa, Jose Luis Rodrigues de, Valenca, Vianna do Castello.—Wine. 660

1472 Simoes, Joaquim Antonio, Figueira, Coimbra.—Red and white wine, brandy, vinegar. 660

1473 Salgado Domingos, Carraseda d'Anciaes, Braganca.—Red wine. 660

1474 Pinto Coelho, Carlos Z., Lisbon. —White and red wine. 660

1475 Pereira, Joaquim, Cadaval, Lisbon.—Red wine. 660

1476 Paulo Jorge, Carcavellos, Lisbon. —Red and white wine. 660

1477 Pereira, Antonio Rodrigues, Peniche, Leiria.—Wine and vinegar. 660

1478 Pinheiro, Antonio Joaquim, Pinamacor, Castello Branco.—Red wine. 660

1479 Pimenta, Jacintho Francisco, Ponte Sor, Portalegre.—Red and white wine. 660

1480 Prego, Joaquim Romao Mendes, Reguengo, Evora.—Red wine. 660

1481 Pinheiro, Joaquim Garcia, Reguengo, Evora.—Vinegar. 660

1482 Pinto, Maria Rita Ramos Borges, Folgosa, Viseu.—Red and white wine. 660

1483 Pereira, Adrianno Rodrigues, Anadia, Aveiro.—Red wine. 660

1484 Portella, Jose Ferreira, Anadia, Aveiro.—Wine. 660

1485 Serrado, Viscount of, Viseu.—Wine. 660

1486 Villafanha, Antonio de, Tondella, Viseu.—Red and white wine. 660

1488 Viseu, Henrique Nunes, Santar, Viseu.—Wine. 660

1489 Gomes, Antonio Luis, Valenca, Vianna do Castello.—Wine and brandy. 660

For classes of exhibits, indicated by numbers at end of entries, see Classification, pp. 12–14.

Animal and Vegetable Products.

1490 Guimaraes, Victorino Barbosa, Penafiel, Oporto.—Wine. 660

1491 Guisado, Joao Baptista Ribeiro, Peniche, Leiria.—Wine and vinegar. 660

1492 Galvao, Sabino Jose M. dos Anjos, Azueira, Lisbon.—Wine. 660

1493 Vasconcellos, Francisco P. Carvalho, Valle Cavez, Braga.—Wine. 660

1495 Vasconcellos, Augusto Cesar Carvalho, Valle Cavez, Braga.—Wine. 660

1496 Vasconcellos, Bento M. Pereira Pita, Monsao, Vianna do Castello.—Wine. 660

1497 Veiga, Jose da Cunha Costa, Povoa de Midoes, Coimbra.—Red wine. 660

1498 Montariol, Viscount of, S. Victor, Braga.—Wine. 660

1499 Vieira, Bernardo de Campos, Taboa, Coimbra.—Red wine. 660

1500 Teixira, Francisco Manuel, Mirandella, Braganca.—Red wine. 660

1502 Teixeira, Jose Luis, Mirandella, Braganca.—Red wine. 660

1503 Teixeira, Joao Firmino, Mirandella, Braganca.—Wine. 660

1504 Themes, Fortunato de Cerqueira, Valdigem, Viseu.—Red wine. 660

1505 Tavares, Jose da Costa Andrade, Alpedrinha, Castello Branco.—Red wine. 660

1506 Tavares, Joao da Silva, Estremos, Evora.—Corkwood. 660

1507 Tavares, Antonio Bernardo Xavier, Portalegre.—Red wine. 660

1508 Torres e Oliveira, Henriqueta Josepha Pereira, Fundao, Castello Branco.—Wine. 660

1509 Tavares, Jose Antonio, Lisbon.—White wine. 660

1510 Telles, Manuel Joaquin, Evora.—Red wine. 660

1511 Themudo, Antonio Dias, Coimbra.—Cognac and liquor. 660

1512 Trigo, Jose Antonio Horta da, Villarica, Braganca.—White wine. 660

1513 Tacho, Jose Maria da Silva, Tragosella, Viseu.—Wine. 660

1514 Teixeira, Joao B. Pacheco, Celorico de Basto, Braga.—Wine. 660

1515 Tavares, Antonio Jose, Covilha, Castello Branco.—Wine and vinegar. 660

1516 Jusarte, Jose Carlos, Parada, Viseu.—White wine. 660

1517 Royal Wine Company of Alto Douro, Oporto.—Vinegar, port wine 1815–1875. 660

1518 Lacerda, Alberto Araujo Figueiro dos, Vinhos, Leiria.—Red wine. 660

1519 Michon & Gussac, Oporto.—Brandy of grains. 660

1520 Madeira, Antonio, Goes, Coimbra.—Brandy. 660

1521 Moreira, Antonio Ignacio, Oporto.—Brandy. 660

1522 Menezes, Jose Rebello Cardoso, Timpeira, Villa Real.—Wine. 660

1523 Machado, Manuel Alves, Celorico de Basto, Braga.—Wine. 660

1524 Magalhaes, Antonio de Barros, Sattam, Viseu.—Wine. 660

1525 Marques, Jacintho, Salgueiros, Viseu.—Red and white wine, brandy. 660

1526 Magalhaes, Manuel Alexandre de, Budiosa, Viseu.—Wine. 660

1527 Machado, Domingas Alves, Celorico de Basto, Braga.—Wine. 660

1528 Moura, Luis Manuel Alves, Celorico de Basto, Braga.—Wine. 660

1529 Moscoso, Simao P. Velho, Monsao, Vianna.—Wine. 660

1530 Moura, Augusto, Celorico de Basto, Braga.—Wine. 660

1531 Moraes, Antonio Carlos, Boelhe, Oporto.—Wine. 660

1532 Moraes, Antonio Fernandes, Abelheira, Vianna do Castello.—Wine. 660

1533 Marques, Jose Parada, jr., Viseu.—Red and white wine. 660

1534 Martins, Manuel Jose, Gondomil, Vianna do Castello.—Wine. 660

1535 Meneses, Manuel Antonio, Horta da Villarica, Braganca.—Wine. 660

1536 Martins, Jose da Veiga, Carrazeda d'Anciaes, Braganza.—Red wine. 660

1537 Magalhaes, Joao da Veiga, Vinhaes, Braganca.—Wine. 660

1538 Moraes, Domingos Alves, Poca, Braganca.—Wine. 660

1539 Miranda, Antonio Bernardino, Horta da Villarica, Braganza.—White wine. 660

1540 Basto, Manuel Jose Teixeira, S. Miguel de Refojo, Braga.
a Wine. 660
b Olive oil. 662

1541 Abecassis Brothers, Lisbon.
a Port wine. 660
b Olive oil. 662

1542 Castro, Luis de Mello T. Soares d'Albegaria, S. Thiago, Coimbra.
a Brandy. 660
b Olive oil. 662

1543 Carvalho, Joao Antonio, Pedrogam, Santarem.
a White wine 660
b Olive oil. 662

1544 Carvalho, Carlos Manuel de, Pedrogam, Santarem.
a White wine. 660
b Olive oil. 662

1545 Caldeira, Joaquim de, Albuquerque, Castello Branco.
a Wines. 660
b Olive oil. 662

1546 Pereira, Eduardo Augusto, Meixamil, Oporto.
a Vinegar. 660
b Olive oil. 662

1547 Casqueiro, Jose Maria, Crato, Portalegre.
a Wine. 660
b Olive oil. 662

1548 Conde da Junqueira, Almeirim, Santarem.
a Wines. 660
b Olive oil. 662

1549 Cardoso, Manuel Gualdino, Gameiro, Torres Nevas, Santarem.
a Brandy and wines. 660
b Olive oil. 662

For classes of exhibits indicated by numbers at end of entries, see Classification, pp. 12–14.

Animal and Vegetable Products.

1550 Carvalho, Luis Xavier do Amaral, Rio de Moinho, Viseu.
a Wine. 660
b Olive oil. 662

1551 Albuquerque, Manuel Lopes, Alvito, Braga.—Wine. 660

1552 Abreu, Honorato Jose Marchado, Zibreira, Lisbon.
a Red wine. 660
b Olive oil. 662

1553 Pygnatelli, Jose da Cunha, Guarda.
a Red and white wine. 660
b Olive oil. 662

1554 Ramalho, Domingos Antonio, Falle Redondo, Evora. 660
a Red and white wine and brandy, vinegar. 660
b Olive oil. 662

1555 Abreu, Carlos de Souza Pinto, Valle de Prazeres, Castello Branco.
a Wine. 660
b Olive oil. 662

1557 Antonio Nunes de Souza & Co., Covilha, Castello Branco.
a Wine. 660
b Olive oil. 662

1558 Athayde, Luis da Silva, Leiria.
a Red and white wine and brandy. 660
b Olive oil. 662

1559 Accioli, Joao da Fonseca, Portalegre.
a Vinegar. 660
b Olive oil. 662

1560 Beltraa, Jose de Gouvea de Lucena, Anca, Coimbra.
a Red wine. 660
b Olive oil. 662

1561 Bogalho, Joao Joaquim, Villa Boim.
a Red and white wine. 660
b Olive oil. 662

1562 Durao, Pedro Manuel, Castello de Vide, Portalegre.
a Vinegar. 660
b Olive oil. 662

1563 Caldas, Manuel Duarte de Silva, Cartaxo, Santarem.
a Wine and vinegar. 660
b Olive oil. 662

1564 Carreira, Joaquim de Salles Simoes, Batalha, Leiria.
a Brandy. 660
b Olive oil. 662

1565 Faro, Joaquim de Carvalho Azevedo, Reizende, Viseu.
a Wine. 660
b Olive oil. 662

1566 Guimaraes, Jose Lopes, Coimbra.
a Red wine and brandy. 660
b Olive oil. 662

1567 Falcao, Luis da Costa, Constanca, Santarem.
a Wine. 660
b Olive oil. 662

1568 Franco, Vital Jose Pereira, Guarda.
a Red wine. 660
b Olive oil. 662

1569 Ferreira, Angusto Dias, Santarem.
a Wine. 660
b Olive oil. 662

1570 Franco, Rev., Francisco Guedes, Portalegre.
a Vinegar. 660
b Olive oil. 662

1571 Francioze, Maria do Carmo, Cartaxo, Santarem.
a Vinegar. 660
b Olive oil. 662

1572 Guerra, Joaquim Jose da, Elvas, Portalegre.
a Wine and brandy. 660
b Olive oil. 662

1573 Villarinho, Viscount of, S. Romas, Oporto.
a Muscadine and other wines. 660
b Olive oil. 662

1574 Prime, Viscount of, Viseu.
a Red and white wine. 660
b Olive oil. 662

1575 Jose Ferreira Pinto Basto, Heirs of, Santa Eulalia de Ferreira, Coimbra.
a Red wine. 660
b Olive oil. 662

1576 Joaquin Guilherme de Vasconcellos & Sons, Elvas, Portalegre.
a Vinegar. 660
b Olive oil. 662

1579 Lima, Jorge Abraham d'Almeida, Aldeia de Paio Pires, Lisbon.
a Red and white wine. 660
b Olive oil. 662

1580 Souza d'Alte, Francisco Rapozo de, Lisbon.
a Wines. 660
b Olive oil. 662

1581 Silva, Eliza Ludovina da, Covilha, Castello Branco.
a Wines. 660
b Olive oil. 662

1582 Silva, Manuel Joaquim da, Redondo, Evora.
a Red wine and vinegar. 660
b Olive oil. 662

1583 Souza, Manuel Lopes de, Guarda.
a Wines and vinegar. 660
b Olive oil. 662

1584 Viva, Barreto, Covilha, Castello Branco.
a Red and white wine. 660
b Olive oil. 662

1585 Alcacer, Viscount of Sal, Lisbon.
a Wine. 660
b Olive oil. 662

1586 Oliveira, Rafael Rodrigues de, Torres Novas, Santarem.
a Red wine. 660
b Olive oil. 661

1587 Castello de Borges, Viscount of, Lisbon.
a Wines. 660
b Olive oil. 662

1588 Vinua Jorge & Sons, Parreiras, Santarem.
a Brandy. 660
b Olive oil. 662

1589 Vidal, Antonio Jose Rodrigues, Vaccarica, Aveiro.
a Red and white wine. 660
b Olive oil. 662

1590 Prime, Viscount of, Viseu.
a Red and white wine. 660
b Olive oil. 662

1591 Caevuo, Viscount of, Gaira, Guarda.
a Wine. 660
b Olive oil. 662

For classes of exhibits, indicated by numbers at end of entries, see Classification, pp. 12–14.

Animal and Vegetable Products.

1592 Macedo, Joaquim Augusto de Thomar, Santarem.
a Wine. 660
b Olive oil. 662

1593 Esperanca, Viscount of, Jose, Evora.
a Brandy, red wine, and vinegar. 660
b Olive oil. 662

1594 S. Sebastiao, Viscount of, Leiria.
a Brandy. 660
b Olive oil. 662

1595 Mesquita, Pedro Jose de, Sinde, Coimbra.
a White wine, vinegar. 660
b Olive oil. 662

1596 Magalhaes, Francisco T., Sinde, Coimbra.
a White wine. 660
b Olive oil. 662

1597 Oliveira, Verissimo Ferreira A. de, Montalvao, Santarem.
a Red wine, vinegar. 660
b Olive oil. 662

1598 Pedrozo, Maria Jose Lopes, Lavos, Coimbra.
a Wine, brandy, and vinegar. 960
b Olive oil. 662

1599 Lopes, Joaquim Emilio, Leiria.
a Wines and brandy. 662
b Olive oil. 662

1600 Le Cocq, Joao Jose, Castello de Vide, Portalegre.
a Wine. 660
b Olive oil. 662

1601 Larcher, Marcal, Ramiro, Portalegre.
a Brandy. 660
b Olive oil. 662

1602 Levita, Jose Eduardo, Portalegre.
a Vinegar and brandy. 660
b Olive oil. 662

1603 Larcher, Maria Jose, Portalegre.
a Vinegar. 660
b Olive oil. 662

1604 Mendes, Carlos da Costa Pereira, Thomar, Santarem.
a Wine. 660
b Olive oil. 662

1605 Machado, Pedro Xavier, Portalegre.
a Wine, brandy, vinegar. 660
b Olive oil. 662

1606 Moraes, Antonio da Silva, Sardoal, Santarem.
a Wine. 660
b Olive oil. 662

1607 Quintanilha, Francisco, Cuba, Beja.
a White and red wine. 660
b Olive oil. 662

1608 Mattoso, Alfredo de Moura, S. Thiago, Coimbra.
a White wine, brandy. 660
b Olive oil. 662

1609 Rangel, Manuel de Souza, Guilhufe, Oporto.
a Wine. 660
b Olive oil. 662

1610 Rangel, Diogo, Torres Novas, Santarem.
a Alcohol and white wine. 660
b Olive oil. 662

1611 Rego, Antonio Profirio Gomes do, Covilha, Castello Branco.
a Wines. 660
b Olive oil. 662

1612 Reis, Antonio Nunes dos, Turcifal, Lisbon.
a Wines. 660
b Olive oil. 662

1613 Relvas, Carlos, Gollega, Santarem.
a Wine. 660
b Olive oil. 662

1614 Ramos, Antonio Maria Taborda, Castello Branco.
a Red wine. 660
b Olive oil. 662

1615 Rodrigues, Joao Antonio, Grandola, Lisbon.
a Wine. 660
b Olive oil. 662

1616 Silva, Francisco Candido da, Torres Novas, Santarem.
a Wine and brandy. 660
b Olive oil. 662

1617 Souza, Pedro Augusto Pereira e Abreu, Santa Marinha, Villa Real.
a Wine. 660
b Olive oil. 662

1618 Sa, Jose Filippe de, Azoia de Baixo, Santarem.
a Wine. 660
b Olive oil. 662

1619 Seixas, Jose Maria Ayres de, Gaviao, Portalegre.
a Wine. 660
b Olive oil. 662

1620 Caires, Manuel A. de Mello Pereira, Penalva do Castello, Viseu.
a Red wine. 660
b Olive oil. 662

1621 Condessa d'Anadia, Santa Clara, Coimbra.
a White and red wine, and vinegar. 660
b Olive oil. 662

1622 Castello Branco, Amelia Pinto de Tavares, Valle de Prareres, Castello Branco.
a White wine. 660
b Olive oil. 662

1623 Castello Branco, Ignacio Cardoso de B. Caldeira, Portalegre.
a Red wine. 660
b Olive oil. 662

1624 Carrilho Bello, Antonio Marcellino, Castello de Vide, Portalegre.
a Red and white wine, and vinegar. 66c
b Olive oil. 662

1625 Castello Branco, Amelia Pinto de Tavares, Valle de Prazeres, Castello Branco.
a White wine. 660
b Olive oil. 662

1626 Barao do Salgueiro, Leiria.
a White and red wine. 660
b Olive oil. 662

1627 Britto, Joao de, Lisbon.
a Red and white wine, vinegar. 660
b Biscuits. 661
c Corn flour. 667

1628 Barao de Mogadouro, Freixeas, Guarda.
a Red and white wine. 660
b Olive oil. 662

For classes of exhibits, indicated by numbers at end of entries, see Classification, pp. 12–14.

Animal and Vegetable Products.

1629 Castro, Miguel Ozorio Cabral de, Santa Clara, Coimbra.
a Red and white wine. 660
b Olive oil. 662

1630 Costeira, Manuel Fernandes, Lamego, Viseu.
a Red wine. 660
b Olive oil. 662

1631 Costa, Lourenco Justiniano da Fonseca, Oliveira do Hospital, Coimbra.
a Wine. 660
b Olive oil. 662

1632 Morao, Maria Emilia d'Almeida, Penamacor, Castello Branco.
a White wine. 660
b Olive oil. 662

1633 Albino Jose de Freitas Almeida & Co., Ega, Coimbra.
a Wines. 660
b Olive oil. 662

1634 Asambuja, Antonio Maria da, Means, Coimbra.
a White wine. 660
b Olive oil. 662

1635 Pontes, Francisco Ferraz Tavares de, Mirando de Corvo, Coimbra.
a Red wine. 660
b Olive oil. 662

1636 Pinto, Antonio Rodrigues, Coimbra.
a Wine and vinegar. 660
b Olive oil. 662

1637 Pinto, Augusto Leal de Gouvea, Miranda do Corvo, Coimbra.
a Red and white wine. 660
b Olive oil. 662

1638 Pereira, Antonio Ignacio, Redondo, Evora.
a Brandy, red wine, vinegar. 660
b Olive oil. 662

1639 Accioli, Joao da Fonseca, Portalegre.
a Vinegar. 660
b Olive oil. 662

1640 Melleiro, Francisco Carmello, Lisbon.—Macaroni. 661

1641 Pinto, Jose Clemente, Sta. Cruz, Coimbra.—Macaroni. 661

1642 Cruz, Jose Francisco da, Coimbra. —Biscuits. 661

1643 Costa, Eduardo Antonio da, Lisbon.—Biscuits. 661

1644 Silva, Eduardo da Conceicao e, Lisbon.—Biscuits. 661

1645 Schurmann, Lisbon.—Biscuits. 661

1646 Silva, Estavao Ribeiro da, Lisbon. —Bread. 661

1647 Aurajo, Antonio Correa de, Coimbra.—Biscuits. 661

1648 Administrator of the Conselho of Guimaraes, Guimaraes, Braga.—Olive oil. 662

1649 Papanca, Manuel Augusto Mendes, Reguengos, Evora.—Olive oil. 662

1650 Pina, Manuel Maria de, Portalegre. —Olive oil. 662

1651 Pereira, Jose Ignacio, Elvas, Portalegre.—Olive oil. 662

1652 Proenca, Francisco Tavares d'Almeida, Castello Branco.—Olive oil. 662

1653 Possidonio, Antonio, Montalvao, Portalegre.—Olive oil. 662

1654 Sobral, Bernardo Moreira Coelho, Parada, Visen.—Olive oil. 662

1655 Almeida, Silva, & Co., Lisbon.— —Olive oil. 662

1656 Almeida, Antonio Joaquim de, Villa Nova de Ourem, Santarem.—Olive oil. 662

1657 Abreu, Francisco Rodrigues de, Abrantes, Santarem.—Olive oil. 662

1659 Almeida, Manuel d', Gafanhao, Visen.—Olive oil. 662

1660 Abreu, Joao Lopes Coelho de, Barcouco, Aveiro.—Olive oil. 662

1661 Almeida, Antonio Ribeiro da Costa e, Sta. Leocadia de Baio, Oporto.—Olive oil. 662

1662 Aragao, Alexandre de, Villa Flor, Braganca.—Olive oil. 662

1663 Sachetti, Cazimiro Barreto, N. S. da Gloria, Aveiro.—Olive oil. 662

1664 Seabra, Alexandre, Arcos, Aveiro.—Olive oil. 662

1665 Santos, Josepha Maria dos, Balasza, Povoa de Varzim.—Olive oil. 662

1666 Silva, Manuel Ribeiro da, Ferreirim, Visen.—Olive oil. 662

1667 Silveira, Manuel Jose da, Arganil, Coimbra.—Olive oil. 662

1668 Brito, Joao Fernandes Soares de, Nisa, Portalegre.—Olive oil. 662

1669 Barros, Luis Xavier de, Portalegre.—Olive oil. 662

1670 Barros Gomes, B., Lisbon.— Olive oil. 662

1671 Castro, Joaquim Jose Paditha de, Abrantes, Santarem.—Olive oil. 662

1672 Costa, Antonio da, Elvas, Portalegre.—Olive oil. 662

1673 Conceiro, Joaquim Rodrigues, Elvas, Portalegre.—Olive oil. 662

1674 Cosoliero, Manuel Goncalves, Valle da Serra, Santarem.—Olive oil. 662

1675 Corinho, Jose Maria, Montargil, Portalegra.—Olive oil. 662

1676 Coelho, Manuel Diogo, Castello de Vide, Portalegra.—Olive oil. 662

1677 Callado jr., Joao da Costa, Alter do Chao, Portalegre.—Olive oil. 662

1678 Cunha Ozorio, Joaquim Felizardo da, Arronches, Portalegre.—Olive oil. 662

1679 Conde, Domingos Lopes, Montalvao, Portalegre.—Olive oil. 662

1680 Peixoto, Jose Nunes de Souza, Penafiel, Oporto.—Olive oil. 662

1681 Continho, Joao da Fonseca, Portalegre.—Olive oil. 662

1682 Chicorro, Antonio Maria, Portalegre.—Olive oil. 662

1683 Carvalho, Antonio Jose de, Elvas, Portalegre.—Olive oil. 662

1684 Correa, Joaquim, Penacova, Coimbra.—Olive oil. 662

1685 Carvalho, Simao Pinto de Mesquita, Sta. Leocadia, Oporto.—Olive oil. 662

1686 Carvalho, Joao Baptista, Valle Passos, Villa Real.—Olive oil. 662

1687 Cardoso, Francisco Antonio Lopes, Monvorio, Braganca.—Olive oil. 662

For classes of exhibits, indicated by numbers at end of entries, see Classification, pp. 12–14.

Animal and Vegetable Products.

1688 Conde da Graciosa, Arcos, Aveiro. —Olive oil. 662

1689 Costa, Lucio Jose da, Salzedas, Visen.—Olive oil. 662

1690 Continho, Fernando Affonso d'Almeida, Sepins, Coimbra.—Olive oil. 662

1691 Souza, Jose d'Andrade e, Portalegre.—Olive oil. 662

1692 Souza, Jose Saldanha Oliveira e. —Olive oil. 662

1693 Santa Clara, Francisco de Paula, Elvas, Portalegre.—Olive oil. 662

1694 Salazar, Manuel Maia, Torres Novas, Santarem.—Olive oil. 662

1695 Reis, Antonio dos, Lisbon.—Olive oil. 662

1696 Rijo, Joaquim Antonio, Elvas, Portalegre.—Olive oil. 662

1697 Ramires, Manuel Peres, Evora.—Olive oil. 662

1698 Regallo, Antonio Meira, Portalegre.—Olive oil. 662

1699 Ratto, Antonio Gonsalves, Barquinha, Santarem.—Olive oil. 662

1700 Ramos, Manuel Nogueira, Goes, Coimbra.—Olive oil. 662

1701 Rodrigues, Manuel Antonio, Ferradosa, Braganca.—Olive oil. 662

1702 Rocha, Serafim de Sousa, Canellas, Oporto.—Olive oil. 662

1703 Rocha, Antonio Coelho da, Gondomar, Oporto.—Olive oil. 662

1704 Mendonca, Joao Themudo de Oliveira, Abrantes, Santarem.—Olive oil. 662

1705 Mendes, Joas Jose Soares, Abrantes, Santarem.—Olive oil. 662

1706 Barao de Casaes do Douro, Casaes do Douro, Visen.—Olive oil. 662

1707 Lemos, Joao Gonsalves de, Souza, Coimbra.—Olive oil. 662

1708 Leite, Joao Baptista de Araujo, Mirandella, Braganca.—Olive oil. 662

1709 Monteiro, Francisco Vaz, Ponte Sor, Portalegre.—Olive oil. 662

1710 Vasconcellos, Francisco Maria de, Sabugal, Guarda.—Olive oil. 662

1711 Vieira, Agostinho Jose, Sto. Ovidio, Porto.—Olive oil. 662

1712 Vassea & Coelho, Oporto.—Olive oil. 662

1713 Vasconcellos, Manuel S. Quaresma, Condeixa, Coimbra.—Olive oil. 662

1714 Veiga, Francisco Antonio, Goes, Coimbra.—Olive oil. 662

1715 Vasconcellos, Joaquim Guilherme de, Elvas, Portalegre.—Olive oil. 662

1716 Varella jr., Jose Gomes, Serpa, Beja.—Olive oil. 662

1717 Oliveira Manuel Joaquim de Sendin, Miranda do Douro.—Olive oil. 662

1718 Oliveira, Jose Duarte, Murca, Villa Real.—Olive oil. 662

1719 Valdez, Antonio de Campos, Alcacer do Sal, Lisbon.—Olive oil. 662

1720 Serpa, Francisco Lopes, Portalegre.—Olive oil. 662

1721 Moran, Jose Antonio Martins, Vianna do Alemtejo.—Olive oil. 662

1722 Osorio, Manuel de Azevedo Ferrao, Monforte, Castello Branco.—Olive oil. 662

1723 Leitao, Joas Paes d'Almeida, Sattam, Visen.—Olive oil, 662

1724 Leite, Jeronymo Augusto Pereira, Cavez, Braga.—Olive oil. 662

1725 Loio, Gaspar, da Silva, Armamar, Viseu.—Olive oil. 662

1726 Lobo, Jose Maria, Guarda.—Olive oil. 662

1727 Neves, Filho, Adelino St. Antonio dos Olivaes, Coimbra.—Olive oil. 662

1728 Negrao, Manuel Nicolau Osorio, Ansede, Oporto.—Olive oil. 662

1729 Pinto, Antonio Thomas da Costa, Bibalonga, Braganca.—Olive oil. 662

1730 Pereira, Jose Sebastiao Martins, S. Thiago, Coimbra.—Olive oil. 662

1731 Lima Meyer & Sons, Lisbon.—Olive oil. 662

1732 Mendes, Raymundo Jose Soares, Abrantes, Santarem.—Olive oil. 662

1733 Mourato, Mathias, Alpalao, Portalegre.—Olive oil. 662

1734 Kempe, Guilherme, Lisbon.—Olive oil. 662

1735 Mendes, Casemiro Esteves, Aviz, Portalegre.—Olive oil. 662

1736 Mocinha, Manuel Jeronymo, Campo Maior, Portalegre.—Olive oil. 662

1737 Moraes, Jose Barzilio, Arronches, Portalegre.—Olive oil. 662

1738 Lima, Andre Avelino de, Cano, Portalegre.—Olive oil. 662

1738*a* Abrantes, Viscount da A., Santarem.—Olive oil. 662

1738*b* Chicorro, Andre G., Monforte, Portalegre.—Olive oil. 662

1739 Lobo, Thomaz Antonio de Araujo, Oporto.—Olive oil. 662

1740 Souza, Jose Antonio Nunes de, Covilha, Castello Branco.—Olive oil. 662

1741 Senna Bello, Manuel Thomar de, Guarda.—Olive oil. 662

1742 Silva, Jose Nunes, Elvas, Portalegre.—Olive oil. 662

1743 Mello, Higino O. de, Queroza, Santarem.—Olive oil. 662

1744 Asevedo, Marianno de Lemos, Villa Nova de Ourem, Santarem.—Olive oil. 662

1745 Araujo, Antonio Joaquim de, Thomar, Santarem.—Olive oil. 662

1746 Almeida, Antonio Mendes, Alcacer do Sal, Lisbon.—Olive oil. 662

1747 Almeida, Sebastiao Saldanha de, Portalegre.—Olive oil. 662

1748 Bentes, Ignacio Jose, Serpa, Beja. —Olive oil. 662

1749 Cardozo, Antonio Augusto Correa da Silva, Cellorico, Guarda.—Olive oil. 662

1750 Castello Branco, Joao da Silva Ferrao de, Villa Franca, Lisbon.—Olive oil. 662

1751 Domingues, Victorino Jose, Faro. —Olive oil. 662

1752 Duarte, Egydio Jose, Castello de Vide, Portalegre.—Olive oil. 662

For classes of exhibits, indicated by numbers at end of entries, see Classification, pp. 12–14.

Animal and Vegetable Products, Textile Substances.

1753 Freire, Jose Luis Ferreira, Lagos, Coimbra.—Olive oil. 662

1754 Fernandes, Justiniano Jose, Mirandella, Braganca.—Olive oil. 662

1755 Figueiredo, Joao Ferreira de, Villa Flor, Braganca.—Olive oil. 662

1756 Ferrenda, Ildefonso Numes, Valdigem, Viseu.—Olive oil. 662

1757 Freixedas, Eduardo, Castello de Vide, Portalegre.—Olive oil. 662

1758 Guimaraes, Manuel Antonio da Costa, Mirandella, Braganca.—Olive oil. 662

1759 Guerra, Thomas Ignacio de Meirelles, Moncorvo, Braganca.—Olive oil. 660

1760 Gomes, Joao Manuel, Portalegre. —Olive oil. 662

1762 Gama, Jose Augusto Sanches, Coimbra.—Olive oil. 662

1763 Gama, Joao Cardoso Lemos da, Casa Branca, Portalegre.—Olive oil. 662

1764 Grillo, Manuel Francisco, Ribeira de Nisa, Portalegre.—Olive oil. 662

1766 Blanco, Andre Faustino Peres, Aldeia Nova, Beja.—Olive oil. 662

1767 Campos, Antonio d'Aranjo Juzarte de, Portalegre.—Olive oil. 662

1768 Avilez, Count of, Portalegre.—Olive oil. 662

1769 Carvalho, Joao Augusto, Portalegre.—Olive oil. 662

1770 Carvalho, Euzebio Nobre de, Lisbon.—Olive oil. 662

1771 Costa, Manuel Joaquim, Portalegre.—Olive oil. 662

1772 Calheiros, Luis d'Oliveira, Lisbon.—Olive oil. 662

1773 Carvalho, Joao Antonio de, Porto de Moz, Leiria.—Olive oil. 662

1774 Castro, Antonio Maria Queiroz de Mello e, Frozoeira, Ferreira do Zezere, Santarem.—Olive oil. 662

1775 Figueiredo, Jose Paulo Teixeira de, Matheus, Villa Real.—Olive oil. 662

1776 Fernandes, Joaquin Pinto, Campello, Oporto.—Olive oil. 662

1777 Falcao, Maximo, Azinhaga, Santarem.—Olive oil. 662

1778 Fernandes, Joaquim, Mogao, Santarem.—Olive oil. 662

1779 Ferreira, Jose Maria, Chamusca, Santarem.—Olive oil. 662

1780 Ferreira, Joaquim da Motta, Rio Maior, Santarem.—Olive oil. 662

1781 Figueira, Manuel Duarte, Castello Branco.—Olive oil. 662

1782 Ferreira, Joaquim Jose, Elvas, Portalegre.—Olive oil. 662

1783 Falcao, Joao Carlos da Costa, Fundao, Alcaide, Castello Branco.—Olive oil. 662

1785 Escobar, Hermenegildo, Portalegre.—Olive oil. 662

1786 Inchado, Jose Antonio Dias, Moura, Portalegre.—Olive oil. 662

1788 Deus, Joao Rodrigues de, & Co., Torres Novas, Santarem.—Olive oil. 662

1789 Vieira, Agostinho Jose, Sto. Ovidio, Oporto.—Olive oil. 662

1791 Teixeira, Carlos Augusto, Grandola, Lisbon.—Olive oil. 662

1792 Tavares, Antonio Jose, Covilha, Castello Branco.—Olive oil. 662

1793 Tierno, Simeon, Elvas, Portalegre. —Olive oil. 662

1794 Teixeira, Manuel Maria, Mirandella, Braganca.—Olive oil. 662

1795 Xavier, Manuel Camillo, Benavente, Santarem.—Olive oil. 662

1796 Yuquete, Jose de Oliveira, Leiria. —Olive oil. 662

1797 Leal, A. Goncalves da Matta, Castanheira.—Olive oil. 662

1798 Mello, Joaquim Jose de, Pampilhosa, Aveiro.—Olive oil. 662

Textile Substances of Vegetable or Animal Origin.

1799 Sarmento, Antonio Ferreira, Vinhaes, Braganca.—Flax. 666

1800 Silva, Domingos d'Almeida e, S. Mamede, Oporto.—National flax. 666

1801 Sencadas, Manuel Gomes Moreira, Amorim, Oporto.—Flax. 666

1802 Louza, Augusto Pereira d'Abreu, Sta. Marinha, Villa Real.—Flax. 666

1803 Pygnatelli, Jose da Cunha, Guarda.—Flax. 666

1804 Cavadas, Jose da Silva, S. Mamede, Oporto.—Flax. 666

1805 Mattos, Rita de, Ponta Delgada. —Linen in various stages of preparation. 666

1806 Castello, Antonio de Gouvea Rebello, Sernache, Viseu.—Flax. 666

1807 Souto, Antonio Duarte da Cunho, Freixinho, Visen.—Flax. 666

1809 Rodrigues, Joaquim, Oporto.—Combed flax. 666

1810 Queiroz, Joaquim Carneiro Leao, Meixomil, Oporto.—Flax. 666

1811 Queiroz, Jose de Sequeira Pinto, S. Sebastiao do Duque, Vianna do Castello.—Flax. 666

1814 Almeida, Joaquim Ribeiro, Campanha, Oporto.—Flax. 666

1815 Albergaria, Thomas Antonio Pinto Soares, Villa Cha, Aveiro.—Flax. 666

1816 Administrator of the Counsello of Alentem, Alentem, Oporto.—Flax. 666

1817 Almeida, Manuel d', Gafanhao. Viseu.—Flax. 666

1818 Coelho, Jose Justino, Villa do Tamega, Villa Real.—Flax. 666

1819 Carvalho, Joaquim Augusto da Silveira, Penafiel, Porto.—Flax. 666

1820 Costa, Manuel Jorge da, Valongo, Oporto.—Flax. 666

1821 Cadaval, Francisco de Sousa, Villa Nova da Cevreria, Vianna do Castello.—Flax. 666

1822 Moraes, Antonio da Silva, Sardoal, Santarem.—Flax. 666

1823 Matta, Anacleto da Fonseca, Sardoal, Santarem.—Hemp. 666

1824 Silva, Jose Diogo da, Lisbon.—Wool. 666

For classes of exhibits, indicated by numbers at end of entries, see Classification, pp. 12–14.

Textile Substances.

1826 Saraiva, Francisco Martins, Belmonte, Castello Branco.
a Flax. 666
b Wool. 667

1827 Basto, Manuel Jose Teixeira, S. Miguel de Refoyos, Braga.—Flax. 666

1828 Pimentel, Jose Reis, Castello de Vide, Portalegre.—Flax. 666

1829 Freitas, Jose Monteiro de, Campello, Oporto.—Flax. 666

1830 Ferreira, Joao Dias, Vallongo, Oporto.—Flax. 666

1831 Frausto, Leandro Pinto, Marvao, Portalegre.—Flax. 666

1832 Franco, Joao, Povoa de Meadas, Portalegre.—Flax. 666

1833 Guerra, Thomas Ignacio de Meirelles, Moncorvo, Braganca.—Flax. 666

1834 Gama, Manuel Telles da, Lisbon. —Wines. 660

1835 Gomes, Antonio Luis, Valenca, Vianna do Castello.—Flax. 666

1836 Guerreiro, Antonio Manuel, Villa Nova da Cerveira, Vianna do Castello.—Flax. 666

1837 Vieira, Pedro Martins, Cabeceiras de Bastro, Braga.—Flax. 666

1838 Torres, Antonio Alves, Arcos, Oporto.—Flax. 666

1839 Moreira, Joao Baptista, Rates, Oporto.—Flax. 666

1840 Machado, Manuel Barcellos, Viseu.—Flax. 666

1841 Soveral, Victorino da Costa, Mondim de Basto.—Flax. 666

1842 Leite, Luis Maria Felgueiras, Mogadouro, Braganca.—Hemp. 666

1843 Leal, Manuel da Cunha, Sobreira, Oporto.—Flax. 666

1844 Nogueira, Francisco Bento, Paredes de Coura, Vianna do Castello.—Flax. 666

1845 Pedroza, Maria Jose Lopes, Lavos, Coimbra.—Flax. 666

1846 Mattos, Rosa de, Island of St. Michaels, Ponta Delgada.—Flax, hemp, and hemp-thread. 666

1847 Mesquita, Pedro Jose de, Sinde, Coimbra.—Flax. 666

1848 Leite, Antonio Bernardo d'Oliveira, Cabeceiras de Basto, Braga.—Flax. 666

1849 Mendes, Luis Antonio Soares, Castello Branco.—Flax. 666

1850 Fernandes, Manuel Ignacio, Telloes, Villa Real.
a Flax. 666
b Wool. 667

1851 Montenegro, Joao Joaquim Pereira Telles de Menezes Mozellos, Vianna do Castello.
a Flax. 666
b Wool. 667

1852 Rapozo, Luis, Miranda do Douro, Braganca.
a Flax. 666
b Wool. 667

1853 Magalhaes, Francisco T., Sinde, Coimbra.
a Flax. 666
b Wool. 667

1854 Silva, Antonio Lopes da, Balasar, Oporto.
a Flax. 666
b Wool. 667

1855 Santos, Ascencio Jose dos, Valenca, Vianna do Castello.
a Flax. 666
c Wool. 667

1855*a* Rosa, Jose da Graca Pereira. Niza, Portalegre.—Wool. 667

1856 Sarmento, Manuel Gomes de, St. Estevao, Villa Real.—Wool. 667

1856*a* Souza, Manuel Lopes de, Guarda.—Wool. 667

1857 Piteira Fernandez, Joaquim Filippe, Reguengo, Evora.—Wool. 667

1857*a* Sardinha, Joao Maria da Silva, Monforte, Portalegre.—Wool. 667

1858 Pinto, Antonio Mascarade, Villa Boim, Portalegre.—Wool. 667

1858*a* Silva, Jose Diogo da, Lisbon.—Wool. 667

1859 Pimenta, Isidoro E. O. C. Margues, Villa Boim, Portalegre.—Wool. 667

1860 Pereira, Jose Francisco, Castello de Vide, Portalegre.—Wool in the fleece. 667

1861 Pereira, Jeronymo, Serpa, Beja.—Wool. 667

1862 Pimentel, Jose Reis, Povoa de Meadas, Portalegre.—Wool. 667

1863 Continho, Fernando Affonso d'Almeida, Sepins, Coimbra.—Wool. 666

1864 Pimentel, Antonio Augusto de Moraes, Castello Branco, Braganca.—Wool. 667

1865 Couraca, Jose de Gouvea, Faia, Viseu.—Wool. 667

1866 Rio, Antonio Manuel, Miranda do Douro, Braganca.—Wool. 665

1867 Montoya, Diogo Lopes, Castello Branco.—Wool. 667

1868 Murteira, Manuel Maria, Campo Maior, Portalegre.—Wool. 667

1869 Lacerda, Antonio Augusto de, Chorindo, Visen.—Wool. 667

1870 Costa, Lourenco Justiniano da Fonseca, Oliveira do Hospital, Coimbra. —Wool. 667

1871 Calca e Pina, Antonio, Souzel, Portalegre.—Wool, 667

1872 Lecocq, Joao Jose, Castello de Vide, Portalegre.—Wool. 667

1873 Pera, Francisco Marcos, Miranda do Douro, Braganca.—Wool. 667

1874 Pascual, Eduardo Augusto, Meixomil, Oporto.—Wool. 667

1875 Lemos, Francisco Antonio Pereira, Villarellos, Braganca.—Wool. 667

1876 Marcal & Bro., Portalegre.—Wool unwashed and washed. 667

1877 Oliveira Soares, M. E. de, Evora. —Wool. 667

1878 Villar, Manuel Pereira, Torroso, Oporto.—Wool. 667

1879 Carneiro, Jose Antonio, Santa Eulalia, Portalegre.—Wool. 667

1880 Casqueiro, Jose Maria, Crato, Portalegre.—Wool. 667

For classes of exhibits, indicated by numbers at end of entries, see Classification, pp. 12–14.

Textile Substances, Engineering and Administration.

1881 **Oliveira, Domingos Manuel,** Miranda do Douro, Braganca.—Wool. 667

1882 **Vasconcellos, Bartholomeu** d'Aragao Costa Tavares de, Fundao, Castello Branco.—Wool. 667

1883 **Miranda, Antonio Augusto Lobo** de, Lagos, Faro.—Wool. 667

1884 **Bogalho, Joao Joaquim, Villa,** Boim.—Wool. 667

1885 **Bello, Francisco Severianno Car**ilho, Castello de Vide, Portalegre.—Wool in the fleece. 667

1886 **Coelho, Luis Pires, Sardoal,** Santarem.—Wool. 667

1887 **Guimaraes, Victorino Barbosa,** Penafiel, Oporto.—Wool. 667

1888 **Migueis, Joao, Ilhavo.**—Wool. 667

1889 **Castel.Branco, Francisco Barreto** Caldeira, Portalegre.—Wool. 667

1890 **Falcao, Lazaro Domingos, Povoa,** Braganca.—Wool. 667

1891 **Geraldes, Manuel Vaz Preto,** Louza, Castello Branco.—Wool. 667

1892 **Veiga, Jose d'Almeida, Anciaes,** Braganca.—Wool. 667

1894 **Costa, Joao Carlos, Elvas, Porta**legre.—Wool. 667

1895 **Cid, Jose Ignacio, Mirandella,** Braganca.—Wool. 667

1896 **Central Commission of the District** of Viseu, Viseu.
a Wool. 667
b Silk balls. 668

1897 **Nunes, Antonio Manuel, Chacim,** Braganca.—Raw silk. 668

1898 **Franqueira, Romao, Carrazede,** Braganca.—Cocoons. 668

1899 **Cabral, Paco F., & Sons, Sernan**cethe, Visen.—Cocoons and raw silk. 668

1900 **Silk Manufacturing Company,** Egyptaniense, Oporto.—Silk balls. 668

Agricultural Engineering and Administration.

1901 **Rocha & Co., Lisbon.**—Artificial guano. 681

1902 **Abattoir of Lisbon, Alcantara,** Lisbon.—Artificial manures. 681

1904 **Phosphorite Company, Mar**vensi, Lisbon.—Phosphate of lime. 681

1905 **Board of Public Forests, Lisbon.** —Garden tools. 700

For classes of exhibits, indicated by numbers at end of entries, see Classification, pp. 12–14.

TURKEY.

(NOTE.—*The Agricultural Exhibit of Turkey is installed in the Main Building, and catalogued in that volume.*)

RUSSIA.

(West of West Aisle, Columns 12 to 15.)

Arboriculture, Pomology, Agricultural Products.

Arboriculture and Forest Products.

1 Sidoroff, Michael, St. Petersburg.—Larch wood, larch and cedar strobils. 6:o

2 Verekha, Peter, St. Petersburg.
a Wild-growing trees; collection of sections. 6)o
b Statistical map of forests (Russia in Europe). 606

3 Ostrom Bros., Uleaborg, Finland.—Willow bark, tanning material. 602

4 Matteissen, Nicolas, Moscow.—Gall-nuts. 602

5 Wagner, Charles, Riga.—**Fir and** pine tree seeds. 605

6 Russian Society of Forestry, St. Petersburg.—Seeds of forest-growing trees. 605

Pomology.

8 Imperial Russian Horticultural Society, St. Petersburg.—Reproduction of apples growing on the island of Walaam, on the Ladogalake. 610

Agricultural Products.

9 Egert, John von Henziany, Government of Warsaw, District of Radimmin.—Oats, barley, in grain and sheaves. 620

10 Dengink, Henrietta, Kishineff, Bessarabia.—American maize. 620

11 Bessarabian Horticultural School, Kishineff.
a Bessarabian wheat, maize, and Indian millet. 620
b Linseed and sunflower seed. 624

12 Bell, David, Alexandrovska Farm, near St. Petersburg.—Wheat, rye, barley, oats, and timothy grass-seed. 620

13 Novossiltseff, John, Voin, Government of Orel.—Rye, barley, oats, red clover, rape, and tares. 620

14 Firsoff, George, Michalafskoe, Government of Voronesh, District of Ostrogoisk.—Wheat and oats. 620

15 Penzin, John, Samara.—Wheat. 620

16 Plighin, Philip, Volks, Government of Saratoff.—Wheat. 620

17 Shatiloff, Joseph, Mokhovoe, Government of Toola, District of Novossil.—Wheat, rye, barley, and oats in grains and sheaves. 620

18 Stichinsky, Simon, Gololobovo, near Voronesh.—Wheat and oats. 620

19 Vassiltchikoff, Prince Victor, Troobetchino, Government of Tambow, District of Lebedian.—Wheat, rye, and oats. 620

20 Warschafsky, A., St. Petersburg.—Wheat, rye, and oats. 620

21 Wickberg, Charles, Sederkylla, Finland, Government of Nyland.—Wheat, rye, barley, and timothy grass-seed. 620

22 Grotenfeld, Nicolas, Finland, St. Michael.—Buckwheat. 620

23 Ermoloff, Alexis, Archangelskoe, near Voronesh.
a Wheat, oats, peas. 620
b Timothy and French grass-seeds 624

24 Institute of Agriculture & Forestry, New Alexandria, Government of Lublin, District of Alexandrovsk.—Wheat. 620

25 Fastrzembsky, Stanislas, Yurkou and Dembiany, Government of Kielce, District of Pintihow.—Wheat, rye, peas, millet, barley, and oats. 620

26 Kazan Model Farm.—Wheat, rye, oats, timothy grass, clover, tares, and cornspurry seed. 620

27 Karamysheff, Nicolas, Polossy, Government of Pskoff, District of Porkhoff.—Wheat, rye, and oats. 620

28 Korf, Baron Michael, Selzo, near St. Petersburg.—Wheat, rye, barley, and oats. 620

29 Krapotkine, Prince Demetrius, Kabylino, Government of Riazan, District of Riaisk.
a Samples of wheat and buckwheat. 620
b Peas. 621

30 Labenski, W., Okence, Government and District of Warsaw.—Wheat and rye. 620

31 Levchine, Theodore, St. Petersburg.—Wheat. 620

32 Maltzoff, Michael, Nikolaevsk, Government of Samara, Belotoorka.—Wheat. 620

33 Mariynska Model Farm, near Saratoff.—Samples of cereals. 620

34 Gorki Model Farm, Government of Moghileff.—Wheat and rye in grain and sheaves. 620

35 Petrovski Rural Academy Model Farm, near Moscow.—Wheat, rye, barley, and oats. 620

36 Mookhin, John, Moscow.—Red clover, timothy grass, white and black tares. 620

37 Nostitz, Count John, Government of Ekaterinoslaw, District of Novo, Moskovsk.—Red wheat and barley. 620

38 Obratnoff, Paul, Uralsk.—Summer wheat. 620

39 Odessa Exchange Committee, Odessa.—Wheat, rye, barley, maize, and millet. 620

40 Ookhin Brothers, Pokrovskoe, Government of Samara, District of Novo, Ovzen.—Wheat. 620

For classes of exhibits, indicated by numbers at end of entries, see Classification, pp. 12–14.

Agricultural, Animal, and Vegetable Products, Fish Culture.

41 **Petrovski, Michael, Stadly, Government** of Radom, District of Sandomir. —Wheat. 620

42 **Pleshanoff, John, Samara.—Wheat.** 620

43 **Zablotskf-Dessetoysky, Paul, Krymki**, Government of Kieff, District of Tchigirin.
a Red wheat. 620
b Leaf tobacco. 623
c Comline and beet seed. 624

44 **Zakrzevsky, Felix, Staro, Government** of Warsaw, District of Gostynin.—Wheat in grain and sheaves. 620

45 **Odessa Exchange Committee.—Peas** and French beans. 621

46 **Mariynska Model Farm, near Saratoff.**—Common and French beans. 621

47 **Levchine, Theodore, St. Petersburg.**
a Peas. 621
b Rape seed. 624

49 **Deugink, Henrietta, Kishineff, Bessarabia.**—Pearl lentils. 621

50 **Bessarabian Agricultural School,** Kishineff.—Sweet French beans, white and red. 621

51 **Dooroontcha, Sadook, Krementchoog**, Government of Poltarvo.—Tobacco and cigarettes. 623

52 **Doonaieff, Nicephore, Moscow.**—Tobacco and cigarettes. 623

53 **Asmoloff & Co., Basil, Rostaff on the** Don.—Tobacco and cigarettes. 623

54 **Abramoff, Moscow.—Tobacco and** cigarettes. 623

55 **Dooroontcha, Moshe, Paltawa.**—Tobacco and cigarettes. 623

56 **Kooshnareff, James, Rostaff on the** Don.—Tobacco and cigarettes. 623

57 **Kraft Brothers, Alexander & Oswald**, St. Petersburg.—Tobacco, cigars, and cigarettes. 623

58 **Laferme, St. Petersburg.—Tobacco** and cigarettes. 623

60 **Rymarenko, Martha, Moscow.**—Leaf tobacco. 623

61 **Petroff Bros., St. Petersburg.—Leaf** tobacco. 623

62 **Philitis, Stephen, Moscow.—Tobacco** and cigarettes. 623

63 **Mylnikoff & Zazoobrin, Irkootsk.**—Tobacco and cigars. 623

64 **Matteisson, Nicolas, Moscow.—Bell** pepper. 623

65 **Weiss, C.A., Riga.—Roasted chicory-**root. 623

66 **Pykhoff Brothers, Rostaff, Govern**ment of Faroslow.—Chicory-root roasted. 623

67 **Meyer, L., St. Petersburg.—Fig-**coffee, and chocolate. 623

68 **Hofmark, Bruno, St. Petersburg.**—Chicory-root, roasted and ground. 623

69 **Harman, G. W., Rija.—Chicory-root** raw and roasted. 623

70 **Maximoff, Basil, Zagorie, Govern**ment of Kostroma, District of Nevekhta. —Bohemian hops. 623

71 **Kharkoff Model Farm.—Bohemian** hops. 623

73 **Tzytzoorin, Theodore, St. Petersburg.**—Leaf tobacco. 623

74 **Sokoloff, John, St. Petersburg.**—Tobacco, cigars, and cigarettes. 623

75 **Saatchi & Mangoobi, St. Petersburg.** —Tobacco and cigarettes. 623

77 **Zapevaloff, Alexander, St. Petersburg.**—Kitchen-garden plants and seeds. 624

78 **Waag & Sons, Doobovka, Govern**ment of Saratoff.—Mustard-seed. 624

79 **Vassiltchikoff, Prince Victor, Troo**betchino, Government of Tamboff, District of Lebedian.—Beet and timothy grass-seeds. 624

80 **Ritter, Leopold, Moscow.—Collec**tion of kitchen-garden plants seeds. 624

81 **Repnin, Prince, Nicolas, Fagotin,** Government of Poltawo, District of Piriatin.—Linseed. 624

82 **Pleshanoff, John, Samara.—Linseed.** 624

83 **Abratnoff, Paul, Uralsk.—Linseed.** 624

84 **Müller, Christian, Doobovka, Gov**ernment of Saratoff, District of Tzaritzin. —Mustard seed. 624

85 **Mariynska Model Farm, near Sara**toff.—Hemp and poppy seed. 624

87 **Karamycheff, Eugene, Toriok, Gov**ernment of Tver.—Linseed. 624

88 **Gratcheff, E., St. Petersburg.**—Grains and vegetables. 624

89 **Dookhinoff Brothers, St. Petersburg.** —Linseed. 624

Water Animals, Fish Culture, and Apparatus.

91 **Sidoroff, Michael, St. Petersburg.**—Fish from the Northern Ocean. 641

92 **Mangold, Charles, St. Petersburg.**—Preserved fish. 641

93 **Sokoloff, Nicolas, St. Petersburg.**—Isinglass and viazingo. 646

94 **Schultz, Alexander, Astrakhan.**—Isinglass and viazingo. 646

96 **Matteisson, Nicolas, Moscow.—Isin**glass. 646

Animal and Vegetable Products.

97 **Odnooshefsky, M., & Sons, St. Pe**tersburg.—Furs, sable, blue fox, etc. 652

98 **Ulich, Gustavus, Warsaw.—Albu**men, dried blood, and blood extract. 652

99 **Sivokhin, E., St. Petersburg.**—Honey. 654

100 **Berlinski, George, Warsaw.—Pre**pared French mustard. 656

101 **Chief Intendancy of War, St. Pe**tersburg.—Preserved meat and vegetables. 656

102 **Yacovleff, John, St. Petersburg.**—Preserved greens and mushrooms. 656

103 **Sivokhin, E., St. Petersburg.**—Preserved greens and mushrooms. 656

104 **Semenkoff, Victor, Oostie, Govern**ment of Vologda.—Meat extract. 656

105 **Sidoroff, Michael, St. Petersburg.** —Salt reindeer tongues from the island of Nova Zembla. 656

For classes of exhibits, indicated by numbers at end of entries, see Classification, pp. 12-14.

Animal and Vegetable Products.

106 Nikitin, Alexander, Smolensk.—Fruit preserves. 656

107 Mangold, Charles, St. Petersburg.—Preserved meats. 656

108 Ninberg, Otto, Uleaborg, Finland.—Preserved game. 656

109 Likhonin, Gregory, St. Petersburg.—Cranberry juice condensed by freezing. 656

110 Foorkhin, Paul, St. Petersburg.—Fruit paste (pastila). 656

111 Martens, Julius, St. Petersburg.—Coffee extract, dry and liquid. 656

112 Company for the Supply of Food, Varonesh and Moscow.—Preserved meat and vegetables for the army. 656

113 Petroff, John, St. Petersburg.—Cranberry juice. 656

114 Abrikosoff's Sons, Moscow.—Preserves, marmalade, fruit-paste. 656

115 Stephany, F., Mitau.—Wheat-flour. 657

116 Waag & Sons, Doobovka, Government of Saratoff.
a Mustard-flour, decorticated mustard-seed and husks. 657
b Mustard-seed oil and cake. 662

117 Verevitin, Alexis, Mzensk, Government of Orel.—Wheat-flour and decorticated grain. 657

118 Taldykin, Catherine, Eletz, Government of Orel.—Wheat-flour and decorticated grain. 657

119 Müller, Christian, Doobovka, Government of Saratoff, District of Tzaritsin.
a Mustard-flour, decorticated seed and husks. 657
b Mustard-seed oil and cakes. 662

120 Matteissen, Nicolas, Moscow.—
a Flour and groats. 657
b Anise and mustard seed oil. 662

122 Golikoff, K. P., Frtzach, Government of Riazan, District of Spassk.—Starch and glycose. 658

123 Tarnoosky, Basil, Parafievka, Government of Tchernigoff, District of Berzna.—Raw sugar. 659

124 Galitzyn, Prince Victor, Slavgorod, Kharkoff, District of Akhtyvke.—Raw beet-root sugar. 659

125 Hermanoff Sugar Manufacturing Company, Government of Warsaw.—Refined sugar in loaves and crystallized. 659

126 Gnevan Sugar Manufacturing Company, Government of Warsaw.—Refined sugar. 659

127 Wassiltchikoff, Prince Victor, Troobetchina, Government of Tamboff, District of Lipetzk.—Raw beet-root sugar. 659

128 Warsaw Sugar Manufacturing Company, Warsaw.—Refined sugar. 659

129 Sokolovka Sugar Manufacturing Company, Government of Podolia, District of Olgopol.—Refined beet-sugar. 659

130 Ostroff Sugar Manufacturing Company, Warsaw.—Sugar refined. 659

131 Sergeieff, Alexis & Apraxin, Count John, Pensa.—Refined beet-root sugar. 659

132 Nathanson, Jacob, Warsaw.—Sugar refined. 659

133 Mlodzescin Sugar Mill, Government of Warsaw.—Sugar refined in loaves and powder. 659

134 Meck, Charles von, Brailovka, Government of Podolia, District of Vinnitza.—Beet-root sugar, raw and refined. 659

135 Lanin, Nicolas, Moscow.—Fruit syrups and juices, effervescent fruit liquors and mineral waters. 659

136 Kümens, Richard, Sobolevka & Tsharnomin, Government of Podolia, District of Gaissin.—Sugar, raw and refined. 659

137 Krasinec Sugar Mill Company, Government of Plock.—Sugar. 659

138 Keshner, Frederic, St. Petersburg.—Refined beet-root sugar. 659

139 Yoozefow Sugar Manufacturing Company, Government of Warsaw.—Refined sugar. 659

140 Goozov Sugar Manufacturing Company, Government of Warsaw.—Refined sugar. 659

141 Dobrozelinsky Sugar Manufacturing Company, Government of Warsaw.—Sugar, raw and refined. 659

142 Maizner, N. Lanenta, & Fzabelin, Sugar Mills, Government of Warsaw.—Beet-root sugar, raw and refined. 659

143 Lysckowice Sugar Manufacturing Company, Government of Warsaw.—Refined sugar. 659

144 Leonoff Sugar Manufacturing Company, Government of Warsaw.—Beet-root sugar, refined. 659

145 Paskevitch, F., Soodak, Crimea.—Wine. 660

146 Doolvetoff, David, Simpheropol, Crimea.—White wine. 660

147 Imperial Nikitzky Garden, Yalta, Crimea.—White and red wine. 660

148 Foondoocley, John, Goorsoof District, Yalta, Crimea.—Wine. 660

149 Kniajevitch, Antoine, Alushta, Crimea.—Crimean wine. 660

150 Lancki, Robert, Soodack, Crimea.—Red and white wine. 660

151 Lanin, Nicolas, Moscow.—Liquors. 660

152 Hartwig, Herman, Malo Danilof brewery near Kharkoff.—Beer, mead, and malt. 660

153 Worontzoff, Prince Simon, Massandra, Crimea.—Red and white wines. 660

154 Bashmakoff, S. D., St. Petersburg.—Spirits and liquors. 660

155 Deshariot, A., Moscow.—Spirits, cordials, and liquors. 660

156 Makaroff, Petrus, Tiflis.—Kakhetian wine, red and white. 660

157 Rajevski, Nicolas, Crimea district, Yalta.—Wines. 660

158 Briantzeff, Victor, Irkoutsk.—Cordials and liquors. 660

159 Fokrath & Co., St. Petersburg.—Cordials and liquors. 660

160 Grevsmül, Alexander, Moscow.—Spirits. 660

For classes of exhibits, indicated by numbers at end of entries, see Classification, pp. 12–14.

Animal and Vegetable Products, Textile Substances.

161 Grote, Alexander von, Lemburg, near Riga.—Cumin liqueur. 660

162 Korf, Baron K., St. Petersburg.—Spirits and liquors. 660

163 Karali, G. N., & Co., St. Petersburg.—Cordials, liquors, and spirits. 660

164 Kalashnikoff, Peter, Pskoff.—Spirits, cordials, and liquors. 660

165 Tankowski, T., Warsaw.—Cordials and liquors. 660

166 Scheierman & Co., Riga.—Vinegars. 660

167 Lutoslavski, T., Drosdovo, Government & District of Lomza.—Bottled beer. 660

168 Krause, W., Warsaw.—Beer. 660

169 Tigezem Brewery Company, near Riga.—Malt extract. 660

170 Doordin, John, St. Petersburg.—Beer. 660

171 Zyzykin, M. Y., Brothers, Moscow.—Cordials, liquors, and artificial champagne. 660

172 Wickel, Y., Helsingfors.—Swedish punch. 660

173 Varaksin, Demetrius, & Sanin, George, Kazan.—Spirits and liquors. 660

174 Traverse, Marquis Alexander de Looga, Government of St. Petersburg.—Cordials and liquors. 660

175 Stemnikovski, A., Warsaw.—Corn brandy and mead. 660

176 Smirnoff, Peter, Moscow.—Cordials, spirits, and liquors. 660

177 Rouget, Pauline, Moscow.—Cordials and liquors. 660

178 Petroff, W., St. Petersburg.—Spirits, cordials, and liquors. 660

179 Natus, T., & Co., St. Petersburg.—Spirits and liquors. 660

180 Martini, G., St. Petersburg.—Spirits, cordials, and liquors. 660

181 Lilieroth, Victor, Helsingfors.—Imperial and fruit punch. 660

182 Landrin, George, St. Petersburg.—Bonbons and chocolate. 661

183 Zaitzeff, Simon, Moscow.—Cakes and gingerbread. 661

184 Sivakhin, E., St. Petersburg.—Gingerbread. 661

185 Meyer L., St. Petersburg.—Gingerbread and bonbons. 661

186 Lapin, N. & A., Brothers, St. Petersburg.—Cakes, marmalade, chocolate, and confectionery. 661

187 Koodriavzeff, A. & G., Brothers, Moscow.—Sweetmeats and sugar candy. 661

188 Ootkin, Basil, Tver.—Cakes. 661

189 Belolipetzky, Michael, Toola.—Cakes. 661

191 Tzelikoff, Theodore, Moscow.—Vegetable oils and linseed oil cakes. 662

193 Zablotsky, Dessetovsky Paul, Kryniki, Government of Kieff, District of Tchigirin.—Camline seed oil. 662

Textile Substances of Vegetable or Animal Origin.

195 Agricultural Museum of the Ministry of Domains, St. Petersburg.—Samples of cotton and cotton seed grown in Turkestan, Central Asia. 665

196 Wishaw, Alfred, St. Petersburg.—Vologda flax. 666

197 Warschafsky, A., St. Petersburg.—Flax. 666

198 Repnin, Prince Nicolas, Fagotin, Government of Poltawo, District of Periatin.—Flax in different stages of preparation. 666

199 Pskoff Statistical Committee.—Flax from the Government of Pskoff. 666

200 Nemiloff, Anthony, Orel.—Hemp cleaned and uncleaned. 666

201 Maximoff, Basil, Zagorye, Government of Kostroma, District of Nerekhta.—Flax raw and clean. 666

202 Kazan Model Farm, Kazan.—Flax. 666

203 Karamysheff, Nicholas, Polossy, Government of Pskoff, District of Porkhoff.—Flax. 666

204 Karamysheff, Eugene, Torjok, Government of Tver.—Flax. 666

205 Gent & Co., Pskoff.—Flax. 666

206 Riga Exchange Committee, Riga.—Flax and hemp. 666

207 Cartau, Robert, Pskoff.—Flax. 666

208 Vassilief, Nicolas, Ovekque.—Flax, clean and half clean, flax tow. 666

209 Bykoff, Theodore, Vologda.—Flax. 666

210 Mariolaki, P., Rostoff on the Don.—Washed wool of the Russian Donskoy breed. 667

211 Stichinsky, Simon, Gololobovo, near Voronesh.—Wool in fleece. 667

212 Orloff, Nicolas, Repievka, Government of Saratoff, District of Balashoff.—Wool in fleece. 667

213 Warschafsky, A., St. Petersburg.—Wool, Rambouillet and Rambouillet Negretti breeds. 667

214 Moshevski, Wladislav, Odessa.—Wool of common Don breed. 667

215 Mariynska Model Farm, near Saratoff.—Wool in fleece. 667

216 Labensky, V., Okence, Government & District of Warsaw.—Samples of wool. 667

217 Karlovka Estate of H. F. H. the Grand Duchess Catharine Mihaelovna, Government of Poltawo, District of Constantinovgrad.—Merino wool for carded and combed wool-stuffs. 667

218 Komarovsky, Count, Government & District of Orel.—Wool in fleece, Russian and Negretti breeds. 667

219 Glinka, Nicolas, Szczavin, Government of Lomza, District of Ostrolenka.—Wool. 667

220 Ganeshin Brothers & Co., Moscow.—Washed wool, Metis and Tzigai breed. 667

221 Fatz, Theodore, Olviopol, Government of Kherson.—Wool in fleece, Spanish breed. 667

For classes of exhibits, indicated by numbers at end of entries, see Classification, pp. 12–14.

Machines, Implements, Engineering, and Administration.

222 **Falz, Fein, Edward, Kakhovka,** Government of Tauride.—Washed and unwashed wool. 667

223 **Baklanoff's, K. K., Sons, Moscow.**—Washed wool, merino breed. 667

224 **Pokrovsky Sisterhood of Charity,** Moscow.—Cocoons of silk-worms, floss and raw silk. 668

225 **Lootchinsky, Laurentius, Oaman,** Government of Kief.—Cocoons, raw and floss silk. 668

226 **Kozishnikoff, Peter, Veliki Oostioog,** Government of Vologda.—Bristles. 669

Machines, Implements, and Processes of Manufacture.

227 **Lilpop, Rau, & Loevenstein, Warsaw.**

a Reaping-machine. 672

b Threshing-machine for corn and clover-seed. 673

228 **Grubinksky, Florain, Warsaw.**—Reaping-machine. 672

229 **Benkovski, Albert, Warsaw.**—Asparagus-digger. 672

230 **Westberg, Nicholas, Kharkoff.**—Threshing-machine. 673

231 **Meshtcherin, John, Orel.**—Winnowing and sorting machine. 673

233 **Fvanoff, Alexander, Kharkoff.**—Winnowing and sorting machines. 673

Agricultural Engineering and Administration.

234 **Calcined Bone Manufacturing Company,** St. Petersburg.—Ground bone and horn, and phosphatic manures. 681

235 **Przeciszewsky, Constantine, Warsaw.**—Pulverized bones for manure. 681

236 **Borissovki, Peter, Moscow.**—Apiary and artificial honey-comb. 683

For classes of exhibits, indicated by numbers at end of entries, see Classification, pp. 12–14.

JAPAN.

Location, South-west Corner of Agricultural Hall.

Arboriculture, Agricultural Products, Fish Culture.

Arboriculture and Forest Products.

1 Kuwangiyo-Riyo (Imperial Board of Agriculture, Industry, & Commerce), Tokio.
a Specimens of trees. 600
b Dyewoods, barks, and galls. 602
c Resins, etc. 603

2 Matsu-o, I., Tokio.—Bamboo. 601

Agricultural Products.

3 Kuwangiyo-Riyo (Imperial Board of Agriculture, Industry, & Commerce), Tokio.
a Rice, millet, wheat, sorghum, Indian corn, etc. 620
b Beans, peas, etc. 621
c Teas, green and black. 623
d Seeds. 624

4 Kaitakushi (Department for the Colonization of the island of Yesso).—Wheat. 620

5 Shirakawa-ken, Local Government of.—Tobacco leaves, cut and uncut. 623

6 Kagoshima-ken, Local Government of.—Tobacco leaves, cut and uncut. 623

7 Shiga-ken, Local Government of.—Tobacco leaves, cut. 623

8 Kiyoto, Municipality of, Kiyoto-fu.—Tobacco leaves, cut and uncut. 623

9 Osaka, Municipality of, Osaka-fu.—Tobacco leaves, cut and uncut. 623

10 Nagasaki-ken, Local Government of.—Cigars. 623

11 Saga-ken, Local Government of.—Tobacco. 623

12 Noda, D., Kumamoto, Province of Higo.—Tobacco leaves and cigars. 623

13 Kiriu-Kosho-Kuwaisha (First Japanese Manufacturing & Trading Company), Tokio.—Cigarettes and tea. 623

14 Susuki, S., Province of Hiuga.—Tea. 623

15 Kuroki, Y., Province of Hiuga.—Tea. 623

16 Otori, M., Province of Hiuga.—Tea. 623

17 Sato, S., Province of Hiuga.—Tea. 623

18 Womura, I., Province of Hiuga.—Tea. 623

19 Watanabe, M., Province of Hitachi.—Green tea. 623

20 Yebihara, Y., Province of Hitachi.—Green tea. 623

21 Katakura, J., Province of Hitachi.—Green tea. 623

22 Kuroda, N., Province of Higo.—Green tea. 623

23 Kamimura, N., Province of Higo.—Green tea. 623

24 Kaku, S., Province of Higo.—Green tea. 623

25 Fujita, H., Province of Higo.—Green tea. 623

26 Kobori, C., Province of Higo.—Green tea. 623

27 Hirano, H., Province of Higo.—Black tea. 624

28 Tanaka, K., Province of Chikugo.—Black tea. 623

29 Kawai, S., Province of Omi.—Green tea. 623

30 Maino, R., Province of Omi.—Green tea. 623

31 Hayashi, Y., Province of Tosa.—Green tea. 623

32 Morikawa, K., Province of Yetchizen.—Green tea. 623

33 Hori, G., Province of Iwami.—Tea. 623

34 Miura, G., Province of Mino.—Tea. 623

35 Miyazaki, T., Province of Hizen.—Green tea. 623

36 Sato, I., Province of Yetshigo.—Green tea. 623

37 Yanagida, K., Province of Yetshigo.—Black tea. 623

38 Imai, K., Province of Totomi.—Green tea. 623

39 Fukukawa, S., Province of Totomi.—Green tea. 623

40 Ozaki, I., Province of Suruga.—Green tea. 624

41 Minobe Chiubeye, Kiyoto.—Green tea. 623

42 Nagaya Buyemon, Kiyoto.—Tea. 623

43 Asada Toyemon, Kiyoto.—Green tea. 623

44 Kambayashi, Sansho & Sannin, Uji, Province of Yamashiro.—Tea; implements and apparatus used for the preparation. 623

45 Kiriu-Kosho-Kuwaisha (First Japanese Manufacturing and Trading Company), Tokio.—Tea. 623

46 Marunaka, M., Kanazawa, Province of Kaga.—Tea. 623

Marine Animals, Fish Culture, and Apparatus.

47 Kuwangiyo-Riyo (Imperial Board of Agriculture, Industry, & Commerce), Tokio.
a Shells. 645
b Shagreen and sturgeon skins. 646

For classes of exhibits, indicated by numbers at end of entries, see Classification, pp. 12–14.

Animal and Vegetable Products, Tnxtile Substances.

48 Kiriu-Kosho-Kuwaisha (First Japanese Manufacturing & Trading Company), Tokio.—Nets, baskets, hooks, rods, lines, and other apparatus used for fishing. 647

49 Nagasaki-ken, Local Government of.—Fishing implement and apparatus. 647

Animal and Vegetable Products.

50 Nagura, O., Kiyoto.—Vegetable isinglass. 650

51 Kuwangiyo-Riyo (Imperial Board of Agriculture, Industry, & Commerce), Tokio.
a Hides, furs, horns. 652
b Feathers of crane and pheasant. 653
c Preserved fruits prepared with sugar. 656
d Flour. 657
e Starch. 658
f Sugar. 659

52 Kumagai, K., Kiyoto.—Vegetable incense. 655

53 Kaitaku-shi (Department for Colonization of the Island of Yesso).—Preserved meat and fish. 656

54 City Chemical Laboratory, Kiyoto.
a Sugar candy. 659
b Mulberry wine, lemonade, punch, and other drinks. 660

55 Kamzaki, Tokio.—Sake, sweet liquors, spirits, and other alcoholic liquors. 660

56 Matsuya, H., Tokio.—Sweet liquors, wines, and malt liquors. 660

57 Sawada, Z., Tomo, Province of Bingo.—Sweet liquors. 660

58 Hashimoto, S., Tokio.—Spirits, sake, sweet liquors, and soy. 660

59 Kitakaze Yu, Hiogo, Province of Setzu.—Vinegars. 660

60 Naga-oka, Z., Tokio.—Soy and sweet liquors. 660

61 Mori, R. & K., Ito, Tokio.—Soy. 660

61*a* Nishi-wo Matsutaro, Kiyoto.—Yatsuhashiyaki (kind of cracknel). 661

Textile Substances of Vegetable or Animal Origin.

62 Government Cotton Factory, Sakai, Province of Setzu.—Cotton in raw state, and in all stages of preparation. 665

63 Maru, T., Province of Iwami.—Ramie, raw and prepared. 666

64 Hattori, Z., Province of Iwami.—China grass, spooled. 666

65 Asaya, T., Tokio.—Hemp, ramie, jute, etc. 666

66 Takamura, R., Province of Totomi.—Fibres. 666

67 Riu-kiu han, Loochoo Island.—Fibres of Musa-Basho, and China grass. 666

68 Kuwangiyo-Riyo-no-yosankakari (Government establishment for Experimental Silkworm-Breeding), Tokio.—Silk in cocoon and reeled. 668

69 Tamamura, Y., Ishi-i-mura, Province of Shimodzuke.—Silk, reeled. 668

70 Marunako, M., Kanazawa, Province of Kaga.—Silk, reeled. 668

Agriculture Engineering and Administration.

71 Kuwangiyo-Riyo (Imperial Board of Agriculture, Industry, & Commerce), Tokio.—Plows, scythes, harrows, and grain cradles. 670

Ornamental Trees, Snrubs, and Flowers.

72 Kuwangiyo-Riyo (Imperial Board of Agriculture, Industry, & Commrrce).
a Evergreen trees and shrubs. 700
b Herbaceous perennial plants. 701
c Lillies. 702
d Ornamental foliage. 703
e Ferns. 707
f New plants, with origin. 708

Garden Tools, Accessories of Gardening.

73 Kuwangiyo-Riyo (Imperial Board of Agriculture, Industry, & Commerce), Tokio.—Fences, gates, etc. 722

Garden Construction.

74 Miyagi, C., Garden laid out by. 733

For classes of exhibits, indicated by numbers at end of entries, see Classification, pp. 12-14.

PHILIPPINE ISLANDS.

Arboriculture, Pomology, Agricultural Products.

Arboriculture and Forest Products.

1 **Asuero, Eduardo, Province of Tarlac.**—Dita bark. 600

2 **Provincial Board, Province of Batangas.**
a Peruvian Guaiacum bark. 600
b Maiden's hair. 604

3 **Inspection-General of Woods and Forests.**
a Timber, lumber, barks, charcoal, etc. 600
b Ornamental woods. 601
c Dye woods and barks. 602
d Gums and resins. 603

4 **Olano, Casto, Manila, Province of Manila.**—Section of Pterocarpus santalinus L. 601

5 **Provincial Board, Province of Samar.**
a Cane. 601
b Balao. 603

6 **Jesus, Francisco de, Province of Pampanga.**—Camanchile bark. 602

7 **Provincial Board, Province of Masbate.**—White pitch. 603

8 **Cortina, Mariano de la, Bawang, Province of Batangas.**—Abilo resin. 603

9 **Orduña, Eduardo, Province of Batangas.**—Resins and gums, macabuhay. 603

10 **Labhart & Co., Province of Manila.**—Mastic. 603

11 **Provincial Board, Province of Tayabas.**—White pitch. 603

12 **Provincial Board, Province of Iloibo.**—Seeds. 605

Pomology.

13 **General Inspection of Woods & Forests.**—Fruits. 611

14 **Provincial Board, Province of Manila.**—Cocoa nuts. 611

Agricultural Products.

15 **Cirer, Manuel, Province of Tarlac.**—Rice. 620

16 **Arque, Benito, Province of Carite.**—Rice. 620

17 **Salivia, Fulgencio, Province of Camarines, S.**—Rice. 620

18 **Santos, Apolinaria, Province of Bulącan.**—Rice. 620

19 **Rico, José, Province of Na Ecya.**—Rice. 620

20 **Otero, Manuel G., Province of Nva, Exija.**—Rice. 620

21 **Rodriguez, Ambrosio, Sariaya, Province of Tayabas.**—Wheat. 620

22 **Liñan, Diego, Province of Tarlac.**
a Rice. 620
b Mongos. 622

23 **Naves, Andres, Province of Bulacan.**
a Anajao. 620
b Angolong hilive, tapican, etc. 622

24 **Provincial Board, Province of Antigue.**
a Rice. 620
b Cocoa and coffee. 623

25 **Provincial Board, Province of Samar.**
a Rice. 620
b Seeds. 624

26 **Provincial Board, Province of Batangas.**
a Maize and rice. 620
b Arbutra root. 622
c Cocoa and coffee. 623

27 **Provincial Board, Province of Benguet.**
a Rice. 620
b Beans. 621
c Coffee. 623
d Seeds. 624

28 **Lorenzo, Catalino, Province of Pampanga.**—Arrowroot. 622

29 **Provincial Board, Province of Samar.**—Cascalote, tabiguig, arbutra root, etc. 622

30 **Valmaceda, Esteban, Province of Bataan.**—Gogo. 622

31 **Provincial Board, Province of Bulacan.**—Matang-ulang and arbutra root. 622

32 **Adriano, Lucia A., Province of Mindoro.**—Yuro. 622

33 **Provincial Board, Province of Masbate.**—Gogo. 622

34 **Reyes, Andres, Province of Samar.**
a Sarsaparilla root. 622
b Laurel. 623

35 **Provincial Board, Province of Mindanao.**
a Gogo. 622
b Cocoa and coffee. 623

36 **Orduña, Eduardo, Province of Batangas.**
a Campuput root. 622
b Tuba and millet seed. 624

37 **Rodo, Luciano P. de, Province of Cavite.**—Coffee. 623

38 **Provincial Board, Province of Mainba.**—Cinnamon, pepper, etc. 623

39 **Lopez, Felix, Province of Cavite.**—Coffee. 623

40 **Temprado, Ramon F., Province of Camarines Sur.**—Coffee. 623

41 **Gallardo, Francisco, Province of Bohol.**—Coffee. 623

42 **Sanz, Victor, San José, Province of Lepanto.**—Coffee. 623

43 **Spanish Nation, Province of Manila.**—Leaf and manufactured tobacco, cigars, and cigarettes. 623

For classes of exhibits, indicated by numbers at end of entries, see Classification, pp. 12–14.

Agricultural, Animal, and Vegetable Products.

44 **Ruiz, Juan, Province of Laguna.**—Coffee. 623

45 **Velarde, Angel, Province of Cavite.**—Cocoa and coffee. 623

46 **Teodoro, Saturnino, Province of** Tarlac.—Cocoa. 623

47 **Mendosa, Gregorio, Province of** Tarlac.—Coffee. 623

48 **Alcántara, Dámasco, Sariaya,** Province of Batangas.—Cocoa. 623

49 **Hernandez, Telesoro, San José,** Province of Batangas.—Coffee. 623

50 **Catigbac, Norverto, Province of** Batangas.—Coffee. 623

51 **Ron, A., & Son, Province of Cebú.**—Coffee. 623

52 **Nieves, Agapito, Province of Albay.**—Cocoa and coffee. 623

53 **Saucian, Ciriló, Guinobatan, Province** of Albay.—Cocoa and coffee. 623

54 **Economical Society, Province of** Benguet.—Tea leaves. 623

55 **Nieves, Agapito, Province of Masbate.**—Tea leaves. 623

56 **Provincial Board, Province of Camarines Sur.**
a Coffee. 623
b Lumbang seed. 624

57 **Peñalosa, Andrés, Province of Batangas.**
a Cocoa. 623
b Lumbang seed. 624

58 **Prieto, Federico, Province of Albay.**
a Coffee. 623
b Pili seed. 624

59 **Rodriguez, Lucía, Province of** Pampanga.—Seeds. 624

60 **Provincial Board, Ilocos Sur.**—Seeds. 625

61 **Mamanal, Luisa, Province of Tarlac.**—Indigo seed. 624

62 **Dairit, Florentino, Province of** Pampanga.—Lumbang seed, sesame seed. 624

63 **Leonarde, Quinton, Province of** Laguña.—Lumbang seed. 624

64 **Baneg, Jo, Province of Bulacan.**—Lumbang seed. 624

65 **Provincial Board, Province of** Pampanga.—Pili seed. 624

66 **Peñaloso, Andres, S. Pablo, Province** of Batangas.—Lumbang seed. 624

67 **Guzman, Miguel de, Province of** Bataan.—Canary seed. 624

68 **Mora, José, Province of Mindoro.**—Castor beans. 624

69 **Liñan, Diego, Province of Tarlac.**—Beneseed. 634

71 **Argoncillo, Ramon, Province of** Batangas.—Coffee. 624

72 **Jesus, Francisco de, Province of** Pampanga.—Indigo seed. 624

Land Animals.

73 **Inspection-General of Woods &** Forests.—Zoological specimens. 630

Water Animals, Fish Culture, and Apparatus.

74 **Provincial Board, Province of Manila.**—Tortoise and other shells. 645

75 **Provincial Board, Province of** Bohol.—Mother-of-pearl shells. 645

76 **Macatangay, Jorgé, Province of** Batangas.—Fishing nets. 647

77 **Garun, Nicolás, Province of Manila.**—Fishing nets. 647

78 **García, Nicolás, Province of Manila.**—Model of fishing net. 647

Animal and Vegetable Products.

79 **Pagdangco, Gavino, Gumaca,** Province of Tayabas.—Sponges. 659

80 **Provincial Board, Province of Bohol.**—Flying-fox skins. 652

81 **Provincial Board, Province of Laguña.**
a Buffalo horns. 652
b Cocoanut oil. 662

82 **Provincial Board, Province of Manila.**
a Varnished cowhides, cut hides, deer skins, shark skin, etc. 652
b Birds' nests and feathers. 652
c Pickled fish. 656

83 **Osmeña, Rita, & Co., Province of** Cebri.
a Buffalo horns and sigay. 652
b Perfume pastilles. 655
c Sugar. 659
d Cocoa oil. 662

84 **Provincial Board, Province of Lepanto.**—Honey. 654

85 **Provincial Board, Province of Calamianes.**—Virgin wax. 654

86 **Estrada, Saturnino, Gumaca, Province** of Tayabas.—Virgin wax. 654

87 **Inspection-General of Woods &** Forests.
a Wax and honey. 654
b Tapioca, sago, arrowroot, and other flours. 657

88 **Casas, Calixta, Province of Cebú.**—Perfume pastilles. 655

89 **García, Regino, Province of Manila, Cavite, Bulacan, Laguña, and Isla** Negros.—Hulled rice. 657

90 **Posar, José, Province of Mindora.**—Hulled rice. 657

91 **Pasig, Agustin, Province of Mindoro.**—Hulled rice. 657

92 **Provincial Board, Province of Cavite.**—Hulled rice. 657

93 **Albir, Benito, Province of Cavite.**—Hulled rice. 657

94 **Ocampo, Benigno de, Province of** Pampanga.—Arrowroot flour. 657

95 **Provincial Board, Ilocos Sur.**—Arrowroot flour. 657

96 **Rodriguez, Lucía, Province of** Pampanga.—Arrowroot flour. 657

97 **Bravo, Antonio, Province of Batangas.**—Sugar. 659

98 **Guisones, Joaquin, Province of** Batangas.—Sugar. 659

99 **Argoncillo, Ramon, Province of** Batangas.—Sugar. 659

For classes of exhibits, indicated by numbers at end of entries, see Classification, pp. 12–14.

Animal and Vegetable Products, Textile Substances.

100 Rico, José, Province of Nueva Erija.—Sugar. 659

101 Macan, Luis, Calumpit, Province of Bulacan.—Sugar. 659

102 Aragon, Inocencia, Malate, Province of Manila.—Fruit syrups. 659

103 Garcia, P., Province of Manila.—Fruit syrups. 659

104 Provincial Board, Tananan, Province of Leyte.—Sugar. 659

105 Gonzalez, Victorina, Province of Antique.—Sugar. 659

106 Lirer, Manuel, Province of Tarlac.—Sugar. 659

107 Liñan, Diego, Province of Tarlac.—Sugar. 659

108 Puig, José, Province of Pampanga.—Sugar. 659

109 Ocampo, Manuel de, Province of Pampango.—Sugar. 659

110 Puig, Andrés, Province of Pampanga.—Sugar. 659

111 Miranda, Bernardo V. de, San Fernando, Province of Pampanga.—Sugar. 659

112 Lorenzo, Catalino, Province of Pampanga.—Sugar. 659

113 Sasatin, Leoncia, Province of Pampanga.—Sugar. 659

114 Buison, Julian, Province of Pampanga.—Sugar. 659

115 Jesus, Laureano, Province of Pampanga.—Sugar. 659

116 Enison, Catalino, Province of Pampanga.—Sugar. 659

117 Ocampo, Benigno de, Province of Pampanga.—Sugar. 659

118 Leon & Santos, José, Province of Pampanga.—Sugar. 659

119 Puig, Andrés, Province of Pampanga.—Sugar. 659

120 Gil, Rafael, Province of Pampanga.—Sugar. 659

121 Tison, José, Province of Pampanga.—Sugar. 659

122 Ker, Benito, Province of Pampanga.—Sugar. 659

123 Rosa & Son, Province of Cebú.—Sugar. 659

124 Onchica, Andrés, Province of Laguña.—Sugar. 659

125 Provincial Board, Province of Antigue.—Sugar. 659

126 Provincial Board, Province of Mindanao.—Sugar. 659

127 Jesus, Francisco de, Province of Pampanga.
a Sugar. 659
b Alcohol. 660

128 Rodriguez, Lucia, Province of Pampanga.
a Sugar. 659
b Sesame and lumbang oils. 662

129 Leon, Celestino de, Province of Pampanga.
a Sugar. 659
b Beneseed oil. 662

130 Inchausti & Co., Province of Manila.—Alcohol. 660

131 Reyes, Vicente, Province of Laguña.—Cocoa wine. 660

132 Besa Santos, Mateo, Province of Manila.—Palo-maria oil. 662

133 Provincial Board, Province of Samar.—Cocoanut oil. 662

134 Maringan, Jocinto, Province of Batangas.—Beneseed oil. 662

135 Provincial Board, Province of Ilocos Sur.—Palo-maria and other vegetable oils. 662

136 Provincial Board, Province of Visayas.—Tagulanag oil. 662

137 Beso Santos, Mateo, Province of Bulacan.—Palo-maria oil. 662

138 Naves, Andrés, Province of Bulacan.—Cocoanut oil. 662

139 Banes, Jo, Province of Bulacan.—Lumbang oil. 662

140 Provincial Board, Province of Camarines N.—Balao oil. 662

141 Dairit, Florentino, Province of Pampanga.—Lumbang oil. 662

142 Tribula, Eleuterio, Province of Pampanga.—Lumbang oil. 662

143 Maceda, Leon, Province of Laguña. Cocoanut oil. 662

144 Provincial Board, Province of Pampanga.—Beneseed oil. 662

145 Orduña, Eduardo, Province of Batangas.—Lausina oil. 662

146 Inspection-General of Woods & Forests.—Vegetable oils. 662

147 Provincial Board, Province of Batangas.—Tuba and cocoanut oil. 662

148 Zugadi, Nicolàs, Provinces of Bulacan, Ilocos Sur, Leite, Batangas, and Camarines N.—Vegetable oils. 662

149 Provincial Board, Province of Bulacan.—Lumbang and beneseed oil. 662

Textile Substances of Vegetable or Animal Origin.

150 Macatangay, Agaton, Province of Batangas.—Cotton. 665

151 Reyes, Juana, Province of Batangas.—Cotton. 665

152 Dimayuga, Procesa, Province of Batangas.—Cotton. 665

153 Reyes, Juan, Province of Bohol.—Raw cotton. 665

154 Roa, A., & Son, Province of Cebú.—Cotton. 665

155 Beluyos, Damian, Province of Bataan.—Cotton. 665

156 Provincial Commission, Province of Benguet.—Cotton. 665

157 Orduña, Eduardo, Province of Batangas.
a Cotton. 665
b Textile vegetable substances. 666

158 Provincial Board, Province of Batangas.
a Coyote cotton. 665
b Textile vegetable substances. 666

159 Provincial Board, Province of Mindanao.
a Cotton. 665
b Balibago cords. 666

160 Gomez, Enrique, Province of Abra.—Textile substances. 666

For classes of exhibits, indicated by numbers at end of entries, see Classification, pp. 12–14.

Textile Substances, Machines, Implements.

161 **Provincial Board, Province of Camarines Sur.**—Abacá fibres. 666

162 **Bravo, Antonio, Guagua, Province** of Pampanga.—Balibago barks. 666

163 **Provincial Board, Province of Samar.**—Bonote. 666

164 **Cortina, Mariano de la, Province** of Batangas.—Maguey plant. 666

165 **Provincial Board, Province of** Manila.—Balibago fibres. 666

166 **Argoncillo, Eustaquio, Lopez,** Province of Tayabas.—Abacá fibres. 666

167 **Figueroa, Andrés, Province of** Albay.—Abacá fibres. 666

168 **Rodriguez, José, Vigan, Province** of Ilocos Sur.—Maguey. 666

169 **Muñoz & Bros., Province of Albay.** —Abacá and cabo-negro. 666

170 **Provincial Board, Province of** Camarines N.—Balibago fibres and abacá. 666

171 **Gallegos, Tomás, Province of** Albay.—Abacá lupiz. 666

172 **Medina, Ildefonso, Province of** Mindora.—Abacá. 666

173 **Garcia, Cirilo, Guinobatan, Province** of Albay.—Abacá. 666

174 **Provincial Board, Burasun, Province** of Leite.—Cabo-negro and Nabó. 669

175 **Parochial Curate, Province of Pangasinan.**—Textile substances. 666

176 **Banson, Nicasio, Province of** Bataan.—Textile vegetable fibres and samples of work. 666

177 **Banson, Arcadio, Province of Bataan.**—Dantin cord. 666

178 **Provincial Board, Province of** Pangasinan.—Textile vegetable fibres and samples of work. 666

179 **Mangataren, Parson of, Pangasinan.**—Alinoa bark and ropes. 666

180 **Provincial Board, Province of** Bohol.—Malacapas. 666

181 **Jesus, Francisco de, Province of** Pampanga.—Cord of thistle fibres. 666

182 **Provincial Board, Province of Pampanga.**—Textile vegetable fibres. 666

183 **Vera, Rosa de, Province of Albay.** —Nito. 666

184 **Provincial Board, Province of Antigue.**—Textile vegetable substances. 666

185 **Llamas, Gabriel, Province of** Manila.—Dugtung-ajas bindweed. 666

186 **Provincial Board, Province of Albay.**—Bark and abacá fibres. 666

187 **Provincial Board, Province of** Laguña.—Abacá. 666

188 **Reyes, Andrés, Province of Samar.** —Abacá. 666

189 **Juan, Fernando, Tanauan, Province** of Leite.—Abacá layajon. 666

190 **Peñaflor, Ines, Province of Cavite.** —Abacá. 666

191 **Nieva, Calixto M., Province of** Mindora.—Abacá. 666

192 **Perfecto, Teodora, Province of** Camarines Sur.—Abacá. 666

193 **Gallegos, Tomás, Province of** Batangas.—Abacá lupiz. 666

194 **Perez, Agustin, Province of** Albay.—Abacá fibres. 666

195 **Rivera, Gregorio, Orion, Province** of Bataan.—Balibago fibres. 666

196 **Reyes, Juana, Lemery, Province of** Batangas.—Prepared abacá. 666

197 **San Isidro, Parson of, Province of** Pangasinan.—Cabulagna roots, and oplit bark. 666

198 **Esteves, Félipe, Province of Albay.** —Nito and piña. 666

199 **Adriatano, Luciano M., Province** of Mindoro.—Cabo negro. 666

200 **Zugadi, Nicolas, Province of Bulacan.**—Nito. 666

201 **Provincial Board, Province of Bohol.**—Textile vegetable fibres, etc. 666

202 **Buison, Julian, Province of Pampanga.**—Bark of the buri palm tree. 666

203 **Peele, Hubbell, & Co., Santa Mesa,** Province of Manila.—Abacá rigging. 666

204 **Villamarzo, Tiburcio, Province of** Tayabas.—Cabo-negro cables, nabo and pasao fibres. 666

205 **Rivera, L. de, Province of Bataan.** —Bark of the malacacas tree. 666

206 **Panda, Corporation of, Province of** Antigue.—Pineapple leaf fibres. 666

Machines, Implements, and Processes of Manufacture.

207 **Provincial Board, Province of Bulacan.**—Plows. 670

208 **García, Nicolas, Province of Manila.**—Model of a sugar cane mill. 673

For classes of exhibits, indicated by numbers at end of entries, see Classification, pp. 12–14.

ANNEXES AND SPECIAL EXHIBITS IN THE DEPARTMENT OF AGRICULTURE.

No. 69. CANADIAN LOG HOUSE.

Size, 40 feet by 64.

CANADIAN COMMISSION.

Is one story high, constructed of logs, and located close by the British Government Buildings. Its materials and contents constitute an exhibit of Canadian arboriculture and forest products.

1 **Quebec Advisory Board, Quebec.**
a White pine logs.
b Sugar maple.
c Ash birch.
d Chestnut elm.
e Hemlock butternut.
f Yellow pine, red cherry.
g Spruce cedar.
h Black walnut.
i Poplar oak.
j Pear wood.

2 **Quereus & Genana, Victoria, B. C.**—Oak.

3 **Canadian Commission, Victoria, B. C.**—Arbutus.

4 **George, D. F., Fredericton, N. B.**—Clapboards.

5 **Moody & Nelson, Victoria.**
a Native woods, etc.
b Shingles.

6 **Layard, W. P., Victoria.**—Oak flooring, etc.

7 **Dawson, W. G., Victoria.**—Axe-handles.

8 **Layard, W. P., Victoria, B. C.**—Pine.

9 **Cusack, H. P., Newberry.**—Flour barrel hoops.

10 **Richardson, Peter, Chatham.**—Hoops.

11 **Lactinbros, Wm., Quebec.**—Yellow pine planks.

12 **Rochester, I., Ottawa.**—Yellow pine, etc.

13 **Head, James S., Ottawa.**—Pine shingles.

14 **Perley & Patton, Ottawa.**—Yellow pine laths.

15 **Silliman, James R., Toronto.**—Pine lumber, etc.

16 **Oliver, John, Toronto.**—Chestnut, ash, oak, etc.

17 **Colwell, H., & Son, Ontario.—Ash.**

18 **Young, Levi, Quebec.**—Board lumber.

19 **Bronsons & Weston, Ontario.**—White pine.

20 **Lachlaw, W., Bros., Arnprior.**—Pine.

21 **Canadian Commission, Victoria, B.C.**
a Daglos pine.
b Dogwood.

22 **Newell, George, Ottawa.**—Ash columns.

23 **New Brunswick Advisory Board.**
a Woods, etc.
b Maple logs.
c Ash logs.
d Birch logs.
e Squared birch.

24 **Canadian Commission, Victoria, B.** C.—Mouldings.

25 **Hayward & Jenkinson, Victoria, B.** C.—Mouldings, etc.

No. 144. CUBAN ACCLIMATION GARDEN.

EMILE LACHAUME, Proprietor.

Contains a variety of tropical plants, etc. Situated south of Horticultural Hall.

No. 165. WAGON BUILDING.

Size, 144 feet by 196 feet.

Constructed of wood, one story high, situated north-east of Agricultural Hall, consists of three lines of sheds. Is used to display wagons, trucks, etc.

Arboriculture, Machines, Engineering, Administration, Vehicles.

Arboriculture and Forest Products.

1 **Reppard, R. B., Savannah, Ga.**—Yellow pine timber. 601

Machines, Implements, and Processes of Manufacture.

2 **Decrow, A. W., Bangor, Maine.**—Scavenger. 674

3 **Lynch, Peter, Mt. Holly, N. J.**—Hog scalders. 674

Agricultural Engineering and Administration.

4 **Wenkenbach, W., & Sons, Philadelphia, Pa.**—Beer wagon. 682

5 **Keiser, Joseph, New York, N. Y.**—Beer wagon. 682

6 **Sebastian, Jacob, New York, N. Y.**—Wagon and truck. 682

7 **Crater, Charles H., North Kingsville, O.**—Vehicle coupling. 682

8 **Lehigh Car Manufacturing Co., Stemton, Pa.**—Platform, spring wagon, truck wagon. 682

9 **Studebaker Bros. Manufacturing Co., South Bend, Ind.**—Farm, lumber, and express wagons. 682

10 **Cortland Wagon Manufacturing Co., Cortland, N. Y.**—Platform spring business wagon. 682

11 **Jarboe, John W., New York, N. Y.**—Paper model of wagon body. 682

12 **Adgate, J. J., New York, N. Y.**—Self-unloading wagon. 682

13 **Carré, W. W., New Orleans, La.**—Lumber wagon. 682

14 **Ressler, H. & G., Philadelphia, Pa.**—Carts and wagons. 682

15 **Server & Brenz, Philadelphia, Pa.**—Wagons. 682

16 **Mills & Combs, Wilmington, Del.**—Wagon. 682

17 **Rech, Jacob, Philadelphia, Pa.**—Milk wagon. 682

18 **Becker, Jacob, jr., Seymour, Ind.**—Farmers' wagon. 682

19 **Beggs, John, & Sons, Philadelphia, Pa.**—Truck and wagon. 682

20 **Lengert, George, & Son, Philadelphia, Pa.**—Express wagons. 682

21 **Winchester & Partridge Manufacturing Co., Whitewater, Wis.**—Wagons. 682

22 **Knickerbocker Ice Co., Philadelphia, Pa.**—Ice wagon, and set of wheels. 682

23 **Wright Spring Co., Denmark, Iowa.**—Wagon springs. 682

24 **Heytler, Frank, Burlington, Iowa.**—Wagon. 682

25 **Wilson, Childs, & Co., Philadelphia, Pa.**—Wagons and carts. 682

26 **Kramer, Jacob, New York, N. Y.**—Dumping wagon. 682

27 **French & Co., Davenport, Ia.**—Piano truck. 682

28 **Schauz, C., Philadelphia, Pa.**—Business and express wagons. 682

29 **Funck & Hertzler, Burlington, Ia.**—Farm wagon. 682

30 **Rauch, Charles, Cleveland, O.**—Ice wagon. 682

31 **Harrison, Lautz Bros., & Co., South Bend, Ind.**—Dump wagon. 682

32 **Austin, Tomlinson, & Webster Manufacturing Co., Jackson, Mich.**—Lumber wagons. 682

33 **Fish Bros. & Co., Racine, Wis.**—Farm and California rack bed wagons. 682

34 **Moline Wagon Co., Moline, Ill.**—Farm and spring wagons. 682

35 **Schuttler, Peter, Chicago, Ills.**—Spring farm and freight wagons. 682

36 **Kansas Manufacturing Co., Leavenworth, Kansas.**—Farm wagons. 682

37 **Milburn Wagon Co., Toledo, O.**—Spring farm and freight wagons, sleds. 682

38 **Stryker, Peter J., New Brunswick, N. J.**—Self-loading excavator. 691

For classes of exhibits, indicated by numbers at end of entries, see Classification, pp. 12–14.

No. 166. POMOLOGICAL BUILDING.

Size, 182 feet by 192 feet.

Constructed of wood, one story high, situated east of Agricultural Hall. Is designed for the exhibit of fruits in season.

No. 167. BREWERS' BUILDING.

Architect, H. J. SCHWARZMANN.—Size, 272 feet by 96 feet.

Erected under the auspices of the United States Brewers' Association.

Constructed of wood in the style of Machinery Hall, and situated on Lansdowne drive, opposite the northeast corner of Agricultural Hall. It contains a model brewery, and exhibits the several processes of manufacturing malt liquors.

Agricultural, Animal, and Vegetable Products.

Agricultural Products.

1 **White, John G., & Co., Philadelphia, Pa.**—Barley and malt. 620

2 **Schere, Solomon, Buffalo, N. Y.**—Barley and malt. 620

3 **Liebman's, S., Sons, Brooklyn, N. Y.**—Malt. 620

4 **Palin, Thomas, Brooklyn, N. Y.**—Malt. 620

5 **Pulling, A. C., New York, N. Y.**—Malt. 620

6 **Committee on Barley & Malt, New York, N. Y.**—Barley and malt. 620

7 **Perot's, Francis, Sons, Philadelphia, Pa.**—Barley and malt. 620

8 **Appleton, Wm., Albany, N. Y.**—Malt. 620

9 **Lill & Bullen, Chicago, Ill.—Malt.** 620

10 **Mueller, H., & Co., Cleveland, O.**—Barley and malt. 620

11 **McCredie, Thomas, Albany, N. Y.**—Malt. 620

12 **Pardee, Charles W., Oswego, N. Y.**—Barley and malt. 620

13 **Lynde, B. A., Buffalo, N. Y.—Malt.** 620

14 **Niagara Malt House, Buffalo, N. Y.**—Malt. 620

15 **Neidlinger, Schmidt, & Co., New York, N. Y.**—Malt. 620

16 **Poke, Charles, Chicago, Ill.—Malt.** 620

17 **Marsh, A. M., Buffalo, N. Y.—Malt.** 620

18 **Schmid, Bernheimer, & Co., Brooklyn, N. Y.**—Malt. 620

19 **White, Rufus P., New York, N. Y.**—Malt and barley. 620

20 **Akin, W. H., & Son, New York, N. Y.**—Hops. 620

21 **Weilbacher & Loewi, New York, N. Y.**—Hops. 623

22 **Franke, Louis, New York, N. Y.**—Yeast. 620

23 **Uhlman, Simon, New York, N. Y.**—Hops. 623

24 **Dole Bros., Boston, Mass.—Hops.** 623

25 **Schlesinger Bros., New York, N. Y.**—Hops. 623

26 **Tyler, George H., New York, N. Y.**—Hops. 623

27 **Scott, John R., & Co., New York, N. Y.**—Hops. 623

28 **Wheeler, Walter G. B., New York, N. Y.**—Isinglass. 646

29 **Howe & French, Boston, Mass.**—Isinglass. 646

30 **Chrisfield, Wm., & Son, New York, N. Y.**—Isinglass. 646

31 **Greenway, John, Syracuse, N. Y.**—Ale and porter. 660

32 **Hartung & Krantz, Honesdale, Pa.**—Beer. 660

33 **Meyerhofer, Carl, Poughkeepsie, N. Y.**—Beer. 660

34 **Miles, W. A., & Co., New York, N. Y.**—Ale. 660

Animal and Vegetable Products.

35 **Liebman, S., & Sons, Williamsburg, N. Y.**—Beer. 660

36 **Grecke, Philip, Philadelphia, Pa.**—Ale, porter, and beer. 660

37 **Hinckel, Frederick, Albany, N. Y.**—Beer. 660

38 **Yuengling & Sons, Pottsville, Pa.**—Ale, porter, and beer. 660

39 **Frauenheim & Vilsack, Pittsburg, Pa.**—Beer. 660

40 **Bergner & Engel, Philadelphia, Pa.**—Beer. 660

41 **Bolton, S., & Sons, Lansingburg, N. Y.**—Ale. 660

42 **Evans, C. H., & Co., Hudson, N. Y.**—Ale. 660

43 **Gardner, John, & Co., Philadelphia, Pa.**—Ale and porter. 660

44 **Smith, Robert, Philadelphia, Pa.**—Ale. 660

45 **Clausen, H., & Son, New York, N. Y.**—Ale and beer. 660

46 **Walker, J., & Co., Cincinnati, O.**—Ale and porter. 660

47 **Baltz, J. & P., Philadelphia, Pa.**—Beer. 660

48 **Blatz, Valentine, Milwaukee, Wis.**—Beer. 660

49 **Reuter & Alley, Boston, Mass.—Ale.** 660

For classes of exhibits, indicated by numbers at end of entries, see Classification, pp. 12–14.

Animal and Vegetable Products, Machines, Implements.

50 **Walker, J., & Co., Cincinnati, O.**—Ale. 660

51 **Clausen, H., & Co., New York, N. Y.**—Beer. 660

52 **Anheuser, E., & Co.'s Brewing Association, St. Louis, Mo.**—Malt liquor. 660

53 **Pfannenstiel, C., Philadelphia, Pa.**—Beer. 660

54 **Ruppert, Jacob, New York, N. Y.**—Beer. 660

55 **Gukes, C., Philadelphia, Pa.**—Ale. 660

56 **Philip Best Brewing Co., Milwaukee, Wis.**—Malt liquor. 660

57 **Jones, David, New York, N. Y.**—Malt. 620

58 **Barbey, Peter, Reading, Pa.**—Beer. 660

59 **Feigh, Adrian, New York, N. Y.**—Beer. 660

60 **Kane, E., & Co., Brooklyn, N. Y.**—Beer. 660

61 **Rulsann & Horrman, Stapleton, N. Y.**—Beer. 660

62 **Hupfel's, A., Sons, New York, N. Y.**—Beer. 660

63 **Ziegele, Albert, Buffalo, N. Y.**—Beer. 660

64 **Schmitle & Kohne, New York, N. Y.**—Beer. 660

65 **Jos. Schlitz Brewing Co., Milwaukee, Wis.**—Beer. 660

66 **Mayer & Bachman, Staten Island, N. Y.**—Beer. 660

67 **Bechtel, George, Staten Island, N. Y.**—Beer. 660

68 **Grasser & Brand, Toledo, O.**—Beer. 660

69 **Ferris, H., & Son, New York, N. Y.**—Ale. 660

70 **Ehrel, George, New York, N. Y.**—Beer. 660

71 **Ebling, Philip & William, Morrisania, N. Y.**—Beer. 660

72 **Hoffman & Merkel, New York, N. Y.**—Beer. 660

73 **Loewer, Valentine, New York, N. Y.**—Beer. 660

74 **Urig, Joseph, St. Louis, Mo.**—Beer. 660

75 **Lemp, Wm. I., St. Louis, Mo.**—Beer. 660

76 **Elias & Betz, New York, N. Y.**—Beer. 660

77 **Mark, J. & F., Brooklyn, N. Y.**—Beer. 660

78 **Finck, A., & Son, New York, N. Y.**—Beer. 660

79 **Voigt, E. W., Detroit, Mich.**—Beer. 660

80 **Kuechle, Joseph, St. Josephs, Mo.**—Beer. 660

81 **Rose, Miss Sophie, Baltimore, Md.**—Beer. 660

82 **Boeuilein, C., Bro., & Co., Bennett's Station, Pa.**—Beer. 660

83 **Seiger, I., Baltimore, Md.**—Beer. 660

84 **Schlotterer, S., Philadelphia, Pa.**—Beer. 660

85 **Howard & Fuller, Brooklyn, N. Y.**—Ale. 660

86 **Schwaner & Amend, New York, N. Y.**—Beer. 660

87 **McKechnie, J. & A., Canandaigua, N. Y.**—Ale and beer. 660

88 **Philip Best Brewing Co., Milwaukee, Wis.**—Beer. 660

89 **Miles, Wm. A., & Co., New York, N. Y.**—Ale. 660

90 **Hughes, H. R. & M., Pittston, Pa.**—Ale. 660

91 **Liebmann's, S., Sons, Brooklyn, N. Y.**—Beer. 660

92 **Hollender & Co., New York, N. Y.**—Beer. 660

93 **Lyman, T. C., & Co., New York, N. Y.**—Ale. 660

94 **Hawkins, Chas. P., New York, N. Y.**—Ale. 660

95 **Anheuser, E., Co.'s Brewing Association, St. Louis, Mo.**—Beer. 660

96 **Flanagan & Wallace, New York, N. Y.**—Ale. 660

97 **Besley's Waukegan Brewing Co., Chicago, Ill.**—Ale. 660

98 **Von der Horst, J. H., Baltimore, Md.**—Beer. 660

99 **Beadleston, Price, & Woerz, New York, N. Y.**—Ale. 660

100 **Stein, Conrad, New York, N. Y.**—Beer. 660

Machines, Implements, and Processes of Manufacture.

101 **Kampf, Stephen, Albany, N. Y.**—Malt-shovels. 670

102 **Lynde, B. A., Buffalo, N. Y.**—Malt-shovels. 670

103 **Knapp, S. P., New York, N. Y.**—Malt shovels. 670

104 **Beardsley, B. A., Waterville, N. Y.**—Hop press. 673

105 **Ingraham & Beard, Chicago, Ill.**—Grain separater and grader. 673

106 **Keastner, Chas., & Co., Chicago, Ill.**—Feed-mills. 674

107 **Haberman, S., New York, N. Y.**—Beer-swimmer. 674

108 **White's N. Y. Malt House, New York, N. Y.**
a Plows, shovels, etc. 670
b Elevator buckets, etc. 674

109 **White, John G., & Co., Philadelphia, Pa.**—Malt-mill. 674

110 **Roos, Aug., New York, N. Y.**—Beer-cooler. 674

111 **Zoller, A., Hoboken, N. J.**—Barrel-washer, valves, and faucets. 674

112 **Steubing, Henry, New York, N. Y.**—Ice-swimmer. 674

113 **Decker, John, & Son, Philadelphia, Pa.**—Ice-swimmers, watering-can, funnels, and yeast-sieve. 674

114 **Iron Clad Can Co., New York, N. Y.**—Apparatus for preserving ales, beer, etc. 674

For classes of exhibits, indicated by numbers at end of entries, see Classification, pp. 12–14.

Machinery, Implements, Engineering, Administration.

115 Trottman & Ott, Philadelphia, Pa. —Cooler. 674

116 Spiess, Fr., New York, N. Y.—Malt-mill. 674

117 Schalk, C.W., Reading, Pa.—Malt-mill. 674

118 Hupfel, Adolf G., New York, N. Y. —Barrel-rolling machine. 674

119 Bergner, Theodore, Philadelphia, Pa.—Cork-driver, valves. 674

120 Otto, John M., Brooklyn, N. Y.—Beer-cooler, ice-swimmer, baskets. 674

121 Union Hardware Co., New York, N. Y.—Beer-coolers. 674

122 Kirby Bung Manufacturing Co., Cincinnati, O.—Bung machine and saw. 674

123 Cornell, G. B., Chicago, Ill.—Bung-bushes. 675

124 Union Machine Works, New York, N. Y.—Malt-mill. 674

125 Haas, Edward, Philadelphia, Pa.—Malt-mill, scourer, and cleaner. 674

126 Stoll, Chas., Brooklyn, N. Y.—Scales, malt-mill. 674

127 Bremer, J. L., Bro., & Co., New York, N. Y.—Grain-bags. 674

128 Littlejohn, L., New York, N. Y.—Bung-bushes and tools. 674

129 Spiess, Fr., New York, N. Y.—Pumps, belt-stretcher, shaving-machine. 674

130 Storms, James, Buffalo, N. Y.—Elevator buckets. 674

131 Gendar, W. F. & T. V., New York, N. Y.—Brewers' instruments. 674

132 Schmahl, Martin, New York, N. Y. —Copper-washing apparatus. 674

133 Woerle, W., Milwaukee, Wis.—Ice-swimmer. 674

134 Murphy, C. J., New York, N. Y.—Testing-still. 674

135 Hupfel, J. C. G., New York, N. Y.—Barrel-rinsing machine. 674

136 Woehrle, Chas., New York, N. Y. —Elevator buckets. 675

137 Burkhardt, G. F., & Co., Philadelphia, Pa.—Steep-tub. 675

138 Morrison, J., Portsmouth, N. H.—Hogshead. 675

139 Burkhardt, G. J., & Co., Philadelphia, Pa.—Vats and tanks. 675

140 Link, John, Cincinnati, O.—Barrels and kegs. 675

141 Fisher & Hall, Philadelphia, Pa.—Cedar tubs. 675

142 Smith, John M., & Son, Philadelphia, Pa.—Steep-tub. 675

143 Dieringer, C., Cincinnati, O.—Coopers' work. 675

144 Lutz, R. F., Wabash, Ind.—Kegs and staves. 675

145 Schwarzwallder & Son, New York, N. Y.—Kegs, barrels, and hogsheads. 675

146 Luckhaupt Bros., Columbus, O.—Kegs. 675

147 Wandelt, Samuel, Brooklyn, N. Y. —Tubs. 675

148 Seligsberg, Arnold, New York, N. Y.—Tubs, vats, malt-holders, and chests. 675

Agricultural Engineering and Administration.

149 White's N. Y. Malt House, New York, N. Y.—Carts. 682

150 Saal & Schlich, Philadelphia, Pa.—Beer wagon and machinery. 682

151 Wenkenbach, W. L., Philadelphia, Pa.—Beer-wagon. 682

152 Kiesler, Joseph, New York, N. Y. —Beer-wagon. 682

153 Brunner, August F., New York, N. Y.—Plan of ice-house. 683

154 Wisker, Aug., Boston, Mass.—Model of brewery. 683

155 Weilbacher, P., New York, N. Y.—Hop-kiln. 683

156 Stoll, Charles, Brooklyn, N. Y.—Model of brewery. 683

157 Holden, D. L., Philadelphia, Pa.—Drawings of ice and refrigerating machines. 683

158 Seligsberg, A., New York, N. Y.—Grain-box. 683

159 White's N. Y. Malt House, New York, N. Y.—Kiln flooring and furnace. 683

160 Bergner, Theodore, Philadelphia, Pa.—Malt turner and kiln. 683

161 Spangenburg, Schroeder, & Co., Milwaukee, Wis.—Wire kiln surface. 683

162 Hughes, W. W., & Son., Philadelphia, Pa.—Malt-kiln, etc. 683

163 Hampel, Otto, New York, N. Y.—Model malt-kiln. 683

164 Lieber, Robert, Boston, Mass.—Model of brewery. 683

165 Korn, George W., Philadelphia, Pa. —Refrigerator. Brewers' store. 683

166 Shada, O. S., Philadelphia, Pa.—Block of coal. 101

167 German Rock Asphalt Co., New York, N. Y.—Cement flooring. 103

168 White's New York Malt House elevator, New York, N. Y.—Cement flooring. 103

169 Mock, Isidor, Brooklyn, N. Y.—Cement floors. 103

170 Meyers, A. G., New York, N. Y.—Compound for lining barrels. 103

171 Wehn, G. H., Philadelphia, Pa.—Artificial stone. 103

172 Doerchuck, Gustav, Brooklyn, N. Y.—Varnish. 202

173 Hatter, Carl, New York, N. Y.—Bottle-stoppers. 215

174 Brown & Jones, Waterville, N. Y. —Stove to dry hops. 222

175 Asten, William B., & Co., New York, N. Y.—Malt-bags. 229

176 Bremer, J. L., Bro. & Co., Philadelphia, Pa.—Seamless bags. 229

177 Tuchfarber, F., & Co., Cincinnati, O.—Show-cards. 262

178 Simon, A., New York, N. Y.—Weather-vanes. 283

For classes of exhibits, indicated by numbers at end of entries, see Classification, pp. 12–14.

Agricultural Engineering and Administration.

179 **Wells, Hope, & Co., Philadelphia,** Pa.—Metallic signs. 283

180 **Trageser, John, New York, N. Y.—** —Copper work. 284

181 **Toope, Charles, New York, N. Y.** —Grate-bars. 513

182 **Brown, A. & F., New York, N. Y.** —Horizontal engine, shafting, pulleys, etc. 552

183 **Vogt, Henry, & Bro., Brooklyn,** N. Y.—Tubular boiler. 552

184 **Brown, A. & F., New York, N. Y.** —Shafting, pulleys, and hangers. 553

185 **Albany Lubricating Compound & Cup Co., New York, N. Y.—Oil cups.** 555

186 **Niagara Steam Pump Works,** Brooklyn, N. Y.—Pumps. 560

187 **Schutte & Goehring, Philadelphia,** Pa.—Pumps. 560

188 **George F. Blake Manufacturing** Co., New York, N. Y.—Steam pumps. 560

189 **Zinsser, Wm., & Co., New York,** N. Y.—Pumps. 560

190 **Knowles Steam Pump Works, New** York, N. Y.—Pumps. 560

191 **Cope & Maxwell Manufacturing** Co., Cincinnati, O.—Air pumps. 561

192 **Krakovicz, F. O., Walkertown, Ind.** —Ventilator. 562

193 **Otis Bros., New York, N. Y.—Ele-** vator. 563

194 **Bawer, E., Brooklyn, New York.—** Racking-off hose. 564

195 **Maegerlein, Chas., Chicago, Ill.—** Hose. 564

196 **Fairbanks & Ewing, Philadelphia,** Pa.—Scales. 571

197 **Haas, Edward, Philadelphia, Pa.—** Scales and hopper, etc. 571

198 **Buffalo Scale Co., Buffalo, N. Y.—** Scales. 571

199 **Willing & Co., New York, N. Y.—** Racking-cock. 587

200 **Schmitz, Theodore, New York,** N. Y.—Britannia measures. 587

201 **Guth, H., New York, N. Y.—Brew-** ers' instruments. 587

202 **Tagliabue, Charles J., New York,** N. Y.—Brewers' instruments. 587

203 **Travis, M. W., New York, N. Y.—** Weighing and measuring implements. 587

204 **Fiederlin, F., New York, N. Y.—** Mashing-machine. 587

205 **Schafhaus, John, New York, N. Y.** —Mashing-machine. 587

206 **Schimper & Immen, Newark N. J.** —Mashing-machine. 587

207 **Spittler & Lang, New York, N. Y.** —Mashing and shaving machine. 587

GREAT BRITAIN.

Animal and Vegetable Products, Engineering, Administration.

Animal and Vegetable Products.

1 **Pickering, Jonathan, Stockton-on-Tees, England.—Must.** 661

Agricultural Engineering and Administration.

2 **Lawrence & Co., London, England.** —Refrigerators. 683

CANADA.

Animal and Vegetable Products.

Animal and Vegetable Products.

1 **Davis, T., & Bro., Toronto, Canada.—Porter and ale.** 661

2 **Keith & Son, Halifax, N. S.—Ale.** 661

GERMANY.

(*West of Nave, Columns 1 to 4.*)

Agricultural Products.

Agricultural Products.

1 **Schlemmer, August von, Hochheim, Germany.—Malt.** 623

For classes of exhibits, indicated by numbers at end of entries, see Classification, pp. 12–14.

No. 168. THE HOUSE APIARY.

Size, 10 feet by 16 feet.

J. S. COE, Montclair, N. J.

Exhibits thirty-two colonies of Italian, Corinthian, and Cyprian bees at work making honey. Situated east of the Pomological Building.

No. 169. GUANO BUILDING.

Situated east of the Women's Pavilion, and north of Fountain Avenue. Is used for the exhibition of fertilizers.

No. 171. WINDMILLS.

1 **Eclipse Windmill Co., Beloit, Wis.** —Three windmills for pumping water, grinding, etc.

2 **U. S. Wind Engine & Pump Co.,** Batavia, Ill.—Two windmills.

3 **Stover Wind Engine Co., Greencastle, Pa.**—One windmill.

4 **Hartford Pump Co., Hartford, Conn.** —One windmill for raising water by compressed air.

No. 172. HEADQUARTERS OF THE "PRACTICAL FARMER."

(Newspaper.)

Size, 10 feet by 16 feet.

J. R. GARRETSON, Proprietor, Rochester, N. Y.

Situated east of the Pomological Building. Office of the paper.

No. 173. HAY PRESS.

Architect, W. P. ROCKAFELLOW, Albany, N. Y.—Size, 48 feet front; wings, 12 by 20 and 12 by 24.

P. K. DEDRICK & CO., Albany, N. Y.

Exhibits the perpetual baling press.

No. 176. BOILER HOUSE.

Size, 40 feet by 100 feet.

Situated directly east of Agricultural Hall, contains two Mast sectional boilers, manufactured at Springfield, Ohio, 100 horse-power each, which furnish steam to the machines in Agricultural Hall.

STATED DISPLAYS.

The Stated Displays in the Agricultural Department of the International Exhibition are as follows:

AGRICULTURAL PRODUCTS.

Pomological Products and Vegetables	May 16th to 24th.
Strawberries	June 7th to 15th.
Early Grass Butter and Cheese	June 26th to July 6th.
Early Summer Vegetables	June 20th to 24th.
Honey	June 20th to 24th.
Raspberries and Blackberries	July 3d to 8th.
Southern Pomological Products	July 18th to 22d.
Melons	August 22d to 26th.
Peaches	September 4th to 9th.
Northern Pomological Products	September 11th to 16th.
Autumn Vegetables	September 19th to 23d.
Cereals	September 25th to 30th.
Potatoes and Feeding Roots	October 2d to 7th.
Grapes	October 10th to 14th.
Autumn Butter and Cheese	October 17th to 21st.
Nuts	October 23d to November 1st.
Autumn Honey and Wax	October 23d to November 1st.

FIELD EXHIBITIONS.

Mowing Machines, Tedders, and Hay Rakes	June 26th to 30th.
Reaping Machines	July 5th to 10th
Fly-Casting Tournament	August 15th.

LIVE STOCK.

Horses	September 1st to 14th.
Dogs	September 1st to 8th.
Neat Cattle	September 21st to October 4th.
Sheep	October 10th to 18th.
Swine	October 10th to 18th.
Poultry	October 27th to November 6th

EXHIBITIONS OF LIVE STOCK.

1. The live stock display at the International Exhibition will be held within the months of September, October, and November, 1876; the periods devoted to each family being as follows: Horses, mules, and asses, from September 1st to 14th. Dogs from September 1st to 8th. Horned cattle, from September 21st to October 4th. Sheep, swine, and goats, from October 10th to 18th. Poultry will be exhibited from October 27th to November 6th.

2. Animals to be eligible for admission to the International Exhibition must be, with the exception of trotting stock, walking horses, matched teams, fat and draught cattle, of such pedigree that the exhibitor can furnish satisfactory evidence to the Chief of Bureau, that as applied to thorough-bred horses, as far back as the fifth generation of ancestors on both sides, they are of pure blood and of the same identical breed. As to short-horned cattle, they are registered in either Allen's, Alexander's, or the English herd-books. As to Holsteins, Herefords, Ayrshires, Devons, Guernseys, Brittanys, Kerrys, and other pure breeds, they are either imported or descended from imported animals on both sides. As to Jerseys, they are entered in the Herd Register of the American Jersey Cattle Club, or in that of the Royal Agricultural Society of Jersey. As to sheep or swine they are imported or descended from imported animals, and that the home-bred shall be of pure blood as far back as the fifth generation.

3. The term breed, as used, is intended to comprehend all family divisions, where the distinction in form and character dates back through years of separation; for instance, it is held that the progeny of a pure-blood Jersey and a pure-blood Guernsey is not a thorough-bred but a cross-bred animal, and, as such, is necessarily excluded.

4. In awarding prizes to animals of pure blood, the judges will take into consideration chiefly the relative merits as to the power of the transmission of their valuable qualities; a cardinal object of the Exhibition being to promote improvement in breeding stock.

5. In case of doubt relative to the age of an animal, satisfactory proof must be furnished or the animal will be subject to examination by a veterinary surgeon; and should the state of dentition indicate that the age has not been correctly stated, the person so entering as an exhibitor will be prohibited from exhibiting in any class.

6. The forms of classification for awards, as given under each head, are intended (except in the case of trotting stock, walking horses, matched teams, fat and draught cattle) to apply to the animals of any pure breed that are entered for competition.

7. The Exhibition being open to the world, it is of the first importance that the best of their kind only be brought forward, as the character of the stock will be judged by the general average of those exhibited.

8. Exhibitors will be expected to furnish their own attendants, on whom all responsibility of the care of feeding, watering, and cleaning the animals, and also of cleaning the stalls, will rest.

9. Forage and grain will be furnished at cost prices, at depots conveniently located within the grounds. Water can be had at all hours, ample facilities being provided for its conveyance and distribution throughout the stock yards.

10. Exhibitors must supply all harness, saddlery, vehicles, and other appointments, and all such must be kept in their appointed places.

11. The Commission will erect ample accommodation for the exhibition and protection of live stock, yet contributors who may desire to make special arrangements for the display of their stock, will be afforded facilities at their own cost. Fractious animals, whether stallions, mares with foals, or bulls, will be provided with stalls of suitable character.

12. All stalls will be regularly and distinctly numbered; corresponding numbers on labels of uniform character will be given to each exhibitor, and no animal will be allowed to pass from its stall without its proper number attached.

13. Numbers alone will distinguish stock in the show yards, preceding the awards of prizes.

14. The judges of live stock will make examination of all animals on the opening day of each serial show, and will for that day have exclusive entrance to the show yard.

15. No premium will be awarded an inferior animal, though there be no competition.

16. All animals will be under the supervision of a veterinary surgeon, who will examine them before admission, to guard against infection, and who will also make a daily inspection and report. In case of sickness the animal will be removed to a suitable inclosure especially prepared for its comfort and medical treatment.

17. When animals are taken sick, the exhibitors may either direct the treatment themselves, or allow the veterinary surgeon appointed by the Commission to treat the case. In this latter event the exhibitor will be charged for all expenses incurred. All possible care will be taken of animals exhibited, but the Commission cannot be held responsible for any injury or accident.

18. A ring will be provided for the display and exercise of horses and cattle.

19. On the last day of each serial show, a public auction may be held of such animals as the exhibitors may desire to sell. Animals may be sold at private sale at any time during their exhibition. During the period of a serial show, no animal, even in the event of being sold, will be allowed to be definitely removed.

20. An official catalogue of the animals exhibited will be published.

21. Exhibitors of thoroughbred animals must, at the time of making their entries, file with the Chief of the Bureau a statement as to their pedigree, affirmed or sworn to before an officer authorized to take affidavits, and the papers so filed shall be furnished to the Jury of Experts.

22. The ages of live stock must be calculated up to the opening day of the exhibition of the class to which they belong.

23. Sheep breeders, desiring to exhibit wool, the produce of the flocks, will display not less than five fleeces.

24. All animals must be entered according to the prescribed rules as given in forms of entry, which forms will be furnished on application to the Chief of the Bureau of Agriculture.

BREEDING HORSES.

Mares entered as breeding animals must have had foals within one year of the show, or if in foal, certificates must be furnished to that effect.

All foals exhibited must be the offspring of the mare with which they are at foot.

Awards will be made to respective breeds for pure bred turf stallions, six years and over; pure bred turf stallions, over four years and under six years; pure bred turf stallions, over two years and under four years; pure bred turf mares, six years and over; pure bred turf mares, over two and under six years.

Awards will be made for trotting stallions, six years and over; trotting stallions, over four years and under six; trotting stallions, over two years and under four; pure bred draught stallions, six years and over; pure bred draught stallions, over four years and under six years; pure bred draught stallions, over two years and under four years; pure bred draught mares, six years and over; pure bred draught mares, over two and under six years; trotting brood mares, six years and over; trotting fillies, over four years, and under six; trotting fillies, over two years and under four.

RUNNING AND TROTTING HORSES

Shall be judged according to their record up to August 15th, 1876, due regard being had to present condition.

Awards will be made for running horses having made fastest record; trotting stallions having trotted a mile within two-thirty; mares and geldings having trotted a mile within two-twenty-five.

WALKING HORSES.

Fast-walking horses, whether bred for agricultural purposes or the saddle, will compete in the ring for awards.

MATCHED TEAMS.

Awards will be made for matched teams having trotted a mile in two-thirty-five; matched stallions for heavy draught, over sixteen hands high, and over fifteen hundred pounds weight each; matched geldings for heavy draught, over sixteen hands high, and over fifteen hundred pounds weight each; matched mares for heavy draught, over fifteen hands high, and over fourteen hundred pounds weight each, matched mules for heavy draught, over fifteen and a half hands high, and over thirteen hundred pounds weight each.

BREEDING ASSES.

Awards will be made to respective breeds of pure bred jacks over six years; pure bred jacks over three years and under six; pure bred she-asses over six years; pure bred she-asses over three years and under six.

NEAT CATTLE.

No cow will be eligible for entry unless accompanied with a certificate that, within fifteen months preceding the show, she had a living calf, or that the calf, if born dead, was born at its proper time. No heifer entered as in calf will be eligible for a prize unless accompanied with a certificate that she had been bulled before the first of April, or presents unmistakable proof of the fact to the judges. No bull above one year old can be entered unless he have a ring in nose, and the attendant be provided with a leading stick, which must be used whenever the animal is taken out of stall.

Awards will be made for the best herd of each respective breed, consisting as follows: one bull, four cows, none under fifteen months.

Neat cattle, of each respective breed, will compete individually for awards: bulls, three years and over; bulls over two years and under three years; bulls over one year and under two years; cows four years and over; cows over three and under four years; cows or heifers in calf, over two years and under three years; yearling heifers. A sweepstake award will be made for the best bull of any breed. A sweepstake award will be made for the best cow of any breed.

FAT AND DRAUGHT CATTLE.

Animals entered as fat and draught cattle need not be of pure blood, but will compete on individual merits. Fat cattle must be weighed, and in general those will be judged best which have the greatest weight with the least surface and offal.

Awards will be made for best fatted steer of any age and breed; best fatted cow of any age or breed; most powerful yoke of oxen; most rapidly walking yoke of oxen; most thoroughly trained yoke of oxen; most thoroughly trained team of three or more yokes of oxen.

BREEDING SHEEP.

All sheep offered for exhibition must be accompanied with certificate to the effect that they have been shorn since the first of April, and the date given. If not fairly shorn, or if clipped so as to conceal defects, or with a view to improve the form or appearance, they will be excluded from competition.

Awards will be made to respective breeds for the best pen of five animals of same flock and including one ram, the ewes all having had living lambs the past spring.

Awards will be made to respective breeds for rams two years and over; shearling rams.

A sweepstake award will be made for the best ram, respectively of long, middle, and fine wooled breeds.

Awards will be made to respective breeds for ewes in pens of three, all having had living lambs; shearlings in pens of three.

A sweepstake award will be made for the best pen of three breeding ewes, respectively of long, middle, and fine wooled breeds.

FAT SHEEP.

Fat sheep entered for competition must be weighed, and in general those will be judged best which have the greatest weight, with the least surface and offal.

Awards will be made for pen of three best fatted sheep of each breed; pen of three best fatted sheep of any breed.

BREEDING SWINE.

Every competing sow above one year old must have had a litter, or be in pig, and the owner must bring proof of these facts if required. If a litter of pigs be sent with a sow, the young pigs must be sucklings, the offspring of the sow, and must not exceed the age of three months.

Awards will be made to respective breeds for the best pen of one boar and two breeding sows; for pen of sow and litter.

Awards will be made to respective breeds for boars two years old and over; boars one year old and under two years; boars between nine months and one year; breeding sows two years old and over; breeding sows one year old and under two years; pen of three sow pigs between nine months and one year.

A sweepstake award will be made for the best boar of any breed. A sweepstake award will be made for the best sow of any breed.

FAT SWINE.

Fat swine entered for competition must be weighed, and, in general, those will be judged best which have the greatest weight, with the least surface and offal.

Awards will be made for pairs of best fatted hogs of each breed; pairs of best fatted hogs of any breed.

DOGS.

Benches will be furnished free of charge. Exhibitors may themselves assume the cost of attendance upon their animals, but to provide for them who cannot conveniently attend the Exhibition, the Commission will assume the expenses of feeding and daily care, upon the payment of an attendance charge of three dollars upon each animal.

Awards will be made to respective breeds for dogs of two years and over; dogs of one year and under two; pups.

A sweepstake award will be made for the best foreign-bred dog of any breed. A sweepstake award will be made for the best home-bred dog of any breed.

Awards will be made to respective breeds for bitches of two years and over; bitches of one year and under two; bitch pups.

A sweepstake award will be made for the best foreign-bred bitch of any breed. A sweepstake award will be made for the best home-bred bitch of any breed.

POULTRY.

Poultry can only be exhibited in coops made after specifications furnished by the Bureau of Agriculture. The Commission will furnish coops and attendance upon payment of one dollar on each bird of the gallinaceous division, and two dollars on each pair of the aquatic division.

Awards will be made to respective breeds for pairs of one year and over, of chickens, turkeys, ducks, geese, swans, pigeons, guineas, and ornamental birds; for pairs under one year.

FISH.

Living fishes will be displayed in both fresh and salt water aquaria.

Awards will be made for largest display of fish of each species; largest display of fish of all species.

Department of Horticulture.

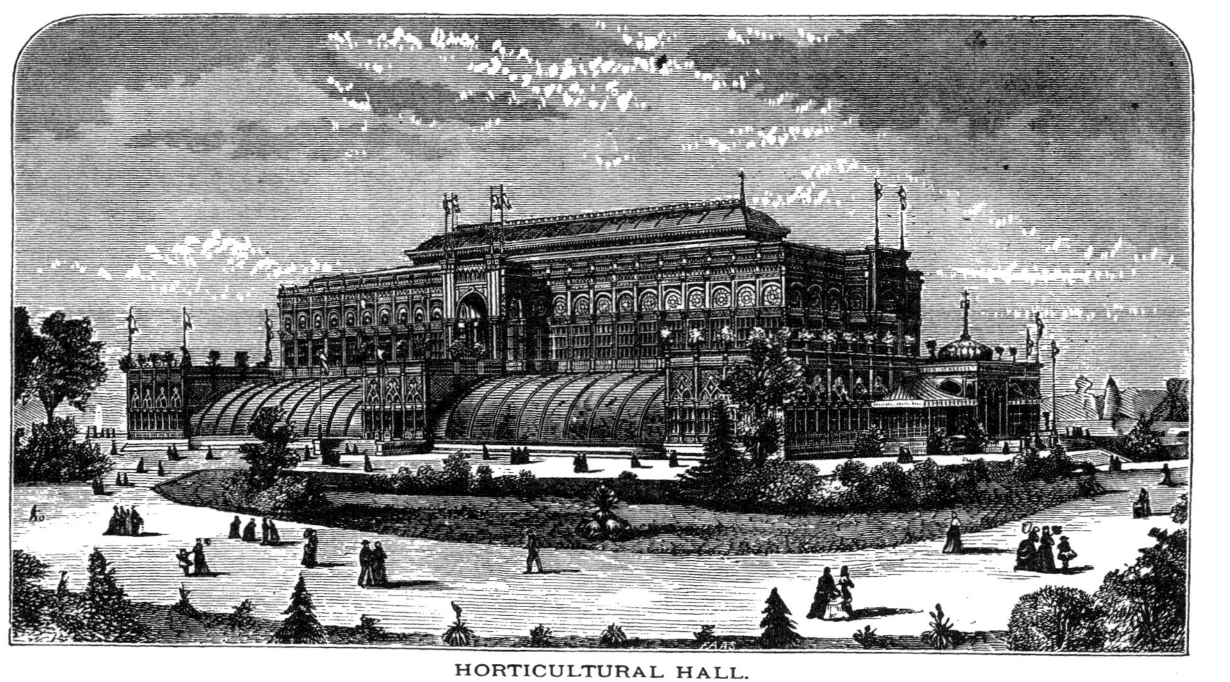

HORTICULTURAL HALL.

No. 151. HORTICULTURAL HALL.

Size 383 by 193 feet.

Architect, H. J. SCHWARZMAN.

Contractor, JOHN RICE, *Philadelphia.*

Wrought iron furnished by KEYSTONE BRIDGE COMPANY, *Pittsburgh, Pa.*

Cast iron furnished by SAMUEL J. CRESSWELL, *Philadelphia.*

Painting by JOSEPH CHAPMAN, *Philadelphia.*

Masonry by MOORE & SCATTERGOOD, *Philadelphia.*

APPROPRIATIONS of the City of Philadelphia have provided the Horticultural Building, which is to remain in permanence as an ornament of Fairmount Park. It is on the Lansdowne Terrace, a short distance north of the Main Building and Art Gallery, and has a commanding view of the Schuylkill river and the northwestern portion of the city. The design is in the Moorish style of architecture of the twelfth century, the principal materials externally being iron and glass. The main floor is occupied by the central conservatory, 230 by 80 feet, and 55 feet high, surmounted by a lantern 170 feet long, 20 feet wide, and 14 feet high. Running entirely around this conservatory, at a height of 20 feet from the floor, is a gallery 5 feet wide. On the north and south sides of this principal room are four forcing houses for the propagation of young plants, each of them 100 by 30 feet, covered with curved roofs of iron and glass. Dividing the two forcing houses in each of these sides is a vestibule 30 feet square. At the centre of the east and west ends are similar vestibules, on either side of which are the restaurants, reception room, offices, etc. From the vestibules ornamental stairways lead to the internal galleries of the conservatory, as well as to the four external galleries, each 100 feet long and 10 feet wide, which surmount the roofs of the forcing houses. These external galleries are connected with a grand promenade, formed by the roofs of the rooms on the ground floor, which has a superficial area of 1800 square yards.

The east and west entrances are approached by flights of blue marble steps from terraces 80 by 20 feet, in the centre of each of which stands an open kiosque 20 feet in diameter. The angles of the main conservatory are adorned with eight ornamental fountains. In the basement, which is of fireproof construction, are the kitchen, storerooms, coal-houses, ash-pits, heating arrangements, etc.

The ground was graded and the foundations of Horticultural Hall laid on May 1st, 1875. The building was finished April 1st, 1876. It covers an area for exhibition purposes of 122,500 square feet, and cost about $300,000. This building will be permanent.

HORTICULTURAL HALL.

Scale, 80 ft. to 1 in.

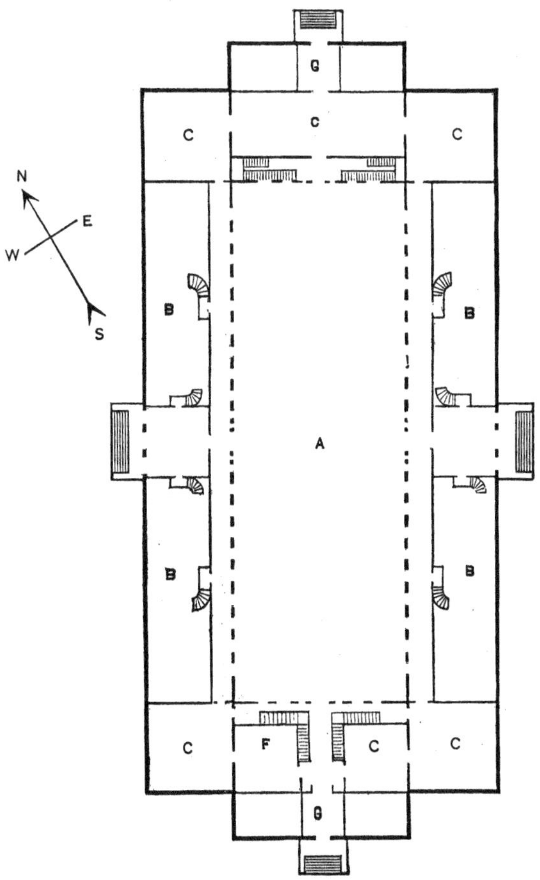

A *Floral Hall.* B *Greenhouse.* C *Exhibits.* F *Offices.* G *Porch.*

Total Length, 350 ft. Width, 160 ft. Height, 65 ft.

CLASSIFICATION.

DEPARTMENT VII.—HORTICULTURE.

ORNAMENTAL TREES, SHRUBS, AND FLOWERS.

CLASS 700.—Ornamental trees and shrubs, evergreens.

CLASS 701.—Herbaceous perennial plants.

CLASS 702.—Bulbous and tuberous rooted plants.

CLASS 703.—Decorative and ornamental foliage plants.

CLASS 704.—Annuals and other soft-wooded plants, to be exhibited in successive periods during the season.

CLASS 705.—Roses.

CLASS 706.—Cactacea.

CLASS 707.—Ferns, their management in the open air and in ferneries, wardian cases, etc.

CLASS 708.—New plants, with statement of their origin.

CLASS 709.—Floral designs, etc.—Cut flowers, bouquets, preserved flowers, leaves, seaweeds. Illustrations of plants and flowers.—Materials for floral designs. Bouquet materials, bouquet holders, bouquet papers, models of fruits, vegetables, and flowers.

HOTHOUSES, CONSERVATORIES, GRAPERIES, AND THEIR MANAGEMENT.

CLASS 710.—Hothouse and conservatory plants.

CLASS 711.—Fruit trees under glass.

CLASS 712.—Orchids and parasitic plants.

CLASS 713.—Forcing and propagation of plants.

CLASS 714.—Aquatic plants under glass, or in aquaria, etc.

CLASS 715.—Horticultural buildings, propagating houses, hotbeds, etc., and modes of heating them. Structures for propagating and forcing small fruits.

CLASS 716.—Portable or movable orchard houses and graperies, without artificial heat. Frames, beds.

GARDEN TOOLS, ACCESSORIES OF GARDENING.

CLASS 720.—Tools and implements.—Machines for the transplanting of trees, shrubs, etc. Portable forcing pumps, for watering plants in greenhouses and methods of watering the garden and lawn.

CLASS 721.—Receptacles for plants.—Flower pots, plant-boxes, tubs, fern cases, jardinieres, etc. Window gardening. Plant and flower stands, ornate designs in iron, wood, and wire.

CLASS 722.—Ornamental wirework, viz.: fences, gates, trellis bordering of flower beds, porches. Park seats, chairs, garden statuary, vases, fountains, etc. Designations, labels, numbers.

GARDEN DESIGNING, CONSTRUCTION, AND MANAGEMENT.

CLASS 730.—Laying out gardens.—Designs for the laying out of gardens, and the improvement of private residences. Designs for commercial gardens, nurseries, graperies. Designs for the parterre. Books on gardening.

CLASS 731.—Treatment of water for ornamental purposes, cascades, fountains, reservoirs, lakes.

CLASS 732.—Formation and after-treatment of lawns.

CLASS 733.—Garden construction, buildings, etc.— Rockwork, grottoes. Rustic constructions and adornments for private gardens and public grounds.

CLASS 734.—Planting, fertilizing, and cultivating.

UNITED STATES.

Trees, Shrubs, Flowers, Hot-House Plants.

Ornamental Trees, Shrubs, Flowers, and Floral Designs.

1 **Wharton, Joseph, Philadelphia, Pa.** —Eucalyptus globulus. 700

1*a* **Bingham, Rodolphus, Camden, N. J.**—Nelumbium luteum; sarracenia purpurea, drosera. 700

1*b* **Bliss, G. K., & Sons, New York, N. Y.**—Gladiolus, brenchleyeasis. 702

2 **Lovering, Joseph S., Philadelphia, Pa.**—Decorative foliage, plants, etc. 703

3 **Graham, Hugh, Philadelphia, Pa.**
a Decorative and ornamental foliage plants, palms, etc. 703
b Begonias, soft-wooded plants, etc. 704
c Ferns, in collection. 707
d Floral designs and cut flowers. 709

4 **Pennock Brothers, Philadelphia, Pa.**
a Foliage plants. 703
b Cut-flower designs. 709

4*a* **Boyle, W. F., Philadelphia, Pa.**—Decorative and ornamental foliage plants. 703

4*b* **Compondu, Louis F., New Brighton, N. Y.**—Variety of colens. 703

4*c* **Eagle, Louis J., Philadelphia, Pa.**—Decorative and ornamental foliage plants. 703

4*d* **Robertson, Thomas, Philadelphia, Pa.**—Decorative and ornamental foliage plants. 703

5 **The Misses Richardson, Philadelphia, Pa.**—Cactus. 706

6 **Fitzgerald, R., Philadelphia, Pa.**—Cactus. 706

7 **Miller & Sievers, San Francisco, Cal.**
a Collection of Pacific coast cactus. 706
b Collection of ferns. 707

8 **Such, George, South Amboy, N. J.**
a Decorative and ornamental foliage plants. 703
b Cactus, in collection. 706
c New plants. 708

9 **Moon, Mahlon, & Son, Morrisville, Pa.**—Collection of ferns. 707

10 **Dick, John, Philadelphia, Pa.**
a Cactus. 706
b Ferns. 707

11 **Miller & Hayes, Philadelphia, Pa.**—Tree ferns from Australia. 707

12 **Parsons, S. B., & Sons, Flushing, N. Y.**
a Varieties of ferns. 707
b Skeleton plants. 709

13 **Sturtevant, Edmund D., Bordentown, N. J.**—Ferns. 707

14 **Saunders, William, Washington, D. C.**—New and rare plants. 708

14*a* **Roehrs, I., New York, N. Y.**—Begonia trœblie; entirely new begonia. 708

15 **Freeman, J. R., Georgetown, D. C.** —Seedling begonia (large leaved species). 708

16 **Dreer, Henry A., Philadelphia, Pa.**
a Ferns in ferneries and in wardian cases. 707
b Floral designs. 709

17 **Henderson, Peter, New York, N. Y.** —Wire designs for cut flowers, bouquet papers, and materials. 709

18 **Marot, Charles H., Philadelphia, Pa.** —"The Gardener's Monthly." 709

19 **Parisian Flower Co., New York, N. Y.**—Artificial tropical leaf-plants and bouquets. 709

20 **Kresken, H. Acosta, Cincinnati, Ohio.**—Preserved flowers, leaves, grasses, bouquets, baskets, crowns, etc. 709

20*a* **Rice, D., & Co., Philadelphia, Pa.**—Michaux and Nuttall's North American Sylva. 709

20*b* **Huss, J. & Francois, Flushing, N. Y.** — Japanese and American skeleton ferns. 709

20*c* **Bayersdorfer, M. M., & Co., Philadelphia, Pa.**—Bouquet fixtures formed in shape of a tree. 709

20*d* **Kift, Joseph, & Son, Philadelphia, Pa.**—Floral designs, cut flowers, bouquets, etc. 709

20*e* **Peple, A., Brooklyn, N. Y.**—Fancy grasses, baskets, etc. 709

20*f* **Ringwalt, G. P. B., Philadelphia, Pa.**—Autumnal leaves. 709

20*g* **Smith, Stephen W., Philadelphia, Pa.**—Preserved natural flowers. 709

20*h* **Iles, F., Philadelphia, Pa.**—Wire floral designs. 709

21 **Cook, Mrs. O. A., San Francisco, Cal.**—Preserved natural flowers. 709

22 **Rolker, August, & Sons, New York, N.Y.**—Preserved flowers and grasses, bouquet papers, tin foil, wire, frames, etc. 709

23 **Leopold, Emil L., New York, N. Y.** —Fancy flower baskets, in straw, different shapes and styles. 709

24 **Le Moult, Adolphe, New York, N. Y.**—Preserved flowers, representation of a lake with natural water lilies. 709

25 **Jansen, Edward, 104 West 18th street, New York, N. Y.**—Fancy flower baskets, imitation coral, white gilt, straw, brown willow, and fancy wire. 709
Fine novelties will be out for the coming fall season. Sample cards and price lists sent on application.

26 **Rue, Miss Lizzie, Philadelphia, Pa.** —Models of fruits and flowers. 709

27 **Williamson, A. & H. A., 438 N. 8th St., Philadelphia, Pa.**—Wax models of fruits, vegetables, flowers, ferns, autumn and foliage leaves. 709
Instructions given and orders executed. 32 premiums awarded.

28 **Moffatt, Isaac, Philadelphia, Pa.**—Models of named American fruits, facsimile of choice specimens. 709

For classes of exhibits, indicated by numbers at end of entries, see Classification, pp. 12–14.

Hot-House Plants and Appliances, Gardening Implements.

29 Brossè, Madame S. C., San Francisco, Cal.—Collection of California sea mosses. 709

30 Long Brothers, Buffalo, N. Y.—Floral designs, comprising monograms, initials, etc. 709

31 Klag, Philip, New York, N. Y.—Preserved natural flowers. 709

31*a* Hazelehurst & Young, Philadelphia, Pa.—Cut flowers. (*Special concession to sell in the Exhibition grounds.*) 709

Hot-Houses, Conservatories, Graperies, and their Management.

32 Saunders, William, Washington, D. C.—Collection of American economic plants. 710

33 Graham, Hugh, Philadelphia, Pa.—Hot-house and conservatory plants, crotons, etc. 710

34 Lovering, Joseph S., Philadelphia, Pa—Hot-house and conservatory plants. 710

35 Price, Stephen S., Philadelphia, Pa.—Hot-house and conservatory plants. 710

36 Committee of the Congressional Library of the United States (Botanic Garden), Washington, D. C.—Officinal, medicinal, tropical, and semi-tropical plants. 710

37 United States Agricultural Department, Washington, D. C.—Officinal and medicinal plants, mahogany, cocoa, chocolate, guava, papaw, rose apple, etc. 710

38 Baldwin, Mrs. M. W., Philadelphia, Pa.—Hot-house and conservatory plants. 710

39 Zoological Society, Philadelphia, Pa.—Australian tree fern. 710

40 Bines, Samuel M., Philadelphia, Pa.—India rubber tree. 710

41 Merryweather, Ann E., Camden, N. J.—Aloe. 710

42 Sellers, John, jr., Philadelphia, Pa.—Hot-house and conservatory plants. 710

43 Cummings, William, Philadelphia, Pa.—Orange tree, banana, ivy, and date palm. 710

44 Faust, William F., Philadelphia, Pa.—Philodendron pertuosum and water lily. 710

45 Mackenzie, Thos. J., Philadelphia, Pa.—Hot-house and conservatory plants, plants of commerce. 710

46 Johnson, Joseph, Philadelphia, Pa.—Wax plant. 710

47 Cuthbert, Allen, Philadelphia, Pa.—Orange tree. 710.

48 Carpenter, Mrs. George W., Philadelphia, Pa.—Collection of conservatory plants. 710

50 Abbott, Charles F., Philadelphia, Pa.—Century plants (green and striped), sago palm. 710

52 Agnew, Hannah M., Philadelphia, Pa.—Banana. 710

53 Morris, Galloway C., Philadelphia, Pa.—Hot-house and conservatory plants. 710

54 Hoffner, Jacob, Cincinnati, Ohio.—Sago palm over 100 years old, belonged to Robert Morris in 1776. 710

55 Stokton, John A., Philadelphia, Pa.—Fig tree. 710

56 Weightman, William, Philadelphia, Pa.—Hot-house and conservatory plants. 710

57 Hance, A., & Sons, Red Bank, N. J.—Cycas revoluta.

58 Schaffer, William L., Philadelphia, Pa.—Sago palms. 710

59 Cope, Alfred, Philadelphia, Pa.—Century plants. 710

60 Such, George, South Amboy, N. J.
a Ferns, hot-house, and conservatory plants. 710
b Orchids, etc. 712

61 Clark, E. W., Philadelphia, Pa.—Century plants. 710

63 Moon, Mahlon, & Son, Morrisville, Pa.—Variegated pineapple. 710

63*a* Sturtevant, Edmund D., Bordentown, N. J.—Orchids and parasitical plants. 712

64 Wilson, John G., New York, N. Y.—Portable green-house boiler, hot water pipe with vapor pan attached. 715

64*a* Myers, Thomas J., & Son, Philadelphia, Pa.—Green-house boiler for heating conservatories. 715

64*b* Dick, John, Philadelphia, Pa.—Boiler for heating green-houses, conservatories, etc. 715

64*c* Warner, James, Philadelphia, Pa.—Boiler for heating green-houses, etc. 715

65 Jordan Horticultural Co., St. Louis, Mo.—Heating apparatus for green-houses. 715

65*a* Hitchings & Co., New York, N. Y.—Corrugated fire-box, boilers, and base-burning water-heater for warming green-houses, conservatories, etc. 715

66 Smith & Lynch, Boston, Mass.—Portable boilers for heating green-houses. 715

67 Ellis, Charles R., New York, N. Y.—Base-burning boilers for heating green-houses, graperies, etc. 715

Garden Tools, Accessories of Gardening.

68 Allen, R. H., & Co., New York, N.Y.—Comstock sower and attachments. 720

69 Jones, John M., Palmyra, N. Y.—Horticultural and floricultural implements of various styles and modifications. 1st. Revolving-staff implements for pruning, transplanting, weeding, and cultivating. 2d. Implements to be used with one hand, for weeding, transplanting, and cultivating, and in one of its forms is very convenient and attractive for ladies' use. 720

69*a* Bliss, B. K., & Sons, New York, N. Y.—Hand seed-sower, fertilizer dropper. 720

69*b* Jenks, George E., Concord, N. H.—Portable sprinkler and fountain for irrigating and ornamenting lawns, etc. 720

69*c* Farra, L. D., Philadelphia, Pa.—Lawn sprinkler. 720

70 Wheeler, W. F., Boston, Mass.—Hose liquid distributor, watering pot, insect annihilator, for garden and field, liquid manure distributor. 720

For classes of exhibits, indicated by numbers at end of entries, see Classification, pp. 13-14.

Garden Ornaments, Accessories, and Designs.

71 Moon, Mahlon, & Son, Morrisville, Pa.
a Wheel hoe. 720
b Vase. 721
c Lead label. 722

72 Dreer, Henry A., Philadelphia, Pa.
a Tools and implements. 720
b Receptacles for plants, fern cases, etc. 721

73 Bingham, O. A., Keene, N. H.—Revolving flower stand. 721

74 Hews, A. H., & Co., North Cambridge, Mass.—Flower pots, hanging pots, ferneries, garden vases, etc. 721

75 Pierce, Mrs. M. R., New York, N.Y.—Window attachments and other improved flower stands with water receptacle, sprinkling pan, and draining saucer. 721

76 Chase, James, Rochester, N. Y.—Combined aquarium, plant stand, bird cage, and fernery. 721

77 McClunie, Thomas, Hartford, Conn.—Drainer and evaporator with globe attachments for pots, vases and hanging baskets. 721

78 Rolker, August, & Sons, New York, N. Y.—Flower pots, boxes, fern cases, flower stands, etc. 721

79 Hills, George, Plainville, Conn.—Revolving flower stand with fountain attachment. For hydrants, self-sprinkling, surplus water caught by drip-pan. 721

80 Perine, M., & Sons, Baltimore, Md.—Flower pots, stone and fancy earthenware. 721

81 Pennock Brothers, Philadelphia, Pa.—Wardian cases, ferneries with shades 721

82 Hess, John M., & Sons, Philadelphia, Pa.—Chandelier designs with baskets, hanging baskets, hanging ferneries, vases, etc. 721

83 Freeman & Smith, Racine, Wis.
a Aquaria, ferneries, fountains, vases, etc. 721
b Plant stands, flower-pot brackets, window boxes and shelves, tree-tub castors, etc. 722
Illustrated catalogues free. Goods packed flat for shipment.

84 Racine Hardware Co., Racine, Wis.
a Plant and flower stands, ferneries, aquariums, etc. 721
b Fountains, vases, settees, etc. 722

85 Galloway & Graff, Philadelphia, Pa.
a Parlor vases, window boxes, pots, fern cases, baskets, etc. 721
b Terra-cotta statuary, vases, tazzas, pedestals. 722

86 Page, W. H., & Co., Greenville, Conn.
a Plant stands. 721
b Trellises. 722

87 Chase, Benj., jr., Derry, N. H.—Round-tapering flower stakes. 722

88 Balderston, George, Colora, Md.—Sectional vases. 722

89 Henderson, Peter, Jersey City, N. J.—Pot, plant, garden, and veranda trellises. 722

90 Harvey & Adamson, Philadelphia, Pa.—Oriental and Japanese garden vases, statuary, etc. 722

91 The Floral Works, 58 Cortlandt st., New York, N. Y., E. A. Reeves, Treasurer.—Crystal self-acting fountains, and self-acting fountain-attachments for aquaria and bird-cages, very simple and reasonable in price. 722

92 Mott, J. L., Iron Works, New York, N. Y.— Garden statuary, vases, etc. 722

93 Sanguinetti, Percy A., Philadelphia, Pa.—Glass-covered metallic labels, tree-protecting boxes. 722

94 Mayer, Charles, Baltimore, Md.—Self-acting water fountain. 722

95 Ebert, John, Philadelphia, Pa.—Parlor self-driving fountain. 722

95*a* Iles, F., Philadelphia, Pa.—Wire baskets, flower stands, etc. 722

96 Mueller, Quackenboss & Co., Philadelphia, Pa.—Vases in artificial stone designs. 722

97 Brown, J. Morton, Philadelphia, Pa.—Grape-vine trellises. 722

98 Moorhead Clay Works, Philadelphia, Pa.—Terra-cotta vases. 722

Garden Designing, Construction, and Management.

99 Miller & Hayes, Philadelphia, Pa.—Designs for laying out gardens and improving country residences. 730

101 Weidenmann, Jacob, New York, N. Y.—Set of plans for beautifying and improving country homes; survey, drainage, planting, and general maps. 730

102 Heissinger, F. X., New York, N. Y.—Designs for landscape gardening. 730

103 McClunie, Thomas, Hartford, Ct.
a Designs for laying out gardens, and the improvement of public grounds. 730
b Essay on formation and after-treatment of lawns. 732
c Metallic lawn gutters, curb, and drain. 733

103*a* Bliss, B. K., & Sons, New York, N. Y.—Globe sun-dial, adapted to any latitude. 320

103*b* Shove, Geo. A., Dighton, Mass.—Designs for a sanatorium. 342

103*c* Phœnix Stone Manufacturing Co., Philadelphia, Pa.—Artificial stone. 715

103*d* Rion, James H., Winsboro', S. C.—Section of cork-oak raised from an acorn. 600

OUT-DOOR EXHIBITS.

Ornamental Trees, Shrubs, and Flowers.

1 Bingham, Rudolphus, Camden, N. J.—Water lilies. 702

1*a* Salt, James, Philadelphia, Pa.—Fig tree. 700

1*b* Bliss, B. K., & Sons, New York, N. Y.—Gladiolus brenchiliensis. 702

2 Mackenzie, Thomas J., Philadelphia, Pa.—Decorative foliage plants. 703

2*a* Wilson, Charles H., Lower Merion, Pa.—Collection of geraniums. 703

Garden Ornaments, Designs, Tools, Ornamental Plants.

2b Gibson & Bennet, Woodbury, N. J. —Collection of verbenas. 703

2c Harris, Wm. K., Philadelphia, Pa. —Collection of geraniums. 703

3 Dreer, Henry A., Philadelphia, Pa.
a Bulbous and tuberous-rooted plants. 702
b Ornamental foliage plants. 703
c Annuals and soft-wooded plants. 704
d Ferns, in ferneries and wardian cases. 707

3a Scott, Robert, Philadelphia, Pa.
a Collection of geraniums; Zonlaes geraniums. 703
b Collection of roses. 705

4 Maginly, Thomas J., Philadelphia, Pa.
a Annuals and other soft-wooded plants. 704
b Roses, in collection. 705

4a Marc, Gabriel, Woodside, N. Y.—Collection of roses. 705

5 Moon, Mahlon, & Son, Morrisville, Pa.
a Ornamental trees, shrubs, etc. 700
b Herbaceous plants. 701
c Gladiolus, dahlias, etc. 702
d Flowering and ornamental plants, etc. 703
e Soft-wooded plants. 704
f Roses, in collection. 705
g New plants. 708
h Allen's new American hybrid gladiolus, raised by C. L. Allen, Long Island, New York. 702
i H. E. Hooker's new grape Brighton, very early, hardy, and excellent.
j E. Y. Teas' new tri-colored cana, and new geraniums. 703
k Wm. H. Moon's collection of new clematis. 703

6 Felton, A. L., Philadelphia, Pa.
a Herbaceous perennial plants. 701
b Bulbous and tuberous-rooted plants. 702
c Annuals and other soft-wooded plants. 704

7 Sturtevant, Edmund D., Bordentown, N. J.
a Herbaceous plants. 701
b Ferns. 707

8 Such, George, South Amboy, N. J.
a Ornamental trees, shrubs, etc. 700
b Herbaceous perennial plants. 701
c Bulbous and tuberous-rooted plants. 702

9 Dick, John, Philadelphia, Pa.
a Ornamental trees, shrubs, etc. 700
b Decorative and ornamental plants. 703
c Soft-wooded plants. 704
d Roses. 705
e New plants. 708

10 Wilson, William C., Astoria (L. I.), N. Y.—Plants for flower beds. 703

11 Henderson, Peter, 35 Courtlandt st., New York, N. Y.—250 varieties of new and rare geraniums, comprising double zonale, silver tri-color and golden tri-color sorts; also a circular bed of 500 plants, representing the "massing" or "ribbon" style of gardening by the use of different colored leaves. Located on and near Agricultural avenue. 704

12 Meehan, Thomas, Philadelphia, Pa.
a Hardy trees and shrubs. 700
b New plants. 708

13 Zeller, Charles, Flatbush, Long Island, N. Y.—Monthly carnations, tropical plants, liliums, and cut-flowers a specialty. 701

14 Compondu, Louis F., New Brighton, N. Y.—Pansies. 708

15 Hance, A., & Son, Red Bank, N. J.—New hardy ornamental plants and trees. 708

16 Parsons, S. B., & Sons, Flushing, N. Y.
a Deciduous trees, evergreens, and shrubs. 700
b New plants from Japan. 708

17 Hoopes, Bro., & Thomas, West Chester, Pa.
a Conifers. 700
b Ivies. 703

18 Parsons, R. B., & Co., Flushing, N. Y.
a Evergreen trees and shrubs, conifers, rhododendrons, kalmias, etc., deciduous trees, magnolias, azaleas, etc. 700
b Roses, in collection. 705

19 Miller & Hayes, Philadelphia, Pa.
a Ornamental trees and shrubs. 700
b Decorative plants. 703
c Roses, in collection; Centennial geranium. 705

20 Buist, Robert, Philadelphia, Pa.
a Ornamental trees and shrubs, abies and retinospora, from Japan. 700
b Roses, in collection; Centennial geranium. 705
c New plants; clematis veronica from Japan. 708

21 Moore, Samuel H., junior, Philadelphia, Pa.—Fig tree. 700

22 Hexamer, F. M., New Castle, N. Y.—Begonia Froebelii, a new bedding plant, Mont Blanc, a new hybrid. 708

Garden Tools, Accessories of Gardening.

23 Peck & Skilton, Westville, Conn.
a Rustic goods for house. 721
b Rustic goods for grounds. 722

24 Mott, J. L., Iron Works, New York, N. Y.—Fountains, vases, statuary, and settees. 722

25 Hanson, F. O., Philadelphia, Pa.—Galvanized railing, fences, gates, seats, vases, etc. 722

26 Gossin, F., Philadelphia, Pa.—Terra-cotta vases. 722

27 Mitchell, Wilson, Philadelphia, Pa.—Potsilica (artificial stone) fountain basins, vases, tiles, etc. 722

28 Walker, M., & Sons, Philadelphia, Pa.—Wrought-iron railing, ornamental gates, farm and hurdle fence, wirework 722

29 Brown, J. Morton, Philadelphia, Pa.—Grape-vine trellises. 722

30 O'Brien Bros., Yonkers, N. Y.
a Hanging baskets, etc. 721
b Rustic gates, settees, chairs, stands, vases, etc. 722

31 Moorhead Clay Works, Philadelphia, Pa.—Terra-cotta vases. 722

31a Elmore, Daniel, Trumansburg, N. Y.—Settees and chairs. 722
(In grounds of American Restaurant.)

Garden Designing, Construction, and Management.

32 Sturtevant, Edmund D., Bordentown, N. J.—Rustic adornments. 733

33 O'Brien Bros., Yonkers, N. Y.—Rustic summer-houses, etc. 733

For classes of exhibits, indicated by numbers at end of entries, see Classification, pp. 12–14.

Garden Designing, Construction, and Management.

34 Peck & Skilton, Westville, Ct.—Rustic buildings. 733

35 Lebanon Building & Paving Block Company, Lebanon, Pa.—Building blocks of annealed slag paving. 733

35*a* Seibrecht, H. A., & Co., New York, N. Y.—Rock-work. 733

35*b* Elmore, Daniel, Trumansburg, N. Y.—Summer-houses and pagodas. 733

36 Pacific Guano Co., Boston, Mass.
a Machines, materials, staple products of the soil of the United States, specimen plants fertilized with guano. 734
b Commercial fertilizers, phosphatic, calcareous, etc. 681

37 Boileau, A., New York, N. Y.—Trained fruit trees. 734

38 Austin, R., Camden, N. J.—Cranberry vines. 734

39 Miller & Sievers, San Francisco, Cal.—Collection of cones of the Pacific coast, coniferæ. 605

For classes of exhibits, indicated by numbers at end of entries, see Classification, pp. 12–14.

GREAT BRITAIN.

Ornamental Trees, Shrubs, Tools, and Accessories of Gardening.

Ornamental Trees and Shrubs.

1 **Veitch, James, & Sons, Royal Exotic** Nursery, London.
a Collection of standard and dwarf rhododendrons, standard and dwarf hollies, standard Portugal laurels 700
b Collection of new Japanese coniferæ. 708

2 **Waterer, Anthony, Knap Hill Nursery**, Woking, Surrey.—Rhododendrons and azaleas (*in tent*). 700

3 **Williams, B. S., Victoria & Paradise** Nurseries, London.—Collection of new and rare plants, orchids, and ferns of recent introduction. 708

4 **Bull, William, Chelsea, London.**—Illustration of new and rare plants. 709

Garden Tools, Accessories of Gardening.

5 **Barnard, Bishop, & Barnard, Nor**folk Iron Works, Norwich.
a Lawn-mowers, garden-rollers, horse-reels, water-barrows, croquet-netting, espalier-trainers, etc. 720
b Garden-chairs. 722

6 **Doulton, H., & Co., Lambeth, Lon**don.—Terra-cotta work, statue of Diana (heroic size), Amazon vase, and sundry other vases. 722

NEW ZEALAND.

Ornamental Trees and Shrubs.

Ornamental Trees and Shrubs.

1 **New Zealand.—Esculent fern root. Will germinate if crushed and planted** in rich soil and shady place; collection of ferns. 707

JAMAICA.

Hot-Houses, Conservatories, and their Management.

Hot-Houses, Conservatories, and their Management.

1 **Thompson, Robert, Jamaica.—Collection of economic plants.** 710

For classes of exhibits, indicated by numbers at end of entries, see Classification, pp. 12-14.

CANADA.

Gardening Appliances.

Garden Tools, Accessories of Gardening.

1 **Wells, William, Beamsville, Ont.**—Flower-pots and saucers. 721

2 **Ahern, J. H., Paris, Ont.**—Flower-pots and saucers. 721

3 **Pratt, Chorless, London, Ont.**—Flower-pots and saucers. 721

4 **Welding, E., Brantford, Ont.**—Flower-pots and saucers. 721

5 **Farrar, G. H. & L. E., St. John, Q.**—Fancy flower-pots. 721

6 **Hobson, Walter, Quebec, Q.**—Flower-pots. 721

FRANCE.

Ornamental Plants, Hot-Houses, Ornaments, Designs.

Ornamental Trees, Shrubs, and Flowers.

1 **Roempler, L., Nancy.**—Ornamental plants. 700

2 **Leroy, Louis, Angers, Maine-and-Loire.**—Ornamental plants and fruit trees. 700

3 **Verdier, E., senior, Paris.**—Gladiolus. 702

4 **Verdier, Charles, Paris.**
a Gladiolus. 702
b Roses. 705

4*a* **Lacharme, Fr., Lyons.**—A collection of roses; thirty-seven varieties originated and grown by exhibitor. 705

4*b* **Allegatoire, Lyons.**—New zonal double geraniums, originated and grown by exhibitor. 708

4*c* **Sisley, Jean, Lyons.**—New zonal geraniums, originated and grown by exhibitor. 708

5 **Vilmorin, Andrieux, & Co., Paris.**—Seeds, flowers, and vegetables. 709

Hot-Houses, Conservatories, Graperies.

6 **Roempler, L., Nancy.**—Hot-house plants. 710

7 **Pinel, C. P., Paris.**—Application of electricity to germination and fructification. 713

8 **Lichtenfelder, Paris.**—Monumental hot-houses. 715

Garden Tools, Accessories of Gardening.

9 **Couette, La Briche, Seine.**—Portable tents, kiosk, and sheds; folding arm-chairs, bedsteads. 722

10 **Durenne, A., Paris.**—Monumental fountain. 722

11 **Lichtenfelder, Paris.**—Garden furniture; elastic seats; iron gates and trellises. 722

12 **Thiry, J., jr., Paris.**—Trellises and galvanized iron fences. 722

13 **Walcker, W., Paris.**—Garden seats. 722

Garden Designing, Construction, and Management.

14 **Bonvoisin, A., Paris.**—Garden plans. 730

15 **Duvillers, F., Paris.**—Park and garden plans; books on parks and gardens. 730

16 **Vilmorin, Andrieux, & Co., Paris.**—Photographs of flowers, vegetables, and plants; samples of seeds. 730

17 **Ratinet, Paris.**—Rocky grotto. 733

For classes of exhibits, indicated by numbers at end of entries, see Classification, pp. 12–14.

GERMANY.

Garden Designing, Construction, and Management.

Garden Designing, Construction, and Management.

2 Eichler, Gustav, Sans Souci.—Plans for gardens. 730

AUSTRIA.

Garden Designing, Construction, and Management.

Garden Designing, Construction, and Management.

1 Pohl, Charles, Austria.—Standard currants and gooseberries. 734

NETHERLANDS.

Fruit Trees, Ornamental Plants, Flowers, Designing.

Ornamental Trees, Shrubs, and Flowers.

1 Galesboot, J. P. R., Amsterdam.—Fruit trees. 700

2 Boer, W. C., Boskoop.—Ornamental trees and shrubs. 700

3 Krelage, J. H., Haarlem.
a Bulbs. 700
b Collection of gladiolus, etc. 702

4 Nes, Az. P. van, Boskoop.—Trees, shrubs, and flowers. 700

6 Groenewegen, A. C., Haarlem.—The flowers of Haarlem. 709

Garden Designing, Construction, and Management.

7 Nes, Az. P. van, Boskoop.—Trained fruit trees. 734

8 Galesboot, J. P. R., Amsterdam.—Trained fruit trees. 734

SWEDEN.

Garden Tools.

Garden Tools, Accessories of Gardening.

1 Von Essen, H. H., Baron, Tidaholm.—Gardeners' Scissors. 720

For classes of exhibits, indicated by numbers at end of entries, see Classification, pp. 12–14.

ITALY.

Garden Decoration.

Garden Tools, Accessories of Gardening.

1 Foley, Margaret A., Rome.—Marble Fountain. 722

LUXEMBURG.

Ornamental Trees.

Ornamental Trees, Shrubs, and Flowers.

1 Suppert & Notting, Limpertsberg, near Luxemburg.—Rose trees. 705

HAWAII.

Ornamental Trees.

Ornamental Trees and Shrubs.

1 Hawaiian Islands.—Ferns. 707

ARGENTINE REPUBLIC.

Ornamental Plants, Designs.

Ornamental Trees, Shrubs, and Flowers.

1 Provincial Commission, Province of Santiago del Estero.—Cacti. 706

2 Fuente, Diego de la, Province of Corrientes.—Caraguata plant. 706

3 Gelos, Martin, Province of La Rioja.—Scarlet oak, coccus cacti. 706

4 Provincial Commission, Province of Mendoza.—Cacti. 706

5 Provincial Commission, Province of Cordoba.—Cacti. 706

Garden Designing, Construction, and Management.

6 Forkel, F., Province of Buenos Ayres.—Projected plan of the park "3d of February." 730

For classes of exhibits, indicated by numbers at end of entries, see Classification, pp. 12–14.

SPAIN.

Ornamental Trees, Shrubs, Flowers, Garden Designing.

Ornamental Trees, Shrubs, Flowers, and Floral Designs.

1 Lachaume, Jules, Havana, Cuba.—Collection of plants, cactus, new plants. 706

Hot Houses, Conservatories, Graperies, and their Management.

2 Lachaume, Jules, Havana, Cuba.—Agaves, euphorbias. 710

3 Poey, Juan, Havana, Cuba.—Forty plants presented to the U. S. Centennial Commission. 710

Garden Designing, Construction, and Management.

4 Lachaume, Jules, Havana, Cuba.—
a Physiology of plants. 730
b Rustic and stone work. 733

PHILIPPINE ISLANDS.

Ornamental Trees and Shrubs.

Ornamental Trees and Shrubs.

1 Philippine Islands.—Ferns. 707

No. 170. HORTICULTURAL ANNEX.

North of Horticultural Hall. Constructed of wood and iron, in the form of a tent, and covered with canvas. Designed for the exhibition of flowers and plants during the season.

For classes of exhibits, indicated by numbers at end of entries, see Classification, pp. 12–14.

STATISTICAL APPENDIX.

STATISTICAL APPENDIX.

UNITED STATES.

THE United States of America occupy the entire width of the central portion of North America, between latitude 24° 30′ and 49° north, and from longitude 66° 50′ and 124° 30′ west. They are bounded, north, by New Brunswick, Canada (from which they are separated by the river St. Lawrence and the great lakes), and British Columbia; on the south, by Mexico and the Gulf of Mexico; east, by the Atlantic; and west, by the Pacific Ocean. Their greatest breadth, from Cape Cod, on the Atlantic, to the Pacific, near the parallel of latitude 42 degrees, is about 2600 miles. Their greatest length, from the northern boundary of Maine to Key West, in Florida, is about 1600 miles. Their mean length, from east to west, is about 1600 miles, and from north to south about 1300 miles. Their area, according to calculations founded on the report of the Commissioner of the General Land Office, for 1867, is 3,057,407 square miles, or 1,956,740,480 acres. This, however, is exclusive of the district of Alaska, in the extreme northwest of the continent, purchased from Russia, and comprising 577,390 square miles, or 369,529,600 acres. Including Alaska, the entire area of the United States and territories is 3,634,797 square miles.

Three mountain ranges, the Appalachian chain towards the east, the Rocky Mountains in the centre, and the Sierra Nevada in the west, divide the United States into four great regions. The first of these is the Atlantic slope, or all that portion lying east of the Appalachian or Alleghany range; the second, lying between the Appalachian and the Rocky Mountains, is known as the basin of the Mississippi and Missouri; the third is the country between the Rocky Mountains on the east and the Sierra Nevada on the west; the fourth extends from the Sierra Nevada to the Pacific Ocean, and is known as the Pacific slope.

The Appalachian or Alleghany mountains extend from the State of Mississippi northeast through the States of Alabama, Georgia, Tennessee, North Carolina, Virginia, Pennsylvania, New York, and Vermont, for about 1200 miles, at a variable distance of from 70 to 300 miles from the Atlantic coast, and with an average breadth of about 100 miles. Their mean height is from 2000 to 3000 feet, half of which consists in the elevation of the mountains over the adjacent plains, and the rest in the elevation of these plains above the sea. The White Mountains of New Hampshire, belonging to this chain, reach a height of 6226 feet, and the Black Mountain, of North Carolina, is 6732 feet above the level of the sea. The Rocky Mountains are a prolongation of the Mexican Cordillera, and some of their highest peaks attain to between 12,000 and 15,000 feet above the level of the sea. Their average altitude is about 8500 feet. The Sierra Nevada, or Snowy Mountains, are 10° to 12° west of the Rocky Mountains. Under different names, and with different altitudes, this range extends from the peninsula of lower California to Alaska, some of its passes being about 9000 feet, and its highest summits about 16,000 feet above the level of the sea.

The rivers of the United States are of great magnitude and importance. Of those flowing east and south the principal are the Mississippi and Missouri, which, with their tributaries, the Ohio, Arkansas, Red, Yellowstone, and Nebraska rivers, give to the interior an extent of inland navigation and a facility of communication unequaled on any other continent. Among the principal rivers flowing into the Atlantic, are the Hudson, Delaware, Susquehanna, Potomac, Savannah, and St. Johns. The Columbia, Sacramento, and Colorado flow into the Pacific Ocean. The Mississippi,

Alabama, Colorado (of Texas), and Rio Grande (the last named forming the boundary between Texas and Mexico), empty into the Gulf of Mexico. The area of the water-basins has been estimated as follows: Rivers flowing into the Pacific, 644,040 square miles; into the Atlantic, 488,877; into the Gulf of Mexico, 1,683,325 square miles, of which 1,257,457 are drained by the Mississippi-Missouri rivers. The coast-line on both oceans has a length of about 13,200 miles, excluding the numerous bays and sounds, besides 3600 miles on the great northern lakes.

The following table shows the area and population of each State and Territory:

STATES.	POPULATION IN 1870.	AREA IN SQUARE MILES.
Alabama,	996,992	50,722
Arkansas,	484,471	52,198
California,	560,247	188,981
Colorado,	39,864	104,000
Connecticut,	537,454	4,750
Delaware,	125,015	2,120
Florida,	187,748	58,268
Georgia,	1,184,109	58,000
Illinois,	2,539,891	55,410
Indiana,	1,680,637	33,809
Iowa,	1,194,020	55,045
Kansas,	364,399	81,318
Kentucky,	1,321,011	37,680
Louisiana,	726,915	41,346
Maine,	626,915	35,000
Maryland,	780,894	11,124
Massachusetts,	1,457,351	7,800
Michigan,	1,184,059	56,451
Minnesota,	439,706	83,531
Mississippi,	827,922	47,156
Missouri,	1,721,295	65,350
Nebraska,	122,993	75,995
Nevada,	42,491	104,125
New Hampshire,	318,300	9,280
New Jersey,	906,096	8,320
New York,	4,382,759	47,000
North Carolina,	1,071,361	50,704
Ohio,	2,665,260	39,964
Oregon,	90,923	95,274
Pennsylvania,	3,521,951	46,000
Rhode Island,	217,353	1,306
South Carolina,	705,606	34,000
Tennessee,	1,258,520	45,600
Texas,	818,579	274,356
Vermont,	330,551	10,212
Virginia,	1,225,163	38,348
West Virginia,	442,014	23,000
Wisconsin,	1,054,670	53,924
ORGANIZED TERRITORIES.		
Arizona,	9,658	113,916
Dakota,	14,181	150,932
District of Columbia,	131,700	64
Idaho,	14,999	86,294
Montana,	20,595	143,776
New Mexico,	91,874	121,291
Utah,	86,786	84,476
Washington,	23,955	69,994
Wyoming,	9,118	97,883
TERRITORIES NOT ORGANIZED.		
Alaska,		577,340
Indian,		68,991
Total,	38,558,351	3,602,424

In a country extending through 24° of latitude, and nearly 60 of longitude, the climate varies considerably. In the north, along the British frontier, the winter is very severe; during this season the snow is sufficiently abundant in New England to admit the use of sleighs, and the ice on the rivers strong enough to bear the passage of horses and wagons. As far south as Pennsylvania and New Jersey, the thermometer falls, in winter, below zero; rising, in summer, to nearly 100° Fahr. Along the Atlantic coast, between latitude 41° and 45°, the climate is colder in winter and warmer in summer, by nearly 10°, than in those parts of Europe which lie under the same parallels. Snow, however, rarely falls south of latitude 30°; nor is it frequently seen south of the Potomac, except on mountains. The mean annual temperature of Albany is about 49°; of New York and Cincinnati, about 51°; of Philadelphia, 54°; of Natchez, 65°, and of Cantonment Brooke, in Florida, 72°. The temperature along the Pacific is much higher than in corresponding latitudes on the eastern coast.

The Mississippi valley is very fertile. In the Eastern States there still exist large forests of valuable timber, such as beech, birch, maple, oak, pine, spruce, elm, ash, walnut; and, in the South, live-oak, water-oak, magnolia, palmetto, tulip tree, cypress, etc., remnants of the wooded region which formerly extended over the whole Atlantic slope, but into which great inroads have been made by advancing civilization. Apples, pears, cherries, and plums flourish in the North; peaches, melons, and grapes in the Middle States; pineapples, pomegranates, figs, almonds, and oranges in the South. Maize is grown from Maine to Louisiana, and wheat throughout the Union; tobacco as far north as Connecticut, and in the Western States south of Ohio. There is not much cotton raised north of 37°, though it grows as far north as 39°. Rice is cultivated in South Carolina, Georgia, Louisiana, and as far north as St. Louis, Mo. The sugar-cane grows as high as 33°, but does not thoroughly succeed beyond 31° 30′. The vine and mulberry tree grow in various parts of the Union; oats, rye, and barley throughout the North and the mountainous parts of the South; and hemp, flax, and hops in the Western and Middle States. The following figures, taken from the report of the ninth census (1870), will convey an idea of the extent of the annual productions of agriculture:

Spring wheat,	112,549,733	bushels
Winter wheat,	175,195,893	"
Rye,	16,918,795	"
Indian corn,	760,944,549	"
Oats,	282,107,157	"
Barley,	29,761,305	"
Buckwheat,	9,821,721	"
Rice,	73,635,021	pounds
Tobacco,	262,735,341	"
Cotton,	3,011,996	bales
Peas and beans,	5,746,027	bushels
Irish potatoes,	143,337,473	"
Sweet potatoes,	21,709,824	"
Wine,	3,092,369	gallons
Hay,	27,316,048	tons
Clover seed,	639,657	bushels
Grass seed,	583,188	"
Sugar (from cane),	87,043	hhds
Maple sugar,	28,443,645	pounds
Molasses,	23,564,469	gallons
Dairy Products.—Butter,	514,092,683	pounds
Cheese,	53,492,153	"
Milk sold,	235,500,599	gallons
Wool,	100,102,387	pounds
Wax,	631,129	"
Honey,	14,702,815	"

The same report gives the cash value of farms in the United States at $9,262,803,861; of farming implements and machinery, at $336,878,429; live stock, at $1,525,276,457.

Total estimated value of all farm productions, including betterments and additions to stock, $2,447,538,658. Value of orchard products, $47,335,189; products of market gardening, $26,719,229.

There were, at the same time, 8,690,219 horses, 28,074,582 cattle, 28,477,951 sheep, and 25,184,540 hogs.

Except a few small isolated fields, all the bituminous coal in the United States lies west of the Appalachian chain, where a vast series of coal beds stretch from the mountains west through Ohio, Indiana, and Illinois, parts of Kentucky and Alabama, into the State of Missouri, and as far as two hundred miles beyond the Mississippi. Anthracite coal is found most extensively in Pennsylvania; also in Western Virginia and the eastern portion of Ohio and Illinois. The oil-wells of northwestern Pennsylvania contain apparently inexhaustible stores of mineral oil or petroleum. Numerous salt-springs exist in New York, Virginia, Pennsylvania, and the Western States. Iron is distributed most abundantly through the coal measures in Pennsylvania, Ohio, Virginia, and Tennessee, the ore containing from 25 to 33 per cent. of metal. Iron ore also abounds in the Northwestern States; and that found in one part of Vermont yields 78 per cent. of iron. A large proportion of the ore found in this part of the Union is magnetic. Lead is found in various places, but more especially in Missouri, Wisconsin, and Illinois. In some parts of Wisconsin this ore yields from 60 to 70 per cent. of lead. Large deposits of copper have been found in Michigan, in the Lake Superior region. Gold, in large quantities, and silver, have been found in the States and Territories west of the Rocky Mountains. Gold has also been found in Virginia, the Carolinas, Georgia, and Tennessee. Quicksilver, zinc, manganese, with lime and building stone, are the other chief mineral products. The following figures are from the Statistics of Mining, Table VIII, Report of the Ninth Census (1870):

	VALUE OF PRODUCTS.
Anthracite coal,	$38,495,745
Bituminous coal,	35,029,247
Copper,	5,201,312
Gold, placer mined,	7,266,613
" hydraulic mined,	2,508,531
Quartz, gold and silver bearing,	16,677,508
Iron ore,	13,204,138
Lead,	736,004
Petroleum,	19,304,224

The mechanical and manufacturing establishments of the Union, in 1870, numbered 252,148, using steam-engines of 1,215,711 horse-power and 1,130,431 horse-power in water-wheels, and employing 2,053,996 hands. The amount of capital invested is $2,118,208,769; annual wages, $775,584,343; material used, $2,488,427,242, and the total products $4,232,325,442. The chief manufacturing States are Pennsylvania, New York, Massachusetts, Ohio, Illinois, New Jersey, Connecticut, and Rhode Island.

The importations for the year ending June 30th, 1875, were:

Merchandise,	$533,005,536
Gold and silver,	20,894,217
Total,	$553,899,753

Foreign exports, merchandise,	$14,157,611
Gold and silver,	8,275,013
Total,	$22,432,624

The gold value of domestic exports, during the same period, was $583,141,229.

In the length of miles of railway open to traffic, the United States exceeds all other nations, although in the proportion of miles of railway to miles of area, it ranks below some of the smaller and more densely populated states of Europe. The following figures, from Poor's "Railway Manual," illustrate the growth of the railway system in the United States:

In 1830, there were	23	miles in operation.
" 1840, " "	2,818	" " "
" 1850, " "	9,021	" " "
" 1860, " "	30,635	" " "
" 1870, " "	52,898	" " "
" 1874, " "	72,623	" " "

During the year 1874, the gross earnings were $520,466,016, of which $379,466,935 was for freight, and $140,999,081 for passengers. Net earnings, $189,570,958; dividends paid, $67,042,942.

The government of the United States is, by the Constitution, intrusted to three separate authorities, the executive, the legislative, and the judicial. The executive power is vested in a President, who is elected every four years, and is eligible for re-election. The legislative power is vested in two houses, the Senate and the House of Representatives, the President having a veto power, which may be overcome by a two-thirds vote of both houses. Two senators from each State are elected by the legislature thereof, for the term of six years; and representatives are chosen in each State, by popular vote, for two years. The number of Representatives for each State is allotted in proportion to its population, one for each 135,239.

The supreme judicial authority is vested in a Chief Justice and eight Associate Justices, who are appointed for life by the President, by and with the consent of the Senate.

The government of each State is on the same model as that of the general government. There is a governor chosen by popular vote, and a State legislature, similarly chosen, composed of two houses. Each State also has a constitution which prescribes its form of government.

The following statistics apply to the army and navy of the United States in 1875: The army consisted, July 1st, 1875, of 2204 commissioned officers, and 25,000 enlisted men; the navy of 175 vessels, with an armament of 1282 guns, 8500 men, 1254 commissioned, and 490 non-commissioned officers on the active list.

The postal service is conducted by the general government. During the fiscal year ending June 30th, 1875, it carried 601,921,520 letters, 117,215,850 stamped wrappers, 13,956,750 newspapers, and 31,094,500 postal cards. The money orders amounted to $75,425,854.

The telegraph lines belong to private corporations. Their total length, in January, 1875, was 75,000 miles; length of wires, 165,000 miles; number of offices, 6172; number of messages transmitted during the year 1874, 13,700,000.

Education is conducted by the separate States. In general the primary schools are supported by a property tax, and nearly all the States have school funds in addition, the income of which is distributed among the towns in proportion to the number of pupils educated. The gifts with which, during late years, private individuals have endowed institutions of learning, prove a growing appreciation of the claims of the higher education.

The following statistics are collated from the report of the ninth census, 1870:

PUBLIC SCHOOLS.

NUMBER OF SCHOOLS.	TEACHERS EMPLOYED.			PUPILS IN ATTENDANCE.		
	MALE.	FEMALE.	TOTAL.	MALE.	FEMALE.	TOTAL.
125,059	74,174	109,024	183,198	3,120,052	3,108,008	6,228,060

The schools "Not Public" are arranged under two headings: "Classical, Professional, and Technical," and "Other Schools."

"NOT PUBLIC" SCHOOLS (Classical, Professional, and Technical).

NUMBER.	TEACHERS.			PUPILS.		
	MALE.	FEMALE.	TOTAL.	MALE.	FEMALE.	TOTAL.
Classical, etc., 2,545	7,766	5,001	12,767	148,810	106,380	255,190
Other Schools, 14,025	11,389	13,688	25,077	353,134	373,554	726,688

INCOME.

PUBLIC.		NOT PUBLIC.	
		CLASSICAL, PROFESSIONAL, AND TECHNICAL.	OTHERS.
From Taxation of Public Funds, ...	$58,855,507	$2,320,250	$570,282
" Endowments, ...	144,533	3,356,003	163,249
" Other Sources, including Tuition, .	5,030,633	11,999,654	12,962,615
	$64,030,673	$17,675,907	$13,696,146

The total number of libraries returned was 163,353, containing 44,539,184 volumes. Of these, 107,673 were private libraries, containing 25,571,503 volumes. In the opinion of the superintendent of the census, these results are "manifestly far below the truth."

The newspaper and periodical press comprised, in 1875, 7870 publications, divided as follows: Daily, 1718; tri-weekly, 80; semi-weekly, 107; weekly, 5957; bi-weekly, 24; semi-monthly, 106; monthly, 802; bi-monthly, 8; quarterly, 68.

GREAT BRITAIN.

THE following brief table is given (approximately) of the area, population, revenue, and commerce of the British Empire. It is not possible to give the exact figures, but for all practical purposes those now given will be sufficient. The colonies which exhibit are treated under their proper names.

NAME OF COUNTRY.	AREA IN SQUARE MILES.	POPULATION.	REVENUE.	PUBLIC DEBT.	IMPORTS AND EXPORTS.
Great Britain and Ireland,	122,518	31,857,338	$389,600,000	$3,555,100,000	$3,262,900,000
Indian Possessions, etc., .	1,558,254	240,000,000	243,500,000	550,310,000	472,390,000
Other Eastern Possessions,	25,264	3,150,000	10,714,000	8,766,000	160,710,000
Australasia, ...	3,087,000	2,105,000	53,570,000	219,150,000	365,250,000
North America, ...	3,620,500	4,000,000	21,915,000	107,140,000	209,410,000
Africa, ...	250,000	1,400,000	4,870,000	7,792,000	43,830,000
West Indies, ...	12,707	1,075,000	535,700	4,870,000	48,700,000
European Possessions, .	120	160,000	1,022,700	1,217,500	73,050,000
Various settlements, . .	96,171	200,000	2,678,500	3,165,500	24,350,000
Totals, ...	8,772,534	283,947,338	$728,405,900	$4,457,511,000	$4,660,590,000

The *United Kingdom of Great Britain and Ireland* is the full designation of the country more generally known as Great Britain or the United Kingdom. It includes the two large islands of Great Britain and Ireland, and the adjacent smaller islands, together with the Channel Islands and the Isle of Man.

The following table exhibits the area, in English square miles, and population, according to the last census of the several constituent parts:

	AREA.	POPULATION.
England, ...	50,922	21,495,131
Wales, ...	7,397	1,217,135
Scotland, ...	31,324	3,360,018
Great Britain, ...	89,648	26,072,284
Ireland, ...	32,481	5,411,416
Isle of Man, and Channel Islands, ...	394	144,638
	122,518	
Army and Navy, and Merchant Seamen, ...		229,000
		31,857,338

The island of Great Britain lies between latitude 49° 57′ 30″ and 58° 40′ 24″ north. and between longitude 1° 46′ east, and 6° 13′ west, and is the largest island in Europe, It is bounded on the north by the Atlantic, on the east by the North Sea, and on the south by the English Channel, and on the west by the Atlantic, the Irish Sea, and St. George's Channel. Its greatest length is about 608 miles, and its greatest breadth (from Land's End to the east coast of Kent), about 300 miles.

England, which may be roughly said to be divided from Scotland on the north by the Cheviot Hills and the Rivers Tyne and Solway, and from Wales by the Severn and Dee, is, except on the west and north, for the most part a level country, so cultivated as to be highly productive. The other districts have mineral riches, as iron, tin, lead, copper, and coal, which make abundant amends for the poverty of their surface. Wales is generally mountainous, and also has great mineral wealth.

The greater part of the surface of Scotland is irregularly distributed into mountains and valleys, a very small proportion spreading into level plains. The eastern coast forms a waving, continuous, and rarely broken line; the western is extremely irregular, being deeply indented with bays and arms of the sea, and exhibiting steep promontories and mountainous islands. The whole country is physically divided into *Highlands* and *Lowlands*—the former comprehending the northwest, west, and central portions; the latter, generally speaking, the east coast and the country south of the Forth and Clyde.

Ireland is an island lying between 51° 26′ and 55° 23′ north latitude, and 5° 20′ and 10° 26′ west longitude. It is about 60 miles to the west of England. On three sides it is washed by the Atlantic Ocean, and on the east by the Irish Sea and St. George's Channel. Its greatest length is, from north to south, 306 miles, and from east to west 120 to 180 miles. Ireland is divided into the four provinces of Ulster, Leinster, Munster, and Connaught, which are again subdivided into 32 counties.

The geology of Great Britain is of peculiar importance. British geologists have given to the world the names whereby the various strata are known, and British rocks form the typical series of the earth's strata. The whole recognized series of stratified deposits occur in Britain, one or two only being more fully developed elsewhere; and it is only in these singular cases that the foreign equivalents are taken as the types. British geology is no less important from the influence it has had in the development of the country, its mineral wealth, especially the coal and iron, being the real sinew of Britain's wealth and power.

In the year 1874, there was produced from the ore nearly 6,000,000 tons of pig iron, value £16,476,372; and 385 ounces of gold were raised, value £1540. Copper, tin, lead, zinc, silver, and other metals brought the total value of metals produced up to £19,539,070. The aggregate value of all the minerals, metals, coal, etc., obtained in the United Kingdom in 1874, was £67,834,313. Included in this were 125,043,257 tons of coal, value £46,849,194.

The climate of Great Britain is mild and equable in a remarkable degree, the winters being considerably warmer and the summers colder than at places within the same parallels of latitude. The mean temperature of England is 49.5°, and of Scotland 47.5°.

Very few species of plants or animals are peculiar to Great Britain. The flora, for the greater part, resembles that of Germany; but in the south of England there is, as might be expected, a closer correspondence with that of the northwest of France; and some plants found in the Channel Islands and on the French coast appear nowhere in Britain but on the southwest coast of England. The mountains of Wales, Cumberland, and Scotland have a vegetation resembling that of Scandinavia more than that of the mountains of central or southern Europe. The state of the case is much the same as to the fauna. There are, however, many remarkable instances both of plants and animals, which, from these apparent relations to continental Europe, might be expected in Great Britain, and which are not indigenous to it; as, for instance, among plants, the Norway spruce, and among animals, the lemming, both common in Scandinavia. The progress of civilization and of cultivation has completely banished from Great Britain many of the animals which were once numerous, as bears, wolves, etc. On the other hand, many plants which were unquestionably introduced by man, have become thoroughly naturalized.

For administrative purposes, Great Britain with its surrounding islands (excepting the Channel Islands and the Isle of Man, which are under peculiar jurisdiction) is divided into 84 counties or shires.

The soil of Great Britain is almost exclusively devoted to the production of the two primary necessities of society,—breadstuffs (chiefly wheat, barley, and oats) and grass, roots, etc., as food for domestic animals. The annual value of the pastures and meadow hay is immense. The total extent of land returned in 1872, as being under all kinds of crops, bare fallow and grass, was 31,004,173 acres in Great Britain, 15,746,547 acres in Ireland, 88,573 in the Isle of Man, 18,026 acres in the island of Jersey, and 12,007 acres in the islands of Guernsey, Alderney, etc., making a total for the United Kingdom of 46,869,326 acres. The number of horses included in the agricultural returns was 1,808,259; the number licensed in Great Britain was 857,048; the number of others than agricultural horses exempt from license duty, was probably about 35,000; and the number belonging to the army at home may be stated at 15,000, which would bring the total number of horses in the United Kingdom up to 2,715,000. The total number of cattle returned for the United Kingdom in 1872, was 9,718,000; sheep, 32,246,000; pigs, 4,178,000.

Constabulary returns, based upon information obtained from farmers and others and received by the Boards of Guardians, show that in the year 1873, Ireland produced 469,563 quarters of wheat, 6,912,765 quarters of oats, 1,016,339 quarters of barley, 25,576 quarters of bere and rye, 48,375 quarters of beans and peas, 2,683,060 tons of potatoes, 4,429,967 tons of turnips, 515,690 tons of mangold wurzel, 278,923 tons of cabbage, 19,843 tons of flax, and 3,306,163 tons of hay. At the end of 1873, Ireland had 4,142,400 head of cattle, 4,482,053 sheep, 532,146 horses and 1,042,244 pigs.

The following table shows the condition of the textile industries of the United Kingdom, 1874:

	NO. OF FACTORIES.	HANDS EMPLOYED.
Cotton	2,655	479,515
Woolen	1,800	135,605
Worsted	692	142,097
Flax	449	128,459
Silk	818	45,559
Shoddy	125	3,431
Hemp	61	5,211
Jute	110	37,920
Hair	27	1,211
Hosiery and other factorys	557	27,667
Total	7,294	1,006,675

The government of Great Britain is of the kind known as a "constitutional monarchy," in which the sovereign accepts of his dignity under an express agreement to abide by certain prescribed conditions. The sovereignty is hereditary in the family of Brunswick, now on the throne, and in the person of either a male or a female. The executive government of the United Kingdom is vested nominally in the crown, but practically in a committee of Ministers, commonly called the Cabinet, which has come to absorb the functions of the ancient Privy Council, the members of which, bearing the title of Right Honorable, are sworn "to advise the king according to the best of their cunning and discretion," and "to help and strengthen the execution of what shall be resolved." Though not the offspring of any formal election, the Cabinet is virtually appointed by Parliament, and more especially by the House of Commons, its existence being dependent on the possession of a majority in the latter body.

The powers of Parliament are politically omnipotent within the United Kingdom, its colonies and dependencies. It can make new laws, and enlarge, alter, or repeal those existing. Its authority extends to all ecclesiastical, temporal, civil, or military matters, as well as to altering or changing the constitution of the realm. Parliament is the highest court of law, over which no other has jurisdiction.

The budget estimates for the financial year 1875–76, laid by the Chancellor of the Exchequer before the House of Commons, April 15th, 1875, was as follows:

Total revenue,	£75,685,000
" expenditure,	75,266,000
" estimated surplus,	£419,000

The following figures show the numerical strength of the military force in the United Kingdom in 1875:

Cavalry,	13,358
Artillery,	19,418
Engineers,	4,020
Infantry,	55,590
Total,	92,386

The army estimates of March 31st, 1876, contain votes of money for four classes of reserves, as follows:

	MEN.
Militia,	139,018
Yeomanry cavalry,	15,130
Volunteers,	161,150
Enrolled pensioners and army reserve force,	32,000

The total force of the British army in India was stated, in the estimates of 1875–76, to amount to 63,197.

On the 1st of December, 1874, the navy consisted of 233 steamers and sailing vessels, manned by crews aggregating 60,000.

The following are the statistics for the year 1874 of the tonnage of British and foreign vessels (sailing and steam) entered and cleared at ports in the United Kingdom from and to foreign countries and British possessions:

	ENTERED.	CLEARED.	TOTAL.
British,	14,833,644	15,256,039	30,089,683
Foreign,	7,534,866	7,804,408	15,339,274
Total,	22,368,510	23,060,447	45,428,957

There were, in 1874, 20,872 vessels, with crews aggregating 203,606, and of a registered tonnage of 5,864,588.

On the 1st of January, 1875, there were 16,448 miles of railway open in the United Kingdom. The statistics of capital, passengers, receipts, and working expenses for the year 1874 were as follows: Total capital paid up (shares, loans), $2,970,456,106; number of passengers, 478,316,701; total of traffic receipts, $277,109,238; working expenses, $158,040,397.

The number of letters delivered in 1874 was, in England and Wales, 804,000,000, in Scotland, 90,000,000, and in Ireland, 73,000,000. Of postal cards there were 66,000,000 delivered in England and Wales; 9,000,000 in Scotland; and 4,000,000 in Ireland; total for the United Kingdom, 79,000,000.

The number of newspapers and book packets delivered in 1874 was 207,000,000 in England and Wales, 29,000,000 in Scotland, and 23,000,000 in Ireland; total, 259,000,000. The number of money orders in 1874, in the whole of the United Kingdom was 15,900,562, of the aggregate value of £26,296,441. At the end of the year the total amount of deposits held by the Post Office Savings Bank was £24,030,711.

There were 19,116,634 telegraph messages forwarded from postal telegraph stations in the year 1874. The number of post offices at the end of 1874 was 12,950. The total number of telegraph offices, at the same date, was 5600, including 1800 railway telegraph offices. The total length of the postal telegraph wires at the end of 1874 was 107,000 miles.

In England, the chief institutions for education are the ancient national universities of Oxford and Cambridge; the more recent institutions of London, Durham, and Lampeter, in Wales; the classical schools of Eton, Westminster, Winchester, Harrow, Charter House, and Rugby; Owens College, Manchester, and other colleges and schools, chiefly for physical science; the various military schools; the colleges of the dissenting denominations; the middle class schools, either started by individual teachers or by associated bodies acting as directors, to whom the teachers are responsible; and the schools of design.

For primary education, a national system has now been established. Under the Elementary Education Act for England, 1870, a popularly elected school board is established in any district where the existing schools are deficient. Schools under the act are supported by school-rates and fees, and by parliamentary grants, varying according to the number of pupils, and their proficiency, as tested by different standards of examination. They are at all times to be open to government inspection. It is left to the discretion of school boards to make education compulsory.

Scotland possesses four universities for the higher branches of education, viz.: Edinburgh, Glasgow, St. Andrew's, and Aberdeen, besides a variety of other minor colleges. The Scotch education act, 1872, is modelled after the English act, but differs from it by enacting that a school board is to be elected in *every* parish and burgh; by making it illegal for parents to omit educating their children, between five and thirteen, in reading, writing, and arithmetic; and by comprehending higher class schools.

The number of the day-schools in Great Britain, inspected in 1871, was 10,700; the daily average attendance throughout the year was 1,434,488; 1,724,689 scholars were present at inspection; 875,298 were examined; and 598,203 passed the prescribed tests. On the registers of the inspected day-schools were 2,055,312 children, of whom 517,344 were under six years of age, 1,332,229 between six and twelve, and 205,739 above twelve; 2709 night-schools, were inspected, having an average attendance of 86,206 each night. In December, 1871, there were in Great Britain 15,605 certificated teachers, 1196 assistant teachers, and 21,854 pupil teachers.

Ireland is well supplied with educational establishments, having three universities, a large number of endowed schools, and an admirable system of mixed schools.

Commission from GREAT BRITAIN and COLONIES to the International Exhibition:

HIS GRACE THE DUKE OF RICHMOND AND GORDON, K. G.,
Lord President of the Council.

THE RT. HON. VISCOUNT SANDON, M. P., Vice-President of the Committee of Council on Education.

THE RT. HON. SIR EDWARD THORNTON, K. C. B., Her Britannic Majesty's Envoy Extraordinary and Minister Plenipotentiary at Washington, Special Commissioner to represent Great Britain at Opening Ceremonies.

Executive Staff:

COL. HERBERT SANDFORD, R. A., Joint Executive Commissioner.

PROF. THOMAS C. ARCHER, F. R. S. E., Joint Executive Commissioner.

A. J. R. TRENDELL, Secretary.

T. A. WRIGHT, Superintendent Industrial Space.

JOHN ANDERSON, LL.D., Superintendent General Machinery.

JOSEPH MIDDLETON JOPLING, Superintendent Fine Arts.

B. T. BRANDRETH GIBBS, Superintendent Agriculture and Horticulture.

J. H. CUNDALL, Assistant General Superintendent and Engineer.

HUGH WILLOUGHBY SWENY, Assistant Superintendent Catalogue and Official Publications.

FREDERICK J. HODGKINSON, Financial Clerk.

E. E. COOPER, Assistant for Machinery.

ERNEST CHARRINGTON, Clerical Assistant.

J. M. BRETT, Clerical Assistant (India Section).

H. A. P. ROOKE, Clerical Assistant (Passenger and Transport Arrangements).

NEW ZEALAND.

NEW ZEALAND, a British colony in the South Pacific Ocean, consists of three principal islands, called, respectively, the North, South, and Stewart Islands. There are several small islets—mostly uninhabited—dependent on the colony; the chief of them are the Chatham Islands and the Auckland Islands. The New Zealand group is situated about 6500 miles west of South America, and about 1200 miles east of Australia. The entire group lies between 34° and 48° south latitude and 166° and 179° east longitude. The three principal islands extend in length 1100 miles, but their breadth is extremely variable, ranging from 46 miles to 250 miles; the average breadth being about 140 miles. The North and South Islands are separated by Cook Strait, which is crossed by steamers in about two hours.

The total area of New Zealand is about 100,000 square miles, or 64,000,000 acres.

According to a census taken March 31st, 1874, the population (exclusive of the aborigines) numbered 299,514 souls. It is estimated that the present white population (April, 1876) is about 400,000. The Maori population, according to an approximate census taken on June 1st, 1874, was 45,470.

The aborigines, called Maoris, who formerly caused much trouble, though a large number have always sided with the British, are now peacefully settling down to agricultural pursuits, and, since 1871, permanent tranquility appears to have been established.

The New Zealand Islands are of primitive rocks and tertiary plains, but a great portion of the entire area is occupied by mountains, among which are many extinct and a few active volcanoes. The mountains are mostly clothed with evergreen forests of luxuriant growth, interspersed with fern-clad ranges, and occasionally with treeless grassy plains. Extensive and rich valleys and sheltered dales abound in the North Island; and in the east of the South Island there are many extensive plains of rich land, admirably adapted either for agriculture or cattle-breeding. Water and water-power are found in great abundance in the colony, and the numerous rivers are subject to sudden floods from the melting of the mountain snows. As a rule, however, the streams are short, and are not navigable for more than 50 miles above their mouths. The chief is the Clutha, in the South Island, and the Waikato river, in the North Island, which latter, issuing from the Taupo lake (30 miles long by 20 broad), flows in a northern direction for 200 miles, and reaches the sea on the west coast.

In the North Island, around Lakes Rotomahana and Rotorua, are a number of grand and beautiful geysers, which throw up water heated to the boiling point. The southwest coast of the South Island is indented with a number of deep sounds, of which Milford Sound is the chief. In this sound the water is unfathomable; the only way of securing a ship being to moor it, stem and stern, to the trees which overhang the water. Steamers of 2000 tons have been thus moored. The geology of New Zealand is remarkable and varied in a high degree. The mountains, which are of every variety of outline, are chiefly composed of the schist and slate-rocks, primary sandstone, and limestone. Extensive beds of coal and lignite exist; the former have been to some extent worked, and are at present being largely developed by the construction of railways and harbor works in their vicinity.

Of the whole surface extent of New Zealand, one-fourth is estimated to consist of dense forest tracts, one-half of excellent soil, and the remainder of waste lands, scoriæ hills, and rugged mountain regions. Nearly 40,000,000 acres are supposed to be more or less suitable for agriculture and cattle-breeding. The soil, though often clayey, has in the volcanic districts more than a medium fertility; but the luxuriant and semi-tropical vegetation is perhaps as much due to excellence of climate as to richness of soil. Owing to the prevalence of light and easily worked soils, all agricultural processes are performed with unusual ease. The climate of New Zealand is one of the finest in the world. The country contains few physical sources of disease; the average temperature is remarkably even at all seasons of the year, and the atmosphere is continually agitated and freshened by winds that blow over an immense expanse of ocean. In the North Island, the mean annual temperature is 57°; in the South Island, 52°. The mean temperature of the hottest month at Auckland, in the northernmost province, is 68°, and at Dunedin, in the most southern province, 58°; of the coldest month, 51° and 40° respectively. The air is very humid, and the fall of rain is greater than in England, but there are more dry days. All the native trees and plants are evergreens. Forests, shrubberies, and plains are clothed in green throughout the year, the results of which are that cattle, as a rule, browse on the herbage and shrubs of the open country all the year round, thus saving great expense to the cattle-breeder; and that the operations of reclaiming and cultivating land can be carried on at all seasons. The seasons in New Zealand are the reverse of ours; January is their hottest month, and June the coldest. All the grains, grasses, fruits, and vegetables grown in England are cultivated in the colony with perfect success, being excellent in quality and heavy in yield; while, besides these, the vine is cultivated in the open air, and maize, the taro (*Caladium esculentum*), and the sweet potato are cultivated with success in the sunny valleys of the North Island.

The temperature, it will be thus observed, is very equable, for while the summers are as cool as those of England, the winters are as warm as those of Italy. The mean annual temperature of Auckland is nearly the same as at Rome; at Wellington, nearly the same as at Milan; at Dunedin, nearly the same as at London. The official reports of the British Army Medical Department show that, where the annual mortality from all diseases out of every 1000 British soldiers quartered in the United Kingdom was 16, it was only 5 out of every 1000 in the troops quartered for more than 25 years in New Zealand. In other words, this colony appears to be peculiarly favorable to the duration of human life.

In connection with this, it may be mentioned, in order to show the redundancy of the population in New Zealand, that in 1874 the births were 40.05 per 1000 of the population, and the death rate was only 12.97 per 1000, while the marriages were 8.81 for every 1000 people.

The entire acreage under crop, in February, 1875, was 1,788,800. Of the crops, the principal were wheat, oats, barley, potatoes, and sown grass. At the same date, the number of holdings was 16,092, the population being 296,018. The average yield of wheat was, in 1875, over 28 bushels per acre.

The live stock of the colony consisted, at the census of March 1st, 1874, of 99,859 horses, 494,917 cattle, 11,704,853 sheep, 123,921 pigs, and 1,058,198 head of poultry.

Large gold fields were discovered in the spring of 1857. In the year 1874, there were 376,388 ounces of gold, of the declared value of $7,526,655, exported from New Zealand, the average annual yield of the gold fields since 1862 being 588,072 ounces, or value of $11,395,140, while from April 1st, 1857, to December 31st, 1875, the total quantity of gold exported was 8,025,676 ounces, valued at $151,271,293 gold.

The principal produce of the colony is wool, 46,848,735 pounds, valued at $14,173,475, having been exported in 1874.

The total imports of the colony during the year 1874 were $40,609,060; the total exports, $26,256,345.

The class of people most required in New Zealand are farmers with a small capital, carpenters, who can earn, according to their skill, from 11 shillings to 15 shillings per diem, and single women, who always gain good wages, and rarely stop in service for a long time, being greatly in demand in the matrimonial market. All classes of laborers find ready employment at remunerative rates.

By an imperial statute, passed in 1852, the legislative power is vested in the Governor and a Parliament of two chambers; the first called the Legislative Council, and the second the House of Representatives, and collectively, the General Assembly. The Legislative Council consists at present of 49 members, nominated by the crown for life; and the House of Representatives of 83 members, elected by the people for five years. Two Maoris sit in the Legislative Council, and 4 in the House of Representatives. Two of the latter also are members of the Executive Council. The Governor is assisted by an Executive Council, composed of the responsible ministers for the time being, and any others he may appoint. Members of both branches receive pay at the rate of $787 for the session, which generally lasts three months. Every owner of a freehold worth $250, or tenant house-holder, in the country at $25, in the town at $50 a year rent, is qualified to vote for members of the House, and is eligible for membership. The seat of government is at Wellington, a town of about 12,000 people, and centrally situated.

The colony is divided into nine provinces; four in the North, and five in the South Island. Each of these provinces is governed by an elected Superintendent and Provincial Council. In 1875, the General Assembly passed a bill declaring that the provincial governments should cease to exist after the close of their next session. The form of local government which is to take the place of provincial government has not been decided upon, but will probably take the shape of legislative powers.

In the year 1874, the total ordinary revenue (including provincial) was $9,367,240, and the territorial revenue, $5,754,500, which, with incidental receipts of $221,320, makes the total general revenue—ordinary, territorial, and incidental—amount to $15,343,060. The total ordinary expenditure by general and provincial governments was $14,803,555.

Beyond the ordinary expenditure, a sum of $13,629,465 was spent, which is charged to the loan account. The public debt of New Zealand amounted, at the end of 1874, to $66,834,680, and as a loan expenditure is still proceeding, it is estimated that the total debt will shortly amount to about $95,000,000. Against this there is a sinking fund already amounting to $5,000,000, and, moreover, a large amount has been spent on reproductive works. In 1870, the sum of $20,000,000 was authorized to be borrowed for the purposes of emigration and public works (such as railways, roads, telegraphs, water-races, bridges, etc.), besides $5,000,000 for defence and other purposes. Since then, further large loans have been contracted for public works. To assist in the development of these works, a vast number of emigrants have been brought into the country, receiving either free passage from England or a grant of land. Railways are now being constructed throughout the islands, 260 miles being open for traffic; 420 miles under construction, of which a good deal is near completion; and 330 miles are authorized to be constructed.

Under the stimulus of the public works and emigration policy, no less than 43,965 emigrants arrived in New Zealand in 1874.

On the 31st of December, 1874, the colony had 2632 miles of telegraph lines, and 5284 miles of wires. The number of telegrams during the year was 844,301, of which total 724,582 were private, and the remainder government messages.

During the year 1874, the post office received 4,339,165 letters, and dispatched 4,719,291. The total number of newspapers received was 3,872,668, and dispatched, 2,434,024. Money orders to the number of 62,712 and the amount of $1,315,820 were issued during 1874.

Grammar and free schools, endowed from the public revenues of the various provinces, several colleges, and two universities, one being established in Otago and the other a corporation endowed by the general government, are the principal educational institutions.

The shipping entered in 1874 consisted of 856 vessels, with a tonnage of 399,296. Of these, 237 vessels, measuring 201,017 tons, were British; 552, measuring 170,303 tons, colonial; and 67, measuring 27,976, were foreign. Of the foreign vessels entered, 50 were American. Coasters are not included in the above statistics. In 1874 the number of vessels entered coastwise was 14,351, and their tonnage 1,353,085.

The number of individual exhibits included in this Catalogue from New Zealand is 1114.

Commission from NEW ZEALAND to the International Exhibition:

THE HON. WALTER BALDOCK DURANT MANTELL, M. L. C., F. G. S., Chairman.
THE HON. WILLIAM GISBORNE.
WILLIAM HORT LEVIN, ESQ.
DANIEL MCINTYRE, ESQ., Consular Agent of the United States Government at Wellington.
JAMES HECTOR, ESQ., C. M. G., M.D., F. R. S., Special Commissioner to Philadelphia.
ARTHUR THOMAS BOTHAMLEY, Secretary.

NEW SOUTH WALES.

NEW SOUTH WALES, a British colony in the southeastern portion of Australia, is bounded on the north by a line which, beginning at Point Danger, in latitude 28° 8′ south, follows several lines of heights across the Dividing Range till it meets the 29th parallel, which forms the rest of the boundary westward; on the west by the 141st meridian; on the east by the Pacific Ocean; and the line separating it from Victoria on the south runs from Cape Howe, at the southeast of the island, northwest to the source of the Murray, and then along that stream, in a direction west by north, to the western boundary of the two colonies.

Its area is 323,437 square miles, and its population in 1874 was, exclusive of aborigines, 584,278. At the same date the population of Sydney, the capital, was 150,000. Within the colony of New South Wales, the mountain range, which girdles nearly the whole island, is most continuous and elevated, and is known as the Dividing Range. The section of this mountain system on the southern boundary of the colony, called the Australian Alps, rises in Mount Kosciusko to 6500 feet. From this the range extends northward, the water-shed being from 50 to 150 miles distant from the east coast, and thus divides the colony into two slopes, with two distinct water systems. The rivers on the eastern side descend with great rapidity, and in oblique tortuous courses, their channels often forming deep ravines. Many of them are navigable in their lower course for sea-going steamers. The principal are the Richmond, Clarence, Macleay, Manning, Hunter, Hawkesbury, and Shoalhaven. The numerous streams that rise on the west side of the water-shed within the colony, all converge and empty their waters into the sea through one channel within the colony of South Australia. The southern and main branch of this great river system is the Murray. The other great trunks of the system are the Murrumbidgee, which is navigable, the Lachlan, at times reduced to a string of ponds, and the Darling. The Macquarie, passing through the rich district of Bathurst, is a large tributary of the Darling, but it reaches it only in the rainy seasons. The coast line from Cape Howe to Point Danger is upwards of 700 miles long, and presents numerous good harbors formed by the estuaries of the rivers. Owing to the great extent of the colony, stretching as it does over eleven degrees of latitude, the climate is very various. In the northern districts, which are the warmest, the climate is tropical, the summer heat occasionally rising in inland districts to 120°, while on the high table-lands weeks of severe frost are sometimes experienced. At Sydney, the mean temperature of the year is about 65°. The mean heat of summer, which lasts here from the beginning of December to the 1st of February, is about 80°, but it is much modified on the coast by the refreshing sea breeze. The annual fall of rain is about 50 inches. Rain sometimes descends in continuous torrents, and causes the rivers to rise to an extraordinary height. Sometimes the rains almost fail for five or six months in succession. Along the coast, for 300 miles from the northern boundary, the soil and climate are admirably adapted for the growth of cotton, and that plant has already been cultivated as far south as the river Manning (latitude 32° south). Farther south the climate is more temperate, and is fitted to produce all the grain products of Europe. Immense tracts of land, admirably adapted for agriculture, occur in the southwestern interior; while in the southeast coast districts the soil is celebrated for its richness and fertility. In the north, the tobacco plant, the vine, and sugar-cane are grown; and pineapples, bananas, guavas, lemons, citrons, and other tropical fruits are produced. In the cooler regions of the south, peaches, apricots, nectarines, oranges, grapes, pears, pomegranates, melons, and all the British fruits are grown in perfection, and sometimes in such abundance that pigs are fed with them. Wheat, barley, oats, and all the cereals and vegetables of Europe are also grown.

In 1875, New South Wales had 22,872,882 sheep, 856,699 horned cattle, 346,691 horses, and 219,958 pigs. The total area of land under cultivation, at the same date, embraced 469,957 acres, of which there were under wheat, 166,911 acres, under barley, 3984 acres, under oats, 17,974, under rye, 1342, under maize, 119,956.

New South Wales is believed to be richer in coal than the other territories of Australia. In 1874 there were 28 mines worked, producing in the year 1,298,400 tons of coal, valued at £786,152.

The gold mines of New South Wales cover a vast area, extending chiefly over the districts called the Western Fields, the Northern Fields, and the Southern Fields. Of these the Western Fields are the most important, furnishing three-fourths of the total supply. The gold exports of 1873 consisted of 200,134 ounces, value £773,439, of gold dust and bar, and of 490 boxes, value £2,151,168, of gold coin. The yield from the copper mines, in 1873, was 6027 tons.

The total exports during the year 1874 were £12,345,603; imports, £11,293,739.

The constitution of New South Wales vests the legislative power in a Parliament of two houses, the first called the Legislative Council, and the second the Legislative Assembly. The Legislative Council consists of not less than 21 members, nominated by the crown, and the Assembly of 72 members, elected by sixty constituencies. To be eligible a man must be of age, a natural-born subject of the Queen, or, if an alien, he must have been naturalized for five years, and resident for two years before election. There is no property qualification for electors, and the votes are taken by secret ballot. The executive is in the hands of a governor, nominated by the crown, who acts under the advice of ministers responsible to Parliament.

The public revenue during 1874 was £4,664,568; the expenditure, £4,426,040. The public debt, chiefly incurred for railways and other public works, amounted, at the end of 1874, to £10,842,415.

New South Wales possesses 436 miles of railways. Of electric telegraph, there were in the colony 8000 miles of wire, at the end of 1874. Number of paid messages transmitted during 1874, 385,000; number of telegraph stations, 105.

The post office of the colony transmitted 9,300,000 letters, 4720 newspapers, and 250,000 packets in 1874.

The number of schools, public and private, in 1872, was 1464, with 106,691 pupils.

Commission from NEW SOUTH WALES to the International Exhibition:

HIS HONOR, SIR JAMES MARTIN KNIGHT, Chief Justice, President.
HON. JOHN HAY, President of the Legislative Council, Vice-President.
HON. GEORGE WIGRAM ALLEN, Speaker of the Legislative Assembly, Vice-President.
HON. SIR EDWARD DEAS THOMSON, C. B., K. C. M. G., M. L. C., Vice-President.

Commissioners:

The Rev. Chas. Badham, D.D.
Samuel Bennett, Esq.
James Byrns, Esq.
R. W. Cameron, Esq., Resident Commissioner, N. Y.
The Hon. G. H. Cox, M. L. C.
J. R. Fairfax, Esq.
Andrew Garran, Esq., LL.D.
Hon. S. D. Gordon, M. L. C.
Henry Halloran, Esq.
Edward S. Hill, Esq.
Hon. Thos. Holt, M. L. C.
P. A. Jennings, Esq.
G. W. Lord, Esq., M. P.
Hon. Sir Wm. Macarthur Knight, M. L. C.
William Macleay, Esq., F. L. S.
T. S. Mort, Esq.
Benjamin Palmer, Mayor of Sydney.
Commander Thos. Stackhouse, R. N.
Alexander Stuart, Esq., M. P.
George Thornton, Esq., J. P.
William Wallis, Esq.
James Watson, Esq., M. P.
Hon. J. B. Watt, M. L. C.
Fitz William Wentworth, Esq.
John Williams, Esq.
W. C. Windeyer, Esq.
Robert Wisdom, Esq., M. P.
John Woods, Esq.
William Wolffen, Esq.
Rev. W. B. Clarke, M. A.
Professor Swersedge.
C. L. Wilkinson, Esq.
Charles Moore, Esq.
P. F. Adams, Esq.
Robert Adams, Esq.
James Powell, Esq.
Archibald Thompson, Esq.
Joseph Thompson, Esq.
P. N. Frebeck, Esq.
James Newton, Esq.
John Leving, Esq.

Resident Commissioners:

Augustus Morris, Esq., of New York, Executive Commissioner.
Marshall Burdekin, Esq., of Sydney.
Roderick William Cameron, Esq., of New York.
Sir Daniel Cooper, Baronet, of London,
Edward Flood, Esq., of Sydney.
Dr. R. W. Forbes, of New York.
Patrick Alfred Jennings, Esq., of Sydney.
The Honorable Jacob Levi Montefiore, of Sydney, a member of the Legislative Council of New South Wales.
George Oakes, Esq., of Sydney.
Joseph James Phelps, Esq.. of Sydney, a member of the Legislative Assembly of New South Wales.
George Russell, Esq., of Scotland.
The Honorable James White, of Sydney, a member of the Legislative Council of New South Wales.
Christopher Rolleston, Esq.
William Morris, Esq.
Charles Robinson, Esq., Secretary.

VICTORIA.

VICTORIA comprises the southeast corner of Australia, at that part where its territory projects furthest into cool southern latitudes. Wilson's Promontory, to the southeast, the most southerly headland, just passes the 39° of south latitude, while the most northern point, which is at the opposite or northwest extreme, is in south latitude 34°. The longitude comprises 9°,—between 141° and 150° east of Greenwich. To the west is the colony of South Australia, separated by the 141° of east longitude, to the north is New South Wales, separated by the line of the Murray river eastwards from 141° east longitude to its source, and thence by a straight line southeast to Cape Howe, and from Cape Howe to South Australia again the colony is bounded on the south by Bass's Strait. The extreme length is east and west, and is about 500 miles, by an extreme width north and south of 300 miles. But a remarkable indentation of both the north and south boundaries opposite each other, about the middle of the colony, reduces the breadth between the head of the Port Phillip inlet and the Murray to only 120 miles. The superficial area is 88,198 English square miles.

Although Victoria may be called mountainous, as compared with the general flatness of Australia, it has much of the quiet and peculiar scenery characteristic of that division of the world. The highest mountain in Australia, Mount Feathertop, is 6303 feet in height. The largest river, which runs throughout its entire course in Victoria, is the Gouldbourn, 230 miles long. The Murray, which winds for a distance of 630 miles along the northern boundary of Victoria, rises in New South Wales, and falls into the sea in South Australia, so that it can scarcely be called a Victorian river.

The climate is on the whole healthful and agreeable. The average temperature of Melbourne is 57.6°, about the same as that of Marseilles, Bordeaux, Bologna, Nice, and Madrid. The common summer heat is from 65° to 80°, with an occasional advance to 90°, and even to 100°, during hot winds and a dry season. The winter range is mostly from 45° to 60°. Ice occasionally occurs in the midwinter of July, but it rarely, except on elevated ground, survives the noonday sun.

The estimated population of Victoria, on the 31st of March, 1875, was returned at 810,442 by the Registrar-general.

In 1875 there were 1,011,776 acres under crops, including 332,936 acres of wheat, 114,921 of oats, 29,505 of barley, 35,183 of potatoes, 119,031 of hay, and 253,129 of green forage. The gross produce was: wheat, 4,850,165 bushels; oats, 2,121,612 bushels; barley, 619,896 bushels; potatoes, 124,310 tons; hay, 157,261 tons; wine, 577,493 gallons. The total number of horses was, in 1875, 180,254; milch cows, 241,137; horned cattle, 717,251; sheep, 11,221,036; pigs, 137,941. The manufactures of Victoria employed 25,000 persons, and the capital invested in machinery and plant was £5,000,000. The number of persons at work in the gold fields, December 31st, 1874, was 45,151, of whom 12,180, or 27 per cent., were Chinese.

The total value of the imports and exports of Victoria, including bullion and specie, for the year 1874, was as follows: Imports, £16,953,985; exports, £15,441,109. The most important, in value, of the imports are woolens, sugar, cotton, apparel and haberdashery, and tea. The two staple articles of export are wool and gold. The total exports of wool in 1874 amounted to 88,662,311 pounds, of the value of £6,373,641. The export of gold, exclusive of specie, was 1,012,153 ounces, of a declared value of £4,053,288.

The number of mercantile vessels on the register of Victoria, at the end of 1874, was 429, with a total tonnage of 70,696, and crews of 3229 men. Of these vessels 47 were steamers.

The constitution of Victoria was established by an act passed by the legislature of the colony in 1854, and subsequently confirmed by the crown. The legislative authority is vested in a parliament of two chambers—the Legislative Council, composed of 30 members, and the Legislative Assembly, composed of 78 members. A property qualification is required both for members and electors of the Legislative Council. No electoral property qualification is required for graduates of British universities, matriculated students of the Melbourne university, religious ministers of all denominations, certificated schoolmasters, lawyers, medical practitioners, and officers of the army and navy. Six members, or a fifth, of the Legislature Council must retire every two years, so that a total change is effected in ten years. The members of the Legislative Assembly are elected by universal suffrage, for the term of three years. The executive consists of a governor appointed by the crown, and a ministry which must contain at least four members of parliament, and must command a majority in the assembly. The revenue for the year 1874–75 was £4,406,906; the expenditure, £4,425,277. The public debt, incurred entirely for the construction of public works, amounted to £12,485,432 on January 1st, 1875.

Victoria has a more extensive system of railways than any other of the Australasian colonies. On the 1st of January, 1875, there were 457½ miles opened for traffic, and 427 more in course of construction. There were, in 1874, 148 telegraph stations, 4464 miles of wires. Number of telegrams forwarded during the year, 701,080. The work of the post office during the same year, 15,732,888 letters, 6,866,918 newspapers, and 1,269,822 packets. Number of post offices, 802.

The following table shows the educational condition of the population above five years of age:

	MALES.	FEMALES	TOTAL.
Able to read and write,	264,665	209,898	474,665
Able to read only,	30,049	36,336	66,385
Unable to read,	25,462	26,315	51,077

The state of education among the children, between 5 and 15, showed that 846 children out of 1000 could read, 640 could read and write, and only 154 were totally uninstructed. Education in Victoria is gratuitous, secular, and compulsory, and the legislature has voted large sums for the primary education of the people.

The total number of schools is 1867, including 908 "common" schools, with an attendance of 154,353 pupils. (Furnished, in part, by the Victoria Commission.)

Commission from VICTORIA to the International Exhibition:

SIR REDMOND BARRY, Acting Chief Justice of the Supreme Court, President.

HON. J. J. CASEY, M. P.
HON. J. F. SULLIVAN, M. P.
HON. C. J. JENNER, M. L. C.
JAMES MUNRO, HON., M. P.
J. MCILWRAITH, ESQ.
L. J. SHERRARD, ESQ.
COUNT DE CASTELNAU.
HON. S. H. BINDON.
JAMES BOSISTO, ESQ., M. P.
JAS. GATEHOUSE, ESQ., Mayor of Melbourne.
JOHN MCINTYRE, ESQ.
J. I. BLEASDALE, D.D.
HON. SIR JOHN O'SHANASSY, K.C.M.G.
HON. SIR JAMES MCCULLOCH, M. P.
HON. JOHN ALEXANDER MACPHERSON, M. P.
HON. JOHN THOMAS SMITH, M. P.
LESLIE JAMES SHERRARD, ESQ.,
JOHN DANKS, ESQ.
GEORGE COLLINS LEVEY, ESQ., Secretary.

SOUTH AUSTRALIA.

THE colony of South Australia embraces 25 degrees of latitude through the centre of the continent of Australia, from the Southern to the Indian Ocean, and is bounded on the east by the colonies of Victoria, New South Wales, and Queensland, and on the west by the colony of Western Australia. Its area is 914,730 square miles, or 585,427,200 acres; being about a third of the area of the United States of America, or ten times that of Great Britain. Its population is 210,699.

Its chief exports are wool, wheat, and copper. In 1875 the exports were valued at £4,442,100—namely: of wool, £1,778,297; of agricultural produce, £1,688,035; of metals, £758,664; and of other products, £217,104. Its revenue in 1875 was £1,143,312, its people not being taxed at a higher rate than 25 shillings a head. The people have purchased land of the government to the extent of 4,634,711 acres, of which 1,400,000 are under cultivation; and the average price paid since 1845 is £1 5*s.* 2*d.* per acre. The public debt is about £3,000,000; but, as an offset, is a sum of £2,225,000 due for lands sold to occupiers, and payable within six years.

The natural wealth of the colony in healthy climate, fruitful soils, and abundant minerals, has been greatly augmented by useful and substantial improvements. In addition to numerous ports made serviceable for coasting trade, inland traffic is facilitated by 884 miles of excellent macadamized roads, which have cost over £2,000,000; and by railways of nearly an equal further cost. The public and private buildings, both in towns and country, are mostly of well-built stone, with slate or iron roofs. Gardens and orchards, pasture and arable fields cover the more settled portions of the colony, whilst over hundreds of miles outside of these some 6,000,000 sheep, 200,000 head of horned cattle, many thousands of horses, and a few hundred camels, thrive at large on the native vegetation, save that their ranches, or runs, are mostly inclosed in areas of from 5 to 50 square miles with good post and wire fencing.

The best of meat and bread, fruit and vegetables, grow in abundance in South Australia. People there live well at little cost. Labor is well rewarded. There are not, or ought not to be, any able-bodied paupers in the colony. At the savings' banks, which are guaranteed by government, the small deposits of the poorer classes approximate £800,000, on which four to five per cent. interest is paid. Immigration is promoted by annual money votes, which, through Mr. F. S. Dutton, C. M. G., Agent-General for the colony in London, supply free or assisted passages for eligible persons.

The government, the laws, and the social institutions, like the people of South Australia, have an Anglo-Saxon character. There is the fullest civil and religious freedom under a vice-regal governor, whose ministers are chosen by, and are responsible to, a majority of two houses of parliament elected by ballot, as to the larger house, of manhood suffrage alone, and, as to the smaller house, by a slightly restricted property qualification. These organizations have worked harmoniously to the contentment of the people.

Churches and schools are numerous. The facilities for acquiring real property in the colony are great, and laws well secure its quiet enjoyment. The public lands are mostly sold on credit: one-tenth per cent. is paid down as interest on the purchase money, which is not less than twenty shillings per acre. The balance is deferred to the sixth year, a second ten per cent. on the purchase money having been paid on the third year as interest. At the sixth year half the balance may be renewed for four years at four per cent. if needed; but that the State may secure certain benefit from the sale of its lands under a credit system, the purchaser is bound to effect annual improvements. All metals, precious or other, go to the purchaser. The title to real estate from the crown is by registration, of which the purchaser gets a certificate in simple form. This system is popular, for it is ready and inexpensive at the outset, and is returnable to the registration office for record on it of all subsequent dealings, or for substituted certificate, or certificate as needed, in the event of sales. At the close of 1874 the value of landed property, which had passed under it, amounted to £9,260,186. Adjoining colonies have adopted this law.

The settled portions of the colony of South Australia are sectioned off into counties, and these counties, when arable cultivation requires it, are subdivided into hundreds, whose municipal governing bodies can be elected for local public works and education. Outside the hundreds, in the southern portion of the colony, the public lands are left for purely pastoral occupation, for which fourteen or twenty-one years' leases can be procured at moderate rents, regulated much by distance from ports of shipment, except that, both as to public lands inside or outside the hundreds, rights to search for and work minerals are readily granted. The rent of a mining lease is fixed at ten shillings an acre per annum, on a fourteen years' term, renewable.

For the northern territory of South Australia, with its tropical climate, the land laws are modified. Land there is open for selection and sale at *7s. 6d.* per acre, or for lease over ten years at *6d.* per acre per annum. And, for the special growth of sugar, cotton, tea, rice, and tobacco, selections varying from 320 to 1280 acres can be made at a rental of *6d.* per acre per annum for five years, when, if the land has been inclosed and one-half under cultivation, a free grant is procurable.

In 1872 South Australia erected 1973 miles of telegraph wire across her territory, and, at a cost of £350,000, connected Australia with India and Europe.

Commission from SOUTH AUSTRALIA (ADELAIDE) to the International Exhibition:

HIS EXCELLENCY, SIR ANTHONY MUSGRAVE, C. M. G., Chairman.

HON. W. EVERARD, Commissioner of Crown Lands.
HON. H. E. BRIGHT, M. L. C., J. P., Commissioner of Public Works.
HON. JOHN CROZIER, M. L. C., J. P.
HON. WENTWOOD CAVANAUGH, ESQ., M. P., J. P.
JOSIAH BOOTHLY, ESQ., J. P.
E. W. ANDREWS, ESQ., J. P.
S. DAVENPORT, ESQ., J. P., Special Commissioner.
GEORGE MCEWEN, ESQ., J. P.
DR. SCHOMBURGH, D. P., J. P.
CALEB PEACOCK, ESQ., J. P.
R. D. ROSS, ESQ., M. P., J. P.
W. E. SMITH, ESQ., M. P., J. P.
WALTER HACKE, ESQ.
J. A. HOLDEN, ESQ., J. P.
JOSEPH CROMPTON, ESQ.
S. V. PIZEY, ESQ.
F. G. WATERHOUSE, ESQ.
W. A. E. WEST ERSKINE, ESQ.
C. J. COATES, ESQ., Commissioner and Honorary Secretary.

CAPE OF GOOD HOPE.

THE colony of the Cape of Good Hope is bounded north and northeast by the Orange river, which divides it, in parts of its course, from the Free State; east and northeast by the Tees, a small tributary of the Orange, the Stormbergen Mountains, and the Indwe and Great Kei, which two rivers separate the Cape Colony from Kaffirland; on the south it is bounded by the Indian Ocean, and on the west by the Atlantic. Latitude 28° 10′ to 34° 51′ south; longitude 16° 20′ to 28° 20′ east. The breadth on the greatest meridian is about 450 miles, the length on the largest parallel about 600 miles, and the total area is about 201,000 square miles. The colony is generally considered as forming two sections, the Western and Eastern Provinces, each divided into 16 electoral divisions, which are again subdivided for fiscal and magisterial purposes. The first regular census (1865) gave the following result as to the numbers of the population:

White, or European,	181,592
Hottentot,	81,598
Kaffir,	100,536
Other colored,	132,655
	496,381

Since the census, the annexation of British Kaffraria, Basutoland, Fingoland, and Normansland, added 5847 whites and 273,930 colored to the population, making the total, 776,158.

Hydrographically, the country, as a whole, is decidedly superior to most parts of Africa. The seaboard presents several comparatively safe and commodious harbors. Of these, however, two—Table Bay in the Western Province, and Algoa Bay in the Eastern—absorb nearly the whole of the foreign trade. Hardly any of the ports command navigable communication with the interior.

The highest range of mountains within the colony is 9000 feet above the sea. The dividing ridge runs parallel with the coast at a distance of 100 miles. Between the principal range and the sea, on the east, there are two other ranges, less continuous and regular; the intermediate one generally more distant from the first than they are from each other.

The prevalent winds—the southeast in summer, and the northeast in winter—mitigate each the rigor, whether heat or cold, of its own season; and, in spite of occasionally sudden and great changes, render the temperature, as a whole, one of the most salubrious and delightful in the world. The mean temperature of the year at Cape Town is about 68° F.; that of the coldest month being 57°, and of the hottest, 79°.

The value of the total exports and imports of the Cape Colony, including British Kaffraria, was, in 1873, as follows:

Imports,	£5,451,927
Exports,	4,011,327

Among the articles of export, wool is the most important, forming nearly nine-tenths of the total. Among the other leading items are copper ore, feathers, and sheepskins.

There were, at the end of 1865, in the colony, 692,514 head of cattle and 9,836,065 sheep. The sheep farms are often of very great extent, comprising from 3000 to 15,000 acres and upwards. Those in tillage are comparatively small. The graziers are, for the most part, proprietors of the farms they occupy, paying a quit rent to government, as the original owner of the soil.

COMPARISON OF TOTAL STOCK IN THE COLONY IN 1865 AND 1875.

	1865.	1875.
Horses	228,465	207,318
Mules and asses	24,267	29,517
Draught oxen	249,291	398,825
Other cattle	443,004	698,681
Wooled sheep	8,426,619	10,064,289
Other sheep	1,465,883	944,050
Angora goats	121,432	972,733
Common goats	2,147,807	2,122,808
Pigs	78,578	110,489
Ostriches	80	22,257

There were lines of railways of a total length of 134 miles at the end of 1874, and a system of other main lines, as well as of telegraphs, was under consideration by the government.

The constitution vests the executive in the Governor and an Executive Council, composed of certain officeholders appointed by the crown. The legislative power rests with a Legislative Council of 21 members, and a House of Assembly of 66 members.

The income and expenditure of the colony, during 1873, were as follows:

Revenue,	£2,078,220
Expenditure,	2,159,658

Included in the above receipts is a loan of £859,000 for public works. The public debt, on the 1st of January, 1875, amounted to £1,723,144.

Commissioner from the CAPE OF GOOD HOPE to the International Exhibition:

MR. H. CRAWFORD COATES, Executive Commissioner.

JAMAICA.

JAMAICA, one of the West India Islands, and by far the most important of those belonging to Great Britain, is about 90 miles to the south of Cuba, and stretches in north latitude between 17° 40′ and 18° 30′, and in west longitude between 76° 15′ and 78° 25′. Area, 6300 square miles; population (in 1871), 506,154, of whom less than three per cent. were white. The greatest length of the island is 150 miles, and its greatest breadth, 50 miles. It is traversed from east to west by a heavily timbered ridge called the Blue Mountains, which rises to about 7000 feet. From this range at least 70 streams descend to the north and south shores; one of these, the Black river, affords for small craft a passage of about 30 miles into the interior. The others, owing to the shortness and declivity of their course, are not navigable. Excellent harbors are everywhere to be found. The best of these is formed by a deep and capacious basin, in the southeast quarter of the island, which washes the most spacious and fertile of the plains between the hill country and the coast. Around this inlet, and within a few miles of each other, are all the considerable centres of population, Port Royal, Kingston, and Spanish Town.

The climate varies considerably, the torrid belt of the coast gradually passing into the temperate region of the central heights. The latter is said to be remarkably favorable to longevity; and, after having long been a retreat for the residents themselves, it has lately begun to attract invalids from the United States. To contrast two positions—the one near Kingston harbor, the other at an intermediate elevation of 4000 feet—their annual mean temperature are stated to be respectively 81° F. and and 68° F.

In 1871 the chief exports were in value as follows: Sugar, £502,193; rum, £271,267; coffee, £147,562; logwood, £115,423; while the chief imports were: Flour, £135,500, and salt-fish, £92,801. During the same year the revenue amounted to £434,564; the expenditure to £430,154.

The sum of £19,403 was devoted to the support of the schools during the year 1872.

Commissioner from JAMAICA to the International Exhibition:
WM. ROBERT THOMSON, ESQ., Kingston.

BAHAMAS.

A CHAIN of islands lying between 21° 42′ and 27° 34′ N. lat., and 72° 40′ and 79° 5′ W. long. The group is composed of about twenty inhabited islands and an immense number of islets and rocks. The principal islands are New Providence (containing the capital, Nassau), Abaco, Harbor Island, Eleuthera, Inagua, Mayaguana, St. Salvador, Andros Island, Great Bahama, Ragged Island, Rum Cay, Exuma, Long Island, Crooked Island, Acklin Island, Long Cay, Watling's Island, the Berry Islands, and the Biminis. In 1848 the Turks and Caicos Islands were separated from the other Bahamas and formed into a distinct government, under the government-in-chief of the governor of Jamaica. The Turks and Caicos Islands lie between 21° and 22° N. lat., and 71° and 72° 37′ W. long.

There are ten colonial custom-houses and ports of entry in the government of the Bahamas—viz., Nassau, Abaco, Eleuthera, Harbor Island, Exuma, Rum Cay, Long Island, Long Cay, Inagua, and Ragged Island. Considerable quantities of pineapples, oranges, and sponges are exported, chiefly to England and the United States. The pineapple crop is very precarious. The industry of salt-raking has ceased to be remunerative, owing to the duties imposed on salt by the United States. Experiments in coffee-planting and other branches of industry have been commenced under the patronage of the present governor.

The public expenditures for 1874 were £37,283; receipts during the same year, £38,374. The total public debt in 1873 was £65,081.

In 1874 the imports were valued at £183,993, and the exports at £130,293. The census of 1871 gave the population of the colony as 39,162.

The colony's staples are salt, fruit, sponge, barks, dye and furniture woods, guano and straw, turtle-shell, fish-scale, and shell-work.

The articles on exhibition fairly represent the productions and manufactures of these islands, and both might be indefinitely extended. But it is not the commercial position of the Bahamas only which should make a knowledge of them general. Their equality and wonderful salubrity of climate commend them to all who seek a genial, healthy, life-giving atmosphere. As a winter home for the afflicted, Peter Henry Bruce wrote nearly a century and half ago, "It is no wonder the sick fly hither for relief, being sure to find a cure here." Modern travelers also testify that, as a resort from damp and cold to sunshine and summer, for those who require change and climatic benefit, the Bahamas offer peculiar advantages. The heat is tempered by an ocean breeze of softness and purity seldom experienced elsewhere. Tropical flowers gladden the eye, and the luscious pineapple, orange, and melon tempt the palate with their freshness and beauty. Fish abound in the clear pellucid waters surrounding these islands, and the northern fowl seek a home on the lakes. In a word, the Bahamas seem by nature fitted as a grand sanitarium for the afflicted from the North American continent, and as a most desirable winter resort for all who wish to escape the rigors of the northern season.

(The above data have been derived from the special Catalogue of the British section.)

Commission from BAHAMAS to the International Exhibition.

DR. EDWARD T. WEBB, Commissioner, Philadelphia.

BERMUDAS,

OR Somers' Islands, are a cluster of about one hundred small islands, situated on the western side of the Atlantic Ocean, in lat. 32° 15′ N. and long. 64° 51′ W., at a distance of about 580 miles from the nearest land—viz., Cape Hatteras, in North Carolina. Fifteen or sixteen of these islands are inhabited; the rest are of inconsiderable size, the largest, or Bermuda proper, containing less than twenty square miles of land, and nowhere exceeding three miles in breadth.

The islands extend from N.E. to S.W. in a curved line for about twenty miles, bending inward at both extremities, so as to enclose spacious and secure harbors.

Besides the main island, on which the town of Hamilton, the present seat of government, is situated, the principal islands are St. George's, where the ancient town of St. George, the former capital, stands; Ireland Island, where the dockyard is established; Boaz and Watford Islands, occupied entirely by a military detachment, formerly a convict establishment; Somerset, St. David's, Smith's, Cooper's, Nonsuch, Godet's, Port's, and River's. With the exception of one break between Somerset and Watford Islands, there is continuous communication by bridges from St. George's to Ireland Island. The climate has been long celebrated for its mildness and salubrity. The islands produce arrowroot of a fine quality, and an indigenous cedar of great durability, well adapted for ship-building and house-timber. A few whales are occasionally taken in the neighboring waters. Turtle are common.

The islands derive their name from Bermudez, a Spaniard, who sighted them in 1527. They were first colonized by Admiral Sir George Somers, who was shipwrecked there in 1609, on his way to Virginia. On his report the Virginia Company claimed them, and obtained a charter for them from James I. in 1612. This company sold their right for £2000 to an association of 120 persons, who obtained a new charter in 1616, incorporating them as the Bermuda Company, and granting them very extensive powers and privileges. Representative government was introduced in 1620. In 1621 the Bermuda Company in London made a Body of Ordinances for the government of the colony. During the civil war great numbers of emigrants from England were attracted thither by the favorable reports of the climate and soil. Toward the end of the reign of Charles II. grave complaints were made by the inhabitants of the misgovernment of the plantation by the company, and its charter was annulled by process of quo warranto, at Westminster, in 1684–85. Since then the governors have been appointed by the Crown, and laws for the colony enacted by a local legislature, consisting of the governor, council, and assembly. The lands belonging to the company were forfeited to the Crown on the annulment of their charter, and, with the exception of some reserved for public uses, were granted in 1759 to purchasers on small quit-rents, extinguishable on the payment of a fixed sum of money.

During the Revolutionary war in North America the inhabitants suffered great privations from the scarcity of food; and although they export largely certain articles of agricultural produce, especially potatoes, onions, tomatoes, and arrowroot, they are still dependent on foreign supplies for all the flour and most of the meat consumed. Early in the present century the importance of the Bermudas as a naval station came to be recognized. Ireland Island was purchased exclusively by the government, and a dockyard established there. By order in council, dated June

28, 1824, the Bermudas were declared a place where male convicts might be kept at hard labor on the public works; but these islands never were made a penal settlement, strictly speaking, where convicts might be discharged. The establishment was broken up in 1863. On the abolition of slavery in 1834, the system of temporary apprenticeship of the emancipated slaves, permitted by the Act of Parliament in the slave-holding colonies, was dispensed with by the local legislature of Bermuda, so as to entitle the slaves to their absolute freedom six years sooner than was required by Parliament. They and their descendants now form more than a numerical half of the entire population.

In 1846 a lighthouse, visible at more than thirty miles' distance, was erected on the highest land in the colony, the light being 362 feet above the sea. A public library was established in 1839. In 1871 the island of St. George's was connected with the main island by a causeway and road two miles in length, commenced in 1866, and completed at a cost of nearly £30,000. An iron-girder swing-bridge still permits the passage of vessels.

The revenue in 1874 was £29,066, the expenditure £29,800, the public debt £13,234, the imports £252,435, the exports £81,585; total tonnage of vessels entered 72,212; cleared, 71,935. The census of 1871 showed a population of 12,121, of whom 4725 were white, 7396 colored.

(The above data have been derived from the special Catalogue of the British section.)

Commission from BERMUDA to the International Exhibition:

HIS HON. THOMAS L. WOOD, Chief Justice, President.
HON. HENRY FOWLER, Receiver-General.
LT. COL. BLAND, R. E.
JAMES TUCKER, ESQ., Colonial Secretary and Honorary Secretary.
CAPT. LOCKHART, R. A., A. D. C.

Assistant Commissioners.

A. H. FRAZER LEFROY, ESQ.
W. S. BARR, ESQ.
H. J. HINSON, ESQ., M. D.
J. B. HEYL, ESQ.
C. C. KEANE, ESQ.

Resident Commissioner—A. A. OUTERBRIDGE, Philadelphia.

BRITISH GUIANA.

THIS colony is a portion of the South American Continent, extending from east to west about two hundred miles. It includes the settlements of Demerara, Essequebo, and Berbice. It is bounded on the east by Dutch Guiana, from which it is divided by the river Corentyn, on the south by Brazil, on the west by Venezuela, and on the north and north-east by the Atlantic Ocean.

This territory was first partially settled by the Dutch West India Company in 1580. It was from time to time held by Holland, France, and England. It was restored to the Dutch in 1802, but in the following year retaken by Great Britain, to whom it was finally ceded in 1814. It is impossible to determine the exact area of the colony, as its precise boundaries are undetermined between Venezuela and Brazil, respectively, but it has been computed to be 76,000 square miles.

Under the Dutch, Demerara and Essequebo constituted one government, and Berbice another, which arrangement indeed continued in force under the British administration down to the year 1831.

The revenue in 1874 was £475,885, the expenditure £485,893, both exclusive of the sums expended on immigration by the planters. The public debt was £426,030, but £400,030 was invested for a sinking fund, or otherwise secured. The exports in 1874 were valued at £1,873,219, the imports at £2,761,837.

The population in 1871 was stated to be 193,491, of whom 113,570 were natives of British Guiana, 13,385 of West India Islands, 7925 of Madeira and the Azores, and 9635 of other places. The estimated population in 1875 was 212,000, including an immigrant population under indenture on estates of 38,597, of whom 33,360 were Indians, 3875 Chinese, and 562 Africans. The aboriginal Indians were estimated in 1851 at about 7000; but Mr. M'Clintock, Superintendent of Rivers and Creeks, an undoubted authority on the subject, carries the number as high as 20,000 or 21,000, but the numbers of the tribes within the British territories vary, and are at all times very uncertain.

(The above data have been derived from the special Catalogue of the British section.)

Commission from BRITISH GUIANA to the International Exhibition.

A. A. OUTERBRIDGE, Commissioner, Philadelphia.

CEYLON.

AN island situated in the Indian Ocean, off the southern extremity of Hindostan, lying between 5° 55′ and 9° 51′ N. lat., and 79° 41′ and 81° 54′ E. long.; its extreme length from north to south—*i. e.*, from Point Palmyra to Dondera Head—is 266 miles; its greatest width 140½ miles, from Colombo on the west coast to Sangemankende on the east.

The climate for a tropical country is comparatively healthy, the heat in the plains, which is nearly the same throughout the year, being much less oppressive than in Hindostan. Along the coast the annual mean temperature is about 80° Fahr.; at Kandy, 1465 feet above the sea level, it is 76° (average of ten years); at Colombo the annual variation is from 76° to 86°; at Galle 70° to 90°; and at Trincomalee 74° to 91°. In the mountain ranges there is of course a great variety of climate, the thermometer at the hill station Nuwara Eliya, which is some 6000 feet above the level of the sea, falling at night as low as 32°.

Ceylon was visited in early days by the Greeks, Romans, and Venetians; in 1505 the Portuguese formed settlements on the west and south of the island; in the next century they were dispossessed by the Dutch. In 1795-6 the British took possession of the Dutch settlements in the island. They were annexed then to the Presidency of Madras, but five years later, in 1801, Ceylon was constituted a separate colony. In 1815 war was declared against the native government of the interior: the Kandyan king was taken prisoner, and the whole island fell under the rule of the British.

By letters patent under the Great Seal, April, 1831, a Council of Government was appointed, and by a supplementary commission to the then governor (March, 1833) the form of government almost as now existing was established.

The public expenditures for 1874 were £1,184,192; receipts, £1,324,328. The total public debt in 1874 was £600,000. In 1874 the total value of imports was £5,691,860, and of exports £4,687,388.

(The above data have been derived from the special Catalogue of the British section.)

STRAITS SETTLEMENTS.

SINGAPORE is an island about 25 miles long by 14 wide, situated at the southern extremity of the Malayan peninsula, from which it is separated by a narrow strait about ¾ of a mile in width. There are a number of small islands adjacent to it which form part of the settlement. The seat of government is the town of Singapore, at the southern point of the island, in lat. 1° 16′ N., and long. 103° 53′ E.

Penang is an island about 20 miles long and 9 broad, containing an area of 107 square miles, situated off the west coast of the Malayan peninsula in 5° N. lat., and at the northern extremity or entrance to the Straits of Malacca. On the opposite shore of the mainland, from which the island is separated by a strait from 2 to 10 miles broad, is Province Wellesley, a strip of territory forming part of the settlement, averaging 8 miles in width, and extending 45 miles along the coast, including 10 miles of newly-acquired territory to the south of the Krean. The chief town is George Town, in 5° 24′ N. lat. and 100° 21′ E. long.

Malacca is situated on the western coast of the peninsula, between Singapore and Penang, about 120 miles from the former and 240 from the latter, and consists of a strip of territory about 42 miles in length, and from 8 to 24½ miles in breadth. The principal town, called Malacca, is 2° 10′ N. lat. and 102° 14′ E. long.

The revenue during the year 1874 was £309,991, and the public expenditures £317,726.

(The above data have been derived from the special Catalogue of the British section.)

GOLD COAST COLONY, WEST AFRICA.

THE Gold Coast Colony, which comprises the British settlements on the Gold Coast and at Lagos, was constituted by a charter under the Great Seal, bearing date the 24th day of July, 1874.

The Gold Coast is the name generally given to a portion of Upper Guinea, between 5° and 4° 20′ E. long., stretching along the Gulf of Guinea from the river Assini on the west to the river Volta on the east, between which points are the settlements of Axim, Dixcove, Secondee, Elmina, Cape Coast Castle, Anamaboe, Accra, and Addah. In 1672 a company was formed, called the Royal African Company, which built forts at Dixcove, Secondee, Commendah, Anamaboe, Winnebah, and Accra, besides strengthening Cape Coast Castle, which was already in existence. This company was succeeded in 1750 by the African Company of Merchants, constituted by Act of Parliament, with liberty to trade and to form establishments on the West Coast of Africa between 20° N. and 20° S. lat. This company was dissolved in 1821 by Act of Parliament, and the forts transferred to the Crown, by whom they were placed under the government of Sierra Leone.

The revenue of the Gold Coast for 1874 was £74,868, the expenditure £47,796. The annual imports were £225,525, the exports, £330,624. It has no public debt. The estimated population, including the protectorate, is 400,000.

The revenue of Lagos for 1874 was £39,350, the expenditure £37,296, the public debt £11,631. The imports for the same year were £348,636, the exports £486,227 The population is 62,021.

(The above data have been derived from the special Catalogue of the British section.)

MAURITIUS.

An island lying in the Indian Ocean, between 57° 17′ and 57° 46′ E long., and 19° 58′ and 20° 32′ S. lat. It is 400 miles east of Madagascar. It comprises an area of 676 square miles.

The Mauritius was discovered by the Portuguese in 1507. They claimed possession of it during nearly the whole of the sixteenth century. The first who made any settlement in it were the Dutch in 1598, who named it Mauritius, in honor of their prince Maurice. It was abandoned by them in 1710, and afterward taken possession of by the French. Mauritius was for a long time during the war a source of great mischief to English merchant-vessels and Indiamen, from the facility with which sorties might be made from it upon traders by French men-of-war and privateers. The British government determined on an expedition for its capture, which was effected in 1810. The possession of the island was ratified by the treaty of Paris, 1814.

Mauritius pays £45,000 per annum to the imperial government as military contribution, but this amount is subject to reduction when the garrison is below the standard fixed upon as necessary for the defence of the colony. The total police force is 849.

The revenue for 1874 was £720,130, the expenditure £727,063, the public debt £895,600, bearing six per cent. interest. The imports were £2,427,813, the exports £2,697,892. The estimated population at the close of 1874 was 3,331,371, of whom 233,017 were Indians.

(The above data have been derived from the special Catalogue of the British section.)

QUEENSLAND.

QUEENSLAND occupies the whole of the northeastern portion of Australia, commencing at a point of the east coast about 400 miles north of Sidney, called Point Danger, in latitude 28° 8′ south. The greater portion of the southern boundary line is formed by the 29th parallel of south latitude. The eastern seaboard extends about 1300 miles to Cape York, the extreme northern point of the continent, in latitude 10° 40′. The mean breadth of the territory is 900 miles from the eastern coast-line to the meridian of 138° east longitude, which forms the western boundary line. This includes the greater portion of the Gulf of Carpentaria, which has a seaboard of about 900 miles. The whole of Queensland comprises 678,000 square miles,—nearly twelve times the area of England and Wales.

The portion of the colony extending along the eastern coast, is indented with numerous bays, which are the outlets of many navigable rivers, having their sources in the cool gorges and deep recesses of a great mountain range, running north and south, parallel with the sea coast, at a distance of from 50 to 100 miles. The summits of this great dividing range rise from 2000 to 6000 feet above the level of the sea. Numerous spurs are given off from the range, in ridges sloping gradually towards the coast. These ridges are generally composed principally of quartz, and in many places form good natural roads for a considerable distance. The ridges are usually covered with a variety of fine and valuable timber. The iron-bark, bloodwood, box, and other descriptions of wood, very valuable to the farmer for fencing and building, are found here in great abundance.

Unlike almost every other portion of Australia, Queensland is correctly described as "a land of rivers and streams." These rivers find an outlet in the many large and beautiful bays and estuaries on the eastern seaboard. One of these, Moreton Bay, receives the waters of five rivers, which are always navigable. The largest of these, the Brisbane, is navigated by good-sized steamers for 75 miles, and is nearly a quarter of a mile wide at a distance of 15 miles from its mouth. The principal rivers on the eastern seaboard are the Logan, the Brisbane, the Mary, the Caliope, the Boyne, the Fitzroy, the Pioneer and the Burdekin. The longest tidal river in Queensland is the Fitzroy, which drains an area of not less than 50,000,000 of acres, and is navigable as far as Yaruba, 60 miles from its estuary in Keppel Bay. It receives as its principal tributaries, the Dawson, Mackenzie, and Isaacs, large streams flowing for several hundred miles from the northwest, west, and southwestern parts of the interior. The tide at Rockhampton (40 miles from the embouchure of the river) rises 4 feet, and the stream is thus navigable for vessels of considerable burden.

The banks of the rivers are usually well elevated, and in many places consist of very rich alluvium, brought down from the great mountain ranges. This alluvial soil is frequently of very great depth, and is marked everywhere by a magnificent growth of timber, very unlike the ordinary Australian wood.

Beyond the Main, or great dividing range, the country presents features of still greater beauty and fertility. Vast plains—60, 70, or 80 miles across—stretch out their level surface, unbroken by a single tree, but covered with luxuriant grass, and often purpled over with fragrant herbage. These great plains are composed of rich, black soil. They are well watered with a network of streams, which trickle down from the gradual slopes of the mountain range. The soil in this locality is admirably adapted for tillage; and within a certain distance of the mountain range the rains fall with great regularity. The land here is lightly timbered, and is cleared with less labor than on the lower lands, and the soil has proved to be peculiarly adapted for the growth of wheat of the finest quality. The yield per acre in this locality has sometimes been as much as 50, and even 60 bushels, of 63 pounds to the bushel. The average yield may be estimated at 30 bushels per acre. Indian corn and other cereals as well as all the European fruits grow luxuriantly, and come to the greatest perfection in this highly favored locality, which has been called the Garden of Queensland.

This country, west of the great dividing range, stretches away in a series of fine plateaux for a distance of 400 or 500 miles westward, and, with the interruptions of other mountain ranges crossing the main range at right angles, for upwards of 1000 miles towards the fertile plains bordering the shores of the Gulf of Carpentaria.

The climate of Queensland is said to closely resemble that of Madeira; the mean annual external shade temperature, taken at Brisbane, being very nearly the same as at Funchal in Madeira, though it is a little hotter in the summer and colder in the winter at Brisbane than at Funchal. Moreton Bay, now Brisbane, has for many years been the resort of invalids from all the other British colonies in the southern hemisphere, and has been called the Montpellier of Australia. The summer season is hot,—the thermometer rising sometimes to 90° or even 100° in the shade; but the air is dry, elastic, and healthy, and the sea breezes temper the heat, and make it perfectly endurable, even to the outdoor laborer, in the hottest time of the year. However hot the day, the night is almost invariably cool, even in the most northern parts of the colony.

The growth of cotton and of the sugar-cane has been attempted in recent years, and both industries are reported to be rapidly advancing. At the end of 1873, there were 9663 acres under cotton, and 14,495 acres under sugar-cane, out of a total of 64,218 acres under cultivation.

The live stock at the end of 1873 numbered 99,243 horses, 1,343,093 cattle, 7,268,946 sheep, and 42,884 pigs. It is estimated that there are, at present, about 17,000,000 sheep in the colony.

There are several coal mines in the colony, the produce of which, in 1873, amounted to 33,613 ounces, valued at £22,052. Gold fields were discovered in 1867, the principal of them at Gympie Creek, which had a digging population of 5010 at the end of 1873. The total gold produce amounted to 163,972 ounces, valued at £555,310, in 1873.

The total value of the imports and exports of Queensland, during the year 1875, was: Imports, £3,881,726; exports, £4,544,513. The principal articles of export are gold, wool, tin ore, and raw cotton.

The form of government of Queensland was established December 10th, 1859, on its separation from New South Wales. The power of making laws and imposing taxes is vested in a Parliament of two houses, the Legislative Council and the Legislative Assembly. The former consists of 21 members, nominated by the crown for life. The House of Assembly comprises 42 deputies, returned from as many districts, for five years, by the ballot vote of all taxpayers. The executive is vested in a governor appointed by the crown.

Queensland is divided into 17 municipalities, the largest of which, as regards population, is Brisbane. It contains the city of Brisbane, the capital of the colony and the seat of government, with a population of 19,413, at the end of 1872.

At the end of 1873, there were 218 miles of railway open for traffic.

The post-office during that year carried 2,459,434 letters, 1,594,792 newspapers, and 93,540 packets. There were 20,998 money orders, to the value of £85,455.

At the end of 1873, there were in the colony, 3609 miles of telegraph wire, with 73 stations. The number of messages sent in 1873, was 156,608.

An excellent system of primary education, which, since 1870, has been made free, is in successful and vigorous operation throughout the colony.

Commission from QUEENSLAND to the International Exhibition:

ANGUS MACKAY, ESQ.	W. R. GORDON, ESQ.
P. A. JENNINGS, ESQ.	C. STRAGER, ESQ.
W. B. TOOTH, ESQ.	T. STOMAN, ESQ.
W. HILL, ESQ.	

SEYCHELLES ARCHIPELAGO.

THE island of Rodrigues, the Seychelles Islands, Diego Garcia, and others, are dependencies of the Mauritius. Rodrigues is situated about 300 miles east of Mauritius. It is 26 miles in length by 12 in breadth. It is cultivated by colonists from Mauritius.

The Seychelles, or Mahe Islands, are situated between the parallels of south latitude 4° and 5°; the total number of acres comprised in this group is 50,120; the distance from Mauritius 940 miles. These islands are under the superintendence of a Chief Civil Commissioner (assisted by a Board of Commissioners) at Mahe, who is appointed by the Secretary of State, but is subordinate to the Governor of Mauritius, from whom he takes instructions.

(The above data have been derived from the special Catalogue of the British section.)

TASMANIA.

TASMANIA, formerly known as Van Diemen's Land, is an island about 100 miles S. E. of Australia, from which it is separated by Bass' Strait. It lies between lat. 40° 45′ and 43° 35′ S., and long. 144° 50′ and 148° 20′ E. Its greatest length from N. to S. is 186 miles, its medium breadth 165 miles. The total area is 16,778,000 acres, of which 3,982,003 acres are alienated from the Crown by grant and sale; 1,348,400 acres are held under depasturing licenses from the Crown; the total area under cultivation is 326,486 acres. Wheat is cultivated on 57,633 acres; barley on 5129; oats on 32,704. Consequent on the high duties enforced on agricultural produce by the other Australian colonies, and the fluctuating state of the intercolonial markets, the attention of Tasmanian agriculturists has of late years been turned to the production of wheat for the English market, and this has become the most important article of strictly agricultural produce. The export of grain in the year 1874 was valued at £115,788.

Salubrity and comparative coldness of climate, owing to higher latitude, make Tasmania a breeding station of stud stock for all the Australian continent. The number of horses in 1874 was 23,208, cattle 110,450, and sheep 1,714,168.

Most of the wool produced is merino, the export during the year 1874 amounting to 5,050,920 lbs., which represented a value of £350,713.

Mining industry for many years was confined to gold and coal, but of late tin, iron, and slate have attracted attention. The yield of gold in 1874, produced by 185 persons, was—alluvial 850 oz., quartz 3800 oz. 14 dwt. The quantity of quartz crushed was 3452½ tons. The average yield per ton of stone was 1 oz. 5 dwt. 8½ grs. The average value of gold per ounce was £3 19*s*. 6*d*. for alluvial; quartz, £3 19*s*. 6*d*. The total value of the produce of gold for 1874 was £18,491. The mineral which occupies the greatest share of attention is tin, the supply of ore being practically unlimited. The total amount raised in 1874 was 490 tons, valued at £78 a ton. The only locality in which silver ore has been worked in Tasmania is Penguin Creek. Of iron the quantity raised during 1874 was 1400 tons; of this quantity 1000 tons were raised at Lempriere, West Tamar, and 400 tons at Lewisham.

The island is intersected by valuable coal-measures. At present the output of Tasmanian coal is not extensive, and the island is mainly supplied from Newcastle, New South Wales, although, for domestic purposes, Tasmanian coal is used to a considerable extent.

Of late years attention has been directed to the slate deposits of Tasmania; the high prices ruling for English slates in the colonial markets has induced the Australian Slate Company to commence work on a fair scale. In 1874 a quarter of a million of slates were prepared for sale at Piper's River.

At Ilfracombe Bay there is an extensive bed of pure white clay which seems very refractory, and which, when mixed with fine quartz (also abundant and close at hand), forms an admirable fire-brick. Common clays are found in all directions and the iron companies are now manufacturing bricks. Kaolin or porcelain clay is also found at Circular Head.

In the West Tamar district limestone quarries have been worked for many years past. There is an immense mountain of blue limestone situated about two miles from the township of Latrobe, on the River Mersey. At the River Don there are very large deposits of pure carbonate of lime, and the eastern districts, especially Fingal, abound with lime of various kinds and qualities.

The principal timber trees of Tasmania—such as blue gum, stringy bark, white gum or gum-topped stringy bark, swamp gum, and peppermint tree—furnish a hard, close-grained, and strong timber. Other useful woods are the huon pine, blackwood, myrtle, swamp gum, sassafras, celery-topped pine, silver wattle, ironwood, native cherry, whitewood, pinkwood, and native pear.

Bark is largely exported to England and New Zealand for tanning purposes. The price of ground bark varies from £4 to £6 per ton at the ports. During the year 1874 about 4870 tons were exported, valued at £22,123. Hops are also largely cultivated. In 1874, 819,145 pounds weight were exported, valued at £42,284.

The principal animals are the kangaroo, wallaby, opossum, and bandicoot, the skins of which are all available for tanning purposes, the fur being highly valuable as rugs, etc. The devil and Tasmanian tiger are formidable beasts, and used to make great havoc among the flocks. The tiger is a low, long-bodied animal with powerful forequarters and a dog-like head, weighing sometimes from sixty to seventy pounds. The devil, though not so large, is more hideous in appearance than the tiger.

Of birds 171 species have been observed, but of these only 20 species are supposed to be peculiar to Tasmania. The notes of many of the birds are very musical, the most remarkable being the reed warbler, the tones of which approach those of the nightingale, the black and white magpie, and the butcher-bird. The principal edible birds are varieties of quail, duck, snipe, golden plover, and pigeons.

There are many species of freshwater fish, the most valuable being the cucumber grayling. Among the estuary fish, those most appreciated as edible are the sole, whiting, garfish, and rock-cod. The best of the deep-sea fish are the trumpeter and kingfish. During the last ten years the salmon trout and brown trout, the tench and perch, have been established in many of the rivers and lakes. Salmon and salmon trout have also succeeded.

The chief industries are brewing, milling, jam-making, fellmongering, tanning, and coopering. Most of the beer is excellent, and is appreciated in the other colonies. In 1874 ale to the quantity of 22,900 gallons was exported. The quantity of jam exported in the same year was 2,648,012 lbs., and 179,762 bushels of fruit, valued together at £120,027. Tasmanian leather is excellent, all varieties from kip to kangaroo being supplied of such quality that a great falling off in the importation of inferior leather from European ports has taken place; and in 1874, £15,513 worth was exported from Hobart Town.

There is one remarkable feature distinguishing Tasmania from all other countries whose statistics have been compared with hers which ought not to be passed by unnoticed—namely, the small mortality among children, particularly those under one year of age. Taking an average of five years, the following results have been arrived at. Out of 100 infants born there died within the first year in Tasmania 9.45; in N. S. Wales, 9.57; in Queensland, 11.07; in Victoria, 11.86; in S. Australia, 14.24; the number in England being about 16; in Scotland about 12½. The percentage of deaths of children under five years was: Tasmania, 20.08; N. S. Wales, 42.14; Victoria, 45.50; Queensland, 46.33; S. Australia, 54.17. The proportion of children under five who died to 1000 children of the same age living was: In Victoria (ten years) about 52¼; in England and Wales (thirty years), about 67½; in Tasmania, less than 27. Thus it appears that the mortality of children under five years of age in Tasmania is little more than half that of the least healthy of the Australian colonies. It is also considerably under that of New Zealand, which, as regards the general death-rate, is the most healthy of all the Australasian group.

In 1870 the population, according to the census then taken, numbered 99,328 souls; the estimated population on the 31st of December, 1874, was 104,176. The revenue for 1874 was £327,925, and the expenditure £318,278. The amount expended for public works, roads, bridges, and railways, inclusive of the expenditure on the Launceston and Western District Railway, amounted during the year 1874 to £45,410. The value of imports during the same period was £1,247,785, while that of exports was £925,325.

(The above data have been in part condensed from the official report of the Victoria Exhibition, 1870.)

Commission from TASMANIA to the International Exhibition.

H. P. WELCH, ESQ., Commissioner. P. A. JENNINGS.

TRINIDAD.

TRINIDAD is an island lying to the eastward of Venezuela, between N. latitude 10° 3′ and 10° 50′, W. longitude 61° and 62° 4′ of Greenwich. Its length is 65 miles on the southern and 53 miles on the northern side of the island, and its breadth, on the eastern and western sides respectively, 48 and 49 miles. It is separated from the continent of America by the Gulf of Paria, into which fall the northern mouths of the Orinoco. The area of the island is 1754½ square miles. Port of Spain, the chief town and port of entry, according to the census of 1871, contains 23,561 inhabitants. The second town and port of entry is San Fernando, 26 miles south from Port of Spain, with a population of 5006 inhabitants. There are also the minor island towns of St. John, St. Joseph, Aronca, and Arima. The harbor is the finest in the West Indies.

The revenue for 1874 was £276,529, the expenditure £294,006. The public debt is £100,000 for railways and £47,500 secured on general revenue, but recoverable by the colony from other parties. The imports in 1874 were £1,342,992, the exports, £1,412,260. The census of 1871 showed a population of 109,638.

(The above data are derived from the "Colonial Office List," 1876.)

INDIA.

BRITISH INDIA is the name given to those parts of Hither and Further India placed under the administration of the viceroy, or governor-general of India. It does not include Ceylon, which, although a British possession, has its government entirely separate from that of Hindustan; but it extends along the eastern coast of the Bay of Bengal to 10° south latitude, and thus includes part of Further India, or Indo-China.

The following table, from the statistical abstract, relating to British India, for 1873 shows the area and population of the provinces under British administration:

TERRITORIES AND PROVINCES UNDER THE ADMINISTRATION OF	AREA IN ENGLISH SQ. MILES.	POPULATION.	AVERAGE POT. PER SQ. MILE.
Governor-general of India:			
Ajmere,	2,672	426,268	159
Coorg,	2,000	168,312	84
Berar,	16,960	2,231,565	132
Mysore,	27,077	5,055,412	187
Governor of Madras,	141,746	31,311,142	220
" " Bombay,	127,532	14,042,596	110
Lieutenant-governor of Bengal,	248,231	66,856,859	269
" " Northwest Provinces,	80,901	30,769,056	380
" " Punjab,	102,001	17,596,752	173
Chief Commissioner of Oude,	23,973	11,220,747	465
" " Central Provinces,	84,162	9,066,038	108
" " British Burmah,	93,664	2,562,323	27
	950,919	191,307,070	201

Cotton is the most important product of Hindustan. Wool will probably soon become a great Indian staple. The chief supply is from the Himalaya and Afghan regions. Hemp and flax, silk from the high lands, coffee, linseed, tobacco, and indigo, are all valuable productions of British India. The leaves and silver blossoms of the tea plant are beginning to cover the Himalaya slopes, and the hilly districts of Bengal, the Northwest Provinces, and the Punjab. Great quantities of rice are raised in Southern India and British Burmah. The Malabar district, Martaban, and Tenasserim furnish thousands of logs of the best teak timber. The cinchona or quinine plant has lately been introduced on the Neilgherries with great success, the original plants having been brought over from Peru.

The total value of the imports of British India, during the year 1874, was as follows:

	IMPORTS.	EXPORTS.
Merchandise,	£32,593,609	£54,960,778
Treasure,	5,792,533	1,914,071
Total,	£38,386,142	£56,874,849

The imports and exports, including treasure, were divided as follows:

	IMPORTS.	EXPORTS.
Bengal,	£17,169,310	£23,201,820
British Burmah,	1,852,459	3,480,407
Madras,	3,861,057	7,258,147
Bombay,	15,054,121	21,694,571

The most important articles of exports from India to the United Kingdom, during 1874, were:

		VALUE.
Cotton,	3,668,928 cwts.	£10,325,630
Jute,	4,260,170 "	3,545,124
Rice,	6,387,966 "	3,236,232
Indigo,	62,203 "	1,661,745
Tea,	17,608,538 lbs.	1,566,128
Hides,	321,299 cwts.	1,351,696

Next to the United Kingdom, the countries having the largest trade with India are China and Japan, the imports from which average £8,500,000 per annum, while the exports to them are of the average value of £12,000,000. Exports of the average value of £5,000,000 are also sent to Egypt, in transit for the United Kingdom.

The following figures show the number and tonnage of vessels, including native craft, which entered and cleared during 1874:

	VESSELS.	TONS.
Entered,	20,435	4,424,454
Cleared,	19,629	4,588,428

The executive authority in India is vested in a Governor-general, or Viceroy, appointed by the crown, and acting under the orders of the Secretary of State for India. The Governor-general, in council, has power to make laws for all persons, whether British or native, foreigners or others, within the Indian territories under the dominion of Her Majesty, and for all subjects of the crown, within the dominions of Indian princes and states in alliance with Her Majesty.

The duties of the Council of State are, under the direction of the Secretary of State, to conduct the business transacted in the United Kingdom in relation to the government of and the correspondence with India. The government in India is exercised by the Council of the Governor-general, consisting of five ordinary members, and one extraordinary member, the latter the commander-in-chief.

The total revenue and expenditure, during the year ending March, 1874, were:

	REVENUE.	EXPENDITURE.
In India,	£49,360,142	£44,637,637
In Great Britain,	238,111	10,321,591
Total,	£49,598,253	£54,959,228

In the army estimates for the British forces in India, in the year 1875–76, their strength was stated as follows:

Royal horse artillery,	2,497
Cavalry of the line,	4,330
Royal artillery and engineers,	10,171
Infantry of the line,	45,852
Total,	62,850

Returns of the year 1874 state that the combined armies of the native chiefs of India number 315,000 men, with an artillery of 5300 large guns.

On December 31, 1874, there were 6273 miles of railway, built at an expense of £97,000,000, open for traffic. A further extent of 2518 miles was in course of construction at the commencement of 1875.

In the fiscal year ending March 31, 1874, the number of letters which passed through the post office of British India was 98,531,628, of newspapers, 8,762,200, of parcels, 605,312, and of books and patterns, 1,336,363, being a total of 109,235,303. The mail traveled over 54,617 miles, of which total 44,857 miles were done by boats and runners, 4003 miles by carts and on horseback, and 5739 miles by railways. Number of post offices and letter boxes, 6805.

There were at the same time 16,436 miles of telegraph lines, 32,148 miles of wires, and 225 telegraph offices. The total number of messages during the year was 788,048.

Efforts for spreading education among the population of India have been made since 1848, in which year the Lieutenant-governor of Agra brought forward a scheme for giving a schoolmaster to every village of at least a hundred families. After three years' discussion, the Court of Directors of the East India Company accepted the groundwork of the plan, and orders were issued directing that a good vernacular school should be established for every cercle of villages, called Hulkabundee, and that the teacher should be paid from a cess of 2 per cent. on the land revenue.

In the year 1871 the number of educational institutions belonging to, aided, or maintained by the government in British India, was 25,147; average attendance of pupils, 799,622; amount expended by government, £749,724; total expenditure from all sources, £1,019,418.

In the northwestern provinces and Madras the foundation has been laid of a national system of education; while the general position for India is that the government has succeeded in establishing a system of public instruction for the upper and middle classes, but has as yet made little or no impression on the middle classes.

CANADA.

THE Dominion of Canada consists of the provinces of Ontario, Quebec—formerly Upper and Lower Canada—Nova Scotia, New Brunswick, Manitoba, British Columbia, and Prince Edward's Island. The two principal provinces, Quebec and Ontario, are almost entirely embraced within the basin of the river St. Lawrence, but occupy only those portions north of the great lakes, and of the river as far as the town of Cornwall (45° north latitude and 74° 45′ west longitude), whence eastward they occupy both banks, and are bounded on the south by the United States. The most westerly limit is the heads of the Pigeon and Arrow rivers, which debouch in Lake Superior. The eastern or maritime provinces embrace no portion of the basin of the great river.

The following table shows the area and population of the various provinces:

	AREA, ENG. SQ. MILES.	POPULATION (1871).
Ontario,	121,260	1,620,851
Quebec,	210,020	1,191,516
Nova Scotia,	18,660	387,800
New Brunswick,	27,105	285,594
Manitoba,	2,891,734	11,953
British Columbia,	213,000	10,586
Prince Edward's Island,	2,173	94,021
Total,	3,483,952	3,602,321

The principal river of Canada is the St. Lawrence. Its most important tributaries are all from the left. The St. Lawrence drains an area of 565,000 miles. The Ottawa, 450 miles long, forms the boundary between Ontario and Quebec. The St. Maurice is nearly 400 miles in length, and the Saguenay, noted for its fine scenery, is 225 miles long. The only affluents from the right worth naming are the Richelieu, the St. Francis, and the Chaudiere.

A great part of Canada, more especially the shores of Lake Superior, is valuable only for mineral resources, such as iron, zinc, lead, copper, silver, gold, cobalt, manganese, gypsum, marl, granite, sandstone, limestone, slate, and marbles of nearly every imaginable color. Considerable portions, also, though heavily timbered, chiefly with pine, are yet but little adapted to settlement and cultivation. Towards the Gulf of the St. Lawrence, again, a considerable section derives importance mainly from the fisheries, being, with partial exceptions in Gaspe, comparatively worthless for every other object. Thus the area for the profitable production of ordinary cereals cannot materially exceed 40,000 square miles, containing, however, within this space a singularly small portion of irreclaimable surface. This cultivable block increases regularly in width and fertility, from its commencement on the lower St. Lawrence to the shores of Lake Huron. Below Quebec—to say nothing of the precarious nature of the crops—there may always be seen, on one or on both sides, the primeval forest. Between that city, again, and the basin of the Ottawa, a gradual improvement shows itself, even on the north side; and towards the south there stretches away to the frontier of the United States a broad belt of generally undulating character, probably the best field in the country for the blending of pasturage and agriculture. From the basin of the Ottawa inclusive, the parallel of the south end of Lake Nipissing may be said to cut off, towards the southwest, the entire residue of the practicable soil, in the shape of a roughly defined triangle, which, as a whole, is at least equal, in the growth of grain in general and of wheat in particular, to any region of the same extent in North America.

The climate of Canada is subject to great extremes of heat and cold, the thermometer ranging between 102° above and 36° below the zero of Fahrenheit.

As Canada slants southwards eight or nine degrees from the mouth of the St Lawrence to that of the Detroit, which communicates between Lakes St. Clair and Erie, the climate of the west must be warmer than that of the east. Besides, the lakes of Upper Canada appear, in a good measure, to neutralize and mitigate the extremes of a Canadian climate. While Quebec in winter ordinarily enjoys five or six months of sleighing, the corresponding season in Toronto ranges from five or six days to five or six weeks. As to summers, the difference in favor of Toronto is rather in point of duration than of intensity. As indications of the climate of Canada, it may be stated that the isle of Orleans, immediately below Quebec, is famous for its plums, and the island of Montreal for its apples; and from the neighborhood of Toronto to the head of Lake Erie, grapes and peaches ripen without any aid whatever. Melons, again, of large size, come to maturity, through the settled parts of the province, in the open air; and pumpkins and squashes attain enormous size, some of them near Toronto having weighed 300 pounds.

The following statistics of the mining, agricultural, and manufacturing industries are taken from the Official Report of the Canadian Census of 1871. They refer only to the provinces of Ontario, Quebec, New Brunswick, and Nova Scotia.

RAW MINERAL PRODUCTS.

Coal,	671,008 tons.	Gold,	22,941 oz.
Iron ore,	129,363 "	Silver,	69,197 "
Copper ore,	13,310 "	Phosphate of lime,	1,980 tons.
Pyrites,	2,800 "	Mica,	4,010 lbs.
Manganese,	635 "	Crude petroleum,	12,969,435 galls.
Other ores,	14,063 "	Grained marble,	8,870 cub. ft.
Peat,	14,772 "	Building stone for dressing,	5,206,796 "
Plumbago,	270 "	Roofing slate,	6,013 sqs.
Lump gypsum,	114,433 "		

The statistics of agriculture are as follows:

Spring wheat,	10,355,912 bushels.	Beans,	220,644 bushels.
Winter wheat,	6,367,961 "	Buckwheat,	3,726,484 "
Barley,	11,496,068 "	Corn,	3,802,830 "
Oats,	42,489,463 "	Potatoes,	47,330,187 "
Rye,	1,064,354 "	Turnips,	24,339,476 "
Peas,	9,905,720 "	Grass and clover seed,	348,605 "
Hay,	3,818,641 tons.		

The principal items of furs are 488,182 muskrats, 49,799 minks, 48,151 beavers, 19,271 moose, cariboo and deer, 17,582 martens, 37,402 seals, 12,861 foxes, 6132 otters, and 2553 bears.

The following are the statistics of manufactures:

Capital invested,	$77,964,020
Number of hands employed,	187,942
Amount of yearly wages,	40,851,009
Value of raw material,	124,907,846
Total value of products,	221,617,773

The statistics of the fisheries are as follows: Vessels, 991, men, 6984; boats, 16,876, men, 25,876; shoremen, 4647; fathoms of nets, 1,879,435.

The leading items of the product of the fisheries were 682,631 quintals of cod, 120,213 quintals of haddock, 417,300 barrels of herring, 77,925 barrels of mackerel, 2491 gallons of cod-liver oil, and 676,403 gallons of other fish oils.

The foreign trade, during 1874, was, including bullion and specie, as follows: Imports, $128,213,582; exports, $89,851,928. The trade of the Dominion of Canada is chiefly with the United States and Great Britain.

The "British North American Act, 1867," orders that the constitution of the Dominion shall be "similar in principle to that of the United Kingdom;" that the executive authority shall be vested in the sovereign of Great Britain and Ireland, and carried on in her name by a Governor-general and Privy Council; and that the legislative power shall be exercised by a Parliament of two Houses, called the Senate and the House of Commons. Provision is made in the act for the admission of Newfoundland, still an independent province of British North America, into the Dominion of Canada. The seven provinces forming the Dominion have each a separate parliament and administration, with a Lieutenant-governor at the head of the executive. They have full power to regulate their own local affairs, dispose of their revenues, and enact such laws as they may deem best for their own internal welfare, provided only they do not interfere with, and are not adverse to, the action and policy of the central administration under the Governor-general.

The public debt of the Dominion, incurred chiefly on account of public works, and the interest on which forms the largest branch of the expenditure, was $116,082,917 on the 1st of July, 1875. The total revenue during the year ending June 30th, 1874. was $39,930,791; the total expenditure during the same period, $36,524,876.

The strength of the troops maintained by the imperial goverment, and forming the garrison of Halifax, was reduced, in 1871, to 2000 men. Besides these, Canada has a large volunteer force, and a newly organized militia. By the terms of the act passed in March, 1868, "to provide for the defence of the Dominion," the militia consists of all British subjects between the ages of 18 and 60, who are called out to serve in four classes, namely: 1st class, 18 to 30, unmarried; 2d, from 30 to 45 unmarried; 3d, 18 to 45, married; 4th, 45 to 60. A general order from the Militia Department, issued in 1874, reduced the active militia force, for the purposes of drill and pay, for the years 1874 and 1875, to 30,000 officers and men. Two schools of military instruction for infantry are established in each of the provinces of Ontario and Quebec, and one in each of the provinces of New Brunswick and Nova Scotia.

The naval forces of Canada consisted, in 1875, of 8 screw steamers, carrying 18 guns. Besides these, the government owned two fast steamers, employed on coast service, not fitted with guns, but available as gunboats.

The total shipping registered on the 31st of December, 1874, was 6930 vessels of a burthen of 1,158,363 tons. Included in this were 634 steamers, of 76,487 tons.

At the end of October, 1874, Canada had a network of railways of a total length of 4022 miles. There were, at the same period, lines of a total length of 1120 miles in course of construction, and 3000 miles more had been surveyed and concesssions granted by the government.

On June 30th, 1875, there were in the Dominion, 3943 post offices. The number of letters and post-cards sent through the mails, during the year, was 34,750,000; of newspapers, 25,480,000.

The provinces of Quebec and Ontario have separate school laws, adapted to the religious element prevailing in either. Each township in Ontario is divided into several school sections, according to the requirements of inhabitants. The common schools are supported partly by the government and partly by local self-imposed taxation, and occasionally by the payment of a small fee for each scholar. All teachers must pass an examination before a county board of educators, or receive a license from the provincial normal school, empowering them to teach, before they can claim the government allowance.

Commission from CANADA to the International Exhibition:

SENATOR LUC LETELLIER DE ST. JUST, Minister of Agriculture, President.

Honorary Commissioners.

HON. S. C. WOOD, Provincial Treasurer.
HON. P. A. GARNEAU Minister of Agriculture.
HON. P. CARTERET HILL, Provincial Secretary.
HON. J. J. FRAZER, Provincial Sect'y.
HON. L. C. OWEN, Attorney-General.
HON. W. J. ARMSTRONG, Minister of Agriculture.
HON. MR. NOLIN, Minister of Agriculture.

Executive Commissioners.

HON. E. G. PENNY, Senator Montreal.
HON. R. D. WILMOT, Senator Sanbury.
D. MACDOUGALL, ESQ., Berlin.
J. PERRAULT, ESQ., Secretary.

FRANCE.

FRANCE is the most westerly state of Central Europe, extending from 42° 20′ to 51° 5′ north latitude, and from 7° 45′ east to 4° 45′ west longitude. It is bounded on the north by the Channel and the Straits of Dover, which separate it from England, by Belgium, the grand duchy of Luxembourg; on the east by Germany, Switzerland, and Italy, on the south by the Mediterranean and Spain, from which it is separated by the Pyrenees, and on the west by the Atlantic Ocean (the Bay of Biscay). The greatest length of France, from Dunkirk, in the north, to the Col de Falguere, in the south, is about 620 miles; its greatest breadth from east to west, from the boundary line in the Vosges to Cape St. Matthieu, in Finisterre, is about 550 miles. The superficial area of France, including the two Savoy provinces and Corsica, is reckoned at about 201,600 square miles. The possessions of France, which are situated in the non-European parts of the world, have a total superficial area of 463,827 square miles, and the largest is Algeria, with an area of 258,310 square miles. France is divided into 86 departments. The total population, exclusive of Algeria and the colonies, was given (in 1872) at 36,102,921.

The colonies and foreign possessions of France in Africa are Algeria, Senegambia, the islands of Bourbon (Reunion), St. Marie, Mayotte, and Nussi-be, in the Indian Ocean, and Gaboon, on the coast of Guinea. The total possessions in Africa cover an area of about 270,000 square miles, with a population of 2,840,000 souls. In America are the islands of Martinique and Guadaloupe in the West Indies, French Guiana, or Cayenne, with St. Pierre and Miquelon, near Newfoundland; forming together an area of 45,000 square miles, with a population of 345,000. In Asia, the Indian settlements of Pondicherry, Mahe, Karikal, Yanaon, and Chaudernagore, comprise 19,600 square miles, with a population of 265,000. A settlement has also been made in Cochin China, embracing 21,700 square miles and 1,336,000 inhabitants, and a protectorate declared over the Empire of Anam. In the Pacific Ocean are two groups, the Marquesas and Tahiti, and New Caledonia, with the Loyalty Isles, the whole forming an area of 11,182 square miles, with 87,000 inhabitants.

The following table gives the population, in 1872, of some of the largest cities in France:

Paris,	1,850,000
Lyons,	323,000
Marseilles,	313,000
Bordeaux,	194,000
Lille,	158,000
Toulouse,	125,000
Nantes,	119,000
St. Etienne,	111,000
Rouen,	102,000

There are four great mountain chains belonging to France—the Pyrenees which separate the French territory from Spain; the Cevenne-Vosgian range, running north and south between the Moselle and the new boundary line; the Alps, which separate the Swiss territory from the provinces of Savoy and Nice; and the Sardo-Corsican range which belongs, as the name implies, to the islands of Sardinia and Corsica. The highest peaks in the Pyrenees are the Maladetta and Mont Perdu (10,886 feet and 10,994 feet); in the Cevenno-Vosgian range, the greatest height (the Widderkalm) does not greatly exceed 7000 feet. The French portion of the Alps now includes several of the highest mountains and most elevated passes of the ranges, as Mont Blanc, 15,744 feet; Mont Iseran, 13,272 feet; Mont Cenis, 11,457 feet; and the pass of Little St. Bernard, 7190 feet, etc. In Corsica, the highest peak rises to an elevation of 9000 feet. The grand water-shed of France is the Cevenno-Vosges chain, which determines the direction of the four great rivers, the Seine, the Loire, the Garonne, and the Rhone; the first three of which flow north-west into the Bay of Biscay and the English Channel, and the fourth into the Gulf of Lyons.

The entire extent of river navigation in France amounts to 5500 miles, or 8,900,000 metres, while the 99 larger canals, which have been constructed either to connect the various river courses or to supply entirely new channels of water communication, extend over a length of 2900 miles, or 4,700,000 metres. The most important of these works are the canals connecting Nantes and Brest, and the Rhone with the Rhine, and those of Berry, Nivernais, and Bourgogne.

France is peculiarly rich in mineral springs, of which there are said to be nearly 1000 in use. Of these, more than 400 are situated in the group of the Pyrenees, where there are 93 establishments for their systematic use. It is estimated that there are, moreover, fully 4000 springs not hitherto employed.

According to M. Maurice Block's estimate, the physical and agricultural character of the soil of France may be comprised under the following heads:

	HECTARES.*
Mountainous districts, heaths, and commons,	9,944,839
Rich land,	7,276,399
Chalk, or lime districts,	9,788,197
Gravel, stony and sandy,	15,951,618
Clay, marshy, miscellaneous,	9,807,577
	52,768,600

The same writer further subdivides the soil of France, according to its actual employment, under the following heads:

	PER CENT. OF THE WHOLE ACRE.
Arable lands,	48.3
Meadow lands,	9.7
Vineyards,	3.7
Cultivated lands,	17.8
Roads, streets, public walks, etc.,	3.7
Forest and unproductive lands,	16.8

France possesses one of the finest climates in Europe, although, owing to its great xtent of area, very considerable diversities of temperature are to be met with. The mean annual temperature of different parts of France has been estimated as follows, by Humboldt: Toulon, 62° F.; Marseilles, 59.5°; Bordeaux, 56°; Nantes, 55.2°; Paris, 51.2°; Dunkirk, 50.5°.

The following are the statistics of agricultural productions for the year 1869:

	HECTOLITRES.†
Wheat,	108,000,000
Rye,	24,000,000
Barley and oats,	90,000,000
Maize,	10,000,000
Potatoes,	100,000,000

The production of beet-root sugar in 1872–73 amounted to 418,000 tons. The average yearly produce of the vineyards of France is estimated at about 50,000,000

* The *hectare* is equal to about 2.47 English acres.

† The *hectolitre* equals 2.75 bushels.

of hectolitres (about 1,000,000,000 of gallons). Of this about one-seventh is made into brandy.

The principal forest trees are the chestnut and beech on the central mountains, the oak and cork tree in the Pyrenees, and the fir in the Landes. The destruction of the national forests has been enormous within the last two centuries, but measures have been taken in recent years to plant wood, in order to protect those mountain slopes which are exposed to inundations from mountain torrents, and to provide a supply for the ever-increasing demand for fuel. About one-seventh of the entire territory of France is still covered with wood. Turf taken from the marshy lands is extensively used, more especially in the rural districts, for fuel.

According to the census of 1866—the most recent in regard to animals—there were in France 3,312,637 horses, 518,000 asses, 350,000 mules, 12,733,000 horned cattle, 30,386,000 sheep, 5,500,000 swine, and 1,680,000 goats. There were, according to the *Statistique Agricole* for 1858, about 3,000,000 of beehives, valued at rather more than 24,000,000 of francs; the mean annual returns are, for honey, 6,670,000, and for wax, 1,620,000 kilogrammes.* Poultry constitutes an important item of farm produce in France, estimated at 45,500,000 of francs, while the eggs and feathers yield 35,250,000 of francs.

The following figures show the condition of the merchant navy of France on the 31st of December, 1873:

		TONNAGE.	MEN.
Sailing vessels,	15,043	882,866	88,541
Steam vessels,	516	185,165	10,448
	15,559	1,068,031	98,989

The *cabotage*, or internal coasting traffic, is a great source of financial wealth to the State, to which all rivers and canals belong. In 1873, it employed 2776 vessels, with a tonnage of 122,850 and an equipment of 10,871.

The chief mineral products of France are coal and iron, in the excavation of which nearly 250,000 men were employed in 1868. The production of coal in 1868 was 132,000,000 of quintals, the quintal being equal to 1.97 hundredweight. During the same year, there were 150 iron mines in operation, yielding 34,500,000 of quintals, more than half of this quantity being obtained from the five departments of Haute-Marne, Haute-Saone, Cher, Moselle, and Nord. Argentiferous galena, a little silver and gold, copper, lead, manganese, antimony, and tin occur, but hitherto their working has not proved very productive. The department of Charento-Inferieure yields the largest amount of salt, the mean annual produce being 1,500,000 of quintals (2,500,000 of francs), which is fully one-third of the entire annual produce of the whole country. France derives about 41,000,000 of francs from its quarries of granite and freestone, its kaolin, marbles, sands, lithographic stones, millstones, etc. Granite and syenite are found in the Alps, Vosges, Corsica, Normandy, and Burgundy; porphyry in the Vosges; and basalt and lava, for pavements, in the mountains of Auvergne. Marble is met with in more than 40 departments; alabaster occurs in the Pyrenees; the largest State quarries are near Cherbourg and St. Lo.

The following list gives an approximate estimate of the value of the chief products of French industry:

	MILLIONS OF FRANCS.
Linen fabrics,	250
Cotton fabrics,	650
Woolen fabrics,	950
Silk fabrics,	1000
Mixed fabrics,	330
Jewelry, watchmaking,	35
Gilt wares	12

* The kilogramme equals 2.2 pounds avoirdupois.

Minerals, mines, salt, etc.,	600
Articles of food, as sugar, wines, etc.,	364
Skins, leather, oils, tobacco,	556
Bone, ivory, isinglass, etc.,	30
Chemical products,	80
Ceramic arts,	86
Paper, printing,	60
Forests, fisheries,	98

The total imports, for 1873, were 4,576,000,000, and the total exports, for the same year, 4,822,000,000 of francs.

France was proclaimed a republic on the 4th of September, 1870. According to the law of February 25th, 1875, the legislative power is vested in the two Houses, the Chamber of Deputies and the Senate. The Chamber of Deputies is elected by universal suffrage. The Senate is composed of 300 members, 225 of whom are elected by the departments and the colonies, and 75 by the National Assembly. The President of the republic is elected by a majority of the votes of the Senate and Chamber of Deputies, united as the National Assembly. His term of office is for seven years, and he is eligible for re-election.

According to the budget for 1876, the estimated receipts for the year are put down at 2,575,028,582 francs, and the expenditures at 2,570,505,513. The public debt is 23,403,000,000 francs.

The nominal strength of the army, on a peace footing, is given in the latest government returns as 490,332 men; on a war footing, 1,750,000.

The navy of France was composed, at the end of 1873, of 62 ironclads, 264 unarmored screw steamers, 62 paddle steamers, and 113 sailing vessels.

According to the official report for December, 1874, the railways in operation measure 20,711 kilometres, or about 12,866 miles. With the exception of less than 500 miles, the railways of France are held by six companies, which are under the superintendence of the State.

The number of letters forwarded by the post office, in 1874, was 341,068,000; newspapers, postal cards, and parcels, 331,786,000.

At the end of 1873, there were 45,942 kilometres of lines of telegraphs, comprising 123,669 kilometres of wire. The number of messages sent, in 1873, was 6,225,000, of which nearly one-fourth were international messages. There were annual deficits since the establishment of the public telegraph department, in March, 1851. There were 2206 telegraph offices at the end of 1873.

Public instruction is presided over in France by a special ministry. Nearly half the expenses connected with it are defrayed by the State, and the remainder by the departments. There are 15 academies, located in the following towns: Aix, Besancon, Bordeaux, Caen, Clermont, Dijon, Douai, Grenoble, Lyon, Montpellier, Nancy, Paris, Poitiers, Rennes, Toulon. These academies are divided into the five faculties of theology, law, medicine, sciences, and literature, and supplemented by various superior and preparatory schools. The professors are paid partly by the State and partly by fees. Secondary instruction has received an immense impetus during the present century. The different departments share very unequally in the diffusion of education, and it may be generally observed that the proportion of the educated is highest in the northern and eastern districts of France. France supports numerous colleges and schools for instruction in special branches of knowledge. There are also numerous agricultural, forest, farming, and veterinary schools, besides the Ecole Polytechnique, specially designed to prepare youths for the public services; and military and naval colleges at St. Cyr, Saumur, Paris, Vincennes, Brest, Toulon, and St. Denis.

Paris possesses several libraries belonging to, and supported by, the State, but freely opened to the public. There are 338 public libraries in the provinces, to all of which access is afforded in the most liberal spirit. France is rich in public galleries of painting, statuary, and articles of *vertu*. The expenses of secondary and primary education, literary and scientific institutions, etc., are charged in the budget for 1876 at 44,912,545 francs.

(Detailed information as to the colonial dependencies of France will be found under the appropriate headings in other portions of the catalogue.)

Commission from FRANCE to the International Exhibition:

M. M. OZENNE, Counsellor of State, Secretary-General of the Ministry of Agriculture and Commerce, Commissioner-General of International Exhibitions.

DU SOMMERARD, Director of the Museums of Thermes and Cluny, Commissioner-General of International Exhibitions.

Committee.

Organized under the Presidency of the Minister of Agriculture and Commerce.

M. DUCLERC, Vice-President of the National Assembly, Member of the Committee on International Exhibitions.
MARQUIS DE TALHOUET, Deputy.
BARON DE SOUBEYRAN, Deputy.
MR. WOLOWSKI, Deputy.
MARQUIS DE LAFAYETTE, Deputy.
M. BONNET, Deputy.
M. FLOTARD, Deputy.
M. LABOULAYE, Deputy.
M. DIETZ-MONIN, Deputy.
M. COUNT DE BOUILLE, Deputy.
VISCOUNT D'HAUSSONVILLE, Deputy.
M. DE CHABROL, Deputy.
M. JULLIEN, Deputy.
The Secretary-General of the Ministry of Agriculture and Commerce.
The Director-General of Customs.
The Director of the Academy of Fine Arts.
The Director of Consulates and Commercial Affairs, at the Ministry of Foreign Affairs.
M. OUTREY, Minister Plenipotentiary.
M. DU SUMMERARD, Director of the Museum of Thermes and Cluny.
The Assistant Director of Foreign Commerce.
The President of the Paris Chamber of Commerce.
M. GUILLAUME, Member of the Institute.
MARQUIS DE ROCHAMBEAU.
BARON ALPHONSE DE ROTHSCHILD.
M. SIEBER.
M. ALFRED MAME.
M. JULES LAVEISSIERE, Dealer in Metals.
M. ROULLEAUX DUGAGE, Secretary.
M. DE FALLOIS, late Chief of Bureau, Ministry of Public Works, Assistant Secretary.

Resident Commissioners.

MR. DE LAFOREST, Consul-General of France, Commissioner-General.
MR. RAVIN D'ELPEUX, Vice-Consul.
CAPT. ANFRYE, Military Attache, French Legation.
MR. BAZERGNE, Attaché.
MR. A. IMBERT GOUZBEYRE, Secretary.

GERMANY.

THE German Empire occupies the central portion of Europe, and extends from 6° to 22° 40′ east longitude and 49° 7′ to 55° 50′ north latitude. It is bounded on the north by the German Ocean, the Danish Peninsula, and the Baltic; on the east by Russia and Austria; on the south by Russia, Austria, and Switzerland, and on the west by France, Belgium, and the Netherlands. The population (1871) is about 41,000,000. Its area is estimated at 208,000 square miles, or about one-sixteenth of that of all Europe. The coast line measures about 950 miles.

Germany is composed of an aggregation of 26 different States. The following list gives the names of these States, their population, area, and the number of members representing each in the Bundesrath, or Federal Council, and the Reichstag, or Imperial Diet:

STATES.	POPULATION IN 1871.	AREA IN SQUARE MILES.	NO. OF MEMBERS IN BUNDESRATH.	NO. OF DEPUTIES IN REICHSTAG.
Kingdoms:				
1. Prussia,	24,691,307	139,751	17	236
2. Bavaria,	4,863,450	29,280	6	48
3. Saxony,	2,556,244	5,780	4	23
4. Wurtemburg,	1,818,539	7,532	4	17
Grand Duchies:				
5. Baden,	1,461,562	5,850	3	14
6. Hesse,	852,894	2,962	3	9
7. Mecklenburg-Schwerin,	557,897	5,136	2	6
8. Saxe-Weimar,	286,183	1,403	1	3
9. Mecklenburg-Strelitz,	96,982	1,130	1	1
10. Oldenburg,	314,777	2,470	1	3
Duchies:				
11. Brunswick,	311,764	1,425	2	3
12. Saxe-Meiningen,	187,884	955	1	2
13. Saxe-Altenburg,	142,122	510	1	1
14. Saxe-Coburg-Gotha,	174,339	760	1	2
15. Anhalt,	203,437	896	1	2
Principalities:				
16. Schwarzburg-Rudolstat,	75,523	367	1	1
17. Schwarzburg-Sondershausen,	67,191	332	1	1
18. Waldeck,	56,224	438	1	1
19. Reuss (altere Linie),	45,094	123	1	1
20. Reuss (jungere Linie),	89,032	320	1	1
21. Schaumburg-Lippe,	32,059	170	1	1
22. Lippe-Detmold,	111,135	438	1	1
Free Towns:				
23. Lubeck,	52,158	110	1	1
24. Bremen,	122,402	97	1	1
25. Hamburg,	338,974	158	1	3
26. Alsace-Lorraine,	1,549,459	5,590		
	41,058,632	208,613	58	382

The *Almanac de Gotha*, for 1876, divides the population of the German Empire, in regard to nationality, as follows: Germans, 37,820,000; Poles, 2,450,000; Wends, 140,000; Czechs, 50,000; Lithuanians and Courlanders, 150,000; Danes, 150,000; French and Walloons, 210,000. The Germans admit of being divided into high and low Germans; the phraseology of the former is the cultivated language of all the German States; that of the latter, known as *Platt-Deutsch*, is spoken in the north and northwest. The Poles are found exclusively in the east and northeast of Prussia; the Czechs in Silesia, about Appeln and Breslau; the Wends, in Silesia, Brandenburg, and Prussian Lusatia; the Lithuanians and Courlanders in east Prussia; the Danes, in Schleswig; the Walloons, about Aix-la-Chapelle, in Rhenish Prussia, and the French, partly in the same region, and in Alsace and Lorraine.

Germany presents two very distinct physical formations. . First, a range of high table land, occupying the centre and southern parts of the country, interspersed with numerous ranges and groups of mountains, the most important of which are the Harz and Teutoburger in the north, the Taunus and Thuringerwald in the middle, and the Schwarzwald and Raube Alps in the south, and containing an area, including Alsace and Lorraine, of 110,000 square miles. Second, a vast sandy plain, which extends from the centre of the empire north to the German Ocean, and including Schleswig-Holstein, contains an area of about 98,000 square miles. This great plain, stretching from the Russian frontier on the east to the Netherlands on the west, is varied by two terrace-like elevations. The one stretches from the Vistula into Mecklenburg, at no great distance from the coast of the Baltic, and has a mean elevation of 500 to 600 feet, rising in one point near Danzig to 1020 feet; the other line of elevations begins in Silesia, and terminates in the moorlands of Luneberg, in Hanover, its course being marked by several summits from 500 to 800 feet in height. A large portion of the plain is occupied by sandy tracts, interspersed with deposits of peat; but other parts are moderately fertile, and admit of successful cultivation.

In respect of drainage the surface of Germany belongs to three different basins. The Danube, from its source in the Schwarzwald to the borders of Austria, belongs to Germany, and through this channel the waters of the greater part of Bavaria are poured into the Black Sea, thus opening up communication with the east. The greater part of the surface, however (about 185,000 square miles), has a northern slope, and belongs partly to the basin of the North Sea, and partly to the basin of the Baltic. The chief German streams flowing into the North Sea are the Rhine, the Weser, and the Elbe; into the Baltic, the Oder and the Vistula.

The most important of the numerous canals of Germany are the Ludwig's canal, in Bavaria, connecting the Danube and Main, and thus opening a communication between the Black Sea and the German Ocean; the Finow and Friedrich Wilhelm's canals, in Brandenburg; the Plaue canal, connecting the Elbe and the Havel; and the Kiel and Eyder canal, uniting the Baltic and the German Ocean. Numerous lakes occur both in the table-land of southern Germany, and in the lowlands of the northern district, but few of them are of any great size. Mineral springs occur principally in Nassau, Wurtemburg, Baden, Bavaria, and Rhenish Prussia. Many of these springs have retained their high reputation from the earliest ages.

The climate of Germany presents less diversity than a first glance at the map might lead one to infer, for the greater heats of the more southern latitudes are considerably modified by the alpine character of the country in those parallels, while the cold of the northern plains is mitigated by their vicinity to the ocean. The average decrease in the mean temperature is in going from south to north, about 1° F. for every 52 miles; and in going from west to east, about 1° F. for every 72 miles. The line of perpetual snow varies from 7200 to 8000 feet above the level of the sea. The mean annual fall of rain is 20 inches.

The following table shows the mean temperature at different points:

	MEAN ANNUAL TEMPERATURE.	SUMMER.	WINTER.
Hamburg,	47.	64	30
Dresden,	48.	67	29
Frankfort-on-the-Main,	48.5	66	31
Berlin,	46.5	66	27
Hanover,	48.	63	33
Königsberg,	43.	62	24

Germany is rich in mineral products, among which the most important are silver, found in the Hartz mountains; iron in numerous mountain ranges; salt in many parts of the country; coal in Rhenish Prussia, Silesia. Cobalt, arsenic, sulphur, saltpetre, alum, gypsum, bismuth, pumice-stone, tripoli-slate, kaolin, emery, ochre, and vitriol, are all among the exports of Germany.

The following figures show the product of the principal mining industries of Germany (exclusive of Alsace and Lorraine) for the year 1870:

	NO. OF WORKS.	PERSONS EMPLOYED.	PRODUCT IN CWT.	VALUE IN THALERS.
Coal (including brown coal),	1362	145,782	680,060,074	61,863,399
Iron ore,	1258	24,793	58,550,539	7,116,828
Zinc ore,	72	9,797	7,335,603	2,315,429
Lead ore,	174	18,057	2,111,810	5,511,235
Copper ore,	3	6,156	4,147,627	1,619,938

The yield of salt, for the same year, was 14,658,990 hundredweight, from 69 works, employing 4610 persons, and valued at 3,926,650 thalers.

The leading products of the metallurgical industries are given as follows:

	WORKS.	PERSONS EMPLOYED.	AMOUNT PRODUCED IN CWT.	VALUE IN THALERS.
Cast iron,	631	39,525	29,942,264	49,251,650
Wrought iron (including wire, bars, and manufactured iron of various kinds),	354	43,849	17,437,766	57,490,284
Steel,	216	12,892	3,399,027	22,747,626
Zinc,	53	6,256	1,727,570	10,212,259
Silver,	10	1,601	(lbs.) 185,847	5 549,943
Lead (products of),	17	1,513	1,195,753	6,951,164
Copper,	28	1,971	174,687	4,667,535

The entire production of mines, furnaces, salt works, etc., is given as 824,965,732 hundredweight, valued (including 186,270 pounds of gold and silver) at 246,482,099 thalers.

The vegetable products comprise a very large proportion of the European flora. All the ordinary cereals are extensively cultivated in the north, and largely exported, chiefly from Wurtemberg and Bavaria; hemp and flax, madder, woad, and saffron grow well in the central districts, where the vine, the cultivation of which extends in suitable localities as far north as 51°, is brought to greater cultivation—the best wine-producing districts being the valleys of the Danube, Rhine, Main, Neckar, and Moselle, which are, moreover, generally noted for the excellence of their fruits and vegetables. Tobacco is grown in sufficient quantities for extensive exportation on the Upper Rhine, the Werra, and Oder. The hops of Bavaria have a high reputation, and the chicory grown in that country and in the district between the Elbe and the Weser finds its way all over Europe as a substitute for coffee. The average annual product of cereals is approximately as follows:

Rye, ...	89,000,000 hectolitres.*
Oats, ...	87,000,000 "
Wheat, ...	34,000,000 "
Barley, ...	30,000,000 "

The average annual potato crop amounts to 272,000,000 hectolitres. The production of beets, in 1872, was over 61,000,000 hundredweight. A fair yield of wine is about 4,500,000 hectolitres, and of tobacco, about 700,000 hundredweight.

The most extensive forests are found in central Germany, and in some parts of Prussia, while the northwestern parts of the great plain are deficient in wood, the place of which is in some degree supplied by the abundance of turf yielded by the marshy lands. Germany has long been noted for the good breed of horses raised in the northern parts of the continent, while Saxony, Silesia, and Brandenburg have an equal reputation for their sheep-flocks, and the fine quality of the wool which they yield. The rich alluvial flats of Mecklenburg and Hanover are celebrated for their cattle; the forests of northern and central Germany abound in swine, and in small game of various kinds; while the Bavarian Alps afford shelter to the larger animals, as the chamois, the red deer and wild goat, the fox, marten, and wolf.

According to the last enumeration of live stock, there were in Germany 3,500,000 horses, 15,000,000 cattle, 30,000,000 sheep, 8,000,000 swine, and 2,000,000 goats. The wool crop for 1869 amounted to 750,000 hundredweight.

Among the fishes of Germany, the most generally distributed are carp, salmon, trout, and eels; the rivers contain also crayfish, pearl-bearing mussels, and leeches. The oyster, herring, and cod fisheries constitute important branches of industry on the German shores of the Baltic and North Seas.

The preservation and cultivation of woods receive almost as much attention in Germany as agriculture, and, like the latter, are elevated to the rank of a science. The larger woods and forests in most of the states belong to the government, and are under the care of special boards of management, which exercise the right of supervision and control over all forest lands, whether public or private. The value of the forests of Germany was, in 1873, estimated at 666,000 thalers.

The oldest and most important of the German industrial arts are the manufactures of linen and woolen goods. The chief localities for the cultivation and preparation of flax, and the weaving of linen fabrics, are the mountain valleys of Silesia, Lusatia, Westphalia, the Harz, and Saxony (for thread laces); while cotton fabrics are principally made in Rhenish Prussia and Saxony. The same districts, together with Pomerania and Bavaria, manufacture the choicest woolen fabrics, including damasks and carpets. Toys, wooden clocks, and wood-carvings, which may be regarded as almost a specialty of Germany industry, are carried to the greatest perfection in the hilly districts of Saxony, Bavaria, and the Black Forest. The best iron and steel manufactures belong to Silesia, Hanover, and Saxony. Silesia probably possesses the finest glass manufactories; while Saxony and Prussia stand pre-eminent for the excellence of their china and earthen wares. Augsburg and Nuremberg dispute with Munich and Berlin the title to pre-eminence in silver, gold, and jewelry work, and in the manufacture of philosophical and musical instruments; while Leipzig and Munich claim the first rank for type foundries, printing, and lithography. The trading cities of northern Germany nearly monopolize the entire business connected with the preparation of tobacco, snuff, etc., the distillation of brandies, and the manufacture of sugar from the beet, potato, and other roots; while vinegar and oils are prepared almost exclusively in central and southern Germany.

The constitution of the empire is confederate, under the presidentship of the King of Prussia, who bears the hereditary title of German Emperor. He has the right

* The hectolitre equals 2.75 bushels.

and duty of representing the empire in all respects of international law, of declaring war in the name of the empire, making peace and treaties, etc. For a declaration of war the consent of the Bundesrath is necessary. He is the commander-in-chief of the whole army and navy, in peace as well as in war, except the military powers of Wurtemberg and Bavaria, which—in times of peace only—form separate corps under the command of their respective kings. He names and dismisses the officers and functionaries of the empire. His orders, issued in the name of the empire, must be countersigned by the Chancellor, who, as the first minister of the empire, is by his signature responsible for them.

The legislative powers lie in the *Bundesrath* and the *Reichstag*. The former consists of the delegates of the confederate governments, representing in all fifty-eight votes. The Reichstag has 382 members directly elected by the secret ballot of the people. The bills promulgated by these two assemblies in accordance are compulsory on all governments of the empire, and annul *eo ipso* all possible institutions contradictory to them in the several States.

The empire has no debt. The debts of the separate States amounted, in 1873, to 1,093,800,000 thalers, 589,300,000 of which sum was for railways.

The army consists, on a peace footing, of about 400,000 men; on a war footing, of about 1,300,000. The navy comprises 51 vessels, of which number 47 are steamers, of 77,130 horse-power, 64,198 tons burthen, and carrying 321 guns; and 4 sailing vessels (1 frigate and 3 brigs) mounting 36 guns.

The multiplicity of small States into which Germany was long broken up, opposed great obstacles to the development of commerce; but the difficulty has to some extent been obviated by the establishment of the *Zollverein*, or "Customs confederation." The Hanse Towns, Hamburg and Bremen, do not belong to it, being free ports; but it comprises all the other states of the empire and the grand duchy of Luxembourg.

The estimated value of goods exported, imported, and in transit (by the customs lines) for 1873 was as follows:

Imports,	4,257,300,000 marks.
Exports,	2,489,000,000 "
In transit,	1,233,000,000 "

The merchant navy comprised, in 1873, 4748 vessels, including 253 steamers, with a total of 1,201,358 tonnage.

The railways measured, in 1871, about 13,310 English miles; but these figures represent the length, not of the lines within the limits of the German Empire, but of those which are under German administration, though extending some way into neighboring States.

The various telegraphic lines of the empire (excepting those of Bavaria and Wurtemburg) are now under a central administration, and, in 1874, the whole measured 42,571 kilometres; length of wires, 149,410 kilometres· number of messages, 13,422,-511; number of offices, 4992.

The post office forwarded in 1874:

Private letters,	521,900,000
Postal cards,	47,900,000
Official letters,	37,700,000
Parcels, etc.,	89,700,000
	697,200,000
Newspapers,	349,600,000
Number of offices,	7,900

Education is more generally diffused in Germany than in any other part of Europe, and is cultivated with an earnest and systematic devotion not met with, to an equal extent, among other nations. The attendance of children at school, for at least four or five years, is made compulsory in nearly all the German States, and hence the proportion of persons who cannot read and write is exceedingly small in Germany.

The elementary schools are 60,000 in number, and are attended by 6,000,000 pupils between the ages of six and fourteen. Of the middle schools, including 330 gymnasia and 214 pro-gymnasia and Latin schools, there were in 1873 over 1000, attended by 177,379 pupils. There are 21 universities, with (in 1873) 1620 instructors and 17,858 students. Of polytechnic schools there are ten, with 360 instructors and 4500 students. Besides these there are numerous special schools of technology, agriculture, commerce, mining, metallurgy, military science, navigation, trades, etc. The German academies of art and sciences and conservatories of music enjoy a world-wide reputation. Public libraries—of which there are more than one hundred and fifty—museums, botanical gardens, art collections, and picture galleries are to be met with in most of the capitals and many of the country towns.

Commission from the GERMAN EMPIRE to the International Exhibition:

DR. JACOBI, Royal Prussian Actual Privy Superior Government Counsellor and Ministerial Director, President.

DR. STUVE, Royal Prussian Privy Government Counsellor and Counsellor in the Ministry of Commerce.

DR. WEDDING, Royal Prussian Counsellor of Mines.

MR. REITHER, Royal Bavarian Counsellor of Legation.

MR. VON NOSTITZ WALWITZ, Royal Saxon Envoy Extraordinary and Minister Plenipotentiary.

BARON VON SPITZEMBERG, Royal Wurtemberg Envoy Extraordinary and Minister Plenipotentiary.

DR. NEIDHARDT, Grand Ducal Hessian Ministerial Counsellor.

MR. KAUFMANN, Royal Prussian Counsellor of Commerce.

DR. KRUGER, Hanseatic Minister, Resident.

MR. VON HOLLOBEN, Royal Prussian Superior Tribunal Counsellor.

MR. NIEBERDING, Counsellor in the Office of the Chancellor of the Empire.

BARON VON ZEDLITZ, Royal Prussian Provincial Counsellor.

MR. F. REULEAUX, Commissioner General.

MR. KNIFFLER, Assistant Engineer.

G. A. RADTKE, Secretary.

Resident Commissioners.

JOHN D. LANKENAU, ESQ.

CHARLES H. MEYER, ESQ., Consul.

GUSTAVUS REMAK, ESQ.

DR. FRED. VOLCK.

MR. BARTELS, Engineer and Architect.

AUSTRIA.

THE Austrian Empire forms, on the whole, a compact territory with a circumference of about 5349 miles. It is included between 42° to 51° north latitude, and between 8° 20′ to 26° 20′ east longitude. The body of the empire lies in the interior of the European continent, though, by means of the southern projection of Dalmatia, it has about 1200 miles of sea-coast on the Adriatic. With the rest of its circumference, it borders on the States of the Church, Modena, Parma, Italy, Switzerland, Bavaria, Saxony, Prussia, Russia, Moldavia, Wallachia, Servia, Turkey, and Montenegro. Its present provinces embrace an area of 241,123 square miles, and a population which, in 1869, amounted to 35,904,435.

The following table gives the area, number of civil inhabitants, and total population, civil and military, of the various provinces of the empire—distinguishing its two great political divisions, the German monarchy, or Cisleithan Austria, and the Hungarian kingdom, or Transleithan Austria, together with the so-called military frontier, placed under the administration of the ministry of war for the whole empire—according to the official returns for 1869:

PROVINCES.	AREA IN ENGLISH SQ. MILES.	CIVIL POPULATION.	TOTAL POPULATION.
GERMAN MONARCHY.			
Lower Austria,	7,658	1,954,251	1,990,708
Upper Austria,	4,634	731,579	736,557
Salzburg,	2,768	151,410	153,159
Styria,	8,674	1,131,309	1,137,990
Carinthia,	4,007	336,400	337,694
Carniola,	3,858	463,273	446,334
Coast Land,	3,085	582,079	600,525
Tyrol and Vorarlberg,	11,321	878,907	885,789
Bohemia,	20,763	5,106,069	5,140,544
Moravia,	8,579	1,997,897	2,017,274
Silesia,	1,988	511,581	513,352
Galicia,	30,320	5,418,016	5,444,683
Bukowena,	4,037	511,964	513,404
Dalmatia,	4,942	442,796	456,961
Total German Monarchy,	116,634	20,217,531	20,934,980
KINGDOM OF HUNGARY.			
Hungary,	82,867	11,117,623	11,118,502
Croatia and Slavonia,	7,445	1,160,085	1,164,806
Transylvania,	21,222	2,101,727	2,115,024
Military Frontier,	12,956	1,037,892	1,041,123
Total Hungary,	124,490	15,417,327	15,509,455
Total Austro-Hungary,	241,124	35,634,858	35,904,435

Three-fourths of Austria is mountainous or hilly, being traversed by three great mountain chains—the Alps, Carpathians, and Sudetes, whose chief ridges are of primitive rock. The Alps are accompanied, north and south, by parallel ranges of calcareous mountains, covering whole provinces with their ramifications. The Carpathians are lapped on their northern side by sandstone formations; mountains of the same character also occupy Transylvania. Springing from the northwest bend of the Carpathians, the Sudetes run through the northeast of Moravia and Bohemia, in which last the range is known as the Riesen gebirge, or Giant mountains. Continuous with this range, and beginning on the left bank of the Elbe, are the Erzgebirge, or Ore mountains, on the confines of Saxony; and veering round to nearly southeast, the range is further prolonged in the Bohemian Forest mountains, between Bohemia and Bavaria. The chief plains of the Austrian empire are: the great plains of Hungary (the smaller of these is in the west, between the offsets of the Alps and Carpathians, and is about 4200 square miles in extent; the other, which is in the east, and traversed by the Danube and the Theiss, has an area of 21,000 square miles), and the plains of Galicia.

From the south point of Dalmatia to the boundary of Italy, Austria has a sea-line of about 1000 miles, not counting the coasts of the numerous islands, the largest of which is Veglia, 23 miles by 12. The chief lakes are: the Platten See, and the Neusiedler See, both in Hungary. The first is navigable by steamers, and both are rich in fish, and have fruitful vineyards around them. The Alps and Carpathians inclose numerous mountain lakes, which are surrounded with wood and rock, and all the other attributes of picturesque scenery. The Long lake in the Tatra mountains lies at an elevation of 6000 feet. The most remarkable of all is the Zirknitz lake, in Illyria. There are extensive swamps or morasses in Hungary. One connected with the Neusiedler See covers some 80 square miles. A good deal has been done in the way of reclaiming lands by draining morasses.

The leading rivers that have navigable tributaries are: the Danube, which has a course of 849 miles within the Austrian dominions, the Vistula, the Elbe, and the Dniester. The Rhine bounds Austria for about fourteen miles above Lake Constance.

The climate of Austria is on the whole very favorable; but from the extent and diversity of surface, it presents great varieties. In the warmest southern region, between 42° to 46° latitude, rice, olives, oranges, and lemons ripen in the better localities; and wine and maize are produced everywhere. In the middle temperate region from 46° to 49°, which has the greatest extent and diversity of surface, the vine and maize still thrive in perfection. In the northern region, beyond 49°, except in favored spots, neither the vine nor maize succeeds; but grain, fruit, flax, and hemp, thrive excellently. The mean temperature of the year is, at Trieste, 58° F.; at Vienna, 51°; at Lemberg, in Galicia, 44°.

The raw products of Austria are abundant and various; and in this respect it is one of the most favored countries in Europe. Its mineral wealth is not surpassed in any European country; it is only lately that Russia has exceeded it in the production of gold and silver. Mining has been a favorite pursuit in Austria for centuries, and has been encouraged and promoted by the government. Bohemia, Hungary, Styria, Carinthia, Salzburg, and Tyrol, take the first place in respect of mineral produce. Except platina, none of the useful metals is wanting. The mines are partly State property, and partly owned by private individuals. Gold is found chiefly in Hungary and Transylvania, and in smaller quantity in Salzburg and Tyrol. The same countries, along with Bohemia, yield silver. The discovery of quicksilver at Idria first brought this branch of mining industry into importance. This metal is now also found in Hungary, Transylvania, Styria, and Carinthia. Copper is found in many districts—tin, in Bohemia alone. Zinc is got chiefly in Cracow and Carinthia. The most productive lead mines are in Carinthia. Iron is found in almost every province of the monarchy, though Styria, Carinthia, and Carniola are chief seats. The production, though great, is not yet equal to the consumption. Antimony is confined to Hungary; arsenic is found in Salzburg and Bohemia; cobalt in Hungary, Styria, and Bohemia; sulphur in Galicia, Bohemia, Hungary, Venice, Salzburg, etc., though not enough to supply home consumption. Graphite is found abundantly in Bohemia, Moravia, Carinthia, etc.

The useful earths and building-stones are to be had in great profusion; all sorts of clay up to the finest porcelain earth (in Moravia, Bohemia, Hungary, Venice), and likewise marble, gypsum, chalk, etc. Of precious and semi-precious stones are the Hungarian opal, which passes in commerce as oriental, Bohemian garnets—the finest in Europe—cornelians, agates, beryl, amethyst, jasper, ruby, sapphire, topaz, etc.

The following table shows the principal metals and minerals produced in Austria in 1867, and their average value in florins at the place of production:

	WEIGHT.	VALUE IN FLORINS.
Gold (Austrian pound)	3,562	2,406,041
Silver "	81,378	3,655,643
Quicksilver (Austrian hundredweight)	5,944	723,958
Tin " "	591	33,812
Zinc " "	40,296	495,956
Copper " "	47,930	2,377,840
Lead and litharge " "	136,668	1,770,884
Iron, raw and cast " "	5,705,761	16,709,039
Graphite " "	279,355	271,123
Mineral coal " "	108,488,390	17,322,283

Austria is peculiarly rich in salt. Rocksalt exists in immense beds on both sides of the Carpathians, chiefly at Wieliczka and Bochnia, in Galicia, and in the country of Marmaros in Hungary, and in Transylvania. The annual produce of rock-salt is greatly above three million hundredweight. Salt is also made at State salt-works by evaporating the water of salt-springs. The chief works are those at Hallstadt, Ischl, Hallein, and Hall in Tryol. From two to three millions hundredweight are thus produced annually. A considerable quantity is also made from sea-water on the coast of the Adriatic. Of other salts, alum, sulphate of iron, and sulphate of copper are the chief. Austria has abundance of mineral springs, frequented for their salubrity; 1600 are enumerated, some of them of European reputation, as the sulphurous baths of Baden, in lower Austria, the saline waters of Karlsbad, Marienbad, and Ofen, etc.

The vegetable productions, as might be expected from the vast diversity in the soil and position of the different provinces, are extremely various. Although three-fourths of the surface is mountainous, more than five-sixths is productive, being used either for tillage, meadows, pasture, or forest. Grain of all kinds is cultivated most abundantly in Hungary and the districts south of it on the Danube, in Bohemia, Moravia, Silesia, and Galicia. Agriculture is not yet far advanced; the prevailing system is still what is called the three-field system, introduced into Germany by Charlemagne, in which a crop of winter wheat is followed by one of summer grain, and that by fallow.

In Hungary, the Magyar adheres to his primitive husbandry; the German and Slave are adopting improved methods. Rice is cultivated in the Banat, but not enough for the consumption. Potatoes are raised everywhere; and in elevated districts, are often the sole subsistence of the inhabitants. Horticulture is carried to great perfection; and the orchards of Bohemia, Austria proper, Tyrol, and many parts of Hungary, produce a profusion of fruit. Great quantities of cider are made in upper Austria and Carinthia, and of plum brandy in Slavonia. In Dalmatia, oranges and lemons are produced, but not sufficient for the requirements of the country; twice as much olive oil is imported as is raised in the monarchy.

In the production of wine, Austria is second only to France. With the exception of Galicia, Silesia, and upper Austria, the vine is cultivated in all the provinces; but Hungary stands first, yielding not only the finest quality of wine, but four-fifths the amount of the whole produce of the empire. The average produce of the whole empire is estimated at about 680 millions of gallons.

Of plants used in manufactures and commerce, the first place is held by flax and hemp. Flax is cultivated almost universally; white hemp in Galicia, Moravia, Hungary, etc. Tobacco is raised in great quantities, especially in Hungary, which also is first in the cultivation of rapeseed. Bohemia raises hops of the first quality, which are partly exported, though other provinces import from abroad. The indigo plant has lately been successfully acclimatized in Dalmatia. More than a third of the productive surface is covered with wood (75,000 square miles), which, besides timber, yields a number of secondary products, as tar, potash, charcoal, bark, cork, etc.

As to animals, bears are found in the Carpathians, Alps, and Dalmatia; wolves, jackals, and lynxes in these same districts, and also in the Banat, Croatia, Slavonia, and the military frontiers. The marmot, otter, and beaver are also found in Dalmatia. Game has of late sensibly diminished. The wild goat lives in the highest, the chamois and white Alpine hare in the middle regions of the Alps and Carpathians. More productive than the chase are the fisheries of the Danube, Theiss, and numerous streams, lakes, and ponds. The chief sea-fishing is in Dalmatia. Leeches, procured chiefly in Hungary and Moravia, form an article of considerable trade. For foreign commerce, the most important branch of rural industry is the rearing of silk.

Austria produces about a quarter a million of silk cocoons annually. The silk trade is very extensive on the Tyrol—the yearly supply of cocoons in that country being about 32,000.

In 1851, the number of horses in the monarchy was stated at 3,229,884 (not including 75,000 belonging to the army); cattle, 10,410,484; sheep, 16,801,545; goats, 2,275,900; and swine, 7,401,300. Nearly three-fourths of the population are engaged in husbandry, so that Austria is decidedly an agricultural State, though its capabilities in this respect have by no means been fully develoved.

The annual value of its manufactures—not including small trades—is estimated at 1000 to 1200 millions of florins, while that of its husbandry may reach 3000 millions. Bohemia takes the lead in this industry; then follow Austria proper, Moravia and Silesia, Hungary. Vienna is the chief seat of manufacture for articles of luxury; Moravia, Silesia, and Bohemia for linen, woolen, and glass wares; Styria and Carinthia for iron and steel wares. The chief manufactured articles of export are silken and woolen; the only others of consequence are linen, twist, glasswares, and cotton goods. The yearly value of manufactured iron is about fifty-four millions of florins. The glasswares of Bohemia are of special excellence. The hemp and flax industry is one of the oldest and still most important.

No branch of industry has risen more rapidly than that of cotton. The annual value of the silk industry is estimated at about sixty millions of florins. The manufacture of tobacco is a State monopoly, and produced a revenue in 1873 of 58,126,000 florins. The salt monopoly secured 18,720,000 florins.

The imports for the year 1874 were 565,600,000 florins; the exports were 452,200,000 florins. This is exclusive of Dalmatia—not within the imperial line of customs. The figures for Dalmatia were, during the same year: 9,600,000 florins imports, and 6,600,000 florins exports.

The merchant navy, at the beginning of 1875, comprised 7203 vessels, with a tonnage of 332,005, and an equipment of 27,381 seamen. Of great importance for the commerce of the empire is the Austrian Lloyds. This company owned, on the 1st of January, 1874, a fleet of seventy-six steamers, of 15,800 horse-power.

Since the year 1867 Austria has been a twofold empire, consisting of a German or "Cisleithan" monarchy—Austria proper; and a Magyar or Transleithan kingdom—Hungary. Each of the two countries has its own laws, parliament, ministers, and government; and the formal tie between them is a body known as the Delegations. These form a parliament of 120 members; one-half is chosen by the legislature of Austria, and the other by that of Hungary, the upper house of each returning twenty, the lower house forty delegates. The delegations have jurisdiction over all matters affecting the common interests of the two countries, especially foreign affairs, war, and finance. The acts of the delegations require to be confirmed by the representative assemblies of their respective countries.

The administration of Austria proper is divided among nine ministries—Foreign Affairs, Police, Public Education, Agriculture and Public Works, Finance, Interior, War and Navy, Commerce, and Justice. The Reichsrath consists of an upper and a lower house. The upper house is constituted by princes, nobles, archbishops, bishops, and life members nominated by the emperor. To give validity to bills passed by the Reichsrath, the consent of both chambers is required, as well as the sanction of the emperor.

The executive of Hungary is carried on in the name of the king by a responsible ministry.

The following figures are extracted from the budget for 1875:

EXPENDITURES.

Austria,	319,916,323	florins.
Hungary,	218,558,301	"
General,	116,364,502	"
	654,839,126	"

RECEIPTS.

Austria,	283,298,975	florins.
Hungary,	209,633,909	"
From duties and other sources,	123,315,125	"
	616,248,009	"

The public debt of Austria, on the 1st of January, 1875, was 2,649,484,475 florins; that of Hungary, January 1st, 1873, was 488,717,380 florins.

According to official returns, Austria possessed, in 1875, a standing army numbering 284,435 men on the peace footing, and 785,649 on the war footing.

The naval forces consisted of seventy-one vessels, of a tonnage of 115,380, carrying 308 heavy and 87 light guns. Of this fleet, 47 vessels were steamers, of 100,260 tons burthen.

The length of railways, at the close of 1875, was

In Austria,	9,823	kilometres.
" Hungary,	6,415	"
Total,	16,238	"

The work of the post office in Austria-Hungary for 1874 was as follows:

Letters,	253,909,000
Postal cards,	28,741,000
Parcels,	31,959,000
Newspapers,	82,085,000
Number of post offices,	6,296

The statistics of telegraphs for the year 1874 are as follows:

Length of lines (Austria-Hungary),	45,441	kilometres.
" " wires " "	129,171	"
Number of offices,	2,923	"
" of dispatches,	5,797,492	"

Education, since 1849, is under the care of a Minister of Public Worship and Instruction. In the major part of German Austria the law enforces the cumpulsory attendance in the "Volksschulen," or National Schools, of all children between the ages of six and twelve, and parents are liable to punishment for neglect. It is rarely, however, that cases occur in which penalties for non-attendance at school have to be enforced. The cost of public education mainly falls on the communes, but of late years the State has come forward to assist in the establishment of schools for primary education.

There are seven universities in the empire. Four of these, the high schools at Vienna, Prague, Graz, and Innsbruck, are called German universities, and were attended as follows, in 1872:

	PROFESSORS AND TEACHERS.	STUDENTS.
Vienna,	200	3881
Prague,	97	1709
Graz,	70	926
Innsbruck,	58	612

Of the other universities, Pesth, the high school of Hungary, had 2500 students at the end of 1873, and Cracow and Lemberg, the high schools for Galicia and the other Slavonian provinces, had, at the same date, together, 1900 students.

Commission from AUSTRIA to the International Exhibition:

RUDOLF ISBARY, Vice-President of the Chamber of Commerce, President.

FRANZ RITTER VON LIEBIG, Member of the Chamber of Commerce, First Vice-President.

MICHAEL MATSCHEKO, Manufacturer, Second Vice-President.

DR. F. MIGERVA, Counsellor to the I. R. Austrian Ministry of Commerce, Commissioner General, and Resident Commissioner.

EUGENE FELIX, President of the Society of Arts.

EDWARD KANITZ, Member of the Chamber of Commerce.

KARL VON OBERLEITNER, Member of the Chamber of Commerce.

OTTO VON BAUER, Member of the Chamber of Commerce.

ERNST VON PONTZEN, Engineer.

DR. EMIL HORNIG, Counsellor.

THEO. A. HAVEMEYER, Austro-Hungarian Consul-General.

SWITZERLAND.

SWITZERLAND is an inland country of Europe, situated between 45° 48′ and 47° 49′ north latitude, and 5° 55′ and 10° 30′ east longitude. Its greatest length from east to west is 180 miles, and its greatest width from north to south, 130 miles.

The following table gives the area and population of each of the 22 cantons, according to the census returns of 1870:

	ENGLISH SQUARE MILES.	POPULATION.
Graubünden,	2,968	91,782
Bern,	2,561.5	506,465
Wallis (Valais),	1,661.6	96,887
Vaud (Waadt),	1,181.9	231,700
Ticino (Tessin),	1,034.7	119,619
St. Gallen,	747.7	191,015
Zurich,	685.3	284,786
Luzern,	587.4	132,338
Fribourg (Freeburg),	563.9	110,832
Aargau,	502.4	198,873
Uri,	420.8	16,107
Schwyz,	338.3	47,705
Neuchatel (Neuenburg),	280.2	97,284
Glarus,	279.8	35,150
Thurgau,	268.3	93,300
Unterwalden,	262.8	26,116
Solothurn,	254.6	74,713
Basle,	184.6	101,887
Appenzell,	152.8	60,635
Schaffhausen,	119.7	37,721
Genève (Genf),	91.3	93,239
Zug,	85.4	20,993
Total,	15,233.0	2,669,147

Switzerland is the most mountainous country of Europe. Its principal chains are the Alps and the Jura. The former run from east to west along its southern or Italian frontier. Their ramifications fill more than one-half the country, and terminate along a line which may be traced from Vevey, on the lake of Geneva, to Mount Moleson and Mount Napf, across Lake Zug, to the southern shores of the lakes of Zurich and Wallenstadt, and Sargans on the Rhine. The mean elevation of the highest chain is from 8000 to 9000 feet. The Jura run northeast from the western corner of Switzerland. They consist of a series of parallel ridges inclosing long and narrow valleys, and their mean elevation does not exceed 4000 feet. In the angle formed between them and the Alps lies the plain of Switzerland, a table-land 100 miles in length, and from 20 to 30 miles in width, with a mean elevation of about 1400 feet above the sea. It is not absolutely level, but covered with elevations which seem very unimportant when contrasted with the huge masses of the Alps and Jura. The communication between the plain of Switzerland and the German valleys of the Danube and Rhine is not continuous. The plain terminates in the east in a third hilly tract, the Thur hill country, which lies between the lakes of Zurich and Constance, and, to some extent, forms a barrier between the plain of Switzerland and Germany. The Jura, the plain, and the hill country, are the three great divisions of northern Switzerland. The divisions in the Alpine region are more strongly marked in nature. They isolate and inclose (1) the valleys drained by the Rhone which connect Switzerland with southern France; (2) Ticino, drained by streams which descend to the Po, and bring this section into communication with Italy; (3) the Grisons, the most sequestered valleys of Switzerland, drained by the tributaries of the Rhine and Danube, and shut out by mountains from the lower basins of these rivers; (4) Bernese Oberland, which slopes towards the western extremity of the Swiss plain; (5) the district of the Forest Cantons, Schwyz, Uri, and Unterwalden, surrounding the Lake of Lucerne.

In Switzerland the climate chiefly varies with the elevation above the sea level. At a height exceeding 9500 feet the mountains are covered with perpetual snow, which descends along the glaciers to a much lower level, and thus covers the elevated part of the country with a vast sea of ice. Below the level of perpetual snow the surface of Switzerland has been divided into a series of belts, characterized by different climates and productions. The highest of these, lying between the snow and the level of 6900 feet, has been called the Upper Alpine region. In it the glaciers fill the valleys, but plants clothe the scanty soil of the ridges. The second or Lower Alpine belt descends to 4800 feet, and is a country of pastures in which shrubs, but no trees, are seen. In the third belt, which descends to 4350 feet, meadows still abound, but forests of firs and maples, in many parts, replace them. The fourth belt sinks to 3000 feet. Here forests still abound, the beech being the prevailing tree; the meadows are excellent, and rye and barley are successfully cultivated. The fifth belt descends to 1800 feet. In it the oak and walnut are the characteristic forest trees. Spelt and the best wheat are cultivated. The last belt sinks to 750 feet. In it the chestnut is the characteristic tree; the mulberry and vine are extensively cultivated, and wheat is the grain chiefly grown. This belt includes the greater part of the Swiss plain, and sinks to its lowest level in the valley of the Rhine, between Constance and Basle, and the banks of Lake Zurich and Lago Maggiore. In the last district the vegetation is that of northern Italy. The most populous part of Switzerland lies between 1250 and 2150 feet. The temperature of this region is fairly represented by that of Zurich, which averages, for the year, 47.95°.

The German language is spoken by the majority of the inhabitants in sixteen cantons, the French in four, and the Italian in two. It is reported in the census returns of 1870 that 384,561 families speak German, 134,183 French, and 30,293 Italian. According to the same returns there were but five towns in Switzerland with more than 20,000 inhabitants, namely, Geneva, seat of the watch and jewelry industry, with 46,783; Basle, centre of the silk industry, with 44,834; Bern, political capital, with 36,001; Lausanne, with 26,520; and Zurich, with 21,199 inhabitants. The soil is pretty equally divided among the population, it being estimated that four-fifths of the inhabitants are land owners. Of every 100 square miles of land 20 are pasture, 17 forest, 11 arable, 20 meadow, 1 vineyard, and 30 uncultivated, or occupied by lakes, rivers, and mountains.

According to the census of 1870 there are 1,095,447 individuals supported, either wholly or in part, by agriculture. At the same date, the manufactories employed 216,468 persons, the handicrafts 241,425. In the canton of Basle the manufacture of silk ribbons employs 6000 persons, with a total annual production valued at $7,000,000. In the canton of Zurich silk stuffs, to the value of about $8,000,000, are made by 12,000 operatives. The manufacture of watches and jewelry in the cantons of Neuchatel, Geneva, Vaud, Bern, and Solothurn, employ 36,000 workmen, who produce annually 500,000 watches—three-sevenths gold, four-sevenths silver—valued at $9,000,000. In the cantons of St. Gall and Appenzell, 6000 workers make $2,000,000 worth of embroidery annually. The printing and dyeing factories of Glarus turn out goods to the value of $3,000,000, per annum. The manufacture of cotton goods occupies upwards of 1,000,000 spindles, 4000 looms, and 20,000 operatives, besides 38,000 hand-loom weavers.

The Federal custom house returns classify all imports and exports under three chief headings, namely, live stock, *ad valorem* goods, and goods taxed per quintal. No returns are published of the value of imports or exports: only the quantities are given. The following table shows the imports and exports during the year 1871:

IMPORTS.

Live stock, ...	256,851 head.
Agricultural instruments, carts, and railway carriages for travelers and merchandise, *ad valorem*, ...	1,043,991 francs.
Goods taxed per quintal, including loads reduced to quintals, ...	25,450,359 quintals.

EXPORTS.

Live stock, ...	127,490 head.
Wood and coal, *ad valorem*, ...	5,351,941 francs.
Goods, per load and quintal, ...	4,086,646 quintals.

The present constitution vests the supreme legislative and executive authority in a parliament of two chambers, a Standerath, or State Council, and a Nationalrath, or National Council. The first is composed of 44 members, chosen by the 22 cantons—2 for each canton. The Nationalrath consists of 135 representatives, chosen by popular vote, at the rate of one deputy for every 20,000 souls. A general election for representatives takes place every three years. Both chambers united are called the Bundesversammlung, or Federal Assembly, and as such represent the supreme government of the republic. The chief executive authority is deputed to a Bundesrath, or Federal Council, consisting of seven members elected for three years by the Federal Assembly. The president and vice-president of the Federal Council are the first magistrates of the republic. Both are elected by the Federal Assembly for the term of one year, and are not re-eligible until after the expiration of another year. Independent of the Federal Assembly, though issuing from the same, is the Bundes-Gericht, or Federal Tribunal, consisting of eleven members, elected for three years. The Federal Tribunal decides, in the last instance, on all matters in dispute between the various cantons, or between the cantons and the Federal government, and acts in general as a high court of appeal. Each of the Swiss cantons and demi-cantons has its local government, different in organization in most instances, but all based on the absolute sovereignty of the people.

In the budget estimates for the year 1875 the total revenue is set down at 39,516,000 francs,* and total expenditure at 39,266,000 francs. The public debt of the republic amounted, at the commencement of 1875, to 30,635,552 francs, as a set-off against which there was a so-called Federal fortune, or property belonging to the State, valued at 31,783,303 francs.

The fundamental laws of the republic forbid the maintenance of a standing army within the limits of the confederation. The troops are divided into three classes: 1, the Bundes-Auszug, or Federal army, consisting of all men able to bear arms from the age of 20 to 30; 2, the army of reserve, consisting of all men who have served in the first class, from the age of 31 to 40; 3, the Landwehr, or militia, comprising all men from the 41st to the completed 44th year. The strength of the armed forces of Switzerland, at the end of 1874, was as follows:

Staff, ...	841
Bundes-auszug, ...	84,369
Reserve, ...	50,069
Landwehr, ...	65,981
Total, ...	201,260

* One franc = 19.3 cts. gold.

From official returns it appears that the railways open for public traffic in Switzerland had, at the end of 1874, a total length of 1024 English miles.

The post office of Switzerland forwarded, during the year 1874, 63,252,884 letters; 19,925,200 packets, and 45,651,344 newspapers.

At the end of September, 1875, there were 3736 miles of telegraph lines and 9538 miles of wires. The number of messages sent, in the year 1874, was 2,625,104; number of offices, 815. The entire telegraph system belongs to the State.

In no country is elementary instruction more widely diffused. Parents are compelled to send their children to school from five to twelve, but not above that age. There are universities on the German model at Basle, Bern, and Zurich, and academies on the French plan at Geneva and Lausanne. The number of clubs for scientific, literary, musical, and social purposes, is remarkable. There are few pursuits to which any class of men can devote themselves which are not represented in Switzerland by societies.

Commission from SWITZERLAND to the International Exhibition;

DR. SCHENK, Member of Federal Council, Chief of the Department of Railways and Commerce, President.
JOHN HITZ, Consul-General of Switzerland.
R. KORADI, Consul, Resident Commissioner.
W. ITSCHNER, Vice-Consul.
DR. ADOLPH HIRSCH, Director of the Observatory.
MR. SAUR-USTERI, Engineer.
MR. SALVISBERG. Architect.
DR. EMILE SCHUMACHER.
COLONEL SIEGFRIED, Chief of Bureau of the General Staff.
MR. STEINMANN BUCHER, Secretary of the Department of Commerce.
DR. FR. DE TSCHUDI, Councillor of State.
DR. WILLI, Secretary of the Federal Department of Commerce, Secretary.

Resident Commission in Switzerland.

COLONEL H. RIETER, Commissioner-General.

Resident Commissioners in Philadelphia.

MR. EDWARD GUYER, Secretary-General.
MR. JOHN E. ICELY, Engineer.
MR. JOSEPH BEELER, Secretary.

BELGIUM.

BELGIUM lies between latitude 49° 27′ and 51° 30′ north, and between longitude 2° 33′ and 6° 5′ east. It is bounded on the north by Holland; on the east by Dutch Limbourg, Luxembourg, and Rhenish Prussia; on the south and southwest by France; and on the northwest by the North Sea. Its greatest length, from northwest to southeast, is 173 English miles; and its greatest breadth, from north to south, 112 English miles. The whole area is 11,313 square miles. The following table gives a list of the provinces in Belgium, with the area, population, and chief town of each:

PROVINCES.	AREA IN SQ. MILES.	POPULATION (1870).	CHIEF CITIES.
Antwerp,	1,094	492,482	Antwerp.
West Flanders,	1,243	668,976	Bruges.
East Flanders,	1,154	837,726	Ghent.
Hainault,	1,430	896,285	Mons.
Liege,	1,111	592,177	Liege.
Brabant,	1,260	879,814	Brussels.
Limbourg,	929	200,336	Hasselt.
Luxembourg,	1,695	205,784	Arlon.
Namur,	1,397	313,525	Namur.
Total,	11,313	5,087,105	

Belgium is the most densely populated country in Europe, the population being about 404 to the square mile; and in the particular provinces of East Flanders, 675; Brabant, 594; Hainault, 537; and West Flanders, 502, respectively, to the square mile. The rural population bears to that of the towns a proportion of about 3 to 1. About 58 per cent. of the inhabitants are Flemish, the rest Walloon and French, with 39,000 Germans in Luxembourg. Belgium is, on the whole, a level and even low-lying country; diversified, however, by hilly districts. In the southeast, a western branch of the Ardennes highlands makes its appearance, separating the basin of the Maas from that of the Moselle, but attains only the moderate elevation of 2000 feet. In Flanders the land becomes so low that in parts where the natural protection afforded by the downs is deficient, dikes, etc., have been raised to check the encroachments of the sea. In the northeast part of Antwerp, a naturally unfertile district named the Campine, and composed of marshes and barren heaths, extends in a line parallel with the coast. The once impassable morasses of the *Morini* and the *Menapii*, which stayed the progress of Cæsar's legions, are now drained, and converted into fertile fields, surrounded by dense plantations, which make the land at a distance look like a vast green forest—though, when more closely regarded, we see only numerous dwellings interspersed among fields, canals, and meadows.

The abundant water-system of Belgium is chiefly supplied by the rivers Scheldt and Maas, both of which rise in France, and have their embouchures in Holland. At Antwerp, the Scheldt, which, like the Maas, is navigable all through Belgium, is 32 feet deep, and about 480 yards wide. Its tributaries are the Lys, Dender, and Rupel. The Maas, or Meuse, receives in its course the waters of the Sambre, the Ourthe, and the Roer. These natural hydrographical advantages are increased by a system of canals which unite Brussels and Louvain with the Rupel, Brussels with Charleroi, Mons with Conde, Ostend with Bruges and Ghent, and this last place with Terneuse. The climate of Belgium, in the plains near the sea, is cool, humid, and somewhat unhealthy; but in the higher southeast districts, hot summers alternate with very cold winters. April and November are always rainy months. The geological formations of Belgium are closely associated with France and Britain. The greater portion of the country is covered with tertiary deposits. A line drawn across the course of the Scheldt, by Mechlin, along the Demer and Maas, will have on its northern and northwestern aspect a tract of tertiary deposits, bounded northwards by the sea. In these tertiary strata the different geological periods are fully represented; but only the second, containing the Pleiocene deposits, is rich in fossils. The secondary deposits occupy an extensive tract in the centre of Belgium, between the Scheldt and the Demer. The most important district, economically, is the southwestern, consisting of palæozoic rocks—Silurian, Devonian, and Carboniferous. These beds have a very complicated structure, from the numerous and extensive flexures and folds they have undergone, and these are often accompanied with great upward shifts, by which beds of many different ages are brought to the same level. Belgium is rich in minerals, which, next to its abundant agriculture, constitute the chief source of its national prosperity. The four provinces in which they are found are Hainault, Namur, Liege, and Luxembourg. They include lead, copper, zinc, calamine, alum, peat, marble, limestone, slate, iron, and coal. Lead is wrought, but only to a small extent, in Liege; copper in Hainault and Liege; manganese in Liege and Namur; black marble at Dinant; slates at Herbemont; and calamine principally at Liege. But these products are insignificant compared to the superabundance of coal—from anthracite to the richest gas coal—and iron.

In the year 1871, the total coal production of Belgium amounted to 13,733,176 tons, of a total value of 153,803,000 francs. Number of hands employed in the coal mines of Belgium, 94,186. The average daily pay of the workmen, in 1871, was 2¾ francs per day; average cost of production, 9½ francs per ton of coal. The Ardennes districts yield a large supply of wood; while the level provinces raise all kinds of grain—wheat, rye, barley, oats, etc., leguminous plants, hemp, flax, colza, tobacco, hops, dye-plants, and chicory. Belgium contains upwards of 7,000,000 acres, of which one-half is arable, rather more than one-fifth in meadow and pasture, the same in woods and forests, and not above 500,000 acres lying waste. Some hundreds of acres are devoted to vineyards, but the wine produced is of an inferior quality. The forests of Ardennes abound in game and other wild animals. Good pasturage is found on the slopes and in the valleys of the hilly districts, and in the rich meadows of the low provinces. Gardening occupies not less than 130,000 acres; indeed, it has been said that the agriculture of Belgium is just gardening on a large scale, so carefully and laboriously is every inch of soil cultivated. The spade is still the principal instrument used. In the Campine, the care of bees is very productive, and the cultivation of the silkworm is encouraged. There are valuable fisheries on the coast, which, in 1871, employed 263 boats, with a tonnage of 8963. Belgium is famous for its horses, and in one year contained 294,537 of these animals, 1,203,891 horned cattle, and 662,508 sheep.

Wool is the object of an immense industry, the woolen manufactures of Verviers and its environs alone employing a population of 50,000 operatives. Flannels, serges, camlets, carpets, flax fabrics, silks, velvets, fine laces, ribbons, hosiery, hats, paper, etc., are extensively and profitably manufactured. The working of metals, as iron, copper, and tin, is very important; the manufacture of cannon, firearms, and locomotive engines being an especial feature of the metallurgical industry of Belgium.

The foreign trade of Belgium is officially divided into "general commerce," including the sum total of all international mercantile intercourse, and "special commerce," comprising such imports as are consumed within and such exports as have been produced in the country. The following table gives the value of both the general and special exports for the year 1873:

General imports,	2,424,800,000	francs.
" exports,	2,164,900,000	"
Special imports,	1,422,700,000	"
" exports,	1,158,600,000	"

The statistics of the Belgian merchant navy for 1873, are—

	NO.	TONNAGE.
Sailing vessels,	41	16,434
Steam "	28	30,005
Total,	69	46,439

Belgium is a constitutional, representative, and hereditary monarchy. The legislative power is vested in the King, the Chamber of Representatives, and the Senate. The Chamber of Representatives is composed of deputies chosen directly by all citizens paying a small amount of direct taxes. The number of deputies is fixed according to the population, and cannot exceed one for every 40,000 inhabitants. The Senate is composed of exactly one-half the number of members composing the other chamber, and are elected by the same citizens who appoint the deputies. The public expenditures of Belgium, for 1875, were 238,281,441 francs; receipts during the same year, 243,032,600 francs. The total public debt, in 1875, was 1,127,040,009 francs. The standing army is formed by conscription, to which every able-bodied man, who has completed his nineteenth year, is liable. Substitution is permitted. The actual number of soldiers under arms, on the 1st of January, 1875, was 103,893.

In Belgium the State is a great railway proprietor, and the State railway is one of the largest sources of national revenue. As each conceded railway lapses gratuitously to the State in 90 years from the period of its construction, the entire system will in time become national property. There were, at the end of 1875, 1953 kilometres of railways owned by the State, and 1479 worked by companies; in all 3432 kilometres. (The kilometre = 1093 yards.)

The work of the post office for 1874, was—

Number of offices,	479
Private letters,	58,036,628
Official "	6,035,861
Newspapers,	58,825,598
Packets (printed matter, etc.),	30,094,027

There were, on the 1st of January, 1875, telegraph lines of a length of 4909 kilometres; length of telegraph wires, 20,512 kilometres; telegraph stations, 574.

Elementary education is not yet generally diffused among the people. The schools are supported by the communes, the provinces, and the State combined. Education is not compulsory. In the budget for the year 1874, the sum voted by the Chamber of Representatives for public education amounted to 9,701,628 francs.

Commission from BELGIUM to the International Exhibition :

HIS ROYAL HIGHNESS, THE COMTE DE FLANDRE, Honorary President.

BARON GUSTAVE DE WOELMONT, Senator, President.

ALEXANDER ROBERT, Historical Painter, Member of the Belgium Academy of Fine Arts, Letters, and Sciences, Vice-President.

CH. DE SMET-DE SMET, Manufacturer, President of the Industrial and Commercial Society, Vice-President.

J. CLERFEYT, Chief of Bureau, Ministry of the Interior, Secretary of the Upper Consul of Industry and Commerce, late Secretary of the Belgium Commission and Juries of the International Exhibition of Paris, London, and Vienna, Secretary.

ALFRED ANCION, Manufacturer of Arms.

JEAN BECO, Mining Engineer.

A. J. BELPAIRE, Inspector-General of Railways and Telegraphs.

L. DE CURTE, Architect, Member of the Royal Commission of Monuments and Council for the Improvement of the Arts of Design.

FELIX DUHAYON, Lace Manufacturer, Judge of the Tribunal of Commerce.

E. DUISBERG, Director of the Paper Manufactories of Messrs. Godin & Co., at Huy, Member of the Chamber of Commerce.

JOS. FAYN, Mining Engineer, Consul of the Netherlands.

P. F. GHYS-BRUNEEL, Lace Manufacturer.

JULES HAVENITH, Shipowner, Consul of Austria-Hungary.

J. KINDT, Inspector-General of Industry, Minister of the Interior.

EUGENE MEEUS, Manufacturer, Member of the Chamber of Representatives.

ALPH. MOREL, Director of the Glass Works, Lodelinsart.

HENRI MOREL, Flax Manufacturer.

REMY PAQUOT, Director of the Company of Bleyburg-es-Montzen.

EDM. PARMENTIER, Manufacturer.

FERDINAND PAUWELS, Historical Painter.

AUG. RONNBERG, Director-General of Agriculture and Manufactures, Ministry of the Interior.

E. SADOINE, Director-General of the Company "John Cockerill."

JULES SAUVEUR, Director-General of Public Instruction, Ministry of the Interior.

E. E. A. SCHARR, Chief Engineer, Director of the Arsenal and Railways of the State.

ALFRED SIMONIS, Cloth Manufacturer, Member of the Chamber of Representatives.

Resident Commissioners in Philadelphia.

COUNT D'OULTREMONT, Director-General.

MR. J. BECO, Delegate of the Belgian Government.

MR. J. VAN BREE, Chief of Fine Art Department.

MR. J. GODY, State Architect, Chief of the Commissioner's Office.

MR. JULIAN DEBY.

NETHERLANDS.

THE Kingdom of the Netherlands lies between 50° 43′ and 53° 36′ north latitude and 3° 22′ and 7° 16′ east longitude, is bounded on the north by the North Sea, east by Hanover and the western part of Prussia, south by Belgium, west by the North Sea. Its greatest length, from north to south, is 195 English miles; its greatest breadth from the west, on the North Sea to the extremity of Overyssel, on the east, 110 English miles. It contains 12,637 square miles, including the grand duchy of Luxembourg (which, although possessed of a separate administration, is connected with the kingdom in the person of the sovereign). The entire population, in 1872, was 3,835,111.

The following table gives the population (1872) and area of the provinces, including the reclaimed Haarlem Lake:

	AREA IN SQUARE MILES.	POPULATION.
North Brabant,	1,985	435,262
Gelderland,	1,972	436,029
South Holland,	1,176	700,499
North Holland,	966	591,338
Zeeland,	642	181,532
Utrecht,	531	175,037
Friesland,	1,267	300,257
Overyssel,	1,308	256,681
Groningen,	907	228,883
Drenthe,	1,029	106,713
Limburg,	854	225,352
	12,637	3,637,583
Grand Duchy of Luxembourg,	990	197,528
Total,	13,627	3,835,111

The land is generally low, much of it being under the level of the sea, rivers, and canals, especially in North and South Holland, Zeeland, the southern part of Gelderland, and Friesland. Along the west coast the low lands are protected from the sea by a line of sand-hills, or dunes, and where that natural defence is wanting strong dykes have been constructed to keep back the waters, and are maintained at great expense. The greatest of these dykes are those of the Helder and of West Kapell, on the east coast of Walcheren. Engineers, called the officers of the Waterstaat, take special charge of the dykes and national hydraulic works. A hilly district stretches from Prussia through Drenthe, Overyssel, the Veluwe, or Arnhem district of Gelderland, the eastern part of Utrecht, into the Betuwe or country between the Maas and the Waal. This tract has many pretty spots, is of a light sandy soil, well watered, and when not cultivated, is covered with heath or oak-coppice. The greater portion of the north is very fertile, the low lands and drained lakes, called Polders, being adapted for pasturing cattle, and the light soils for cereals and fruits; but in some districts there are sandy heath-clad plains, extensive peat-lands, and undrained morasses, which industry is rapidly bringing under cultivation.

The islands may be divided into two groups, of which the southern, formed by the mouths of the Schelde and Maas, contains Walcheren, South and North Beveland, Schouwen, Duiveland, Tholen, St. Philipsland, Goeree, Voorne, Putten, Beyerland, Ysselmonde Rozenburg, and the island of Dordrecht. The northern group contains the islands at the entrance of the Zuyder Zee and along the coast of Groningen and Friesland, as Wieringen, Texel, Vlieland, Terschelling, Ameland, Schiermonnikoog, and Rottum. In the Zuyder Zee are Marken, Urk, and Schokland. The chief rivers are the Rhine, Maas, and Scheldt. Important branches of these are the Waal, Lek, Yssel, Roer, etc.

Water ways are more numerous than in any other European country, the immense tracts of meadow-land and the fertile polders being girdled by large canals, and cut in all directions by smaller ones for drainage and communication. Those of most importance to the national trade are, the North Holland canal, constructed 1819–1825, to connect the port of Amsterdam with the North Sea; the Voorne canal, from the north side of Voorne to Hellevoetsluis, which shortens the outlet from Rotterdam; the South Willemsvaart, through North Brabant, Dutch and Belgian Limburg, from Hertogenbosch to Maastricht, being 71½ English miles in length, and having 24 locks. Besides these, there are numerous important canals, connecting rivers, and cutting the kingdom into a network of water-courses. To improve the entrances to the Maas, the Hock, of Holland, has lately been cut. The new canal through the Y will be nowhere less than 80 yards broad, with sluices nearly 400 feet in length, and a depth of nearly 23 feet. It will reduce the distance from Amsterdam to the sea to about 15 miles, and gives a safe way for large ships.

The climate of the Netherlands is variable, chilly colds often closely succeeding high temperatures, inducing various forms of fever and ague, and requiring peculiar care as to clothing, etc. In summer, the thermometer sometimes rises above 80°, and even to 90° F. in the shade, and a winter of great severity usually occurs every fifth year, when carriages and heavily laden wagons cross the rivers and the Y on the ice, and thousands enjoy the national pastime of skating.

The farms are generally small and well cultivated. The leading agricultural products of Zeeland are wheat and madder; in South Holland, madder, hemp, butter, and cheese; in North Holland, butter and cheese are extensively made, and cattle, sheep, and pigs reared and exported. The horses of Friesland, Zeeland, and Gelderland are of first-rate quality. The exportation of butter from Holland and Friesland, and of Edam, Leyden, Gonda, and Frisian cheese, is quite large. Fruit is abundant, and in several provinces, as Gelderland, Utrecht, and Drenthe, much attention is paid to bees. In Haarlem and neighborhood, tulips and hyacinths are much cultivated, realizing a large annual amount. Wild ducks, snipes, plovers, and hares are plentiful; and there are also conies, partridges, pheasants, and deer—game forming an article of export.

The Netherlands are of recent formation, and consist of an alluvial deposit, chiefly of a deep, rich clayey soil, superimposed on banks of sand, marine shells, and beds of peat and clay. It appears that at some distant period there has been a depression of the land below its former level, enabling the sea to burst through its sand-banks, submerge the land, and form new deposits. The higher districts are composed of sand-drift mingled with fertile earths, and resting on a bed of clay. Coal is worked in Limburg; and a soft sandstone, which becomes fit for building purposes after having been some time exposed to the atmosphere, is quarried in the southern part of that province, which has also pipe and other clays. Valuable clays for pottery, tile, and brick making, abound in the various provinces.

The chief manufactures are linen, woolen, cotton, and silk fabrics; paper, leather, glass, etc. Leyden and Tilburg are famed for woolen blankets, wool-dyed pilot, fine cloths, and friezes; Hertogenbosch for linens and rich damasks; calicoes, shirtings, drills, tablecloths, striped dimities are made at Almelo, Amersfort, and in the leading towns of Overyssel. Good imitation Smyrna and Scotch carpets, and carpets of hair and wool, are manufactured at Deventer, Delft, Arnhem, Hilversum, Utrecht, and Breda; Turkey-red yarns, dyed silks, and silk stuffs at Roermond, Utrecht, Haarlem, etc.; leather, glass, firearms, at Maastricht and Delft; iron-founding, rolling and hammering of lead and copper, cannon-founding are carried on at the Hague, etc.; and powder-mills at Muiden; Oudenkerk, Middelburg, Hertogenbosch, Amsterdam, Nymegen, etc., have important breweries. Waalwyk, Heusden, and surrounding districts, manufacture boots and shoes, of which Heusden sends to North and South Holland 1,000,000 pairs annually. Gin is distilled at Schiedam, Delft, Rotterdam, and Weesp. Amsterdam has the largest diamond-cutting trade in the world, 10,000 persons depending on that branch of industry. Sugar refining is largely carried on at Amsterdam, Rotterdam, and Dordrecht, from all of which sugar is exported to Russia, the Levant, and countries of Europe. Paper is chiefly made in Holland and Gelderland. The leading letter-type founders are at Amsterdam and Haarlem. Manufactures of every kind are being rapidly increased in number, and adding to the material prosperity of the Netherlands. The chief motive power is the windmill, which forms a never-failing element in the scenery; but of late years steam is becoming more general.

Fishing, not only in the inland waters, the coasts and bays of the North Sea, but also on the coast of Scotland, is vigorously pursued. In 1872 the total value of the herrings taken in the North Sea was about $450,000, 108 vessels having been employed; on the Netherland coasts, to the value of about $250,000, and in the Zuyder Zee, additional, 18,052,000 herrings were taken. The anchovy take, almost exclusively in the Zuyder Zee, amounted to 9000 anker, valued at about $90,000. There are productive oyster beds, besides extensive fishings of cod, ling, turbot, flounders, soles, shrimps, haddock, etc.; and from the rivers, salmon, eels, perch, etc.

The foreign commerce of the Netherlands, during the year 1873, was as follows:

	IMPORTS. IN GUILDERS.	EXPORTS. IN GUILDERS.*
Europe,	533,390,000	459,799,000
America,	39,838,000	8,125,000
Asia,	23,207,000	435,000
Africa,	2,747,000	890,000
Other countries,	298,000	1,000
	599,480,000	469,250,000
COLONIAL POSSESSIONS.		
Java,	82,485,000	45,083,000
West Indies,	119,000	302,000
	682,084,000	514,635,000

The Guinea coast is not included in the above, the statistics for 1873 not being at command. During 1872, the imports 26,000, the exports 137,000 guilders. At the end of 1874 the merchant navy numbered 1827 vessels of 511,982 tons.

The constitution vests the whole legislative authority in a parliament composed of two chambers, called the States-General. The Upper House, or First Chamber, consists of 39 members, elected by the provincial states, from among the most highly assessed inhabitants of the various counties. The Second Chamber of the States-General, elected by ballot, at the rate of one deputy to every 45,000 souls, numbered 80 members in 1875. All citizens, natives of the Netherlands, not deprived of civil rights, and paying assessed taxes to the amount of not less than 20 guilders, are voters. Clergymen, judges of the High Court of Justice, and governors of provinces, are debarred from being elected. Every two years one-half the members of the Second Chamber, and every three years one-third of the members of the Upper House, retire by rotation. The Second Chamber has the initiative of new laws, and the functions of the Upper House are restricted to either approving or rejecting them, without the right of inserting amendments. The king has full veto power, but it is rarely, if ever, exercised. The executive authority is, under the

* The guilder equals 40 cents gold.

sovereign, exercised by a responsible council of ministers. The budget estimates for the year 1874, were as follows: Total revenue, 93,742,144 guilders; total expenditure, 93,742,144; estimated deficit, 6,244,740 guilders. The financial estitmates are always framed with great moderation, generally showing a deficit, which, in the final account, becomes a surplus. There is a separate budget for the great colonial possessions in the East Indies. The Netherlands East India estimates, for 1874, are thus summarized:

	GUILDERS.
Revenue from receipts in the Netherlands,	48,958,967
" " " in India,	74,639,232
	123,598,199
Expenditure in the Netherlands,	17,956,922
" " India,	95,096,698
	113,053,620
Contribution in aid of the Home Government, for 1874,	10,544,579
	123,598,199

At the commencement of the year 1874, the national debt was represented by a capital of 927,320,076 guilders. The regular army stationed in the Netherlands comprised, on the 1st of July, 1875, 1935 officers and 59,491 men. The colonial army, on the 1st of January, 1875, comprised 27,475 men, 12,310 of whom were Europeans, and 15,165 natives. The navy, on the 1st of July, 1875, consisted of 88 steamers, carrying 474 guns, and 27 sailing vessels, with 195 guns. At the beginning of the year 1875, there were 1668 kilometres of railway opened for traffic. Of these, 853 belonged to private companies and 815 to the State. The number of post offices at the commencement of 1875 was 1241; the number of letters carried during the year, 44,396,330. The length of telegraph lines, January 1st, 1875, was 3431 kilometres; the length of wires, 12,365 kilometres; the number of offices, 328. During the year 1874 the number of telegrams carried was 2,084,121. Under the working of the primary instruction law, there were, in January, 1871, according to government returns, 2608 public schools, with 6538 schoolmasters and 477 schoolmistresses, and 1119 private schools with 2332 schoolmasters and 1565 schoolmistresses. At the same date the pupils in the public schools numbered 390,129, and the pupils in the private schools, 111,762. There were, also, in 1871, 81 schools of middle instruction, with 7047 pupils, and 55 Latin schools, with 1128 pupils. There are three universities, Leyden, Groningen, and Utrecht, with 1339 students in January, 1871, and a polytechnic institution, at Delft, with 171 pupils.

Colonies.

The colonial possessions of the Netherlands embrace an area of 666,756 English square miles. The total population, according to the last returns, was 24,386,991.

The East Indian island of Java, possessing, with the adjoining Madura, an area of 51,336 English square miles, and a population, at the end of 1872, of 17,298,200, is by far the most important of the colonial possessions of the Netherlands. The whole of the other Netherlands possessions in the East Indies are administered as dependencies of Java.

Almost the entire trade of Java and Madura is with the Netherlands, and there is comparatively little commercial intercourse with other countries. The total imports, including specie, for 1873, were 108,304,000 guilders; total exports, including specie, 155,881,000 guilders. The principal articles of export from Java are sugar, coffee, rice, indigo, and tobacco. The imports of the other East Indian possessions, during 1873, were 42,486,000 guilders; the exports, 41,869,000 guilders.

The Dutch West India Islands, of which Curacoa is the most important, have a total population of 36,160, and an area of about 400 square miles. Surinam, with an area of about 45,000 square miles has a population of 69,834.

Commission from the NETHERLANDS to the International Exhibition:

DR. E. H. VON BOMHAUER, Honorary Professor, Secretary of the Dutch Society of Sciences, Director of the Society for the Advancement of Industry in the Netherlands, President.

F. DE CASEMBROOT, Rear Admiral, Aid-de-camp in Extraordinary Service to His Majesty the King of the Netherlands, and member of the States-General, 2d Chamber.

A. H. EIGEMAN, Industrial President of the Society of Dutch Industrials.

P. HARTSEN, Chairman of the Amsterdam Board of Commerce.

J. E. VAN HEEMSKERCK VAN BEEST, Artist.

DR. W. T. A. JONCKBLOET, President of the Committee of Superintendence of the Academy of Imitative Arts.

D. VAN DER KELLEN, JR., Member of Administration Society Arti et Amicitiæ.

L. C. VAN KERKWYK, Pensioned Lieutenant-colonel, Corps of Engineering, Member of the Council of Administration of the Royal Institution of Engineers.

M. M. DE MONCHY, President of the Board of Commerce.

DR. J. TH. MOULTON, Vice-President of the Society to Promote Manufactures and Trade Industry in the Netherlands.

C. T. VAN DER OUDERMEULEN, President of the Dutch Society of Agriculture.

BARON W. G. BRANTSEN VAN DE ZYP, LL.D., Lord in Waiting to His Majesty the King of the Netherlands.

DR. M. W. C. GORI, Doctor of Medicine, late Medical Officer of the Netherlands Army, Ophthalmic Surgeon.

R. C. BURLAGE, Consul-general of the Netherlands.

L. WESTERGAARD, Consul of the Netherlands.

D. D. KRUSEMAN VAN ELTEN.

C. MUYSKEN, Civil Engineer, Secretary.

DENMARK.

DENMARK is situated between 54° 23′ and 57° 54′ 50″ north latitude, and 8° 5′ and 12′ 45′ east longitude, excepting the small island of Bornholm in the Baltic, about ninety miles east of Seeland, which lies in 15° east longitude. Denmark is bounded on the north by the Skager Rack, a gulf of the North Sea; on the east by the Cattegat, the Sound, and the Baltic; on the south by the German Empire; and on the west by the North Sea, which the Danes call the "Western Ocean."

The kingdom of Denmark has an area of 14,553 English square miles, and a population (in 1874) of about	1,860,000
Faroe Islands,	128,000
Iceland,	
Greenland,	
Danish possessions in the West Indies,	
Total,	1,988,000

The chief pursuits are agriculture, cattle-breeding, navigation, and fishing, about one-half of the population being engaged in these industries.

The annual yield of grain may be calculated at about 100,000,000 bushels, beside 200,000,000 barrels of potatoes, beans, etc. About three-fourths of the whole country is under cultivation. The raising of horses and cattle is quite an important interest; the statistics of live stock are, approximately, as follows: horses, 350,000; cattle, 1,250,000; sheep, 1,900,000; hogs, 450,000.

The exports consist mainly of grain, flour, horses, cattle, hogs, meat, pork, butter, wool, hides and skins, beer, brandy, train oil, etc. The principal imports are iron, coal, salt, sugar, coffee, tea, wood, cotton cloth, tobacco, rice, etc.

Of manufactures, the most important are china ware, terra cotta, tiles, crockery, glass, tobacco, linen, cloth, paper, and soap. There are large woolen mills, sugar refineries, iron foundries, machine shops, dockyards, distilleries, tanneries, etc.; flour mills can be found in all sections of the country. The commerce is not inconsiderable, and Danish joiners' work, gold and silver ware, watches, gloves, terra cotta, etc., find ready sale abroad.

The merchant navy consisted, in 1875, of 2766 sailing vessels of 183,740 registered tons; 114 steamships of 24,323 registered tons, making a total of 2880 vessels of 208,063 registered tons.

The national wealth of Denmark is estimated at 4500 millions of crowns,* of which 3400 millions is real estate and 1100 millions capital, or about 2200 crowns to each individual.

In the 350 savings banks of the country, there were deposited, at the end of 1874, 194,308,902 crowns.

The army numbers, in all, 52,000 men. The navy consists of three iron-clad frigates and eight iron-clad corvettes, carrying 79 guns; three frigates, three corvettes, and five schooners, carrying 136 guns; twelve iron gunboats, carrying 17 guns. Also, transports, etc.

The budget for 1876–77 estimated the revenue at 50,008,843 crowns against an expenditure of 46,885,045 crowns. The public debt, April 1st, 1876, was 181,117,700 crowns against 262,034,296 crowns in 1869. The debt has, in five years, been reduced by more than 80,000,000 crowns.

(The foregoing statistics are furnished by the Danish Commission.)

* The Danish crown = 26 4-5 cents, gold.

The length of railways in the kingdom, at the end of 1874, was 1024.5 kilometres, of which 665 belonged to the State and 359.5 to companies.

The work of the post office for the year 1873–74 was 16,487,777 letters, and 15,134,-812 newspapers.

The length of telegraph lines, 2545 kilometres; length of wires, 7049 kilometres; number of offices, 174; messages in 1874, 762,609.

Elementary education is widely diffused in Denmark, attendance at schools being obligatory from the age of seven to fourteen. Instruction is furnished gratuitously in the public schools to children whose parents cannot afford to pay for their teaching. Besides the university of Copenhagen, there are thirteen public gymnasia in the principal towns of the kingdom, which afford a classical education, and under them are a large number of middle schools, for the children of the trading and higher working classes. Instruction at the public expense is given in the parochial schools, of which there were, in August, 1869, 28 in Copenhagen, 132 in the towns, and 2780 in the rural districts.

Denmark is a constitutional monarchy. The people are efficiently represented, and have a voice in all public matters. The press is virtually free, and only answerable to law. The national assembly consists of the Folksthing and Landsthing, and is invested with very extensive powers; it meets annually for two months, but the deputies are elected triennially, and receive a fixed allowance during their sittings. The several colonies are governed by governors or high bailiffs, nominated by and alone responsible to the crown. The king has a privy council, in which there are associated with him the heir-apparent and eight members.

Commission from DENMARK to the International Exhibition:

JACOB HOLMBLAD, Manufacturer, President.
OLAF HANSEN, United States Vice-Consul, Vice-President.
JOH HANSEN, Austrian Consul-General, Treasurer.
TH. GREEN, Secretary.
C. C. BURMEISTER, Manufacturer.
V. CHRISTESEN, Manufacturer.
V. FIELDSKOV, Sculptor.
CHAS. HANSEN, Manufacturer.
WM. HAMMER, Artist.
CHR. HETSCH, Artist.
THOMAS SCHMIDT, Commissioner.

SWEDEN.

SWEDEN and Norway (Sverige and Norge), two independent kingdoms, but under a common king, form the Scandinavian peninsula, whose shores are washed by the waters of the Gulf of Bothnia, the Baltic, the Sound, the Kattegat, the Skager-Rack, the North Sea, the Atlantic and Arctic Oceans, and is thus completely separated from the mainland, with the exception of its northeastern part. The length of its coast, which is indented with numerous bays and fiords, and protected from the brunt of the sea by innumerable islands and rocks, may be estimated at about 3200 English miles, each kingdom possessing about one-half. The Scandinavian peninsula, of which Sweden forms the eastern and southern part (58 per cent.), while Norway makes up the rest (42 per cent.), embraces an area of 13,830 geographical square miles (294,000 English square miles). The united kingdoms have a population of rather more than six millions, of which 70 per cent. belong to Sweden, and 30 per cent. to Norway. The statistics of Norway are given elsewhere in this catalogue.

Although Sweden extends northward to latitude 69° 3′ 21.1″, thus passing beyond the Arctic circle, it reaches southward to latitude 55° 20′ 18″, coming within the latitude of its neighboring state, Denmark, and even further south than that part of Prussia which projects northward along the eastern shore of the Baltic. The total length of Sweden, from north to south, is about 950 English miles, and the width from 200 to 250 English miles. The observatory of Sockholm lies 18° 3′ 29.85″ east of Greenwich.

The läns (governments or departments) are the largest administrative divisions of the country, and frequently have two names, one of which is derived from the seat of government, the other usually from the old division of the provinces. The geographic division of the kingdom into three parts stands in intimate relation with the old provincial division. The three geographical divisions are as follows: Svealand (the central), Götaland (the southern), and Norrland (the northern); and though the boundaries of the läns and the provinces do not quite correspond, the following may on the whole be stated as correct:

Svealand has six provinces: Uppland, Södermanland, Westmanland, Nerike, Vermland, and Dalecarlia (or Dalarne).

Görland has nine provinces: Ostergötland, Westergötland, Dalsland, Smäland, Gottland, Blekinge, Scania or Skäne, Halland, and Bohnslaw.

Norrland comprises Gestrickland, Helsingland, Medelpad, Angermanland, Jemtland, Herjedalen, and Westerbotton, together with Lapland.

Lapland, the most northern part of Sweden, bordering on Norway, has an area of about 40,000 English square miles, and, together with Norrland, forms more than one-half the whole area. This vast territory is, of all the Swedish provinces, the least adapted to agriculture, and is but sparsely populated.

In 1874, the population of Sweden was divided among the different läns, as follows:

NAMES.	POPULATION.
The town of Stockhom,	150,446
Län of Stockholm,	134,620
" Uppsala,	103,282
" Södermanland,	139,216
" Ostergötland,	262,872
" Jönköping,	186,841
" Kronoberg,	163,793
" Kalmar,	238,399
" Gottland,	54,499
" Blekinje,	130,921
" Kristianstad,	228,498
" Malmöhus,	330,115
" Halland,	130,802
" Göteb, and Bohus,	241,936
Län of Elfsborg,	285,217
" Skaraborg,	250,257
" Vermland,	266,362
" Orebro,	177,084
" Westmanland,	121,018
" Kopparberg,	184,330
" Gefleborg,	160,487
" Westernorrland,	147,212
" Jemtland,	74,758
" Westerbotten,	96,607
" Norrbotten,	81,987
Total,	4,341,559

The area is stated at 171,749 English square miles.

Sweden is generally less mountainous than Norway, and the highest mountains are found just on the border of that country. The boundary line itself is supposed to run along a mountain chain, which is called by geographers the Kölen, though in reality there is no mountain of that name. The highest mountain in Sweden, Sulitelma (6315 Swedish feet above the level of the sea), lies in Lapland, and is the only alpine elevation in Sweden where, as far as is known, glaciers are found, but there are other mountains in these districts, and still further south along the frontier of the kingdom, in Jemtland and Herjedalen, with an elevation of from 4000 to 5000 feet, whose peaks are dotted with patches of snow the whole year round.

About eight per cent. of the area of Sweden is considered to lie upwards of 2000 feet above the level of the sea. Those parts which sometimes extend beyond the tree-line are exclusively in Norrland and Dalarne, and border upon Norway. The coast-line along the Gulf of Bothnia, and the whole of the central and southern parts of Sweden, lie, with few exceptions, lower than 800 feet above the level of the sea. Of the whole area of the kingdom, a third part does not lie 300 feet above the level of the sea, and it is within these lower lying districts that the most highly cultivated parts of the country are found, as well as the largest plains, such as the Uppland, the Ostgöta, the Westgöta, and the Skane plains. With the exception of these, the plains are neither numerous nor large, for, though there are extensive tracts of land which attain a height of only a few hundred feet above the level of the sea, these are generally intersected by numerous hills and valleys.

Sweden, next to Finland, is the best irrigated country in Europe, as her lakes and rivers cover an area of 14,428 English square miles, or 8.4 per cent. of her whole territory, while she has a sea coast of 1500 English miles. The water of the Swedish lakes, as well as that of the rivers, is generally clear and drinkable. Lake Wetter is especially known for its clear, but at the same time turbulent, body of water, as well as for its great depth—420 feet. Of the numerous rivers (or elfs) which flow into the Gulf of Bothnia, the Angerman elf is the best known, not only for its volume, but for its natural beauty. The Dal elf, which is usually considered as the dividing line between Norrland and the southern part of Sweden, empties further to the south. On the west coast flows the Göta elf, the outlet of Lake Wener, famed for the Trollhätta waterfall.

Almost every river or stream forms a foaming current or roaring cataracts, and there are thousands of them. Even the Trollhätta finds a rival in the Njommelsaska (Hare's Leap), in Lapland. One of the peculiarities of these lakes is that they are sometimes interrupted by an almost perpendicular fall—the water then spreading out, forming a second part of the lake. The nation possesses in these numerous falls an almost inexhaustible water power, which has not, as yet, been utilized to that extent which it might be. This character of the Swedish rivers carries with it, however, the disadvantage of rendering them innavigable, many of the rivers (the Dal elf, for instance) being barred at their very mouths by a fall; and, as a rule, they are navigable only for a mile or two, except for rafts and small boats, unless, as in the case of the Göta elf, they are provided with canals

The climate of Sweden is mild in comparison to its high latitude, a fact which is attributed to the influence of the Gulf Stream. There are dense forests; and barley and rye mature in the province of Norrland, while its most southern part lies in the same latitude as the ice fields of Greenland, and its northern in that of barren Iceland. The country, extending through so many degrees of latitude, has a great variety of climate. The mean yearly temperature of the northern parts along the coast is 34° F., while that of the southern is 44° to 46° F. The mean yearly temperature of Stockholm is 41° F. The wells which serve as a measure of the earth's temperature, give about the same figures, the average temperature of a deep well in central Sweden being 43° F., while it is not unusual in Lapland to find a deep well covered with ice in midsummer, or a bog, 5 to 6 feet deep, frozen at its bottom; nevertheless, the cereals and potatoes mature in these districts, for although the summer is short, it is very warm and clear. There can scarcely be said to be any night here during the summer, only a twilight, so that vegetation, even in this high latitude, receives the light and heat necessary for its ripening. The temperature of the southern parts is also subject to very great changes.

The farmers' worst enemy in Sweden is the frost, which in a single clear night, perhaps, after a warm summer day, will destroy his brightest prospects; but it is hoped that the increase of tillage, the draining of the bogs, and like causes, will at least mitigate its severity, if not altogether prevent it. Such severe frosts are very rare in the central and southern parts of Sweden.

(The greater portion of the foregoing was furnished by the Swedish commission.)

Mining is one of the most important departments of Swedish industry, and the working of the iron mines in particular is making constant progress by the introduction of new machinery. There were raised, in the year 1873, 19,458,339 hundredweight of iron ore from mines, besides 126,147 hundredweight from lake and bog. The pig iron produced amounted to 7,987,646 hundredweight, the cast goods to 501,350 hundredweight, the bar iron to 4,125,915 hundredweight, and the steel to 1,290,907 hundredweight. There were also raised, in the same year, 1660 pounds of silver, 26,152 hundredweight of copper, and 645,631 hundredweight of zinc ore. There are large veins of coal in various parts of Sweden, but no systematic working of them has as yet taken place.

The principal articles of cultivation are, in addition to the various cereals, potatoes, hemp, flax, tobacco, and hops, which are generally grown in sufficient quantities for home consumption. The forests are of great extent, covering nearly one-fourth of the whole surface, and, in some spots, rising to an elevation of 3000 feet above the level of the sea. The birch, fir, pine, and beech are of great importance, not only for the timber, tar, and pitch which they yield, but also for their supplying charcoal and firewood. The common fruit trees, as cherries, apples, and pears, grow as far north as 60°, but the fruit seldom comes to great perfection except in the southern provinces; cranberries and other berries abound in all parts of the country.

In 1870, there were in Sweden, 428,446 horses, 1,965,800 horned cattle, 1,780,000 sheep and goats, and 354,303 swine.

In 1873, there were 2549 factories, with a production valued at 146,869,000 crowns.* Mines and mining establishments are not included in these figures. Ship building forms an extensive branch of industry.

According to the "Statesman's Year Book for 1876," the commercial navy of Sweden, at the end of 1873, numbered 1865 registered vessels for foreign trade, of a total burthen of 366,370 tons. The total imports, for the same year, were 271,440,-000 riksdalers,† and the exports, 221,904,000.

Sweden is a constitutional monarchy, based on the fundamental law of 1809, by which it was decreed that the succession should be in the male line; that the sovereign should profess the Lutheran faith, and have sworn fidelity to the laws. The diet, which meets every year, and remains sitting for three or four months, is composed of two chambers, which are both elected by the people. The members of the first chamber serve for nine years, and those of the second for three. The diet exercises a strict control over the expenditure of the revenue, fixes the budget, and has power to take cognizance of the acts of the ministers and crown officers. The king's person is inviolable, and he can exercise a veto on the decrees of the diet. He is assisted by a Council of State, composed of ten members, who are responsible to the diet.

The budget estimates for 1875 place the receipts at 64,775,900, and the expenditures at 71,885,798 riksdalers. At the end of October, 1875, the public liabilities of the kingdom were 130,477,920 riksdalers.

* The Swedish crown equals 26.8 cents. † One riksdaler equals one crown.

The total strength of the armed forces of Sweden, at the end of September, 1875, was 132,775. The navy consists of 131 vessels, of 3183 horse-power, carrying 394 guns, and with crews aggregating 4693.

At the end of September, 1875, the total length of railways opened for traffic was 2237 English miles, of which 938 miles belonged to the State. All the telegraphs, with the exception of those of private railway companies, belong to the State. The total length of telegraph lines, at the end of 1874, was 4981 English miles; the total length of wires, 10,980 English miles. The total number of dispatches sent, in the year 1874, was 986,397.

The Swedish post office carried 16,711,100 letters in the year 1873. The number of post offices, at the end of the year, was 641.

Education is well advanced in Sweden. Public instruction is gratuitous and compulsory, and children not attending schools under the supervision of the government must furnish proofs of having been privately educated. In the year 1871 nearly 97 per cent. of all the children between eight and fifteen years visited the public schools.

Commission from SWEDEN to the International Exhibition:

P. A. BERGSTROM, late Minister of Interior, President Board of Domains, President.
C. O. TROILIUS, Director-General of Public Railways, Vice-President.
F. L. VON DARDEL, Director-General Board of Public Buildings
CH. DICKSON, M.D.
BARON A. H. E. FOCK, Chief of Board of Controls.
F. W. SCHOLANDER, Professor, Academy of Fine Arts.
C. F. LUNDSTROM, Manufacturer.
N. H. ELFVING, Consul-General.
S. STENBERG, Professor, Carolinian Medico-Chirurgical Institution.
A. R. AKERMAN, Professor School of Mines.
J. BOLINDER, Manufacturer.
J. LENNING, Manufacturer.
C. L. LUNDSTROM, Manufacturer.
CL. G. BREITHOLTZ, Colonel of Artillery.
K. PEYRON, Captain in the Navy, Chamberlain.
E. WIDMARK, Chief of the Board of Public Education.
H. WIDEGREN, Superintendent of Fisheries.
P. E. SIDENBLADH, Secretary of the Central Board of Statistics.
V. NORMAN, Captain of Engineers, Secretary.

Resident Commissioners in Philadelphia.

C. JUHLIN DANNFELT, Commissioner-General.
CHARLES BILDT, Chamberlain, Assistant Commissioner.
L. WESTERGAARD, Consul, Assistant Commissioner.
DR. J. LINDAHL, Ph., Secretary.
DR. WM. P. HEADDEN, Ph., Assistant Secretary.
W. HOFFSTEDT, Engineer, Secretary of the Judges.
M. ISÆUS, Architect.
COUNT FR. POSSE, Engineer.

Special Commissioners.

G. W. BERGMAN, Captain of Artillery, Army Department.
E. BRUSEWITZ, Engineer, Metallurgical Department.
BARON O. HERMELIN, Fine Art Department.
A. E. JACOBI, Engineer, Machinery Department.
C. J. MEIJERBERG, Professor Educational Department.

NORWAY.

NORWAY, the western portion of the Scandinavian peninsula, is situated between 57° 58′ and 71° 10′ north latitude, and between 5° and 28° east longitude. It is bounded to the east by Sweden and Russia, and on every other side is surrounded by water, having the Skagerrak to the south, the German Ocean to the west, and the Arctic Sea to the north. Its length is about 1100 miles, and its greatest width about 250 miles; but between the latitudes of 67° and 68° it measures little more than 25 miles in breadth. The area is given as 121,779 square miles, and the population as 1,800,000. Only 1.6 per cent. of the whole area can be cultivated; natural pastures occupy about 1.5 per cent; forests, about 20.2 per cent.; mountains, glaciers, lakes, rivers, and land, etc., about 76.7 per cent. The whole of the Scandinavian peninsula consists of a connected mountain mass, which, in the southern and western parts of Norway, constitutes one continuous tract of rocky highlands, with steep declivities dipping into the sea, and only here and there broken by narrow tracts of arable land. South of Trondjem (63° north latitude) the rocky ridge expands nearly the entire breadth of Norway. The northern portions of the range, known as the Kiöllen Fielle, occupy a space of about 25 miles in width, and form, as far north as 69°, the boundary line between Sweden and Norway. South of 63° north latitude the range of the Scandinavian mountains is known as the Norske, or Dovre Fielle, although the latter name belongs properly only to the part immediately in contact with the Kiöllen. This range, about 360 miles in length, attains its greatest elevation at the Sogne Fjord, where it is known as the Hurungerne. Here the highest summits are 8000 and 8400 feet above the sea, while the contiguous snowfields of Justedal, the largest in Europe, and covering an area of 600 square miles, have probably an elevation of nearly 7000 feet. From these and other vast snowfields, averaging more than 10 miles in width, vast glaciers descend to within 2000 feet above the sea, where they often terminate in deep lakes, some of which are very extensive. The upper valleys of this range, although generally too high for cultivation, contain the best timber that is exported from Norway, and afford good pasturage in the height of the summer, when the flocks and herds are driven thither from the lowlands near the entrance of the fjords. The general elevation of the Norska Fielle does not rise above the line of perpetual snow, whose average height in these latitudes is 5000 feet, but it ranges above that of the growth of trees, which may be stated to lie 1000 feet lower. The most northern part of the Norska Fielle, which is known as the Dovrefield, and includes Sneehätten, nearly 7500 feet above the sea, presents a broken surface, rent with ravines and narrow valleys, which admit of cultivation, but are difficult of access from the configuration of the land around them.

The Scandinavian range consists principally of primitive and transition rock, and exhibits almost everywhere the effect of glacial action, the glaciers and moraines presenting the same appearances as in the Swiss alpine district. The numerous islands which skirt the coast of Norway, and must be regarded as portions of the range, present the same characters as the continental mass. Some of these, as the islands of Alsten and Dunnoe, rise perpendicularly from the sea with peaks penetrating beyond the snowline, which lies here at an elevation of 4000 feet. Norway abounds in lakes and streams; according to some topographers, there are upwards of 30,000 of the former, of which the majority are small, while none have an area exceeding 400 square miles. The chief rivers of Norway are the Glommen, Lougen, Louven, Drammen, Otter, and Wormen. The first of these has a course of 400 miles, but the majority of the Norwegian streams, all of which rise at great elevations, have a comparatively short course, and are unfit for navigation, although they are extensively used to float down timber to the fjords, whence the wood is exported in native ships to foreign ports. These fjords, or inlets of the sea, which form so characteristic a feature of Norwegian scenery, and give with their various sinuosities a coast-line of upwards of 8000 miles, form the outlet to numerous rapid streams and waterfalls, which leap or trickle down the edges of the treeless fields or mountain flats above.

The peculiar physical character of Norway necessarily gives rise to great varieties of climate in different parts of the country. The influence of the sea and of the Gulf Stream, and the penetration into the interior of deep inlets, greatly modify the severity of the climate on the western shores, and render it far superior to that of the other Scandinavian countries in the same latitude. In Norway proper, the winters, as a rule, are long and cold, and the summers, which rapidly follow the melting of the snows in April and May, are warm and pleasant. On the islands, however, the heats of summer are often insufficient to ripen corn.

Norway had, in 1875, 150,000 horses, 950,000 oxen and cows, 1,710,000 sheep and goats, 110,000 pigs, and 102,000 reindeer. The value of the annual product is about $25,000,000.

The principal cereals cultivated in Norway are oats, barley, corn, rye, and wheat; the yearly produce is about 11,160,000 bushels, besides 14,100,000 bushels of potatoes. The value of the harvest amounts to about $16,000,000 per annum.

The products of agriculture and cattle-breeding being insufficient to supply the wants of the country, considerable quantities are imported.

Forestry is of great importance. As stated above, the forests of Norway cover more than one-fifth of its entire area. They supply considerable quantities of timber, both for home consumption and exportation. The average annual exports of timber amount to about $16,000,000.

The fisheries of Norway employ about 27,000 men, and yield about $16,000,000 per annum. They are of great importance, and not only yield one of the most important articles of home consumption, but at the same time constitute one of the most profitable sources of foreign export. Fish are caught in almost every stream and lake of the interior, as well as in the fjords of the coast, and in the bays and channels which encircle the numerous islands skirting the long sea-line of Norway. These fish are principally cod and herring. Cod, prepared as stock-fish or dried salt fish, is exported to Spain and Italy; herring to the Baltic ports.

The merchant marine of Norway had, in 1875, a tonnage of 1,220,000, and was manned by 53,000 seamen.

The following statistics apply to the exports and imports of Norway in 1873:

Value of goods exported,	$33,000,000	
Gross freight of goods carried in Norwegian vessels,	28,400,000	
Receipts from various sources,	800,000	
		$62,200,000
Value of goods imported,	$45,800,000	
Expenses of Norwegian vessels in foreign countries,	11,400,000	
Other expenses,	2,400,000	
		59,600,000
Balance,		$2,600,000

The principal articles of export were, in 1873: Products of the fisheries, $11,600,000; of forestry, $15,500,000; of agriculture and cattle-breeding, $1,300,000; metals and minerals, $1,800,000; textile fabrics, $660,000.

The imports were principally: Articles of food, $13,500,000; coffee, $3,500,000; liquors, $1,000,000; textile fabrics and dry goods, $8,300,000; hardware, $3,300,000; hides, $1,200,000; coal, $1,700,000; vessels, $4,400,000.

Manufactures have made some progress during the last few years, but are, as yet, inconsiderable. About 32,000 persons are employed, mainly in sawmills, planing mills, brick factories, shipbuilding, and metallurgical and textile industries.

The mineral products comprise silver, copper, cobalt, iron, chrome, ironstone, etc., and yield an annual income of nearly $1,000,000.

Education is compulsory, parents being bound to let their children, between the ages of seven and fourteen, receive public instruction; 241,000 children attend the common schools, and 16,500 receive a higher instruction. The expenses of the higher schools were, in 1873, $827,000.

The public revenue, in 1873, was $6,870,000, and the expenditures $7,277,000, of which amount $865,000 was for the construction of railways. The public debt amounts to $9,200,000.

Norway has 12,432 miles of highways and district roads, 304 miles of railways, and 147 miles of canals. There are 719 post offices, which distribute 7,500,000 letters per annum.

(The foregoing statistics are furnished by the Norwegian Commission.)

According to "Martin's Year Book," there were, at the end of 1873, telegraph lines of the length of 3745 miles, and wires of the length of 5845 miles.

The government of Norway is a constitutional monarchy. The executive is represented by the king, who exercises his authority through a Council of State, composed of one minister of state and nine councillors. The legislative power of the realm is the Storthing, or Great Court, the representative of the sovereign people.

On the 1st of January, 1874, the troops of the land numbered 13,000 men. The reserve forces at the same time numbered 19,000, and the landwaern 11,000 men. The naval force comprised, at the same date, twenty vessels, all steamers, with an armament of 149 guns.

Commission from NORWAY to the International Exhibition:

HERMAN BAARS. WM. C. CHRISTOPHERSEN.

GERHARD GADE, U. S. Consul.

ITALY.

THE geographical territory comprised under the name of Italy consists of a considerable stretch of peninsular mainland, besides several islands, situated in Southern Europe, between latitude 36° 35′ and 47° north, and between longitude 6° 35′ and 18° 35′ east. From the southern extremity of Sicily to the Alps its maximum length is about 600 miles, its utmost breadth being 300 miles. Its boundaries on the north are Austria and Switzerland, on the south the Mediterranean, on the west France and the Mediterranean, and on the east the Ionian and Adriatic seas, while its natural limits are strongly defined by the Alps and the sea.

The first general census of the kingdom of Italy was taken by the government on the 31st of December, 1871, on which date the population numbered 26,796,073 souls, living on an area of 296,013 square chilos, or 112,677 English square miles. The density of population was 237 per English square mile.

The kingdom of Italy is administratively divided in 69 provinces, as follows:

	POPULATION.	
PIEDMONT AND LIGURIA.		
1. Alessandria,	683,361	
2. Cuneo,	617,232	
3. Genoa,	716,284	
4. Novara,	624,969	
5. Porto Maurizio,	127,042	
6. Turin,	972,988	
		3,741,876
ISLAND OF SARDINIA.		
7. Cagliari,	392,981	
8. Sassari,	243,274	
		636,255
LOMBARDY.		
9. Bergamo,	368,152	
10. Brescia,	456,023	
11. Como,	477,642	
12. Cremona,	300,595	
13. Milan,	1,009,794	
14. Pavia,	448,357	
15. Sondrio,	111,240	
		3,171,803
EMILIA.		
16. Bologna,	439,232	
17. Ferrara,	216,545	
18. Forli,	234,090	
19. Massac Carrare,	161,944	
20. Modena,	273,231	
21. Parma,	264,509	
22. Piacenza,	225,775	
23. Ravenna,	220,801	
24. Reggio,	240,635	
		2,276,762

	POPULATION.	
THE MARCHES.		
25. Ancona,	262,369	
26. Ascoli Picerio,	203,008	
27. Macerata,	236,994	
28. Pesaro e Urbino,	213,072	
		915,443
UMBRIA.		
29. Perugia,		549,833
TUSCANY.		
31. Arezzo,	234,645	
31. Florence,	766,611	
32. Grosseto,	107,457	
33. Leghorn,	118,851	
34. Lucca,	280,399	
35. Pisa,	265,959	
36. Sienna,	206,446	
		1,980,368
NEAPOLITAN PROVINCES.		
37. Aquila,	332,782	
38. Avellino,	375,237	
39. Bari,	604,540	
40. Benevento,	232,012	
41. Campobasso,	364,843	
42. Caserta,	695,754	
43. Catanzaro,	412,226	
44. Chisti,	340,299	
45. Cosenza,	440,272	
46. Foggia,	322,754	
47. Lecce,	493,574	
48. Naples,	908,029	
49. Potenza,	509,202	
50. Reggio,	353,606	
51. Salerno,	541,739	
52. Teramo,	245,684	
		7,171,553
SICILY.		
53. Caltainisetta,	230,066	
54. Catania,	495,240	
55. Girgenti,	289,018	
56. Messina,	420,649	
57. Palermo,	617,660	
58. Siracusa,	294,915	
59. Trapani,	236,388	
		2,583,936
VENETIA.		
60. Belluno.	175,370	
61. Mantua,	288,942	
62. Padua,	364,355	
63. Rovigo,	200,835	
64. Trevise,	352,538	
65. Udine,	481,787	
66. Venezia,	337,539	
67. Verona,	367,426	
68. Vicenza,	363,161	
		2,931,953
69. ROME,		836,291

According to the old political division, the population is divided as follows:

iedmont and Liguria,	3,741,876
Island of Sardinia,	636,255
Lombardy,	3,171,803
Emilia,	2,276,762
The Marches,	915,443
Umbria,	549,833
Tuscany,	1,980,368
Neapolitan Provinces,	7,171,553
Sicily,	2,583,936
Venice,	2,931,953
Rome (States of the Church),	836,291
	26,796,073

The physical aspect presented by the surface of Italy is diversified in the extreme. Northern Italy is, for the most part, composed of one great plain—the basin of the Po, comprising all Lombardy and a considerable portion of Piedmont and Venice, bounded on the northwest and partly on the south by different alpine ranges. Throughout Central Italy, the great Apennine chain gives a picturesque irregularity to the physical configuration of the country, which in the southern extremity of Italy assumes still wilder forms. In the highland districts of Naples in which the Apennine ridge reaches its maximum elevation (10,000 feet), the scenery exhibits a savage grandeur. Along the extensive coast plains, as well as in the sub-Apennine valleys, the rural charms of this portion of Italy are extreme, while the brilliant flora and vegetation impart to it a novel character of beauty. The chief mountain system of Italy is the frontier ridge of the Alps, and their noble continuation, the Apennines.

Italy likewise comprises a considerable stretch of volcanic zone, which traverses the peninsula from the centre to the south in a line parallel with that of the Apennines, and of which the most remarkable active summits are Vesuvius, adjoining Naples, Ætna in Sicily, and Stromboli in the Lipari Isles.

The great plains of Italy are those of Lombardy, which stretch from the Mincio to the Ticino and the Po; of Piedmont; the Venetian plains; the plain of the Roman legations; the plain of the Campo Felice, on which stands Vesuvius; the Apulian plain; the long, narrow Neapolitan plain of the Basilicata, 100 miles in length, and 24 miles in breadth, stretching along the Gulf of Tarento.

The great majority of the rivers of Italy are only navigable for small coasting boats or barges. By far the most important is the Po, which rises on the borders of France, and flows into the Adriatic. It has numerous tributaries. Among the others may be mentioned the Adige, Brenta, Piave, Tagliamento, Aterno, Sangro, Metauro, Ofanto, Bradano, also belonging to the Adriatic basin; the Arno, the Tiber, the Ombrone, the Garigliano, and the Volturno, which belong to the Mediterranean basin.

The canal system of Italy is most extensive in the north. Nine principal canals in Lombardy administer to the irrigation of the plains and to the purposes of commercial communication, contributing in no small degree to the prosperity of the district. The Naviglio Grande or Ticinello is the finest hydraulic construction in Italy; it communicates between the Ticino and Milan, and has a course of 28 miles, navigable for vessels of large size. It was begun in 1179. The Naviglio Martesana, 38 miles long, unites Concesa on the Adea with Milan; the Naviglio di Pavia is 18 miles in length; the bifurcated Naviglio d'Ostiglia unites the Po with the Adige. 253 canals intersect Piedmont, extending over a length of 1932 kilometres. Venice comprises 203 navigable, and 40 minor canals. Numerous canals have been constructed for the drainage of the Pontine Marshes. This system of water communication was early carried to a high degree of efficiency in Italy, and is of incalculable service in the agricultural districts.

The mountain lakes of Italy are famed for their picturesque beauty. They are mostly in the northern provinces of Lombardy and Venetia. The principal are Maggiore, Lugano, Como, Iseo, and Garda. The Roman lakes of Perugia, Bolseno, and Bracciano, that of Castiglione in Tuscany, and Celano in Naples, also deserve mention.

The mineral and thermal springs of Italy are innumerable, and possess a great variety of curative and sanitary properties.

In the northern provinces, the climate is temperate, salubrious, and frequently severe in winter; in the centre, it assumes a more genial and sunny character: while the heat of the southern extremity is almost of a tropical intensity. The singular clearness of the atmosphere sets off the landscape and monumental beauties of Italy with brilliant effect. The drawbacks of Italy's climate are the piercing tramontana or mountain winds; the deadly sirocco, which blights all nature at seasons along the western coast; and the malaria or noxious miasmata which issues from the Maremma of Tuscany, the Pontine Marshes, and the Venetian lagoons, generating pestilential fevers and aguish diseases in the summer season. The mean temperature of the leading divisions of the country throughout a whole year was as follows: Milan, 55° 4′ of Fahrenheit's scale; Rome, 59°; Palermo, 62° 5′; and in Sardinia, 60° 5′. The highest temperature at Rome rises to 95°, and in Sicily from 97° to 104°.

The staple products of Italy are corn, wine, oil, raw silk, rice, olives, and fruits. Hemp, flax, and cotton are also largely grown. The sugar-cane is successfully cultivated in the two Sicilies. Agriculture, except in the north, is in a very backward condition. It is calculated that only two-thirds of the area of the kingdom capable of production are cultivated, and that the rest lies waste. The superficial extent of the productive soil of Italy is 23,017,096 ellaras,* divided thus:

	ELLARAS.
Arable land,	11,003,061
Meadow land,	1,173,436
Rice ground,	144,903
Olive plantations,	554,767
Chestnut plantations,	585,132
Woods and forests,	4,158,349
Pastures,	5,397,448
Total,	23,017,096

There are, besides, 3,997,059 ellaras of rock and marsh. Of the land capable of cultivation, more than half is devoted to the growth of cereals, mainly wheat. The average crop is insufficient for the supply of the country. The wines of Naples are esteemed the best, small quantities of the famous *Lachrima Christi* and the *Vind d'Asti* being exported, while the Sicilian wines of Marsala form a considerable item of export. The best oil and olives are furnished by Tuscany, Lucca, and Naples. Silk is chiefly manufactured in the northern provinces, the cultivation of the mulberry and the rearing of the silkworm forming, in Lombardy, a most important interest. The best manufactured silk comes from Piedmont, Tuscany, and the Roman provinces. The fruits of the two Sicilies are exquisite in flavor, and embrace several tropical species. Oranges, lemons, almonds, figs, dates, melons, and the pistachio nut, are common to all orchards, and are largely exported. A considerable cheese trade exists in the northern provinces.

The sea and fresh water fisheries of Italy are considerable, the Mediterranean furnishing immense quantities of tunny, anchovies, sardines, mullets, pelchards, and mackerel. The export of anchovies and of sardines is of immense extent. The

* One ellara equals 2.47 acres,

river fisheries yield salmon, trout, sturgeon, lampreys, tench, barbel, etc. The crustaceans and shell fish of the Italian seas are of great variety and delicate flavor, and are a favorite article of Italian consumption.

The total exports of the kingdom, during the year 1874, were 1,304,994,328 lire;* the imports, during the same year, 985,458,532 lire.

The number and tonnage of merchant vesssls belonging to the kingdom, on January 1st, 1874, were as follows: 17,562 sailing vessels, aggregating 925,337 tons burthen; and 103 steamers, of a total burthen of 24,476 tons. Of the sailing vessels, 9074 were under 6 tons each.

According to the present constitution of Italy, the executive power belongs exclusively to the sovereign, and is exercised by him through responsible ministers. The legislative authority vests conjointly in the king and parliament, the latter consisting of two chambers, a Senate and a Chamber of Deputies. The Senate is composed of the princes of the royal house who are of age, and of an unlimited number of members, above forty years old, who are nominated by the king for life; a condition of the nomination being that the person should either fill a high office, or have acquired fame in science, literature, or any other pursuit tending to the benefit of the nation: or, finally, should pay taxes to the annual amount of 3000 lire. The members of the Chamber of Deputies are elected by a majority of all citizens who are twenty-five years of age and pay taxes to the amount of 40 lire. A deputy must be thirty years old, and must have the requisites demanded by the electoral law, among them a slight property qualification. Neither senators nor deputies receive any salary.

The following are the budget estimates for 1875:

Estimated revenue,	1,344,164,158 lire.
Estimated expenditures,	1,575,487,190 "

The entire public debt, at the end of 1873, was 9,757,613,267 lire.

The actual strength of the army, at the end of December, 1873, was:

Number of men under arms (peace footing),	199,557
Number of men on unlimited furlough,	244,952
Total (war footing),	444,509

The navy, at the commencement of 1875, consisted of 95 ships of war, carrying 1256 guns. Of these, 9 were ironclads, carrying 346 guns, 46 were screw steamers, carrying 693 guns, and 32 paddle steamers, carrying 113 guns.

The total length of railways opened for traffic, at the end of 1874, was 4607 English miles.

The number of post offices at the commencement of 1874 was 2709. In the year 1873 the post office carried 504,402,431 letters and 94,402,596 printed parcels.

The length of telegraphic lines, on the 1st of January, 1874, was 12,622 English miles, nearly two-thirds of the whole belonging to the government. There were, at the same date, 1408 telegraphic offices. The number of private telegrams during 1873 was 4,670,090, and of official telegrams, 163,852.

Under the new Italian government, a great part of the property confiscated from the monastic establishments has been devoted to the cause of public education. In addition to this, the Parliament votes an annual credit of 15,000,000 lire for the same purpose. Since the commencement of the year 1860 there were opened throughout the kingdom thirty-three model schools. Notwithstanding these important aids to instruction, education still stands very low. According to the census of 1864, out of a total population of 21,703,710 souls, there were about 17,000,000 who could neither read nor write. Piedmont occupied the first place, Sicily the last, on the register of knowledge. In the Basilicata, Calabria, and Sicily, more than nine-tenths of the population could neither read nor write.

* One lire equals 19.3 cents gold.

There are twenty-two universities in Italy, many of them of ancient foundation. By a decree of the Minister of Public Instruction, issued in 1871, six high-schools—Naples, Pavia, Turin, Bologna, Florence, and Parma—were declared first-class universities of the kingdom. The number of students at all the universities was returned as 10,524 in 1871.

Commission from ITALY to the International Exhibition:

H. E. BARON BLANC, Minister Plenipotentiary.
COUNT B. LITTA, First Secretary of Legation.
CHEVALIER ALONZO M. VITI, Vice-Consul.
A. PADOVANI, President of the Central Committee.
JOSEPH DASSI.
N. CANTALAMESSA PAPOTTI.
PIO BACCARANI.
G. VIGNA DEL FERRO.
G. CONARI.
ANGELO GIANELLO, General Agent.

EGYPT.

THE territories under the rule of the sovereign of Egypt, including those on the Upper Nile and Central Africa, are vaguely estimated to embrace an area of 4,777,830 square kilometres, and to be inhabited by a population of 16,952,000, of whom about one-third are in Egypt proper. The following tabular statement gives the area and population of the various divisions of the kingdom, and its recent annexation, according to government estmate, of the year 1875:

DIVISIONS.	AREA, SQ. KILOMETRES.	POPULATION.
Egypt proper,	550,630	5,252,000
Nubia,	864,500	1,000,000
Former kingdom of Ethiopia,	2,918,000	5,000,000
Darfur, and other annexed territories,	444,700	5,700,000
	4,777,830	16,952,000

The great physical peculiarity of Egypt is the absence of rain, the land being only irrigated by the annual overflow of the Nile. The climate is remarkably mild and sound, especially south of the Delta; and in the desert, from Cairo to Alexandria, the air contains more moisture than to the south, From the middle of August to December, west winds prevail; east winds from that time till March; after that, unhealthy south winds or Khamsin till June; and from June till August the north or Etesian winds. Earthquakes are occasionally felt, and the temperature varies from 84° F. to 32°. The most remarkable phenomenon is, however, the regular increase of the Nile, fed by the fall of the tropical rains, which commence in 11° north latitude, in the spring; and falling first into the White, and then Blue Nile, reach Egypt in the middle, and the Delta in the end of June. In the middle of July, the red water appears, and the rise may be dated from that time it attains its maximum at the end of September, and begins to decline visibly in the middle of October, and subsides to its minimum in April. At the end of November, the irrigated land has dried, and is sown, and is covered with green crops, which last till the end of February. In March is the harvest. The state of the Nile, in fact, marks the season more accurately than the variation of temperature. Egypt is by no means remarkably healthy, as, in addition to the visitations of plague and cholera, ophthalmia, diarrhœa, dysentery, and boils often prevail, and European, and even Nigritic races cannot be acclimatized.

Many of the European trees and plants are found in Egypt; the date-palm, the doom-palm, the sycamore, acacias, tamarisks, etc., are among its more peculiar botanical productions. The extensive culture of papyrus has been, in modern times, replaced by that of the sugar-cane, cotton, indigo, and tobacco, and the plant has almost disappeared. Gourds and melons have always abounded. To the wheat and barley of antiquity have been added maize and durra. Egypt is very deficient in timber trees. The rocks of Egypt afforded the stones used in its edifices and sculptures; granite, syenite, breccia (in the Cossier Rood), porphyry (from the quarries of Gebel Dokhan, opened in the reign of the Emperor Claudius), sandstone, and limestone. Alabaster (found at Middle Egypt) **has been used from** the earliest periods to the present day. Emeralds are produced by the mines of Gebel Zabara; salt, natron, and—since 1850—sulphur, are among the other mineral productions of Egypt.

Egypt proper is divided into three great districts, namely: Masr-el-Bahri, or Lower Egypt; El-Wustani, or Middle Egypt; and El-Said, or Upper Egypt—designations drawn from the course of the river Nile. These three geographical districts, subdivided into eleven administrative provinces, had, according to an enumeration made by the government in March, 1872, a rural population of 4,603,660, and an urban population of 648,340, dispersed over six towns, as follows:

Cairo,	349,983	Tanta,	28,500
Alexandria,	212,054	Rosetta,	15,002
Damietta,	29,383	Suez,	13,498

The Khedive is absolute sovereign or king. The administration is carried on by a Council of State of four military and four civil dignitaries.

The revenue of Egypt for the financial year ending September 10th, 1874, was calculated in the official budget at 1,982,394 purses;* the expenditures at 1,763,128 purses.

The public debt of Egypt consists chiefly of foreign loans. These are divided into two classes, namely, general loans, contracted by the State, and loans of the Khedive, as greatest of land-owners, raised on his individual responsibility.

The following table shows the actual state of the debt:

Funded debt,	£49,270,380
Floating debt,	7,600,000
	£56,870,380
Personal debt of the Khedive,	13,174,360
Total,	£70,044,740

The army is raised by conscription. It consisted, in January, 1875, of four regiments of infantry, of 3000 men each; of a battalion of chasseurs, of 1000 men; of 3500 cavalry, 1500 artillery, and two battalions of engineers, of 1500 each. There are, besides, two regiments of black troops, of Sudan, numbering 5000 men.

The Egyptian navy comprised, in 1875, 7 ships of the line, 6 frigates, 9 corvettes, 7 brigs, 18 gunboats and smaller vessels, and 27 transports.

The commerce of Egypt is very large, but consists, to some extent, of goods carried in transit. The total exports for the year 1873 amounted to about 1,450,000,000 piastres the imports to about 600,000,000 piastres. The merchant navy, in 1872, comprised 585 vessels of a total burthen of 59,874 tons.

The commerce of the world has been greatly benefited by the Suez Canal, which connects the Mediterranean with the Red Sea. Starting from Port Said, forty miles east of the Damietta mouth of the Nile, it proceeds across the isthmus and through lakes Menzaleh, El Ballah, and Timsah, on the shores of which latter stands the new town of Ismailia, and through the Bitter lakes to Suez. Its total length is 92 miles. Its actual width over the greater part of its length, does not permit of two vessels passing or crossing each other in the canal itself; but there are numerous sidings, by which vessels are enabled to cross one another; vessels measuring 430 feet in length and drawing 25 feet 9 inches of water have passed safely through the canal. Its actual cost, according to the report for the year 1875, was £17,518,729, exclusive of £1,360,000 bonds issued to pay for coupons on shares in arrear during part of the period of construction.

* 1 purse = 500 piastres = $25 gold

The number and tonnage of vessels which passed through the canal in each of the five years, 1870 to 1874, were as follows:

YEAR.	VESSELS.	TONNAGE.
1870,	491	436,618
1871,	761	761,875
1872,	1082	1,439,169
1873,	1171	2,085,270
1874,	1264	2,423,672

Egypt had, on the 1st of January, 1875, a railway system of a total length of 955 English miles, open for traffic, with 502 miles under construction. With the exception of a short line of about 5 miles, all of the Egyptian railways are tate property.

The telegraphs of Egypt were, at the commencement of 1875, of a total length of 4094 miles, the length of wires being 8690 miles. The whole of the telegraphs are State property.

Commission from EGYPT to the International Exhibition:

HIS HIGHNESS, PRINCE MOHAMMED TAWFIC PACHA, President.
HIS EXCELLENCY, RAGHIB PACHA, Minister of Commerce, Vice-President.
H. BRUGSCH BEY, Commissioner-General.

Commissioners.

GENERAL STONE.
M. MAHMOUD BEY, Astronomer.
M. MARIETTE BEY, Director of the Museums of Antiquities.
M. GASTINEL BEY, Professor in the Medical School.
M. ROGERS, Director in the Ministry of Public Instruction.
M. ACTON, Chief of Division, Ministry of Commerce
M. BAUDRY, Architect.
M. DELCHEVALERIE, Attachè.

Resident Members in Philadelphia.

H. BRUGSCH BEY, Commissioner-General.
E. BRUGSCH, Chief of Transportation and Installation.
A. BEHMERSD, Attaché. Secretary.
EDWARD ELIAS, Secretary and Interpreter.
M. DANINOS, Attaché for Special Mission.

TUNIS.

TUNIS, a country of Africa, and one of the Barbary States, is bounded on the north by the Mediterranean, on the west by Algeria, on the south by the Desert, and on the east by Tripoli and the Mediterranean. Its greatest length from north to south is about 440 miles; its average breadth, 160; area, upwards of 75,000 square miles; population, according to latest authorities, 1,200,000. Tunis is traversed by branches of the great Atlas range, which, in fact, has its proper termination here. The northern coast is rocky and steep, with numerous bays, of which the largest is the Gulf of Tunis; and two of its promontories, Capes Blanco (Ras-el-Abid) and Bon, are the most northern in Africa. The eastern coast, on the other hand, is flat, sandy, and infertile, like that of Tripoli, but has two large gulfs, Hammamet and Cabes. The southern part of Tunis belongs to the desert steppe known as Belud-el-Jerid. There is only one fresh water lake of any consequence, that of Biserta or Bensart, near the north coast. The brooks and torrents of Tunis either lose themselves in the sand, or find their way to the sea after a short course. None are navigable. The longest is the Mejerdah, which flows in a generally northeastern direction into the Gulf of Tunis. Other streams are the Ved-el-Milianah and the Ved-el-Kebir. There are several mineral springs in the country. The climate of Tunis is fine, and the soil exceedingly fertile, so that, in spite of a very poor knowledge of agriculture, wheat, barley, maize, dhurra, pulse, olives, oranges, figs, grapes, pomegranates, almonds, and dates are abundantly produced. The culture of oil is more attended to, and is very lucrative. Great herds of cattle are fed on the plains; the sheep are famous for their wool; and the horses and dromedaries are no less celebrated. The chief mineral products are sea-salt, saltpetre, lead ore, and quicksilver. In the vicinity of the sea-coasts, considerable manufacturing and trading industry is manifested, more particularly in the cities of Tunis and Susa. Wool, olive oil, wax, honey, soap, hides, coral, sponges, dates, wheat, and barley are the principal exports. Cloth, leather, silks, muslins, spices, cochineal, and arms are transported by means of caravans to the interior of Africa, whence in exchange are brought for exportation to European and other countries, senna, gums, ostrich feathers, gold, and ivory. Total exports in 1874, valued at 28,815,358 francs; imports, 25,193,785 francs. During the same year the entries at the port of Tunis (Goulette) were 779 vessels, 116,927 tons burthen; departures, 768, of 108,031 tons burthen.

The Bey of Tunis receives his investiture from Constantinople; without the Sultan's authority he can neither declare war, conclude peace, nor cede territory; the Sultan's name must appear on all the coinage; the army must be at the disposal of the Sublime Porte. In internal matters the power of the Bey remains absolute.

The Tunisian army comprises about 4000 regulars, 5000 Karouglis (descendants of the Turkish janissaries), 5000 Zouaves (infantry), and 1500 spahis (cavalry). In time of war the irregular cavalry can be increased to about 3000. The navy consists of two vessels, carrying 10 guns, and crews aggregating 250 men. The merchant navy comprises 300 vessels, ranging from 10 to 150 tons burthen.

There are about forty miles of railways in operation. There is at Tunis, a French, and also an Italian post office.

French telegraph lines connect the city of Tunis with various towns within the borders of the regency, as well as with Algiers and Europe.

Commission from TUNIS to the International Exhibition:

HIS EXCELLENCY SIDI HEUSSEIN, General of Division, Minister of Instruction and Public Works, President.

G. H. HEAP, U. S. Consul, Resident Commissioner.

ORANGE FREE STATE.

THE republic of the Orange Free State is situated on the northeast boundary of Cape Colony, and is bounded as follows: On the west and northwest by the territory claimed for the chief, Nicholas Waterboer, under the name of Griqualand West, and by Betchuanaland, respectively, on the north and northeast by the Transvaal republic, on the east by the colony of Natal, and on the south by British Basutoland, the Native Reserve Lands, and the Cape Colonial divisions of Albert and Colesberg.

Its area is roughly taken to be about 70,000 square miles, but no accurate computation has hitherto been made, and the probability is that the actual extent will be found considerably greater.

The country consists of extensive undulating plains, which slope from the great Watershed, northward and westward, respectively, to the Vaal and Orange rivers, and is intersected at varying intervals by the Wilge, Rhenoster, Valsch, Vet, and Riet rivers, all of which empty their waters into the Vaal river, and the Caledon river, which empties into the Orange river. The courses of the large rivers are extremely tortuous and hollow, their banks being for the greater part very precipitous, and generally lined with water-willow, mimosa, and other trees indigenous to this country. The streams are usually fordable; during the rainy season, however, they become swollen and impassable.

The Orange Free State is, for the greater part, a grazing country, and though agriculture is everywhere attended to on a larger or smaller scale, according to the natural capabilities of the farms, still it is chiefly in the southern and eastern districts that it is carried on as the principal source of production, and it is almost exclusively from the districts of Rouxville, Lady Brand, Winburg, Bethlehem, and Harrismith, that grain is brought into the markets of the other districts.

Neither is it altogether without mineral wealth, as diamonds, rubies, and other precious stones have been discovered in various parts of the country. Coal also of a very good quality, and in paying quantities, has been found in the Winburg district, as well as on farms in the Lady Brand and Harrismith districts.

In the early days of this republic the distribution of animal life was a subject of great interest, from the fact of the immense variety of wild animals inhabiting the country. Even now the lion still frequents some sections of it. But, owing to the advance of civilization and human industry, all the larger animals, as the elephant, rhinoceros, hippopotamus, and giraffe, have retreated far away. Upon its vast undulating plains, however, a large and splendid variety of the antelope tribe roams in countless numbers. The country being favorable for the rearing of horses, cattle, and wooled sheep, the number of the latter contained therein may be estimated by millions.

Birds abound in great variety, particularly those of the larger kinds, among which might be enumerated the ostrich, eagle, vulture, pelican, hawk, and various species of crane.

The staple articles of export from the Orange Free State are wool and skins, and of late years diamonds and other precious stones, while owing to the mining population in the disputed territories along the Vaal river, a large trade in grain and other agricultural produce has been productive of great wealth to the country.

From the same cause, although more indirectly, trade in all articles of import, such as ironware implements, and manufactures in woolen, cotton, and silk goods, and articles for consumption, either as necessaries or luxuries, has received a great stimulus, and the commercial community is to all appearance in a healthy and prosperous condition.

The average height of the Orange Free State above the level of the sea is about 5000 feet, and the climate is generally salubrious. The winter here is cold but dry, the summer usually warm and moist, though droughts are sometimes experienced in the summer months. The air, however, is healthy and dry, as a rule, and this is particularly felt at Bloemfontein and its vicinity; consequently numbers of invalids suffering from pulmonary affections resort to Bloemfontein, and experience much benefit from a residence is this part of the country.

In other respects it has been noticed that the changes of the seasons are to a greater or less degree, according to their duration, accompanied by a greater liability to colds and fevers, generally of a typhoid type, and inflammatory affections, especially amongst children.

The government of the Orange Free State is republican, and its constitution vests the legislative powers in the Volksraad, the members of which are elected by their constituents for four consecutive years. The whole number of representatives (there being one for each chief town of a district, and one for each field cornetcy) is fifty-two. Of this number, the half retire by rotation every two years, and a new election takes place to fill up the vacancies.

The educational department of the country is only now receiving that vital attention which a subject of so vast importance to any country ought to have; and the legislature has only of late years been impressed with the absolute necessity of placing this department on the best possible footing. Accordingly, a fund is gradually being raised for educational purposes, which in 1876 will place at the disposal of the government an amount of £56,000.

Meantime, in accordance with an order made in 1872, an inspector of education has been appointed, who has already entered upon the task of remodeling the whole educational system. It is only right, nevertheless, to state that a government allowance of £90 a year has for years past been given to each district town, on condition of its subscribing at least one-half more, and attempts to establish good schools have everywhere been made by the district school committees, comprising the Landdrost, Dutch Reformed Church, and three elected members, with varying success in some places, but in others only to meet with failure, which is principally to be attributed to the defective system hitherto pursued.

The pricipal support hitherto afforded by the government consists in the liberal allowances made for the salaries of teachers in the Grey College; but owing to the short time that has elapsed since the arrival of one of them, and various other circumstances beyond the control of the government, the desired results are still to be looked for. Very praiseworthy efforts have also been made on behalf of education by the Anglican Church, in schools established at Bloemfontein and at Smithfield, and this latter has already shown very satisfactory results.

The revenue of the State, for the year 1874–75, was £190,958; the expenditure, during the same year, £98,242.

The government lands of the Orange Free State are still very considerable, though as nought compared with their original size, owing to the sales of farms which have been held from time to time. The value of fixed property of all kinds has increased greatly within the last few years. Even in the districts of Harrismith and Kroonstad, where land formerly was almost valueless, farms are now eagerly sought after, and change hands at very high rates. The average price of land throughout the whole State may now be fixed at 10*s.* per morgen. A rough estimate fixes the number of farms throughout the country as between 6000 and 7000. Fixed property changes ownership by registration. The population of the State is estimated at about 75,000 white, and 25,000 colored or native.

Commission from ORANGE FREE STATE to the International Exhibition:

CHARLES W. RILEY, Consul-General.

LUXEMBOURG.

THE Grand Duchy of Luxembourg is connected with the Netherlands in the person of the sovereign, but has a constitution and administration of its own. The King of Holland, as Grand Duke, appoints a deputy-governor. Dutch Luxembourg was a part of the Germanic Confederation from its formation, in 1815, till its dissolution, in 1866. In 1867 its neutrality was guaranteed by the great powers. Its present constitution dates from 1868. The chamber of deputies consists of 40 members chosen for 6 years by direct vote in the electoral districts. Area, 990 Eng. sq. miles. Population (1871) 197,528, the most of whom are engaged in agriculture. The chief products are wine, corn, hops, hemp, and flax. In the eastern districts there are iron mines, and lime and slate quarries. The majority of the inhabitants are Walloons, the rest mainly Germans. The capital is Luxembourg. By the law of 1868, the army consists of 13 officers, 500 under-officers and privates, besides 110 gensdarmes.

CHINA.

THE following table gives the area and population of the various divisions comprising the Chinese empire:

	AREA IN ENGLISH SQ. MILES.	POPULATION.
China proper,	1,534,953	405,213,152
DEPENDENCIES.		
Mandchuria,	362,313	3,000,000
Mongolia,	1,288,035	2,000,000
Thibet,	643,734	6,000,000
Corea,	90,300	8,000,000
Lieukhien Islands,	2,310	
Liaotong,	2,982	1,000,000
Total,	3,924,727	425,213,152

China proper is included between 18° 15′ and 43° 15′ north latitude and 98° and 122° 40′ east longitude. Its coast-line exceeds 2500 miles, and its land frontier 4400 miles. It is divided into eighteen provinces, and includes the two large islands of Formosa and Hainan. The administration of the empire is parceled out into separate governments, corresponding with the provincial divisions, each of which has a complete organization, exchequer, army, and naval force of its own. Besides providing for the cost of its own administration, each province is required to remit annually to Peking a certain portion of its revenue to meet the expenses of the court, central government, and garrison of Peking, as well as to provide for exigencies arising in other provinces, and for the requirements of the garrisons in Turkestan, Mongolia, and Mandchuria, which are administered by military governors.

According to the latest reports, the imperial army comprises a total of 850,000 men, including 678 companies of Tartar troops, 211 companies of Mongols, and native Chinese infantry, a kind of militia, numbering 120,000 men. The native soldiers do not live in barracks, but in their own houses, mostly pursuing some civil occupation.

The Chinese are pre-eminent for their indefatigable industry. Of the immense territory peopled by them, there is scarcely a rood of arable ground that is not assiduously cultivated. Unfortunately, however, their husbandry is, to a great extent, nullified by the rude and ill-adapted implements employed. Therefore scientific agriculture is but slightly advanced in China, although the Chinese system of land irrigation is superior to that of any other people. As a manufacturing nation the Chinese are highly distinguished; porcelain originated entirely with them, and the art of spinning silk they also gave to the West. The lacquered ware produced in China, though very beautiful, must be considered inferior to that of Japan, but in the more minute arts of carving and inlaying, the Chinese have no superiors. Their ivory and mother of pearl industry is too well known to need description. Gunpowder, though a Chinese invention, is little manufactured, and that little of indifferent quality. Paper is ingeniously made of various materials; it is, in general, thin, silky, and highly absorbent of ink.

Chinese trade has the peculiarity of being, for the most part, internal, the country supplying most articles of subsistence or luxury, and is carried on by means of canal and river navigation. The principal exports are tea, porcelain, raw and spun silk, sugar, rhubarb, embroidery, lacquered wares, and carved articles of domestic ornament. The imports consist mainly of cotton and woolen goods, opium, raw cotton, furs, and edible birds' nests, which form an expensive luxury, and are held in high esteem. The total value of commodities exported from China, in 1865, reached the figure of $173,609,085, as against imports of $238,504,520. Of the exports, tea is the chief, showing a total quantity of 223,679,182 pounds shipped. The export of raw silk for the same year aggregated 40,726 bales, and of cotton, 35,855,792 pounds.

The grand canal, about 700 miles in length, has greatly facilitated the internal trade of the country. China is traversed in all directions by 20,000 imperial roads, most of which are badly kept. There is a postal service, but of a very rude kind.

Education, as the high road to official employment, to rank, wealth, and influence, is eagerly sought by all classes. Literary proficiency commands everywhere respect and consideration, and primary instruction penetrates to the remotest villages. Self-supporting day-schools are universal throughout the country, and the office of teacher is followed by a great number of the *literati*. Government provides state examiners, but does not otherwise assist in the education of the people.

The Chinese executive system is based on those noteworthy competetive examinations which are intended to sift out from the millions of educated Chinese the best and ablest for the public service.

Commission for CHINA to the International Exhibition:

ROBERT HART, ESQ., Inspector General of Imperial Maritime Customs.
G. DETRING, ESQ., Commissioner of Customs.
E. B. DREW, ESQ., Commissioner of Customs.
W. SCOTT FITZ, ESQ.
H. SEYMOUR GEARY, ESQ.

Resident Commissioners in Philadelphia.

JAMES H. HART, ESQ., Commissioner of Customs.
ALFRED HUBER, ESQ., Commissioner of Customs.
J. L. HAMMOND, ESQ., Commissioner of Customs.
EDWARD CUNNINGHAM, ESQ.
W. W. PARKIN, ESQ.
F. P. KNIGHT, ESQ.
W. NOYES MOREHOUSE, ESQ., Imperial Maritime Customs, Secretary.

JAPAN.

JAPAN proper comprehends four large islands, viz.: Niphon (the Japanese mainland), Sikok or Sikopf, Kiusiu, and Yesso, and extends from 31° to 45° 30′ north latitude. The empire of Japan includes about 3800 small islands and islets besides the four larger ones, and is situated between 26° and 52° north latitude, and 128° and 151° east longitude. It is bounded on the north by the Sea of Okotsk, on the east by the north Pacific Ocean, on the south by the eastern Sea of China, and on the west by the Sea of Japan. The islands of Japan appear to be of volcanic origin, and that part of the Pacific on which they rest is still intensely affected by volcanic action. Earthquakes occur very frequently in Japan, although certain parts of the country are exempt. Japan has been called the land of mountains: but though these are very numerous, and many of them volcanic, they are of moderate elevation, and rarely attain the limits of perpetual snow. The country generally is of moderate elevation, with fertile valleys, picturesque landscapes, and a coast indented with magnificent harbors; the soil is productive, rich in mineral wealth, and teeming with every variety of agricultural produce. Springs, lakes, and rivers are numerous; but the last, being sand-choked, are valuable chiefly for the purposes of irrigation.

Our knowledge of the climate of Japan is yearly increasing. June, July, and August are the months of rain, which sometimes descends in unceasing torrents. The months of October and November are the pleasantest and most genial of the twelve, when fine weather is enjoyed without the scorching heat of summer. The summers are very hot, and the winters in the northern parts almost Siberian; the thermometer rising to 96° in the shade in the former, and sinking to 18° below zero in the latter season. Alcock says: "The thermometer in the shade (during the summer) ranges from 70° to 85°, and averages 80° between the morning and the evening, while it is sometimes below 70° at night." Hurricanes and waterspouts are frequent; dense fogs hide the sun, sometimes for four or five days together; and about the change of the monsoons, typhoons and equinoctial gales frequently sweep the Japanese seas.

The following figures are furnished by the Japanese commission:

Area,	23,740 ris (the ri equals 2¼ miles).
Population.—Male,	16,891,729
Female,	16,408,946
Total,	33,300,675
Imports,	22,841,166.93 yens.*
Exports,	18,367,259.29 "
Revenue,	81,552,294. "
Expenditure,	79,881,820. "
Army,	42,073 men

The navy consists of 20 vessels, manned by 3757 men.

The country is rich in minerals, gold, silver, iron, sulphur, and especially copper abound. There are also large quantities of coal. Amongst the most remarkable of its vegetable productions is the camphor tree, the varnish or lacquer tree, the paper mulberry tree, the vegetable wax tree, the tea shrub, the tobacco plant, and the rice plant. The principal manufactures are those of silk and cotton. The internal trade is very extensive, and rigid regulations are in force to protect and encourage home industry. In the mechanical arts the Japanese have attained great excellence, especially in metallurgy, and in the manufacture of porcelain, lacquer ware, and silk fabrics. In some of these departments works are produced so exquisite in design and execution, as to more than rival the best products of Europe

* The yen equals 99.7 cents gold.

The Japanese government is organized on a basis which is partly European. The Mikado is supreme in temporal and spiritual matters, but the work of government is carried on by the Great Council, which is divided into three sections, denominated Centre, Right, and Left. The Centre is composed of the Prime Minister, Vice Prime Minister, and five advisers. The left is made up exclusively of the Council of State, the functions of which are analogous to those of the French Conseil d'Etat, so far as the preparation and discussion of laws is concerned. The Right includes all the ministers and vice-ministers of eight departments into which the administration is divided. The ministers, either individually or united in a Cabinet, decide all ordinary questions; but points of real importance are reserved for the Great Council, presided over by the Mikado. The local administration in the provinces is in the hands of prefects, one of them residing in each of the 75 districts into which Japan is divided.

Education is very general in Japan. In 1871 a Ministry of Instruction was created, and as a result of its efforts, public primary schools are increasing rapidly, especially in the towns; but the movement is far more marked in the western provinces and on the coast than in the interior. Private schools are more abundant still, and any person being at liberty to establish them,—subject to a permission, which is always given,—they spring up with facility wherever wanted. In order to facilitate the acquirement of foreign languages, the government has engaged European professors, and has also sent, at public expense, a large number of students to America and Europe. The first line of railway, from Yokahama to Yeddo, 17 miles long, was opened for traffic on the 12th of June 1875, and other lines were in progress at that date.

The post office carried 17,095,842 letters in 1874. The number of post offices at that date was 3244.

Commission from the JAPANESE EMPIRE to the International Exhibition:

HIS EXCELLENCY OKUBO TOSHIMICHI, Minister of the Interior and Privy Counsellor, President.

HIS EXCELLENCY LIEUTENANT-GENERAL SAIGO TSUKUMICHI, Imperial Army, Vice-President.

MR. KAWASE HIDEHARU, Vice-President Bureau of Agriculture and Industry, Commissioner-General.

MR. TANAKA YOSHIO, Ministry of the Interior.
MR. SEKIZAWA AKEKIO, Bureau of Agriculture and Industry.
MR. YAMATAKA NOBUAKIRA, Bureau of Agriculture and Industry.
MR. SHIODA MASASHI, Bureau of Agriculture and Industry.
MR. SUZUKI TOSHINOBU, Bureau of Agriculture and Industry.
MR. SUGIYAMA KADZUNARI, Bureau of Agriculture and Industry.
MR. HIDAKA LIRO, Lieutenant Imperial Army.
MR. AMORI KORENAKA, Bureau of Agriculture and Industry.
MR. ISHIHARA TOYOYASU, Bureau of Agriculture and Industry.
MR. ISHIDA TAMETAKE, Bureau of Agriculture and Industry.
MR. YAMAO TSUNETARO, Bureau of Agriculture and Industry.
MR. KUBO HIROMICHI, Bureau of Agriculture and Industry.
MR. FUKUI MAKOTO, Bureau of Agriculture and Industry.
MR. SHIBATA HIROSHI, Bureau of Agriculture and Industry.
MR. MAKIYAMA KOHEI, Bureau of Agriculture and Industry.
MR. ASMI TCHUGA, Bureau of Agriculture and Industry.
MR. ISHII YOSHITAKA, Bureau of Agriculture and Industry.
MR. ASAHI SUSUMU, Bureau of Agriculture and Industry.
MR. YOSHIO NAGAMASA, Bureau of Agriculture and Industry.
MR. SASASE MOTOAKIRA, Bureau of Agriculture and Industry.
MR. TSUCHIYA SHIGENAO, Attache.
MR. YOSHIKAWA NISUKE, Attache.
MR. AKUSAWA SUSUMU, Attache.
MR. SANDA TADASHI.
MR. TAWARA WAKICHIRO, Attache.

HAWAII.

THE islands forming the kingdom of Hawaii are eight in number, exclusive of one or two small islets. The chain runs from southeast to northwest, and lies in the middle of the Pacific Ocean, in latitude 19°—22° north, and longitude 155°—160° west. Area 7400 square miles; population (1872), 56,897, of whom 2539 were Europeans. The names, with the areas, of the respective islands are: Hawaii (formerly Oghyhee), 4210 square miles; Maui, 760; Oahu, 600; Kaui, 590; Molokai, 270; Lanai, 150; Niihau, 97; and Kahoolawe, 65 square miles.

Situated near the middle of the Pacific Ocean, about half the distance from San Francisco in North America that they are from Melbourne in Australia and Canton in China, the Sandwich Islands form an oasis in the middle of a wide ocean waste, and offer convenient stations for the refreshment and repair of the merchantmen and whalers that traverse the Pacific. They are of volcanic origin, and contain the largest volcanoes, both active and quiescent, in the world. The most prominent physical features of the group are the two lofty mountain peaks of Hawaii, Mauna Kea and Mauna Loa, each of which is 14,000 feet in height, or within 1860 feet of the loftiest of the Alps. Besides those two chief peaks, which stand apart from each other, and one of which is covered with perpetual snow, the island is traversed by other mountains, which give it a rugged and picturesque outline, and in some cases front the sea in bold, perpendicular precipices, from 1000 to 2000 feet in height. In general, the islands are lofty—the small islet of Lehua is 109 feet high, and the upland regions of Kaui are, on an average, 4000 feet above sea level. Within the coral reefs, which, in single, and more rarely in double ridges, skirt portions of the coasts, sandy shores, leading up to rich pasture-lands, and occasionally to productive valleys, are frequently seen. Everywhere, however, the configuration of the surface betrays the volcanic origin of the islands. Extinct volcanoes occur in most of the islands. Kilauea, on the Mauna Loa mountain in Hawaii, the largest active volcano in the world, has an oval-shaped crater nine miles in circumference, and is 6000 feet above sea level. In the centre of this immense caldron is a red sea of lava, always in a state of fusion. At intervals, the lava is thrown to a great height, and rolls in rivers down the mountain sides. On Maui, the crater of Mauna Haleakala (House of the Sun), by far the largest known, is from 25 to 30 miles in circumference, from 2000 to 3000 feet deep, and stands 10,000 feet above sea level. Within this huge pit, about 16 basins of old volcanoes, whose ridges formed concentric circles, have been counted. Good harbors are few. The chief is that of Honolulu, in Oahu, with 22½ feet of water in its shallowest parts. On the same island is Puuloa, an immense basin, with 12 feet of water on the bar at low tides. During the prevalence of the trade wind, which blows southwest for about nine months of the year, the south shores of the islands afford safe anchorage almost everywhere.

At Honolulu, the extremes of temperature in the shade during the 12 months are 90° and 50°, and the diurnal range is 12°. Rains brought by the northeast tradewind are frequent on the mountains; but on the leeward side of the islands little rain falls, and the sun is rarely obscured by the clouds. The soil, the constituent parts of which are mainly scoriæ, decomposed lava, and sand, is generally thin and poor. This, however, is not universally the case. At the bases of the mountains and in the valleys, where abrasion, disintegration, and the accumulation of vegetable mould have gone on for ages, there are extensive tracts as fertile as they are beautiful. The islands produce fine pasturage in abundance, and large herds are bred and fattened to supply meat to the whalers and merchant ships. The upland slopes of the mountains are clothed with dense forests; and lower down are grassy plains and sugar and coffee plantations. Basalt, compact lava, coral rock, and sandstone are used for building purposes. No metals occur. Several of the islands, especially Hawaii and Kaui, are well supplied with rivers, which, from the size and conformation of the group, are necessarily small, but afford great facilities for irrigation. Vast numbers of semi-wild horses roam the islands, and while they consume the pasturage and break down the fences, are of little use. The indigenous fauna is small, and consists mainly of swine, dogs, rats, a bat that flies by day, birds of beautiful plumage, but for the most part songless. Among the indigenous trees and plants are the sugar-cane, banana, plantain, cocoanut, candle-nut, various palms, the taro, a succulent root which formed the staple of the food of the natives, and is still generally used, the cloth-plant, and the *ti*, the roots of which were baked and eaten, while the leaves were used for thatching huts. Cattle and other useful and foreign animals and plants were introduced by Vancouver and other navigators. In 1860 there were 30,000 mules and semi-wild horses in the kingdom.

The government of Hawaii is a constitutional monarchy.

The public revenue during the biennial period ending March 31, 1874, was 1,136,524 dollars; the public expenditure, 1,192,512 dollars. The public debt, at the same date, 355,050 dollars.

The principal exports during the year 1874 were: Sugar, 24,567,000 pounds; rice, 1,188,000 pounds; coffee, 75,000 pounds; pulu, 418,000 pounds; tallow, 126,000 pounds; wool, 400,000 pounds; hides, 94,575. Total value, 1,839,000 dollars. The imports during the same year amounted in value to 1,310,000 dollars.

Of 115 vessels that entered the port of Honolulu during 1874, 64 were American, 30 English, 15 Hawaiian, etc.

Commission from THE HAWAIIAN ISLANDS to the International Exhibition:

W. L. MOEHONUA, Minister of the Interior and President of the Commission.
HON. S. G. WILDER, Privy Councillor of State.
HON. J. U. KAWAINUI, Privy Councillor of State.
ELISHA H. ALLEN, JR., Hawaiian Consul General, New York.
H. R. HITCHCOCK, Inspector General of Schools, Hawaiian Islands, and Special Agent of Hawaii on Centennial Commission.
REV. SAMUEL C. DAMAN.
MR. WILLIAM TUFTS BRIGHAM.

BRAZIL.

BRAZIL is the most extensive state of South America. Towards the interior, it borders on all the other states of that continent except Chili and Buenos Ayres—on Uruguay, the Argentine Confederation, Paraguay, Bolivia, Peru, Ecuador, New Granada, Venezuela, and English, Dutch, and French Guiana; while its seaboard, beginning about 200 miles to the north of the Amazon, and reaching to within the same distance of the Plata, projects into the Atlantic fully 1000 miles to the east of the direct line between its two extremes. This immense country extends between latitude 5° 10′ north and 46° 10′ south, and between longitude 35° and 70° west, being, in round numbers, 2600 miles long and 2500 broad. The area, according to official accounts, is 3,100,000 square miles, with a population, in 1872, of 12,000,000. including 1,683,684 slaves, and consisting of aboriginals, Africans, and Europeans, the first being proportionately fewer than in most parts of America.

Brazil differs in many respects from most of the other divisions of the new continent. It knows nothing of the volcanoes and earthquakes of the Pacific coast; with winds blowing constantly from the Atlantic Ocean, it is exempted from those droughts which are always blighting one or other of the slopes of the Andes, the remoter slope in Peru and Chili, and the nearer in Buenos Ayres and Patagonia; its mines, again, are as famous for gold and diamonds as those of the western Cordilleras for silver. In its hydrography, Brazil contrasts unfavorably with the other divisions. While the Amazon and the Plata, the Mississippi and the St. Lawrence—not to mention countless rivers of inferior magnitude on both shores—are for the most part practicable almost to their sources, the streams of Brazil, with the exception of the Amazon, are mostly impeded throughout by cataracts and shallows, thus counterbalancing, as it were, its matchless seaward facilities by the deficiencies of its inland communications. Further, the most navigable of these streams, instead of entering the open sea, mingle their waters with those of the Plata or of the Amazon—the Parana and the Uruguay joining the former, and the Madeira, the Tapojos, the Zingu, and the Tocantins, the latter; and even among those that do send their tribute at once to the ocean, a similar direction is sometimes impressed by the dividing ridges—the San Francisco, for instance, by far the largest of them, running to the northward parallel with the southeast coast through 11° of latitude, and leaving only 4° of longitude for its remaining course to the Atlantic. These hydrographic peculiarities must be the more strongly felt, inasmuch as a humid surface and a luxuriant vegetation conspire to render ordinary roads all but impossible.

Among the mineral treasures, besides gold and diamonds, already mentioned, iron of superior quality is abundant; and salt, also, is extensively produced in saline marshes by the alternate processes, according to the season, of inundation and evaporation. The productions of the soil are, of course, equally various and rich. The cotton is naturally excellent, and the tea-plant of China has been introduced, though hitherto with indifferent success. The exports necessarily vary in different sections of the country. From the north, they are coffee, cotton, cocoa, sugar, and tobacco; from the south, hides, tallow, horns, etc.; and from the middle, drugs, diamonds, gold dust, dyes, rice, manioc, tapioca, spirits, and rosewood.

The total value of the imports into Brazil, including bullion and specie, averaged about $91,000,000 in the five years 1869—1873, and that of the exports, during the same period, likewise including bullion and specie, about $110,000,000.

The executive authority is vested in the Emperor, who, besides being aided by a council of state, must act through responsible ministers. The legislature consists of two chambers, which sit four months every year. Both the deputies and the senators, who must have annual incomes respectively of 800 milrees and 1600, are indirectly elected by voters who must possess 200 milrees per annum—the former for four years, and the latter for life. The senate, however, appears to represent the crown as well as the people, inasmuch as each constituency merely nominates three individuals for his majesty's choice of one. Justices of the peace, also, are appointed by the respective communities; and in the courts generally, whether civil or criminal, there prevails trial by jury.

The budget for the year ending June 30th, 1876, calculates the receipts at 107,-133,070 milrees, and the expenditures at 102,634,053 milrees.* The public debt, on the 1st of April, 1875, was, including paper money, 664,739,395 milrees.

In a vote passed by the House of Congress, June, 1869, the strength of the standing army was fixed at 30,000 on the peace footing, and at 60,000 on the war footing. There were actually under arms, according to official reports, at the end of April, 1874, 28,933 troops, of which number 2397 were in garrison in Paraguay.

The imperial navy consisted, in 1875, of 61 men-of-war, carrying 230 guns, and crews aggregating 4136.

The empire possessed, at the end of 1873, railways of a total length of 714 English miles, open for traffic. There were railways of an aggregate length of 397 miles in course of construction at the end of June, 1874. There were, at the beginning of the year 1874, telegraph lines to the extent of 3375 miles. The number of offices was 74 at the same date. The post office carried 12,251,000 letters in the year 1873, of which number 6,548,000 came from or to Rio de Janeiro, the capital.

Commission from BRAZIL to the International Exhibition:

HIS HIGHNESS, GASTON D'CRLEANS, Conde d' Eu, Marshal of the Army, President.
VISCOUNT DE JAGUARY, 1st Vice-President.
VISCOUNT DE BONN-RETIRO, 2d Vice-President.
VISCOUNT DE SOUZA FRANCO.
JOAQUIN ANTONIO DE AZEVEDO.
HIS EXCELLENCY, A. P. DE CARVALHO BORGES, Envoy Extraordinary and Minister Plenipotentiary of His Majesty the Emperor of Brazil.
FELLIPE LOPES NETTO, Vice-President.
DR. JOSE DE SALDANHA.
DR. NICOLAS JOAQUIM MOREIRO.
PEDRO PAES LEME.
CAPT. LUIZ DE SALDANHA, Naval Attaché.
DR. J. M. DE SILVA COUTINHA.
MR. B. F. TORREAS DE BANOS, Secretary of Legation.

* The milreis = 1000 reis, 54½ cents.

ARGENTINE REPUBLIC.

THE Argentine Republic—the confederation of the Rio de la Plata, or River of Silver, South America—is a federal union of fourteen provinces and three large territories, covering an almost unbroken plain of 1,200,000 square miles, with a population of about 2,000,000 inhabitants. It extends from 22° south latitude to the straits of Magellan, and from 59° west longitude to the Andes.

Each province has its own legislature, courts of justice, and political government; but civil, penal, and commercial laws are common to all the provinces, codes of such laws having been issued by the congress of the confederation.

The President of the republic is elected for a term of six years by the representatives of the provinces, and is not eligible for re-election. The Vice-president, elected in the same manner, fills the office of chairman of the Senate, but has otherwise no political power. The President is commander-in-chief of the troops, and appoints to all civil, military, and judicial offices; but he and his ministers are responsible for their acts, and liable to impeachment before the Senate by accusation of the House of Representatives. Legislative power is vested in a Senate, of members elected by the provincial legislatures, two from each province, and a House of Representatives, elected by the people, and apportioned to each province according to population. The senators hold their office for nine years, and the representatives for three.

The chief exports of the country are wool, hides, salt beef, and tallow; but its resources embrace all the products of the tropical and temperate zones, as may be seen by the catalogue of its exhibits.

The farming stock of the republic is estimated at 15,000,000 horned cattle, 4,000,000 horses, and 80,000,000 sheep, whose aggregate value cannot fall short of $200,000,000, gold, yielding about $50,000,000 of export produce per annum.

The total trade may be estimated at $100,000,000 per annum. In 1874 the imports amounted to $55,961,117, against over $71,000,000 in the previous year. The exports amounted to $43,104,712, against $45,869,314 in 1873. The decrease in imports and exports was caused by a severe commercial crisis, from which the country is just recovering.

The annual revenue amounted to $20,217,231 in 1873, but the crisis reduced it in 1874 to $16,090,661, or over $2,000,000 less than in 1872, and nearly $4,500,000 less than in 1873. The general expenditures in 1874 reached the sum of $28,596,006. The total debt in January, 1875, was $68,416,043.

The regular army numbers 10,807 men, divided as follows: cavalry 4800, infantry 4400, artillery 400, and 1173 special troops. The navy is composed of 26 vessels, among them 2 ironclads and 6 gunboats, with crews amounting in all to 900.

The capital of the republic is provisionally situated at the city of Buenos Ayres, capital of the province of the same name.

(The statistics given above have been furnished by the commission of the Argentine Republic.)

A network of railways, constructed mainly at the expense of the State, has been in progress for several years. At the end of the year 1873 there were 664 miles open for traffic, and 642 miles of State railways in course of construction. There were besides, at the end of 1873, railways of a total length of 1997 miles, sanctioned by the government, including an international line from Buenos Ayres to Chili, of 894 miles.

At the end of September, 1873, there were 4170 miles of telegraph lines in operation. The total length of telegraph wires at the same date was 8267 miles. The number of telegraphic dispatches during the same year was 170,079.

The post office, in the year 1873, carried 1,493,700 parcels and packets, and 4,574,188 letters. The number of letters carried doubled in the five years from 1869 to 1873.

Commission from the ARGENTINE REPUBLIC to the International Exhibition:

CARLOS CARRANZA, President.
EDWARD SHIPPEN, Vice-President.
EDW. T. DAVISON, Treasurer, Consul-General.
DIEGO DE CASTRO, Secretary.
E. MARA DAVISON, Deputy Member.

Central Committee.

ERNESTO OLLENDORF, President.
JULIO VICTORICA, Secretary.

EDUARDO OLIVERA,
ONESIMO LEGUIZAMON,
DIEGO DE LA FUENTE,
LINO PALCOIS.

RICARDO NEWTON,
LEONARDO PEREYRA,
JOSE M. JURAFDO,
EMILIO DUPORTAL.

CHILI.

CHILI lies wholly between the water-shed of the Andes and the shores of the Pacific, stretching coastwise from Bolivia to Patagonia, in latitude 25° 30′ to 43° 20′ south, and longitude 69° to 74° west, having an extreme length of about 1240 miles and an average breadth of fully 120. Within these limits, however, lies the virtually independent Araucania, comprising most of the mainland to the left of the Biobio, while the southern portion is confined chiefly to Chiloe and its archipelago. Chili is divided into thirteen provinces, of which, including certain outlying dependencies in Patagonia, the aggregate area has been officially stated at nearly 140,000 square miles, and the population in 1874 at 2,068,447. Chiloe, the insular province of Chili, is separated from the rest of the republic, or rather from Patagonia, by the Gulf of Ancud, extending in south latitude from 41° 40′ to 43° 20′, and in west longitude from 73° to 74°. The province, which, in 1874, numbered 64,536 inhabitants, contains, in addition to Chili proper, about 60 islets, of which some 30 are uninhabited. The predominant rocks of Chili are crystalline and metamorphic. They form the range of the Andes, except in those districts in which active volcanoes exist, where they are covered with recent volcanic rocks. They occupy also the whole of the level ground between the mountain range and the shores of the Pacific, with the exception of a narrow stretch of palæozoic fossiliferous strata which run along the coast south from Santiago for a distance of 300 miles. The coast-line of Chili is being continually altered from the elevation of the whole country to an extent of at least 1200 miles along the Pacific shores, produced by volcanic agency.

Physically, the continental portion of the republic presents many singularities. Of all the maritime regions on the globe, it is perhaps the most isolated. On every side but the sea, and that sea very remote from the main thoroughfares of commerce, it is beset by difficulties of communication. With the lonely wilderness of Patagonia to the south, and the dreary desert of Atacama on the north, it is bounded on the east by a mountain chain which, altogether impracticable in winter, can be crossed, even in summer, only by a few passes ranging between 12,450 feet and 14,370 feet in elevation. Moreover, this strip between the Andes and the Pacific is broken into plateaus in the interior, and valleys on the coast, by two longitudinal ranges, with numerous lateral spurs; while, throughout the length and breadth, the general level gradually descends, as well to the south as to the west. In point of mere temperature, so rugged a surface, covering fully 15° of latitude, and attaining an altitude of more than four miles within about 2° of longitude, must present nearly every possible variety. Through the reciprocal action of the Andes and the prevailing winds, the rain-fall graduates itself, with something of mathematical regularity, from the parching skies of the north to the drenching clouds of the south, a graduation which, disturbed merely by the melting of the mountain snows, is, in a great measure, necessarily reflected in the condition and magnitude of the countless water-courses. Hence the rivers to the north of the Maypo, which enters the Pacific near latitude 34°, are but inconsiderable streams; while, further to the south, the Maule, the Biobio, and the Calacalla are all to some extent navigable.

From the cause last mentioned, different districts vary remarkably in their productions. To the north of the Coquimbo, about latitude 30°, is chiefly an arid waste, redeemed, however, from being valueless by its mines; and to the south of the Biobio, about latitude 37°, timber and pasturage divide the soil between them. The intermediate centre alone is fitted for agriculture, yielding, besides maize and hemp, European grains and fruits in abundance. Notwithstanding all the varieties and vicissitudes of climate, the country may claim to be, on the whole, extremely healthy. The manufactures are earthenwares, copperwares, linens, cordage, soap, leather, and brandy; and, in addition to the wheat and metals already specified, the exports, especially from the south, embrace tallow, hides, jerked beef, and live stock.

The public debt of Chili, at the beginning of 1874, was 48,149,850 pesos (or doilars). The budget for 1875 stated the expenditures at 16,474,890, and the receipts at 16,440,000 pesos.

The army consisted, in 1874, of 3516 men, the force comprising 2000 infantry, 712 cavalry, and 804 artillery. The navy numbered 10 vessels, carrying 34 guns.

The imports, for 1874, were 38,810,000 pesos, and the exports, during the same year, were 36,510,000 pesos. The commercial navy of Chili consisted, in 1872, of 250 vessels of 58,230 tons burthen, with 2900 sailors.

In 1875 there were 991 kilometres of railway in operation; of these, 628.6 belonged to the State and 362.4 to companies.

The work of the post office, for 1873, was 5,116,797 letters and 6,233,916 newspapers, etc.

There were, at the same time, 55 telegraph offices. The length of lines was 3729 kilometres; of wires, 4909 kilometres. Number of despatches, in 1873, 265,318.

Commission from CHILI to the International Exhibition:

Resident Commissioners.

SR. DON ADOLFO YBANEZ, Envoy Extraordinary and Minister Plenipotentiary of Chili.

EDWARD SHIPPEN, ESQ., Consul and President.

DR. J. PATTERSON Burd, Secretary and Treasurer.

SR. FRANCISCO GONALEZ ERRAZURIZ, Secretary of Chilian Legation.

Special Commissioners.

SR. DON EDUARDO SEVE,
SR. RAFAEL MASEULLI,
SR. E. GERRA,
SR. LOUIS BUFFE.

Home Commission.

SR. RAFAEL LARRAIN, President.
SR. MAXIMIANO ERRAZURIZ.
SR. IGNACIO DOMEYKO.
SR. ARMANDO PHILLIPPI.
FRANCISCO SOLANO ASTA BURUAGO.
SR. RAMON BARROS.
SR. EUGENIO FIGUEORA.

PERU.

PERU is an important maritime republic in South America, bounded on the N. by Ecuador, on the W. by the Pacific, on the S. and S.E. by Bolivia, and on the E. by Brazil. It lies in lat. 3° 25′ to 21° 30′ S., and in long. 68° to 81° 20′ W. The general outline resembles a triangle, the base of which is formed by the boundary-line between Peru and Ecuador on the north. Its area is estimated at upward of 500,000 square miles, and its population at 2,500,000. The area of Peru, however, can only be given approximately, as, on the east side of the Andes and between the Amazon and the Purus, there is a wide and unexplored expanse of country, upon which both Peru and Brazil have claims which have not yet been determined. The country is 1100 miles in length, 780 miles in extreme breadth along the northern boundary, but is little more than 50 miles wide in the extreme south. Following the general direction, and not including windings, the coast-line is 1660 miles in length. The shores are in general rocky and steep ; in the south lofty cliffs rise from the sea, and in some places the water close inshore has a depth of from 70 to 80 fathoms. Farther north, however, sandy beaches occur, and in the extreme north the shores are often low and sandy and covered with brushwood. Owing to the comparative unfrequency of bays and inlets along the coast, the harbors are few and unimportant. Those of Callao (the port of Lima) and Payta afford the most secure anchorage, and the others are Trujiilo, Cañete, Pisco, Cammaná, Islay, Ilo, Arica and Inquique.

The islands on the Peruvian coast, although valuable, are extremely few in number and small in extent. In the north are the Lobos Islands; on their eastern and more sheltered sides they are covered with guano. The Chincha Islands, famous as a source of supply for guano, also form a group of three, and are situated in the Bay of Pisco, about twelve miles from the mainland, and in lat. 13° to 14° S., long. 76° and 77° W. They lie in a line running north and south, and are called the North, Middle, and South Islands, respectively. Each island presents, on the eastern side, a wall of precipitous rock, with rocky pinnacles in the centre, and with a general slope toward the western shore. The cavities and inequalities of the surface are filled with guano, and this material covers the western slopes of the islands to within a few feet of the water's edge. There is no vegetation.

The surface of Peru is divided into three distinct and well-defined tracts or belts, the climates of which are of every variety from torrid heat to arctic cold, and the productions of which range from the stunted herbage of the high mountain-slopes, to the oranges and citrons, the sugar-canes and cottons, of the luxuriant tropical valleys. These three regions are the *Coast*, the *Sierra*, and the *Montaña*, The *Coast* is a narrow strip of sandy desert between the base of the Western Cordillera and the sea, and extending along the whole length of the country. This tract, varying in breadth from thirty to sixty miles, slopes to the shore with an uneven surface, marked by arid ridges from the Cordillera, and with a rapid descent.

It is, for the most part, a barren waste of sand, traversed, however, by numerous valleys of astonishing fertility, most of which are watered by streams that have their sources high on the slopes of the Cordillera. In the coast-region, properly so called, rain is unknown. This is caused by the coast of Peru being within the region of perpetual south-east trade-winds. The want of rain is compensated for, to some extent, by abundant and refreshing dews which fall during the night. The climate of the coast is modified by the cool winds. In the valleys the heat, though considerable, is not oppressive. The highest temperature observed at Lima in summer is 85°, the lowest in winter is 61° Fahr.

The *Sierra* embraces all the mountainous region between the western base of the maritime Cordillera and the eastern base of the Andes, or the Eastern Cordillera. The principal physical features of the *Sierra* are: 1. The plain of Titicaca, partly in Peru and partly in Bolivia. It is enclosed between the two main ridges of the Andes, and is said to have an area of 30,000 miles. In its centre is the great Lake Titicaca, 12,846 feet above sea-level, or 1600 feet above the loftiest mountain pass (the Col of Mont Cervin) of Europe. The lake is 115 miles long, from 30 to 60 miles broad, from 70 to 180 feet deep, and 400 miles in circumference. Its shape is irregular; it contains many islands, and several peninsulas abut upon its waters. 2. The Knot of Cuzco. The mountain-chains which girdle the plain of Titicaca trend toward the north-west, and form what is called the Knot of Cuzco. The Knot comprises six minor mountain chains, and has an area thrice larger than that of Switzerland. Here the valleys enjoy an Indian climate and are rich in tropical productions; to the north and east of the Knot extend luxuriant tropical forests, while the numberless mountain slopes are covered with waving crops of wheat, barley, and other cereals, and with potatoes, and higher up extend pasture-lands, where the vicuña and alpaca feed.

The *Montaña* or central region has an elevation of 12,000 feet above the sea-level, and forms a portion of the great central plain of South America. The virgin soil of the Montaña is of amazing fertility, while its climate, though not oppressively hot, is healthy. The forests consist of huge trees, of which some are remarkable for the beauty of their wood, others for their valuable gums and resins, and others as timber trees. A rank undergrowth of vegetation covers the country, and the trees are often chained together and festooned with parasites and closely-matted creepers. In this region, for the most part undisturbed by the voice of man, civilized or savage, animal life flourishes in endless variety, and birds of the brightest plumage flit among the foliage. Among the products which are yielded here in spontaneous abundance are the inestimable Peruvian bark, India-rubber, gum-copal, vanilla, indigo, copaiba, balsam, cinnamon, sarsaparilla, ipecacuanha, vegetable wax, etc. On the western fringe of the Montana, where there are still a few settlements, tobacco, sugar, coffee, cotton, and chocolate are cultivated with complete success.

The hydrography of Peru may be said to be divided into three systems—those of Lake Titicaca, the Pacific, and the Amazon. The streams that flow into Lake Titicaca are few and inconsiderable. The rivers, which, having their sources in the Western Cordillera, flow west into the Pacific, are about sixty in number; but many of them are dry in summer, and even the more important are rapid and shallow, have a short course, are not navigable even for canoes, and are mainly used for the purpose of irrigation. All the great rivers of Peru are tributaries of the Amazon. The Marañon, rising between the Eastern and Western Cordilleras, and flowing tortuously to the north-north-west, is generally considered to be the headwater of the Amazon. The Huallaga rises near the town of Huanuco, and flows northward to the Amazon. It is navigable for 600 miles, the head of its navigation (for canoes) being at Tingo Maria, within 100 miles of its source. The Yucayali, or Ucayali, an immense river, enters the Amazon 210 miles below the Huallaga. Its tributaries and upper waters, among which are the Pampas and the Apurimac, drain the greater portion of the Peruvian Sierra. The Purus, which reaches to the valleys of Paucartambo, within sixty miles of Cuzco, has not yet been explored. The Andes abound in mines of gold, silver, copper, lead, bismuth, etc.; and in the Montaña gold is said to exist in abundance in veins, and in pools on the margins of rivers.

But besides the precious metals, Peru possesses other most important mineral resources. In addition to the guano, to which allusion has already been made, another important article of national wealth is nitrate of soda, which is found in immense quantities in the province of Tarapaca. This substance, which is a powerful fertilizer, is calculated to cover, in this province alone, an area of fifty square leagues. Here, also, great quantities of borax are found. The trade in guano, nitre, and borax is entirely in the hands of the government.

The vegetable productions of Peru are of every variety, embracing all the products both of temperate and tropical climes. The European cereals and vegetables are grown with perfect success, together with maize, rice, pumpkins, tobacco, coffee, sugar-cane, cotton, etc. Fruits of the most delicious flavor are grown in endless variety. Cotton, for which the soil and climate of Peru are admirably adapted, is now produced here in gradually increasing quantity. The land suited to the cultivation of this plant is of immense extent, and the quality of the cotton grown is excellent. The animals comprise those of Europe, together with the lama and its allied species.

The principal items of export in 1870 were: Guano, 482,299 tons; nitrate of soda, 147,200 quintals, valued at 6,624,000 soles;* quinine, 11,921 quintals, valued at 810,641 soles; silver, 1,120,118 soles; hides and skins valued at 530,403 soles; wool valued at 396,610 soles.

The merchant navy in 1869 comprised 95 vessels, aggregating 9596 tons burden; included in this were 11 steamers of a total burden of 435 tons.

The constitution of Peru is modeled on that of the United States, the legislative power being vested in a Senate and House of Representatives, the former composed of deputies of the provinces, two for each, and the latter of representatives nominated by the electoral colleges of provinces and parishes, at the rate of one member for every 20,000 inhabitants. The parochial electoral colleges choose deputies to the provincial colleges, who in turn send representatives to Congress. In the session of 1875 the Senate was composed of 44 and the House of Representatives of 110 members.

The executive power is entrusted to a president, assisted by a vice-president, both elected by popular vote and serving for a term of four years.

By the terms of the constitution of 1867 there exists absolute political but not religious freedom, the charter prohibiting the public exercise of any other religion than the Roman Catholic, which is declared the religion of the State.

The public debt is divided into an internal debt, which in 1872 was about £2,500,000, and the foreign debt, which in 1875 amounted to £34,713,980. The public income during 1872 was 58,982,851 soles; the public expenditures during the same year 57,913,764 soles.

The army comprises: Infantry, 5600; cavalry, 1200; artillery, 2000; total, 8800 men. The navy consists of 6 iron-clads, one of which is a 14-gun frigate, 2 monitors of 3 guns each, and 3 other vessels of 2, 2, and 14 guns respectively; besides which there are 6 steamships of 2, 2, 4, 4, 14, and 30 guns.

A system of railways designed mainly to develop the exploitation of the mineral wealth of the country, including important mines of nitrate of soda, has been in course of construction for several years. At the end of June, 1875, there were open for traffic or in course of construction lines of State railways of a total length of 1097 English miles. There were also in course of construction at the end of June, 1875, railways of a total length of 600 English miles, to be completed in 1877–80. The most important of these are a line from Lima to Oroya, 222 miles in length, and another, offering vast engineering difficulties, 187 miles long, from Arequipa to Puno, across the summit of the Cordillera de los Andes.

There were in 1874 telegraph lines of a total length of 608 miles.

Commission from PERU to the International Exhibition:

JOSE CARLOS TRACY, President.	ANTONIO HERNANDEZ, Chief of Installation.
JUAN JOSE BARRIL.	ENRIQUE VALIENTE, Secretary.
WILLIAM RUSSELL GRACE.	

* One sol = 96½ cents, gold.

MEXICO.

THE Mexican Republic extends between latitude 15° to 32° 42′ north, and from 88° 54′ 30″ to 119° 25′ 30″ west longitude (meridian of Paris), or from 12° 21′ on the east to 18° on the west of the City of Mexico, and is bounded on the north by the United States, on the south by Guatemala, on the east by the Gulf of Mexico, and on the west by the Pacific Ocean.

The country measures in its greatest length, from the conflux of the Gila and Colorado Rivers to the bar of Ocos, which is the lower end of the State of Chiapas, 2933 kilometres, by 1733.2 kilometres in width, from the mouth of the Rio Grande to that of the Rio del Fuerte. Its coast-line embraces 8272.47 kilometres. The area of the Mexican territory amounts to 1,972,648 square kilometres.

Mexico is a mountainous country. The *Cordillera*, which can be considered as a development of the Andes, that start in Patagonia, South America, occupies all the country, forming, in its gradual descent toward the coasts, large table-lands and fertile valleys. At the point where this Cordillera reaches the territory of New Mexico it is divided into two ramifications, the eastern one parallel to that of Lower California, its principal summits being the *Pico de Orizava* and *Cofre de Perote*, and the western one, which becomes entangled with the other chains running toward the Nevado de Toluca. This point of intersection is marked by the volcano of *Colima*. The eastern chain has its nucleus in the *Zempoaltépec*, whose several ramifications extend over the State of Oaxaca, with the exception of the principal branch, which stretches over the State of Guerrero. Between these two mountainous chains there is another of no less importance, which includes the beautiful mountains Popocatapetl and Ixtaccihuatl. The latter, the Cofre de Perote, and the White Pick of Toluca are the highest peaks of the Mexican Andes.

The northern part of the republic, between latitude 23° 30′ and 32° 42′ north, belongs to the temperate zone, and the southern portion, included between 15° and 32° 30′, to the torrid zone. Owing partially to this division and to the difference in the level of the soil, there is in Mexico a great variety of climate. The warm temperature is observed in the region extending from the coast to the height of 3000 feet; the temperate, from the height of 3000 feet to 5000 feet; and the cold climate, from 5000 feet to the highest summits.

The population of Mexico amounts to 8,743,000, in the following proportions:

European,	2,331,000
Indigenous,	1,750,000
Of a mixed origin,	4,662,000
Total,	8,743,000

The following list shows which are the principal centres of population:

CITIES.	STATES.	POPULATION.
Mexico,	District of Mexico,	200,000
Leon,	Guanajuato,	90,000
Guadalajara,	Jalisco,	75,000
Puebla,	Puebla,	65,000
Guanajuato.	Guanajuato,	63,000
Queretaro,	Queretaro,	48,000
Celaya,	Guanajuato,	37,000
Orizaba,	Vera Cruz,	37,000
San Miguel Allende,	Guanajuato.	35,000

A more complete idea of the manner in which the population is distributed can be arrived at by the following statistical table:

NAME OF STATES IN THEIR GEOGRAPHICAL ORDER.	SQUARE LEAGUES.	POPULATION.	INHABITANTS PER SQUARE LEAGUE.
Souvra,	11,953	147,133	12
Chihuahua,	15,534	179,971	11
Coahuila,	8,692	67,691	8
Nuevo Leon,	2,119	171,000	81
Tamaulipas,	4,228	108,514	26
San Luis Potosi,	4,262	397,735	93
Zacatecas,	3,922	398,977	101
Aguas Calientes,	327	86,576	264
Durango,	6,921	173,942	27
Sinaloa,	3,825	161,157	42
Jalisco,	7,224	924,580	128
Colima,	353	48,649	137
Michoacan,	3,188	618,072	193
Guanajuato,	1,642	874,000	532
Queretaro,	506	166,643	329
Mexico,	1,416	599,810	323
Hidalgo,	1,251	404,207	323
Morelos,	280	121,409	433
Guerrero,	3,574	270,000	76
Puebla,	1,735	830,000	478
Tlaxacala,	221	117,941	533
Vera Cruz,	4,047	380,976	94
Oaxaca,	4,035	601,850	149
Tabasco,	1,876	83,707	44
Chiapas,	2,474	193,987	78
Campeche,	3,848	86,453	22
Yucatan,	4,818	282,634	59
Federal District,	12.56	225,000	
Lower California Territory,	8,709	21,000	2
	112,362.56	8,743,614	

The sugar and coffee culture, and the industries of which the agave plant is a basis, deserve particular mention. Numerous metalliferous veins are found in the mountains of the Sierra Madre and its different ramifications. These mineral districts contain not only the precious ores for which Mexico has been particularly noted, but also iron, tin, copper, and some other metals of great industrial value. Bismuth, having become scarce in former years, was found at last in the States of San Luis Potosi, Sinaloa, Queretaro, and Zacatecas. Discoveries of coal, precious opals, and quicksilver ores have also been made, the former in the States of Puebla and Vera Cruz, the latter in the States of Queretaro and Guerrero. The district of Huitzuco has proved the most abundant in mercury, and during the last year has supplied the Mexican market with large quantities of this useful metal.

The geological formations which are found in the mineral veins of Mexico consist chiefly of the three following classes of rocks:

1. Compact mesozoic limestone.
2. Slate and sandstone.
3. Metalliferous porphyry, which probably corresponds to the Tertiary period.

As types of these three formations should be mentioned those found respectively in the States of Queretaro, Guanajuato, and Hidalgo. Many mountains of the above-mentioned types, and containing metalliferous veins, can be seen in almost all the States of the Republic. The argentiferous galenite and tetrahedrite prevail in the first of the aforesaid formations; the polybasite and the pyrargirite in the second; and sulphuret of silver, argentiferous galenite, and blende in the third. The collections exhibited in the Mexican Department of the Main Building include some samples of these mineral compounds, and of rocks useful as building and ornamental materials, among which the beautiful calcareous slates from the District of Tecali (State of Puebla) are worthy of especial mention.

Among the advantages which industry and trade have secured in Mexico, the double line of railroad from the principal port to the capital, and the exceptional and liberal tariffs established for goods intended for exportation, ought to be considered as the most beneficial. One of the aforesaid lines (via Orizaba) is complete, and has been in operation for several years; the other, which connects Vera Cruz with the town of Jalapa and with some of the agricultural districts of the State of Puebla, will soon be completed. The Mexican Congress has made very liberal grants for the construction of three railways intended to connect the city of Mexico with the northern frontier, and the districts more abundant in tropical products with the city of Puebla. Between this city and the trunk line of the Vera Cruz Railroad there is a branch line in operation. Another railroad connecting the capital with the city of Toluca is under construction, and in operation as far as the town of Tlalnepantla. Another line connects the port of Vera Cruz with the town of Medellin. The capital is connected by electric wires with the principal cities and with the ports and coasts of the republic.

The United States of Mexico maintain an active trade with the following nations, viz.: England, France, United States, Germany, Spain and Cuba, New Granada, Guatemala, Nicaragua, and on smaller scale with Belgium, Ecuador, and Italy.

The imports of foreign goods during the fiscal year ending June, 1873, amounted to $29,062,406.94, taking as a basis the market value of the articles. All the articles are registered in the custom-house tariff of duties under eleven heads, viz.:

	INVOICE VALUE.	MARKET VALUE.	DUTIES.
1. Cottons,	$7,311,646.03	$10,531,970.15	$4,734,340.87
2. Groceries,	3,437,525.43	5,191,788.62	2,012,509.30
3. Articles free from duty,	2,411,593.73	3,354,259.77	
4. Mercury,	1,356,600.31	2,184,014.56	763,908.87
5. Miscellaneous,	1,434,216.56	2,035,609.63	1,055,828.05
6. Linen and hemp,	993,362.76	1,452,978.28	564,125.89
7. Wools,	1,038,044.31	1,427,867.58	644,496.77
8. Mixtures,	998,831.81	1,417,427.61	605,146.49
9. Silks,	419,017.10	588,911.32	267,404.71
10. Earthenware, crystal, and glass	344,936.45	577,510.82	206,547.31
11. Drugs,	173,852.32	300,069.05	131,011.38
	$19,919,632.81	$29,062,406.94	$10,989,319.64

The value of goods exported amounts to $31,473,607.24. The exports are arranged under two heads:

Minerals and metals,	$25,373,673.78
Agricultural and industrial products,	6,317,477.06
Total,	$31,691,150.84

Under the first heading are:

Silver coin,	$22,602,493.33
Solid silver,	1,512,616.94
Gold coin,	640,270.97
Solid gold,	288,578.21
Ores and mineral earths,	222,854.00
Silver amalgam,	39,251.78
Lead,	30,831.00
Copper,	17,137.94

Under the second heading:

Skins,	$1,546,869.43
Henequen,	1,049,202.58
Building and color woods,	1,042,586.31
Coffee,	532,912.86
Vanilla,	414,038.40
Cochineal,	276,699.30
Cattle,	209,960.00
Tobacco,	132,984.75
Orchilla (Rocsella tintorea),	128,450.09
Precious pearls,	109,300.00
Caoutchouc,	93,052.88
Sarsaparilla,	90.862.18
Wool,	88,635.72
Indigo,	80,229.87
Jalap,	77.517.40
Cocoanuts,	46,000.00

The revenue of the General Government and the expenses of the Federal Administration amount to a yearly average of 20,000,000 dollars.

There have been 8103 schools established by the Government for the primary instruction of the people. In eighteen of the States attendance has been made compulsory.

The official data in regard to secondary and higher instruction are condensed in the following figures relating to the institutions of these two degrees, maintained by the Mexican government:

26 Preparatory Schools.
18 Colleges of Jurisprudence.
12 " " Engineering.
11 " " Medicine.
9 " " Pharmacy.
2 " " Navigation.
2 " " Agriculture.
2 " " Mining.
2 Conservatories of Art.
3 " " Music.
15 Ladies' Colleges.

The above list does not include a large number of establishments conducted by the clergy, benevolent societies, or private teachers.

Commission from MEXICO to the International Exhibition:

Commissioners.

MANUEL M. DE ZAMACONA.
MARIANO BARCENA.
ELENTERIO AVILA.
MANUEL CORELLA, Attache.
AURTRO YBANEZ, Engineer.
EDITH BORZELL, Engineer.
LLUTARCO ORNELAS, Acting Sect'y.
FERNANDO CAMACHO, Employe.
J. LEON CALDERON, Employe.

LIBERIA.

THE Republic of Liberia is situated on the West Coast of Africa, between the fourth and eighth degrees of north latitude, and extends along five hundred and twenty miles of the coast, from the English colony of Sierra Leone to the mouth of the San Pedro River. Its most interior settlement is some thirty miles from the sea-board. The land has been purchased in an open and honorable manner from the aboriginal owners, and there is no obstacle to the acquisition of additional territory inland until the heart of the great continent is reached.

Immediately on the sea-shore the land is generally low, but very soon becomes elevated, rising in gentle undulations or swells. The whole country is well wooded and watered. Timber suitable for building purposes, cabinet-work, and shipbuilding is abundant, as is also good water.

All tropical productions are readily raised in Liberia, many of them the entire year, and dug from the earth every month for use. The Lima bean, tomato, and egg-plant are indigenous and of several varieties, and yield abundantly. Fruits grow in a wild state and under cultivation. Oranges are especially fine. Nowhere is a better quality of sugar-cane produced. Liberia coffee is the richest known, always commanding the highest market price. Cotton, ginger, ground-nuts, arrow-root, pepper, and indigo are mainly raised by the American settlers. Palm-oil, made by the natives, ivory, camwood, gums, and hides are valuable articles of commerce exported from Liberia. Horses are little used on the coast, but are plentiful in the interior. Cows, goats, hogs, ducks, turkeys, and fowls are abundant. The rivers abound in shell and other fish.

The climate is uniformly sultry and moist, but the heat is not excessive; the thermometer in the wet season stands at about 71°, and in the dry at about 82°.

A very great impulse is perceptible in Liberian industry during the last thirteen years. The greatest success has, however, resulted from a natural capacity for agriculture, which is growing rapidly and promises at an early day to make the whole territory a vast coffee grove. A very superior quality of iron ore is found in all parts of the country and worked by the natives, and will be of great use in manufacture and trade. Three years ago a volcanic eruption disclosed many valuable minerals.

The American Colonization Society, to which Liberia owes its origin, was founded in Washington, D. C., December 21st, 1816. It has given passage more or less every year for the last fifty-five years to 15,098 persons of color, and it induced the government of the United States to settle in Liberia 5722 recaptured Africans, making a grand total of 20,820 persons to whom the society has given homes in that republic. Monrovia, at the mouth of the river Mesurado, is the capital, and has about 7000 inhabitants.

Some 600,000 natives residing on the territory of Liberia live mostly in their own towns, subject to their own headmen and their own laws, yet amenable to Liberian authority and having all the protection and privileges of citizens. Not a few have become such and creditably fill various public offices, while all are gradually acquiring the arts, comforts, and conveniences of civilized life.

The last tabular statement issued shows the previous year's imports of Liberia to have reached $209,423.88, and the exports $171,351.47. Since then Edward S.

Morris & Co., of Philadelphia, Pa., have introduced improved and patented coffee-hulling machinery and a steamer, the first on the St. Paul's River, thus greatly stimulating not only the production and transportation of coffee, but other valuable articles, for export. They have also there begun the manufacture of palm-oil soap and indigo. The commercial statistics of Liberia would therefore, if presented now, appear far more advantageously.

There are two Liberia newspapers, the "Liberia Advocate" and the "Interior." The former aims to discuss principles and point facts that will be useful to the country in every particular; the other is especially devoted to assisting intercourse and amity with the strange interior tribes, most of whom can read, while all are anxious for an English education. By a law of Liberia all parents are required to send their children to school. In some of the settlements the schools are good. A college, the materials and erection of which cost $20,000, is in operation at Monrovia. All the professors are colored men.

The State has good patent laws, hospitals, and saw-mills and lighthouses. All religious denominations are allowed, and there are several in each of the settlements. Quite a number of vessels have been built in the country and are owned, manned, and managed wholly by Liberians. Some of these have appeared in American and European ports loaded with Liberian and other African products.

The Constitution of Liberia very closely resembles that of the United States, and was adopted in convention on the 26th of July, 1847. The powers of government are vested in three departments, legislative, executive, and judicial. The legislative authority consists of a House of Representatives and a Senate, each of which has a negative on the other. The election of representatives is for two years. Two members from each county constitute the Senate, and are elected for four years. The executive power is vested in a President, chosen every two years. He is commander-in-chief of the army and navy, and makes treaties, two-thirds of the Senate concurring. With the advice and control of the Senate he appoints all public officers for whose appointment special provision is not made by law. There is also a Vice-president elected in the same manner, who is president of the Senate. The judicial power is placed in a Supreme Court and such subordinate courts as the legislature may from time to time establish.

Among the miscellaneous provisions of this Constitution is the following: "Section 13. The great object of founding these colonies being to provide a home for the despised and oppressed children of Africa, and to regenerate and enlighten that benighted continent, none but persons of color shall be admitted to citizenship in this republic."

Liberia has an earnest hope that this exhibition of her products will attract the attention of colored Americans and draw the large immigration needed. The country needs this more than anything else, and with it could be powerful and rich in ten years.

SPAIN.

SPAIN occupies the larger portion of the great peninsula which forms the southwest corner of the European continent, reaching farther south than any other European country, and farther west than any except Portugal. It is bounded on the north by the Bay of Biscay and by France, from which it is separated by the mountain ridge of the Pyrenees, on the east and south by the Mediterranean and Atlantic, and on the west by the Atlantic and Portugal. Greatest length, from Fuenterrabia on the north to Tarifa on the south, 560 miles; greatest breadth, from Cape Finisterre (Land's End), the extreme point on the west, to Cape Creuze, the extreme point on the east, about 650 miles; average breadth about 380 miles. Area, including the Balearic and Canary Isles, 196,031 English square miles; population (1870), 16,835,506. The country, including the Balearic and Canary Isles, was divided, in 1834, into 49 modern provinces, though the former division, into 14 kingdoms, states, or provinces, is still sometimes used.

The entire perimeter of the country is 2080 English miles, and the coast line, exclusive of windings, is 1317 miles long, of which 712 miles are formed by the Mediterranean, and 605 miles by the Atlantic. The north coast, from Fuenterrabia west to Cape Ortegal, is unbroken by any considerable indentation. A wall of rocks, varying in height from 30 to 300 feet, runs along this shore; but the water, which retains considerable depth close to the beach, is not interrupted to any unusual extent by islands or rocks. The northwest coast, from Cape Ortegal south to the mouth of the river Minho—which separates the Spanish province of Galicia from Portugal—though rock-bound, is less elevated, and is much more broken than the shores washed by the Bay of Biscay; and the indentations, the chief of which are Noya Arosa and Vigo Bays, form secure and spacious harbors. From the mouth of the Guadiana, on the south, to the Strait of Gibraltar, the coast line, though well defined, is low, sandy, and occasionally swampy. From Gibraltar to Cape Palos the shores, which are backed in part by the mountain range of the Sierra Nevada, are rocky and high (though flats occur at intervals), are unbroken by indentations, and comprise only two harbors, those of Cartagena and Malaga. A low, and for the most part sandy, coast extends north from Cape Palos, rising into rocky cliffs and bluffs in the vicinity of Denia, but extending in sandy flats from Denia to the mouth of the Ebro. From the mouth of this river north to the frontier of France the coast is alternately high and low, and its principal harbors are Barcelona and Rosas. The compactness and the isolation of this country, and its position between two seas, the most famous and commercially the most important in the world, are not more in its favor than the character of its surface, which is more diversified than that of any other country in Europe of equal extent. An immense plateau, the loftiest in the continent, occupies the central regions of Spain, and is bounded on the north and west by mountainous tracts, and on the northeast by the valley of the Ebro; on the east by tracts of land frequently low, but in some parts traversed by hill ranges; on the south by the valley of the Guadalquivir, which intervenes between it and the Sierra Nevada. This great plateau rises to the height of from 2000 to 3000 feet, and occupies upward of 90,000 square miles, or about half of the entire area of the country. The whole of the Pyrenean peninsula is divided by Spanish geographers into seven mountain ranges, of which the chief are: 1. The Cantabrian mountains and the Pyrenees, forming the most northern range; 2. The

Sierra de Guadarrama, separating Leon and Old Castile from Estremadura and New Castile, and rising in the peak of Penalara 7764 feet above sea level; 3. The Montes de Toledo, forming a part of the water-shed between the Tagus and the Guadiana; 4. The Sierra Morena, between the upper waters of the Guadiana and Guadalquivir; 5. The Sierra Nevada, running parallel with the shores of the Mediterranean, through Southern Murcia and Andalucia, and rising in its chief summits to loftier elevations than are found in any mountain system of Europe except that of the Alps. The several mountain ridges, or as they are called Cordilleras, of Spain, have a general east and west direction, and between them run, in the same direction, the nearly parallel valleys or basins of the great rivers of the country, the Douro, Tagus, Guadiana, and Guadalquivir, each of which is described in its proper place.

The climate of Spain, owing to extent and configuration of the country, is exceedingly various. In the northwest (maritime) provinces it is damp and rainy during the greater part of the year; at Madrid, which is situated about 11° south of London, and only 5° north of the shores of Africa, winters have occurred of such severity that sentinels while on duty have been frozen to death, while the south and east provinces are warm in winter, and are exposed to burning winds from the south, and to an almost tropical heat, in summer. Both ancient and modern geographers have adopted difference of climate as the rule for dividing the peninsula into tracts distinct as well in soil and vegetation as in temperature. Of these tracts or zones the first and most northern may be considered as embracing Galicia, Asturias, the Basque Provinces, Navarre, Catalonia, and the northern districts of Old Castile and Aragon. In this tract the winters are long and the springs and autumns rainy, while north and northeast winds blow cold from the snow-covered Pyrenees. The middle zone is formed mainly by the great central plateau, and embraces Northern Valencia, New Castile, Leon, and Estremadura, with the south parts of Old Castile and Aragon. The climate of the great part of this region is pleasant only in spring and autumn. The soil is generally fertile, and corn and wine are most abundantly produced. The southern or Bætican zone, comprising the rich country that extends between the southern wall of the central plateau and the Mediterranean shores, includes Andalucia, Murcia, and Southern Valencia. The stony rampart on the north protects it from the chilly winds of the central zone; but it is unprotected against the hot winds which in summer blow north from Africa and render this season intolerable to northern Europeans. Here the winter is temperate, and the spring and autumn delightful beyond description. The soil, which is artificially irrigated, is well adapted to agriculture and the cultivation of heat-loving fruits. The products comprise sugar, cotton, and rice, and the orange, lemon, and date.

The vast mountains of the country, affording, for the most part, only scanty crops of herbage, are utilized as pasture-grounds and are divided into large farms. But in the warm and fertile plains, especially where water is abundant, the farms are small. In 1860 there were 3,426,083 farms of all sizes, of which 750,000 were occupied by tenants, and the others by proprietors.

The cotton manufactures of Spain have been making considerable progress, and silk stuffs are largely fabricated. The principal cotton factories are at Barcelona. Excellent paper is made at Tolosa and Valladolid, and in the last-named town there are a few minor manufactures. The manufactures of tobacco, arms, and gunpowder are carried on by the government exclusively. Though neither the agricultural nor mineral resources of Spain are properly developed, a great advance has been evident within the last ten years, chiefly in mining, and more especially so in the working of lead and copper mines. Lead, copper, and tin are abundant, and there are large deposits of good coal and iron ore. The quicksilver mines of Almaden have been long celebrated and are still worked.

The merchant navy consisted in 1873 of 3069 vessels, of a total burden of 678,886 tons. Of these 202 were steam-vessels, 138,670 tons burden. The imports during the year 1874 amounted to 382,000,000 pesetas,* the exports to 403,000,000 pesetas. The principal imports are sugar, yarn, woolen fabrics, raw cotton, iron, machinery, coals, and dried fish; the principal exports are wine, metals, dried fruit, flour, bullion, green fruits, olive-oil, minerals, wool, grain, vegetation, and seeds, cork, and salt.

At the end of 1875 Spain had no constitution, but it was resolved by the government of King Alfonso XII. that a charter should be drawn up by a Cortes Constituyentes, to be called together in the spring of 1876. As a preliminary measure a committee of senators and deputies of the last Cortes, dissolved in 1874, had been called together July, 1875, at Madrid, which meeting resulted in the production of a constitutional scheme which was adopted by the government, and from which are to spring the future fundamental laws of Spain. The projected constitution provides that the power to make laws shall reside "in the Cortes with the king," and that the Cortes shall be composed of a Senate and Congress equal in faculties.

The various provinces of Spain, districts and communes, are governed by their own municipal laws, with strongly pronounced local administration. Neither the national executive nor the Cortes have the right to interfere in the established municipal and provincial self-government, except in case the action of the provincial parliaments or municipal councils (ayuntamientos) goes beyond the locally limited sphere to the injury of general and permanent interests.

The public debt, June 1, 1874, was 10,120,285,220 pesetas; the estimated public receipts for the financial year 1874–75, 609,541,141; estimated expenditures for the same year, 605,125,569. The army statistics are as follows:

	ON A PEACE FOOTING.	ON A WAR FOOTING.
Infantry,	56,000	178,000
Cavalry,	10,900	10,900
Artillery,	9,300	11,900
Engineers,	2,200	2,200
Carabineers,	13,000	13,000
Totals,	91,400	216,000

The navy consists of 123 steam-vessels, carrying 755 guns and aggregating 21,161 horse-power. Besides these, there are 3 school-ships, carrying 54 guns, and 2 sailing-vessels. The Spanish fleet is manned by 14,000 seamen and 5500 marines.

The length of railways in operation January, 1875, was 3810 English miles, and 1264 English miles were in course of construction. The whole of the Spanish railways belong to private companies, but nearly all have obtained guarantees or subventions from the government.

The post-office carried 75,300,000 letters in the year 1874. There were 2365 post-offices on the 1st of January, 1875.

The length of lines of telegraph on the 1st of January, 1875, was 7510 English miles, and the total length of wires 16,950 English miles. In the year 1874 the number of messages was 937,845.

COLONIES.

	AREA IN ENGLISH SQ. MILES.	POPULATION.
AMERICA.		
Cuba,	43,225	1,400,000
Puerto Rico,	3,544	625,000
ASIA.		
Philippine Islands and adjacent archipelago	66,423	6,034,410
AFRICA.		
Fernando Po, Annobon, etc.,	483	35,000
Total,	113,675	8,094,410

* The peseta = 19.3 cents.

The following figures show the production of sugar and molasses and amount exported from Cuba during the year 1873:

	PRODUCTION.	EXPORTED.
Sugar,	796,179 tons.	714,960 tons.
Molasses,	242,308 "	189,333 "
Total,	1,038,487 "	904,293 "

About two-thirds of the sugar and about nine-tenths of the molasses are sent to the United States.

The exports from the port of Havana during the year 1873 included 1412 tierces of honey, 19,574 pipes of rum, 46,216 lbs. of wax, 13,387,652 lbs. of tobacco, and 224,765,000 cigars. The number of vessels entered at the port of Havana during 1873 was 2194, with a total tonnage of 921,632.

During the same year Porto Rico exported 2,032,913 quintals of sugar, 6,082,539 gallons of molasses, 270,895 quintals of coffee, 51,766 quintals of tobacco, 2484 quintals of cotton, and 32,782 gallons of rum.

The exports of the Philippine Islands are principally sugar, hemp, tobacco, cigars, and coffee, and amounted in 1873 to 15,216,000 pesos.*

(The above statistics were furnished in part by the Spanish Commission.)

Commission from SPAIN to the International Exhibition:

COLONEL F. LOPEZ FABRA, Royal Commissioner-General.
COLONEL JUAN J. MARIN, Engineer Corps, Royal Spanish Commissioner.
DON JOAQUIN OLIVER, Secretary.
DON ALVARO DE LA GANDARA, Director of the Industrial Department.
COUNT DEL DONADIO, Director of the Department of Fine Arts.
DON JOSE JORDANA Y MORERA, Director of the Agricultural Department.
DON JUAN MORPHY, Consul-General of Spain, Member of the Commission.
DON JULIAN A PRINCIPE, Vice-Consul, Attache.
DON MIGUEL GONZALEZ, Attache.
DON JOSE FONRODONA, Attache.

Chiefs of Bureaus.

DON ENRIQUE BROTONS.
DON ALFREDO ESCOBAR.
DON ENRIQUE BORRELL.

Chiefs of Installation.

DON BERNARDO FORZANO.
DON FRANCISCO FORZANO.
DON FRANCISCO PARODY, Interpreter.

* The peso = 92½ cents.

PORTUGAL.

PORTUGAL, the most westerly kingdom of Europe, is a part of the great Spanish peninsula, and lies in 36° 55′ to 42° 8′ N. lat., and 6° 15′ to 9° 30′ W. long. Its greatest length from north to south is 368 miles, and its average breadth from east to west about 100 miles. It is bounded by the Atlantic on the south and west, and by Spain on the north and east.

Portugal is divided into six provinces, the area of which and population, according to the last census (1868), is given in the subjoined table:

PROVINCES.	AREA IN ENGLISH SQ. MILES.	POPULATION.
Minho,	2,671	988,985
Tras-os-Montes,	4,065	370,144
Beira	8,586	1,288,994
Estremadura,	8,834	837,451
Alemtejo,	10,255	332,237
Algarve,	2,099	177,342
	36,510	3,995,153

The insular appendages of Portugal are, the Azores, 1133.79 sq. miles, pop. (1868) 252,480; Madeira, etc., 330.75 sq. miles, pop. 113,341. The total area of the home possessions of Portugal is, therefore, 37,510.83 sq. miles, and the population 4,360,974.

Portugal must be regarded as essentially a littoral country, forming the Atlantic or western part of the Spanish peninsula, from which it is separated by political rather than physical boundaries. Its mountains and rivers are, with few exceptions, mere western prolongations of those of Spain. The principal mountain ranges lie about halfway inland, leaving almost the whole of its 500 miles of coast-line a flat sandy tract, with few rocky headlands, and hence there are scarcely any harbors or places of safe anchorage, except at the embouchures of the larger rivers. The highest range is the Serra de Estrella, which, passing from north-north-east to south-south-west, through Beira and Estremadura, terminates in the steep acclivities of Cintra and Cap la Rocca, near Lisbon. The principal chain, which is also known as the Serra da Junto, merges in a series of ridges, which cover a tract thirty miles in length between the Tagus and the sea. Another mountain range, named the Serra de Calderao and the Serra de Monchique, but constituting a mere continuation of the Spanish Sierra Morena, crosses the southern part of Portugal from east to west, and terminates in its most southern promontory of Cape St. Vincent. These ranges, with the numerous mountain-spurs that intersect the northern districts in every direction, so thoroughly occupy the area of Portugal that there are only two or three plains of any extent in the whole country, and these are situated to the west of the Guadiana, in Alemtejo, and in Beira and Estremadura, near the Tagus and Vouga. The valleys are very numerous, and by their great fruitfulness present a striking contrast to the barren and rugged mountains by which they are enclosed. The principal rivers enter Portugal from Spain. Of these, the largest are the Guadiana, which, leaving Spain near Badajoz, forms in part the boundary between the southern provinces of the neighboring kingdom, while the Minho and Douro, flowing west, form a part of the boundary in the north and north-east. The Tagus, or Tejo, intersects Portugal from its northern frontier to the southern termination of the Estrella Mountains, where it enters the sea a little below Lisbon. The Mondego, the largest river belonging entirely to Portugal, after receiving numerous affluents in its course, falls into the sea about midway between the Douro and the Tagus. The larger rivers, although obstructed at their mouth with dangerous bars, afford admirable means of internal navigation, together with the numerous lesser streams, and might through canals be connected into one great system of water routes; but hitherto nothing has been done to improve these great natural advantages. Except a few mountain tarns, Portugal has no lakes. It has salt marshes on the coast near Setubal, in Estremadura, and Aveiro, in Beira, whence large quantities of salt are annually obtained by evaporation. Mineral springs are abundant in many parts of the country, but hitherto they have been almost wholly neglected.

The vicinity to the western ocean tempers the climate of Portugal and exempts it from the dry heat by which Spain is visited. The great inequalities of the surface produce, however, great diversities of climate; for while snow falls abundantly on the mountains in the northern provinces, it is never seen in the lowlands of the southern districts, where spring begins with the new year and harvest is over by midsummer. Rain falls abundantly, especially on the coast, from October to March, and as a general rule the climate is healthy in the elevated districts even of the southern provinces; but malaria and fever prevail in low, flat lands and near the salt marshes. The mean annual temperature at Lisbon is 61° Fahr.

The natural products correspond to the diversity of the physical and climatic conditions; for while barley, oats and wheat, maize, flax, and hemp are grown in the more elevated tracts, rice is cultivated in the lowlands, the oak thrives in the northern, the chestnut in the central, and the cork, date, and American aloe in the southern parts, while every species of European and various kinds of semi-tropical fruits and vegetables are grown in different parts of the country. The soil is generally rich, but agriculture is everywhere neglected, and is scarcely made subservient to the wants of the population. The cultivation of the vine and that of the olive are almost the sole branches of industry; from the former is derived the rich red wine familiarly known to us as Port, from its being shipped at *O Porto*, "the port." The mineral products include gold, antimony, lead, copper, marble, slate, coal, iron, and salt, but of these the last is alone worked in sufficient quantity for exportation, and is in eager demand for the British market on account of its superior hardness, which adapts it specially for the salting of meat for ships. The commercial industry of the country falls very far below its physical capabilities, and Oporto and Lisbon are the only centres of manufacture and trade, the former of which has important silk and glove manufactories, and produces an inconsiderable quantity of linen, cotton, and wool fabrics, metal and earthenware goods, tobacco, cigars, leather, etc.

The external trade of Portugal is as follows: Imports 34,047,000 milreis, exports 23,609,000 milreis. (The milreis equals $1.08 in gold.)

The commercial navy of Portugal consisted on the 1st of January, 1872, of 813 vessels, of a total burden of 88,510 tons.

The fundamental law of the kingdom is the "Carta Constitutional," granted by King Pedro IV. April 29th, 1826, and altered by an additional act, dated July 5th, 1852. The crown is hereditary in the female as well as male line, but with preference of male in case of equal birthright. The constitution recognizes four powers in the state, the legislative, the executive, the judicial, and the "moderating" authority, the last of which is vested in the sovereign. There are two legislative chambers, the "Camera dos Pares," or House of Peers, and the "Camera dos Deputados," or House of Commons, which are conjunctively called the Cortes Geraes. The peers, unlimited in numbers, but actually comprising 133, are named for life by the sovereign, by whom also the president and vice-president of the first chamber are nominated. The members of the second chamber are chosen in direct election by all citizens having a clear annual income of 133 milreis. The deputies must have an income of at least 390 milreis, but lawyers, professors, physicians, or the graduates of any of the learned professions need no property qualification. Continental Portugal is divided into ninety-four electoral districts, returning as many deputies. The General Cortes meet and separate at specified periods, without the intervention of the sovereign, and the latter has no veto on a law passed twice by both Houses. All laws relating to the army or general taxation must originate in the Chamber of Deputies. The executive authority vests, under the sovereign, in a responsible ministry.

The budget of the financial year 1875-76 gives the estimated revenue at 23,152,000 milreis, and the expenditure at 24,129,000 milreis.

About one-half of the total liabilities of Portugal rank as an external debt, contracted for mainly in Great Britain, the rest being a home debt. The entire public debt amounted November 30, 1873, to £72,833,000. The army, in time of peace, numbers 31,826 men.

The navy of Portugal comprised, at the end of 1875, 21 steamers and 11 sailing-vessels, most of the latter laid up in harbor. The steamers comprise 9 corvettes, 8 sloops, and 7 gunboats, with a total of 170 guns and 4906 horse-power. The navy is officered by 1 vice-admiral, 5 rear-admirals, and 31 captains, and manned by 3493 sailors and marines.

The total length of railways in Portugal at the commencement of 1875 was 523 English miles. All the railways receive subventions from the state.

The number of post-offices in the kingdom at the beginning of 1872 was 599, and the number of telegraph offices 121. There were at the same time 1944 miles of telegraph lines. The number of telegrams despatched in the year 1871 was 698,700, nearly one-fifth for foreign countries. An international service by submarine cables was opened June 11, 1870.

Public education is entirely free from the supervision and control of the Church. By a law enacted in 1844 it is compulsory on parents to send their children to a place of public instruction, but this prescription is far from being enforced.

There are at present—

Scientific establishments for higher education,	9
For secondary education,	19
Elementary schools,	2445
For especial instruction,	6
	2479

The sum voted in 1875 for public instruction amounted to 902,730 milreis. The sum expended by private persons is estimated at about 300,000 more.

Colonies.

The colonial possessions of Portugal, situated in Asia and Africa, embrace a total area of 713,225 English square miles, or 34,820 geographical square miles. The latest official returns, based mainly on estimates, state the area and population as follows:

	AREA IN GEOG. SQ. MILES.	POPULATION.
1. POSSESSIONS IN ASIA:		
Settlements at Goa, Salcete, etc.,	68.60	474,233
" Damas and Diu,	7.45	53,284
Indian Archipelago,	260.	850,300
Macao,	.56	100,000
Total Asia,	336.61	1,477,817
2. POSSESSIONS IN AFRICA:		
Cape Verde Islands,	77.64	67,347
Settlements in Senegambia and Guinea,	1,687.	8,500
Islands of St. Thomas and Principe,	21.36	19,295
Angola, Benguela, and Mossamedas,	14,700	2,000,000
Mozambique and Sofala,	18,000	300,000
Total Africa,	34,486	2,395,142
Total Possessions,	34,822	3,872,959

Although of small extent, the Cape Verde Islands are estimated as the most important colonial possession of Portugal, politically and commercially. There are nine principal or inhabited islands that form the archipelago of the Cape de Verdes. Five of these islands—viz., St. Nicholas, Bona Vista, San Antonio, St. Vincent, and Sal—compose the Windward, and the four remaining islands—St. Jago, Fogo, Brava, and Maio—the Leeward, group. The island of St. Vincent, 70 English square miles in extent, but with not more than 1700 inhabitants, is possessed of a deep and excellent harbor, affording a secure anchorage at all seasons for vessels of the largest size. In the year 1871 there entered St. Vincent harbor 317 vessels of all nations. These islands, being in the direct route of European steamers bound to the coast of Brazil, the river Plate, and the west coast of South America, are of great value as affording a convenient resting-place for coaling and renewing provisions and water.

By the terms of a law passed by the Cortes Geraes of Portugal in 1858, domestic slavery is to cease in all the Portuguese colonies and settlements on the 29th of April, 1878.

Commission from PORTUGAL to the International Exhibition:

The preliminary works of the International Exhibition of Philadelphia were committed by the Portuguese Government to different corporations, these being helped by the authorities of the country.

EXECUTIVE COMMITTEES IN PORTUGAL.

DEPARTMENT I.

Bureau of Mines. JOAO BAPTISTA SCHIAPPA D'AZEVEDO, Chief.

Mining Engineers.

JOAO FERREIRA BRAGA.
LOURENCO MALHEIRO.
FRANCISCO FERREIRA ROQUETTE.
PEDRO VICTOR DA COSTA SEQUEIRA.

DEPARTMENTS II., III., IV., AND V.

Committee of the Society for the Encouragement of Manufacturing Industry.

ANTONIO AUGUSTO D'AGUIAR, Director of the Industrial Institute of Lisbon, President.
DANIEL CORDEIRO FEIO.
JOAQUIM MOREIRA MARQUES.
MANUEL DE CARVALHO RIBEIRO VIANNA.
IZIDORO THOMAZ DE MOURA CARVALHO.
MANUEL GOMES DA SILVA.
JOSE CAETANO D'ALMEIDA NAVARRO.
ANTONIO ADRIANO DA COSTA.
FIRMINO SEIXAS.
FRANCISCO JOSE LOPES FERREIRA.
MATHEUS FERREIRA.
ANTONIO DOS SANTOS MIGUEIS.
JULIO JOSE PIRES.
HENRIQUE PEREIRA TAVEIRA.

AT OPORTO.

GUSTAVO ADOLPHO GONCALVES E SOUZA, Director of the Industrial Institute of Oporto.

DEPARTMENTS VI. AND VII.

Committee of the Royal Central Society of Portuguese Agriculture.

VISCOUNT OF CARNIDE, President.
MANUEL JOSE RIBEIRO.
CAETANO DA SILVA LUZ.
JAYME BATALHA REIS.

ALFREDO DE QUEIROZ GUEDES, Treasurer.
LUIS AUGUSTO MARTINS D'ANDRADE, Secretary.

Committee of the Agricultural Society of Oporto.
BENTO DE FREITAS SOARES, President.
BARON OF ROEDA.
VISCOUNT OF VILLARINHO DE S. ROMAO.
VISCOUNT OF VILLAR ALLEN.
CONSTANTINO VANZELLER.
ARNALDO AMANDIO PEREIRA DE FARIA.
ALFREDO CARLOS LE COCQ.
JOAQUIM TAIBNER DE MORAES, Secretary.

COMMISSION IN PHILADELPHIA.

BARON OF SANT' ANNA, Royal General Commissioner.

DEPARTMENTS I., II., III., IV., AND V.

LOURENCO MALHEIRO, Commissioner.
ANTONIO JOSE ANTUNES NAVARRO.
FORGE CANDIDO BERKELEY COTTER.
THOMAZ VICTOR DA COSTA SEQUEIRA.

DEPARTMENTS VI. AND VII.

JAYME BATALHA REIS, Commissioner.
ALFREDO CARLOS LE COCQ.
MEM RODRIGUES DE VASCONCELLOS.
CAETANO OLYMPIO ROVERE.

TURKEY.

TURKEY, or the Ottoman Empire, includes large portions of the continents of Europe, Asia, and Africa, and consists of Turkey Proper, which is under the direct rule of the sultan, and of numerous dependent and tributary states, governed by their own princes. Turkey Proper is partly in Europe and partly in Asia, and is divided into a number of provinces, or *eyalets*.

The total area of the empire comprises 1,812,048 square miles, divided as follows:

	AREA.	POPULATION.
Turkey in Europe,	207,438	9,800,000
" " Asia,	660,870	16,750,000
" " Africa,	943,740	600,000
	1,812,048	27,150,000

The states dependent upon Turkey are either subject to hereditary chiefs — as in Egypt, Servia, and Montenegro — to elective rulers, or to viceroys appointed by the Sultan; and these chiefs, of whatever sort, must, on their accession, be approved of by the sultan, must acknowledge his suzerainty, and pay tribute; in all other respects they are on the footing of independent rulers.

Turkey Proper, as the immediate possessions of the sultan are called, is bounded by the Austrian dominions, Roumania, and the Black Sea on the north; by Persia, the Persian Gulf, and the Arabian Desert on the east; and by the Red Sea and its outlet, Egypt, the Mediterranean, Greece, the Adriatic Sea, and the Austrian empire on the south and west.

Turkey in Europe, the smaller of the two divisions of Turkey Proper, is generally hilly and undulating, traversed by a mountain system which has its origin in the Alps, whose eastern extension, the Julian Alps, enters the country at its north-west corner, runs in a south-west direction as the Dinaric Alps, keeping parallel to the coast-line, and after entering Albania, where it becomes Mount Pindus, assumes an almost southern direction till it reaches the Greek frontier. This range, which forms the water-shed between the Adriatic and Ægean Seas, has its culminating point in Mount Dinara (7458 feet), and sends out numerous offshoots over Montenegro and Albania.

The great river of Turkey is the Danube, which, with its tributary, the Save, forms the northern boundary, and receives in Turkey the Bosna and Drin from Bosnia, the Morava from Servia, and the Isker and Osma from Bulgaria. The Maritza, whose basin is formed by the Great Balkan and its two south-eastern branches, and the Strumo and Vardar, in Macedonia, are also considerable rivers, but those which are situated to the west of the Dinaric-Pindus range are, from the proximity of that water-shed to the sea-coast, insignificant in size; chief of them are the Narenta, Drin, and Voyutza. The Primitive rocks predominate in Macedonia, the Secondary group in the western provinces and to the north of the Balkan, and Tertiary deposits in the basins of the Save and Maritza, and in Suli.

On the high lands the cold is excessive in winter, owing to the north-east winds, which blow from the bleak and icy steppes of Southern Russia; and the heat of summer is almost insupportable in the western valleys. Violent climatic change is, on the whole, the rule in European Turkey; but those districts which are sheltered from the cold winds, as the Albanian valleys, enjoy a comparatively equable temperature. Although the soil is for the most part very fertile, but little progress has been made in the art of agriculture, and the most primitive implements are in common use. The cultivated products are maize in the south; rice, cotton, rye, barley in the centre, and millet in the north; the natural products are the pine, beech, oak, lime, and ash, with the apple, pear, cherry, and apricot in the Danube basin; the palm, maple, almond, sycamore, walnut, chestnut, carob, box, myrtle, laurel, etc., in the provinces south of the Balkan; large forests of fir and pine in the north-west; the olive, orange, citron, vine, peach, plum, and other fruit trees in Albania; and abundance of roses in the valley of the Maritza. The mineral products are, iron in abundance, argentiferous lead ore, copper, sulphur, salt, alum, and a little gold, but no coal. The wild animals are the wild boar, bear, wolf, wild dog, civet, chamois, wild ox, and those others which are generally distributed in Europe. The lion was formerly an inhabitant of the Thessalian Mountains.

TURKEY IN ASIA.—This portion of the Turkish Empire is more hilly than the other; the two almost parallel ranges Taurus and Anti-Taurus, which are the basis of its mountain system, cover almost the whole of the peninsula of Asia Minor or Anatolia, with their ramifications and offshoots, forming the surface into elevated plateaux, deep valleys, and enclosed plains. From the Taurus chain the Lebanon range proceeds southward parallel to the coast of Syria, and diminishing in elevation in Palestine terminates on the Red Sea coast at Sinai. Besides the Euphrates, Tigris, and Orontes, the only important rivers of Turkey in Asia are the Kizil-Ermak, which rises on the borders of Cilicia, and after a devious course across the peninsula falls into the Black Sea near Samsoun; the Mæander and Sarabat, which flow to the Ægean; and the Sakaria, which empties itself into the Euxine. On the whole, Turkey in Asia is ill-supplied with water; and though the mountain slopes afford abundance of excellent pasture, the plains and many of the valleys, especially those of the Euphrates, Tigris, and Jordan, are reduced by the parching droughts of summer to the condition of sandy deserts.

The fertile portions produce abundance of wheat, barley, rice, maize, tobacco, hemp, flax, and cotton; the cedar, cypress, and evergreen oak flourish on the mountain slopes; the sycamore and mulberry on the lower hills; and the olive, fig, citron, orange, pomegranate, and vine on the low lands. The mineral products are iron, copper, lead, alum, silver, rock salt, coal (in Syria), and limestone. The fauna includes the lion (east of the Euphrates), the hyena, lynx, panther, leopard, buffalo, wild boar, wild ass, bear, wolf, jackal, jerboa, and many others; and the camel and dromedary increase the ordinary list of domestic animals.

Notwithstanding the primitive state of agriculture in Turkey, the extreme fertility of the soil, which returns from twenty-five fold to one hundred fold, makes ample amends for this defect, and supplies materials for the comparatively unimportant manufactures and industries of the country. The products are wax, raisins, dried figs, olive oil, silks, red cloth, dressed goat-skins, excellent morocco, saddlery, swords of superior quality, shawls, carpets, dye-stuffs, embroidery, essential oils, attar of roses, plum brandy, etc. The commerce of Turkey is extensive and important, and under the influence of judicious regulations is rapidly increasing. Detailed statistics are not obtainable. The average annual value of the imports of Turkey in Europe is estimated at £18,500,000; and of the exports at £10,000,000. The exports are the surplus of the above-mentioned natural and manufactured products of the country, also wool, goats' hair, meerschaum clay, honey, sponges, drugs, madder, gall-nuts, various gums and resins, and excellent wines; the imports are manufactured goods of all kinds, glass, pottery, arms, paper, cutlery, steel, amber, etc.

The merchant navy included, in 1873, 224 sailing-vessels of a total burden of

34,711 tons, and 9 steamers, aggregating 3049 tons. The total tonnage of the merchant navy is estimated at 180,000.

The sovereign is commonly styled sultan, but has also the titles padishah, grand seignior, khan, and hunkiar; though nominally absolute, his power is much limited by the *sheikh-ul-islam*, the chief of the *Ulemas*, who has the power of objecting to any of the sultan's decrees, and frequently possesses more authority over the people than his sovereign. The supreme head of the administration, and the next in rank to the sultan, is the grand vizier (*sadri-azam*), under whom are the members of the cabinet or divan (*menasybi-divaniie*), namely, the presidents of the supreme council of state (*alkiami-adlie*) and of the Tanzimat, the *Seraskier*, the *capudan pasha*, or high-admiral, and the other heads of departments of the administration. The governors of the *eyalets*, or provinces, are styled *walis;* each eyalet is divided into *sanjaks* or *livas*, ruled by *kaimakams*, each liva containing a number of *cazas*, or districts, and each caza a number of *nahiyehs*, composed of villages and hamlets.

According to the budget for 1875-76 (the year 1291, according to the Turkish calendar), the estimated public revenue was 4,776,588 purses* of 500 piastres each; the expenditure, 5,785,819 purses. The foreign debt of Turkey amounted in 1875 to £184,981,783; the internal and floating debt has been estimated variously at from £13,000,000 to £30,000,000.

The military forces of Turkey were officially estimated as follows in 1875: on a peace footing, 157,667 men; on a war footing, 586,100.

The navy consisted at the end of 1875 of 20 iron-clad ships and 70 other steamers. In addition to these there were 4 steam transports and a number of old sailing-vessels not fit for service. The total length of railways open for traffic on January 1st, 1875, was 825 English miles, of which 654 were in Europe and 171 in Asiatic Turkey. The length of telegraph lines on the 1st of January, 1875, was 17,597 miles. The total number of despatches carried in the year 1874 was 910,130, of which number 102,987 were international messages.

Education was long neglected, but in 1847 a new system was introduced; and since then schools for elementary instruction have been established throughout Turkey, and middle schools for higher education and colleges for the teaching of medicine, agriculture, naval and military science, etc. In 1870, Constantinople had 415 public schools, which were attended by 24,000 pupils.

Commission from TURKEY to the International Exhibition:

HIS EXCELLENCY G. D'ARISTARCHI BEY, Minister Plenipotentiary, President.
BALTAZZI EFFENDI, First Secretary of Legation.
RUSTEM EFFENDI, Second Secretary of Legation.
COUNT DELLA SALA, Acting Consul of Turkey.
MR. EDWARD SHERER.
MR. AUGUSTE GIESE, Honorary Member.

* One purse of 300 piasters = $25, gold.

RUSSIA.

THE empire of Russia, extending over a large proportion of the northern regions of the globe, includes the eastern part of Europe, the whole of Northern Asia, and a part of Central Asia. Lat. 38° 30′ to 78° N.; long. 17° 19′ E. to 190° E. (170° W.). Russia is bounded on the N. by the Arctic Ocean; on the E. by the Pacific Ocean; on the S. by the Chinese Empire, Turkestan, Caspian Sea, Persia, Asiatic and European Turkey, and the Black Sea; on the W. by Austria, Prussia, the Baltic, and Sweden.

The following table, showing the area and population of the Russian empire, is from the *Almanach de Gotha* for 1876:

	AREA IN SQUARE KILOMETRES.	POPULATION.
Russia,	4,909,194	65,704,559 (1870)
Poland,	127,316	6,026,421 (1870)
Grand Duchy of Finland,	373,536	1,832,138 (1872)
Lieutenancy of Caucasus,	447,645	4,893,332 (1871)
Siberia,	12,500,083	3,428,867 (1870)
Central Asia,	3,307,953	5,800,628
Total,	21,665,727	87,685,945

The northern shores of the Russian territories, which are washed by the Arctic Ocean, are deeply indented. The White Sea, an immense arm of the Arctic Ocean, penetrates 350 miles into the mainland, and is subdivided into the gulfs of Onega and Archangel or Dwina. The other chief inlets on the north of Russia are the Kara Sea and the gulfs of Obi and Yenisei. Westward from Nova Zembla the Arctic Ocean is navigable for three months of the year; east from that island the sea, even at the mildest season, is encumbered with floating icebergs. The chief islands in this ocean are the Kolguef, Waigatz, Nova Zembla, and Spitzbergen isles. The eastern shores of Russia are washed by the Pacific, subdivided into the Behring, Okhotsk, and Japan Seas, and the islands belonging to this country in these seas are Sakhalin and the northern part of the Kuriles. On the south are the Black Sea and the Sea of Azov, the latter communicating with the former by the Strait of Kertch, and so shallow that it is navigable for small craft only. Of the Caspian Sea, Russia commands the whole, with the exception of the south shore, which belongs to Persia. The northern and eastern banks of the Caspian are the seats of the chief fisheries of the empire. On the north-west of Russia are the Baltic Sea, with the gulfs of Riga, Finland, and Bothnia; and in these waters the islands of Aland, Esel, and Dago belong to the empire. The freezing of the water near the shores of the Baltic renders the navigation of this sea impracticable during five months of the year, although a few ports are accessible throughout the whole year. Possessing means of easy communication with the most fertile governments of the interior, and sustaining chiefly the commerce of the Russian empire with the other parts of Europe and with America, the Baltic is of the highest commercial importance.

European Russia consists of a vast plain bordered with mountains. On the east are the Ural Mountains, forming a broad range of no great elevation, ending on the north on the shores of the Arctic Ocean, and on the south in a range of elevated plains on the left bank of the Volga. On the south-east of the great plain is the lofty range of the Caucasus, crossed by the Pass of Derbend and the so-called Military Georgian Road. The Crimean Mountains, a continuation of the Caucasian chain, rise to 5000 feet in their highest summit. The districts in the south-west of Russia, between the Vistula and the Pruth, are covered by hilly ranges from the Carpathian Mountains, which in Poland are known as the Sandomir Mountains. The Finland Mountains, on the north-west, are ranges of granite rocks, embracing numerous lakes, and not rising higher than 600 feet. The Alaunsky table-land, which connects itself with the Ural Mountains by a chain of hills in latitude about 62° N., is the key to the configuration of European Russia. From this table-land, with an elevation of about 1200 feet, the country, with gradually declining slopes, falls away in four directions—north to the Arctic, north-west to the Baltic, south to the Black, and south-east to the Caspian Seas. The sloping country on the north of the Alaunsky heights is called, from its eastern and western limits, the Ural-Baltic table-land; that on the south of the same dividing heights is called, for the same reason, the Ural-Carpathian table-land. The Alaunsky heights form the great water-shed, and regulate the course of all the great rivers of the Russian empire. To the north they throw off the Petchora, the Northern Dwina, and the Onega; to the south, the Dniester, Bug, Dnieper, Don, and Kouban; to the south-east, the Volga, with its great affluents the Oka and Kama. The Western Dwina, the Niemen, and the Vistula fall into the Baltic Sea. At the foot of the north-west slope from the central terrace is the lake country of European Russia, and the great lakes are Ladoga, Onega, Ilmen, Peipus, and Pskov. The plain of European Russia naturally divides itself into three tracts or zones, each of which differs from the others in the nature and quality of its soil. The northern zone extends between the Arctic Ocean and the Ural-Baltic table-land, the middle zone between the Ural-Baltic and the Ural-Carpathian table-lands, and the southern zone between the Ural-Carpathian table-land and the Black and Caspian Seas. The soil of the northern zone is marshy and the climate inclement. In its middle part, between the rivers Onega and Mezen, and especially along the banks of the Northern Dwina, forests of fir-wood and large tracts of fodder-grass occur. Toward the east of this tract the woods disappear, and vast marshes, frozen the greater part of the year, cover the country. The middle zone reaches south-west to the government of Volhynia and the South of Poland, and north-east to the Ural Mountains. In the west it consists of an extensive hollow, covered with woods and with marshes, the chief of which are those of Pinsk. In the middle part of this zone the soil is partly heavy and covered with mould, and toward the north sandy. Beyond the Oka luxuriant meadows abound, and on the east, beyond the Volga, this tract forms an extensive valley, covered with a thick layer of mould, abounding in woods, and rising into hills in the vicinity of the Ural range. The southern zone consists of steppes extending along the shores of the Black and Caspian Seas. The steppes of the Black Sea have mostly a mouldy soil covered with grass, but in the south-east shifting sands and salt marshes predominate. The steppes of the Caspian consist of sand, salt marshes, and salt lakes, the Elton lake, yielding nearly 4,000,000 pouds (about 1,290,000 hundred weights) of salt annually, being the most remarkable.

Owing to its vast extent, the Russian empire presents great varieties of climate. At Archangel the mean temperature of the year is 32° Fahr.; at Yalta, in the Crimea, 52°; and at Kutais, in the Caucasus, 58°. Consisting of an immense area of dry land, the climate of the empire is essentially continental, and the climate of localities in its interior is much more rigorous than that of places on the western shores of Europe in the same latitudes. The rigor of the climate of the empire increases not only with the latitude, but as you advance eastward; thus, the mean winter temperature of the town of Abo, on the Gulf of Bothnia, is the same as that of Astrakhan, viz., 23° Fahr., although the former is in lat. 61° and the other in lat. 47°, or 14° nearer the equator. The difference of the mean summer temperature under the same latitudes is, on the contrary, not very considerable. The isothermal line of Astrakhan (60° Fahr.) passes through Lublin, in Poland, and Ekaterinoslav. In the east the maximum heat is even greater than in the west, and such heat-loving plants as the watermelon are grown more successfully in the south-east of Russia than in the west of Europe under the same latitude. The dryness of the atmosphere increases in the direction from north-west to south-east. On the banks of the Baltic the average number of rainy and snowy days is 150 and the annual rainfall is 20 inches, while near the Caspian the number of such days is 70 and the rainfall only 4 inches. The climate of Russia is in general healthy, but there are several places where diseases seem to be localized, as the shores of the Frozen Ocean, where scurvy is common, the marshes along the Niemen and Vistula, where the pica polonica is the chief disease, and the marshy lands on the Black, Azof, and Caspian Seas, where ague always prevails.

Russia is an eminently agricultural country, although only a comparatively small portion is under cultivation. In the central zone the soil is almost entirely black mould, extremely fertile, and hardly ever requiring manure. The system of husbandry most extensively practiced is what is called the "three-field system," in the working of which one-third of the land is always in fallow. In the south and south-east a system of agriculture peculiar in Russia is in operation; it is called the "fallow system," and consists in raising three or four consecutive crops from the same land, and afterward allowing it to lie fallow for five or six years, after which time it begins to grow feather-grass (*Stipa pennata*), which is considered a token of returning fertility. A great drawback to the development of agriculture is the want of proper means of communication, and consequently the low price of corn in the locality in which it is grown. Fodder-grass is rarely cultivated, as a sufficient supply of fodder is afforded by the extensive natural meadows. The chief cereals are wheat, which is grown as far north as lat. 62°, rye, barley, and oats. Buckwheat and millet are grown in the south, and from these, but specially from rye, the staple food of the inhabitants is made. Hemp and flax are extensively cultivated, and the oil extracted from the seeds of the former is an indispensable article of the peasant's household, as it is used for food during the fasts, which, taken together, extend over about half the year. Tobacco crops cover about 16,000 acres. Beet-root and maize are also cultivated, and there are numerous vineyards in the Crimea, Bessarabia, and along the Don. Gardening is an important branch of industry, the products being cucumbers, onions, cabbages, and other vegetables and fruits. An area of 486,000,000 acres is covered with woods, but the quantity of timber, from which material the peasant supplies almost all his wants, is at present suffering diminution. Coniferous trees are the chief in the northern districts, but in the central tracts oaks, limes, maples, and ashes are the chief. Timber is the chief article of internal commerce, and is floated down the rivers from the well-wooded districts to those which are destitute of wood.

ANIMALS AND ANIMAL PRODUCTS.—In the northern and central provinces cattle are kept chiefly for the purpose of obtaining manure, but in other parts cattle-breeding is an important branch of industry. On an average there are 30,000,000 head of cattle in Russia. Of horses the best, chiefly trotters, are reared in breeding-stables in the southern central governments, but the great bulk of the horses are obtained from the half-wild studs of the Cossacks, Kalmucks, and Kirghiz. The horses of Viatka, Kazan, and Finland are strong and hardy. The total number of the horses in Russia is about 18,000,000. Sheep-breeding is carried on extensively on the southern steppes. The sheep number 10,000,000, of which upward of 1,000,000 are of the fine merino breed. Besides these animals, there are camels in the south of Russia, reindeer in the north, and hogs and poultry in great abundance everywhere. A breed of the urus—a huge and rare animal which does not occur in any other country—is preserved in a forest of the government of Grodno. Among the wild animals are (chiefly in the north) the bear, wolf, elk, fox, and marten; on the northern coasts are found the seal and walrus and the eider-duck and other wild-fowl. The more expensive kinds of furs are procured from Siberia.

The most important Russian fisheries are those of the Caspian and Black Seas and the Sea of Azof and their tributaries. The Baltic Sea is not remarkably rich in fish, but the produce of the adjoining lakes is much more considerable. The herrings, cod-fish, and salmon, caught in abundance in the White Sea, constitute the chief resources of the inhabitants of the adjoining districts. Bee-culture is very general in Russia. Silkworms are reared chiefly in the Caucasus.

During the year 1874, according to official returns, the state foundries smelted 1,225,000 Russian pouds* of bronze, 557,000 pouds of iron, and 1000 pouds of steel; 89,000 pouds weight of articles in bronze were cast, and 508,000 pouds weight of ammunition, 9000 pouds weight of steel cannon and 15,000 pouds weight of iron cannon, besides which 15,000 pouds of lead and 6600 pouds of zinc were smelted. There were also made 7800 pouds weight of iron articles, 10,000 pouds sheet-iron, and 7500 roubles'† worth of iron for use in shipbuilding, and 46,700 side-arms, 20,000 blades, and 5725 gun-barrels. The amount of metal passing through private factories is given approximately in the same official returns. They state the estimated products of the smelting establishments of the Ural at 13,200,000 pouds of bronze, 1,017,000 pouds of iron, 69,000 pouds of steel, and 100,000 pouds of copper. Those around Moscow are supposed to have produced 3,360,000 pouds of bronze and 1,830,000 pouds of iron. South Russian produce is estimated at 430,000 pouds of bronze and 440,000 pouds of iron; that of the Polish provinces at 1,370,000 pouds of bronze, 800,000 of iron, and 120,000 of zinc. Lastly, 44,000 pouds of copper is estimated as the return from the Caucasus. During 1874 gold to the amount of 1806 pouds was extracted, without reckoning the districts of Altai and Nerchmst, which yield an annual average of 165 pouds. The total amount of coal raised in 1874 was 83,375,000 pouds. The extraction of mineral oils in the Caucasus shows a great increase, and oil-wells have lately been discovered in the government of Kielce, Poland. Small handicraft manufacturing establishments abound in all the central governments, especially in the neighborhood of Moscow, where whole villages during the winter season are employed in some special industry, as weaving, tanning, fur-dressing, joiners' work, shoemaking, etc. The chief manufacture is spinning and weaving flax and hemp. Linen is manufactured to the value of 100,000,000 roubles, chiefly in hand-looms, although the finer qualities are manufactured by power-looms, mostly in the governments of Jaroslav and Kostroma and the capitals. Hemp is manufactured into sailcloth and ropes, which articles are largely exported. Woolen and worsted stuffs are made to the value of 50,000,000 roubles, and the quantity is on the increase. Fine cloths and mixed fabrics are made in the capitals, and in the governments of Livonia and Tchernigov. Silk-spinning and weaving are carried on in the factories of Moscow, which is renowned for its brocades and gold and silver embroideries.

In 1870 there were 158 cotton-spinning mills, producing goods to the value of 53,350,000 roubles, and weaving establishments with an annual product of 13,000,000 roubles. The next most important branch of industry is tanning, the products of which amount to 20,000,000 roubles. Other important branches of industry are cutlery, pottery, and glass-works. The produce of the machine-factories in 1870 did not exceed 15,000,000 roubles; of the sugar-refineries 27,250,000 roubles; of the paper-mills 5,750,000 roubles.

The following table shows the imports and exports during the year 1873:

* The *pud* or *poud* = 36 lbs. avoirdupois. † One rouble = 77 cents, gold.

	IMPORTS ROUBLES.	EXPORTS. ROUBLES.
Baltic ports,	232,900,000	140,494,000
White Sea ports,	981,000	7,913,000
Southern Sea ports,	61,070,000	89,343,000
Land frontier,	117,524,000	108,108,000
Total, Europe,	412,475,000	345,858,000
" Asia,	20,958,000	9,757,000
	433,433,000	355,615,000

By far the largest portion of exports consisted of cereals.

The merchant navy of Russia consisted, at the end of the year 1874, of 2512 sea-going vessels, of an aggregate burden of 521,008 tons. Included in the total were 621 ships engaged in trading to foreign countries, and 1672 coasting-vessels, many of them belonging to Greeks, but sailing under the Russian flag. Not included in the return were 385 river and lake steames.

The government of Russia is an unlimited monarchy, the head of which is the emperor, who unites in himself every authority and power—that is to say, is the head of the military, the legislative, and the judicial systems, and is also the ecclesiastical chief of the orthodox Greek Church. The order of succession is by primogeniture, hereditary in heirs-male, and in females in default of males. Every military or civil officer of the crown is required to take an oath of allegiance. The council of state is the highest branch of the executive, and comprehends the legislative, judicial, and administrative powers. The president and members — among whom are always included the ministers of the crown — are appointed by the emperor. A secretary of state, whose duty it is to report the opinion of the council to the emperor, is attached to this body. The estimates of expenditure and income, and every proposition introducing an addition to or a modification of the laws, are considered and revised by this council.

European Russia is divided into 50 provinces, over each of which is a governor appointed by the emperor. Some of these provinces, although administered by governors, are united under a governor-general. The governor-generalships are generally the remote frontier regions.

The nominal strength of the various divisions of the Russian army, according to the returns of the ministry of war, was as follows in 1874:

	PEACE FOOTING.	WAR FOOTING.
Regular army,	457,872	808,670
Army of first reserve,	180,740	127,923
Army of second reserve,	207,812	276,664
Total,	846,424	1,213,257

The navy comprised, in 1875, 223 vessels, of 188,120 tons burden, and carrying 561 guns. This included an iron-clad fleet of 29 vessels, of 9210 horse-power, 74,793 tons burden, and carrying 184 guns.

In the budget for 1875, the revenue is estimated at 559,361,193 roubles, and the expenditure at 556,105,410 roubles.

In 1875 the public debt was stated as 2,409,739,996 roubles, against which there was a credit, consisting of advances made to railway companies, etc., of 634,489,942 roubles.

The total length of railways at the end of the year 1874 was 13,227 English miles. Nearly one-half of the railway property was held by the government.

The post-office, in the year 1874, conveyed 59,529,000 letters, 1,300,000 post-cards, 2,218,000 wrappers, 1,493,000 parcels, and 29,020,000 newspapers. There were 3191 post-offices. The total receipts for the year 1874 did not cover the expenditure.

The length of telegraph lines, Jan. 1st, 1875, was 31,459 English miles, and the length of wires 58,675 miles. About five-sixths of the total belonged to the state. The total number of telegrams in 1874 was 3,512,003.

The following table shows, after official returns, the number of educational establishments in Russia, maintained either wholly or in part by the government, and placed under the Minister of Public Instruction, at the end of the year 1870:

	NUMBER.	PUPILS.
Universities,	8	7,275
Lyceums,	2	262
Veterinary schools,	2	154
Gymnasia and progymnasia, for males,	153	58,478
Gymnasia and progymnasia, for females,	173	
Training schools for teachers,	39	1,274
District schools,	419	27,508
Primary schools,	22,827	831,402
Total,	23,623	926,353

Commission from RUSSIA to the International Exhibition:

ALEXANDRE BUTOWSKY, Privy Councillor, Director of the Department of Commerce and Manufactures, President.

DMITRI KOBEKO, Privy Councillor; Chief of Cabinet; Ministry of Finance.

NICOLAS YERMAKOFF, Actual Councillor of State; Vice-Director of the Department of Commerce and Manufactures.

CHARLES DE BIELSKY, Actual Councillor of State; Commissioner-General.

ICAN WISCHNEGRADSKY, Actual Councillor of State; Director of the Technological Institute of St. Petersburg.

MICHEL PODOBEDOFF, Actual Councillor of State; Ministry of Finance.

ALEXIS BEHR, Actual Councillor of State; Ministry of Finance.

NICOLAS ILJINE, Councillor of State; Professor in Technological Institute of St. Petersburg.

DMITRI TIMIRIASEF, Councillor of State; Ministry of Finance.

Executive Committee at Philadelphia.

CHARLES DE BILLSKY, Actual Councillor of State, Commissioner-General.

BARON GUSTAV NOLCKEN, Delegate; Ministry of Finance.

EMILE DE LERCHE, Delegate; Ministry of Finance.

ALEXANDRE GOLDECHEN, Delegate; Ministry of Finance.

CHARLES BRECKMANN, Delegate; Ministry of Finance.

LEON WARSCHAWSKY, Delegate; Ministry of Finance.

ALEXANDRE PLETNEFF, Delegate; Ministry of Finance.

PIERRE ORLOFF, Secretary.

CHARLES SCHOENICH, Engineer, Inspector of the Russian Section.

OTTO KITZING, Special Secretary.

ERNEST PELLETIER, Attaché.

INDEX OF EXHIBITORS.

DEPARTMENTS VI., VII.

A.

C.

D.

E.

F.

G.

H.

K.

M.

N.

O.

Q.

R.

T.

U.

W.

X.

Y.

Z.